FUTURES GUIDE
2020

The Top Prospects For Every MLB Team and more

Edited by Craig Brown and Nick Schaefer

Mark Anderson, Mark Barry, Demetrius Bell, Sydney Bergman, Jacob Bickman, J.P. Breen, Smith Brickner, Craig Brown, Ben Carsley, Kevin Carter, Alexis Collins, Ricky Conti, Spring Marie Cullen, Scott Delp, Patrick Dubuque, Steve Givarz, Nathan Graham, Samuel Hale, Wilson Karaman, Keanan Lamb, David Lee, Allison McCague, Tyler Oringer, Jeffrey Paternostro, Keith Rader, Jen Mac Ramos, Jesse Roche, Bret Sayre, Ginny Searle, Jarrett Seidler, Ben Spanier, Tyler Stafford, Forest Stulting, Matt Sussman, Matt Trueblood, Collin Whitchurch, Brandon Williams, Matt Winkleman, Jeff Wiser, Kazuto Yamazaki

Dave Pease, Consultant Editor
Robert Au, Harry Pavlidis and Amy Pircher, Statistics Editors

Library of Congress Cataloging-in-Publication Data:
paperback
ISBN-10: 1732355584
ISBN-13: 978-1732355583

Project Credits
Cover Design: Michael Byzewski at Aesthetic Apparatus
Interior Design and Production: Jeff Pease, Dave Pease
Layout: Jeff Pease, Dave Pease

Cover Photos
Front Cover: Jo Adell. © Mark J. Rebilas-USA TODAY Sports

Baseball icon courtesy of Uberux, from https://www.shareicon.net/author/uberux

Manufactured in the United States of America
10 9 8 7 6 5 4 3 2 1

Table of Contents

Top 101 Prospects

by Jeffrey Paternostro and Jarrett Seidler

1. Wander Franco, SS, Tampa Bay Rays

Franco is a switch-hitting shortstop who we think will either stay there or end up at second. He has a high chance at a plus hit/plus power outcome. He hit .327/.398/.487 as an 18-year-old playing at Low-A and High-A, and walked more than he struck out at both levels. If it wasn't for Nick Madrigal, we'd be talking about how he has the best bat-to-ball skills of any top prospect, despite his youth. He's been the best player in his age cohort for years now, with the signing bonus and past rankings to prove it. While he's not quite as toolsy as some of the players just below him on this list, he's still pretty toolsy, and he's blending it with dominant performance. He's the boring choice to be the best prospect in baseball, but clearly the right one.

2. Jo Adell, OF, Los Angeles Angels

Baseball is an entertainment business. That often gets lost beneath a haze of $/WARP analysis, four-and-a-half hour playoff games with picture-in-picture ads from Jaguar and arguments over whether the inconsistent seam height of baseballs has been purposeful. Now, generally speaking, good baseball is more entertaining than bad baseball, and good players more entertaining than bad. And Adell is going to be a very good baseball player. But he also gets that this is an entertainment business, and if that means staying past his allotted time in the batter's box during Futures Game batting practice to try and hit a ball off the scoreboard at Progressive Field—despite the wind blowing in—he's happy to oblige. Adell came up just a few rows short in the end, but it's one of our abiding memories of the 2019 season. And fair play, given his 70-grade raw power he had a shot at it. There's a potential plus hit tool that could carry that pop into major league games as soon as April 1st. And no foolin', while Franco has a better chance to be a very good player for a long time, Adell has the most upside of anyone on this list. He may not get there, but it sure will be entertaining to watch him try.

3. Gavin Lux, SS/2B, Los Angeles Dodgers

We have a lot of pithy little sayings here on the Baseball Prospectus prospect team. "Catchers are weird," "There's no such thing as a number three starter" and "Jo Adell is an icon" to name just a few. "Player development is not linear" is another one. It sure wasn't for Lux. He was in the mix for the back of our 2019 Top 101, but missed for merely being a polished middle infielder with a strong collection of average or solid-average tools. Very early in 2019, it became clear something had changed. He had grown into a stronger, but no less athletic frame. He looked more like a sure-shot shortstop, but with the flexibility to be above-average at other spots. The doubles power grew into over-the-fence power without giving up any plate coverage or sacrificing a patient approach. All of a sudden, Lux was slugging .719 in Triple-A and made the Dodgers playoff roster—where he mashed a pinch-hit home run in NLDS Game 1. We still think he's polished and high probability, but now he's probably going to make a few All-Star games. There wasn't a single tool breakout here, everything just got a little bit better. Put that mix of plus tools in a shortstop and, well, that's a heady brew.

4. Adley Rutschman, C, Baltimore Orioles

This is the highest the previous summer's 1-1 has landed on the 101 in quite some time. The circumstantial evidence from the draft process supports it; Rutschman was the consensus top player in the draft process from start to finish and set a record bonus number, under a system that incentivizes teams to shave money with the top pick to go after big-bonus preps later. Our looks at Rutschman after the draft flashed the expected offensive tools, led by two mirrored and near-perfect swings geared for power. We also saw a strong, polished base of defensive abilities, and we firmly believe that he will excel in the soft factors of catching as well. Will blowing up a highly-drafted switch-hitting Orioles catching prospect inevitably lead to Matt Wieters jokes? You bet. But Wieters is a four-time All-Star who has compiled over 20 WARP, so is that actually that bad?

5. MacKenzie Gore, LHP, San Diego Padres

As best pitching prospects in baseball go, Gore is not the most exciting example to write about. It's not his fault. He's a very good pitching prospect. We are literally saying he's the best pitching prospect. There just isn't an easy hook—although there is a very easy hook. Gore got a full, blister-free season under his belt, with the stipulation that "full" in our modern times means 20 judiciously spaced starts of 55-75 pitches, totaling 101 innings. So, it's still not clear exactly what the stuff will look like as a traditional 180-inning, every fifth day, starter. It's clear what it looks like now, though, and it's dang impressive. Gore boasts a deep arsenal of pitches led by a mid-90s fastball from the left side that he commands well for a 20-year-old with fewer than 200 pro innings under his belt. A plus-or-better curve—the aforementioned easy hook—and potentially above-average slider and change round out the repertoire. He gets good extension and deception from his funky delivery right out of the Ministry of Silly Walks. So there's no need to always look on the bright side of life to see that Gore is one of the elite pitching prospects in all of baseball.

6. Luis Robert, OF, Chicago White Sox

Professional baseball is a game for all shapes and sizes. Prospects on this list will range from 5-foot-7 (Nick Madrigal, allegedly) to 6-foot-7 (Oneil Cruz). There are beanpole pitchers and BIG BOY SZN corner mashers. There is no perfect baseball body. However, if there was a perfect baseball body, it might be Robert's. Built like an NFL wideout with the plus-plus run times to match, everything just looks easy when he's on the field or in the batter's box. The 21-year-old blitzed three levels to the tune of .328 and 32 home runs in 122 games, finishing the year on the doorstep of the South side. He looks like he should be a corner outfielder, but is perfectly fine roaming center. The offensive tools are All-Star level. The one question left: Can Robert's "see ball, hit ball" approach work against the best pitchers in the world? We'll find out in 2020.

7. Jarred Kelenic, OF, Seattle Mariners

We said last year that "in a year or two [Kelenic] might be the sort of prospect the Mets will sorely wish they still had." Well, here we go. The difference between projecting a player for a bunch of 55 tools and a bunch of 6 tools isn't huge. For hit and power, a half-grade jump is only one extra single and homer a month. And yet, that slight across-the-board uptick is the main difference driving Kelenic's 50-plus spot rise. That's not the whole story, of course; he's moving faster than we expected, subverting prior concerns about him being an older prep draftee into reaching Double-A less than a month after his 20th birthday and he's sticking in center, for now. He remains more likely to be a well-rounded star than a superstar, but every team in baseball could use this type of crown jewel prospect. Especially the Mets.

8. Dustin May, RHP, Los Angeles Dodgers

The "Gingergaard" sobriquet was supposed to stay between us, dear reader. It was meant mostly in jest, a nod to the long line of projectable Texas prep arms—with or without flowing locks—that get drafted every spring. But ESPN's Jeff Passan had to go and mention it in a column about May's call-up, and next it was on national broadcasts. Then both May and Syndergaard had to comment, and now it is just awkward for

everyone. May can exist as his own pitcher sans glib comps, and he took another step forward in 2019. The velocity ticked up again into the high-90s without the fastball losing any of its frightening arm-side run. May added a hard cutter for a different glove-side look to pair with his aesthetically-pleasing power curve. Okay, okay, perhaps this does sound a little bit familiar. May isn't quite there yet, as he struggled to command his offspeed stuff during his major-league cameo. But he announced his presence with all the fury of Heimdallr blowing the Gjallar-Horn. As for what shall come to pass afterward, "when all the world is burned, and dead are all the gods and all the champions and all mankind?" Well, probably a number two starter. Yeah, I mean anything was going to be an anti-climax after the apocalypse. But given all the postseason *Fimbulwinters* the Dodgers have gone through recently, May might be exactly the hero they need.

9. Jesus Luzardo, LHP, Oakland Athletics

Recency bias is a necessary evil in our line of work. Prospects can change rapidly, and the most recent look might be the most representative one of what player they can be. Watching Luzardo carve up major-league lineups down the stretch with a potent three-pitch mix could make one think they were watching the best pitching prospect in baseball. Upper-90s heat, a potential plus curve and change, enough command to make it all work—yeah that's a recipe for a top pitching prospect. Look a bit further back though, and you'll note Luzardo only threw 55 innings this year due to a lat issue, and missed a year after being drafted due to Tommy John surgery. And really the *most* recent version you saw was him dominating in relief. It would be awfully tempting to let Luzardo continue to rip off strikeouts with maxed out stuff in the late innings, but we'd like to see a full North American tour of 32 starts from The Jesus Lizard before consigning him to a supporting act in the bullpen.

10. Julio Rodriguez, OF, Seattle Mariners

For all we just waxed poetic about Jarred Kelenic, he's not even the highest-upside outfield prospect in Seattle's system. Forest Stulting saw Rodriguez's first series of the season in the South Atlantic League—literally Rodriguez's first stateside at-bats—and immediately sounded the claxons, stating he was one of the best outfield prospects in the game. By the end of the season, there was no debate about that, as Rodriguez laid waste to lower-minors pitching before holding his own in the Arizona Fall League, all as an 18-year-old. He has a quick, compact swing that is geared for hard contact, and already touts an advanced plate approach for a teenager with such limited experience. We expect that as he matures, he will start lifting the ball more and ultimately grow into significant game power. Simply put, he's a potential offensive monster in the making.

11. Carter Kieboom, IF, Washington Nationals

There are a few "prospect fatigue" entries every year on this list, and Kieboom will be the first. Development *isn't* always linear, but he's gone year-over-year from a late first-round pick with potential, to the 71st-best prospect in baseball after a strong full-season debut, to the 16th-best prospect in baseball upon reaching Double-A, to the 11th-best prospect in baseball after hitting .300 with some pop in Triple-A as a 21-year-old. Kieboom is a slow burn despite his top prospect status, who maintained his potential plus hit/power combo and strong approach at every minor-league stop, against better and better pitching. He's played all around the infield and should slot in somewhere on the dirt for the 2020 Nationals. This should be our last chance to write "Kieboom goes the dynamite," so let's get that in print at least.

12. Casey Mize, RHP, Detroit Tigers

Mize looked like the best pitching prospect in baseball early in 2019, breezing through the minors with four plus-or-better pitches. That version of Mize would rank no worse than fourth on this list. But from the moment he walked off the mound in mid-June with shoulder inflammation, he simply didn't look like a budding ace anymore. When he came back a month later, his full breadth of stuff didn't come back with him, and he got shelled until he was shut down in mid-August. If we were only considering that version of Mize, without his priors, he wouldn't be a candidate for this list at all. Shoulder injuries are notoriously tricky, and the delta is now massive even though he's something like a present No. 2 starter on talent. We're taking an optimistic line for now, hoping he's back to full form, or something close to it, come spring.

13. Nick Madrigal, 2B, Chicago White Sox

In an era where strikeouts are more prevalent than ever, Madrigal struck out just 16 times in 532 plate appearances across three levels of the minors, a ludicrous stat that you'd only expect to find in pre-war baseball. Unlike fellow unicorn Willians Astudillo, the only other hitter in affiliated baseball demonstrating anything close to this kind of contact ability, Madrigal combines his bat-to-ball skills with an excellent approach. This allows him to walk at a reasonable rate even though he makes contact with nearly everything he swings at. He also offers quality second base defense and plus speed which, combined with his unusual hitting abilities, gives him a high probability of being a solid regular or better. His reasonable ceiling involves multiple batting titles and endless "how did he square *that* up?" GIFs on Twitter.

14. Marco Luciano, SS, San Francisco Giants

This might feel aggressive for a player with nine games above complex ball, but it shouldn't. Luciano signed for $2.6 million last summer and already had heat on him when he landed in Arizona that fall for instructs. It's easy to point to seven-figure IFAs who flopped quickly once stateside. We've even ranked some of them in the Top 101 in the past, but organized baseball—even in the complex—will give you a better feel for these bonus babies. The Vlad Juniors and Wander Francos separate themselves out from the Kevin Maitans and Gilbert Laras quickly. Luciano looks closer to the former, with potential plus-plus raw power generated by a swing that's a leveraged blur through the zone. He's already pretty yoked up for a 17-year-old, and he could still grow off of shortstop. It's a potential power/speed combo that could play anywhere on the diamond though. His path through the minors as an 18-year-old might not look all that different from Julio Rodriguez's and in some ways we have already baked that into this year's ranking. Like we said: it might feel aggressive, but it's justified.

15. Luis Patiño, RHP, San Diego Padres

There is a writer or two on staff that actually prefers Patiño to MacKenzie Gore among Padres prospects, and it's not crazy. Patiño is a bit less cerebral, a bit more visceral. While Gore's virtues require more focus as they unfurl over 90 or so minutes, like Schoenberg's *Erwartung*, Patiño is an easier scout. He has an explosive fastball/slider combo that announces itself early in starts, like Beethoven's Fifth Symphony—famously described by the composer as "the sound of fate knocking at the door." Patiño made it to Double-A as a 19-year-old, striking out over 30 percent of batters along the way; a Cal League batter's fate was often a quick return to the dugout. Like Gore, Patiño rounds out his arsenal with two more above-average secondaries, including a potentially impact changeup. On the other hand, Patiño hasn't even thrown 100 innings in a season yet and is a shorter righty as opposed to the tall, well-built, left-handed M Gore. Sometimes it does come down to a matter of taste, and this time we will side with the atonal opera buffs. Although we usually prefer five-tool-technique to 12-tone.

16. Kristian Robinson, OF, Arizona Diamondbacks

It wasn't an accident that Robinson snuck on the end of the 2019 101, but even we didn't think the profile would pay large dividends so quickly. He torched the Northwest League as an 18-year-old, earning a late-season promotion to the Midwest League where he hit a few bombs to dead center for Kane County on cool, late summer nights. There's plus raw power to all fields, a loose swing with plus-plus bat speed that stays in the zone, and an already advanced approach for a teenager. Robinson shows extreme athleticism both at the plate and in the field, although his large frame might end up better served in a corner outfield spot than center as it fills out. There's little question now that he will have the bat—and the arm—to carry a right field profile. Normally that would put a damper on the overall ceiling, as right fielders really have to hit. But, well, Robinson is really going to hit.

17. A.J. Puk, LHP, Oakland Athletics

The other oft-injured lefty prospect with huge stuff for Oakland, Puk's Tommy John "rehab" was storming through a few levels of the minors, and then taking a few relief innings for the Athletics in a playoff race. Like Jesus Luzardo, there's reliever risk here. In addition to the elbow scar, Puk has struggled with his control and command due to "tall pitcher problems" in his mechanics. But that delivery also gives him frightening extension on a fastball that can touch triple digits. It's a tough angle to pick up out of his hand as well, helping his upper-90s heat get on you faster than you'd think—and you'd think it would get there pretty fast. Puk pairs the fastball with a wipeout slider that sits around 90. He doesn't need much more than that to start—assuming his left elbow and command cooperate—but there's some feel for a changeup and a "slower" low-80s curve as well. There will always be the temptation to let him loose in the pen with the two 70-grade offerings as the next Andrew Miller or Josh Hader. But even if that happens, we ranked Hader around this spot a couple years ago and he's justified the ranking even in relief.

18. Dylan Carlson, OF, St. Louis Cardinals

In the interest of full disclosure, the signing scout on Carlson was Zach Mortimer, a former Baseball Prospectus prospect team member. With 20-plus alumni scattered among scouting and player development departments, this is going to happen more and more. It's easy to see why Mort got hired though, as his eye was dead on here. Carlson flashed big tools as a pro, but didn't consistently get them into games in 2018 during his time as a teenager in Peoria and Palm Beach. In 2019, everything popped. The plus raw power exploded into games. Then the Cardinals—being the Cardinals—decided he was a full-time center fielder now after playing mostly right in 2018. And wouldn't you know it, Carlson at worst could battle it to a draw, and there's above-average possibilities with more reps. You line up the updated reports—potential plus hit and power, solid arm, sneaky speed, improving glove, and all of a sudden you've got a five-tool center fielder and a top-20 prospect.

19. Nate Pearson, RHP, Toronto Blue Jays

Do you like big dudes that throw triple-digit gas with a wipeout slider? Is there anyone who doesn't? Pearson is famous as the hardest-throwing starting pitcher in baseball, and he is certainly that. He's also one of the best overall pitching prospects now, following a season of general dominance. He also finally logged a full season of innings after an injury-laden 2018, and we're a bit more confident that he can stick as a starter now. The "fallback" option here might be more fun, if not quite as valuable. Able to dump it out for a single inning in the 2019 Futures Game, Pearson sat a lively 99-101 and flashed an 80-grade slider, putting an alternate outcome where he ends up as an elite closer squarely in the mind's eye.

20. Michael Kopech, RHP, Chicago White Sox

After ranking 24th last year knowing he'd just had Tommy John surgery, this was a bit of a foregone conclusion. By all accounts, Kopech has had an uneventful rehab and should be a full go for spring training. Assuming full health—and there's always some risk with Tommy John rehabs until they're all the way back—Kopech possesses one of the most gifted arms around. Even the dialed back version of his fastball he was throwing in the majors in 2018 is a heavy pitch in the upper-90s, and he hit 100 multiple times for Steve Givarz while rehabbing in instructs last October. Command often lags behind after elbow reconstructions, and Kopech's command was inconsistent before all this, so that's something to watch early this season.

21. Royce Lewis, SS, Minnesota Twins

Another bit of favored shorthand around the Prospect Team offices, er, Slack Channel, is "it just looks right." Eventually, most, if not all, of these prospects will make the majors and their performance will be laid bare for you in the preceding pages of this tome. Until then though, aesthetics can count for almost as much as stats. A lot of evaluation is running through a mental catalog of comparisons to major leaguers past and present, and we can't think of a major leaguer that makes Lewis' current swing work. The fact that he wasn't completely underwater statistically in 2019 is a testament to his hand/eye coordination and incredible hand speed, but he struggled mightily to stay in sync and get his bat through the zone last season, something chronicled in depth by Keanan Lamb out of the Florida State League. Lewis is a premium athlete, and he's maybe only a couple tweaks away from unlocking an All-Star upside. For right now, it doesn't look right.

22. Cristian Pache, OF, Atlanta Braves

Pache is the best defensive outfield prospect in the game, with plus-plus tools on the grass. That was true last year too, but what's changed in the interim is the offensive projection. Not all that long ago, Pache combined being a wild free swinger with limited strength; this led to a whole lot of off-balance, weak contact. He's added substantial upper-body strength over the past year while also gaining control over his swing. This has led to not just better present offensive outcomes but much better projection. If you combine his defensive profile with even an average offensive outcome, he's a first-division regular. If he's just a bit more than that with the stick, he's going to be a star, and that's firmly in play now.

23. Nolan Gorman, 3B, St. Louis Cardinals

Third-base profiles are tricky. The best third base prospects may be present shortstops—glance up to Kieboom, Luciano, or Royce Lewis above—and Gorman is a large enough human that there's going to be moderate concern he might slide further down the defensive spectrum in his 20s. But while third base is considered to be somewhere in the middle of the defensive spectrum, it carries a high offensive bar as well. In 2019 third basemen slugged .455, right in line with both corner outfield spots and first base. Wherever he ends up, the slugging should not be a problem for Gorman who has plus-plus raw power and should be able to get to all of it in major-league games given time to refine his swing and approach. At that point it's less important where he stands, but he's athletic for his size and passable at the hot corner with a plus arm. He may not end up the best third baseman on this list, but the present package is the best third base prospect in baseball.

24. Deivi Garcia, RHP, New York Yankees

As pitching roles in the majors have become amorphous, so too have role projections for pitching prospects. In the past, even the recent past, Garcia would've been consigned to a relief projection and likely been further down this list for it. He's extremely short—listed at 5-foot-9—and when ranking pitchers that short, it was largely assumed they'd be relievers until evidence proved otherwise. It's possible Garcia won't be able to handle a full starting workload as we envisioned it even a decade ago, but those workloads are petering out already. He threw over 110 innings in the minors last year, and even if he caps out around there, teams have gotten much more creative on how to leverage those innings. If he gets to much more than that, he's pretty close to a modern starting workload. Garcia certainly has the stuff, with a new slider combining with his explosive mid-90s fastball, sharp curve and developing change to give him four pitches that project to above-average or better.

25. Joey Bart, C, San Francisco Giants

Bart's reign as best catching prospect in baseball lasted for precisely one year, right up until Rob Manfred announced Adley Rutschman's name as the first-overall pick from the podium in Secaucus last summer. Mr. Congeniality acquitted himself well in 2019, although he missed time with a fracture on his left hand, and then had his AFL campaign ended early by a fractured thumb on his right. In between, he showcased plus power and promising defense behind the plate, the calling cards as an amateur that made him the second overall pick in 2018. There's some stiffness in the swing, and Bart is unlikely to contend for batting titles, but the offensive bar for catchers is low and he should easily hop over it via 20-plus bombs, while providing plus defense. Oh, and in case you didn't know, unlike Rutschman, he did call his own games in college.

26. Forrest Whitley, RHP, Houston Astros

A thorough albeit not exhaustive timeline of Whitley's last two seasons:

- Suspended 50 games for using a banned stimulant to help him drive back from a college basketball game during the 2017 offseason
- Suffers a left oblique injury a month into his delayed 2018 campaign, is limited to 26 1/3 innings overall
- Looks like the best pitching prospect in baseball in the Arizona Fall League
- Shut down with shoulder fatigue two months into a disastrous 2019 campaign
- Struggles on rehab in the GCL where his mechanics look like a mess
- Slowly rounds back into form in Double-A, although control and command issues continue
- Looks like the best pitching prospect in baseball in the Arizona Fall League...again

We held the line after 2018, but this is now two functionally lost seasons for Whitley, who has thrown a total of 138 innings over the last two calendar years, and has added arm issues to go with the inconsistent stuff. When he's right—usually in Arizona in front of half the baseball universe—he's got four plus-or-better pitches, not all that dissimilar from Casey Mize. We have our concerns about Mize as well, outlined above, but he's been better and healthier more recently than Whitley. With a pitcher this talented, you run it back again in 2020, but we really weren't expecting to still be writing about him at this point.

27. Sixto Sánchez, RHP, Miami Marlins

If you're going to give up the best catcher in baseball in his age-28 season for a short pitching prospect, it better be a hell of a short pitching prospect. The Marlins flipped J.T. Realmuto to the Phillies last February for a prospect package led by Sánchez, who is indeed a hell of a pitching prospect of any size. Sánchez sits in the high-90s and regularly gets into triple-digits with his fastball. He also throws a changeup, which he gives a few different looks to, and multiple breaking balls, all of which show as at least average offerings. Earlier in his career it looked like he'd be able to push one of those many offerings into plus-or-better territory. Instead, he's rounding into having a bundle of average-to-above-average offspeed pitches that confuse hitters without necessarily dominating them—that shows up in strikeout rates that have trended towards good instead of great. It's worth waiting another year or two to see if something jumps, because there's absolutely ace upside here. He maintains No. 2 starter or high-end closer potential even if the fastball velocity remains the flashiest part.

28. Brendan McKay, LHP/DH, Tampa Bay Rays

It has been obvious for a few years now that McKay was more promising as a pitcher than a hitter, but 2019 made Tampa Bay's intentions fully clear. He's major-league ready there, a polished lefty with a beautiful curveball and strong command. His velocity ticked up a notch or two in 2019, and he was more regularly hitting the mid-90s than he had in the past by the time he was in the majors. The Rays repossessed McKay's first base glove early in spring training, deciding to only use him as a pitcher and a designated hitter. While still in the minors, he was the DH around three or four times a week, on quiet days in his pitching cycle. While in the majors, he barely hit at all. He did get one spot start and a handful of appearances as a pinch-hitter, but for the most part he was used as a normal AL starting pitcher. For now, we'll consider McKay a ready, high-probability mid-rotation lefty with a touch of additional upside on the chance his bat catches up.

29. Bobby Witt Jr., SS, Kansas City Royals

Sometimes, baseball bloodlines manifest in profile similarities. There's exactly one shared trait between Bobby Witt, Jr. and his famous baseball father: draft pedigree. Bobby Witt, Sr. was the drafted third overall by the Texas Rangers in 1985, 34 years before his son went second overall to the Royals. Past that, well, there's not a lot in common. Senior was a college pitcher who quickly made The Show on his way to an itinerant career as a fourth starter type. Junior is a toolsy prep shortstop with plus power, a quick bat and the defensive chops for short. He's also raw, and is going to need substantial time in the minors to develop his hit tool. Senior never made the All-Star Game and while Junior has all the ability needed to reach that level and beyond, past prospect lists are littered with hitters who had everything else but never hit.

30. Shane Baz, RHP, Tampa Bay Rays

The Chris Archer trade is, uh, not working out well for the Pirates. Austin Meadows made the All-Star game, hitting .290 and swatting 33 home runs. The Rays waved a magic wand over Tyler Glasnow, which erased his control issues and left a dominant—when healthy—starter. Baz was the player to be named later in the deal, and all he managed in 2019 was a breakout season that places him just outside the top 10 pitching prospects in baseball. This was somewhat foreseeable: He was an intriguing power arm as a Texas prep that went 12th overall in the 2017 draft. On the back of mid-90s heat and a polished-for-his-age slider. The fastball bumps the upper 90s consistently now, and the slider is plus, flashing higher. His other offerings lag behind the first two,

understandably, but his frame is that of a starting pitcher and he should be able to stick in the rotation if he can get a third pitch to the vicinity of average.

31. Andrew Vaughn, 1B, Chicago White Sox

Player development has been getting more scientific of late, with teams increasingly relying on data gathered from Trackman, Rapsodo, Edgertronic and the like as inputs. Evaluation has historically tended more towards art, but those same developmental systems are put to use for evaluation by analytics departments. Most of that information is not made public, and what is publicized is often lacking context. Vaughn is a short, hit-first, right-handed college first baseman, which is a profile that really has to hit to make it because there's no path to substantial secondary value. That he was drafted third overall despite the "limited" profile is a valuable bit of data. The expected leaks about elite exit velocity and batted ball profile have since come to fruition, and Ben Spanier projected him as a plus hit, plus power player in his Carolina League coverage following the draft. Hit tool projection is perhaps the last remaining art form when it comes to player evaluation, and even its days avoiding data are dwindling. Whether Vaughn ends up above-average, plus, or plus-plus will make a dramatic difference in his overall profile, but there's reason to be confident it will play despite the high baseline for his position.

32. Brusdar Graterol, RHP, Minnesota Twins

It's easy to look at the short, stocky right-hander with a checkered injury history—including a Tommy John as a teenager—and just chuck him in the reliever bin. The Twins thought as much and used him as a reliever after he came back from a shoulder impingement last summer. And, hey, Brusdar would likely be a dominant late-inning reliever. He boasts an easy upper-90s fastball with movement as a starter, and his sinker *sat* 99 in a late-season relief cameo in the Twin Cities. He pairs it with a firm, upper-80s slider that snaps off late on bewildered batters. The change is fringy but there's enough feel for it for it to at least keep lefties honest, and he's surprisingly athletic for a listed 265 pounds. So yeah, maybe he's just a reliever. We're still okay with ranking him here if that's the case, but we'd like to see what he can do with the ball in his hand every fifth day. And it's not like the 2020 Twins have a plethora of more interesting options.

33. CJ Abrams, SS, San Diego Padres

Abrams was one of the higher-variance prospects at the top of the 2019 Draft, and he slipped to the sixth pick, despite an insane athletic projection, due to concerns that he might not drive the ball enough against professional pitching. He proceeded to go out and hit over .400 with power in the Arizona League, and while complex league stats don't engender much faith, doing that is certainly better than not doing it. More importantly, our feedback from his time in the AZL indicated he was, indeed, driving the ball more and that some of the concerns from before the draft had already been allayed. Abrams might ultimately end up in center field à la Billy Hamilton, where he has some amateur experience, and we'd expect him to be quite good out there if it comes to pass. He doesn't quite have Hamilton's speed—nobody does—but he has a swing far more suited to gap power and perhaps a touch beyond.

34. Heliot Ramos, OF, San Francisco Giants

Prospect development isn't linear; often it isn't even unidirectional. Ramos has been a bit of a sine curve since being drafted. Strong post-draft reports in 2017—flagging all his tools as average-or-better—came quickly from the complex and an aggressive ranking for a late first-round draft pick followed. Ramos scuffled a bit in the South Atlantic League the following season as an 18-year-old, and the tools our staff saw were a bit more muted. The power/speed combo was still there, but so was an overly-aggressive approach exploited by full-season college arms. Everything also looked a little more corner outfield like. Something clicked in 2019 though, and from the first reports in the Cal League in April, the five tools were flashing again. Ramos is likely to end up in right field—although he should be quite good there—but with the volume turned back up, and possible 30-home-run pop to come, he sure looks like a Top 50 prospect in baseball. And we are happy to co-sign that.

35. JJ Bleday, OF, Miami Marlins

Bleday is the archetypal top college bat. A potential plus/hit power combo from a sweet lefty swing, experience up-the-middle in the NCAA, but athletic tools that fit better in a corner, and a long track record of mashing in a major conference. A middle-of-the-order stalwart for the College World Series champs, Vanderbilt, Bleday's junior year was marked by the raw power that was promised by his swing finding its way into games. There isn't as much upside as some of the prep bats drafted around him, but Bleday is very likely to be a high-quality player for five or six years, with a leisurely decline as an average starter, then bench bat. When David Roth is remembering some guys in 2045 or so, Bleday will be one of them, and the memories will be fond, perhaps Ryan Klesko-esque.

36. Spencer Howard, RHP, Philadelphia Phillies

Howard was one of the most painful cuts from this list last year. There is never enough room for all that could stick at the bottom: balancing high-upside players on the precipice of breaking out into national names and high-floor players likely to provide a significant contribution is a tricky one to strike. Howard certainly broke out in 2019, dominating two levels and the Arizona Fall League with a mid-to-high-90s fastball and a plus slider/changeup combo. Were it not for a

shoulder injury that cost him a couple months in the early part of the summer, he probably would've reached the majors, and he might've anyway if the Phillies had been stronger contenders in September. He's close to ready on talent, but he might not have enough stamina built up to be a mid-rotation starter for the entirety of 2020.

37. Leody Taveras, OF, Texas Rangers

The Baseball Prospectus Top 101 List is a team effort generated by discussion amongst 20 or so writers and evaluators. This is not one writer's pref list. It is not beholden to industry consensus. It's the product of the prospect *team*. So we use "we" when writing these blurbs. However, Leody Taveras's spot—Top 50 prospect for three years running now—is mostly the doing of our Lead Prospect Writer, Jeffrey Paternostro. It's very likely he wrote the blurb you are reading now. The offensive performance has never been amazing, even after adjusting for how young Taveras has been for his levels. This year he got to Double-A as a 20-year-old and held his own, and there were accompanying good reports from our Texas League staffers. And even if he doesn't hit much more than he has so far, the defensive profile is strong. Taveras is a plus center fielder with a plus arm and foot speed to spare. Ender Inciarte has been worth almost 20 WARP for his career with slash lines that look similar to what Taveras has done so far. Perhaps the glove isn't quite *that* good, and maybe Inciarte isn't exactly what you are looking for in the 37th best prospect in baseball, but that outcome is above the median for this spot, and Taveras will still flash plus raw from both sides. It's getting less likely it will all click for him at the plate each year it doesn't. But we (I) am still going to hold out hope.

38. Ian Anderson, RHP, Atlanta Braves

For the second year in a row, Anderson was right on the border for our OFP (Overall Future Potential) grades, with our team debating whether he was a "soft 70" or a "hard 60." We have considered the OFP grade to represent a reasonable future ceiling projection, something akin to a 75th-percentile outcome for a projection system. (All of the prospects on the list this year are in the 70 OFP to 55 OFP band, and there are some 55s who didn't make it.) Translated from scout speak, a 70 for pitchers represents a No. 2 starter and a 60 represents a No. 3 starter. Anderson still has a shot for top-of-the-rotation outcomes, and we're not really down on him in any substantial way from last year. We just think he's a touch less likely to hit a top-of-the-rotation outcome (perhaps 20 percent instead of 25 percent) since he hasn't taken a major step forward in stuff and the command hasn't sharpened out yet. As our former Minor League Editor and current Editor-In-Chief Craig Goldstein has imparted on us many times: if you have to ask yourself this hard if a guy is a 70, he's probably a 60.

39. Logan Gilbert, RHP, Seattle Mariners

Have you ever heard of Stetson University? It's a private school nestled between Orlando and Daytona Beach—not a small school per se, but on the smaller side for Division I baseball. They play baseball in the mid-major Sun Belt Conference, and they've been pretty successful in recent years. In 2018, they made the NCAA World Series Super-Regionals for the first time ever behind staff ace Gilbert. He would soon become the highest draft pick in school history, 14th overall that year to the Mariners. He's a prototypical strong mid-rotation prospect: tall with advanced command and pitchability, moving through the minors quickly with a four pitch-mix. Despite being the best *prospect* the school has ever produced, Gilbert has next-to-no chance to be the best *pitcher* the school has produced, for the group of 10 Stetson alums that have made the majors includes both Jacob deGrom and Corey Kluber. Good luck living up to that legacy.

40. Alec Bohm, 3B, Philadelphia Phillies

Baseball teams have gotten better at fitting square pegs into round holes recently. Bohm has the body and defensive skills that would, under normal circumstances, best lend themselves to playing first base. Except the Phillies have Rhys Hoskins at first base, and they've already tried Hoskins in the outfield to dubious results. Bohm isn't great at third base either, and he has the limited range you'd expect from someone around his height (6-foot-5) who isn't named "Scott Rolen." But despite mediocre footwork, he projects to around fringe-average there thanks to a solid arm and improving instincts. That's exactly the kind of infielder you can hide with aggressive shifting and perhaps a defensive caddy, and he's athletic enough overall to make the corner outfield a future option if things become untenable at third. Bohm is a disciplined, advanced hitter on the verge of getting to all of his plus-plus raw power, and is going to force his way to the big leagues pretty soon.

41. Nico Hoerner, SS/2B/OF, Chicago Cubs

When Javier Baez broke his thumb at the beginning of September, the Cubs turned to Hoerner to man shortstop for the home stretch. He wasn't ready—he'd only had 375 professional plate appearances total, and he was putting up a 104 DRC+ in the Southern League, barely above league-average—but the Cubs lacked a shortstop on their 40-man in a desperate pennant race. Given the less-than-ideal circumstances, Hoerner performed with aplomb, giving the Cubs steady defense and competitive at-bats. He has a short swing with excellent bat-to-ball skills, projecting for a future plus hit tool, and those skills kept him above water in the majors. With Baez entrenched at short in Wrigley for the foreseeable future, the Cubs started working Hoerner at second base and center field in 2019, which are also good fits for his speed and athleticism. His power...well, the good

news is that he hit as many homers in the majors as he did in a half-season in Double-A, and the bad news is that the number was three. He should be back in the bigs to stay at some point in 2020.

42. Drew Waters, OF, Atlanta Braves

"Waters or Pache?" has been a popular Braves prospect parlor game ever since Waters was drafted as a prep bat in 2017. They're both tool-laden center fielders who were born about a month apart, so it's an easy connection to make. Pache has pulled away for now, but that's no knock on Waters, who has done nothing but hit. Waters has blown through all four full-season minor-league levels, reaching Triple-A last August at just 20 years old. He has an advanced hit tool, especially from the left side, but we're still unsure if he's ever going to loft the ball enough to get above-average game power. He played almost all of the 2019 season alongside Pache, and they split time between center and the corners, with Pache spending a bit more time in center. Waters would have a chance to carry the position elsewhere, but in an organization with Ronald Acuña and Pache that defensive projection for center is going to be purely academic.

43. Jordan Groshans, SS, Toronto Blue Jays

Groshans was one of the big early-season breakout prospects of 2019. The 12th-overall pick in 2018 made the jump to full-season ball as a teenager and dominated in April, looking more like a college draftee than a 19-year-old prep. Then he suffered a foot injury in May and had a series of setbacks that ultimately ended his season. Groshans was already likely to slide from shortstop to third base because of size and lack of foot speed, and we reckon that process will be sped up by the injury. He has a strong hit-and-power profile and surprising offensive polish for his age, but that he missed so much time is a bit alarming. The tools that he was flashing warrant a top-25 placement, if not higher, and he's expected to be ready for spring training, so some aggression is still warranted.

44. Sean Murphy, C, Oakland Athletics

The skillset of the major-league backstop is broad, and while traditionally they were evaluated on pop time and bat—framing and game calling are the current water cooler subjects—there's also a host of soft skills they need to manage a modern pitching staff. Murphy checks pretty much every catcher-skill box and he has a major-league cameo under his belt. There is, however, a top line concern remaining: We don't know if he's durable enough to handle the physical rigors of the everyday catcher. He is already dealing with knee issues in his mid-20s and, well, the job requires a lot of squatting. Murphy has never caught more than 91 games in a season, and this year managed only 53. If there was more certainty he could spend the next six to eight years catching 100-120 games a season, he'd be further up this list; the glove (an easy plus) and power (ditto) could land him on a few All-Star teams. Catcher can be a war of attrition, and Murphy has yet to fortify a Maginot Line.

45. Grayson Rodriguez, RHP, Baltimore Orioles

Rodriguez is straight off the touted assembly line of prep pitchers from Texas: a tall and sturdy righty flashing big stuff. He went a long way towards actualizing his projection in the 2019 season, showing marked improvement as the season wore on, sitting 94-97 and throwing five pitches in a late-August showing. There's still a bit of rawness present in the profile: There's enough bleed between his curveball and slider to the point where he'd be best off picking one or the other, and a new hard cutter is only in the nascent stages of development. The late-season Rodriguez/Rutschman battery that the Orioles assembled in Delmarva points to a tantalizing future for a team that has little hope in the present.

46. Jasson Dominguez, OF, New York Yankees

The hype surrounding Dominguez is as out of this world as his nickname, "The Martian." He's billed as a five-tool outfielder, prodigiously advanced for his age. The Yankees dumped out nearly their entire 2019-20 international pool to sign him. The comps are lofty and colorful; Mike Trout was repeatedly brought up in an article by ESPN's Jeff Passan before Dominguez signed, and that's as lofty a comp as you can get in modern baseball. He's yet to play an official game, but he excelled in instructs, and the video we've reviewed supports the hype. Yet we just don't have the depth of information about Dominguez that we have about every other player on this list, and that makes him the trickiest player of all to rank. He doesn't have the extensive amateur foundation that similarly touted draftees do, let alone any significant pro foundation. It was only three years ago that we ranked Kevin Maitan at a similar stage of development and hype, and Maitan is perilously close to being an out-and-out bust. If Dominguez comes stateside this year and is as advertised, he'll surely be dozens of spots up the 101 next year. We're going to need to see it happen, though.

47. Matt Manning, RHP, Detroit Tigers

Another year, another step toward the majors. Manning passed the Double-A test with relative ease in 2019, although our in-person reports continue to be just a touch below the overall hype on him. He's a tall pitcher who extends well, which might cause the mid-90s fastball to play up a bit from the raw velocity. He throws a plus curveball already, an advanced pitch with true two-plane break. The changeup is coming along insomuch as it flashes usefulness—or even more—now, whereas in prior years it was a straight show-me pitch. In many ways, this is our first "plus fastball and breaking ball, but he needs to improve the changeup or

command" third-starter entry of this list, although Manning has better command and less relief risk than most in that class. Which is why he's the highest-ranked of them.

48. Ronny Mauricio, SS, New York Mets

Mauricio's slash line in the South Atlantic League looks like a player just keeping his head above water, but our staff reports describe a projectable teenager with a potential plus hit/power combo due to good bat speed and enough hand-eye to cover for a presently raw approach. Mauricio may slide over to third as he ages, but he'd be above-average there with a plus arm, and it's not a lock he moves off the six. The overeager approach needs to be ironed out or he'll generate more bad contact than is ideal, making the power play down to average-or-a-tick-above. If the downside comp sounds a little like Wilmer Flores, well, that's a little lazy, but not wildly inaccurate, and Flores ranked in this range on prospect lists once upon a time.

49. Riley Greene, OF, Detroit Tigers

If there is a central casting office for "fifth-overall pick prep outfielder," Riley Greene would be the top headshot on the pile. He has a lean, projectable frame; one you can see growing into plus power, which he already flashes pull side in batting practice. There's also plus bat speed with lift and the contact makes *that* sound. He's an above-average runner, although his present routes in the outfield are crude and as he grows into his body he might be sliding to a corner, regardless. Greene showed some rawness against same-side spin, and he can get long with his swing, but that's all expected for a high schooler figuring things out during his first pro summer. There's nothing too loud here—if that were the case he'd be cast as "first overall prep outfielder"—but as 18-year-olds go, Greene is a high-probability regular with some first-division upside.

50. Matthew Liberatore, LHP, Tampa Bay Rays

In evaluating Liberatore's fortunes for 2019 we said he'd "shoot pretty far up the list with 120 healthy innings." He came up about 40 innings short. The Rays held him back in extended spring to start the season and abbreviated his outings late in the season, both in the name of load management. In between, he was one of the most advanced arms in the Low-A Midwest League, despite pitching the entire season as a 19-year-old. Liberatore possesses a full four-pitch arsenal and, as a smooth lefty with a plus overhand curve, he certainly has fine aesthetics for a pitching prospect. He lacks the high upside or certainty necessary to be higher than this, but a small jump in his stuff or continued strong performance and health would propel him into the top tier of pitching prospects.

51. Brandon Marsh, OF, Los Angeles Angels

The Angels have a type in the draft and it's "athletic high school football players." Marsh was a highly-recruited wide receiver out of Buford High School in Georgia, and although his long-term future was always likely on the diamond, he retains a lot of his football athleticism. The multi-sport prep prospect—Marsh played basketball as well—implies a certain amount of baseball rawness in this era of early specialization, but Marsh is already a polished hitter as well with advanced bat-to-ball skills. He's a plus runner of course, with a shot to stick in center field—although he's unlikely to man it in Angel Stadium. The one missing tool at the moment is game power. Although Marsh is tall and strong, he doesn't consistently elevate the ball. If he can unlock some of his plus raw power in games, the 2022 *Angels in the Outfield* remake might feature a trio of All-Stars on the movie poster.

52. Jazz Chisholm, SS, Miami Marlins

Double-A can be a real Point of Departure for even good hitting prospects. The jump from the low minors is tricky; better velocity, better breaking stuff, older arms with major-league experience who knows exactly how to leave you feeling Kind of Blue. Jazz swings hard and often, and while his raw power can boom like Heavy Weather, Double-A pitchers figured out how to pitch to him on his Maiden Voyage at the level. Prospects always deserve Time Out to adjust though, and Chisholm hit .257/.340/.459 after June 1st. That will play, and gives a feel for what The Shape of Jazz to Come might look like. "Might" is doing some heavy lifting there though, as Double-A to the majors requires some Giant Steps. The shortstop glove is just about ready for the bigs though, and if the bat catches up in the next year or two, Marlins fans will be Moanin' in anticipation of his arrival in Miami. And I will Speak No Evil about Jazz either, because his power stroke is one of My Favorite Things. You've heard The Best of the Hot 5 and 7, and Jazz is a Hot 6.

53. Mitch Keller, RHP, Pittsburgh Pirates

Keller was two innings from graduating from this list, which would've saved a difficult discussion about how much we have to consider the context in which he's failing to blossom. His major-league performance was one part disastrous (the airplane ERA) and two parts okay (an above-average DRA and plenty of strikeouts). The fastball was still mid-90s and touching 98, but it got absolutely tattooed; opposing hitters hit .461 and slugged .719 off it. The curveball still flashes huge, but he didn't throw it all that much. Instead, Keller favored a slider that mostly replaced his underdeveloped and mediocre changeup, and it's not clear that's the right answer either. The Pirates have had long-standing issues developing pitchers and Keller's recent lack of progress sure looks like the latest manifestation of that. It may be overly cheeky to suggest that his most likely path to success is to end up on a smarter team, but... [**waves in the direction of Gerrit Cole and Tyler Glasnow**]

54. Alek Thomas, OF, Arizona Diamondbacks

Prospect writers love three things above all else: two-and-a-half hour games with no mid-inning pitching changes, a Panera Bread just off the interstate and sweet lefty swings. There's just something more aesthetically pleasing about the perfect southpaw swat. In Thomas' case, function follows form as everything is balanced and in sync, and his controlled aggression at the plate rips line drives from gap-to-gap. It's not an emphatic batting practice, punctuated by 400-foot bombs—and the power projection is fringy at present—but there's a pleasant rhythm at the plate, a Chopin piano concerto. Yeah, it just looks right (and just sounds right). The swing plays at seven o'clock too, as the 19-year-old hit .300 between two A-ball levels. Oh yeah, and Thomas is a potential plus center fielder with plus speed. It's an intriguing package of tools, but we are happy just to watch him take some hacks as the sun starts to set, the rest of the game blurring at the edges and then fading into the background, as he fires another ball to right-center to the strains of a faintly heard Steinway.

55. Oneil Cruz, SS, Pittsburgh Pirates

Cruz is 6-foot-7, about three inches taller than what we usually think of as the upper-bound for shortstop height. Athletically, he more resembles an ACC power forward or SEC defensive end than a shortstop prospect. Yet he's played every game over the past two seasons at short, and is fairly rangy and nimble at present. There is no real comp for where he might ultimately land defensively; there's never been a left-side infielder this tall, let alone a shortstop, and he's filling out as he ages. At the plate, he has long levers with titanic raw power and better natural feel for hitting than you'd otherwise expect. The most likely outcome by his mid-20s remains a power-hitting corner outfielder, but truly weird prospects are the ones that break the mold, and Cruz certainly qualifies.

56. Brendan Rodgers, SS, Colorado Rockies

Eons ago in prospect terms, when Taylor Swift's "Bad Blood" topped the charts, Rodgers was selected third overall in the draft behind fellow shortstops Dansby Swanson and Alex Bregman. Since then, Bregman won a World Series ring and scored himself a nine-figure contract extension. Swanson doesn't boast quite the same CV, but he's a solid regular with amazing hair. Rodgers is afforded a longer lead time as a prep product, but it's been a rocky road (sorry) even in the upper minors. He still touts a potential plus hit/power combination, but has been limited by an aggressive approach, and a labrum tear ended his 2019 early after a less-than-inspiring cup of coffee. There is probably some prospect fatigue, but it would be nice to see him dominate a level for an extended period of time. If that comes to pass, he won't be ranked here—or at all.

57. Ryan Mountcastle, 1B, Baltimore Orioles

Mountcastle has become a bit of a meme for our prospect team. Every list, midseason 50 or offseason 101, team or national, we end up staring at our final draft wondering how he ended up so high. Over five list cycles, he's moved from shortstop to third base—was there some outfield in there, we don't recall—and now finally, inevitably to first. And over the last few years he's ranked somewhere in this general range as a national prospect because every time we are finalizing a list, we look down at the names below him and ask "are they really going to hit more than Ryan Mountcastle?" The answer is inevitably no. Because wherever he stands on the field, he hits. Mountcastle capped off his minor league career by batting .312 with 25 bombs and 35 doubles as a 22-year-old in Triple-A. It's an effective swing from the right side, good bat speed, good feel for the barrel, some loft. And while we may roll our eyes internally every time he ends up ahead of a toolsy shortstop in A-ball or projectable draftee with a big fastball and hook, but there isn't really a better list-making strategy than "bet on the guy who you think will hit."

58. George Valera, OF, Cleveland Indians

Valera came stateside in 2018 after signing a $1.3 million dollar IFA deal the previous summer. He mashed for a week before promptly breaking his hamate bone, which ended his season. He struggled at times in 2019, following a tough assignment to the New York-Penn League. His swing features some moving parts—including a bit of waggle and a large step in to close his wide open stance—but he flashed more game power than you'd expect given the present frame and swing plane. The setup may be a bit unorthodox, but once Valera starts to move his hands forward, the bat speed is ferocious and…well, just looks right. There's enough hand-eye and barrel velocity that he can hang back on offspeed, although he's still developing an eye for spin generally. So while it's unusual to project a .300 hitter from a prospect that just hit .230 in short-season, Valera has a swing to dream on.

59. Nick Lodolo, LHP, Cincinnati Reds

A rare two-time first-rounder (unsigned in the compensatory first by the Pirates in 2016, signed as the seventh pick by the Reds last year), Lodolo was outrageously good in a small sample after signing, striking out 30 and walking none in 18 1/3 innings. Over the course of a three-year starting run at TCU, he grew from a tall, skinny kid with projection to a polished, well-rounded starting prospect that can hold velocity in the mid-90s and projects for two above-average-to-plus offspeed pitches. He was used lightly after the draft following a college campaign where he went over 100 innings, but he was far too good for hitters at the short-

season or Low-A levels. Lodolo is a high probability No. 3 starter prospect, and is expected to move pretty quickly once stretched out as a pro.

60. Kyle Muller, LHP, Atlanta Braves

When drafted in 2016, Muller was your classic projectable prep arm with promising feel for spin, and he took a few seasons to get going in the minors. After several offseasons working with Driveline—one of the epicenters of rapid and significant change within player development—on velocity maximization, he's now consistently in the mid-to-high-90s from the left side with two average-or-better secondaries, a true power starter or closer in the making. Muller is not the only pitcher on this list who is affiliated with Driveline, but he epitomizes current industry trends of players seeking to improve themselves outside of the team player development system and actually doing so.

61. Josiah Gray, RHP, Los Angeles Dodgers

Gray is the perfect pitching prospect to kick off a little game we like to call: future mid-rotation starter or closer? He has a plus fastball—mid-90s, heavy with run. He has a potential plus breaker too—a firm, mid-80s slider with sweep that can miss bats in the minors, but needs a bit more two-plane action to project as a bat misser in the majors. The change flashes, but is seldom used with less than ideal velocity separation off the heater. The command is actually okay, but he can have his rough patches. He's still a bit of a raw arm, as he converted from shortstop at small, cold-weather LeMoyne College, and was only a full-time pitcher his junior year. That might mean there's a bit more upside in his lightly-worn right arm. It also means there is a fair bit of bullpen risk. Same as it ever was.

62. Evan White, 1B, Seattle Mariners

The natural endgame to service time manipulation is the type of contract White signed last fall. The former first-rounder made significant gains at Double-A last year and now projects as an above-average hitter with unusual defensive prowess for the position. He's added game power over the past two seasons, getting to average from fringe, though average power is still not a lot for first base. He's almost ready, but the Mariners stood to claw back an extra year of team control by keeping him down just a few weeks this spring. Instead, he signed a long-term contract that has options extending through 2028. The team gets a huge bargain if White becomes a star and a moderate one as long as he's a solid regular, and White locks in $24 million guaranteed before playing a game in Triple-A, much less the majors. That's generational wealth and financial security for his family, years before he'd have otherwise seen the money, and all of a sudden he has a strong shot at being the Opening Day first baseman. It's easy to understand all the motivations here, and it is a win/win deal, if only one ignores all the coercive factors of baseball's economic structure for young players.

63. Ke'Bryan Hayes, 3B, Pittsburgh Pirates

It felt like this was going to be the year Hayes started hitting for power and staked his claim as one of the best position player prospects in baseball. And that was before there were any signs that the Triple-A ball was going to travel like a V-2 rocket. Instead he went out and had another very Ke'Bryan Hayes season—plenty of doubles and great defense at third base, but not much over-the-fence power. That's a useful player, but as mentioned previously, there is a certain slugging standard for the hot corner. Hayes can make up the gap in other ways—that plus-plus glove certainly helps—but the wait continues to see if he can adjust the launch angle on those laser beams off his bat. Even if he doesn't, Hayes projects as a solid everyday guy at third, but—fair or unfair—it feels a bit disappointing.

64. Brady Singer, RHP, Kansas City Royals

Singer is a bit of a different bird. Usually it's command and third pitch concerns keeping prospects in this range from the next tier up. Singer's stuff isn't quite as good as Gray or Muller's, but his command and ability to mix pitches makes everything play up. The stuff isn't fringy by any means, he can touch 95 and move the fastball this way and that, and there's a solid-average slider he can manipulate the action on. The change can be a bit fringy, so that fits with his list cohort at least. Singer has a good frame and a track record of durability. Nothing jumps off the scouting report, but it just all works. "He just knows how to pitch" is a meaningless cliche—nebulous and imprecise—but when you watch Singer, you get what it means.

65. Miguel Vargas, 3B, Los Angeles Dodgers

When you think of 14-year-old prodigies, you might think of Bobby Fischer or Samuel Barber or Jennifer Capriati. Fischer was a U.S. Chess Champion at 14, Barber was at the Curtis School of Music studying piano, Capriati made the semifinals of the French Open. Miguel Vargas was playing in the Cuban Serie Nacional de Béisbol, nearly 13 years younger than the average player. He went a fairly anemic 3-for-26, which might give him more in common with Joe Nuxhall, another famous teenaged baseball debutante. Nuxhall returned to the majors nine years later and carved out a 15-year career, even making a couple All-Star Games. It shouldn't take Vargas that long to find his way to Los Angeles. At 19, he hit .300 between two A-ball levels and the offensive prowess is every bit as precocious as that makes it sound. In fact every tool here grades out as average-or-better. Vargas is a smooth third baseman with soft hands and quick reflexes. He should grow into above-average power in his twenties to pair with the plus hit tool. He's a true two-way third-baseman, and he might make a couple All-Star Games himself.

66. Nolan Jones, 3B, Cleveland Indians

On the opposite side of the spectrum, Jones is not a true two-way third baseman. He might not even be a third baseman; he has a plus arm, but the hands have yet to improve enough to stick at the hot corner. His body is filling out such that he might end up just being a better fit in an outfield corner or even first base. He has the outer contours of an elite patience-and-power approach, with a vicious uppercut swing geared to tap into plus-plus raw and bat speed. The barrel control isn't there yet, and the resulting swing-and-miss both limits his hit tool projection and the ability to get to all of the raw power in games at present. There are building blocks here for stardom, but he's a few major adjustments away from actually getting there.

67. Luis Campusano, C, San Diego Padres

At present, any time we talk about the defensive skill set for a catcher, first and foremost is their ability to frame strikes. Robot umps, with which the MLB Umpires Association recently agreed to cooperate, obliterate the need for that skill set. This comes far too late for the Ryan Doumits of the world—perhaps just in time for the Zack Collinses—but Campusano might be a beneficiary, albeit in an indirect way. Although his defensive skills have been improving, he is an offensive-minded catcher with above-average hit and power tools. He's an athletic backstop and good at blocking balls, and will regularly pop 1.8 or 1.9 on throws. His throwing mechanics and actions can get out of sorts though, which has allowed baserunners in the minors to run a bit rampant on him. If he only had to focus on the man on first when the pitch is coming in, rather than his body and hand positions, it might allow him to clean up those caught-stealing rates, which are poised to become a bigger part of overall catching defense in our Post-Skynet world. This is all a hypothetical intellectual exercise, and either way, Campusano would be of the top catching prospects in baseball, but this could be a seismic change for catcher development and evaluation going forward.

68. Hunter Bishop, OF, San Francisco Giants

Bill James had a theory that the younger brother of a baseball-playing family disproportionately ended up with the most talent of his siblings. Hunter's older brother Braden never made a 101—although he has already debuted in the majors—but this one will take a while to play out. They certainly are very different kinds of baseball players though. Hunter has four inches and 20 pounds on his older sibling, and smashed 22 home runs in 57 games for Arizona State this year, rocketing him up draft boards and making him a top-10 pick. He's got speed, but is still raw in the outfield, so he might end up in more of a corner slugger role, albeit with an intriguing power/speed combo. While Hunter may manage to take the baseball crown in the Bishop family, he is quite unlikely to be remembered as the best baseball player in his high school or college's history, as both institutions count Barry Bonds among their alumni.

69. Taylor Trammell, OF, San Diego Padres

"It is, moreover, evident from what has been said, that it is not the function of the poet to relate what has happened, but what may happen—what is possible according to the law of probability or necessity. The poet and the historian differ not by writing in verse or in prose. The work of Herodotus might be put into verse, and it would still be a species of history, with meter no less than without it. The true difference is that one relates what has happened, the other what may happen."

-Aristotle, Poetics

What happened: Trammell hit .234/.340/.349 in Double-A. His swing and approach were messy at the best of times. At others he looked more like a left fielder than a center fielder despite his easy plus speed. His game power remains mostly theoretical.

What may happen: It's a stretch to imply that a prospect writer is a poet, but by Aristotle's definition it seems to fit (and who are we to argue with Aristotle?). What is probable is not what is possible, and we are choosing to focus on what is possible for Trammell for another year—a two-way center fielder with above-average hit and power tools.

But the Greeks also knew that there is a real danger of falling into a well while gazing at the stars.

70. Josh Jung, 3B, Texas Rangers

A top-10 draft position presents a rebuttable presumption that the player will be on the following winter's 101. It means that smart, experienced player evaluators thought that the draftee was a 101-level prospect. Which brings us to Jung, who Texas popped with the eighth pick last June. He's basically what one would expect if all you knew about him was that he was a power conference third baseman drafted towards the back of the top 10: He has the potential to hit for average and power after he adjusts more to pro pitching and wood bats, solid defense but a touch unreliable, fairly polished. The presumption here that he's good hasn't been rebutted.

71. Shane McClanahan, LHP, Tampa Bay Rays

I'm hard-throwing but a little wild
I'm effort in the delivery but not too bad
I'm electric stuff but not always on, yeah
I'm a knee-buckling curve but not all the time
I'm a flashing change but inconsistent
I'm starting now but I might close

And what it all comes down to
Is that everything's gonna be fine, fine, fine
Cause I've got one outcome as a mid-rotation starter
And the other one is closin' games

72. Jordyn Adams, OF, Los Angeles Angels

Adams was a four-star wide receiver recruit signed to UNC, whom the Angels lured away with a first-round bonus in 2018. He has the extreme athleticism, speed, range and projection you'd expect to see in a top wide receiver recruit. He also showed off a fairly advanced approach for a teenager in full-season ball, with an all-fields approach suited for likely gap power. Adams is the third of four Angels in the outfield on this year's list, but his defensive prowess might ultimately be what knocks Mike Trout from center some years down the line.

73. Vidal Brujan, 2B, Tampa Bay Rays

Brujan is one of the fastest prospects around, in a system that picked up two more fellow notable speed demons last year, Xavier Edwards in the Tommy Pham trade and Greg Jones in the first round. He's a second baseman who is already picking up other positions; he played 29 games at short last year, his first appearances there since complex ball. We expect that at some point his speed will lend itself to picking up the outfield, although he hasn't seen game time there yet. And he has one of the best hit tool projections on this entire list. Steve Givarz gave it plus-plus potential last May, and if he ends up as a .300-plus hitter he's going to be a star (especially a fantasy one) despite lacking power. If he lands a bit below that projection, he'll still be quite useful. The Rays might be better than any other organization at maximizing the value of versatile players who do a few things very well, so he's in the right place.

74. Nick Solak, Hitter, Texas Rangers

We could list a bunch of positions for Solak, and they'd be correct in some technical sense. He played second and third in the majors, and also played all three outfield positions in the minors in 2019. Yet listing him as a 2B/3B/OF would imply a certain level of defensive value, wouldn't it? Well, he spent nearly half of his time in the majors as the DH. Like Willie Calhoun before him, picking a defensive home for Solak is more of a matter of where his glove would be acceptably hidden than finding somewhere for him to excel. The excelling part, that's going to be at the plate. He's long been a Professional Hitter with a short swing geared for hard contact that projected for strong average and on-base ability. In 2019, he suddenly showed up with plus game power, hitting 27 homers in 477 Triple-A plate appearances, all sandwiched around a rare midseason prospect-for-prospect challenge trade when he was swapped for pitcher Peter Fairbanks. The rabbit ball conditions at Triple-A carry some cause for skepticism when it comes to sudden homer barrages there. But it kept looking right in the majors after his August promotion, and even if he caps out at a 20-home run bat, that's a heck of a hitter.

75. Adrian Morejon, LHP, San Diego Padres

Morejon has nearly every kind of prospect risk imaginable. He's never hit 70 innings in a season. He's undersized, listed at 6-foot-even (and few who are listed at that height actually are). He's had recurring shoulder problems. He only threw more than three innings three times in 2019, all in April. There's durability risk, there's injury risk, there's relief risk, there's command-and-control risk. There's one of the most talented lefty arms in baseball present and accounted for, too. Morejon is a dynamo with a strong chance for three plus pitches who reached the majors at the tender age of 20. Despite all the risks, we can't lose this thread: he might be really good.

76. Tarik Skubal, LHP, Detroit Tigers

One of the biggest debates about prospect rankings is how reactive we should be to new information. It's always a tightrope walk, comparing priors and past information to new things demonstrated in the present. Skubal was on the radar a year ago as a live-armed seventh-round pick who got well over slot but presented heavy risk because of command woes and a long Tommy John recovery. He broke out in 2019, slicing his way up to and through Double-A with a three-pitch mix that, when on, rivals nearly any lefty in the minors. In a vacuum, Skubal's 2019 would support a higher ranking than this, but it does not exist sans context. Prior command and injury risks factor in when assessing his overall future career path. The further he leaves those in the distance, the more confident we'll be. Right now, though, they're still in plain sight.

77. Shea Langeliers, C, Atlanta Braves

Of all the catchers on this list other than Rutschman, Langeliers projects for the highest floor thanks to a strong, well-rounded defensive profile. He has a strong arm, receives the ball well, has a solid frame and athleticism for the position and by reputation is a good leader and game caller. How much catcher defense evaluation is likely to change during this decade has already been discussed, and if we're this deep into a comment without mentioning a hitter's offense, that's pretty telling. Langeliers doesn't project to be useless with the bat, but he also doesn't project much above solid-average, and high floors for catchers are subject to cave in quickly due to the rigors of the position.

78. Miguel Amaya, C, Chicago Cubs

Amaya produced at roughly the same clip as he did last year, but did so at a level closer to the majors and in a tough home park to hit in. There were little improvements along the way for Amaya too. The batting practices were a little louder, and he's grown into plus raw power. The swing can be a bit short and upper-body heavy, so he might not get to all of it, but he should get to enough to be an average major-league hitter on balance. The defense is similarly competent if not spectacular. He's a solid receiver with an above-average arm. A collection of 50 and 55s on the scouting sheet usually isn't 101 worthy, but a catcher with this broad base of skills is rare, and Amaya already has a fair bit of polish for a 20-year-old backstop.

79. Keibert Ruiz, C, Los Angeles Dodgers

While Amaya took a small step forward in 2019, Ruiz scuffled. His aggressive approach outweighed his natural feel for the barrel, and, while he walked more than he struck out, he consistently made suboptimal contact. He continued to show good receiving skills and an above-average arm, but he struggles to move laterally and the athleticism has gone backwards a bit. He's also 21 now, which, while still young in prospect terms, is not as young as he used to be (and so it goes). Amaya and Ruiz went in different directions this year, but they now have similar profiles as catching prospects. That could end up meaning both just lack a carrying tool, but often just being able to don the tools of ignorance 115 times a year is the only one you need.

80. Jesús Sánchez, OF, Miami Marlins

Two years ago we wrote: "Sánchez is an A-ball left fielder...so he's going to have to hit. He's going to have to hit for average, and he's going to have to hit for power. So far, so good, and the underlying tools are there for a plus-hit/plus-power left fielder." Well, the underlying tools are still there, but they remain a little too underlying. The raw power is plus-plus, but he's yet to top 15 home runs in a season. His free-swinging ways haven't been tamed, either, and the hit tool now looks more average despite excellent hand-eye and bat control. A .260, 30-homer bat would fit nicely in any team's outfield corner, but until those offensive tools appear reliably in games, his stock will trend downward.

81. Tony Gonsolin, RHP, Los Angeles Dodgers

Gonsolin has a very good shot to be the most successful straight senior sign under the current capped draft bonus system. He was a two-way player at St. Mary's, primarily an outfielder who dabbled on the mound. The Dodgers selected him in the ninth round in 2016 as a soft-tossing senior reliever (read: a low-priority prospect) and signed him for $2,500. By 2018, he was a four-pitch starter with a mid-90s fastball and a ridiculous splitter that falls off the table as well as two distinct and usable breaking balls. He's an oddball profile, already entering his age-26 season but still improving rapidly, and he looked like he belonged in the majors last summer and fall.

82. Jose Urquidy, RHP, Houston Astros

Urquidy is among the most famous prospects on this list, thanks to his five shutout innings in Game 4 of the 2019 World Series. A year ago, you wouldn't have found him anywhere on here. For starters, he was known as Jose Luis Hernandez up until last spring, and under that name he was a middling prospect who passed through the Rule 5 draft after missing more than a season with Tommy John surgery. After changing his preferred presentation to his mother's family name, Urquidy quickly made major gains across his entire profile, and he was a key pitcher for the Astros down the stretch. He's ready to contribute now as a mid-rotation starter, and has one of the highest floors of any pitcher on the list since he's already had significant big-league success. Something to watch for early in the 2020 season: Urquidy started leaning heavily on his slider in the playoffs, and it was flashing plus, significantly better than earlier reports.

83. Alek Manoah, RHP, Toronto Blue Jays

Manoah is a hulking monster with a high-end fastball/slider combo that needs more changeup and command to stick in the rotation. Basically, he's a potential mid-rotation starter with caveats, just like a lot of his ranking brethren, which makes it tough to describe him in original terms. We'll just cut to the feeling: The macro outcomes for this kind of pitcher are good enough that they get ranked every year, but accurately predicting exactly which one is going to learn a new changeup grip or mesh with the right pitching guru is a river we may never ford.

84. Brailyn Marquez, LHP, Chicago Cubs

No prospect on this list shows just how good pitchers have gotten as a group more than Marquez. He's a tall and physically projectable lefty who regularly sits 100-plus with his fastball and supplements it with a potential wipeout slider and a usable changeup—oh, and he's already been successful in full-season ball. Even with significant command and relief risk, that's a profile that would've been much more touted, even in the fairly recent past. Marquez still possesses special arm talent—triple-digits from the left side is always going to be triple-digits from the left side and the slider is a second potential out pitch—but, at present, it's more likely than not that he's going to end up a reliever.

85. Trevor Larnach, OF, Minnesota Twins

Larnach hit more home runs in the third of the season he spent at Double-A than the two-thirds he spent in High-A, which is both a fun quirk and a testament to the difficulties hitters face in the Florida State League. He had a fine season adjusted for context, hitting well at both stops and starting to bring his plus-plus raw power into games. He's a big, maxed-out corner dude, so he's going to have to *hit* for it all to play, just like the next name on this list...

86. Alex Kirilloff, 1B/OF, Minnesota Twins

Hey, another Twin corner bat—sometimes it's nice to compare apples to apples instead of weighing them against kumquats. Like Larnach, Kirilloff has a lot of offensive upside, driven by a tantalizing combination of advanced bat-to-ball skills and impressive raw power. His swing did get exploited more by upper-minors pitching, and it isn't geared to lift the ball enough, bringing into question whether he will ever maximize that raw. He's also sliding down the defensive spectrum towards first base, putting even more pressure on the bat to develop.

87. Daulton Varsho, C, Arizona Diamondbacks

Backstop prospects are tricky to rank, because defensive development can lag behind a major-league-ready bat, and because the rigors of catching every day can grind down above-average offensive tools to fringy nubs. Varsho has hit and power to spare, mashing 18 home runs while batting .300 in just over 100 games in Double-A. The defensive development continues to, uh, develop though. Varsho is a good athlete—he'll post an average run time down the line—with the underlying actions to be a good receiver. But the catching is still rough around the edges, which brings us to the last problem with ranking catching prospects: We don't have great insight into the soft skills—game calling, pitcher management—that often makes or breaks "average" gloves. Should the worst-case scenario arise Varsho is athletic enough to handle a bit of third and corner outfield as well; even if he remains in the squat, he could benefit from some time spent elsewhere to give his knees a rest. And he, more than any other catching prospect on this list, might benefit from the robot umps.

88. Francisco Alvarez, C, New York Mets

Young catchers are the riskiest prospect demographic in the game, a horror show littered with examples of what John Sickels once dubbed "Young Catcher Offensive Stagnation Syndrome." While we're aware of the general risks of the profile, we *really* like Alvarez. He was one of the top prospects in the 2018 international free agent class, and he spent only seven games in complex ball last summer before being promoted to the Appy League. That's a brutal assignment for a 17-year-old adjusting to being a professional player in an unfamiliar country, yet Alvarez handled it with aplomb, showing off advanced and projectable hitting talent. He has the raw ability and frame to stay behind the plate, though a million little things can (and, perhaps) will happen to knock his course off track between here and the majors. Other than that, Alvarez is about as safe as a catching prospect below full-season ball can be.

89. Kyle Wright, RHP, Atlanta Braves

Wright was 42nd on this list two years ago and 58th last year. From a wide lens, he remains close to the ideal pitching prospect—a four-pitch starter with an optimal frame and classic motion. Zoomed in, he's shown less command than hoped and there's been a concerning lack of development on his slower stuff. The relief risk is creeping, and while he'd be a good reliever—airing out the fastball and hard slider/cutter— he lacks the overwhelming stuff that would land a pure reliever on the101. Wright is still just some small gains away from a solid rotation outcome, but so are a lot of similar arms who end up pitching relief.

90. Andrés Giménez, SS, New York Mets

When swing changes are discussed in these pages, it is almost always in a positive context—"hey, this undersized middle infielder is launching the ball and now might hit 20 home runs." That was likely the intention when the Mets gave Giménez's stroke the ol' stomp-and-lift makeover, but he never really adjusted to it and instead scuffled in a repeat engagement in Double-A. The half-grade or so boost he saw in raw power negatively affected his hit tool, and he struggled to find a balance between the two. To make matters worse, he didn't even hit for that much power. The slick glove and plus speed are still present, which gives him a decent floor, and the reports from the AFL were improved enough to keep him on the back of this list. It's a bit confusing why they messed with a solid, if unspectacular offensive profile, but it's a reminder that not every swing change is a good one. You just don't usually find the bad ones on a top prospect list.

91. Geraldo Perdomo, SS, Arizona Diamondbacks

Last year's Giménez is a fairly good match for this year's Perdomo despite very different body types and approaches at the plate. Perdomo is a plus defender at the six with a polished hit tool and approach, though there is less power projection, and it might truly be a glove-driven profile. You don't have to hit much to be a decent shortstop prospect, especially when you have Perdomo's eye, but it would be nice to see Perdomo maintain his hitting line against Double-A arms or start filling out his lanky frame before projecting him as a plus regular. If he starts selling out for pull-side power in Jackson, we might have to worry we are in some sort of *Star Trek* temporal loop—or, perhaps it's just evidence that player-development staffs have become too infatuated with launch-angle swings.

92. Brennen Davis, OF, Chicago Cubs

Davis got held back in extended spring training for six weeks, and missed time after getting hit in the hand on two separate occasions, but he did enough in his 50 games on the field that necessitated a spot on this list. Davis was considered raw for a second-round prep outfielder, but he adjusted well to the Midwest League across the summer, flashing above-average hit and power tools. He's a plus runner who should maintain his speed as he ages, and he has enough speed to stick in center where he already shows advanced instincts. This might look low in a year if Davis can avoid being plunked in the hand and continue to refine his swing and approach in the Carolina League.

93. Daniel Lynch, LHP, Kansas City Royals

Lefty heat
Ninety-nine, short relief?
Slider bites,
Change, all right
Command concerns, such great height
Third starter, repeat

94. Gabriel Arias, SS, San Diego Padres

Now, for the inverse of the Ryan Mountcastle principle: "Bet on the plus-plus shortstop and hope he hits a little bit." Arias has one of the best shortstop gloves in the minors and is a complete defender with a plus arm. He does everything well one needs to do at shortstop, and it's not a brief list of skills. And it isn't like he's an offensive zero, either. Arias, 19, hit .302/.339/.470 in the Cal League last season. Yes, it's the Cal League, filled with offensive paradises, but there's some real pop from the still-wiry Arias. The trade-off is his swing has some length and a lot of timing mechanisms. Couple that with a grip-it-and-rip-it approach at the plate, and the hit and power tools may play fringy against better competition. There's a fair bit of offensive upside, and if Arias keeps hitting in Double-A, then next year's blurb won't be in the 90s.

95. Xavier Edwards, 2B/SS, Tampa Bay Rays

If you're looking at this list to find out who the potential fantasy stars are, you need to know that Edwards possesses game-changing speed in the middle infield, and is extremely relevant to your interests, even if he doesn't develop much at the plate or in the field. For real baseball interests, Edwards is a bit more divisive as a prospect. He has good contact ability and some bat speed, so there are the makings for a plus hit outcome. We're concerned about his ability to get there because at present he's a slap hitter with minimal power projection. Our staff had a *lot* of looks on him between the Midwest and California Leagues, and is relatively split on his offensive upside, as is wont to happen when a hitting profile is hit tool-reliant. Defensively, Edwards has the physical ability to stay at short or second, but needs to develop greater reliability. He was playing both positions in the Padres system in 2019, and he's likely to continue expanding his versatility now that he's been traded to the Rays.

96. Kris Bubic, LHP, Kansas City Royals

Bubic is a potential mid-rotation starter who should stick there. His fastball has ticked up since the draft, now sitting low-90s more consistently. The breaking ball has improved as well, from a slurvy, show-me pitch to solid-average offering. The change is still plus, with huge velocity separation and good fade. There's deception due to his hitchy, stop-start delivery and high slot. His command profile is better than that description of his mechanics would lead one to believe. Bubic has an ideal starter's build and threw 150 highly effective innings in A-ball last year. And that's how you go from a back-of-the-rotation starting pitching prospect to a mid-rotation starting pitching prospect. Easy peasy, right? Double-A will be a test perhaps, but the only real finishing school for this combination of stuff and polish is major-league hitters.

97. Edward Cabrera, RHP, Miami Marlins

The Marlins system is dotted with boom-or-bust prospects. Cabrera perhaps has a higher floor, with a fastball that sits mid-90s and touched 100, plus two potential above-average secondary offerings. Like many pitching prospects nowadays, however, we don't know what he will look like fully stretched out. He's never thrown more than 100 innings in a season. Will the fastball really sit mid-90s across 100 pitches and 32 starts? Are the curve and change good enough to turn over a lineup a second time? These are the kind of questions that arise in regards to dozens of pitching prospects every offseason. But hey, if you are 6-foot-4 with three above-average pitches, you are probably going to make this list. We'll figure out the rest as we go.

98. Brayan Rocchio, SS, Cleveland Indians

Man, last year's Mahoning Valley team had a fun collection of prospects. In addition to Valera and Rocchio, they had two first-round picks in Ethan Hankins and Daniel Espino and a late-season appearance by seven-figure IFA second baseman Aaron Bracho. (Plus, the coolest alternate jersey in the minors, the Mahoning Valley Peppers in Oil, featuring an appropriately cranky-looking Italian *nonna* mascot.) Rocchio spent all of last summer about an hour away from Progessive Field, but if you had dropped him in The Cleve, he might have been able to handle the defensive responsibilities. Rocchio is as smooth a shortstop you will see in the low minors with good range and quick hands. The offensive stuff is going to be more of a slow burn. He's a switch-hitter with an approach and quick bat, although he's never going to show much in the way of pop. Rocchio is a good runner and canny on the bases though, and should add a bit of value that way. It might end up a bit of a glove-first profile, but it's a heckuva glove.

99. D'Shawn Knowles, OF, Los Angeles Angels

To promote the start of the 2019 season, MLB put together another "Let the kids play" commercial featuring some of the best young stars in baseball. There were World Series predictions, home run predictions, general trash talking and Francisco Lindor bat flipping a microphone. It was fun without being unserious. The 2019 season itself still featured the standard tension between on-field joy and the unwritten rules, moderated by the usual cranky coterie of columnists and color commentators with graying goatees. This is another reminder that baseball is an entertainment business, and Knowles is remarkably fun. He has the talent to someday be up on the dais with the stars, and he looks like a dude that has a mean microphone bat flip. Power isn't a huge part of the teenager's game yet, but he flashes plus bat speed from both sides. He makes it look easy in center field and is a joy to watch on the base paths. He's still pretty raw and spent all of last season as an 18-year-old in rookie ball, but we have a bit of a reputation for chasing upside, and Knowles doesn't lack for star potential. He's fun, but a serious talent.

100. Jeremy Pena, SS, Houston Astros

Dozens of prospects could credibly slot into this part of the list, where tiers are mushy and subjectivity plays a larger role than ever—101 is an arbitrary endpoint, and cuts off Jose Garcia or Brice Turang or Will Wilson, none of whom are that far off Pena as a prospect. Sometimes it comes down to a question as simple as "who do you want to get on the list?" We wanted Pena. It's not to get a marker down for 2020. His skillset is broad and solid on both sides of the ball, but he's unlikely to rocket up the 2021 edition. It's just that every member of the prospect team that has seen him—going back to college—likes him. There won't be much power coming, but he can hit a little, run a little and play a good everyday shortstop. You can move him around the infield if you like, and he will be a solid hand wherever he's positioned. Pena is unlikely to be a star, but sometimes you just want to nod in a prospect's general direction and say "we like the dude."

101. James Karinchak, RHP, Cleveland Indians

The term "video game pitcher" is used to describe pitchers whose repertoires resemble a maxed-out created player. Karinchak is more like a Super Baseball Simulator 1.000 pitcher throwing the ultra pitches; his arsenal is beyond belief on raw power stuff. He combines an explosive high-90s fastball with an absolutely ridiculous curveball that is a true 12-to-6 breaker at mid-80s velocity, and it all comes from an extreme overhand arm slot that is difficult to pick up. Because of that combination, he's posted nearly unprecedented strikeout rates in the minors. He continued to absolutely baffle hitters in a September call-up, quickly becoming a Pitching Ninja favorite. There's enough uncertainty about command and injuries to stop us from running Karinchak any further up this list, and we'd be remiss to not mention once more that he's a two-pitch reliever. But it might be a better two pitches than anyone else on this list. That's the kind of overwhelming stuff that gets a pure reliever on the 101.

An additional note on Noah Song, RHP, Boston Red Sox

Song has one of the most unique backgrounds you'll ever see. He was a minor prospect coming out of high school, and his only Division I scholarship offer was from the Naval Academy. Over the course of his four years there, he unexpectedly developed into one of the best pitchers in college baseball and a serious pro prospect, with a fastball scraping the high-90s and a quality variety of other offerings. But he committed to serving in the Navy by staying until

graduation. It was unclear at the time of the 2019 draft whether he'd be able to pursue a professional career; despite first-round talent, he slipped to the fourth round as a Red Sox priority senior sign. Song looked every bit the part of a top pitching prospect after the draft, and was so impressive that he would have ranked in the 80s if he received a deferral from his commitment. But as of press time, the likelihood is that he will miss some or all of the 2020 and 2021 seasons while serving as a flight officer. He's the best prospect to be facing years off for military service in recent memory, so it's quite an edge case for us as prospect evaluators. We feel comfortable saying it increases the chances he'll end up in the bullpen and substantially inflates his overall risk, enough to discourage us from placing him on the list proper.

Arizona Diamondbacks

The State of the System

Seven draft picks in the first 75 will improve your system health quite quickly. A few breakout teenaged IFAs don't hurt either, and the Diamondbacks now have one of the deeper systems in baseball.

The Top Ten

★ ★ ★ *2020 Top 101 Prospect* **#16** ★ ★ ★

1 **Kristian Robinson** **OF** OFP: 70 ETA: Late 2022

Born: 12/11/00 Age: 19 Bats: R Throws: R Height: 6'3" Weight: 190 Origin: International Free Agent, 2017

YEAR	TEAM	LVL	AGE	PA	R	2B	3B	HR	RBI	BB	K	SB	CS	AVG/OBP/SLG	DRC+	VORP	BABIP	BRR	FRAA	WARP	PF
2018	DIA	RK	17	182	35	11	0	4	31	16	46	7	5	.272/.341/.414	126	9.5	.351	1.3	CF(26) -5.3, LF(6) -0.9	0.7	91
2018	MSO	RK	17	74	13	1	0	3	10	11	21	5	3	.300/.419/.467	119	6.0	.405	0.5	CF(10) -2.3, LF(7) 0.4	0.0	108
2019	YAK	A-	18	189	29	10	1	9	35	23	47	14	3	.319/.407/.558	208	24.4	.398	-0.1	CF(21) 1.6, RF(18) 3.8	2.8	94
2019	KNC	A	18	102	14	3	1	5	16	8	30	3	2	.217/.294/.435	91	3.0	.263	-0.3	CF(18) 0.6, RF(5) 0.2	0.2	101
2020	ARI	MLB	19	251	25	12	1	7	27	22	85	5	3	.228/.302/.371	80	0.0	.332	-0.1	CF 1, RF 1	0.4	101

Comparables: Ronald Acuña Jr., Fernando Tatis Jr., Yorman Rodriguez

The Report: Robinson is an intimidating presence. His extra-large frame and long, strong legs make for a dynamic athlete. And at just 19, he already has great body control for his size. During batting practice Robinson shows off prodigious power to all fields. He can consistently get the ball in the air, and although in-game power is a work in progress due to his still-developing hit tool, he hit some mammoth shots with Kane County. Robinson is a patient hitter, rarely swinging at first pitches, but at this stage he does tend to expand the zone quite a bit with two strikes, and has also struggled against breakers. His swing is loose, highlighting a lightning-quick bat that stays through the zone a long time. Robinson has solid balance and rhythm in the box, and he uses his lower half well.

On the basepaths, he runs like a deer. His long strides, paired with improving agility, will lead to stolen bases once he understands how to swipe a bag. Patrolling the outfield Robinson flashes the ability to be a plus center fielder, making numerous impressive catches. He still needs to refine his jumps and route efficiency, but when he learns the position better he should have no problem contending for Gold Gloves. His arm already sits plus. Even when on the move he is able to get his lower half engaged and throw a strike to any base. Once Robinson improves his instincts with reps he has the potential to be a true five-tool outfielder with a long and successful big-league career.

Variance: High. Robinson is very young and still needs to develop quite a bit, especially his hit tool in order to max-out his power game.

Mark Barry's Fantasy Take: Athletic. Potential five-tool stud. Upside. Bahamas. And that, my friends, is Kristian Robinson bingo. To be fair, though, it's hard to discuss Robinson without most, if not all of these descriptors, as the 18-year-old hit 14 homers and stole 17 bags in just under 300 trips to the plate. There are plenty of swings and misses in his game, but if everything clicks, hooooo boy. Robinson is a pretty clear top-25 dynasty guy right now.

★ ★ ★ *2020 Top 101 Prospect* **#54** ★ ★ ★

2 Alek Thomas OF   OFP: 60   ETA: 2022

Born: 04/28/00   Age: 20   Bats: L   Throws: L   Height: 5'11"   Weight: 175   Origin: Round 2, 2018 Draft (#63 overall)

YEAR	TEAM	LVL	AGE	PA	R	2B	3B	HR	RBI	BB	K	SB	CS	AVG/OBP/SLG	DRC+	VORP	BABIP	BRR	FRAA	WARP	PF
2018	DIA	RK	18	138	24	3	5	0	10	13	18	8	2	.325/.394/.431	162	15.2	.381	1.6	CF(13) -2.1, LF(11) -2.4	0.8	93
2018	MSO	RK	18	134	26	11	1	2	17	11	19	4	3	.341/.396/.496	160	7.9	.392	-1.0	CF(21) 0.1, LF(7) 0.5	0.8	110
2019	KNC	A	19	402	63	21	7	8	48	43	72	11	6	.312/.393/.479	153	32.4	.372	0.4	CF(75) -10.1, RF(7) 0.8	2.5	100
2019	VIS	A+	19	104	13	2	0	2	7	9	33	4	5	.255/.327/.340	90	3.7	.373	0.4	CF(23) 2.6	0.6	100
2020	ARI	MLB	20	251	25	12	2	6	27	20	64	3	1	.256/.320/.394	90	0.0	.332	-0.2	CF -2, LF 0	0.3	101

Comparables: Victor Robles, Billy McKinney, Byron Buxton

The Report: Thomas might end up being the best pure hitter from the 2018 draft class. As a teenager he excelled in the Midwest League, earning a place on the Futures Game roster and a late season promotion to High-A. Offensively, his sweet, left-handed swing is quick and compact and he shows a disciplined approach. The bat speed and strength provide some sneaky pop, but it's presently geared mostly for gap-to-gap, line-drive power. After contact, he accelerates quickly out of the box and has plus raw speed. It's the type of acceleration that allows for extra bases and eventually, as he becomes more experienced, the occasional stolen base. Defensively, his quick-twitch athleticism allows him to cover plenty of ground in center field. That plus range and solid instincts make for a future above-average outfielder.

Variance: High. Thomas' athleticism and defensive ability give a fairly high floor but he's still a teenager who has yet to face advanced pitching.

Mark Barry's Fantasy Take: Thomas is a plus runner who hits tons of line drives with gap power which makes him extremely #myjam. He doesn't need to hit a ton of homers to be useful in fantasy circles, but if the ball stays juiced, Thomas is a guy who could certainly benefit. He doesn't quite have Robinson's ceiling, but he's still a top-40ish dynasty prospect.

★ ★ ★ *2020 Top 101 Prospect* **#87** ★ ★ ★

3 Daulton Varsho C   OFP: 55   ETA: Early 2021

Born: 07/02/96   Age: 23   Bats: L   Throws: R   Height: 5'10"   Weight: 190   Origin: Round 2, 2017 Draft (#68 overall)

YEAR	TEAM	LVL	AGE	PA	R	2B	3B	HR	RBI	BB	K	SB	CS	AVG/OBP/SLG	DRC+	VORP	BABIP	BRR	FRAA	WARP	PF
2017	YAK	A-	20	212	36	16	3	7	39	17	30	7	2	.311/.368/.534	156	24.2	.338	2.4	C(36) 0.8	2.3	94
2018	VIS	A+	21	342	44	11	3	11	44	30	71	19	3	.286/.363/.451	131	30.5	.341	2.5	C(55) 1.4	2.7	96
2019	WTN	AA	22	452	85	25	4	18	58	42	63	21	5	.301/.378/.520	156	52.6	.317	5.9	C(75) -5.7, CF(4) -1.2	4.3	101
2020	ARI	MLB	23	70	9	4	1	3	10	5	15	1	0	.271/.332/.498	114	0.0	.304	0.2	C -1, CF 0	0.3	101

Comparables: Max Stassi, Kyle Lewis, Nate Lowe

The Report: Varsho's bat took another step forward in the Southern League in 2019. He got less pull-happy, improving both his approach and contact rate, while putting more balls over the fence due to his strong, fireplug frame. Both the hit and power tools here are potentially above-average.

Varsho is deceptively quick and athletic and that helps him both on the basepaths and behind the plate, although his receiving remains a work in progress. He has a plus, accurate arm, and he's improved year-over-year defensively as a pro. The bat is likely to be major-league-ready well before the glove though.

Variance: High. So the offensive variance here is, at worst, medium. We think Varsho will be an above-average hitter in the majors, which gets him well over the bar for catcher offense. Catcher defense is trickier though, and he's never caught more than 76 games in a season. He has the frame for it, but the defensive chops aren't there yet, and that could make the ultimate projection trickier. If he even gets to average defensively though, the bat could make him an occasional All-Star behind the dish.

Mark Barry's Fantasy Take: If you're going to trust a catching prospect (and generally, you probably should not) Varsho isn't a bad one to roll with, offering a potent power/speed combo rarely seen behind the dish. He's not a great defender though, so he'll need to continue progressing with the glove to keep that sweet, sweet catcher eligibility. He has the offensive chops to be a top-five backstop, if he sticks, though.

★ ★ ★ *2020 Top 101 Prospect* **#91** ★ ★ ★

4 Geraldo Perdomo SS   OFP: 55   ETA: 2021

Born: 10/22/99   Age: 20   Bats: B   Throws: R   Height: 6'3"   Weight: 184   Origin: International Free Agent, 2016

YEAR	TEAM	LVL	AGE	PA	R	2B	3B	HR	RBI	BB	K	SB	CS	AVG/OBP/SLG	DRC+	VORP	BABIP	BRR	FRAA	WARP	PF
2017	DDI	RK	17	278	42	3	2	1	11	60	37	16	8	.238/.410/.285	135	18.4	.282	1.4	SS(63) 11.9	3.5	101
2018	DIA	RK	18	101	20	4	2	1	8	14	17	14	1	.314/.416/.442	168	14.9	.382	2.6	SS(14) 2.6, 2B(8) 0.5	1.6	92
2018	MSO	RK	18	29	3	0	1	0	2	7	4	1	1	.455/.586/.545	248	6.6	.556	0.4	SS(5) 0.3, 2B(1) -0.2	0.5	106
2018	YAK	A-	18	127	20	3	2	3	14	18	23	9	4	.301/.421/.456	149	16.1	.359	1.4	SS(30) 3.9	1.7	103
2019	KNC	A	19	385	48	16	3	2	36	56	56	20	8	.268/.394/.357	127	25.7	.318	-2.2	SS(80) 2.1, 2B(11) -0.1	2.7	101
2019	VIS	A+	19	114	15	5	0	1	11	14	11	6	5	.301/.407/.387	128	7.8	.325	-0.2	SS(25) -1.0	0.6	100
2020	ARI	MLB	20	251	25	10	1	4	23	27	51	6	3	.237/.329/.346	83	0.0	.292	0.0	SS 2, 2B 0	0.5	101

Comparables: Victor Robles, J.P. Crawford, Jorge Polanco

The Report: The 19-year-old shortstop slashed .275/.397/364 with 21 doubles and 26 steals while playing 116 games at two different levels of A-ball in the 2019 season. The switch-hitting Perdomo stays inside the baseball exceptionally well, and utilizes a high rate of contact to generate line drives gap-to-gap. He's displayed more power from the left side of the plate in the minors, hitting all eight of his career home runs against right-handed pitching. He shows advanced strike-zone awareness (169 BB/148 K in 1034 PAs as pro) and a proclivity to lay down bunts, further showcasing his adept control of the box and the bat.

The plus runner utilizes long strides to gather ground between bases, and on defense where he's demonstrated good range and mobility at shortstop. His exceptional hand-eye coordination and receptive hands eat up grounders and pair with a solid throwing arm, allowing him to make most plays at shortstop. His athleticism and advanced baseball acumen would enable him to succeed at any defensive position in the infield or outfield, perhaps making him most valuable as a super-utility player. Perdomo's advanced offensive game, defensive versatility, and baseball instincts allow him to impact a game in a multitude of ways. He should be on the fast-track to Arizona.

Variance: Medium. Perdomo's still in A-ball, but his advanced offensive game and baseball savvy increase his value and set a high-floor.

Mark Barry's Fantasy Take: In the Midseason Top 50, Bret tabbed Perdomo as having Elvis Andrus + Walks upside. Bret is the boss, so I won't argue with him. I like Perdomo quite a bit.

5 Corbin Carroll OF   OFP: 55   ETA: 2023

Born: 08/21/00   Age: 19   Bats: L   Throws: L   Height: 5'10"   Weight: 165   Origin: Round 1, 2019 Draft (#16 overall)

YEAR	TEAM	LVL	AGE	PA	R	2B	3B	HR	RBI	BB	K	SB	CS	AVG/OBP/SLG	DRC+	VORP	BABIP	BRR	FRAA	WARP	PF
2019	DIA	RK	18	137	23	6	3	2	14	24	29	16	1	.288/.409/.450	161	22.7	.366	2.7	CF(23) -0.1, LF(5) -0.6	1.3	94
2019	YAK	A-	18	49	13	3	4	0	6	5	12	2	0	.326/.408/.581	116	6.4	.452	0.8	CF(11) 0.0	0.3	110
2020	ARI	MLB	19	251	22	12	2	3	22	25	77	3	1	.221/.302/.335	73	0.0	.321	0.0	CF 0, LF 0	0.0	101

Comparables: Teoscar Hernández, Jason Martin, Victor Robles

The Report: Despite being an undersized prep outfielder, and a bit of a throwback profile, Carroll had first-round buzz all spring, and didn't make it past the first of the Diamondbacks' plethora of picks. For the 16th-overall pick Arizona got a quick-twitch, up-the-middle defender, with good wrists and above-average bat speed. Carroll has a flat swing plane, generating line drives and ground balls. He's strong enough to put some sting into them, though, and his high-end plus speed will rack up both infield hits and extra bases in the gaps. Carroll should stick in center field and has an above-average arm. The lack of power might ultimately limit the upside here, but it's an intriguing package overall as a hit-and-speed top of the order bat that can go get it at a premium defensive position.

Variance: High. This is a hit-tool driven profile offensively, and we are a ways away from knowing if he can handle upper minors velocity, let alone major league stuff. If he does grow into a bit of pop—he's gotten some Brett Gardner comps—he could be...well, Brett Gardner I guess. But there's some risk he's just another slappy fourth outfielder type in three years. Which was also said about Brett Gardner as a prospect.

Mark Barry's Fantasy Take: If you're wondering where all the steals went, apparently they're all in this system. Carroll is going to steal a lot of bases. He's a little guy, so we still don't know if there will ever be any power, but if it comes, he could be a Lorenzo Cain-y-type guy.

6   Brennan Malone   RHP   OFP: 60   ETA: 2022/23

Born: 09/08/00   Age: 19   Bats: R   Throws: R   Height: 6'4"   Weight: 205   Origin: Round 1C, 2019 Draft (#33 overall)

YEAR	TEAM	LVL	AGE	W	L	SV	G	GS	IP	H	HR	BB/9	K/9	K	GB%	BABIP	WHIP	ERA	DRA	WARP	PF
2019	DIA	RK	18	1	2	0	6	3	7	4	0	6.4	9.0	7	29%	.176	1.29	5.14	3.32	0.2	97
2020	ARI	MLB	19	2	2	0	33	0	35	35	5	3.9	7.4	29	42%	.288	1.43	4.79	4.92	0.2	101

Comparables: Elvin Ramirez, Touki Toussaint, Devin Williams

The Report: In the mix to be the first prep arm taken in this past year's draft, Malone fell into the compensation round as the fourth high school hurler taken. Given his mature, athletic body, repeatable mechanics, and advanced stuff for his age, it was a surprise he lasted as long as he did. Playing for one of the most prospect-laden teams we've seen in quite a while, he stood out as the go-to prospect on the squad.

He's able to locate his mid-90s fastball and does so early in games to set the tone. While the command isn't perfect, there is an effort to paint the corners and work all quadrants of the zone unlike a typical hard-thrower; there is moxy to his gameplan. Once the hitters attempt to speed up their bat, he's able to counter with a solid slider that works in the low 80s and has a sharp break to the glove-side. A decent 12-to-6 curveball is also employed, but it doesn't have the current ability to both land for strikes and chase swings like the slider does. There's even some feel for a changeup, but with such a solid foundation in all other parts of his game, it is the asset in need of most work.

Variance: Very high. Like any mature-bodied pitcher fresh out of high school, there is so much that can happen to a talented arm once it adjusts to a professional schedule.

Mark Barry's Fantasy Take: It's hard not to be intrigued by Malone's combination of a controllable slider and a fastball that flirts with triple digits. He's also a huge dude, and has a pair of developing secondaries that could firmly entrench him as a mid-rotation starter. He's also a pitching prospect, which as we all know can go horribly awry at a moment's notice. For now, let's call him rosterable in 200-prospect leagues.

7   Blake Walston   LHP   OFP: 60   ETA: 2023/24

Born: 06/28/01   Age: 19   Bats: L   Throws: L   Height: 6'5"   Weight: 175   Origin: Round 1, 2019 Draft (#26 overall)

YEAR	TEAM	LVL	AGE	W	L	SV	G	GS	IP	H	HR	BB/9	K/9	K	GB%	BABIP	WHIP	ERA	DRA	WARP	PF
2019	YAK	A-	18	0	0	0	3	3	6	6	0	3.0	9.0	6	41%	.353	1.33	3.00	5.95	-0.1	100
2020	ARI	MLB	19	2	2	0	33	0	35	35	5	4.0	9.4	36	40%	.311	1.45	4.86	4.95	0.2	101

Comparables: Logan Webb, Chris Volstad, Alex Sanabia

The Report: Walston got picked a few spots ahead of Malone, and we prefer the surety of the latter at present, but it's a reasonably close call and could look very different after Walston gets a year of pro instruction. He's a tall, projectable lefty who's already touching 95 and flashes good sink and explosive life when he elevates armside. The combination of his quick arm and slingy three-quarters slot gets the fastball on you faster than you'd think low 90s would arrive. It might be mid 90s in time. There is a bit of upper body effort in the delivery at times, I'd expect that all to smooth out some as he fills out. Overall, it's a relatively clean delivery given his size.

Walston's secondaries are a bit raw, but there's some feel for a curveball that can show high spin and good 12-6 depth, although it does tend to flatten out and get slurvy at times. The changeup is rough, but it's a discernible changeup and advanced for a prep arm. He's confident throwing it in games, and can run it in to righties where it will flash some sink and fade, although he tends to guide and really cast it to turn it over. Walston is going to be a bit more of a project than Malone, but there's a smidge more upside if it all comes together.

Variance: Very high. Walston is just now focusing solely on baseball, and while the raw materials are all there, a lot has to go right for him to reach the projection. There's a decent reliever fallback as a fastball/curve lefty, but even that would be half a decade away.

Mark Barry's Fantasy Take: Walston is a fun guy to keep on the radar, and was arguably the best prep arm in the 2019 draft, but he's very, very far away, and you probably need around 250-300 prospects in your league for him to be rostered.

8 Corbin Martin RHP   OFP: 55   ETA: 2019

Born: 12/28/95   Age: 24   Bats: R   Throws: R   Height: 6'2"   Weight: 200   Origin: Round 2, 2017 Draft (#56 overall)

YEAR	TEAM	LVL	AGE	W	L	SV	G	GS	IP	H	HR	BB/9	K/9	K	GB%	BABIP	WHIP	ERA	DRA	WARP	PF
2017	TCV	A-	21	0	1	1	8	3	27²	20	1	2.6	12.4	38	63%	.297	1.01	2.60	2.42	0.8	98
2018	BCA	A+	22	2	0	1	4	3	19	4	0	3.3	12.3	26	64%	.111	0.58	0.00	1.74	0.8	91
2018	CCH	AA	22	7	2	0	21	18	103	84	7	2.4	8.4	96	48%	.277	1.09	2.97	3.34	2.3	104
2019	ROU	AAA	23	2	1	0	9	8	37¹	33	2	4.3	10.8	45	42%	.341	1.37	3.13	3.00	1.3	94
2019	HOU	MLB	23	1	1	0	5	5	19¹	23	8	5.6	8.8	19	43%	.283	1.81	5.59	7.18	-0.3	103
2020	ARI	MLB	24	1	2	0	14	3	24	27	5	4.2	8.1	22	42%	.314	1.60	6.03	5.91	-0.1	101

Comparables: Jess Todd, Aaron Blair, Andrew Moore

The Report: Martin got off to a good start in the PCL, got bombed a bit in the Astros rotation, and then went down with a UCL tear. Shortly after surgery he was dealt to the Diamondbacks as part of the Zack Greinke trade. The stuff looked major-league-quality despite the command and long ball issues. Martin sits in the mid 90s and touched as high as 98. The fastball can run a little true but is explosive with "rise" when he elevates it. Both his slider and curve are potentially above-average, and while his change can be a bit firm, there's enough fade to make it a crossover option, even if it lacks the consistent tumble to miss bats. Will that all still be there eighteen months from now? How long will it take the command to come back? It's a cliche, but in this case literally only time will tell.

Variance: High. Well, I mean he's not likely to pitch again until 2021, and while Tommy John surgery is fairly common now, it's not by any means routine. Martin was major-league-ready with four average-or-better pitches, but until we see it back on the mound, there's going to be known unknowns here.

Mark Barry's Fantasy Take: Martin was fine in his five-start cup of coffee with the big club this season, but surrendered too many walks and dingers to be anything more than a fantasy SP6-7. Then he had Tommy John surgery, so we won't see him at all until 2021. Again, he's fine, but a preexisting lack of control doesn't bode well for his return to the bump. On a side note, there are way too many Corbins in this top 10.

9 Liover Peguero SS   OFP: 60   ETA: 2023

Born: 12/31/00   Age: 19   Bats: R   Throws: R   Height: 6'1"   Weight: 160   Origin: International Free Agent, 2017

YEAR	TEAM	LVL	AGE	PA	R	2B	3B	HR	RBI	BB	K	SB	CS	AVG/OBP/SLG	DRC+	VORP	BABIP	BRR	FRAA	WARP	PF
2018	DDI	RK	17	90	14	3	3	1	16	6	12	4	1	.309/.356/.457	128	8.4	.343	-0.3	SS(21) 0.9	0.7	102
2018	DIA	RK	17	71	8	0	0	0	5	5	17	3	2	.197/.254/.197	76	-4.5	.265	-0.9	SS(19) 2.2	0.3	91
2019	MSO	RK+	18	156	34	7	3	5	27	12	34	8	1	.364/.410/.559	154	22.1	.448	1.7		1.6	104
2019	YAK	A-	18	93	13	4	2	0	11	8	17	3	1	.262/.333/.357	104	3.5	.328	0.1	SS(18) -0.1	0.4	101
2020	ARI	MLB	19	251	22	11	2	4	23	16	71	3	1	.239/.291/.343	68	0.0	.328	0.0	SS 1	0.0	101

Comparables: Amed Rosario, Enrique Hernández, Willi Castro

The Report: A mid-six-figure bonus baby from the Diamondbacks' 2017 IFA class, Peguero is already paying dividends as a pro. It's one of the best frames to bet on out there—lean and strong, high-waisted and athletic, projectable, but not likely to grow off shortstop. It's the kind of body that my predecessor—who also happens to be the pro scouting director here—would gush over in these pages.

This isn't a mere projection bet on a Dominican teenager, though. Despite a little bit of an unorthodox swing—it's reminiscent of Jung-Ho Kang with his hands loaded out in front and a big leg kick—Peguero shows advanced barrel control for his age. Coupled with good wrists and explosive bat speed, there's potential for above-average hit and above-average power in the profile as he adds strength.

Peguero is a smooth shortstop and a plus runner at present. I'd expect him to bleed some of that speed as he fills out, but the frame is on the narrow side, and he's likely to stick and settle in at average or maybe a tick-above at the 6. The bat will carry the profile, but hey, it's a potentially special bat.

Variance: Extreme. He's an 18-year-old with a limited short-season resume.

Mark Barry's Fantasy Take: We talk a lot about getting in early on guys flashing loud tools in short-season league, and Peguero is one of the better examples of the type. He's a ways away, but he's above-average pretty much everywhere with the stick, and if he replicates his 2019 campaign, he absolutely won't be under the radar any longer.

10   Jon Duplantier   RHP   OFP: 55   ETA: 2019

Born: 07/11/94   Age: 25   Bats: L   Throws: R   Height: 6'4"   Weight: 225   Origin: Round 3, 2016 Draft (#89 overall)

YEAR	TEAM	LVL	AGE	W	L	SV	G	GS	IP	H	HR	BB/9	K/9	K	GB%	BABIP	WHIP	ERA	DRA	WARP	PF
2017	KNC	A	22	6	1	0	13	12	72²	45	4	1.9	9.7	78	52%	.240	0.83	1.24	2.23	2.6	98
2017	VIS	A+	22	6	2	0	12	12	63¹	46	2	3.8	12.4	87	53%	.324	1.15	1.56	3.49	1.3	98
2018	DIA	RK	23	0	0	0	2	2	7	5	0	2.6	11.6	9	44%	.312	1.00	1.29	3.05	0.2	102
2018	WTN	AA	23	5	1	0	14	14	67	52	4	3.8	9.1	68	56%	.282	1.19	2.69	3.79	1.2	103
2019	RNO	AAA	24	1	2	0	13	11	38	31	1	6.6	10.4	44	47%	.323	1.55	5.21	2.93	1.4	113
2019	ARI	MLB	24	1	1	1	15	3	36²	39	2	4.4	8.3	34	44%	.356	1.55	4.42	5.73	-0.1	100
2020	ARI	MLB	25	2	2	0	19	3	31	32	5	4.6	7.5	26	46%	.299	1.54	5.24	5.17	0.2	101

Comparables: Yefry Ramírez, Alex Meyer, Jordan Montgomery

The Report: Duplantier's durability concerns continue. After a bout of bicep tendinitis in 2018, shoulder inflammation cost him significant time in 2019. Those are two fairly concerning injuries for a pitching prospect, and the Diamondbacks used Duplantier solely in relief after his return to the big club in September. Honestly, he's not a bad fit there. He can lean on a power 12-6 curveball to miss bats and although his velocity dipped a bit this year into the low 90s, it's still a lively fastball with run. Duplantier offers a hard slider and serviceable change as well, but the command profile and delivery have always had strong bullpen markers, and while he has a full four-pitch mix, that may merely make him an option to go once through the lineup or so out of the pen. That's a useful arm though, assuming he can stay healthy.

Variance: Low. Duplantier is not without risks mind you, they are just known risks of the reliever and injury variety. He's major-league-ready.

Mark Barry's Fantasy Take: I would like Duplantier better if he struck out more guys, walked fewer and didn't get hurt so much. It's a bummer, and probably a little reductive, but his is a profile that's hard to bet on long-term.

The Next Ten

11   J.B. Bukauskas   RHP

Born: 10/11/96   Age: 23   Bats: R   Throws: R   Height: 6'0"   Weight: 196   Origin: Round 1, 2017 Draft (#15 overall)

YEAR	TEAM	LVL	AGE	W	L	SV	G	GS	IP	H	HR	BB/9	K/9	K	GB%	BABIP	WHIP	ERA	DRA	WARP	PF
2017	TCV	A-	20	0	0	0	2	2	6	4	0	6.0	9.0	6	53%	.267	1.33	4.50	5.10	0.0	102
2018	TCV	A-	21	0	0	0	3	3	8¹	8	0	2.2	9.7	9	46%	.364	1.20	0.00	4.27	0.1	98
2018	QUD	A	21	1	2	0	4	4	15	15	0	4.2	12.6	21	55%	.395	1.47	4.20	3.95	0.2	104
2018	BCA	A+	21	3	0	0	5	5	28	13	1	4.2	10.0	31	59%	.194	0.93	1.61	2.72	0.9	89
2018	CCH	AA	21	0	0	0	1	1	6	1	0	3.0	12.0	8	60%	.100	0.50	0.00	2.56	0.2	93
2019	WTN	AA	22	0	1	0	2	2	7	10	0	6.4	14.1	11	39%	.556	2.14	7.71	7.33	-0.2	109
2019	CCH	AA	22	2	4	1	20	14	85²	81	8	5.7	10.3	98	48%	.332	1.58	5.25	6.11	-1.3	102
2020	ARI	MLB	23	1	1	0	11	0	11	11	2	3.7	8.8	11	44%	.299	1.37	4.34	4.51	0.1	101

Comparables: Logan Webb, Jorge Alcala, Nick Tropeano

In the 2019 Annual, Bukauskas' blurb posited that if he "can just stay healthy and throw strikes, he's one of the few pitchers in the minors with top-of-the-rotation potential." He promptly missed a chunk of the season with elbow soreness and walked 14 percent of batters when he was on the mound. The stuff is still tantalizing enough that he was a key piece of the Diamondbacks' return for Zack Greinke, but his future looks more like that of a key bullpen piece now. Bukauskas remains a short, physically maxed righty with a potential plus fastball/slider combo. The fastball is lively, but sits in more of an average velocity band when he's stretched out, although it's mid 90s in short bursts. The slider is a true out pitch, firm with late dive. There's a cutter and a serviceable change as well, so like Duplantier, you can squint and see a rotation piece, but also like Duplantier, the consistent command and injury issues as a pro make late-inning relief the likely outcome.

12 Blaze Alexander SS

Born: 06/11/99 Age: 21 Bats: R Throws: R Height: 6'0" Weight: 160 Origin: Round 11, 2018 Draft (#339 overall)

YEAR	TEAM	LVL	AGE	PA	R	2B	3B	HR	RBI	BB	K	SB	CS	AVG/OBP/SLG	DRC+	VORP	BABIP	BRR	FRAA	WARP	PF
2018	DIA	RK	19	118	25	10	2	2	25	19	21	7	3	.362/.475/.574	209	21.5	.438	-0.9	2B(11) 0.5, SS(10) -3.5	1.3	91
2018	MSO	RK	19	129	27	9	3	3	17	12	31	3	0	.302/.364/.509	113	11.4	.386	1.5	SS(24) 3.6, 2B(4) 0.9	0.9	109
2019	KNC	A	20	406	56	12	4	7	47	42	89	14	4	.262/.355/.382	120	24.8	.324	0.2	SS(49) 1.9, 2B(31) -0.5	2.5	101
2020	ARI	MLB	21	251	25	12	1	6	26	21	71	2	1	.236/.310/.376	83	0.0	.317	-0.1	SS 0, 2B 0	0.3	101

Comparables: Isan Díaz, Roman Quinn, Mat Gamel

Short but with a medium frame, Alexander is a pure athlete with plus body control. His solid footwork and quick-twitch movements stand out—especially in the field, where he is strongest. He has the ability to play shortstop, second and third base at premium levels, though he primarily profiles as an up-the-middle type player. Working around the bag at second, Alexander shows impressive instincts, reads and fundamentals. His hands are quick and smooth, which match his swift footwork. But Alexander's arm strength and accuracy are the most impressive part of his game. There aren't many guys in the minors that showcase the amount of carry on throws as Alexander does. In the box is where the question marks begin. Overall, he has slightly above-average bat to ball skills and a short swing with small uppercut, but his pitch selection needs refinement. There also is not much, if any, power in the tank. And with his frame I don't see him ever hitting for power. Alexander has above-average wheels and knows how to swipe a bag. The profile fits as a defensive specialist.

13 Seth Beer OF

Born: 09/18/96 Age: 23 Bats: L Throws: R Height: 6'3" Weight: 195 Origin: Round 1, 2018 Draft (#28 overall)

YEAR	TEAM	LVL	AGE	PA	R	2B	3B	HR	RBI	BB	K	SB	CS	AVG/OBP/SLG	DRC+	VORP	BABIP	BRR	FRAA	WARP	PF
2018	TCV	A-	21	51	9	3	0	4	7	6	10	0	0	.293/.431/.659	188	7.7	.296	-0.8	LF(7) -1.0, 1B(4) -0.1	0.3	93
2018	QUD	A	21	132	15	7	0	3	16	15	17	1	0	.348/.443/.491	166	11.6	.391	-1.2	RF(10) -0.9, LF(9) -1.1	0.8	102
2018	BCA	A+	21	114	15	4	0	5	19	4	22	0	1	.262/.307/.439	110	1.1	.288	-2.2	LF(13) -1.4, 1B(6) -0.2	-0.1	94
2019	BCA	A+	22	152	24	8	0	9	34	14	30	0	3	.328/.414/.602	189	14.6	.359	-1.6	1B(16) 0.0, LF(15) -0.7	1.3	104
2019	CCH	AA	22	280	40	9	0	16	52	24	58	0	0	.299/.407/.543	177	21.5	.333	-3.1	1B(46) 0.8, LF(8) -0.6	2.1	103
2019	WTN	AA	22	101	8	7	0	1	17	8	25	0	1	.205/.297/.318	74	-0.2	.270	0.0	1B(14) -0.7, LF(9) -0.4	-0.2	105
2020	ARI	MLB	23	42	6	2	0	2	6	3	11	0	0	.268/.347/.505	124	0.0	.320	-0.1	LF 0	0.2	101

Comparables: Nate Lowe, Anthony Santander, Ryan O'Hearn

Once upon a time, Beer was considered to be a lock to go first overall in the 2018 draft. He had a strong junior campaign in a tough conference, but his slide down the draft board started the previous fall and went through the spring, eventually landing him with the Astros at pick 28. There's obvious limitations to the profile. Beer is unathletic at both corner outfield and first base. While he's not a complete zero there, he's comfortably below-average and best suited to DH.

You'd be expecting a long and strong power profile at the plate based on the above, and there's some truth to that. Beer only has average bat speed and it's not a true launch angle uppercut, but he's strong enough to muscle balls out to the pull side and he's a better pure hitter than you'd think. He has good barrel control despite the stiff swing, and a strong approach at the plate. He can get pull-happy, leading to swing-and-miss in the zone, especially against offspeed, but as three true outcome sluggers go, Beer is a better bet to hit .270 or .280 than most. That might not be enough to make him more than a second-division corner bat, but he's hit everywhere so far, and the PCL isn't likely to offer him much more of a challenge.

14   Wilderd Patino   OF

Born: 07/18/01   Age: 18   Bats: R   Throws: R   Height: 6'1"   Weight: 175   Origin: International Free Agent, 2017

YEAR	TEAM	LVL	AGE	PA	R	2B	3B	HR	RBI	BB	K	SB	CS	AVG/OBP/SLG	DRC+	VORP	BABIP	BRR	FRAA	WARP	PF
2018	DDB	RK	16	111	10	5	0	0	7	14	19	2	3	.225/.360/.281	123	4.7	.278	1.1	CF(21) 2.9	1.0	94
2018	DDI	RK	16	27	4	1	0	0	2	2	5	4	2	.409/.519/.455	123	4.5	.529	-0.1	CF(6) -0.6	0.4	103
2019	DIA	RK	17	125	18	4	3	1	21	11	32	13	3	.349/.403/.472	147	13.3	.462	1.0	CF(22) 1.1, RF(5) -0.3	1.1	96
2019	MSO	RK+	17	40	6	1	2	0	4	2	14	1	1	.229/.300/.371	43	1.2	.364	0.1		-0.1	101
2020	ARI	MLB	18	251	22	11	1	3	22	20	91	4	2	.229/.304/.333	70	0.0	.369	0.0	CF 1, RF 0	0.1	101

Comparables: Franmil Reyes, Yorman Rodriguez, Ronald Acuña Jr.

Patino is even more of a physical freak than Liover Peguero, although the overall game is much rawer. Patino is a pure burner on the bases and in center field, with plus speed he can get to quickly and enough present feel on the grass to project a plus center fielder at maturity. At the plate, it's raw, with an aggressive approach and some issues with pitch recognition. There's also good hand speed and a projectable frame. Like with Peguero, the wrists just work. Patino tends to think he's more of a power hitter than he is at present and swings like it. But there's some room to fill out and get stronger in his upper body at least, so fringe pop might come, rounding out the profile and making him a top-of-the-order weapon.

15   Levi Kelly   RHP

Born: 05/14/99   Age: 21   Bats: R   Throws: R   Height: 6'4"   Weight: 205   Origin: Round 8, 2018 Draft (#249 overall)

YEAR	TEAM	LVL	AGE	W	L	SV	G	GS	IP	H	HR	BB/9	K/9	K	GB%	BABIP	WHIP	ERA	DRA	WARP	PF
2018	DIA	RK	19	0	0	0	4	4	6	3	0	3.0	9.0	6	47%	.200	0.83	0.00	2.79	0.2	83
2019	KNC	A	20	5	1	0	22	22	100¹	72	4	3.5	11.3	126	48%	.292	1.11	2.15	3.17	2.4	100
2020	ARI	MLB	21	2	2	0	33	0	35	34	5	3.8	9.3	36	44%	.308	1.41	4.63	4.72	0.3	101

Comparables: Neftalí Feliz, Miguel Almonte, Keyvius Sampson

In his first full-season assignment, Kelly turned himself from a probable future bullpen arm to a potential rotation piece. The delivery was simplified and overall control cleaned up by a transition to working out of the stretch exclusively. He also took a big step with the development of his secondaries, most notably the slider. He has confidence in it and it is a true weapon, showing two-plane movement and fading away from right-handed hitters. It plays well off of the fastball which sits in the mid 90s and has some late life. That fastball/slider combination gives Kelly a solid floor of a late-inning reliever. However, he was unhittable at times last year and if another secondary develops he'll solidify his role as a starter.

16   Drey Jameson   RHP

Born: 08/17/97   Age: 22   Bats: R   Throws: R   Height: 6'0"   Weight: 165   Origin: Round 1C, 2019 Draft (#34 overall)

YEAR	TEAM	LVL	AGE	W	L	SV	G	GS	IP	H	HR	BB/9	K/9	K	GB%	BABIP	WHIP	ERA	DRA	WARP	PF
2019	YAK	A-	21	0	0	0	8	8	11²	14	1	6.9	9.3	12	42%	.371	1.97	6.17	7.64	-0.3	99
2020	ARI	MLB	22	2	2	0	33	0	35	35	6	4.1	6.9	27	40%	.283	1.46	5.00	5.10	0.1	101

Comparables: Taylor Cole, Tyler Cloyd, Ryan Cook

After a dominant sophomore season at Ball State, the draft-eligible Jameson became yet another first-round pick for Arizona. He's an undersized righty—listed at 6-foot, 165 pounds—with an uptempo, effortful delivery, so there's strong reliever risk here. His fastball sat comfortably in the mid 90s when starting, though, and there may be more in short bursts. He pairs the fastball with a tight 12-6 curve which gives him the second pitch for late-inning work. There's a hard slider and a changeup—both potentially average—as well, but the mechanics, size, and overall command profile might limit him to late-inning pen work.

17 Luis Frias   RHP

Born: 05/23/98   Age: 22   Bats: R   Throws: R   Height: 6'3"   Weight: 180   Origin: International Free Agent, 2015

YEAR	TEAM	LVL	AGE	W	L	SV	G	GS	IP	H	HR	BB/9	K/9	K	GB%	BABIP	WHIP	ERA	DRA	WARP	PF
2018	DIA	RK	20	1	1	0	7	6	29	17	1	3.4	9.6	31	51%	.229	0.97	2.48	2.27	1.2	92
2018	YAK	A-	20	0	4	0	7	7	25²	21	0	5.3	9.5	27	32%	.309	1.40	3.16	4.38	0.3	97
2019	YAK	A-	21	3	3	0	10	10	49²	36	0	3.1	13.0	72	42%	.340	1.07	1.99	3.56	0.9	87
2019	KNC	A	21	3	1	0	6	6	26²	22	1	4.1	9.8	29	37%	.300	1.27	4.39	4.78	0.1	100
2020	ARI	MLB	22	2	2	0	33	0	35	34	5	3.8	9.4	37	35%	.312	1.40	4.49	4.62	0.3	101

Comparables: Domingo Germán, Touki Toussaint, Victor Alcántara

Originally signed as a third baseman in 2015 out of the Dominican Republic, the D'Backs moved the extra-large-framed but athletic Frias to the mound a year later. So far, the move has paid off as he fanned 101 batters over 76 1/3 innings between short-season and Low-A. Frias is in the conversation for the most electric stuff in Arizona's system. His four-pitch mix offers two potential plus pitches. Frias' straight fastball sits mid 90s and can touch 98 mph. He creates a steep downhill plane with it as he throws almost straight over the top. At times fastball command can be elusive when he overthrows, but overall control isn't an issue. Frias' best pitch is his 12-6 hammer curveball—one of the best I saw all year. Thrown in the low 80s, it has sharp, late bite and plenty of depth to it. He shows plus command of the breaker, throwing it for strikes or inducing chases and hitters from both sides of the plate look flabbergasted when trying to attack it. Frias also offers a mid-80s slider that has inconsistent shape but showed solid horizontal movement, and a high-80s split-changeup with hard tumble. Better feel and command for both of these secondaries is needed, but his split-changeup has a chance to be another big whiff pitch. With two plus swing-and-miss pitches, Frias has a solid floor as a relief arm and an intriguingly high ceiling if the rest of the arsenal rounds out with more mound experience.

18 Tommy Henry   LHP

Born: 07/29/97   Age: 22   Bats: L   Throws: L   Height: 6'3"   Weight: 205   Origin: Round 2, 2019 Draft (#74 overall)

YEAR	TEAM	LVL	AGE	W	L	SV	G	GS	IP	H	HR	BB/9	K/9	K	GB%	BABIP	WHIP	ERA	DRA	WARP	PF
2020	ARI	MLB	22	2	2	0	33	0	35	35	5	3.6	7.7	30	41%	.291	1.40	4.70	4.84	0.2	101

Comparables: Andrew Moore, Nick Margevicius, Matt Hall

Another 2019 draft pick to cover. Unlike the other new arms in the system, Henry is more of a polish guy than a stuff guy. A typical good college lefty in a lot of ways, he mixes a low-90s fastball in with an above-average changeup with solid dive and a short and slurvy slider that he commands well. It's a solid starter's frame, and Henry might even have a smidge of projection left despite being on the older side for a college pick. He was used heavily at Michigan during their College World Series run, so he only made a few one-inning appearances as a pro. We'll have more info on whether or not his command of averageish stuff plays against pro hitters next year, but for now he looks like your typical OFP 50 / No. 4 starter type, which is impressive to still be finding this deep in a system list.

19 Dominic Fletcher   OF

Born: 09/02/97   Age: 22   Bats: L   Throws: L   Height: 5'9"   Weight: 185   Origin: Round 2, 2019 Draft (#75 overall)

YEAR	TEAM	LVL	AGE	PA	R	2B	3B	HR	RBI	BB	K	SB	CS	AVG/OBP/SLG	DRC+	VORP	BABIP	BRR	FRAA	WARP	PF
2019	KNC	A	21	239	33	14	1	5	28	22	50	1	1	.318/.389/.463	145	21.1	.396	2.3	CF(25) -2.1, RF(22) 4.0	2.2	100
2020	ARI	MLB	22	251	24	12	1	6	27	15	71	3	1	.245/.296/.383	80	0.0	.326	0.0	CF 0, RF 1	0.3	101

Comparables: Darren Ford, Harrison Bader, Whit Merrifield

David Fletcher's younger brother was drafted out of Arkansas in 2019's Competitive Balance Round. Fletcher, Dominic that is, has an extra-large frame with thick, strong legs. The D'Backs pushed him to High-A Kane County and he was not overmatched. At the plate Fletcher controls the zone well with above-average plate coverage, displaying plus barrel control most of the time. He can spray it line-to-line, making him more of a contact guy than a true home run threat, but he has above-average raw power; his ability to transfer that power into games is still up for debate. Fletcher's swing is reminiscent of Brett Gardner's. He uses a lot of his upper half and doesn't engage his lower half fully, resulting in a long swing on occasion, especially on pitches up in the zone. Fletcher's slightly above-average speed should make him a marginal stolen base threat.

Defensively, he can play all three outfield spots. The 5-foot-9, 185-pounder moves with ease and swiftness, showing fluid movements and routes—a plus defender. His arm flashes plus at times but sits comfortably in the above-average range. Fletcher is a grinder, and profiles as an average, everyday center fielder with a floor as a platoon outfielder.

20 Andy Young IF

Born: 05/10/94   Age: 26   Bats: R   Throws: R   Height: 6'0"   Weight: 195   Origin: Round 37, 2016 Draft (#1126 overall)

YEAR	TEAM	LVL	AGE	PA	R	2B	3B	HR	RBI	BB	K	SB	CS	AVG/OBP/SLG	DRC+	VORP	BABIP	BRR	FRAA	WARP	PF
2017	PEO	A	23	244	31	11	4	12	38	22	54	5	2	.284/.379/.545	152	26.2	.331	0.7	2B(28) -2.3, 3B(15) 0.0	2.1	96
2017	PMB	A+	23	221	24	9	0	5	20	10	49	3	0	.265/.327/.388	111	11.7	.322	0.7	2B(30) -2.0, SS(13) 0.0	0.6	92
2018	PMB	A+	24	351	43	10	2	12	34	31	59	4	0	.276/.372/.444	141	29.4	.304	-0.1	2B(73) -4.5, 3B(7) -0.5	1.9	94
2018	SFD	AA	24	152	18	3	1	9	24	7	26	0	2	.319/.395/.556	149	14.4	.340	-0.9	2B(30) -2.8, 3B(7) -0.7	0.7	105
2019	WTN	AA	25	263	36	15	2	8	28	18	53	1	1	.260/.363/.453	128	18.2	.305	-0.3	2B(47) -2.5, SS(8) -1.1	1.2	99
2019	RNO	AAA	25	277	53	10	3	21	53	24	68	2	2	.280/.373/.611	110	21.2	.305	0.9	SS(25) 1.3, 3B(23) -1.0	1.5	109
2020	ARI	MLB	26	112	14	5	1	6	17	7	32	0	0	.247/.324/.481	116	2.0	.300	-0.2	2B -1, 3B 0	0.4	101

Comparables: Jonathan Davis, Jack Mayfield, Steve Pearce

The other, other part of the Paul Goldschmidt deal, there was plenty of residual Cardinals Devil Magic left in the former 37th-round small college infielder. There might not be a prospect who enjoyed the new PCL ball more than Young, who smashed 21 home runs in just 68 games for Reno. That overstates his power projection, but there's solid raw with some feel to hit. The plate approach and glove are limiting factors here and probably make Young more of a useful bench piece than an everyday guy, but he can stand at a bunch of infield spots and is a potentially better-than-average bat. Those guys tend to get 300 PA here and there for a while.

Personal Cheeseball

PC Domingo Leyba 2B

Born: 09/11/95   Age: 24   Bats: B   Throws: R   Height: 5'11"   Weight: 160   Origin: International Free Agent, 2006

YEAR	TEAM	LVL	AGE	PA	R	2B	3B	HR	RBI	BB	K	SB	CS	AVG/OBP/SLG	DRC+	VORP	BABIP	BRR	FRAA	WARP	PF
2017	YAK	A-	21	32	4	1	0	1	6	4	2	0	0	.286/.375/.429	123	2.0	.280	0.1	SS(6) 2.0	0.4	105
2017	WTN	AA	21	64	11	4	0	2	9	5	6	0	0	.276/.344/.448	121	5.5	.280	1.9	SS(14) -2.2	0.4	105
2018	WTN	AA	22	358	43	17	2	5	30	35	46	5	2	.269/.344/.381	116	14.0	.300	-1.7	2B(72) -2.9, SS(8) 0.5	1.3	101
2019	RNO	AAA	23	498	85	37	3	19	77	32	78	0	2	.300/.351/.519	92	23.9	.325	2.9	SS(66) -4.0, 2B(42) 2.9	1.7	110
2019	ARI	MLB	23	30	6	2	1	0	5	4	9	0	0	.280/.367/.440	84	0.4	.412	0.0	2B(8) 0.4, SS(2) 0.1	0.1	98
2020	ARI	MLB	24	112	11	5	1	3	12	7	23	1	0	.233/.286/.381	70	2.0	.270	0.1	2B 0, SS 0	0.0	101

Comparables: Cole Tucker, Enrique Hernández, Ben Taylor

Man, I really wanted to get Leyba on this list. It's just too deep and laden with upside to justify it. I still think he can be a second-division starter at the keystone, and at worst he's a useful extra infielder with a broad base of skills. Mostly he's a link back to when this system wasn't, uh, quite this good and he was top-five, but at least a little interesting to write about. Now the system is far more up my alley, loaded with interesting prep arms, and high-waisted teenaged athlete bats. Leyba is extremely neither of those, a 24-year-old middle infielder who's stretched at short, not particularly athletic, and missed chunks of 2017 and 2018 while the system improved around him. He can hit a bit though, and while he's likely squeezed out of a clear 2020 role with Arizona despite a solid September cameo, Leyba is clearly the system's cheeseball.

Low Minors Sleeper

LMS Jeferson Espinal OF
Born: 06/07/02   Age: 18   Bats: L   Throws: L   Height: 6'0"   Weight: 180   Origin: International Free Agent, 2018

YEAR	TEAM	LVL	AGE	PA	R	2B	3B	HR	RBI	BB	K	SB	CS	AVG/OBP/SLG	DRC+	VORP	BABIP	BRR	FRAA	WARP	PF
2019	DIA	RK	17	43	6	1	0	0	7	8	11	4	1	.286/.419/.314	127	4.3	.417	0.7	CF(7) 0.7, LF(2) -0.2	0.4	96
2020	ARI	MLB	18	251	23	11	1	3	20	31	94	3	1	.220/.321/.312	76	0.0	.373	0.0	CF 1, LF 0	0.2	101

Comparables: Jason Martin, Ronald Acuña Jr., José Martínez

We leave my favorite (not best, Rays fans, calm down) system with one more toolsy teenager for the road. Espinal is a lesser version of Patino at present although he carries a similar center field profile. He's more likely to project as the bench outfielder version, as he lacks some of Patino's physicality, and may be more of a slash and burn guy. Check back in two years, though by then I am sure all your dynasty league mates will have rostered him due to his Northwest League steal totals.

Top Talents 25 and Under (as of 4/1/2020)

1. Kristian Robinson
2. Carson Kelly
3. Zac Gallen
4. Alek Thomas
5. Daulton Varsho
6. Geraldo Perdomo
7. Corbin Carroll
8. Brennan Malone
9. Blake Walston
10. Corbin Martin

There are few talents in baseball, let alone inside the Diamondbacks' organization, that boast the kind of impact talent that Kristian Robinson is capable of deploying at peak. He's got plus-plus physicality that looks more applicable to a college football field more than a baseball diamond. But he has a good idea of what he's doing with both the bat and the glove and if he can get to most of his projection, he's going to be a very good one. If he gets to all of it, well, let's not go there just yet because he just turned 19.

Carson Kelly's ability to catch has never been in question, but he used 2019 to prove that all of those forecasts about his hitting weren't in vain. He ate lefties for lunch but had a much tougher time against arm-side pitching. He's still a tremendous asset who's already proven his worth. And, given his lack of consistent big league experience, may have yet another gear to grab. Zac Gallen came to Arizona mid-season in a swap for Jazz Chisholm and immediately looked the part of a controllable mid-rotation starter. There isn't one particular carrying tool or pitch in his arsenal that jumps off the page. The changeup is the best of the bunch, however, and the control is there for him to keep up this kind of profile with a chance to take another step forward.

Alek Thomas has pushed himself into comfortable top-100 territory with his monster 2019 campaign. An advanced approach has served him well and there's enough physical strength in his compact frame to allow for more pop to come than might meet the eye at first glance. Staying in center field would help his stock, but he could also be a real asset in left should it come to that down the line. You're probably well aware that Daulton Varsho can hit. Where he lines up remains the question. An electronic strike zone could allow him to stay behind the dish, but he should be able to slide into left field easily enough or even, perhaps, take some reps at second if he doesn't catch much. A super-utility guy with his hitting ability should allow Torey Lovullo to get creative on a nightly basis.

Geraldo Perdomo popped up in the summer of 2018 then impressed that fall. Since then, he has performed well in full season ball, High-A and the Arizona Fall League (almost all of that production came at the age of 19, by the way). Corbin Carroll made his presence felt immediately after being drafted and has a chance to wind up the best outfielder in this system, depending on how he and his soon-to-be teammates mature. Brennan Malone was a luxury with the 33rd overall pick in June, thanks in part to all of those draft picks, and has plenty of upside. Arizona was all over Walston pre-draft and popped him 26th overall. The lanky lefty didn't pitch much in his debut but is a player development bet with a high rate of return should he pay off. Corbin Martin joined the organization in the Greinke deal and, despite his ongoing TJ rehab, should be a solid asset for the D-backs long-term.

The Diamondbacks' big league squad is intriguing in how age is currently distributed across the roster. Arizona should feature a bunch of guys playing in their age-26 through age-31 seasons. That's to say, the team won't be especially young, but not especially old, either. As the list above shows, however, there's another wave on the way. While the D-backs intend to compete in 2020, there should be plenty of rolling turnover in the next few years as these prospects matriculate to the majors. The Diamondbacks' roster should get collectively younger in the process, but that's still a year or two off.

Eyewitness Reports

Eyewitness Report: Kristian Robinson

Evaluator: Forest Stulting
Report Date: 11/19/2019
Dates Seen: June-August 2019
Risk Factor: Medium
Physical/Health: XL frame, athletic, lean, room to grow muscle, tall, strong and long legs, plus body control, quick twitch, agile, explosive, confident, gamer.

Tool	Future Grade	Report
Hit	55	Slight bat wiggle and swaying with lower body preload, settles as pitcher comes set, hands at shoulder with bat at 45 degree angle, high elbow, small stride, rubber band effect, not much movement in upper body in load, stays balanced and in rhythm, plus bat speed and barrel control, short stroke, easy swing, barrel stays through the zone on fairly flat path, uses lower half well, solid rotation in back hip, one-armed follow through, takes first pitch a lot, lunges at off speed occasionally, shows flashes of controlling the zone but needs improvement seeing breaking pitches earlier, will swing and miss, expands with two strikes a lot, approach is mainly pull and up the middle, has shown ability to go with outside pitches with authority, can hit any fastball, hunts fastball, ball jumps off bat.
Power	70	Future power to all fields, approach is to left and center field, plus-plus raw power, see flashes of in-game power to left and center, strength to hit low and high launch angle homers, knows how to get the ball in the air.
Baserunning/Speed	60	Stolen base potential, needs to improve stolen base instincts, long strides, minimal effort, slightly above-average instincts on bases, gets out of box quickly, agile, glides.
Glove	60	Athletic enough to make almost any play, confident going to wall, plus range, route efficiency needs improvement, can get turned around at times, smooth fielding ground balls in OF, average and inconsistent jumps, shown ability to make diving catches in all directions.
Arm	60	Plays plus in any outfield slot, plus velocity, plus carry, on a line, accurate, sets feet well, fluid release.

Conclusion: Once Robinson improves his instincts with reps he has the potential to be a true five-tool player with a long and successful big-league career.

Eyewitness Report: Alek Thomas

Evaluator: Nathan Graham
Report Date: 07/16/2019
Dates Seen: 6/18/19; 7/11/19
Risk Factor: High
Physical/Health: Smaller frame but strong, athletic with some quick twitch; mild projection left in the frame.

Tool	Future Grade	Report
Hit	60	Upright balanced stance with a mild load and leg kick, incorporates lower half well; Has good bat to barrel skills, shows an advanced approach at the plate, will attack in hitter's counts, recognizes spin and does not often expand the zone.
Power	45	Strong and compact frame and above average bat speed generate sneaky pop; makes loud contact to all fields, mostly line drives; Not going to be a slugger but power will play fringe average at maturity.
Baserunning/ Speed	60	Plus runner with a quick start up; 3.97 clock on a dig to first; not a huge threat to steal bases but is aggressive and smart on the base paths.
Glove	60	Has the tools and instincts to be a plus defender in center field; speed and athleticism give plus range, gets good jumps.
Arm	45	Accurate, but lacks arm strength, not a ton of carry on throws; will be stretched to handle center.

Conclusion: Speed and defense give a major league floor for Thomas. A projected plus hit tool and his ability to stick in center field give a profile of a future everyday outfielder.

Atlanta Braves

The State of the System

There are a lot of familiar names here, but they're still good prospects, and they are now close to helping a good major-league team.

The Top Ten

★ ★ ★ *2020 Top 101 Prospect* **#22** ★ ★ ★

1 **Cristian Pache** **OF** OFP: 70 ETA: 2020
Born: 11/19/98 Age: 21 Bats: R Throws: R Height: 6'2" Weight: 185 Origin: International Free Agent, 2015

YEAR	TEAM	LVL	AGE	PA	R	2B	3B	HR	RBI	BB	K	SB	CS	AVG/OBP/SLG	DRC+	VORP	BABIP	BRR	FRAA	WARP	PF
2017	ROM	A	18	514	60	13	8	0	42	39	104	32	14	.281/.335/.343	100	22.0	.360	5.8	CF(116) 27.8, RF(2) 0.0	5.2	103
2018	BRV	A+	19	387	46	20	5	8	40	15	69	7	6	.285/.311/.431	114	14.7	.330	-1.1	CF(93) 3.9	2.1	98
2018	MIS	AA	19	109	10	3	1	1	7	5	28	0	2	.260/.294/.337	69	-0.6	.347	-0.5	CF(28) 1.3	0.1	97
2019	MIS	AA	20	433	50	28	8	11	53	34	104	8	11	.278/.340/.474	139	30.2	.351	-1.7	CF(57) 1.6, RF(23) 3.3	3.3	95
2019	GWN	AAA	20	105	13	8	1	1	8	9	18	0	0	.274/.337/.411	90	1.2	.329	-0.9	CF(23) -3.2, RF(3) 3.3	0.2	101
2020	ATL	MLB	21	147	14	7	1	4	16	9	37	3	2	.251/.299/.402	80	0.0	.320	-0.1	CF 1, RF 1	0.3	103

Comparables: Ronald Acuña Jr., Jake Bauers, Freddie Freeman

The Report: Signed as a raw, yet toolsy outfielder with an elite predilection defensively, Pache has improved each year offensively to round out his game as the top prospect in the organization and one of the best in baseball. It helps having an abundance of athleticism to draw from, as he's been able to maintain his dynamic body while adding strength. In the span of one season he put on 10-15 pounds of muscle on what was once a very thin frame, with still some room left to completely fill out.

It's always been a free-swinging approach that produces a lot of contact, but now the power is becoming more pronounced with the added strength. He's a fastball hunter with relatively quiet movements, employing a modest leg kick in fastball counts and shortening up against offspeed. Previously, he had a tendency to swing out of his shoes to generate more power, but as the body developed, he's been able to stay balanced through contact better without sacrificing power and also allowing to see the ball better.

The strikeouts will always be a concern given his approach, but the latest signs of improved plate discipline would be the finishing touches on the makings of a true five-tool player. With plus speed, a double-plus glove and throwing arm, Pache should be roaming the outfield very early in 2020. He saw time in all three outfield spots last season because of the current deployment of outfielders in Atlanta, but center field would be a natural fit. Alongside Ronald Acuña (and another prospect not much further down this list), Pache is poised to be part of an exciting trio of outfielders for years to come.

Variance: High. He has unteachable talent, but what remains to be taught is a honed approach that will inevitably determine just how high the ceiling is.

Mark Barry's Fantasy Take: *Finally* a super-toolsy and exciting outfielder in Atlanta. It's about time. Pache's defense is the marquee quality for sure, but for our purposes, his ceiling will depend on two things—1) whether he can curtail the Ks enough to unlock his power whilst (damn right, whilst) not sapping batting average, and 2) whether his elite speed can translate to stolen bases. That second part might be the most important, as Pache can definitely run, but snagged just eight bags in 19 tries this season. Upside is perhaps peak Ender Inciarte with 20+ homer pop. Downside is 2019 Ender Inciarte without steals.

★ ★ ★ *2020 Top 101 Prospect* **#38** ★ ★ ★

2 Ian Anderson RHP   OFP: 60   ETA: 2020
Born: 05/02/98   Age: 22   Bats: R   Throws: R   Height: 6'3"   Weight: 170   Origin: Round 1, 2016 Draft (#3 overall)

YEAR	TEAM	LVL	AGE	W	L	SV	G	GS	IP	H	HR	BB/9	K/9	K	GB%	BABIP	WHIP	ERA	DRA	WARP	PF
2017	ROM	A	19	4	5	0	20	20	83	69	0	4.7	11.0	101	50%	.345	1.35	3.14	3.80	1.4	103
2018	BRV	A+	20	2	6	0	20	20	100	73	2	3.6	10.6	118	47%	.282	1.13	2.52	2.75	3.0	96
2018	MIS	AA	20	2	1	0	4	4	19¹	14	0	4.2	11.2	24	48%	.304	1.19	2.33	3.29	0.5	94
2019	MIS	AA	21	7	5	0	21	21	111	82	8	3.8	11.9	147	46%	.287	1.16	2.68	3.80	1.6	94
2019	GWN	AAA	21	1	2	0	5	5	24²	23	5	6.6	9.1	25	39%	.277	1.66	6.57	4.87	0.4	103
2020	ATL	MLB	22	3	4	0	22	11	57	55	7	3.6	9.9	62	42%	.316	1.37	4.12	4.24	0.9	103

Comparables: Alex Reyes, Archie Bradley, Jake Thompson

The Report: The crown jewel of a deep pitching pipeline that Braves' player development keeps producing is tall righty Ian Anderson. He's one of a slough of pitching prospects drafted and developed in relatively short order, part of a talent class that ascended together to all reach Triple-A around their age-21 season. While his five-start stint in Gwinnett wasn't glamorous due to giving up the longball at an uncharacteristic clip, he's quietly amassed an impressive minor league resume chalking up strikeouts and preventing runs.

He stands much taller on the hill than his listed 6-foot-3, and with long levers and a high three-quarters arm slot he is able to get excellent plane on his fastball that sits 92-94 but can top out at 96 mph. The arm slot is key to Anderson's success, as it makes it difficult to square up the heater and also provides the unconventional shape he gets from his secondary offerings. The curveball is his best present offspeed pitch, and it has good tumbling finish in the zone, but the changeup flashes equal promise despite its inconsistencies with late sink.

What is left to accomplish prior to cracking the big league roster? He tends to nibble around the strike zone, which can lead to deep counts and inflated walk totals. The stuff is good enough to attack hitters and have more efficient outings, rather than relying on trying to strike out everybody. His late season struggle was one of the first of his professional career, so how he handles adversity will be something to monitor.

Variance: Medium. The mechanics are clean, even with a high delivery, and there's no history of arm issues. Like any young pitcher, especially one who is enduring a heavy innings workload for the first time in his life, there is always mild risk involved.

Mark Barry's Fantasy Take: When Anderson was drafted, I remember thinking "Huh, that seems like a reach. I don't know about that one, Braves." Well, I'm big enough to tell you that Past Mark is a dumb idiot. The extra walks are troubling, yes, but I can't think of five dynasty hurlers I'd rather have than Anderson.

★ ★ ★ *2020 Top 101 Prospect* **#42** ★ ★ ★

3 Drew Waters OF   OFP: 60   ETA: 2020
Born: 12/30/98   Age: 21   Bats: B   Throws: R   Height: 6'2"   Weight: 183   Origin: Round 2, 2017 Draft (#41 overall)

YEAR	TEAM	LVL	AGE	PA	R	2B	3B	HR	RBI	BB	K	SB	CS	AVG/OBP/SLG	DRC+	VORP	BABIP	BRR	FRAA	WARP	PF
2017	BRA	RK	18	58	13	3	1	2	10	7	11	2	1	.347/.448/.571	126	7.9	.417	0.8	CF(9) -1.6, RF(3) 0.7	0.2	104
2017	DNV	RK	18	166	20	11	1	2	14	16	59	4	2	.255/.331/.383	84	5.9	.409	-1.3	CF(35) -4.6	-0.3	91
2018	ROM	A	19	365	58	32	6	9	36	21	72	20	5	.303/.353/.513	143	31.6	.362	3.9	CF(83) -0.6	3.2	99
2018	BRV	A+	19	133	14	7	3	0	3	8	33	3	0	.268/.316/.374	92	4.6	.363	0.0	CF(30) -1.5, RF(1) -0.1	0.2	97
2019	MIS	AA	20	454	63	35	9	5	41	28	121	13	6	.319/.366/.481	143	36.7	.436	-3.3	LF(54) 6.3, CF(38) 7.0	4.2	94
2019	GWN	AAA	20	119	17	5	0	2	11	11	43	3	0	.271/.336/.374	79	-1.1	.429	0.7	RF(16) 2.1, LF(7) 0.4	0.3	101
2020	ATL	MLB	21	105	10	7	1	2	12	6	35	2	1	.259/.310/.418	87	0.0	.381	0.1	LF 2, RF 1	0.4	103

Comparables: Jorge Bonifacio, Travis Snider, Andrew Lambo

The Report: Selected as one of the youngest players in the 2017 draft, Waters has done nothing but hit since joining the Braves, reaching Triple-A last year at 20 years old. The accelerated path is a product of his offensive potential as a switch-hitting doubles machine who is still tapping into his power. The question that confounds evaluators is whether the game power will ever be fully realized given his flat bat path and propensity to be out on his front leg, which saps potential power out of the swing. Regardless, he led the Southern League in hitting as one of its youngest players before his late season promotion to Gwinnett.

His hyper-aggressive approach leads to either hard contact early in the at-bat, or gets him quickly behind in the count where he's forced to battle. There's more fluidity from the left side where he's able to drop his hands quickly to meet the ball, whereas from the right-handed batter's box he looks more stiff and out of sync. It's fair to question how long he will continue switch-hitting given the disparity in platoon splits that are evident in each of his pro seasons.

Defensively, he is passable in every outfield spot, but given a future triumvirate of Cristian Pache and Ronald Acuña in Atlanta, he would likely be relegated to left field as the weakest glove of the three. He is far from a polished product, but the natural talent to hit line drives with regularity will have him knocking on the door of the majors in short order.

Variance: Very high. Depending on who you ask, Waters will either be a star at his peak or an average, everyday player. It all boils down to if the power arrives and the doubles turn into homers.

Mark Barry's Fantasy Take: I guess I shouldn't penalize Waters for not knowing who he is at 20 years old. In a dynasty setting, it would be nice to figure it out though. If he can scale back on the strikeouts while maintaining his efficiency on the bases, he's got OF2 upside. If he doesn't, well, he doesn't. He's still a top-20 dynasty prospect, so we're grading on a big curve here, but there is some downside if things don't click.

★ ★ ★ *2020 Top 101 Prospect* **#60** ★ ★ ★

4 | **Kyle Muller LHP** | OFP: 60 | ETA: 2020
Born: 10/07/97 Age: 22 Bats: R Throws: L Height: 6'6" Weight: 225 Origin: Round 2, 2016 Draft (#44 overall)

YEAR	TEAM	LVL	AGE	W	L	SV	G	GS	IP	H	HR	BB/9	K/9	K	GB%	BABIP	WHIP	ERA	DRA	WARP	PF
2017	DNV	RK	19	1	1	0	11	11	47²	43	5	3.4	9.3	49	40%	.284	1.28	4.15	3.39	1.4	96
2018	ROM	A	20	3	0	0	6	6	30	24	3	2.4	6.9	23	54%	.253	1.07	2.40	4.18	0.4	98
2018	BRV	A+	20	4	2	0	14	14	80²	80	2	3.6	8.8	79	42%	.350	1.39	3.24	4.91	0.4	98
2018	MIS	AA	20	4	1	0	5	5	29	22	3	1.9	8.4	27	40%	.244	0.97	3.10	3.48	0.6	94
2019	MIS	AA	21	7	6	0	22	22	111²	81	5	5.5	9.7	120	41%	.284	1.33	3.14	4.85	0.1	92
2020	ATL	MLB	22	1	1	0	3	3	16	16	2	3.8	8.4	15	39%	.302	1.43	4.59	4.71	0.2	103

Comparables: Eduardo Rodriguez, Jake Thompson, Génesis Cabrera

The Report: Big man, big fastball, big strikeouts, but also big walks. "Big" is the appropriate word when describing Kyle Muller—including his potential—but within a good 2019 campaign a troubling trend lurked. A slight up-tick in fastball velocity led to elevated strikeout totals but also an alarmingly high amount of walks issued compared to his previous body of work.

Regularly working in the mid-to-upper 90s, the southpaw unquestionably has a live arm, but the extra effort exerted to reach the high 90s more consistently has had a negative effect on his command. The overall package is that of a potential starter, with a breaking ball he can manipulate to have a slurvy break or tighter slider shape, and a changeup that took a big step forward to perhaps become his best secondary offering.

The frame is prototypical workhorse material, the stuff is obvious, but unless the walk totals go back to their pre-2019 average ratings, the question of a potential reliever profile begins to creep into the discussion.

Variance: Very high. The upside in Muller's game could push his grade even higher, but with the sudden increase in velocity and subsequent drop in command there is risk regarding his future role and inherent injury risk, too.

Mark Barry's Fantasy Take: If I had to guess, Muller's favorite Lou Reed song is "Walk on the Wild Side." I bet he also really enjoyed the White Walkers in *Game of Thrones*. He walks a lot of people, is what I'm saying. The talent is absolutely there for a top-100 dynasty prospect, but the extra free passes lead me to believe he could be a liability in the rate stats, expanding his floor to fantasy SP6ish or *gasp* a reliever.

──────────────────── ★ ★ ★ *2020 Top 101 Prospect* **#77** ★ ★ ★ ────────────────────

5 Shea Langeliers   C   OFP: 55   ETA: 2021

Born: 11/18/97   Age: 22   Bats: R   Throws: R   Height: 6'0"   Weight: 190   Origin: Round 1, 2019 Draft (#9 overall)

YEAR	TEAM	LVL	AGE	PA	R	2B	3B	HR	RBI	BB	K	SB	CS	AVG/OBP/SLG	DRC+	VORP	BABIP	BRR	FRAA	WARP	PF
2019	ROM	A	21	239	27	13	0	2	34	17	55	0	0	.255/.310/.343	100	4.9	.325	-1.3	C(41) 0.8	0.9	103
2020	ATL	MLB	22	251	21	12	1	4	23	15	76	2	1	.219/.271/.330	58	0.0	.304	0.0	C 0	-0.4	103

Comparables: Eddy Rodriguez, Tomás Nido, Elias Díaz

The Report: Atlanta was high on Langeliers and went all-in on the top defensive catcher in the 2019 draft class. He would've been the first backstop taken if not for a certain No. 1 overall pick. No catcher is ever a certainty coming through the minor leagues, but even a small hint of a productive bat will push Langeliers to the upper levels because of an impressive set of defensive tools. He has the makings of a plus glove with a strong feel to receive, solid footwork and an advanced ability to handle a game and pitching staff. He's a leader on the field. It also helps that he flashes plus-plus pop times and has an easy plus arm as one of the biggest weapons on the field. He has a strong catcher's frame with a durable lower half, but he's also more athletic than the typical backstop. At the plate, Langeliers has a surprisingly quick bat and sound swing geared for contact and gap power. His above-average raw power produces loud contact, but his first taste of pro ball left him between pitches at times and he pressed himself into over-aggressiveness. A quick, short stroke and aptitude are on his side and should be enough to reach average hit and power. That's enough to make Langeliers a glove-first starter.

Variance: Medium. Catchers can take a million different directions developmentally, but Langeliers can put you a little more at ease because of advanced, standout defense that will carry his profile.

Mark Barry's Fantasy Take: Glove-first, dynasty-catching prospects rank somewhere between Hall of Fame arguments and the Cleveland baseball team's spending habits on my list of least favorite things. Sure, he could eventually be a top-five backstop on the NL, but according to valuations czar Mike Gianella that's only good for the 91st most valuable hitter on the Senior Circuit. I like Langeliers more than the next catcher we'll get to on this list, but it's a low bar.

──────────────────── ★ ★ ★ *2020 Top 101 Prospect* **#89** ★ ★ ★ ────────────────────

6 Kyle Wright   RHP   OFP: 60   ETA: 2018

Born: 10/02/95   Age: 24   Bats: R   Throws: R   Height: 6'4"   Weight: 200   Origin: Round 1, 2017 Draft (#5 overall)

YEAR	TEAM	LVL	AGE	W	L	SV	G	GS	IP	H	HR	BB/9	K/9	K	GB%	BABIP	WHIP	ERA	DRA	WARP	PF
2017	BRV	A+	21	0	1	0	6	6	11¹	8	0	3.2	7.9	10	61%	.258	1.06	3.18	3.01	0.3	102
2018	MIS	AA	22	6	8	0	20	20	109¹	103	6	3.5	8.6	105	56%	.311	1.34	3.70	4.12	1.6	94
2018	GWN	AAA	22	2	1	0	7	4	28²	15	2	2.5	8.8	28	51%	.183	0.80	2.51	2.15	1.1	98
2018	ATL	MLB	22	0	0	0	4	0	6	4	2	9.0	7.5	5	41%	.133	1.67	4.50	4.98	0.0	92
2019	GWN	AAA	23	11	4	0	21	21	112¹	107	13	2.8	9.3	116	48%	.313	1.26	4.17	3.54	3.4	101
2019	ATL	MLB	23	0	3	0	7	4	19²	24	4	5.9	8.2	18	43%	.351	1.88	8.69	6.33	-0.1	103
2020	ATL	MLB	24	4	5	0	37	10	78	83	12	3.7	7.8	68	47%	.308	1.48	5.09	5.08	0.5	103

Comparables: Reynaldo López, Zack Wheeler, Zack Littell

The Report: David noted in this space last year that Wright is, on paper, "the ideal pitching prospect." He's certainly got an ideal build. He has the full four-pitch mix, and he's added a sinker. His mechanics are visually impressive and repeatable. He pitched well for three years in the SEC and went in the top five in his draft year. He moved through the minors quickly, making his major-league debut just fifteen months after he was drafted. Why, then, has he been slipping just a little each year for us?

The whole is adding up to be a bit less than the sum of the parts, I suppose, and it might be sending Wright on a different path than we expected. The fastball is still in the same 92-96 velocity band where it's always been, touching a tick or two higher. Yet his fastball command has never advanced far enough for it to play up, and it gets hit just a little more than you'd like. His slider velocity has ticked up into the 88-90 range, and it's gotten more cuttery, to the point that Wright has referred to it as both a slider and a cutter. It's his best offspeed, a true out pitch…and also the only one that projects as an above-average pitch right now. Neither his curve nor his change has advanced to be a reliable third offering.

So what we have, as he's on the precipice of fully graduating to the majors, is a pitcher reliant on his mid-90s fastball and power slider, with command and third pitch questions, who looked generally dominant in September short relief. Let's pretend he's not Kyle Wright, former Vanderbilt ace and fifth-overall pick and mound adonis, and just Kyle Wright, pitching prospect. Doesn't that sound a whole lot like a future closer instead of a mid-rotation starter to you?

Variance: Medium. Wright has already reached an up-and-down role, and he's likely to be at least a decent major-league pitcher as soon as 2020. There's some volatility in terms of role, and to some extent there's the whole "mid-rotation prospects rarely end up exactly turning into mid-rotation pitchers" thing going on here.

Mark Barry's Fantasy Take: One person that's probably psyched by the Braves signing ALL OF THE RELIEVERS this offseason has to be Wright. After getting rocked in his first big-league taste as a starter, he was relegated to a bullpen role down the stretch, and really has the stuff to be a late-inning star. He'll likely get the chance to start again now, and if he can hone a third pitch (which is, like, super easy, right?), fantasy SP4 is still the upside.

7 Bryse Wilson RHP   OFP: 55   ETA: 2018

Born: 12/20/97   Age: 22   Bats: R   Throws: R   Height: 6'1"   Weight: 225   Origin: Round 4, 2016 Draft (#109 overall)

YEAR	TEAM	LVL	AGE	W	L	SV	G	GS	IP	H	HR	BB/9	K/9	K	GB%	BABIP	WHIP	ERA	DRA	WARP	PF
2017	ROM	A	19	10	7	0	26	26	137	105	8	2.4	9.1	139	54%	.272	1.04	2.50	3.33	3.1	101
2018	BRV	A+	20	2	0	0	5	5	26²	16	0	2.4	8.8	26	60%	.229	0.86	0.34	2.48	0.9	95
2018	MIS	AA	20	3	5	0	15	15	77	77	3	3.0	10.4	89	44%	.347	1.34	3.97	4.63	0.6	93
2018	GWN	AAA	20	3	0	0	5	3	22	20	6	1.2	11.5	28	45%	.280	1.05	5.32	3.38	0.5	98
2018	ATL	MLB	20	1	0	0	3	1	7	8	0	7.7	7.7	6	29%	.381	2.00	6.43	5.37	0.0	94
2019	GWN	AAA	21	10	7	0	21	21	121	120	12	1.9	8.8	118	46%	.316	1.21	3.42	3.27	4.0	102
2019	ATL	MLB	21	1	1	0	6	4	20	26	5	4.5	7.2	16	34%	.339	1.80	7.20	7.30	-0.3	100
2020	ATL	MLB	22	3	3	0	37	5	58	60	10	2.9	7.9	51	40%	.294	1.35	4.60	4.80	0.5	103

Comparables: Lucas Giolito, Jaime Barria, Jake Thompson

The Report: Wilson shot up from A-ball to the majors in 2018. 2019 was more of a consolidation year; he pitched well in Triple-A, but struggled in a handful of stints in the majors. In many ways, he's been in a similar pattern to Wright over the last year: he's slipped a little more in that he's failed to take a step forward. That said, unlike Wright, before 2019 he did actually make big strides from where he was on draft day.

He remains an extremely fastball-reliant pitcher at present, throwing it around 70 percent of the time in the majors so far. It's a very good fastball, thrown in the mid 90s with late life. But it's hard to thrive as a starting pitcher with that level of fastball usage. The slider and changeup both flash above-average, but neither is consistently there, and he doesn't reliably lean on either as a primary offspeed quite yet. Like Wright, it is possible that his future home is more in a late-inning relief role, especially given organizational pitching depth.

Wilson doesn't turn 22 until next month. There isn't a lot left for him to show in Triple-A. The Braves, who have four rotation spots locked up already by Mike Soroka, Mike Foltynewicz, Max Fried, and Cole Hamels, have multiple other Opening Day rotation candidates, including Wright, Touki Toussaint, and Sean Newcomb. So Wilson might get squeezed into the bullpen or even back to Triple-A; the 2020 Braves present a case where the needs of player development and a contending major-league roster might be at cross purposes.

Variance: Medium. Wilson has also reached an up-or-down role, and also is about ready. We do think he's a bit less likely to put it all together and end up higher than a mid-rotation type than Wright, which explains why he's behind him here.

Mark Barry's Fantasy Take: Wilson might be a prisoner of his organization, as he's probably ready to pitch full time in the big leagues, but the Braves are overflowing with options for back of the rotation starters. I think that's his role, though, as a sixth starter and a fantasy streamer. There's always going to be a guy like this on the wire.

8 William Contreras C   OFP: 55   ETA: 2021

Born: 12/24/97   Age: 22   Bats: R   Throws: R   Height: 6'0"   Weight: 180   Origin: International Free Agent, 2015

YEAR	TEAM	LVL	AGE	PA	R	2B	3B	HR	RBI	BB	K	SB	CS	AVG/OBP/SLG	DRC+	VORP	BABIP	BRR	FRAA	WARP	PF
2017	DNV	RK	19	198	29	10	1	4	25	24	30	1	0	.290/.379/.432	133	19.2	.326	-0.4	C(35) -0.5	1.4	92
2018	ROM	A	20	342	54	17	1	11	39	29	73	1	1	.293/.360/.463	138	23.3	.351	-0.9	C(43) -0.3	2.2	98
2018	BRV	A+	20	90	3	7	0	0	10	6	16	0	0	.253/.300/.337	103	2.5	.309	-0.3	C(20) -0.4	0.3	97
2019	BRV	A+	21	207	26	11	0	3	22	14	44	0	0	.263/.324/.368	112	6.6	.329	-0.2	C(43) -0.8	1.0	96
2019	MIS	AA	21	209	24	9	0	3	17	15	40	0	0	.246/.306/.340	99	8.4	.295	0.8	C(52) -1.1	0.9	91
2020	ATL	MLB	22	251	24	13	1	6	27	15	64	0	0	.245/.296/.383	75	0.0	.312	-0.4	C -3	-0.3	103

Comparables: Abiatal Avelino, Meibrys Viloria, Jacob Nottingham

The Report: The start of Contreras's season in High-A and the latter part in Double-A was a study in contrasts largely driven by confidence. In High-A, Contreras had a swagger that carried into every part of his game. He was an energetic and athletic player who led with his attitude and his play. His Double-A performance was an example of how important confidence is in a player's performance as he was noticeably more subdued in every area and his results suffered.

When at his best, Contreras has the makings of a solid defensive catcher. His arm is his best tool and he uses it liberally to keep runners honest. He has some work to do to refine his framing and blocking, but he has soft hands and quick feet and shows a willingness to work to improve. He projects as an above-average defender.

Offensively, Contreras has an athletic approach with a solid foundation. He has quick hands and slightly above-average bat speed. He struggles with timing and he likely needs an adjustment to get to more loft in his swing to access his power more efficiently.

Again, the difference in levels was interesting. At High-A, he was aggressive and that made him susceptible to offspeed pitches, especially in higher-leverage at-bats. At Double-A, he was less aggressive, took more pitches and had less swing-and-miss, but the quality of his contact was not as consistent.

Contreras is just a few adjustments away from becoming a catcher who can make an impact on both sides of the ball. If he can also rediscover that swagger from early in the 2019 season, he will be on his way to becoming an above-average backstop.

Variance: High. Catching has a lot of moving parts.

Mark Barry's Fantasy Take: Is this the Golden Age for dynasty catching prospects? Almost certainly not, but also maybe. That's damning with faint praise, sure, as Contreras is probably a top-10 dynasty prospect behind the dish but probably doesn't have that same top-10 big-league upside.

9 Braden Shewmake SS   OFP: 50   ETA: 2021

Born: 11/19/97   Age: 22   Bats: L   Throws: R   Height: 6'4"   Weight: 190   Origin: Round 1, 2019 Draft (#21 overall)

YEAR	TEAM	LVL	AGE	PA	R	2B	3B	HR	RBI	BB	K	SB	CS	AVG/OBP/SLG	DRC+	VORP	BABIP	BRR	FRAA	WARP	PF
2019	ROM	A	21	226	37	18	2	3	39	21	29	11	3	.318/.389/.473	162	25.7	.359	3.5	SS(38) 0.0	2.5	103
2019	MIS	AA	21	52	7	0	0	0	1	4	11	2	0	.217/.288/.217	58	-0.9	.278	0.7	SS(14) 1.8	0.3	87
2020	ATL	MLB	22	251	22	12	1	4	24	15	54	2	1	.234/.288/.350	69	0.0	.286	0.0	SS 2	0.1	103

Comparables: Darnell Sweeney, Donovan Solano, Gift Ngoepe

The Report: The Braves surprised many by drafting Shewmake with their second first-round pick in 2019, but his early play appeared to vindicate the selection, as he garnered louder post-draft reports. The pre-draft grades seemed especially light on his defense, where he showed excellent feel at shortstop in his first pro assignment. The lanky Aggie has soft hands and ranges well for his length, helped in part by good instincts, and there's enough arm for any infield position. He'll always be lean and long, but he does enough on the first step and has the hands to play anywhere on the infield, more so on a regular basis at second or third and in a pinch at short. It's the same on the basepaths, where he's surprisingly quick down the line for solid-average run. Shewmake's top tool is a potential above-average hit based on excellent feel for the barrel. It's a simple, contact-oriented swing and approach that limits his game power to fringe-average, but he'll make consistent, hard contact and shoot the gaps often while running into the occasional blast. This is a pretty straightforward profile with fringe- to above-average tools across the board and the instincts to make them play at the highest level. It's not sexy but it's worthy of super-utility potential, and it shouldn't take long to happen.

Variance: Medium. He hasn't passed the upper-level test yet, but the advanced bat will play pretty quickly and get him to the majors.

Mark Barry's Fantasy Take: Shewmake seems to be missing a few letters from his name, but he didn't miss the chance to fly through the organization, reaching Double-A by the end of his draft year. If he continues the trajectory to super-utility stardom, he's an interesting name for deeper or onlies, but he's not shallow-mixed league relevant right now.

10 Jasseel De La Cruz RHP OFP: 50 ETA: 2020

Born: 06/26/97   Age: 23   Bats: R   Throws: R   Height: 6'1"   Weight: 215   Origin: International Free Agent, 2015

YEAR	TEAM	LVL	AGE	W	L	SV	G	GS	IP	H	HR	BB/9	K/9	K	GB%	BABIP	WHIP	ERA	DRA	WARP	PF
2017	BRA	RK	20	2	1	0	4	4	19	13	1	3.3	8.1	17	49%	.231	1.05	1.89	2.52	0.7	95
2017	DNV	RK	20	0	2	0	7	6	23²	25	1	4.2	7.2	19	57%	.316	1.52	5.32	5.03	0.3	91
2018	ROM	A	21	3	4	0	15	13	69	65	6	4.4	8.5	65	64%	.309	1.43	4.83	5.81	-0.5	98
2019	ROM	A	22	0	1	0	4	4	18	19	1	2.5	11.0	22	53%	.391	1.33	2.50	4.67	0.1	97
2019	BRV	A+	22	3	1	0	4	4	28	12	0	2.2	8.4	26	52%	.174	0.68	1.93	2.44	0.9	92
2019	MIS	AA	22	4	7	0	17	16	87	71	7	3.8	7.6	73	46%	.262	1.24	3.83	4.67	0.3	92
2020	ATL	MLB	23	2	2	0	33	0	35	35	5	4.2	7.3	28	43%	.289	1.47	4.82	4.89	0.2	103

Comparables: Josh Sborz, Chad Bettis, Scott Barlow

The Report: De La Cruz struggled with injuries in 2018 and was described on last year's Braves list by David Lee as "a raw power arm who could go in a million directions." Well, he was healthy in 2019, tossed 133 pretty good innings across three levels, and signs are pointing up. The underlying stuff profile is mostly the same, we just saw it across a longer body of work. De La Cruz pumps mid-90s heat with good extension and some deception, although there is a lot of effort to hit the upper end of that velocity range. The fastball command and control can be erratic, and the pitch can run a bit true. Despite his height, the extension and higher slot gives the pitch some plane, at least.

De La Cruz pairs the heater with a power slider that flashes plus and has gotten more consistent in 2019. It's easy to see it as a swing-and-miss pitch in the majors. His changeup is firm, regularly hitting 90 or higher, and he struggles to get it down in the zone, although on the rare occasions he does the pitch will show average dive. De La Cruz is still a raw power arm in some ways, but he's started to see on-field results. The reliever risk here is high, but he'd be a good reliever, and he's still young enough to project some command and changeup gains if so inclined.

Variance: Medium. De La Cruz's fastball/slider combo gives him a decent shot at some sort of major-league pen work, even with the quibbles about the command. He's already had Double-A success as well. Still, the overall profile is pretty raw and there's significant reliever risk given the delivery, command, and present changeup. That risk might manifest in making him merely an up-and-down frustrating pen arm that flashes for a month here and there.

Mark Barry's Fantasy Take: The range of outcomes for De La Cruz is breathtaking. If things shake right, he's a sneaky-good, mid-rotation option. If things break (hopefully not literally) wrong, he pitches a handful of middling innings out of the pen when called upon as an injury fill-in. I'd take a flier on him in leagues with 250 prospects or more, betting on continued development now that he's stringing together better health.

The Next Ten

11 Freddy Tarnok RHP

Born: 11/24/98   Age: 21   Bats: R   Throws: R   Height: 6'3"   Weight: 185   Origin: Round 3, 2017 Draft (#80 overall)

YEAR	TEAM	LVL	AGE	W	L	SV	G	GS	IP	H	HR	BB/9	K/9	K	GB%	BABIP	WHIP	ERA	DRA	WARP	PF
2017	BRA	RK	18	0	3	0	8	8	14	11	0	1.9	6.4	10	36%	.250	1.00	2.57	2.69	0.5	99
2018	ROM	A	19	5	5	0	27	11	77¹	70	5	4.8	9.7	83	40%	.297	1.44	3.96	5.25	-0.2	93
2019	BRA	RK	20	0	1	0	3	3	8	3	1	1.1	10.1	9	50%	.118	0.50	3.38	1.00	0.4	108
2019	BRV	A+	20	3	7	0	19	19	98	105	6	3.3	7.5	82	38%	.329	1.44	4.87	6.06	-1.2	93
2020	ATL	MLB	21	2	2	0	33	0	35	35	5	3.6	6.4	25	37%	.278	1.39	4.50	4.81	0.2	103

Comparables: Victor Arano, Jeanmar Gómez, Edgar Garcia

Last year's report on Tarnok called him more of a "slow burn" than the pitching prospects ranked above him. That still fits him well after almost 100 innings of mixed results at High-A Florida this past season. He just turned 21 in November 2019, but it seems like he's been around longer because the Braves have worked him slowly after he didn't even turn to pitching until late in his prep days. He's still raw, but he's still throwing with an ideal pitcher's frame, and he still has stuff. The fastball has plus potential with mid-90s velocity in short bursts, while the curveball flashes above-average and can settle a tick below with further refinement. He's worked to get his changeup on par and it's always had that potential, but it's still a work in progress along with the ability to repeat his delivery. None of this sounds particularly thrilling, but one can see why the Braves are taking the time with Tarnok. He has standout arm strength and a great frame with fewer innings on the arm. The ceiling is still very high, like, impact starter high, but the gap is still very large and could ultimately push him to the bullpen.

12 Bryce Ball 1B

Born: 07/08/98   Age: 21   Bats: L   Throws: R   Height: 6'6"   Weight: 235   Origin: Round 24, 2019 Draft (#727 overall)

YEAR	TEAM	LVL	AGE	PA	R	2B	3B	HR	RBI	BB	K	SB	CS	AVG/OBP/SLG	DRC+	VORP	BABIP	BRR	FRAA	WARP	PF
2019	DNV	RK+	20	173	37	12	0	13	38	22	30	0	0	.324/.410/.676	173	25.5	.321	0.3		1.5	94
2019	ROM	A	20	90	14	6	0	4	14	4	20	0	0	.337/.367/.547	154	5.2	.403	-0.7	1B(11) -1.3	0.4	102
2020	ATL	MLB	21	251	23	13	0	6	26	16	69	2	1	.227/.280/.367	69	1.0	.295	0.0	1B -2	-0.3	103

Comparables: Juan Francisco, Keston Hiura, Jacob Nottingham

It's understandable if the first question that crosses your mind after watching Ball is how he ended up lasting until the 24th round. This is a massive kid who already has the biggest raw power in the system, perhaps alongside Alex Jackson. It's quite the find when an organization drafts a player that late and he immediately has a system's best tool, pushing 70. That high grade comes from size and natural strength, but it's not a muscled swing. His bat speed approaches above-average with good lift and separation. The bat speed can play down at times when he settles for contact to all fields, but it's a positive that he's capable of covering the plate well for his size and profile. It's not a boom-or-bust power profile because he's shown a feel to hit. Ball's defense is a different matter. He shows a lack of feel for first base with a hard glove and inconsistent footwork. It'll take time to develop his glove enough to be serviceable, and first base is his only option because of bottom-of-the-scale speed. Regardless of his defense, Ball has more than enough potential in his bat and power to force an organization to find a lineup spot for him. First base profiles are a tricky business for prospects, but the Braves found themselves a super-intriguing slugger who should rocket up this list in short order. It's not crazy to say he can become the best first base prospect in the game at some point.

13 Huascar Ynoa RHP

Born: 05/28/98   Age: 22   Bats: R   Throws: R   Height: 6'3"   Weight: 175   Origin: International Free Agent, 2014

YEAR	TEAM	LVL	AGE	W	L	SV	G	GS	IP	H	HR	BB/9	K/9	K	GB%	BABIP	WHIP	ERA	DRA	WARP	PF
2017	ELZ	RK	19	0	1	0	6	6	25²	28	1	4.9	8.1	23	38%	.346	1.64	5.26	5.65	0.1	102
2017	DNV	RK	19	0	3	0	7	7	25²	24	1	5.3	9.5	27	53%	.315	1.52	5.26	5.55	0.1	87
2018	ROM	A	20	7	8	0	18	18	91²	69	7	4.1	9.8	100	47%	.264	1.21	3.63	4.07	1.2	96
2018	BRV	A+	20	1	4	0	6	6	24²	33	1	4.4	11.3	31	46%	.438	1.82	8.03	6.47	-0.3	98
2019	BRV	A+	21	0	1	0	3	3	11	10	0	4.9	13.1	16	59%	.370	1.45	3.27	3.91	0.2	101
2019	MIS	AA	21	1	2	1	6	0	13²	17	2	3.3	9.9	15	67%	.366	1.61	5.27	5.49	-0.1	100
2019	GWN	AAA	21	3	5	0	17	14	72²	80	14	4.2	9.8	79	43%	.332	1.57	5.33	5.06	1.1	102
2019	ATL	MLB	21	0	0	0	2	0	3	6	1	3.0	9.0	3	42%	.455	2.33	18.00	6.70	0.0	98
2020	ATL	MLB	22	1	1	0	16	0	17	20	3	4.8	6.8	13	46%	.313	1.70	6.23	5.88	-0.1	103

Comparables: Joel Payamps, Brock Burke, Jonathan Hernández

On June 16th, Ynoa made his major-league debut in Atlanta, mopping up the last two innings of a 15-1 blowout win over the Phillies. He spiked his first fastball at 98—nerves no doubt—and then proceeded to work his way through the Phillies lineup, pumping upper-90s heat, touching 99, and breaking off what Brooks thinks are a bunch of 86 and 87 mph curves, one of which ended up a nice souvenir—his first professional strikeout against Rhys Hoskins.

On July 17th, he found himself back in the majors, and promptly got shelled to the tune of six runs in one inning of work. Christian Yelich hit a laser beam grand slam off one of those power breakers that only bent. Major League Baseball is hard, my man.

Aside from those two games, Ynoa found himself starting at three levels of Braves affiliates, struggling to throw strikes, but missing plenty of bats when he was in the zone. It's power stuff—similar to De La Cruz—but even less refined and with greater command issues. Ynoa looks more like a reliever long term, but that fastball/breaking ball combo is deadly when he's right, and he only turned 21 a couple weeks before his major-league debut. That debut was perhaps a bit premature—Ynoa was added to the 40-man last season and the Braves needed an arm, but that June afternoon could be a preview of coming attractions and the trailer won't be misleading.

44 - Atlanta Braves

14   Alex Jackson   C

Born: 12/25/95   Age: 24   Bats: R   Throws: R   Height: 6'2"   Weight: 215   Origin: Round 1, 2014 Draft (#6 overall)

YEAR	TEAM	LVL	AGE	PA	R	2B	3B	HR	RBI	BB	K	SB	CS	AVG/OBP/SLG	DRC+	VORP	BABIP	BRR	FRAA	WARP	PF
2017	BRV	A+	21	282	44	17	0	14	45	13	74	0	1	.272/.333/.502	140	20.5	.329	-1.3	C(33) -2.1	1.4	100
2017	MIS	AA	21	120	12	4	0	5	20	10	32	0	0	.255/.317/.427	113	5.0	.315	-0.1	C(23) -1.3	0.5	95
2018	MIS	AA	22	252	27	12	1	5	24	20	78	0	0	.200/.282/.329	67	3.7	.280	-0.9	C(61) -2.1	0.1	94
2018	GWN	AAA	22	125	15	11	2	3	17	12	42	0	0	.204/.296/.426	86	5.4	.292	0.2	C(29) 2.7	0.7	100
2019	GWN	AAA	23	345	52	9	0	28	65	20	118	1	0	.229/.313/.533	106	13.6	.261	-2.8	C(78) 17.9	3.1	101
2019	ATL	MLB	23	15	0	0	0	0	0	1	5	0	0	.000/.133/.000	77	0.4	.000	0.0	C(4) 0.5	0.1	110
2020	ATL	MLB	24	119	12	5	0	4	13	7	45	0	0	.190/.263/.351	57	0.0	.276	-0.3	C 2	0.1	103

Comparables: Ed Bailey, Michael Chavis, Kyle Skipworth

This has been quite a journey. You may remember Jackson as the sixth-overall pick in the 2014 Draft by the Mariners. He was a prep catcher then, but was immediately converted to the outfield under the idea that his bat was ahead of his glove. He ranked 94th on the 2015 101, and then proceeded to go out and hit .157 in his full-season debut in 2015, getting demoted back to extended spring training in late May. Suddenly the bat wasn't so advanced anymore, and after another season of slightly better muddling in 2016, the Mariners offloaded him to the Braves for well under sticker price. Atlanta immediately converted him back to catcher, and he's slowly filtered up through their system for the past three years, getting a couple cups of coffee in 2019. On some levels, the story has remained the same since his later days in the Seattle farm; he's still a good athlete with a big, strong frame and plus raw power, but major questions about his ability to make contact and hit for any average. It's a long swing and not always on balance. Yet two markers from his 2019 statistical performance paint a more optimistic picture: he hit 28 homers in just 345 Triple-A plate appearances, which is still a lot even given the Super Happy Fun Ball. Perhaps even more interestingly, he graded out as the best defensive catcher in Triple-A by FRAA. That's a level where we have pretty sticky framing stats. He also gunned out 50 percent of baserunners. That's enough pop and defense to give him some substantial upside, perhaps even still a good regular if he can keep the average high enough.

15   Victor Vodnik   RHP

Born: 10/09/99   Age: 20   Bats: R   Throws: R   Height: 6'0"   Weight: 200   Origin: Round 14, 2018 Draft (#412 overall)

YEAR	TEAM	LVL	AGE	W	L	SV	G	GS	IP	H	HR	BB/9	K/9	K	GB%	BABIP	WHIP	ERA	DRA	WARP	PF
2019	ROM	A	19	1	3	3	23	3	67^1	55	1	3.2	9.2	69	53%	.303	1.17	2.94	4.44	0.4	95
2020	ATL	MLB	20	2	2	0	33	0	35	34	5	3.9	7.8	30	48%	.289	1.41	4.41	4.72	0.3	103

Comparables: Eduardo Sanchez, Edgar Garcia, Dustin Antolin

Vodnik is an easy pick for future mover in the system because of a combination of impending graduations and his own rise in the minors. He doesn't get much love because he's a 6-foot right-hander with a bullpen future, but he has major-league stuff, enough command to make it work, and the mound presence to match. He was kept on a throwing schedule in his first full season and missed July but still threw 67 innings because of his multi-inning role, which serves him well as the type of arm that can toss a couple innings at the time. His fastball is 93-96 and touches 97 with riding life and effectiveness up and down the zone. He mixes two breaking balls between a short, hard slider and a power curve with downward break and solid-average depth, the latter flashing above-average. He'll also toss the occasional show-me changeup. Vodnik lacks height advantage but attacks hitters in all four quadrants with lively stuff and a quick arm. The easy call is middle relief, but he has the chance for late-innings impact.

16 Michael Harris OF

Born: 03/07/01   Age: 19   Bats: L   Throws: L   Height: 6'0"   Weight: 195   Origin: Round 3, 2019 Draft (#98 overall)

YEAR	TEAM	LVL	AGE	PA	R	2B	3B	HR	RBI	BB	K	SB	CS	AVG/OBP/SLG	DRC+	VORP	BABIP	BRR	FRAA	WARP	PF
2019	BRA	RK	18	119	15	6	3	2	16	9	20	5	2	.349/.403/.514	138	11.3	.414	0.3	CF(19) 1.4, RF(3) -0.5	0.8	100
2019	ROM	A	18	93	11	2	1	0	11	9	22	3	0	.183/.269/.232	58	-4.5	.246	-0.7	RF(18) 5.1, CF(4) 0.8	0.4	102
2020	ATL	MLB	19	251	22	11	1	3	22	23	72	3	1	.230/.304/.336	72	0.0	.322	0.0	CF 1, RF 1	0.2	103

Comparables: Justin Williams, J.P. Crawford, David Dahl

After taking the high-floor college route with their first three picks in the 2019 draft, the Braves went back to their Georgia prep athlete roots by popping Harris in the third round and convincing him to pass on a Texas Tech commitment that probably would've led to two-way stardom. The Braves liked him at the plate and put him in right field full-time, where he was aggressively pushed to Low-A Rome for the final few weeks and he struggled to stay afloat. Harris is a raw product with the bat, at times getting caught between pitches and showing wrap and inconsistent bat paths. There's a lot to like, though, especially a feel for the barrel and loose hands that should help as he works to iron out his swing. His contact is loud and he'll grow into above-average raw power despite an average frame, a testament to his quick bat and strong wrists. Harris is a good athlete but not a burner, featuring average run times and solid- to above-average range in the outfield. A move to center field would boost his stock tremendously, but if he stays in right the bat and power will need to max out. His standout tool is at least a plus arm that profiles as a weapon in center or right. It's going to be a level-by-level process that'll take time and patience, but there's a lot to like with Harris, namely athleticism, a feel for the game, and a cannon for an arm.

17 Tucker Davidson LHP

Born: 03/25/96   Age: 24   Bats: L   Throws: L   Height: 6'2"   Weight: 215   Origin: Round 19, 2016 Draft (#559 overall)

YEAR	TEAM	LVL	AGE	W	L	SV	G	GS	IP	H	HR	BB/9	K/9	K	GB%	BABIP	WHIP	ERA	DRA	WARP	PF
2017	ROM	A	21	5	4	2	31	12	103²	96	4	2.6	8.8	101	56%	.322	1.22	2.60	4.05	1.3	101
2018	BRV	A+	22	7	10	0	24	24	118¹	120	5	4.4	7.5	99	48%	.332	1.50	4.18	5.63	-0.4	98
2019	MIS	AA	23	7	6	0	21	21	110²	88	5	3.7	9.9	122	51%	.304	1.20	2.03	4.43	0.7	93
2019	GWN	AAA	23	1	1	0	4	4	19	20	0	4.3	5.7	12	51%	.339	1.53	2.84	5.48	0.2	102
2020	ATL	MLB	24	2	2	0	28	2	36	35	5	3.9	8.2	33	47%	.295	1.40	4.25	4.38	0.5	103

Comparables: Duane Below, Matt Hall, Jalen Beeks

Perhaps no pitcher in the system, besides maybe De La Cruz, increased his stock this past season more than Davidson. Credit to the left-hander for recognizing that the full-time starter experiment was in danger of going off the rails. He put in the work to improve his arm strength and durability, and his stuff held deeper in starts this past season, resulting in a great year between the two highest levels of the minors and a 40-man roster spot. He saw an uptick in fastball velocity to pump mid-90s more often and he mixed his stuff more effectively between an average curve that flashes above and an improved changeup. There was little reason in 2018 to believe that Davidson had a chance to be a starter, but he's worked his way into that conversation. The fallback plan is still a lefty reliever with a hard fastball and solid curve, which could happen as soon as 2020, but he's now given the Braves a reason to see if he sticks as a starter at the highest level.

18 Patrick Weigel RHP

Born: 07/08/94   Age: 25   Bats: R   Throws: R   Height: 6'6"   Weight: 240   Origin: Round 7, 2015 Draft (#210 overall)

YEAR	TEAM	LVL	AGE	W	L	SV	G	GS	IP	H	HR	BB/9	K/9	K	GB%	BABIP	WHIP	ERA	DRA	WARP	PF
2017	MIS	AA	22	3	0	0	7	7	37¹	32	2	2.7	9.2	38	37%	.300	1.15	2.89	4.26	0.4	94
2017	GWN	AAA	22	3	2	0	8	8	41	42	5	3.7	6.6	30	44%	.301	1.44	5.27	5.28	0.2	97
2019	MIS	AA	24	0	1	0	7	7	15²	8	0	5.2	9.2	16	54%	.205	1.09	1.72	3.21	0.3	90
2019	GWN	AAA	24	6	1	0	21	11	63¹	42	9	4.5	7.8	55	40%	.208	1.17	2.98	3.03	2.2	100
2020	ATL	MLB	25	1	2	0	14	3	28	28	4	3.9	7.9	24	40%	.300	1.46	5.08	5.09	0.2	103

Comparables: Keyvius Sampson, Stephen Gonsalves, Ryan Helsley

If you're looking for someone to root for in this system, I recommend Weigel. He was an immediate seventh-round steal with explosive stuff who was knocking on the major-league door until he succumbed to Tommy John surgery and fell by the wayside. He reappeared late in 2018 with his velocity mostly back, but he was understandably rusty and expectations were all over the map entering 2019. He responded to Atlanta's faith (and a 40-man roster addition) by returning to the precipice of the majors with his mid-to-upper-90s fastball in short bursts and a sharp slider. It was never a given that Weigel would be a starter in the majors, and it now seems more likely that his ultimate role is in relief where he can let his velocity fly and cut his arsenal down. Weigel's stuff is late-innings worthy and he has nothing left to prove in Triple-A.

19 Greyson Jenista OF

Born: 12/07/96   Age: 23   Bats: L   Throws: R   Height: 6'3"   Weight: 210   Origin: Round 2, 2018 Draft (#49 overall)

YEAR	TEAM	LVL	AGE	PA	R	2B	3B	HR	RBI	BB	K	SB	CS	AVG/OBP/SLG	DRC+	VORP	BABIP	BRR	FRAA	WARP	PF
2018	DNV	RK	21	47	10	1	0	3	7	6	9	0	1	.250/.348/.500	128	2.2	.250	0.0	RF(7) 2.6, LF(2) 0.6	0.5	99
2018	ROM	A	21	130	20	5	3	1	23	10	17	4	1	.333/.377/.453	143	7.5	.373	0.2	RF(30) -0.4	0.8	100
2018	BRV	A+	21	74	3	3	1	0	4	7	15	0	0	.152/.230/.227	33	-5.8	.192	-0.6	RF(14) -0.8, CF(1) 0.0	-0.5	97
2019	BRV	A+	22	231	24	14	1	4	29	27	70	1	4	.223/.312/.361	100	1.5	.315	-3.1	RF(40) -1.6, CF(8) -0.1	-0.1	96
2019	MIS	AA	22	256	18	4	1	5	26	27	75	2	4	.243/.324/.338	98	5.8	.333	-2.9	LF(30) -4.4, RF(27) 0.4	-0.3	92
2020	ATL	MLB	23	251	23	11	1	6	25	19	83	2	1	.219/.281/.351	66	0.0	.315	-0.4	RF 1, LF -1	-0.3	103

Comparables: Bubba Starling, Michael Hermosillo, Joe Benson

Jenista is a big, strong lefty-swinging power hitter. Though he is a bit more athletic than many other players with that physical profile, the power is his only standout tool and his development as a prospect is going to be all about how well he is able to get to that power in games. The other tools are mostly average. Defensively, he can play center in a pinch and he has just enough arm to play in right, but he's mostly a left fielder who should be able to make most of the plays there. He could see some time at first base at some point down the road as well.

At the plate, he starts with his hands very high and that leaves him a lot to accomplish to get his bat to the ball at the proper launch angle to find that plus raw power. To this point in his career, he has struggled to find the correct timing to do that with any consistency. When it does work, it's a thing of beauty. It is going to take a major adjustment, though, for him to get quicker to the ball, create a more power-efficient bat path and better manage what are becoming alarmingly high strikeout rates. Without that adjustment, Jenista's ceiling drops to just that of a platoon bat.

20 Trey Riley RHP

Born: 04/21/98   Age: 22   Bats: L   Throws: R   Height: 6'3"   Weight: 205   Origin: Round 5, 2018 Draft (#142 overall)

YEAR	TEAM	LVL	AGE	W	L	SV	G	GS	IP	H	HR	BB/9	K/9	K	GB%	BABIP	WHIP	ERA	DRA	WARP	PF
2018	DNV	RK	20	0	0	0	6	2	9	10	1	10.0	13.0	13	44%	.409	2.22	8.00	5.65	0.0	108
2019	ROM	A	21	2	7	0	17	12	58²	71	4	7.1	6.3	41	47%	.354	1.99	7.67	8.24	-2.2	96
2020	ATL	MLB	22	2	2	0	33	0	35	35	6	4.7	5.2	20	43%	.268	1.53	5.14	5.34	0.0	103

Comparables: Chad Sobotka, Paul Clemens, Justin Hancock

The fifth-round pick in 2018 had a tough go-round in his first year of full-season ball. Riley struggled mightily with command throughout his abbreviated injury-riddled season, issuing 46 walks against 41 punchouts over 58 2/3 innings. His fastball sits 92-95 mph and comes in fairly straight. However, violent mechanics can lead to major command issues. Riley has fast arm action with a max-effort delivery, and he struggles to engage his lower half to take full advantage of his 6-foot-3 frame. An above-average 85-86 mph slider with hard, late break shows flashes of a true swing-and-miss pitch. Riley's other breaking pitch is an 11-5 power curveball that sits 77-80 mph featuring late bite. This pitch also has plus whiff potential. He also offers a mid-80s average changeup. Riley's ceiling will depend on how he develops his fastball command and employs his lower half more efficiently. With two potential plus offspeed pitches, he certainly has a solid base to build on.

Personal Cheeseball

PC **Trey Harris** OF
Born: 01/15/96   Age: 24   Bats: R   Throws: R   Height: 5'8"   Weight: 215   Origin: Round 32, 2018 Draft (#952 overall)

YEAR	TEAM	LVL	AGE	PA	R	2B	3B	HR	RBI	BB	K	SB	CS	AVG/OBP/SLG	DRC+	VORP	BABIP	BRR	FRAA	WARP	PF
2018	BRA	RK	22	132	24	9	2	1	18	21	13	4	3	.314/.450/.467	186	13.8	.352	0.2	CF(13)-0.9, RF(13)1.1	1.3	103
2018	ROM	A	22	94	10	9	0	0	11	7	13	3	0	.286/.351/.393	137	5.2	.333	0.1	RF(18)2.4, LF(1)0.9	0.9	94
2019	ROM	A	23	230	38	14	4	8	44	20	32	4	4	.366/.437/.594	207	32.3	.405	1.3	RF(27)-1.4, LF(17)-2.1	2.7	95
2019	BRV	A+	23	139	20	5	0	4	17	12	26	3	0	.303/.388/.443	145	5.6	.359	-2.5	RF(20)1.4, LF(9)-0.4	0.7	98
2019	MIS	AA	23	156	15	7	3	2	12	4	33	1	2	.281/.318/.411	91	6.7	.351	-1.1	RF(36)-1.3	-0.1	91
2020	ATL	MLB	24	251	26	13	1	7	29	13	57	1	0	.264/.316/.420	95	0.0	.323	-0.3	RF-1, LF 0	0.5	103

Comparables: Lane Adams, Mike Tauchman, Mike Yastrzemski

One of the most fun things in what we do is to watch the development of a player like Harris. He got a $10,000 bonus as a senior sign 32nd-round pick out of the University of Missouri in the 2018 draft, but he quickly rose above the expectations that might have come with that background. When I went to see the Mississippi Braves play this season, I was interested to see all of the big name prospects on that roster, but the guy who stood out most to me was Harris.

He has a compact, athletic build at 5-foot-10 and 215 pounds and a collection of mostly average-to-a-tick-above tools. What he does is put all of those tools together in a way that makes him at least a bit intriguing. Harris is balanced at the plate with good timing, though he is a free-swinger and he seems to be focused on making contact to the middle of the field. In 14 at-bats, he put the ball in play 13 times, with all of them going from right-center to left-center. It wasn't just defensive contact, either, as he hit three balls to deep left-center, including one of only two balls I've seen go out to that part of the park in Jacksonville in four seasons of watching games there.

Defensively, Harris' arm is just average, but it seemed at least adequate for right field and he did take good routes to fly balls. He needs to figure out how to combine his aggressiveness with just a bit more selectivity to help him improve his walk rates and give him a better opportunity to recognize when he can turn on pitches and do more damage to the pull side. If he can find that happy medium, he has a floor of a short-side platoon player and if it all comes together, he could find regular at-bats. That's a nice outcome for a 32nd-round pick.

Low Minors Sleeper

LMS **Vaughn Grissom** SS
Born: 01/05/01   Age: 19   Bats: R   Throws: R   Height: 6'3"   Weight: 180   Origin: Round 11, 2019 Draft (#337 overall)

YEAR	TEAM	LVL	AGE	PA	R	2B	3B	HR	RBI	BB	K	SB	CS	AVG/OBP/SLG	DRC+	VORP	BABIP	BRR	FRAA	WARP	PF
2019	BRA	RK	18	184	22	7	1	3	23	16	27	3	0	.288/.361/.400	146	11.0	.323	-2.5	SS(42)-2.5	1.0	102
2020	ATL	MLB	19	251	22	11	1	3	21	20	64	3	1	.223/.294/.321	66	0.0	.296	0.0	SS-1	-0.3	103

There were a few options for Atlanta's low minors sleeper pick this year, because the organization drafted several projectable prep athletes after the 10th round this past June in an effort to shore up lower-level depth. A year from now we may be discussing names like Tyler Owens and Jared Johnson as the next system risers, but Grissom gets the nod right now for his exciting potential with the bat. He earned one of the highest signing bonuses of the 11th round for his highly-projectable frame and potential to be a corner masher. He'll likely move off shortstop as he grows and they'll need to evaluate his arm strength going forward for a potential fit at third, but second base or the outfield could also be possibilities down the road. Grissom's bat is the big draw, showing a feel to hit with a loose, quick stroke and present strength when he catches one out front. As he grows, he could develop impact power along with solid barrel awareness and plate discipline. His eventual defensive home is a bit up in the air, but it's easy to get excited about the bat as he develops.

Top Talents 25 and Under (as of 4/1/2020)

1. Ronald Acuña Jr.
2. Mike Soroka

3. Ozzie Albies
4. Cristian Pache
5. Ian Anderson
6. Drew Waters
7. Austin Riley
8. Kyle Muller
9. Shea Langeliers
10. Kyle Wright

You know things are going well for you when you produce the runner-up in NL Rookie of the Year voting the year after you produce the actual winner of the thing. That's where the Braves are when it comes to their young talent, and it's absolutely conceivable that another wave is on the way to complement the wave that has already hit Atlanta and is thriving as well.

Both Ronald Acuña and Mike Soroka are going to be on top of this list for a while. Soroka is coming off of a rookie season where he eventually established himself at the top of the rotation and should be there for years to come. Then there's Acuña, who squashed any rumors of a "sophomore slump" by making a serious run at a 40/40 season. Both of those players were in their age-21 season, which means that they've still got plenty of potential left to realize.

Ozzie Albies may be a couple of years older, but he's still just as dynamic as the two aforementioned players. The most pleasant surprise about Ozzie has been his bat, as he's hit 48 home runs over the past couple of seasons. This was after he earned a reputation as a light-hitting, defense-first infielder during his time on the farm. Now he's got the bat and the defense is just as good, so he is absolutely in a good place right now.

While Austin Riley came onto the major-league scene like a lion, he eventually calmed down and was forced to transform into a lamb once the pitchers caught up to his approach on the plate. The flashes of potential he showed during his early days as a major leaguer were brilliant and if he can come anywhere close to that on a consistent basis, then he could go up in this ranking as he gets closer to reaching the age limit here.

However, the next wave of talent that is still plying their craft in Atlanta's farm system is worth dreaming about if you're a Braves fan. Cristian Pache has truly come into his own as a professional and it seems inevitable that the defensive dynamo will be joining Acuña in the outfield at some point in 2020. The same could be said for Drew Waters, who had a wonderful season in the minors and is also primed to make an arrival in the upcoming season. If those two live up to the lofty level of play that Acuña has set, then Atlanta's outfield could be set in stone for a long time.

Then there's the pitching. During the initial stages of their relatively quick rebuild, the Braves loaded up on pitching prospects and that was initially the star of this farm system's story. As the position players developed, the pitching prospects seemed to fall off. However, there's still good stuff to be excited about, as Kyle Wright and Kyle Muller are still projected to be solid arms and Ian Anderson continues to stand tall (both literally and figuratively) as the top hurler in the farm system.

While Atlanta's minor league strength may not be as formidable as it once was, it also comes with the understandable caveat that a lot of the stars of this system are graduating to become stars at the big league level. The first big wave of young talent has already shown its stuff at the top level, and we're getting closer to the day when the second big wave gets its chance as well.

Eyewitness Reports

Eyewitness Report: Shea Langeliers

Evaluator: David Lee
Report Date: 09/10/2019
Dates Seen: 6/29-30/19; 8/16/19; 8/18/19
Risk Factor: Medium
Physical/Health: Strong catcher's frame with mature build, slight squat and strong lower half. Maxed physically. More athletic than typical squat catchers, including quick actions.

Tool	Future Grade	Report
Hit	50	Above-average bat speed is the surprising quality here. He shows solid lower-half fire and gets to the zone with a short, quick stroke and simple mechanics. He's been caught between pitches at times and has to adjust his plate discipline and occasional over-aggressiveness to avoid getting stuck with a fringe hit future. Aptitude and a quick stroke are on his side.
Power	50	Above-average raw power. Gets to power from quick swing that produces above-average explosiveness and lift. Hit tool will limit to average in-game power but will produce consistent extra-base pop.
Baserunning/ Speed	30	He's not a clog on the bases and is a good athlete for his stature and position, but he won't impact the run game.
Glove	55	This grade could end up on the low end if he progresses beyond expectations. The position comes naturally to him with leadership qualities, instincts, agility behind the plate and a feel to receive. He has a soft mitt and quiet body that receives well. He's an athlete for the position with quick actions and good shifting ability on pitches in the dirt.
Arm	60	Consistent plus arm that flashes 70 pop times. This is his carrying tool and will be one of the biggest weapons on the field every time he plays. He has quick footwork to support at least a plus arm and his throws are accurate. He can control a run game with this tool.

Conclusion: Langeliers is a definite defense-first catcher with at least above-average defense and a plus arm, flashing higher for both. There's a reason he was considered the top defensive catcher in his draft class. That part of his game is basically ready now. His hit tool remains the question. He has the swing mechanics to produce consistent contact and the strength and quick stroke to tap into above-average raw power. The question is how high the hit tool will go based on his eye. An average hit is a real possibility because of his feel and swing. The tools are there to be a major-league starter behind the plate with impact defense and enough hit.

Baltimore Orioles

The State of the System

The 2020 Orioles system is much deeper than recent vintages, but it lacks impact talent beyond the first few names on the list below.

The Top Ten

─────────────── ★ ★ ★ *2020 Top 101 Prospect* **#4** ★ ★ ★ ───────────────

1 **Adley Rutschman C**   OFP: 70   ETA: Early 2021
Born: 02/06/98   Age: 22   Bats: B   Throws: R   Height: 6'2"   Weight: 216   Origin: Round 1, 2019 Draft (#1 overall)

YEAR	TEAM	LVL	AGE	PA	R	2B	3B	HR	RBI	BB	K	SB	CS	AVG/OBP/SLG	DRC+	VORP	BABIP	BRR	FRAA	WARP	PF
2019	ABE	A-	21	92	11	7	1	1	15	12	16	0	0	.325/.413/.481	177	11.5	.387	-0.1	C(9) -0.2	0.8	98
2019	DEL	A	21	47	5	1	0	2	8	6	9	0	0	.154/.261/.333	85	1.2	.138	0.1	C(6) 0.1	0.1	88
2020	BAL	MLB	22	251	24	12	1	7	27	18	65	2	1	.219/.281/.364	72	0.0	.275	0.0	C 0	0.0	110

Comparables: Lucas Duda, Chris McGuiness, Christian Walker

The Report: There isn't much he can't do on a baseball field. He has a beautiful swing that is basically identical from both sides of the plate. It's also a swing that's made for modern baseball with lots of loft, owing to quick hips and fast hands. His approach is a plus. He projects for plus or better game power. He pairs a catcher's frame with excellent athleticism. He's an average runner down the line—not an average runner for a catcher but an actual average runner. While he needs more reps calling games and handling professional baseball in general, he has all of the skills present to project as an excellent defensive catcher: hands, agility, arm, and perhaps most importantly, leadership. This is one of the best college position player prospects in recent memory, and he has a chance for some really big outcomes.

Variance: Low. There's always risk inherent to the tools of ignorance, and he didn't actually hit all that well coming off mono after his college season ended. Then again, he was coming off mono and his season started in February. It's extremely hard to see an outcome where he stays reasonably healthy and isn't at least a first-division starting catcher.

Mark Barry's Fantasy Take: The Pros: Great hitter, excellent plate discipline, 70 name.

The Cons: He's a catcher—that's kinda it.

This is one of the many "better in real life than fantasy" guys you'll find in this book. Rutschman is a top-25 dynasty guy, to be sure, and could easily be a top-three catcher in any format. He's still a catcher, though, which likely lowers his ceiling in comparison to other top-25 names.

★ ★ ★ *2020 Top 101 Prospect* **#45** ★ ★ ★

2 Grayson Rodriguez RHP OFP: 60 ETA: Late 2021

Born: 11/16/99 Age: 20 Bats: L Throws: R Height: 6'5" Weight: 220 Origin: Round 1, 2018 Draft (#11 overall)

YEAR	TEAM	LVL	AGE	W	L	SV	G	GS	IP	H	HR	BB/9	K/9	K	GB%	BABIP	WHIP	ERA	DRA	WARP	PF
2018	ORI	RK	18	0	2	0	9	8	19¹	17	0	3.3	9.3	20	43%	.321	1.24	1.40	2.89	0.7	97
2019	DEL	A	19	10	4	0	20	20	94	57	4	3.4	12.4	129	45%	.262	0.99	2.68	2.69	2.8	93
2020	BAL	MLB	20	2	2	0	33	0	35	34	5	3.5	10.1	39	42%	.317	1.37	4.66	4.52	0.3	110

Comparables: Tyler Glasnow, Clayton Kershaw, Lucas Giolito

The Report: Imagine a big Texas prep pitcher who got picked pretty high in the first round last year. Your mental image is probably close enough for horseshoes here. Rodriguez started the season more in the low-to-mid 90s—occasionally scraping higher—but by the time the weather started cooling down again he was throwing hand grenades in the mid-to-upper 90s, frequently hitting 97 and 98. Rodriguez generates good plane and movement from his big frame. At various points in the season he showed the ability for three above-average-to-plus offspeed pitches. The slider was flashing as the best of these by the end of the season, a big sweeper in the low-80s that projects as a plus offering. The change more consistently projected as plus over the course of the full season, with strong dive and the potential to play pretty well in the same velocity band as the slider. The curve doesn't have a ton of velocity separation from the slider, leading to the potential for the pitches to run together in slurviness, but it has a nice shape to it on its own. Rodriguez also started throwing a cutter a tick or two on either side of 90 towards the end of the season, and that's a good pitch for his arm slot and arm speed. While the OFP here is technically the same as it was a year ago, it's gone from a soft 60 to a hard 60, and his chances of getting there have risen greatly as projectability becomes reality. If only 65 were a real grade…

Variance: Medium. There's inconsistency in his offspeed offerings. He's probably going to end up having to figure out which three pitches play best and work better on sequencing and tunneling; he's clustered his offerings from outing-to-outing and even inning-by-inning. There's all the general relief and durability risk you'd associate with a teenage pitcher here, too.

Mark Barry's Fantasy Take: With the regime change in Baltimore it's probably unfair to just type "Orioles pitcher LOL," which is certainly less fun. Even with the plague of his predecessors in mind, Rodriguez offers enough to potentially buck the trend. He's still a couple years away, but high-90s gas paired with a combo of potentially plus offspeed pitches is a perfect start to an SP2 upside.

★ ★ ★ *2020 Top 101 Prospect* **#57** ★ ★ ★

3 Ryan Mountcastle 1B OFP: 60 ETA: Early 2020

Born: 02/18/97 Age: 23 Bats: R Throws: R Height: 6'3" Weight: 195 Origin: Round 1, 2015 Draft (#36 overall)

YEAR	TEAM	LVL	AGE	PA	R	2B	3B	HR	RBI	BB	K	SB	CS	AVG/OBP/SLG	DRC+	VORP	BABIP	BRR	FRAA	WARP	PF
2017	FRD	A+	20	379	63	35	1	15	47	14	61	8	2	.314/.343/.542	137	28.3	.343	1.5	SS(82) -12.1	1.8	109
2017	BOW	AA	20	159	18	13	0	3	15	3	35	0	0	.222/.239/.366	56	-0.4	.265	0.5	3B(37) -1.1	-0.3	106
2018	BOW	AA	21	428	63	19	4	13	59	26	79	2	0	.297/.341/.464	119	22.2	.339	-1.5	3B(81) -4.9	1.6	100
2019	NOR	AAA	22	553	81	35	1	25	83	24	130	2	1	.312/.344/.527	115	18.2	.370	-0.9	1B(84) -6.1, LF(25) 2.1	1.3	101
2020	BAL	MLB	23	385	44	22	1	17	54	15	104	2	1	.266/.299/.472	93	3.0	.327	-0.6	3B -2, 1B 0	0.2	110

Comparables: Brendan Rodgers, Richard Ureña, Justin Williams

The Report: He just keeps hitting while sliding down the defensive spectrum. We don't usually describe right-handed swings as pretty, and while Mountcastle's swing may not get an exhibit in The Prado, he might hit like Martin. Mountcastle has plus bat speed, and can make loud contact in all four quadrants of the zone. He does tend to expand a bit too much, leading to a higher K-rate and lower quality of contact than you'd prefer in your bat-first prospect, but assuming some continued adjustments, it's an easy plus hit tool. Mountcastle always had a plus raw power projection, but found the Triple-A baseball particularly to his liking, knocking 35 doubles and 25 bombs in about three-quarters of a full season. That's about where I'd peg his potential major league production, but he will need to temper the approach to get to that level of pop in *Las Grandes Ligas*. That's a bit better than Martin Prado I suppose. It will need to be since we've made it 150 words into this blurb and haven't mentioned his glove yet. Mountcastle is finally, officially a first baseman. He's fine there.

Variance: Medium. The phrase "we really think Mountcastle will hit" may have been written more times than any other sequence of words at Baseball Prospectus over the last couple years (other than, perhaps, "the ball is juiced"). The Triple-A performance as a 22-year-old is nothing to sneeze at, even with the rabbit ball, but the aggressive approach may cause Mountcastle issues in the majors, barring an adjustment. And he's going to have to hit a lot.

Mark Barry's Fantasy Take: Last year, Ben comped Mountcastle to Nicholas Castellanos, and while I'd love nothing more to come up with a perfect replacement example of Mountcastle's future prospects, Castellanos just feels too right. The downgrade on the positional spectrum hurts a touch, but only a touch.

4 DL Hall LHP   OFP: 60   ETA: Late 2021
Born: 09/19/98 Age: 21 Bats: L Throws: L Height: 6'2" Weight: 195 Origin: Round 1, 2017 Draft (#21 overall)

YEAR	TEAM	LVL	AGE	W	L	SV	G	GS	IP	H	HR	BB/9	K/9	K	GB%	BABIP	WHIP	ERA	DRA	WARP	PF
2017	ORI	RK	18	0	0	0	5	5	10¹	10	1	8.7	10.5	12	58%	.360	1.94	6.97	6.58	-0.1	110
2018	DEL	A	19	2	7	0	22	20	94¹	68	6	4.0	9.5	100	46%	.262	1.17	2.10	3.80	1.5	90
2019	FRD	A+	20	4	5	1	19	17	80²	53	3	6.0	12.9	116	36%	.299	1.33	3.46	3.72	1.3	101
2020	BAL	MLB	21	2	2	0	33	0	35	35	5	4.2	10.5	41	39%	.327	1.47	5.16	4.91	0.1	110

Comparables: Jeremy Jeffress, Alex Reyes, Jesse Biddle

The Report: Hall may have been lapped by Grayson Rodriguez as the organization's best pitching prospect, but that has more to do with the latter's excellence than the former's performance. Hall matched his success as a teenager in the Sally League with an equally impressive campaign as a 20-year-old in the Carolina League, and bettered it measuring by some of the peripherals. He was on pace to surpass his debut innings total when he was shelved with a lat strain in mid-August. The 2017 first-rounder's best pitch is undoubtedly his fastball, which sits 94-96 touching 97 and explodes up in the zone, carrying enough life when lower to still get swings and misses or weak contact. His low-80s curveball features good depth and sharp bite. It's his best secondary, and he can use it in any count. It's equally effective getting called strikes early to set up the fastball or as a put-away pitch down and glove-side.

Hall rounds out the mix with a better-than-decent change and the occasional slider. He's altered his approach this season to be more curve-heavy, and his K rate has jumped to nearly 13 per 9. He did have problems with his control that are worth tempering enthusiasm going forward, but Hall is athletic and the delivery is simple enough that he should have the ability to improve his command. All in all he's the same high-end mid-rotation starter prospect with high reliever risk that he was last year. Hall is going to contribute one way or another in the big leagues some day, but if it is going to be as a starter there are still some hurdles to clear.

Variance: Medium. He's got impact stuff from the left side but runs into issues with control and command that can look like markers of a move to the bullpen. Hall has a strong build and an athletic motion, but isn't tall, it isn't the prototypical pitcher's build, and he just went down with a season-ending lat injury. There's a lot that could happen in either direction, but it is tough to complain about his stuff or performance so far, and he's a 21-year-old ticketed for Double-A.

Mark Barry's Fantasy Take: There's something about Hall that just screams (how do I not say poor man's?) less-advantaged Robbie Ray. In a sense, that's great news for the O's. On the other hand, Ray never walked as many guys in the minors as Hall has. There's upside, yes, but as always, it comes with flame-out/relief potential.

5 Ryan McKenna OF   OFP: 55   ETA: Late 2020
Born: 02/14/97 Age: 23 Bats: R Throws: R Height: 5'11" Weight: 185 Origin: Round 4, 2015 Draft (#133 overall)

YEAR	TEAM	LVL	AGE	PA	R	2B	3B	HR	RBI	BB	K	SB	CS	AVG/OBP/SLG	DRC+	VORP	BABIP	BRR	FRAA	WARP	PF
2017	DEL	A	20	530	62	33	2	7	42	43	128	20	2	.256/.331/.380	117	28.3	.336	-0.2	CF(124) -7.6	1.8	93
2018	FRD	A+	21	301	60	18	2	8	37	37	45	5	6	.377/.467/.556	218	46.2	.436	2.5	CF(64) -6.2, LF(2) -0.2	4.1	105
2018	BOW	AA	21	250	35	8	2	3	16	29	56	4	1	.239/.341/.338	90	10.7	.312	2.6	CF(55) 3.4, RF(3) 2.1	1.4	100
2019	BOW	AA	22	567	78	26	6	9	54	59	121	25	11	.232/.321/.365	112	21.5	.287	1.9	CF(98) -4.1, LF(18) 0.6	2.3	100
2020	BAL	MLB	23	175	17	9	1	4	18	14	47	2	1	.226/.299/.367	75	0.0	.294	0.1	CF 0, LF 1	0.1	110

Comparables: Brandon Nimmo, Brett Phillips, Rey Fuentes

The Report: McKenna's top line numbers as a 22-year-old in the Eastern League don't look amazing, but he heated up in the second half, and there's no real weakness on the scouting sheet. McKenna generates sneaky pop from minimal load and length, although he can get a bit pull-happy at times, which I suspect will limit the hit tool to average at the highest level. When he stays back and takes what he's given, he can drive the ball to the opposite field gap as well. There's the potential for 30-40 doubles in the profile, and McKenna should see enough fastballs on the inner half which he can yank to add double-digit home run totals to the back of his baseball card most years. He's a plus runner and should hold the speed, so while he's unlikely to challenge for Gold Gloves in center field, he's at worst average there. The only tool that doesn't grade out at least as a 5 is his arm, which is fringe, but accurate. There's not really a carrying tool in the profile though, and if McKenna doesn't temper his approach in the majors he may end up more as a fourth/extra outfielder.

Variance: Medium. The speed/glove up-the-middle gives him at least a bench outfielder downside projection, but he hasn't really hit in Double-A as much as you'd like to project an average hit tool. Don't scout that stat line, but the stat line indicates some approach/aggression issues that will need to be ironed out before McKenna can be a regular in the majors.

Mark Barry's Fantasy Take: Welcome to the first of many "Let's See What Happens With the Ball" guys, as McKenna likely won't really pop unless he adds a little, uh, power. The whole is greater than the sum of the parts, and McKenna does everything kinda/sorta well on the field. His proximity to the big leagues makes him an interesting dude in deeper formats, but the ceiling is relatively low here.

6 Yusniel Díaz OF   OFP: 55   ETA: Late 2020
Born: 10/07/96   Age: 23   Bats: R   Throws: R   Height: 6'1"   Weight: 195   Origin: International Free Agent, 2015

YEAR	TEAM	LVL	AGE	PA	R	2B	3B	HR	RBI	BB	K	SB	CS	AVG/OBP/SLG	DRC+	VORP	BABIP	BRR	FRAA	WARP	PF
2017	RCU	A+	20	374	42	15	3	8	39	35	73	7	9	.278/.343/.414	95	8.9	.328	-1.0	CF(29) 1.8, RF(26) -1.2	0.7	108
2017	TUL	AA	20	118	15	8	0	3	13	10	29	2	5	.333/.390/.491	155	7.0	.434	-0.8	RF(26) -0.6, CF(5) -0.1	0.7	99
2018	TUL	AA	21	264	36	10	4	6	30	41	39	8	8	.314/.428/.477	163	21.5	.360	1.8	CF(29) -1.7, RF(28) -1.6	2.1	110
2018	BOW	AA	21	152	23	5	1	5	15	18	28	4	5	.239/.329/.403	96	4.6	.267	-0.5	RF(29) 0.3, CF(6) -0.5	0.2	99
2019	FRD	A+	22	25	0	0	0	0	2	3	7	0	0	.273/.360/.273	88	-0.7	.400	-0.6	CF(5) -0.4	-0.1	110
2019	BOW	AA	22	322	45	19	4	11	53	32	67	0	3	.262/.335/.472	150	19.7	.303	0.6	RF(53) 1.4, CF(5) 0.3	2.5	99
2020	BAL	MLB	23	35	4	2	0	1	4	3	9	0	0	.239/.306/.411	85	0.0	.300	-0.1	RF 0	0.0	110

Comparables: Billy McKinney, Gary Sánchez, Jorge Bonifacio

The Report: Díaz was the prospect centerpiece of the Manny Machado trade last summer, but a year-plus later it's not a slam dunk he'll end up the best major-league piece in the deal. Díaz missed almost all of May with an undisclosed injury, and then dealt with a quad issue late in the season. When he was on the field, he didn't dominate Double-A like you'd hope a top-50 prospect corner bat would. The raw pop is certainly still there. Díaz is strong enough, and has enough of an idea what pitches to drive, that you can still dream on 25-plus bombs in the majors. However, the swing has gotten stiffer and more grooved, leading to more bad contact in the zone. Everything looks a bit less athletic in the box this year, and Díaz's body has gotten a bit softer as well. He's still perfectly fine in right field, but that won't mean much if the bat doesn't carry its weight. You can still wishcast a .260 or .270 hitter with 25 bombs in a couple years, but Díaz now looks less like he will play up past the sum of his solid-average tools, and more like, well…maybe Stephen Piscotty?

Variance: Medium. Díaz and McKenna make a nifty side-by-side for this list. Díaz has more upside if the power plays in the majors, but he's less likely to sustain a major-league career if the hit tool lands at a 40 or 45. He's generally performed better in the minors though, so the risk factor ends up about the same, even though the shape of the risk is very different. Basically we think Díaz has less margin for error with the bat, but is less likely to just not hit at all.

Mark Barry's Fantasy Take: It's a little concerning that Díaz was more or less "fine" last season at Double-A Bowie and didn't really sniff a promotion to Norfolk, let alone Baltimore. Díaz isn't a write off by any means (.270 and 25-30 homers is still the ceiling), but the reports are trending in the wrong direction for him to live up to the Top Prospect in the organization billing he enjoyed just a year ago. He's basically variance-edition Ryan McKenna.

7 Adam Hall 2B/SS   OFP: 50   ETA: 2022
Born: 05/22/99   Age: 21   Bats: R   Throws: R   Height: 6'0"   Weight: 170   Origin: Round 2, 2017 Draft (#60 overall)

YEAR	TEAM	LVL	AGE	PA	R	2B	3B	HR	RBI	BB	K	SB	CS	AVG/OBP/SLG	DRC+	VORP	BABIP	BRR	FRAA	WARP	PF
2018	ABE	A-	19	256	35	9	3	1	24	17	58	22	5	.293/.368/.374	138	24.8	.386	2.6	SS(59) -3.0, 2B(4) 0.4	1.9	92
2019	DEL	A	20	534	78	22	4	5	45	45	117	33	9	.298/.385/.395	140	52.3	.387	3.1	SS(79) 0.4, 2B(39) 0.2	4.5	93
2020	BAL	MLB	21	251	23	11	1	3	22	16	71	10	3	.249/.316/.347	79	0.0	.350	0.5	SS 1, 2B 0	0.3	110

Comparables: Eugenio Suárez, Roman Quinn, Jake Smolinski

The Report: There's been a lot of excitement up to this point on this list. This year's 1.1! First-round pitchers with big arms! Toolsy hitters! Well, Adam Hall will…not be one of those reports. He's a good prospect, don't get me wrong. He's a solid, professional hitter. He's got solid bat-to-ball ability and drives the ball into the gaps a bit. He's got a solid approach and wasn't overmatched at all in an aggressive full-season assignment in his first full season as a Canadian prep. He's a solid defender in the middle infield with solid actions. You've probably noticed by now that I've used solid five times in the last four sentences, and you've probably correctly inferred there isn't anything particularly flashy here. There isn't huge tools upside anywhere in the profile, and he's more polished than projectable. But the guy with all of the 5s and 55s on the report and good performance is a good prospect too, even if he's terribly unlikely to ever bust out into a superstar. He is, in a word, solid.

Variance: Medium. This profile depends a lot on the hit tool projection, and the hit tool is one of the hardest things to project in A-ball hitters, generally. The rest of the skills are low variance.

Mark Barry's Fantasy Take: Hall's calling card for fantasy relevance will be his speed (he swiped 33 bags last season), but he'll need to be able to hit for the speed to play. I'm not overly optimistic that will happen. There are visions of a (way) less fast, less efficient Billy Hamilton dancing in my head, and that makes Hall a little less solid for fantasy purposes.

8   Dean Kremer   RHP   OFP: 50   ETA: 2020

Born: 01/07/96   Age: 24   Bats: R   Throws: R   Height: 6'3"   Weight: 180   Origin: Round 14, 2016 Draft (#431 overall)

YEAR	TEAM	LVL	AGE	W	L	SV	G	GS	IP	H	HR	BB/9	K/9	K	GB%	BABIP	WHIP	ERA	DRA	WARP	PF
2017	RCU	A+	21	1	4	3	33	6	80	86	6	3.8	10.8	96	43%	.369	1.50	5.18	4.78	0.2	102
2018	RCU	A+	22	5	3	0	16	16	79	67	7	3.0	13.0	114	40%	.351	1.18	3.30	2.94	2.2	107
2018	TUL	AA	22	1	0	0	1	1	7	3	0	3.9	14.1	11	75%	.250	0.86	0.00	2.53	0.2	115
2018	BOW	AA	22	4	2	0	8	8	45¹	38	3	3.4	10.5	53	41%	.310	1.21	2.58	3.10	1.2	102
2019	FRD	A+	23	0	0	0	2	2	9²	6	0	3.7	13.0	14	20%	.300	1.03	0.00	3.56	0.2	89
2019	BOW	AA	23	9	4	0	15	15	84²	75	9	3.1	9.2	87	42%	.297	1.23	2.98	4.68	0.3	99
2019	NOR	AAA	23	0	2	0	4	4	19¹	30	2	1.9	9.8	21	38%	.459	1.76	8.84	7.58	-0.2	98
2020	BAL	MLB	24	6	6	0	19	19	97	97	16	3.2	8.8	95	40%	.303	1.36	4.72	4.45	1.2	110

Comparables: Ryan Helsley, Robert Dugger, Hunter Wood

The Report: Kremer has continued to dominate since his conversion back to starting pitching in 2018. Ironically, the success has come mostly because of his reliance on his two best pitches. Kremer's fastball sat in the mid-90s during his days as a reliever. It's more low-90s as a starter, but it has some nice plane and batters tend to see it late due to a deceptive arm action. He can pop it up in the zone effectively, which pairs well off his mid-70s curveball with 12-6 dive. It's not a true power breaker at that velocity band, but it's an effective pitch with an above-average projection. Kremer does show occasional issues moving it east-west in the zone, and will twist it off or use a bit of head whack to get it glove-side against righties. That would be less of an issue if his slider were more consistent, but the mid-80s offering tends to cut and ride up, lacking true two-plane movement. He has a straight change in the same velo band that he sells well, but tends to be overly firm. If Kremer can refine his third and fourth offerings a bit more, there's potential for a league-average starter here, but there might be more upside in seeing if he can find mid-90s velocity in the pen again and let him pair that with the above-average curve in a late-innings role.

Variance: Low. He has two quality major-league offerings in his repertoire already, now it's just a matter of what role he ends up in.

Mark Barry's Fantasy Take: Going out on a limb here, but I've always liked Kremer a little bit. He's still under-the-radar enough where you can keep him on the watch list for now, but you should definitely nab him if he can start to loosen up that change.

9 Michael Baumann RHP   OFP: 50   ETA: 2020

Born: 09/10/95   Age: 24   Bats: R   Throws: R   Height: 6'4"   Weight: 225   Origin: Round 3, 2017 Draft (#98 overall)

YEAR	TEAM	LVL	AGE	W	L	SV	G	GS	IP	H	HR	BB/9	K/9	K	GB%	BABIP	WHIP	ERA	DRA	WARP	PF
2017	ABE	A-	21	4	2	0	10	9	41¹	25	2	4.1	8.9	41	48%	.217	1.06	1.31	3.01	1.1	98
2018	DEL	A	22	5	0	0	7	7	38	23	0	3.1	11.1	47	53%	.277	0.95	1.42	2.78	1.1	85
2018	FRD	A+	22	8	5	0	17	17	92²	82	9	3.9	5.7	59	35%	.261	1.32	3.88	4.69	0.7	106
2019	FRD	A+	23	1	4	0	11	11	54	40	2	4.0	12.8	77	46%	.314	1.19	3.83	3.79	0.8	102
2019	BOW	AA	23	6	2	1	13	11	70	45	2	2.7	8.4	65	43%	.229	0.94	2.31	2.79	1.8	100
2020	BAL	MLB	24	3	3	0	10	10	49	48	7	3.5	9.0	48	41%	.303	1.37	4.61	4.36	0.7	110

Comparables: Brandon Woodruff, André Rienzo, Corey Kluber

The Report: Everyone's favorite doppelgänger of everyone's favorite *Ringer* writer jumped from personal cheeseball to a real prospect arm in 2019. An improved changeup and slider give him four fringe-to-average offerings, and Baumann has a frame built to log innings in a major-league rotation. There's some effort in the delivery to get the fastball up to 95—and some outings he will sit more low 90s—but it shows good life above the hands due to his over-the-top slot. Down in the zone the heater can run a bit true, although he occasionally bores it in on lefties. Accidental cut? Who's to say nowadays.

The slider can run from slurvy to cutterish, but the Goldilocks-approved version around 85 has sharp two-plane action. Baumann's true curveball is a bit soft in the mid 70s, but the 12-6 downer action gives a different breaking ball look. His change can vacillate as well between circle and split action, but he's comfortable throwing it against lefties and sells the offering well enough for it to be more than a show-me pitch. Baumann might lack a true out pitch in the majors, making him more of a swingman or middle reliever, but the improving secondaries give him a shot to stick in the back of a rotation.

Variance: Low. There's not much left to project in the frame or the stuff, and there might not be sustained major league success in the rotation, but Baumann doesn't have much left to prove in the minors either.

Mark Barry's Fantasy Take: DRA might like Baumann more than Kremer, but a range of outcomes such as fringy starter, swingman and middle reliever doesn't inspire a ton of confidence for our purposes. So I guess, Orioles pitcher LOL (old habits die hard).

10 Cadyn Grenier SS   OFP: 50   ETA: 2021

Born: 10/31/96   Age: 23   Bats: R   Throws: R   Height: 5'11"   Weight: 188   Origin: Round 1, 2018 Draft (#37 overall)

YEAR	TEAM	LVL	AGE	PA	R	2B	3B	HR	RBI	BB	K	SB	CS	AVG/OBP/SLG	DRC+	VORP	BABIP	BRR	FRAA	WARP	PF
2018	DEL	A	21	183	23	12	2	1	13	17	53	3	2	.216/.297/.333	84	9.9	.312	-0.5	SS(39) 2.7	0.7	87
2019	DEL	A	22	364	49	18	3	7	39	48	107	5	1	.253/.360/.399	123	29.3	.360	3.0	SS(54) 6.1, 2B(26) -2.2	2.9	96
2019	FRD	A+	22	92	11	4	1	1	4	11	31	2	1	.208/.337/.325	72	2.4	.333	0.9	SS(22) 2.7	0.5	103
2020	BAL	MLB	23	251	22	12	1	6	25	17	93	1	0	.208/.271/.342	59	0.0	.322	-0.3	SS 4, 2B 0	-0.1	110

Comparables: Michael Perez, Jeremy Hazelbaker, Jaylin Davis

The Report: He's *really* good defensively. Good enough that he pushed Nick Madrigal to second at Oregon State. Good enough that he mostly pushed Hall—a better prospect—to second when they were together in Delmarva. Good enough that he was a first-rounder last year even with critical questions about his hitting ability. Suffice to say, those questions remain. Grenier has some bat speed and pop, so he's not hopeless on offense. But he chases too much and doesn't adjust his bat path well, which leads to the potentially-fatal combination of too much swing-and-miss and too much poor contact when he does connect. As hinted at above, he can really go pick it at both short and second, so there's a high "floor" in that he should at least have some sort of utility player career even if he fails to hit much. He could probably be that already, frankly. There's just enough hitting ability to get him to a regular at present if you're optimistic, and, given the secondary abilities and general baseball feel, you can hope it gels if you're extremely optimistic. We're always known for our optimism here at the Baseball Prospectus Prospect Team, right?

Variance: Medium. He's very likely to make the majors and have a real career given his versatility, but there's a lot of room between the lower-side realistic outcomes where he's an up-and-down sixth infielder type and the OFP.

Mark Barry's Fantasy Take: Grenier is a great choice if your league only awards points for defensive stats or variations of the -adyn, -aydan, -aiden forename.

The Next Ten

11 Gunnar Henderson   SS

Born: 06/29/01   Age: 19   Bats: L   Throws: R   Height: 6'3"   Weight: 195   Origin: Round 2, 2019 Draft (#42 overall)

YEAR	TEAM	LVL	AGE	PA	R	2B	3B	HR	RBI	BB	K	SB	CS	AVG/OBP/SLG	DRC+	VORP	BABIP	BRR	FRAA	WARP	PF
2019	ORI	RK	18	121	21	5	2	1	11	11	28	2	2	.259/.331/.370	65	2.7	.338	0.4	SS(21) -1.6	0.0	96
2020	BAL	MLB	19	251	21	11	1	4	22	21	85	3	1	.215/.285/.324	64	0.0	.324	0.0	SS 0	-0.3	110

Comparables: Gavin Lux, Junior Lake, Brendan Rodgers

Henderson, the Orioles second-round pick, got Mark Vientos comps around draft time. I can kind of see it physically, and he has the same kind of length to his swing, but without the same present raw that Vientos had as a teenager due to a pretty flat swing plane. There's better present athleticism, although Henderson might slide over to third himself as he fills out, and his actions can be a bit sluggish for the 6. He was also a youngish prep draftee, so he might eventually catch up to Vientos on the pop with some added strength and a swing tweak. It's an intriguing tool set overall, but 2020 will give us more data on what exactly the shape of the player might look like in a few years. For now, there's a major league OFP somewhere on the left side of the infield, but a much higher variance than even the upper-minors arms above him.

12 Austin Hays   OF

Born: 07/05/95   Age: 24   Bats: R   Throws: R   Height: 6'1"   Weight: 195   Origin: Round 3, 2016 Draft (#91 overall)

YEAR	TEAM	LVL	AGE	PA	R	2B	3B	HR	RBI	BB	K	SB	CS	AVG/OBP/SLG	DRC+	VORP	BABIP	BRR	FRAA	WARP	PF
2017	FRD	A+	21	280	42	15	3	16	41	12	40	4	6	.328/.364/.592	149	25.5	.337	0.7	CF(57) 8.1, RF(4) -0.6	3.1	110
2017	BOW	AA	21	283	39	17	2	16	54	13	45	1	1	.330/.367/.594	157	31.3	.345	3.2	CF(32) -3.3, RF(29) -0.4	2.4	105
2017	BAL	MLB	21	63	4	3	0	1	8	2	16	0	0	.217/.238/.317	70	-3.3	.273	-0.4	RF(14) -1.6, CF(8) -1.3	-0.4	102
2018	ABE	A-	22	39	6	2	0	0	3	2	7	0	0	.189/.231/.243	92	-2.9	.233	0.0	RF(5) -0.6	0.0	88
2018	BOW	AA	22	288	34	12	2	12	43	12	59	6	3	.242/.271/.432	89	8.3	.263	0.9	RF(36) 6.7, LF(16) -0.3	1.1	98
2019	FRD	A+	23	40	3	0	0	2	6	1	11	0	0	.162/.200/.324	41	-1.0	.160	0.2	CF(7) -0.7	-0.2	94
2019	BOW	AA	23	61	9	5	0	3	11	5	11	3	1	.268/.328/.518	142	3.2	.286	-1.1	RF(7) 1.2, CF(4) 0.0	0.4	103
2019	NOR	AAA	23	257	43	16	1	10	27	11	61	6	4	.254/.304/.454	93	10.1	.302	4.2	CF(38) 4.8, RF(16) 0.0	1.3	100
2019	BAL	MLB	23	75	12	6	0	4	13	7	13	2	0	.309/.373/.574	111	3.9	.333	0.8	CF(20) 2.3	0.7	106
2020	BAL	MLB	24	350	43	19	1	19	54	16	85	2	1	.253/.293/.490	99	0.0	.283	-0.4	CF 4	1.6	110

Comparables: Christian Yelich, Nomar Mazara, Tyler Colvin

Austin Hays. Boy, I don't know. Some players just peak at 21. That neat parabola arcing at Age 26-28 is a composite of thousands of player's careers. So it's not impossible the best season of his career came when he was torching a couple minor league levels. There were of course the two years of injuries that followed—ankle, thumb, hamstring—and rumors that the previous administration weren't as high on Hays as the prospect list makers were. He's been a beneficiary of the giant reset button in Charm City and found himself with a second chance to make a September impression. Hays has always been more of a broad base of skills type rather than an outfielder with a clear carrying tool, so there is the risk that the injuries may have eroded those skills to fringy. He's also never *really* hit above Double-A. On the other hand, it's a potential average hit/power profile and the ability to battle center field to a draw some days. Hays is not the trickiest "prospect" on this list to rank—that's still to come—but he has the weirdest variance profile in this glut of OFP 50 names.

13 Keegan Akin LHP

Born: 04/01/95   Age: 25   Bats: L   Throws: L   Height: 6'0"   Weight: 225   Origin: Round 2, 2016 Draft (#54 overall)

YEAR	TEAM	LVL	AGE	W	L	SV	G	GS	IP	H	HR	BB/9	K/9	K	GB%	BABIP	WHIP	ERA	DRA	WARP	PF
2017	FRD	A+	22	7	8	0	21	21	100	89	12	4.1	10.0	111	38%	.307	1.35	4.14	3.96	1.5	108
2018	BOW	AA	23	14	7	0	25	25	137²	114	16	3.8	9.3	142	32%	.278	1.25	3.27	3.76	2.5	102
2019	NOR	AAA	24	6	7	0	25	24	112¹	109	10	4.9	10.5	131	34%	.331	1.51	4.73	4.36	2.6	101
2020	BAL	MLB	25	4	5	0	16	16	68	71	12	3.7	9.1	68	34%	.310	1.45	5.30	4.90	0.5	110

Comparables: Matt Hall, Brad Mills, Taylor Hearn

It was more of the same for Akin this season, for good and ill. He gave back a tick or so of the mid-90s heat that popped up in 2018, but he still touches 95 with boring action in on righties, and can vary the fastball look with two-seam action in the low-90s. He has difficulty repeating his arm path, though, and continues to struggle with command and control of the fastball. The raw velocity from the left side, plus some deception, allows him to get swings and misses with the fastball, which is good because both secondaries remain below-average. He throws his low-80s slider a fair bit now, but it tends to slide down barrels rather than miss bats due to a lack of depth and general slurviness. The 2019 Orioles used 40 pitchers in 2019 and Akin is likely to be one of the multitudes in 2020, but he's more likely to fit as a reliever than a starter.

14 Alex Wells LHP

Born: 02/27/97   Age: 23   Bats: L   Throws: L   Height: 6'1"   Weight: 190   Origin: International Free Agent, 2015

YEAR	TEAM	LVL	AGE	W	L	SV	G	GS	IP	H	HR	BB/9	K/9	K	GB%	BABIP	WHIP	ERA	DRA	WARP	PF
2017	DEL	A	20	11	5	0	25	25	140	118	16	0.6	7.3	113	43%	.251	0.91	2.38	3.48	2.9	93
2018	FRD	A+	21	7	8	0	24	24	135	142	19	2.2	6.7	101	36%	.301	1.30	3.47	5.21	0.2	105
2019	BOW	AA	22	8	6	0	24	24	137¹	123	10	1.6	6.9	105	43%	.274	1.07	2.95	4.56	0.7	100
2020	BAL	MLB	23	2	2	0	33	0	35	35	6	3.2	6.2	24	41%	.274	1.37	4.94	4.86	0.1	110

Comparables: Gabriel Ynoa, José Ureña, Paul Blackburn

I see—conservatively—two dozen different "soft-tossing lefties" over the course of the season, and I'll be the first to admit that I like Wells more than I should. I liked him more when he topped out at 90 in the Penn League though. It was 88 this year, but he manipulates the pitch well and will sink or cut it. There's 70 control and 60 command to boot. His best secondary is an average changeup that he throws a lot. It doesn't have ideal velocity separation, sitting in the low 80s, but there's enough late fade to miss bats or induce weak contact. I'd like him more if I could really get it to a plus projection, but for as much as he throws it there's too many hittable ones. He shows a slider and a curve. I actually prefer the slider as a left-on-left option, as his low-70s curve tends to be a bit loopy and obvious out of the hand. But the curve comes in from an incredibly difficult angle as Wells releases everything from as close to first base as possible for a southpaw with a relatively high slot. Despite the funk and crossfire, Wells is just playing catch out there and repeats everything well. I just wish the everything popped off the scouting sheet a little bit more. I'm not gonna bet against him doing enough to be a backend starter, but he looks more like a swingman or crossover lefty pen arm.

15 Zac Lowther LHP

Born: 04/30/96   Age: 24   Bats: L   Throws: L   Height: 6'2"   Weight: 235   Origin: Round 2, 2017 Draft (#74 overall)

YEAR	TEAM	LVL	AGE	W	L	SV	G	GS	IP	H	HR	BB/9	K/9	K	GB%	BABIP	WHIP	ERA	DRA	WARP	PF
2017	ABE	A-	21	2	2	0	12	11	54¹	35	1	1.8	12.4	75	47%	.283	0.85	1.66	1.95	2.1	101
2018	DEL	A	22	3	1	0	6	6	31	12	2	2.6	14.8	51	33%	.192	0.68	1.16	1.45	1.4	94
2018	FRD	A+	22	5	3	0	17	16	92²	74	6	2.5	9.7	100	40%	.288	1.08	2.53	3.30	2.2	105
2019	BOW	AA	23	13	7	0	26	26	148	102	8	3.8	9.4	154	41%	.259	1.11	2.55	4.16	1.4	98
2020	BAL	MLB	24	3	3	0	10	10	49	48	7	3.5	8.9	48	40%	.305	1.38	4.73	4.49	0.6	110

Comparables: Matt Hall, Taylor Hearn, Jordan Montgomery

You can shake up the names of the lefty arms in the Next Ten in a tombola and draw them out at random and I'd mostly shrug and then sign off on the results. Lowther has a better fastball than Wells in that he more regularly touches 90-91. He offers late, almost wiffle ball, movement on the pitch, along with even more deception, but less command. It's a tough angle for lefties, and Lowther has some success boring both the fastball and the change in on righties. The change is firm in the low 80s, but has enough fade to be effective, and Lowther can spot it to either side. He has two below-average breaking balls in the arsenal as well. There was internal discussion around the idea that a dude with that kind of natural fastball movement should be able to pick up some kind of breaking ball or cutter with a bit of "pitch design," but we also can't really project that. What we can project is another lefty swingman or fifth starter type.

16 Rylan Bannon   IF

Born: 04/22/96   Age: 24   Bats: R   Throws: R   Height: 5'7"   Weight: 180   Origin: Round 8, 2017 Draft (#250 overall)

YEAR	TEAM	LVL	AGE	PA	R	2B	3B	HR	RBI	BB	K	SB	CS	AVG/OBP/SLG	DRC+	VORP	BABIP	BRR	FRAA	WARP	PF
2017	OGD	RK	21	175	39	8	0	10	30	19	29	5	0	.336/.425/.591	161	19.7	.360	0.8	3B(34) 5.9	1.9	117
2018	RCU	A+	22	403	58	17	6	20	61	59	103	4	4	.296/.402/.559	160	35.9	.367	0.0	3B(54) 2.9, 2B(22) 0.2	4.0	109
2018	BOW	AA	22	122	16	6	0	2	11	22	24	0	0	.204/.344/.327	98	2.5	.243	-1.4	2B(30) -0.9, 3B(2) -0.1	0.1	97
2019	BOW	AA	23	444	45	22	4	8	42	47	72	8	4	.255/.345/.394	124	19.4	.294	-0.4	3B(68) 1.8, 2B(38) 1.4	2.8	100
2019	NOR	AAA	23	90	18	10	0	3	17	3	14	0	1	.317/.344/.549	119	6.1	.338	-0.3	3B(20) 3.1	0.7	100
2020	BAL	MLB	24	251	25	12	1	7	27	20	59	1	0	.229/.300/.381	79	3.0	.280	-0.3	3B 2, 2B 0	0.4	110

Comparables: Alex Blandino, Adam Eaton, Yonder Alonso

Bannon doesn't have the slick glove of Grenier, the overall up-the-middle tool set of Hall, or the amateur pedigree of either. What he has done is hit at every level, showing surprising pop from an undersized frame. There won't be the 20+ home run power he showed in Rancho, because that's Rancho, but it's better-than-average raw, and he has the ability to stand at a few different infield spots (and could likely hack it in corner outfield as well). Yes, it's a grindy, Day 2 college bat that can't play a premium defensive spot. But Bannon doesn't have much left to prove in the minors, and while issues with spin might limit him to an extra infielder role, sometimes these guys show enough secondary skills that the whole profile plays up despite below-average batting averages.

17 Hunter Harvey   RHP

Born: 12/09/94   Age: 25   Bats: R   Throws: R   Height: 6'3"   Weight: 175   Origin: Round 1, 2013 Draft (#22 overall)

YEAR	TEAM	LVL	AGE	W	L	SV	G	GS	IP	H	HR	BB/9	K/9	K	GB%	BABIP	WHIP	ERA	DRA	WARP	PF
2017	DEL	A	22	0	1	0	3	3	8²	4	0	3.1	14.5	14	31%	.250	0.81	2.08	2.21	0.3	92
2018	BOW	AA	23	1	2	0	9	9	32¹	36	3	2.5	8.4	30	36%	.351	1.39	5.57	5.07	0.1	95
2019	BOW	AA	24	2	5	1	14	11	59	63	14	3.2	9.3	61	40%	.316	1.42	5.19	6.42	-1.1	99
2019	NOR	AAA	24	1	1	0	12	0	16²	13	2	2.7	11.9	22	43%	.275	1.08	4.32	2.97	0.5	100
2019	BAL	MLB	24	1	0	0	7	0	6¹	3	1	5.7	15.6	11	55%	.200	1.11	1.42	3.70	0.1	106
2020	BAL	MLB	25	3	3	10	54	0	57	49	8	3.6	10.1	64	39%	.286	1.26	4.09	3.86	0.8	110

Comparables: Keury Mella, Michael Blazek, Wilfredo Boscan

What a long, strange trip it has been. Hunter Harvey remains—much to my consternation—both still eligible for this list and functionally impossible to rank. He finally made his major-league debut in 2019. This comes after three years as a Top 101 arm which ended halfway into six injury-plagued minor league seasons where he threw just 250 innings total. Harvey is strictly a reliever now, but he's pumping 99 mph fastballs and a power curve to go with it. So it's badass late-inning stuff. He also was used sparingly in September because of "soreness." If the health record were a little better and the fastball a little less true he'd be a top 10 prospect in the system, but there's little evidence Harvey can handle even a 50-inning-a-year reliever workload at this point.

18 Bruce Zimmermann LHP

Born: 02/09/95 Age: 25 Bats: L Throws: L Height: 6'2" Weight: 215 Origin: Round 5, 2017 Draft (#140 overall)

YEAR	TEAM	LVL	AGE	W	L	SV	G	GS	IP	H	HR	BB/9	K/9	K	GB%	BABIP	WHIP	ERA	DRA	WARP	PF
2017	DNV	RK	22	0	1	0	11	11	23^1	21	0	3.5	10.8	28	58%	.350	1.29	3.09	3.64	0.6	90
2018	ROM	A	23	7	3	0	14	14	84^2	74	5	1.9	10.5	99	48%	.319	1.09	2.76	3.79	1.4	97
2018	MIS	AA	23	2	1	0	6	6	28^2	25	3	6.0	8.2	26	41%	.286	1.53	3.14	5.44	0.0	92
2018	BOW	AA	23	2	3	0	5	5	21^1	25	2	3.0	6.8	16	30%	.324	1.50	5.06	6.52	-0.3	99
2019	BOW	AA	24	5	3	0	18	17	101^1	88	9	3.0	9.0	101	41%	.283	1.20	2.58	4.38	0.7	100
2019	NOR	AAA	24	2	3	0	7	7	38^2	44	3	4.2	7.7	33	49%	.352	1.60	4.89	5.69	0.4	101
2020	BAL	MLB	25	2	2	0	33	0	35	34	5	3.5	7.6	29	41%	.287	1.36	4.63	4.54	0.3	110

Comparables: Alex Young, Drake Britton, Scott Barlow

Zimmerman slides from 11 to 18 due to an improving system, but this southpaw varietal more or less held serve in 2019. He conquered Double-A the second time around, missing bats consistently with a sneaky fast ~90 mph heater and potentially average change. The change shows tight, late fade, and Zimmerman sells it well with the arm action. Is this starting to sound a lot like Zac Lowther? Well, sure. Zimmerman's slider is a tick better than Lowther's breaking balls—inconsistent, but flashing razorblade action in the low 80s. There's a humpy, low-70s curve as well, for a different look or to steal a strike. If you preferred Zimmerman over Lowther—or frankly some of the other arms in the Next Ten—that'd be fine by us, but the 24-year-old senior sign is more or less what he is right now, and Triple-A and the majors might be a bit rude to the profile.

19 Drew Rom LHP

Born: 12/15/99 Age: 20 Bats: L Throws: L Height: 6'2" Weight: 170 Origin: Round 4, 2018 Draft (#115 overall)

YEAR	TEAM	LVL	AGE	W	L	SV	G	GS	IP	H	HR	BB/9	K/9	K	GB%	BABIP	WHIP	ERA	DRA	WARP	PF
2018	ORI	RK	18	0	2	0	10	9	30^2	20	1	1.8	8.2	28	49%	.232	0.85	1.76	1.17	1.6	98
2019	DEL	A	19	6	3	1	21	15	95^1	83	5	3.1	11.5	122	47%	.328	1.22	2.93	4.17	1.0	95
2020	BAL	MLB	20	2	2	0	33	0	35	35	5	4.1	9.2	36	43%	.307	1.45	5.05	4.84	0.1	110

Rom was quite solid in his full-season debut in the South Atlantic League. This was an aggressive assignment for a 19-year-old, fourth-round prep arm. Rom thrived with a four-pitch mix he can throw for strikes, including a solid slider. The fastball sits in the low 90s and while he repeats well, the command of the arsenal is merely average. Rom lacks a clear out pitch or above-average velocity, and developing either would leapfrog him over the long list of backend starters ahead of him. For now he remains more intriguing, but also further away than that cohort.

20 Brenan Hanifee RHP

Born: 05/29/98 Age: 22 Bats: R Throws: R Height: 6'5" Weight: 215 Origin: Round 4, 2016 Draft (#121 overall)

YEAR	TEAM	LVL	AGE	W	L	SV	G	GS	IP	H	HR	BB/9	K/9	K	GB%	BABIP	WHIP	ERA	DRA	WARP	PF
2017	ABE	A-	19	7	3	0	12	12	68^2	65	2	1.6	5.8	44	59%	.289	1.12	2.75	3.92	1.1	96
2018	DEL	A	20	8	6	0	23	23	132	120	8	1.5	5.8	85	55%	.275	1.08	2.86	4.36	1.3	90
2019	FRD	A+	21	9	10	0	24	22	129	126	12	4.0	5.4	78	51%	.280	1.42	4.60	5.56	-0.9	102
2020	BAL	MLB	22	2	2	0	33	0	35	34	5	3.7	4.6	18	50%	.257	1.39	4.89	4.82	0.1	110

Hanifee is your typical sinker-slider guy, relying on a steady supply of grounders to get outs and holding his breath every time he elevates a pitch anywhere near the middle. He sits around 90-92 with a two-seamer that pretty consistently shows late arm-side run and sink. This pitch is especially effective against same-side hitters and generates its share of weak rollers to the left side of the infield. His low-80s slider is above-average, and he often uses it to sneak strikes on lefties via the backdoor. Sometimes short and tight and sometimes slurvier, he'll also use it for a swing-and-miss from a righty every now and then. The changeup is his third pitch at the moment, but if he can improve it it would be a very useful weapon against lefties. He by and large improved as the season went on but 2019 was a step back overall, and while the command is fine the stuff really isn't overwhelming. Next he'll either look to conquer Advanced-A or corral Double-A on the fly.

Personal Cheeseball

PC **Mason McCoy** **IF**
Born: 03/31/95   Age: 25   Bats: R   Throws: R   Height: 6'0"   Weight: 175   Origin: Round 6, 2017 Draft (#188 overall)

YEAR	TEAM	LVL	AGE	PA	R	2B	3B	HR	RBI	BB	K	SB	CS	AVG/OBP/SLG	DRC+	VORP	BABIP	BRR	FRAA	WARP	PF
2017	ABE	A-	22	220	34	11	3	1	29	26	28	4	3	.301/.382/.409	157	20.9	.342	1.8	SS(48) -1.1	2.0	99
2018	DEL	A	23	536	66	18	10	4	47	45	95	13	2	.266/.331/.369	116	33.5	.321	3.2	SS(89) 8.2, 2B(32) -0.2	4.2	88
2019	FRD	A+	24	125	21	9	0	2	17	8	16	3	0	.379/.416/.509	186	15.7	.424	0.2	SS(17) 0.7, 2B(10) 1.4	1.7	105
2019	BOW	AA	24	471	60	13	7	2	31	36	84	10	3	.266/.326/.343	115	21.8	.326	3.9	SS(86) -1.6, 2B(16) 0.7	3.0	99
2020	BAL	MLB	25	251	21	11	2	3	23	16	55	1	0	.250/.301/.351	74	0.0	.315	0.0	SS 1, 2B 0	0.1	110

On these pages, there will be sidearming relievers, lefties with a change, Wilson's favorite beefy sluggers, and grind-em-out utility infielders. Mason McCoy is the last of those types, and the answer to the question, "What if Cadyn Grenier weren't good enough defensively to go in the first round of the draft?" Perhaps that's a bit harsh on McCoy, who was a priority senior sign who has had to prove it at every level of the minors. So far, so good, as he's hit enough, and held down both middle infield spots to make it to Double-A. There's not much in the way of power projection here, and he's merely passable at shortstop, but McCoy grinds out at-bats and makes enough good contact that his level-by-level progress could very well keep going until he finds himself with a major league bench spot.

Low Minors Sleeper

LMS **Toby Welk** **3B/1B**
Born: 05/02/97   Age: 23   Bats: R   Throws: R   Height: 6'2"   Weight: 205   Origin: Round 21, 2019 Draft (#618 overall)

YEAR	TEAM	LVL	AGE	PA	R	2B	3B	HR	RBI	BB	K	SB	CS	AVG/OBP/SLG	DRC+	VORP	BABIP	BRR	FRAA	WARP	PF
2019	ABE	A-	22	204	22	12	2	4	28	16	42	2	2	.344/.397/.500	166	22.1	.417	-1.1	3B(41) -4.4	1.1	99
2019	DEL	A	22	36	2	1	0	0	2	4	8	1	0	.250/.333/.281	118	0.4	.333	-0.3	3B(6) -1.1	0.0	87
2020	BAL	MLB	23	251	25	12	1	6	27	16	73	3	1	.250/.303/.388	83	3.0	.338	0.0	3B -3	0.0	110

Welk is the first player drafted from the rather prolix school of Penn State Berks, a college of Pennsylvania State University. He's more athletic than the "21st round Div. III corner infield senior sign" biography would suggest. There's feel for contact too, but Welk is going to have to hit at every level from here to Bowie just to even end up in Mason McCoy territory. But given that the author first came to fame on the prospect internet for suggesting Josh Satin had a major-league future, Welk will at worst remain a personal cheeseball for years to come.

Top Talents 25 and Under (as of 4/1/2020)

1. Adley Rutschman
2. Grayson Rodriguez
3. Ryan Mountcastle
4. DL Hall
5. Ryan McKenna
6. Yusniel Díaz
7. Anthony Santander
8. Renato Núñez
9. Chance Sisco
10. Adam Hall

The top four names on the prospect list are the slam-dunk top four under-25 talents in the organization as well. I'll leave it up to the reader to decide whether that's due in greater part to the star potential at the top of the system (which is real) or the dearth of foundational talent currently at the big league level. Adley Rutschman was the clearest-cut first overall pick in several years, and Grayson Rodriguez, Ryan Mountcastle, and DL Hall should all eventually end up high-level big leaguers in some form. Rutschman of course looks like an excellent two-way catcher, while Rodriguez and Hall look like mid-rotation arms or more, and high-leverage relievers even if some things go awry. Mountcastle has never really had a position but the bat's always played and there's an opening in Baltimore at the cold corner.

Ryan McKenna and Yusniel Díaz show enough upside that even given the risks in their profiles they deserve to slot in ahead of outfielder Anthony Santander and corner-infielder Renato Núñez, who emerged amid the rubble of the 2019 Orioles as solid contributors, but are likely not a lot more than that. Chance Sisco was nearer to the top of this list a few years ago, but he's never truly managed to assuage concerns about his work behind the plate. He split time between Baltimore and Triple-A Norfolk last season, and his bat suffered when he was with the big club. Adam Hall isn't dripping with upside like some of the names higher up on the list, but he's a decent middle-infielder who can hit more than a little and seems a safe bet to be a part of conversation in the coming years.

Eyewitness Reports

Eyewitness Report: Adley Rutschman

Evaluator: Keanan Lamb
Report Date: 06/01/2019
Dates Seen: 5/10-12/19
Risk Factor: Medium

Physical/Health: Well built, fully formed 6-foot-2 backstop that has both good strength and mobility. Not too big or too tall for the position; he's perfectly suited for the role. Better athlete than many would give credit for, but well above average for a catcher.

Tool	Future Grade	Report
Hit	60	At present, he is nearly identical from both sides of the plate ability-wise as a switch-hitter. His compact setup and swing is best suited for a contact approach, despite his power ability. Even if the game power doesn't fully come around, his knowledge of the zone and handspeed should equate to a plus batting average regardless of position, and double-plus relative to the position.
Power	60	The power has really improved as his approach has refined. He is able to get into hitter's counts and wait for his pitch, unloading with plus batspeed and adding leverage to his swing when necessary. At minimum, he is able to barrel the ball with regularity with easy gap-to-gap power with a contact approach without having to sellout for power.
Baserunning/ Speed	50	A better runner than many would think, he can at least be an average runner -- which is far better than most catchers. While certainly no burner, he is a very good baserunner and gets very good reads off balls put in play and in the dirt.
Glove	60	From a fundamental standpoint, his receiving skills are clean with decent framing ability. His lateral movement is very good at anything bounced at the plate, and is especially excellent at pop-ups. One concern while playing at Oregon State: he never called his own games even though he was a three year starter. He may be able to work in tandem with a pitching staff, but it is an unknown.
Arm	70	While the arm is certainly plus, his footwork and release routinely give him pop times in the 1.8-1.9 range which helps play up the arm grade. Throws are regularly strong and accurate, with very few runners willing to test him this season.

Conclusion: Rutschman does everything well, if not above average on all his tools with very few holes. There are so many commitments to balance as a professional catcher: handling a staff, scouting an opponent, and then putting in time in the batting cages from both sides of the plate. If anything suffers, maybe it's the bat, but the defense alone is consistent enough to make him an everyday catcher on a first division team with a high floor. However, if the bat continues to play, he is a regular all-star caliber player given the positional scarcity. Given the physical demands of the position and high attrition rates, there is enough risk involved to prevent a higher OFP, although a 70 grade in the future is not out of the question.

Eyewitness Report: Grayson Rodriguez

Evaluator: Jarrett Seidler
Report Date: 07/02/2019
Dates Seen: 7/1/2019
Risk Factor: High
Delivery: Big and fully developed frame. Substantial leg kick out of windup with moderate tempo motion. High three-quarters arm slot, bordering on overhand. Medium effort in delivery. Generates substantial plane with armslot, extension, and size. Did not appear to be fully comfortable in stretch, and velocity was down from there. Was clustering his offspeed pitches in particular innings.

Pitch Type	Future Grade	Sitting Velocity	Peak Velocity	Report
Fastball	60	91-96	96	Sat 95-96 in the first inning, but never hit 96 again after, and pitched much of the game 92-94. Generates big plane and has some natural cut. He was able to get it past most of the hitters in the Lakewood lineup. Had the best command of any of his offerings, but he's still going to have to improve. Although he probably doesn't have a ton of physical projectability left, wouldn't be surprised if he could be more consistently towards the top of this band or even higher with further development.
Slider	60	80-83	84	Didn't have feel for the pitch at all in the first inning, when he mostly leaned on his curveball, but unleashed it with full force in the second inning, and then sporadically through the rest of the game. Big, sweeping break, and more of a classic slider than the hard, cutter-like "Warthen slider" that many hard-throwers have adopted. This is a potential plus, swing-and-miss offering if he can refine and gain greater command of it.
Curveball	55	76-78	79	Pitch has plus potential on its own, but I am downgrading it a half-grade because it ran together some with the slider, which I think is probably a better pitch. Classic 11-to-5 two plane break when it was right. Didn't have stellar command of the pitch, and hung a few.
Changeup	50	80-81	81	Rodriguez worked this pitch in the third inning and beyond as an offering to get through the order the second and third times. It works as a change of pace in that it's broadly in the same velocity band as the breaking balls, and runs the opposite way of the rest of his arsenal. It's a bit firm, and nothing to write home about, but as a third or fourth offering it'll do.

Conclusion: Rodriguez is the prototype for a Texas prep pitcher drafted in the top half of the first round: big, hard-throwing, and somewhat unpolished. He needs to gain command and consistency, especially out of the stretch. His breaking balls are also running together, and I expect that he'll either need to create greater separation between the pitches or he'll be best off scrapping one. Overall, Rodriguez is one of the better A-ball pitching prospects in the game, despite high risk factors that are typical for the cohort. Reasonable outcomes here include a no. 3 starter or late-inning reliever if everything pulls together.

Boston Red Sox

The State of the System
The 2019 draft class gave the system a much needed injection of talent, but the Sox still lack for impact prospects.

The Top Ten

1 **Triston Casas   1B**   OFP: 55   ETA: Late 2022
Born: 01/15/00   Age: 20   Bats: L   Throws: R   Height: 6'4"   Weight: 238   Origin: Round 1, 2018 Draft (#26 overall)

YEAR	TEAM	LVL	AGE	PA	R	2B	3B	HR	RBI	BB	K	SB	CS	AVG/OBP/SLG	DRC+	VORP	BABIP	BRR	FRAA	WARP	PF
2019	GRN	A	19	493	64	25	5	19	78	58	116	3	2	.254/.349/.472	145	24.1	.300	-0.9	1B(94) -4.7, 3B(8) -1.2	2.1	101
2020	BOS	MLB	20	251	26	12	1	9	30	20	74	3	1	.220/.290/.398	81	1.0	.283	-0.4	1B -2, 3B 0	0.0	112

Comparables: Matt Olson, Mike Carp, Trayce Thompson

The Report: It was an up-and-down year for the 2018 first-rounder. Casas showed off his plus power tool to the tune of 19 home runs and 25 doubles, but the extra-base pop came in spurts. His power stroke is best utilized when he shoots the ball to the left-center field gap. However, he would fall into spells where he would try to pull everything, exacerbating his swing-and-miss tendencies and raising questions about the hit tool projection. But even with those concerns, Casas still has the potential to flirt with 40 home runs on a yearly basis, due to his strength and quick bat. His load is very quiet, employing a minimal leg kick and no movement in his upper half, meaning he only needs a change to his approach and not an overhaul of the swing mechanics. Defensively Casas made positive strides throughout the season. It isn't always smooth at first base, but he possesses the basic tools to be an average fielder. His backhand impressed me on multiple occasions. His best attribute in the field is his plus arm. What keeps me optimistic about Casas is his makeup. From multiple sources, he is teachable, a competitor and someone who puts in the extra work–all traits that will help him reach his potential.

Variance: Medium. His power tool and ability to play an average first base gives Casas a fairly high floor. But his full potential in the bigs hinges on improvements to his approach, which will turn him from an average player into a potential All-Star.

Ben Carsley's Fantasy Take: It's always fun when the best guy in a system is a first baseman in the low minors! I actually like Casas quite a bit for a player with his profile; it's just not a terribly enticing fantasy skill set. The dream is Casas improves his approach and turns into a .270/30/100-type on the regular. There's plenty of value in that, of course, but a) it's gonna come at first base and b) please remember that's indicative of Casas' upside, and not a promise of what's to come. It's awfully early to be talking about rankings, but Casas strikes me as the type of dude who'll get knocked off our top-101 in favor of toolsier teenagers, stuck in the dreaded "honorable mentions" until he's closer to the bigs. That still makes him worth rostering in most dynasty leagues, though.

2 **Noah Song   RHP**   OFP: 55   ETA: ??
Born: 05/28/97   Age: 23   Bats: R   Throws: R   Height: 6'4"   Weight: 200   Origin: Round 4, 2019 Draft (#137 overall)

YEAR	TEAM	LVL	AGE	W	L	SV	G	GS	IP	H	HR	BB/9	K/9	K	GB%	BABIP	WHIP	ERA	DRA	WARP	PF
2019	LOW	A-	22	0	0	0	7	7	17	10	0	2.6	10.1	19	42%	.244	0.88	1.06	2.49	0.5	95
2020	BOS	MLB	23	2	2	0	33	0	35	35	5	3.5	7.9	31	40%	.293	1.38	4.52	4.69	0.2	112

Comparables: Troy Scribner, Jesse Hahn, Daniel Ponce de Leon

The Report: Song has one of the most unusual backgrounds of any prospect in recent memory, as a top pitching prospect currently facing an obligation to serve at least two years in the armed forces. He pitched collegiately at the Naval Academy and stayed until graduation; the Red Sox drafted him in the fourth round last summer despite an unclear future in baseball.

After Song played for Team USA in Olympic qualifying last fall, he sought a waiver to postpone his military commitment to the end of his pro career. As of press time, the waiver has not been granted, and it is increasingly likely that he will miss most or all of the 2020 and 2021 seasons while serving as a Naval flight officer.

If Song were free and clear from those military commitments, he'd rank first on this list and would've made the 101. It's a testament to his talent that he still ranks where he does even building in the risk that he's iced for several years. In terms of baseball functionality, he's an advanced first-round talent college arm with big stuff, the type of player who is a real boon to the system. He manipulates a low-to-mid-90s fastball with aplomb, touching 98 as a starter and a tick or two higher in relief. His plus slider was far too much for New York-Penn League hitters after the draft, and he mixes in a change and curve as well. He could move quickly as an impact starter or reliever... if only he gets a chance to pitch.

Variance: Unusual, because of the risk that he'll be unavailable for most or all of the early-2020s.

Ben Carsley's Fantasy Take: How is this for a hot take: until we have a better understanding of how long his military commitment will keep him from the mound, Song shouldn't be owned at all. Yes, at all. Consider how much risk the average starting pitcher prospect comes with. Now add in the unique circumstances surrounding Song's career, and you can see how I'd come to that conclusion. I understand that Song is probably a top-150 guy on talent alone, but the risk-to-reward payoff is just much, much too high for me. Unless my league rosters ~300-plus prospects—at which point I have much bigger problems—I'm letting Song serve as someone else's gamble.

3 Bobby Dalbec 3B   OFP: 55   ETA: Second half 2020

Born: 06/29/95   Age: 25   Bats: R   Throws: R   Height: 6'4"   Weight: 225   Origin: Round 4, 2016 Draft (#118 overall)

YEAR	TEAM	LVL	AGE	PA	R	2B	3B	HR	RBI	BB	K	SB	CS	AVG/OBP/SLG	DRC+	VORP	BABIP	BRR	FRAA	WARP	PF
2017	RSX	RK	22	32	3	1	0	0	2	5	9	1	0	.259/.375/.296	62	-0.1	.389	0.7	3B(4) -0.5	0.0	115
2017	GRN	A	22	329	48	15	0	13	39	36	123	4	5	.246/.345/.437	113	13.2	.383	-2.0	3B(67) -2.3	1.0	105
2018	SLM	A+	23	419	59	27	2	26	85	60	130	3	1	.256/.372/.573	161	44.2	.318	0.9	3B(91) 5.2, SS(1) 0.0	4.5	102
2018	PME	AA	23	124	14	8	1	6	24	6	46	0	0	.261/.323/.514	96	7.1	.377	-0.1	3B(18) -3.9, 1B(2) -0.3	-0.2	103
2019	PME	AA	24	439	57	15	2	20	57	68	110	6	4	.234/.371/.454	151	31.4	.278	-2.2	3B(90) 7.2, 1B(13) 0.9	4.2	100
2019	PAW	AAA	24	123	12	4	0	7	16	5	29	0	2	.257/.301/.478	83	3.8	.278	0.3	3B(17) 2.0, 1B(11) -1.3	0.2	90
2020	BOS	MLB	25	350	39	17	1	14	45	32	113	1	0	.220/.305/.415	91	1.0	.296	-0.6	1B -2, 3B 0	0.0	112

Comparables: Jabari Blash, Josh Bell, Taylor Teagarden

The Report: Shortly after Dalbec was drafted, some doofus suggested his best shot at the major leagues might come with a move back to the mound. The K-rates continue to be high, but they have improved as Dalbec has moved up the minor-league ladder, and he's gotten enough of his 70 raw power into games to perhaps fit as the kind of Three True Outcomes slugger that's in vogue in 2019 (and probably 2020) baseball. The power comes from length and leverage, and there's some stiffness to the swing, but Dalbec is a big, strong human, and if he can make enough good contact, the slash line will take care of itself. The Red Sox ran this profile in 2019 with Michael Chavis, and it's a similar set of strengths and weaknesses, although Dalbec is a little bit better defensively at the hot corner, with—as you'd expect—a much better arm. But the margins for this profile are thin, as Chavis found out last year. As always the line between Pete Alonso and C.J. Cron is slim for the R/R corner mashers.

Variance: Medium. He might just be 2019 Michael Chavis instead.

Ben Carsley's Fantasy Take: If you looked at Chavis in 2019 and thought "I wish I could dial up the good *and* the bad by about 20 percent," Dalbec is the prospect for you. To be fair, I really never even thought he'd make it this far given the insane swing-and-miss. I'm still not convinced it's gonna work at the major league level, though. Dalbec should be owned in TDGX-sized leagues (~200 prospects rostered) because of his proximity and his crazy power upside. There's a chance you'll get a few "the good Mark Reynolds" years out of him. That being said, he's not gonna sniff my personal top-101.

4 Jarren Duran OF   OFP: 50   ETA: Late 2020

Born: 09/05/96   Age: 23   Bats: L   Throws: R   Height: 6'2"   Weight: 200   Origin: Round 7, 2018 Draft (#220 overall)

YEAR	TEAM	LVL	AGE	PA	R	2B	3B	HR	RBI	BB	K	SB	CS	AVG/OBP/SLG	DRC+	VORP	BABIP	BRR	FRAA	WARP	PF
2018	LOW	A-	21	168	28	5	10	2	20	11	26	12	4	.348/.393/.548	177	19.6	.406	0.4	2B(20) 4.9, CF(15) 0.1	2.2	101
2018	GRN	A	21	134	24	9	1	1	15	5	22	12	6	.367/.396/.477	167	12.2	.438	1.6	RF(30) 0.0	1.3	97
2019	SLM	A+	22	226	49	13	3	4	19	23	44	18	5	.387/.456/.543	201	30.5	.480	3.4	CF(50) 0.2	3.3	103
2019	PME	AA	22	352	41	11	5	1	19	23	84	28	8	.250/.309/.325	76	9.9	.335	5.1	CF(79) -3.3	0.5	99
2020	BOS	MLB	23	251	24	11	2	4	24	13	67	11	6	.264/.309/.380	80	0.0	.355	1.1	CF -1, RF 0	0.3	112

Comparables: Jedd Gyorko, Andrew Stevenson, Eddie Rosario

The Report: In a system that desperately needed a breakout prospect, Duran took the bull by the horns and ran with it. He obliterated High-A arms with his combination of a solid hitting approach and plus speed. At the plate Duran shows average bat speed with a smooth, line-drive stroke that he uses to shoot ball to all fields. While the home run power is well below average, he drives the gaps well, and his speed allows him to turn singles into doubles, and some doubles into triples. After playing second base in college and his first year in pro ball, Duran has transitioned well to center. His plus speed allows him to cover plenty of grass and he has a good first step and already has solid instincts. His arm is fringe-average, so while he can stand anywhere in the outfield, it only plays in left and center on an every day basis.

Variance: Medium. His first introduction to Double-A did not go smoothly, the power doesn't really play over-the-fence, and the bat could be knocked out of his hands against better arms. There is still a floor of a defensive contributor/pinch-runner even if the bat doesn't play at a high level.

Ben Carsley's Fantasy Take: Ah, now here's a guy I probably *am* too high on! I wish Duran had performed better once promoted to Portland, of course, but if you know anything about me, you know I fall head-over-heels for speedy hitters with contact skills. Sometimes that means I'm sitting alone in a dark room in a Jose Peraza shirsey (thanks, Bret), but other times it means I get in on the ground floor of your Ender Inciarte types. That's the dream for Duran–a dude who can fight his way to .280-plus averages with 30-plus steals without getting the bat knocked out of his hands. Given his proximity to the big leagues, he should be considered a top-150 fantasy prospect, even if there's more risk here than his High-A numbers would have you believe.

5 Thad Ward RHP   OFP: 50   ETA: 2021

Born: 01/16/97   Age: 23   Bats: R   Throws: R   Height: 6'3"   Weight: 182   Origin: Round 5, 2018 Draft (#160 overall)

YEAR	TEAM	LVL	AGE	W	L	SV	G	GS	IP	H	HR	BB/9	K/9	K	GB%	BABIP	WHIP	ERA	DRA	WARP	PF
2018	LOW	A-	21	0	3	0	11	11	31	33	2	3.5	7.8	27	54%	.337	1.45	3.77	5.89	-0.2	96
2019	GRN	A	22	5	2	0	13	13	72¹	51	2	3.1	10.8	87	48%	.280	1.05	1.99	3.25	1.7	100
2019	SLM	A+	22	3	3	0	12	12	54	38	4	5.3	11.7	70	48%	.296	1.30	2.33	4.35	0.5	103
2020	BOS	MLB	23	2	2	0	33	0	35	35	5	4.2	9.3	36	45%	.309	1.47	4.99	4.97	0.1	112

Comparables: Parker Bridwell, Dinelson Lamet, Tyler Thornburg

The Report: The 2018 fifth-round choice enjoyed one of the more notable breakout campaigns of 2019, collecting 157 strikeouts in 126 1/3 innings between Low- and High-A. Ward's watershed year was aided by the addition of an 87-88 mph cutter that has plus, sharp horizontal action. He also employs a straight four-seamer and a two-seamer that has tail, both sitting between 92-95 mph.

Beyond the firm stuff, Ward also throws two breaking balls. His low-80s slider is a sweepy pitch with plus horizontal break and it's one of his swing-and-miss pitches, along with the cutter. He also throws an upper-70s, 12-6 curveball sparingly. Ward rounds out his deep arsenal with a high-80s sinking changeup that has late, hard downward action.

What makes this right-hander even more effective is his deceptive mechanics. Throwing from a three-quarters angle, Ward creates an unusual slot with his cross-fire delivery. This makes his cutter/slider combo even harder to hit. There is a lot to like in Ward's profile. But he has a long way to go, plus the possibility of becoming a reliever still lingers until he can prove his wiry frame can make it as a starter long-term.

Variance: High. We've seen a few college arms in the Red Sox system fizzle out after dominating the lower minors.

Ben Carsley's Fantasy Take: Two things can be true at once: Ward has dramatically increased in fantasy value since he was drafted, and Ward's fantasy value still isn't that high. If you're the type of masochist who plays in dynasty AL-only leagues or if your league rosters 300 prospects or something, then sure, Ward is worth buying. Otherwise, we're looking at a back-end starter or reliever in a system that's had quite a bit of trouble developing either. Barring another improvement that leads us to believe he's got a higher upside, Ward won't be fantasy-relevant until he's knocking on the door.

6 Jay Groome LHP   OFP: 50   ETA: 2022

Born: 08/23/98 Age: 21 Bats: L Throws: L Height: 6'6" Weight: 220 Origin: Round 1, 2016 Draft (#12 overall)

YEAR	TEAM	LVL	AGE	W	L	SV	G	GS	IP	H	HR	BB/9	K/9	K	GB%	BABIP	WHIP	ERA	DRA	WARP	PF
2017	LOW	A-	18	0	2	0	3	3	11	5	0	4.1	11.5	14	58%	.208	0.91	1.64	2.65	0.3	102
2017	GRN	A	18	3	7	0	11	11	44¹	44	6	5.1	11.8	58	55%	.355	1.56	6.70	4.49	0.4	105
2020	BOS	MLB	21	2	2	0	33	0	35	35	6	4.1	9.0	35	47%	.304	1.47	4.98	5.09	0.0	112

Comparables: Lewis Thorpe, Jordan Lyles, Mike Soroka

The Report: Groome did get back on the mound for few rehab outings coming off his Tommy John surgery last May. Fifteen months later, there are no real red flags. The fastball velocity isn't all the way back to his pre-surgery mid 90s, but he sits in the low 90s with some plane and arm-side wiggle. Unsurprisingly the fastball command isn't all there at present, but there's no obvious cause for concern long term, despite some effort and a bit of crossbody action to the delivery.

The curve still flashes at the top of the scale, but again, there are consistency issues with the pitch coming out of a long injury layoff. Groome threw his change a fair bit in the rehab outing I caught, but it's well below average. He struggled to turn it over, although it would flash fringe tumble. He's filled out some from his listed weight, maybe 20 or 30 pounds, but the build is more solid than soft, with a good, thick lower half. This ranking feels low, but there's enough uncertainty that it also might end up high. Groome has shown 70-grade stuff, and it's the body of a mid-rotation starter, but he has pitched fewer innings in four pro seasons than your average seventh-inning guy does in a year. Throw a dart.

Variance: Xtreme (which is higher than extreme). Groome has thrown 66 pro innings. He was drafted in 2016. There were some durability and command concerns before Tommy John. The stuff is already flashing back to where it was pre-surgery, but he's a long way away from the majors, and not much has gone right for him so far. That all said, if stuff starts going right, this OFP could get bumped up by midseason next year. There's also a chance he never pitches above Double-A. We told you it was xtreme.

Ben Carsley's Fantasy Take: Call me crazy, but until we have a better understanding of Song's military commitment and until Ward carries less reliever risk, I still think Groome is actually the best fantasy pitching prospect in this system. There's ridiculous risk in the profile, as mentioned above, but if it all clicks we're looking at a potential top-25 fantasy prospect and bona fide fantasy SP2. It also kind of feels like he'll emerge as a late-inning weapon for, like, the A's in 2024 at this point, so do with this type of variance what you will.

7 Bryan Mata RHP   OFP: 50   ETA: Late 2020

Born: 05/03/99 Age: 21 Bats: R Throws: R Height: 6'3" Weight: 160 Origin: International Free Agent, 2016

YEAR	TEAM	LVL	AGE	W	L	SV	G	GS	IP	H	HR	BB/9	K/9	K	GB%	BABIP	WHIP	ERA	DRA	WARP	PF
2017	GRN	A	18	5	6	0	17	17	77	75	3	3.0	8.6	74	53%	.333	1.31	3.74	4.67	0.5	105
2018	SLM	A+	19	6	3	0	17	17	72	58	1	7.2	7.6	61	59%	.292	1.61	3.50	5.71	-0.3	103
2019	SLM	A+	20	3	1	0	10	10	51¹	38	1	3.2	9.1	52	67%	.268	1.09	1.75	3.68	0.8	103
2019	PME	AA	20	4	6	0	11	11	53²	54	6	4.0	9.9	59	54%	.340	1.45	5.03	5.42	-0.3	97
2020	BOS	MLB	21	2	2	0	33	0	35	34	5	3.7	7.9	31	47%	.292	1.39	4.54	4.69	0.2	112

Comparables: Carlos Martínez, Junior Fernandez, David Holmberg

The Report: Mata cleaned up his control and command a bit in 2019, cutting his walk rate in half and making it to Double-A before he was old enough to hit up Cascade Barrel House. The fastball sits mid 90s, and is a bit of a bowling ball, but the offering plays down as Mata still isn't sure where it's going much of the time. After all, cutting his walk rate in half merely got the control to below-average, and the command a step below that. The slider is the best of the present secondaries, it can be a bit cutterish in the low 90s, but will flash razor blade action, and is the offspeed pitch most likely to end up above average. His curveball is a bit of an up-and-under thing from his lower slot, and on the short side, but every once in a while he will pop one to the backfoot of a lefty that makes you go, "hmm." The changeup lags behind the rest of the arsenal, lacking ideal velocity separation or much fade. The change and command issues may limit Mata to the pen, and neither of the breaking balls might end up good enough to make up for the command wobbles, further limiting him to middle relief. However, you don't have to squint too hard to see a good fastball/slider late inning arm. And there's a non-zero chance he sticks as a starter at least for a bit.

Variance: Medium. There's a lot of reliever risk, but I'm also willing to be patient with a 20-year-old who missed as many bats as he did in Double-A. There's enough feel for all three secondaries that you could bet on one or two of them getting to at least average—making Mata a low-end No. 3 or high-end No. 4 starter—but I wouldn't lay your mortgage payment on it.

Ben Carsley's Fantasy Take: It feels as though the general Prospect Industrial Complex has been praising Mata's stuff while lamenting his results for about four decades now. Mostly I just want him to exhaust his rookie eligibility so I can stop writing about him. You'll want to own him if he ends up closing, but if he doesn't, you … won't. Please continue to subscribe to Baseball Prospectus for our fantasy analysis.

8 Tanner Houck   RHP   OFP: 50   ETA: 2020 as needed

Born: 06/29/96   Age: 24   Bats: R   Throws: R   Height: 6'4"   Weight: 210   Origin: Round 1, 2017 Draft (#24 overall)

YEAR	TEAM	LVL	AGE	W	L	SV	G	GS	IP	H	HR	BB/9	K/9	K	GB%	BABIP	WHIP	ERA	DRA	WARP	PF
2017	LOW	A-	21	0	3	0	10	10	22¹	21	0	3.2	10.1	25	49%	.333	1.30	3.63	4.91	0.1	104
2018	SLM	A+	22	7	11	0	23	23	119	110	11	4.5	8.4	111	50%	.298	1.43	4.24	4.96	0.5	103
2019	PME	AA	23	8	6	0	17	15	82²	86	4	3.5	8.7	80	50%	.346	1.43	4.25	5.45	-0.5	99
2019	PAW	AAA	23	0	0	1	16	2	25	19	3	5.0	9.7	27	48%	.250	1.32	3.24	3.52	0.7	85
2020	BOS	MLB	24	1	1	0	3	3	15	14	2	3.9	7.7	12	46%	.292	1.43	4.82	4.86	0.1	112

Comparables: Reed Garrett, Hansel Robles, Corey Kluber

The Report: Houck finally made the transition to the bullpen in July, allowing him to lean heavily on his two best pitches. The fastball is a power two-seamer in the mid 90s with both sink and run and, when his command is right, it's very effective movement. He pairs it with a mid-80s slider that tunnels well off the fastball then makes a late, sharp left turn with good depth despite a low-three-quarters slot. It's a high-effort arm action, so the command can be a little loose on both offerings, and the changeup never really got there—hence the move to the pen—but Houck is a major-league ready pen arm with late-inning potential.

Variance: Low. Houck looks to be a reliever for the foreseeable future, but it's a plus/plus two-pitch mix, so that makes him a fairly safe bet to be a solid relief arm, command and control permitting.

Ben Carsley's Fantasy Take: The rare pitching prospect who I actually hope heads to the bullpen instead of sticking in the rotation, thereby enabling us to make "Houck: A ROOGY" jokes. Barring some injuries that lead to save changes, that figures to be about the extent of Houck's fantasy relevance as well.

9 Gilberto Jimenez   OF   OFP: 50   ETA: 2023

Born: 07/08/00   Age: 19   Bats: B   Throws: R   Height: 5'11"   Weight: 160   Origin: International Free Agent, 2017

YEAR	TEAM	LVL	AGE	PA	R	2B	3B	HR	RBI	BB	K	SB	CS	AVG/OBP/SLG	DRC+	VORP	BABIP	BRR	FRAA	WARP	PF
2018	DRS	RK	17	284	42	10	8	0	22	19	40	16	14	.319/.384/.420	146	25.1	.378	-1.0	CF(64) 3.4	2.5	90
2019	LOW	A-	18	254	35	11	3	3	19	13	38	14	6	.359/.393/.470	191	30.7	.413	1.2	CF(57) -9.8, RF(1) -0.1	1.9	97
2020	BOS	MLB	19	251	23	12	2	3	23	15	57	6	5	.272/.321/.370	86	0.0	.349	-0.2	CF -3, RF 0	0.1	112

Comparables: Victor Robles, Harold Ramirez, Enrique Hernández

The Report: An under-the-radar $10,000 IFA signing, Jimenez came stateside quickly and thrived during an aggressive 2019 assignment to the Penn League. The left-handed swing is ahead of the right-handed one at the moment, but even that is flat, contact-oriented and bordering on defensive or slappy at times. On better swings, you'd call Jimenez "effectively short to the ball," but he lacks present physicality, or much in the way of projection—he's athletic but a tad stocky. Power is never going to be a part of his game past legging out some extra bases on balls into the gaps. The right-handed swing is longer with more of a leg lift, but also with additional sync and timing issues. Jimenez is aggressive at the plate, but generally knows what he can get the barrel on, so there's the outline of an above-average hit tool here. I'd just like to see the swing get less slappy and to see him drive the ball against better velocity and location than he saw in the Penn League before I fully sign off.

I have no such quibbles with the footspeed. Jimenez is a plus-plus runner who posts above-average run times even when he's not even busting it. The speed plays down on the basepaths, as Jimenez's instincts are raw and he's hyper aggressive with his leads and baserunning. In the outfield, though, his instincts and footspeed give him plus range in center. He knows where to run to, can adjust his routes on the fly, and has the closing speed to get balls coming in or going out, gap to gap. Jimenez's arm strength is just average, but he gets throws out quickly and accurately.

Variance: High. Jimenez is a long way from the majors, and I'm not as convinced by the hit tool as the .360 batting average might make you think. The speed and glove give him a good base for some sort of major-league contribution, but that might end up being more extra outfielder.

Ben Carsley's Fantasy Take: A good one for your watch list, as he is very fast. A bad one to invest in heavily now, as he is very far away.

10 Matthew Lugo SS   OFP: 50   ETA: 2023
Born: 05/09/01   Age: 19   Bats: R   Throws: R   Height: 6'1"   Weight: 185   Origin: Round 2, 2019 Draft (#69 overall)

YEAR	TEAM	LVL	AGE	PA	R	2B	3B	HR	RBI	BB	K	SB	CS	AVG/OBP/SLG	DRC+	VORP	BABIP	BRR	FRAA	WARP	PF
2019	RSX	RK	18	157	19	5	1	1	12	15	36	3	0	.257/.342/.331	125	6.0	.340	1.0	SS(30) 1.7	1.2	101
2020	BOS	MLB	19	251	22	11	1	4	23	21	84	3	1	.221/.292/.329	66	0.0	.331	0.0	SS 0	-0.3	112

Comparables: Isan Díaz, Gavin Cecchini, Dawel Lugo

The Report: The second of Boston's second-rounders in the 2019 draft, Lugo is a good projection bet, but pretty raw at present. He has a lithe, athletic frame that should grow into average power in his 20s and will flash some pop pull-side already from a bit of loft and above-average bat speed. Lugo can lack physicality at the plate, and the swing can get a little choppy against better velo. There's some natural inside-out when he's worked away, and he's quick inside if you try to bust him there. You don't have to squint too hard to see an average hit/power combo at maturity, although "maturity" is gonna be a long ways off. Lugo is an above-average runner, heady and aggressive on the basepaths. He can be a bit mechanical at shortstop at present, and I'm curious to see if some of the effort in the field gets smoothed out with more pro reps. The portrait of his future is more Monet than Courbet at present, but the upside is intriguing.

Variance: Very High. There's very little pro track record here and the overall profile is raw. Far from a lock to stick at shortstop or hit against better pitching.

Ben Carsley's Fantasy Take: Look, we all realize this isn't the most exciting system in the world, but I actually like Lugo as a flyer for those of you in super deep leagues despite his ranking here. For our purposes, better a good hitter who's not a lock to stick at short than a lock to stick at short who can't hit. Plus, what could go wrong when you bet on a Red Sox shortstop named Lugo?

The Next Ten

11 Ryan Zeferjahn RHP
Born: 02/28/98   Age: 22   Bats: R   Throws: R   Height: 6'5"   Weight: 225   Origin: Round 3, 2019 Draft (#107 overall)

YEAR	TEAM	LVL	AGE	W	L	SV	G	GS	IP	H	HR	BB/9	K/9	K	GB%	BABIP	WHIP	ERA	DRA	WARP	PF
2019	LOW	A-	21	0	2	0	12	12	22	24	2	4.9	12.7	31	40%	.415	1.64	4.50	6.45	-0.3	96
2020	BOS	MLB	22	2	2	0	33	0	35	36	6	4.0	8.8	34	38%	.306	1.46	5.03	5.11	0.0	112

Comparables: Drew Steckenrider, James Karinchak, Tyler Cloyd

Zeferjahn was drafted in the third round by the Red Sox after three years of racking up strikeouts for the Jayhawks. He is a large human being, cutting a towering figure even while throwing a bullpen three hundred feet away. Once he's within 60 feet and six inches, you quickly figure out why he racked up plenty of walks as well. Although he gets over his lower half well, a twisting, torquey delivery with a long arm action negatively impacts his ability to throw strikes with his fastball or consistently start his slider in the zone. It's not traditional "tall pitcher problems," but results in the similar issues. The stuff may end up good enough to make the command a mere unfortunate footnote. The power fastball/slider combination got our attention in the Cape a couple summers ago, the heater still sits mid 90s, and the breaker still flashes plus-or-better. The Sox kept Zeferjahn somewhat stretched out in short-season ball, but given the present delivery issues, and a curve and change that lag behind the rest of the repertoire, he profiles best as a late inning reliever. However, he could be an impact pen arm quickly, as long as he can keep his Brooks Baseball page from looking like a Mondrian painting.

12 C.J. Chatham   SS

Born: 12/22/94   Age: 25   Bats: R   Throws: R   Height: 6'3"   Weight: 185   Origin: Round 2, 2016 Draft (#51 overall)

YEAR	TEAM	LVL	AGE	PA	R	2B	3B	HR	RBI	BB	K	SB	CS	AVG/OBP/SLG	DRC+	VORP	BABIP	BRR	FRAA	WARP	PF
2018	GRN	A	23	80	13	6	1	0	9	3	14	1	1	.307/.329/.413	120	1.6	.371	0.6	SS(4) -0.2	0.4	103
2018	SLM	A+	23	392	42	14	1	3	43	21	72	10	4	.315/.355/.384	110	16.4	.380	2.7	SS(67) -3.6	1.7	102
2019	PME	AA	24	376	39	26	1	3	36	18	66	7	1	.297/.333/.403	126	18.1	.354	-2.2	SS(77) -1.4, 2B(7) 2.3	2.3	100
2019	PAW	AAA	24	91	11	5	0	2	10	4	21	0	0	.302/.330/.430	109	3.2	.375	0.3	SS(15) -0.6, 2B(5) -0.7	0.4	90
2020	BOS	MLB	25	35	3	2	0	1	3	1	9	0	0	.248/.285/.360	67	0.0	.320	-0.1	SS 0	-0.1	112

Comparables: Wilmer Difo, Ryan Goins, Kevin Pillar

Chatham keeps hitting around .300 at every level, and that skill didn't fade for him this season in Double-A and a late-season Triple-A trial. As you'd expect, the former second-rounder has strong bat-to-ball ability and excellent barrel control in general; he can dunk singles about as well as any prospect this side of Nick Madrigal. He also plays a fine shortstop, with exposure to the other infield positions, and he's athletic in general. What he doesn't do is drive the ball for anything more than fringe gap power, and that limits the profile. We don't expect that to improve at this stage of the game for him, because his bat speed is limited. Overall, he projects to bring enough defensive versatility/value and hit tool to be a contributor in a utility or second-division role. He needs to keep hitting close to .300 to profile as a first-division starter, which is a tough ask given his lack of secondary offensive skills, but not impossible.

13 Durbin Feltman   RHP

Born: 04/18/97   Age: 23   Bats: R   Throws: R   Height: 6'0"   Weight: 205   Origin: Round 3, 2018 Draft (#100 overall)

YEAR	TEAM	LVL	AGE	W	L	SV	G	GS	IP	H	HR	BB/9	K/9	K	GB%	BABIP	WHIP	ERA	DRA	WARP	PF
2018	GRN	A	21	0	1	3	7	0	7	6	0	1.3	18.0	14	43%	.429	1.00	2.57	2.65	0.2	100
2018	SLM	A+	21	1	0	1	11	0	12¹	12	0	2.9	10.9	15	58%	.364	1.30	2.19	3.68	0.2	100
2019	PME	AA	22	2	3	3	43	0	51¹	42	8	5.4	9.5	54	43%	.266	1.42	5.26	5.14	-0.3	100
2020	BOS	MLB	23	2	2	0	33	0	35	35	6	3.7	8.7	34	41%	.302	1.41	4.72	4.89	0.1	112

Comparables: Shawn Armstrong, Evan Phillips, Trevor Gott

When I saw Feltman in April for Portland, I really didn't expect him to remain list-eligible down here. He ranked fifth on this list last year, and he just looked far too good for the Eastern League. He was throwing 95 with movement — a few ticks down from where he'd been in college, but still impressive, and sometimes velocities aren't all the way there in the first couple weeks of the season. He mixed in a big, impressive sweeping slider. It had some slurviness too it, but not in a bad way. With Boston's bullpen woes, he looked like he'd be in the majors within months, if not weeks. Instead, Feltman struggled with walks at Double-A, and the fastball never truly came around. He didn't make it to Triple-A, let alone the majors. It's still impressive enough stuff to make this list, and he could still very easily be a late-innings arm soon. But his ranking speaks just as much to the weakness of the system depth as it does Feltman.

14 Antoni Flores   SS

Born: 10/14/00   Age: 19   Bats: R   Throws: R   Height: 6'1"   Weight: 190   Origin: International Free Agent, 2017

YEAR	TEAM	LVL	AGE	PA	R	2B	3B	HR	RBI	BB	K	SB	CS	AVG/OBP/SLG	DRC+	VORP	BABIP	BRR	FRAA	WARP	PF
2018	DRX	RK	17	57	10	3	1	1	14	8	7	0	1	.347/.439/.510	163	9.7	.390	0.3	SS(13) -1.7	0.5	88
2019	LOW	A-	18	208	14	4	1	0	12	25	59	1	3	.193/.293/.227	84	-2.5	.285	-1.9	SS(47) 4.8, 2B(6) -0.1	0.8	97
2020	BOS	MLB	19	251	21	11	1	4	21	21	84	1	0	.206/.276/.308	55	0.0	.307	-0.4	SS 1, 2B 0	-0.5	112

Comparables: Manuel Margot, Franklin Barreto, Francisco Mejía

Flores did not perform nearly as well as Jimenez during the pair's aggressive Penn League assignments, but I wouldn't quibble too much with you if you thought the Venezuelan shortstop was the better long term performance bet. The bat is much rawer, but there's a potential average hit and power combo if Flores fills out and shortens up a little. He flashed some gap power and above-average bat speed early in the Penn League campaign, but the swing had gotten long and out of sync by the end of it, showing none of the bat control or pop he flashed in June. In the field, Flores is a pretty smooth shortstop, with enough arm for the six. His actions could be a little rough at times, but he's got a good shot to stick assuming he doesn't fill out too much more. The present frame reminds me a bit of a more physical Andrés Giménez at times. It's significantly less polish than Giménez though, and the bat is a huge risk until we see a more consistent swing and better performance stateside.

15 Nick Decker OF

Born: 10/02/99   Age: 20   Bats: L   Throws: L   Height: 6'0"   Weight: 200   Origin: Round 2, 2018 Draft (#64 overall)

YEAR	TEAM	LVL	AGE	PA	R	2B	3B	HR	RBI	BB	K	SB	CS	AVG/OBP/SLG	DRC+	VORP	BABIP	BRR	FRAA	WARP	PF
2019	LOW	A-	19	197	23	10	5	6	25	21	59	4	5	.247/.328/.471	121	13.3	.333	1.7	RF(50) -5.1, CF(2) -0.2	0.4	96
2020	BOS	MLB	20	251	22	12	2	6	25	18	92	2	1	.204/.266/.349	61	0.0	.309	0.0	RF -2, CF 0	-0.6	112

Comparables: Alex Jackson, Dylan Cozens, Zach Green

A year after being drafted in the second round, Decker still has some of the rawness you'd associate with a cold weather prep outfielder. But there is also some decent feel to hit here, and while the swing can wrap some and get long, he shows plus bat speed and above-average raw power as well. The defensive tools on the grass are all a bit fringy—especially for center—and his routes can be a bit ugly at times. Other days he'd look perfectly passable up-the-middle, but I expect he will fill out enough to force him to a corner regardless. The arm strength is fringe as well, so left is more likely than right, but most likely of all is a little bit of all three spots as a fourth outfielder with some pop. But keep an eye on how the bat develops here, because cold weather preps can also have slower development curves.

16 Jaxx Groshans C

Born: 07/20/98   Age: 21   Bats: R   Throws: R   Height: 6'0"   Weight: 209   Origin: Round 5, 2019 Draft (#167 overall)

YEAR	TEAM	LVL	AGE	PA	R	2B	3B	HR	RBI	BB	K	SB	CS	AVG/OBP/SLG	DRC+	VORP	BABIP	BRR	FRAA	WARP	PF
2019	LOW	A-	20	175	15	5	1	4	23	23	34	1	1	.216/.314/.345	113	7.2	.246	0.1	C(33) -0.8	0.8	97
2020	BOS	MLB	21	251	22	11	1	6	25	16	70	2	1	.205/.260/.334	56	0.0	.266	0.0	C 0	-0.6	112

Groshans was divisive internally on the prospect team, and this is a bit of a compromise ranking. Evaluating college catchers post-draft is tricky. It's a long season and a lot of hours squatting behind the plate. Groshans is an athletic receiver, excellent moving laterally to block balls in the dirt, and flashes an easy plus arm. His frame is a bit on the slight side at present, reminding me some of Francisco Mejia's, so you will have to continue monitoring how the body holds up under a more rigorous pro workload behind the plate. The bat is decidedly not Mejia's, but Groshans is short to the ball, and will make hard, mostly line drive contact despite only average bat speed. There's a little loft in the swing too, so more power might come in the pros when he hasn't been catching for six straight months. You'd like to see him fill out a bit—he was relatively young for his draft class—and get that true fire hydrant catcher body, but I kind of like the Kevin Plawecki comp I heard put on him recently.

17 Cameron Cannon IF

Born: 10/16/97   Age: 22   Bats: R   Throws: R   Height: 5'10"   Weight: 196   Origin: Round 2, 2019 Draft (#43 overall)

YEAR	TEAM	LVL	AGE	PA	R	2B	3B	HR	RBI	BB	K	SB	CS	AVG/OBP/SLG	DRC+	VORP	BABIP	BRR	FRAA	WARP	PF
2019	LOW	A-	21	180	17	12	0	3	21	12	37	1	0	.205/.289/.335	101	2.6	.248	0.2	2B(19) 1.8, SS(18) -0.8	0.7	96
2020	BOS	MLB	22	251	22	12	1	6	26	14	76	2	1	.204/.261/.344	57	0.0	.275	0.0	SS 0, 2B 0	-0.5	112

Comparables: David Adams, Taylor Featherston, Sheldon Neuse

Cannon's swing and body type will remind you a bit of Colton Welker's. He presently lacks Welker's physicality and bat speed—although it's solid enough—but the approach is similar, swing hard with some loft and let God sort 'em out. He can make loud contact, but was vulnerable to pulling off offspeed moving down and/or away. He also doesn't have Welker's pro track record despite being almost exactly the same age. Cannon does have a chance to stick up the middle, although I suspect the foot speed and actions will limit him primarily to second base, but he'd likely be fine at third too. Ultimately Cannon will go as far as the bat takes him, and he'll need to adjust to offspeed stuff to get the most out of his swing, but a good bench infielder with plenty of doubles seems a plausible result.

18   Dedgar Jimenez   LHP

Born: 03/06/96   Age: 24   Bats: L   Throws: L   Height: 6'3"   Weight: 240   Origin: International Free Agent, 2012

YEAR	TEAM	LVL	AGE	W	L	SV	G	GS	IP	H	HR	BB/9	K/9	K	GB%	BABIP	WHIP	ERA	DRA	WARP	PF
2017	SLM	A+	21	10	3	0	18	17	99²	97	2	2.1	8.4	93	48%	.332	1.20	3.07	3.90	1.6	101
2017	PME	AA	21	5	0	0	8	8	46¹	45	4	3.5	4.9	25	41%	.272	1.36	2.91	4.59	0.3	103
2018	PME	AA	22	10	7	0	25	24	137¹	124	18	3.6	7.6	116	42%	.275	1.30	4.39	4.51	1.3	103
2018	PAW	AAA	22	1	0	0	1	1	6	5	0	1.5	6.0	4	39%	.278	1.00	3.00	3.96	0.1	90
2019	PME	AA	23	4	5	10	29	12	85²	75	9	4.3	7.8	74	42%	.278	1.35	3.78	5.05	-0.2	101
2019	PAW	AAA	23	0	1	0	2	2	7²	10	2	11.7	8.2	7	36%	.348	2.61	14.09	8.65	-0.1	84
2020	BOS	MLB	24	2	2	0	33	0	35	35	5	3.6	6.6	26	40%	.279	1.39	4.61	4.75	0.2	112

I am a noted Dedgar enthusiast, and even I was surprised that Jeffrey asked me to write up Dedgar for this list, because I'm genuinely surprised that Dedgar made a list. Basically, imagine a burly lefty throwing a kitchen sink's worth of fringy-to-average stuff, with a low-90s fastball and a slider leading the way, and your mental image is probably about right on this one. He's really entertaining and fun to watch, but there's no projectability and he's not at all a typical top-20 system talent even given that he's still only 23. After 44 starts over three seasons in Double-A, the Red Sox gave Jimenez a shot in Triple-A in June, where he got shelled for two starts. He was demoted back and moved to the bullpen, where he pitched very well and soon picked up the closer's role. If this all sounds like he's going to be somewhere on the utility pitcher to LOOGY spectrum, well, he probably is. If this also sounds like we could've stopped writing about the system already as to not end up ranking members of the Future LOOGYs of Baseball, well, that's probably true too, but uniformity and all.

19   Yoan Aybar   LHP

Born: 07/03/97   Age: 22   Bats: L   Throws: L   Height: 6'3"   Weight: 165   Origin: International Free Agent, 2013

YEAR	TEAM	LVL	AGE	W	L	SV	G	GS	IP	H	HR	BB/9	K/9	K	GB%	BABIP	WHIP	ERA	DRA	WARP	PF
2018	RSX	RK	20	1	1	0	15	0	26¹	23	0	4.1	9.2	27	53%	.315	1.33	4.10	3.61	0.6	100
2019	GRN	A	21	1	3	0	40	0	51²	34	1	7.0	11.7	67	53%	.266	1.43	4.88	4.37	0.3	100
2020	BOS	MLB	22	1	1	0	11	0	11	11	2	4.0	8.2	10	44%	.295	1.42	4.56	4.69	0.1	112

Comparables: Paul Fry, Jaye Chapman, Jorge Alcala

A former outfielder who could barely hit his weight, Aybar was transitioned to relief pitcher around the middle of 2018. And, in flashes, has shown why. The lefty sits 94-96 mph with 98 mph in his pocket when he needs it. He also offers an 84-87 mph wipeout slider with plus tilt, giving him a dominant fastball/slider combination. However, the reason why his 2019 ERA (4.61) looks the way it does is because of major control issues, as he walked 41 batters over 56 2/3 innings. That said, he also struck out 70. His delivery and electric arsenal remind me of Aroldis Chapman, with his high leg kick towards the stomach with similar arm motion and release point. But repeating his delivery and release point are a concern. His athleticism on the mound gives me hope he can harness those issues and alleviate his high walk rate.

20   Aldo Ramirez   RHP

Born: 05/06/01   Age: 19   Bats: R   Throws: R   Height: 6'0"   Weight: 180   Origin: International Free Agent, 2018

YEAR	TEAM	LVL	AGE	W	L	SV	G	GS	IP	H	HR	BB/9	K/9	K	GB%	BABIP	WHIP	ERA	DRA	WARP	PF
2018	DRS	RK	17	1	2	0	5	5	23	10	0	1.2	6.7	17	60%	.159	0.57	0.39	1.70	1.1	88
2019	LOW	A-	18	2	3	0	14	13	61²	59	5	2.3	9.2	63	48%	.309	1.22	3.94	4.78	0.3	97
2020	BOS	MLB	19	2	2	0	33	0	35	35	6	4.1	7.1	28	43%	.285	1.46	4.89	5.05	0.1	112

Comparables: Alex Sanabia, Antonio Senzatela, JC Ramírez

Ramirez is an undersized Mexican righty who signed late and lacks much physical projection, but showed feel for pitching far beyond what you'd expect from functionally a high school senior. The fastball sat in the low 90s for the most part, although he could ramp it into an average velocity band in the early innings. Ramirez can struggle to locate the fastball arm-side due to some natural cut and crossfire in his delivery, but the velocity comes relatively easily. The curveball is very projectable, mid-70s with good shape and command at present, although he doesn't always get tight, late break with it. He's confident enough to throw it early in counts, when he's behind, or in jams. Ramirez can manipulate it for strikes or to chase, and it's advanced feel for spin, even if the pitch only projects as average. The change is firm, without ideal velocity separation, but he'll flash some some decent circle action when he can keep the cambio around 85. It's well behind the curve at present, but also projectable. The overall package here is three potential average offerings, but there's a long way to get there, and the more likely outcome is an up-and-down swing/middle reliever type. Still, Ramirez is definitely worth a follow as he heads to full-season ball next year.

Personal Cheeseball

PC **Jenrry Mejia RHP**
Born: 10/11/89   Age: 30   Bats: R   Throws: R   Height: 6'0"   Weight: 205   Origin: International Free Agent, 2007

YEAR	TEAM	LVL	AGE	W	L	SV	G	GS	IP	H	HR	BB/9	K/9	K	GB%	BABIP	WHIP	ERA	DRA	WARP	PF
2019	LOW	A-	29	0	1	1	6	0	6¹	7	1	1.4	11.4	8	63%	.333	1.26	4.26	3.91	0.1	100
2019	PAW	AAA	29	2	7	7	42	0	48	52	9	3.0	9.2	49	42%	.321	1.42	6.38	5.27	0.4	100
2020	BOS	MLB	30	2	2	0	33	0	35	35	5	3.6	8.5	33	45%	.299	1.40	4.60	4.75	0.2	112

Comparables: Rubby De La Rosa, Collin Balester, Randall Delgado

I passed the New Jersey bar exam in July 2013. It was the culmination of a winding path towards being an attorney that saw me go to law school and then decide not to practice and then change my mind a few years later and decide to take the exam. (Aspiring attorneys, I don't recommend having to relearn all of law school three years later.)

Anyways, Jenrry Mejia started for the Mets in Miami on the night in between the MBE and the essays. I watched the game while trying with mixed success to control terrible anxiety, and I have memories of him pitching very well. Looking it up, these are apparently the lies your brain tells you six-and-a-half years later. It was the start before the one during my bar exam where he came up off Tommy John surgery and pitched seven shutout innings. In the start I remember from that night he actually gave up three runs over six and was tagged with the loss.

It's been an up and down journey for both of us. My time practising wasn't any kind of success; I hated doing bankruptcy and foreclosure work, which was the best job I could find at the time, and ended up back in my previous real-world profession within a year. I consider everything in that period in my life to have ended up being really expensive training for being a baseball writer.

Mejia's career would be on a rollercoaster too. His starting pitching promise never panned out, whether due to lack of durability or mishandling by the Mets or something else. He'd eventually land as the team's closer, and held that role for much of the 2014 season. Warming up for his first save in 2015, he tweaked his elbow, and shortly thereafter, he was suspended for the first time for PEDs. He failed twice more for steroids over the next year, and ended up permanently banned from MLB.

After some wild accusations against Major League Baseball, he'd fade into the background, popping up every offseason for unaffiliated winter ball and the annual oddity of agreeing to a Mets contract that he couldn't fulfill. He was quietly reinstated with conditions attached late in 2018, and the Red Sox signed him to a minor-league deal before 2019. He didn't pitch well in the minors, but he did pitch most of the season, and he's back down pitching for Toros del Este in the Dominican at press time. And I'll always remember him for being the guy on the mound when I had to control a panic attack during the bar exam, and root for him to make it back, which is about as cheesy as it gets.

Low Minors Sleeper

LMS **Brendan Cellucci RHP**
Born: 06/30/98   Age: 22   Bats: L   Throws: L   Height: 6'4"   Weight: 201   Origin: Round 12, 2019 Draft (#377 overall)

YEAR	TEAM	LVL	AGE	W	L	SV	G	GS	IP	H	HR	BB/9	K/9	K	GB%	BABIP	WHIP	ERA	DRA	WARP	PF
2019	LOW	A-	21	1	0	0	8	0	12	14	1	5.2	12.8	17	38%	.464	1.75	5.25	7.76	-0.4	100
2020	BOS	MLB	22	2	2	0	33	0	35	35	6	3.9	8.3	32	39%	.299	1.44	4.88	5.02	0.1	112

Well we have already put a bunch of Boston's 2019 draft on this list so let's continue. I considered Chris Murphy—their sixth-round pick—for this spot. He's your standard fifth starter type with below-average fastball velo and three polished secondary options, with one or two that might bump average, but let's go with the lefty power arm instead. Cellucci got $345k as a 12th-round draft-eligible sophomore, because you don't find too many southpaws that touch 96 with a potential plus slider on Day Three. The curve might end up above-average as well, while the command and change are existent, but will limit him to the reliever-only track. He could be a fast mover on the strength of his top two pitches though, and adds another intriguing relief option to the Red Sox system. Normally we wouldn't call relief prospects "intriguing" as a rule, but then again did you watch the 2019 Boston bullpen?

Top Talents 25 and Under (as of 4/1/2020)

1. Rafael Devers
2. Andrew Benintendi
3. Michael Chavis
4. Triston Casas
5. Noah Song
6. Bobby Dalbec
7. Jarren Duran
8. Darwinzon Hernandez
9. Thad Ward
10. Jay Groome

The Red Sox apologist's take is that "25 and Under" is an arbitrary designation. Were this, say a "27 and under" list, we could include Mookie Betts, Xander Bogaerts, and Eduardo Rodriguez, and we'd feel much better about the depth of this group. In fact, it'd still be in the running for one of the best such collections of talent in the game. Yes, Boston's farm system has been terrible for a few seasons now, but that's in part because it had graduated a tremendous amount of young talent. Any budding narrative that the Sox will be unable to compete because of their desolate farm–that new "Chief Baseball Officer" Chaim Bloom needs to rebuild this talent base from scratch–willfully overlooks that a whole lot of Boston's best players are under 30.

And yet, a consequence of Boston's offensive core being so good while so young is that they're getting very expensive as they peak. Betts, as you may have heard, is entering his walk year. So too is Jackie Bradley, Jr. Bogaerts signed a six-year, $120 million deal that, while perhaps a bargain compared to what similar talents make, still pays him $20 million a year. E-Rod is entering his second arbitration year. Benintendi is now arbitration-eligible. When those players were all making, like, $30 million combined, it was easy to support them with megastars like Chris Sale, J.D. Martinez, and David Price. Now that the members of the young core are being paid as stars themselves, the Red Sox are going to need to supplement them with new homegrown talent.

That might be a problem, because aside from Devers and Benintendi, their 25U list ain't so hot.

We'll start with the good news. Devers took the much anticipated leap in 2019, emerging as one of the best young hitters in the game and improving his defense at third. He finished 11th in all of baseball in BWARP. He's only just turned 23. He's an absolute stud, and should bat in the middle of Boston's lineup for the next half-decade.

While Devers got much, much better in 2019, Benintendi got worse. His slugging percentage declined despite the hitter-friendly balls. His average dropped despite a career-best BABIP. He walked less, struck out more, and even had a rough season in left field, per FRAA. Everything about Benny's past performance and overall profile suggests this was more a bump in the road than a sign of anything of lasting regression, but still it is, to use a scouting term, not what you want.

The final two non-prospect members of the 25U list, Chavis and Hernandez, have not yet convincingly displayed that they deserve prominent roles on first-division clubs, though it's clear they belong in some capacity. After setting the world on fire in his first six weeks in the majors, Chavis struggled badly, striking out a ton as pitchers exploited the hole in his swing. He has power, can capably man either spot on the left side of the infield, and is adorably enthusiastic, but we still don't know if he'll make enough contact to play every day. Hernandez was often dominant when on the mound, but also issued more walks than Rover and he dispelled any notion that he can start. He's so talented that there's a chance he's Josh Hader-lite, but he's so wild that there's also a chance he's, like, a left-handed Tayron Guerrero.

That's where the Red Sox are with their truly young talent, then: a group that includes one of the game's best players, a role-6 outfielder coming off a down year, two wild-cards and then the top-six members of a bottom-five system. It's a collection of talent that's a long ways away from the terrible Angels 25U lists of a few seasons ago, but perhaps even farther away from a time when Boston's young core was considered the envy of the league.

Odds are one of Bloom's chief directives is to improve the young talent in Boston's organization. The real question is: can he do so without dramatically lowering his current squad's ceiling?

Eyewitness Reports

Eyewitness Report: Noah Song

Evaluator: Jarrett Seidler
Report Date: 08/19/2019
Dates Seen: 8/10/2019
Risk Factor: Unusual
Delivery: Arm is a little late coming through the delivery, which generates arm speed and deception, but adds a little reliever risk. Repeated well and showed an advanced command profile overall. Song is thin and athletic, and might be more projectable than you'd think for a pitcher who had four years of college.

Pitch Type	Future Grade	Sitting Velocity	Peak Velocity	Report
Fastball	60	92-95	95	Song sat 92-95 for two innings and dipped into a few 91s in the third inning. Excellent pitch manipulation to both sides of the plate, and rode in pretty hard on righties. Heavy and creates plane with high arm slot. There's some additional velocity projection here even just from my look, and an industry source confirmed he's topped out at 98 in other starts.
Slider	60	82-85	85	Way, way too much for Penn League hitters. Looked like he was pulling the strings on a wiffle ball. Tight break. Potential MLB out pitch.
Changeup	50	82-86	86	Consistently flashed average potential. Turned over a few in the third inning that hinted at potential for a little more. Did not command as well as his fastball or slider. Development of this pitch will be critical to his future as a starter.
Curveball	0	78	78	Song threw one curveball in this look, which obviously isn't anywhere near enough to hazard a grade. But I can confirm that it does exist as at least a show-me pitch.

Conclusion: Song was on paper a priority senior sign in this year's draft out of the Naval Academy, and the Red Sox nabbed him for $100k at the end of the fourth round. Yet he's a completely unique case, caught in the middle of a strange political situation. It's unclear at present whether he can defer his commitment to Naval flight school past November, and he may have to serve two to four years before continuing his professional career. If he stays on the mound, the Red Sox have an absolute steal. On talent, Song is more like a first round pitcher than fourth round pitcher, a potential no. 3 starter or weapon out of the bullpen. He was one of the best pitchers in college baseball over the last two seasons, and displays command and pitchability common to advanced college arms. I've pegged him at a 55 OFP for now, which is something of a default until we know what circumstances under which his career might continue on; he might rise to a 60 if we knew it was a normal career arc.

Eyewitness Report: Jarren Duran

Evaluator: Steve Givarz
Report Date: 10/12/2019
Dates Seen: 10/2, 10/4-10/6, 10/8, 10/11
Risk Factor: High
Physical/Health: Large frame with a well-proportioned, physical body, mature.

Tool	Future Grade	Report
Hit	50	Hits from a tall stance, small stride and load with average bat speed but above-average hands and trigger, smooth one-plane swing, not a lot of effort, works all fields. While over the fence power only plays pullside, can work the gaps for doubles. Patient at the plate, will work pitchers but is suspect against early in the count against off speed. Can have spells of weak contact, but makes enough contact ability to project as an average hitter.
Power	30	Below-average raw power, lacks strength in body, swing is more of the line drive variety, not over the fence power. Can really only take a ball out pullside, power will be more of the doubles and triples variety.
Baserunning/ Speed	60	Plus runner, 4.11-4.19 home-to-first, gets up to speed quick, gets good jumps and reads pitchers well, plus baserunner.
Glove	55	Have seen play all three outfield spots, takes good reads and routes to the ball and covers a lot of ground, quality first step which helps range play above his run speed, future above-average defender in all three spots.
Arm	45	Fringe-average arm, not a weapon, gets to cutoff men quick but isn't a threat from the outfield.

Conclusion: See as a glove-first regular in center field. 23 y/o L/R outfielder, average hit, above-average run/field, well-below-average raw pop and a fringe arm that could limit him to LF in the long run, moderate interest.

Chicago Cubs

The State of the System

The Cubs are a fairly generic, below-average system. Not close to the worst, and with some interesting names outside the top six, but lacking generally in potential impact talent.

The Top Ten

1 **Nico Hoerner SS**   OFP: 60   ETA: 2019

Born: 05/13/97 Age: 23 Bats: R Throws: R Height: 5'11" Weight: 200 Origin: Round 1, 2018 Draft (#24 overall)

YEAR	TEAM	LVL	AGE	PA	R	2B	3B	HR	RBI	BB	K	SB	CS	AVG/OBP/SLG	DRC+	VORP	BABIP	BRR	FRAA	WARP	PF
2018	EUG	A-	21	28	6	0	1	1	2	5	3	4	1	.318/.464/.545	170	4.1	.333	-0.5	SS(5) -0.4	0.2	91
2019	TEN	AA	22	294	37	16	3	3	22	21	31	8	4	.284/.344/.399	104	16.5	.311	1.6	SS(44) -2.6, 2B(15) 0.5	1.5	102
2019	CHN	MLB	22	82	13	1	1	3	17	3	11	0	0	.282/.305/.436	95	3.3	.292	0.3	SS(17) 0.6, CF(1) -0.1	0.4	96
2020	CHN	MLB	23	420	42	19	3	10	46	24	64	7	3	.260/.309/.402	88	2.0	.287	0.0	2B 3, SS 0	1.4	98

Comparables: *Andrelton Simmons, Willi Castro, Milt Bolling*

The Report: Hoerner had a very solid first full professional season. It was not the kind of performance that would normally merit a late season call-up, but a series of unfortunate events to the Cubs middle infielders impressed him into major league service. While it was a big jump for a prospect with only 70 games of upper minors experience—all in Double-A—Hoerner didn't look overmatched at all in the bigs. He has a preternatural feel for contact, with enough bat speed and barrel control to drive a ball wherever it's pitched. He's happy to spray line drives, but he's quick enough inside to yank your fastball out to left field if you try to beat him there. He was sacrificing power for contact some as he tried to stay afloat in the majors—and there probably isn't even average game power here anyway—but I'd expect him to find low-double-digit home run pop with plenty of doubles once he gets his sea legs under him. Hoerner is a plus runner, but not a particularly aggressive base stealer, and a perfectly acceptable shortstop. The bat is what carried him to the majors though and will keep him there for a long time.

Variance: Low. The hit tool is plus, and he might have years where he hits .300, but the rest of the profile doesn't exactly pop.

Ben Carsley's Fantasy Take: Hoerner is ready to contribute now, will play with a good supporting cast and has the type of carrying fantasy tool (average) you'd like to see. On those merits alone, he's a top-101 dynasty prospect. Just don't confuse Hoerner's meteoric rise as a sign of more offensive upside to come, because at the end of the day, Hoerner's fantasy profile isn't really all that different from, like, Kevin Newman's. That's perhaps a bit harsh, but helps to illustrate that you should only be counting on Hoerner as an MI or depth bat in most moderately sized leagues. He's very safe, but he's not a future fantasy star.

★ ★ ★ *2020 Top 101 Prospect* **#78** ★ ★ ★

2 **Miguel Amaya** C OFP: 60 ETA: Late 2021/22

Born: 03/09/99 Age: 21 Bats: R Throws: R Height: 6'1" Weight: 185 Origin: International Free Agent, 2015

YEAR	TEAM	LVL	AGE	PA	R	2B	3B	HR	RBI	BB	K	SB	CS	AVG/OBP/SLG	DRC+	VORP	BABIP	BRR	FRAA	WARP	PF
2017	EUG	A-	18	244	21	14	1	3	26	11	49	1	0	.228/.266/.338	69	1.6	.274	-1.5	C(43) -0.5, 1B(8) -0.4	-0.1	92
2018	SBN	A	19	479	54	21	2	12	52	50	91	1	0	.256/.349/.403	119	31.5	.298	0.6	C(95) 2.5, 1B(9) -0.7	3.1	98
2019	MYR	A+	20	410	50	24	0	11	57	54	69	2	0	.235/.351/.402	124	20.9	.259	-3.6	C(90) 2.8	2.7	99
2020	CHN	MLB	21	251	24	13	0	7	27	18	57	1	0	.212/.279/.364	69	0.0	.251	-0.5	C 0, 1B 0	-0.1	98

Comparables: *Francisco Mejía, Victor Robles, Manuel Margot*

The Report: Amaya more or less xeroxed his 2018 at a higher level—and in a brutal home park—so that's good all on its own, but he also continued to improve his defensive skills and now projects as a plus glove behind the plate. He moves well laterally and hoovers up anything in the dirt, and he's an above-average receiver with enough catch-and-throw skills to control the running game. The swing is compact with good pound-for-pound pop, and he has consistently demonstrated a strong approach at the plate. There's enough power to keep upper minors arms from feeling too great about challenging him in the zone, so I'd expect the high walk rates to continue and prop up what might be a fringy hit tool. It's not an exciting offensive profile, but it's potentially average, and with the quality of glove he's flashing now, it doesn't need to be much more than that.

Variance: High. Catchers are weird, and Amaya is still has to prove himself in the upper minors.

Ben Carsley's Fantasy Take: As I have discussed ad nauseum, catchers need to have insanely special offensive upsides for me to consider them of any real interest in all in dynasty leagues. Amaya lacks that, and as such I'd be staying away unless your league rosters 200+ prospects.

★ ★ ★ *2020 Top 101 Prospect* **#84** ★ ★ ★

3 **Brailyn Marquez** LHP OFP: 60 ETA: 2021

Born: 01/30/99 Age: 21 Bats: L Throws: L Height: 6'4" Weight: 185 Origin: International Free Agent, 2015

YEAR	TEAM	LVL	AGE	W	L	SV	G	GS	IP	H	HR	BB/9	K/9	K	GB%	BABIP	WHIP	ERA	DRA	WARP	PF
2017	CUB	RK	18	2	1	0	11	9	44	50	3	2.5	10.6	52	52%	.367	1.41	5.52	4.75	0.6	103
2018	EUG	A-	19	1	4	0	10	10	47²	46	5	2.6	9.8	52	52%	.333	1.26	3.21	4.75	0.3	88
2018	SBN	A	19	0	0	0	2	2	7	7	0	2.6	9.0	7	33%	.333	1.29	2.57	5.06	0.0	93
2019	SBN	A	20	5	4	0	17	17	77¹	64	4	5.0	11.9	102	51%	.335	1.38	3.61	5.25	-0.1	100
2019	MYR	A+	20	4	1	0	5	5	26¹	21	1	2.4	8.9	26	44%	.282	1.06	1.71	3.98	0.3	93
2020	CHN	MLB	21	2	2	0	33	0	35	35	5	3.7	8.8	34	45%	.302	1.40	4.63	4.79	0.2	98

Comparables: *Brad Keller, Justus Sheffield, Jesse Biddle*

The Report: Last offseason, Marquez developed from a flamethrower to a pitcher with multiple secondaries, and the results were noticeable. He returned to South Bend, after a brief two-game 2018 cameo and dominated Midwest League hitters, striking out 102 in just 77 innings. The fastball had ticked up a notch, sitting in the high 90s and even touching triple digits on occasion. The heater played up more due to the development of his off speed pitches, most notably his slider. It's still raw and inconsistent at times, but it flashes big bite, diving in to the back foot of right-handed hitters. He will also mix in an occasional changeup as a change of pace. It lacks movement but the velocity separation and arm replication will eventually make it an average offering. A year ago it looked like Marquez was destined for a future bullpen role. Now the Cubs finally have what they have been lacking since the current front office took over: a high ceiling, home-grown pitching prospect.

Variance: High. There's still a chance he ends up being a late-inning bullpen arm. The offspeed might not develop much past fringe average and the mechanical inconsistencies could return.

Ben Carsley's Fantasy Take: You know it's a weird system when I speak more positively about an arm than the bats surrounding him, but I really like Marquez. Yes, there's plenty of risk in the portfolio, but there's also sky-high fantasy upside, and that's what I'm going for when I'm investing in a dynasty pitching prospect. Plus, Marzquez is left-handed, which means he'll be given approximately 25,345 chances to succeed! Give me dudes with this profile over your generic SP5/6 prospects any day of the week.

★ ★ ★ *2020 Top 101 Prospect* **#92** ★ ★ ★

4 Brennen Davis OF OFP: 55 ETA: 2022
Born: 11/02/99 Age: 20 Bats: R Throws: R Height: 6'4" Weight: 175 Origin: Round 2, 2018 Draft (#62 overall)

YEAR	TEAM	LVL	AGE	PA	R	2B	3B	HR	RBI	BB	K	SB	CS	AVG/OBP/SLG	DRC+	VORP	BABIP	BRR	FRAA	WARP	PF
2018	CUT	RK	18	72	9	2	0	0	3	10	12	6	1	.298/.431/.333	156	4.4	.370	0.0	CF(10) 0.6, RF(4) -0.6	0.5	102
2019	SBN	A	19	204	33	9	3	8	30	18	38	4	1	.305/.381/.525	155	19.9	.346	-0.6	LF(23) -1.2, CF(23) -2.1	1.4	99
2020	CHN	MLB	20	251	27	11	1	8	30	19	64	5	1	.245/.315/.410	93	0.0	.306	-0.1	CF 0, LF 0	0.6	98

Comparables: Trent Grisham, Trayce Thompson, Abraham Almonte

The Report: Davis' prospect stock got a helium injection during his 50-game stint in Low-A, and he's poised for a further breakout in 2020 for Myrtle Beach. A former prep basketball star, he's built like a small forward with the potential for good weight to be added in the future without sacrificing athleticism. Despite limited game time due to a late start out of spring training and then a hand injury, the bat showed significant development. Davis shortened up his stroke and improved his ability to control the zone. There's natural loft in the swing, and it combines with his quick bat to produce some pop that plays in-game. The game power will continue to grow as he matures physically. He's not much of a threat to steal bases but his long strides and solid instincts make him an above-average baserunner. Those same long strides help him cover a lot of ground in the outfield. The arm is a little light for right field but he's currently a capable defender and his athleticism will make him above average as he gains experience.

Variance: High. He's still very raw and if the power doesn't develop as he matures he might end up profiling as Albert Almora 2.0.

Ben Carsley's Fantasy Take: Few prospects seem to have gained as much helium over the last year or so as Davis. To be honest, his lack of premium power or speed upside makes me think he's a touch overrated in fantasy circles. That being said his athleticism and hit tool combine to make him a relatively easy top-101 prospect. I don't think you should expect true fantasy superstardom, but if you want to dream on an Eddie Rosario-ish OF3 profile, be my guest.

5 Adbert Alzolay RHP OFP: 55 ETA: 2019
Born: 03/01/95 Age: 25 Bats: R Throws: R Height: 6'0" Weight: 179 Origin: International Free Agent, 2012

YEAR	TEAM	LVL	AGE	W	L	SV	G	GS	IP	H	HR	BB/9	K/9	K	GB%	BABIP	WHIP	ERA	DRA	WARP	PF
2017	MYR	A+	22	7	1	0	15	15	81²	65	8	2.4	8.6	78	39%	.263	1.07	2.98	3.26	1.9	97
2017	TEN	AA	22	0	3	0	7	7	32²	27	0	3.3	8.3	30	36%	.297	1.19	3.03	3.58	0.6	101
2018	IOW	AAA	23	2	4	0	8	8	39²	43	4	2.9	6.1	27	37%	.307	1.41	4.76	5.29	0.1	90
2019	IOW	AAA	24	2	4	0	15	15	65¹	53	10	4.3	12.5	91	32%	.295	1.29	4.41	2.70	2.5	93
2019	CHN	MLB	24	1	1	0	4	2	12¹	13	4	6.6	9.5	13	32%	.273	1.78	7.30	5.52	0.0	98
2020	CHN	MLB	25	5	5	0	47	10	88	89	16	4.3	9.0	87	34%	.301	1.49	5.22	5.30	0.3	98

Comparables: John Gant, Jakob Junis, Corbin Burnes

The Report: Alzolay looked like he might be a key piece of the Cubs pitching staff this year after he got off to a hot, if delayed, start to his season in Triple-A. Sure enough, he got called up for a few spot starts, but then optioned back down and went through a bout of ineffectiveness back in the PCL that ended with a brief IL stint for bicep soreness. The rest of the season was spent in "load management mode," and although he got a September recall, he only made one appearance for the big club after rosters expanded. His 2018 was similarly abridged, as a lat strain ended Alzolay's season in May.

When healthy last year, Alzolay flashed three above-average pitches. His fastball is a lively, mid-90s offering. His low-80s curve has short, late, tight break, and he will throw a power sinking change to both lefties and righties. The warts on the profile remain durability—both in-game and across a season—and command. The fastball has some arm-side movement, but it can flatten out when he overthrows and it too often finds too much of the plate. His delivery involves a glove tap and a fair bit of upper body effort. The reliever markers have been there for a while, and it might be time to just let him loose in the pen.

Variance: Medium. The main risks here are health as he's spent enough time in the minors and flashed solid stuff in the majors. The health risks are not insignificant though.

Ben Carsley's Fantasy Take: Alzolay might be a damn good reliever prospect, but he's still a reliever prospect. If you really love him you can keep holding on for a bit to wait for official word that he's going to the bullpen, but the smarter move is to cut bait now. Seriously, you don't want to gamble on reliever prospects *glares at Joe Jimenez.*

6 Kohl Franklin   RHP   OFP: 55   ETA: 2023

Born: 09/09/99   Age: 20   Bats: R   Throws: R   Height: 6'4"   Weight: 190   Origin: Round 6, 2018 Draft (#188 overall)

YEAR	TEAM	LVL	AGE	W	L	SV	G	GS	IP	H	HR	BB/9	K/9	K	GB%	BABIP	WHIP	ERA	DRA	WARP	PF
2018	CUT	RK	18	0	1	0	5	3	8²	5	0	6.2	8.3	8	33%	.208	1.27	6.23	3.40	0.2	107
2019	EUG	A-	19	1	3	0	10	10	39	31	2	3.2	11.3	49	48%	.302	1.15	2.31	3.32	0.9	105
2020	CHN	MLB	20	2	2	0	33	0	35	35	5	4.2	8.5	33	42%	.300	1.47	4.96	5.03	0.2	98

The Report: The Cubs have struggled for years to internally develop starting pitching, but Franklin is definitely an arm to keep an eye on for 2020 and beyond. The tall prep righty has filled out some and looks maybe 10 or 20 pounds over his listed 190. The fastball runs up into the mid 90s from a simple, repeatable delivery. There's potential above-average command of the pitch with more pro reps, and his high-three-quarters slot creates some plane as well. You could even see a smidge more projection left here as he could take on some more good weight.

Oh, and Franklin has one of the better breaking balls you'll see in short-season. It's inconsistent—as you'd expect at this level of experience—but it flashes power 12-6 action at it's best, and he's comfortable throwing it early in counts, not just to put away batters. It's a second potential plus pitch in the arsenal. He has some feel for a change as well, but it's a bit firm and straight and still in the nascent stage. Next year I expect we will be writing Franklin as the standard good mid-rotation pitching prospect who needs change and command improvements to really stick in a rotation. So why don't we just do it now?

Variance: High. I'm not opposed to maybe being a year early. You want to see this type of arm in full-season ball, but I expect the fastball/curve combo will be more than enough there as well. There's still a long way between Franklin and the majors though, and also, he's a pitcher.

Ben Carsley's Fantasy Take: Our squad admits this is probably a year too early to be in on Franklin, and I suggest fantasy owners take note. Pay attention to how Franklin does in full-season ball if you're looking to round out your roster, but there's not a particularly compelling reason to dive in yet. This is just not a very deep system.

7 Pedro Martinez   IF   OFP: 55   ETA: 2024

Born: 01/28/01   Age: 19   Bats: B   Throws: R   Height: 5'11"   Weight: 165   Origin: International Free Agent, 2018

YEAR	TEAM	LVL	AGE	PA	R	2B	3B	HR	RBI	BB	K	SB	CS	AVG/OBP/SLG	DRC+	VORP	BABIP	BRR	FRAA	WARP	PF
2018	DCH	RK	17	228	37	3	5	2	25	26	26	31	9	.310/.398/.406	150	27.4	.349	3.0	SS(34) 2.6, 3B(16) -0.9	2.6	98
2019	CUB	RK	18	121	12	6	3	2	17	12	27	8	5	.352/.417/.519	144	11.0	.456	-0.2	SS(16) -0.4, 2B(9) -2.1	0.7	108
2019	EUG	A-	18	112	15	2	3	0	7	12	36	11	5	.265/.357/.347	83	3.8	.419	1.1	2B(14) 1.7, SS(11) -1.2	0.4	103
2020	CHN	MLB	19	251	23	10	2	3	21	22	83	15	5	.239/.311/.333	73	0.0	.365	0.7	SS 0, 2B 0	0.1	98

Comparables: Thairo Estrada, Abiatal Avelino, Ozzie Albies

The Report: He'll never see his own player page come up first on a baseball-reference search, but this Pedro is a pretty fun prospect himself. A switch-hitter with a mirrored, if noisy, setup and swing, Martinez shows sneaky pop from the left side and feel for the barrel from both. He has a typical teenager-in-the-low-minors frame and could fill out and end up with fringe power at maturity. He's raw at present and has a tendency to overswing and pull his head off a bit, and he struggled with short-season level breaking stuff as well. That means the offensive profile is going to be risky, but the underlying swing looks good and some of this might get smoothed out with reps and more physical strength.

Martinez is an above-average runner with a high motor, and he moves well in the infield. The hands and actions are smooth and work well at short, although the arm isn't ideal for the left side. He does get the ball out quickly though, and his throws come in shoulder high from a variety of angles. He's not a sure shot shortstop, but there is a shot, and he should be playable there a couple times a week in a utility role at worst. Ideally, an 18-year-old who might lack a carrying tool is not this high in your system, but this isn't an ideal system, and Martinez is a fun prospect if nothing else.

Variance: Extreme. Short-season resume, swing-and-miss and spin issues in the Northwest League, might be more of a second baseman than a shortstop.

Ben Carsley's Fantasy Take: Listen, I am absolutely the wrong person to ask about speedy middle infield prospects with notable names. This is my kryptonite. Martinez is really nothing more than an interesting flier at this point, but I look forward to overdrafting him in a majority of my leagues.

8 Ryan Jensen RHP   OFP: 55   ETA: 2021
Born: 11/23/97   Age: 22   Bats: R   Throws: R   Height: 6'0"   Weight: 180   Origin: Round 1, 2019 Draft (#27 overall)

YEAR	TEAM	LVL	AGE	W	L	SV	G	GS	IP	H	HR	BB/9	K/9	K	GB%	BABIP	WHIP	ERA	DRA	WARP	PF
2019	EUG	A-	21	0	0	0	6	6	12	7	0	10.5	14.2	19	68%	.318	1.75	2.25	6.90	-0.2	102
2020	CHN	MLB	22	2	2	0	33	0	35	35	5	3.7	8.7	34	47%	.300	1.40	4.68	4.83	0.2	98

Comparables: CD Pelham, Drew Steckenrider, Cole Kimball

The Report: Jensen was a bit of a surprise pick when the Cubs popped him in the first round. He offers a big fastball, but it comes with an undersized frame and enough effort in the mechanics to indicate a likely bullpen future. The fastball has plus-plus velocity and explodes out of his hand, but the delivery is high effort and features a rather long arm stroke that Jensen can struggle to repeat, so the occasional bouts of wildness in his pro debut may not be a mere blip after a long college season. Jensen's slider flashes plus, a power, two-plane breaker he can run up to 90, but it can get softer or slurvier, the shape inconsistent from pitch to pitch. There's a theoretical changeup as well, but with a two pitch combination like the fastball/slider, he didn't need much else in college or the Northwest League.

So the two million dollar question: Can Jensen start long term? I'd be lying if I said I was particularly bullish. If you want to play the comp game it's hard to think of a right-handed starter with those kind of mechanics, even before considering whether his frame will hold up across 100 pitches a start for 32 starts. Now we're in an era where starting pitching roles are shifting and perhaps you can carve one out to work for Jensen. But since we are playing the comp game, he looks like a late-inning reliever. He might be a good enough one to justify the late-first-round pick anyway.

Variance: High. It's a very good fastball, but the slider will need to improve to even give him a second pitch for high-leverage work. There's also a limited pro track record in any role.

Ben Carsley's Fantasy Take: Unless Jansen ends up with a better chance to start or close, he's of relatively little interest to us. That's it. That's the analysis.

9 Christopher Morel 3B   OFP: 50   ETA: 2023
Born: 06/24/99   Age: 21   Bats: R   Throws: R   Height: 6'0"   Weight: 140   Origin: International Free Agent, 2015

YEAR	TEAM	LVL	AGE	PA	R	2B	3B	HR	RBI	BB	K	SB	CS	AVG/OBP/SLG	DRC+	VORP	BABIP	BRR	FRAA	WARP	PF
2017	DCU	RK	18	268	44	6	2	7	40	35	37	23	10	.220/.332/.359	79	16.1	.228	1.6	SS(49) -8.2, 3B(12) 0.7	0.1	87
2018	CUB	RK	19	128	20	6	0	2	12	11	28	1	4	.257/.331/.363	105	8.3	.321	0.5	3B(19) 0.1, SS(9) 2.9	0.9	94
2018	EUG	A-	19	93	7	2	0	1	8	0	29	0	1	.165/.172/.220	-7	-6.1	.226	1.7	3B(17) -2.1, SS(6) -0.7	-0.7	98
2019	SBN	A	20	278	36	15	7	6	31	11	60	9	6	.284/.320/.467	113	16.3	.345	0.2	3B(72) 2.2, LF(1) 0.4	1.6	101
2020	CHN	MLB	21	251	22	11	1	5	24	16	72	5	3	.215/.272/.341	60	3.0	.287	-0.2	3B 1, SS 0	-0.4	98

Comparables: Brett Phillips, Jesmuel Valentín, Drew Robinson

The Report: Morel is more than a bit heftier than his listed 140 pounds, but he remains fairly lean even now. That is not a deterrent to believing he is a future power hitter though, and the man swings with bad intentions. There's plus bat speed that generates plus raw pull-side pop, and I wouldn't recommend trying to beat him inside with a fastball, but it comes at the price of some barrel control and with an overaggressive approach. Some added strength would add balance to his swing, and additional game reps might tame the approach some. While we are squinting a bit to see an average hit/pop combo, it's in there.

Morel was signed as a shortstop, and he plays third base like one. He's rangy with a good first step and has a plus, accurate arm. There are the occasional bouts of rawness on the defensive side as well, but I'm more confident in the above-average projection on the glove than the bat. Although that got cloudier too after a July knee injury that ended his season early.

Variance: High. Limited pro experience, needs to add some physicality and tame down the approach against better pitching. There's also the question of how he returns from the knee injury.

Ben Carsley's Fantasy Take: Morel has enough bat speed, power projection and potential positional value to occupy a spot on your watch list, but not enough of any of the above to warrant serious investment just yet. I do prefer him to the non-Marquez pitchers on this list, though.

10   Riley Thompson   RHP   OFP: 50   ETA: 2022

Born: 07/09/96   Age: 23   Bats: L   Throws: R   Height: 6'3"   Weight: 205   Origin: Round 11, 2018 Draft (#338 overall)

YEAR	TEAM	LVL	AGE	W	L	SV	G	GS	IP	H	HR	BB/9	K/9	K	GB%	BABIP	WHIP	ERA	DRA	WARP	PF
2018	EUG	A-	21	0	2	0	9	8	25¹	24	1	3.2	8.9	25	49%	.324	1.30	2.84	4.80	0.1	99
2019	SBN	A	22	8	6	0	21	21	94	85	9	3.0	8.3	87	45%	.290	1.23	3.06	4.77	0.5	99
2020	CHN	MLB	23	2	2	0	33	0	35	35	6	3.9	6.8	26	42%	.281	1.44	4.81	4.90	0.2	98

Comparables: Chris Stratton, David Phelps, Joel Carreno

The Report: The Cubs took an 11th-round flyer on Thompson, who was coming off of a disappointing stint at Louisville that saw him lose a year to Tommy John and fail to live up to his billing as a former top prep arm. Since then, the high effort delivery has been replaced by a more in-line and in control motion. It's caused a dip in velocity (92-93) but has resulted in above-average command. Thompson's also developed a devastating changeup, which has the potential to be a true swing-and-miss pitch. It shows good velocity separation, sitting mid 80s, and fades away from right-handed hitters. He will also mix in the occasional curve. They lack consistency, but when he gets it right it's sharp and has some bite. Blessed with the classic starting pitcher frame, advanced secondaries, and above average command, Thompson profiles as a future back-of-the-rotation piece.

Variance: High. Thompson has only one good year of full-season baseball under his belt. There's a lot that can go wrong between South Bend and Chicago.

Ben Carsley's Fantasy Take: A back-of-the-rotation prospect who isn't ready right now and already has TJ on his resume! Don't sign me up. Don't sign me up at all.

The Next Ten

11   Chase Strumpf   2B

Born: 03/08/98   Age: 22   Bats: R   Throws: R   Height: 6'1"   Weight: 191   Origin: Round 2, 2019 Draft (#64 overall)

YEAR	TEAM	LVL	AGE	PA	R	2B	3B	HR	RBI	BB	K	SB	CS	AVG/OBP/SLG	DRC+	VORP	BABIP	BRR	FRAA	WARP	PF
2019	CUT	RK	21	32	5	3	0	0	1	7	7	0	0	.182/.406/.318	116	2.1	.250	0.2	2B(5) 0.4	0.2	95
2019	EUG	A-	21	111	17	8	0	2	14	15	28	2	0	.292/.405/.449	151	9.9	.387	-1.3	2B(24) -3.4	0.3	101
2019	SBN	A	21	28	3	1	0	1	2	1	7	0	0	.125/.214/.292	50	-0.9	.118	0.0	2B(6) 0.2	-0.1	100
2020	CHN	MLB	22	251	24	12	1	7	26	18	82	2	1	.211/.283/.358	71	2.0	.297	0.0	2B -1	-0.2	98

Comparables: Vince Belnome, Jake Rogers, David Bote

If you are taking a college second baseman, you'd better be confident he's going to hit. Fortunately, the first thing that pops out with Strumpf is his ability to square up his pitch—not just any pitch. It's a sweet approach and even sweeter swing—quick wrists and compact to the ball. Strumpf hits the ball hard enough to rack up some doubles, and there might be some sneaky home run pop as well. Nothing here really stands out as above-average, and he's only passable at the keystone, but there is certainly a chance that advanced approach carries him into a starting second base role somewhere down the line.

12   Cole Roederer   OF

Born: 09/24/99   Age: 20   Bats: L   Throws: L   Height: 6'0"   Weight: 175   Origin: Round 2C, 2018 Draft (#77 overall)

YEAR	TEAM	LVL	AGE	PA	R	2B	3B	HR	RBI	BB	K	SB	CS	AVG/OBP/SLG	DRC+	VORP	BABIP	BRR	FRAA	WARP	PF
2018	CUT	RK	18	161	30	4	4	5	24	18	37	13	4	.275/.354/.465	122	13.6	.337	2.1	CF(29) -1.3, RF(4) -1.1	0.7	102
2019	SBN	A	19	448	45	19	4	9	60	52	112	16	5	.224/.319/.365	91	13.6	.285	1.6	CF(94) 3.3, LF(9) -0.7	1.4	101
2020	CHN	MLB	20	251	23	11	1	6	24	18	79	7	3	.204/.268/.337	57	0.0	.284	0.3	CF 3, LF 0	-0.2	98

Comparables: Joe Benson, Trent Grisham, Abraham Almonte

Roederer struggled out of the gate in his first full-season assignment, slashing just .218/.290/.339 prior to the All-Star break. The teenager at times looked overmatched, especially against left-handed pitching. It wasn't completely a lost season however, as there were still some bright spots. Defensively, he played an above-average center field, covering plenty of range with his plus speed. That speed and athleticism also made him an efficient base stealer. Late in the year, Roederer appeared to be more comfortable and locked in at the plate allowing some surprising pop to play in game. It's too early to write him off as a non-prospect, there are intriguing tools and he could be poised to rebound next season.

13 Richard Gallardo RHP
Born: 09/06/01 Age: 18 Bats: R Throws: R Height: 6'1" Weight: 187 Origin: International Free Agent, 2018

YEAR	TEAM	LVL	AGE	W	L	SV	G	GS	IP	H	HR	BB/9	K/9	K	GB%	BABIP	WHIP	ERA	DRA	WARP	PF
2019	CUB	RK	17	0	2	0	11	9	30¹	32	1	3.6	6.8	23	55%	.316	1.45	4.15	4.16	0.6	108
2020	CHN	MLB	18	2	2	0	33	0	35	35	5	3.8	5.6	22	41%	.268	1.42	4.65	4.83	0.2	98

Comparables: Emmanuel Clase, Elieser Hernandez, Chris Flexen

Gallardo was one of the top IFA arms available in the 2018 and one of the prizes of the Cubs J2 class. He's not super projectable with a big fastball like you might expect. Rather Gallardo is a short, somewhat stocky righty who's probably close to already maxed out in an average velocity band. He has advanced command and an easy, almost slinky delivery. And if Franklin has one of the better curveballs you will see in short-season, Gallardo's wasn't far behind his. Gallardo's curve has more 11-5 break, but he commands the pitch well and it should end up a plus offering. Gallardo held his own stateside at 17, but may lack a gaudy OFP for how far away he is from the majors. You're hoping he develops a solid changeup and the pitchability and command make him a third or fourth starter.

14 Michael McAvene RHP
Born: 08/24/97 Age: 22 Bats: R Throws: R Height: 6'3" Weight: 210 Origin: Round 3, 2019 Draft (#103 overall)

YEAR	TEAM	LVL	AGE	W	L	SV	G	GS	IP	H	HR	BB/9	K/9	K	GB%	BABIP	WHIP	ERA	DRA	WARP	PF
2019	EUG	A-	21	0	0	0	6	6	12²	5	0	2.8	14.2	20	29%	.238	0.71	1.42	2.28	0.4	99
2020	CHN	MLB	22	2	2	0	33	0	35	35	5	3.7	8.9	35	37%	.306	1.41	4.70	4.82	0.2	98

Comparables: Radhames Liz, Tobi Stoner, Michael Stutes

The Cubs' third-round pick closed for Louisville last spring and already has an elbow scar, but Chicago appears to be at least toying with the idea of stretching him back out as a starter. I'm skeptical given the health history and level of effort in the delivery, and McAvene could move quickly as a fastball/slider power arm. His fastball gets up into the mid 90s and has some run and ride to it. The slider can get slurvy, but will flash good depth. Neither pitch pops enough to project a closer-level relief arm in the majors, but he could be a seventh or eighth inning arm for the Cubs as soon as 2021 if they elect to keep him in the pen.

15 Cory Abbott RHP
Born: 09/20/95 Age: 24 Bats: R Throws: R Height: 6'2" Weight: 220 Origin: Round 2, 2017 Draft (#67 overall)

YEAR	TEAM	LVL	AGE	W	L	SV	G	GS	IP	H	HR	BB/9	K/9	K	GB%	BABIP	WHIP	ERA	DRA	WARP	PF
2017	EUG	A-	21	0	0	0	5	5	14	14	1	1.9	11.6	18	31%	.371	1.21	3.86	3.86	0.2	100
2018	SBN	A	22	4	1	0	9	9	47¹	35	5	2.5	10.8	57	39%	.275	1.01	2.47	2.73	1.4	99
2018	MYR	A+	22	4	5	0	13	13	67²	59	3	3.5	9.8	74	46%	.316	1.26	2.53	3.93	1.1	96
2019	TEN	AA	23	8	8	0	26	26	146²	112	15	3.2	10.2	166	38%	.274	1.12	3.01	4.19	1.4	103
2020	CHN	MLB	24	2	2	0	33	0	35	35	6	3.5	9.2	36	38%	.308	1.40	4.64	4.79	0.2	98

Comparables: Jon Duplantier, Rogelio Armenteros, Cody Martin

The Cubs' second-round pick in 2017 out of Loyola Marymount, Abbott has taken a slightly sluggardly pace up the minor league ladder for a polished college arm. He works primarily off of a low-90s fastball and high-80s cutter, which tunnel well out of his three-quarters slot, and mixes in a short, downer 12-6 curve with average projection. The cutter and curve give him options against lefties as the change hasn't really developed in the pros, and while nothing here is above-average, everything can miss bats when deployed judiciously. A long and somewhat funky arm action can lead to bouts of wildness or command issues, but Abbott has enough stuff to fit at the back of a rotation, and the frame and durability track record to log innings.

16 Zack Short IF

Born: 05/29/95   Age: 25   Bats: R   Throws: R   Height: 5'10"   Weight: 180   Origin: Round 17, 2016 Draft (#524 overall)

YEAR	TEAM	LVL	AGE	PA	R	2B	3B	HR	RBI	BB	K	SB	CS	AVG/OBP/SLG	DRC+	VORP	BABIP	BRR	FRAA	WARP	PF
2017	SBN	A	22	300	50	17	3	7	26	54	54	15	5	.237/.393/.424	144	27.2	.278	2.5	SS(26) 0.2, 3B(23) -0.2	2.8	99
2017	MYR	A+	22	277	34	11	3	6	21	40	50	3	5	.263/.372/.414	130	20.4	.307	-2.7	SS(61) -1.9	1.5	97
2018	TEN	AA	23	524	68	28	2	17	59	82	136	8	3	.227/.356/.417	129	35.1	.290	-0.2	SS(117) 4.8, 2B(4) 0.4	4.4	94
2019	CUB	RK	24	25	5	2	0	0	3	8	4	0	0	.375/.600/.500	180	3.4	.500	-0.7	SS(3) 0.5, 2B(2) -0.1	0.2	112
2019	TEN	AA	24	74	7	3	2	0	5	9	18	0	1	.250/.338/.359	86	4.3	.340	0.4	SS(13) -0.7, 2B(2) -0.2	0.2	104
2019	IOW	AAA	24	160	22	9	0	6	17	21	50	2	1	.211/.338/.414	76	3.3	.282	-1.9	SS(27) 1.2, 2B(13) -0.1	0.1	94
2020	CHN	MLB	25	251	27	12	1	8	29	30	76	3	1	.215/.318/.387	90	0.0	.291	-0.2	SS 0, 2B 0	0.5	98

Comparables: Jake Rogers, Alex Blandino, Joe Benson

Like Chase Strumpf, Short possesses a strong approach and ability to track pitches. However, his swing mechanics don't allow him to take advantage of his pitch as well as Strumpf does. Short, ironically, has a long stride with a lot of pre-pitch motion, which has him sacrificing some barrel control and leaves the hit tool closer to a 4 than a 5. Defensively, well there his surname is appropriate. He's a smooth fielder with good actions and he can make throws from a variety of angles. Short has played a fair bit of second base as a pro too, and spent some time at the hot corner on the Cape. Defensive flexibility and a bit of on-base and sneaky pop will be what punches his ticket to a bench role in the majors.

17 Brendon Little LHP

Born: 08/11/96   Age: 23   Bats: L   Throws: L   Height: 6'1"   Weight: 195   Origin: Round 1, 2017 Draft (#27 overall)

YEAR	TEAM	LVL	AGE	W	L	SV	G	GS	IP	H	HR	BB/9	K/9	K	GB%	BABIP	WHIP	ERA	DRA	WARP	PF
2017	EUG	A-	20	0	2	0	6	6	16¹	21	2	5.0	6.6	12	45%	.339	1.84	9.37	7.64	-0.5	96
2018	SBN	A	21	5	11	0	22	21	101¹	106	8	3.8	8.0	90	49%	.317	1.47	5.15	5.16	0.0	97
2019	CUB	RK	22	0	0	0	2	2	7¹	4	2	4.9	11.0	9	31%	.143	1.09	3.68	2.18	0.3	116
2019	SBN	A	22	0	1	0	6	6	28¹	18	0	4.1	7.9	25	52%	.241	1.09	1.91	3.80	0.5	102
2019	MYR	A+	22	2	1	0	4	4	19²	21	2	4.1	10.5	23	40%	.345	1.53	5.95	5.61	-0.1	99
2020	CHN	MLB	23	2	2	0	33	0	35	35	6	3.8	7.5	29	44%	.287	1.43	4.84	4.93	0.2	98

The Cubs' 2017 first-rounder has struggled to get his feet under him in pro ball. A lat strain cost him the first half of 2019, but there were at least some improvements to the offspeed stuff once he got back on the mound. His upper-80s curve shows good 12-6 depth and is a potential future plus pitch and his low-80s change has improved enough to get some swings-and-misses against righties as well. The fastball velocity is down from his breakout summer on the Cape, sitting more low-90s now, but Little can cut and run the pitch. He has a fairly simple delivery, but still has too many command and control blips, given the stuff is mostly averagish. A full, healthy 2020 and some command refinements would get him back on course for a future back-end starter or swingman role.

18 Keegan Thompson RHP

Born: 03/13/95   Age: 25   Bats: R   Throws: R   Height: 6'1"   Weight: 210   Origin: Round 3, 2017 Draft (#105 overall)

YEAR	TEAM	LVL	AGE	W	L	SV	G	GS	IP	H	HR	BB/9	K/9	K	GB%	BABIP	WHIP	ERA	DRA	WARP	PF
2017	EUG	A-	22	1	2	0	7	1	19	15	1	1.9	10.9	23	40%	.298	1.00	2.37	2.11	0.6	117
2018	MYR	A+	23	3	3	0	12	12	67²	49	6	1.7	8.1	61	36%	.239	0.92	3.19	2.74	2.0	98
2018	TEN	AA	23	6	3	0	13	13	62	66	3	3.0	7.8	54	36%	.333	1.40	4.06	4.95	0.3	94
2020	CHN	MLB	25	2	2	0	33	0	35	35	5	3.5	8.4	32	39%	.298	1.38	4.61	4.79	0.2	98

Thompson missed almost the whole season with injuries, but popped back up for reps in the AFL, showing an average low-90s fastball that he could take a couple ticks off of for some additional run. He also has an average hard slider that can get cutterish, and a fringy curve and change. Thompson gets by on pitch mix and his ability to throw all four pitches for strikes. He looked like a quick-moving, polished, back-end arm in 2018. The lost developmental time in 2019 derailed that a bit, but he could be an option to take major league innings in some capacity by the end of this season. The lack of a swing-and-miss offering in the arsenal could leave him more as a spot starter or swingman though.

19 Jack Patterson LHP
Born: 08/03/95   Age: 24   Bats: L   Throws: L   Height: 6'0"   Weight: 210   Origin: Round 32, 2018 Draft (#968 overall)

YEAR	TEAM	LVL	AGE	W	L	SV	G	GS	IP	H	HR	BB/9	K/9	K	GB%	BABIP	WHIP	ERA	DRA	WARP	PF
2018	CUT	RK	22	2	1	0	7	5	26¹	28	3	2.4	8.2	24	46%	.321	1.33	3.08	3.46	0.7	97
2019	SBN	A	23	5	1	1	16	1	42¹	29	0	3.8	10.0	47	62%	.279	1.11	2.34	3.43	0.7	96
2019	MYR	A+	23	2	0	0	5	5	23²	8	0	3.0	9.1	24	66%	.151	0.68	0.00	2.03	0.9	103
2019	TEN	AA	23	1	0	0	3	3	13²	11	1	4.0	5.9	9	58%	.270	1.24	2.63	5.38	-0.1	105
2020	CHN	MLB	24	2	2	0	33	0	35	34	5	3.4	7.7	30	45%	.287	1.35	4.32	4.51	0.3	98

Patterson has been a quick mover in the system since being drafted in the 32nd round in 2018. After an excellent first half working out of the bullpen in Low-A South Bend, the Cubs began to transition him to a starting role. The stuff is not electric and there is not much projection left, but he's got a good mix of secondaries and knows how to use them. The fastball sits around 93 and has some arm side run that allows him to miss bats. It plays up due to the offspeed that he'll throw at any count. His low-80s change is currently the most advanced and shows quality velocity separation, but the slider and curve both grade out to future average pitches as well. Ultimately, he's likely a future bullpen arm, but that's not a bad outcome for someone drafted that late in the draft.

20 Chris Clarke RHP
Born: 05/13/98   Age: 22   Bats: R   Throws: R   Height: 6'7"   Weight: 212   Origin: Round 4, 2019 Draft (#132 overall)

YEAR	TEAM	LVL	AGE	W	L	SV	G	GS	IP	H	HR	BB/9	K/9	K	GB%	BABIP	WHIP	ERA	DRA	WARP	PF
2019	EUG	A-	21	0	1	0	9	8	23	20	2	1.6	10.2	26	51%	.305	1.04	1.96	3.24	0.5	102
2020	CHN	MLB	22	2	2	0	33	0	35	35	6	3.6	8.0	31	44%	.292	1.40	4.70	4.86	0.2	98

Clarke is a massive human, listed at 6-foot-7 and 212 pounds. He was a dominant multi-inning reliever for USC his junior year and was popped by Chicago in the fourth round of the draft. He isn't a flamethrower despite his size, but he does sit low 90s, can dial it up to 95 and it comes from a steep angle with sink. Clarke's delivery looks a little awkward at times given the sheer volume of limbs he has to corral, but he repeats his mechanics fairly well. A big breaking, potential plus curveball complements the fastball, and Clarke is effective moving it down into or down out of the zone. This is among the lazier comps I will offer this year, but I do get some Rauchian vibes, although Clarke doesn't use his height quite as well as Rauch did. I cannot speak to his tattoo game.

Personal Cheeseball

PC Trevor Clifton RHP
Born: 05/11/95   Age: 25   Bats: R   Throws: R   Height: 6'4"   Weight: 170   Origin: Round 12, 2013 Draft (#348 overall)

YEAR	TEAM	LVL	AGE	W	L	SV	G	GS	IP	H	HR	BB/9	K/9	K	GB%	BABIP	WHIP	ERA	DRA	WARP	PF
2017	TEN	AA	22	5	8	0	21	21	100¹	112	8	4.0	7.7	86	36%	.343	1.56	5.20	6.26	-1.3	98
2018	TEN	AA	23	3	4	0	12	12	56²	41	0	3.7	7.1	45	36%	.255	1.13	2.86	3.36	1.3	96
2018	IOW	AAA	23	4	3	0	14	12	69¹	65	8	3.8	7.3	56	38%	.292	1.36	3.89	4.91	0.5	94
2019	IOW	AAA	24	4	8	0	24	20	99	98	20	4.5	7.6	84	35%	.270	1.49	5.18	5.07	1.5	93
2020	CHN	MLB	25	2	2	0	33	0	35	36	5	3.8	6.7	26	35%	.286	1.44	5.09	5.12	0.1	98

As we enter our final division for the website lists, I start to get philosophical. Eh, maybe I'm just out of ideas. Anyway, before the 2017 season, we ranked Trevor Clifton as the 87th-best prospect in baseball. I got a fun Tony Clifton riff in the Annual out of it too. Sometimes I will look back at a ranking and think, "well, we weren't really wrong at the time." Prospects change. Well, in this case we were probably wrong at the time. And there it will stand forever, an orphan on his baseball-reference page. It happens. I know why it happened. And, he did suffer a fairly significant velocity dip the season after, which didn't help, mind you.

The low-90s velocity is back now, but the good sink is intermittent, and a near 50% flyball rate is going to do him no favors with the Triple-A baseballs. Regardless I still root for him to make the majors. Not to prove me right, that ship has sailed, but you end up forming weird rooting interests in your mind when you start putting names onto ordinal lists.

Low Minors Sleeper

LMS **Nelson Velazquez** **OF**
Born: 12/26/98 Age: 21 Bats: R Throws: R Height: 6'0" Weight: 190 Origin: Round 5, 2017 Draft (#165 overall)

YEAR	TEAM	LVL	AGE	PA	R	2B	3B	HR	RBI	BB	K	SB	CS	AVG/OBP/SLG	DRC+	VORP	BABIP	BRR	FRAA	WARP	PF
2017	CUB	RK	18	126	26	5	2	8	17	15	39	5	2	.236/.333/.536	112	6.0	.286	0.0	LF(16) 0.8, CF(8) -2.1	0.3	101
2018	EUG	A-	19	293	35	18	2	11	33	23	81	12	4	.250/.322/.458	106	14.3	.320	-1.2	LF(28) -0.7, RF(20) -1.3	0.1	97
2018	SBN	A	19	120	6	1	0	0	7	7	43	3	0	.188/.242/.196	25	-9.8	.304	-0.1	RF(20) -1.6, LF(5) 0.9	-0.7	96
2019	SBN	A	20	285	33	16	4	4	34	21	77	5	3	.286/.338/.424	126	12.7	.390	-1.3	RF(41) 2.0, LF(14) -0.3	1.5	101
2020	CHN	MLB	21	251	22	12	1	6	25	16	87	3	1	.215/.269/.346	59	0.0	.318	0.0	RF 0, LF 1	-0.4	98

Velazquez struggled badly in his first cup of coffee in full-season ball at the end of 2018, but he made improvements both year-over-year and throughout 2019. He's a strong kid with above-average bat speed, so there is the potential for above-average power, but his approach and pitch recognition issues made it difficult for him to unlock the pop in games. Velazquez showed a more patient approach and willingness to use all fields as the year wore on, and after missing two months with a strained oblique he slugged .472 in August. His slow first step and general lack of range will limit him to a corner, so hopefully his late-season adjustments have unlocked something going forward, because he will really need to hit.

Top Talents 25 and Under (born 4/1/93 or later)

1. Nico Hoerner
2. Miguel Amaya
3. Ian Happ
4. Brailyn Marquez
5. Brennen Davis
6. Adbert Alzolay
7. Albert Almora
8. Kohl Franklin
9. Pedro Martinez
10. Ryan Jensen

This list would look a lot better if the arbitrary cut off were 28-and-under, but there's no getting around the fact that the Cubs are an exceedingly veteran team at this point. I'm as lost with where to slot in Ian Happ as the Cubs are, especially since I'm particularly fond of both Marquez and Davis. Still, Happ has recorded a season and change of .500-plus slugging percentages (yes, both during rocket ball seasons of 2017 and 2019), with one league-average offensive line in between. DRC+ (113) isn't as complimentary to Happ's offensive prowess as stats like OPS+ (126) for 2019, but above-average production at the plate from a guy who can stand in a bunch of places (FRAA of 1.0 in 2019) is pretty useful.

Almora makes the list, mostly by dint of a weak system. His superlative glove is keeping his overall profile afloat, but just barely. He's seen his DRC+ go from 93 in 2017 to 85 in 2018 to last year's 72. That's more fifth outfielder than fourth, and many teams have stopped carrying five full-time outfielders. It's possible the 26th spot that's coming in 2020 will save Almora for a bit, but he's proven his inability with the lumber to the point that I'd rather gamble on the upside of the prospects ahead of him.

Eyewitness Reports

Eyewitness Report: Brailyn Marquez

Evaluator: Nathan Graham
Report Date: 08/16/2019
Dates Seen: 4X, 2018-2019
Risk Factor: High
Delivery: Extra-Large frame with a thick lower half and projection remaining in the upper body, bigger than listed height and weight; Semi-windup, with 3/4 arm slot, stays online well with a clean landing, easy delivery.

Pitch Type	Future Grade	Sitting Velocity	Peak Velocity	Report
Fastball	70	96-99	100	Fastball has become a weapon for Marquez this year, he's cleaned up the delivery and become more consistent with the arm slot using his height to get good plane; The pitch is straight but has life and explodes on hitters; Velocity dipped after 4 innings.
Changeup	50	85-86	86	Recently added to his mix of pitches, currently lacks feel and consistency, pitch lacks movement but has good velocity separation and Marquez replicates his arm action well.
Slider	60	87-91	92	Primary off speed offering, still has some inconsistency and will get loose, in my most recent looks he missed armside early but gained feel deeper into the game, will bury on the back boot of right handed hitters; 2/8 movement, has swing and miss potential.

Conclusion: Marquez has always had the physical tools, an extra large frame to go along with a strong arm, but it did not always translate to in game performance. It's beginning to click this year as he's cleaned up the delivery and is more under control allowing the fastball to be his centerpiece pitch. The secondaries are still lacking feel but they have the look of at least major league average offerings. The Cubs will keep him in a starting role as long as possible but will eventually be a late inning closer type.

Eyewitness Report: Brennen Davis

Evaluator: Nathan Graham
Report Date: 09/17/2019
Dates Seen: multiple 2019
Risk Factor: High
Physical/Health: Extra large build, athletic and lean with long legs; projectable upper body.

Tool	Future Grade	Report
Hit	55	Crouched stance, with high hands. Still raw but has made improvements through the year shortening the swing and staying in the zone longer; will get out of sync at times and can be exploited by high velocity. Above average hand/eye coordination and bat-to-ball skills.
Power	55	Produces power with plus bat speed and natural loft in the swing. Future added growth and strength will make the pop play above-average in game.
Baserunning/ Speed	60	4.19 average home to first on multiple clocks; slow to accelerate due to long strides but has plus raw speed once he gets going. He won't steal a ton of bases but is a smart base runner, selectively aggressive. Athletic enough to maintain speed with physical maturity.
Glove	50	Shows good instincts and looks natural in the outfield, takes good routes; athleticism allows for plenty of ground to be covered.
Arm	45	Throws lack carry, would be fine for left but fringe average for center field.

Conclusion: Davis is still raw but has plenty of potential. I was impressed with the strides made as a teenager facing more advanced pitching in the Midwest League. The arm is on the light side but he should be able to stick in center. He's still a long way off but the potential speed/power combination gives a high ceiling.

Chicago White Sox

The State of the System

The White Sox still have a few close-to-ready high-end prospect cards to play as they transition to AL Central contenders, but past that things thin out more quickly than recent years.

The Top Ten

★ ★ ★ *2020 Top 101 Prospect* **#6** ★ ★ ★

1 Luis Robert OF OFP: 70 ETA: 2020
Born: 08/03/97 Age: 22 Bats: R Throws: R Height: 6'3" Weight: 185 Origin: International Free Agent, 2017

YEAR	TEAM	LVL	AGE	PA	R	2B	3B	HR	RBI	BB	K	SB	CS	AVG/OBP/SLG	DRC+	VORP	BABIP	BRR	FRAA	WARP	PF
2017	DWS	RK	19	114	17	8	1	3	14	22	23	12	3	.310/.491/.536	203	20.6	.397	2.5	CF(19) -0.5	1.7	100
2018	KAN	A	20	50	5	3	1	0	4	4	12	4	2	.289/.360/.400	105	3.0	.394	-0.2	CF(10) 0.0	0.1	96
2018	WNS	A+	20	140	21	6	1	0	11	8	37	8	2	.244/.317/.309	83	3.1	.341	0.5	CF(27) 3.1, RF(4) -0.4	0.5	103
2019	WNS	A+	21	84	21	5	3	8	24	4	20	8	2	.453/.512/.920	273	18.3	.553	-1.2	CF(13) 1.9	1.6	107
2019	BIR	AA	21	244	43	16	3	8	29	13	54	21	6	.314/.362/.518	128	20.2	.384	2.5	CF(36) 1.9, RF(7) -0.8	1.8	104
2019	CHR	AAA	21	223	44	10	5	16	39	11	55	7	3	.297/.341/.634	114	13.2	.324	1.2	CF(46) 6.5	1.7	112
2020	CHA	MLB	22	595	74	30	4	29	86	30	175	18	6	.262/.315/.487	111	0.0	.334	1.9	CF 8, RF 0	3.8	100

Comparables: Brett Phillips, Lewis Brinson, Greg Golson

The Report: Watching him scuffle through an injury-plagued 2018, there was an air of creeping disappointment unable yet to stifle great hopes and expectations. Watching him swing through hittable pitches and lousy breaking balls, unable to tap into his power, one knew there had to be something there that had made Robert the most talked about international talent in years. Just wait until he's right.

Well, he healed up in 2019 and proved all he had to at the minor league level. A true five-tool player with a whiff of purely hypothetical uncertainty about the hit, La Pantera preyed on pitchers across three levels while playing a beautiful center field and swiping bases by the bundle. An incredible athlete, Robert has excellent speed underway but typically makes the plays simply by gliding. He's similarly quiet and assured at the plate with a smooth swing that produces good bat speed and has some lift to it for easy plus power. He can catch up to the hard stuff and his approach against breaking balls has taken leaps; he is now able to lay off spin when it is out of the zone while reserving the ability to adjust, wait back, and drive to all fields when he finds one to his liking.

If there is one ephemeral worry surrounding Robert it is that old demons could crop up when he is faced with top shelf breaking stuff, and that this could dampen his hit tool a bit. Still, he's shown the aptitude to make adjustments when necessary and is strong enough everywhere else that the profile can overcome a slight lag in his fifth tool. At this time, it is a very select group of prospects we'd take over this cat.

Variance: Low. He's big-league ready and probably has been since midseason. His hit tool carries risk but he will contribute even if he ends up hitting for a low average.

Ben Carsley's Fantasy Take: That pesky Jo Adell guy keeps Robert from earning the distinction of the top outfield prospect in dynasty, but our protagonist ranks only one spot behind. Aside from some boo boos on his resume, Robert has everything you could want in a prospect: A high upside, a high floor and a fantasy-friendly ETA (even more so post-contract extension). If it all clicks, we're looking at a bonafide OF1 capable of contributing substantially across all five categories. But even if Robert's hit tool fails to fully actualize, he's got enough power and speed to serve as a fine OF3. Congrats if you bought in on the hype way back when; it looks justified.

★ ★ ★ *2020 Top 101 Prospect* **#13** ★ ★ ★

2   Nick Madrigal   2B   OFP: 70   ETA: 2020

Born: 03/05/97   Age: 23   Bats: R   Throws: R   Height: 5'7"   Weight: 165   Origin: Round 1, 2018 Draft (#4 overall)

YEAR	TEAM	LVL	AGE	PA	R	2B	3B	HR	RBI	BB	K	SB	CS	AVG/OBP/SLG	DRC+	VORP	BABIP	BRR	FRAA	WARP	PF
2018	KAN	A	21	49	9	3	0	0	6	1	0	2	2	.341/.347/.409	145	5.3	.319	1.1	2B(12) 0.9	0.6	97
2018	WNS	A+	21	107	14	4	0	0	9	5	5	6	3	.306/.355/.347	121	2.7	.319	0.0	2B(25) -1.8	0.3	103
2019	WNS	A+	22	218	20	10	2	2	27	17	6	17	4	.272/.346/.377	114	11.5	.269	3.6	2B(41) 3.4	1.6	106
2019	BIR	AA	22	180	30	11	2	1	16	14	5	14	6	.341/.400/.451	154	14.0	.348	0.3	2B(39) 0.1	1.6	103
2019	CHR	AAA	22	134	26	6	1	1	12	13	5	4	3	.331/.398/.424	103	6.0	.336	0.5	2B(27) 1.5	0.6	112
2020	CHA	MLB	23	420	39	20	1	6	38	26	29	12	6	.259/.315/.359	82	2.0	.268	0.2	2B 2	1.0	100

Comparables: Kevin Newman, Dixon Machado, Steve Clevenger

The Report: Madrigal has extreme, extreme bat-to-ball ability, essentially off the charts; he struck out a grand total of 16 times across 532 plate appearances this season. He doesn't do that by constantly hacking away at bad pitches either, like Willians Astudillo has, and Astudillo is the only other current affiliated player who has demonstrated this level of contact ability. Madrigal's walk and swing rates are more or less normal. He just doesn't miss when he swings, and it doesn't lead to off-balance or poor contact.

What Madrigal doesn't do yet is hit the ball consistently hard. He has below-average raw, and he's yet to attempt the trade-off to even get to that in games. His offensive game is to shoot the ball between the defense, not over it, and that's unusual for today's game of optimized launch angles and focus on exit velocity. He will provide secondary value with his defense (he's quite good at second base, and the White Sox have made prior noise about trying him at short) and speed (plus-plus, and he uses it well on the basepaths). But we can't project him for much more than 40 game power, and he's not even there yet.

So what should you make of all this? We see an outlier profile with a good shot for a batting average that is consistently starting with 3 and carries the rest of the profile. If you're a little less sanguine about his ability to hit 'em where they ain't, that's going to be closer to a David Eckstein or late-career Marco Scutaro offensive profile, but that isn't so bad either.

Variance: Low, although the fair over/under on batting crowns is probably more like 0.5 on his median outcome. He's one of the highest floor prospects in the game, an unusually safe bet to be at least a decent regular because of his already existent contact/defense/speed.

Ben Carsley's Fantasy Take: Only 21 batters stole 20 or more bases last season, and only 10 of those batters had infield eligibility. Only 19 (qualified) batters hit above .300 last season, and only 11 of them had infield eligibility. Madrigal lacks pop, it's true, but he's a genuine threat to hit .300 with 25-plus steals on a regular basis, and he could score a ton of runs, too. There's some slight Fancy Dog Jose Peraza risk in the profile, but there's a better chance that Madrigal is the spiritual successor to some of those early day Elvis Andrus stat lines. He's an easy top-20 dynasty prospect.

★ ★ ★ *2020 Top 101 Prospect* **#20** ★ ★ ★

3   Michael Kopech   RHP   OFP: 70   ETA: 2018

Born: 04/30/96   Age: 24   Bats: R   Throws: R   Height: 6'3"   Weight: 205   Origin: Round 1, 2014 Draft (#33 overall)

YEAR	TEAM	LVL	AGE	W	L	SV	G	GS	IP	H	HR	BB/9	K/9	K	GB%	BABIP	WHIP	ERA	DRA	WARP	PF
2017	BIR	AA	21	8	7	0	22	22	119¹	77	6	4.5	11.7	155	42%	.272	1.15	2.87	3.15	2.9	97
2017	CHR	AAA	21	1	1	0	3	3	15	15	0	3.0	10.2	17	35%	.375	1.33	3.00	4.18	0.3	96
2018	CHR	AAA	22	7	7	0	24	24	126¹	101	9	4.3	12.1	170	40%	.316	1.27	3.70	3.75	2.6	104
2018	CHA	MLB	22	1	1	0	4	4	14¹	20	4	1.3	9.4	15	28%	.381	1.53	5.02	6.84	-0.3	103
2020	CHA	MLB	24	5	6	0	40	13	91	97	20	4.2	7.8	78	36%	.294	1.55	6.02	5.78	-0.3	100

Comparables: Tyler Glasnow, Eric Hurley, Logan Allen

The Report: As expected, Kopech missed the entire year recovering from Tommy John surgery. Steve Givarz saw him rehabbing in instructs in the fall, and he was sitting 97-98 and touched 101. So, basically, he looked like Michael Kopech. He's expected to have a relatively normal spring and should be a rotation factor again during the first half.

When healthy, Kopech sits in the mid-to-high-90s with his fastball and regularly touches triple-digits; he hit 105 mph on a Boston charting gun in 2016, and he's said his goal is to hit 107. His best offspeed pitch is a nasty, wipeout slider in the low-to-mid-80s. That pitch has sharp, two-plane break, and it's a true swing-and-miss pitch and a potential plus-plus offering. He also supplements with a changeup that was improving to more of a true third pitch from a prior show-me level, and flashes a nice slower curve from time to time.

Kopech has battled significant bouts of wildness in the past, and at times has dialed his stuff a bit back to get better command and control. Steve noted in his instructs look that Kopech's command wasn't all the way back yet, and that's going to be a key storyline to follow with him early in the season.

Variance: Medium. Kopech was in the majors when he got hurt and is generally pretty fully-formed. The wildness and Tommy John do add a dash of relief risk, although he'd be a monster there.

Ben Carsley's Fantasy Take: This system is fun. I have long served as the BP Fantasy Team's resident Kopech apologist, and I'm not jumping off the bandwagon now. Few if any arms in the minors can match Kopech's pure strikeout potential, and he should see significant MLB time in 2020. The catch of course is that Kopech is likely to take in WHIP what he gives in Ks, and there's still enough command/control risk that he could end up a reliever. My personal bet is that Kopech reigns it in just enough to serve as a (Tampa Bay Rays) Chris Archer-esque fantasy SP3 who provides you with 200-plus strikeouts. That makes him a top-30ish fantasy prospect in my book, but if you're lower on him you're not crazy.

★ ★ ★ *2020 Top 101 Prospect* **#31** ★ ★ ★

4 Andrew Vaughn 1B   OFP: 60   ETA: 2021
Born: 04/03/98   Age: 22   Bats: R   Throws: R   Height: 6'0"   Weight: 214   Origin: Round 1, 2019 Draft (#3 overall)

YEAR	TEAM	LVL	AGE	PA	R	2B	3B	HR	RBI	BB	K	SB	CS	AVG/OBP/SLG	DRC+	VORP	BABIP	BRR	FRAA	WARP	PF
2019	KAN	A	21	103	14	7	0	2	11	14	18	0	0	.253/.388/.410	137	6.0	.297	1.2	1B(19) -0.5	0.6	99
2019	WNS	A+	21	126	16	8	0	3	21	16	17	0	1	.252/.349/.411	140	6.0	.270	-0.3	1B(15) -0.3	0.5	109
2020	CHA	MLB	22	251	24	13	0	6	26	19	56	3	1	.223/.295/.360	75	1.0	.271	0.0	1B -2	-0.1	100

Comparables: Ty France, Mike Ford, Patrick Wisdom

The Report: Vaughn isn't the most viscerally thrilling of top five picks, but he is a pretty safe bet to be a productive if unglamourous big leaguer. He didn't have a particularly strong professional debut, but this is understandable. Asked to jump into full-season ball almost immediately after the conclusion of his college campaign, the 21-year-old was saddled with big expectations and asked to make big adjustments on the fly while presumably dealing with some level of fatigue. His tools at the plate were apparent anyway, led by excellent discipline that doesn't waver when he slumps and allows him to limit swing-and-miss while zeroing in on pitches in particular zones where he does damage. Pair this with his barrel control and you have a plus hit tool with low strikeout rates and a lot of hard contact. The power is also plus, driven by a quick bat and strength that is easily visible in both the upper and lower halves. He's fine at first but won't add a lot of value with his defense.

Variance: Low. Offensive game is well-developed, just needs to prove it at the upper levels.

Ben Carsley's Fantasy Take: Yes, Vaughn is a first base prospect, but he's easily the best one in the minors, and his combination of floor, ETA, and reasonable ceiling make him a very strong fantasy asset. We have Vaughn as the best player available in first-year supplemental drafts—ahead even of Adley Rutschman, because catchers are weird—as well as a top-10 overall fantasy prospect. I know—I was surprised when I saw the rankings, too—but the more you hear about Vaughn's bat, the more you understand it. Don't overthink this one; pursue Vaughn aggressively wherever you can.

5 Jonathan Stiever RHP   OFP: 55   ETA: 2021
Born: 05/12/97   Age: 23   Bats: R   Throws: R   Height: 6'2"   Weight: 205   Origin: Round 5, 2018 Draft (#138 overall)

YEAR	TEAM	LVL	AGE	W	L	SV	G	GS	IP	H	HR	BB/9	K/9	K	GB%	BABIP	WHIP	ERA	DRA	WARP	PF
2018	GRF	RK	21	0	1	0	13	13	28	23	3	2.9	12.5	39	48%	.323	1.14	4.18	2.71	1.0	101
2019	KAN	A	22	4	6	0	14	14	74	88	10	1.7	9.4	77	46%	.361	1.38	4.74	6.02	-0.7	98
2019	WNS	A+	22	6	4	0	12	12	71	56	7	1.6	9.8	77	41%	.278	0.97	2.15	3.11	1.7	110
2020	CHA	MLB	23	2	2	0	33	0	35	36	6	3.4	8.2	32	41%	.297	1.40	4.82	4.97	0.1	100

Comparables: Trent Thornton, Felix Jorge, Jordan Smith

The Report: A fifth-rounder from a cold-weather state, Stiever began his professional career slowly but caused a lot of antennae to fly up with an excellent three months or so in the Carolina League following a June promotion. The Hoosier dominated High-A hitters with a plus fastball that explodes up in the zone and gets some sink down, sitting a lively 95 and topping out at 97. The curve is a potential plus pitch as well, a powerful offering in the low-to-mid 80s. This pitch is best when he hits a particular sweet spot of velocity and movement; he can get both horizontal and lateral movement on the pitch, with about a 10-4 break and sharp downward action paired with slider-like glove-side cut. He'll also throw a change-of-pace curve in the mid-70s and a decent mid-80s change, and he would do well to make the latter more prominent in his arsenal. He's a joy to watch, outwardly competitive and a great athlete with a sound delivery that portends future strides in fastball command.

Variance: Medium. Has many of the characteristics of a mid-rotation starter or possibly even a No. 2, but at present he is essentially a two-pitch pitcher whose command is a work in progress.

Ben Carsley's Fantasy Take: And now the fun ends. Stiever is a nice filler prospect for those of you in deeper leagues, as he has reasonable upside and pretty much no name value right now. That being said, he's still just somewhere in the giant glut of potential fantasy SP5/6 prospects who need a third pitch, better command, or both. Don't consider biting unless your league rosters around 200 dudes.

6 Dane Dunning RHP   OFP: 55   ETA: Late 2020

Born: 12/20/94   Age: 25   Bats: R   Throws: R   Height: 6'4"   Weight: 200   Origin: Round 1, 2016 Draft (#29 overall)

YEAR	TEAM	LVL	AGE	W	L	SV	G	GS	IP	H	HR	BB/9	K/9	K	GB%	BABIP	WHIP	ERA	DRA	WARP	PF
2017	KAN	A	22	2	0	0	4	4	26	13	0	0.7	11.4	33	64%	.224	0.58	0.35	1.74	1.1	108
2017	WNS	A+	22	6	8	0	22	22	118	114	15	2.7	10.3	135	52%	.316	1.27	3.51	4.30	1.3	105
2018	WNS	A+	23	1	1	0	4	4	24^1	20	2	1.1	11.5	31	61%	.300	0.95	2.59	3.20	0.6	103
2018	BIR	AA	23	5	2	0	11	11	62	57	0	3.3	10.0	69	49%	.343	1.29	2.76	4.55	0.6	93
2020	CHA	MLB	25	2	1	0	14	3	26	25	4	3.4	8.9	26	44%	.297	1.35	4.46	4.65	0.2	100

Comparables: Tyler Wilson, Kendry Flores, Rogelio Armenteros

The Report: Dunning was one of last spring's Tommy John blowouts after missing time at the end of 2018 with arm problems. He's going to be behind Kopech on his rehab schedule, but he's throwing off a mound already and should be back in game action at some point in 2020, barring setbacks. He was knocking on the door of the majors before going down, so if he comes back early and at full strength, he could be up quickly.

Before going down, Dunning had established himself as a four-pitch, back of the 101-quality mid-rotation starting prospect. His fastball is in the low-90s, which is close to average velocity these days, but has heavy sink and run. That movement, along with plus command, cause the pitch to play up from its velocity a bit. Dunning throws two breaking balls: A hard, nearly-cutterish slider that has a shot to get to plus, and a big bendy curveball that should settle in at average or a touch above. He also mixes in a changeup that flashes, but needs improvement.

Variance: Medium. Tommy John rehab is a risk factor, and he's going to be returning as 25-year-old with a total of 62 innings in the high-minors, but Dunning is relatively "safe" as mid-rotation prospects go.

Ben Carsley's Fantasy Take: See Stiever, Jon, but factor in that Dunning has some more name value since he's been around longer. If someone (reasonably) cut bait after his Tommy John, feel free to re-add him if you're in a TDGX-sized (200-plus prospects) league. Just don't expect front-end SP production.

7 Luis Alexander Basabe OF   OFP: 50   ETA: 2020/21

Born: 08/26/96   Age: 23   Bats: B   Throws: R   Height: 6'0"   Weight: 160   Origin: International Free Agent, 2012

YEAR	TEAM	LVL	AGE	PA	R	2B	3B	HR	RBI	BB	K	SB	CS	AVG/OBP/SLG	DRC+	VORP	BABIP	BRR	FRAA	WARP	PF
2017	WNS	A+	20	435	52	12	5	5	36	49	104	17	6	.221/.320/.320	85	9.6	.292	4.4	CF(92) 0.1, RF(12) -0.4	1.1	104
2018	WNS	A+	21	245	36	12	5	9	30	34	64	7	8	.266/.370/.502	144	19.7	.341	-2.0	CF(28) 2.2, LF(16) 1.5	2.0	103
2018	BIR	AA	21	270	41	9	3	6	26	30	76	9	4	.251/.340/.394	108	13.3	.344	2.1	CF(42) -1.9, RF(15) 0.3	1.1	92
2019	BIR	AA	22	291	31	12	1	3	30	29	85	9	4	.246/.324/.336	92	3.3	.355	1.4	CF(25) 0.3, LF(22) -2.7	0.6	100
2020	CHA	MLB	23	105	11	4	1	3	12	9	35	2	1	.217/.286/.370	71	0.0	.308	0.2	LF 0, CF 0	0.0	100

Comparables: Daniel Fields, Lewis Brinson, Jeimer Candelario

The Report: We are still waiting for Basabe to put it all together, and that's beginning to become a problem. To be fair, injuries have plagued his pro career. Last year, a broken hamate in spring training and a quad injury in June limited him to just 75 games. At a certain point—perhaps right around when you turn 23 or so—those patterns of injuries start to become "durability concerns." And yes, hamate injuries tend to sap power, which would explain some of why Basabe only hit three home runs in a half-season in Birmingham despite above-average raw power, but in total he's hit .248/.345/.392 across 130 Double-A games. He'll be 24 next year and projection only takes you so far now.

The thing is, the underlying prospect still looks pretty good. Basabe offers bat speed from both sides of the plate, although an aggressive approach undermines him too often. There's power potential from the left side, although he can get longer to tap into it, while his right-handed swing shoots the gaps more. He continues to see time at all three outfield spots, but should have enough foot speed for center and enough arm for right. The whole package looks more like a good fourth outfielder now—which was the risk with the profile going back to his Red Sox days—but you can still squint and blame the injuries some and see a starter if you'd like. At least for one more year.

Variance: High. Basabe may just not hit enough for anything more than an extra bench outfielder role. The injuries have sapped the tools a bit at this point as well. But then he will have games where he looks like a sure shot outfield starter, so you keep squinting to see it during the IL stints and bad weeks.

Ben Carsley's Fantasy Take: I'm about ready to hop off the Basabe bandwagon, which probably means he's about to turn into Mike Trout. The lack of power doesn't concern me given his hamate injury. I'm more worried about Basabe's hit tool, and in total the upside here just isn't high enough to justify the risk. He's close enough that he's arguably still worth rostering if you keep 200-250 prospects, but I'd also be fine cutting bait. It's hard to see him as more than a fourth or fifth outfielder at this point.

8   Zack Collins   C   OFP: 45   ETA: 2019

Born: 02/06/95   Age: 25   Bats: L   Throws: R   Height: 6'3"   Weight: 220   Origin: Round 1, 2016 Draft (#10 overall)

YEAR	TEAM	LVL	AGE	PA	R	2B	3B	HR	RBI	BB	K	SB	CS	AVG/OBP/SLG	DRC+	VORP	BABIP	BRR	FRAA	WARP	PF
2017	WNS	A+	22	426	63	18	3	17	48	76	118	0	2	.223/.365/.443	119	21.9	.282	-2.6	C(76) 1.5	2.4	104
2017	BIR	AA	22	45	7	2	0	2	5	11	11	0	0	.235/.422/.471	164	4.7	.286	-0.1	C(11) -2.4	0.2	95
2018	BIR	AA	23	531	58	24	1	15	68	101	158	5	0	.234/.382/.404	126	33.7	.329	-3.2	C(74) -14.4	1.5	94
2019	CHR	AAA	24	367	56	19	1	19	74	62	98	0	0	.282/.403/.548	134	27.1	.346	0.8	C(50) -4.6, 1B(19) -1.6	2.1	110
2019	CHA	MLB	24	102	10	3	1	3	12	14	39	0	0	.186/.307/.349	79	0.3	.295	0.0	C(10) -3.0, 1B(1) -0.1	-0.3	101
2020	CHA	MLB	25	140	16	6	0	6	17	19	48	0	0	.209/.320/.397	88	1.0	.295	-0.3	1B -1, C -1	-0.1	100

Comparables: Will Smith, Ryan O'Hearn, Derek Norris

The Report: As his 2019 Annual comment suggests, Collins came around about a decade too late to be a top catching prospect. In another era he'd be ranked with the Jeff Clements and J.P. Arenecibias of the prospect world. Power hitters with plus arms, not much else to catching, right? Collins' power is real, and although the rabbit ball certainly helped him, he's always had plus raw power and enough of an idea what he could pull 400 feet to get to it in games. There's stiffness and bat wrap as well though, meaning strikeouts come in bunches, but if he could stick behind the plate and hit .230 or .240 or so, he'd be a viable starter given how low the bar for catcher offense is.

The bar for catcher defense however, has changed a lot since the mid-2000s. Even coming out of college, the grade on Collins glove was—to put it kindly—"needs improvement." He's a big lad, and a stiff receiver at best. His CSAA rate stat in the majors—in an admittedly small sample—was bottom 10 among the 113 catchers in baseball last year. His Triple-A numbers were not much better. He spent more time at first base and DH in the majors than he did behind the plate, and he might be best suited as a Sunday backup who you can start elsewhere during the week.

Variance: Low. Collins' bat is as ready for the majors as it will ever be, although his first go-round featured a fair bit of flailing at stuff on the outer half. He also might be the one player in baseball who would be helped the most by an automated strike zone, although that may come too late to help him stick behind the plate.

Ben Carsley's Fantasy Take: I told you to stay away from catching prospects. Stay away from catching prospects.

9 Gavin Sheets 1B   OFP: 50   ETA: 2020/21

Born: 04/23/96   Age: 24   Bats: L   Throws: L   Height: 6'4"   Weight: 230   Origin: Round 2, 2017 Draft (#49 overall)

YEAR	TEAM	LVL	AGE	PA	R	2B	3B	HR	RBI	BB	K	SB	CS	AVG/OBP/SLG	DRC+	VORP	BABIP	BRR	FRAA	WARP	PF
2017	KAN	A	21	218	16	10	0	3	25	20	34	0	0	.266/.346/.365	112	2.1	.308	-2.4	1B(50) -2.1	0.0	102
2018	WNS	A+	22	497	58	28	2	6	61	52	81	1	0	.293/.368/.407	134	10.5	.344	-3.9	1B(108) -4.3	1.4	104
2019	BIR	AA	23	527	56	18	1	16	83	54	99	3	1	.267/.345/.414	129	10.4	.305	-6.3	1B(109) 3.8	1.9	100
2020	CHA	MLB	24	251	26	12	0	8	29	20	58	0	0	.249/.314/.402	89	1.0	.303	-0.5	1B 0	0.5	100

Comparables: Russ Canzler, Matt Thaiss, David Cooper

The Report: Sheets has maintained a slow but steady climb up the organizational ladder since he was a second-round pick in 2017. He finally showed positionally appropriate game pop in Double-A, which is a positive sign. He has the strength and physicality for 20 home runs in the majors despite keeping everything relatively quiet and compact through the zone for a hitter of his size. Sheets does tend to get pull-happy and doesn't lift the ball as consistently as you'd like to feel confident in a plus power projection, and it's more likely to play merely above-average. The hit tool is average-ish due to the aforementioned propensity to try and pull everything to right field, and some issues with spin generally. There isn't anything particularly positive or negative to say about his first base defense. He moves well for a dude with a XXL frame, and shows good hands in the field and on scoops.

Variance: Medium. There's not so much game power in here that he can survive seeing the hit tool diminished against better arms, and he was merely fine, not spectacular against Double-A ones.

Ben Carsley's Fantasy Take: I will never be free of this pain.

10 Lenyn Sosa SS   OFP: 50   ETA: 2022

Born: 01/25/00   Age: 20   Bats: R   Throws: R   Height: 6'0"   Weight: 180   Origin: International Free Agent, 2016

YEAR	TEAM	LVL	AGE	PA	R	2B	3B	HR	RBI	BB	K	SB	CS	AVG/OBP/SLG	DRC+	VORP	BABIP	BRR	FRAA	WARP	PF
2017	WSX	RK	17	180	19	4	2	2	23	14	24	3	4	.270/.330/.358	100	6.6	.304	-0.1	SS(22) 1.0, 2B(20) 8.0	1.5	96
2018	GRF	RK	18	291	44	13	3	4	35	7	36	2	2	.293/.317/.406	105	13.0	.322	-0.6	SS(49) -5.2, 3B(13) -1.1	0.0	103
2019	KAN	A	19	536	72	35	2	7	51	27	102	6	6	.251/.292/.371	110	24.3	.301	-0.1	SS(116) 12.8, 2B(3) -0.3	4.1	97
2020	CHA	MLB	20	251	21	12	1	4	23	16	58	1	0	.228/.280/.337	63	0.0	.287	0.0	SS 2, 2B 0	-0.1	100

The Report: Sosa has generated some hype in White Sox prospect fan circles over the last year or so, and the reasons for this are understandable enough. He has a name that rolls off the tongue and is easily memorable, and he has the look of a type of high-upside youth that the Sox haven't quite filled lists with in recent years. It might surprise some to hear it, but the main question in the profile is probably how high this upside actually is. The 20-year-old isn't really physically projectible, standing at about 6-foot and listed at a mostly filled-out 180 lbs. His game doesn't really have glaring weaknesses. He's very sound at short with the range, hands, action and arm to cover the rest of the diamond. He's a pretty good contact hitter who can adjust to different pitch types, fast and breaking. The bat speed is fine and he has some pop. I wouldn't be concerned with the pedestrian production considering age and level but I'd like to see one or two of these skills develop into a carrying tool, and this is far from a guarantee.

Variance: High. There is a lot that needs to happen here but he's still very young.

Ben Carsley's Fantasy Take: Too far away and with too meh of a ceiling (industry term) to be of interest to us. Add him to your watch list if you must.

The Next Ten

11 Andrew Dalquist RHP

Born: 11/13/00   Age: 19   Bats: R   Throws: R   Height: 6'1"   Weight: 175   Origin: Round 3, 2019 Draft (#81 overall)

12 Matthew Thompson RHP

Born: 08/11/00 Age: 19 Bats: R Throws: R Height: 6'3" Weight: 195 Origin: Round 2, 2019 Draft (#45 overall)

Take your pick of projectable prep arms. The White Sox took them a round apart and gave both around $2 million to sign. We prefer Dalquist—the third-round pick—a smidge more at present due to his combination of present stuff and future projection. He already shows average fastball velocity, and will flash good two-seam run on the pitch. It's not hard to see a 55 or better pitch as he fills out and adds strength. The curveball is the best present secondary. Dalquist has advanced feel for the mid-70s breaker although he can snap it off at times. He also shows a slider and changeup. The delivery is uptempo with a bit of late effort, but it shouldn't be hard to smooth out if he stays a starter.

Thompson is a tall, high-waisted, athletic Texas prep arm right out of central casting. He's at times shown a bit more velocity than Dalquist, and he's got big arm speed, but his radar readings have been more inconsistent as an amateur. He offers the same four-pitch mix, but neither breaker is as advanced as Dalquist's curve, although both have the potential to be above-average. There's a bit more torque and head whack in the delivery when he's ramping up on the fastball, so there's a bit more command and reliever risk here.

Both pitchers made brief pro cameos in the complex and are conservatively four years away from the bigs. It's perhaps a bit of a punt to cast them both as potential No. 3 or 4 starters or late inning relievers, as their profiles will no doubt ebb and flow over the balance of the half-decade. Pitches will improve, injuries will happen, sands will pass through the hourglass, but that's where we are for this particular snapshot in time.

13 Luis González OF

Born: 09/10/95 Age: 24 Bats: L Throws: L Height: 6'1" Weight: 195 Origin: Round 3, 2017 Draft (#87 overall)

YEAR	TEAM	LVL	AGE	PA	R	2B	3B	HR	RBI	BB	K	SB	CS	AVG/OBP/SLG	DRC+	VORP	BABIP	BRR	FRAA	WARP	PF
2017	KAN	A	21	277	26	13	4	2	12	38	50	2	3	.245/.356/.361	116	10.9	.302	-0.2	CF(31) -2.9, LF(18) -0.1	0.8	101
2018	KAN	A	22	255	35	16	2	8	26	21	57	7	2	.300/.358/.491	147	19.8	.365	-0.6	CF(39) -1.0, RF(13) -1.9	1.6	96
2018	WNS	A+	22	288	50	24	3	6	45	27	46	3	5	.313/.376/.504	150	26.8	.354	5.8	CF(31) 3.9, LF(14) 0.2	3.1	104
2019	BIR	AA	23	535	63	18	4	9	59	47	89	17	9	.247/.316/.359	103	13.0	.281	1.0	CF(60) 0.7, RF(29) 1.1	2.1	100
2020	CHA	MLB	24	251	24	12	1	6	27	18	57	1	1	.234/.293/.380	77	0.0	.285	-0.3	CF 1, RF 0	0.4	100

Comparables: Gary Brown, Danny Ortiz, Lane Adams

González struggled a bit with the jump to Double-A after a minor breakout in 2018. The profile remains broadly the same. Despite a bit of a noisy set-up and double toe tap, González makes a decent amount of contact from the left side with gap power. The swing plane is fairly flat, and can be geared for all-fields contact, so the game power is likely to top out in the low double-digits. He's an average runner, perhaps a tick above, and has experience at all three outfield spots, and often played center last year over both Basabe and Blake Rutherford. He's passable there for now, but there remain a lot of tweener/fourth outfield profile markers here.

14 Jimmy Lambert LHP

Born: 11/18/94 Age: 25 Bats: R Throws: R Height: 6'2" Weight: 190 Origin: Round 5, 2016 Draft (#146 overall)

YEAR	TEAM	LVL	AGE	W	L	SV	G	GS	IP	H	HR	BB/9	K/9	K	GB%	BABIP	WHIP	ERA	DRA	WARP	PF
2017	KAN	A	22	7	2	0	12	12	74	77	1	1.3	5.2	43	57%	.315	1.19	2.19	4.78	0.4	100
2017	WNS	A+	22	5	4	0	14	14	76	86	10	3.4	7.0	59	50%	.326	1.51	5.45	6.08	-0.7	106
2018	WNS	A+	23	5	7	0	13	13	70²	57	5	2.7	10.2	80	46%	.292	1.10	3.95	3.67	1.4	103
2018	BIR	AA	23	3	1	0	5	5	25	20	2	2.2	10.8	30	40%	.286	1.04	2.88	3.07	0.7	94
2019	BIR	AA	24	3	4	0	11	11	59¹	62	11	4.1	10.6	70	38%	.338	1.50	4.55	5.57	-0.4	99
2020	CHA	MLB	25	2	2	0	33	0	35	35	6	3.4	8.8	34	38%	.299	1.38	4.65	4.83	0.1	100

Comparables: Dylan Covey, Brandon Woodruff, Travis Lakins

Lambert looked to continue his 2018 breakout into 2019, and despite the velocity dipping back into the low-90s, he got off to a strong start in Double-A mixing in his above-average curve and average change. Toward the end of May he started to lose the strike zone and give up some bombs, and then came the dreaded discovery of a UCL tear. Lambert had Tommy John surgery in the summer and will likely miss all of 2020 as well. He will be 26 before he throws another pitch, but the potential four-pitch mix here remains intriguing—if backend starterish—assuming a normal rehab.

15   Yolbert Sanchez   SS

Born: 03/03/97   Age: 23   Bats: R   Throws: R   Height: 5'11"   Weight: 176   Origin: International Free Agent, 2019

Signed out of Cuba last July for $2.5 million, Sanchez is already 22 and has three seasons under his belt in Serie Nacional. Far from a tools monster, Sanchez is a polished contact hitter with a potential plus shortstop glove. There's almost no power in the profile, so how well the bat translates to professional pitching in the minors will dictate whether he's more of a defensive specialist bench piece or a potential everyday player at the 6. Sanchez only played in the DSL last summer—likely for tax purposes—but 2020 should clear up some things with regards to his future projection.

16   Micker Adolfo   OF

Born: 09/11/96   Age: 23   Bats: R   Throws: R   Height: 6'4"   Weight: 255   Origin: International Free Agent, 2013

YEAR	TEAM	LVL	AGE	PA	R	2B	3B	HR	RBI	BB	K	SB	CS	AVG/OBP/SLG	DRC+	VORP	BABIP	BRR	FRAA	WARP	PF
2017	KAN	A	20	473	60	28	2	16	68	31	149	2	0	.264/.331/.453	117	16.8	.366	-4.1	RF(102) -12.1	0.0	100
2018	WNS	A+	21	336	48	18	1	11	50	34	92	2	1	.282/.369/.464	140	14.6	.372	-1.5		1.6	104
2019	WSX	RK	22	58	8	5	0	2	3	7	21	0	0	.260/.362/.480	86	-0.2	.407	-3.1		-0.3	103
2019	BIR	AA	22	95	5	7	0	0	9	14	36	0	3	.205/.337/.295	95	-2.7	.372	-3.3		-0.3	96
2020	CHA	MLB	23	251	24	13	0	8	28	18	107	1	0	.213/.280/.374	71	0.0	.360	-0.5	RF -5	-0.6	100

Comparables: Trayce Thompson, Steven Moya, Michael Chavis

As a remix of all the pitchers in this organization coming off Tommy John surgery, here's a hitter coming off the surgery. Elbow damage has marred Adolfo's last two seasons. He suffered a partial UCL tear early in 2018 spring training, which limited him to DH duties until he underwent surgery late that summer. He was DHing again in Double-A this April when he went down with complications in his elbow that kept him out until complex action in August. He did show up in the Arizona Fall League and finally played some outfield, which is a good sign. Adolfo has absolutely massive raw power and has a crazy athletic frame, so there remains a lot to dream on here. But he's struggled to get to all of his raw into games because of persistent swing-and-miss problems, and missing as much developmental time as he has missed presents a big hurdle. At the very least, he might be an awful lot of fun in Triple-A if the rocket ball remains.

17   Bryce Bush   3B/OF

Born: 12/14/99   Age: 20   Bats: R   Throws: R   Height: 6'0"   Weight: 200   Origin: Round 33, 2018 Draft (#978 overall)

YEAR	TEAM	LVL	AGE	PA	R	2B	3B	HR	RBI	BB	K	SB	CS	AVG/OBP/SLG	DRC+	VORP	BABIP	BRR	FRAA	WARP	PF
2018	WSX	RK	18	52	8	4	0	1	8	8	4	1	2	.442/.538/.605	228	10.4	.474	0.4	3B(12) 2.3	1.0	101
2018	GRF	RK	18	108	16	5	1	2	10	10	21	3	0	.250/.327/.385	73	4.4	.301	1.0	3B(18) -2.1	-0.3	102
2019	KAN	A	19	288	29	12	5	5	33	27	92	4	1	.201/.285/.346	89	1.8	.288	0.5	RF(33) -2.2, 3B(10) -1.4	-0.1	98
2020	CHA	MLB	20	251	21	11	1	5	23	18	86	1	0	.198/.263/.323	53	3.0	.292	0.0	3B 0, RF 0	-0.7	100

Bush wasn't expected to sign as a 33th-round pick in the 2018 draft, but the White Sox offered him Day 2 money and bought him out of his college commitment to Mississippi State. The results have been mixed so far, although the South Atlantic League was an aggressive assignment for Bush in his first full pro season. The raw power and bat speed are still obvious, but he's moved off third base—not unexpectedly—to right field. The tools profile is a better fit there, but he struggled with full-season spin, and a bout of bronchitis kept him off the field most of the summer. There was always going to be a long developmental window with Bush, but the overall forecast of his bat remains a bit cloudier than you'd like after 2019.

18 Bernardo Flores LHP

Born: 08/23/95   Age: 24   Bats: L   Throws: L   Height: 6'2"   Weight: 190   Origin: Round 7, 2016 Draft (#206 overall)

YEAR	TEAM	LVL	AGE	W	L	SV	G	GS	IP	H	HR	BB/9	K/9	K	GB%	BABIP	WHIP	ERA	DRA	WARP	PF
2017	KAN	A	21	8	4	0	14	14	78	73	5	1.5	8.1	70	50%	.308	1.10	3.00	4.16	1.0	97
2017	WNS	A+	21	2	3	0	9	9	40¹	43	5	4.2	7.4	33	41%	.309	1.54	4.24	5.44	-0.1	101
2018	WNS	A+	22	5	4	0	12	12	77²	75	5	2.0	6.7	58	56%	.294	1.18	2.55	4.43	0.8	104
2018	BIR	AA	22	3	5	0	13	13	78¹	79	5	1.6	5.4	47	52%	.301	1.19	2.76	4.80	0.5	93
2019	WSX	RK	23	0	0	0	4	4	12	17	2	0.8	9.8	13	54%	.455	1.50	3.75	5.77	0.0	109
2019	BIR	AA	23	3	8	0	15	15	78¹	74	10	1.7	7.9	69	55%	.282	1.14	3.33	4.40	0.5	98
2020	CHA	MLB	24	2	1	0	14	3	26	25	5	3.3	6.6	19	49%	.271	1.35	4.47	4.69	0.2	100

Comparables: Jayson Aquino, Jarlin García, Josh Rogers

Either side of a mid-season oblique injury, Flores kept on puttering through the minors mixing his pitches and keeping baseballs off the fat part of the bat. A solidly built lefty with an uptempo delivery with a bit of funk, he pounds both sides of the plate with a low-90s fastball that he uses to set up his array of secondaries. The changeup is his best offspeed pitch, with 10+ mph of velocity separation and arm speed that sells it as the fastball. He can steal a strike with his humpy, low-70s curve and a short, cutterish slider offers a different breaking ball look to lefties. Nothing here grades out all that better than average, and Flores has been consistently old for his levels, but he's a durable, useful utility arm who could fit in a bunch of different roles on a modern major-league staff most likely as a bulk innings guy or swingman.

19 Konnor Pilkington LHP

Born: 09/12/97   Age: 22   Bats: L   Throws: L   Height: 6'3"   Weight: 225   Origin: Round 3, 2018 Draft (#81 overall)

YEAR	TEAM	LVL	AGE	W	L	SV	G	GS	IP	H	HR	BB/9	K/9	K	GB%	BABIP	WHIP	ERA	DRA	WARP	PF
2018	GRF	RK	20	0	1	0	6	6	12	14	1	3.0	6.8	9	52%	.333	1.50	5.25	4.25	0.2	103
2019	KAN	A	21	1	0	0	6	6	33¹	15	2	3.0	11.3	42	35%	.186	0.78	1.62	2.18	1.2	100
2019	WNS	A+	21	4	9	0	19	19	95²	99	7	3.7	9.0	96	38%	.341	1.44	4.99	5.69	-0.8	108
2020	CHA	MLB	22	2	2	0	33	0	35	35	5	4.1	7.9	31	35%	.296	1.46	4.89	4.98	0.1	100

Comparables: Ranger Suárez, Henry Sosa, Jayson Aquino

A third-rounder in 2018 out of Mississippi State, Pilkington was known early in his collegiate career for a mid-90s heater that he could pair with decent secondaries. The stuff has backed up since then, and his reputation as a prospect has ebbed significantly throughout his pro career. The 22-year-old dominated Low-A Kannapolis early this season but struggled after a promotion to High-A Winston-Salem. Currently sitting around 88-91 and flashing occasional run and sink, the fastball gets hit when it is not located precisely and will require a command bump if it is to be effective against hitters at the higher levels. The curve is interesting, ranging from the mid-70s to the mid-80s and showing varying types of break. The pitch comes in around 10-4 or 11-5 on the lower end and is almost a distinct offering in the upper velo bands, featuring short cutter-like movement that could turn it into a weapon against opposite-hand hitters. The change is fine and has a bit of split-action, but nothing that will propel his arsenal to another level. With command refinements he might be able to make it as a back-end starter, but the lack of any premium ingredients makes Pilkington a risky proposition.

20 Blake Rutherford OF

Born: 05/02/97   Age: 23   Bats: L   Throws: R   Height: 6'2"   Weight: 210   Origin: Round 1, 2016 Draft (#18 overall)

YEAR	TEAM	LVL	AGE	PA	R	2B	3B	HR	RBI	BB	K	SB	CS	AVG/OBP/SLG	DRC+	VORP	BABIP	BRR	FRAA	WARP	PF
2017	CSC	A	20	304	41	20	2	2	30	25	55	9	4	.281/.342/.391	98	10.8	.341	-2.6	CF(39) -5.6, LF(13) -0.5	-0.3	96
2017	KAN	A	20	136	11	5	0	0	5	13	21	1	0	.213/.289/.254	98	-4.9	.257	-0.1	CF(13) -1.3, LF(10) -0.3	0.1	103
2018	WNS	A+	21	487	67	25	9	7	78	34	90	15	8	.293/.345/.436	121	18.7	.351	1.1	RF(74) -2.5, LF(15) -2.7	1.4	104
2019	BIR	AA	22	480	50	17	3	7	49	37	118	9	2	.265/.319/.365	95	7.1	.343	2.4	RF(67) 1.7, LF(29) -1.7	1.0	100
2020	CHA	MLB	23	251	23	11	1	5	25	16	72	3	1	.237/.289/.363	73	0.0	.319	-0.1	RF -1, LF -1	-0.4	100

Comparables: Destin Hood, Sócrates Brito, Eddie Rosario

On 2016 draft day, it seemed likely Rutherford and Mickey Moniak would be linked together as prep outfield prospects much the way Clint Frazier and Austin Meadows were. I guess it's worked out that way...sort of, as both have been relatively disappointing as pros. Rutherford and Moniak were considered two of the safest prep bats in recent memory. Rutherford was older as a prep pick and more likely to move to a corner, perhaps two reasons—along with bonus demands—that he fell out of the top half of the first round, but we always thought he'd hit. More swing-and-miss creeped into his game in Double-A and Rutherford continues to struggle against same-side pitching. The swing lacks loft and at this point it's hard to predict Rutherford growing into more power without a fairly significant swing change. Like Moniak, he looks more like a bench outfielder than a starter, but he lacks his draft counterparts center field glove, making it a tougher profile in the majors.

Personal Cheeseball

PC Alec Hansen RHP
Born: 10/10/94   Age: 25   Bats: R   Throws: R   Height: 6'7"   Weight: 235   Origin: Round 2, 2016 Draft (#49 overall)

YEAR	TEAM	LVL	AGE	W	L	SV	G	GS	IP	H	HR	BB/9	K/9	K	GB%	BABIP	WHIP	ERA	DRA	WARP	PF
2017	KAN	A	22	7	3	0	13	13	72²	57	3	2.8	11.4	92	32%	.292	1.10	2.48	2.80	2.1	101
2017	WNS	A+	22	4	5	0	11	11	58¹	42	5	3.9	12.7	82	38%	.296	1.15	2.93	2.79	1.7	101
2017	BIR	AA	22	0	0	0	2	2	10¹	15	0	2.6	14.8	17	36%	.536	1.74	4.35	5.44	0.0	92
2018	WNS	A+	23	0	1	0	5	5	15²	14	0	9.8	11.5	20	27%	.378	1.98	5.74	6.08	-0.1	106
2018	BIR	AA	23	0	4	0	9	9	35²	30	3	10.6	8.8	35	33%	.293	2.02	6.56	7.09	-0.7	91
2019	WNS	A+	24	1	0	0	9	0	12²	1	0	5.0	14.9	21	63%	.053	0.63	2.13	1.95	0.4	100
2019	BIR	AA	24	1	2	1	30	1	39²	43	5	8.4	10.2	45	38%	.362	2.02	5.45	7.21	-1.3	98
2020	CHA	MLB	25	2	2	0	33	0	35	35	5	4.0	9.2	36	37%	.309	1.44	4.68	4.79	0.2	100

Comparables: Josh Ravin, Thomas Pannone, Adbert Alzolay

Well, this hasn't gone so well recently. Just two offseasons ago, Hansen was a top 50 global prospect coming off an utterly dominant season as a starter. He was still a little riskier than most advanced college arms who tore through A-ball with premium stuff because of a history of wildness, but it looked like just that: history. Then he came into spring in 2018 and suffered a forearm injury, and he's largely been unable to throw strikes since. He converted to relief in 2019, and mixed flashes of dominance there with the same control problems. He's a giant, and we comped Dellin Betances here last year as another tall mid-90s fastball/power breaking ball prospect who couldn't throw strikes in the high-minors but eventually got it together to become an elite reliever. Every year Hansen doesn't pull it together, that sort of outcome gets a little further away, but he's only 25 and the stuff is still there somewhere…

Low Minors Sleeper

LMS James Beard OF
Born: 09/24/00   Age: 19   Bats: R   Throws: R   Height: 5'10"   Weight: 170   Origin: Round 4, 2019 Draft (#110 overall)

YEAR	TEAM	LVL	AGE	PA	R	2B	3B	HR	RBI	BB	K	SB	CS	AVG/OBP/SLG	DRC+	VORP	BABIP	BRR	FRAA	WARP	PF
2019	WSX	RK	18	138	19	4	1	2	12	8	54	9	3	.213/.270/.307	40	-2.3	.352	0.7	CF(31) -9.0	-1.1	103
2020	CHA	MLB	19	251	18	11	1	3	20	15	115	2	1	.196/.250/.287	40	0.0	.369	0.0	CF -2	-1.3	100

Comparables: Michael Reed, Willy García, Jorge Bonifacio

Potentially the fastest player in the 2020 draft class, the White Sox fourth-round pick is an 80-grade runner who will need significant development time on the rest of the profile. Because of the speed, you'll likely hear some Billy Hamilton comps, but he reminds me a bit more of a stronger Anfrenee Seymour at present. Whether that added physicality allows him to generate more game power than Hamilton or Seymour have been able to will be key to his professional development. The hit tool is extremely raw at present as well. Despite his speed he still needs some work on the grass as well, but players with that kind of straight line speed almost always end up of above-average in center field.

Top Talents 25 and Under (as of 4/1/2020)

1. Yoan Moncada
2. Lucas Giolito
3. Eloy Jimenez
4. Luis Robert

5. Nick Madrigal
6. Michael Kopech
7. Dylan Cease
8. Andrew Vaughn
9. Jonathan Stiever
10. Dane Dunning

Robert rightfully ranks highly on the Top 101, so the fact that three names appear ahead of his speaks to the young talent the White Sox have graduated to the major-league level in recent years.

It's kind of hard to fathom, but amid Tim Anderson's bat flips and batting title, and Lucas Giolito's bounce-back All-Star season, Moncada's 2019 performance seemed to fly under-the-radar. The former top prospect was the White Sox best player, putting up a 123 DRC+ and 5.1 WARP season despite missing 30 games. He hit 25 home runs, stole 10 bags, and proved more than competent defensively after a move back to third base. He turned into the type of talent we'd long anticipated.

Giolito's turnaround from one of the worst pitchers in baseball to legitimate ace was close to unprecedented. The right-hander abandoned his sinker entirely and upped his fastball usage while turning his changeup into a devastating weapon. He doubled his strikeout rate (16 percent to 32 percent) and chopped three percentage points off his walk rate. About the only thing he didn't accomplish was crossing the 200-inning mark, as the White Sox played it safe with him down the stretch after a minor injury and shut him down for the last month.

Jimenez's season mirrored Moncada's 2018 in a way, as the slugger we ranked as the fourth-best prospect in baseball before last year showed plenty of potential while enduring injuries and growing pains in an uneven rookie year. The power played as expected—his HR/FB was the eighth-highest mark in the majors—but he also whiffed a ton and hardly walked (he finished the year with 31 home runs and 30 walks) while his defense in left field was … adventurous, to put it kindly. Jimenez still has all the makings of the middle-of-the-order masher many envisioned, he just hasn't put it all together quite yet.

The only other non-prospect-eligible player on the list is Cease, who missed a lot of bats and a lot of the plate in a 14-start rookie year following a midseason call-up. He has elite stuff, but didn't always know where it was going. He slots in behind Kopech based solely on ceiling despite Kopech's uncertainty following Tommy John surgery.

Eyewitness Reports

Eyewitness Report: Andrew Vaughn

Evaluator: Ben Spanier
Report Date: 08/28/2019
Dates Seen: 7/26, 7/27, 7/29, 8/3, 8/16, 8/26, 8/27
Risk Factor: Low
Physical/Health: Stocky with strength throughout; already maxed. Not overly athletic, profile reliant on bat.

Tool	Future Grade	Report
Hit	60	Excellent plate discipline and barrel control allow Vaughn to limit swing/miss and maximize hard contact. Did not see him at what I believe to be the best of his ability during most of my looks, but even when timing is off he takes good at-bats; spits on bad pitches and will not expand zone even when slumping and still makes hard contact into outs. Ability to wait for and attack pitch paired with contact ability is a nice combination.
Power	60	Didn't really see him tap into his raw much in-game, but am given to understand he has hit at least one very impressive homer this season. The power is easily visible due to the strength in both his upper and lower body as well as his quick bat, solid mechanics, and controlled yet aggressive swing. Plus power that works hand-in-hand with his plus hit. Ability to zero in on pitch to drive will help here too.
Baserunning/ Speed	30	Pretty slow runner and not getting any faster; neutral effect at best on the bases.
Glove	40	Solid enough around the bag but doesn't add much with his range or hands and doesn't really exude smoothness.
Arm	40	Did not see him make many throws but arm looked fine.

Conclusion: Plus hit and power are both obviously apparent, and it is also well known that Vaughn is a bat-first prospect with a bat-first profile. Despite his slow start in the Carolina League, there is little doubt that he will hit at the higher levels. It is quite possible that he is worn down from a long season and I believe quite likely that he will hit the ground running next season, seeing Triple-A Charlotte in no time. Wouldn't be surprised if he makes my hit/power projections look low. Not much risk but will need to produce a lot with the bat to come close to the value provided by other top prospects in the organization.

Eyewitness Report: Jonathan Stiever

Evaluator: Ben Spanier
Report Date: 07/23/2019
Dates Seen: 7/9/19, 7/20/19
Risk Factor: Low
Delivery: Strong, high-waisted build on medium frame. Repeats delivery and stays strong throughout the game. High 3/4 release, springy and athletic wind that really drives off back leg. Has a confident bearing and is very outwardly competitive.

Pitch Type	Future Grade	Sitting Velocity	Peak Velocity	Report
FB	60	93-95	97	True plus pitch fastball that flashes better; gets some glove-side run, slight sink down and great life and "rise" up in the zone that generates weak contact and swing-and-miss. Can live around 95-97 in the early innings but settles into a mid-90s rhythm by the middle innings. Command is decent but could be better.
CV	55	82-84	87	Varies the shape on his power curve, the mid-80s variation more like a slider that is effective running down and away from RHH. The slightly slower version of this pitch has more of a 10-4 break, and he likes to use both to front-door RHH and get called strikes. This pitch flashes plus when he hits the sweet spot therein, with late and sharp downward action and just enough lateral movement. He also throws a much slower true curve on occasion, going 12-6 in the low-70s for a drastic change of pace.
CH	50	84-85	86	Doesn't throw the change often, but looks to be at least an average offering.

Conclusion: Stuff jumps out at you, as does athleticism and competitiveness. All of this makes him a joy to watch, but there are areas to iron out as Stiever climbs the ladder. Fastball command could improve, and I believe it will as the athleticism is there and the mechanics are sound enough. While the ability to vary the speed and shape on his curve is an asset, it doesn't always seem like there is a purpose to the alterations or that he has fully harnessed the potential of the pitch. He hasn't really needed a third pitch at this level, but he should use and refine the change as it will be necessary at some point. I believe the ingredients are here for a back end to mid-rotation starter in the big leagues.

Cincinnati Reds

The State of the System

Trades, injuries and stagnation leave the Reds system adrift somewhere in the bottom ten orgs.

The Top Ten

───────────── ★ ★ ★ *2020 Top 101 Prospect* **#59** ★ ★ ★ ─────────────

1   **Nick Lodolo**   **LHP**   OFP: 60   ETA: 2020/21

Born: 02/05/98   Age: 22   Bats: L   Throws: L   Height: 6'6"   Weight: 202   Origin: Round 1, 2019 Draft (#7 overall)

YEAR	TEAM	LVL	AGE	W	L	SV	G	GS	IP	H	HR	BB/9	K/9	K	GB%	BABIP	WHIP	ERA	DRA	WARP	PF
2019	BIL	RK+	21	0	1	0	6	6	11¹	12	1	0.0	16.7	21	36%	.458	1.06	2.38	2.41	0.5	98
2019	DYT	A	21	0	0	0	2	2	7	6	0	0.0	11.6	9	50%	.333	0.86	2.57	3.40	0.1	104
2020	CIN	MLB	22	2	2	0	33	0	35	35	5	3.6	8.2	32	43%	.295	1.39	4.64	4.84	0.2	97

Comparables: Josh Rogers, Devin Smeltzer, Eric Surkamp

The Report: The Pirates drafted Lodolo with the 41st choice of the 2016 draft, but the sides couldn't make a deal, and Lodolo enrolled at TCU where he toed the rubber for three years. As an amateur, he improved his K-rate each season until he topped out at 11.4 per nine his Junior year, when he also managed a 2.36 ERA. That performance was enough for the Reds to make the lefty the number seven overall pick in last year's draft. He's only thrown 18 ⅓ innings since his pro debut, but he's been impressive in that sample, striking out 30 without walking a single batter.

Lodolo is tall and lanky with very long limbs and a high waist. He has three plus pitches and he throws all of them for strikes. He fires from a true three-quarters arm slot and gets downhill, but can cut off his extension a bit. It's not the smoothest delivery out there, and he gets big time hand separation with his glove side getting in front early. His slider is consistent, sharp, and tough to pick up. He commands the slider and change well. Lodolo has good athleticism and controls his long frame well. His release point is incredibly consistent and it's virtually impossible to differentiate between the slider and fastball until it's too late for hitters.

As mentioned, Lodolo has thrown fewer than 20 professional innings, but it's almost impossible to be more impressive than he was in 2019 on the whole. He's an advanced college arm, and he isn't far off from the majors. I don't think it's probable, but I wouldn't be shocked if he is logging innings for the Reds if they are in contention in late in 2020. While he is in the minors, Lodolo starts are ones that you're going to want to get on your calendar.

Variance: Medium. It's tough to be more impressive than Lodolo was in his small 2019 sample in the pros. He's a college lefty with an advanced feel for pitching. If for any reason he's unable to stick in the rotation, he will still be a difference maker out of the bullpen.

Mark Barry's Fantasy Take: Do you like guys with walk totals that are literally "LOL, no thanks"? Lodolo couldn't have been better in his first pro taste, and although all the standard caveats apply, I like him quite a bit and think he's an easy add into my top-75 or so.

2 Jose Garcia SS   OFP: 55   ETA: 2022

Born: 04/05/98   Age: 22   Bats: R   Throws: R   Height: 6'2"   Weight: 175   Origin: International Free Agent, 2017

YEAR	TEAM	LVL	AGE	PA	R	2B	3B	HR	RBI	BB	K	SB	CS	AVG/OBP/SLG	DRC+	VORP	BABIP	BRR	FRAA	WARP	PF
2018	DYT	A	20	517	61	22	4	6	53	19	112	13	9	.245/.290/.344	83	10.3	.307	1.8	SS(93) -0.7, 2B(29) -1.8	1.0	102
2019	DAY	A+	21	452	58	37	1	8	55	25	83	15	2	.280/.343/.436	143	27.5	.329	-0.8	SS(99) 0.7	3.8	103
2020	CIN	MLB	22	251	23	14	1	5	25	15	63	3	2	.229/.291/.359	73	0.0	.294	0.0	SS 0, 2B 0	0.0	97

Comparables: Lucas May, Billy Hamilton, Chris Nelson

The Report: The Reds gave Garcia a five million dollar bonus in the 2016-17 signing period. At the time the club was already over their international spending limit and were forced to pay a 100% tax on the signing. He then didn't play for the organization for almost a full year after, but Cincinnati threw him directly into full-season ball with Dayton in 2018. The first half of his stateside debut was rough, but Garcia has shown steady improvement since that point.

In last year's Reds top-10 list, Nathan Graham wrote that Garcia was poised for a breakout in 2019, and he couldn't have been more right. If you go to a game without knowing the rosters, Garcia is the one that will stand out immediately. He's long and lean with a high waist, and he's always going to be one of the most athletic players in any given game. Don't expect an elite defender at short, but he should finish as an above-average shortstop. He's smooth with good footwork and has a plus arm. He's a heady player with the glove and has plus speed on the basepaths. The swing is smooth and pretty, and the hit tool could end up plus, Garcis shows a solid approach and improving barrel control. Power is the biggest shortcoming in the profile, but it still projects to 10+ home runs. Don't expect a flashy player when he climbs the organizational ladder, but you can expect a prospect who does everything well without any weakness to his game.

Variance: Medium. Garcia projects to be a four tool contributor. He's young and hasn't escaped the low minors, but he's already displayed an ability to adjust and improve.

Mark Barry's Fantasy Take: I'm getting strong Cesar Hernandez-vibes from Garcia, which may seem like an unspectacular for the number-two prospect in an organization, but I swear, that's a compliment. He's not terribly close, though, and the low ceiling points to relevance in deeper formats or only leagues.

3 Tyler Stephenson C   OFP: 55   ETA: 2021

Born: 08/16/96   Age: 23   Bats: R   Throws: R   Height: 6'4"   Weight: 225   Origin: Round 1, 2015 Draft (#11 overall)

YEAR	TEAM	LVL	AGE	PA	R	2B	3B	HR	RBI	BB	K	SB	CS	AVG/OBP/SLG	DRC+	VORP	BABIP	BRR	FRAA	WARP	PF
2017	DYT	A	20	348	39	22	0	6	50	44	58	2	1	.278/.374/.414	138	20.4	.322	-2.6	C(53) -4.0	2.0	100
2018	DAY	A+	21	450	60	20	1	11	59	45	98	1	0	.250/.338/.392	118	24.3	.301	0.2	C(97) -3.3	2.4	104
2019	CHT	AA	22	363	47	19	1	6	44	37	60	0	0	.285/.372/.410	128	23.3	.331	-2.1	C(85) -11.8	1.3	109
2020	CIN	MLB	23	251	26	13	0	7	29	19	63	0	0	.240/.309/.397	86	0.0	.300	-0.5	C -8	-0.5	97

Comparables: Christian Vázquez, Victor Caratini, Meibrys Viloria

The Report: We now have two seasons of mostly healthy Tyler Stephenson, and the projection of a potential above-average everyday catcher has come more into focus. The track record of high pick prep catchers is abysmal, but after a successful season in Double-A, Stephenson looks like he might be able to buck the trends of his cohort. The main issue with high school backstops is just so much can go wrong given how long and complex the development track is. But for Stephenson the issues were simple, injuries marred his first few pro seasons, and he still hasn't caught 100 games in a season, which is slightly worrisome. He is on the large side for catcher, but moves well behind the plate. The catch and throw skills remain a bit rough, but projectable. Stephenson sets a big, quiet target, but can get a bit snatchy at the top and bottom of the zone. He has average arm strength, and a quick release for a big dude, but doesn't always get great carry on his throws. He has a good approach at the plate and despite some stiffness in the swing, projects for an 50/55 hit/power combination. If he can continue to refine his defense and stay on the field, he could be the first good prep catcher since...uh...Brian McCann?

Variance: High. Durability concerns still abound. If the hit tool plays down a bit up the ladder and takes some of the power with it, he might be more of a fringe starter.

Mark Barry's Fantasy Take: Don't look now, but we might be restarting the Tyler Stephenson Hype Train. Of course that train is sure to run off the tracks and spend countless days repairing its engine, but still. Despite his first-round pedigree, I wouldn't expect star-level performance from Stephenson, but he could flirt with a few fantasy top-10 seasons in his career.

4 Jonathan India 3B   OFP: 55   ETA: 2021
Born: 12/15/96 Age: 23 Bats: R Throws: R Height: 6'0" Weight: 200 Origin: Round 1, 2018 Draft (#5 overall)

YEAR	TEAM	LVL	AGE	PA	R	2B	3B	HR	RBI	BB	K	SB	CS	AVG/OBP/SLG	DRC+	VORP	BABIP	BRR	FRAA	WARP	PF
2018	GRV	RK	21	62	11	2	1	3	12	15	12	1	0	.261/.452/.543	150	6.3	.290	0.6	3B(12) -0.6, SS(2) -0.2	0.5	101
2018	DYT	A	21	112	17	7	0	3	11	13	28	5	0	.229/.339/.396	104	7.0	.292	1.5	3B(21) 2.4, SS(4) -0.1	0.8	101
2019	DAY	A+	22	367	50	15	5	8	30	37	84	7	5	.256/.346/.410	130	18.1	.319	-1.8	3B(74) -9.2, 2B(5) 0.0	1.0	101
2019	CHT	AA	22	145	24	3	0	3	14	22	26	4	0	.270/.414/.378	141	11.0	.314	0.2	3B(31) -0.4	1.1	108
2020	CIN	MLB	23	251	28	11	1	8	29	25	70	4	1	.232/.326/.399	95	3.0	.303	-0.1	3B -2, SS 0	0.4	97

Comparables: Alex Blandino, Hunter Dozier, Kyle Kubitza

The Report: Calling a player "polished" isn't usually a pejorative, but in India's case it's a mixed blessing. He has an above-average glove at third with the arm to match. The glove there isn't so good that it's a carrying tool, mind you, and his performance at the plate in 2019 was uneven. India can struggle to strike a balance between patience and passivity, hit and power. He has above-average bat speed and feel for contact, but while he will rip one pull side on occasion, he tends to play more gap to gap, and it's not always the loudest contact. You'd like to give the offensive profile higher praise than "polished" at this point. India was drafted that high in the first round in part due to his "high floor," but what does that floor realistically look like? .270, plenty of walks, 10 HR, with a pretty good third base glove and the ability to play passable defense at a few other spots? There's more than that in the tank of course. And if that looks more like .280 with 15-20 home runs. You pencil him in every day in the second spot in your lineup. I'm just not fully convinced he gets there, and the lack of a carrying tool in this kind of profile is always a little concerning.

Variance: Medium. There's an obvious outline of a major leaguer here as you recite the tools, but when you look a little deeper, he doesn't play a premium defensive position and may not hit for a ton of power.

Mark Barry's Fantasy Take: I like India more than Garcia for fantasy purposes, but it's a similar high-floor, low-ceiling profile. India probably has better plate discipline, which gives him more room for error, but it sure would be nice if he could hit for *slightly* more power.

5 Hunter Greene RHP   OFP: 60   ETA: 2022
Born: 08/06/99 Age: 20 Bats: R Throws: R Height: 6'4" Weight: 215 Origin: Round 1, 2017 Draft (#2 overall)

YEAR	TEAM	LVL	AGE	W	L	SV	G	GS	IP	H	HR	BB/9	K/9	K	GB%	BABIP	WHIP	ERA	DRA	WARP	PF
2018	DYT	A	18	3	7	0	18	18	68^1	66	6	3.0	11.7	89	43%	.353	1.30	4.48	4.58	0.5	103
2020	CIN	MLB	20	2	2	0	33	0	35	36	6	4.2	9.1	35	40%	.310	1.49	5.14	5.16	0.1	97

Comparables: Jordan Lyles, Roberto Osuna, Mike Soroka

The Report: I was in attendance for Hunter Greene's most recent start. The good news: He hit 100 on my gun on three consecutive pitches and ended the first with a 101 mph fastball. The bad news: he only threw two innings and the start took place on July 26th, 2018. It has been a long time since Greene saw game action. Technically he was removed from that start due to an "upset stomach", but it was later revealed that he was dealing with elbow issues. Finally in April of 2019 it was announced that he undergo Tommy John surgery after sustaining new UCL damage while throwing live batting practice.

The second overall pick in the 2017 amateur draft, Greene was very briefly a two-way prospect and received 30 rookie-level at-bats in his draft year. He has been solely a pitching prospect since and is heavily reliant on his fastball. When you have an 80 fastball though, you throw the 80 fastball. You never know how a player, especially someone so young and fastball dependent, is going to bounce back after Tommy John Surgery and what will be nearly two years removed from game action.

On last year's Reds list, we wrote that Greene was a "pitch-and-a-half prep arm," and even when healthy he was a fairly raw pitcher. He is blessed with elite arm speed and plus athleticism. It's going to take a while to get him up to speed when he returns to the mound, and even longer to develop into a pitcher from a thrower. Greene has incredible tools, so I certainly won't count him out, but he has thrown only 72 professional innings and is not as young as he once was.

Variance: Extreme. It was a volatile profile prior to his surgery, and even more so at this point. The Reds will give him every opportunity to develop and become a rotation piece in the majors. If he recoups his velocity he will have a job in a bullpen even if a starting role doesn't pan out.

Mark Barry's Fantasy Take: On one hand, it might be a good idea to see if Greene has any name value still left on the trade market. On the other hand, after going under the knife for Tommy John surgery last April, I'm not sure his value can get lower. I'd be ok moving on from the fireballer in shallower formats, but if you've waited this long to cut bait in deeper leagues, you might as well hang on and see how Greene looks upon his return to the bump.

6 Tony Santillan RHP   OFP: 55   ETA: 2021

Born: 04/15/97   Age: 23   Bats: R   Throws: R   Height: 6'3"   Weight: 240   Origin: Round 2, 2015 Draft (#49 overall)

YEAR	TEAM	LVL	AGE	W	L	SV	G	GS	IP	H	HR	BB/9	K/9	K	GB%	BABIP	WHIP	ERA	DRA	WARP	PF
2017	DYT	A	20	9	8	0	25	24	128	104	9	3.9	9.0	128	45%	.281	1.25	3.38	3.44	2.7	99
2018	DAY	A+	21	6	4	0	15	15	86^2	81	5	2.3	7.6	73	44%	.298	1.19	2.70	4.25	1.1	102
2018	PEN	AA	21	4	3	0	11	11	62^1	65	8	2.3	8.8	61	46%	.315	1.30	3.61	4.68	0.5	97
2019	CHT	AA	22	2	8	0	21	21	102^1	110	8	4.7	8.1	92	37%	.333	1.60	4.84	5.75	-1.0	112
2020	CIN	MLB	23	2	3	0	25	5	46	47	8	3.7	6.8	35	38%	.284	1.43	4.90	4.91	0.4	97

Comparables: Touki Toussaint, Sean Reid-Foley, Jonathan Hernández

The Report: Santillan struggled more in his second time around the Southern League as his command and control went backwards. The stuff is still pretty solid, a low-90s fastball, a plus-flashing slider with two-plane action he commands well gloveside, and a potentially average change that will show some tumble. The change-up is 45ish enough now that it wouldn't be a bar to starting, but the command remains an issue. Santillan has a fairly simple, if uptempo, delivery, so there should be some command projection here, but he's also not the most athletic of moundsmen which can affect his mechanics and efficiency. I'd say the reliever risk has bumped a little bit as his command continues to scuffle, but it would be a potential plus fastball/slider combo in short bursts, so there are worse fallbacks. And there's still a decent chance he sorts the command issues out enough to be an innings-eating, if somewhat frustrating, mid-rotation starter.

Variance: Medium. The strikeout and walk rates went in the wrong direction in Double-A, and the reliever risk is up as well.

Mark Barry's Fantasy Take: Santillan's control seriously backed up this season, and I can't say it doesn't scare me a little. If you start from a middle-of-the-rotation upside there aren't a lot of fantasy-relevant places to fall to.

7 Mariel Bautista OF   OFP: 55   ETA: 2023

Born: 10/15/97   Age: 22   Bats: R   Throws: R   Height: 6'3"   Weight: 194   Origin: International Free Agent, 2014

YEAR	TEAM	LVL	AGE	PA	R	2B	3B	HR	RBI	BB	K	SB	CS	AVG/OBP/SLG	DRC+	VORP	BABIP	BRR	FRAA	WARP	PF
2017	CIN	RK	19	157	29	9	1	0	20	5	24	16	1	.320/.353/.395	119	14.8	.379	3.5	LF(24) -1.7, CF(10) 3.2	1.1	102
2018	BIL	RK	20	233	43	12	4	8	37	16	29	16	3	.330/.386/.541	139	28.0	.349	2.3	CF(40) -4.4, LF(6) -1.3	0.6	96
2019	DYT	A	21	433	43	10	2	8	33	28	88	19	11	.233/.303/.332	88	5.5	.278	1.9	LF(42) -3.0, RF(36) 0.9	0.2	104
2020	CIN	MLB	22	251	22	11	1	4	23	12	66	4	2	.227/.276/.340	62	0.0	.299	0.1	LF -1, CF -1	-0.5	97

Comparables: Victor Robles, Aristides Aquino, Michael Hermosillo

The Report: Bautista has been in the Reds system since being signed out of the Dominican Republic in 2014, but didn't make his way stateside until 2017, and he finally got his first taste of full-season ball in 2019. The Reds have been moving Bautista along with kid gloves. He put up big rookie-ball numbers in 2018, and it appeared he was primed to break out in 2019, but instead he floundered. Bautista was hot out of the gate lin 2019, but after the first month of the season he really struggled. In the second half of the season, he looked completely lost at the plate and showed a complete inability to lay off breaking stuff beneath the zone.

Bautista has a wiry frame which should benefit from added mass and strength as he ages. He is a tool shed with 70 speed and 60 raw power. He's quick-twitch and shows big-time athleticism. There is plus bat speed, and he handles pitches up in the zone like he was born to do it. He doesn't look out of place in center field, but he might be a better fit in a corner despite his speed. Bautista has all the gifts and tools needed to become an All-Star, but there is still a lot to piece together. He has been brought along slowly and is still raw for a 22-year-old. At some point there is going to need a swing reset and hit tool improvements. If he can retool to better handle the lower half the zone, he will be well on his way to realizing his potential. The Reds organization doesn't have the best player development track record in this regard, but there have been some positive changes there. Bautista has a long way to go, but the building blocks are in place.

Variance: Extreme. Bautista has yet to impress in full-season ball and is still extremely raw. The changes he needs to make are not minor. All the tools are there, but the clock is ticking.

Mark Barry's Fantasy Take: Bautista has been in the Reds organization for five seasons and and his ETA is 2023. Pass.

8 Jose Siri CF   OFP: 50   ETA: 2020/21
Born: 07/22/95 Age: 24 Bats: R Throws: R Height: 6'2" Weight: 175 Origin: International Free Agent, 2012

YEAR	TEAM	LVL	AGE	PA	R	2B	3B	HR	RBI	BB	K	SB	CS	AVG/OBP/SLG	DRC+	VORP	BABIP	BRR	FRAA	WARP	PF
2017	DYT	A	21	552	92	24	11	24	76	33	130	46	12	.293/.341/.530	137	50.5	.349	7.4	CF(103) 15.7, RF(9) 1.5	6.4	102
2018	DAY	A+	22	126	15	9	2	1	9	4	32	9	1	.261/.280/.395	89	2.2	.341	1.1	CF(26) 0.4	0.4	101
2018	PEN	AA	22	283	42	8	9	12	34	24	91	14	5	.229/.300/.474	91	15.0	.301	2.2	CF(59) -3.9	0.5	97
2019	CHT	AA	23	405	46	15	1	11	50	33	126	21	6	.251/.313/.388	84	8.0	.349	-0.1	CF(98) 22.8, RF(1) 0.0	3.2	111
2019	LOU	AAA	23	112	10	4	1	0	3	9	39	5	2	.186/.252/.245	42	-6.0	.302	1.6	CF(26) 2.3, RF(4) -0.1	0.0	99
2020	CIN	MLB	24	35	4	2	0	1	4	2	13	1	1	.224/.272/.389	68	0.0	.333	0.1	CF 1	0.1	97

Comparables: Zoilo Almonte, Jeremy Moore, Aristides Aquino

The Report: Jose Siri the prospect gives me a bit of a headache. It's not from the stress of coming up with the evaluation—the strengths and weaknesses are both very apparent—but rather the process of them slotting him into a broader context, in this case the Reds system. Our OFP is supposed to be a 75th percentile outcome. But pegging Siri to a single number is imprecise to a degree that...well, gives me a headache. Admittedly there will be a degree of false precision in any single number ranking. There's a plethora of possibilities higher or lower for any prospect that we write up in these pages. We cover some of those in our variance section. For Siri, a short paragraph there feels insufficient.

He has tremendous bat speed, lightning-quick wrists that generate plus raw despite a still-lean frame. He's a plus runner and gets to his top gear quickly. He should end up above-average in center field. He has enough arm for right. Nothing particularly interesting so far. I mean the tools are interesting, but there's nothing unusual about a four-tool up-the-middle guy with hit tool questions. Siri won't be the first or last written up in these pages, but he feels like a series of discrete outcomes more than a continuum. It will either click or it doesn't. Some teams are using what I'd call "bucket reports" now, where you give a percentage likelihood for each outcome 2-8. And Siri feels like a prospect that is more likely to be a 7 or a 3 than a 5, which makes him particularly confounding to rank.

Variance: Still really high. He's 24 and struck out 32% of the time in Double-A. He didn't hit a home run in 112 PA in Triple-A with the coward ball (©Bradford William Davis). The tools are still there but as the years go by the lack of performance carries more and more weight.

Mark Barry's Fantasy Take: Look, I get it. It's hard to find steals. Having said that, if you strike out over a third of the time and walk at a clip less than nine percent, it's awfully hard snag those bags. Such is the Siri Dilemma (also, I feel like Vegas had a "Hey, Siri" reference at -350, so sorry to disappoint).

9 Michael Siani CF   OFP: 50   ETA: 2024
Born: 07/16/99 Age: 20 Bats: L Throws: L Height: 6'1" Weight: 188 Origin: Round 4, 2018 Draft (#109 overall)

YEAR	TEAM	LVL	AGE	PA	R	2B	3B	HR	RBI	BB	K	SB	CS	AVG/OBP/SLG	DRC+	VORP	BABIP	BRR	FRAA	WARP	PF
2018	GRV	RK	18	205	24	6	3	2	13	16	35	6	4	.288/.351/.386	115	10.8	.342	-0.1	CF(45) 6.5	1.6	103
2019	DYT	A	19	531	75	10	6	6	39	46	109	45	15	.253/.333/.339	96	22.0	.318	7.4	CF(111) 24.7, RF(5) -0.7	4.8	103
2020	CIN	MLB	20	251	22	10	1	4	22	16	65	4	2	.231/.289/.330	64	0.0	.306	0.4	CF 6, RF 0	0.3	97

Comparables: Kyle Tucker, Abraham Almonte, Xavier Avery

The Report: The Reds made Siani their fourth round selection in the 2018 amateur draft as a Philadelphia prep. That Summer, he put up decent numbers in rookie ball, albeit without much in the way of power. So coming into last season, he was a trendy breakout candidate as he began his first year of full-season baseball. Well, Siani looked pretty bad to begin the year and awful in the middle of the season. He was too passive at the plate and struggled to make good contact. For most of 2019 he looked like he didn't belong in the level, but things turned around toward the end of the year—his passivity turned into patience and he started hitting more line drives.

The way Siani ended the year gave me some optimism about his chances to find his way to the big leagues at some point. He is a good defender with plus speed and should able to handle centerfield. He also has a plus-plus arm which would play anywhere on the grass and even stand out in right. The questions are at the plate. I don't expect him to develop much power. It's not there presently, and the body is close to mature. Siani has a compact swing and is short to the ball, but he still struggles with pitches up in the zone. The glove is going to play and if he's able find some consistency at the dish, he could blossom into a potential regular. At worst he is likely an up-and-down extra outfielder that will provide a club a solid glove that they can plug into any outfield position.

Variance: High. Siani is young and hasn't proven he can hit at this point. The glove should carry him up the organizational ladder and will keep his floor relatively high for a player with major offensive questions.

Mark Barry's Fantasy Take: Bret preached Siani's virtues in this spot last season, and hipster prospect hounds followed suit, touting him as a stealthy pickup. It didn't necessarily happen, but like Keith mentioned above, he started to find a rhythm toward the end of the season. As a guy that was really young for his level, that's definitely something to build on. Oh, he also stole 45 bases, which is nice. Toss Siani on the watch list, in shallower leagues, but he's rosterable in 300-prospect leagues.

10 Lyon Richardson RHP OFP: 50 ETA: 2022

Born: 01/18/00 Age: 20 Bats: B Throws: R Height: 6'2" Weight: 192 Origin: Round 2, 2018 Draft (#47 overall)

YEAR	TEAM	LVL	AGE	W	L	SV	G	GS	IP	H	HR	BB/9	K/9	K	GB%	BABIP	WHIP	ERA	DRA	WARP	PF
2018	GRV	RK	18	0	5	0	11	11	29	37	3	5.0	7.4	24	41%	.362	1.83	7.14	6.54	-0.1	104
2019	DYT	A	19	3	9	0	26	26	112²	126	10	2.6	8.5	106	41%	.340	1.41	4.15	5.70	-0.7	105
2020	CIN	MLB	20	2	2	0	33	0	35	36	6	4.2	6.5	25	38%	.280	1.49	5.13	5.24	0.1	97

Comparables: Joe Ross, Tyrell Jenkins, Jeanmar Gómez

The Report: Richardson plays with a chip on his shoulder and is going to challenge every single hitter he faces in his career. He pitches with a faster tempo than most, but does slow things down a bit when he puts a runner on base. He's athletic and repeats his delivery well despite some violence and herky-jerky mechanics. Richardson has a lightning quick move to first and should hold runners well. He typically works in the low-to-mid-90's, but has touched as high as 97. The changeup is inconsistent, but you'll see a good one on occasion. The breaking ball is a nice compliment to his fastball and will show sharp break when it's right. I expect Richardson is a reliever in the long run - he has the demeanor for it, and I don't think he'll ever have a consistent third pitch.

Variance: High—thus far he hasn't shown a great propensity for strikeouts, and with the bullpen a likely destination that is a bit of a concern. He hasn't thrown a professional pitch as a 20-year-old, so there is plenty of time for development, but the outcomes are wide-ranging.

Mark Barry's Fantasy Take: If Richardson is unlikely to ever develop a third pitch, his already low strikeout numbers make him unlikely to be fantasy relevant. As this was my last fantasy blurb for list season, I'd be Lyon if I said this wasn't a disappointing one to end on.

The Next Ten

11 Stuart Fairchild OF

Born: 03/17/96 Age: 24 Bats: R Throws: R Height: 6'0" Weight: 190 Origin: Round 2, 2017 Draft (#38 overall)

YEAR	TEAM	LVL	AGE	PA	R	2B	3B	HR	RBI	BB	K	SB	CS	AVG/OBP/SLG	DRC+	VORP	BABIP	BRR	FRAA	WARP	PF
2017	BIL	RK	21	234	36	5	4	3	23	19	35	12	4	.304/.393/.412	107	14.9	.355	1.8	CF(43) -9.4, RF(5) -0.6	-0.3	105
2018	DYT	A	22	276	40	12	5	7	37	31	65	17	4	.277/.377/.460	138	20.2	.352	2.3	CF(30) -2.3, LF(26) -0.4	1.8	104
2018	DAY	A+	22	242	25	14	1	2	20	17	63	6	2	.250/.306/.350	98	-4.2	.335	-4.4	LF(31) 0.1, CF(30) -2.4	-0.1	104
2019	DAY	A+	23	281	32	17	2	8	37	25	60	3	5	.258/.335/.440	148	16.5	.306	-1.1	CF(39) -3.3, LF(15) 3.5	1.9	101
2019	CHT	AA	23	179	25	12	1	4	17	19	23	3	2	.275/.380/.444	132	11.4	.302	-1.1	CF(28) 0.2, RF(10) 1.6	1.2	107
2020	CIN	MLB	24	251	26	12	1	7	28	18	62	4	1	.235/.303/.394	85	0.0	.291	-0.1	CF -1, LF 0	0.3	97

Comparables: Lane Adams, Drew Stubbs, Jaylin Davis

Fairchild has always had a broad collection of averagish tools, but his game could lack refinement at times. He'd get overly aggressive at the plate and try to tap into his merely average raw power, leading to Ks or poor quality of contact. It's an unorthodox swing, as he starts with his hands straight out over the plate and loads in and back, so there can be some stiffness and barrel control issues. But Fairchild has refined his approach and his above-average bat speed generates hard contact to all fields. He's found a decent balance between his hit and power tools now, and while he won't be a middle-of-the-order force, something like .260 and 15 home runs is perfectly plausible. Fairchild is an above-average runner that should stick in center, and has enough speed and arm to play any outfield spot. The bat might end up just short of an every day role, but Fairchild does a little of everything, and that should be enough to keep him employed in the majors for a while.

12 Jameson Hannah OF

Born: 08/10/97　Age: 22　Bats: L　Throws: L　Height: 5'9"　Weight: 185　Origin: Round 2, 2018 Draft (#50 overall)

YEAR	TEAM	LVL	AGE	PA	R	2B	3B	HR	RBI	BB	K	SB	CS	AVG/OBP/SLG	DRC+	VORP	BABIP	BRR	FRAA	WARP	PF
2018	VER	A-	20	95	14	4	1	1	10	9	24	6	0	.279/.347/.384	128	7.5	.377	1.1	CF(18) -2.4	0.4	100
2019	STO	A+	21	414	48	25	3	2	31	29	88	6	7	.283/.341/.381	111	12.7	.361	-3.2	RF(49) -0.8, CF(41) -2.4	0.7	100
2019	DAY	A+	21	78	6	3	1	0	6	9	16	2	1	.224/.325/.299	70	-1.4	.294	-0.3	CF(13) -0.3, RF(2) 0.1	-0.1	107
2020	CIN	MLB	22	251	20	12	1	3	21	15	70	4	1	.230/.284/.326	61	0.0	.318	-0.3	CF -1, RF 0	-0.5	97

Comparables: Zoilo Almonte, Alfredo Marte, Fernando Martinez

Acquired from the Athletics for a Tanner Roark rental, Hannah doesn't have a ton of upside due to some tweenerish tendencies in the profile, but he should have a productive major league career. He's a smaller guy with minimal stride and load, so it's very much a hit-over-power profile, although he can fire some balls into the gaps for you. There's an above-average hit tool, although the approach is still raw. Hannah shows good instincts in the outfield, although he may not have the sheer foot speed to play every day in center, and his arm is fringy enough to be a better fit in left. That said, he could handle all three spots in the outfield, hit a little bit, run a little bit, and there's a non-zero chance he develops enough pop to be a second-division starter type. The likely outcome here is fourth/bench outfielder though.

13 Tyler Callihan 2B/3B

Born: 06/22/00　Age: 20　Bats: L　Throws: R　Height: 6'1"　Weight: 205　Origin: Round 3, 2019 Draft (#85 overall)

YEAR	TEAM	LVL	AGE	PA	R	2B	3B	HR	RBI	BB	K	SB	CS	AVG/OBP/SLG	DRC+	VORP	BABIP	BRR	FRAA	WARP	PF
2019	GRV	RK+	19	217	27	10	5	5	26	9	46	9	3	.250/.286/.422	86	3.9	.297	-0.4		0.3	91
2020	CIN	MLB	20	251	20	11	2	4	23	15	73	2	1	.213/.265/.330	55	0.0	.291	0.0		-0.6	97

Callihan slid to the third round of the draft from a late-first-round projection, and the Reds were more than happy to give him almost double slot to sign him away from South Carolina. He's a bat-first prospect with plus power projection, and if that all plays out you will find a spot in the field for him to stand. The Reds have tried him at both second and third base. Third base is a better fit, although his hands and transfer can be a bit rough, the actions somewhat mechanical. That is something you can smooth out, but I don't expect he'll ever be a good infield glove. You're here for the bat though, and Callihan offers a sweet, rotational lefty swing with plenty of bat speed and loft. The usual non-elite prep bat risks apply to the hit tool here, but there's above-average every day upside with 20+ home runs possible.

14 Rece Hinds SS

Born: 09/05/00　Age: 19　Bats: R　Throws: R　Height: 6'4"　Weight: 215　Origin: Round 2, 2019 Draft (#49 overall)

YEAR	TEAM	LVL	AGE	PA	R	2B	3B	HR	RBI	BB	K	SB	CS	AVG/OBP/SLG	DRC+	VORP	BABIP	BRR	FRAA	WARP	PF
2020	CIN	MLB	19	251	20	11	1	4	21	20	89	2	1	.200/.270/.303	54	0.0	.310	0.0		-0.6	97

Without much debate, Hinds possessed the best raw power of any prep prospect entering the 2019 draft. What tools he possesses beyond the pop is an entirely different debate. After winning several home run derbies in the summer showcase circuit, he was edged-out by Bobby Witt Jr. in the All-Star Game edition that is played in-between rounds of the MLB derby. While Witt was chosen second overall, Hinds was selected 47 picks later due to his one-dimensional profile. Playing for one of the most stacked high school teams in recent memory, he was relegated to the designated hitter role and spent time at both third base and the corner outfield spots because of his defensive liabilities. The arm is strong -- as is the theme for most of his skill-set -- but he lacks finesse and precision to handle a position like shortstop, and the max effort swinging may cause him trouble. On the bright side, with some refinement to his game, there is a lot of room for development in a young power-hitting archetype.

15 Joel Kuhnel RHP

Born: 02/19/95   Age: 25   Bats: R   Throws: R   Height: 6'5"   Weight: 260   Origin: Round 11, 2016 Draft (#318 overall)

YEAR	TEAM	LVL	AGE	W	L	SV	G	GS	IP	H	HR	BB/9	K/9	K	GB%	BABIP	WHIP	ERA	DRA	WARP	PF
2017	DYT	A	22	2	4	11	48	0	64	78	6	1.4	7.6	54	54%	.353	1.38	4.36	5.10	-0.1	100
2018	DAY	A+	23	1	4	17	44	0	53¹	54	2	1.9	9.4	56	54%	.340	1.22	3.04	3.84	0.7	100
2019	CHT	AA	24	3	2	10	25	0	35²	26	5	2.0	7.6	30	39%	.212	0.95	2.27	3.23	0.6	100
2019	LOU	AAA	24	2	1	4	16	0	18	13	1	4.0	10.0	20	38%	.273	1.17	2.00	3.41	0.5	100
2019	CIN	MLB	24	1	0	0	11	0	9²	8	1	4.7	8.4	9	54%	.259	1.34	4.66	4.37	0.1	98
2020	CIN	MLB	25	2	2	0	31	0	32	31	5	3.8	9.9	36	42%	.303	1.37	4.32	4.36	0.4	97

Comparables: Chasen Bradford, Dan Slania, Sam Tuivailala

Kuhnel somewhat anonymously climbed the ranks of the Reds organization after converting to the bullpen following the 2016 draft. He's never dominated quite as much or rose quite as quickly as you'd expect from a college arm with a two-pitch mix as good as his fastball and slider. The fastball sits mid-90s and the four-seam has some giddy-up when he elevates it, and he'll throw a sinker down in the zone with decent run as well. The slider is a plus two-plane breaker in the upper-80s. Kuhnel works with an easy tempo and uses a short arm action that means hitters see the ball late. He lacks athleticism, but repeats well enough and fills up the zone, and he certainly doesn't lack for arm strength. A plus fastball/slider reliever is more common than it used to be, but you can still use on in the seventh or eighth inning.

16 Ryan Hendrix RHP

Born: 12/16/94   Age: 25   Bats: R   Throws: R   Height: 6'3"   Weight: 185   Origin: Round 5, 2016 Draft (#138 overall)

YEAR	TEAM	LVL	AGE	W	L	SV	G	GS	IP	H	HR	BB/9	K/9	K	GB%	BABIP	WHIP	ERA	DRA	WARP	PF
2017	DYT	A	22	4	1	6	23	0	34¹	19	2	2.6	16.0	61	49%	.298	0.84	2.36	1.92	1.2	100
2017	DAY	A+	22	1	4	2	24	0	27²	29	4	6.2	8.8	27	49%	.309	1.73	3.58	5.95	-0.3	100
2018	DAY	A+	23	4	4	12	44	0	51	38	2	4.6	13.9	79	55%	.330	1.25	1.76	3.12	1.1	100
2019	CHT	AA	24	3	0	2	16	0	19¹	14	0	3.7	10.7	23	46%	.292	1.14	2.33	4.00	0.1	100
2020	CIN	MLB	25	2	2	0	33	0	35	35	5	4.0	10.6	41	42%	.327	1.44	4.71	4.73	0.3	97

Comparables: David Bednar, Stephen Nogosek, Cory Gearrin

Hendrix missed three months in the middle of the year due to injury, but when he was on the mound in Chattanooga, Southern League hitters struggled to deal with his fastball/curve combo. The fastball sits in the mid-90s and gets decent plane from the combination of Hendrix's height and high slot. The curve gets heavily-used, and it's not hard to see why he'd want to spam it—it's a power, 12-6 mid-80s breaker. He commands the hook better than the heater as well. Hendrix doesn't have much of a track record of throwing strikes, going all the way back to his time in the Texas A&M bullpen, so the wildness and lack of wiggle on the fastball may make him more of a middle reliever than late-inning fireman. Then again, the curve might be good enough that a high-leverage role is on the table regardless.

17 Packy Naughton RHP

Born: 04/16/96   Age: 24   Bats: R   Throws: L   Height: 6'2"   Weight: 195   Origin: Round 9, 2017 Draft (#257 overall)

YEAR	TEAM	LVL	AGE	W	L	SV	G	GS	IP	H	HR	BB/9	K/9	K	GB%	BABIP	WHIP	ERA	DRA	WARP	PF
2017	BIL	RK	21	3	3	0	14	12	60	58	5	3.0	9.4	63	55%	.325	1.30	3.15	2.59	2.2	104
2018	DYT	A	22	5	10	0	28	28	154	168	12	2.0	8.0	137	39%	.343	1.31	4.03	5.31	-0.2	101
2019	DAY	A+	23	5	2	0	9	9	51¹	49	2	1.6	8.8	50	45%	.320	1.13	2.63	4.20	0.5	99
2019	CHT	AA	23	6	10	0	19	19	105²	109	8	2.2	6.9	81	40%	.299	1.28	3.66	4.91	0.1	108
2020	CIN	MLB	24	2	2	0	33	0	35	35	5	3.4	6.6	26	39%	.278	1.37	4.48	4.68	0.3	97

Comparables: Taylor Rogers, Dillon Overton, Aaron Brooks

A somewhat generic college lefty when the Reds popped him late on Day 2 of the 2017 draft, Naughton has developed into a solid, if not spectacular pitching prospect. One of a growing group of young southpaws that emulate Cole Hamels, Naughton works primarily off a low-90s fastball and potential plus change. His fastball has ticked up into the low-90s since college, and he commands the pitch well enough to keep hitters from doing too much damage. The added velocity has helped separate it even further off his low-80s change. The cambio shows good fade and he commands it well as well. It will be his out pitch at higher levels as Naughton's curveball is below-average. Despite lacking premium stuff, Naughton handled Double-A in 2019 with aplomb. The profile is more backend starter or swingman without a breaking ball jump.

18 TJ Friedl OF

Born: 08/14/95   Age: 24   Bats: L   Throws: L   Height: 5'10"   Weight: 180   Origin: Undrafted Free Agent, 2016

YEAR	TEAM	LVL	AGE	PA	R	2B	3B	HR	RBI	BB	K	SB	CS	AVG/OBP/SLG	DRC+	VORP	BABIP	BRR	FRAA	WARP	PF
2017	DYT	A	21	292	47	20	6	5	25	29	46	14	8	.284/.378/.472	138	25.6	.328	4.1	RF(22) 0.7, CF(18) -3.0	1.9	100
2017	DAY	A+	21	199	15	6	2	2	13	10	39	2	1	.257/.313/.346	80	3.3	.317	0.0	CF(20) -1.3, RF(18) -2.5	0.2	101
2018	DAY	A+	22	274	40	10	4	3	35	38	44	11	4	.294/.405/.412	138	23.4	.350	4.7	LF(39) 2.0, CF(19) -1.0	2.3	103
2018	PEN	AA	22	296	47	10	3	2	16	28	56	19	5	.276/.359/.360	112	12.7	.345	3.3	LF(53) 5.1, CF(9) -1.0	1.9	98
2019	CHT	AA	23	269	38	11	4	5	28	29	50	13	4	.235/.347/.385	113	9.4	.277	1.3	RF(42) 2.4, LF(14) -1.4	1.1	111
2020	CIN	MLB	24	251	24	11	2	5	25	20	60	6	2	.227/.306/.363	78	0.0	.286	0.4	LF 2, CF -2	0.2	97

Comparables: Matt Szczur, Ty France, Zoilo Almonte

The story of how Friedl came to be a Red is a fun fact—he was signed as an undrafted free agent for $732,500 after no one realized he had been eligible for the 2016 draft—but his pro career turned out more or less how you'd expect a third or fourth round college outfielder's to go. It's more bench outfielder than starter; Friedl can play all three spots although his arm is a bit short for right and he has to grind it out in center. He won't hit for much power, but will be a pesky at-bat and get on base just enough to make himself useful if you have to start him for a month. Almost four years on from his signing, the circumstances add some nice color to what is a solid, if somewhat generic fourth outfielder prospect.

19 Vladimir Gutierrez RHP

Born: 09/18/95   Age: 24   Bats: R   Throws: R   Height: 6'0"   Weight: 190   Origin: International Free Agent, 2016

YEAR	TEAM	LVL	AGE	W	L	SV	G	GS	IP	H	HR	BB/9	K/9	K	GB%	BABIP	WHIP	ERA	DRA	WARP	PF
2017	DAY	A+	21	7	8	0	19	19	103	108	10	1.7	8.2	94	42%	.320	1.23	4.46	3.84	1.7	106
2018	PEN	AA	22	9	10	0	27	27	147	139	18	2.3	8.9	145	46%	.298	1.20	4.35	4.18	2.0	96
2019	LOU	AAA	23	6	11	0	27	27	137	144	26	3.2	7.7	117	41%	.291	1.40	6.04	4.93	2.4	99
2020	CIN	MLB	24	2	2	0	33	0	35	37	7	3.5	6.9	27	41%	.286	1.44	5.28	5.34	0.0	97

Comparables: José Ureña, Hunter Wood, Jackson Stephens

You don't scout the stat line, but there really isn't any way to sugarcoat Guttierrez's 6+ ERA. Can you blame some of the 26 bombs in 137 Triple-A innings on the new baseball? Perhaps, but the horsehide isn't any different in the majors, and the intermittent fastball command issues, loopy curves that stay up, and flat change-ups bare some of the responsibility as well. Your management consultant will tell you not to mix praise in with criticism, and tt was a bad year, but nevertheless let's try to find some good in here. Gutierrez's low-90s fastball can get up to 95 and there's run when he's down in the zone with the pitch. If he is spotting the heater around the knees, batters will just beat it into the ground. A mid-to-upper-70s curve ball is inconsistent, and doesn't always have good late, downer action. It can be a bit humpy, but the best flash above-average. His low-80s change has plenty of velocity separation but can be flat with some tail, although he'll show you one with fade on occasion. Overall the profile was just far too hittable as a starter in the upper minors, but there might be something to be gained out of a move to the pen where Gutierrez can max out the fastball and try to throw the good version of the curve more.

20   Lorenzo Cedrola   OF

Born: 01/12/98   Age: 22   Bats: R   Throws: R   Height: 5'8"   Weight: 152   Origin: International Free Agent, 2015

YEAR	TEAM	LVL	AGE	PA	R	2B	3B	HR	RBI	BB	K	SB	CS	AVG/OBP/SLG	DRC+	VORP	BABIP	BRR	FRAA	WARP	PF
2017	GRN	A	19	379	47	18	3	4	34	11	48	19	7	.285/.322/.387	111	17.7	.319	1.2	CF(75) -7.1, RF(14) 3.0	1.2	104
2018	GRN	A	20	229	40	17	3	0	22	5	29	10	8	.318/.350/.427	120	17.2	.362	3.4	CF(29) 8.5, RF(10) 1.6	2.5	101
2018	DYT	A	20	188	13	4	2	1	11	9	28	13	7	.260/.310/.325	86	1.2	.303	-0.5	CF(44) -2.7	0.0	101
2019	DAY	A+	21	381	41	10	7	1	28	17	43	18	10	.277/.330/.356	112	10.3	.310	-1.4	CF(42) -4.6, LF(31) 4.1	1.0	102
2020	CIN	MLB	22	251	22	11	2	3	22	13	44	7	3	.249/.304/.345	74	0.0	.298	0.0	CF -1, RF 0	0.0	97

And one more bench outfielder for the road. Cedrola has a bit more defensive value than Friedl—he's a bit better center fielder and has a stronger arm—but lacks even Freidl's power and physicality at the plate. Cedrola looks like he hasn't really grown out of his complex-league body, and while he controls the zone well enough, the swing can lack some oomph. It's really hard to be Ben Revere in 2020, and Cedrola likely isn't that good a hitter either. Well, maybe as good as the fourth outfielder version.

Personal Cheeseball

PC   Jimmy Herget   RHP

Born: 09/09/93   Age: 26   Bats: R   Throws: R   Height: 6'3"   Weight: 170   Origin: Round 6, 2015 Draft (#175 overall)

YEAR	TEAM	LVL	AGE	W	L	SV	G	GS	IP	H	HR	BB/9	K/9	K	GB%	BABIP	WHIP	ERA	DRA	WARP	PF
2017	PEN	AA	23	1	3	16	24	0	29²	22	1	3.6	13.3	44	32%	.323	1.15	2.73	2.76	0.7	100
2017	LOU	AAA	23	3	1	9	28	0	32¹	30	4	2.5	7.8	28	38%	.283	1.21	3.06	3.94	0.5	100
2018	LOU	AAA	24	1	3	0	50	0	59²	59	5	3.2	9.8	65	36%	.327	1.34	3.47	4.95	0.1	100
2019	LOU	AAA	25	3	4	2	48	0	58²	41	7	5.5	10.4	68	37%	.246	1.31	2.91	3.12	1.8	100
2019	CIN	MLB	25	0	0	0	5	0	6¹	8	2	4.3	0.0	0	22%	.286	1.74	4.26	8.49	-0.2	97
2020	CIN	MLB	26	1	2	0	33	0	35	54	12	5.1	8.9	35	35%	.382	2.12	10.22	6.94	-0.7	97

Comparables: Chandler Shepherd, Akeel Morris, Heath Hembree

He looks like the best over-30 rec league basketball player in your nearest medium-sized city (he's 26). He wears stirrups, of course. His mechanics wouldn't look out of place in the dead ball era, but he throws a heckuva lot harder than Kid Nichols. He's a sidearmer, naturally, but can get it up to 95. The slider's not bad either. It's a tough at-bat for righties, but the weird funk in his delivery means he might never throw enough strikes to keep him from logging a lot of miles between Louisville and Cincinnati. The aesthetics are different though and a reminder that baseball is a weird sport that you can occasionally bend to your will in odd ways.

Low Minors Sleeper

LMS   Ivan Johnson   SS/2B

Born: 10/11/98   Age: 21   Bats: B   Throws: R   Height: 6'0"   Weight: 190   Origin: Round 4, 2019 Draft (#114 overall)

YEAR	TEAM	LVL	AGE	PA	R	2B	3B	HR	RBI	BB	K	SB	CS	AVG/OBP/SLG	DRC+	VORP	BABIP	BRR	FRAA	WARP	PF
2019	GRV	RK+	20	210	27	10	1	6	22	18	46	11	4	.255/.327/.415	106	11.9	.309	2.6		1.2	92
2020	CIN	MLB	21	251	20	12	1	4	22	14	78	2	1	.205/.256/.312	48	0.0	.290	0.0		-0.8	97

After going over slot for Hinds and Callihan, the Reds turned their attention to Johnson, a JuCo second baseman in Round 4. He's likely an inch or two shorter than his listed six-foot, but it's a solid, athletic frame. It's a well-balanced swing from both sides of the plate with solid bat control, but he might lack even an average offensive tool and is a better fit at second base than shortstop. Keep an eye on how the bat develops or doesn't in full-season ball.

Top Talents 25 and Under (as of 4/1/2020)

1. Nick Senzel
2. Nick Lodolo

3. Aristedes Aquino
4. Jose Garcia
5. Tyler Stephenson
6. Jonathan India
7. Hunter Greene
8. Tyler Mahle
9. Tony Santillan
10. Lucas Sims

For a team in theory opening its competitive window, the Reds sure are old on the "established major leaguer" side. Of 16 Reds producing at least a win in 2019, just two, Tyler Mahle and Aristedes Aquino, are 25 or younger. With value distrubuted by age of like an inverted bell curve, the Reds are going to have to thread a needle with their limited cohort who are both young and presently major league ready.

Part of the team's future success depends on what's around the next bend for Nick Senzel, who still has plenty of luster but also perhaps some twigs and dirt from barreling through the forest. Far outstripping rookie limits and approaching the qualified threshold in 2019, he middled on both the offensive (.742 OPS, 88 DRC+) and defensive sides. He's essentially without a position moving forward, with starting roles at his natural third base and adopted center field homes presumably blocked by Eugenio Suárez and new addition Shogo Akiyama. Still, there remain flashes of the player who was in 2016 the second overall pick, and the hope he might yet deliver on his star billing. As long as he is eligible for the 25U, there's room for dreaming on Senzel.

Aquino, too, gave plenty of reasons for Reds faithful to believe in him; exploding onto the scene with 11 home runs in his first 16 games. His 225 plate appearances as a whole pro-rated him as nearly a three-win player, and while it's unclear if the 25-year-old—eligible for this list by just three weeks—without a prospect pedrigree is truly of that caliber, his small sample of a rookie campaign alone was more a showcase than many players ever get.

Mahle, meanwhile, has shown himself a much more average contributor: In 2019, his DRA- sat at 99, and that represented a step up after struggling in two previous majors stints. It's not an exciting profile, and as it stands now Maile is sixth in the rotation at best, but he has started 48 games across the past two seasons to replacement-level results, with indications he could do more in the future. Maile's not just some bit of junk mail, even if he's not what most Cincinnati fans have waited for.

Sims might appear a strange choice—in his last season of eligibility here, everyone's favorite simulated reality video game is the old man in the room by another measure: he was drafted all the way back in 2012 (in the first round). Finally making the move to the bullpen, he struck out nearly 12 per nine across 43 innings. To take the step beyond mid-leverage piece, the walks and home run rate need to come down, but as to the latter there will likely be a patch to the Sims (and everyone else) next season helping draw it down.

Eyewitness Reports

Eyewitness Report: Nick Lodolo

Evaluator: Samuel Hale
Report Date: 06/02/2019
Dates Seen: 3/22/2019
Risk Factor: Moderate

Delivery: Delivery features a medium leg kick and length to a three-quarter slot that results in issues repeating his release point. It's not high effort, but it doesn't look as smooth as it could. It's a slow progression from the full windup, but his tempo improves when he works out of the stretch. Part of the full windup issues can be chalked up to his size; it takes time getting everything synced and moving in the right direction, and he'll lose his progressions from time to time.

Pitch Type	Future Grade	Sitting Velocity	Peak Velocity	Report
FB	60	92-95	96	Four seamer with minimal cut. Command was above-average. Velo maintained through late game also, staying consistent through 100+ pitches
CH	50	87-89	89	A lot of 88s on the gun, with sink that kept hitters off balance. Generated swinging strikeouts and weak contact, though was more effective against RHB.
CB	60	80-82	83	Good 12-5 movement, good velo separation with fastball. Command improved as game progressed. When it missed, it missed arm side against both RH and LHBs. Wasn't afraid to use it early or late in counts.

Conclusion: Lodolo is a lanky left-handed pitcher with a three-pitch mix and decent athleticism. He used the fastball as his primary weapon, with minimal breaking ball usage early. As the game wore on, he found feel and began working in the curveball more to start off hitters and set up later-count fastballs to finish them off. His windup isn't unusual, but his long arm swing to slot leads to some drag and errant pitches arm side. Overall his fastball is his best pitch, but the curveball showed signs of taking that crown with more time, and it's a deep enough arsenal to top out in the middle of a big-league rotation. Lodolo has a high floor as a big-league arm, but the ceiling is harder to peg on account of baseball's shifting landscape. While he'll begin his career as a starter, the stuff may ultimately play best in a multi-inning relief role, a la playoff Andrew Miller.

Eyewitness Report: Mariel Bautista

Evaluator: Keith Rader
Report Date: 04/30/2019
Dates Seen: 4/4-4/5, 4/25-4/28
Risk Factor: High
Physical/Health: Tall and lanky with plenty of room to add good weight, projectable frame with high and thin waist, expect a Gary Matthews Jr. body comp as he physically matures, walks with a slouch and his head tilted forward, much more athletic than he appears at first glance, quick twitch speedster who should age well.

Tool	Future Grade	Report
Hit	60	Makes a lot of contact; has a plan at the plate; aggressive hitter, but shows a solid awareness of the strike zone; will walk enough, but not a lot; hits off front foot and ends up off balance more than I'd like; susceptible to breaking stuff down; really handles pitches up well, and is short to the ball there; swing lengthens on pitches down in zone; does a good job spoiling pitches when fooled; bat stays in the zone a long time without much loft in bat path; mechanical and swing adjustments will be needed to reach his potential and patch holes in the swing; if he can solve the bottom part of the zone, its an easy plus hit tool
Power	60	Plus bat speed; long arms create plus leverage when extended; ball really jumps off the bat when he gets a pitch he can handle; can hit the ball out to any part of the yard; quick hands on balls up; has the speed/aggressiveness to turn some singles into doubles; balance issues reduce power on pitches down in zone; will hit some really long homers
Baserunning/ Speed	70	Gets out of the box as fast as any RHH and with near elite speed; reaches top speed early; clocked sub-4 once and another 4.00; wants the extra base; eye-catching wheels on the offensive side of the game, but runs a bit more upright with a glove on his hand; will put loads of pressure on opposing infields, and make an impact in the run game
Glove	50	Currently being moved around the outfield, but has the skill set to play anywhere in the grass; takes good routes; gets good reads on balls off the bat, but isn't as explosive in the field as he is running the bases; good closing speed; should improve as a defender with reps and a consistent outfield home; has the speed to make up for a lot of missteps
Arm	50	Easily the weakest part of his game; arm strength may be above average but has struggles to put throws on line; doesn't get great extension; the strength is there, but he has some mechanical work ahead to reach a 5; below average arm for right, but will work well in left or center

Conclusion: Bautista is a five-tool contributor, and has a lot of potential with the bat. He has a nice combination of speed and power, and is eye catching on the diamond. He will have to make a swing adjustment at some point if he's going to cover the bottom part of the zone and reach that potential. It's never a good thing to need a revamped swing to succeed, but Bautista is athletic enough that he should be able to handle it. He's more raw than I'd like from a 21-year-old making his first foray into full-season baseball, but with some patience you don't need to squint to see an impactful everyday player who is a serious threat at the dish.

Cleveland Indians

The State of the System

It's not a bad system by any means, but it does say something that the first prospect we have a photo of ranks fourth.

The Top Ten

★ ★ ★ *2020 Top 101 Prospect* **#58** ★ ★ ★

1 George Valera OF OFP: 60 ETA: 2023

Born: 11/13/00 Age: 19 Bats: L Throws: L Height: 5'10" Weight: 160 Origin: International Free Agent, 2017

YEAR	TEAM	LVL	AGE	PA	R	2B	3B	HR	RBI	BB	K	SB	CS	AVG/OBP/SLG	DRC+	VORP	BABIP	BRR	FRAA	WARP	PF
2019	MHV	A-	18	188	22	7	1	8	29	29	52	6	2	.236/.356/.446	132	11.8	.296	-0.3	CF(25) 0.7, RF(11) -3.5	1.1	100
2019	LKC	A	18	26	1	0	1	0	3	2	9	0	2	.087/.192/.174	35	-3.4	.143	-1.0	RF(3) 1.2, LF(2) 1.6	0.0	106
2020	CLE	MLB	19	251	24	11	1	7	26	22	85	3	2	.203/.278/.346	67	0.0	.291	-0.5	CF -1, RF -1	-0.4	98

Comparables: Ronald Acuña Jr., Carson Kelly, Victor Robles

The Report: There are few in the minor leagues who possess the collection of tools Valera has, and it only takes one look to get a feel for why he's so highly thought of by many in the industry: He has plus hit and power tools thanks to a beautiful, compact swing that delivers hard contact to all fields. The excellent barrel control is a credit to his exceptional balance, as it enables him to make contact with pitches thrown anywhere in the strike zone. He might hit a few too many grounders and still has some pitch recognition kinks to work out, but he nonetheless posted a 132 DRC+ in a league where he was three years younger than the average player: that's special.

While he was listed at 160 pounds for the 2019 season, that admittedly looks rather light (as in, at least 20 pounds light). He has a well-built frame, particularly in the lower half which hasn't impeded his ability to play adequate defense in center, but it could force him into a corner role if he continues to thicken. Still, the fact he earns sufficient defensive grades in center speaks to his athleticism. Should Valera move to a corner spot, he has more than enough bat to profile there.

We want to see how he handles a full season's workload before we full-send on the Valera bandwagon, as his past injuries and load management have sapped him of important reps. Expect him to begin the year with Lake County, where he will once again play against older competition.

Variance: High. Still young, some whiff issues, and non-ideal frame, but he can hit.

Mark Barry's Fantasy Take: The numbers for Valera in 2019 were definitely ugly—he struck out a lot more and generally hit a lot less, neither of which is very encouraging. That said, he'll be 19 years old for the entirety of the 2020 campaign and all of the tools we fell in love with upon his signing are still in the repertoire. Now is the time to see if you can "buy low," as Valera's upside of .290-.300 with decent pop hasn't changed.

★ ★ ★ *2020 Top 101 Prospect* **#66** ★ ★ ★

2 Nolan Jones 3B   OFP: 55   ETA: 2021

Born: 05/07/98   Age: 22   Bats: L   Throws: R   Height: 6'2"   Weight: 185   Origin: Round 2, 2016 Draft (#55 overall)

YEAR	TEAM	LVL	AGE	PA	R	2B	3B	HR	RBI	BB	K	SB	CS	AVG/OBP/SLG	DRC+	VORP	BABIP	BRR	FRAA	WARP	PF
2017	MHV	A-	19	265	41	18	3	4	33	43	60	1	0	.317/.430/.482	182	28.6	.417	1.7	3B(53) 0.0	2.8	104
2018	LKC	A	20	389	46	12	0	16	49	63	97	2	1	.279/.393/.464	155	33.5	.347	-0.9	3B(77) -4.1	2.9	102
2018	LYN	A+	20	130	23	9	0	3	17	26	34	0	0	.298/.438/.471	159	12.7	.418	0.1	3B(28) -0.3	1.1	100
2019	LYN	A+	21	324	48	12	1	7	41	65	85	5	3	.286/.435/.425	172	28.7	.399	-1.4	3B(72) -3.4	2.8	101
2019	AKR	AA	21	211	33	10	2	8	22	31	63	2	0	.253/.370/.466	150	17.0	.346	0.8	3B(43) 0.0	1.8	97
2020	CLE	MLB	22	251	28	12	1	8	29	29	85	0	0	.240/.333/.406	97	3.0	.352	-0.3	3B -1	0.6	98

Comparables: Drew Robinson, Lewis Brinson, Shed Long

The Report: The report on Jones remains mostly the same, for good and for ill. It's an unabashed good that he maintained his pop into the upper minors. There's plus-plus raw power, but you are far more likely to see it at 5 p.m, as a lot has to go right for him to get it into games. He will sell out for pull-side pop too often, and the swing gets long and steep, leading to swing-and-miss and a below-average-to-fringe hit tool projection.

That's still enough hit to get 20-odd bombs on the back of the baseball card, but if Jones can refine some things, it might more look like Matt Chapman on the offensive side. It will distinctly not look like Matt Chapman at the hot corner. The arm is plus, but Jones lacks lateral range or great instincts, and although he grinds it out at third, he might be a better fit in an outfield corner as he still runs pretty well. He has enough power for anywhere on the defensive spectrum, but it remains an open question how much the swing and approach will allow it to play in games up the ladder.

Variance: High. It's a good approach, but there's a lot of swing-and-miss in the zone, and he doesn't track breaking balls well. That means the hit tool is going to be high variance, and thus the profile as well.

Mark Barry's Fantasy Take: There are a few too many strikeouts in Jones's arsenal for me to feel really good about paying a premium for him in dynasty leagues. His advanced ability to draw a walk should offset a portion of the strikeout issues, but sitting down to strikes around 30 percent of the time will significantly affect his ability to be even mediocre in the batting average category. He drew a Matt Chapman-upside comp in our Dynasty Midseason 50, but I worry he'll be a less fun 2019 Daniel Vogelbach on the strong side of a platoon.

★ ★ ★ *2020 Top 101 Prospect* **#98** ★ ★ ★

3 Brayan Rocchio SS   OFP: 55   ETA: 2023

Born: 01/13/01   Age: 19   Bats: B   Throws: R   Height: 5'10"   Weight: 150   Origin: International Free Agent, 2017

YEAR	TEAM	LVL	AGE	PA	R	2B	3B	HR	RBI	BB	K	SB	CS	AVG/OBP/SLG	DRC+	VORP	BABIP	BRR	FRAA	WARP	PF
2018	DIN	RK	17	111	19	2	3	1	12	5	14	8	5	.323/.391/.434	136	9.7	.369	-1.0	SS(15) -0.2, 2B(8) 0.6	0.8	90
2018	CLT	RK	17	158	21	10	1	1	17	10	17	14	8	.343/.389/.448	161	15.0	.378	1.2	SS(26) 5.2, 3B(8) -1.1	2.0	107
2019	MHV	A-	18	295	33	12	3	5	27	20	40	14	8	.250/.310/.373	107	12.8	.276	-1.8	SS(62) 5.5, 2B(6) 0.6	1.8	100
2020	CLE	MLB	19	251	25	12	1	5	25	17	53	9	5	.242/.302/.369	78	0.0	.294	-0.1	SS 2, 2B 0	0.3	98

Comparables: Enrique Hernández, Amed Rosario, Juniel Querecuto

The Report: Like Valera, Rocchio joined the Indians during the 2017 signing period, although with far less fanfare. Yet he immediately showed signs of being a bargain signing. Despite being joined at the hip by Valera and Aaron Bracho for much of his professional career, his style of play is vastly different. Rocchio displays a plus hit tool from both sides of the plate thanks to a sound approach and really good hand-eye coordination. Hitting for power is not his game, however, as his small frame and average bat speed point to more of a line-drive approach. There is no harm in experimenting with elevating the ball at this point in his development timeline: He began lifting the ball with Mahoning Valley more than he'd done in the past. Even if he fails to make progress in lifting the ball, he has more than enough gap-to-gap power to be effective.

Along with his well-regarded hit tool, Rocchio has the makings of a plus defensive shortstop: He displays good instincts and has no problem going to his left or right. His arm might be the only thing which limits him as a shortstop, though, as it's currently borderline for the position. It's possible the arm improves as he adds much-needed muscle, but as things currently stand there is a non-zero chance he moves to the keystone. To that point, however, he played a handful of games at the position this year and looked rather comfortable, so it should be a seamless transition should it come to that.

Rocchio is not as exciting as some of the other names on this list, yet he still could be a solid ballplayer, one who contributes in a multitude of ways even if there may not be a single standout tool. He earned an aggressive placement in 2019 and likely will do so again in 2020, where he figures to begin the year with Lake County.

Variance: Medium. He is what he is. He just needs more reps and muscle.

Mark Barry's Fantasy Take: This version of Rocchio is the standard "better in real life than in fantasy" dude, blending strong defensive chops with an elite knack for contact at the dish. The good news, for Rocchio and dynasty managers alike, is that he's not a finished product by any stretch, and he has the tools and know-how to develop into a real stolen-base threat while not killing you in power categories. He's super far away, but should still slot into that top-200ish range.

★ ★ ★ *2020 Top 101 Prospect* **#101** ★ ★ ★

4 | **James Karinchak** **RHP** OFP: 60 ETA: 2019
Born: 09/22/95 Age: 24 Bats: R Throws: R Height: 6'3" Weight: 230 Origin: Round 9, 2017 Draft (#282 overall)

YEAR	TEAM	LVL	AGE	W	L	SV	G	GS	IP	H	HR	BB/9	K/9	K	GB%	BABIP	WHIP	ERA	DRA	WARP	PF
2017	MHV	A-	21	2	2	0	10	6	23¹	30	1	3.5	12.0	31	30%	.468	1.67	5.79	7.07	-0.5	101
2018	LKC	A	22	3	0	1	7	0	11¹	8	0	5.6	15.9	20	55%	.400	1.32	0.79	3.41	0.2	100
2018	LYN	A+	22	1	1	13	25	0	27	14	1	5.7	15.0	45	40%	.295	1.15	1.00	2.77	0.7	100
2018	AKR	AA	22	0	1	0	10	0	10¹	7	1	10.5	13.9	16	29%	.300	1.84	2.61	5.59	-0.1	100
2019	AKR	AA	23	0	0	6	10	0	10	2	0	1.8	21.6	24	56%	.222	0.40	0.00	1.80	0.3	100
2019	COH	AAA	23	1	1	2	17	0	17¹	14	2	6.8	21.8	42	48%	.571	1.56	4.67	2.12	0.7	100
2019	CLE	MLB	23	0	0	0	5	0	5¹	3	0	1.7	13.5	8	38%	.231	0.75	1.69	3.89	0.1	100
2020	CLE	MLB	24	2	2	0	45	0	48	42	7	4.5	8.3	44	42%	.270	1.37	4.02	4.24	0.5	98

Comparables: Jensen Lewis, Rogelio Armenteros, Aaron Blair

The Report: It's hard to describe Karinchak without resorting to complete hyperbole. His fastball and curveball are both true plus-plus offerings bordering on 8s. His strikeout rate went from "very impressive" to "playing The Show on rookie mode" last year, and he continued his dominance in a September cameo.

Karinchak's fastball is a weapon. He throws it at 96-99 from a very tough, extremely high arm slot reminiscent of former major-leaguer Josh Collmenter. It is difficult to pick up, and comes in with plane and life. It's even tougher to jump on because it's paired with Karinchak's curveball, which is frankly just one of the craziest pitches in the minors. It's a power curve, thrown at slider velocity in the mid 80s, but it moves with classic curveball break. The curve just dives out of sight from that high overhand release and leaves batters looking hapless trying to chase it. The two pitches play off each other quite well, and they leave batters looking foolish.

Karinchak does get out of whack mechanically and has walked more batters than you'd like. That was mostly—but not entirely—contained to the period immediately after he came back from a hamstring injury in 2019, and he did tighten his command more broadly year-over-year. But he might still go through wild spells that will give managers fits.

Variance: Medium. Karinchak might already be a very good or great MLB reliever, but he is a reliever with a spotty command history and that profile can be highly variant.

Mark Barry's Fantasy Take: Karinchak debuted in 2019 and got swinging strikes on 16 percent of his pitches. For a full season, that would slot in as one of the top-20 swinging-strike rates in the game, nuzzling up nicely to guys like Kenley Jansen, Kirby Yates, and Will Smith. That will likely be his role in Cleveland too, as a high-strikeout, high-leverage, bullpen arm. It's hard to go crazy for these guys, but Karinchak could be a mainstay in the top-20 relievers as early as 2021.

5 Daniel Espino RHP   OFP: 60   ETA: 2023/24

Born: 01/05/01   Age: 19   Bats: R   Throws: R   Height: 6'2"   Weight: 205   Origin: Round 1, 2019 Draft (#24 overall)

YEAR	TEAM	LVL	AGE	W	L	SV	G	GS	IP	H	HR	BB/9	K/9	K	GB%	BABIP	WHIP	ERA	DRA	WARP	PF
2019	CLE	RK	18	0	1	0	6	6	13²	7	1	3.3	10.5	16	50%	.207	0.88	1.98	1.65	0.6	104
2019	MHV	A-	18	0	2	0	3	3	10	9	1	4.5	16.2	18	32%	.381	1.40	6.30	2.96	0.3	97
2020	CLE	MLB	19	2	2	0	33	0	35	36	6	3.7	9.3	36	38%	.311	1.43	4.75	4.95	0.1	98

Comparables: Pedro Avila, Jake Thompson, Jenrry Mejia

The Report: There were a handful of high schoolers who had a case for best prep arm in the 2019 draft, and Espino was among them. His case rests primarily on the strength of his fastball, which sits mid 90s and routinely touched higher. The pitch showed explosive life and run up in the zone, and he can switch it up to a two-seamer with good sink as well. Espino isn't a pure arm strength play, as he also features two breaking balls with a chance to get to above-average. There's the usual high school pitcher changeup as well. The need for secondary improvements are one of the reasons Espino was merely a candidate for best prep arm and not the consensus pick. He's also fairly close to physically maxed compared to his cohort, and he can struggle with his command and control at times due to a long arm action he doesn't always repeat as well as you'd like. The fastball is good enough that the low minors shouldn't prove much of a challenge. Past there, the offspeed and command developments will determine whether he's a mid-rotation starter or reliever long term.

Variance: High. Espino is a prep pick with a limited pro track record, less projection than usual, and need of secondary development. The usual stuff.

Mark Barry's Fantasy Take: Your mileage may vary on Espino's potential, but it's not difficult to imagine a fantasy SP2 upside for the prep righty. With a heater that flirts with triple digits and three secondaries that flash better than average, perhaps only injuries and control could keep him from hitting that ceiling.

6 Emmanuel Clase RHP   OFP: 60   ETA: 2019

Born: 03/18/98   Age: 22   Bats: R   Throws: R   Height: 6'2"   Weight: 206   Origin: International Free Agent, 2015

YEAR	TEAM	LVL	AGE	W	L	SV	G	GS	IP	H	HR	BB/9	K/9	K	GB%	BABIP	WHIP	ERA	DRA	WARP	PF
2017	SDP	RK	19	2	4	0	9	6	35²	40	4	5.6	10.6	42	48%	.360	1.74	5.30	6.12	-0.1	101
2018	SPO	A-	20	1	1	12	22	0	28¹	16	0	1.9	8.6	27	62%	.222	0.78	0.64	2.25	0.9	100
2019	DEB	A+	21	2	0	1	6	0	7	4	0	1.3	14.1	11	77%	.308	0.71	0.00	2.98	0.1	100
2019	FRI	AA	21	1	2	11	33	1	37²	34	1	1.9	9.3	39	62%	.314	1.12	3.35	3.70	0.4	95
2019	TEX	MLB	21	2	3	1	21	1	23¹	20	2	2.3	8.1	21	59%	.281	1.11	2.31	3.91	0.4	109
2020	CLE	MLB	22	2	2	4	45	0	48	46	7	3.4	8.8	46	55%	.296	1.34	4.06	4.29	0.5	98

Comparables: Yennsy Diaz, Jake Newberry, Michael Feliz

The Report: Emmanuel Clase throws a 100 mph cutter. It's wild. He blitzed High-A and Double-A with the pitch and jumped right to the majors and was a perfectly fine late-inning arm immediately. Brooks Baseball will at times refer to pitches as being "borderline unfair." Well, there's nothing borderline about Clase's fastball. When he's on you have no idea how anyone ever makes contact with it. He pairs it with a pretty good slider as well that sits in the low 90s. If it weren't for the existence of James Karinchak, Clase would be clearly the best pure relief prospect in the minors. Cleveland now has both and hoo boy, is that pen going to be fun to watch for the next few years, health permitting.

Variance: Low. Clase is ready for a late-inning bullpen role now..

Mark Barry's Fantasy Take: If you've ever been on Twitter dot com, you've heard that Clase throws very hard. This is, in fact, true. He'll join Karinchak to form one of the most potent, young bullpen duos in baseball, boasting the skills that will play up in deeper formats or holds leagues. Unfortunately for Clase, he'll need to excel to avoid being relegated to a "Not Corey Kluber" Players Weekend jersey.

7 Logan Allen LHP — OFP: 55 — ETA: 2019

Born: 05/23/97 Age: 23 Bats: R Throws: L Height: 6'3" Weight: 200 Origin: Round 8, 2015 Draft (#231 overall)

YEAR	TEAM	LVL	AGE	W	L	SV	G	GS	IP	H	HR	BB/9	K/9	K	GB%	BABIP	WHIP	ERA	DRA	WARP	PF
2017	FTW	A	20	5	4	0	13	13	68¹	49	1	3.4	11.2	85	43%	.294	1.10	2.11	2.52	2.2	103
2017	LEL	A+	20	2	5	0	11	10	56²	60	2	2.9	9.1	57	50%	.352	1.38	3.97	3.95	0.9	102
2018	SAN	AA	21	10	6	0	20	19	121	89	7	2.8	9.3	125	43%	.269	1.05	2.75	3.22	3.0	102
2018	ELP	AAA	21	4	0	0	5	5	27²	21	4	4.2	8.5	26	38%	.236	1.23	1.63	3.24	0.7	107
2019	ELP	AAA	22	4	3	0	13	13	57²	61	8	3.4	9.8	63	47%	.338	1.44	5.15	3.84	1.6	109
2019	COH	AAA	22	1	1	0	5	5	22¹	31	6	4.8	7.3	18	24%	.362	1.93	7.66	8.48	-0.4	99
2019	SDN	MLB	22	2	3	0	8	4	25¹	33	4	4.6	5.0	14	54%	.341	1.82	6.75	6.71	-0.3	97
2019	CLE	MLB	22	0	0	0	1	0	2¹	3	0	0.0	11.6	3	17%	.500	1.29	0.00	8.06	-0.1	98
2020	CLE	MLB	23	5	6	0	41	11	88	99	14	3.8	6.9	68	43%	.310	1.55	5.49	5.43	0.0	98

Comparables: Brett Cecil, Peter Lambert, Stephen Gonsalves

The Report: Allen made his major league debut in 2019—winning a one dollar bet with John Cena in the process—but his overall campaign was uneven. Given San Diego's pitching depth, he couldn't really win a rotation spot, and was used a fair bit in long relief. He struggled out of the pen, but the stuff that made him a top 101 prospect remains intact. He got the fastball as high as 97, and the velocity sits a tick above-average from the left side generally. There's a full four-pitch arsenal that he mixes liberally, a good sinking change, a 1-7 breaking ball that's tough on lefties, and an average slider as well. There's nothing here that grades out as plus, which could make him a bit hittable at times in the majors, but there's no real weakness in the repertoire either, as all four pitches are MLB-quality. Cleveland gives him a slightly cleaner shot at a rotation spot, especially if they end up moving Mike Clevinger for some reason, and if he irons out the control and command blips, he remains a high-probability solid stating pitcher.

Variance: Low. Allen had an up-and-down year between Triple-A in the majors across two orgs, and the command issues are a little concerning, but he's a perfectly cromulent 2020 rotation option for Cleveland otherwise.

Mark Barry's Fantasy Take: After being traded to Cleveland, Allen struck out 33 percent of batters faced, walking zero. If he keeps that up, he will be very good. That statline came in just two and a third innings, however, so it might be difficult to rely on that sample. Let's call the lefty a borderline fantasy SP4-5, with upside for a little better if he figures out his command.

8 Ethan Hankins RHP — OFP: 55 — ETA: 2022

Born: 05/23/00 Age: 20 Bats: R Throws: R Height: 6'6" Weight: 200 Origin: Round 1C, 2018 Draft (#35 overall)

YEAR	TEAM	LVL	AGE	W	L	SV	G	GS	IP	H	HR	BB/9	K/9	K	GB%	BABIP	WHIP	ERA	DRA	WARP	PF
2019	MHV	A-	19	0	0	0	9	8	38²	23	1	4.2	10.0	43	61%	.232	1.06	1.40	3.30	0.8	98
2019	LKC	A	19	0	3	0	5	5	21¹	20	3	5.1	11.8	28	49%	.340	1.50	4.64	5.49	-0.1	101
2020	CLE	MLB	20	2	2	0	33	0	35	35	6	3.7	8.4	33	49%	.297	1.41	4.67	4.89	0.1	98

Comparables: Pedro Avila, Joe Ross, Jake Thompson

The Report: Some might forget that heading into the 2018 draft, Hankins was in consideration for the first overall pick, but a slow spring and some medical issues limited teams' interest. Despite that, he began 2019 with an aggressive assignment to Mahoning Valley and had some success before receiving an even-more-aggressive promotion to Lake County. I wrote up Hankins after one of his starts against Staten Island, where he displayed some fire-breathing stuff: The fastball was 94-97 with late life, the curve broke late and tunneled real well with the heater, and the slider was a distant yet sufficient third pitch. He has seldom used his changeup, though it's shown enough tumbling action for us to consider it another legitimate pitch in the repertoire.

Despite this impressive arsenal, there are some red flags we can't ignore. Most notably, Hankins started losing velocity on his heater and command of his secondaries once he got into the third inning of his outings. We believe this is the result of his cross-body throwing motion: Such arm action has been known to cause inconsistent release points that lead to decreased velocity and diminished command over the course of an appearance. This, in combination with his suspect injury history, leads some to believe he might be a future reliever (albeit a darn good one).

But like many of the prospects on this list, Hankins has enjoyed some success against older competition, and another year removed from injuries could help him unleash his obvious talent on a more consistent basis. We'd be remiss to not point out that Cleveland is one of the best at extracting max value from pitchers like this, so Hankins is in an ideal development spot. The educated guess is he starts in Lake County, though don't count out the club aggressively assigning him to Lynchburg.

Variance: Extreme. The mechanics and injury history are worrisome.

Mark Barry's Fantasy Take: A classic "High Ceiling/Low Floor" guy, Hankins's profile is awfully similar to Espino's, and dips slightly thanks to more recent injury woes. If he can stay healthy, and in turn throw more strikes, he could be a top-25 starter. He's a long way away from both, however.

9 Daniel Johnson OF   OFP: 50   ETA: 2020

Born: 07/11/95   Age: 24   Bats: L   Throws: L   Height: 5'10"   Weight: 200   Origin: Round 5, 2016 Draft (#154 overall)

YEAR	TEAM	LVL	AGE	PA	R	2B	3B	HR	RBI	BB	K	SB	CS	AVG/OBP/SLG	DRC+	VORP	BABIP	BRR	FRAA	WARP	PF
2017	HAG	A	21	364	61	16	4	17	52	22	70	12	9	.300/.361/.529	142	30.7	.333	-0.5	RF(51)-1.1, CF(15)0.3	2.3	101
2017	POT	A+	21	185	22	13	0	5	20	13	30	10	2	.294/.346/.459	119	10.2	.331	1.7	CF(30)-3.2, RF(9)3.5	1.1	104
2018	HAR	AA	22	391	48	19	7	6	31	23	90	21	4	.267/.321/.410	96	7.6	.338	-2.3	RF(54)6.3, CF(33)-2.9	0.9	101
2019	AKR	AA	23	167	25	7	2	10	33	16	39	6	3	.253/.337/.534	122	12.0	.276	-2.3	CF(24)-2.3, RF(10)-0.3	0.2	95
2019	COH	AAA	23	380	51	27	5	9	44	34	79	6	7	.306/.371/.496	123	18.0	.370	-1.5	RF(47)6.4, CF(21)1.2	2.4	100
2020	CLE	MLB	24	105	11	5	1	4	13	7	27	3	1	.245/.305/.426	92	0.0	.305	-0.1	CF-1, RF 0	0.2	98

Comparables: Zoilo Almonte, Cedric Mullins, Austin Hays

The Report: Johnson remains equal parts tantalizing and frustrating as an outfield prospect. He made some adjustments to Double-A in his second try, and continued to hit for solid power with the Triple-A baseball. He's always had impressive pound-for-pound raw power, but has tended to be limited in terms of how much he gets it into games due to a violent uppercut and his free-swinging ways. When we were watching his Futures Game batting practice, Chris Blessing noted to me that his swing is more or less perfect for depositing balls about five rows deep in the right field stands at Progessive Field, so if he can tame his approach some, he could pop 20+ home runs in the bigs. Johnson has thickened up some and slowed down and now splits his time between center field and right. He has one of the best outfield arms in the minors, and can handle any of the three outfield spots. The variance here remains sneakily high for a prospect about ready for the majors, but if Johnson can hit .250 or so, he'll be a useful major leaguer for a good while.

Variance: Medium. Hit tool questions remain even after a strong upper minors performance, but Johnson's pop and ability to handle all three outfield spots give him a reasonably safe bench outfielder floor.

Mark Barry's Fantasy Take: In another organization, Johnson might be destined for a role as a platoon bat at best, never getting a chance to develop with regular reps. Luckily for Johnson, Cleveland has roughly 1.5 viable, big-league outfielders, so he should get plenty of opportunities to prove his worth. If his plate discipline improvements from 2019 are real, he should stick as a fantasy OF5.

10 Bo Naylor C   OFP: 50   ETA: 2022

Born: 02/21/00   Age: 20   Bats: L   Throws: R   Height: 6'0"   Weight: 195   Origin: Round 1, 2018 Draft (#29 overall)

YEAR	TEAM	LVL	AGE	PA	R	2B	3B	HR	RBI	BB	K	SB	CS	AVG/OBP/SLG	DRC+	VORP	BABIP	BRR	FRAA	WARP	PF
2018	CLT	RK	18	139	17	3	3	2	17	21	28	5	1	.274/.381/.402	124	12.2	.341	0.3	C(19)-0.4, 3B(5)-0.7	0.7	107
2019	LKC	A	19	453	60	18	10	11	65	43	104	7	5	.243/.313/.421	98	20.9	.296	0.9	C(85)3.4	2.2	105
2020	CLE	MLB	20	251	23	11	2	6	26	22	72	1	0	.217/.289/.361	73	0.0	.291	-0.1	C 0, 3B 0	0.0	98

Comparables: Rio Ruiz, Kyle Skipworth, Joe Benson

The Report: Nabbed by the Indians at the end of the first round in 2018, Naylor held his own in his first full season assignment. As one of the youngest position players in the Midwest League he struggled offensively in the early cold weather but seemed to find his stroke as the season warmed. He's a tough out from the left side with innate bat to ball skills and a good knowledge of the strike zone. There's still room in the frame for good weight to be added as he matures. That added strength and his existing bat speed will get the pop to eventually play as average in-game. Defensively, he will get every opportunity to remain behind the plate but will eventually land elsewhere on the diamond. Athletic and nimble, he moves well showing the ability to block pitches in the dirt. However, the arm strength is lacking and can be a liability against speedy teams.

Variance: High. It's likely Naylor ends up somewhere on the right side of the infield. That's going to put a ton of pressure on the bat to continue to develop.

Mark Barry's Fantasy Take: As far as catching prospects go, I kinda/sorta like Naylor. He spent his age-19 season in full-season ball, which portends well to him sticking behind the dish. If he does, Naylor could be a top-10 catcher. If he doesn't, he'll still be useful-ish as a .260ish guy with 20-25 homers.

The Next Ten

11 Triston McKenzie RHP

Born: 08/02/97 Age: 22 Bats: R Throws: R Height: 6'5" Weight: 165 Origin: Round 1, 2015 Draft (#42 overall)

YEAR	TEAM	LVL	AGE	W	L	SV	G	GS	IP	H	HR	BB/9	K/9	K	GB%	BABIP	WHIP	ERA	DRA	WARP	PF
2017	LYN	A+	19	12	6	0	25	25	143	105	14	2.8	11.7	186	43%	.283	1.05	3.46	3.21	3.5	93
2018	AKR	AA	20	7	4	0	16	16	90²	63	8	2.8	8.6	87	34%	.234	1.00	2.68	3.05	2.4	87
2020	CLE	MLB	22	2	2	0	33	0	35	35	6	3.2	8.9	35	36%	.303	1.37	4.51	4.74	0.2	98

Comparables: Adrian Morejon, Chris Tillman, Arodys Vizcaíno

Two years ago, McKenzie threw 143 innings as a 19-year-old, so despite the string bean physique, he'd shown a fair amount of durability for a pitching prospect. Since then, he missed the first few months of 2018 with a forearm issue, and then all of 2019 with a back issue. Pitchers, man. So a mere 24 months later we have a 21-year-old string bean who hasn't shown he can really handle the rigors of pitching once every 5-6 days. Now, he will be just 22 in 2020, and with experience in Double-A. We know the fastball/curve combo is already major-league quality, assuming it's still there next time he steps on the mound. As for where to rank McKenzie? Well, that we were less sure of. There's an argument he's still the best pitching prospect in this system, but ontologically speaking, you have to pitch to be a pitching prospect.

12 Tyler Freeman SS

Born: 05/21/99 Age: 21 Bats: R Throws: R Height: 6'0" Weight: 170 Origin: Round 2, 2017 Draft (#71 overall)

YEAR	TEAM	LVL	AGE	PA	R	2B	3B	HR	RBI	BB	K	SB	CS	AVG/OBP/SLG	DRC+	VORP	BABIP	BRR	FRAA	WARP	PF
2017	CLE	RK	18	144	19	9	0	2	14	7	12	5	1	.297/.364/.414	117	12.9	.313	1.8	SS(29) -0.1, 2B(4) -0.9	0.9	107
2018	MHV	A-	19	301	49	29	4	2	38	8	22	14	3	.352/.405/.511	189	37.7	.372	3.5	SS(52) -0.1, 2B(10) -0.2	3.7	100
2019	LKC	A	20	272	51	16	3	3	24	18	28	11	4	.292/.382/.424	142	25.1	.320	2.6	SS(57) 0.5, 2B(3) -0.2	2.6	106
2019	LYN	A+	20	275	38	16	2	0	20	8	25	8	1	.319/.354/.397	129	16.7	.350	1.2	SS(56) -1.0, 2B(3) 0.1	1.9	103
2020	CLE	MLB	21	251	24	14	1	3	24	14	35	4	1	.268/.331/.381	92	0.0	.305	0.0	SS 1, 2B 0	0.7	98

Comparables: Isiah Kiner-Falefa, Thairo Estrada, José Altuve

Occasionally my aesthetic preferences will lead me astray. I haven't been a huge fan of Freeman's swing. It isn't merely art, though, there's some science, as it uses a bunch of timing mechanisms including a double toe tap. But look, it works. Kid can hit. He's compact once he gets going with good barrel control, although given his lack of physicality and loft, power is never going to be a big part of the game. That limits the upside, but he can hit a bit, run a bit, and play a passable shortstop. That's potentially a solid major leaguer. I'm a stubborn Italian though, so I still want to see how he does in Double-A first before I sign off on his being in the top 10 in an improving Cleveland system.

13 Sam Hentges LHP

Born: 07/18/96 Age: 23 Bats: L Throws: L Height: 6'8" Weight: 245 Origin: Round 4, 2014 Draft (#128 overall)

YEAR	TEAM	LVL	AGE	W	L	SV	G	GS	IP	H	HR	BB/9	K/9	K	GB%	BABIP	WHIP	ERA	DRA	WARP	PF
2017	CLE	RK	20	0	3	0	6	6	13	16	2	2.1	12.5	18	43%	.400	1.46	4.85	4.23	0.3	106
2017	MHV	A-	20	0	1	0	5	5	17²	5	1	6.1	11.7	23	65%	.121	0.96	2.04	2.22	0.6	102
2018	LYN	A+	21	6	6	0	23	23	118¹	114	4	4.0	9.3	122	41%	.343	1.41	3.27	4.49	1.2	102
2019	AKR	AA	22	2	13	0	26	26	128²	148	11	4.5	8.8	126	36%	.358	1.65	5.11	7.13	-3.4	97
2020	CLE	MLB	23	2	2	0	33	0	35	35	6	3.7	7.3	29	36%	.285	1.41	4.65	4.87	0.1	98

Comparables: Chris Flexen, Sal Romano, Kyle Ryan

Ordinally speaking, dropping from fifth to 13th is pretty significant, but it overstates how badly Hentges' 2019 went in Double-A. It was a rough transition to be sure, and he struggled to throw enough good strikes—or even strikes generally—with his mid-90s fastball, but it is a mid-90s fastball from the left side. We can work with that. Hentges added a cutter in 2018 and it gives him a wrinkle to get inside against righties as his fastball can run a little true. He has good feel for the curveball, although it could lack depth at times and get a little sweepy from his three-quarters slot. The command and control need to get tightened up to avoid a future bullpen role, but the needle hasn't moved down that much on Hentges this year—there's a bit more relief risk, but still No. 4 starter OFP—it's more a matter of an improving system around him.

14 Aaron Bracho 2B

Born: 04/24/01 Age: 19 Bats: B Throws: R Height: 5'11" Weight: 175 Origin: International Free Agent, 2017

YEAR	TEAM	LVL	AGE	PA	R	2B	3B	HR	RBI	BB	K	SB	CS	AVG/OBP/SLG	DRC+	VORP	BABIP	BRR	FRAA	WARP	PF
2019	CLT	RK	18	137	25	10	2	6	29	23	21	4	1	.296/.416/.593	186	22.8	.306	0.9	2B(22) 1.0	1.5	101
2019	MHV	A-	18	32	5	1	0	2	4	5	8	0	0	.222/.344/.481	93	2.3	.235	0.3	2B(8) -1.4	0.0	100
2020	CLE	MLB	19	251	25	12	1	5	25	30	69	3	1	.210/.311/.348	81	2.0	.282	0.0	2B 0	0.3	98

Comparables: Joey Gallo, Daniel Robertson, Logan Morrison

Bracho got a larger bonus than Valera and Rocchio combined, netting $1.5 million when he signed out of Venezuela in 2017. Like Rocchio, he is a switch-hitting middle infielder with more polish than projection. Unlike Rocchio he is already playing almost exclusively second base. The frame and swing remind me a bit of Andrés Giménez at the same age, although Bracho is a bit stouter and less quick-twitch. That could portend more power down the line, but Bracho may lack a carrying tool, and as a second baseman there's less upside and floor. Then again, the 18-year-old version of Giménez went in a slightly different direction than I expected, and Bracho can really hit. There's a shot for a solid regular here, but we'll need to see him out of the complex first.

15 Luis Oviedo RHP

Born: 05/15/99 Age: 21 Bats: R Throws: R Height: 6'4" Weight: 170 Origin: International Free Agent, 2015

YEAR	TEAM	LVL	AGE	W	L	SV	G	GS	IP	H	HR	BB/9	K/9	K	GB%	BABIP	WHIP	ERA	DRA	WARP	PF
2017	CLE	RK	18	4	2	0	14	7	51²	62	2	3.8	12.2	70	52%	.411	1.63	7.14	3.24	1.5	106
2018	MHV	A-	19	4	2	0	9	9	48	34	3	1.9	11.4	61	52%	.274	0.92	1.88	1.94	1.8	102
2018	LKC	A	19	1	0	0	2	2	9	5	0	7.0	6.0	6	44%	.217	1.33	3.00	5.54	0.0	93
2019	LKC	A	20	6	6	0	19	19	87	80	6	4.1	7.4	72	43%	.294	1.38	5.38	4.98	0.2	105
2020	CLE	MLB	21	2	2	0	33	0	35	35	5	4.1	6.4	25	41%	.279	1.45	4.84	4.99	0.1	98

Comparables: Chris Flexen, Chris Archer, Touki Toussaint

We stuck Oviedo at the back of last year's 101 on the strength of his mid-90s fastball and rapidly-developing slider. He promptly came out in 2019 in full-season ball sitting a little over 90 and with the slider looking a bit slurvy. Pitchers, man. It's not uncommon for pop-up velocity guys—Oviedo was a little below 90 mph when he signed—to give back the velocity in subsequent years, but it's still disappointing. Oviedo has a nearly ideal starting pitcher's frame, a well-proportioned 6-foot-4, and a fairly simple, repeatable delivery. Fastball velocity isn't everything, mind you, but the rest of the package isn't going to carry low-90s heat. On what he showed in 2019, this ranking would be too high, but we know a plus fastball is in there somewhere. And Oviedo won't turn 21 until six weeks into the 2020 season, so we can hope the stuff returns. Wait 'til next year, I guess.

16 Yu Chang IF

Born: 08/18/95 Age: 24 Bats: R Throws: R Height: 6'1" Weight: 180 Origin: International Free Agent, 2013

YEAR	TEAM	LVL	AGE	PA	R	2B	3B	HR	RBI	BB	K	SB	CS	AVG/OBP/SLG	DRC+	VORP	BABIP	BRR	FRAA	WARP	PF
2017	AKR	AA	21	508	72	24	5	24	66	52	134	11	4	.220/.312/.461	102	33.9	.254	2.3	SS(122) 20.3	4.8	99
2018	COH	AAA	22	518	56	28	2	13	62	44	144	4	3	.256/.330/.411	104	16.6	.341	-3.3	SS(94) -7.3, 3B(23) -0.7	1.1	99
2019	COH	AAA	23	283	45	15	1	9	39	26	67	4	1	.253/.322/.427	93	8.2	.306	0.9	SS(22) 0.2, 2B(22) 0.4	0.8	100
2019	CLE	MLB	23	84	8	2	1	1	6	11	22	0	0	.178/.286/.274	77	0.7	.240	-0.9	3B(25) -0.3, SS(8) -0.1	-0.1	99
2020	CLE	MLB	24	140	14	6	1	5	16	11	39	1	0	.205/.277/.371	67	0.0	.257	0.0	SS 1, 3B -1	-0.1	98

Comparables: Gil McDougald, Jonathan Villar, Daniel Robertson

You know what you are getting from Chang at this point—medium pop from a fairly long swing, the ability to play multiple infield positions, sneaky speed, and a below-average hit tool, due to the aforementioned length. It likely doesn't all add up to a major league starter, especially given—well, at the time of publication—Cleveland's infield depth. But there's value in a right-handed bat with pop that can handle second, third, and short. If one of your starters has to miss a month, Chang will keep you above water. It's not sexy, but it's a major leaguer. Well…probably. His first pass against major league pitching exposed some issues with the swing, and it's a fine line between hitting .240 or .250 with enough pop to be useful, and hitting .220 and having to shell out for a bunch of $100 Uber rides from Columbus to Cleveland.

17 Will Benson OF
Born: 06/16/98   Age: 22   Bats: L   Throws: L   Height: 6'5"   Weight: 225   Origin: Round 1, 2016 Draft (#14 overall)

YEAR	TEAM	LVL	AGE	PA	R	2B	3B	HR	RBI	BB	K	SB	CS	AVG/OBP/SLG	DRC+	VORP	BABIP	BRR	FRAA	WARP	PF
2017	MHV	A-	19	236	29	8	5	10	36	31	80	7	1	.238/.347/.475	108	11.6	.339	0.1	RF(56) -2.5	0.3	104
2018	LKC	A	20	506	54	11	1	22	58	82	152	12	6	.180/.324/.370	89	5.6	.218	-0.4	RF(113) 5.4, CF(4) -0.2	0.9	102
2019	LKC	A	21	259	44	12	3	18	55	37	78	18	2	.272/.371/.604	140	25.6	.325	1.5	RF(21) -0.8, LF(20) 0.7	1.6	105
2019	LYN	A+	21	255	29	9	2	4	23	31	73	9	2	.189/.290/.304	79	1.3	.255	3.5	LF(37) -3.0, RF(15) -1.1	-0.1	104
2020	CLE	MLB	22	251	23	10	1	7	26	21	94	2	1	.180/.253/.333	51	0.0	.264	0.2	RF -1, LF 0	-0.8	98

Comparables: Jamie Romak, Derek Norris, Tommy Pham

It's a cliche to say we are not selling jeans here. It's even a cliche now to turn that around and suggest that Benson could definitely sell a pair of Levi's 501s. He has a physique equal parts hulking and athletic. Even stooped over some at the plate, he dwarfs most everyone else in A-ball. The raw power is top of the scale, and he's worth getting to the park early to see take a batting practice session when he's in town. In addition to being built like an NFL wideout, he runs like one, too. Unfortunately, the swing-and-miss remains a major impediment to getting the raw power into games. Benson has long levers and struggles when he can't hunt a fastball. Despite his speed, the defensive profile works better in a corner. He adjusted second time through the Midwest League, but once again ended up on the interstate post-promotion to the Carolina League. You have to always keep an eye on him given the physical tools here, but three years since he was drafted in the first round, the performance just hasn't been there.

18 Lenny Torres RHP
Born: 10/15/00   Age: 19   Bats: R   Throws: R   Height: 6'1"   Weight: 190   Origin: Round 1, 2018 Draft (#41 overall)

YEAR	TEAM	LVL	AGE	W	L	SV	G	GS	IP	H	HR	BB/9	K/9	K	GB%	BABIP	WHIP	ERA	DRA	WARP	PF
2018	CLT	RK	17	0	0	0	6	5	15¹	14	0	2.3	12.9	22	51%	.400	1.17	1.76	4.51	0.2	112

Last year I said I would have had Torres ahead of Ethan Hankins on a personal pref list because he hadn't had a bout of shoulder soreness yet. Sorry about that, Cleveland fans. Torres had Tommy John surgery last May and will likely not see a mound again until the middle of next season at the earliest. He was a raw, cold-weather prep arm coming out of the 2018 draft, so the lost development time hurts even more and will only amplify the relief risk in the profile. We may not have a good feel for what Torres is until well into 2021 at this point, but there was a potential plus fastball/slider combo here this time last year.

19 Oscar Gonzalez OF
Born: 01/10/98   Age: 22   Bats: R   Throws: R   Height: 6'2"   Weight: 180   Origin: International Free Agent, 2014

YEAR	TEAM	LVL	AGE	PA	R	2B	3B	HR	RBI	BB	K	SB	CS	AVG/OBP/SLG	DRC+	VORP	BABIP	BRR	FRAA	WARP	PF
2017	MHV	A-	19	246	20	16	0	3	34	5	61	0	0	.283/.301/.388	99	0.5	.366	-1.7	LF(38) -3.2, RF(15) 2.1	0.2	104
2018	LKC	A	20	480	52	25	1	13	52	12	107	5	6	.292/.310/.435	113	12.2	.353	-1.6	LF(76) 7.5, RF(24) -1.5	2.1	102
2019	LYN	A+	21	402	46	22	3	8	61	12	66	7	5	.319/.342/.455	137	14.5	.367	-1.2	LF(48) 4.1, RF(22) 4.5	3.0	102
2019	AKR	AA	21	100	7	5	0	1	9	3	17	0	0	.188/.210/.271	59	-4.7	.215	0.8	LF(13) -0.1, RF(9) 2.8	0.2	96
2020	CLE	MLB	22	251	23	13	1	6	27	12	67	0	0	.246/.284/.382	72	0.0	.318	0.0	LF 1, RF 1	0.2	98

With his strengths and weaknesses, González is an entertaining prospect whose ultimate destination is difficult to pin down. He's a natural hitter who uses his excellent hand-eye coordination and feel for the barrel to square up pitches of all types and locations, or deploys his long arms to foul them away if they're not quite to his liking. He also doesn't have an approach. Not only does he not draw walks, he can seem loath to take a pitch at all. This tendency could create a lot of weak contact as he jumps levels and is faced with pitchers possessed of better command. It also lowers his ultimate ceiling; more selectivity would give him a better chance to tap into his above-average raw power. His defense should be fine, but he's already marooned in the less glamorous corner. Let's see how he hits in Double-A.

20   Nick Sandlin   RHP

Born: 01/10/97   Age: 23   Bats: R   Throws: R   Height: 5'11"   Weight: 175   Origin: Round 2, 2018 Draft (#67 overall)

YEAR	TEAM	LVL	AGE	W	L	SV	G	GS	IP	H	HR	BB/9	K/9	K	GB%	BABIP	WHIP	ERA	DRA	WARP	PF
2018	LKC	A	21	0	0	1	10	0	10¹	9	0	0.0	13.1	15	52%	.391	0.87	1.74	3.09	0.2	100
2018	LYN	A+	21	1	0	4	7	0	6¹	2	0	2.8	14.2	10	50%	.167	0.63	1.42	1.94	0.2	100
2019	AKR	AA	22	0	0	2	15	0	17¹	13	2	4.2	14.0	27	49%	.314	1.21	1.56	4.22	0.1	100
2019	COH	AAA	22	1	0	0	9	0	9	5	2	7.0	11.0	11	53%	.176	1.33	4.00	3.56	0.2	100
2020	CLE	MLB	23	2	2	0	33	0	35	35	5	3.5	10.9	42	43%	.329	1.39	4.60	4.73	0.2	98

Comparables: Evan Phillips, Eduardo Paredes, Trevor Gott

Sandlin could give the 2020 Cleveland bullpen quite the three-headed monster along with Karinchak and Clase, health permitting. The 2018 second-round pick continued to miss bats in the upper minors with his low-90s fastball/low-80s slider combo from a deceptive sidearm slot. The fastball sinks and runs, and the slider tunnels well in the opposite direction. The funk can lead to bouts of wildness, but he's a tough at-bat, especially for righties. "Health permitting" is doing a lot of heavy lifting though, as he got a late start to his season while dealing with a forearm issue that ended up as a strain in late June, ending his season early. A healthy Sandlin has setup arm potential, so check back in a month or so.

Personal Cheeseball

PC   Bobby Bradley   1B/DH

Born: 05/29/96   Age: 24   Bats: L   Throws: R   Height: 6'1"   Weight: 225   Origin: Round 3, 2014 Draft (#97 overall)

YEAR	TEAM	LVL	AGE	PA	R	2B	3B	HR	RBI	BB	K	SB	CS	AVG/OBP/SLG	DRC+	VORP	BABIP	BRR	FRAA	WARP	PF
2017	AKR	AA	21	532	66	25	3	23	89	55	122	3	3	.251/.331/.465	120	17.4	.287	-2.6	1B(125) -6.3	0.9	99
2018	AKR	AA	22	421	49	19	3	24	64	45	105	1	0	.214/.304/.477	109	17.0	.226	-2.3	1B(97) 1.4	0.8	90
2018	COH	AAA	22	128	11	7	2	3	19	11	43	0	0	.254/.323/.430	101	2.8	.377	0.3	1B(29) 1.5	0.3	99
2019	COH	AAA	23	453	65	23	0	33	74	46	153	0	0	.264/.344/.567	124	16.7	.336	-2.5	1B(97) 1.9	1.7	99
2019	CLE	MLB	23	49	4	5	0	1	4	4	20	0	0	.178/.245/.356	54	-2.2	.292	-0.1	1B(5) -0.2	-0.2	101
2020	CLE	MLB	24	105	11	5	0	4	13	8	39	0	0	.200/.271/.385	70	1.0	.285	-0.2	1B 0	-0.3	98

Comparables: Dick Gernert, Tyler O'Neill, Ryan McMahon

Bradley's major-league OPS barely topped his Triple-A slugging in 2019, so the Quad-A warning light has begun to blink brighter now. He struggled mightily against offspeed moving down and/or away from him—a recurring theme throughout his pro career—and his stiff, leveraged swing really needs fastballs up and out over the plate. When he gets one…well go look up the video of his first major league home run. Despite 70 raw power, he's not going to see enough of those to carry a DH profile, and the OFP now might be "2022 KBO home run champ," but until then you can rest assured Bradley will never get cheated in any MLB at-bat to come.

Low Minors Sleeper

LMS   Jose Fermin   SS

Born: 03/29/99   Age: 21   Bats: R   Throws: R   Height: 5'11"   Weight: 160   Origin: International Free Agent, 2015

YEAR	TEAM	LVL	AGE	PA	R	2B	3B	HR	RBI	BB	K	SB	CS	AVG/OBP/SLG	DRC+	VORP	BABIP	BRR	FRAA	WARP	PF
2017	CLE	RK	18	182	24	11	1	1	14	5	19	5	2	.229/.278/.325	64	0.3	.250	1.3	SS(27) -3.2, 2B(18) 0.7	0.1	106
2018	MHV	A-	19	308	47	12	4	2	26	39	26	17	4	.279/.391/.382	159	25.7	.301	-0.2	2B(37) 2.8, SS(22) -4.5	2.3	100
2019	LKC	A	20	456	75	12	2	6	41	42	40	28	9	.293/.374/.379	140	33.6	.311	3.9	2B(63) 0.2, SS(39) 0.8	3.9	105
2020	CLE	MLB	21	251	21	11	1	3	22	15	38	3	1	.234/.291/.333	67	2.0	.267	0.0	2B 1, SS 0	-0.1	98

Fermin was a multiple-time entrant in the "What Scouts are Saying" column this year, and it's no surprise he got plaudits from the area guys. He's exactly the type of prospect who endears himself quickly. He's a plus runner in the middle infield, smooth and sure-handed, although the arm is a better fit for second than short. At the plate he has a good eye and good plate coverage, in part due to a big leg kick that lets him dive for the outside pitch. He's still quick enough inside to pull base hits when you try to beat him there, and there's a bit of sneaky pop in there too, although it's likely to play mostly for doubles. Fermin is the kind of guy you gush about behind the plate and then write up as a 40 or a 45, but hey, that's a major league grade.

Top Talents 25 and Under (as of 4/1/2020)

1. Shane Bieber
2. Franmil Reyes
3. Oscar Mercado
4. George Valera
5. Nolan Jones
6. Brayan Rocchio
7. James Karinchak
8. Daniel Espino
9. Jake Bauers
10. Emmanuel Clase

It really wasn't very long ago that the Indians played extra innings in Game 7 of the World Series. Even more recently, they seemingly had a stranglehold on the American League Central, without a legit challenger in sight. A lacking sense of urgency led to a handful of consecutive complacent offseasons, culminating last year, with a $2.5 million renewal of the ageless wonder Oliver Perez serving as their crowning achievement in free agency. Since that World Series, the team payroll has dropped precipitously, currently checking in as the 25th highest in the league—cool for the bottom line, but less enticing for a team with "serious" championship aspirations.

The payroll purge continued into this offseason, with veteran-ace Corey Kluber jettisoned for a reliever and fourth outfielder while Mike Clevinger and Francisco Lindor have both been hot names on the trade market. You could even rationalize a Clevinger move in a vacuum—he's older than you think and despite gaudy strikeout numbers, he has been recently banged up. Trading Lindor would be the ultimate betrayal. Not only is he one of the five-ish best players in the league, he's a guy who's super easy to root for in a sports landscape that doesn't always churn out likable dudes. Sure the haul would be sizable, but there's really only one reason why you would trade a 26-year-old franchise cornerstone and it doesn't have much to do with competing for postseason success (at least the fans will see tickets and concessions become more affordable—wait…).

Even though things seem less than ideal in the organization, and the Twins (and maybe the White Sox) have cruised past the Indians in their competitive cycle, there are still some positives to build upon. As of this writing, Lindor is still on the team, and he'll remain one-half of baseball's best left side with Jose Ramirez, who after a truly puzzling stretch at the plate, slashed .327/.365/.739 in the second half before a broken hamate bone ended his season. Even without Kluber and the dearly departed Trevor Bauer, the Tribe's rotation is still formidable with U25 star and newly-minted staff ace Shane Bieber seeking to build on his first 200+ inning campaign. After a season spent fighting Leukemia, Carlos Carrasco slots in nicely as a No. 3 starter, providing rotation stability in addition to a ridiculously good story that is super easy to root for. And while most people rolled their eyes at the Kluber return, tossing Clase into a bullpen that already features Karinchak and Brad Hand, late-inning relief in Cleveland should be awfully fun to watch.

On the farm, there isn't a ton of immediate help on the way. Johnson should see some time in the big-league outfield, and there's an outside chance Jones could make an appearance if he cleans up a few of his strikeout tendencies. Even though proximity might not be one of the standout characteristics of most Cleveland prospects, the system is super deep with dudes who could provide solid production with the big club. The organization is oozing with talented middle-infield prospects with strong hit tools, led by Rocchio, with guys like Aaron Bracho, Tyler Freeman and Gabriel Rodriguez not far behind. And speaking of hit tools, Valera and Bo Naylor could both be plus hitters up the middle. Based on how Cleveland has been able to develop pitchers over the last handful of seasons, it seems unfair that both Espino and Ethan Hankins are in this organization, as both could mature to be frontline starters. There are a lot of "could be" and "potential to"s in this organization, and with some development, this system could float through org ranks with a Padres-like speed. Hopefully some of these young studs get the opportunity to play with Lindor.

Eyewitness Reports

Eyewitness Report: Nolan Jones

Evaluator: Ricky Conti
Report Date: 09/25/2019
Dates Seen: 9/19, 9/20
Risk Factor: High
Physical/Health: Medium overall frame with only a touch of room to grow. Decent mobility, but body could be more explosive.

Tool	Future Grade	Report
Hit	45	Very selective/disciplined with solid zone judgment, which should allow him to continue to walk at all levels. Really high hand set that comes down with long stride. Bat head really dipping at the moment, causing him to foul off tons of hittable pitches. That, plus his high selectivity, cause him to strikeout a lot. Struggled to consistently square up the ball in batting practice.
Power	55	Plus to the pull side, but didn't show the ability to go to all fields. Everything (timing, wheelhouse, good swing) needs to come together for it to show.
Baserunning/Speed	45	Was average coming out of high school, and has most certainly dipped below average. Struggled to accelerate out of the box.
Glove	45	Working really hard to improve here. The fundamentals are good, but it seemed to be more of a facade than ability. Made several fielding errors, as hands struggled to react to mid hops. Slow to react on slow rollers.
Arm	60	Throws have great carry across the diamond, more than enough for a corner spot somewhere.

Conclusion: There is more corner outfield risk here than I previously thought. Being a below-average runner is fine for third, but the hands really need to improve.

Eyewitness Report: James Karinchak

Evaluator: Jarrett Seidler
Report Date: 04/25/2019
Dates Seen: 4/16/2019
Risk Factor: High
Delivery: Deceptive and odd. Looks like he's coming at you from 3/4 but then releases high overhand, which aides both his curveball and fastball plane. Easy to understand how repeatability and effort led to a relief outcome. Somewhat similar to former MLBer Josh Collmenter.

Pitch Type	Future Grade	Sitting Velocity	Peak Velocity	Report
Fastball	80	96-99	99	Elite fastball velocity combined with more than enough run to keep batters off balance. Command had been a significant problem in past, manifesting in too many walks, but he put it where he wanted well enough in my look, and walk trend is positive as well. Velocity has been ticking up over last two years; was sitting 91-93 as a starter in 2017 and 95-97 as a reliever in 2018. Might have another tick or two left. Way, way too much for Double-A hitters and will continue to be for all hitters so long as he maintains velocity and command upticks.
Curveball	70	83-85	86	True 12-to-6 curveball action at slider velocity. Has been his out pitch and a plus offering dating back to starting days in college. Has added substantial velocity without sacrificing movement or getting too slurvy. Swing-and-miss offering.

Conclusion: With improvements in command and another significant jump in his stuff, Karinchak is now one of the top relief prospects in the game. He has been video game dominant so far in Double-A, striking out 18 of the 25 batters he's faced early in 2019, without allowing a hit. Potential of first-division closer or elite setup man, and he could get there very fast. Retains a high risk factor for grade due to volatility of relievers and past control issues.

Colorado Rockies

The State of the System

Well, this de-escalated quickly. There's some interesting relief arms, and intriguing low minors guys, but the Rockies system is about as thin as the air up there now.

The Top Ten

★ ★ ★ *2020 Top 101 Prospect* **#56** ★ ★ ★

1 Brendan Rodgers SS   OFP: 55   ETA: 2019

Born: 08/09/96   Age: 23   Bats: R   Throws: R   Height: 6'0"   Weight: 180   Origin: Round 1, 2015 Draft (#3 overall)

YEAR	TEAM	LVL	AGE	PA	R	2B	3B	HR	RBI	BB	K	SB	CS	AVG/OBP/SLG	DRC+	VORP	BABIP	BRR	FRAA	WARP	PF
2017	LNC	A+	20	236	44	21	3	12	47	6	35	2	1	.387/.407/.671	173	26.5	.413	0.9	SS(47) -5.6, 2B(4) -0.6	2.2	122
2017	HFD	AA	20	164	20	5	0	6	17	8	36	0	2	.260/.323/.413	100	6.5	.306	-0.5	SS(33) -1.2, 2B(6) 0.3	0.5	103
2018	HFD	AA	21	402	49	23	2	17	62	30	76	12	3	.275/.342/.493	112	27.4	.301	0.6	SS(58) -6.7, 2B(21) -2.1	1.5	106
2018	ABQ	AAA	21	72	5	4	0	0	5	1	16	0	0	.232/.264/.290	52	-2.8	.302	-0.3	SS(11) -1.8, 3B(4) -0.2	-0.4	121
2019	ABQ	AAA	22	160	34	10	1	9	21	14	27	0	0	.350/.413/.622	130	20.2	.380	2.0	2B(27) -1.9, SS(6) -0.1	1.2	109
2019	COL	MLB	22	81	8	2	0	0	7	4	27	0	0	.224/.272/.250	47	-2.7	.347	1.5	2B(16) 1.1, SS(9) -1.1	-0.1	116
2020	COL	MLB	23	154	17	7	1	6	20	9	41	1	0	.258/.310/.436	83	2.0	.323	-0.1	2B 0, SS -1	0.1	139

Comparables: Jonathan Villar, Alen Hanson, Richard Ureña

The Report: Rodgers started out the year by torching the Pacific Coast League. Yes, it was in Albuquerque, and yes it was with the major league rabbit ball, but it still quelled some of the concerns you might have had after two just okay seasons in Double-A—and Hartford is far from a pitcher's park itself. He blitzed his way to the majors where he had some initial struggles, although some of those can no doubt be chalked up to the right labrum tear that ended his season in June. It's unknown exactly how he will come back from a fairly major surgery. It might force him to the right side of the infield, but he was already the third-best shortstop glove on the roster behind Trevor Story and Garrett Hampson. And that won't matter if the bat plays to its potential in the majors.

That's still an open question, though. Rodgers has plus raw power and an above-average hit projection. It's not an easy, loose swing, but he shows solid barrel control. He has just never developed enough of an approach against offspeed to consistently put himself in position to do damage. He expands when behind and can be overly aggressive generally, something major league arms were able to exploit during his debut. When he's right, you can dream on a .270, 25-home-run middle infielder—before the Coors boost—with a solid enough glove, but we aren't living in dreams anymore with the 23-year-old Rodgers, and the major league reality is a bit more complicated now.

Variance: Higher than you'd like. There remain questions about the hit tool and approach, and he's had some durability issues. A labrum tear is a non-trivial injury for a hitter as well.

Ben Carsley's Fantasy Take: It's crazy to think that I just turned 30, yet this is the 45th year in a row I've written about Brendan Rodgers: Fantasy Prospect. It's true that Rodgers is not the potential fantasy franchise savior we once saw visions of back in, say, 2016. It's also true that he is as prime a prospect fatigue candidate as I can perhaps ever recall. Just because his ceiling isn't "Carlos Correa at Coors" doesn't mean Rodgers can't help your squad in very short order. A well-rounded infielder in Coors is always going to be of supreme interest to us. Thirty-homer middle infielders aren't as in short supply as they were a decade ago, but they're still mighty nice to own.

2 Ryan Rolison LHP   OFP: 55   ETA: 2020-21
Born: 07/11/97 Age: 22 Bats: R Throws: L Height: 6'2" Weight: 195 Origin: Round 1, 2018 Draft (#22 overall)

YEAR	TEAM	LVL	AGE	W	L	SV	G	GS	IP	H	HR	BB/9	K/9	K	GB%	BABIP	WHIP	ERA	DRA	WARP	PF
2018	GJR	RK	20	0	1	0	9	9	29	15	2	2.5	10.6	34	66%	.200	0.79	1.86	0.65	1.7	107
2019	ASH	A	21	2	1	0	3	3	14²	8	0	1.2	8.6	14	40%	.216	0.68	0.61	2.43	0.5	125
2019	LNC	A+	21	6	7	0	22	22	116¹	129	22	2.9	9.1	118	46%	.320	1.44	4.87	4.61	0.6	122
2020	COL	MLB	22	2	2	0	33	0	35	36	6	3.5	7.5	29	42%	.288	1.41	4.77	5.04	0.1	139

Comparables: Josh Rogers, Devin Smeltzer, Scott Diamond

The Report: The Rockies' first-round pick of the 2018 draft, Rolison needed just three starts at Low-A Asheville (14 2/3 IP, 0.61 ERA, 14 K) before earning a promotion to pitcher-unfriendly Lancaster of the High-A California League. The home confines weren't cozy for the lefty, as he posted a 6.06 ERA and opponents hit for a .320 BA in 65 1/3 innings pitched (13 starts). On the road, however, Rolison limited opponents to a .215 BA, struck out 57 batters, and held a 3.35 ERA in 51 IP over nine starts. The 22-year-old left-hander utilizes plus-athleticism and a controlled delivery to command his low-90's fastball, a developing low-80s changeup, and a stellar curveball that can also bump into the low 80s.

Rolison fields his position well, demonstrates good poise, and generally works quickly when on the mound. His game is similar to Barry Zito's in that he'll compete with a well-executed arsenal of quality pitches, rather than overpowering stuff. He profiles long term as a middle-of-the-rotation starting pitcher, but his versatility and advanced pitching acumen would allow him to contribute from a bullpen role as soon as 2020.

Variance: Medium. The low-90's fastball puts added importance on the offspeed offerings, pitch command, and overall execution.

Ben Carsley's Fantasy Take: Every year we struggle to make fantasy writeups for Rockies pitchers interesting. The short answer remains that you should stay away from 99.99 percent of them, Rolison included. However, in very deep leagues, Rolison has some potential utility as a SP5/6 or streamer you may want to occasionally start on the road. That's not worth rostering at present in most formats, but if your league generally sees 250-plus prospects owned, Rolison should be among them.

3 Ryan Vilade SS   OFP: 55   ETA: 2021
Born: 02/18/99 Age: 21 Bats: R Throws: R Height: 6'2" Weight: 194 Origin: Round 2, 2017 Draft (#48 overall)

YEAR	TEAM	LVL	AGE	PA	R	2B	3B	HR	RBI	BB	K	SB	CS	AVG/OBP/SLG	DRC+	VORP	BABIP	BRR	FRAA	WARP	PF
2017	GJR	RK	18	146	23	3	2	5	21	27	31	5	5	.308/.438/.496	130	14.0	.378	0.4	SS(30) -2.1	0.6	120
2018	ASH	A	19	533	77	20	4	5	44	49	96	17	13	.274/.353/.368	114	25.8	.333	-1.9	SS(116) -6.3	2.1	107
2019	LNC	A+	20	587	92	27	10	12	71	56	95	24	7	.303/.367/.466	118	33.5	.342	2.5	SS(82) -4.0, 3B(46) -4.3	2.6	118
2020	COL	MLB	21	251	23	11	2	4	23	23	56	4	2	.238/.314/.349	78	0.0	.302	0.0	SS -2, 3B 0	-0.1	139

Comparables: Gavin Lux, Daniel Robertson, Carlos Rivero

The Report: After a slow start to the 2019 season—Vilade hit .250 in April and May—the 20-year-old infielder slashed .330 and hit all but one of his 12 home runs in his final 80 games at High-A Lancaster. He has a relatively flat stroke, but stays inside the ball well and generates consistent hard contact to all fields. He ultimately led the California League with 10 triples, which along with his 27 doubles—fifth most—and 24 stolen bases, showcase his natural strength and athleticism. At 6-foot-2 and 195-pounds, he's demonstrated adequate range and ability as a shortstop, but appears best-suited for the hot corner, where he played 46 games in 2019. He prefers to throw from a low, side-arm slot, enabling a quick release, but also affecting the carry and accuracy on longer throws, contributing to his 37 errors in 128 games last season. Vilade's combination of advanced skills and raw athleticism set a high-floor for the 20-year-old prospect. The ceiling may be an all-star caliber, five-tool third baseman.

Variance: Medium. The combo of baseball skills and raw tools is exciting, but he's just 20-years-old and will need to continue to adapt to the better competition.

Ben Carsley's Fantasy Take: I have a long and troubled history of overrating Rockies infield prospects, but I just can't help myself; I really like Vilade. I have some concerns about him sticking at third base–especially if the Rockies decide to commit to the bold team-building strategy of, uh, not trading their best player–but I'm pretty convinced he's going to hit. Add in plus power and enough athleticism to swipe 10-plus bags a year, and you've got a mighty well-rounded fantasy player. Now imagine that package in Coors! I'll be fighting with Bret to try and get Vilade on the Top-101.

4 Terrin Vavra SS   OFP: 50   ETA: 2021-22

Born: 05/12/97   Age: 23   Bats: L   Throws: R   Height: 6'1"   Weight: 185   Origin: Round 3, 2018 Draft (#96 overall)

YEAR	TEAM	LVL	AGE	PA	R	2B	3B	HR	RBI	BB	K	SB	CS	AVG/OBP/SLG	DRC+	VORP	BABIP	BRR	FRAA	WARP	PF
2018	BOI	A-	21	199	22	8	4	4	26	26	40	9	1	.302/.396/.467	143	15.7	.373	-0.5	SS(28) 0.8, 2B(16) -2.0	1.4	113
2019	ASH	A	22	453	79	32	1	10	52	62	62	18	9	.318/.409/.489	152	33.2	.350	0.4	SS(53) -1.4, 2B(40) 2.7	4.0	119
2020	COL	MLB	23	251	23	12	1	5	25	17	55	4	1	.234/.289/.359	71	0.0	.287	0.0	SS 0, 2B 1	0.0	139

Comparables: Jason Donald, Cole Figueroa, Wilmer Difo

The Report: Vavra is a polished offensive contributor with enough glove to stick up the middle. In his first full professional season, he showed good control of the zone and the barrel, with a simple, relatively flat swing plane that hit line drives to all fields. There is some pull-side power in the profile, although almost all of Vavra's 2019 pop came at home with the short right field porch in Asheville. Given his size and swing, the power is more likely to play in the 10-15 home run range, albeit along with a potentially plus hit tool. On the dirt, Vavra is rangy enough for shortstop, but his arm strength might limit him to the right side of the infield.

Variance: Medium. The advanced hit tool should let Vavra carve out a fairly quick path to the majors, but he has limited pro experience and may not stick on the left side of the infield.

Ben Carsley's Fantasy Take: As you can probably glean from the writeup above, Vavra is a better real life prospect than a fantasy one. If he stays in this organization, he's likely to be a utility infielder buried behind more talented options. If he leaves the organization, well, half of his games won't come at Coors. Either way, it's tough to see Vavra as anything more than an accumulator. Given his modest ceiling and that he's not even knocking on the door right now, it's tough to consider him even a top-200 dynasty prospect.

5 Sam Hilliard OF   OFP: 50   ETA: 2019

Born: 02/21/94   Age: 26   Bats: L   Throws: L   Height: 6'5"   Weight: 238   Origin: Round 15, 2015 Draft (#437 overall)

YEAR	TEAM	LVL	AGE	PA	R	2B	3B	HR	RBI	BB	K	SB	CS	AVG/OBP/SLG	DRC+	VORP	BABIP	BRR	FRAA	WARP	PF
2017	LNC	A+	23	597	95	23	7	21	92	50	154	37	17	.300/.360/.487	121	25.1	.384	3.9	RF(85) 6.6, LF(30) 5.1	4.1	122
2018	HFD	AA	24	484	58	22	3	9	40	41	151	23	14	.262/.327/.389	97	9.1	.379	0.3	RF(70) 3.5, LF(29) -1.8	1.1	106
2019	ABQ	AAA	25	559	109	29	7	35	101	54	164	22	5	.262/.335/.558	98	17.0	.316	0.5	RF(82) -0.2, CF(33) 5.2	1.8	112
2019	COL	MLB	25	87	13	4	2	7	13	9	23	2	0	.273/.356/.649	109	3.8	.298	0.7	CF(17) 0.6, RF(6) 1.7	0.5	118
2020	COL	MLB	26	154	16	7	1	5	17	12	51	4	2	.222/.285/.388	68	0.0	.311	0.4	CF 2, LF 0	0.1	139

Comparables: Jared Walsh, Aristides Aquino, Donald Lutz

The Report: Hilliard has always looked like a player who should hit for more power than he has as a pro. When you consider that he's built like a football player and has played his home games in Asheville, Lancaster, and Hartford, you'd have expected a season like his 2019 before now. Yes, it's Albuquerque and Coors, but 40 bombs is 40 bombs. Hilliard has some fairly obvious warts to the profile. The swing has some length and stiffness to it, and he's struggled left-on-left. He looked a bit shorter to the ball in the majors, but there's still some swing-and-miss in the zone, especially if you can elevate above his hands, due to a steep swing path.

There's some good stuff here that might be less obvious too. Despite his size, he's a sneaky athlete, an average runner with a big arm who can hack it in center a couple days a week. Hilliard is also a smart baserunner, and he has an idea of what to take his huge hacks at. This feels like the kind of profile the Rockies give too many at-bats to, as he's more of a long-side platoon outfielder, but Hilliard is major-league-ready and no mere lumbering corner slugger. He will hit some majestic bombs playing in Coors too, and that's always fun.

Variance: Low. He's probably not going to hit .260 long term in the majors, but there's enough pop and athleticism to make him a useful major leaguer of some sort.

Ben Carsley's Fantasy Take: If you're going to be a platoon player with pop, there's no better organization for you to be with than the Colorado Rockies. Hilliard probably *should* only be a fourth outfielder or second-division starter, but his power could make him usable in deeper leagues if he finds himself getting more plate appearances than his skill level and ceiling would suggest he should. He's more of an NL Only bet at this point, but a potentially worthwhile one.

6   Michael Toglia 1B   OFP: 50   ETA: 2021-22

Born: 08/16/98   Age: 21   Bats: B   Throws: L   Height: 6'5"   Weight: 226   Origin: Round 1, 2019 Draft (#23 overall)

YEAR	TEAM	LVL	AGE	PA	R	2B	3B	HR	RBI	BB	K	SB	CS	AVG/OBP/SLG	DRC+	VORP	BABIP	BRR	FRAA	WARP	PF
2019	BOI	A-	20	176	25	7	0	9	26	28	45	1	1	.248/.369/.483	132	10.2	.290	0.3	1B(38) -0.2	0.6	115
2020	COL	MLB	21	251	21	11	1	5	24	17	84	2	1	.199/.259/.323	53	1.0	.285	0.0	1B 0	-0.7	139

Comparables: Abraham Toro, Ian Happ, Russ Canzler

The Report: A switch-hitting power threat from both sides of the plate, Toglia's big junior season for UCLA stamped him as a first-round pick despite the defensive limitations in the profile. He's played a fair bit of corner outfield and has plenty of arm for right field, but has primarily played first base as a pro so far. That's going to put a lot of pressure on his bat, but there's plus bat speed and plenty of raw pop to carry the weight of the cold corner. Toglia is tall with long levers in his swing, so there may be swing-and-miss in the zone, but he knows what to swing at and profiles as an everyday Three True Outcomes corner bat with potential 30+ bombs in the majors.

Variance: Medium. The bat should play, but we haven't seen him extensively with wood against better competition yet, and if the offensive profile slides even a bit, it's a tough path to bench bat given the defensive limitations.

Ben Carsley's Fantasy Take: Bret Sayre come get your mans. All jokes about my Internet Dad's affinity for first basemen aside, I like Toglia more than lots of other first-base-only bats. The bat speed checks out, he might offer just enough defensive versatility to eke out extra playing time, and the power upside is high. Toglia isn't a top-101 dynasty prospect–or even terribly close to it–but if you're in the thirdish round of your supplemental draft, you could do worse.

7   Aaron Schunk 3B   OFP: 50   ETA: 2021-22

Born: 07/24/97   Age: 22   Bats: R   Throws: R   Height: 6'2"   Weight: 205   Origin: Round 2, 2019 Draft (#62 overall)

YEAR	TEAM	LVL	AGE	PA	R	2B	3B	HR	RBI	BB	K	SB	CS	AVG/OBP/SLG	DRC+	VORP	BABIP	BRR	FRAA	WARP	PF
2019	BOI	A-	21	192	31	12	2	6	23	14	25	4	1	.306/.370/.503	138	14.4	.329	1.8	3B(37) 7.4	2.2	115
2020	COL	MLB	22	251	23	12	1	6	26	15	55	2	1	.231/.283/.367	72	3.0	.277	0.0	3B 2	0.2	139

Comparables: Cord Phelps, J.D. Martinez, Allen Craig

The Report: Schunk won the John Olerud Award for best two-way college player, but his future is on the position player side. He added a bunch of game power his junior year and it should carry over to wood bats, as he will show off plus raw to all fields. He's not a mere corner masher either, as there's a potential above-average hit tool in the profile based on his bat speed and present feel for the barrel. At third base, Schunk is athletic with a good first step and solid hands, with plenty of arm for the hot corner. David Lee saw some Austin Riley potential in the profile this Spring, although Schunk is only three months younger than Riley right now.

Variance: Medium. There's a limited pro track record and the power will need to continue to play up the levels given the corner profile.

Ben Carsley's Fantasy Take: Schunk is just one for your watch list at present, but maybe for the first half of it? Maybe underline his name or something?

8   Colton Welker 3B   OFP: 50   ETA: 2020-21

Born: 10/09/97   Age: 22   Bats: R   Throws: R   Height: 6'1"   Weight: 195   Origin: Round 4, 2016 Draft (#110 overall)

YEAR	TEAM	LVL	AGE	PA	R	2B	3B	HR	RBI	BB	K	SB	CS	AVG/OBP/SLG	DRC+	VORP	BABIP	BRR	FRAA	WARP	PF
2017	ASH	A	19	279	32	18	1	6	33	18	42	5	7	.350/.401/.500	156	19.4	.399	-1.6	3B(52) -7.3	1.5	110
2018	LNC	A+	20	509	74	32	0	13	82	42	103	5	1	.333/.383/.489	138	30.1	.395	1.1	3B(92) -9.3, 1B(6) -0.7	2.6	117
2019	HFD	AA	21	394	37	23	1	10	53	32	68	2	1	.252/.313/.408	113	6.9	.281	-2.8	3B(63) -1.5, 1B(27) 2.2	1.3	104
2020	COL	MLB	22	251	24	13	0	6	27	16	57	1	0	.245/.296/.385	78	3.0	.299	-0.5	3B -4, 1B 0	-0.3	139

Comparables: Renato Núñez, Nolan Arenado, Gabriel Guerrero

The Report: Welker's first season in Double-A was uneven. The raw power is obvious. It's easy—well, not easy—plus from a violent uppercut hack. There's commensurate plus bat speed, but he can get long and tends to be overly aggressive. Welker only really had one mode against Eastern League arms and he could be exploited by more advanced arms even if they didn't have huge stuff. He struggled to adjust to offspeed and tended to pull off breaking stuff. He'd expand with two strikes and couldn't really cut down. When he made contact, the ball went far, but I wonder how much of the raw pop will get into games. You are basically betting on him making adjustments here, and while there's a good pro track record before this year, it's a tough swing to bet on.

I'd feel better about the overall profile if I were more certain he'd stick at third. The frame is rectangular-ish and he struggled coming in on balls, although he has a decent first step and fine lateral range, the arm is just okay at third base, and overall Welker looked more comfortable across the diamond at first. That would make him a right/right first baseman with a fringe hit tool. That's a tough fit.

Variance: High. There's some risk Welker doesn't hit enough to be more than a corner bench bat. If he does adjust to upper minors pitching and develop a better two-strike approach, he could be a solid regular.

Ben Carsley's Fantasy Take: I've historically been pretty high on Welker, but the scouting reports haven't been trending in his favor for 18-or-so months now. It's a very Michael Chavis profile, and while that can be more useful for fantasy than for actual major league teams, it still makes Welker a relatively poor bet to earn a ton of playing time in Coors. I'm stubborn enough that I'm leaving Welker in my top-200 for now, but I admit that at this point you're basically SOL if either the power or the third base eligibility fall by the wayside. (Now that I'm willing to give up on him, he'll absolutely hit .453 this season).

9 Grant Lavigne 1B   OFP: 50   ETA: 2022-23
Born: 08/27/99 Age: 20 Bats: L Throws: R Height: 6'4" Weight: 220 Origin: Round 1, 2018 Draft (#42 overall)

YEAR	TEAM	LVL	AGE	PA	R	2B	3B	HR	RBI	BB	K	SB	CS	AVG/OBP/SLG	DRC+	VORP	BABIP	BRR	FRAA	WARP	PF
2018	GJR	RK	18	258	45	13	2	6	38	45	40	12	7	.350/.477/.519	190	27.4	.410	-0.6	1B(53) -6.8	1.1	109
2019	ASH	A	19	526	52	19	0	7	64	68	129	8	9	.236/.347/.327	87	-9.0	.314	-4.4	1B(111) 0.9	-0.5	118
2020	COL	MLB	20	251	21	11	0	3	21	23	73	2	1	.215/.296/.308	62	1.0	.305	-0.6	1B -1	-0.5	139

Comparables: Dominic Smith, Aaron Hicks, Trent Grisham

The Report: Yet another corner bat with plus raw power and hit tool questions. Lavigne is the youngest of the group, but has also struggled the most with the transition to the pro game and wood bats so far. He gets good hand-hip separation from his leg kick, but can get out of sync and end up cutting off some of that prodigious raw power due to poor quality of contact. He was at times swinging to stay afloat against South Atlantic League stuff this year, which was a somewhat aggressive assignment for a cold-weather prep bat. Lavigne also struggled with spin, but then there would be an at-bat here or there that he would just swat with a big uppercut and watch the baseball soar. It may take some time for the bat to click, and it might never click, but there's big power upside here. Lavigne is a below-average runner, but athletic enough, not a base clogger or anything, though he's still raw at first base. That should come with reps, and the profile is going to depend far more on the bat than the glove anyway.

Variance: High. Lavigne struggled in his initial full-season assignment and will need to translate his big raw power into games to make it as a starting first baseman. This one is going to take some time to play out too.

Ben Carsley's Fantasy Take: Whereas there's just enough in Toglia's profile to intrigue me despite the first base profile, Lavigne is too limited to a power-only play for my tastes. He's worth monitoring as he ascends the minors, but I'm not ready to invest yet.

10 Karl Kauffmann RHP   OFP: 50   ETA: 2021-22
Born: 08/15/97 Age: 22 Bats: R Throws: R Height: 6'2" Weight: 200 Origin: Round 2, 2019 Draft (#77 overall)

The Report: The Rockies Comp Balance B pick, Kauffmann is a bulldog who attacked Big Ten hitters with a power sinker/slider combo. The fastball generally sits in an average velocity band, although he can tick it up into the mid-90s, and it features good sink and run down in the zone. His mid-80s slider features good late tilt and plays well off the fastball, and Kauffmann is comfortable throwing either pitch to either side of the plate. There's not really a changeup at present, and there's a bit of late effort in the delivery that might eventually doom Kauffmann to relief, but he has two present, quality major league offerings and should move quickly in whatever role that Rockies tab for him.

Variance: Medium. Kauffmann pitched deep into the summer during Michigan's College World Series run, so he has no pro track record to speak of yet. There's the usual pitcher risks here, but it's a very polished two-pitch repertoire already.

Ben Carsley's Fantasy Take: First of all, terrible name. Second of all, this is a hard no for dynasty leaguers. A hard no.

The Next Ten

11   Brenton Doyle   OF

Born: 05/14/98   Age: 22   Bats: R   Throws: R   Height: 6'3"   Weight: 200   Origin: Round 4, 2019 Draft (#129 overall)

YEAR	TEAM	LVL	AGE	PA	R	2B	3B	HR	RBI	BB	K	SB	CS	AVG/OBP/SLG	DRC+	VORP	BABIP	BRR	FRAA	WARP	PF
2019	GJR	RK+	21	215	42	11	3	8	33	31	47	17	3	.383/.477/.611	198	38.0	.484	7.1		3.1	106
2020	COL	MLB	22	251	21	12	1	3	22	19	78	3	1	.233/.295/.331	67	0.0	.339	0.0		-0.2	139

A fourth rounder out of Division II Shepherd University, Doyle absolutely dominated the Mountain East Conference his junior year. It's a bit of an unusual swing, as the tall, lanky outfielder is almost stooped over at the plate in an open stance. It's unorthodox, but Doyle is athletic enough to make it work. He struggled some with pro spin, but overall offers a solid power/speed combo that reminds me a little bit of Brandon Marsh. Doyle's on the raw side compared to Marsh—and he's only six months younger—so there may be a bit of longer lead time here than your typical college outfield pick, but the rewards might be an every day outfielder, and we might find more in the tank once he gets additional pro reps under his belt.

12   Julio Carreras   IF

Born: 01/12/00   Age: 20   Bats: R   Throws: R   Height: 6'2"   Weight: 190   Origin: International Free Agent, 2018

YEAR	TEAM	LVL	AGE	PA	R	2B	3B	HR	RBI	BB	K	SB	CS	AVG/OBP/SLG	DRC+	VORP	BABIP	BRR	FRAA	WARP	PF
2018	DRO	RK	18	168	32	5	3	3	14	23	28	8	6	.252/.392/.400	134	11.4	.298	0.3	3B(23) 2.6, SS(15) 0.3	1.9	108
2018	DCR	RK	18	113	26	6	4	3	17	8	18	8	7	.344/.407/.591	135	16.3	.387	-0.4	3B(16) 1.1, SS(6) 1.5	1.7	101
2019	GJR	RK+	19	307	51	14	8	5	38	25	63	14	8	.294/.369/.466	115	24.4	.362	3.6		1.8	106
2020	COL	MLB	20	251	22	11	2	3	22	18	71	6	4	.219/.286/.332	63	3.0	.304	-0.3	3B 0, SS 0	-0.3	139

Comparables: Ronald Acuña Jr., Lane Thomas, Dilson Herrera

It's a bit of a double standard that I am intrigued by Carreras's profile. You could levy many of the same charges here that I did for Colton Welker above. The swing features a big leg kick and a violent uppercut, coupled with plus bat speed. Carreras is rawer at the plate than Welker—not that it should be surprising given their relative experience levels—and struggles with spin both in and out of the zone. It may look a lot like Colton Welker in a few years if he makes it to Double-A. He may not make it to Double-A. I think Carreras does though.

I'm more willing to bet on this swing when it's attached to this kind of athletic, projectable frame. Carreras is quick-twitch and an above-average runner. Despite the rawness at the plate, he's a smooth infielder with the arm for the left side. The variance is extreme here given his lack of pro reps or amateur pedigree, but he's already started to get results on the field and the tools aren't too shabby either.

13   Jacob Wallace   RHP

Born: 08/13/98   Age: 21   Bats: R   Throws: R   Height: 6'1"   Weight: 190   Origin: Round 3, 2019 Draft (#100 overall)

YEAR	TEAM	LVL	AGE	W	L	SV	G	GS	IP	H	HR	BB/9	K/9	K	GB%	BABIP	WHIP	ERA	DRA	WARP	PF
2019	BOI	A-	20	0	0	12	22	0	21	9	1	3.9	12.4	29	34%	.200	0.86	1.29	1.76	0.8	100
2020	COL	MLB	21	2	2	0	33	0	35	35	6	3.9	9.7	38	37%	.316	1.45	4.80	4.94	0.2	139

Wallace puts every bit of his 6-foot-1, 190-pound frame into every pitch. He can ramp it up mid-90s and higher with the fastball, but the uptempo delivery, and long, bordering on violent arm action, means his fastball command will struggle to bump average. He offers a power slider that flashes good depth as well, so yeah, we are already in the 95-and-a-slider part of this list. Wallace should move fast as a pen arm, and could help the MLB bullpen as soon as this year, although as a UConn pitcher, he was used very heavily late into last spring, so it's worth monitoring his stuff and health going forward. Assuming he stays healthy though, he could be an eighth inning arm in short order.

14 Riley Pint RHP [this space left intentionally blank]

Born: 11/06/97 Age: 22 Bats: R Throws: R Height: 6'5" Weight: 225 Origin: Round 1, 2016 Draft (#4 overall)

YEAR	TEAM	LVL	AGE	W	L	SV	G	GS	IP	H	HR	BB/9	K/9	K	GB%	BABIP	WHIP	ERA	DRA	WARP	PF
2017	ASH	A	19	2	11	0	22	22	93	96	3	5.7	7.6	79	60%	.325	1.67	5.42	5.67	-0.4	111
2018	BOI	A-	20	0	2	0	3	3	8	4	0	10.1	9.0	8	47%	.235	1.62	1.12	5.39	0.0	112
2019	ASH	A	21	0	1	0	21	3	17²	12	0	15.8	11.7	23	50%	.316	2.43	8.66	7.50	-0.6	129
2020	COL	MLB	22	2	2	0	33	0	35	34	5	4.5	7.2	28	51%	.285	1.48	4.89	5.00	0.2	139

Comparables: Sal Romano, Nate Adcock, Tyrell Jenkins

Man, f*** if I know. We've slotted Pint in with a group of relief prospects without closer upside, which represents a precipitous fall for the former fourth-overall pick. He came back from a 2018 forearm injury and promptly walked 31 batters in 23 innings before being shut down in June with shoulder tendonitis. The control issues aren't hard to spot. Pint's delivery is max effort and he struggles badly to find a consistent release point. If he ever does figure it out, he has far more late-inning upside than those around him with triple-digit heat and a plus breaker in his holster. But for a second straight year we must confess, he probably isn't exactly the 14th-best prospect in the system, or if he is, one standard deviation could put him fourth or 44th. In a better system I'd write him off the list until there's some glimmer that it might maybe, possibly, sort of be coming together, but even a longshot upside bet is worth it in Colorado.

15 Ashton Goudeau RHP

Born: 07/23/92 Age: 27 Bats: R Throws: R Height: 6'6" Weight: 205 Origin: Round 27, 2012 Draft (#823 overall)

YEAR	TEAM	LVL	AGE	W	L	SV	G	GS	IP	H	HR	BB/9	K/9	K	GB%	BABIP	WHIP	ERA	DRA	WARP	PF
2017	NWA	AA	24	3	7	1	21	7	57	78	7	2.7	6.8	43	41%	.366	1.67	5.37	6.28	-0.9	96
2018	MOD	A+	25	1	1	0	3	3	14	14	2	3.9	7.7	12	43%	.300	1.43	4.50	5.30	0.0	104
2018	ARK	AA	25	4	5	0	9	9	51¹	51	5	2.5	6.1	35	45%	.299	1.27	4.38	4.83	0.3	104
2018	TAC	AAA	25	1	5	0	20	2	37¹	59	6	4.6	7.5	31	44%	.417	2.09	8.20	8.29	-1.3	113
2019	HFD	AA	26	3	3	0	16	16	78¹	60	4	1.4	10.5	91	45%	.292	0.92	2.07	3.18	1.7	107
2020	COL	MLB	27	1	1	0	22	0	23	26	4	3.1	9.2	24	42%	.325	1.44	5.15	4.76	0.2	139

Comparables: Zach Neal, Drew Gagnon, Phillips Valdez

Now, putting a 27-year-old, recent minor league free agent on your prospect list generally signals to the reader that this is not a very good system. And yes, this is not a very good system, but Goudeau is a prospect, and age ain't nothing but a number. I tend to be less concerned about age-relative-to-league with pitchers, but yeah, a 27-year-old who spent most of the season as a Double-A starter is not usually going to keep my notebook open for that long. But Goudeau found something in his third organization, dominating upper minors hitters with a lively plus fastball that comes from a tough angle given his 6-foot-6 height and high-three-quarters slot. There's some deception in the delivery as well. Goudeau pairs it with an 11-6 curve with late bite that's effective at the bottom of the zone when playing off the riding fastball. The below-average change, occasional command problems, and violent at times mechanics probably limit Goudeau to the pen, and the Rockies moved him there shortly after his promotion to Triple-A, but there's setup potential in the stuff at present. That's useful even if he might technically qualify as an older millennial.

16 Ben Bowden LHP

Born: 10/21/94 Age: 25 Bats: L Throws: L Height: 6'4" Weight: 235 Origin: Round 2, 2016 Draft (#45 overall)

YEAR	TEAM	LVL	AGE	W	L	SV	G	GS	IP	H	HR	BB/9	K/9	K	GB%	BABIP	WHIP	ERA	DRA	WARP	PF
2018	ASH	A	23	3	0	0	15	0	15¹	17	2	2.9	14.7	25	43%	.429	1.43	3.52	3.64	0.2	100
2018	LNC	A+	23	4	2	0	34	0	36²	35	6	3.7	13.0	53	35%	.337	1.36	4.17	3.48	0.6	100
2019	HFD	AA	24	0	0	20	26	0	25²	8	1	2.5	14.7	42	38%	.171	0.58	1.05	1.94	0.8	100
2019	ABQ	AAA	24	1	3	1	22	0	26	29	4	5.9	12.8	37	34%	.379	1.77	5.88	4.49	0.4	100
2020	COL	MLB	25	1	1	0	11	0	12	13	2	3.5	12.1	16	38%	.366	1.49	5.19	4.73	0.1	139

Comparables: Paul Fry, Andrew Vasquez, James Pazos

Bowden is in some ways the left-handed version of Wallace, all the way down to both being from Massachusetts. Bowden is the much larger of the two, and gets to his 95 mph heat a bit easier, from a slingy delivery that's tough on lefties. He dominated Double-A hitters with the fastball and a potential plus tumbling changeup, although he struggled to have consistent feel for the pitch. There's a slurvy slider as well. Bowden's stuff is more low-end setup than high-end, with potential LOOGY risk, but he's also close to ready for the Rockies pen, and continued to miss bats despite getting knocked around in the PCL.

17 Tommy Doyle RHP

Born: 05/01/96   Age: 24   Bats: R   Throws: R   Height: 6'6"   Weight: 235   Origin: Round 2, 2017 Draft (#70 overall)

YEAR	TEAM	LVL	AGE	W	L	SV	G	GS	IP	H	HR	BB/9	K/9	K	GB%	BABIP	WHIP	ERA	DRA	WARP	PF
2017	GJR	RK	21	3	3	3	20	0	21	29	2	4.3	7.7	18	59%	.365	1.86	5.14	3.77	0.4	100
2018	ASH	A	22	7	6	18	52	0	58¹	52	2	1.9	10.2	66	54%	.312	1.10	2.31	3.47	0.9	100
2019	LNC	A+	23	2	3	19	38	0	36	24	4	3.2	12.0	48	58%	.250	1.03	3.25	1.83	1.2	100
2020	COL	MLB	24	2	2	0	33	0	35	34	6	3.5	9.4	37	50%	.306	1.37	4.42	4.68	0.3	139

Doyle was taken in the second round in 2017 as a college closer out of Virginia, but his pace through the minors has been slow-going. The stuff all checks out. He is a massive human who can run it up into the upper-90s and pairs it with a mid-80s slider that has touched 90 and can be a wipeout swing-and-miss offering when it's on. The command is just okay, the slider rolls sometimes, there's only a theoretical change, and plenty of effort in the delivery. There's—you guessed it—late inning potential here, but Doyle is a bit further away than the relief-only arms ahead of him.

18 Ryan Feltner RHP

Born: 09/02/96   Age: 23   Bats: R   Throws: R   Height: 6'4"   Weight: 190   Origin: Round 4, 2018 Draft (#126 overall)

YEAR	TEAM	LVL	AGE	W	L	SV	G	GS	IP	H	HR	BB/9	K/9	K	GB%	BABIP	WHIP	ERA	DRA	WARP	PF
2018	GJR	RK	21	0	0	0	9	9	30²	16	1	1.2	11.4	39	60%	.242	0.65	0.88	0.40	1.9	109
2019	ASH	A	22	9	9	0	25	25	119	137	12	3.5	8.8	116	52%	.357	1.54	5.07	5.18	0.0	122
2020	COL	MLB	23	2	2	0	33	0	35	35	6	3.6	6.9	27	47%	.280	1.39	4.57	4.81	0.2	139

The Rockies fourth-round pick out of Ohio State in 2018, Feltner struggled in his pro debut for Asheville, but the stuff was better than the performance—which was a recurring theme for him in college as well. He offers easy mid-90s heat as a starter, with a fastball that could play up in relief—where he's likely to end up. There's a potential above-average, low-80s slider with late two-plane action as well. Is it another 95-and-a-slider guy? Yes it sure is. You'd have preferred to see Feltner handle the South Atlantic League better as a major college arm, so there is more risk in this profile than some of the other reliever arms ahead of him, but he generally slots in the same "potential setup guy" band otherwise.

19 Antonio Santos RHP

Born: 10/06/96   Age: 23   Bats: R   Throws: R   Height: 6'3"   Weight: 180   Origin: International Free Agent, 2015

YEAR	TEAM	LVL	AGE	W	L	SV	G	GS	IP	H	HR	BB/9	K/9	K	GB%	BABIP	WHIP	ERA	DRA	WARP	PF
2017	ASH	A	20	9	10	0	27	27	147	200	17	1.6	6.5	106	53%	.373	1.54	5.39	6.48	-2.1	111
2018	ASH	A	21	1	10	0	15	15	86¹	100	8	1.3	9.0	86	53%	.351	1.30	4.48	5.05	0.2	103
2018	LNC	A+	21	4	3	0	12	12	65²	74	15	2.9	7.7	56	37%	.301	1.45	5.21	4.62	0.5	122
2019	LNC	A+	22	3	6	0	18	18	99¹	116	11	1.6	8.7	96	42%	.348	1.35	4.35	5.17	-0.2	111
2019	HFD	AA	22	3	3	0	8	8	45²	47	3	2.0	8.7	44	41%	.342	1.25	4.93	5.09	-0.1	108
2020	COL	MLB	23	2	2	0	33	0	35	39	7	3.5	7.3	28	40%	.304	1.52	5.59	5.16	0.1	139

Comparables: Myles Jaye, Chase De Jong, Victor Arano

Santos is an interesting arm strength flyer. He can run his fastball up into the upper 90s—and sit mid-90s in short bursts—but the pitch tends to run a little true, and a violent finish to his delivery suggests the command profile may not be fine enough to start. He does have a little hitch/hesitation which can create timing issues for the hitters, and he's effectively wild with the heater.

Santos has a full four-pitch mix, but both breaking balls are below-average—a slurvy curveball will occasionally flash decent tilt—and the changeup is inconsistent. The change will at least flash some hard fade and dive, but it's firm, and fastball/changeup relievers are a rare bird. There's some swing/spot start potential here and maybe you can get one of the breakers to average to give him a shot at middle relief, but it's a tough major league profile even before you consider his future home park.

20 Eddy Diaz IF

Born: 02/14/00 Age: 20 Bats: R Throws: R Height: 6'0" Weight: 175 Origin: International Free Agent, 2017

YEAR	TEAM	LVL	AGE	PA	R	2B	3B	HR	RBI	BB	K	SB	CS	AVG/OBP/SLG	DRC+	VORP	BABIP	BRR	FRAA	WARP	PF
2017	DRO	RK	17	155	22	7	4	0	10	19	21	30	6	.311/.403/.424	137	12.0	.366	2.1	SS(23) 0.6, 2B(13) 0.7	1.5	110
2018	DCR	RK	18	223	57	13	5	0	24	31	17	54	8	.309/.417/.436	151	33.5	.337	8.6	SS(39) -1.4, 2B(13) -0.7	2.7	100
2019	GJR	RK+	19	177	32	12	3	0	10	8	33	20	9	.331/.366/.440	131	13.4	.414	2.4		1.3	107
2020	COL	MLB	20	251	23	13	2	3	21	17	61	21	5	.246/.302/.350	73	0.0	.322	2.3	SS 0, 2B 0	0.3	139

Comparables: Abiatal Avelino, José Rondón, Thairo Estrada

Diaz was signed out of Cuba for $750,000 in 2017 and made his stateside debut this year in the Pioneer League. He has a slim frame and should fill out some, but he's not a projection monster. He's likely to remain a bit undersized and be a slash and burn guy at the plate, although the wrists are strong and keep the bat from getting knocked out of his hands at present. He's been splitting his time between second and short, although the arm is a better fit for the keystone. He's a smooth, rangy fielder, who should hold his plus speed as he ages. The lack of physicality limits the upside here, and there's a risk that better velocity beats him as he moves up the organizational ladder, but there's a potential speedy bench infielder here at maturity.

Personal Cheeseball

PC Alan Trejo SS

Born: 05/30/96 Age: 24 Bats: R Throws: R Height: 6'2" Weight: 185 Origin: Round 16, 2017 Draft (#476 overall)

YEAR	TEAM	LVL	AGE	PA	R	2B	3B	HR	RBI	BB	K	SB	CS	AVG/OBP/SLG	DRC+	VORP	BABIP	BRR	FRAA	WARP	PF
2017	GJR	RK	21	190	30	13	2	7	32	9	28	7	4	.347/.388/.566	123	19.1	.379	0.9	SS(21) 1.0, 3B(17) 3.0	1.2	120
2018	LNC	A+	22	497	65	28	4	10	67	31	113	3	6	.278/.329/.425	96	21.8	.346	2.1	SS(80) 6.0, 3B(28) 2.2	2.9	117
2019	HFD	AA	23	476	45	20	0	15	49	25	105	5	4	.243/.290/.391	87	9.6	.285	1.6	SS(91) -5.4, 2B(24) 0.0	0.9	105
2020	COL	MLB	24	251	22	12	1	6	26	12	69	1	1	.226/.269/.363	62	0.0	.292	0.0	SS 0, 3B 1	-0.3	139

It was pretty slim pickings at my full-season home park this year, but Trejo caught my eye early on as at least a player worth keeping tabs on. He's a pretty slick defensive shortstop with some pop, and the Rockies continued to get him reps at second and third. The hit and power tools are both on the wrong side of average, but he's a good athlete and smart baserunner. He can be a bit of a red ass, as he has strong opinions on things like "the strike zone" and "whether or not that was a check swing." It does liven up the proceedings on a cold spring night in Hartford. It's a crowded infield in Coors right now even before you get to the Rox bevvy of infield prospects above Trejo on this list, but the shortstop glove gives him a chance for major league employment at some point.

Low Minors Sleeper

LMS Mitchell Kilkenny RHP

Born: 03/24/97 Age: 23 Bats: R Throws: R Height: 6'4" Weight: 206 Origin: Round 2C, 2018 Draft (#76 overall)

YEAR	TEAM	LVL	AGE	W	L	SV	G	GS	IP	H	HR	BB/9	K/9	K	GB%	BABIP	WHIP	ERA	DRA	WARP	PF
2019	GJR	RK+	22	2	3	0	12	12	42	44	3	2.1	7.9	37	56%	.328	1.29	4.50	4.21	0.9	105

Kilkenny, the Rockies second-round pick in 2018, had Tommy John surgery shortly after the draft. He was back on a Pioneer League mound in 2019 for what amounted to more or less an extended rehab assignment. The command down in the zone of the sinking fastball and slider were solid for a pitcher only a little over a year removed from going under the knife. 2020 will put him over 20 months out TJ, and we'll have more of an idea of what the stuff will look like going forward with a full-season ball assignment and fewer restrictions on his usage. If the low-90s, touch 95 velocity comes all the way back, Kilkenny profiles as a backend starter or setup man out of the pen.

Top Talents 25 and Under (as of 4/1/2020)

1. German Marquez
2. Brendan Rodgers

3. Ryan McMahon
4. Garrett Hampson
5. Ryan Rolison
6. Ryan Vilade
7. Terrin Vavra
8. Peter Lambert
9. Antonio Senzatela
10. Michael Toglia

Folks, I won't lie to you—it's bleak. How bleak? So bleak I considered bending the rules to allow David Dahl (who, celebrating his 26th birthday on April 1st, is by the barest measure ineligible for this exercise) on the list. So bleak that when the deed was done I briefly panicked with Craig about if the Rockies are the next Orioles. So bleak that after having been reassured things aren't quite there yet, I still initially titled my google doc "Orioles 25U."

How did we get here? Fitting for the Rockies, let's go bottom up:

Lambert and Senzatela are here and in their quests for rotation spots united—as massive underperformers who remain in the running by default, being that there is no one in the wings to supplant them and wake up the Rockies from their Evanescence-backed nightmare.

If you think Hampson is where McMahon stood a year ago, there's good and bad news—after flirting with replacement-level in parts of two seasons, McMahon broke through last season as an average regular. The downside? It doesn't look like McMahon, in his last year of eligibility for this list, has another gear in him. With Hampson lumped into the same age bracket, time is running out for him to prove even that capability.

Finally, Marquez is almost everything a team wants atop its rotation—young, great and showing flashes of more to come, cost-controlled on a deal that now looks ludicrously team-friendly—all Marquez can do to improve in 2020 is stay healthy (and ideally benefit from better batted ball luck).

At least there's one legitimate star in this group. But friends, I just don't see it.

Eyewitness Reports

Eyewitness Report: Ashton Goudeau

Evaluator: Steve Givarz
Report Date: 10/12/2019
Dates Seen: 10/1, 10/5, 10/9
Risk Factor: High

Delivery: XL frame with a lean body, looks like he can add physicality, but is on older side. Pitches from the middle of the rubber, semi-wind-up, long deep arm action with average arm speed to a high 3/4 slot. Hides the ball well behind body, stays in control of long levers, good downhill plane and angle.

Pitch Type	Future Grade	Sitting Velocity	Peak Velocity	Report
Fastball	60	93-94	94	While lacking much life, it is deceptive and gets on hitters quick due to extension and deception. Throws quality strikes with it, works both sides of the plate as well as north and south. Pitch is best in the upper part of the strike zone where it got most of the swings and misses. Plays above velocity to a plus offering.
Curveball	50	78-80	80	Primary off speed pitch, 12/6 shape, big breaker with good depth, not particularly sharp but effective at bottom of the zone for strikes. Can get chases as well, average offering.
Changeup	45	85-87	87	Third pitch but shows good feel and arm speed, fringe-average sink, but throws strikes and keeps away from barrels of lefty hitters, fringe-average offering.

Conclusion: See as a multi-inning reliever with chance for back of rotation work. 27 y/o RHP, quality year after being picked up as a MILB FA, plus fastball with average curveball and fringe change, but arsenal plays up with above-average control and average command. Moderate interest.

Detroit Tigers

The State of the System

It's a very good top three, a pretty good top five, and then, well the system is not nearly as deep as you'd want at this point in the uh "planned reconstruction process."

The Top Ten

───────────────── ★　★　★ *2020 Top 101 Prospect* **#12** ★　★　★ ─────────────────

1　**Casey Mize**　**RHP**　　　OFP: 70　　ETA: 2020
　　Born: 05/01/97　Age: 23　Bats: R　Throws: R　Height: 6'3"　Weight: 220　Origin: Round 1, 2018 Draft (#1 overall)

YEAR	TEAM	LVL	AGE	W	L	SV	G	GS	IP	H	HR	BB/9	K/9	K	GB%	BABIP	WHIP	ERA	DRA	WARP	PF
2018	LAK	A+	21	0	1	0	4	4	11²	13	2	1.5	7.7	10	44%	.344	1.29	4.63	5.08	0.0	95
2019	LAK	A+	22	2	0	0	6	6	30²	11	0	1.5	8.8	30	48%	.155	0.52	0.88	1.83	1.2	94
2019	ERI	AA	22	6	3	0	15	15	78²	69	5	2.1	8.7	76	42%	.294	1.11	3.20	4.17	0.8	103
2020	DET	MLB	23	2	2	0	33	0	35	34	5	3.0	7.9	31	40%	.292	1.32	4.33	4.54	0.2	104

Comparables: Jackson Stephens, Brett Kennedy, Robert Dugger

The Report: Healthy 2019 Casey Mize had a strong argument for the best pitching prospect in baseball. He'll show four plus pitches, and each of the fastball, cutter, slider and split will flash plus-plus at times. The fastball can sit around 94, but there's 97 with life when he needs it. He'll manipulate a mid-80s slider from a true 11-5 bat misser, to a slurvier low-80s option to spot. The mid-80s split has good fade and tumble. The cutter is around 90 and has tight, late cut to induce weak contact. There's plus command of everything. Every prospect writer on staff that saw Mize preferred a different secondary, which means it could all come together one day as a monster top-of-the-rotation starter.

Then in June Mize was shut down for a month with what was termed "shoulder inflammation." There were arm concerns going back to his college days, and his arm action has some late effort. I'm not a huge fan of it generally, although he repeats it fine enough. Mize didn't look like the same pitcher after coming back and was shut down a few weeks early. If we had high confidence he would have a healthy, full 2020, he'd rank as the best pitching prospect in baseball. But we don't. If he'd been healthy all of 2019, he might have pitched himself to the majors and out of prospect list consideration. He didn't. Pitchers, man.

Variance: High. Is he healthy? Tune in during spring training to maybe find out!

Mark Barry's Fantasy Take: Yikes. Mize might represent the biggest chasm between ceiling and floor in the minors. That's hyperbole, sure, but with health he could be one of the five best arms in the league. The problem is he's a pitcher and in addition to possessing the skills to get dudes out he also has a knack for picking up nagging arm injuries. He's still one of the best pitching prospects in the game, but the risk is high enough to keep him out of the top spot.

★ ★ ★ *2020 Top 101 Prospect* **#47** ★ ★ ★

2 Matt Manning RHP

OFP: 60   ETA: 2020/21

Born: 01/28/98   Age: 22   Bats: R   Throws: R   Height: 6'6"   Weight: 215   Origin: Round 1, 2016 Draft (#9 overall)

YEAR	TEAM	LVL	AGE	W	L	SV	G	GS	IP	H	HR	BB/9	K/9	K	GB%	BABIP	WHIP	ERA	DRA	WARP	PF
2017	ONE	A-	19	2	2	0	9	9	33¹	27	0	3.8	9.7	36	31%	.310	1.23	1.89	4.32	0.4	95
2017	WMI	A	19	2	0	0	5	5	17²	14	0	5.6	13.2	26	49%	.341	1.42	5.60	3.60	0.3	96
2018	WMI	A	20	3	3	0	11	11	55²	47	3	4.5	12.3	76	43%	.344	1.35	3.40	3.77	0.9	96
2018	LAK	A+	20	4	4	0	9	9	51¹	32	4	3.3	11.4	65	47%	.241	0.99	2.98	2.71	1.6	98
2018	ERI	AA	20	0	1	0	2	2	10²	11	0	3.4	11.0	13	46%	.393	1.41	4.22	4.39	0.1	105
2019	ERI	AA	21	11	5	0	24	24	133²	93	7	2.6	10.0	148	48%	.259	0.98	2.56	2.75	3.6	104
2020	DET	MLB	22	2	2	0	33	0	35	34	5	3.6	9.4	37	44%	.307	1.36	4.27	4.42	0.3	104

Comparables: José Berríos, Jake Thompson, Dustin May

The Report: Three years after drafting Manning as a somewhat baseball-raw, very projectable prep arm, you'd imagine the Tigers have to be fairly pleased with where he is now. It wasn't the most direct route to top-50 prospectdom, mind you. His delivery has vastly changed over the last 24 months from uptempo, uphill, drop and drive mechanics that didn't make good use of his height—and that he couldn't consistently repeat—to a smoother, more upright and repeatable delivery that makes better use of all of his 6-foot-6 length. His fastball generally sits in an average velo band, touching 96 or occasionally higher, but the serious extension and tough angle make it play up. Manning can throw the fastball to both sides of the plate consistently, and move it in or out. The curve can get humpy and he will still slow his arm action on it at times, but it will also flash plus-plus in the upper 70s, and he can manipulate the shape from a true 12-6 downer to a backfoot 12-5 to lefties. The change remains the third pitch, too firm with below-average command. He'll turn over a few nice ones, but it's still in the "needs a grade jump to start" range. We think he'll get close enough with it, and he's a better bet to be a mid-rotation arm now than this time last year.

Variance: Medium. There's still some relief risk. The change might not get there, he's got a lot of limbs to keep in line, and mechanical inconsistency has been a problem in the past. He's shown more fastball occasionally in the past though, and it's not impossible the fastball jumps as he continues to figure things out and the profile plays up past this.

Mark Barry's Fantasy Take: Wait, did I already do to "huge discrepancy between floor and ceiling" bit? Manning's bugaboo is a little less injury-related than Mize's (although there's injury risk because, you know, pitchers) and pertains more to his changeup. He can still be effective with a mediocre change, but as a 2.5-pitch pitcher, his fantasy upside slides to back-end starter or late-inning reliever. His proximity and potential keeps him in the top-50ish, however.

★ ★ ★ *2020 Top 101 Prospect* **#49** ★ ★ ★

3 Riley Greene OF

OFP: 60   ETA: 2023

Born: 09/28/00   Age: 19   Bats: L   Throws: L   Height: 6'3"   Weight: 200   Origin: Round 1, 2019 Draft (#5 overall)

YEAR	TEAM	LVL	AGE	PA	R	2B	3B	HR	RBI	BB	K	SB	CS	AVG/OBP/SLG	DRC+	VORP	BABIP	BRR	FRAA	WARP	PF
2019	TGW	RK	18	43	9	3	0	2	8	5	12	0	0	.351/.442/.595	165	4.9	.478	-1.6	CF(9) -1.9	0.1	92
2019	ONE	A-	18	100	12	3	1	1	7	11	25	1	0	.295/.380/.386	128	5.7	.403	-1.5	CF(21) 3.5	0.7	96
2019	WMI	A	18	108	13	2	2	2	13	6	26	4	0	.219/.278/.344	62	1.9	.268	0.8	CF(20) 1.9, RF(4) 0.0	0.2	98
2020	DET	MLB	19	251	22	11	1	4	22	19	79	3	1	.222/.288/.328	64	0.0	.322	0.0	CF 3, RF 0	0.0	104

Comparables: Addison Russell, Harold Ramirez, Anthony Gose

The Report: Greene is a toolsy prep outfielder with a better present hit tool than the average member of that cohort. He loads late but keeps everything in sync well, and has plus bat speed with slight lift to his swing. The contact makes that sound and while he has a crude approach against offspeed at present, it is projectable, and he'll foul off a tough curve here and there, or stay back on a change and flick it into right field. You'll get enough glimpses to project a plus hit tool at maturity. There's above-average pull-side raw—which will end up plus—and he may grow into all-fields power in his twenties. Greene is not going to sell out for pop—when he does the swing gets long with some wrap—so projects more as a 20-homer guy than a 30-homer guy. He's an above-average runner at present, but is likely to slow down as he ages, and his routes and reads in the outfield are very rough. This might force him to left field—due to below-average arm strength—by the majors. That will put added pressure on the bat, but it's a very good bat.

Variance: High. He may end up in a corner, and it's not a huge power projection play, more a well-balanced offensive skill set, and one that hasn't really been tested as a pro yet.

Mark Barry's Fantasy Take: Spreading your age-18 season across three levels is likely quite the whirlwind, so let's take Greene's stat lines with a grain of salt. I like this guy quite a bit, and am looking forward to him sticking to a level for longer than 108 plate appearances. At his peak, he'll flirt with .300 with 20-25 homers and could even sneak in double-digit steals until he grows out of it. For fantasy purposes, I might have Greene slightly higher Manning.

★ ★ ★ *2020 Top 101 Prospect* **#76** ★ ★ ★

4 Tarik Skubal LHP   OFP: 55   ETA: 2020
Born: 11/20/96   Age: 23   Bats: L   Throws: L   Height: 6'3"   Weight: 215   Origin: Round 9, 2018 Draft (#255 overall)

YEAR	TEAM	LVL	AGE	W	L	SV	G	GS	IP	H	HR	BB/9	K/9	K	GB%	BABIP	WHIP	ERA	DRA	WARP	PF
2018	ONE	A-	21	0	0	1	4	0	12	8	0	1.5	12.8	17	46%	.333	0.83	0.75	3.08	0.2	100
2018	WMI	A	21	2	0	1	3	0	7¹	5	0	1.2	13.5	11	29%	.357	0.82	0.00	2.52	0.2	100
2019	LAK	A+	22	4	5	0	15	15	80¹	62	5	2.1	10.9	97	40%	.292	1.01	2.58	3.31	1.7	94
2019	ERI	AA	22	2	3	0	9	9	42¹	25	2	3.8	17.4	82	41%	.343	1.02	2.13	2.40	1.3	100
2020	DET	MLB	23	2	2	0	33	0	35	34	5	3.4	11.8	46	40%	.341	1.36	4.35	4.46	0.3	104

Comparables: Taylor Rogers, Adam Morgan, Dylan Cease

The Report: Skubal was a bit of an afterthought as a ninth-round pick in 2018, but the Tigers were taking a flyer on a lefty still recovering from Tommy John surgery in 2017. That gamble paid off in spades as Skubal showed off a mid-90s fastball with plenty of movement and improved command across two levels last year. His slider also flashed plus, giving him a dynamic two-pitch mix that gives him both excellent potential as a starter and a floor as an impact reliever. There's potential in his changeup that flashes above-average, but he needs consistency in his second full season. Skubal will also mix a curveball in a times, showing a slower upper-70s bender that proves effective working off his harder fastball and slider. Proving his command improvement is here to stay and allowing an additional tick on his changeup could still push Skubal slightly past this OFP.

Variance: Medium. His pro track record is still pretty short and there's work to do with the changeup, but the lightning fast gain in command has improved this portion of the profile dramatically.

Mark Barry's Fantasy Take: It's a bit of a cliché that the command is the last thing to come back after Tommy John surgery, and it's also a bit of a cliché to say that these things are clichés for a reason. Anyway, now that a semblance of Skubal's command has returned, we can dream on him being a high-strikeout SP3-type, which is probably good for the back end of the 101.

5 Joey Wentz LHP   OFP: 55   ETA: 2020
Born: 10/06/97   Age: 22   Bats: L   Throws: L   Height: 6'5"   Weight: 210   Origin: Round 1, 2016 Draft (#40 overall)

YEAR	TEAM	LVL	AGE	W	L	SV	G	GS	IP	H	HR	BB/9	K/9	K	GB%	BABIP	WHIP	ERA	DRA	WARP	PF
2017	ROM	A	19	8	3	0	26	26	131²	99	4	3.1	10.4	152	41%	.293	1.10	2.60	2.78	3.9	102
2018	BRV	A+	20	3	4	0	16	16	67	49	3	3.2	7.1	53	46%	.250	1.09	2.28	3.46	1.5	98
2019	ERI	AA	21	2	0	0	5	5	25²	20	3	1.4	13.0	37	19%	.315	0.94	2.10	3.28	0.5	103
2019	MIS	AA	21	5	8	0	20	20	103	90	13	3.9	8.7	100	35%	.280	1.31	4.72	5.50	-0.7	93
2020	DET	MLB	22	2	2	0	33	0	35	35	5	3.7	8.4	33	34%	.300	1.40	4.54	4.67	0.2	104

Comparables: Danny Duffy, Giovanni Soto, Alex Torres

The Report: After an injury-plagued 2018 campaign during which he often didn't have a good fastball, Wentz bounced back last year in Double-A. Now healthy, he sat low 90s again with late arm-side run. He is effective changing eye levels with the pitch, and it has some riding life up due to his height and high-three-quarters slot. A deceptive arm action adds to the effective velocity of the fastball as well. Wentz can struggle at times with the consistency of his breaking ball. It will vacillate between a 12-6 curve and something slurvier. The command of the breaker will come and go as well, but it does flash above-average when he's on top of it. The changeup has become a real weapon against righties and he can fade it off the plate away or cut and sink it inside. There may not be a future plus pitch here anymore, but it's a solid-average arsenal from the southpaw and he looked especially effective mixing his stuff post-trade.

Variance: Medium. Outside of his injury-plagued 2018, Wentz has been fairly durable and held his own as a 21-year-old in Double-A. He may not quite have the same upside we saw two years ago in A-ball, but he's a good bet to be a useful major league rotation piece of the Tigers.

Mark Barry's Fantasy Take: Wentz was awesome in five starts after infiltrating the Tigers organization, but I'm still not sure he has quite the same upside as the three arms above him on this list. Solid fantasy SP4, yes. More? Perhaps not.

6 Isaac Paredes SS   OFP: 50   ETA: 2021

Born: 02/18/99   Age: 21   Bats: R   Throws: R   Height: 5'11"   Weight: 225   Origin: International Free Agent, 2015

YEAR	TEAM	LVL	AGE	PA	R	2B	3B	HR	RBI	BB	K	SB	CS	AVG/OBP/SLG	DRC+	VORP	BABIP	BRR	FRAA	WARP	PF
2017	SBN	A	18	384	49	25	0	7	49	29	54	2	1	.264/.343/.401	111	18.2	.294	-1.0	SS(70) -2.7, 3B(7) 2.5	1.9	99
2017	WMI	A	18	133	16	3	0	4	21	13	13	0	0	.217/.323/.348	111	0.3	.214	-0.5	SS(22) -2.4, 3B(5) 1.4	1.1	98
2018	LAK	A+	19	347	50	19	2	12	48	32	54	1	0	.259/.338/.455	130	24.2	.274	0.3	SS(59) 3.2, 2B(22) 0.5	2.8	96
2018	ERI	AA	19	155	20	9	0	3	22	19	22	1	0	.321/.406/.458	145	13.7	.358	0.3	3B(18) 0.6, SS(15) 0.9	1.5	102
2019	ERI	AA	20	552	63	23	1	13	66	57	61	5	3	.282/.368/.416	138	33.2	.298	-2.3	3B(81) -3.4, SS(31) 0.1	3.4	103
2020	DET	MLB	21	35	4	2	0	1	4	3	6	0	0	.251/.332/.396	92	0.0	.282	-0.1	SS 0	0.1	104

Comparables: Jake Bauers, Ozzie Albies, Cheslor Cuthbert

The Report: Paredes was the centerpiece of a 2017 deadline deal that shipped two journeymen players to the Cubs for the stretch run. He's hit at every level thanks to an exceptional ability to recognize spin and detailed knowledge of the strike zone. His ability to track pitches allows him to find hitter's counts and utilize his barrel control to drive the ball. The contact isn't often loud enough to project him as a future plus-plus hitter, but it wouldn't be a stretch to see an above-average hitter with average pop, mostly to the pull side. A below-average runner with below-average range on the dirt, Paredes doesn't project to stay up the middle, putting additional pressure on his solid, if unspectacular, bat. Though he continues to play shortstop, he has seen time at both second and third base, where his ability flashes a touch better, but still inconsistently. Paredes owns a difficult profile where he must walk a fine line to play enough of a defensive position for his bat to hold up and make him a worthwhile regular.

Variance: Medium. His defensive home remains an open question and the bat may not completely support a move too far down the defensive spectrum.

Mark Barry's Fantasy Take: It feels like Paredes has been around forever (or maybe that's just me), but somehow he's still just 20 years old. Lucky for us, we're not too concerned with defense and I get serious Jhonny Peralta, Eduardo Escobar (thanks, Ben) and good-Mark Derosa-y vibes here. While .275 with 20 homers doesn't knock your socks off, it's still pretty useful, especially in deeper and only leagues.

7 Alex Faedo RHP   OFP: 50   ETA: 2020

Born: 11/12/95   Age: 24   Bats: R   Throws: R   Height: 6'5"   Weight: 230   Origin: Round 1, 2017 Draft (#18 overall)

YEAR	TEAM	LVL	AGE	W	L	SV	G	GS	IP	H	HR	BB/9	K/9	K	GB%	BABIP	WHIP	ERA	DRA	WARP	PF
2018	LAK	A+	22	2	4	0	12	12	61	49	3	1.9	7.5	51	33%	.263	1.02	3.10	3.20	1.5	94
2018	ERI	AA	22	3	6	0	12	12	60	54	15	3.3	8.9	59	28%	.250	1.27	4.95	5.14	0.1	102
2019	ERI	AA	23	6	7	0	22	22	115¹	104	17	2.0	10.5	134	33%	.293	1.12	3.90	3.75	1.7	105
2020	DET	MLB	24	2	2	0	33	0	35	37	7	3.3	9.1	35	33%	.312	1.41	5.08	5.17	0.0	104

Comparables: Matt Harvey, Jakob Junis, Robert Dugger

The Report: Faedo's prospect stock has taken a tumble the last two years largely because he hasn't proven to be the pitcher fans fell in love with during the College World Series. Once you get past those memories and focus on what he is today, Faedo is a perfectly acceptable back-end pitching prospect. His fastball sits consistently in the 89-91 mph range, though he will reach for 93 or 94 on occasion. That said, those extra ticks are largely unnecessary as long as he is commanding the fastball and manipulating his slider toward the plus range that it routinely flashes. The package is rounded out by a passable changeup he can locate to both sides of the plate with movement. Faedo earns excellent marks for his competitiveness on the mound. He mixes his pitches well and has a chance to walk the fine line that comes with a profile that is more moxie than raw stuff.

Variance: Low. Little is likely to change in Faedo's profile at this point, and as long as nothing regresses significantly, he should be able to handle big league innings every fifth day.

Mark Barry's Fantasy Take: If you look at Faedo's 2019 stats, you might be a little confused as to why he's not getting more buzz. And that's fair—he was incredible in his second spin through Double-A. Even if the numbers have changed, the skills haven't, so it's tough to envision him breaking through as more than a fantasy SP5.

8 Daz Cameron OF   OFP: 45   ETA: 2020

Born: 01/15/97   Age: 23   Bats: R   Throws: R   Height: 6'2"   Weight: 195   Origin: Round 1, 2015 Draft (#37 overall)

YEAR	TEAM	LVL	AGE	PA	R	2B	3B	HR	RBI	BB	K	SB	CS	AVG/OBP/SLG	DRC+	VORP	BABIP	BRR	FRAA	WARP	PF
2017	QUD	A	20	511	79	29	8	14	73	45	108	32	12	.271/.349/.466	132	38.5	.323	3.1	CF(110) 1.8, LF(4) -0.7	3.9	102
2018	LAK	A+	21	246	35	9	3	3	20	25	69	10	4	.259/.346/.370	119	9.9	.366	2.5	CF(38) 1.9, RF(18) 0.9	1.7	95
2018	ERI	AA	21	226	32	12	5	5	35	25	53	12	5	.285/.367/.470	126	11.4	.366	3.4	CF(34) -7.0, RF(16) 1.5	1.1	102
2018	TOL	AAA	21	62	8	4	1	0	6	2	15	2	2	.211/.246/.316	52	-1.1	.279	0.7	CF(14) 0.3, RF(1) 0.0	0.0	94
2019	TOL	AAA	22	528	68	22	6	13	43	62	152	17	8	.214/.330/.377	86	13.1	.291	2.4	CF(92) -1.0, RF(19) 5.4	1.3	94
2020	DET	MLB	23	251	24	12	2	5	25	22	84	9	4	.216/.298/.357	70	0.0	.318	0.4	CF 0, RF 1	0.1	104

Comparables: Brett Phillips, Alex Jackson, Rymer Liriano

The Report: Cameron has been on the radar for quite some time as the son of a former big leaguer, but his performance has yet to consistently catch up with the name recognition he enjoys. At his best, he shows a broad array of average tools that can play well in game situations. His glove is the most consistent part of his game, with quality defense in center field thanks to above-average speed, an above-average arm, and excellent instincts and feel for the game. He moves well to both sides and reads the ball well off the bat on those hit directly at him. His glove is enough to get him to the big leagues, but the path would be much easier if he were able to make any kind of consistent contact. Cameron's pitch recognition continues to lag behind his instincts in the box, leaving him prone to chasing pitches and leading to too much weak contact. As a result, his average raw power only finds game situations on occasion, leaving his plate appearances too empty, too often, to carve out a regular role. Cameron will need to take advantage of a return trip to Triple-A in order to force his way to Detroit amidst the Tigers rebuild.

Variance: High. The hit tool could go any number of directions, including further off a cliff and completely derailing his future. There's enough other near-average tools to manage a big league role, regardless of the bat, but things get a lot easier if he hits just a little bit.

Mark Barry's Fantasy Take: Learning to hit is hard. Learning to hit against big-league pitching is near impossible. It seems like that's where we're headed with Cameron. He has hit enough in the minors to warrant a look, but with a strikeout rate approaching 30 percent at Triple-A, it will be a tall order to find fantasy usefulness from Cameron, outside of perhaps a handful of steals.

9 Beau Burrows RHP   OFP: 45   ETA: 2020

Born: 09/18/96   Age: 23   Bats: R   Throws: R   Height: 6'2"   Weight: 215   Origin: Round 1, 2015 Draft (#22 overall)

YEAR	TEAM	LVL	AGE	W	L	SV	G	GS	IP	H	HR	BB/9	K/9	K	GB%	BABIP	WHIP	ERA	DRA	WARP	PF
2017	LAK	A+	20	4	3	0	11	11	58²	45	3	1.7	9.5	62	45%	.298	0.95	1.23	3.38	1.3	85
2017	ERI	AA	20	6	4	0	15	15	76¹	79	5	3.9	8.8	75	40%	.339	1.47	4.72	5.12	0.0	105
2018	ERI	AA	21	10	9	0	26	26	134	126	12	3.8	8.5	127	32%	.310	1.36	4.10	4.58	1.2	99
2019	TOL	AAA	22	2	6	0	15	15	65¹	68	12	4.4	8.4	61	34%	.303	1.53	5.51	5.70	0.6	92
2020	DET	MLB	23	2	2	0	16	5	34	35	5	3.7	7.6	29	35%	.296	1.44	4.91	4.83	0.2	104

Comparables: Luis Ortiz, Lucas Giolito, Zach Lee

The Report: Burrows missed significant time on the mound last season due to a variety of injuries, including biceps tendinitis, shoulder inflammation and finally an oblique injury. That lost development time was critical for Burrows as he tried to cement himself as a future rotation workhorse and find his way to the big leagues. Instead, Burrows' command regressed, his changeup failed to progress and whispers of a move to the bullpen grew louder and louder. When healthy, Burrows shows a low-90s fastball that bumps 95-96 mph early in starts. His slider is his best breaking pitch, showing regularly as an above-average mid-80s pitch, while his curveball lacks consistent shape and quality. A below-average changeup completes the pitch mix, though he has yet to discover enough consistency with the change to take the next step. Burrows shows flashes of throwing consistent strikes, but he has yet to move the ball around to the edges of the zone with any regularity. The lack of consistent command and two inconsistent secondary pitches leaves Burrows trending toward the bullpen where he could see a slight tick in power on his fastball and slider, something that would play well in the middle to late innings.

Variance: Medium. Burrows has yet to develop a consistent third pitch or make overwhelming strides with his command, leaving his future in the rotation up in the air. In addition, his ultimate bullpen role is still debatable.

Mark Barry's Fantasy Take: Biceps tendinitis, shoulder inflammation and an oblique injury. Cool, cool, cool. I don't have enough faith in Burrows's stuff to keep him around and wait out his injuries. He's a deep leaguer or AL-only guy that you'll likely find a reasonable facsimile of on the waiver wire.

10 Parker Meadows OF   OFP: 50   ETA: 2022

Born: 11/02/99   Age: 20   Bats: L   Throws: R   Height: 6'5"   Weight: 205   Origin: Round 2, 2018 Draft (#44 overall)

YEAR	TEAM	LVL	AGE	PA	R	2B	3B	HR	RBI	BB	K	SB	CS	AVG/OBP/SLG	DRC+	VORP	BABIP	BRR	FRAA	WARP	PF
2018	TGW	RK	18	85	16	2	1	4	8	8	25	3	1	.284/.376/.500	126	6.1	.378	0.0	CF(20) -3.1	0.2	98
2019	WMI	A	19	504	52	15	2	7	40	47	113	14	8	.221/.296/.312	78	3.6	.277	-1.1	CF(100) -2.3, RF(16) 0.8	0.0	97
2020	DET	MLB	20	251	20	10	1	4	22	17	76	2	1	.209/.267/.311	51	0.0	.291	-0.1	CF 0, RF 0	-0.7	104

Comparables: Michael Saunders, Joe Benson, Abraham Almonte

The Report: The stat line for Meadows took a hit due to some bad luck and a cold Michigan spring, but he still impressed with his raw talent and high upside. There's tons of projection remaining and it's not difficult to see five future above-average tools. The bat's still a ways away from major league ready but it's a pretty left-handed swing that has some natural loft. Physical maturity will bring some natural strength that will make the power play up in game. Meadow's speed and defense will mean the organization will give him plenty of time for the offense to develop. He's not a quick-twitch base stealing threat but there's plus-plus speed which, along with good natural instincts, make him an exceptional base runner. He is also one of the top outfield defenders in the organization, able to handle all three spots. There's a high ceiling in Meadow's profile and a solid 2020 season at High-A Lakeland will catapult him up next year's prospect rankings.

Variance: High. The gap between Meadows' projection and his A-ball performance is significant. On the other side of the coin, you can see the tools flash past this OFP from time to time already.

Mark Barry's Fantasy Take: Meadows is basically his older brother, just more raw and less likely to hit his upside. It's like the reverse Preston/Kyle Tucker dynamic. Even though maximizing his tools might be unlikely, they're still there and they're easy to dream on. We'll know more after this season, but for now, I'm only rostering him in leagues with at least 250 prospects.

The Next Ten

11 Jake Rogers C

Born: 04/18/95   Age: 25   Bats: R   Throws: R   Height: 6'1"   Weight: 205   Origin: Round 3, 2016 Draft (#97 overall)

YEAR	TEAM	LVL	AGE	PA	R	2B	3B	HR	RBI	BB	K	SB	CS	AVG/OBP/SLG	DRC+	VORP	BABIP	BRR	FRAA	WARP	PF
2017	QUD	A	22	116	17	7	1	6	15	9	28	1	0	.255/.336/.520	130	10.3	.290	0.3	C(21) 0.9	1.0	102
2017	BCA	A+	22	367	43	18	3	12	55	44	72	13	8	.265/.357/.457	135	29.4	.302	-0.8	C(63) 1.4	2.8	94
2018	ERI	AA	23	408	57	15	1	17	56	41	112	7	1	.219/.305/.412	88	20.8	.261	2.7	C(98) 29.4, 1B(1) 0.0	4.9	101
2019	ERI	AA	24	112	17	3	1	5	21	19	26	0	0	.302/.429/.535	164	13.6	.356	-1.7	C(21) 2.3	1.2	104
2019	TOL	AAA	24	191	29	10	1	9	31	18	53	0	0	.223/.321/.458	88	6.0	.269	-2.7	C(48) 9.5	1.3	95
2019	DET	MLB	24	128	11	3	0	4	8	13	51	0	0	.125/.222/.259	53	-1.3	.175	-0.4	C(34) -4.0	-0.6	102
2020	DET	MLB	25	70	7	3	0	2	8	6	24	1	0	.197/.281/.362	65	0.0	.271	-0.1	C 0	0.0	104

Comparables: Will Smith, Tom Murphy, Johnny Field

Rogers is going to be a backup catcher for a while on the strength of his glove. He's been one of the elite framers in the upper minors and offers a plus arm that will curtail the running game when he's behind the plate. His first pass against major-league arms didn't go so great though. Rogers has some country strong pop, but the combination of a stiff, pull-happy swing and fringe bat speed led to his getting exploited on the outer half of the plate. If he can make some secondary adjustments, he'll run into enough home runs to kick around a major league bench for six or seven years on the strength of the defensive profile.

12 Wilkel Hernandez RHP

Born: 04/13/99   Age: 21   Bats: R   Throws: R   Height: 6'3"   Weight: 195   Origin: International Free Agent, 2015

YEAR	TEAM	LVL	AGE	W	L	SV	G	GS	IP	H	HR	BB/9	K/9	K	GB%	BABIP	WHIP	ERA	DRA	WARP	PF
2017	ANG	RK	18	3	1	0	11	7	41¹	23	1	4.4	9.1	42	44%	.216	1.04	2.61	1.28	2.0	98
2018	WMI	A	19	2	5	0	10	10	42	40	4	3.4	7.3	34	30%	.288	1.33	4.71	4.68	0.3	96
2019	WMI	A	20	9	7	0	21	21	101¹	97	5	2.3	8.0	90	40%	.302	1.21	3.73	4.05	1.4	96
2020	DET	MLB	21	2	2	0	33	0	35	36	5	4.3	6.6	26	34%	.283	1.49	5.13	5.10	0.0	104

Comparables: Zack Littell, Chris Flexen, Joe Ross

Hernandez remains a bit of a project as a pitching prospect, but there's stuff to like here. It's an ideal starter's frame, long and lean, with plenty of projection left. He's smoothed out his delivery and sits low 90s with good run. He has surprising feel for spin given his experience level, and his curveball could grow into an above-average pitch with refinement. His change remains crude however, and he still struggles to hold his velocity into games. He's not starting off in the mid 90s as often either. The shape of the OFP here remains amorphous though, with both fourth starter and bullpen outcomes in play. There's upside past that too, which is why he slots at the top of this run of arms for now. He's also less likely to pitch in the majors at all compared to the names below him. Weight the variance as you see fit.

13 Logan Shore RHP

Born: 12/28/94   Age: 25   Bats: R   Throws: R   Height: 6'2"   Weight: 215   Origin: Round 2, 2016 Draft (#47 overall)

YEAR	TEAM	LVL	AGE	W	L	SV	G	GS	IP	H	HR	BB/9	K/9	K	GB%	BABIP	WHIP	ERA	DRA	WARP	PF
2017	ATH	RK	22	0	0	0	3	3	8	2	0	0.0	14.6	13	62%	.154	0.25	0.00	0.00	0.6	90
2017	STO	A+	22	2	5	1	17	14	72²	81	5	2.0	9.2	74	54%	.350	1.33	4.09	4.80	0.3	103
2018	STO	A+	23	2	0	0	4	4	22¹	18	0	0.8	10.1	25	63%	.316	0.90	1.21	2.37	0.8	93
2018	MID	AA	23	1	6	0	13	13	68²	85	7	2.5	6.4	49	50%	.342	1.51	5.50	5.59	-0.2	109
2019	ERI	AA	24	4	7	0	23	16	97	91	8	3.6	5.4	58	40%	.279	1.34	3.43	5.13	-0.3	103
2020	DET	MLB	25	2	2	0	33	0	35	34	5	3.3	5.3	21	40%	.265	1.34	4.37	4.57	0.2	104

Shore was arguably the best pitcher on an absolutely loaded 2016 Florida Gators staff. Nowadays he's the seventh-best pitching prospect from that team. Well, technically sixth I guess since their closer, Shaun Anderson, is no longer list-eligible. We often make note of how even your OFP 45 prospects like Shore were usually the best pitcher on their high school and college teams, and occasionally on their minor league teams as well. The Erie rotation was just as loaded as that Gators team, though—and both included Alex Faedo. So it's easy for him to get lost in the shuffle behind Mize, Manning, and Faedo. The stuff won't stand out next to those three, but he offers an effective sinker either side of 90, a potential above-average change, and a potentially average slider. It's very back-of-the-rotation—hence the OFP 45—and he has struggled to miss bats even in Double-A. There may not be much room for him in the Detroit rotation due to…well, Mize, Manning, and Faedo, but a major-league grade is a major-league grade.

14 Kyle Funkhouser RHP

Born: 03/16/94   Age: 26   Bats: R   Throws: R   Height: 6'2"   Weight: 230   Origin: Round 4, 2016 Draft (#115 overall)

YEAR	TEAM	LVL	AGE	W	L	SV	G	GS	IP	H	HR	BB/9	K/9	K	GB%	BABIP	WHIP	ERA	DRA	WARP	PF
2017	WMI	A	23	4	1	0	7	7	31¹	30	3	3.7	14.1	49	56%	.403	1.37	3.16	3.79	0.5	94
2017	LAK	A+	23	1	1	0	5	5	31¹	23	1	1.7	9.8	34	57%	.275	0.93	1.72	2.86	0.9	80
2018	ERI	AA	24	4	5	0	17	17	89	88	10	3.9	9.0	89	44%	.326	1.43	3.74	4.89	0.5	101
2018	TOL	AAA	24	0	2	0	2	2	8²	8	0	10.4	7.3	7	54%	.333	2.08	6.23	8.15	-0.3	90
2019	ERI	AA	25	3	1	0	4	4	23²	16	2	1.1	11.0	29	45%	.275	0.80	1.90	2.81	0.6	97
2019	TOL	AAA	25	3	7	0	18	18	63¹	79	3	7.7	9.2	65	54%	.396	2.10	8.53	7.79	-0.7	95
2020	DET	MLB	26	2	3	0	28	5	46	46	7	3.9	8.1	42	46%	.296	1.42	4.68	4.62	0.4	104

Comparables: Spencer Turnbull, Erick Fedde, Daniel Wright

Funkhouser will be 26 before Opening Day 2020 and hasn't thrown 100 innings in a season since 2016. Elbow inflammation in 2017, a freak broken foot in 2018 and a shoulder impingement in 2019 have all limited his time on a professional mound. The scouting report hasn't changed much since I saw him in short-season. He has a fastball he can get up to 95, but sits more 92-94 and runs a little true. The slider is the best secondary now, mid-80s with short, late depth to it. The change is too firm and lacks ideal velocity separation. Control and command issues bubble up too often. The Tigers have used Funkhouser exclusively as a starter as a pro, but it's probably about time to move him to the pen, even if he didn't have durability concerns. The fastball could be more mid 90s when he's airing it out for an inning, and paired with the above-average slider, he could be a perfectly fine fastball/slider middle reliever, maybe even a seventh-inning guy.

15 Franklin Perez RHP

Born: 12/06/97   Age: 22   Bats: R   Throws: R   Height: 6'3"   Weight: 197   Origin: International Free Agent, 2014

YEAR	TEAM	LVL	AGE	W	L	SV	G	GS	IP	H	HR	BB/9	K/9	K	GB%	BABIP	WHIP	ERA	DRA	WARP	PF
2017	BCA	A+	19	4	2	2	12	10	54¹	38	4	2.7	8.8	53	38%	.236	0.99	2.98	2.76	1.6	95
2017	CCH	AA	19	2	1	1	7	6	32	33	2	3.1	7.0	25	35%	.316	1.38	3.09	4.89	0.1	99
2018	TGR	RK	20	0	1	0	3	3	8	3	0	0.0	5.6	5	27%	.136	0.38	4.50	1.08	0.4	94
2018	LAK	A+	20	0	1	0	4	4	11¹	15	2	6.4	7.1	9	43%	.371	2.03	7.94	7.67	-0.3	99
2019	LAK	A+	21	0	0	0	2	2	7²	7	1	5.9	7.0	6	46%	.286	1.57	2.35	6.15	-0.1	104
2020	DET	MLB	22	2	2	0	33	0	35	35	5	3.6	7.0	27	38%	.287	1.40	4.60	4.64	0.2	104

Comparables: Francis Martes, Brady Lail, Mike Soroka

On our 2017 lists, every risk section for every pitching prospect included some variation on "Also, he's a pitcher." The audience got bored with this quickly and moved to actively annoyed later on, but as an Irony Level 5, I'm not going to give up on a bit. There was a broader point to all of it, too. Pitchers are volatile. And you don't know if a pitcher can maintain a workload through a full season, or season over season, until they do it. There's no doubt that Franklin Perez has significantly higher upside than Funkhouser or Shore. You could argue he has more upside than Wentz even now. Perez threw seven innings this year due to shoulder issues. The same barking shoulder limited him to 19 1/3 innings in 2018. There's a chance he never throws a meaningful full professional season again, despite being only 22. That's a downside outcome, but it's in play. The upside outcome is he shows up healthy in 2020 and looks like the dude in Mauricio's report from 2016. But the best predictor of future pitcher injuries is past pitcher injuries, so perhaps you don't want Anton Chigurh flipping that coin.

16 Paul Richan RHP

Born: 03/26/97   Age: 23   Bats: R   Throws: R   Height: 6'2"   Weight: 200   Origin: Round 2C, 2018 Draft (#78 overall)

YEAR	TEAM	LVL	AGE	W	L	SV	G	GS	IP	H	HR	BB/9	K/9	K	GB%	BABIP	WHIP	ERA	DRA	WARP	PF
2018	EUG	A-	21	0	2	0	10	9	29²	19	2	1.5	9.4	31	40%	.233	0.81	2.12	2.07	1.1	99
2019	MYR	A+	22	10	5	0	17	17	93	96	10	1.7	8.3	86	40%	.315	1.23	3.97	4.90	0.1	97
2019	LAK	A+	22	2	2	0	5	5	30²	39	2	0.6	8.5	29	43%	.398	1.34	4.11	6.73	-0.6	93
2020	DET	MLB	23	2	2	0	33	0	35	35	6	3.4	7.1	28	38%	.285	1.38	4.63	4.76	0.2	104

Comparables: Mike Mayers, Taylor Williams, William Cuevas

Richan, one of the two prospect arms acquired for Nicholas Castellanos, is your standard polished, college strike-thrower. Drafted in the second round by the Cubs out of San Diego in 2018, he throws buckets of strikes with the standard four-pitch mix. The fastball sits in the low 90s but he can move it around the zone and elevate it for Ks when he's ahead. The best of the secondaries is an average slider that has more sweep than tilt, but comes out of the hand like the fastball and offers enough late movement to miss High-A bats. Richan throws a slurvy curve for a different breaking ball look, and a below-average change with occasional fade. It's a good frame, and an easy, repeatable delivery. He has gotten by so far on control and command and may not have an out pitch against better hitters, but so far so good on his road to backend starterdom. Double-A in 2020 will be a stern test of the profile.

17 Nick Quintana   SS

Born: 10/13/97   Age: 22   Bats: R   Throws: R   Height: 5'10"   Weight: 187   Origin: Round 2, 2019 Draft (#47 overall)

YEAR	TEAM	LVL	AGE	PA	R	2B	3B	HR	RBI	BB	K	SB	CS	AVG/OBP/SLG	DRC+	VORP	BABIP	BRR	FRAA	WARP	PF
2019	ONE	A-	21	98	12	7	0	1	4	12	31	1	0	.256/.347/.372	130	4.5	.389	0.4	3B(25) -2.9	0.3	94
2019	WMI	A	21	162	14	5	1	1	13	13	51	3	1	.158/.228/.226	37	-4.3	.229	0.6	3B(38) 3.4	-0.1	97
2020	DET	MLB	22	251	19	12	1	4	21	16	97	2	1	.191/.245/.291	38	3.0	.307	0.0	3B 0	-1.1	104

Comparables: Adrian Nieto, David Bote, Mike Olt

The Tigers second-round pick looks a little like an Asylum Films version of Bo Bichette, which is an aesthetic I can get behind. He tries to hit bombs like Bo too, which really isn't his game. There's a big leg kick that hangs in the air for a bit, and a power-hitter swing without the frame or bat speed to back it up. He manages to handle the barrel pretty well despite all of that, and there's some projection in the offensive profile if he can add some strength or calm down some of the swing elements. Quintana looks more athletic in the field than at the plate, showing good hands and lateral range and enough arm for the left side of the infield. He could probably play a fringe shortstop a couple times a week too. He did look pretty gassed by the time he got to Connecticut in August. Forest saw more power potential in the Midwest League earlier in the Summer, so this might be a case of non-representative looks after a long season, but the profile felt more utility infielder than starter.

18 Derek Hill   OF

Born: 12/30/95   Age: 24   Bats: R   Throws: R   Height: 6'2"   Weight: 195   Origin: Round 1, 2014 Draft (#23 overall)

YEAR	TEAM	LVL	AGE	PA	R	2B	3B	HR	RBI	BB	K	SB	CS	AVG/OBP/SLG	DRC+	VORP	BABIP	BRR	FRAA	WARP	PF
2017	TGW	RK	21	61	11	1	1	1	7	10	15	7	0	.163/.300/.286	70	2.2	.206	1.2	CF(7) 0.6	0.2	95
2017	WMI	A	21	168	28	8	6	1	21	16	38	12	5	.285/.367/.444	115	15.2	.374	2.2	CF(23) 0.1	1.0	98
2017	LAK	A+	21	38	3	1	0	0	2	5	10	10	0	.194/.324/.226	84	3.1	.286	1.5	CF(6) -0.1	0.2	85
2018	LAK	A+	22	383	45	9	3	4	33	33	109	35	12	.239/.307/.318	81	5.3	.338	3.7	CF(55) -2.5, LF(27) -2.1	0.3	96
2019	ERI	AA	23	526	78	19	5	14	45	38	147	21	13	.243/.311/.394	92	16.3	.321	0.7	CF(79) 1.4, RF(37) 7.8	2.2	103
2020	DET	MLB	24	251	23	10	2	5	23	17	83	13	4	.221/.280/.341	58	0.0	.323	1.1	CF 0, RF 1	-0.2	104

Comparables: Aaron Altherr, Joe Benson, Keon Broxton

19 Jose Azocar   OF

Born: 05/11/96   Age: 24   Bats: R   Throws: R   Height: 6'0"   Weight: 185   Origin: International Free Agent, 2012

YEAR	TEAM	LVL	AGE	PA	R	2B	3B	HR	RBI	BB	K	SB	CS	AVG/OBP/SLG	DRC+	VORP	BABIP	BRR	FRAA	WARP	PF
2017	LAK	A+	21	456	38	10	6	3	37	14	122	12	6	.220/.246/.292	45	-14.3	.297	0.9	CF(81) -5.2, RF(38) 0.1	-1.4	87
2018	WMI	A	22	110	19	3	6	1	16	5	21	6	2	.317/.355/.490	131	10.6	.390	1.0	CF(24) -0.5, RF(2) -0.5	0.7	96
2018	LAK	A+	22	318	34	14	3	1	34	9	64	5	2	.290/.308/.367	107	-0.1	.355	-1.7	RF(61) -0.7, CF(9) 0.7	0.6	97
2019	ERI	AA	23	538	65	21	3	10	58	21	132	10	3	.286/.317/.399	103	12.8	.363	0.7	RF(81) 2.1, CF(47) 3.8	2.3	103
2020	DET	MLB	24	251	20	11	2	3	22	9	74	2	1	.243/.274/.342	58	0.0	.339	0.0	RF 0, CF 1	-0.4	104

Hill and Azocar make a neatly matched pair in my mind as potential fourth outfielders with some obvious tools, but some obvious warts as well. Hill is the more traditional up-the-middle type, a plus runner with a lean frame and plenty of quick-twitch athleticism. He's a potential plus center fielder so he got the lion's share of the reps there over Azocar, who would likely be fine there and is an above-average runner himself. Azocar has a borderline plus-plus arm though, so naturally he slots into right field more often than not.

At the plate there are issues as both players strike out more than you'd like given both offensive profiles project as hit-over-power. Hill is inconsistent with his setup and hands and struggles with pitches running off the plate. Azocar's setup is very noisy and he's vulnerable to spin and lacks Hill's bat speed. Both are likely extra outfielders in the end.

20 Anthony Castro   RHP

Born: 04/13/95   Age: 25   Bats: R   Throws: R   Height: 6'2"   Weight: 190   Origin: International Free Agent, 2011

YEAR	TEAM	LVL	AGE	W	L	SV	G	GS	IP	H	HR	BB/9	K/9	K	GB%	BABIP	WHIP	ERA	DRA	WARP	PF
2017	WMI	A	22	10	6	0	21	21	108¹	91	4	2.9	7.9	95	59%	.280	1.16	2.49	4.20	1.4	95
2018	LAK	A+	23	9	4	0	22	20	116²	112	8	3.3	7.8	101	50%	.309	1.33	2.93	4.86	0.6	97
2018	ERI	AA	23	0	0	0	3	3	10	8	1	10.8	3.6	4	50%	.226	2.00	8.10	7.24	-0.2	96
2019	ERI	AA	24	5	3	1	27	18	102¹	75	9	5.7	10.2	116	45%	.273	1.37	4.40	4.78	0.2	102
2020	DET	MLB	25	2	2	0	16	5	34	34	5	3.8	8.7	33	42%	.305	1.42	4.73	4.67	0.3	104

Comparables: Erik Goeddel, Chris Stratton, Josh James

Castro has been bouncing around the Tigers system since signing before the 2012 season, all the while showing flashes of intrigue that enticed onlookers. On his best days he runs his fastball up to 97 mph with plenty of life and his slider can miss bats both in and out of the zone. The emergence of an above-average split-finger has breathed new life into his arsenal and put some shine back on his prospect star. The Tigers tried Castro in the bullpen to start last season before he dazzled as part of a high-profile Erie rotation down the stretch. Castro is a reliever long term and if he can successfully transition to the role throughout 2020, he could be an interesting bullpen piece down the line.

A note about Roberto Campos

Given the shallowness of the organization, and despite my own personal misgivings about aggressively ranking recent J2 signings, this would normally be a system and situation where we'd find a spot for the $2.85 million IFA. Campos provides a particularly difficult time for our evaluation and ranking model however. Even inside the game he was barely known after defecting from Cuba as a 13-year-old. He was largely an unknown quantity while training with ex-Tiger Alex Sanchez in the Dominican. Thus, there is little consensus on where he should have ranked as an IFA even by the specialists in that area, so we will wait until there are more pro looks to go around.

Personal Cheeseball

PC Jack O'Loughlin   LHP

Born: 03/14/00   Age: 20   Bats: L   Throws: L   Height: 6'5"   Weight: 210   Origin: International Free Agent, 2016

YEAR	TEAM	LVL	AGE	W	L	SV	G	GS	IP	H	HR	BB/9	K/9	K	GB%	BABIP	WHIP	ERA	DRA	WARP	PF
2018	ONE	A-	18	0	1	1	7	1	20²	15	1	5.2	10.9	25	52%	.298	1.31	4.35	5.09	0.0	108
2019	ONE	A-	19	2	4	0	13	12	60¹	57	1	3.6	7.3	49	50%	.315	1.34	3.13	5.71	-0.4	94
2020	DET	MLB	20	2	2	0	33	0	35	34	5	4.0	6.2	24	44%	.275	1.43	4.76	4.91	0.1	104

O'Loughlin returned to Norwich this summer looking noticeably slimmer and more athletic and with a few more ticks on the fastball to boot. It now sits either side of 90, with some sink and run at the high end and a distinct cutter at the low. There's deception from the cross-body mechanics, although he's smoothed out the control and command issues somewhat. The curve improved as well, ticking up to the mid 70s with more consistent 1-7 break that he could get gloveside or backdoor. The change shows a circle and split look with 10 mph of velocity separation off the fastball. He's more comfortable throwing the split in on righties and he will lean on the pitch heavily, although it only has an average projection. O'Loughlin is still a teenager, and while he lacks projection in both body and stuff, and the delivery has some effort and whack to it, the year-over-year improvements are a good marker. And I'm still a sucker for a lefty with a fun change.

Low Minors Sleeper

LMS Ryan Kreidler SS

Born: 11/12/97   Age: 22   Bats: R   Throws: R   Height: 6'4"   Weight: 208   Origin: Round 4, 2019 Draft (#112 overall)

YEAR	TEAM	LVL	AGE	PA	R	2B	3B	HR	RBI	BB	K	SB	CS	AVG/OBP/SLG	DRC+	VORP	BABIP	BRR	FRAA	WARP	PF
2019	ONE	A-	21	257	28	13	4	2	20	20	61	9	4	.232/.307/.351	102	8.9	.304	0.3	SS(57) 0.9	1.2	95
2020	DET	MLB	22	251	21	12	1	5	23	15	80	2	1	.207/.262/.328	55	0.0	.293	0.0	SS 0	-0.6	104

After my first couple of looks at Kreidler, I wrote "feels like a Mets fourth-round pick" in my notebook. That is not a compliment given the Mets' lack of success with Day Two college bats over the last, oh, decade or so. He grew on me over the course of subsequent games. The collection of tools are mostly on the fringy side of average, but he gets it done at short and will show some ability to stay inside the ball and use all fields. He struggled a bit with spin at times and there is below-average power production at best, as his contact can lack oomph despite average bat speed. Kreidler has a little less projection and athleticism than Quintana, but looked like the better player at present.

Top Talents 25 and Under (as of 4/1/2020)

1. Casey Mize
2. Matt Manning
3. Riley Greene
4. Tarik Skubal
5. Joey Wentz
6. Joe Jimenez
7. Isaac Paredes
8. Alex Faedo
9. Daz Cameron
10. Victor Reyes

We could easily copy-paste the prospects list and be done here, and not a jury of editors in the tri-state area would convict. Still.

A team this far into a generational cryogenic nap usually transitions the first call-ups from a status of "this will be interesting to see" to "no not like that," and Jake Rogers, a top 10 talent last year, literally hit .125 in two months with the Tigers and missed the cut. Likewise, 26-year-old Jeimer Candelario graduates, but unfortunately with a philosophy degree, hence the lack of a guaranteed job for 2020.

The Packard plant blossom in this garden is Jimenez. One would think he would have recorded more than 12 saves by now. He ought to double it this season and his career should go another five years. He's the same age as Joel Zumaya when his arm could no longer generate velocity, so the habitual eye-rolling on all paragraphs with respect to budding Tigers relievers are understandable. Hence, he'll age off the list a success story.

That leaves us with two options: comprise the 25U list with prospects plus Jimenez or throw a bone to one of those young deer in the headlights who merely got nicked by a side mirror, and that was Reyes. He was an easy out during his 2018 Rule 5 stash year but progressed on all his strengths (contact, baserunning, defense). He's a corner outfielder who can't hit home runs, which is a dying species for a reason. But his 89 DRC+ was a better metric than anyone else in his dugout's age bracket. It wasn't a bright spot, nor a reason for hope. But it definitely happened.

For Detroit, the prospect list started out ghastly. Then the entire major league roster was housed inside Janet's boundless void. Now it's this list. Before you know it, the growing pains will properly shift to all these promising right-handers in the major league rotation, getting early showers thanks to [checks notes] the Royals, again.

Eyewitness Reports

Eyewitness Report: Casey Mize

Evaluator: Spring Marie Cullen
Report Date: 05/08/2019
Dates Seen: 04/29/2019
Risk Factor: Moderate
Delivery: Tall, athletic frame with a thick lower half. Great balance and body control. Clean, repeatable motion from a high 3/4 arm slot and a deceptive high leg kick. Mature mound presence, calm and composed, controls pace of the game. Confident.

Pitch Type	Future Grade	Sitting Velocity	Peak Velocity	Report
Fastball	60	92-95	96	Struggled to hit location early in game, but I believe command will play better than what I saw. In later innings it showed serious flashes of a plus pitch. Velocity plays up due to advanced sequencing and ability to work off his secondaries. Most effective throwing armside. Capable of maintaining velocity late in game.
Slider	60	85-88	88	Commands extremely well. Changes speed to give it two different shapes. At lower velocities it shows slurve qualities with late break. The higher end of the velocity band takes on a more traditional shape, breaking down and away from righties. Throws both versions for strikes, and induces swings and misses. Utilized as a strikeout pitch, making batters chase.
Cutter	60	89-91	92	Consistent. Tight break with moderate horizontal movement. A plus offering he used to get ahead in the count and produce weak contact. Relied on it heavily.
Splitter	60	83-87	88	Deceptive, coming from the same arm slot as his other pitches, appears to be a fastball then breaks late. Occasionally takes a little something off of it for a different look, fading away from batters.

Conclusion: Mize is a potential future ace. His impressive repertoire features plus pitches that compliment each other and his advanced command allows him to continually throw them for strikes. His adept knowledge of sequencing, working counts and pitching in general showcase a high baseball IQ and natural ability to turn in quality starts.

Eyewitness Report: Matt Manning

Evaluator: Jeffrey Paternostro
Report Date: 05/28/2019
Dates Seen: 5/21/19
Risk Factor: Medium
Delivery: Easier tempo than in the past, full arc to HTQ, average arm speed, still a slight lower half hitch, but smoother and more upright, much improved extension and mechanics. Looks like he's playing catch when he's going well.

Pitch Type	Future Grade	Sitting Velocity	Peak Velocity	Report
FB	60	92-94	96	Serious extension and angle, above average command to both sides, will cut or run. Batters were uncomfortable, got on them in a hurry. Flattened a bit and lost some command as he tired but he didn't really bleed velo. Could get to 7, but I don't really see the consistent plus velocity to go with the command and extension
CU	60	77-80	80	Command was loose early, humpy, tightened up as the game went on and showed a 12-6 chase and 12-5 backfoot. Again, best were 7s, but it's not quite tight enough a power curve to get me there at present.
CH	50	85-88	88	Below-average command, turned over a couple nice ones down, but firm and inconsistent for the most part. It's the change of the mid-rotation guy that needs a grade jump to start. Probably gets there?

Conclusion: Much improved mechanics have led to a command jump with both the fastball and curve for Manning. He grew into the start, flashing better secondaries second and third time through the order. Fairly safe number three starter type, will need some secondary improvements to get past that projection. Injury and durability risks are low, although he's still a pitcher. Some reliever risk if the change-up doesn't continue to develop, but I'm not hugely concerned at present. He has a short track record of keeping the delivery together so there may be some hidden risk there. He's a Midseason 50 candidate barring injury or steep regression.

Houston Astros

The State of the System

The system has thinned out across the contention cycle, and the 'stros haven't been able to develop the kind of solid major league arms that would keep them from running bullpen games in the playoffs.

The Top Ten

─────────────── ★ ★ ★ *2020 Top 101 Prospect* **#26** ★ ★ ★ ───────────────

1. Forrest Whitley   RHP   OFP: 70   ETA: 2020

Born: 09/15/97   Age: 22   Bats: R   Throws: R   Height: 6'7"   Weight: 195   Origin: Round 1, 2016 Draft (#17 overall)

YEAR	TEAM	LVL	AGE	W	L	SV	G	GS	IP	H	HR	BB/9	K/9	K	GB%	BABIP	WHIP	ERA	DRA	WARP	PF
2017	QUD	A	19	2	3	0	12	10	46¹	42	2	4.1	13.0	67	37%	.388	1.36	2.91	3.98	0.7	101
2017	BCA	A+	19	3	1	0	7	6	31¹	28	2	2.6	14.4	50	40%	.394	1.18	3.16	3.17	0.8	94
2017	CCH	AA	19	0	0	0	4	2	14²	8	1	2.5	16.0	26	48%	.292	0.82	1.84	2.28	0.5	105
2018	CCH	AA	20	0	2	0	8	8	26¹	15	2	3.8	11.6	34	39%	.220	0.99	3.76	2.29	0.9	101
2019	BCA	A+	21	1	0	0	2	2	8¹	4	0	1.1	11.9	11	44%	.222	0.60	2.16	2.27	0.3	88
2019	CCH	AA	21	2	2	0	6	6	22²	18	2	7.5	14.3	36	47%	.372	1.63	5.56	5.46	-0.1	93
2019	ROU	AAA	21	0	3	0	8	5	24¹	35	9	5.5	10.7	29	32%	.394	2.05	12.21	7.64	-0.2	92
2020	HOU	MLB	22	2	2	0	33	0	35	36	6	4.0	10.9	42	38%	.332	1.47	5.16	5.01	0.1	103

Comparables: Lucas Sims, Clayton Kershaw, Alex Reyes

The Report: It was yet another abbreviated year for 2016's 17th-overall selection due to shoulder fatigue and mechanical issues. The tall right-hander only managed to hurl 59 2/3 innings across four levels, including four rehab starts, and walked 44 batters in those outings. Even with the setbacks and command issues, Whitley still showed plenty of upside with his 86 combined punchouts. He looked much better during his second consecutive trip to the Arizona Fall League, where he led the league in strikeouts once again, showing off his baffling four-pitch mix.

Whitley's mid-90s fastball features plenty of life, and although he struggles to command it more than the secondaries, it is a plus, swing-and-miss offering. A devastating mid-80s changeup with sink and fade pairs extremely well the fastball, and he's not afraid to throw it to both right- and left-handed batters. He has shown excellent feel and command for the "cambio." Both of Whitley's breaking pitches are swing-and-miss offerings as well. His power slider displays late, sharp horizontal break with plus tilt and can hit 90 mph. A 12-6 low-80s curveball is a wipeout pitch with depth and late bite. With four pitches that he can get strikes with in any count, Whitley has the potential to be a dominant starter.

Variance: Higher than ideal at this stage of his development. Health issues have persisted throughout Whitley's four-year professional career, leaving serious doubts as to whether his body can hold up. He has also battled mechanical issues that still seem to flare up from time-to-time.

Mark Barry's Fantasy Take: The Comp: James Bond, *James Bond Franchise*

We're starting with the biggest name, and perhaps the most flashy talent. Whitley opened the season as the game's most promising pitching prospect, and managed to get himself into quite the predicament, battling injuries and his mechanics en route to the worst statistical season of his career. Luckily he has plenty of gadgets that can help him succeed in an organization that should be able to maximize his immense talent—by any means necessary. The hurler is a good buy low (or at least lower, he'll likely still be quite highly valued) candidate this offseason, especially if other managers are queasy looking at this season's ratios as the potential for a top-line fantasy starter is still there. The 2019 volatility might have unseated Whitley as the top pitching prospect in baseball, but our collective fantasy confidence in the 22-year-old should be shaken, not stirred (ah well, I tried).

★ ★ ★ *2020 Top 101 Prospect* **#82** ★ ★ ★

2 Jose Urquidy RHP   OFP: 60   ETA: 2019

Born: 05/01/95   Age: 25   Bats: R   Throws: R   Height: 6'0"   Weight: 180   Origin: International Free Agent, 2015

YEAR	TEAM	LVL	AGE	W	L	SV	G	GS	IP	H	HR	BB/9	K/9	K	GB%	BABIP	WHIP	ERA	DRA	WARP	PF
2018	TCV	A-	23	0	0	0	4	4	11¹	15	0	1.6	7.9	10	42%	.395	1.50	2.38	5.83	-0.1	99
2018	BCA	A+	23	2	2	0	9	7	46	40	2	1.6	7.4	38	52%	.281	1.04	2.35	3.26	1.1	96
2019	CCH	AA	24	2	2	0	7	6	33	28	2	1.4	10.9	40	43%	.302	1.00	4.09	3.07	0.7	98
2019	ROU	AAA	24	5	3	0	13	12	70	67	15	2.1	12.1	94	34%	.311	1.19	4.63	2.87	2.6	98
2019	HOU	MLB	24	2	1	0	9	7	41	38	6	1.5	8.8	40	38%	.281	1.10	3.95	4.33	0.6	103
2020	HOU	MLB	25	9	5	0	21	21	112	101	18	2.6	9.0	112	37%	.282	1.20	3.72	3.82	2.2	103

Comparables: Domingo Germán, Jharel Cotton, Rafael Montero

The Report: You're probably already familiar with Urquidy, who pitched one of the best games of the 2019 postseason, five dominant innings in what was supposed to be a bullpen game in Game 4 of the World Series. He throws a solid fastball, sitting in the 92-94 range and touching 96, that he gets the most out of due to plus command. His primary offspeed has typically been a plus changeup, but he started relying on a slider as his out-pitch more and more as the playoffs progressed, and it was flashing huge. You may have seen the GIFs of said slider making batters look completely ridiculous on Twitter. He also mixes in a curveball for a fourth look.

You may be less familiar with his background. It's a bit of an exaggeration to say he came out of nowhere—he came up in research for this list last offseason, although he wasn't close at all to making it, and he was exposed to and went unpicked in the Rule 5 Draft. He was a known prospect, but not a top one, and it was under a different name; he played as Jose Luis Hernandez until this past spring.

Why was Urquidy overlooked for so long? He didn't make his pro debut until he was 20, which is on the old side even as overaged international signings go. Just when he was starting to get going as a prospect, he underwent Tommy John surgery, which wiped out his entire 2017 and the first half of 2018. He's a short right-hander without an electric fastball, which is a demographic that is easy to overlook and tends to end up in relief.

He's not overlooked anymore. He's very likely to start 2020 in Houston's rotation, and could stick there for a long time.

Variance: Medium. Urquidy is obviously already MLB-ready, and threw 154 innings total this year. He's still a short pitcher with a recent Tommy John in his background. There's also positive variance here if the slider goes from "flashing huge" to "consistently huge." We're trying not to overreact too much to what might've just been the game of his life, but everyone saw it…

Mark Barry's Fantasy Take: The Comp: Jason Bourne, *The Bourne Franchise*

As mentioned above, you might recall Urquidy as Jose Luis Hernandez, just like you might remember Bourne as David Webb. Also like Bourne, Urquidy beasted in the World Series, putting a bow on a breakout 2019 campaign. The gaudy minor-league strikeout numbers didn't completely follow Urquidy to Houston, but his swinging-strike rate was better than league average, and most of his near-4.00 ERA came from two rocky outings against the Indians and Angels. I like Urquidy quite a bit, and could see an SP3 upside, with an SP5 floor. He'll be eminently useful in all formats.

★ ★ ★ *2020 Top 101 Prospect* **#100** ★ ★ ★

3 Jeremy Pena SS   OFP: 55   ETA: 2021

Born: 09/22/97   Age: 22   Bats: R   Throws: R   Height: 6'0"   Weight: 179   Origin: Round 3, 2018 Draft (#102 overall)

YEAR	TEAM	LVL	AGE	PA	R	2B	3B	HR	RBI	BB	K	SB	CS	AVG/OBP/SLG	DRC+	VORP	BABIP	BRR	FRAA	WARP	PF
2018	TCV	A-	20	156	22	5	0	1	10	18	19	3	0	.250/.340/.309	137	10.7	.282	-1.0	SS(32) -0.5, 2B(4) 0.0	1.0	95
2019	QUD	A	21	289	44	8	4	5	41	35	57	17	6	.293/.389/.421	154	33.9	.357	3.3	SS(60) -2.1, 2B(2) -0.3	2.9	101
2019	BCA	A+	21	185	28	13	3	2	13	12	33	3	4	.317/.378/.467	144	16.6	.383	1.8	SS(29) -0.2, 2B(11) 0.1	1.7	105
2020	HOU	MLB	22	251	23	11	1	5	25	17	61	2	1	.243/.303/.366	80	0.0	.311	-0.1	SS -3, 2B 0	-0.1	103

Comparables: Ty France, Patrick Wisdom, Nate Lowe

The Report: No prospect in the Astros' system gained more helium this season than Pena. The former University of Maine star dazzled in the field, showing off one of the top gloves in the organization. An athletic frame, great instincts, and a strong, accurate arm combine to give Pena the tools to not only stick at the six for the foreseeable future, but to develop into an asset there. The offensive strides he made in 2019 really proved a separator for him in the system, however, helping him leapfrog other more-heralded prospects in the organizational food chain. He shows natural bat-to-ball skills and he controlled the zone well in both of his stops at A-ball. The swing is geared mostly for line drives, but the power should develop into something close to fringe-average for a middle infielder. On the bases, Pena is a threat to steal or take an extra base thanks to above-average foot speed and an aggressive nature.

Variance: Medium. One breakout season in the low minors is all Pena has under his belt, and he's yet to face advanced pitching to test out the offensive gains. The glove and speed combination make for a high-floor utility player, though.

Mark Barry's Fantasy Take: The Comp: Philip Jennings, *The Americans*

There are no frills with Jennings, just as there are no frills with Pena. "The glove and speed combination make for a high-floor utility player"—not really the stuff fantasy dreams are made of. Both are better in real life than they are in fantasy. Jennings rose to the occasion when challenged with high-level competition, and Pena should get the opportunity to do just that this season. Perhaps some of Pena's line drives clear the wall, and perhaps his aggression manifests itself into double-digit steals. Even then, that's not a terribly exciting offensive profile.

4 Abraham Toro 3B   OFP: 55   ETA: 2019
Born: 12/20/96   Age: 23   Bats: B   Throws: R   Height: 6'1"   Weight: 190   Origin: Round 5, 2016 Draft (#157 overall)

YEAR	TEAM	LVL	AGE	PA	R	2B	3B	HR	RBI	BB	K	SB	CS	AVG/OBP/SLG	DRC+	VORP	BABIP	BRR	FRAA	WARP	PF
2017	TCV	A-	20	128	21	8	0	6	16	19	21	1	3	.292/.414/.538	190	14.2	.316	-2.1	3B(25) -2.5, C(6) -0.1	0.9	100
2017	QUD	A	20	158	25	3	2	9	17	21	30	2	0	.209/.323/.463	113	11.2	.198	1.1	3B(17) 0.8, C(9) -0.2	0.9	102
2018	BCA	A+	21	349	54	20	1	14	56	45	62	5	1	.257/.361/.473	156	31.2	.278	1.7	3B(81) 3.4	3.6	95
2018	CCH	AA	21	202	16	15	2	2	22	17	46	3	3	.230/.317/.371	89	1.1	.298	-2.6	3B(43) -0.7	0.1	103
2019	CCH	AA	22	435	65	22	4	16	70	48	77	4	1	.306/.393/.513	161	40.4	.346	-0.6	3B(85) 6.3, 2B(11) 0.2	4.6	103
2019	ROU	AAA	22	79	17	9	0	1	10	10	5	0	1	.424/.506/.606	174	15.3	.443	1.9	3B(7) -0.7, 2B(4) -0.2	1.0	103
2019	HOU	MLB	22	89	13	3	2	2	9	9	19	1	1	.218/.303/.385	79	1.0	.259	-0.1	3B(24) -0.8, 1B(1) 0.0	0.0	101
2020	HOU	MLB	23	105	12	4	1	4	14	9	23	0	0	.241/.313/.432	95	3.0	.273	0.0	3B 1	0.3	103

Comparables: Andy LaRoche, Dalton Pompey, Ryan Kalish

The Report: Toro's ascent to the big leagues has bubbled under the surface of the system a bit, but outside of a bumpy Double-A debut a couple years ago he's made steady, consistent progress on his path to the majors. A switch-hitter, his left-handed stroke is the more fluid of the two, featuring good balance, fluidity, and enough plane to lift balls with carry to the pull side. His right-handed stroke gets a little less out of the legs, and he's run into some trouble against high-level pitching from that side, but he still shows solid barrel control and a nice approach. Above-average raw should settle in around average game power, and the hit tool projects similarly.

A former catcher, Toro boasts a carrying tool in his arm, the strength of which helps him cover some for uneven reads and slower actions at the hot corner. He's made progress with his footwork and agility, though, to where an average glove is within reach. It's not an especially sexy profile, as prospect ceilings go, but he's more or less ready now and can evolve quickly into a steady, consistent starting third baseman with the upside of an above-average regular who gets on base, hits for a little pop, and doesn't hurt you on the dirt.

Variance: Medium. He's still young and may struggle to find opportunities to establish himself early in his career, but it's a relatively well-rounded skill set that should ultimately play just fine.

Mark Barry's Fantasy Take: The Comp: Natasha Romanoff, *Marvel Cinematic Universe*

When you're dealing with the Avengers, sometimes it's tough to stand out among the big names and personalities. Similarly, in an organization which recently churned out guys like Bregman, Alvarez, Tucker and Whitley, unheralded guys like Toro fall by the wayside. I'm in on the 22-year-old, whose biggest knock is really just a lack of playing time. I'm encouraged by his ability to functionally play three infield positions, and his plate discipline seems to have translated to the big-league level, albeit in an ultra-small sample. If Toro can find his way onto the field, in this organization or another, I like him as a top 50-75ish dynasty prospect (which might be a little bullish, but whatever). Underappreciated, but gets the job done, just like Black Widow. Let's just hope {redacted for spoilers}.

5 Bryan Abreu RHP OFP: 55 ETA: 2019

Born: 04/22/97 Age: 23 Bats: R Throws: R Height: 6'1" Weight: 204 Origin: International Free Agent, 2013

YEAR	TEAM	LVL	AGE	W	L	SV	G	GS	IP	H	HR	BB/9	K/9	K	GB%	BABIP	WHIP	ERA	DRA	WARP	PF
2017	GRV	RK	20	1	3	0	8	6	29¹	29	4	6.4	12.3	40	38%	.357	1.70	7.98	5.52	0.2	95
2018	TCV	A-	21	2	0	0	4	2	16	11	2	3.4	12.4	22	35%	.281	1.06	1.12	2.93	0.4	93
2018	QUD	A	21	4	1	3	10	5	38¹	22	2	4.0	16.0	68	50%	.312	1.02	1.64	1.89	1.4	102
2019	BCA	A+	22	1	0	0	3	3	14²	9	2	3.7	15.3	25	38%	.292	1.02	3.68	3.09	0.3	108
2019	CCH	AA	22	6	2	2	20	13	76²	60	6	5.6	11.9	101	43%	.309	1.41	5.05	4.24	0.6	103
2019	HOU	MLB	22	0	0	0	7	0	8²	4	0	3.1	13.5	13	50%	.250	0.81	1.04	4.66	0.1	101
2020	HOU	MLB	23	3	2	0	42	3	55	41	6	4.4	13.1	80	42%	.299	1.24	3.43	3.46	1.1	103

Comparables: Dylan Cease, Jorge Alcala, Victor Alcántara

The Report: Abreu spent a good part of 2019 before his big-league debut as a starter, making 16 starts out of 23 total appearances. It's a role that doesn't fit him long term though. Abreu's future impact will be as a bullpen arm. His fastball touches 95-96, mixed with a pair of fringier breaking pitches. The slider at 82-85 has a ton of movement, like a frisbee from right to left. He has a couple extra notches on the slider velo too, tuning it up to 87 at times. The curveball is 81-83, but the shape and command are both below average. With better command of the fastball and slider, Abreu presents a reasonable late innings option for the Astros, but lacks the elite fastball velocity and slider command to be the premier pitcher in a bullpen. Even marginal improvement in both can make Abreu a stalwart in bullpens for years to come.

Variance: Medium. The command takes Abreu out of contention as a starter, putting him into the bullpen. As a reliever, the command issues are workable. Right now, it's good enough to maintain the profile of a late innings reliever. However, should it degrade for any reason that would knock Abreu into last man in the pen/fringe major league status.

Mark Barry's Fantasy Take: The Comp: Jack Ryan, *Jack Ryan Universe*

Though Abreu was impressive in his big-league debut, getting a ton of whiffs and a decent amount of grounders, he's still a long-term reliever, and one without the guarantee of high-leverage use. If you play in a league rostering 250+ prospects or leagues that use holds as a stat, that could be useful, but it limits the upside. It's sort of like taking a highly respected, feature-film character once played by Harrison Ford and shifting him to a streaming service while casting Jim Halpert as the lead. Significantly lower upside (fine, so maybe this one is a stretch, but to be fair, I didn't realize how hard it would be to come up with spy comps for everyone on this list when I started).

6 Korey Lee C OFP: 55 ETA: Late 2021

Born: 07/25/98 Age: 21 Bats: R Throws: R Height: 6'2" Weight: 205 Origin: Round 1, 2019 Draft (#32 overall)

YEAR	TEAM	LVL	AGE	PA	R	2B	3B	HR	RBI	BB	K	SB	CS	AVG/OBP/SLG	DRC+	VORP	BABIP	BRR	FRAA	WARP	PF
2019	TCV	A-	20	259	31	6	4	3	28	28	49	8	5	.268/.359/.371	140	18.8	.328	2.5	C(30) 0.7, LF(5) -0.9	1.8	97
2020	HOU	MLB	21	251	21	10	1	4	23	16	69	3	1	.224/.282/.332	64	0.0	.301	0.0	C 0, LF 0	-0.3	103

Comparables: Sandy León, Francisco Cervelli, Jordan Luplow

The Report: Lee was one of the biggest benefactors of being Andrew Vaughn's college teammate, as scouts got to see more of him than perhaps they otherwise would've. Regardless, he was one of the most sought after catchers in the draft not named Adley Rutschman, and it became pretty apparent why after watching just a few innings. Lee is a big-bodied catcher with solid all-around potential who lacks a standout tool. It starts with above-average raw power that plays to all fields, and he also exhibited average game power throughout the entire New York-Penn League season. He does a really good job of not expanding the strike zone on offspeed and breaking pitches, thus forcing pitchers to throw strikes to get him out. As a result, he raked against a weak NYPL pitching class all season long. If he continues forcing pitchers to throw strikes, Lee could be a 15-20 homer catcher who gets on base at a 33 percent clip.

Lee complements his intriguing offensive profile with solid defense behind the dish. He has athletic motions for a 6-foot-2 catcher, including a plus arm that nabbed 33 percent of base stealers. There were times where he looked gassed from the long season, but such is the case for many recently-drafted catchers. Nonetheless, if everything comes together, you've got yourself a very solid catcher capable of playing 120 above-average games behind the dish.

Variance: Medium. Catchers who show defensive ability and even a hint of offensive promise usually find their way to the bigs.

Mark Barry's Fantasy Take: The Comp: Harry Hart, *Kingsman Franchise*

Lee had a 1.034 OPS while cloaked in the gentleman's armour in his final season at Cal, earning him a first-round selection. Much like Harry Hart, he's probably better in fantasy than reality. Lee could be a decent starter behind the dish, and in fantasy circles, "decent" in real life probably translates to top-10 in fantasy. I have a lot of trouble relying on the development path of dudes that don the tools of ignorance (and Ben has chronicled catching prospects, like, a lot), but Lee's athleticism leaves me at least a little optimistic. He's a top-200ish guy, but even that feels a little bold for a guy with only Low-A experience.

7 Rogelio Armenteros RHP   OFP: 50   ETA: 2019

Born: 06/30/94   Age: 26   Bats: R   Throws: R   Height: 6'1"   Weight: 215   Origin: International Free Agent, 2014

YEAR	TEAM	LVL	AGE	W	L	SV	G	GS	IP	H	HR	BB/9	K/9	K	GB%	BABIP	WHIP	ERA	DRA	WARP	PF
2017	CCH	AA	23	2	3	1	14	10	65¹	49	3	2.6	10.2	74	42%	.284	1.04	1.93	3.08	1.6	97
2017	FRE	AAA	23	8	1	0	10	10	58¹	42	5	2.9	11.1	72	50%	.276	1.05	2.16	2.24	2.2	102
2018	FRE	AAA	24	8	1	1	22	21	118	106	15	3.7	10.2	134	38%	.301	1.31	3.74	3.97	2.1	100
2019	ROU	AAA	25	6	7	0	19	18	84¹	90	14	3.3	9.1	85	35%	.325	1.43	4.80	4.61	1.7	95
2019	HOU	MLB	25	1	1	1	5	2	18	17	1	2.5	9.0	18	38%	.314	1.22	4.00	5.23	0.1	100
2020	HOU	MLB	26	5	4	0	32	10	70	68	13	3.5	8.1	63	36%	.280	1.36	4.76	4.71	0.6	103

Comparables: Nick Tropeano, Aaron Blair, Dan Straily

The Report: Ah sweet Rogelio. Another year, and you remain in our hearts and on our list. Armenteros did what he does last year, including a representative 18-inning sample in Houston that saw him whiff a batter every frame while staying off barrels at an even more impressive clip. The burly right-hander is an aggressive attacker of the zone in spite of a modest fastball that sits around 92. The pitch plays up on account of his advanced pitchability, however, and both the curve and especially the change work as competent secondaries. He fiddled with a slider down the stretch that could extend his already deep arsenal that much further. He pitches forwards, backwards, and in all directions, and he generally commands well enough to keep hitters appropriately off-balance. There is both present and future big-league staff utility here, with a multi-inning and spot-start role probably best-suited for his particular skill set. A reliable 100 innings of league-average production at controlled cost is a highly valuable commodity in today's game, and Rogelio is capable of performing in that kind of role as soon as next season.

Variance: Relatively low. He's fully cooked and ready to serve big-league hitters.

Mark Barry's Fantasy Take: The Comp: Cassian Andor, *Rogue One*

For Cassian, he's best when he's motivated and focused on a cause. For Armenteros, well, I hope that's what was going on, as he spent parts of three seasons at Triple-A Round Rock with diminishing returns. The profile isn't overly exciting—the upside of a good spot starter isn't really what you're hoping for outside of the deepest of dynasties or AL-only leagues. Toss Andor, er, Armenteros on the watch list and cross your fingers for a spot in the rotation.

8 Freudis Nova SS   OFP: 50   ETA: 2022

Born: 01/12/00   Age: 20   Bats: R   Throws: R   Height: 6'1"   Weight: 180   Origin: International Free Agent, 2016

YEAR	TEAM	LVL	AGE	PA	R	2B	3B	HR	RBI	BB	K	SB	CS	AVG/OBP/SLG	DRC+	VORP	BABIP	BRR	FRAA	WARP	PF
2017	DAR	ROK	17	190	30	6	0	4	16	15	33	8	3	.247/.342/.355	108	10.6	.287	-2.1		0.5	87
2018	AST	RK	18	157	21	3	1	6	28	6	21	9	5	.308/.331/.466	127	9.8	.317	0.4	SS(24) -0.8, 2B(9) 0.0	0.9	102
2019	QUD	A	19	299	35	20	1	3	29	15	68	10	7	.259/.301/.369	105	8.6	.332	-0.4	SS(31) -3.0, 2B(23) 0.0	0.8	99
2020	HOU	MLB	20	251	22	12	1	5	24	16	67	4	2	.232/.284/.350	66	0.0	.305	-0.1	SS -2, 2B 0	-0.5	103

Comparables: Tim Beckham, Thairo Estrada, Jorge Polanco

The Report: Signed for seven figures out of the Dominican Republic in 2016, Nova has yet to make a big splash stateside. The wiry-framed infielder even took a small step back over 75 games with Quad Cities this year. His strengths are clearly his glove and speed. However, he wasn't even the best shortstop on Quad Cities for most of the year. Jeremy Pena manned the six until he got promoted. That forced Nova to third base, a position where he did not look comfortable. When he did get the chance to play short, he flashed impressive range and athletic ability, along with a plus arm.

On the bases he shows slightly better than average quick-twitch motions and gets solid jumps, making him a base stealing threat as he matures. At the dish, Nova is still very inconsistent. He will flash good bat speed, but catching up to even average heaters on the inner-half gives him trouble. Currently, there isn't much, if any, power at his disposal. And there doesn't seem to be much room for growth either.

Variance: High. There is still a lot of offensive development needed for Nova. Between inconsistent bat speed and an ensuing lack of power, it will be an uphill battle to become an even average threat in the box, which keeps a reserve infielder projection on the table.

Mark Barry's Fantasy Take: The Comp: Cody Banks, *Agent Cody Banks*

The youngest super-spy of all time meets the youngest prospect on our list (we're reaching here, I know). It's almost always too early to write off a dude who can't legally drink for another year-plus, but Nova's 2019 production doesn't really inspire a ton of confidence. Let's monitor him for now, and pounce if/when he shows some consistent power or consistent speed or consistent, well, offense.

9 Cristian Javier RHP   OFP: 50   ETA: 2020
Born: 03/26/97   Age: 23   Bats: R   Throws: R   Height: 6'1"   Weight: 204   Origin: International Free Agent, 2015

YEAR	TEAM	LVL	AGE	W	L	SV	G	GS	IP	H	HR	BB/9	K/9	K	GB%	BABIP	WHIP	ERA	DRA	WARP	PF
2017	TCV	A-	20	0	0	0	4	2	16²	11	0	4.9	13.0	24	41%	.282	1.20	2.70	2.97	0.4	103
2017	QUD	A	20	2	0	1	8	7	37²	25	3	3.6	11.2	47	17%	.265	1.06	2.39	3.40	0.8	101
2018	QUD	A	21	2	2	1	11	7	49¹	28	3	4.2	14.6	80	32%	.281	1.03	1.82	2.36	1.6	102
2018	BCA	A+	21	5	4	0	14	11	60²	44	6	4.0	9.8	66	33%	.257	1.17	3.41	3.89	1.0	93
2019	BCA	A+	22	2	0	1	7	5	28²	15	1	5.0	12.6	40	33%	.226	1.08	0.94	2.87	0.7	99
2019	CCH	AA	22	6	3	3	17	11	74	31	5	4.7	13.9	114	31%	.197	0.95	2.07	2.11	2.5	104
2019	ROU	AAA	22	0	0	0	2	2	11	5	1	3.3	13.1	16	17%	.182	0.82	1.64	2.66	0.4	93
2020	HOU	MLB	23	2	1	0	5	5	21	21	3	4.1	12.6	29	33%	.359	1.48	5.14	4.96	0.1	103

Comparables: Hunter Wood, Dylan Cease, Freddy Peralta

The Report: Javier is one of the sneakier pop up arms in the Astros system, as he doesn't exactly fit the typical "Astroball" prototype. Javier stands a hair shorter than his listed 6-foot-1 height, but his list weight appears accurate. He has longer legs and levers with a sturdy backside, and he is a good athlete with quality body control.

The righty's velocity sits in the low 90s with plus arm-side life, and at times he will show average command of the offering; it's more of a craft pitch, as opposed to the typical Astros power arm. He has a true plus low-80s curveball with a tight, slurvy shape that boasts plus spin and depth. Javier also mixes in an average-flashing 83-84 mph changeup with good arm speed and some tumble, although it lacks true swing-and-miss fade. You'll occasionally see a mid-80s slider-ish pitch that he seems to have little feel for, as well.

Javier's command of a quality fastball/curve combo with solid pitchability and command should carry him to a 6th starter or low setup role. If he's unable to iron out the changeup consistency he might settle into more of a middle relief role, but an improvement there along with a half a tick in command and he could see himself in the back of an MLB rotation.

Variance: Medium. Javier's advanced feel for fastball/curve combo gives him a major league outcome on the low end, but his ability to refine the changeup and find another improvement to command will be important to his future development.

Mark Barry's Fantasy Take: The Comp: Varys, *Game of Thrones*

Sometimes spies are crafty and unconventional. Take Varys for instance. By looking at him, you wouldn't necessarily think he'd be a master strategist, capable of high-leverage results (something something book and its cover). Same goes for Javier. He's on the small-ish end and doesn't have premium gas in the tank, so it's easy to underestimate him. I'd take a flier on him in AL-onlys and in leagues with 150-200 prospects or so, betting on the come for the changeup.

10 Jairo Solis RHP   OFP: 50   ETA: 2023

Born: 12/22/99   Age: 20   Bats: R   Throws: R   Height: 6'2"   Weight: 160   Origin: International Free Agent, 2016

YEAR	TEAM	LVL	AGE	W	L	SV	G	GS	IP	H	HR	BB/9	K/9	K	GB%	BABIP	WHIP	ERA	DRA	WARP	PF
2017	DAR	ROK	17	1	1	0	6	4	26¹	20	2	2.7	9.6	28	57%	.277	1.06	2.73			87
2017	AST	RK	17	1	0	0	5	4	21	19	1	3.0	10.3	24	43%	.305	1.24	3.00	2.22	0.8	107
2017	GRV	RK	17	1	1	0	4	2	14	12	0	3.9	10.9	17	36%	.333	1.29	1.93	3.29	0.4	99
2018	QUD	A	18	2	5	0	13	11	50²	49	1	5.7	9.1	51	47%	.345	1.60	3.55	5.65	-0.3	100
2020	HOU	MLB	20	2	2	0	33	0	35	35	5	4.1	7.7	30	43%	.290	1.44	4.89	4.84	0.1	103

Comparables: Jordan Lyles, Lewis Thorpe, Felix Jorge

The Report: Solis missed the entire 2019 season while recovering from Tommy John surgery. He moves up within the rankings here anyway because the Astros traded or graduated a lot of their depth and we had already built his surgery into last year's ranking. Going back to 2018 looks, he had the foundations of a three-pitch starting pitcher's arsenal with an above-average fastball supplemented by the makings of a plus curve and average-to-above-average change. The lost year of development time isn't great, but it's not a killer, as Solis had already pitched well in full-season ball at 18. He will pitch the entire 2020 season at 20, so there's plenty of time. We need to see him back on a mound before we get too excited, and he needs to hold up under a starting workload (he was handled very lightly in 2018 and still blew out), but there's a real chance to shoot up the list next year.

Variance: High. He's a young pitcher who just missed an entire year and could be nearly anything.

Mark Barry's Fantasy Take: The Comp: Bran Stark, *Game of Thrones*

No spoilers here, but let's not forget that he took Season 5 off before downloading the entire history of the world through the Weirwood trees and changing the course of Westerosi history. Of course, you have to ignore the whole "he can't walk" thing, as Solis proved plenty capable of that in his 2018 campaign. He's an interesting flier to keep your eye on, just like the Three-Eyed Raven.

The Next Ten

11 Myles Straw SS/CF

Born: 10/17/94   Age: 25   Bats: R   Throws: R   Height: 5'10"   Weight: 180   Origin: Round 12, 2015 Draft (#349 overall)

YEAR	TEAM	LVL	AGE	PA	R	2B	3B	HR	RBI	BB	K	SB	CS	AVG/OBP/SLG	DRC+	VORP	BABIP	BRR	FRAA	WARP	PF
2017	BCA	A+	22	533	81	17	7	1	41	87	70	36	9	.295/.412/.373	152	52.8	.347	5.5	CF(72) 6.9, RF(31) 7.2	6.6	94
2017	CCH	AA	22	54	9	0	0	0	3	7	9	2	0	.239/.340/.239	92	1.8	.297	0.6	CF(11) -1.1, LF(2) 0.7	0.2	93
2018	CCH	AA	23	294	47	7	3	1	17	35	42	35	6	.327/.414/.390	142	24.5	.386	4.4	CF(58) 6.0, RF(6) 2.0	3.4	103
2018	FRE	AAA	23	304	48	10	3	0	14	38	60	35	3	.257/.349/.317	96	8.1	.330	3.8	CF(43) 4.9, RF(25) 1.4	1.8	95
2018	HOU	MLB	23	10	4	0	0	1	1	1	0	2	0	.333/.400/.667	108	1.8	.250	0.7	RF(5) -0.1, CF(3) 0.0	0.1	107
2019	ROU	AAA	24	313	46	11	3	1	33	32	50	19	4	.321/.391/.394	105	20.2	.386	2.5	CF(31) 4.9, SS(30) -1.1	1.9	95
2019	HOU	MLB	24	128	27	4	2	0	7	19	24	8	1	.269/.378/.343	92	4.0	.345	3.5	SS(26) 1.4, CF(11) -0.8	0.8	103
2020	HOU	MLB	25	245	24	11	2	2	21	24	52	12	4	.274/.348/.366	94	0.0	.350	0.8	CF 4, SS 0	1.3	103

Comparables: David Dellucci, Mallex Smith, Denard Span

Straw was a pain in the ass for opposing pitchers in his first Showtime look last season. He rarely swung, forcing an obscene number of pitches in his plate appearances, and then when he finally did offer he flashed elite contact skills in and out of the zone. That tracks with a career-long profile now, as Straw has steadily progressed through the minors on the back of a successful execution of that exact offensive strategy. There is absolutely no power whatsoever, though, and that limits the overall ceiling here. But added defensive versatility, including wholly competent play at the six, pairs intriguingly with on-base skills and elite 80-grade speed that has shown no signs of slipping. He's a fun and valuable player for the depth chart, and there's enough in the raw tools that he can provide average value with a little luck and enough opportunity.

12 Brandon Bielak RHP

Born: 04/02/96   Age: 24   Bats: L   Throws: R   Height: 6'1"   Weight: 210   Origin: Round 11, 2017 Draft (#331 overall)

YEAR	TEAM	LVL	AGE	W	L	SV	G	GS	IP	H	HR	BB/9	K/9	K	GB%	BABIP	WHIP	ERA	DRA	WARP	PF
2017	TCV	A-	21	1	1	1	8	4	29^1	18	0	1.2	11.4	37	54%	.261	0.75	0.92	1.98	1.1	102
2018	BCA	A+	22	5	3	2	14	7	55^2	44	2	2.7	12.0	74	43%	.331	1.10	2.10	3.31	1.2	90
2018	CCH	AA	22	2	5	0	11	10	61^1	52	4	3.2	8.4	57	51%	.294	1.21	2.35	4.15	0.8	102
2019	CCH	AA	23	3	0	0	8	6	36	29	3	3.5	8.2	33	53%	.268	1.19	3.75	4.03	0.4	118
2019	ROU	AAA	23	8	4	0	15	14	85^2	69	10	3.8	9.0	86	44%	.269	1.23	4.41	2.73	3.3	96
2020	HOU	MLB	24	2	2	0	33	0	35	34	5	3.7	8.3	32	45%	.294	1.38	4.49	4.51	0.3	103

Comparables: J.R. Graham, Aaron Blair, Brett Kennedy

Bielak is one of my favorite "under the radar" arms due to his impressive four-pitch mix. He throws from the right side as he sits 92-94 with a four-seam fastball that tends to be a bit flat. His primary secondary is a true plus curveball in the upper 70s with plus depth and spin. He mixes in a harder mid-80s, above-average slider with more horizontal shape and above-average break. His mid-80s changeup has the makings of an average pitch with good deception and some tumble, but his command of it comes and goes.

Bielak is comfortable throwing any of his offerings in any count, which makes him fun to watch when he's able to command his fastball. Pitchability is a utilized strength for Bielak and if he's able to limit his main flaw, it could carry him well-beyond his current projection as a 6th starter. His fastball command wobbles, which combined with it being generally a hittable pitch creates significant reliance on his secondaries. If he can find a way to bump the fastball command high enough to allow his secondaries to mix more effectively, Bielak could find himself as a No. 5 starter in a major league rotation.

13 Jordan Brewer OF

Born: 08/01/97   Age: 22   Bats: R   Throws: R   Height: 6'1"   Weight: 195   Origin: Round 3, 2019 Draft (#106 overall)

YEAR	TEAM	LVL	AGE	PA	R	2B	3B	HR	RBI	BB	K	SB	CS	AVG/OBP/SLG	DRC+	VORP	BABIP	BRR	FRAA	WARP	PF
2019	TCV	A-	21	56	5	0	0	1	3	2	6	2	0	.130/.161/.185	31	-4.3	.128	-0.3	RF(8) -0.9, CF(3) -0.4	-0.3	98
2020	HOU	MLB	22	251	20	11	1	5	23	14	61	2	1	.202/.250/.320	48	0.0	.249	0.0	RF 0, CF 0	-0.8	103

Comparables: Quintin Berry, Cody Asche, Scott Cousins

A wide receiver recruit out of high school who went from Indiana JuCo to Michigan for his junior year, Brewer has premium athleticism you don't normally find in a third-round college pick, but it's paired with fairly raw present baseball skills. As you'd expect given the background, Brewer is a plus runner with explosive burst. There's plus raw power potential—he's built like a D1 slot receiver—although the loft and plane is inconsistent and he can get long while trying to tap into it. He has enough arm for all three outfield spots, but should stick in center field with more reps. Brewer dealt with turf toe towards the end of the college season, and had a poor and abbreviated pro debut, and there are wildly variant opinions on important topics like "will he actually hit at all?" He's a bit of a mystery box going forward, but the positive variance would be exciting. The progress to any sort of a major league role is more sous vide than flash fry, though.

14 Garrett Stubbs C

Born: 05/26/93   Age: 27   Bats: L   Throws: R   Height: 5'10"   Weight: 175   Origin: Round 8, 2015 Draft (#229 overall)

YEAR	TEAM	LVL	AGE	PA	R	2B	3B	HR	RBI	BB	K	SB	CS	AVG/OBP/SLG	DRC+	VORP	BABIP	BRR	FRAA	WARP	PF
2017	CCH	AA	24	300	36	13	0	4	25	32	44	8	0	.236/.324/.331	94	10.9	.269	2.3	C(64) 8.8	2.3	97
2017	FRE	AAA	24	91	11	5	0	0	12	11	15	3	0	.221/.341/.286	80	1.8	.274	1.9	C(19) 0.5	0.4	108
2018	FRE	AAA	25	340	60	19	6	4	38	35	53	6	0	.310/.382/.455	116	30.6	.361	3.0	C(75) 10.5, RF(2) -0.2	3.6	100
2019	ROU	AAA	26	235	33	11	0	7	23	24	38	12	2	.240/.332/.397	85	9.8	.261	0.7	C(54) 8.8, 2B(5) -0.8	1.5	94
2019	HOU	MLB	26	39	8	3	0	0	2	4	7	1	0	.200/.282/.286	79	0.8	.250	0.2	C(11) -1.5, LF(7) -0.1	-0.1	100
2020	HOU	MLB	27	140	14	7	0	3	14	13	26	2	0	.225/.303/.361	75	0.0	.258	0.0	C -3	-0.1	103

Comparables: Joe Ginsberg, John Jaso, Chris Herrmann

Stubbs is getting a little long in the tooth for a list like this, but he found his way into a big-league uniform last year and should see more opportunities in the year ahead. We've long been fans of his athleticism, if wary of his frame and lack of pop, and those all remain defining pieces of the puzzle. He moves extremely well behind the dish, with a fluid blocking technique and quick pop that helps his arm play above-average. After years of speculation, Houston did indeed begin to deploy him for game reps at second and in left field last season, and adding that positional versatility should help his chances of sticking for stretches on a 25-man roster. He's a disciplined hitter with solid bat-to-ball skills, but the lack of power has become a problem at higher levels, as pitchers have attacked him at will in the zone to generate favorable counts. Still, he has continued to get on base at a solid clip at just about every turn, and if that holds along with his newfound defensive utility he'll be able to carve out a nice, long career for himself as a valuable bench piece and second-division starter.

15 Tyler Ivey RHP

Born: 05/12/96 Age: 24 Bats: R Throws: R Height: 6'4" Weight: 195 Origin: Round 3, 2017 Draft (#91 overall)

YEAR	TEAM	LVL	AGE	W	L	SV	G	GS	IP	H	HR	BB/9	K/9	K	GB%	BABIP	WHIP	ERA	DRA	WARP	PF
2017	TCV	A-	21	0	3	0	11	7	36¹	41	2	3.0	10.2	41	47%	.368	1.46	5.94	5.40	-0.1	98
2018	QUD	A	22	1	3	2	9	6	41²	36	2	1.7	11.4	53	50%	.315	1.06	3.46	2.99	1.0	105
2018	BCA	A+	22	3	3	1	15	12	70¹	50	3	2.7	10.5	82	56%	.267	1.01	2.69	3.02	1.8	91
2019	CCH	AA	23	4	0	0	11	8	46	28	5	3.1	11.9	61	39%	.228	0.96	1.57	2.84	1.1	102
2020	HOU	MLB	24	2	2	0	33	0	35	35	5	3.3	10.3	40	39%	.320	1.36	4.52	4.54	0.2	103

Comparables: Tyler Wilson, Ian Kennedy, Jon Duplantier

Ivey is an athletic, high-effort mess of a 6-foot-4 right-handed pitcher with wild limbs and jerky movements. Despite that description, he actually has a lot more control of his body during the delivery than you'd expect. Ivey works between 92-95 with his four-seam fastball. The pitch shows plus life and sets up his hard upper-80s slider. That pitch shows plus horizontal break and hard dive when he's on top of it and down in the zone. Ivey's low-80s 11-5 curveball flashes plus with above-average depth. A fringy mid-80s changeup rounds out the repertoire. He maintains his arm speed well on the change, but it remains fairly lifeless through the zone. Ivey has present fringy command, which actually suggests truly impressive body control given his loud delivery, but that delivery does make it hard to project further refinement.

The arsenal is ideal for a low setup role where he can unleash a potent three-pitch mix in short bursts to buzzsaw through a tough group of righties. There's potential rotation upside here if he can somehow manage to add an improved changeup, but he hasn't yet shown it.

16 Grae Kessinger SS

Born: 08/25/97 Age: 22 Bats: R Throws: R Height: 6'2" Weight: 200 Origin: Round 2, 2019 Draft (#68 overall)

YEAR	TEAM	LVL	AGE	PA	R	2B	3B	HR	RBI	BB	K	SB	CS	AVG/OBP/SLG	DRC+	VORP	BABIP	BRR	FRAA	WARP	PF
2019	TCV	A-	21	45	5	4	0	0	3	3	4	1	1	.268/.333/.366	136	2.9	.297	-0.2	SS(10) 0.9, 3B(1) 0.0	0.4	99
2019	QUD	A	21	201	25	6	0	2	17	26	32	8	2	.224/.333/.294	105	3.9	.261	0.2	SS(23) -2.5, 3B(18) 2.4	0.8	98
2020	HOU	MLB	22	251	22	11	0	5	24	16	56	2	1	.216/.272/.335	60	0.0	.263	0.0	SS -1, 3B 1	-0.4	103

Comparables: Josh Prince, Kevin Kramer, Tony Kemp

The grandson of former Cubs' great, Don Kessinger, Grae shot up draft boards last year after putting together a breakout offensive season at Ole Miss. There were some struggles in his first taste of professional ball which could easily be attributed to fatigue after a deep run in the college playoffs. Expect the bat to eventually play close to average. He has a patient approach and knows the strike zone. The swing is compact and quick, geared toward line drives, but he's athletic enough to develop some pop down the road. Defensively, he's serviceable at short in a pinch but is likely to eventually find a home elsewhere in the infield. None of the tools are loud, but it's a profile that should move quickly through the system and could eventually find its way onto a big league roster.

17 Jose Alberto Rivera   RHP

Born: 02/14/97   Age: 23   Bats: R   Throws: R   Height: 6'3"   Weight: 160   Origin: International Free Agent, 2016

YEAR	TEAM	LVL	AGE	W	L	SV	G	GS	IP	H	HR	BB/9	K/9	K	GB%	BABIP	WHIP	ERA	DRA	WARP	PF
2017	DAR	ROK	20	2	3	0	12	5	36²	20	3	5.9	9.1	37	48%	.189	1.20	3.44			88
2018	AST	RK	21	1	2	0	10	4	39	30	4	1.4	9.0	39	58%	.252	0.92	3.23	1.57	1.8	102
2018	TCV	A-	21	1	2	0	4	1	10	9	2	7.2	12.6	14	31%	.292	1.70	4.50	4.70	0.0	100
2019	QUD	A	22	5	5	1	18	11	75²	61	2	4.3	11.3	95	44%	.322	1.28	3.81	4.14	0.8	100
2020	HOU	MLB	23	2	2	0	33	0	35	35	6	3.9	9.0	35	39%	.306	1.45	5.05	4.97	0.1	103

Comparables: Justin Haley, Corey Kluber, Jeff Beliveau

Rivera was an overaged signee in 2016 and his pro debut came in the Dominican complex at age 20. This is exactly the kind of prospect who might get squeezed out of organizations under the proposed minor league reshuffling, and that would be a shame. Not every arm develops at the same pace, and yes, Rivera is 22 and in the Midwest League. But fastball don't lie, and Rivera's stuff could get him to the majors quickly. He pumps 95 mph heaters and has two usable secondaries in a diving changeup and big breaking slider with 11-6 depth. The command profile is still rough given his paucity of pro reps, but if the Astros iron that out he could be a useful Swiss-Army-type arm on a modern pitching staff.

18 Luis Santana   INF

Born: 07/20/99   Age: 20   Bats: R   Throws: R   Height: 5'8"   Weight: 175   Origin: International Free Agent, 2016

YEAR	TEAM	LVL	AGE	PA	R	2B	3B	HR	RBI	BB	K	SB	CS	AVG/OBP/SLG	DRC+	VORP	BABIP	BRR	FRAA	WARP	PF
2017	MET	RK	17	287	47	12	8	3	52	34	22	16	4	.325/.430/.481	166	27.4	.346	2.4	2B(61) 1.0, SS(4) 0.4	3.1	104
2018	KNG	RK	18	242	34	13	0	4	35	27	23	8	3	.348/.446/.471	170	26.7	.376	-0.4	2B(51) -1.5, 3B(1) -0.1	2.3	105
2019	TCV	A-	19	186	19	8	0	2	15	14	24	4	2	.267/.339/.352	139	13.1	.298	0.2	2B(37) -2.2, 3B(15) -0.6	0.9	97
2019	CCH	AA	19	66	5	2	0	0	2	6	9	0	0	.228/.333/.263	93	0.5	.271	-0.3	2B(17) -2.0, 3B(1) 0.2	-0.1	97
2020	HOU	MLB	20	251	23	12	1	4	24	17	45	2	1	.247/.311/.362	80	2.0	.291	-0.3	2B -3, 3B 0	-0.1	103

Comparables: Luis Arraez, Thairo Estrada, Abiatal Avelino

After coming over to Houston as part of the trade that sent J.D. Davis to the Mets, the 5'8" second baseman got an aggressive May fill-in assignment in Double-A before the New York-Penn League season began. Santana was only somewhat overmatched in Double-A, instead of completely so, because of his plus bat-to-ball skills and knowledge of the zone. He starts open and crouched, utilizing a moderate leg kick to effectively time his swings, though sometimes his hands start moving towards the ball before the hips and torso do, leading to occasional weak contact. At his best, Santana effectively uses his stocky frame to help drive balls to the pull-side gap. Yet despite his mature frame, he is not a power hitter, and he will have to spray the ball more if he's to be a successful gap hitter in the bigs. As an average runner and defender at second, Santana doesn't fit your prototypical utilityman mold, but he may hit enough where it doesn't matter. If the hit tool continues to develop and he maintains the weight, I get lots of right-handed Luis Arraez vibes here.

19 Ronnie Dawson   OF

Born: 05/19/95   Age: 25   Bats: L   Throws: R   Height: 6'2"   Weight: 225   Origin: Round 2, 2016 Draft (#61 overall)

YEAR	TEAM	LVL	AGE	PA	R	2B	3B	HR	RBI	BB	K	SB	CS	AVG/OBP/SLG	DRC+	VORP	BABIP	BRR	FRAA	WARP	PF
2017	QUD	A	22	505	81	23	4	14	62	55	101	17	8	.272/.362/.438	124	27.0	.322	0.3	LF(75) -10.5, RF(24) -0.7	1.2	102
2017	BCA	A+	22	57	7	3	1	0	5	4	9	1	3	.327/.368/.423	130	2.8	.386	-0.3	RF(13) -0.7	0.2	92
2018	BCA	A+	23	376	51	18	1	10	49	39	96	29	11	.247/.331/.398	118	11.8	.317	-2.3	CF(88) 4.8	2.1	95
2018	CCH	AA	23	123	18	6	1	6	14	6	34	6	3	.289/.341/.518	116	10.4	.365	1.9	CF(24) 0.1, RF(5) -0.4	0.7	102
2019	CCH	AA	24	459	71	20	2	17	50	47	141	13	10	.212/.320/.403	98	18.8	.281	1.1	CF(78) -2.6, RF(10) -0.7	1.3	103
2019	ROU	AAA	24	39	1	1	0	0	3	3	11	1	0	.147/.231/.176	26	-3.5	.208	0.1	CF(6) -0.5, RF(4) 0.0	-0.2	92
2020	HOU	MLB	25	251	26	12	1	9	29	19	85	6	3	.211/.285/.382	73	0.0	.294	0.0	CF 2, LF 0	0.2	103

Comparables: Johnny Field, Jaylin Davis, Lane Adams

Dawson has an ideal athlete's build at 6-foot-1, 230 pounds of pure athletic muscle. He has a strong lower half and impressively-built torso and arms. No mere strongman, Dawson is also a good athlete with some quick-twitch and body control. Unfortunately, his offensive profile was almost exactly the kind of profile that tends to over-promise and under-deliver.

Dawson generates plus bat speed and has some barrel control, which leads to a lot of good-quality contact when he gets a hold of a ball. He sees fastball, he hits fastball, for a hard line drive or deep fly ball. He has plus raw power and he swings like it, so he can hit some truly majestic dingers. However, Dawson struggles to recognize breaking balls or offspeed of any kind and regularly misdiagnoses before taking a strong hack at a pitch out of the zone. That's not to say he's overly aggressive, as he actually will lay off pitches he does read, but that doesn't happen enough to make the overall offensive profile play in a corner.

Dawson's an average defender in right despite some inconsistent jumps and routes due to good closing speed and a plus arm. Despite the loud physical tools and a decent defensive profile, Dawson looks to be a better bet to bust than boom. Without marginal improvement with pitch recognition he's unlikely to have much of a major league career and only with significant improvement will be able to settle into a regular role.

20 J.J. Matijevic 1B

Born: 11/14/95 Age: 24 Bats: L Throws: R Height: 6'0" Weight: 206 Origin: Round 2, 2017 Draft (#75 overall)

YEAR	TEAM	LVL	AGE	PA	R	2B	3B	HR	RBI	BB	K	SB	CS	AVG/OBP/SLG	DRC+	VORP	BABIP	BRR	FRAA	WARP	PF
2017	TCV	A-	21	222	34	14	0	6	27	18	60	11	3	.240/.302/.400	120	4.7	.307	0.8	LF(44) -5.3, 1B(1) 0.0	0.3	101
2017	QUD	A	21	26	2	0	0	1	4	1	9	0	1	.125/.192/.250	35	-2.6	.143	-0.2		-0.2	98
2018	QUD	A	22	56	8	6	1	3	5	8	10	3	0	.354/.446/.708	194	7.4	.400	0.0	LF(12) -1.6	0.5	103
2018	BCA	A+	22	376	58	20	3	19	57	36	103	10	13	.266/.335/.513	141	25.3	.323	-2.0	LF(49) -2.1	1.8	94
2019	CCH	AA	23	312	41	21	1	9	35	27	97	8	0	.246/.314/.423	107	5.6	.339	2.3	1B(48) -0.2, LF(21) 2.4	1.2	104
2020	HOU	MLB	24	251	28	14	1	10	33	18	89	5	3	.226/.284/.425	85	0.0	.319	0.0	LF 2, 1B 0	0.5	103

Comparables: Matt Clark, Peter O'Brien, Bryce Brentz

Previously an outfielder, Matijevic started primarily playing first base this year after his promotion to Double-A, and played it nearly exclusively during the Fall League. He was always headed in that direction, dating back to when he was drafted in 2017 as one of the picks the Astros recouped from the Cardinals as a result of the Chris Correa hacking scandal. His defense in the outfield was rough, and he's still not all the way there at first base yet, but it's a better fit for him moving forward defensively with a maxed out frame. What is still to be determined is whether his bat is a fit at first; he possesses plus raw power that he hasn't yet gotten fully into games, and the swing is on the stiff and pull-happy side. He hits the ball hard and has an idea at the plate, so he's interesting, but the offensive bar at first base is high.

Personal Cheeseball

PC Ross Adolph OF

Born: 12/17/96 Age: 23 Bats: L Throws: R Height: 6'1" Weight: 203 Origin: Round 12, 2018 Draft (#350 overall)

YEAR	TEAM	LVL	AGE	PA	R	2B	3B	HR	RBI	BB	K	SB	CS	AVG/OBP/SLG	DRC+	VORP	BABIP	BRR	FRAA	WARP	PF
2018	BRO	A-	21	264	47	9	12	7	35	21	52	14	3	.276/.348/.509	150	26.3	.322	4.4	CF(27) 1.2, LF(18) -0.5	2.3	94
2019	QUD	A	22	288	45	15	5	6	24	37	99	9	8	.223/.354/.403	114	17.9	.351	2.1	CF(51) -3.3, LF(9) 1.8	1.4	101
2019	BCA	A+	22	172	24	5	1	1	16	24	43	2	1	.236/.360/.306	112	4.4	.330	1.2	CF(20) -0.2, LF(15) -0.9	0.6	104
2020	HOU	MLB	23	251	23	11	2	6	25	17	89	5	1	.207/.276/.351	64	0.0	.311	0.0	CF 0, LF -1	-0.4	103

Comparables: Jake Rogers, Chris McGuiness, Brent Lillibridge

The other piece of the J.D. Davis deal, Adolph had a weird and uneven season. Part of that was due to being banged up early, but the outfielder warmed up with the temperature in Quad Cities and managed to get a promotion to High-A before the end of the season. Honestly, I expected him to do better as a polished college bat in A-ball, even a Day Three for-slot one, but he struggled with spin from full-season arms, and despite an overall strong approach, chased a bit too much. There's still interesting tools here—sneaky solid raw and a potential above-average glove in center most noteworthy among them—but until Adolph shows he can consistently hit full-season arms, the major league fourth outfielder projection is a lot murkier than it was this time last year.

Low Minors Sleeper

LMS Blair Henley RHP

Born: 05/14/97 Age: 23 Bats: R Throws: R Height: 6'3" Weight: 190 Origin: Round 7, 2019 Draft (#226 overall)

YEAR	TEAM	LVL	AGE	W	L	SV	G	GS	IP	H	HR	BB/9	K/9	K	GB%	BABIP	WHIP	ERA	DRA	WARP	PF
2019	TCV	A-	22	1	1	1	11	2	33²	29	1	2.1	12.3	46	54%	.346	1.10	1.60	3.45	0.6	99
2020	HOU	MLB	23	2	2	0	33	0	35	35	5	3.7	9.4	37	45%	.309	1.40	4.75	4.71	0.2	103

Drafted but unsigned by the Yankees in 2016, Henley first gained national recognition when he threw three consecutive no-hitters in high school. Henley then attended the University of Texas where he became a respectable starter for the Longhorns en route to being drafted by Houston in the seventh round this past summer. Standing at 6-foot-3, Henley is a lanky, athletic righty with a three-quarters arm slot, who throws enough strikes and utilizes a somewhat funky delivery that can make for an uncomfortable at-bat for fellow righties.

The fastball comes in at 89-93, though it has nice rising action and generates its fair share of swings and misses high in the zone. What makes Henley especially interesting, however, is a plus curveball that displays really nice 11-5 tilt. He can manipulate the pitch inside and outside the zone rather well, and it was consequently one of the best individual pitches in the Penn League this Summer. The change is fringe-average as of now, but he has time to either work on it or experiment with other pitches. The curveball alone will allow him to move up in the minor league ranks, but pair that with his athleticism, a workable heater and solid strike-throwing ability, and he makes for a fun project in an organization which is arguably the best at developing this kind of talent.

Top Talents 25 and Under (as of 4/1/2020)

1. Carlos Correa
2. Yordan Alvarez
3. Forrest Whitley
4. Roberto Osuna
5. Kyle Tucker
6. Jose Urquidy
7. Jeremy Pena
8. Abraham Toro
9. Bryan Abreu
10. Korey Lee

The cutoff for the 25 and Under list is April 1. Alex Bregman, an MVP finalist after finishing with the fourth-highest DRC+ (157) in baseball, turns 26 on March 30. So he is not eligible, but he is there in spirit. Meanwhile, the owner of MLB's seventh-highest DRC+ (Yordan Alvarez, 149) doesn't even top the Astros list.

Houston, like the rest of us, keeps getting older. George Springer and Jose Altuve, both entering their age-30 seasons, are no longer the youthful stars they once were. But the Astros are still loaded with young talent. Correa is a generational star whose only knock has been durability. When he is healthy, there are only a handful of players in the same tier as him. Since his debut in 2015, Correa has a 123 DRC+, the best among all shortstops during that time and a full six points above second place Francisco Lindor.

Alvarez had what the kids are calling, "a year." In 143 combined games between Triple-A and the majors, he hit 50 home runs and drove in 149. His complete lack of defensive value limits his ultimate ceiling, but he's a better baserunner than his frame would lead you to believe and his offensive performance looks as predictable as any other player's, which is to say, who even knows, man.

Tucker and Urquidy will certainly see their roles expand in the 2020 season after shorts stints of varying success levels in 2019. Tucker feasted on fastballs to the tune of a .418 wOBA, but has still shown vulnerability to offspeed stuff, especially backfoot breaking balls from righties. Urquidy blew well past his innings limit but was exactly what the Astros needed with the implosion of Wade Miley down the stretch.

Toro helped Justin Verlander throw a no-hitter with a t-shirt to commemorate the moment and Abreu was as magical as anyone can be in 8 2/3 innings. Pena, as you just read, had a phenomenal year showcasing his glove and his bat. Second, short, and third certainly seem blocked in Houston, but Jack Mayfield appeared in 26 games this year, so anything can happen. The Astros have leapfrogged between short-term catching options ever since Jason Castro left in 2016, so Lee will get his chance to stick soon.

There isn't a ton potential to dream on down the road, but with a championship window wide open right now, having this much young talent ready to contribute at the major leagues is never a bad thing.

Eyewitness Reports

Eyewitness Report: Forrest Whitley

Evaluator: Forest Stulting
Report Date: 10/17/2019
Dates Seen: Oct. 11 2019
Risk Factor: High
Delivery: Large frame, tall, lanky, skinny. Shows emotion on mound. Throws out of stretch only, high leg kick with knee slightly above waist at apex, high three-quarter arm slot, long arm motion, goes below waist and completes a circle at release point, under control till release, hard finish, right leg will occasionally swing hard to first base after release. Repeatable delivery, good extension.

Pitch Type	Future Grade	Sitting Velocity	Peak Velocity	Report
Fastball	60	94-96	97	Four-seam, flashes life, straight. Swing-and-miss pitch. Had some command issues in my look, overthrew occasionally, worked both sides of plate.
Changeup	60	84-85	85	Late sinking action with some fade. Plus command and feel, swing-and-miss pitch, doesn't slow arm down, throws to both RHH and LHH.
Slider	60	88-90	90	Sharp, late horizontal bite, shows tilt, power, swing-and-miss pitch, mainly used as chase pitch but can throw for strike, average command, throws to both LHH and RHH, good arm action.
Curveball	60	80-82	83	12/6, depth, power, late bite, medium hump, swing-and-miss pitch, mainly throws in dirt, throws to both RHH and LHH.

Conclusion: With four pitches that can produce whiffs in any count, Whitley has the potential to be a dominant starter. But injury concerns and a mechanical change this year slowed those expectations. However, the 22-year-old still shows plenty of upside and should be given every opportunity to max out his potential.

Eyewitness Report: Jeremy Pena

Evaluator: Steve Givarz
Report Date: 10/07/2019
Dates Seen: 10/2/19, 10/4-10/6/19
Risk Factor: High
Physical/Health: Medium frame and body, athletic build that is unlikely to fill out, mature.

Tool	Future Grade	Report
Hit	50	Hits from a slightly crouched, even stance, average bat speed, hands are low at set, so can be suspect against pitches up. Tendency to cut himself off in swing, can get over-aggressive at times and swing at early pitches in the count. Made hard contact in viewing, lacked discipline and can doesn't work many counts, future average hitter.
Power	30	Below-average raw power, lacks strength in frame as well as wrists/hands, can take a ball out pullside but most power will be of the extra-base variety.
Baserunning/Speed	55	Above-average runner, consistent 4.25 down the line, have not seen steal a base, gets up to speed quickly and runs the bases well.
Glove	60	Quality defender at short. Quick reactions and instincts at the position, gets self into position with quality footwork and soft hands, works well on the backhand, seen in one game in outfield, did not look comfortable and had not appeared at position in minors.
Arm	60	Plus throwing arm, strong arc and line on throws, has arm strength to play other positions if needed.

Conclusion: See as an everyday glove-first regular at shortstop, 22 y/o R/R, plus defender that can make all the plays and can appear at other positions if needed. Bat won't ever be known for power but project as an average hitter, moderate interest, would acquire.

Kansas City Royals

The State of the System

The pitchers all took a step forward. The hitters all took a step back. Not the ideal Kansas City two-step.

The Top Ten

★ ★ ★ *2020 Top 101 Prospect* **#29** ★ ★ ★

1 Bobby Witt Jr. SS

OFP: 70   ETA: 2022/23

Born: 06/14/00   Age: 20   Bats: R   Throws: R   Height: 6'1"   Weight: 190   Origin: Round 1, 2019 Draft (#2 overall)

YEAR	TEAM	LVL	AGE	PA	R	2B	3B	HR	RBI	BB	K	SB	CS	AVG/OBP/SLG	DRC+	VORP	BABIP	BRR	FRAA	WARP	PF
2019	ROY	RK	19	180	30	2	5	1	27	13	35	9	1	.262/.317/.354	94	4.2	.323	-0.1	SS(26) 3.3	0.8	104
2020	KCA	MLB	20	251	19	10	1	3	20	16	72	2	1	.216/.270/.306	54	0.0	.302	0.0	SS 1	-0.5	100

Comparables: Humberto Arteaga, Niko Goodrum, Leury García

The Report: Some baseball families have more than just the job running through their bloodlines. The Bells all had roughly the same kind of offensive profile. You don't have to squint to see a bit of Mike Cameron in Daz's game. Vlad Jr. doesn't look like his father physically, but the swing is a dead ringer. Then you have Bobby Witt, who was a journeyman right-hander. His son and namesake? A potential five-tool shortstop. Witt has plus-plus athleticism and three potential 60-grade tools on the defensive side. His plus speed works whether ranging in the field or running the bases. The arm will play comfortably from deep in the 5.5 hole. And his actions, hands and instincts all portend a plus shortstop in the majors.

At the plate we can add a fourth plus tool: raw power. Witt has quick hands, quality bat speed and is strong enough to drive the ball over the fence when he gets extended. Well, only one tool to go: hit. And as usual, it's a tricky one for the prep bat. There's positive markers here. He'll show good barrel feel and the ability to adjust to pitches where they are thrown, but he also gets aggressive and you can beat him up with fastballs. His propensity to try to get long and drive the ball could make him vulnerable inside as well. An even average hit tool would allow most of the power to play and for Witt to be a perennial all-star, but if the profile ends up more like 4.50-tool, he'll just be a solid regular.

Variance: Extreme. Complex-league resume, the hit tool may play as fringe-or-below-average, limiting how much the power gets into games and blunting some of the upside.

Mark Barry's Fantasy Take: This dude is pretty far away, but there's a Trea Turner-y whiff with Witt's profile, albeit with slightly less speed and slightly more power. Does that make him another eponymous offspring like Fernando Tatis Jr.? Who's to say. What we can say is that Witt is already a top-30 or so dynasty prospect and could see time atop that list in the foreseeable future.

★ ★ ★ *2020 Top 101 Prospect* **#64** ★ ★ ★

2 Brady Singer RHP   OFP: 60   ETA: 2020
Born: 08/04/96   Age: 23   Bats: R   Throws: R   Height: 6'5"   Weight: 210   Origin: Round 1, 2018 Draft (#18 overall)

YEAR	TEAM	LVL	AGE	W	L	SV	G	GS	IP	H	HR	BB/9	K/9	K	GB%	BABIP	WHIP	ERA	DRA	WARP	PF
2019	WIL	A+	22	5	2	0	10	10	57²	51	1	2.0	8.3	53	56%	.325	1.11	1.87	5.14	-0.1	93
2019	NWA	AA	22	7	3	0	16	16	90²	86	8	2.6	8.4	85	51%	.301	1.24	3.47	3.97	1.1	102
2020	KCA	MLB	23	1	2	0	5	5	24	24	3	3.7	7.4	20	46%	.292	1.41	4.82	4.78	0.2	100

Comparables: Jeff Hoffman, Zach Stewart, Jon Gray

The Report: Let's make something really clear from the get-go: Singer is not ranked second in this system for his upside. He is a healthy, durable, consistent, strike-throwing, polished arm with an excellent performance track record and pedigree. He is a fiery competitor with advanced pitchability. Many pitchers boast some of these qualities, but Singer has pretty much all of them, and that is why he is here.

The fastball sits low-90s, up to 95 with run and sink, generating plenty of groundballs. His command of the pitch is plus, allowing it to play up past the average velocity readings. Singer's best secondary is a firm, low-80s slider that is above-average, but lacks elite movement, and is not consistently a swing and miss pitch. He is excellent at manipulating the shape of both the fastball and slider, allowing him to consistently give hitters different looks. There is a changeup as a third offering, but he rarely uses it, and it doesn't feature any kind of above-average action.

As I mentioned, Singer is theoretically everything you could want in a pitching prospect, minus the blemish of not really having a plus, swing-and-miss pitch.

That particular hole in his game was exposed a bit more in Double-A after he received a midseason promotion on the back of his dominance of the Carolina League. Some have qualms with Singer's mechanics, but to his credit, he still displays consistency and plus command, even with the whole inverted-W and low arm slot thing.

Variance: Medium. More reliever risk than you'd expect given his durability, but definitely a major league arm in some capacity.

Mark Barry's Fantasy Take: There's room for guys like Singer on fantasy rosters, but it's hard to imagine breaking the bank for a Tanner Roark-type or say, Jake Odorizzi pre-2019 strikeout surge. Singer should be a serviceable, back-end fantasy starter, which is certainly useful if not terribly exciting.

★ ★ ★ *2020 Top 101 Prospect* **#93** ★ ★ ★

3 Daniel Lynch LHP   OFP: 60   ETA: 2021
Born: 11/17/96   Age: 23   Bats: L   Throws: L   Height: 6'6"   Weight: 190   Origin: Round 1C, 2018 Draft (#34 overall)

YEAR	TEAM	LVL	AGE	W	L	SV	G	GS	IP	H	HR	BB/9	K/9	K	GB%	BABIP	WHIP	ERA	DRA	WARP	PF
2018	BNC	RK	21	0	0	0	3	3	11¹	9	0	1.6	11.1	14	59%	.310	0.97	1.59	3.08	0.4	95
2018	LEX	A	21	5	1	0	9	9	40	35	1	1.4	10.6	47	51%	.343	1.02	1.58	3.37	0.9	105
2019	ROY	RK	22	0	0	0	3	3	9	6	0	3.0	12.0	12	65%	.294	1.00	1.00	2.09	0.4	112
2019	BNC	RK+	22	1	0	0	2	2	9	13	1	3.0	7.0	7	59%	.429	1.78	4.00	8.31	-0.2	103
2019	WIL	A+	22	5	2	0	15	15	78¹	76	4	2.6	8.8	77	49%	.324	1.26	3.10	4.47	0.5	91
2020	KCA	MLB	23	2	2	0	33	0	35	34	5	3.5	8.1	31	46%	.290	1.35	4.31	4.43	0.3	100

Comparables: Nick Maronde, Eric Skoglund, Taylor Rogers

The Report: Upon being drafted the general consensus was that Lynch was the weakest of the Royals day one selections; most outlets considered him a backend starter at best. Couple that with the history of arm troubles from Virginia draftees and there wasn't much room for optimism. Lynch forced a paradigm shift, and he did it in a hurry. His professional numbers have been impressive from the outset and his ERA has been better as a pro than it ever was in college. His strikeouts are down from his amateur days, but he's still a shade over one per inning and has upside beyond a mere backend arm.

Lynch is tall and lanky with a long torso and narrow frame throughout. He slings the ball to the plate and throws across his body a bit. He works mostly down in the zone with his fastball. In my looks Lynch worked up to 96 with the heater, but he's touched even higher. The fastball has life and is going to generate a lot of groundballs. His slider and changeup are both above-average pitches with the slider as the pitch with the most potential. It's inconsistent at present, but is an easy plus pitch when it's going well. Lynch will mix in a curveball occasionally, but it has shown to be a fairly lazy pitch in my looks. It's something he could use to steal a strike or two, but I don't see it as a legitimate part of his arsenal.

Lynch's mechanics aren't exactly ideal, and the history of arm troubles from Virginia alums is a legitimate thing to keep in mind, but that's a fairly short list of concerns. On the whole, he has a quality arsenal and has shown the ability to strike out professional hitters and get groudballs otherwise. If his command takes a step forward it's easy to see him as a staple of the Royals rotation as soon as the club is ready to start his clock.

Variance: Medium. Lynch has shown an advanced feel for pitching. He has three above-average pitches and there haven't been any hiccups as a professional. If he doesn't make it as a starter, he still stands to serve an important role in the bullpen.

Mark Barry's Fantasy Take: The lack of consistent secondaries screams reliever, in which case Lynch is definitely less interesting. I'm apprehensive in writing him off, however, as a huge velocity spike from college to the pros could portend other unforeseeable jumps in skills. Oh, and being a huge lefty also helps. I'll be monitoring Lynch early in 2020, but I'm not taking the plunge just yet.

★ ★ ★ *2020 Top 101 Prospect* **#96** ★ ★ ★

4   **Kris Bubic   RHP**   OFP: 55   ETA: 2021

Born: 08/19/97   Age: 22   Bats: L   Throws: L   Height: 6'3"   Weight: 220   Origin: Round 1, 2018 Draft (#40 overall)

YEAR	TEAM	LVL	AGE	W	L	SV	G	GS	IP	H	HR	BB/9	K/9	K	GB%	BABIP	WHIP	ERA	DRA	WARP	PF
2018	IDA	RK	20	2	3	0	10	10	38	38	2	4.5	12.6	53	47%	.379	1.50	4.03	4.28	0.7	100
2019	LEX	A	21	4	1	0	9	9	47²	27	3	2.8	14.2	75	49%	.270	0.88	2.08	2.40	1.6	94
2019	WIL	A+	21	7	4	0	17	17	101²	76	3	2.4	9.7	110	43%	.286	1.01	2.30	3.52	1.9	89
2020	KCA	MLB	22	2	2	0	33	0	35	35	5	3.7	10.1	39	42%	.318	1.40	4.63	4.61	0.2	100

Comparables: Andrew Faulkner, Anthony Banda, Nestor Cortes Jr.

The Report: A high pick who nonetheless surprised some with his breakout this year, Bubic showed a combo of stuff and pitchability that proved far too much for A-ball opposition. How well it plays at the upper levels and beyond is more of an open question though. I think he'll be able to get outs in the big leagues, thanks to an effective three-pitch arsenal and a good feel for attacking hitters.

Bubic sits low-90s with his fastball, touching as high as 94 with sink and run. There is sneaky swing and miss here, and he can also generate weak contact in multiple ways; grounders when he locates down and soft pop-ups when he saws someone off. The latter helps him neutralize righties and set up his secondaries. His low-to-mid 80s changeup is reputed to be plus-plus, and the fact that he struck out 11 on my look despite it being almost a non-factor on that particular night is encouraging, especially as regards to his curve. I really liked the pitch, especially the tighter version around 80 mph that plays as an out pitch with its late and sharp break. He'll also drop in a truer version in the low-to-mid 70s as a change of pace. Bubic has has a slightly unorthodox motion but is anchored by a strong lower half and generally repeats his delivery enough to command his pitches.

Variance: Medium. His arsenal is pretty well-established and he knows how to pitch, the margins are tight at the highest level and he'll need to be proficient and efficient with his curve and change.

Mark Barry's Fantasy Take: A personal favorite of mine, Bubic struck out almost literally everyone this season. Even though the K totals are gaudy, he hasn't really been tested by advanced hitters, so the lefty's ultimate upside is still TBD. For now, I'm viewing Bubic as a mid-rotation starter in real life or a fantasy SP4-5. He might not be elite, but he's easily better than a streamer and there's upside for more.

5   **Jackson Kowar   RHP**   OFP: 55   ETA: 2020/21

Born: 10/04/96   Age: 23   Bats: R   Throws: R   Height: 6'5"   Weight: 180   Origin: Round 1C, 2018 Draft (#33 overall)

YEAR	TEAM	LVL	AGE	W	L	SV	G	GS	IP	H	HR	BB/9	K/9	K	GB%	BABIP	WHIP	ERA	DRA	WARP	PF
2018	LEX	A	21	0	1	0	9	9	26¹	19	2	4.1	7.5	22	59%	.239	1.18	3.42	3.71	0.5	108
2019	WIL	A+	22	5	3	0	13	13	74	68	4	2.7	8.0	66	46%	.305	1.22	3.53	4.72	0.3	91
2019	NWA	AA	22	2	7	0	13	13	74¹	73	8	2.5	9.4	78	46%	.323	1.26	3.51	4.67	0.3	99
2020	KCA	MLB	23	2	2	0	33	0	35	35	5	3.8	7.5	29	43%	.288	1.43	4.93	4.94	0.1	100

Comparables: Michael Ynoa, Esmil Rogers, Victor Alcántara

The Report: All in all it was a productive year for the ex-Gator across two levels of the minors. Kowar's fastball ticked back up into the mid-90s, and despite less than ideal movement, it's an above-average pitch. His mid-80s change-up has plus projection, showing fade and dive and good velocity separation off the fastball. The curve remains on the fringy side, as it's a bit humpy and he can struggle to command it. Kowar has some effort in his mechanics and he be a bit stiff and upright, but he throws enough strikes and offers average command that could get to solid-average. It's not a sexy starting pitching profile, due to the lack of a breaking pitch—I wonder if a slider might work better here long term—but there's enough command and stuff that he should stick in a rotation.

Variance: Medium. Despite the plus velocity, Kowar would be a weird pen fit as a righty fastball/change guy, so he's going to have to make his way as a starter. Breaking ball development will determine how good a pitcher he ends up, even an average one could bump the projection to more of a true number three starter.

Mark Barry's Fantasy Take: Meh, I'm starting to gain an appreciation for the origins of Ben's deep disdain for back-end starters. Kowar looks like a back-end starter, is what I 'm saying.

6 Kyle Isbel OF   OFP: 55   ETA: 2021
Born: 03/03/97   Age: 23   Bats: L   Throws: R   Height: 5'11"   Weight: 183   Origin: Round 3, 2018 Draft (#94 overall)

YEAR	TEAM	LVL	AGE	PA	R	2B	3B	HR	RBI	BB	K	SB	CS	AVG/OBP/SLG	DRC+	VORP	BABIP	BRR	FRAA	WARP	PF
2018	IDA	RK	21	119	27	10	1	4	18	14	17	12	3	.381/.454/.610	195	18.0	.429	-0.8	CF(19) 4.5, RF(2) 1.1	1.6	105
2018	LEX	A	21	174	30	12	1	3	14	12	43	12	3	.289/.345/.434	111	7.0	.377	2.8	CF(27) 0.8, LF(11) -0.5	1.0	109
2019	ROY	RK	22	27	9	2	0	2	7	2	5	3	1	.360/.407/.680	155	5.4	.389	1.0	CF(6) 1.6	0.5	96
2019	WIL	A+	22	214	26	7	3	5	23	15	44	8	3	.216/.282/.361	86	5.5	.253	1.8	CF(32) -2.3, RF(11) 0.5	0.2	91
2020	KCA	MLB	23	251	23	12	1	5	24	16	67	9	3	.223/.277/.349	63	0.0	.292	0.6	CF 0, RF 0	-0.2	100

Comparables: Andrew Toles, Alex Presley, Clete Thomas

The Report: Isbel started off 2019 scorching hot, slashing .348/.423/.630 through this first 13 games before fracturing his hamate bone, putting him out until July. A hamate injury is pesky in that it takes much longer than just the rehab time to get that feel and confidence in your swing back. This probably explains some of his slumped July (.118/.132/.235) and August (.206/.287/.299). Isbel made up some of the lost reps in the AFL where he looked more like the early-season version. He was one of the best all-around hitters in the AFL and homered on the bigger stage of the Fall Stars Game.

Isbel displays good pitch recognition and discipline, which should allow him to continue to walk at healthy clips at higher levels. The swing has some length, and while there is some bat speed, it is by no means elite. Nonetheless, there is an excellent feel for hitting, and many signs point towards him being an above-average hitter at the big league level.

The best way to describe Isbel is that he is sneaky good at just about everything. He is an above-average athlete, with significant amateur experience in the infield. Although the swing isn't geared for home runs, there is enough strength to hit 10-15 per year. He is one of the best all-around prospects in this system.

Variance: Medium. Isbel's hit tool gives him a solid floor, but we didn't get to see him play a full season in 2019. If he ends up hitting for power, it's a versatile 20-20 contributor.

Mark Barry's Fantasy Take: Potential 20/20, you say? The speed alone makes Isbel interesting and rosterable in 200ish-prospect leagues, but if he stays healthy this season, and maintains his current level of production, he'll jump right into top-100 conversation.

7 Khalil Lee OF   OFP: 55   ETA: 2021
Born: 06/26/98   Age: 22   Bats: L   Throws: L   Height: 5'10"   Weight: 170   Origin: Round 3, 2016 Draft (#103 overall)

YEAR	TEAM	LVL	AGE	PA	R	2B	3B	HR	RBI	BB	K	SB	CS	AVG/OBP/SLG	DRC+	VORP	BABIP	BRR	FRAA	WARP	PF
2017	LEX	A	19	532	71	24	6	17	61	65	171	20	18	.237/.344/.430	109	19.6	.338	-2.2	CF(67) -6.2, RF(52) 4.3	1.5	106
2018	WIL	A+	20	301	42	13	4	4	41	48	75	14	3	.270/.402/.406	142	26.4	.371	2.2	CF(57) 3.8, RF(9) 0.3	2.8	99
2018	NWA	AA	20	118	15	5	0	2	10	11	28	2	2	.245/.330/.353	81	1.2	.319	0.6	CF(17) 0.3, LF(9) 0.7	0.3	105
2019	NWA	AA	21	546	74	21	3	8	51	65	154	53	12	.264/.363/.372	117	26.4	.374	3.7	RF(54) -6.0, CF(45) -5.7	1.2	101
2020	KCA	MLB	22	251	23	11	1	4	23	24	86	5	3	.221/.307/.337	72	0.0	.340	0.2	CF -3, RF -1	-0.4	100

Comparables: Clint Frazier, Byron Buxton, Jaff Decker

The Report: It seems less and less likely that the power Lee flashed in the Appy League three years ago is going to find its way back into games at higher levels. The above-average raw remains, and Lee looks like he should hit for more pop, given the bat speed and good hips. But his approach often leaves him making less than ideal contact. His swing can get long and out of sync, and while he tracks breaking balls well enough, there can be too much swing-and-miss in the zone.

Lee has filled out a fair bit and is still a plus runner, although the speed can play down in center field as his instincts and routes make him more of an average glove up-the-middle. He feels like a guy where it could just click and he'd be a 20/40 center fielder that gets on base a bunch, but every year it doesn't happen, he looks more like a fourth outfielder.

Variance: High. Lee held his own as a 20/21-year-old in Double-A, but it feels like his hit tool is constantly walking a tightrope, and you are just waiting for it to take a plunge. It's an impressive collection of physical tools when he is going right though, and if Lee ever figures out how to get a bit more of his raw pop into games, he could be a plus regular.

Mark Barry's Fantasy Take: Life is what happens when you wait on the "If He Puts it All Together" guys, and I'm definitely guilty of holding on too long when the skills are tantalizing, like Lee's. For a guy who will ultimately be defined by the steals, the upticks in strikeouts and groundballs are troubling. Sure, he could put it all together, but I'd be taking the temperature on the trade market, hoping there's still some name value left to capitalize upon.

8 MJ Melendez C   OFP: 55   ETA: 2023
Born: 11/29/98   Age: 21   Bats: L   Throws: R   Height: 6'1"   Weight: 185   Origin: Round 2, 2017 Draft (#52 overall)

YEAR	TEAM	LVL	AGE	PA	R	2B	3B	HR	RBI	BB	K	SB	CS	AVG/OBP/SLG	DRC+	VORP	BABIP	BRR	FRAA	WARP	PF
2017	ROY	RK	18	198	25	8	3	4	30	26	60	4	2	.262/.374/.417	113	11.7	.385	0.1	C(30) 0.5	1.0	102
2018	LEX	A	19	472	52	26	9	19	73	43	143	4	6	.251/.322/.492	103	24.5	.327	-1.7	C(73) 1.4	1.7	109
2019	WIL	A+	20	419	34	23	2	9	54	44	165	7	5	.163/.260/.311	51	-2.7	.259	-0.9	C(71) 2.4	-0.4	91
2020	KCA	MLB	21	251	20	13	1	6	24	19	107	0	0	.176/.245/.313	43	0.0	.299	-0.3	C 0	-1.0	100

Comparables: Austin Riley, Bobby Bradley, Lewis Brinson

The Report: The offensive output at Wilmington in 2019 was…not good. It was a throwaway season for Royals High-A bats, and Melendez was no exception. He was absolutely awful at the plate last year, and there is no way around that. The fact that every hitter in Wilmington struggled means something, but you can decide for yourself exactly what it means.

In 2017 the Royals paid overslot to pry Melendez away from Florida International University where father is the manager. The question with Melendez has always been the hit tool, and obviously his 2019 numbers didn't do anything to quell those concerns. If you disregard the hit tool Melendez looks like a star. He has plus raw power, a plus arm, and average speed—plus baserunning smarts and base stealing ability accompany it. He's more athletic than just about anyone behind the dish, he has soft hands, receives the ball well, and has a quick transfer to go with the plus arm. The problem is that the hit tool might be bad enough to prevent him from even getting over the low offensive bar for catchers. He has significant timing issues. He really struggles to see the ball against lefties and takes more than his share of ugly swings. Melendez's ceiling is high, but there are serious concerns about his ability to get there.

Should Melendez continue to struggle at the dish, there's still a major league future behind it. His power and defensive abilities will be enough to land him a backup catcher role at worst. He's a likeable guy and handles the staff well. I hear nothing but good things about his leadership abilities. He's going to be the kind of player you want in your clubhouse even if he doesn't play every day. If the hit tool ends up a 4 or 5 then you have a player who could be a star. Unfortunately it has a long, long way to go.

Variance: Extreme. Again, it's all about the hit tool here. If he puts 2019 behind him and ends up with an average hit tool, the Royals have a star on their hands. If 2019 is a sign of things to come, Melendez is a backup catcher.

Mark Barry's Fantasy Take: "But catcher development is the nonlinear-iest of nonlinear developments," he said, hugging his knees while rocking back and forth in the corner. Fantasy catchers are bad, so the bar is pretty low, but a 40 percent strikeout rate and sub-.600 OPS at High-A is extremely not what you want. Until there are *any* hit-tool improvements, Melendez is off my radar.

9 Zach Haake RHP   OFP: 55   ETA: 2021/22
Born: 10/08/96   Age: 23   Bats: R   Throws: R   Height: 6'4"   Weight: 186   Origin: Round 6, 2018 Draft (#182 overall)

YEAR	TEAM	LVL	AGE	W	L	SV	G	GS	IP	H	HR	BB/9	K/9	K	GB%	BABIP	WHIP	ERA	DRA	WARP	PF
2018	ROY	RK	21	0	0	0	5	4	9²	7	1	1.9	9.3	10	40%	.250	0.93	1.86	2.45	0.4	102
2019	LEX	A	22	4	6	0	18	18	75²	60	2	4.3	10.7	90	40%	.314	1.27	2.85	4.28	0.8	99
2020	KCA	MLB	23	2	2	0	33	0	35	35	5	3.7	8.5	33	38%	.299	1.39	4.60	4.63	0.2	100

Comparables: Steven Matz, Jake Jewell, Jeff Stevens

The Report: Much like fellow 2018 draftee Daniel Lynch, Haake has put up much better numbers as a professional than as an amateur; however, he didn't have anywhere to go but up. Haake attended three colleges in three years and only put up respectable numbers at John A. Logan College (JUCO). His numbers at Arkansas State and Kentucky are not for the faint of heart. As a professional, Haake has managed a 2.55 ERA across 95.1 innings while striking out 108 batters. He wasn't originally mentioned in the same breath as the rest of the college arms the Royals drafted in 2018, but he has finally worked his way into the top ten alongside them.

Haake's fastball is his best offering. It shows plenty of arm side life, and he'll work it up to 97, although it sits more in the 94-95 range. His slider flashes plus, but it's a tease pitch. When he uncorks a good one it's tight and explosive, but he'll mix in more lazy and loopy offerings than you'd like to see. The change is an above-average pitch and his most consistent offspeed offering at present, and I've seen it make several good hitters look bad.

Haake is much rawer than you'd prefer an 23-year-old, ex-SEC arm to be. He shows poor posture on the mound and his stuff flattens out late in starts. His secondary offerings are near elite at times, but his fastball is the only consistent pitch at present. He has some mechanical issues to iron out on his developmental path, but he has a simple delivery and he already made major strides since being drafted.

Variance: High. He's a raw 23-year-old and there are things to clean up mechanically and with the secondary pitches, but if his development stalls he should be a safe bet to contribute in the bullpen.

Mark Barry's Fantasy Take: Whether due to injuries or an over-reliance on his heater, Haake sure sounds like a reliever to me. He could be useful in that role for onlies, but otherwise, not as much.

10 Erick Pena OF   OFP: 55   ETA: 2025
Born: 02/20/03   Age: 17   Bats: L   Throws: R   Height: 6'3"   Weight: 180   Origin: International Free Agent, 2019

The Report: The Royals gave Pena the fourth-largest signing bonus of the 2019 IFA period, and he certainly looks the part of a potential five-tool center fielder. Often these (literal children) can look like the bat is swinging them as they try to max out for raw power because that's what gets paid. However, Pena's swing is already quite physical with good balance, bat speed and barrel control, and his frame could easily take 30-40 more pounds of good weight. The building blocks are all here, but it will be a while before we know if he sticks in center field or how much power he develops, or if he can actually hit professional pitching. It's hard to argue there isn't 3.8 million bucks worth of tools and projection here though.

Variance: Extreme. He was born the week Old School was released and has yet to take a professional at-bat.

Mark Barry's Fantasy Take: If you miss out on Jasson Dominguez, Pena might be a decent fallback. It's impossible to accurately project what the landscape will look like by the time this kid is ready (or really by the time this kid can legally buy lottery tickets), but I'd rather dream on someone like Pena than maybe six dudes on this list. If your roster depth can stand the wait, go for it.

The Next Ten

11 Carlos Hernandez RHP

Born: 03/11/97 Age: 23 Bats: R Throws: R Height: 6'4" Weight: 175 Origin: International Free Agent, 2016

YEAR	TEAM	LVL	AGE	W	L	SV	G	GS	IP	H	HR	BB/9	K/9	K	GB%	BABIP	WHIP	ERA	DRA	WARP	PF
2017	BNC	RK	20	1	4	0	12	11	62^1	64	6	3.9	9.0	62	44%	.322	1.46	5.49	5.12	0.6	98
2018	LEX	A	21	6	5	0	15	15	79^1	71	7	2.6	9.3	82	44%	.298	1.18	3.29	4.24	0.9	108
2019	ROY	RK	22	0	2	0	5	5	11	14	1	2.5	9.8	12	41%	.387	1.55	7.36	2.90	0.4	106
2019	BNC	RK+	22	0	0	0	3	3	10^2	11	1	10.1	11.0	13	33%	.345	2.16	9.28	6.11	0.0	98
2019	LEX	A	22	3	3	0	7	7	36	34	5	2.2	10.8	43	40%	.326	1.19	3.50	4.19	0.4	103
2020	KCA	MLB	23	2	2	0	33	0	35	37	6	3.9	8.4	33	39%	.308	1.49	5.32	5.26	0.0	100

Comparables: Scott Barlow, Seranthony Domínguez, Alec Mills

Hernandez missed the first half of the season due to a stress fracture in his ribcage making it something of a lost year. He made 15 starts for Lexington in 2018 and finished 2019 again in Lexington having made seven starts for the Legends. He strikes out more than one batter per inning, and he does it with a fastball in the 95-97 range, an above-average low-80's slider, and a respectable change. Hernandez isn't very athletic, doesn't field his position well, and he's bad at holding runners on base. That said, he repeats his delivery surprisingly well and he holds his velocity deep into games. The warts are undeniable, but there is also a lot to like here. He signed out of Venezuela at the unheard of age of 19. His body has not developed well which is leading to some durability concerns, but he does a decent job throwing strikes and the raw stuff is good. If he can put together a string of healthy seasons and work on the body a bit, you'll see him creep up these lists.

12 Nick Pratto 1B

Born: 10/06/98 Age: 21 Bats: L Throws: L Height: 6'1" Weight: 195 Origin: Round 1, 2017 Draft (#14 overall)

YEAR	TEAM	LVL	AGE	PA	R	2B	3B	HR	RBI	BB	K	SB	CS	AVG/OBP/SLG	DRC+	VORP	BABIP	BRR	FRAA	WARP	PF
2017	ROY	RK	18	230	25	15	3	4	34	24	58	10	4	.247/.330/.414	108	5.0	.319	-0.8	1B(51) 5.2	0.8	101
2018	LEX	A	19	537	79	33	2	14	62	45	150	22	5	.280/.343/.443	111	14.4	.375	1.4	1B(125) -0.6	1.3	110
2019	WIL	A+	20	472	48	21	1	9	46	49	164	17	7	.191/.278/.310	64	-7.1	.286	0.5	1B(122) 5.2	-0.5	91
2020	KCA	MLB	21	251	21	13	1	5	24	18	98	4	1	.200/.259/.330	51	1.0	.317	0.2	1B 2	-0.5	100

Comparables: Trevor Story, Cody Bellinger, Willy García

Just like the rest of the Wilmington crew, Pratto struggled at the dish. A full-season under the Mendoza line at High-A isn't what you want from your 20-year-old former first rounder—even in one of the worst parks in the minors to hit—but there were some positives as well. Despite his struggles with the bat, Pratto still managed to walk at a healthy clip (just over 10%), and four of his nine homers were hit in Wilmington, where power goes to die. He's a full two-and-a-half years younger than the Carolina league average. He managed 21 doubles despite his paltry batting average. Plus, he's still stealing plenty of bases (17) despite below-average speed. If I'd not mentioned his batting average in this blurb, it would sound like a respectable season. There is something in the water in Wilmington.

Pratto might not have the highest ceiling of the first base prospects you'll come across, but despite the down year, there is still plenty to like. He has big wrists and forearms and a strong build throughout. He's calm and controlled at the plate and he sees the ball incredibly well. He doesn't take many ugly swings. He may very well develop more power, and I don't think future 6 pop is out of the question. In the past I've said that I see Pratto as Eric Hosmer 2.0, but with quality baserunning ability, and I still stand by that sentiment. Don't write off Pratto just yet—he has the tools to figure things out as he develops.

13 Seuly Matias   OF

Born: 09/04/98   Age: 21   Bats: R   Throws: R   Height: 6'3"   Weight: 198   Origin: International Free Agent, 2015

YEAR	TEAM	LVL	AGE	PA	R	2B	3B	HR	RBI	BB	K	SB	CS	AVG/OBP/SLG	DRC+	VORP	BABIP	BRR	FRAA	WARP	PF
2017	BNC	RK	18	246	27	13	3	7	36	16	72	2	1	.243/.297/.423	84	7.4	.318	0.7	RF(52) 9.0	1.0	94
2018	LEX	A	19	376	62	13	1	31	63	24	131	6	0	.231/.303/.550	97	18.8	.264	0.7	RF(75) -2.1	0.4	113
2019	WIL	A+	20	221	23	10	4	4	22	25	98	2	4	.148/.259/.307	48	-4.5	.270	-0.6	RF(51) 5.6	-0.2	92
2020	KCA	MLB	21	251	17	11	1	3	19	17	117	0	0	.156/.224/.259	23	0.0	.296	-0.3	RF 1	-1.5	100

Comparables: Miguel Sanó, Lewis Brinson, Tyler O'Neill

It has already been an odyssey with Matías and, at the risk of sounding trite, I must say that it is hard to believe that he is still only 21 years old. His first year stateside was 2017, with Burlington in the Appy League. He came in hyped and he struggled, showing only brief and rare glimpses of the promise that preceded him. The tools played in his 2018 Sally League campaign as he managed to crack over 30 homers in under 100 games, though he still continued to be plagued with approach issues and swing-and-miss tendencies. 2019 was a lost season, as he struggled horrifically in about two months of Carolina League action before going down with an injury in June. I saw him early this year and was blown away by both the potential positives and the ascendent negatives in his profile. Watching him take BP is a sight; his bat speed and natural strength produce easy plus-plus raw power to all fields, and when he makes contact it plays in game too. He's got a huge arm and plays a decent right field. Unfortunately none of this will matter if he doesn't start hitting the ball with more regularity. His swing often gets long and I saw him get tied up on fastballs in and go flailing at breaking balls down and away. His tendency toward a grooved swing is made even worse when his front foot starts bailing, and it all seems to have a tumbling effect on his confidence. The funny thing is that I actually don't think his underlying mechanics are all that bad; he has quiet hands, a soft load, and minimal stride. It might look bleak at the moment but there have been late bloomers with this sort of profile, and his alluring power potential should allow for one or two more fresh starts.

14 Kelvin Gutierrez   3B

Born: 08/28/94   Age: 25   Bats: R   Throws: R   Height: 6'3"   Weight: 215   Origin: International Free Agent, 2013

YEAR	TEAM	LVL	AGE	PA	R	2B	3B	HR	RBI	BB	K	SB	CS	AVG/OBP/SLG	DRC+	VORP	BABIP	BRR	FRAA	WARP	PF
2017	NAT	RK	22	37	6	3	1	0	1	4	7	2	0	.212/.297/.364	65	0.5	.269	0.8	3B(8) -1.1	0.0	102
2017	POT	A+	22	245	34	10	6	2	16	19	59	3	0	.288/.347/.414	121	12.5	.380	2.0	3B(57) 6.4	2.2	99
2018	HAR	AA	23	249	36	6	3	5	26	16	62	10	1	.274/.321/.391	96	9.3	.352	1.0	3B(56) 12.7, SS(1) 0.1	2.2	102
2018	NWA	AA	23	264	29	8	3	6	40	20	46	10	3	.277/.337/.409	103	9.8	.321	1.3	3B(62) -0.7, SS(2) -0.2	1.0	109
2019	OMA	AAA	24	327	41	9	2	9	43	35	71	12	1	.287/.367/.427	97	13.9	.349	2.3	3B(62) -3.3, 1B(7) -0.7	0.8	95
2019	KCA	MLB	24	79	4	2	1	1	11	5	24	1	0	.260/.304/.356	67	-0.4	.367	-0.8	3B(18) -0.1	-0.1	101
2020	KCA	MLB	25	70	6	3	0	1	7	5	19	1	0	.250/.307/.361	75	3.0	.342	0.1	3B 0, 1B -1	-0.1	100

Comparables: Erik González, Brent Morel, Zoilo Almonte

Gutiérrez got a three-week cup of coffee early in the season, but otherwise had the Kelvin Gutiérrez season in Triple-A—decent batting average, not much pop. Even the Pacific Coast League and Triple-A baseballs couldn't coax much power out of his relatively flat, contact-oriented swing. While power comes later, the unspoken qualifier to that is "if it comes at all." That leaves Gutiérrez as a bit of a square peg on a modern major league roster. He's a very good defensive third baseman, but one that hasn't really played anywhere else. His physical strength and feel for contact means should be able to hit .270 or so—although he was overly aggressive and woefully ineffective against major league breaking stuff—but there just won't be much in the way of secondary skills or defensive flexibility. On the merit of his skill set he's a 45 OFP, a fringe regular. Gutiérrez is an averagish runner so he might be able to handle an outfield corner, and he'd probably be fine at first given more reps. We just don't know, and neither do the Royals. He's already 25 and more or less is what he is.

15 Brady McConnell SS

Born: 05/24/98   Age: 22   Bats: R   Throws: R   Height: 6'3"   Weight: 195   Origin: Round 2, 2019 Draft (#44 overall)

YEAR	TEAM	LVL	AGE	PA	R	2B	3B	HR	RBI	BB	K	SB	CS	AVG/OBP/SLG	DRC+	VORP	BABIP	BRR	FRAA	WARP	PF
2019	IDA	RK+	21	169	25	12	1	4	22	14	66	5	3	.211/.286/.382	58	0.2	.341	0.5		0.0	105
2020	KCA	MLB	22	251	18	12	1	4	20	15	114	2	1	.177/.231/.280	31	0.0	.323	0.0		-1.3	100

Comparables: Brandon Hicks, Steve Tolleson, Jerry Sands

McConnell does not look like your traditional second-round college shortstop. This is a class of prospects that tend to be around 6-foot and 180 pounds, good bat-to-ball, can run a little bit, more polish than projection, and might actually be second basemen. McConnell is listed at 6-foot-3, 195 lbs, and almost all that weight is in his lats, deltoids, and traps. He's broad, projectable and a premium athlete with above-average raw power. If he does have to move off shortstop, it will likely be to third, but he has a decent shot to stick. It's a first-round frame, and he performed well for the Gators his Junior year, hitting .332 with 15 bombs. The main issue with the profile—which was the case in college, but became more obvious in the Pioneer League where he posted a 39% K-rate—is that he doesn't have much of an approach at the plate. McConnell can be a pure guess hitter at times, and it's only going to get harder to guess right in the pros. This can improve with reps to a certain extent, but McConnell is also going to be more boom-or-bust than your traditional second-round college shortstop.

16 Wilmin Candelario SS

Born: 09/11/01   Age: 18   Bats: B   Throws: R   Height: 5'11"   Weight: 165   Origin: International Free Agent, 2018

Candelario signed for 850k out of the Dominican in 2018. Most of your six-figure IFAs are going to be signed as shortstops or center fielders, no matter how likely or unlikely it is they stick up the middle as they proceed up the organizational ladder (or even by the time they head stateside). Candelario is a shortstop. That's not going to be an issue. He's a potential plus one as well, with about the smoothest hands and actions you will see. He lacks physicality at present, so he will need to add strength to avoid having the bat knocked out of his hands against better velocity. It's not a frame that's likely to add that much bulk though, which is both good and bad. He should keep the quick-twitch athleticism you need at the 6, but he is unlikely to make the kind of hard contact with lift to be much of a power threat. Then again, projecting a 17-year-old's physical development with any sort of confidence is more soothsay than science.

17 Austin Cox LHP

Born: 03/28/97   Age: 23   Bats: L   Throws: L   Height: 6'4"   Weight: 185   Origin: Round 5, 2018 Draft (#152 overall)

YEAR	TEAM	LVL	AGE	W	L	SV	G	GS	IP	H	HR	BB/9	K/9	K	GB%	BABIP	WHIP	ERA	DRA	WARP	PF
2018	BNC	RK	21	1	1	0	9	9	33¹	29	1	4.1	13.8	51	42%	.373	1.32	3.78	3.15	1.1	97
2019	LEX	A	22	5	3	0	13	13	75¹	59	5	2.6	9.2	77	42%	.262	1.08	2.75	3.86	1.2	93
2019	WIL	A+	22	3	3	0	11	10	55¹	53	6	2.6	8.5	52	34%	.318	1.25	2.77	5.23	-0.2	93
2020	KCA	MLB	23	2	2	0	33	0	35	35	5	3.6	7.8	30	37%	.292	1.40	4.73	4.79	0.2	100

Comparables: Alex Young, Eric Jokisch, Adam Conley

Cox is a fifth-rounder out of a small college, who I like more than some similar profiles with bigger names. He's a six-foot-four lefty with a solid pitcher's frame, although he's pretty well filled out and doesn't offer much in the way of projection. The fastball sits either side of 90, but he can hit 94 when he needs to. He commands the heater pretty well, especially glove-side where he uses it to get ahead against righties. He throws what looked to me like three distinct and viable breaking balls, all of which work to neutralize the platoon advantage. The strongest of them is a sharp power curve around 80 mph that flashed plus for me, with its late 1-7 action. Cox also likes to mix in a hard slider around 83-86 with almost cutter-like movement and a mid-70s 12-6 curve. These three offerings could all be lumped into an omnibus "breaking ball" category if you like, but each serves in its own purpose. The mid-80s change looked decent as well, with some split action to it. The stuff might be a bit short as he advances, but he's done well with it thus far.

18 Alec Marsh RHP

Born: 05/14/98   Age: 22   Bats: R   Throws: R   Height: 6'2"   Weight: 220   Origin: Round 2, 2019 Draft (#70 overall)

YEAR	TEAM	LVL	AGE	W	L	SV	G	GS	IP	H	HR	BB/9	K/9	K	GB%	BABIP	WHIP	ERA	DRA	WARP	PF
2019	IDA	RK+	21	0	1	0	13	13	33¹	30	5	1.1	10.3	38	46%	.294	1.02	4.05	2.73	1.2	107

Marsh on the other hand is very much your traditional second-round college pick. He's a sturdy lad who lacks much in the way of future projection and will throw four pitches for strikes, all within a half grade or so of average. He works primarily off a low-90s fastball which will flash decent sink from his high-three-quarters slot. There's two breaking balls, a slider and a curve that can smush together a bit around 80 mph, but tease out more distinctively in the mid-70s or low-80s. Both have average potential, but are more likely to end up fringy. The change is a bit crude as he has to really work to turn it over at present. Marsh has a chance to be a backend starter if he can refine the secondaries, but may lack a bat-missing option at higher levels and settle in more as a swingman or middle relief option.

19 Grant Gambrell RHP

Born: 11/21/97   Age: 22   Bats: L   Throws: R   Height: 6'4"   Weight: 225   Origin: Round 3, 2019 Draft (#80 overall)

YEAR	TEAM	LVL	AGE	W	L	SV	G	GS	IP	H	HR	BB/9	K/9	K	GB%	BABIP	WHIP	ERA	DRA	WARP	PF
2019	IDA	RK+	21	1	6	0	11	10	27	41	5	3.7	9.3	28	52%	.419	1.93	6.67	8.28	-0.6	103

Gambrell was taken ten spots after Marsh in the 2019 draft and that might overstate the gap between them as pitching prospects. Gambrell is a bit taller, but just as sturdy of frame. He will show a little more velocity at times, getting up to 95 occasionally, but his fastball was inconsistent across his junior year at Oregon State and first pro summer. His secondaries are a bit less advanced than Marsh as well, although he flashed a potentially average slider in the pros. There's some feel for the change, but it's inconsistent. Gambrell has a chance to be a backend starter if he can refine the secondaries, but may lack a bat-missing option at higher levels and settle in more as a swingman or middle relief option.

20 Richard Lovelady LHP

Born: 07/07/95   Age: 24   Bats: L   Throws: L   Height: 6'0"   Weight: 175   Origin: Round 10, 2016 Draft (#313 overall)

YEAR	TEAM	LVL	AGE	W	L	SV	G	GS	IP	H	HR	BB/9	K/9	K	GB%	BABIP	WHIP	ERA	DRA	WARP	PF
2017	WIL	A+	21	1	0	7	21	0	33¹	18	0	1.1	11.1	41	70%	.237	0.66	1.08	1.86	1.2	100
2017	NWA	AA	21	3	2	3	21	0	33¹	28	1	3.5	9.7	36	50%	.310	1.23	2.16	3.28	0.6	100
2018	OMA	AAA	22	3	3	9	46	0	73	53	3	2.6	8.8	71	51%	.262	1.01	2.47	2.32	2.3	100
2019	OMA	AAA	23	1	2	4	24	0	26¹	26	1	2.4	9.9	29	57%	.342	1.25	3.08	1.86	1.1	100
2019	KCA	MLB	23	0	3	0	25	0	20	30	2	3.6	7.7	17	53%	.412	1.90	7.65	5.62	-0.1	102
2020	KCA	MLB	24	1	1	0	11	0	11	13	2	2.8	6.5	8	50%	.306	1.43	5.07	5.01	0.0	100

Comparables: Eduardo Paredes, José Quijada, Alex Claudio

Lovelady is a 95-and-a-slider guy, but he's a lefty 95-and-a-slider guy. The stuff got worn out a bit in his first outings in las grandes ligas, as the low slot and long arm action give righties an awfully long look at the baseball, and the slider doesn't always have ideal depth to cross over. This was his first real performance blip, and several of your favorite advanced metrics suggest he was maybe a tad unlucky. There's always going to be thin margins and potential platoon issues for Lovelady, but he should get plenty more shots at a meaningful bullpen role since he's a lefty 95-and-a-slider guy.

Personal Cheeseball

PC **Michael Gigliotti OF**
Born: 02/14/96   Age: 24   Bats: L   Throws: L   Height: 6'1"   Weight: 180   Origin: Round 4, 2017 Draft (#120 overall)

YEAR	TEAM	LVL	AGE	PA	R	2B	3B	HR	RBI	BB	K	SB	CS	AVG/OBP/SLG	DRC+	VORP	BABIP	BRR	FRAA	WARP	PF
2017	BNC	RK	21	191	30	8	3	3	30	32	21	15	5	.329/.442/.477	168	27.2	.361	0.7	CF(39) -5.8	1.5	94
2017	LEX	A	21	100	14	5	1	1	8	8	20	7	5	.302/.378/.419	131	6.3	.379	0.3	CF(18) 1.7	0.8	109
2019	LEX	A	23	279	42	19	1	1	23	27	49	29	7	.309/.394/.411	148	27.8	.381	2.0	CF(59) 1.4	2.5	94
2019	WIL	A+	23	99	8	2	1	0	5	8	23	5	3	.184/.268/.230	40	-2.5	.250	1.5	CF(16) -1.6, RF(6) 1.1	-0.2	91
2020	KCA	MLB	24	251	23	12	1	3	21	21	62	9	5	.234/.307/.333	71	0.0	.310	0.4	CF 1, RF 0	0.0	100

Comparables: Taylor Motter, Adam Engel, Lane Adams

Gigliotti has been hanging around these lists for a long time for someone who has yet to accrue 100 at-bats above Low-A. He was really looking to hit his stride at the outset of the 2018 season, but a knee injury six games into the year put an end to that campaign. Gigliotti will be 24 when the 2020 season begins. As with the rest of the Blue Rocks he'll be happy to put 2019 in the rearview. All told, as a professional he is slashing a very respectable .296/.392/.407. The hit tool, speed, and glove are going to be the tools to make or break him. He is short to the ball with a flat, handsy swing, and he's one of the few players in baseball still looking to keep the ball out of the air. Only once has he hit more than one home run as a professional. He's speedy—near plus-plus—and can be expected to tame centerfield at Kauffman should he get there, as the glove won't be the question. If the hit tool doesn't do the trick, Gigliotti may not make it to Kansas City.

Low Minors Sleeper

LMS **Brewer Hicklen OF**
Born: 02/09/96   Age: 24   Bats: R   Throws: R   Height: 6'2"   Weight: 208   Origin: Round 7, 2017 Draft (#210 overall)

YEAR	TEAM	LVL	AGE	PA	R	2B	3B	HR	RBI	BB	K	SB	CS	AVG/OBP/SLG	DRC+	VORP	BABIP	BRR	FRAA	WARP	PF
2017	ROY	RK	21	82	19	3	3	3	13	9	24	13	3	.348/.439/.609	173	11.1	.488	1.4		0.8	103
2017	IDA	RK	21	99	19	8	2	1	10	9	22	3	1	.299/.384/.471	111	5.4	.391	0.4	LF(13) 0.7	0.2	117
2018	LEX	A	22	347	59	18	3	17	65	24	98	29	6	.307/.378/.552	132	26.0	.395	-0.1	LF(43) -0.9, CF(28) -2.9	1.6	109
2018	WIL	A+	22	78	11	4	0	1	3	4	26	6	0	.211/.263/.310	67	-0.4	.318	0.0	LF(13) 2.0, RF(9) 0.4	0.2	97
2019	WIL	A+	23	494	70	13	7	14	51	55	140	39	14	.263/.363/.427	132	38.3	.358	4.6	LF(64) 4.1, CF(20) -3.8	3.3	91
2020	KCA	MLB	24	251	26	11	2	7	28	16	88	11	3	.232/.296/.390	80	0.0	.342	1.2	LF 0, CF -1	0.2	100

Comparables: Corey Dickerson, Jarrett Parker, Alex Castellanos

Hicklen is an athletic guy who shows an impressive combination of plus speed and plus raw power. He committed to UAB out of high school to play both football and baseball, and he looks exactly as you'd expect a two-way commit to look, checking in at 6-foot-2 and 208-pounds. Hicklen was virtually the only Wilmington bat to put up respectable numbers last year when he slashed .263/.363/.427 while stealing an impressive 39 bags. He's a three true outcomes sort of player with a 9.2 percent walk rate and 28 percent k-rate as a professional. He'll make some really impressive plays in the outfield, but will sometimes make routine plays more challenging than they are. He has solid bat speed, but it's mostly strength-based power. He will be 24 when the 2020 season begins, and will likely be given his first crack at upper minors competition. Swing-and-miss will be the big limiting factor for Hicklen, and his 26 K's in 47 at-bats in the 2019 AFL didn't do anything to calm those concerns. Cutting down on the whiffs should be his main concern moving forward.

Top Talents 25 and Under (as of 4/1/2020)

1. Adalberto Mondesi
2. Bobby Witt Jr.
3. Brady Singer
4. Daniel Lynch
5. Kris Bubic

6. Jackson Kowar
7. Brad Keller
8. Kyle Isbel
9. Khalil Lee
10. Nicky Lopez

This is probably what a 25U list should look like for a rebuilding club: Light on big league talent while tilting heavily toward potential on the farm.

Adalberto Mondesi has been a mainstay on this list since 2013. 2013! He debuted at number six that year and, as the World Championship generation graduated off this list, moved his way to the top. It's a perch he's occupied for three consecutive seasons. And with good reason. He's an impact player with the glove and the wheels, along with plenty of potential in the bat. However, Mondesi took a step back with a 75 DRC+ in 2019 in a season that saw his power regress and his OBP dip below .300. The Royals were aggressive with his movement through the system, but even with the offensive struggles he finally feels at home at the 6 at Kauffman Stadium. Another lingering question is his durability. He played just 102 games last season and ended the year on the IL.

Following last summer's number one pick and the Class of 2018 college arms is Keller, a former Rule 5 selection from the Diamondbacks organization. (That kind of says something about the state of the Royals, doesn't it?) Keller generates a ground ball on nearly half the balls put in play against him, which in the age of defensive shifts is a very good thing. Keller also doesn't miss many bats and his 6.6 K/9 was the sixth lowest strikeout rate among qualified starters. He's been the Royals' best starter in each of the last two seasons but should slide his way further back in the rotation as the young arms ahead of him on this list arrive in Kansas City.

Lopez saw a steady diet of inside fastballs in his major league debut and struggled to adjust. A wrist injury didn't help the cause, but neither did an approach that yielded a 4.5 percent walk rate. At every stop along the way to The Show, Lopez has routinely walked in over 10 percent of his plate appearances. He's spent the winter bulking up to help the former issue. Time will tell how he will handle the latter.

It's not an especially optimistic assessment of the major league talent on this U25 list, but that's not the really aim for a rebuilding club. The future, the Royals hope, is in the development of their pitching prospects.

Eyewitness Reports

Eyewitness Report: Brady Singer

Evaluator: Ricky Conti
Report Date: 05/09/2019
Dates Seen: 5/3/2019
Risk Factor: Medium

Delivery: Starts motion with hips already closed to home. Uses a super quick delivery, with a cross over leg kick to create some momentum towards home. Collapses back side a tad. Long arm circles that come back to an inverted-W when landed, stays on line towards home well. Low-3/4 arm slot. Surprising amount of balance throughout delivery given the number of moving parts.

Pitch Type	Future Grade	Sitting Velocity	Peak Velocity	Report
Fastball	55	92-94	95	Mostly 93, topping 95. Excellent arm side run and sink, movement can be more vertical or more horizontal at times. Plus command and feel for the pitch, works to both sides of the plate with ease. Quick delivery and low arm slot helps the pitch play up. Excellent ground ball pitch, especially when down in the zone.
Slider	55	81-83	84	Super firm pitch with good albeit little two-plane break, not a big time swing-and-miss pitch, shows good command of the pitch, but not at the same level as the FB, flashes two variations of the pitch that are very subtle in their difference, both with firm, late break, but one with a bit more vertical movement. Might not be different enough to be truly different pitch.
Changeup	45	84	84	Only flashed a handful of times second time through the order. Still a developing pitch that didn't show much bite or fade at the moment.

Conclusion: Singer's strengths are well known: a track record of durability, performance in the SEC, fastball command, and ability to mix pitches. That causes the package to play up in overall projection more than you might expect from the individual pitch grades, even lacking a true plus-plus pitch. The movement and command of the fastball give him a high floor as a back-end major league starter, but an underdeveloped changeup and no swing-and-miss breaking ball will limit his reasonable upside to a no. 3 starter. An uptick in velocity isn't out of the question, as his lean 6'5" frame definitely has room to add muscle, although the touch of effort in his delivery and low-3/4 arm slot might complicate things. It's no secret that Singer is a big-time competitor with the mental strength to be a big-leaguer.

Eyewitness Report: Zach Haake

Evaluator: Keith Rader
Report Date: 09/08/2019
Dates Seen: 8/29/2019 and 9/6/2019
Risk Factor: Very High

Delivery: Tall and lanky with room to develop; long legs and arms. Poor posture--hunched forward throughout windup and delivery; wrist wrap. Inconsistent mechanics; arm slot will range between high 3/4 to 3/4 and drops more often when throwing slider. Mechanics get loose as he tires. Very quick arm; finishes delivery well. Works quickly; smooth delivery with a touch of violence at the end.

Pitch Type	Future Grade	Sitting Velocity	Peak Velocity	Report
Fastball	70	94-96	97	Explosive arm-side life with moderate sink; locates the pitch well early to both sides of plate. Elevates for K's at top end velo when needed; love the arm speed. Pitch takes a step back late in starts and from stretch. Will break a lot of RHH bats; solid command and control of pitch.
Slider	60	84-87	0	Tease; least consistent pitch in the arsenal, but nearly unhittable when right. Tight pitch that can be explosive but can also be lazy and loopy. Darting explosive break when finished well. Shape will vary even when thrown well; will get hitters whiffing in dirt when sharp.
Changeup	55	84-87	0	Will throw to hitters on either side of plate; also inconsistent, but more reliable than SL. Arm-side fade and depth when right; will make hitters look silly intermittently. Will telegraph and slow delivery periodically; commands pitch well and does a good job keeping it down.

Conclusion: Haake is raw. At present the fastball is the only reliable pitch in the arsenal, but the off-speed stuff flashes near elite at times. The future consistency of off-speed pitches will determine his ultimate role. He could end up as a solid mid-rotation piece, but could also end up in the bullpen if things don't progress well. His simple delivery should make it relatively easy to clean up his mechanical inconsistencies. He has near elite arm speed that will make for a dependable fastball regardless of his future home.

Los Angeles Angels

The State of the System

Still significantly improved compared to a couple years ago, but beyond the icon up top it remains a fairly shallow system reliant on untapped upside at the lower levels eventually bearing fruit.

The Top Ten

──────────────────── ★ ★ ★ *2020 Top 101 Prospect* **#2** ★ ★ ★ ────────────────────

1 **Jo Adell** **OF**   OFP: 70   ETA: 2020

Born: 04/08/99   Age: 21   Bats: R   Throws: R   Height: 6'3"   Weight: 215   Origin: Round 1, 2017 Draft (#10 overall)

YEAR	TEAM	LVL	AGE	PA	R	2B	3B	HR	RBI	BB	K	SB	CS	AVG/OBP/SLG	DRC+	VORP	BABIP	BRR	FRAA	WARP	PF
2017	ANG	RK	18	132	18	6	6	4	21	10	32	5	0	.288/.351/.542	117	13.4	.361	1.9		0.5	98
2017	ORM	RK	18	90	25	5	2	1	9	4	17	3	2	.376/.411/.518	133	7.3	.463	0.4		0.3	119
2018	BUR	A	19	108	23	7	1	6	29	11	26	4	1	.326/.398/.611	164	12.4	.391	1.2	CF(16) -0.4, RF(3) -0.9	1.0	107
2018	INL	A+	19	262	46	19	3	12	42	15	63	9	2	.290/.345/.546	142	21.9	.345	2.0	CF(36) -5.6, RF(8) -1.1	1.4	101
2018	MOB	AA	19	71	14	6	0	2	6	6	22	2	0	.238/.324/.429	100	4.5	.333	-0.3	CF(17) -1.9	0.0	100
2019	INL	A+	20	27	4	1	0	2	5	1	10	0	0	.280/.333/.560	115	3.0	.385	0.3	CF(3) 0.5, RF(2) -0.1	0.2	98
2019	MOB	AA	20	182	28	15	0	8	23	19	41	6	0	.308/.390/.553	168	14.6	.369	0.5	RF(19) -1.2, CF(17) -3.5	1.5	106
2019	SLC	AAA	20	132	22	11	0	0	8	10	43	1	0	.264/.321/.355	66	0.3	.410	2.5	RF(12) -0.5, LF(9) 0.6	0.0	108
2020	LAA	MLB	21	245	26	15	1	8	29	19	77	3	1	.248/.313/.426	93	0.0	.345	0.0	RF -6	-0.3	100

Comparables: Corey Seager, Ronald Acuña Jr., Austin Riley

The Report: There aren't many pages of Adell's prospect story left to read that aren't already slathered in drool, and he will enter the 2020 season perched again—for a final time—among the best couple prospects in the entire world. That he is even still eligible for this list resulted not from a lack of level-appropriate offensive prowess, but from lost developmental time after a gruesome leg injury in the spring and the negative subsequent effects that shelving allegedly had on his ability to track fly balls in a corner spot. This is a true five-tool talent, however, and those types don't wallow well or for long against Triple-A competition. He'll flank Mike Trout in Anaheim rather than supplant him in center, but the glove and speed for a theoretical up-the-middle assignment remain. The bat is now seasoned and cooked to perfection, and he'll have as much of a chance as any rookie to hit the ground hitting against the best pitchers in the game. On-base skills, power, and value-added baserunning and defense is some kind of package.

Variance: Low, at least insofar as any young player's risk factor can be discounted. Loads of talent and plenty of track record make him one of the "safer" high-end prospects around, and it would be quite a shock to the system if a healthy Adell does not go on to at least a first-division career.

Ben Carsley's Fantasy Take: *[Extremely James Blake voice]: You're beautiful. You're beautiful. You're beautiful, it's true.*

Wander Franco is a perfectly reasonable choice, but for my money, Adell is the top dynasty prospect in baseball. .300/30/100 with 20-plus steals will be within his reach some day. Treasure him.

★ ★ ★ *2020 Top 101 Prospect* **#51** ★ ★ ★

2 Brandon Marsh OF   OFP: 60   ETA: Late 2020

Born: 12/18/97   Age: 22   Bats: L   Throws: R   Height: 6'4"   Weight: 215   Origin: Round 2, 2016 Draft (#60 overall)

YEAR	TEAM	LVL	AGE	PA	R	2B	3B	HR	RBI	BB	K	SB	CS	AVG/OBP/SLG	DRC+	VORP	BABIP	BRR	FRAA	WARP	PF
2017	ORM	RK	19	192	47	13	5	4	44	9	35	10	2	.350/.396/.548	120	18.4	.417	3.2	RF(26) -1.9, CF(11) 1.5	0.7	118
2018	BUR	A	20	154	26	12	1	3	24	21	40	4	0	.295/.390/.470	139	12.2	.400	2.9	CF(14) 1.2, RF(13) -1.3	1.4	110
2018	INL	A+	20	426	59	15	6	7	46	52	118	10	4	.256/.348/.385	107	21.3	.356	4.3	CF(50) -0.8, RF(33) 3.0	2.2	99
2019	MOB	AA	21	412	48	21	2	7	43	47	92	18	5	.300/.383/.428	141	27.8	.384	2.6	CF(54) -0.7, RF(19) 1.8	2.9	105
2020	LAA	MLB	22	251	24	13	1	5	25	19	77	3	1	.246/.308/.375	81	0.0	.347	0.0	CF 0, RF 1	0.4	100

Comparables: Tyler Austin, Jordan Schafer, Brett Jackson

The Report: Selected in the second round in 2016, Marsh is an intimidating and agile athlete, standing 6-foot-4 with an extra-large frame. He missed a bunch of Double-A seasoning in 2019 due to a leg injury, but showed off his improving hit tool when healthy. His bat-to-ball skills make him a true gap-to-gap hitter, and plenty of strength lets him drive the ball with some sizzle. Once he finds a gap, his plus wheels are a sight to see. He moves very well for his size, and should remain a threat to swipe a few bags through maturity. His power tool is tracking to play about average, but there is plenty of muscle and strength that points to some potential for swing-change-induced growth with launch angle adjustments. Patrolling the outfield, Marsh can play all three spots, with plus potential in the corners. There's enough to profile as a true center fielder, but as with Adell it might not be enough to supplant Trout, and he will likely slide to right in Anaheim. That challenge will not be a problem, as he has a plus arm to keep runners at bay. Marsh has an intriguing tool set that retains some room for growth and projection. He could very well find himself in an outfield next to Trout and Adell one day.

Variance: High. As mentioned, his ability to make hard contact has been impressive of late. But with just average power, Marsh will need to max out his hit tool to be a consistent threat offensively.

Ben Carsley's Fantasy Take: For how toolsy he is and how close he is to the majors, I'm not sure why Marsh doesn't get more love in fantasy circles. Even if the power never fully materializes and he's only a 15-homer guy, Marsh has the bat and legs to serve as a well-rounded OF4. If he is able to leverage his big boy frame into more pop, we could be looking at a high-end OF3 instead. Given that he should challenge for MLB plate appearances late this year or early next, that makes Marsh a borderline top-50 dynasty prospect for me. I'm a fan, even if part of me still worries the Angels will block him by re-signing Kole Calhoun to a 12-year extension.

★ ★ ★ *2020 Top 101 Prospect* **#72** ★ ★ ★

3 Jordyn Adams OF   OFP: 60   ETA: 2021

Born: 10/18/99   Age: 20   Bats: R   Throws: R   Height: 6'2"   Weight: 180   Origin: Round 1, 2018 Draft (#17 overall)

YEAR	TEAM	LVL	AGE	PA	R	2B	3B	HR	RBI	BB	K	SB	CS	AVG/OBP/SLG	DRC+	VORP	BABIP	BRR	FRAA	WARP	PF
2018	ANG	RK	18	82	8	2	2	0	5	10	23	5	2	.243/.354/.329	84	2.3	.362	0.9	CF(14) -4.2, RF(1) 0.0	-0.2	100
2018	ORM	RK	18	40	5	4	1	0	8	4	7	0	1	.314/.375/.486	113	1.3	.379	-0.8	CF(8) 3.1	0.3	115
2019	BUR	A	19	428	52	15	2	7	31	50	94	12	5	.250/.346/.358	123	20.6	.316	2.4	CF(73) -1.2, LF(9) 2.5	2.6	103
2019	INL	A+	19	40	7	1	1	1	1	5	14	0	1	.229/.325/.400	94	2.0	.350	0.2	CF(4) 0.4, RF(2) -0.3	0.1	116
2020	LAA	MLB	20	251	23	11	1	5	24	20	76	3	1	.226/.292/.343	70	0.0	.318	-0.2	CF 0, LF 0	-0.1	100

Comparables: Trent Grisham, Joe Benson, Victor Robles

The Report: The Angels' 2018 first-round pick passed on a UNC football scholarship for professional baseball and his first full pro season went well, ending with a cup of coffee at High-A Inland Empire. Adams utilizes his exceptional athleticism to roam the outfield with plus-range, while also showing an above-average throwing arm and the direct routes and nose for the ball that you'd expect from a heavily-recruited wide receiver. His 70-grade speed is progressively adapting to the basepaths, as he found success on 16-of-22 stolen base attempts last season. Adams has shown an advanced process and approach at the plate, evidenced in his career .353 OBP and his willingness to drive the ball to all fields. After not homering in 105 at-bats in the 2018 season, Adams left the yard eight times as a 19-year-old—most of it spent in the pitcher's paradise of the Midwest League—flashing the power potential to be a middle-of-the-order, run producing bat. His defense and baserunning set a high floor, and could immediately add value to almost any ballclub. The continued progression of his bat-to-ball skills could put him on a fast-track to the big leagues.

Variance: Medium. The tools and athleticism are enticing to project, but Adams has to continue to develop at the plate to make our projection realistic.

Ben Carsley's Fantasy Take: It's always a little worrisome when the utility of the hit tool is the biggest question about a dynasty prospect, but I like the rest of Adams' game too much to be dissuaded from hyping him up here. Besides, even if it does take Adams a while to hit well at the MLB level, his speed and defense should give him a long leash. In short, I really like Adams as a potential speed-based OF3/4 in his prime, even if he gets trapped in more of a fourth outfielder role for the first year or two of his career. He's remains a top-101 dude for me.

★ ★ ★ *2020 Top 101 Prospect* **#99** ★ ★ ★

4   D'Shawn Knowles   OF   OFP: 55   ETA: 2023

Born: 01/16/01   Age: 19   Bats: B   Throws: R   Height: 6'0"   Weight: 165   Origin: International Free Agent, 2017

YEAR	TEAM	LVL	AGE	PA	R	2B	3B	HR	RBI	BB	K	SB	CS	AVG/OBP/SLG	DRC+	VORP	BABIP	BRR	FRAA	WARP	PF
2018	ANG	RK	17	130	19	4	1	1	14	15	27	7	4	.301/.385/.381	132	9.6	.384	1.1	LF(13) -3.1, CF(9) -0.5	0.4	100
2018	ORM	RK	17	123	27	9	2	4	15	13	38	2	3	.321/.398/.550	123	8.7	.463	0.3	CF(17) -1.2, RF(9) 1.8	0.4	112
2019	ORM	RK+	18	290	38	11	4	6	28	26	76	5	4	.241/.310/.387	70	2.0	.307	-0.3		0.0	107
2020	LAA	MLB	19	251	22	11	1	4	22	24	89	3	2	.210/.292/.320	65	0.0	.329	-0.4	CF 0, RF 0	-0.4	100

Comparables: Mike Trout, Anthony Santander, Juan Soto

The Report: Knowles ticks every box for me when it comes to low-low minors bats. He has a loose and lean, athletic frame that should add some good weight, but that eventuality is unlikely to sap his plus-or-better speed or affect his ability to roam in center. Everything's quick twitch, and he already has some feel for routes on the grass. The swing is a bit raw and awkward at times—especially from the right side—but there's plus bat speed and some feel for the barrel to all four quadrants. And even from his weaker side, Knowles can still rip an inside fastball. There's enough underlying athleticism and barrel feel here for me to be…well, not "comfortable," so let's go with "mildly aggressive" in projecting a plus hit tool. The plate approach is also solid given his limited pro experience. Knowles tracks spin all right, and lays off stuff east-west, although he will expand up for the fastball with two strikes.

His swing is geared more for up-the-middle line drives at present, and I don't see a ton of raw power developing long term even as he adds strength over the balance of his teens and early 20s. It might look a bit like 2019 Taylor Trammell in games—as opposed to Taylor Trammell in batting practice—in 2022 or so. And, well, I do like Taylor Trammell. I often say this product isn't a personal pref list, but this is one instance where it is. You could make stronger cases for alternative orders of 4-7 in this system I'm sure, but Knowles is my guy.

Variance: Very high. He's miles from the majors and although the underlying elements of a plus hit tool are there, he hasn't uh, hit much yet.

Ben Carsley's Fantasy Take: Man I love this system. Bret and I sneaked Knowles in at the very end of our top-101 list last season and he justified our faith by holding his own in short-season ball while continuing to display plus tools. Knowles is definitely a slow burn guy, but when in doubt, bet on the plus hit tool. He may lack Adell-ian upside, but Knowles still has all the ingredients of a well-rounded OF3. I'm happy we're somewhat out in front of him.

5   Jeremiah Jackson   SS   OFP: 55   ETA: 2022

Born: 03/26/00   Age: 20   Bats: R   Throws: R   Height: 6'0"   Weight: 165   Origin: Round 2, 2018 Draft (#57 overall)

YEAR	TEAM	LVL	AGE	PA	R	2B	3B	HR	RBI	BB	K	SB	CS	AVG/OBP/SLG	DRC+	VORP	BABIP	BRR	FRAA	WARP	PF
2018	ANG	RK	18	91	13	4	2	5	14	7	25	6	1	.317/.374/.598	147	13.9	.396	1.3	SS(21) -1.3	0.8	100
2018	ORM	RK	18	100	13	6	3	2	9	8	34	4	1	.198/.260/.396	26	-1.4	.286	-0.3	SS(21) -1.7, 2B(1) 0.0	-0.7	113
2019	ORM	RK+	19	291	47	14	2	23	60	24	96	5	1	.266/.333/.605	111	22.4	.315	1.0		1.3	108
2020	LAA	MLB	20	251	20	12	1	5	22	18	102	5	2	.182/.245/.305	42	0.0	.297	0.3	SS -1, 2B 0	-1.1	100

Comparables: Carter Kieboom, Lewis Brinson, Clint Frazier

The Report: The Angels have taken to calibrating their young hitters off an exaggerated hand hitch before introducing the lower half and hinge as their short-season schedule progresses, and Jackson struggled at times to find pitches or consistent fluidity in his swing as he worked through those adjustments. That said, when he did square pitches up they went a long way. He led the Pioneer League in homers thanks to ample lift and twitchy athleticism that lets him whip the barrel through the zone with a good amount of snap. The approach remained highly aggressive, and questionable pitch selection will be an area of needed developmental focus. The defensive future is somewhat in question as well; the jumps and reads off contact remain fairly raw at short, although there is plenty of pure athleticism and arm strength to allow him to keep developing there. The raw foot speed is solid-average and should hold as he continues to fill out a projectable frame.

Variance: High. The ceiling is exciting, but everything is still very raw, especially the hit tool. It will help our confidence in his OFP projection if the mechanics smooth out and the approach starts to show signs of needed progress next season.

Ben Carsley's Fantasy Take: If I had to pick between rolling the dice on one of the Angels' young shortstops, I'd take Jackson over Wilson without much thought. His floor might be a lot lower, sure, but he's also got a Didi Gregorius-esque upside as a power-first shortstop who does enough of everything else to fight for top-10 SS finishes. We're a long ways away from such a future of course, and unlike Gregorius, Jackson isn't a lock to stick at shortstop. But you don't have to squint *too* hard to see a really solid fantasy asset here.

6 Patrick Sandoval LHP   OFP: 55   ETA: 2019

Born: 10/18/96   Age: 23   Bats: L   Throws: L   Height: 6'3"   Weight: 190   Origin: Round 11, 2015 Draft (#319 overall)

YEAR	TEAM	LVL	AGE	W	L	SV	G	GS	IP	H	HR	BB/9	K/9	K	GB%	BABIP	WHIP	ERA	DRA	WARP	PF
2017	TCV	A-	20	1	1	0	4	4	19	19	0	2.8	13.3	28	47%	.404	1.32	3.79	3.86	0.3	98
2017	QUD	A	20	2	2	1	9	7	40	38	1	3.6	10.8	48	48%	.333	1.35	3.83	4.65	0.3	102
2018	QUD	A	21	7	1	1	14	10	65	58	4	1.5	9.8	71	48%	.305	1.06	2.49	3.25	1.4	99
2018	BCA	A+	21	2	0	1	5	3	23	12	1	1.6	10.2	26	46%	.216	0.70	2.74	2.28	0.8	86
2018	INL	A+	21	1	0	0	3	3	14²	6	0	3.7	12.9	21	47%	.200	0.82	0.00	2.30	0.5	92
2018	MOB	AA	21	1	0	0	4	4	19²	12	0	3.7	12.4	27	40%	.286	1.02	1.37	2.89	0.6	101
2019	MOB	AA	22	0	3	0	5	4	20	14	1	3.2	14.4	32	52%	.302	1.05	3.60	2.55	0.6	104
2019	SLC	AAA	22	4	4	0	15	15	60¹	84	7	5.2	9.8	66	47%	.401	1.97	6.41	6.86	-0.1	108
2019	ANA	MLB	22	0	4	0	10	9	39¹	35	6	4.3	9.6	42	50%	.287	1.37	5.03	4.35	0.6	102
2020	LAA	MLB	23	4	3	0	31	8	61	51	8	4.2	9.9	67	46%	.282	1.31	3.78	3.89	1.0	100

Comparables: Hunter Wood, Jake Faria, Mitch Keller

The Report: The Triple-A super ball combined with some ongoing command issues that carried over into a bumpy-at-times major league debut to obscure some positive developments in Sandoval's game. Most notably he refined his changeup, and the pitch played really well against hitters at all levels. A long lefty with a high slot, he's always been able to spin the ball pretty well, and the curve continued to miss bats effectively in 2019, while an occasional slider offered serviceable utility. The fastball is a limiting factor, however, with below-average movement and wandering command that too often resulted in fat pitches on a liftable plane. There's enough in the secondary arsenal here to hold out hope for a starting role, at least a nouveau-back-end one who takes you through an order one to two times, but Sandoval will need additional refinement with the hard stuff to get there. Barring a significant overhaul of the Angels depth chart this winter, he should enter the season comfortably in the mix for early-season starts.

Variance: Medium. He's big-league ready and has the tools to compile solid innings and provide 25-man value in the coming season.

Ben Carsley's Fantasy Take: Well, Sandoval isn't very exciting, but at least he's ready to contribute now. I'd worry less about his dynasty value and more about his ability to provide you with some quality innings now if you're in a very deep league. But again, you should be able to replace Sandoval's production with a bunch of dudes on waivers, so don't hesitate to drop him if a more exciting option comes your way or if you're rebuilding.

7 Kyren Paris SS   OFP: 50   ETA: ??

Born: 11/11/01   Age: 18   Bats: R   Throws: R   Height: 6'0"   Weight: 165   Origin: Round 2, 2019 Draft (#55 overall)

YEAR	TEAM	LVL	AGE	PA	R	2B	3B	HR	RBI	BB	K	SB	CS	AVG/OBP/SLG	DRC+	VORP	BABIP	BRR	FRAA	WARP	PF
2020	LAA	MLB	18	251	21	11	1	3	21	23	95	3	1	.208/.288/.306	61	0.0	.344	0.0	SS 0	-0.4	100

Comparables: Nomar Mazara, Engel Beltre, Juan Lagares

The Report: The Angels plucked Paris 55th overall last summer and signed him to a marginally over-slot deal to buy him out of a Cal commitment. He's extremely young, and the physicality remains quite raw, with happy feet at short and an unorthodox swing that doesn't really engage his lower half yet. The athleticism and projection are both notable, however, and he shows outstanding quickness and strong agility on the dirt. The throwing motion is higher-effort, but there's solid velocity already and he should grow into enough to keep him on the left side of the infield.

Paris shows an advanced and patient approach at the plate, and quick wrists help him spray the ball line to line. There's very little ability at present to drive anything with loft, though expected physical gains should result in at least some raw power developing down the line. It's a sum-of-parts profile with value tied to his ability to actualize his physical tools at the six.

Variance: Extreme. Paris was one of the youngest players selected in last summer's draft, and he logged all of 10 plate appearances in the AZL after signing. The package remains highly theoretical at this point, with a significant gap between present and future physicality.

Ben Carsley's Fantasy Take: A total lottery ticket, but one where the payout is like $50 instead of just $2, at least. Honestly, Paris is the type of way-too-far-away, uber-risky prospect who I think is overvalued in dynasty leagues at present, but if you like him in particular for any reason, you need to get in soon. Such is life in dynasty leagues in 2019.

8 Jose Soriano RHP OFP: 50 ETA: 2021/22
Born: 10/20/98 Age: 21 Bats: R Throws: R Height: 6'3" Weight: 168 Origin: International Free Agent, 2016

YEAR	TEAM	LVL	AGE	W	L	SV	G	GS	IP	H	HR	BB/9	K/9	K	GB%	BABIP	WHIP	ERA	DRA	WARP	PF
2017	ANG	RK	18	2	2	0	12	10	49	43	2	2.6	6.8	37	57%	.281	1.16	2.94	3.50	1.3	96
2018	BUR	A	19	1	6	0	14	14	46¹	34	1	6.8	8.2	42	45%	.284	1.49	4.47	5.22	0.0	109
2019	BUR	A	20	5	6	0	17	15	77²	53	5	5.6	9.7	84	55%	.261	1.30	2.55	4.40	0.7	103
2020	LAA	MLB	21	2	2	0	33	0	35	34	5	4.3	7.9	31	47%	.291	1.46	4.85	4.87	0.1	100

Comparables: Chris Archer, Joel Payamps, Chris Flexen

The Report: Soriano's big boy body has started to grind into being, as his thicker lower and middle sections have filled out considerably and his shoulders have started to carry some adult muscle. He remains somewhat floppy in his movements, though, and has a ways to go in growing into comfort with, and command of, the frame. The delivery's cadence is correspondingly raw, with a noticeably quickened, up-tempo motion producing inconsistent timing and release points that lead to wandering command. The raw stuff is impressive: a mid-90s fastball with some life and finish, combined with a sharp upper-70s curve and signs of changeup utility. The arm is pretty free and easy, and there's some elastic athleticism that lends hope that he can eventually shape it all into a workable starter's mix with enough command. And if he can't, a synced, mature fastball should be able to climb to the top of the double digits and play nicely with an equally amped hook out of the pen.

Variance: High. There's a long path ahead and a lot of maturation to come. The OFP remains firmly in the theoretical stage of things.

Ben Carsley's Fantasy Take: I feel personally attacked by the first two sentences of Soriano's writeup. Unfortunately, the rest doesn't move the needle for me much in terms of dynasty value.

9 Orlando Martinez SS OFP: 50 ETA: 2021
Born: 02/17/98 Age: 22 Bats: L Throws: L Height: 6'0" Weight: 185 Origin: International Free Agent, 2017

YEAR	TEAM	LVL	AGE	PA	R	2B	3B	HR	RBI	BB	K	SB	CS	AVG/OBP/SLG	DRC+	VORP	BABIP	BRR	FRAA	WARP	PF
2018	ORM	RK	20	53	11	5	0	2	10	4	9	3	2	.375/.415/.604	144	6.7	.421	1.0	LF(9) -1.0, RF(1) -0.1	0.2	114
2018	BUR	A	20	238	27	12	1	3	25	17	56	6	5	.289/.340/.394	107	2.9	.373	-1.2	RF(20) 1.9, LF(18) -1.0	0.7	110
2019	INL	A+	21	422	55	21	4	12	49	36	79	5	4	.263/.325/.434	111	20.7	.299	1.4	CF(41) 3.4, LF(20) 1.6	1.9	100
2020	LAA	MLB	22	251	24	13	1	7	27	15	65	3	2	.236/.286/.385	77	0.0	.298	-0.3	CF 2, LF 0	0.3	100

Comparables: Rafael Ortega, Raimel Tapia, Destin Hood

The Report: The 21-year-old Cuban outfielder missed seven weeks due to injury this season, but still managed to put up 47 extra-base hits in his 88 games played. The 6-foot, 185-pound Martinez is an above-average athlete with good body control and a solid physique. Offensively, he utilizes a gap-to-gap approach and generates a high rate of hard contact. There's some pop in the bat, primarily to right-center field, although he did take top left-handed pitching prospect MacKenzie Gore deep to the opposite field earlier this season. Martinez runs well and is capable of stealing a base, but is not a prolific thief. His advanced baseball instincts and feel for the game ensure astute defensive reads, efficient routes to the ball, and an accurate throwing arm, making him a good defender at all three outfield positions. Martinez is an all-around ballplayer, capable of contributing to the team in a variety of ways. He could be an everyday player, or a valuable fourth outfielder/pinch hitter off the bench.

Variance: Medium. Martinez's defensive versatility and all-around game should allow him to contribute to most ball clubs. It may not be easy to find a starting role initially, especially in a crowded outfield, but the quality of Martinez's contributions should warrant a spot on most rosters, and there's potential for a major-league regular with opportunity.

Ben Carsley's Fantasy Take: Martinez is worth keeping an eye on as he climbs the MiLB ladder, but given the borderline fourth OF profile and how much organizational talent sits in front of him in Orange County, he's best left on watch lists for now.

10 Oliver Ortega RHP   OFP: 50   ETA: 2021

Born: 10/02/96 Age: 23 Bats: R Throws: R Height: 6'0" Weight: 165 Origin: International Free Agent, 2015

YEAR	TEAM	LVL	AGE	W	L	SV	G	GS	IP	H	HR	BB/9	K/9	K	GB%	BABIP	WHIP	ERA	DRA	WARP	PF
2018	BUR	A	21	4	5	0	19	18	82	64	6	4.5	9.4	86	34%	.275	1.28	3.51	3.71	1.4	110
2019	INL	A+	22	4	5	2	21	16	94¹	67	8	4.7	11.5	121	44%	.277	1.23	3.34	3.43	1.7	98
2019	MOB	AA	22	0	3	0	5	5	16²	23	0	4.3	7.6	14	51%	.390	1.86	8.64	6.73	-0.4	108
2020	LAA	MLB	23	2	2	0	33	0	35	34	5	3.9	8.9	35	44%	.301	1.41	4.58	4.66	0.2	100

Signed by the Angels in 2015, the 6-foot tall, 165-pound Dominican is a quick-twitch athlete with a live right-arm and a max-effort delivery. Ortega pitches confidently, attacking the zone with a power mid-90s fastball, an 11-5 power curveball either side of 80, and a seldom-used but effective low-to-mid-80s changeup. Ortega racked up 121 strikeouts while registering a 3.34 ERA in 94 1/3 innings in the Cal League in 2019. Control can be an issue for the right-hander, as his 49 walks issued detracted from his sparkling .198 opponents batting average. Armed with a power repertoire that can be utilized as a starter, middle reliever, or as a high-leverage fireman, Ortega should be able to work his way to the big leagues if he can command his potent offerings more consistently.

The Next Ten

11 Jahmai Jones 2B

Born: 08/04/97 Age: 22 Bats: R Throws: R Height: 5'11" Weight: 205 Origin: Round 2, 2015 Draft (#70 overall)

YEAR	TEAM	LVL	AGE	PA	R	2B	3B	HR	RBI	BB	K	SB	CS	AVG/OBP/SLG	DRC+	VORP	BABIP	BRR	FRAA	WARP	PF
2017	BUR	A	19	387	54	18	4	9	30	32	63	18	7	.272/.338/.425	115	27.5	.309	5.7	CF(65) -3.4, LF(16) 0.5	2.1	101
2017	INL	A+	19	191	32	11	3	5	17	13	43	9	6	.302/.368/.488	124	17.9	.379	2.0	CF(37) -9.7, LF(3) -0.5	0.2	103
2018	INL	A+	20	347	47	10	5	8	35	43	63	13	3	.235/.338/.383	111	12.6	.272	1.5	2B(70) -6.9	0.8	100
2018	MOB	AA	20	212	33	10	4	2	20	24	51	11	1	.245/.335/.375	104	5.7	.323	-1.5	2B(45) -1.7	0.4	101
2019	MOB	AA	21	544	66	22	3	5	50	50	109	9	11	.234/.308/.324	79	2.8	.288	2.3	2B(108) 14.4, CF(7) 0.3	2.3	105
2020	LAA	MLB	22	251	24	12	1	5	25	19	62	6	2	.228/.292/.362	72	2.0	.290	0.0	2B 1, CF -2	-0.1	100

Comparables: Victor Robles, Cole Tucker, Billy McKinney

It was a tough year for Jones, who struggled to produce or advance his skills in a full-season stint at Double-A. He remains an impressive pure athlete with strength and some quick-burst into fluid movement patterns, but none of it has really translated to baseball skills as of yet in spite of a renowned work ethic. The organization has fiddled with his swing several times, but the most recent fruits of those labors have all been stiff and lacking for the kind of quickness or plane to juice his all-too-rare barrelled balls. The approach is okay, but the hit tool remains lagging and he struggles to maximize bat speed or attack hittable pitches the way he needs to. His play at the keystone hasn't progressed as hoped, either, with actions that haven't yet morphed into more natural or nuanced play. Jones still deserves a "he's only 22" pass on some of this, but the lack of progress in refining it all into a coherent MLB-quality package at this point is starting to get concerning.

12 Trent Deveaux OF

Born: 05/04/00 Age: 20 Bats: R Throws: R Height: 6'0" Weight: 160 Origin: International Free Agent, 2017

YEAR	TEAM	LVL	AGE	PA	R	2B	3B	HR	RBI	BB	K	SB	CS	AVG/OBP/SLG	DRC+	VORP	BABIP	BRR	FRAA	WARP	PF
2018	ANG	RK	18	194	20	5	0	1	11	24	68	7	4	.199/.309/.247	67	-1.5	.327	1.4	CF(26) -6.1, RF(14) -0.3	-0.4	100
2019	ANG	RK	19	244	38	15	4	6	23	24	76	14	6	.247/.332/.437	105	13.6	.351	0.3	CF(28) -5.0, LF(14) 0.1	0.4	102
2019	ORM	RK+	19	31	4	1	0	1	2	2	15	1	0	.172/.226/.310	29	-1.7	.308	0.1		-0.1	107
2020	LAA	MLB	20	251	20	12	1	4	22	19	108	2	1	.193/.260/.308	48	0.0	.340	0.0	CF -2, RF 0	-1.0	100

Comparables: Brett Phillips, Aristides Aquino, Derrick Robinson

This list is peppered with high-end athletes and Deveaux might be the best of the lot. The frame reminds me of high school Jo Adell and he was an Olympic-caliber sprinter prospect in the Bahamas. It's a body to dream on and there's some bat speed here as well. But if you thought Jeremiah Jackson had an exaggerated hitch, well, Deveaux has to churn an entire crock of creamery butter during his hand path. It's a long load, and it often leaves him late on hard stuff that isn't center cut and he's unable to adjust to offspeed. The overall baseball profile is rawer than Jackson and Knowles too, and the speed plays down in the outfield at present. The bat control isn't hopeless despite the multiple exaggerated timing mechanisms—there's a Jo Adellish leg kick in the mix too—so I'm going to give Deveaux a long leash as we are entering the part of this list that lacks much in the way of upside. But the low end of the extreme variance here is "never gets out of A-ball."

13 Leonardo Rivas SS

Born: 10/10/97 Age: 22 Bats: B Throws: R Height: 5'10" Weight: 150 Origin: International Free Agent, 2014

YEAR	TEAM	LVL	AGE	PA	R	2B	3B	HR	RBI	BB	K	SB	CS	AVG/OBP/SLG	DRC+	VORP	BABIP	BRR	FRAA	WARP	PF
2017	ORM	RK	19	183	37	6	4	2	29	39	22	11	0	.299/.462/.445	144	19.8	.339	1.7	SS(28) 3.3, 2B(8) -0.2	1.6	115
2017	BUR	A	19	116	24	5	0	0	7	20	22	8	1	.267/.412/.322	131	12.7	.348	2.8	SS(21) 1.7, 2B(4) -0.2	1.3	99
2018	BUR	A	20	547	62	16	7	4	34	84	138	16	10	.233/.355/.326	107	16.1	.325	-0.3	SS(92) 4.6, 2B(26) 1.1	3.1	108
2019	ANG	RK	21	25	6	0	0	0	0	8	4	1	0	.063/.375/.063	109	0.3	.083	0.9	SS(6) -0.2	0.2	105
2019	INL	A+	21	338	44	14	5	6	26	39	90	4	2	.236/.328/.377	101	16.0	.318	0.3	SS(46) 1.0, CF(9) 0.4	1.3	97
2020	LAA	MLB	22	251	23	11	2	4	23	27	77	6	3	.212/.304/.332	71	0.0	.306	0.0	SS 1, 2B 0	0.0	100

Listed at 5-foot-10 and 150 pounds, the 22-year-old infielder doesn't possess much power, but that appears to be Rivas' only weakness in an otherwise solid all-around skill set. A strong arm, soft hands, and good range make him a potential plus defender in the middle of the infield, and he was also impressive in nine starts in center field this season, adding defensive versatility to his resume. The switch-hitting infielder from Venezuela was limited to 73 games due to injury, but managed to post an average offensive effort while young for High-A.

For the second consecutive season, Rivas has performed drastically differently from each side of the plate. Whereas the right-handed swing is quick and compact, he whiffs on far too many pitches in the zone from the other side of the plate. As skilled as Rivas is defensively, hitting from the right side full-time may help focus that development and expedite his progress toward the major leagues.

14 Jared Walsh 1B/LHP

Born: 07/30/93 Age: 26 Bats: L Throws: L Height: 6'0" Weight: 210 Origin: Round 39, 2015 Draft (#1185 overall)

YEAR	TEAM	LVL	AGE	PA	R	2B	3B	HR	RBI	BB	K	SB	CS	AVG/OBP/SLG	DRC+	VORP	BABIP	BRR	FRAA	WARP	PF
2017	INL	A+	23	306	43	29	1	8	52	26	72	1	0	.331/.395/.531	157	20.5	.423	-1.9	1B(51) 1.5, RF(12) -1.7	2.0	105
2017	MOB	AA	23	74	7	3	0	3	9	3	29	1	0	.232/.274/.406	76	-0.5	.351	-0.7	1B(18) -1.1, RF(1) -0.1	-0.3	93
2018	INL	A+	24	178	28	8	1	13	36	24	50	0	1	.275/.365/.604	166	15.3	.308	-0.6	1B(26) 0.3, RF(5) 0.7	1.4	98
2018	MOB	AA	24	173	26	13	0	8	26	21	48	1	0	.289/.382/.537	132	9.6	.372	-0.8	1B(37) 2.0, P(2) 0.0	0.9	101
2018	SLC	AAA	24	198	32	13	0	8	37	16	56	0	0	.270/.333/.478	114	7.1	.345	1.8	RF(27) -5.7, LF(14) -1.7	0.2	117
2019	SLC	AAA	25	454	90	30	0	36	86	59	115	0	0	.325/.423/.686	145	45.4	.374	0.7	1B(58) 4.6, P(12) 0.5	3.6	110
2019	ANA	MLB	25	87	6	5	1	1	5	6	35	0	0	.203/.276/.329	59	-3.3	.349	-0.2		-0.3	99
2020	LAA	MLB	26	35	4	2	0	2	5	3	11	0	0	.237/.310/.454	97	1.0	.308	-0.1	1B 0	0.1	100

Comparables: Harry Agganis, Trey Mancini, Dale Long

YEAR	TEAM	LVL	AGE	W	L	SV	G	GS	IP	H	HR	BB/9	K/9	K	GB%	BABIP	WHIP	ERA	DRA	WARP	PF
2019	SLC	AAA	25	1	0	1	13	0	13	16	0	3.5	6.2	9	68%	.364	1.62	4.15	3.97	0.3	100
2019	ANA	MLB	25	0	0	0	5	0	5	3	0	10.8	9.0	5	83%	.250	1.80	1.80	5.28	0.0	96

Walsh plays both ways, baby, and he rode that two-way street right on up to the big leagues last year, which already constitutes an 80-grade effort for a guy drafted 1,185th overall. Walsh's strength and plus raw power have been interesting for a while now, particularly once he started bringing it into games against better competition in 2018. He continued the power onslaught with the goofy ball at Triple-A last year, though major league arms ate his lunch across his sporadic at-bats against the best of the best. The swing is fluid in spite of stiffness, but a deficit of bat speed fed his destruction by premium velocity in The Show. Given time to adjust, there's enough baseline of bat-to-ball and approach to warrant controlled optimism that he can hit some dingers while offering first base/corner outfield versatility.

That's mildly interesting on its own but he also just so happens to spin it pretty good off the bump. His hook plays well off a low-90s fastball that features quality sink from the left side. He's still expectedly raw as far as mechanical consistency goes, though the delivery is simple enough that he retains some command projection. If he hits enough to offer bench depth on that side of the ball there's a nice little bit of value to be found in his 26th-man profile.

15 Chris Rodriguez   RHP

Born: 07/20/98   Age: 21   Bats: R   Throws: R   Height: 6'2"   Weight: 185   Origin: Round 4, 2016 Draft (#126 overall)

YEAR	TEAM	LVL	AGE	W	L	SV	G	GS	IP	H	HR	BB/9	K/9	K	GB%	BABIP	WHIP	ERA	DRA	WARP	PF
2017	ORM	RK	18	4	1	0	8	8	32¹	35	1	1.9	8.9	32	46%	.343	1.30	6.40	2.86	1.1	115
2017	BUR	A	18	1	2	0	6	6	24²	32	1	2.6	8.8	24	54%	.403	1.58	5.84	6.09	-0.2	99
2019	INL	A+	20	0	0	0	3	3	9¹	6	0	3.9	12.5	13	68%	.316	1.07	0.00	3.14	0.2	91
2020	LAA	MLB	21	2	2	0	33	0	35	34	5	3.6	9.1	35	48%	.304	1.38	4.57	4.68	0.2	100

Comparables: Julio Teheran, Lucas Giolito, Aaron Sanchez

The Floridian fireballer was drafted out of high school by the Angels in the fourth round of the 2016 Draft, and after showing an intriguing four-pitch mix in the low minors he missed the entire 2018 season with a back injury. The 20-year-old made his 2019 debut at Inland Empire and again showcased the same electric four-pitch arsenal seemingly no worse for the wear. The stuff is headlined by a mid-90s heater that moves well in two directions. He also throws a nasty, hard slider, along with both a changeup in the mid 80s and a solid 11-to-5 curveball that'll both flash as above-average offerings. In three Cal League appearances Rodriguez whiffed a bunch of guys and stayed off barrels effectively, but unfortunately his back issues resurfaced and the young righty underwent a procedure that prematurely ended his 2019 campaign. Rodriguez's talent is apparent, as he's demonstrated big-league ability when healthy enough to take the mound. The Angels will certainly hope to get him back on the field and working again towards that OFP in 2020.

16 Luis Madero   RHP

Born: 04/15/97   Age: 23   Bats: R   Throws: R   Height: 6'3"   Weight: 185   Origin: International Free Agent, 2013

YEAR	TEAM	LVL	AGE	W	L	SV	G	GS	IP	H	HR	BB/9	K/9	K	GB%	BABIP	WHIP	ERA	DRA	WARP	PF
2017	MSO	RK	20	3	1	0	5	5	29¹	29	3	1.8	8.6	28	41%	.310	1.19	3.99	3.31	0.9	110
2017	YAK	A-	20	1	1	0	4	4	19²	28	2	2.3	7.8	17	51%	.377	1.68	8.24	6.67	-0.3	100
2017	BUR	A	20	1	2	0	6	6	26²	42	3	3.0	6.1	18	44%	.398	1.91	7.76	8.31	-0.9	100
2018	BUR	A	21	2	7	0	14	14	61¹	69	5	2.2	7.2	49	46%	.332	1.37	4.26	5.81	-0.4	108
2018	INL	A+	21	2	1	0	9	9	44¹	41	3	2.4	9.3	46	40%	.314	1.20	2.44	4.86	0.2	91
2019	INL	A+	22	1	0	0	4	3	16	15	0	3.9	12.9	23	40%	.395	1.38	1.12	4.98	0.0	94
2019	MOB	AA	22	5	11	0	20	19	89²	117	11	2.4	7.5	75	49%	.362	1.57	5.72	6.41	-1.6	106
2020	LAA	MLB	23	2	2	0	33	0	35	35	6	3.5	6.7	26	45%	.278	1.38	4.65	4.82	0.1	100

Comparables: Myles Jaye, Felix Jorge, Keury Mella

The 22-year-old Venezuelan began the 2019 season in the California League but needed just four appearances to earn a promotion to Double-A. The 6-foot-3 Madero pairs quick-twitch athleticism with a low-three-quarters arm slot, attacking hitters with a 92-93 mph fastball, a slurvy 80 mph breaking ball that darts across the strike zone, and a developing mid-80s changeup. His delivery, which includes a waist-high leg kick, can get long, and that leads to occasionally inconsistent command. After posting a 3.79 ERA and limiting opponents to a .253 batting average in his initial 40 1/3 Southern League innings pitched, hitters figured him out in the second half and the performance hit a wall. The righty's three-pitch attack may ultimately be best suited for the bullpen, where his versatility and durability could allow him to pitch multiple innings per appearance and contribute valuable depth across a 162-game season.

17 Hector Yan   LHP

Born: 04/26/99   Age: 21   Bats: L   Throws: L   Height: 5'11"   Weight: 180   Origin: International Free Agent, 2015

YEAR	TEAM	LVL	AGE	W	L	SV	G	GS	IP	H	HR	BB/9	K/9	K	GB%	BABIP	WHIP	ERA	DRA	WARP	PF
2017	ANG	RK	18	0	1	1	10	5	16¹	10	0	6.1	11.6	21	37%	.286	1.29	4.96	2.88	0.5	94
2018	ORM	RK	19	0	4	0	10	10	29²	29	3	6.1	8.8	29	47%	.342	1.65	4.55	5.56	0.2	112
2019	BUR	A	20	4	5	1	26	20	109	74	5	4.3	12.2	148	41%	.298	1.16	3.39	3.76	1.7	103
2020	LAA	MLB	21	2	2	0	33	0	35	36	5	4.0	10.0	39	38%	.323	1.46	5.11	5.09	0.0	100

Comparables: Huascar Ynoa, Randy Rosario, Akeel Morris

Signed out of the Dominican in 2015, Yan made his full-season debut at Burlington and promptly led the Midwest League in K% as one of the younger arms in the league. Unfortunately, he also came close to leading the circuit in walk rate, and that's where our plot thickens. A shorter, physically maxed southpaw, Yan's raw stuff is highly intriguing: a mid-90s fastball that'll top at 97, a biting slider that can take hitters out of the zone, and a hard splitter that offers utility as a second chase pitch. To get the stuff to play against better hitters, however, he'll have to overcome an unorthodox delivery with a low, sweeping leg kick and extreme crossfire; neither the control nor command currently project to approach average. The stuff is good enough that with standard refinement he can get very good hitters out, but absent a jump in command projection a useful if frustrating middle relief track is the one he's on.

18 Nathan Bates   RHP

Born: 03/01/94   Age: 26   Bats: R   Throws: R   Height: 6'6"   Weight: 205   Origin: Round 15, 2015 Draft (#465 overall)

YEAR	TEAM	LVL	AGE	W	L	SV	G	GS	IP	H	HR	BB/9	K/9	K	GB%	BABIP	WHIP	ERA	DRA	WARP	PF
2017	BUR	A	23	0	1	1	8	0	13¹	9	0	4.1	12.1	18	64%	.290	1.12	2.03	3.33	0.2	100
2017	INL	A+	23	0	5	7	33	0	51	65	5	3.9	10.2	58	49%	.403	1.71	6.53	6.20	-0.8	100
2019	INL	A+	25	0	0	0	8	1	10¹	5	0	4.4	13.9	16	59%	.227	0.97	2.61	3.69	0.1	94
2020	LAA	MLB	26	2	2	0	33	0	35	34	5	3.6	9.6	37	42%	.311	1.38	4.51	4.65	0.2	100

The 6-foot-6 right-hander has the look of a major leaguer when he toes the rubber and fires his mid-90s fastball and hard curve from a high three-quarters slot. The "when he toes the rubber" part is the lede, however; Bates has been limited to just 108 1/3 innings in the five years since the Angels popped him in the 15th round on account of both injury and suspension. He looked good in eight late-season appearances for Inland Empire in 2019, and if he can stay healthy and on the field going forward, the hard-throwing Bates could become a valuable one- or two-inning reliever out of the bullpen.

19 Livan Soto   SS

Born: 06/22/00   Age: 20   Bats: L   Throws: R   Height: 6'0"   Weight: 160   Origin: International Free Agent, 2017

YEAR	TEAM	LVL	AGE	PA	R	2B	3B	HR	RBI	BB	K	SB	CS	AVG/OBP/SLG	DRC+	VORP	BABIP	BRR	FRAA	WARP	PF
2017	BRA	RK	17	208	24	5	0	0	14	27	26	7	3	.225/.332/.254	101	6.4	.260	1.2	SS(44) -3.1, 2B(3) -0.9	0.7	102
2018	ORM	RK	18	200	31	10	0	0	11	24	24	9	3	.291/.385/.349	110	8.3	.336	1.6	SS(28) 2.7, 2B(18) -1.1	0.8	111
2019	ANG	RK	19	29	4	2	0	0	1	1	4	0	2	.214/.241/.286	87	0.2	.250	0.2	2B(4) 0.0, SS(3) 0.0	0.1	102
2019	BUR	A	19	282	24	5	0	1	20	32	40	6	2	.220/.311/.253	82	-0.9	.257	-0.6	SS(45) -3.0, 2B(15) -1.5	-0.1	102
2020	LAA	MLB	20	251	22	10	0	3	21	22	50	2	1	.223/.294/.315	63	0.0	.271	-0.4	SS -2, 2B -1	-0.6	100

Comparables: Luis Guillorme, Abiatal Avelino, Engelb Vielma

One of the prospects caught up in the Braves' international signing scandal a few years back, Soto signed a contract with Anaheim for $850k two winters ago and made his way to the Midwest League this year on the back of a solid defensive starter kit at the six. The arm is plenty for the left side, and his lateral movement is the low and quick kind that lends to quality range. He's started filling out his 6-foot frame, but rounded shoulders don't suggest a ton of brute strength development is forthcoming, and there is no power at all in the offensive game. A quick load and flat bat at launch produce minimal plane on his swings, though he has shown quality strike zone awareness and his quick stroke produces a lot of contact. There are some pieces to build with here, though he lacks sufficient straight-line speed to make the offensive profile work as a slap-and-dasher.

20 Michael Hermosillo OF

Born: 01/17/95   Age: 25   Bats: R   Throws: R   Height: 6'0"   Weight: 205   Origin: Round 28, 2013 Draft (#847 overall)

YEAR	TEAM	LVL	AGE	PA	R	2B	3B	HR	RBI	BB	K	SB	CS	AVG/OBP/SLG	DRC+	VORP	BABIP	BRR	FRAA	WARP	PF
2017	INL	A+	22	64	5	6	0	0	2	9	15	5	2	.321/.438/.434	161	4.3	.447	-1.3	CF(9) -2.3, LF(3) -0.3	0.2	97
2017	MOB	AA	22	340	40	13	2	4	26	40	73	21	9	.248/.361/.353	119	14.5	.316	-2.0	CF(52) -2.3, RF(13) 2.3	1.5	94
2017	SLC	AAA	22	129	20	6	1	5	16	7	28	9	2	.287/.341/.487	91	5.7	.337	0.3	LF(14) -0.1, CF(10) 0.6	0.4	103
2018	SLC	AAA	23	323	43	14	4	12	46	30	87	10	5	.267/.357/.480	91	11.6	.341	-0.4	CF(36) 5.5, RF(19) 0.3	1.4	121
2018	ANA	MLB	23	62	7	4	0	1	1	3	17	0	1	.211/.274/.333	61	-1.3	.282	-0.5		0.1	100
2019	SLC	AAA	24	296	51	8	3	15	43	26	88	6	4	.243/.331/.471	72	11.1	.304	0.4	CF(40) 3.4, RF(11) -0.3	0.4	107
2019	ANA	MLB	24	46	7	1	1	0	3	5	19	2	0	.139/.304/.222	62	-0.9	.278	0.8		0.0	100
2020	LAA	MLB	25	210	21	9	1	5	21	17	67	6	3	.214/.297/.351	72	0.0	.302	0.0	CF 0, LF 0	0.0	100

Comparables: Mallex Smith, Brandon Nimmo, Billy McKinney

So it's going to be hard to finagle playing time in the Angels outfield in the coming years. Hermosillo has struggled to capitalize on his 2017 breakout year, dealing with injuries the past two seasons. His recovery from sports hernia surgery cost him the first two months of 2019, and while he's continued to hit in Triple-A, his brief MLB cameos haven't gone well. The hit tool was the big question as a prospect, and Hermosillo has struggled with offspeed in the majors and can't always catch up to better velocity. He's strong enough to do damage when he does connect and is a plus runner that can handle all three outfield spots, so if he refines some stuff with more MLB reps, there's a perfectly fine bench outfielder here. It's going to be tough to get those reps, although I suppose even Mike Trout needs a day off now and again.

Personal Cheeseball

PC Gareth Morgan OF

Born: 04/12/96   Age: 24   Bats: R   Throws: R   Height: 6'4"   Weight: 265   Origin: Round 2, 2014 Draft (#74 overall)

YEAR	TEAM	LVL	AGE	PA	R	2B	3B	HR	RBI	BB	K	SB	CS	AVG/OBP/SLG	DRC+	VORP	BABIP	BRR	FRAA	WARP	PF
2017	CLN	A	21	462	55	21	3	17	61	53	185	14	5	.230/.320/.422	98	17.4	.371	2.7	RF(82) 13.4, LF(28) -0.8	2.4	99
2018	MOD	A+	22	334	42	7	2	19	39	30	180	7	1	.158/.249/.386	62	-2.5	.283	1.2	CF(31) 0.1, LF(29) -3.4	-0.3	98
2019	MOD	A+	23	32	2	0	0	1	3	5	20	1	0	.074/.219/.185	103	-2.3	.167	0.1	LF(1) -0.1	0.1	114
2019	INL	A+	23	196	32	5	0	20	49	9	95	0	1	.290/.327/.645	118	18.0	.471	0.3	RF(18) -0.2, LF(12) -1.7	0.5	101
2019	MOB	AA	23	116	5	3	0	1	10	8	55	1	1	.206/.267/.262	17	-8.5	.412	-1.0	RF(22) -3.2, LF(2) -0.4	-1.2	106
2020	LAA	MLB	24	251	28	10	1	13	35	14	137	2	1	.208/.257/.424	71	0.0	.422	0.0	RF 0, LF -1	-0.1	100

Morgan's displays of immense raw power as a Canadian prep enamored the Mariners enough to select him with the 74th-overall pick in the 2014 Draft. After struggling to develop offensively, including striking out 180+ times in the 2017 and 2018 seasons, the Mariners released Morgan eight games into the 2019 season. The Angels quickly signed him and sent him to their own Cal League affiliate in Inland Empire, where the change of scenery energized Morgan into a power surge as he hit .290 with 20 home runs in his first 44 games in the Angels organization. After earning a promotion to Double-A, the advanced pitching stymied the big fella, as he homered only once while striking out 55 times in 27 games at the higher level. Listed at 6-foot-4 and 265 pounds, Morgan is somewhat shockingly mobile on the basepaths and even demonstrates okay athleticism in the outfield (he managed to log 11 games of center field reps this season). Although he's adequate in the field, this is a brawny, old school DHing slugger profile. With continued development of his bat-to-ball abilities, Morgan could be a fun power bat with a best-case scenario looking not unlike Franmil Reyes.

Low Minors Sleeper

LMS Alexander Ramirez OF

Born: 08/29/02   Age: 17   Bats: R   Throws: R   Height: 6'2"   Weight: 180   Origin: International Free Agent, 2018

Ramirez was a seven-figure J2 signing as one of the younger high-end prospects in the 2018 IFA class, and at the time of his signing listed out at 6-foot-1 and 180 pounds. That's as a 16-year-old, born in the second half of 2002. The body is obscenely projectable, and there's a whole bunch of present strength already to build on. He shows a quiet, balanced swing from the right side with outstanding extension and plane to drive pitches. It's a prototypical power-hitting corner outfield profile, and after he logged 39 games in the DSL last season it'll be interesting to see how aggressive the club gets as far as potentially bringing him stateside in 2020. He is approximately 4.3 light years away from making a Major League roster if it all comes together, but there's a non-zero chance he grows into a physical monster and destroys worlds one day.

Top Talents 25 and Under (as of 4/1/2020)

1. Shohei Ohtani
2. Jo Adell
3. Griffin Canning
4. Brandon Marsh
5. Jordyn Adams
6. David Fletcher
7. D'Shawn Knowles
8. Matt Thaiss
9. José Suarez
10. Jeremiah Jackson

Was there some concern that Adell evangelist (Adellvangelist? Quick, take it before Adele does) Craig Goldstein would summarily fire me when I submitted this list with Ohtani at the perch? No, not at all! Silly you'd even ask. Ridiculous, really…

As to why Ohtani ranks first, I would point dually to his present body of work and the potential he retains to be so much more. As a first-season NPB import and 23-year-old, Ohtani was 22 percent better than league average with the bat and 23 percent from the mound. He was called a "high school hitter" that spring training and then proceeded to win Rookie of the Year with his bat when his arm gave out—an arm that comes easy 97 plus and got 63 punchouts in 50 2/3 innings. Last season held regression at the plate, yes, but Ohtani also spent the entire campaign in grueling rehabilitation from Tommy John surgery, a surgery whose effects on batters is underappreciated. We've seen quite a lot from Ohtani, but there's ample reason to believe the best is yet to come.

Canning was 22 when he debuted and was more okay-good than good-great, but he was nevertheless basically the ace of an Angels rotation that depressed in multiple ways. The major concern that caused the second-round draft pick to fall to California/Anaheim/Los Angeles was durability, and though he was shut down in August with elbow inflammation, it's still looking like the UCLA product will live up to his mid-rotation potential.

Fletcher is one of those diminutive infielders who seems destined to be underrated; his six home runs in 653 plate appearances were both the league's second-worst rate (only Yolmer Sánchez had fewer home runs per at-bat among qualified players) and, given the rocket ball, likely near the limit of his output. He still managed to be a league-average batter thanks to 30 doubles, a three percent hike in walk rate (to an acceptable eight percent), and a dip in strikeout rate (from 11 to 10 percent). Combined with positional versatility, Fletch has proved himself a valuable piece.

The Angels raised eyebrows in 2016 when they selected defensively marginal catcher Thaiss with the 16th overall pick, and got them up into "you're going to give yourself wrinkles" territory when they immediately shifted him to first and tagged him with a host of other issues to overcome. Blocked by Albert Pujols, Thaiss now needs to prove he can handle the hot corner, and likely also bat a bit better than his 91 DRC+ last season, but it's not hard to see him quickly developing into a plus platoon/bench piece or average regular.

Suarez is difficult to rank here, being that he was one of MLB's worst starters last season. Ranking a pitcher who posted nearly negative three wins and a DRA 84 percent worse than average might seem both optimistic and an indictment of the Angels' system, but several caveats are useful. Suarez pitched the entire season at 21, almost certainly would have spent more time developing in the minors had not circumstance conscripted him, and simply cannot surrender 2.6 homers per nine again. The only place to go is up, there's just a ways to climb. Which feels like a metaphor for some team…

Eyewitness Reports

Eyewitness Report: Jo Adell

Evaluator: Ricky Conti
Report Date: 09/24/2019
Dates Seen: 9/19, 9/20
Risk Factor: Medium
Physical/Health: Thick, but athletic legs. Insane present strength from head to toe. Premier speed/strength combo.

Tool	Future Grade	Report
Hit	50	As much hype as he has, the hit tool isn't perfect. There's some swing and miss to his game, and the front side will sometimes pull out too early, causing him to foul off hittable pitches. He was also frozen by a handful of curveballs. Nonetheless, the discipline and plate awareness are solid. There isn't much loft to the swing at the moment. The bat speed is top-tier. The swing is powerful and explosive. Even when he doesn't swing, you can just see the energy build up in his load. It's dangerous.
Power	70	Usually the hit tool unlocks the power tool, but in Adell's case it might be the other way around. He hits the ball so hard, so often, that the baseball is bound to find holes in the field. In batting practice, he launches baseballs to all fields well beyond the outfield fence. It's truly a show, but mainly for your safety, you need to be paying attention when he's hitting, because he will smash baseballs at distances you didn't think a baseball could go.
Baserunning/ Speed	60	He's currently a plus runner with good acceleration. The legs are thick, so there is some risk he will regress to 55, but either way, it'll be enough.
Glove	55	Showed some drift on routine plays, but takes great routes with solid reads. The footwork in the outfield is really good and will give him a chance to throw runners out.
Arm	55	Showed very average in pregame, but at low effort. Can imagine it shows above-average to plus at full effort in-game.

Conclusion: When a prospect has multiple carrying tools, that is what usually puts him on the map. Adell not only has four carrying tools, but one of them is 70 grade, and there's still a chance for a fifth. Part of what makes Adell special is how quick he's made it to the upper minors, how he's been able to accomplish so much for his age, and the legitimate potential for five tools.

Eyewitness Report: Orlando Martinez

Evaluator: Brandon Williams
Report Date: 08/01/2019
Dates Seen: 20+ imes in 2019
Risk Factor: Medium
Physical/Health: Listed at 6-feet and 185-pounds, Martinez retains good athleticism in a strong, stocky physique. Similar build to Melky Cabrera.

Tool	Future Grade	Report
Hit	60	A flat stroke and plus bat-to-ball contact skills generate hard contact from line-to-line. He can occasionally get too pull-oriented, but at his best when utilizing middle-of-the-field approach.
Power	55	Sneaky pop in a compact frame. Good power to right-center field and enough strength to drive the ball to the opposite field. Hit oppo-HR against top LH pitching prospect MacKenzie Gore on 6/20/19.
Baserunning/ Speed	55	Not a burner, but good quickness and moves well around bags. Good instincts and can steal the occasional base.
Glove	55	Can play all three OF positions, but may be best suited in a corner. Good routes and aggressive pursuit of the baseball maximize his range. Willing to sacrifice his body to make a play.
Arm	55	Good accuracy and a quick release will make runners think twice about taking the extra-base.

Conclusion: Martinez is an all-around ballplayer who can help his team win in a multitude of ways. He's able to provide plus-contact and on-base abilities at the top of a lineup, and be a plus-defender at any outfield position. He'd be a great "glue-guy" on a talented roster.

Los Angeles Dodgers

The State of the System

The Dodgers system is shallower and more top-heavy than the last few years, but still has a lot of impact, major-league-ready talent ready for a win-now club.

The Top Ten

★ ★ ★ *2020 Top 101 Prospect* **#3** ★ ★ ★

1 Gavin Lux SS   OFP: 70   ETA: 2019

Born: 11/23/97   Age: 22   Bats: L   Throws: R   Height: 6'2"   Weight: 190   Origin: Round 1, 2016 Draft (#20 overall)

YEAR	TEAM	LVL	AGE	PA	R	2B	3B	HR	RBI	BB	K	SB	CS	AVG/OBP/SLG	DRC+	VORP	BABIP	BRR	FRAA	WARP	PF
2017	GRL	A	19	501	68	14	8	7	39	56	88	27	10	.244/.331/.362	97	20.4	.288	3.4	SS(65) 3.8, 2B(43) 4.0	2.8	97
2018	RCU	A+	20	404	64	23	7	11	48	43	68	11	7	.324/.396/.520	144	34.4	.374	-1.8	SS(66) -0.6, 2B(17) 0.8	3.2	109
2018	TUL	AA	20	120	21	4	1	4	9	14	20	2	2	.324/.408/.495	153	11.6	.370	1.3	SS(26) -0.6	1.2	107
2019	TUL	AA	21	291	45	7	4	13	37	28	60	7	3	.313/.375/.521	166	28.9	.358	-2.6	SS(55) -3.0, 2B(7) 0.5	2.4	99
2019	OKL	AAA	21	232	54	18	4	13	39	33	42	3	3	.392/.478/.719	176	41.2	.451	-1.2	SS(35) -2.8, 2B(12) -0.3	2.7	101
2019	LAN	MLB	21	82	12	4	1	2	9	7	24	2	0	.240/.305/.400	75	0.1	.327	0.1	2B(22) -0.9	-0.1	92
2020	*LAN*	*MLB*	*22*	*462*	*54*	*21*	*3*	*17*	*60*	*40*	*118*	*8*	*4*	*.267/.333/.453*	*107*	*2.0*	*.334*	*-0.2*	*2B 0*	*2.3*	*91*

Comparables: Corey Seager, Brendan Rodgers, Dilson Herrera

The Report: I've written a lot about Lux this year, and the tl;dr version is that sometimes you see a player and you know. Lux showed an elite approach at a young age in Double-A, with advanced pitch recognition that heralded his ability to translate a quality hit tool to the highest level. It's a legitimate shortstop profile, and when you see that play with flashes of plus power in games, it's a special sight. Lux continued to impress around the diamond as his athleticism, body control, and instincts manifested themselves in all facets of his game on through the high minors to ultimately force a big-league promotion at 21.

He generates plus bat speed with the ability to get his bat to the ball with strength and quickness anywhere in the zone. Lux attacks the meat of the zone aggressively while remaining patient on pitchers' pitches early in the count. He's happy to take a free pass, and his selectiveness allows him to tap into his plus power to launch the ball out of the park. He also is adept at going with a pitch to drive the ball to left-center. To round out the profile, Lux is a plus runner, and while he hasn't shown as an especially efficient base-stealer, his excellent instincts and speed allow him to add baserunning value in other ways.

As of now Lux fits well at shortstop, where his clean hands, plus reactions and lateral range make up for an average arm. He plays with an aggressive, high-effort style rather than smooth, natural grace, and he may have to move off the position down the line on account of a frame that should continue to add bulk as he ages. Lux can play as an average shortstop until then, or slide over to the keystone with above-average defense.

When you put the package together, you have yourself one of the best prospects in baseball. Lux should be a plus regular at the major league level, and there's a relatively high chance (as these things go) he's an impact player and All-Star.

Variance: Low. There is a decent chance he fills out and needs to move to second or third on the sooner side of later. But the bat should provide impact value at any infield position, so long as the pitch recognition carries over to the majors.

Ben Carsley's Fantasy Take: Few players offer a better combination of floor and upside than Lux, who will seemingly "bottom out" as a top-12 third baseman but who's got a shot to place as a top-10 second basemen or shortstop as well. Even a modest projection for Lux sees him as a four-category fantasy contributor, and I still think his speed and athleticism could eventually translate to 10-plus steals a year as well. History has proven time and time again that there's no such thing as a truly "safe" prospect, but given Lux's well-roundedness, ETA, and organization, he's about as close to safe as we can possibly hope for.

★ ★ ★ *2020 Top 101 Prospect* **#8** ★ ★ ★

2 **Dustin May** **RHP**   OFP: 70   ETA: 2019
Born: 09/06/97   Age: 22   Bats: R   Throws: R   Height: 6'6"   Weight: 180   Origin: Round 3, 2016 Draft (#101 overall)

YEAR	TEAM	LVL	AGE	W	L	SV	G	GS	IP	H	HR	BB/9	K/9	K	GB%	BABIP	WHIP	ERA	DRA	WARP	PF
2017	GRL	A	19	9	6	0	23	23	123	121	8	1.9	8.3	113	52%	.306	1.20	3.88	4.28	1.4	97
2017	RCU	A+	19	0	0	0	2	1	11	6	0	0.8	12.3	15	60%	.240	0.64	0.82	1.81	0.4	108
2018	RCU	A+	20	7	3	0	17	17	98¹	91	9	1.6	8.6	94	58%	.294	1.10	3.29	2.98	2.7	108
2018	TUL	AA	20	2	2	0	6	6	34¹	27	0	3.1	7.3	28	54%	.267	1.14	3.67	3.50	0.7	106
2019	TUL	AA	21	3	5	0	15	15	79¹	71	5	2.3	9.8	86	52%	.307	1.15	3.74	3.84	1.1	97
2019	OKL	AAA	21	3	0	0	5	5	27¹	21	0	3.0	7.9	24	60%	.276	1.10	2.30	1.90	1.3	95
2019	LAN	MLB	21	2	3	0	14	4	34²	33	2	1.3	8.3	32	46%	.316	1.10	3.63	4.55	0.4	93
2020	LAN	MLB	22	6	5	0	27	16	95	97	13	2.7	7.7	82	50%	.301	1.31	4.09	4.42	1.4	91

Comparables: José Berríos, Jake Thompson, Lucas Giolito

The Report: The lanky redhead's rise to the big leagues has been well documented here at BP, and he is a great example of a player who is unorthodox and well represents the value of eyes-on scouting.

May brings a big fastball to the party. He'll sit mid 90s with it, and he was topping out in triple digits out of LA's pen down the stretch last year. He pairs it with a devastating curveball that spins like a top, though he'll lack consistency with the pitch's shape. Also in the arsenal is a hard slider-ish cutter in the low 90s, and every now and again he'll turn over a changeup in the low 80s that can fool hitters with its movement. The stuff itself is electric, and while the command could unsurprisingly stand to improve, he actually controls his frame quite effectively.

Despite being 6-foot-6, May's mechanics aren't awkward like you might expect; he works out of a three-quarters slot with a smooth arm action and release, and those Go-Go Gadget limbs help give him quality extension towards the plate. There's some room for May to gain additional muscle, though it's unlikely to be the bulky kind.

Variance: Low. There are things May needs to work on, the command first and foremost, but even if he never maxes out on that front the stuff is such that he'll be a valuable pitcher in the big leagues barring calamity.

Ben Carsley's Fantasy Take: As good as May is, he lacks the truly elite strikeout upside that fantasy's true No. 1 starters need. Thus concludes the negative things we can say about Dustin May: Dynasty Prospect. He's already reached the majors. He's got favorable contextual factors. He misses bats, he won't kill your WHIP, and he should earn a ton of wins on the Dodgers unless they get weird with their usage. They get there in very different ways, but from a pure output standpoint, he could end up being a similar fantasy asset to Aaron Nola. History has proven time and time again that there's no such thing as a truly "safe" pitching prospect, but given May's well-roundedness, ETA, and organization, he's about as close to safe as we can possibly hope for.

★ ★ ★ *2020 Top 101 Prospect* **#61** ★ ★ ★

3 **Josiah Gray** **RHP**   OFP: 60   ETA: 2021
Born: 12/21/97   Age: 22   Bats: R   Throws: R   Height: 6'1"   Weight: 190   Origin: Round 2, 2018 Draft (#72 overall)

YEAR	TEAM	LVL	AGE	W	L	SV	G	GS	IP	H	HR	BB/9	K/9	K	GB%	BABIP	WHIP	ERA	DRA	WARP	PF
2018	GRV	RK	20	2	2	0	12	12	52¹	29	1	2.9	10.1	59	38%	.219	0.88	2.58	0.91	2.9	102
2019	GRL	A	21	1	0	0	5	5	23¹	13	0	2.7	10.0	26	41%	.241	0.86	1.93	2.26	0.8	97
2019	RCU	A+	21	7	0	0	12	12	67¹	52	3	1.7	10.7	80	40%	.292	0.97	2.14	2.29	2.2	110
2019	TUL	AA	21	3	2	0	9	8	39¹	33	0	2.5	9.4	41	35%	.314	1.12	2.75	3.27	0.8	101
2020	LAN	MLB	22	1	1	0	10	0	11	11	1	3.2	8.9	11	38%	.302	1.33	3.93	4.36	0.1	91

Comparables: Chance Adams, Rafael Montero, Jorge Alcala

The Report: The Cincinnati Reds selected Gray with the 72nd-overall pick of the 2018 draft, then promptly shipped him to Los Angeles as part of the Yasiel Puig trade several months later. In his first season in the Dodgers' system, the right-hander excelled across three levels and was named the organization's Minor League Pitcher of the Year. A former college shortstop turned hurler, he proved durable in 2019, throwing 130 combined innings across his three stops. Gray attacks the strike zone with no-nonsense efficiency and plus command of a heavy, mid-90s fastball. He sets the tone with that pitch getting ahead with it, or generating quick outs. A tight slider that can sit as high as 85 plays well off of the heater, and a developing mid-to-upper-80s changeup rounds out what projects as a solid three-pitch mix. Although none of his pitches grade out better than plus, Gray's confidence to attack with all of them keeps pressure on opposing hitters. He's a competitor on the mound, with a good work ethic and live arm that combine to set a high floor.

Variance: Medium. The secondaries are still work-in-progress stage, with room for improved command and consistency.

Ben Carsley's Fantasy Take: On the one hand, the Dodgers are about as good an organization as a pitching prospect can ask to be in; their track record with recent prospects speaks for itself, and they offer a favorable home ballpark and good supporting team upon reaching the majors. On the other hand, the Dodgers have a lot of pitching talent right now, and Gray lacks the upside needed to assure himself of a full-time spot in the rotation. Thus, we're presented with a quandary: is it better if Gray sticks with the Dodgers and reaps the organizational benefits, or is it better if he gets shipped to an org in which he'd have a clearer path to start? Either way, if your dynasty league rosters 100 prospects, you should be willing to burn a roster spot to find out.

★ ★ ★ *2020 Top 101 Prospect* **#65** ★ ★ ★

4 Miguel Vargas 3B   OFP: 60   ETA: 2021

Born: 11/17/99   Age: 20   Bats: R   Throws: R   Height: 6'3"   Weight: 205   Origin: International Free Agent, 2017

YEAR	TEAM	LVL	AGE	PA	R	2B	3B	HR	RBI	BB	K	SB	CS	AVG/OBP/SLG	DRC+	VORP	BABIP	BRR	FRAA	WARP	PF
2018	DOD	RK	18	37	6	3	1	0	2	5	3	1	0	.419/.514/.581	196	4.6	.464	-0.7	1B(5) 0.8, 3B(4) 1.1	0.5	96
2018	OGD	RK	18	103	25	11	1	2	22	8	13	6	1	.394/.447/.596	203	13.0	.443	1.2	3B(13) 0.5, 1B(6) -0.4	1.2	112
2018	GRL	A	18	89	4	1	1	0	6	10	20	0	0	.213/.307/.253	66	-1.0	.281	-0.5	3B(19) 3.1	0.2	94
2019	GRL	A	19	323	53	20	2	5	45	35	43	9	1	.325/.399/.464	162	27.6	.363	-2.5	3B(59) 2.2, 1B(2) 0.4	3.1	99
2019	RCU	A+	19	236	23	18	1	2	32	20	40	4	3	.284/.353/.408	127	8.9	.341	-2.3	3B(43) -1.9, 1B(6) 0.4	0.8	103
2020	LAN	MLB	20	251	25	14	1	5	26	20	51	1	0	.259/.324/.394	91	3.0	.314	-0.3	3B 0, 1B 0	0.6	91

Comparables: Jeimer Candelario, Delino DeShields, J.P. Crawford

The Report: Signed by the Dodgers after defecting with his father in 2017, the now-20-year-old Cuban infielder impressed as a wee 19-year-old across two levels of A-ball. He plays a savvy defensive third base, displaying soft hands, a strong throwing arm, and impressive mobility and body control. At 6-foot-3 and 205 pounds, Vargas shows quality athleticism in a frame that is in the process of getting stronger. The raw power is growing right along with him. His exceptional hand-eye coordination, bat-to-ball ability, and professional gap-to-gap hitting approach stand out; his at-bats have a plan, and he executes a quality swing when he gets his pitch. He's surprisingly fleet of foot at present, keenly cutting the basepaths with solid acceleration. It was a season of exciting growth for Vargas, and he ends it as the biggest mover in the system.

Variance: High. He's talented, but he's young, and he's on an aggressive trajectory.

Ben Carsley's Fantasy Take: The time to get in on Vargas in most dynasty leagues has come and gone, but if you play in a shallower setting you might still be able to capitalize on his relative lack of fantasy buzz. Vargas' ceiling isn't sky-high, but at the end of the day, is he really that different from Ke'Bryan Hayes? I don't think he is, yet Hayes seems to have a lot more name value at this point. That should change.

★ ★ ★ *2020 Top 101 Prospect* **#79** ★ ★ ★

5 Keibert Ruiz C   OFP: 55   ETA: 2022

Born: 07/20/98   Age: 21   Bats: B   Throws: R   Height: 6'0"   Weight: 200   Origin: International Free Agent, 2015

YEAR	TEAM	LVL	AGE	PA	R	2B	3B	HR	RBI	BB	K	SB	CS	AVG/OBP/SLG	DRC+	VORP	BABIP	BRR	FRAA	WARP	PF
2017	GRL	A	18	251	34	16	1	2	24	18	30	0	0	.317/.372/.423	127	16.2	.355	-3.2	C(49) -0.9	1.3	96
2017	RCU	A+	18	160	24	7	1	6	27	7	23	0	0	.315/.344/.497	127	13.2	.333	0.0	C(37) -0.3	1.2	106
2018	TUL	AA	19	415	44	14	0	12	47	26	33	0	1	.268/.328/.401	91	8.3	.266	-3.8	C(86) 3.5	1.4	109
2019	TUL	AA	20	310	33	9	0	4	25	28	21	0	0	.254/.329/.330	105	4.1	.261	-3.5	C(61) 0.5	1.1	99
2019	OKL	AAA	20	40	6	0	0	2	9	2	1	0	0	.316/.350/.474	87	-0.5	.286	0.9	C(8) -0.5	0.2	104
2020	LAN	MLB	21	35	4	2	0	1	4	2	5	0	0	.259/.311/.394	86	0.0	.279	-0.1	C 0	0.1	91

Comparables: Jake Bauers, Jose Tabata, Wilmer Flores

The Report: After breaking out across two levels in 2017 then holding his own as a 19-year-old in Double-A in 2018, Ruiz nearly cracked the top 30 of last winter's 101. 2019 saw the backstop take a couple steps back, however. Ruiz is a bat-first catcher whose best tool is his ability to make contact from both sides, and we've had evaluators put a comfortable 6 on the hit. The approach has stagnated, however, and one of Ruiz's flaws has been an inability to develop enough selectivity at the plate. His free-swinging tendencies are mitigated some by the superior bat-to-ball skill, but he hasn't yet been able to optimize his contact against higher-end pitching. To that end, the power has also revealed as a bit of a concern; he'll show average raw with flashes of in-game, but the right-handed swing in particular is flatter and lacks explosiveness through the ball at present.

Behind the plate, Ruiz still remains a work in progress. His ability to smother balls and handle things around the plate is notable, as is a firm glove hand on receipt. But he has struggled on plays that require him to come out of the crouch and move laterally. Some of those struggles are simply the product of his general lack of experience—bear in mind he is still just 21—but the frame is also on the bulkier side, and the body thickened up by a few more pounds this season. Ruiz's arm is a solid-average tool, and he has the raw tools he needs to stay behind the plate; it's all about refinement in both ability and physique.

Variance: High. This is less about the risk Ruiz carries and more about the ceiling. If Ruiz becomes more selective at the plate, matures his body to develop more power and athleticism while cleaning up his issues on defense he's an above-average major league catcher. He's young enough, and he has advanced quickly enough, that there remains an expectation that he can make these adjustments.

Ben Carsley's Fantasy Take: Ruiz was my test case. After years of "missing" (or at least not being able to accept the opportunity cost associated with rostering) on guys like Blake Swihart, Francisco Mejia, Chance Sisco, et al., Ruiz was where I decided to draw the line. I'm out on catching prospects for dynasty now, even when they're as promising with the bat as Ruiz is. The lead times are too unpredictable, the developmental hurdles too numerous, the gaps between MLB ETA and fantasy ETA too wide. Ruiz is a fun prospect, and I fully respect those who'll choose to dive in on him; they may be rewarded with a Willson Contreras-esque fantasy asset. To me, that upside isn't worth the risk.

★ ★ ★ 2020 Top 101 Prospect **#81** ★ ★ ★

6 Tony Gonsolin RHP   OFP: 55   ETA: 2019

Born: 05/14/94   Age: 26   Bats: R   Throws: R   Height: 6'3"   Weight: 205   Origin: Round 9, 2016 Draft (#281 overall)

YEAR	TEAM	LVL	AGE	W	L	SV	G	GS	IP	H	HR	BB/9	K/9	K	GB%	BABIP	WHIP	ERA	DRA	WARP	PF
2017	GRL	A	23	0	1	1	3	0	8	8	2	0.0	13.5	12	38%	.316	1.00	3.38	3.29	0.2	100
2017	RCU	A+	23	7	5	5	39	0	62	61	5	2.6	10.6	73	43%	.344	1.27	3.92	3.30	1.2	100
2018	RCU	A+	24	4	2	0	17	17	83²	72	5	2.8	11.4	106	38%	.319	1.17	2.69	2.72	2.5	110
2018	TUL	AA	24	6	0	0	9	9	44¹	32	3	3.2	9.9	49	39%	.261	1.08	2.44	3.00	1.2	108
2019	OKL	AAA	25	2	4	0	13	13	41¹	41	4	4.6	10.9	50	37%	.327	1.50	4.35	2.98	1.5	101
2019	LAN	MLB	25	4	2	1	11	6	40	26	4	3.4	8.3	37	43%	.208	1.02	2.92	4.19	0.6	101
2020	LAN	MLB	26	4	3	0	25	10	65	58	9	3.7	8.7	63	39%	.275	1.29	3.68	4.04	1.2	91

Comparables: John Curtiss, Brock Stewart, Trevor Richards

The Report: A former ninth-round senior sign back when he threw 89-90, Gonsolin has just kept right on keepin' on as a professional, ultimately battling his way through 40 successful debut innings in Los Angeles last year after surviving the Triple-A moon ball. His four pitches all play up off each other, starting with a fastball that nowadays will sit 93-95 and tickle 96. There isn't a ton of movement or explosiveness to it, but a nasty trap-door splitter tunnels really well off its line, and there's deception in his slow-building delivery to add some sneaky perceived velocity to the heater. A noted cat lover, he can miss bats with two distinct spinners, and has shown an aptitude for carving off weak fly-ball contact with both of those offerings. He's a good athlete who shows fluidity and solid balance in his delivery, though there's some herk-and-jerk and stab to his arm action that continues to wobble the command. First-look deception and pitchability helped him get away with some looseness around the zone in his debut, but free passes and wandering fastballs will threaten his peripherals and pose the biggest threat to his ceiling as an above-average member of a first-division staff.

Variance: Low. He's big league-ready, and already showed he could hang with the big boys last year.

Ben Carsley's Fantasy Take: Take all the concerns we mentioned with Gray, now dial down the upside even more. Gonsolin might make for an acceptable spot starter/depth guy if you're competing in 2020, but otherwise you should be aiming for profiles with more impact potential.

7 Diego Cartaya C   OFP: 60   ETA: 2023
Born: 09/07/01 Age: 18 Bats: R Throws: R Height: 6'2" Weight: 199 Origin: International Free Agent, 2018

YEAR	TEAM	LVL	AGE	PA	R	2B	3B	HR	RBI	BB	K	SB	CS	AVG/OBP/SLG	DRC+	VORP	BABIP	BRR	FRAA	WARP	PF
2019	DOD	RK	17	150	25	10	0	3	13	11	31	1	0	.296/.353/.437	126	12.3	.359	1.9	C(28) -0.2	1.1	98
2020	LAN	MLB	18	251	22	12	1	5	24	19	79	3	1	.225/.288/.341	67	0.0	.323	0.0	C 0	-0.2	91

Comparables: Francisco Mejía, Chris Marrero, Cheslor Cuthbert

The Report: One of the top international prospects in the 2018 class, Cartaya showed well enough in his professional debut in the Dominican that the notoriously-aggressive Los Angeles front office brought him stateside as a 17-year-old. He's got a thick, mature frame, but there's exciting baseline athleticism. Cartaya already moves well behind the dish, and there's an overall physicality that's fun to dream on. His hands are a little stiff right now, but they're quick, strong, and accurate to the ball, and there's cause for cautious optimism that he can develop into a solid receiver. The swing is already very pretty; he'll drift into the zone a bit, but he takes fluid, strong rips from the right side, and could grow into above-average power. Everything's to the pull-side right now, but he sees pitches well and puts good wood on the ball. He is obviously eons away from being anywhere close to a finished product, but the early returns on the club's substantial investment are good, and it should surprise nobody if he finds his way to Great Lakes next season.

Variance: Extreme. The range of outcomes is as enormous as the timeline for him to actualize his exciting starter's set of tools. Catcher development is frequently disjointed and weird, even in organizations with strong recent track records of developing the position.

Ben Carsley's Fantasy Take: If I'm not super in on Ruiz, you can imagine how I feel about Cartaya. If you opt to invest in dynasty catching prospects, more power to you. I'll be using my roster spots differently.

8 Jeter Downs SS   OFP: 55   ETA: 2021
Born: 07/27/98 Age: 21 Bats: R Throws: R Height: 5'11" Weight: 180 Origin: Round 1, 2017 Draft (#32 overall)

YEAR	TEAM	LVL	AGE	PA	R	2B	3B	HR	RBI	BB	K	SB	CS	AVG/OBP/SLG	DRC+	VORP	BABIP	BRR	FRAA	WARP	PF
2017	BIL	RK	18	209	31	3	3	6	29	27	32	8	5	.267/.370/.424	97	12.8	.288	-1.5	SS(50) -4.5	-0.1	105
2018	DYT	A	19	524	63	23	2	13	47	52	103	37	10	.257/.351/.402	124	23.2	.306	-1.6	2B(73) -2.9, SS(43) -9.3	1.6	102
2019	RCU	A+	20	479	78	33	4	19	75	54	97	23	8	.269/.354/.507	127	44.3	.304	4.1	SS(90) -4.0, 2B(10) -1.1	2.9	107
2019	TUL	AA	20	56	14	2	0	5	11	6	10	1	0	.333/.429/.688	167	7.9	.333	0.8	SS(11) -0.4, 2B(1) 0.0	0.6	111
2020	LAN	MLB	21	251	30	12	1	11	34	20	63	7	3	.236/.306/.445	96	0.0	.276	0.4	SS -4, 2B -1	0.3	91

Comparables: Gavin Lux, Carter Kieboom, Alen Hanson

The Report: The second prospect coming back to the sunshine state for Yasiel Puig last winter, Downs showed a solid power-and-speed combination from the shortstop position in his age-20 season. He led the California League with 33 doubles, then continued to rake during a cameo at Double-A, tying off his season with a three-homer game in the Texas League playoffs. After a pull-happy first half, Downs made adjustments to better utilize the opposite field in the second half, and both the hit and game power tools flourished. There isn't really a carrying tool in the offensive toolbag; he's got a decent approach and there's solid-average pop, but he stills cuts off the outer half too often. He's an above-average runner whose instincts play amplify his baserunning skill and should allow him to continue stealing bases at a solid clip. Defensively, the athletic 5-foot-10 middle infielder has good mobility and receptive hands, along with a 50-grade arm that is reasonable enough to cut it at the six, if not ideal for the role. It's more comfortable as a second base projection, but he should be able to stay up the middle and add occasional shortstop utility. The bat will lead him to the big leagues, however, and while the Dodgers' depth may delay Downs' debut, he should be scratching at the major league door by 2021.

Variance: Medium-to-High. The bat-to-ball consistency will dictate whether he's a toolsy bench asset or an everyday contributor.

Ben Carsley's Fantasy Take: Downs might actually be a better dynasty prospect than an IRL one thanks to his power and speed combo. That being said, I'm lower on him than some of my dynasty-loving colleagues, as I think he has utility infielder written all over him if he stays in this org. Downs is more interesting than most players with this profile because of the potential for modest contributions in every category but average. Even so, the upside remains fairly modest.

9 Kody Hoese 3B OFP: 50 ETA: 2021

Born: 07/13/97 Age: 22 Bats: R Throws: R Height: 6'4" Weight: 200 Origin: Round 1, 2019 Draft (#25 overall)

YEAR	TEAM	LVL	AGE	PA	R	2B	3B	HR	RBI	BB	K	SB	CS	AVG/OBP/SLG	DRC+	VORP	BABIP	BRR	FRAA	WARP	PF
2019	DOD	RK	21	68	14	5	1	3	13	10	11	1	0	.357/.456/.643	185	11.1	.395	1.9	3B(6) -0.5	0.8	98
2019	GRL	A	21	103	15	3	1	2	16	8	14	0	0	.264/.330/.385	103	3.6	.286	-0.2	3B(11) 0.7	0.3	95
2020	LAN	MLB	22	251	22	12	1	5	24	16	60	2	1	.226/.283/.344	66	3.0	.285	0.0	3B 0	-0.2	91

Comparables: Matt Thaiss, Hunter Dozier, Erik Komatsu

The Report: The first of the Dodgers' two first-rounders last summer, Hoese is a big, strong kid who pounded the ball during his junior season at Tulane and then kept right on hitting after signing. The stance is rigid and muscley, but he's a fluid mover whose strength translates into a quick burst at first move. He'll drift deep and lengthen his leveraged swing, so there's swing-and-miss risk here that can threaten the utility of his plus raw power. He's a patient hitter, however, and he showed an encouraging ability to stay in the zone in his debut. A sore elbow limited him defensively down the stretch, and there is some variance in the early defensive reports, with some seeing an instinctual player who will provide value at the hot corner, while others see a stiffer, fringe-averagier contributor with more limited range.

Variance: High. He'll give us more of a clue about how his later-popping college bat will translate to pro pitching next year.

Ben Carsley's Fantasy Take: Honestly, it's been like two years since Max Muncy and they're already gonna move forward with a remake?

10 Gerardo Carrillo RHP OFP: 50 ETA: 2021

Born: 09/13/98 Age: 21 Bats: R Throws: R Height: 5'10" Weight: 154 Origin: International Free Agent, 2016

YEAR	TEAM	LVL	AGE	W	L	SV	G	GS	IP	H	HR	BB/9	K/9	K	GB%	BABIP	WHIP	ERA	DRA	WARP	PF
2017	DDG	RK	18	5	2	0	14	10	48¹	44	1	2.6	6.0	32	58%	.277	1.20	2.79	5.23	0.4	80
2018	DOD	RK	19	2	0	1	4	1	11	6	0	1.6	10.6	13	58%	.231	0.73	0.82	1.71	0.5	77
2018	GRL	A	19	2	1	0	9	9	49	35	3	2.8	6.8	37	50%	.235	1.02	1.65	3.26	1.1	98
2019	RCU	A+	20	5	9	0	23	21	86	87	3	5.3	9.0	86	54%	.338	1.60	5.44	5.22	-0.2	108
2020	LAN	MLB	21	2	2	0	33	0	35	34	5	3.8	7.0	27	48%	.283	1.41	4.59	4.87	0.2	91

Comparables: Jeanmar Gómez, Lance McCullers Jr., German Márquez

The Report: Carrillo spent all of this season in the California League as a slight 20-year-old, but while the placement may have been a bit aggressive, he threw well enough at Great Lakes in 2018 to make it a reasonable challenge. He didn't fare well production-wise, pitching to a 5.22 DRA while walking 51 across 86 innings, but he showed plenty of raw material to get excited about.

He's not a big guy, at all, but the carrying tool is effortless mid-90s gas that ran up to 98 during the season and wandered into triple digits during his stint in the Arizona Fall League. The pitch features some run and sink, allowing him to get under barrels and generate plenty of ground-ball contact. A curve in the 78-82 band breaks with big—though early—vertical action. He sells the pitch well, but it does hump enough for some of the better hitters in the league to identify and lay off. His third pitch is a mid-80s slider that remains in the developmental stage; he's still trying to get a feel for it, but it tunnels well with the fastball, and has the chance to develop into an average pitch down the line. There is a changeup, but it's a distant fourth pitch with modest action.

He missed time with a shoulder injury that didn't sound great at the time, but he looked healthy and strong in the fall. There is enough athleticism, youth, and room for improvement in the mechanics to project some growth for his underwhelming present command, and he can grow into a devastating double-plus fastball with an above-average breaking ball.

Variance: Very High, bordering on extreme. His impressive showing in the AFL gave a glimpse of his potential if and when healthy, but here's a significant developmental road still ahead.

Ben Carsley's Fantasy Take: t's hard to imagine he's anything other than a reliever in this system. Pass.

The Next Ten

11 Michael Busch 2B

Born: 11/09/97   Age: 22   Bats: L   Throws: R   Height: 6'0"   Weight: 207   Origin: Round 1, 2019 Draft (#31 overall)

YEAR	TEAM	LVL	AGE	PA	R	2B	3B	HR	RBI	BB	K	SB	CS	AVG/OBP/SLG	DRC+	VORP	BABIP	BRR	FRAA	WARP	PF
2020	LAN	MLB	22	251	23	11	1	6	25	19	68	2	1	.210/.283/.345	69	2.0	.271	0.0	2B 0	-0.1	91

Comparables: Wilmer Difo, Josh Prince, Lane Adams

The Dodgers' other first-rounder last summer (compensation for not signing J.T. Ginn in 2018), Busch is a thick, athletic left-handed college bat with a solid offensive pedigree. It's a pretty swing with nice balance and loft, and while the bat speed doesn't stand out, he's strong and carves a tight path to the ball. He's also a disciplined hitter, with quality pitch recognition and the willingness and ability to drive pitches to the opposite field. It looks the part of eventually-above-average hit and game power tools. The defensive future is less clear; he played a bunch of first base and outfield as an amateur, and there's some lumber to the stride that suggests a future home at the former. The Dodgers are unconvinced, however, as they shifted him over to the keystone after he signed. The early returns on that experiment didn't look great, though some leeway is warranted given the newness of it all. He crammed in a couple games at Great Lakes down the stretch, and that'll be his likely landing spot to start 2020.

12 DJ Peters OF

Born: 12/12/95   Age: 24   Bats: R   Throws: R   Height: 6'6"   Weight: 225   Origin: Round 4, 2016 Draft (#131 overall)

YEAR	TEAM	LVL	AGE	PA	R	2B	3B	HR	RBI	BB	K	SB	CS	AVG/OBP/SLG	DRC+	VORP	BABIP	BRR	FRAA	WARP	PF
2017	RCU	A+	21	587	91	29	5	27	82	64	189	3	3	.276/.372/.514	118	43.2	.385	0.9	CF(80) -3.5, LF(18) -1.0	2.3	107
2018	TUL	AA	22	559	79	23	3	29	60	45	192	1	2	.236/.320/.473	97	20.6	.316	-3.6	CF(96) -3.1, RF(29) 1.4	0.9	110
2019	TUL	AA	23	288	31	10	1	11	42	28	93	1	0	.241/.331/.422	104	15.7	.331	-0.6	CF(48) -1.2, RF(20) 1.1	0.9	100
2019	OKL	AAA	23	255	40	10	1	12	39	33	75	1	1	.260/.388/.490	120	19.6	.341	0.0	CF(55) -0.9	1.4	100
2020	LAN	MLB	24	251	25	10	1	7	27	21	91	0	0	.210/.293/.355	72	0.0	.317	-0.3	CF -1, RF 0	-0.1	91

Comparables: Ryan O'Hearn, Joe Benson, Brett Jackson

At 6-foot-6 and 235 pounds Peters has the ideal build for a power forward, or perhaps a Greek god if you're feeling classical. He's on the large side for a baseball player, and the athleticism took a small step back last year, though he's still a very good athlete with the ability to control his body and generate quick-twitchy movements.

At the plate this physicality translates to plus bat speed and the ability to find the barrel for tremendous exit velocities when he makes contact. It's plus-plus raw power, which is a good starting point, but he has extremely long levers and despite the speed of his barrel acceleration he'll struggle to catch up to premium velocity. He has also consistently struggled to recognize breaking balls and offspeed, and significant strikeout issues cap the hit tool and take a bite out of the in-game power. On the bright side, Peters has maintained a quality approach into the high minors, off-setting his whiffs with strong walk rates.

He's shown the ability to hang as a fringy centerfielder and may retain some utility there in the early years of his major league career, but he's a better fit as a potentially above-average defender in one of the corners. He's got the tools and talent to add value as a fourth outfielder, and if enough of the power plays the profile will carry him to an major league regular spot.

13 Jacob Amaya   IF

Born: 09/03/98   Age: 21   Bats: R   Throws: R   Height: 6'0"   Weight: 180   Origin: Round 11, 2017 Draft (#340 overall)

YEAR	TEAM	LVL	AGE	PA	R	2B	3B	HR	RBI	BB	K	SB	CS	AVG/OBP/SLG	DRC+	VORP	BABIP	BRR	FRAA	WARP	PF
2017	DOD	RK	18	140	17	4	1	2	14	19	25	4	2	.254/.364/.356	116	5.4	.304	-0.3	SS(25) 2.4, 2B(7) 0.4	1.0	102
2018	OGD	RK	19	155	41	9	3	3	24	27	29	11	4	.346/.465/.535	181	23.7	.432	3.2	SS(27) -0.7, 2B(8) -2.0	1.5	111
2018	GRL	A	19	119	13	1	0	1	5	20	18	3	3	.265/.390/.306	132	5.0	.316	-1.8	SS(21) 2.2, 2B(5) -0.2	0.9	94
2019	GRL	A	20	470	68	25	4	6	58	74	83	4	4	.262/.381/.394	146	41.0	.314	-0.5	SS(50) -3.8, 2B(49) 1.9	3.6	99
2019	RCU	A+	20	89	14	3	2	1	13	7	15	1	3	.250/.307/.375	99	5.3	.292	0.3	SS(14) -2.1, 2B(4) 1.0	0.2	100
2020	LAN	MLB	21	251	23	11	1	4	23	25	61	2	1	.225/.305/.341	74	0.0	.291	-0.4	SS 0, 2B 1	0.0	91

Comparables: Abiatal Avelino, Victor Robles, Ehire Adrianza

Amaya is just a fundamentally solid ball player. The feel and instincts for the infield are impeccable; his hands are silky smooth, and he consistently makes firm, accurate throws. He might not have the high-end quickness you want to see from a shortstop, but he makes up for it with sound execution and there's a broad enough defensive skill set that he can add value all over the dirt. At the plate, he has a modest leg kick, and uses it well to generate solid bat speed. There are elements of a solid hitter here, starting with an excellent approach that keeps him in the zone and in solid hitting counts, and the pop is sneaky to the gaps. There's a bit of tweener risk here, but he plays well above his tools and he finds enough ways to positively impact the game that he can grow into a valuable member of someone's 25-man roster in the next couple years.

14 Omar Estevez   IF

Born: 02/25/98   Age: 22   Bats: R   Throws: R   Height: 5'10"   Weight: 185   Origin: International Free Agent, 2015

YEAR	TEAM	LVL	AGE	PA	R	2B	3B	HR	RBI	BB	K	SB	CS	AVG/OBP/SLG	DRC+	VORP	BABIP	BRR	FRAA	WARP	PF
2017	RCU	A+	19	502	56	24	3	4	47	33	97	2	2	.256/.309/.348	71	10.2	.314	1.0	SS(98) 2.7, 2B(22) 0.4	1.0	106
2018	RCU	A+	20	577	87	43	2	15	84	45	138	3	1	.278/.336/.456	104	36.2	.344	1.2	SS(74) 2.6, 2B(47) 1.7	2.9	108
2019	TUL	AA	21	336	34	24	0	6	36	31	70	0	2	.291/.352/.431	118	15.5	.355	-0.2	2B(50) -2.6, SS(23) -0.4	1.3	100
2020	LAN	MLB	22	251	24	14	0	6	27	18	70	0	0	.239/.298/.381	77	0.0	.317	-0.6	SS 1, 2B 0	0.2	91

Comparables: Cole Tucker, Domingo Leyba, Cheslor Cuthbert

Estevez has never lacked for a notable swing, and the hit tool took another cautious step forward last year at Double-A before he ran out of gas in the AFL. Nothing's changed a ton about the profile. The swing's unconventional, with an early hip turn that helps him put some juice into it and create some loft to the pull side. He's aggressive in the zone, but he does a decent job recognizing spin and offspeed, and he should get to the fringe-average power in games. His whiff and walk rates both went the right way last year, but he'll show vulnerability away, and pitchers may exploit it going forward. He split time between short and second again, though he played almost exclusively the latter in the second half. He's better-suited to the keystone, where his average arm can play and he can better cover his inconsistent reactions. He's still very young, and while his development to date has jerked and halted, he's made encouraging progress on a relatively short timeline. There's no carrying tool here, but he can be a nice middle-of-the-infield player to have around.

15 Mitchell White   RHP

Born: 12/28/94   Age: 25   Bats: R   Throws: R   Height: 6'3"   Weight: 210   Origin: Round 2, 2016 Draft (#65 overall)

YEAR	TEAM	LVL	AGE	W	L	SV	G	GS	IP	H	HR	BB/9	K/9	K	GB%	BABIP	WHIP	ERA	DRA	WARP	PF
2017	DOD	RK	22	0	0	0	3	3	7	2	0	2.6	10.3	8	53%	.133	0.57	0.00	0.72	0.4	95
2017	RCU	A+	22	2	1	0	9	9	38²	26	0	3.7	11.4	49	64%	.286	1.09	3.72	2.41	1.3	108
2017	TUL	AA	22	1	1	0	7	7	28	17	2	4.2	10.0	31	51%	.217	1.07	2.57	2.83	0.8	104
2018	TUL	AA	23	6	7	0	22	22	105¹	114	12	2.9	7.5	88	49%	.317	1.41	4.53	5.57	-0.3	107
2019	TUL	AA	24	1	0	0	7	7	30	18	3	2.1	11.1	37	43%	.217	0.83	2.10	2.97	0.7	92
2019	OKL	AAA	24	3	6	0	16	13	63²	73	13	3.4	9.6	68	43%	.349	1.52	6.50	4.94	1.0	103
2020	LAN	MLB	25	1	1	0	14	3	26	26	4	3.7	8.9	25	43%	.302	1.41	4.53	4.86	0.2	91

Comparables: Hunter Wood, Ben Lively, Jerad Eickhoff

You tell me you've got an idea of what Mitchell White turns into at this point, and I'll tell you yer a dang liar. It was another in an increasingly long line of injury-interrupted, inconsistent seasons for the now-24-year-old. While he managed to avoid any major maladies, he found the injured list on three separate occasions over the course of a season that saw him dominate

Double-A (third time's a charm) before running headlong into the Triple-A ball. Despite a good dose of athleticism, White's never been able to key in on consistent mechanics, and his velocity will fluctuate pretty significantly from start to start. He actually pitched pretty well in the majority of his 16 PCL appearances last season, but his clunkers—including a gruesome 11-run start in August—underscore the volatility of his stuff on any given day. A low-90s cutter and downer curveball both show above-average potential, with the latter laying claim among the system's best when it's on. The durability concerns are significant, as are questions as to whether he'll ever develop something to round out an arsenal that once again got rolled pretty hard by left-handed hitters. Assuming he's physically able, he should enter the mix for big-league innings at some point next year, and how it all turns out from here…well, we'll all learn together.

16 Connor Wong   C

Born: 05/19/96   Age: 24   Bats: R   Throws: R   Height: 6'1"   Weight: 181   Origin: Round 3, 2017 Draft (#100 overall)

YEAR	TEAM	LVL	AGE	PA	R	2B	3B	HR	RBI	BB	K	SB	CS	AVG/OBP/SLG	DRC+	VORP	BABIP	BRR	FRAA	WARP	PF
2017	GRL	A	21	107	19	6	0	5	18	7	26	1	1	.278/.336/.495	125	7.4	.328	0.0	C(27) 0.2	0.8	99
2018	RCU	A+	22	431	64	20	2	19	60	38	138	6	2	.269/.350/.480	113	27.8	.372	0.9	C(71) 0.7, 2B(11) -0.5	2.4	108
2019	RCU	A+	23	302	39	15	6	15	51	21	93	9	2	.245/.306/.507	102	22.6	.310	1.3	C(59) 0.7, 2B(10) 1.3	1.7	105
2019	TUL	AA	23	163	17	9	1	9	31	11	50	2	1	.349/.393/.604	163	18.1	.467	0.3	C(23) 0.1, 3B(10) -0.8	1.5	104
2020	LAN	MLB	24	251	25	12	1	9	30	15	91	1	0	.227/.281/.400	75	0.0	.331	-0.2	C -3, 2B 0	-0.2	91

Comparables: Xavier Scruggs, Eric Haase, Jamie Romak

Wong has interesting physical and defensive profiles that offset some severe flaws enough to make him a fun wildcard in the system. The right/right catcher is 23 and just finished terrorizing Double-A in a short 40-game stint after spending the better part of two seasons at High-A.

Wong has excellent coordination that allows him to make hard line drive contact consistently, but the combination of an extreme arm bar, aggressive approach, and trouble recognizing breaking balls lead to outlandishly high strikeout rates that threaten to derail the offensive profile. The arm bar helps him generate power, but it also creates huge holes up and on the inner third. He's athletic enough to bet on an ability to integrate mechanical changes, but there's work ahead.

Defensively, Wong has solid hands behind the plate, and while he doesn't always have a smooth path to the ball, he performs well enough vertically and on the edges of the zone to add some value with his receiving. He has good footwork on blocks and a quick transition out of the crouch, which helps an average arm to play. The organization has flirted with second- and third-base reps for him, as well.

Wong currently projects to a tandem catching role at the major league level if he can shorten up the upper half of his swing and continue to bring his pop into games against experienced arms.

17 Michael Grove   RHP

Born: 12/18/96   Age: 23   Bats: R   Throws: R   Height: 6'3"   Weight: 200   Origin: Round 2, 2018 Draft (#68 overall)

YEAR	TEAM	LVL	AGE	W	L	SV	G	GS	IP	H	HR	BB/9	K/9	K	GB%	BABIP	WHIP	ERA	DRA	WARP	PF
2019	RCU	A+	22	0	5	0	21	21	51²	61	7	3.3	12.7	73	30%	.412	1.55	6.10	5.38	-0.2	107
2020	LAN	MLB	23	2	2	0	33	0	35	36	6	4.2	10.0	39	32%	.323	1.50	4.97	5.20	0.1	91

Comparables: Mike Mayers, Taylor Williams, Zach Stewart

After recovering from Tommy John surgery, the club's second-rounder in 2018 eased into his professional debut with 51 2/3 very interesting innings in the California League. He got pummeled by terrible luck on batted balls all year, but the progress of his stuff is the real story. Grove is lean, strong, and extremely athletic, with good body control that should allow him to repeat a clean delivery, though his deep drop onto his backside caused timing issues as he knocked off rust all year. He comes from a high, over-the-top slot that gives his tight breaker a bunch of vertical action. The fastball sits 91-93, topping at 95, and while it doesn't feature tremendous life, it spins hard and he locates it to both sides of the plate with two-way movement. Grove doesn't presently have a plus pitch, but you can tell there is plenty of confidence in what he does have, and given the physicality it shouldn't surprise anyone if the velocity takes another step forward and pushes the heater into plus range assuming improved command. He's a prime candidate to move up this list with another healthy season in Double-A next year.

18 Dennis Santana RHP

Born: 04/12/96 Age: 24 Bats: R Throws: R Height: 6'2" Weight: 190 Origin: International Free Agent, 2013

YEAR	TEAM	LVL	AGE	W	L	SV	G	GS	IP	H	HR	BB/9	K/9	K	GB%	BABIP	WHIP	ERA	DRA	WARP	PF
2017	RCU	A+	21	5	6	0	17	14	85²	87	5	2.3	9.7	92	50%	.340	1.27	3.57	3.88	1.3	113
2017	TUL	AA	21	3	1	0	7	7	32²	32	2	6.3	10.2	37	52%	.337	1.68	5.51	4.93	0.1	104
2018	TUL	AA	22	0	2	0	8	8	38²	26	3	3.3	11.9	51	56%	.258	1.03	2.56	2.44	1.3	111
2018	OKL	AAA	22	1	1	0	2	2	11	10	0	1.6	11.5	14	45%	.345	1.09	2.45	2.93	0.3	91
2018	LAN	MLB	22	1	0	0	1	0	3²	6	0	2.5	9.8	4	31%	.462	1.91	12.27	3.78	0.0	125
2019	OKL	AAA	23	5	9	0	27	17	93¹	111	16	5.1	10.1	105	44%	.364	1.76	6.94	6.51	0.1	102
2019	LAN	MLB	23	0	0	0	3	0	5	6	1	7.2	10.8	6	47%	.357	2.00	7.20	5.24	0.0	113
2020	LAN	MLB	24	2	1	0	14	3	27	24	4	4.5	9.5	29	43%	.282	1.38	4.10	4.34	0.4	91

Comparables: Touki Toussaint, Rob Whalen, Miguel Almonte

A year ago Santana capped a storybook rise with a major league debut, but then he hurt his rotator cuff and never looked quite all the way back to form in 2019. The fastball dropped a couple ticks, and he couldn't find the handle on its still-well-above-average movement. The poor command and diminished velocity proved a dangerous combination with the Triple-A ball, and he got absolutely pummeled in 17 starts to the tune of a ghastly 8.00 ERA. That precipitated a perhaps inevitable transition to the bullpen, where he settled things down a bit in spite of ongoing control issues. The club has worked hard to streamline what was once a significant crossfire, but he has struggled to sync up his timing and attack the zone consistently, even as he has continued to miss bats at a solid clip. At its best his four-seamer moves an obscene amount and pairs with a slider that flashes above-average and works effectively as a chase pitch, and the hope is that as he gets farther away from the shoulder issue he'll get back on track and into the mix for important relief innings in LA in 2020.

19 Cristian Santana 3B/1B

Born: 02/24/97 Age: 23 Bats: R Throws: R Height: 6'2" Weight: 175 Origin: International Free Agent, 2014

YEAR	TEAM	LVL	AGE	PA	R	2B	3B	HR	RBI	BB	K	SB	CS	AVG/OBP/SLG	DRC+	VORP	BABIP	BRR	FRAA	WARP	PF
2017	OGD	RK	20	48	18	2	1	5	16	6	6	0	0	.537/.583/1.000	296	12.1	.548	0.7	3B(5) 0.4, 2B(3) 0.4	1.1	120
2017	GRL	A	20	180	18	9	0	5	25	5	42	0	1	.322/.339/.460	131	11.7	.398	0.1	3B(31) 1.2, 1B(9) -0.5	1.2	98
2018	RCU	A+	21	580	75	23	0	24	109	20	143	2	2	.274/.302/.447	87	14.5	.325	-0.7	3B(76) 2.8, 1B(42) -0.1	0.9	109
2019	TUL	AA	22	413	45	22	1	10	57	10	88	0	0	.301/.320/.436	96	13.8	.363	-2.6	3B(82) -2.1, 1B(14) -0.7	0.5	98
2020	LAN	MLB	23	251	24	12	0	7	28	8	72	0	0	.253/.281/.394	75	3.0	.333	-0.6	3B 1, 1B 0	0.0	91

Comparables: Humberto Arteaga, Edmundo Sosa, Juan Francisco

Signed by the Dodgers in 2014 out of the Dominican Republic, the 22-year-old third baseman ranked third in the Texas League with a .301 batting average last season while improving his strikeout rate in spite of the difficult jump to Double-A. He's done a lot of work to tone down some seriously wild-swinging ways, but even as he now stays in better control of his ferocious hacks, he has remained an extremely aggressive hitter. It's really not a profile that typically yields confidence in the bat holding up, though Santana has defied the odds to this point. The former shortstop has good mobility and receptive hands when guarding the corners, and it's more likely today than it was at this time last year that he'll be able to stick at third (at least most of the time). His strong throwing arm is well-suited for the hot corner, and he can compensate for the occasional lapse in technique with plus raw arm strength. The good outcome here is an Adam Jones freak who hangs on to play a passable D on the left side, and there's cult favorite potential if that happens on account of a dynamic Puig-like electricity to his game.

20   Brett de Geus   RHP

Born: 11/04/97   Age: 22   Bats: R   Throws: R   Height: 6'2"   Weight: 190   Origin: Round 33, 2017 Draft (#1000 overall)

YEAR	TEAM	LVL	AGE	W	L	SV	G	GS	IP	H	HR	BB/9	K/9	K	GB%	BABIP	WHIP	ERA	DRA	WARP	PF
2018	OGD	RK	20	4	5	0	15	14	62	78	10	3.9	8.4	58	56%	.354	1.69	7.26	6.20	-0.1	112
2019	GRL	A	21	4	2	4	19	0	30²	17	0	1.8	10.6	36	49%	.239	0.75	2.35	2.22	0.9	100
2019	RCU	A+	21	2	0	4	20	0	31	28	0	2.0	10.5	36	65%	.341	1.13	1.16	3.23	0.5	100
2020	LAN	MLB	22	2	2	0	33	0	35	35	6	3.5	8.5	33	51%	.295	1.38	4.37	4.73	0.3	91

Comparables: Kris Medlen, Trevor Gott, Jacob Rhame

Drafted by the Dodgers out of Cabrillo Community College in the 33rd-round of the 2017 draft (the 1000th overall selection!), de Geus had a breakout season in 2019 after transitioning from starting to relief work. The 21-year-old held Midwest League hitters to a .163 average across 19 outings and didn't miss a beat after a promotion to the California League, where he struck out 36 batters with a 1.16 ERA in 20 appearances out of the bullpen. The 6-foot-2 righty aggressively attacks the strike-zone with a 94-96 mph sinking fastball, an 87-89 mph slider/cutter thing, and a hard-biting 81-83 mph curveball with 11-to-5 shape. His low three-quarters slot is efficient and repeatable, and his advanced command of three quality pitches could have him contributing to the big club's bullpen as soon as late-2020.

Personal Cheeseball

PC   Edwin Ríos   4C

Born: 04/21/94   Age: 26   Bats: L   Throws: R   Height: 6'3"   Weight: 220   Origin: Round 6, 2015 Draft (#192 overall)

YEAR	TEAM	LVL	AGE	PA	R	2B	3B	HR	RBI	BB	K	SB	CS	AVG/OBP/SLG	DRC+	VORP	BABIP	BRR	FRAA	WARP	PF
2017	TUL	AA	23	332	47	21	0	15	62	17	69	1	1	.317/.358/.533	144	24.9	.363	0.9	3B(38) -4.1, 1B(28) 1.8	2.0	105
2017	OKL	AAA	23	190	23	13	0	9	29	18	42	0	1	.296/.368/.533	121	8.6	.345	-2.6	1B(33) 0.6, 3B(9) -1.0	0.6	104
2018	OKL	AAA	24	341	45	25	0	10	55	23	110	0	1	.304/.355/.482	116	16.6	.433	-2.4	3B(38) -4.2, 1B(28) -1.3	0.6	97
2019	OKL	AAA	25	444	72	23	2	31	91	37	153	2	2	.270/.340/.575	106	24.4	.349	-2.6	3B(66) 1.7, 1B(25) 0.6	1.8	101
2019	LAN	MLB	25	56	10	2	1	4	8	9	21	0	0	.277/.393/.617	87	0.5	.409	-0.2	1B(12) -0.4, 3B(5) -0.5	-0.1	102
2020	LAN	MLB	26	77	8	4	0	3	10	5	29	0	0	.227/.287/.414	80	0.0	.337	-0.2	LF 1, 1B 0	0.0	91

Comparables: Chris Shaw, Ryan O'Hearn, Tyler Austin

I've spun many a tantalizing yarn about Edwin Ríos' majestic power on these pages, and he didn't disappoint in his long-anticipated major league debut. It was a tiny, meaningless sample, but dude's exit velocity was up there in Judge/Sanó range in his limited looks at big-league pitching, and that's fun! Not much of anything has changed in his profile or projection; he is smooth and sure-handed in the field, but he's also slower than a spoon of molasses slathered onto a sloth's fur coat, and it's just not a realistic third-base future. That means he's gotta hit. And keep hitting. And then hit some more. And he's going to have to do that in spite of an approach that gets C.J. Cron a little flushed. He's made it work at just about every step along the way, which is why we continue to write about him. But it's a narrow, fraught path to generating enough positive value with the bat to justify a 26-man slot on a modern roster. The hope here, obviously, is that he does just that.

Low Minors Sleeper

LMS Andy Pages OF
Born: 12/08/00   Age: 19   Bats: R   Throws: R   Height: 6'1"   Weight: 180   Origin: International Free Agent, 2018

YEAR	TEAM	LVL	AGE	PA	R	2B	3B	HR	RBI	BB	K	SB	CS	AVG/OBP/SLG	DRC+	VORP	BABIP	BRR	FRAA	WARP	PF
2018	DDG	RK	17	178	34	8	0	9	33	23	31	9	6	.236/.393/.486	157	18.8	.238	-0.8	RF(20) 0.0, LF(9) 2.3	1.3	89
2018	DOD	RK	17	34	5	1	0	1	3	6	4	1	1	.192/.382/.346	109	1.8	.190	0.3	RF(6) 0.2, LF(3) -0.5	0.1	92
2019	OGD	RK+	18	279	57	22	2	19	55	26	79	7	6	.298/.398/.651	173	33.8	.364	-0.2		2.6	104
2020	LAN	MLB	19	251	24	13	1	6	24	21	86	4	2	.194/.284/.334	66	0.0	.285	-0.3	RF 1, LF 0	-0.2	91

Comparables: Cody Bellinger, Juan Lagares, José Martínez

Pages was a late 2017-18 sign out of the Dominican, where he made a successful debut last year before migrating to Extended last spring and the Pioneer League last summer. And by gum, if you squinted and adjusted your old-man spectacles up and down just so, that right there was a young Justin Turner in the batter's box! Pages' frame is mature for a kid who just turned 19, and he channels his strength into a lofted swing with quality bat speed. The stance is vertical, the hands show signs of loading consistently off a large leg kick, and he explodes through the hitting zone. There isn't as much physical projection remaining as your typical teenager, but the raw power should grow into plus territory. He's struck out a good bit in his young career, but that's not necessarily surprising given the complex hitting mechanics, and it's consistently loud contact when he makes it. He's an entertaining, confident hitter in the box. He played center for the majority of his reps last summer in the Pioneer League, but it's a corner profile with heavier legs that produce average-at-best foot speed. Given the advanced offensive development he's likely to see full-season ball next year, and he'll be a fun one to monitor once he does.

Top Talents 25 and Under (as of 4/1/2020)

1. Cody Bellinger
2. Walker Buehler
3. Corey Seager
4. Gavin Lux
5. Dustin May
6. Will Smith
7. Julio Urias
8. Alex Verdugo
9. Josiah Gray
10. Miguel Vargas

The first two names on this list should come as a surprise to no one. Bellinger just authored an MVP season while spending time at first base in addition to fields center and right, and graded out to a cumulative +15 FRAA. His 158 DRC+ was second to only Christian Yelich (167) in the National League. Given that his greatest competition for the top spot on this list is a pitcher with Tommy John surgery on his resume, it wasn't a difficult call. That pitcher, Buehler, assumed the mantle of staff ace from Clayton Kershaw this year, even if he was statistically overshadowed by Hyun-Jin Ryu for much of it. There's no one Manager Dave Roberts and company trust more with the season on the line than the flamethrower with the coat-hanger frame. With good reason, too: Buehler produced a 2.89 DRA to go with his 215 strikeouts in 182 1/3 innings–good for 5.7 WARP, which ranked 7th in the National League and 11th in MLB.

The biggest pain point in this process was slotting in Seager. The Dodgers' current shortstop produced a three-win season, but much of that was based on solid fielding from a valuable position, given his mild 106 DRC+. Given how much positioning factors in to Seager's ability to man the position, it's fair to wonder how much credit is really his to claim. Seager has also produced two four-win seasons in recent memory, but injuries took away most of 2018 while striking just as his bat started to heat up a couple times in 2019. It's not unfair to prefer the shiny new option (Lux), but Seager topped our prospect list back in 2015, speaking to the upside present in a guy who has produced 13 wins already in his career. There's nothing to say Lux won't meet the same or similar obstacles as Seager has, even if recency bias has us wishcasting that he doesn't. Seager earns the spot here due to actually doing at the top level, but if you prefer the risk proposition that Lux offers, we won't blame you.

May vs. Smith offers a similarly intriguing argument, especially since the latter has "done it" in the majors a bit more than the former. Still, as good as Smith was overall, it's easy to use some admittedly arbitrary endpoints to call into question whether the league adjusted or he tired. He became the full-time catcher around July 27th. Over his first 19 games, Smith slashed .339/.411/.887. Over his next 26 games (until the end of the season), he nosedived down to .183/.277/.305. He ended the season with a .907 OPS and was solid, if not better, behind the dish. This ranking is a bet that he sees some offensive regression as he starts consistently over the course of a full season, though we're still quite high on the overall package he offers.

For his part, May flashed in his brief major-league stint. He recorded some solid overall surface stats that bely an uglier DRA (4.55) but shiny FIP (2.85). His stuff was tremendous, though, as his fastball demonstrated enough run that it could viably Beat the Freeze, and a useful cut fastball that tricked batters because they had to consider the running two-seamer. His vaunted curveball came and went, and it seems like the different grip/seams on the major-league (and Triple-A) ball might have played a part there. Slotting May in over Smith is a gamble that he figures that out and ascends to mid-rotation status while flashing more over the course of the next season.

Urias fails to join May above Smith only because it isn't at all clear how many innings he can muster. He accrued just shy of 80 in 2019, which doesn't exactly forebode a full season in the rotation. He also needs to demonstrate his progress as a human being after earning a 20-game suspension after he was arrested for suspicion of domestic violence, where witnesses allege he shoved his girlfriend to the ground in a parking lot.

Verdugo is a logical endpoint for the eligible major leaguers on this list. He started out quite hot, tailed off, and then missed most of August and all of September due to injury. He's limited to the corner outfield, so there is significant pressure on the bat to produce enough value to justify his playing time. That said, his (limited) success in the big leagues is enough to easily earn him a spot ahead of the third- and fourth-ranked prospects in the system.

Eyewitness Reports

Eyewitness Report: Gavin Lux

Evaluator: Kevin Carter
Report Date: 06/26/2019
Dates Seen: 6/11/2019
Risk Factor: Low
Physical/Health: Mature average frame with lean athletic muscle throughout build. Quality strength in legs and hips with a high waist. Excellent athlete with plus quick twitch and plus coordination/Body control. Instinctual feel for movements and adjusting body to get power where needed.

Tool	Future Grade	Report
Hit	60	Plus barrel acceleration, excellent feel for barrel, plus coordination, adjusts swing to location, stays back when fooled, lower and upper body stay in sync. Hits the hard to all fields. Punishes pitches in zone aggressively, tracks spin, understands the zone and doesn't chase often.
Power	55	Plus raw power with powerful legs and hips. Lower body mechanics are clean and stay in sync with upper body and allows him to generate significant barrel velocity at the point of contact. Line drive approach may mean a very high double rate, but he will still put them into the seats at an above average rate.
Baserunning/ Speed	55	Above average runner who accelerates well and has an above average top speed. Excellent base-runner with great instincts and reads, but likely won't steal many bases.
Glove	55	Quick physical reactions and good closing speed in the gap. Good hands and clean mechanics should lead to relatively few miscues. Good footwork and body control allows him to adapt to balls that lead to strange body positioning. Current reads and instincts should improve a bit with more reps.
Arm	50	Might be a hair below average arm strength, but quick transitions and an accurate arm lead to more than enough ability to get the ball into 1B in time on the vast majority of plays.

Conclusion: Gavin Lux profiles as a plus shortstop at the MLB level. Lux possesses a plus offensive skillset including impressive physical hit tool markers, a quality approach with spin recognition, and above average game power. He should be a slight positive both on the basepaths and defensively compared to the average MLB shortstop. Even if he doesn't reach his potential as an above average defensive shortstop, being able to field the position competently with his offense is more than enough to provide significant value. Lux has all-star shortstop upside if he continues to refine his approach to include more patience and taps into more of his plus raw power.

Eyewitness Report: Josiah Gray

Evaluator: Brandon Williams
Report Date: 06/11/2019
Dates Seen: 5/29 ; 6/9
Risk Factor: Medium
Delivery: The converted shortstop operates with an efficient, easily repeatable, drop-and-drive delivery with a natural three-quarters release point.

Pitch Type	Future Grade	Sitting Velocity	Peak Velocity	Report
Fastball	60	94	96	Gray throws a heavy 93-96 MPH fastball with natural arm-side run emanating from his three-quarters release. He adroitly commands the pitch with effectiveness to all quadrants of the zone.
Slider	55	85	86	A firm 84-86 MPH slider sweeps away from right-handed batters with slight vertical drop. Thrown with good command to the outer-half of the plate versus righties, Gray utilizes the pitch for the punchout and to keep hitters from sitting on his fastball.
Changeup	50	86	88	Gray's 84-88 MPH changeup is his least used offering, although it too flashes plus-potential. Thrown with good arm-action, hitters anxiously anticipating the 95 MPH heater are helpless as the deceptive cambio tumbles beneath their swings.

Conclusion: Gray's athleticism, efficient mechanics, and solid three pitch arsenal establish a high-floor for the 21-year-old right-hander. Still relatively new to pitching, the converted shortstop's potential is high. With continued development and mastery of his craft, Gray could eventually be a no. 2 or 3 starter or a vital bullpen component.

Miami Marlins

The State of the System

Hi kids, do you like upside?

The Top Ten

★ ★ ★ *2020 Top 101 Prospect* **#27** ★ ★ ★

1 Sixto Sanchez RHP OFP: 70 ETA: 2020

Born: 07/29/98 Age: 21 Bats: R Throws: R Height: 6'0" Weight: 185 Origin: International Free Agent, 2015

YEAR	TEAM	LVL	AGE	W	L	SV	G	GS	IP	H	HR	BB/9	K/9	K	GB%	BABIP	WHIP	ERA	DRA	WARP	PF
2017	LWD	A	18	5	3	0	13	13	67¹	46	1	1.2	8.6	64	49%	.251	0.82	2.41	2.72	2.0	82
2017	CLR	A+	18	0	4	0	5	5	27²	27	1	2.9	6.5	20	42%	.295	1.30	4.55	4.83	0.1	90
2018	CLR	A+	19	4	3	0	8	8	46²	39	1	2.1	8.7	45	52%	.295	1.07	2.51	3.48	1.0	99
2019	JUP	A+	20	0	2	0	2	2	11	14	1	1.6	4.9	6	60%	.351	1.45	4.91	5.73	-0.1	90
2019	JAX	AA	20	8	4	0	18	18	103	87	5	1.7	8.5	97	49%	.286	1.03	2.53	4.06	1.1	94
2020	MIA	MLB	21	2	3	0	17	6	44	42	5	3.1	7.3	36	45%	.285	1.29	3.71	4.05	0.8	91

Comparables: David Holmberg, Deolis Guerra, Mike Soroka

The Report: If you are one of the top pitching prospects in all of baseball, the cornerstone trade return for arguably the best catcher in the game, and having just finished the season injury-free in Double-A, you should feel pretty good, right? If you're Sixto Sanchez, there is plenty to be excited about, yet some prominent questions remain as the scrutiny of the big leagues looms.

Standing just 6-foot even, Sanchez is unquestionably blessed with a power arm that few others his stature can feature. Routinely running it up into the high-90s and above, he uses a stout lower half in his delivery to generate extra velocity as he torques over his front hip. The fastball is, well, fast. However, it lacks complementary life, movement, and finish despite its elite velocity. While his command is better than you'd expect from a generic triple-digit fireballer—if such a thing exists—it's not a pitch he consistently controls in the zone.

The secondaries are good—not great—with the ability to throw off the timing of the hitter if he tries to cheat on the heater. The slider is short and snappy, used primarily to the glove-side where it breaks more, as opposed to flattening out on the arm-side. His changeup took a big step forward in 2019, touching 90 regularly with good sinking action as it approaches the plate. But neither the slider nor the changeup are formidable punch-out pitches.

With the straightness of the fastball, Sanchez has had to rely more on getting outs in the field than someone of his pedigree. Of the pitchers listed in our midseason top 50, and the rough draft of our forthcoming Top 101, nobody has a lower strikeout percentage than Sanchez. Given his injury history, diminutive size, low walks (good) and low strikeouts (bad), you have to begin to wonder if his future is destined for an electric late-inning relief role.

Variance: Extreme. This can go any number of directions. He could be a No. 2 or 3 starter, he could be a high-leverage reliever, he could be a star when healthy or have his playing time cut short. Such is the life of a 21-year-old who throws really hard and doesn't have a long track record of sustained success.

Mark Barry's Fantasy Take: Please don't tell any of my bosses, but for some reason I'm lukewarm on Sixto. For a guy with triple-digit heat and one-and-a-half plus secondaries, it really feels like he should strike more dudes out. Seeing Sanchez eclipse the 100-inning mark for the first time is certainly encouraging, but he has yet to punch out a batter per inning at any level, despite premium stuff. I'm obviously not saying Sanchez is bad, far from it, but I am concerned about his trajectory into fantasy acedom.

★ ★ ★ *2020 Top 101 Prospect* **#35** ★ ★ ★

2 **JJ Bleday** **OF**   OFP: 60   ETA: 2021
Born: 11/10/97   Age: 22   Bats: L   Throws: L   Height: 6'3"   Weight: 205   Origin: Round 1, 2019 Draft (#4 overall)

YEAR	TEAM	LVL	AGE	PA	R	2B	3B	HR	RBI	BB	K	SB	CS	AVG/OBP/SLG	DRC+	VORP	BABIP	BRR	FRAA	WARP	PF
2019	JUP	A+	21	151	13	8	0	3	19	11	29	0	0	.257/.311/.379	105	2.1	.306	-1.1	RF(32) -0.9	0.1	91
2020	MIA	MLB	22	251	23	12	1	6	25	16	66	2	1	.225/.277/.355	67	0.0	.288	0.0	RF -5	-0.7	91

Comparables: Yangervis Solarte, Rymer Liriano, Abraham Almonte

The Report: Bleday is not the most exciting 2019 draftee to write about. Adley Rutschman could be a generational catching prospect, Andrew Vaughn might be the best pure bat we've seen in a bit, and Bobby Witt, Riley Greene and CJ Abrams—to name three—arguably have more upside. Bleday is merely a very good, polished, college corner outfielder. He's got more than enough arm for right field and should be above-average there, but man that is not an exciting lede for the fourth-overall pick in the draft. Frankly the lede has been buried here already, so let's dig up, stupid. While Vaughn might be the best pure bat in this year's draft class, Bleday isn't that far behind. He actually lapped Vaughn on game power his junior year, swatting 26 home runs for Vanderbilt. This was an important development for Bleday, who was on follow lists for a while due to his hitting ability and power potential, but it wasn't until last summer on the Cape that he started dragging that plus pop into games. Now he's a potential plus hit/plus power right fielder who could move quickly—the Marlins sent him to the Florida State League right out of the draft—and he has a relatively high floor. There's plus bat speed and good strength out of his broad, athletic frame. He has a solid command of the strike zone and enough barrel control to flick a base hit if he gets fooled. Bleday might not have the most upside in the 2019 draft class, but he's very likely to be somewhere in the middle of the lineup on the next good Marlins team.

Variance: Medium. We think he will hit, but with a corner outfield profile, he'll need to really hit to be a plus regular.

Mark Barry's Fantasy Take: As it turns out, folding a little power into an already strong offensive profile is, uh, good. Bleday smashed 26 homers and slugged over .700 as a junior at Vanderbilt before heading straight to High-A after the draft. The power retention will dictate his ceiling, but if some version of the breakout sticks, Bleday has OF2 upside.

★ ★ ★ *2020 Top 101 Prospect* **#52** ★ ★ ★

3 **Jazz Chisholm** **SS**   OFP: 60   ETA: 2021
Born: 02/01/98   Age: 22   Bats: L   Throws: R   Height: 5'11"   Weight: 165   Origin: International Free Agent, 2015

YEAR	TEAM	LVL	AGE	PA	R	2B	3B	HR	RBI	BB	K	SB	CS	AVG/OBP/SLG	DRC+	VORP	BABIP	BRR	FRAA	WARP	PF
2017	KNC	A	19	125	14	5	2	1	12	10	39	3	0	.248/.325/.358	92	6.4	.371	0.7	SS(29) 0.8	0.6	97
2018	KNC	A	20	341	52	17	4	15	43	30	97	8	2	.244/.311/.472	102	17.7	.303	-1.4	SS(75) -0.3	1.3	106
2018	VIS	A+	20	160	27	6	2	10	27	9	52	9	2	.329/.369/.597	139	21.1	.443	0.5	SS(36) -0.7	1.3	98
2019	JAX	AA	21	94	6	4	2	3	10	11	24	3	0	.284/.383/.494	104	10.2	.370	-0.5	SS(21) -1.8	0.4	96
2019	WTN	AA	21	364	51	6	5	18	44	41	123	13	4	.204/.305/.427	108	19.9	.261	2.9	SS(88) -5.8	1.7	101
2020	MIA	MLB	22	35	3	1	0	1	4	3	13	1	0	.206/.279/.367	68	0.0	.312	0.0	SS 0	0.0	91

Comparables: Yu Chang, Michael Chavis, Trevor Story

The Report: Another top prospect brought in from outside the organization, Chisholm was a breakout name after a dominant 2018 season that had him slashing .272/.329/.513 with 25 dingers between two levels of A-ball. Yes, there were strikeouts. In fact, there were a lot of them. But with that kind of offensive production, as well as plus athleticism with commensurate defensive ability, it was worth overlooking all the whiffs.

That is, until the first half of 2019 where he struckout 85 times in 59 games at Double-A Jackson and saw his batting average dip below .200 until the Fourth of July. The power was still present, as Chisholm jacked 13 homers in a notoriously difficult hitting environment. He also swiped a handful of bases, and improved his walk rate compared to prior years. With those tools still present, Arizona and Miami pulled off a rare double-prospect trade.

Chisholm was largely the same player in the final month of the season with his new organization, with slightly fewer strikeouts that will hopefully provide some distance from the projection of a rare non-first-base/DH Three True Outcomes offensive player. He is a dynamic, quick-twitch player that you can tell is having fun when out on the diamond. If the approach can continue to tighten up, he can be one of the better all-around middle infield prospects in the game.

Variance: Very high. It all boils down to how much will he strikeout. Because he will strikeout; probably a lot. If it's down closer to 25 percent of the time, it will be overshadowed by the damage inflicted with the bat.

Mark Barry's Fantasy Take: Because I'm ever the rosy optimist, let's start with the good: Jazz hit 21 dingers and snagged 16 bags in 2019, while drawing walks over 11 percent of the time. The bad: there were strikeouts, oh so many strikeouts. Chisholm could be a 20/20 guy, a feat only nine big leaguers achieved in 2019, but there's substantial risk that he'll strike out too much to reach that upside. He's a top-50 guy still, but the variance is immense.

★ ★ ★ *2020 Top 101 Prospect* **#80** ★ ★ ★

4 Jesús Sánchez OF   OFP: 60   ETA: 2021

Born: 10/07/97   Age: 22   Bats: L   Throws: R   Height: 6'3"   Weight: 230   Origin: International Free Agent, 2014

YEAR	TEAM	LVL	AGE	PA	R	2B	3B	HR	RBI	BB	K	SB	CS	AVG/OBP/SLG	DRC+	VORP	BABIP	BRR	FRAA	WARP	PF
2017	BGR	A	19	512	81	29	4	15	82	32	91	7	2	.305/.348/.478	127	29.7	.349	3.4	LF(78) 14.0, RF(19) -0.5	4.3	104
2018	PCH	A+	20	378	56	24	2	10	64	15	71	6	3	.301/.331/.462	137	19.9	.350	-1.5	RF(78) 1.8, CF(7) -1.4	2.0	99
2018	MNT	AA	20	110	14	8	0	1	11	11	21	1	1	.214/.300/.327	92	-0.8	.263	0.7	RF(26) -0.8, CF(1) 0.0	0.1	94
2019	MNT	AA	21	316	32	11	1	8	49	24	65	5	4	.275/.332/.404	122	10.2	.327	0.1	RF(72) 0.0	1.4	97
2019	DUR	AAA	21	71	6	2	1	1	5	6	20	0	0	.206/.282/.317	52	-6.2	.279	-0.3	RF(15) 0.7	-0.2	97
2019	NWO	AAA	21	78	11	1	0	4	9	9	15	0	0	.246/.338/.446	74	-2.5	.250	0.3	CF(8) -1.6, RF(7) 3.6	0.2	97
2020	MIA	MLB	22	42	4	2	0	1	4	3	11	0	0	.240/.289/.379	77	0.0	.309	-0.1	RF 0	0.0	91

Comparables: Jorge Bonifacio, Justin Williams, Gabriel Guerrero

The Report: Selling high on a lofty reliever and depth starter, the Marlins were able to nab quite the haul in Jesús Sánchez from Tampa in their midseason trade. At every stop in his professional matriculation up the Rays organization, Sánchez did nothing but hit for high average year after year. The questions were—and still are to some degree—is the hit tool sustainable, and will the power develop?

It's a compact setup that relies on his excellent hands and barrel control to meet the ball, casting the bat instead of engaging his core to invoke more power. The bat-speed isn't elite, which leads evaluators to wonder whether his strength gains will help turn more doubles into home runs. One positive trend, despite lackluster numbers in Triple-A, is his propensity to adapt to a level change. Even after struggles, he's shown an ability to learn and improve, coming back better the second time around. It stems from a desire to compete which is evident in every at-bat: he wants to beat you.

So much of the projection is reliant upon the offensive upside, but he's also an average runner and won't hurt you in the field, featuring a strong arm perfectly suited for right field. If for some reason the stick never fulfills its full potential, he's at worst a very good option off the bench. At best? He's a corner outfielder with middle of the order run production attributes.

Variance: High. He could be an All-Star, he really could. But there is a plateau effect in play, that if you keep thinking something will happen in development and it hasn't yet, you wonder if it ever will.

Mark Barry's Fantasy Take: Sánchez was better after changing Florida zip codes at the deadline, but still hasn't lived up to the promise of his breakout 2017 campaign. His proximity to the big club keeps him in the dynasty consciousness, but he still needs some work offensively to be better than an OF5.

★ ★ ★ *2020 Top 101 Prospect* **#97** ★ ★ ★

5 Edward Cabrera RHP   OFP: 55   ETA: 2021

Born: 04/13/98   Age: 22   Bats: R   Throws: R   Height: 6'4"   Weight: 175   Origin: International Free Agent, 2015

YEAR	TEAM	LVL	AGE	W	L	SV	G	GS	IP	H	HR	BB/9	K/9	K	GB%	BABIP	WHIP	ERA	DRA	WARP	PF
2017	BAT	A-	19	1	3	0	13	6	35²	42	1	2.0	8.1	32	55%	.350	1.40	5.30	6.17	-0.4	104
2018	GRB	A	20	4	8	0	22	22	100¹	105	11	3.8	8.3	93	44%	.329	1.47	4.22	5.33	-0.2	100
2019	JUP	A+	21	5	3	0	11	11	58	37	1	2.8	11.3	73	49%	.277	0.95	2.02	3.04	1.4	91
2019	JAX	AA	21	4	1	0	8	8	38²	28	6	3.0	10.0	43	50%	.242	1.06	2.56	3.43	0.7	99
2020	MIA	MLB	22	2	2	0	29	2	37	37	6	3.9	9.3	38	44%	.313	1.45	4.81	4.96	0.2	91

Comparables: Jake Faria, Yordano Ventura, Gerrit Cole

The Report: Cabrera had a breakout campaign in 2019, adding improved command to his plus-plus velocity. His fastball sat at 94-96 and touched 100 several times. He has good feel for spinning his curve, though the movement can still be inconsistent. Cabrera improved his change this season, and it now has the potential to be a third above-average pitch. He mixes his pitches well and can keep hitters off-balance with changes in velocity and movement.

The biggest challenge for Cabrera going forward is to continue to refine the secondary stuff and command, and to prove he can handle a starter's workload, as he has never thrown more than 100 1/3 innings in a season. That's not uncommon for a young pitcher moving quickly through the minors, it does increase the risk factor. But the improvements Cabrera showed in 2019 were uniformly positive markers.

Variance: Medium. Durability and stamina concerns remain, but the stuff is starter-quality, and he has some Double-A success under his belt.

Mark Barry's Fantasy Take: It must be nice adding around 10 percentage points to your strikeout rate as you ascend through the system as Cabrera did in 2019. If this trend continues, Cabrera could be punching out 100 percent of batters by 2027. For real, though, Cabrera is a legit dude, with the potential to have the "D" capitalized. I'd have him in the top-150, and he could even flirt with the top-100.

6 Monte Harrison OF   OFP: 55   ETA: 2020

Born: 08/10/95 Age: 24 Bats: R Throws: R Height: 6'3" Weight: 220 Origin: Round 2, 2014 Draft (#50 overall)

YEAR	TEAM	LVL	AGE	PA	R	2B	3B	HR	RBI	BB	K	SB	CS	AVG/OBP/SLG	DRC+	VORP	BABIP	BRR	FRAA	WARP	PF
2017	WIS	A	21	261	32	12	1	11	32	29	70	11	3	.265/.359/.475	132	22.1	.333	1.3	CF(62) 1.6	2.1	101
2017	CAR	A+	21	252	41	16	1	10	35	14	69	16	1	.278/.341/.487	127	20.5	.358	3.3	CF(32) -1.8, RF(24) 2.1	1.8	102
2018	JAX	AA	22	583	85	20	3	19	48	44	215	28	9	.240/.316/.399	96	28.5	.368	3.6	CF(121) -8.0, RF(14) 0.4	1.3	95
2019	NWO	AAA	23	244	41	7	2	9	24	25	73	20	2	.274/.357/.451	94	12.5	.373	3.2	CF(32) 2.6, RF(19) -2.4	0.9	94
2020	MIA	MLB	24	112	10	5	1	2	11	8	41	3	1	.215/.289/.344	65	0.0	.333	0.3	CF 0, RF 0	-0.1	91

Comparables: Lane Thomas, Brett Phillips, Teoscar Hernández

The Report: Harrison missed a bunch of time this year with a wrist injury that required some summer surgery, but overall he bounced back some from a poor 2018 campaign in Double-A. He's tinkered with his setup and swing during his recent pro struggles, but seems to have returned to a similar setup and the small leg lift that he employed during his 2017 breakout. He's filled out some in the lower half, but it's still a very athletic, high-waisted frame.

Harrison still looks the part of a five-tool center fielder. The bat doesn't look quite as quick and whippy as it once did, and his feel for spin can remain raw, but the hand-eye is good enough to project an average hit tool, which should allow enough of the raw power to manifest in games to give him a shot to be an outfield regular. That hit tool is still projection-heavy for a guy in Triple-A, though.

Harrison glides out there in center, and he's improved his reads and routes enough that he's not just getting by on pure foot speed. He could use some more consolidation time in Triple-A, and while he's older now than you might think—he turned 24 at the end of last season—the upside remains tantalizing. However, it's now more in the mold of a solid power/speed everyday outfielder, not quite the same all-star heights we dreamt of after 2017.

Variance: High. You know the drill by now. The swing-and-miss here could lead to a lot of hit tool variance. See Lewis Brinson or Isan Díaz's issues in the majors so far (the Marlins sure have a type). On the other hand, all five tools still pop up from time to time, and if he comes back from his wrist injury in 2020 without issue, it's still a profile I'd like to bet on.

Mark Barry's Fantasy Take: Harrison swiped 23 bags in 25 tries this season, a mix of speed and skill that portends well for his future in base thievery. That alone keeps him in the top-100 or so, and his proximity to the big leagues probably has him closer to the top-50. The strikeouts are concerning and have always been Harrison's biggest obstacle irl and in fantasy, keeping his range of outcomes wide.

7 Jorge Guzman RHP   OFP: 55   ETA: Late 2020

Born: 01/28/96 Age: 24 Bats: R Throws: R Height: 6'2" Weight: 182 Origin: International Free Agent, 2014

YEAR	TEAM	LVL	AGE	W	L	SV	G	GS	IP	H	HR	BB/9	K/9	K	GB%	BABIP	WHIP	ERA	DRA	WARP	PF
2017	STA	A-	21	5	3	0	13	13	66²	51	4	2.4	11.9	88	55%	.311	1.03	2.30	3.42	1.4	90
2018	JUP	A+	22	0	9	0	21	21	96	84	7	6.0	9.5	101	40%	.303	1.54	4.03	5.77	-0.5	91
2019	JAX	AA	23	7	11	0	25	24	138²	96	13	4.6	8.2	127	34%	.241	1.20	3.50	4.16	1.3	94
2020	MIA	MLB	24	2	2	0	33	0	35	36	5	3.9	7.8	30	35%	.298	1.46	4.77	4.97	0.2	91

Comparables: Matt Hall, Hansel Robles, André Rienzo

The Report: There is a lot to like about Guzman. He has a plus fastball that sits 95-97 and occasionally hits triple digits. His slider and change both flash above average. But that makes him just about every decent pitching prospect nowadays. Guzman's failure to rise above the crowd is largely due to his inability to consistently repeat his delivery. The resulting command issues have hounded him throughout his career, and though there were hints of improvement at times in 2019, it is looking more and more like a relief profile long-term. The good news is that it should be a high-leverage role as the fastball is definitely a weapon. A move to the pen would allow Guzman to focus on just his change as the only secondary pitch he would need. That pitch improved over the course of the season and could develop into a swing-and-miss offering. It's time for the Marlins to make Guzman a reliever and let him help in Miami quickly.

Variance: High. There remains significant relief risk here and the command might make him just a frustrating and tantalizing setup guy.

Mark Barry's Fantasy Take: As Bret mentioned in Guzman's write up from last season, the former Yankee prospect still has more name value than fantasy value, mostly due to him being, well, a former Yankee prospect. The stuff still dazzles in flashes, but for me the control is spotty enough to keep him outside the top-200.

8 Lewin Diaz 1B   OFP: 55   ETA: 2021

Born: 11/19/96   Age: 23   Bats: L   Throws: L   Height: 6'4"   Weight: 225   Origin: International Free Agent, 2013

YEAR	TEAM	LVL	AGE	PA	R	2B	3B	HR	RBI	BB	K	SB	CS	AVG/OBP/SLG	DRC+	VORP	BABIP	BRR	FRAA	WARP	PF
2017	CDR	A	20	508	47	33	1	12	68	25	80	2	1	.292/.329/.444	109	11.8	.322	-2.2	1B(110) 3.0	1.2	102
2018	FTM	A+	21	310	21	11	3	6	35	10	56	1	0	.224/.255/.344	65	-14.6	.255	-1.8	1B(74) 2.7	-0.6	99
2019	FTM	A+	22	234	34	11	1	13	36	14	40	0	0	.290/.333/.533	157	15.5	.297	-1.3	1B(52) 4.9	2.0	95
2019	PEN	AA	22	138	12	16	1	6	26	8	23	0	0	.302/.341/.587	130	10.2	.320	-0.6	1B(31) -0.2	0.9	96
2019	JAX	AA	22	129	16	6	0	8	14	11	28	0	1	.200/.279/.461	122	-0.5	.188	-0.2	1B(29) -2.2	0.5	96
2020	MIA	MLB	23	251	27	13	1	11	33	15	61	0	0	.227/.280/.429	85	1.0	.263	-0.4	1B 1	0.5	91

Comparables: Max Kepler, Abiatal Avelino, Zach Green

The Report: Diaz was acquired for Sergio Romo in the midst of what was a breakout season for him in the Twins organization. He has plus raw power and his swing is becoming more efficient in translating that to games. He starts with his hands low and he generates good loft and bat speed. He also shows a rapidly-improving hit tool, with good pitch recognition. He can effectively use the whole field and he makes a lot of contact for a power hitter. Diaz has worked to make himself a good player defensively. He has good hands and range and improving footwork around the bag. The development needs to continue as the margins on this profile are razor-thin, but Diaz seems like the perfect addition to a system that had been very pitcher-heavy.

Variance: Medium. The progression of power development could break down at any time and/or the hit tool could disappear into the power-sellout vortex.

Mark Barry's Fantasy Take: I'm a big fan of this guy, especially the way he walked around in the cold with the cat and, like, sang folk songs and stuff. I don't know, I kind of fell asleep during that one. Aside from his vocals, Diaz has some budding pop, which is cool, but is otherwise a 1B-only prospect in the NL, which means those budding skills will have to bloom in a big way for him to be fantasy useful.

9 Trevor Rogers LHP   OFP: 55   ETA: 2021

Born: 11/13/97   Age: 22   Bats: L   Throws: L   Height: 6'6"   Weight: 185   Origin: Round 1, 2017 Draft (#13 overall)

YEAR	TEAM	LVL	AGE	W	L	SV	G	GS	IP	H	HR	BB/9	K/9	K	GB%	BABIP	WHIP	ERA	DRA	WARP	PF
2018	GRB	A	20	2	7	0	17	17	72²	86	4	3.3	10.5	85	48%	.394	1.56	5.82	5.89	-0.6	102
2019	JUP	A+	21	5	8	0	18	18	110¹	97	7	2.0	10.0	122	44%	.303	1.10	2.53	3.93	1.5	94
2019	JAX	AA	21	1	2	0	5	5	26	25	3	3.1	9.7	28	34%	.314	1.31	4.50	4.96	0.0	99
2020	MIA	MLB	22	2	2	0	33	0	35	35	5	3.3	8.4	33	38%	.298	1.36	4.29	4.62	0.3	91

Comparables: Andrew Faulkner, Anthony Banda, Yordano Ventura

The Report: Depending on who you asked before the 2017 draft, Trevor Rogers fell somewhere in the 25-50 range of best available players, yet was selected 13th overall by Miami. Ignoring the competition level of rural New Mexico, his older draft age as a high schooler—and a very scrawny 6-foot-6 frame—his selection was considered somewhat surprising at the time. After a breakout 2019 campaign, most detractors have been silenced.

The tall lefty is all arms and legs, utilizing those long levers in a surprisingly repeatable delivery that has good tempo. Spotting to either corner of the plate, the fastball has late arm-side finish in the low-90s, bumping as high as 95 when needed. The breaking ball is a tad slurvy with side-to-side break but flashes plus when thrown in the lower 80s. And his changeup shows good feel and depth that, with more consistency, could be another plus offering.

With a late season taste of Double-A in just his second full season as a pro, Rogers will likely remain in the Southern League for most of 2020 for further maturation, yet his trajectory is certainly trending upwards.

Variance: High. From both an evaluation and statistical standpoints, Rogers has done everything and more in his first two full years. Even with a "high" risk that comes with a young pitcher, it's a fairly mild risk given his ability to log innings at an advanced rate for his experience.

Mark Barry's Fantasy Take: Rogers could be a decent starting pitcher occupying the middle or back-end of a rotation. That's good for a real-life baseball club, but it's less good for dynasty leagues.

10   Kameron Misner   OF   OFP: 55   ETA: 2023

Born: 01/08/98   Age: 22   Bats: L   Throws: L   Height: 6'4"   Weight: 219   Origin: Round 1, 2019 Draft (#35 overall)

YEAR	TEAM	LVL	AGE	PA	R	2B	3B	HR	RBI	BB	K	SB	CS	AVG/OBP/SLG	DRC+	VORP	BABIP	BRR	FRAA	WARP	PF
2019	MRL	RK	21	38	2	2	0	0	4	9	7	3	0	.241/.421/.310	139	3.7	.318	0.4	CF(5) -0.1, RF(3) -0.2	0.2	98
2019	CLN	A	21	158	25	7	0	2	20	21	35	8	0	.276/.380/.373	137	11.1	.357	2.2	CF(30) 7.1	2.0	102
2020	MIA	MLB	22	251	24	12	1	5	24	23	73	3	1	.226/.304/.345	75	0.0	.312	0.0	CF 7, RF 0	0.8	91

Comparables: Darrell Ceciliani, Mitch Haniger, Jacob May

The Report: Misner possesses an extra-large frame, lean muscle, and displays tons of athleticism with plus speed. There is true five-tool potential here. At the plate, he employs a short and quick stroke with a fairly flat bat path. The lefty rarely expands the zone and owns a patient, selective approach. During batting practice, he shows plenty of power, but mainly to the pull side. Misner can spray it line-to-line, just not for round-trippers yet. When he finds a gap, his wheels take over. His ability to regularly swipe bags highlight plus instincts on the basepaths. He profiles as an above-average center fielder down the road. Coming in on fly balls is Misner's strength, but he can improve on going back to the wall and getting quicker jumps. He has outstanding body control, and exhibits great footwork to gather himself to make strong throws, an easy plus arm in any situation. It seems as though Misner is a more polished—with a higher ceiling—version of Connor Scott.

Variance: High. The only real concern is translating his raw power into games. Even if power doesn't come, he still has four plus tools to work with, but then he falls into the mold of every typical center fielder.

Mark Barry's Fantasy Take: How lucky do you feel? Misner is an uber-athlete with 25/25 upside and a great patience at the dish. His floor feels poor-man's Jake Marisnick-y, however, which is far less appealing.

The Next Ten

11   Braxton Garrett   LHP

Born: 08/05/97   Age: 22   Bats: L   Throws: L   Height: 6'3"   Weight: 190   Origin: Round 1, 2016 Draft (#7 overall)

YEAR	TEAM	LVL	AGE	W	L	SV	G	GS	IP	H	HR	BB/9	K/9	K	GB%	BABIP	WHIP	ERA	DRA	WARP	PF
2017	GRB	A	19	1	0	0	4	4	15¹	13	3	3.5	9.4	16	49%	.250	1.24	2.93	4.86	0.1	109
2019	JUP	A+	21	6	6	0	20	20	105	92	13	3.2	10.1	118	54%	.294	1.23	3.34	4.85	0.2	93
2020	MIA	MLB	22	2	2	0	33	0	35	36	6	4.1	8.5	33	42%	.300	1.48	4.98	5.18	0.1	91

Comparables: Sal Romano, Kyle Ryan, Victor Arano

Having nearly fully recovered from Tommy John surgery that cost him all of 2018, Garrett had a big bounce-back year in 2019, pitching well enough in High-A to eclipse the 100-inning mark and earning a final start to the season in Double-A. Following surgery, velocity is typically the first to return after strength rehab, and command typically the last thing to develop. While not to be confused as a hard-thrower pre-surgery, Garrett struck out over a batter an inning and kept modest walk totals. The fastball velocity for both the two-seamer and four-seamer with natural cut, seems to be a tick down, but it's balanced out by a very good curveball.

The hammer curve was its usual self, showing good 12-6 finish. Garrett can throw the hook in any count with abundant confidence. The changeup is still lagging behind, while fastball command is coming along, but given the low expectations for the former first round pick for this season, his successes were a welcome sight as he heads into what should be a fully healthy 2020 campaign. It will be interesting to see what off-season strength gains have been made, and whether the kid-gloves will be off for the next step of development.

12 Víctor Víctor Mesa OF

Born: 07/20/96 Age: 23 Bats: R Throws: R Height: 5'10" Weight: 165 Origin: International Free Agent, 2018

YEAR	TEAM	LVL	AGE	PA	R	2B	3B	HR	RBI	BB	K	SB	CS	AVG/OBP/SLG	DRC+	VORP	BABIP	BRR	FRAA	WARP	PF
2019	JUP	A+	22	390	37	5	3	0	26	19	48	15	2	.252/.295/.283	90	1.2	.287	-0.9	CF(75) -3.3	0.3	92
2019	JAX	AA	22	113	8	2	0	0	3	3	16	3	0	.178/.200/.196	16	-6.9	.209	-0.4	CF(25) 6.0	0.1	96
2020	MIA	MLB	23	35	3	1	0	0	3	2	7	1	0	.227/.268/.300	46	0.0	.275	0.0	CF 0	-0.1	91

Comparables: Rafael Bautista, Engelb Vielma, David Fletcher

Craig recently asked me if Mesa was the biggest one-year drop for a team number one prospect. I don't really have the time to research it right now, Craig, but I can try to contextualize it. Mainly, it's a set of circumstances which are unlikely to reoccur. Mesa was a soft number one in a shallow system last year, and he'd have been unseated by Sixto if that trade hadn't happened just after the Futures Guide cutoff. We also had far less info on him than I'd like when ranking a prospect at the top of a system. Mesa hadn't played any sort of pro baseball in over a year, and was more akin to a top dollar J2 IFA, who I would tend to be more conservative with in terms of ranking. But he was 21, not 16, the reports were good, and the Serie Nacional ain't the Dominican showcase circuit.

But we do have a lot more information now. Last year's Almora comp looks about right on the glove and speed, and less so on the bat…well, actually Almora was pretty bad last year wasn't he? Maybe it still works offensively too, but comping 2019 Albert Almora is not what you want. Mesa is already a major league quality center fielder, with an arm that will play in any outfield spot, and he's a plus baserunner. However, he has struggled to make quality contact in his first year in pro ball, and hasn't looked the part at the plate at all. Mesa deserves (and needs) time to adjust, but the profile here looks more bench outfielder than starter at present.

13 Nick Neidert RHP

Born: 11/20/96 Age: 23 Bats: R Throws: R Height: 6'1" Weight: 202 Origin: Round 2, 2015 Draft (#60 overall)

YEAR	TEAM	LVL	AGE	W	L	SV	G	GS	IP	H	HR	BB/9	K/9	K	GB%	BABIP	WHIP	ERA	DRA	WARP	PF
2017	MOD	A+	20	10	3	0	19	19	104¹	95	7	1.5	9.4	109	43%	.318	1.07	2.76	3.40	2.3	98
2017	ARK	AA	20	1	3	0	6	6	23¹	33	4	1.9	5.0	13	47%	.341	1.63	6.56	6.40	-0.3	94
2018	JAX	AA	21	12	7	0	26	26	152²	142	17	1.8	9.1	154	47%	.309	1.13	3.24	4.21	2.0	96
2019	JUP	A+	22	0	1	0	2	2	9¹	10	1	3.9	5.8	6	29%	.300	1.50	4.82	5.38	0.0	90
2019	NWO	AAA	22	3	4	0	9	9	41	45	4	4.8	8.1	37	25%	.336	1.63	5.05	5.70	0.4	95
2020	MIA	MLB	23	3	3	0	28	6	52	53	8	3.3	7.3	42	36%	.292	1.39	4.59	4.88	0.4	91

Comparables: Zach Lee, Luis Ortiz, Ronald Herrera

We usually associate prospect fatigue with top prospects we've just run out of things to say about to the point where it a prime example. But it can strike lesser prospects as well. This is the fifth time we've included Neidert on a team list at Baseball Prospectus. He went from a backend starting pitching prospect in a bad Mariners system, to a backend starting pitching prospect in a bad Marlins system, to a backend starting pitching prospect in a much-improved Marlins system. The organizational improvements around him account for much of his slide down the list since last year, although he did miss significant time in 2019 with knee tendinitis.

When he was on the mound he was still extremely Nick Neidert. A low-90s fastball with enough movement and command to play a tick above-average. The changeup is clearly above-average with plus sinking action and good arm speed. Neither breaking ball is anything to write home about—or a blurb about, but he throws strikes with everything. Everything can also be a bit too hittable in the zone. This is rarely a profile that excites me, the 90-mph, good-change righty. But Neidert has a little bit better fastball command and a little bit better change than the average member of this not-very-exclusive club. I'm still not sold that he's much more than a backend/swing type, but I have now conjured enough words to fight off the fatigue for one more list cycle.

14 Jose Devers IF
Born: 12/07/99 Age: 20 Bats: L Throws: R Height: 6'0" Weight: 155 Origin: International Free Agent, 2016

YEAR	TEAM	LVL	AGE	PA	R	2B	3B	HR	RBI	BB	K	SB	CS	AVG/OBP/SLG	DRC+	VORP	BABIP	BRR	FRAA	WARP	PF
2017	DYA	RK	17	47	4	2	1	0	7	0	16	1	0	.239/.255/.326	56	-2.6	.367	-0.7	SS(7) 0.2, 2B(3) -0.1	-0.1	113
2017	YAN	RK	17	169	17	7	2	1	9	18	21	15	3	.246/.359/.348	124	10.6	.277	-2.9	SS(39) -0.4	0.7	91
2018	GRB	A	18	362	46	12	4	0	24	15	49	13	6	.273/.313/.332	91	4.0	.318	-2.6	SS(59) 2.2, 2B(15) 0.0	0.9	104
2019	MRL	RK	19	46	7	3	1	0	2	4	4	3	1	.275/.370/.400	83	3.1	.306	1.5	SS(1) -0.1	0.1	98
2019	JUP	A+	19	138	13	3	1	0	3	8	20	5	0	.325/.384/.365	128	7.8	.387	-1.8	SS(32) -1.9	0.6	91
2020	MIA	MLB	20	251	21	11	1	2	21	15	52	5	2	.244/.302/.332	70	0.0	.306	0.0	SS -1, 2B 0	-0.2	91

Part of the Marlins' return in exchange for Giancarlo Stanton, Devers was known mostly for his glove at the time of the trade. He's still an above-average defender at the six. Fluid and athletic, he has soft hands and shows a natural feel in the field. The bat, formerly an afterthought, took a major step forward last season as Devers held his own as a teenager in the Florida State League. The swing is geared for line drives and he shows an above-average ability to make contact. There's also a discipline in his approach which is rare in younger players as he controls the zone and recognizes spin well. He is never going to hit for much power but the trifecta of hit tool, speed, and defense give him a pretty high floor. Another strong year of offensive development and Devers could be a fast mover in the organization.

15 Connor Scott OF
Born: 10/08/99 Age: 20 Bats: L Throws: L Height: 6'4" Weight: 180 Origin: Round 1, 2018 Draft (#13 overall)

YEAR	TEAM	LVL	AGE	PA	R	2B	3B	HR	RBI	BB	K	SB	CS	AVG/OBP/SLG	DRC+	VORP	BABIP	BRR	FRAA	WARP	PF
2018	MRL	RK	18	119	15	1	4	0	8	14	29	8	5	.223/.319/.311	90	0.5	.307	-1.2	CF(22) -1.6	0.0	104
2018	GRB	A	18	89	4	2	0	1	5	10	27	1	3	.211/.295/.276	56	-2.5	.300	-1.9	CF(22) -3.0	-0.7	104
2019	CLN	A	19	413	56	24	4	4	36	31	91	21	9	.251/.311/.368	98	12.6	.322	1.6	CF(85) -2.6, LF(1) -0.1	1.1	102
2019	JUP	A+	19	111	12	4	1	1	5	11	26	2	1	.235/.306/.327	85	3.0	.301	0.9	CF(24) -1.5	0.1	89
2020	MIA	MLB	20	251	21	11	1	3	21	20	73	4	3	.214/.280/.317	58	0.0	.299	-0.2	CF -2, LF 0	-0.7	91

Comparables: Carlos Tocci, Anthony Gose, Joe Benson

A first-round selection in 2018, Scott has an athletic, tall and lean frame. So far in his pro career, he's impressed more with his defense than his bat. Playing center field, the lefty shows plus range in every direction, while taking efficient routes to the ball. Scott also displays a natural feel and smoothness for the position. The arm strength is plus with an easy throwing motion. At the plate Scott's disciplined and patient approach helps him control the zone well. However, he doesn't have the quickest bat and struggles to barrel inside fastballs on occasion. He also lacks consistent over-the-fence power, but is strong enough to run in to a few. His plus wheels do make him an extra- and stolen-base threat, although his running technique is odd with very long strides and arms that flail out. The defense and speed give Scott a higher floor, but his ceiling is limited because of his offensive profile. He will need to make more consistent hard contact to swim with the fish in Miami.

16 Jerar Encarnacion OF
Born: 10/22/97 Age: 22 Bats: R Throws: R Height: 6'4" Weight: 219 Origin: International Free Agent, 2015

YEAR	TEAM	LVL	AGE	PA	R	2B	3B	HR	RBI	BB	K	SB	CS	AVG/OBP/SLG	DRC+	VORP	BABIP	BRR	FRAA	WARP	PF
2017	MRL	RK	19	167	25	7	3	5	26	10	51	3	3	.266/.323/.448		0.0	.367	0.0		0.0	100
2018	BAT	A-	20	190	30	14	2	4	24	4	57	1	1	.284/.305/.448		0.0	.390	0.0		0.0	100
2018	GRB	A	20	59	3	0	0	0	2	5	23	0	0	.074/.153/.074		0.0	.129	0.0		0.0	100
2019	CLN	A	21	281	34	16	0	10	43	23	69	3	1	.298/.363/.478		0.0	.375	0.0		0.0	100
2019	JUP	A+	21	272	27	10	1	6	28	17	71	3	2	.253/.298/.372		0.0	.326	0.0		0.0	100

You'll be hard-pressed to find a bigger internal development success story for the Marlins than Encarnacion. As an 18-year-old signee out of the Dominican, little had been accomplished in his career prior to 2019 with only two facts being aboundingly clear: he was big and strong. The 6-foot-4 masher destroyed the Midwest League in the first half of the season, hitting .298/.363/.478 with 10 bombs, promptly earning a promotion to High-A. The batting stance elicits memories of former Marlins slugger Giancarlo Stanton, closing his front-side off at delivery to keep his shoulder inside the ball before uncorking a powerful hip pivot that explodes the bat through the zone. He isn't the most fleet of foot, so he may not be long for the outfield, likely ending up at first base. After a strong showing in the Arizona Fall League—including a grand slam in the championship game—Encarnacion will attempt to follow up in 2020 with an equally impressive year; a welcome sight for the higher-ups that want to see more right-handed power in their system.

17 Alex Vesia LHP

Born: 04/11/96 Age: 24 Bats: L Throws: L Height: 6'2" Weight: 195 Origin: Round 17, 2018 Draft (#507 overall)

YEAR	TEAM	LVL	AGE	W	L	SV	G	GS	IP	H	HR	BB/9	K/9	K	GB%	BABIP	WHIP	ERA	DRA	WARP	PF
2018	MRL	RK	22	1	0	0	4	0	8²	4	0	3.1	7.3	7	52%	.174	0.81	0.00	1.80	0.4	100
2018	BAT	A-	22	3	0	0	10	0	24²	27	1	1.5	11.3	31	34%	.394	1.26	1.82	3.70	0.3	100
2019	CLN	A	23	1	2	3	19	1	31²	24	1	4.8	14.5	51	30%	.354	1.29	2.56	3.47	0.5	102
2019	JUP	A+	23	4	0	1	10	0	18²	12	2	0.5	11.6	24	48%	.238	0.70	1.93	2.42	0.5	100
2019	JAX	AA	23	2	0	1	9	0	16¹	8	0	0.6	13.8	25	46%	.286	0.55	0.00	2.62	0.4	100
2020	MIA	MLB	24	2	2	0	33	0	35	34	5	3.4	11.0	43	42%	.329	1.36	4.22	4.52	0.3	91

Comparables: Ryne Harper, John Gaub, Andrew Vasquez

When last draft's 17th-round senior sign out of Cal State-East Bay—the Pioneers, if you were wondering—makes your prospect list, it usually means one of two things: 1) You have a very, very bad system, like late 00's Astros bad, or 2) you pulled off a very nice bit of draft and development work. Vesia is the latter. The fastball velocity is only average, but emerges from a deceptive arm action and a high slot, while generating plenty of sink to keep the heater off of barrels. He commands the fastball well east-west, and it plays up to above-average from the left side. He pairs it with a mid-80s slider that he can manipulate to either side of the plate. It will flash plus with late depth when he wants to come in with it against righties and is good enough to crossover, given how well he commands it generally. There's a change for a different look against righties, too, although it acts more like a firm two-seamer. Vesia goes right after hitters, but the stuff and command make him no mere minor league southpaw strike-thrower who gets found out when you add on the third deck. The upside here isn't huge, but Vesia is a quality relief prospect.

18 Jordan Holloway RHP

Born: 06/13/96 Age: 24 Bats: R Throws: R Height: 6'6" Weight: 215 Origin: Round 20, 2014 Draft (#587 overall)

YEAR	TEAM	LVL	AGE	W	L	SV	G	GS	IP	H	HR	BB/9	K/9	K	GB%	BABIP	WHIP	ERA	DRA	WARP	PF
2017	GRB	A	21	1	2	0	11	11	50	41	10	4.0	9.0	50	50%	.244	1.26	5.22	4.38	0.5	104
2019	JUP	A+	23	4	11	0	21	21	95	77	6	6.3	8.8	93	51%	.281	1.51	4.45	5.74	-0.8	89
2020	MIA	MLB	24	2	2	0	33	0	35	36	6	4.3	7.1	28	46%	.287	1.49	4.94	5.13	0.1	91

Comparables: Parker Bridwell, Shane Greene, José Castillo

Selected as a physically projectable right-hander in the 20th round of the 2014 draft, it has been a rough road to present day for the power arm from Colorado. He missed the second half of 2017 and all of 2018 after Tommy John surgery. Despite the missed time, he was protected from the Rule 5 draft and added to the 40-man roster last year, showing just how much the Miami brass believed in the talent. His live arm was back in full effect for 2019, but so were some of the command problems that plagued him prior to his surgery. The profile has far more upside as a reliever, where he can sit in the upper-90s and touch 100, while featuring a power breaker as a true swing-and-miss pitch.

19 Nasim Nunez SS

Born: 08/18/00 Age: 19 Bats: B Throws: R Height: 5'9" Weight: 160 Origin: Round 2, 2019 Draft (#46 overall)

YEAR	TEAM	LVL	AGE	PA	R	2B	3B	HR	RBI	BB	K	SB	CS	AVG/OBP/SLG	DRC+	VORP	BABIP	BRR	FRAA	WARP	PF
2019	MRL	RK	18	214	37	5	1	0	12	34	43	28	2	.211/.340/.251	88	13.3	.276	3.2	SS(48) 1.7	1.2	98
2020	MIA	MLB	19	251	19	11	1	2	18	23	77	2	1	.191/.269/.270	45	0.0	.278	0.0	SS 1, 2B 0	-0.8	91

Comparables: Jesmuel Valentín, Yairo Muñoz, Erick Mejia

Nunez—the Marlins second-round pick this past summer—lacks for some present strength or physical projection, but he's a polished, quick-twitch shortstop, who should not only stick at the 6, but be above-average there. He's athletic and rangy in the field, with a plus arm that can make all the throws. He's a plus-plus runner down the line, and the speed will be a weapon on the basepaths. There's good markers in the hit tool here too, as Nunez has a loose, line drive swing with good feel for the barrel considering his age and limited pro experience. The main question on the offensive side is whether he will be strong enough to keep the bat from getting knocked out of his hands against better velocity up the ladder. The speed and defensive tools should earn him a bench role regardless, but if he can show some sting in the bat when he sees 95+, he could carve out a starting role as a tablesetter type.

20 Robert Dugger RHP
Born: 07/03/95   Age: 24   Bats: R   Throws: R   Height: 6'2"   Weight: 180   Origin: Round 18, 2016 Draft (#537 overall)

YEAR	TEAM	LVL	AGE	W	L	SV	G	GS	IP	H	HR	BB/9	K/9	K	GB%	BABIP	WHIP	ERA	DRA	WARP	PF
2017	CLN	A	21	4	1	2	22	9	72	55	4	2.0	8.6	69	51%	.263	0.99	2.00	2.87	1.9	97
2017	MOD	A+	21	2	5	0	9	9	45²	49	4	3.2	9.3	47	40%	.341	1.42	3.94	5.40	-0.1	100
2018	JUP	A+	22	3	1	0	7	7	41¹	40	2	1.5	7.4	34	57%	.306	1.14	2.40	3.83	0.7	89
2018	JAX	AA	22	7	6	0	18	18	109¹	100	13	3.0	8.8	107	36%	.296	1.24	3.79	4.42	1.2	94
2019	JAX	AA	23	6	6	0	13	13	70²	57	6	2.7	9.3	73	48%	.276	1.10	3.31	3.93	0.9	92
2019	NWO	AAA	23	2	4	0	10	10	53¹	74	12	2.9	8.3	49	38%	.376	1.71	7.59	8.50	-0.9	95
2019	MIA	MLB	23	0	4	0	7	7	34¹	33	6	4.5	6.6	25	39%	.262	1.46	5.77	6.38	-0.2	92
2020	MIA	MLB	24	4	6	0	15	15	74	79	15	3.5	6.7	55	40%	.285	1.45	5.29	5.44	0.3	91

Comparables: Hunter Wood, Justin Dunn, Jorge Alcala

When you get down to the 24-year-old, 20th prospect on the team, you kind of know what the description will be. Duggar handled Double-A hitters pretty well with a repertoire that can best be described as average. His fastball rarely topped 90 and he had no standout secondary pitches. He did it all with decent command and an understanding of his craft. He mixed pitches, changed speeds, changed eye levels and kept inexperienced hitters off balance. Then he went to Triple-A and, later, to the major leagues. It didn't work quite as well at those levels. Fly-ball pitchers without overpowering stuff do not find a friend in the Triple-A/MLB baseball and Dugger was no exception. There is still time for him to figure out how he can pitch effectively at the upper levels, but the likely outcome is looking like an up-and-down starter or long reliever.

Personal Cheeseball

PC Evan Edwards 1B
Born: 06/21/97   Age: 23   Bats: L   Throws: L   Height: 6'0"   Weight: 200   Origin: Round 4, 2019 Draft (#111 overall)

YEAR	TEAM	LVL	AGE	PA	R	2B	3B	HR	RBI	BB	K	SB	CS	AVG/OBP/SLG	DRC+	VORP	BABIP	BRR	FRAA	WARP	PF
2019	CLN	A	22	288	32	14	1	8	48	28	74	3	0	.285/.361/.441	135	17.9	.371	0.8	1B(66) 0.3	1.5	102
2020	MIA	MLB	23	251	23	12	1	6	25	15	87	2	1	.227/.278/.356	67	1.0	.333	0.0	1B 0	-0.2	91

Okay, so 6-foot, left/left first basemen and I have a bit of a checkered history. It's not my favorite profile. And while Edwards is stout, even bordering on rectangular of frame, he is not yet a big enough boy to pique Wilson's interest. He does have a quality beard, actually paying attention to shape and lines without being overly finicky about it, a rarity among baseball players. He has big forearms, the whole aesthetics of the look just work with the profile. And the profile isn't that bad. I could easily slip Edwards into the Low Minors Sleeper spot as well. He's aggressive and swings hard. There's some stiffness as well, and he may never make enough contact to consistently get his power from those forearms into games, but it's intriguing pop and he's a very good defender at first base. A defense-first, shorter first baseman with bat questions. Yeah, not exactly filling out a bingo card of my predilections here, but sometimes you surprise yourself.

Low Minors Sleeper

LMS Will Banfield C

Born: 11/18/99   Age: 20   Bats: R   Throws: R   Height: 6'0"   Weight: 200   Origin: Round 2, 2018 Draft (#69 overall)

YEAR	TEAM	LVL	AGE	PA	R	2B	3B	HR	RBI	BB	K	SB	CS	AVG/OBP/SLG	DRC+	VORP	BABIP	BRR	FRAA	WARP	PF
2018	MRL	RK	18	94	7	8	1	0	14	7	28	0	1	.256/.330/.378	82	1.8	.375	-0.9	C(22) 1.2	0.3	105
2018	GRB	A	18	52	5	0	0	3	4	4	15	0	0	.208/.269/.396	76	0.7	.233	0.1	C(14) 0.1	0.1	105
2019	CLN	A	19	433	44	13	2	9	55	25	121	0	0	.199/.252/.310	53	-1.4	.256	-1.7	C(91) 5.5	0.2	102
2020	MIA	MLB	20	251	21	11	1	6	24	16	88	1	0	.198/.257/.322	50	0.0	.291	-0.3	C 0	-0.8	91

Comparables: Kyle Skipworth, Justin Williams, Deivy Grullon

The Midwest League is an aggressive assignment for a prep catcher, even for one that was a second-round pick. His long swing was overmatched by full-season stuff, and while there's some power in the profile, Banfield will need a lot of refinement at the dish to tap into it. The picture is brighter on the defensive side. He's built like a catcher, with a sturdy but athletic frame. He blocks well, he has a cannon for an arm, and projects well as a receiver. He's going to have to hit some to make the majors, but there's the outline of a catch-and-throw backup with some pop already, and he was only 19 in Clinton last year.

Top Talents 25 and Under (as of 4/1/2020)

1. Sixto Sanchez
2. JJ Bleday
3. Sandy Alcantara
4. Jazz Chisholm
5. Jesús Sánchez
6. Isan Díaz
7. Jordan Yamamoto
8. Edward Cabrera
9. Monte Harrison
10. Jorge Guzman

Alcantara threw 197 1/3 innings with a 3.88 ERA and a 45 percent groundball rate in his first extended look at major-league action. He threw two complete game shutouts. He also had games where he struggled to complete five innings and couldn't find the plate. All told, he was a 2.6-WARP pitcher who looked the part of a mid-rotation workhorse who does just enough to stick around but not enough to anchor a rotation. That's great, but doesn't quite trump the upside of the likes of Sanchez and Bleday. In conclusion, Alcantara is a pitcher of contrasts. The only two other players on the list who exhausted their prospect eligibility are Díaz and Yamamoto. Díaz checked in at No. 4 in the system a year ago and laid waste to the PCL to earn an August call-up, after which he struggled mightily. He still projects to have above-average pop and can hold his own at second, the question is if the hit tool and plate discipline come around to the point where the profile isn't entirely reliant on him hitting bombs. 30+ homers with no OBP doesn't buy what it used to. Yamamoto made the jump from Double-A to the majors in June and found himself with a Jacob deGrom-ian 1.59 ERA through his first six starts. He regressed as expected, but a DRA of 3.56 says he was actually significantly better than the 4.46 ERA. His upside is somewhere in the No. 3 or 4 starter range, but that's not too shabby for the fourth piece in the now-infamous Christian Yelich trade.

Eyewitness Reports

Eyewitness Report: Sixto Sanchez

Evaluator: Keanan Lamb
Report Date: 08/01/2019
Dates Seen: 6/11, 6/22, 7/13, 7/29/19
Risk Factor: Very High
Delivery: Front leg actually takes a step back behind the rubber to begin momentum driving down the mound. Hands get maximum separation with ball stabbing down slightly at the bottom of his arm circle. A lot of effort to the delivery, often over-throwing and falling off. True 3/4 slot and tunnels each of his pitches very effectively.

Pitch Type	Future Grade	Sitting Velocity	Peak Velocity	Report
Fastball	70	98	100	Pure gas. Some riding life, explodes out of the hand. Throws a lot of strikes but is more of a strike controller than someone who can command it. With so much effort in the delivery to generate velocity, would likely need to back off a tick to achieve better command. As a starter he can maintain his velo deep into games, so it's a question of just how effective the fastball can be at triple digits if it's getting too much of the plate.
Slider	50	85	87	Sharp, late breaking, can be thrown for strikes and better used in the zone as opposed to a chase pitch. Flattens out at the belt. Gets caught over-throwing with extra effort to spin. Better located to arm-side but not as effective with backdoor break, gets lost glove-side but could be a better swing-and-miss option if precisely thrown. Needs to be more consistent.
Changeup	60	88	90	Firm, but plays almost as a bowling ball sinker with the bottom really falling out at the knees. Excellent arm action plays very well off the fastball with hitters speeding up their bats against the velocity. Confident with pitch, can be used effectively against both righties and lefties.

Conclusion: Sixto is an exciting talent, no doubt about it. However, the track record for 6-foot fireballers who rely on big fastballs isn't exactly great. For someone who has already lost some time due to an arm injury, the Marlins are being very, very careful with slowly building his starter's innings as he is topping the 100 inning mark for the first time in a season during his career. The fastball is top of the scale, and the changeup is a very good plus offering. But the slider is just okay with its inconsistencies, combined with his physical stature and injury history, there is enough concern to question whether he is a starter long-term.

Eyewitness Report: Jesús Sánchez

Evaluator: Keanan Lamb
Report Date: 06/11/2019
Dates Seen: 5/16-20/19, 6/7-8/19
Risk Factor: High
Physical/Health: Tall, muscular build especially in the lower half, maybe a little more room left to add strength in the upper body. Good flexibility and fluid movements; has a certain rhythm to the way he moves. Not overly athletic, at least average to a tick better.

Tool	Future Grade	Report
Hit	50	Excellent hand-eye coordination. Has superb bat control and barreling abilities. More of a dead fastball hitter, always on time, but with such good hands he can lay back on off-speed pitches and still put good contact into the field. Still a bit of a free-swinger with below average strike zone awareness, will likely see strikeout numbers go up as he plays against better competition.
Power	60	Raw power is closer to a 70, and still tapping into his game power with more frequency. Routinely hits the ball with authority and with power to all fields. It is plausible that if he is able to tighten his approach at the plate and be more selective, the power numbers could top out a grade higher.
Baserunning/ Speed	50	Average running ability at present and shouldn't regress much, if at all, even if he does add some weight it shouldn't make too much a difference.
Glove	50	Takes good routes in flight, plays caroms off the wall very well. Good reaction time although a tad hesitant on liners hit directly at him. Doesn't have great top-end speed so range is somewhat limited.
Arm	60	Very strong arm, suited for right field. Sometimes too aggressive with it, needs to reign it in and make the proper throw with accuracy rather than airing it out. Definitely has plus potential.

Conclusion: A hitter first and foremost. Will be a run-producing corner outfielder that fits the profile, chance to have all-star caliber years of production. Still young and refining his game, leading to potential of even more projection. His natural born skills will take him very far, and as he matures could become a special player. Only risk involved is the swing-and-miss to his game, but if that devolves, the rest of his value as a player is sapped.

Milwaukee Brewers

The State of the System

Every year, somebody has to be the worst system in baseball. At least the big league team is good.

The Top Ten

1 **Brice Turang SS**   OFP: 55   ETA: 2021/22

Born: 11/21/99   Age: 20   Bats: L   Throws: R   Height: 6'0"   Weight: 173   Origin: Round 1, 2018 Draft (#21 overall)

YEAR	TEAM	LVL	AGE	PA	R	2B	3B	HR	RBI	BB	K	SB	CS	AVG/OBP/SLG	DRC+	VORP	BABIP	BRR	FRAA	WARP	PF
2018	BRR	RK	18	57	11	2	0	0	7	9	6	8	1	.319/.421/.362	153	4.5	.357	0.0	SS(12) 2.0	0.7	99
2018	HEL	RK	18	135	26	4	1	1	11	22	28	6	1	.268/.385/.348	119	9.8	.345	1.7	SS(23) -0.1, 2B(5) -0.1	0.6	105
2019	WIS	A	19	357	57	13	4	2	31	49	54	21	4	.287/.384/.376	142	25.1	.339	3.2	SS(43) 0.6, 2B(28) 0.9	3.2	103
2019	CAR	A+	19	207	25	6	2	1	6	34	47	9	1	.200/.338/.276	99	2.4	.268	1.6	SS(35) -2.6, 2B(5) -0.8	0.6	108
2020	MIL	MLB	20	251	23	10	1	4	23	25	60	5	1	.231/.310/.339	75	0.0	.298	0.4	SS -1, 2B -1	0.0	93

Comparables: J.P. Crawford, Gavin Lux, Ehire Adrianza

The Report: Turang is one of a handful of Top 101 candidate shortstops this year with a good speed/glove profile, but a long horizon to an MLB role and perhaps limited offensive upside. First the good: Turang is an above-average shortstop with plus range to both sides. He's fluid with his hands and actions, and shows present good instincts on the dirt as a teenager. The arm strength is merely above-average and not a true howitzer, but he's accurate and gets it out quick.

Turang is a plus runner with strong baserunning instincts that will garner him additional value through both traditional thievery and taking the extra base. At the plate there is a potential plus hit tool. He's selective without being passive, and has a line drive swing that stays in the zone a long time. He has enough bat speed to handle better velocity and will drive balls line-to-line. Turang is wiry but not particularly projectable, so power is unlikely ever to be a major part of his game, although he will hit his fair share of doubles. If he hits .270 or .280 consistently he'll be a solid regular, but any erosion of the hit tool might make him more of a fifth infielder.

Variance: High. The lack of power might lead to him getting challenged more in the upper minors. Speed/glove combo make for a realistic bench floor, but the bat is still high variance since it's hit tool/batting average driven.

Ben Carsley's Fantasy Take: Oh god, this is where we're starting, eh? Turang's speed and positional value combine to make him a borderline top-150 dynasty prospect, but you'd be hard pressed to convince me he's more exciting than that. If it all breaks right, maybe he's pre-power Elvis Andrus, but it seems more likely he's a Jose Peraza who can actually play shortstop. Is that worth rostering? Some years. Is that worth punting a prospect roster spot for for a few seasons? It is not.

2   Tristen Lutz   OF   OFP: 55   ETA: 2022

Born: 08/22/98   Age: 21   Bats: R   Throws: R   Height: 6'2"   Weight: 210   Origin: Round 1, 2017 Draft (#34 overall)

YEAR	TEAM	LVL	AGE	PA	R	2B	3B	HR	RBI	BB	K	SB	CS	AVG/OBP/SLG	DRC+	VORP	BABIP	BRR	FRAA	WARP	PF
2017	HEL	RK	18	111	23	1	1	6	16	12	21	2	4	.333/.432/.559	141	11.5	.373	-1.1	CF(22) -1.7	0.3	110
2017	BRR	RK	18	76	12	4	3	3	11	4	21	1	0	.279/.347/.559	116	3.9	.364	0.1	CF(11) 0.5, LF(4) -1.2	0.3	103
2018	WIS	A	19	503	63	33	3	13	63	46	139	9	3	.245/.321/.421	116	13.2	.322	-0.9	RF(68) -11.4, LF(29) 1.9	0.5	103
2019	CAR	A+	20	477	62	24	3	13	54	46	137	3	2	.255/.335/.419	109	17.4	.343	-1.5	CF(70) -3.0, RF(39) -2.4	0.9	109
2020	MIL	MLB	21	251	25	12	1	8	29	15	86	1	0	.222/.279/.392	73	0.0	.312	-0.3	CF -1, RF -2	-0.4	93

Comparables: Clint Frazier, Chris Parmelee, Austin Riley

The Report: Strong, athletic, and oozing *Friday Night Lights* vibes, Lutz has a lot to offer tools-wise, but you still are asking questions about how important baseball skills are developing. He's well-muscled throughout his body, and is just about completely filled out at 21. The arm is his big tool on defense, and though I think right field is his ultimate position, he covers enough ground to man center ably.

Lutz's obvious physical strength and quick bat generate at least plus raw power, but we haven't seen it in games to the extent we'd like. This is a casualty of his contact issues, currently the main weakness in his profile. The approach isn't bad, but he lacks fluidity in the box and harbors some mechanical issues that lead to swing-and-miss and suboptimal contact. Lutz sort of hunches over in the box and dips his shoulder, which results in him missing pitches up in the zone or on the outer half and popping up those that are more in his groove path. If he is going to reach this OFP, he will need to keep his K-rate from soaring against upper-level pitching and make enough good contact that his plus power plays more in games.

Variance: High. There are hit tool questions that currently hamper the efficacy of his plus power.

Ben Carsley's Fantasy Take: Lutz is the top dynasty prospect in this system for my money, but he's a scary one to invest in given the hit tool concerns. If he can make contact even slightly more frequently, he could emerge as a Hunter Renfroe-esque power-hitting OF4. If not, he profiles as more of a fourth or fifth outfielder type who'll probably commit a devastating error for the Brewers in a playoff game.

3   Aaron Ashby   LHP   OFP: 55   ETA: 2021

Born: 05/24/98   Age: 22   Bats: R   Throws: L   Height: 6'2"   Weight: 181   Origin: Round 4, 2018 Draft (#125 overall)

YEAR	TEAM	LVL	AGE	W	L	SV	G	GS	IP	H	HR	BB/9	K/9	K	GB%	BABIP	WHIP	ERA	DRA	WARP	PF
2018	HEL	RK	20	1	2	1	6	3	20¹	18	3	3.5	8.4	19	52%	.273	1.28	6.20	2.95	0.7	102
2018	WIS	A	20	1	1	0	7	7	37¹	40	1	2.2	11.3	47	52%	.398	1.31	2.17	4.19	0.5	102
2019	WIS	A	21	3	4	0	11	10	61	47	4	4.1	11.8	80	49%	.319	1.23	3.54	4.45	0.5	102
2019	CAR	A+	21	2	6	0	13	13	65	54	1	4.4	7.6	55	50%	.283	1.32	3.46	4.81	0.2	111
2020	MIL	MLB	22	2	2	0	33	0	35	34	5	4.1	8.1	32	46%	.293	1.43	4.79	4.83	0.2	93

Comparables: Justin Wilson, Blake Snell, Yennsy Diaz

The Report: Ah, every system has to have one crafty lefty with a plus curveball, don't they? Ashby's lanky and long and excitedly brings one of the better lefty curveballs in the minors. That's something that a fairly thin pitching pipeline in Milwaukee can use. He has a clean delivery and his ability to use his limbs and tunnel his four pitches off an above-average fastball makes Ashby an exciting young prospect in a system mostly bereft of them. He needs to iron out his command issues to quiet whispers that he will be a future bullpen arm, and improving on a fringy slider and change wouldn't hurt either, but the curve is good enough that he should get every chance to start, especially in an organization that could leverage that fastball/curve combo in a more non-traditional starting pitching ways.

Variance: Medium. No real injury history and pretty filled out physically, but does need to work on command.

Ben Carsley's Fantasy Take: He's gonna get Jalen Beeks-ed, isn't he? Until Ashby is a safer bet to remain a starter, much closer to the majors or both, you needn't concern yourself with him.

4 Ethan Small LHP OFP: 55 ETA: 2021

Born: 02/14/97 Age: 23 Bats: L Throws: L Height: 6'3" Weight: 214 Origin: Round 1, 2019 Draft (#28 overall)

YEAR	TEAM	LVL	AGE	W	L	SV	G	GS	IP	H	HR	BB/9	K/9	K	GB%	BABIP	WHIP	ERA	DRA	WARP	PF
2019	WIS	A	22	0	2	0	5	5	18	11	0	2.0	15.5	31	32%	.286	0.83	1.00	2.50	0.6	105
2020	MIL	MLB	23	2	2	0	33	0	35	35	5	3.9	11.5	45	38%	.340	1.44	4.87	4.84	0.2	93

Comparables: Carlos Torres, Andrew Vasquez, Framber Valdez

The Report: It was a bit of a surprise when the Brewers popped Small at the end of the first round this past Summer. And a dry recitation of the arsenal—a fastball that sits either side of 90, a potentially average curve and solid-average change, average command of it all—well, it doesn't sound like a first round pick. The stuff is better than my rather banal description due to a very deceptive delivery and big extension from his overhead slot.

Small will vary his speed out of the windup, using big or repeated hesitations to disrupt the pitchers timing. This does limit the command projection some—although he fills up the zone—but it does put hitters off. The fastball has some riding life up and good plane down, getting far more swings and misses than a 90 mph fastball should. And he makes professional hitters look bad flailing at fringy fastball velocity. The changeup has good separation off the heater and above-average fade. The breaker is below-average at present, but will flash 50. Honestly, I don't think it's first round stuff myself, but if pitching is disrupting hitter's timing as Warren Spahn opined, Small has at least one plus-plus tool in his locker.

Variance: High. Deception isn't an out pitch. Maybe it makes the fastball one, but Small is going to have to prove it at every level.

Ben Carsley's Fantasy Take: Don't let the first-round pedigree fool you: this is a Brian Johnson-ass dynasty prospect. What's that: Johnson was a first-rounder too? As I said: you can pass.

5 Mario Feliciano C OFP: 55 ETA: 2021

Born: 11/20/98 Age: 21 Bats: R Throws: R Height: 6'1" Weight: 195 Origin: Round 2, 2016 Draft (#75 overall)

YEAR	TEAM	LVL	AGE	PA	R	2B	3B	HR	RBI	BB	K	SB	CS	AVG/OBP/SLG	DRC+	VORP	BABIP	BRR	FRAA	WARP	PF
2017	WIS	A	18	446	47	16	2	4	36	34	72	10	2	.251/.320/.331	88	11.2	.297	1.4	C(78) -2.8	0.9	101
2018	CAR	A+	19	165	20	7	1	3	12	13	59	2	0	.205/.282/.329	51	0.4	.318	0.5	C(25) -0.6	-0.2	103
2019	CAR	A+	20	482	62	25	4	19	81	29	139	2	1	.273/.324/.477	119	19.0	.351	-5.1	C(60) -0.4	1.7	109
2020	MIL	MLB	21	251	23	11	1	7	27	15	78	1	0	.223/.277/.368	69	0.0	.304	-0.3	C -1	-0.2	93

Comparables: Cole Tucker, Gary Sánchez, Engel Beltre

The Report: Feliciano's potential with the bat started materializing last year, as he put up impressive numbers in High-A and showed interesting skills at the plate. He is still working on his approach, and at present has some swing/miss and strikeout issues. There's something here though, as he has a direct inside-out type swing that allows him to spray the ball to all fields and often leads to hard line drives. He will flash surprising power to all fields too, as I saw him hit several balls deep into right-center. Short and stocky-ish with plenty of strength in the lower half, Feliciano is a pretty good athlete who has the archetypical catcher's body. He is still familiarizing himself with the position, however, and how strong he ends up becoming behind the dish will have a lot to say about how his profile eventually shakes out.

Variance: High. He's begun to break out with the bat, but there are still all the risks associated with catching prospects, and he's still developing defensively.

Ben Carsley's Fantasy Take: I think the dream is that we'd value him next year the way we value Daulton Varsho now? If you think that sort of modest but meaningful ceiling is enough to consider Feliciano a top-200 dynasty prospect, I'd listen. Anything more than that and you're just encouraging me to go on another anti-catcher diatribe.

6 Carlos Rodriguez OF

OFP: 50   ETA: 2024

Born: 12/07/00   Age: 19   Bats: L   Throws: L   Height: 5'10"   Weight: 150   Origin: International Free Agent, 2017

YEAR	TEAM	LVL	AGE	PA	R	2B	3B	HR	RBI	BB	K	SB	CS	AVG/OBP/SLG	DRC+	VORP	BABIP	BRR	FRAA	WARP	PF
2018	DBW	RK	17	230	38	13	1	2	32	7	19	12	8	.323/.358/.419	129	16.9	.347	2.6	CF(27) 7.1, LF(21) 2.6	2.5	96
2019	CSP	RK+	18	157	20	3	1	3	12	4	20	4	6	.331/.350/.424	120	8.9	.364	-0.5		0.7	100
2020	MIL	MLB	19	251	24	11	1	4	25	11	48	6	3	.270/.308/.376	81	0.0	.322	-0.3	CF 0, LF 1	0.4	93

Comparables: Raimel Tapia, Harold Castro, Luis Sardiñas

The Report: Rodriguez has one of the more unorthodox swings you will see. He uses a hokey-pokey leg kick—you put your right foot in, you take your right foot out—that somehow doesn't lead to as many timing issues as you'd think. That said, he can get out on his front foot or out of sync, but generally the swing works well enough due to very advanced bat control and above-average, slashy bat speed. It might be the weirdest above-average hit tool I will ever project, and I'll probably never feel comfortable about it.

The 5-foot-10 listing is probably a bit generous and he's not particularly physical or projectable so any power here will be mostly of the doubles variety. Rodriguez is fast enough to stretch some of those into triples, and that speed should allow him to comfortably stick in center, although he can drift through his routes at present. It's a fairly polished up-the-middle package all in all for a teenaged outfielder, but there isn't much projection or upside, and he's a long way from the majors.

Variance: Extreme. Short-season resume only, it's kind of a wonky swing that might have issues when he sees better velocity/spin combos up the ranks.

Ben Carsley's Fantasy Take: A small teenage outfield prospect with an unorthodox yet plus hit tool and good speed? Carlos Rodriguez is Raimel Tapia, confirmed. You can add him to your watch lists, at least.

7 Corey Ray OF

OFP: 45   ETA: 2020

Born: 09/22/94   Age: 25   Bats: L   Throws: L   Height: 6'0"   Weight: 195   Origin: Round 1, 2016 Draft (#5 overall)

YEAR	TEAM	LVL	AGE	PA	R	2B	3B	HR	RBI	BB	K	SB	CS	AVG/OBP/SLG	DRC+	VORP	BABIP	BRR	FRAA	WARP	PF
2017	CAR	A+	22	503	56	29	4	7	48	48	156	24	10	.238/.311/.367	96	7.1	.346	-2.5	CF(80) 5.5, RF(24) 0.9	1.6	103
2018	BLX	AA	23	600	86	32	7	27	74	60	176	37	7	.239/.323/.477	119	35.8	.303	0.5	CF(126) 1.8, LF(6) 1.4	3.6	97
2019	BLX	AA	24	46	5	3	0	0	0	6	14	3	2	.250/.348/.325	116	1.0	.385	0.1	CF(10) 1.6, LF(1) -0.2	0.4	104
2019	SAN	AAA	24	230	23	8	0	7	21	20	89	3	1	.188/.261/.329	45	-1.2	.283	-0.4	CF(40) -5.0, RF(8) -1.3	-1.2	95
2020	MIL	MLB	25	251	23	13	1	6	24	19	98	8	3	.197/.263/.336	56	0.0	.313	0.5	CF 2, RF 0	-0.3	93

Comparables: Joe Benson, Michael A. Taylor, Anthony Alford

The Report: Third, tenth, fourth, and now back to seventh in the rankings for the former fifth overall pick in the 2016 draft. After four years, even though his ranking in the organization has ebbed and flowed, he largely remains the same player with no significant improvements. Selected as a potential five-tool player, he has failed to hit over .250 in a season with eye-popping strikeout numbers, inconsistencies playing the field and a lackluster arm. There are many who believe Ray's value might be tapped out as a fourth outfielder with pop. Coming off a successful 2018 campaign where he was the Southern League MVP and led the circuit in home runs, extra base hits, total bases, and stolen bases, 2019 got off to a rough start with a jammed finger in the first month of the season at Triple-A San Antonio. A re-aggravation of the injury shelved him for nearly six weeks and sapped the power from his swing, which relies mostly on his hips flying open to generate bat speed. The combination of holes in the swing and lack of hand strength left his offensive output close to null. Even at full health, the ceiling seems to have been lowered.

Variance: Low. He is what he mostly is. He can launch one out, swipe a bag, play left or center field, but the flaws in his game are too big to expect a consistent starting role.

Ben Carsley's Fantasy Take: It would be cruel of you to do so, but if you want to try and sell high on Ray to the guy in your fantasy league who just emerged from a three-year coma, this is probably your last chance.

8 Zack Brown RHP   OFP: 45   ETA: 2020
Born: 12/15/94 Age: 25 Bats: R Throws: R Height: 6'1" Weight: 180 Origin: Round 5, 2016 Draft (#141 overall)

YEAR	TEAM	LVL	AGE	W	L	SV	G	GS	IP	H	HR	BB/9	K/9	K	GB%	BABIP	WHIP	ERA	DRA	WARP	PF
2017	WIS	A	22	4	5	0	18	13	85	78	7	3.6	8.9	84	47%	.316	1.32	3.39	4.75	0.4	99
2017	CAR	A+	22	3	0	0	4	4	25	24	1	0.7	8.3	23	56%	.319	1.04	2.16	3.76	0.4	101
2018	BLX	AA	23	9	1	0	22	21	125²	95	8	2.6	8.3	116	57%	.257	1.04	2.44	3.80	2.2	97
2019	SAN	AAA	24	3	7	0	25	23	116²	138	16	4.9	7.6	98	54%	.342	1.73	5.79	6.53	0.2	93
2020	MIL	MLB	25	1	1	0	11	0	12	12	2	3.7	6.5	9	51%	.270	1.38	4.66	4.74	0.1	93

Comparables: Erik Johnson, Matt Bowman, Tyler Wilson

The Report: After a breakout season in 2019 that saw him named Most Outstanding Pitcher in the Southern League, Brown had to take his array of mostly average stuff to the PCL. It did not go as well. Some of the wounds were self-inflicted, as Brown went through periods where he struggled to throw strikes, and Triple-A hitters could sit on and punish his low-90s fastball when it was in the zone. His curve too often was a less effective slurvy thing, and the changeup remains inconsistent, although it will flash good fade and dive even if it's firmer than you'd like. Brown's Triple-A campaign was bad enough that the Brewers left him exposed to the Rule 5 draft. But he went unselected and remains with Milwaukee. He will likely have another chance to sort himself out in the Pacific Coast League. His high effort delivery might be better suited to short bursts where the fastball can play closer to 95 and he might be able to find an above-average breaker again.

Variance: Medium. Brown's stuff isn't good enough to afford the kind of command and control wobbles he had in 2019, but he's also a good month in 2020 away from being a potential major leaguer.

Ben Carsley's Fantasy Take: A good rule of thumb is that if a dude is exposed to and unclaimed in the Rule 5 draft, you don't need to worry about his fantasy outlook.

9 Antoine Kelly LHP   OFP: 50   ETA: 2022/23
Born: 12/05/99 Age: 20 Bats: L Throws: L Height: 6'6" Weight: 205 Origin: Round 2, 2019 Draft (#65 overall)

YEAR	TEAM	LVL	AGE	W	L	SV	G	GS	IP	H	HR	BB/9	K/9	K	GB%	BABIP	WHIP	ERA	DRA	WARP	PF
2019	BRB	RK	19	0	0	0	9	9	28²	21	0	1.6	12.9	41	47%	.333	0.91	1.26	1.57	1.4	100
2020	MIL	MLB	20	2	2	0	33	0	35	35	6	4.0	10.2	40	43%	.320	1.44	4.91	4.88	0.2	93

Comparables: Robert Stephenson, Matt Moore, César Vargas

The Report: Kelly is a big, tall lefty with a big fastball. He sits mid-90s, but has reportedly touched triple digits, and when he's going well, it looks like he's playing catch. The frame has some projection in it too, although I'd expect him to remain fairly lean. The delivery has some mechanical inconsistencies exacerbated by his tendency to throw across his body, especially out of the windup. There's a potential above-average slider here, although that takes a fair bit of squinting and projection at present. He's a cold weather JuCo arm still growing into his body, so it's going to be a bit of a project. Mid-90s velocity from a southpaw is a good place to start though.

Variance: High. There's potential power stuff from the left side, but the command and secondaries are going to need some work.

Ben Carsley's Fantasy Take: Wait, a guy with an impact fastball but poor secondaries and spotty command? Folks, it seems like maybe Antoine Kelly Has Great Stu/[is hit by a train.]

10   Devin Williams   RHP   OFP: 45   ETA: 2019

Born: 09/21/94   Age: 25   Bats: R   Throws: R   Height: 6'3"   Weight: 165   Origin: Round 2, 2013 Draft (#54 overall)

YEAR	TEAM	LVL	AGE	W	L	SV	G	GS	IP	H	HR	BB/9	K/9	K	GB%	BABIP	WHIP	ERA	DRA	WARP	PF
2018	CAR	A+	23	0	3	0	14	14	34	40	2	5.8	9.3	35	38%	.380	1.82	5.82	6.33	-0.4	100
2019	BLX	AA	24	7	2	4	31	0	53^1	34	3	4.9	12.8	76	48%	.279	1.18	2.36	3.88	0.5	100
2019	MIL	MLB	24	0	0	0	13	0	13^2	18	2	4.0	9.2	14	42%	.372	1.76	3.95	5.15	0.0	97
2020	MIL	MLB	25	2	2	0	39	0	42	41	7	3.9	8.6	40	44%	.292	1.42	4.94	4.92	0.2	93

Comparables: Elieser Hernandez, Domingo Germán, Jake Newberry

The Report: After years of injury issues including missing an entire season after Tommy John surgery, Williams finally put together a healthy season after a shift to relief and dominated the Southern League. He made a brief stop in San Antonio before spending the last two months of the year in the major league pen. Williams sits mid-90s in short bursts and can dial it up to 97-98. The pitch can pop up in the zone, but does run a bit true otherwise. His primary secondary is actually a little scroogie change that mostly works off the 10 mph velocity difference from the fastball, although Williams generally does a good job keeping it down in the zone and away from both righties and lefties. There's a slider as well. It's not true late inning or closer stuff, but Williams should have a solid career as a pen arm, perhaps as soon as this year if he can win a job in camp.

Variance: Low. It's a good fastball and he has made the majors.

Ben Carsley's Fantasy Take: Is...is Devin Williams a top-5 dynasty prospect in this system? Oh god. Make it stop.

The Next Ten

11   Drew Rasmussen   RHP

Born: 07/27/95   Age: 24   Bats: R   Throws: R   Height: 6'1"   Weight: 225   Origin: Round 6, 2018 Draft (#185 overall)

YEAR	TEAM	LVL	AGE	W	L	SV	G	GS	IP	H	HR	BB/9	K/9	K	GB%	BABIP	WHIP	ERA	DRA	WARP	PF
2019	CAR	A+	23	0	0	0	4	4	11^1	7	0	1.6	12.7	16	52%	.280	0.79	1.59	2.57	0.3	102
2019	BLX	AA	23	1	3	0	22	18	61	49	4	4.3	11.4	77	48%	.317	1.28	3.54	4.29	0.5	98
2020	MIL	MLB	24	2	2	0	33	0	35	34	5	3.6	10.0	39	44%	.316	1.39	4.60	4.63	0.3	93

Comparables: Jharel Cotton, Cesar Valdez, Ben Taylor

It's pretty amazing Rassmussen is back on a pro mound at all, let alone showing the stuff he did in 2019. He hadn't pitched more than 37 innings in a season since his Freshman year at Oregon State back in 2015. He's had two Tommy John surgeries in the interim, but came out in 2019 pumping mid-to-upper-90s heat past batters at three levels. Rasmussen's fastball can lack wiggle at times, but it's easy plus, bordering on plus-plus. His primary secondary is a hard, short slider he can run up to 90, and a sinking change in the upper-80s. Given his health track record, the Brewers were very cautious with his usage—while technically a starting pitcher, he never threw more than four innings or 64 pitches in an outing, and occasionally was used out of the pen to further manage his workload. The Brewers still seem interested in trying to develop him as a starter, but with this level of health risk, it almost feels like those bullets should be spent getting outs in a major league pen. Rassmussen could quickly slot into a high leverage role there too.

12   Micah Bello   OF

Born: 07/21/00   Age: 19   Bats: R   Throws: R   Height: 5'11"   Weight: 165   Origin: Round 2, 2018 Draft (#73 overall)

YEAR	TEAM	LVL	AGE	PA	R	2B	3B	HR	RBI	BB	K	SB	CS	AVG/OBP/SLG	DRC+	VORP	BABIP	BRR	FRAA	WARP	PF
2018	BRR	RK	17	174	25	4	3	1	15	18	41	10	1	.240/.324/.325	94	0.6	.321	0.2	CF(26) 0.7, LF(13) -0.9	0.4	102
2019	CSP	RK+	18	198	30	9	3	6	20	18	47	5	4	.232/.308/.418	73	7.2	.280	2.4		0.2	100
2020	MIL	MLB	19	251	21	11	1	4	22	20	81	4	1	.201/.268/.316	54	0.0	.290	0.2	CF 0, LF 0	-0.5	93

Comparables: Eloy Jiménez, César Puello, Wilin Rosario

One of the younger prep bats available, the Brewers selected Bello in the second round of the 2018 draft. There was—and still is—plenty of baseball rawness and Milwaukee has him on a fairly conservative development track. He looks about an inch or two taller than his listed 5-foot-11 and more filled out than 165 lbs. Bello stands very upright at the plate with a medium leg kick followed by a violent uncoiling of an uppercut swing. Bello's plus bat speed makes up for some of the length, and the total package shows easy plus raw power. He's growing into a right field profile but may have the pop to match. Bello has better control of the barrel than the description of his swing implies, but the swing really only has one gear, so the hit tool may struggle against better arms. And there were already swing-and-miss and quality of contact issues against Pioneer League arms.

13 Nick Kahle C
Born: 02/28/98   Age: 22   Bats: R   Throws: R   Height: 5'10"   Weight: 210   Origin: Round 4, 2019 Draft (#133 overall)

YEAR	TEAM	LVL	AGE	PA	R	2B	3B	HR	RBI	BB	K	SB	CS	AVG/OBP/SLG	DRC+	VORP	BABIP	BRR	FRAA	WARP	PF
2019	CSP	RK+	21	163	25	11	1	6	25	20	36	2	1	.255/.350/.475	125	9.0	.300	-1.6		0.7	101
2020	MIL	MLB	22	251	21	12	1	5	23	18	80	2	1	.198/.261/.318	53	0.0	.279	0.0	C 0	-0.7	93

Comparables: Miguel Perez, Martín Prado, Pete Kozma

In a strong year for draft prospects, who finished third in the Pac-12 conference in on-base percentage behind only Adley Rutschman and Andrew Vaughn? None other than this stocky catcher from Washington selected in the fourth round. While Kahle's defensive abilities are so-so, the potential of an offensive-minded backstop with a keen eye for the zone is a welcome sight in any system. There are improvements to the swing that could be made, as he tends to get his hands locked when firing and bars out his lead arm, adding length to the bat path. After previously struggling in wood-bat summer leagues, a strong showing in the rookie-level Pioneer League for his pro debut put to rest worries of a rough transition, before he finished his year in Hi-A.

14 Payton Henry C
Born: 06/24/97   Age: 23   Bats: R   Throws: R   Height: 6'1"   Weight: 215   Origin: Round 6, 2016 Draft (#171 overall)

YEAR	TEAM	LVL	AGE	PA	R	2B	3B	HR	RBI	BB	K	SB	CS	AVG/OBP/SLG	DRC+	VORP	BABIP	BRR	FRAA	WARP	PF
2017	HEL	RK	20	241	38	17	1	7	33	30	69	1	0	.242/.344/.435	83	13.5	.326	-2.2	C(42) -1.1, 1B(1) -0.1	-0.2	108
2018	WIS	A	21	389	44	15	2	10	41	38	124	1	3	.234/.327/.380	100	13.5	.335	-2.5	C(93) 1.4	1.7	102
2019	CAR	A+	22	482	49	22	1	14	75	26	142	1	1	.242/.315/.395	98	6.6	.324	-2.5	C(67) 2.4	1.4	109
2020	MIL	MLB	23	251	25	12	0	8	28	15	91	0	0	.214/.281/.374	72	0.0	.315	-0.5	C -1, 1B 0	-0.2	93

Comparables: Carson Blair, Jeremy Moore, Aristides Aquino

A large catcher with a strong, muscular build, Henry has long had a positive defensive reputation. 2019 looks gave us nothing that contradicts that; he moves around well behind the plate, and has enough arm to deter the running game. His standout tool at the plate is above-average power, which is a trait that will serve him well in the Fraternal Order of Backup Catchers. The problem here is with the hit tool. Henry's approach isn't great and his stiff, uphill swing results in a lot of whiffs and weak contact. There's more leeway on the offensive profile given his strong backstop defense, but he'll need to tighten things up to be a viable big league option.

15 Joe Gray OF
Born: 03/12/00   Age: 20   Bats: R   Throws: R   Height: 6'1"   Weight: 195   Origin: Round 2, 2018 Draft (#60 overall)

YEAR	TEAM	LVL	AGE	PA	R	2B	3B	HR	RBI	BB	K	SB	CS	AVG/OBP/SLG	DRC+	VORP	BABIP	BRR	FRAA	WARP	PF
2018	BRR	RK	18	98	14	5	0	2	9	18	25	6	0	.182/.347/.325	108	3.5	.235	2.0	CF(18) -1.0, LF(4) 0.4	0.5	101
2019	CSP	RK+	19	129	19	4	1	3	9	13	36	3	2	.164/.279/.300	36	-3.1	.208	-0.1		-0.4	103
2020	MIL	MLB	20	251	22	11	1	5	22	25	90	4	1	.182/.273/.301	55	0.0	.279	0.0	CF 1, LF 0	-0.5	93

Believed by many as a first-round talent entering the 2018 draft, Gray slid into the second round and hasn't had much success as a pro…yet. Despite having an idyllic baseball body with loads of projection, the rawness in his game has been exposed in the pros, especially at the plate. As a prep in Mississippi he utilized a high leg kick and decent bat-to-ball skills to feast on lesser competition. Against better velocity as a pro, the length in the swing and tardiness of his timing has left him struggling against better competition. This past season, an earnest attempt to work on his swing by switching to a stride at setup and slightly opening up did not produce better results, but with more reps using the tuned-up swing we'll see how much improvement has been made in 2020 in what will likely be his first foray into full-season ball.

16 Cooper Hummel OF

Born: 11/28/94 Age: 25 Bats: B Throws: R Height: 5'10" Weight: 198 Origin: Round 18, 2016 Draft (#531 overall)

YEAR	TEAM	LVL	AGE	PA	R	2B	3B	HR	RBI	BB	K	SB	CS	AVG/OBP/SLG	DRC+	VORP	BABIP	BRR	FRAA	WARP	PF
2017	CAR	A+	22	239	26	11	2	4	25	38	42	2	2	.244/.368/.381	117	11.1	.288	0.8	C(44) 0.2	1.4	103
2018	CAR	A+	23	404	51	25	0	8	50	63	93	3	1	.260/.397/.410	140	22.9	.339	-1.5	LF(28) -1.8, RF(23) -0.5	1.9	103
2019	BLX	AA	24	419	62	8	5	17	56	62	100	4	7	.249/.384/.450	138	25.5	.301	-1.1	LF(74) 6.3, RF(4) 0.5	3.2	100
2020	MIL	MLB	25	251	29	11	1	9	30	28	74	1	0	.226/.328/.407	97	0.0	.299	0.0	LF 2, C 0	0.9	93

A former catcher, the stocky 5-foot-10 outfielder possesses one of the better eyes and approaches in the Brewers system. Hummel appears very relaxed in his stance and features a leg kick that helps generate above-average power. The swing is best-suited for hunting down in the zone as he drops his hands pretty low to engage the ball. The switch-hitting Hummel doesn't really have a carrying tool—other than his eye—and his defense leaves a bit to be desired, although there is room for improvement given his lack of reps in the outfield. It's hard for ex-catchers to remain prospects after moving out from behind the dish, but if Hummel can continue to generate decent game power and work counts the way he does, he could be a platoon outfielder for the Brewers in future years.

17 Eduardo Garcia SS

Born: 07/10/02 Age: 17 Bats: R Throws: R Height: 6'2" Weight: 160 Origin: International Free Agent, 2019

Garcia was one of the big names from Milwaukee's 2018 J2 class, but went down with a fractured right ankle shortly into his Dominican Summer League debut. His carrying tool was his defense at shortstop, so how serious the ankle injury is and how his recovery goes injects even more variance into the profile of a 17-year-old who hasn't even come state side yet. We're still ranking him though, because...yeah.

18 Braden Webb RHP

Born: 04/25/95 Age: 25 Bats: R Throws: R Height: 6'3" Weight: 200 Origin: Round 3, 2016 Draft (#82 overall)

YEAR	TEAM	LVL	AGE	W	L	SV	G	GS	IP	H	HR	BB/9	K/9	K	GB%	BABIP	WHIP	ERA	DRA	WARP	PF
2017	WIS	A	22	6	7	3	22	13	86²	72	8	4.1	9.3	90	45%	.281	1.28	4.36	4.39	0.8	103
2018	CAR	A+	23	5	8	0	21	21	100²	89	9	5.0	9.3	104	45%	.302	1.44	4.20	4.86	0.6	102
2018	BLX	AA	23	1	0	0	4	3	20	13	0	4.5	10.8	24	39%	.283	1.15	1.80	3.99	0.3	98
2019	BRR	RK	24	0	1	0	5	5	8	1	0	5.6	14.6	13	46%	.077	0.75	2.25	0.94	0.4	97
2019	CAR	A+	24	1	2	0	8	8	36²	23	2	6.1	7.6	31	35%	.226	1.31	3.44	3.69	0.6	113
2019	BLX	AA	24	1	4	0	6	5	15	15	2	9.0	7.8	13	32%	.289	2.00	9.00	7.52	-0.5	99
2020	MIL	MLB	25	2	2	0	33	0	35	35	6	4.1	7.6	29	38%	.291	1.47	5.10	5.07	0.1	93

Comparables: Jeff Brigham, Jake Esch, Kevin McGowan

A former third-rounder out of South Carolina, the now 24-year-old Webb has struggled to gain traction in the upper levels and spent most of last year marooned at High-A. The stuff is pretty pedestrian overall, though if you squint you can see a major league arm. His fastball sits low-90s with some sink when he locates down, but his command can waver and when he leaves the fastball up it gets hit. He has three secondaries, two breakers and a sparsely-used change. His 12-6 curve is effective at generating weak contact, but it doesn't always miss bats. He'll also mix in a shorter slider in the mid-80s. The pitch mix is solid but the command still isn't there and the stuff isn't loud enough to overcome that at present.

19   Je'Von Ward   OF

Born: 10/25/99   Age: 20   Bats: L   Throws: R   Height: 6'5"   Weight: 190   Origin: Round 12, 2017 Draft (#354 overall)

YEAR	TEAM	LVL	AGE	PA	R	2B	3B	HR	RBI	BB	K	SB	CS	AVG/OBP/SLG	DRC+	VORP	BABIP	BRR	FRAA	WARP	PF
2017	BRR	RK	17	132	15	6	0	0	15	9	39	2	7	.276/.326/.325	104	-2.0	.405	-1.5	LF(15) -1.0, RF(11) -2.2	-0.2	104
2018	HEL	RK	18	271	40	13	2	2	21	32	57	13	5	.307/.391/.403	120	12.3	.397	0.5	LF(55) -12.7, RF(2) -0.2	-0.8	103
2019	WIS	A	19	423	35	16	7	2	46	47	107	7	6	.225/.311/.322	85	1.3	.309	-0.7	LF(47) -9.3, RF(36) -1.3	-1.1	103
2020	MIL	MLB	20	251	19	11	1	3	20	18	80	3	1	.213/.271/.307	51	0.0	.312	0.0	LF -5, RF 0	-1.2	93

If you want a, oh let's say 35th percentile outcome for Bello in 24 months, it might look a bit like Ward. Ward was also quite young for his draft class, and has a classic long and lean projectable frame even now at 20-years-old. He's taller and even toolsier than Bello but has struggled to make consistent contact do to issues with spin and a leveraged, muscley swing. His physical strength hasn't actually led to game power either, as he has hit just four home runs in 205 professional games. He's an above-average runner underway, but it can take a while for his long strides to get up to speed and he's played almost exclusively in a corner outfield spot as a pro. The chance the tools pop at some point keeps him at the back of this list, but it's one of the few he'd make.

20   Lucas Erceg   3B

Born: 05/01/95   Age: 25   Bats: L   Throws: R   Height: 6'3"   Weight: 210   Origin: Round 2, 2016 Draft (#46 overall)

YEAR	TEAM	LVL	AGE	PA	R	2B	3B	HR	RBI	BB	K	SB	CS	AVG/OBP/SLG	DRC+	VORP	BABIP	BRR	FRAA	WARP	PF
2017	CAR	A+	22	538	66	33	1	15	81	35	95	2	3	.256/.307/.417	100	11.3	.287	-1.6	3B(97) -0.6	1.3	104
2018	BLX	AA	23	508	52	21	1	13	51	37	82	3	1	.248/.306/.382	96	8.5	.274	-0.4	3B(117) -0.7	1.5	97
2019	SAN	AAA	24	406	55	17	1	15	52	44	102	2	2	.218/.305/.398	65	-1.6	.259	-2.0	3B(84) 7.9, 1B(18) 1.8	0.4	95
2020	MIL	MLB	25	251	26	12	1	9	30	19	69	0	0	.224/.285/.394	76	3.0	.280	-0.4	3B 1, 1B 0	0.2	93

Comparables: Kelvin Gutierrez, Jordy Mercer, Jefry Marte

This is one of those "what you see is *probably* what you get" type of guys. There's a long swing, with a sizable stride towards the mound. Unfortunately, Erceg isn't as disciplined as one would like given the below-average barrel control and length to contact. The former second-rounder's best tool is his arm, no question about it. You could tell he was a former pitcher on his throws across the diamond. And I would not be shocked to see him grade out as an average third baseman given his range and solid reads on balls to both sides. Erceg is still fairly athletic and there were some tools here in the not-so-distant past. It's a lefty bat with potential 20+ homers. You can find a place for that, but there is a lot of work still to do to get there for a guy in Triple-A.

Personal Cheeseball

PC   Max Lazar   RHP

Born: 06/03/99   Age: 21   Bats: R   Throws: R   Height: 6'3"   Weight: 185   Origin: Round 11, 2017 Draft (#324 overall)

YEAR	TEAM	LVL	AGE	W	L	SV	G	GS	IP	H	HR	BB/9	K/9	K	GB%	BABIP	WHIP	ERA	DRA	WARP	PF
2017	BRR	RK	18	0	2	0	7	1	13²	16	2	0.7	9.2	14	51%	.359	1.24	5.93	3.85	0.3	96
2018	HEL	RK	19	3	3	0	14	14	68	74	7	2.0	7.3	55	44%	.312	1.31	4.37	3.92	1.6	103
2019	BRR	RK	20	0	1	0	3	3	6	4	0	0.0	15.0	10	27%	.364	0.67	1.50	0.90	0.3	105
2019	WIS	A	20	7	3	1	19	10	79	67	5	1.7	12.4	109	39%	.353	1.04	2.39	3.63	1.3	103
2020	MIL	MLB	21	2	2	0	33	0	35	36	6	3.6	9.7	38	37%	.316	1.43	4.99	5.00	0.2	93

Back during one of Carlos Tocci's three seasons in Lakewood, Jarrett Seidler coined the term "jeans buddy" to describe his physique. This is a prospect that could wear the same jeans size as me, and as I'm presently around a 30/32, this isn't generally the frame or physicality you find in future major leaguers. There have been several since, usually undersized, lean, sometimes projectable position players. Nick Gordon is the best present example. They aren't usually pitchers, but Max Lazar might fit. I'd have to roll the cuffs since he is listed at 6-foot-3, but the uniform literally hangs off the 20-year-old. Nevertheless, he can dial it up into the low-90s, but sits more upper-80s. There's low spin, creating some sink. He has a potentially average change and a fringy, mid-70s breaker. He throws strikes with everything and it was more than enough to overwhelm A-ball at first time of asking, which I guess is more than Carlos Tocci could say. Lazar has some projection left and will have to add more strength and velocity though, as the overall stuff profile is a bit underwhelming at present.

Low Minors Sleeper

LMS Nick Bennett LHP

Born: 09/01/97   Age: 22   Bats: L   Throws: L   Height: 6'4"   Weight: 210   Origin: Round 6, 2019 Draft (#193 overall)

YEAR	TEAM	LVL	AGE	W	L	SV	G	GS	IP	H	HR	BB/9	K/9	K	GB%	BABIP	WHIP	ERA	DRA	WARP	PF
2019	CSP	RK+	21	0	0	0	6	3	12²	13	0	4.3	13.5	19	45%	.419	1.50	1.42	3.98	0.3	102
2019	WIS	A	21	1	0	0	5	3	20¹	15	1	1.8	10.6	24	52%	.264	0.93	2.21	3.41	0.4	101
2020	MIL	MLB	22	2	2	0	33	0	35	35	6	4.4	8.3	32	45%	.297	1.48	5.08	5.06	0.1	93

The sixth round of the draft is a bit deeper than we'd normally go for a low minors sleeper, but you have probably figured out by now that this Brewers system is pretty thin. Bennett's a sturdy college southpaw with a high-spin fastball around 90. There's some lefty funk and deception that helps the pitch play up without significantly impacting his ability to throw strikes. His mid-70s 1-7 curve has average projection and comes in at a tough angle for lefties to deal with. There's some risk he's just a LOOGY in an era of baseball where that role has been functionally eliminated, but the curve may be good enough to cross over.

Top Talents 25 and Under (as of 4/1/2020)

1. Keston Hiura
2. Josh Hader
3. Luis Urias
4. Corbin Burnes
5. Brice Turang
6. Eric Lauer
7. Tristen Lutz
8. Aaron Ashby
9. Ethan Small
10. Freddy Peralta

The Brewers organization got sneaky old rather quickly, and they're now trying to fill multiple big-league holes with major-league veterans on short contracts because the farm system has dried up after some trades and promotions. Hader has proven himself to be one of the most dominant relievers in baseball, striking out almost 50 percent of opposing batters and posting 2.6- and 2.7-win seasons in 2018 and 2019, respectively. Still, Hiura hit .303/.368/.570 in his big-league debut. Even with questionable defense, he would've matched Hader's WARP over the course of an entire season. Hiura is more valuable to the Brewers than Hader due to the fact that Hiura is younger, has more years of control, and has less risk (before you argue, consider Edwin Díaz in 2019). Regardless, it's a nice one-two punch to have atop a 25U list, especially given modern bullpen usage.

Things then crater in a hurry. Luis Urias has the prospect pedigree and the bat-to-ball skills to be a significant big-league contributor at shortstop, but he simply hasn't hit the ball very hard in the majors. Perhaps he develops a bit more strength—as Urias is only 22 years old—but guys who rely on a premium hit tool and show up with below-average exit velocities aren't safe prospects. Luckily, he's there to replace Orlando Arcia, who was the second-worst hitter among qualified hitters in 2019 and was second-worst among hitters with at least 300 PA in 2018. Urias will get his chances.

After Urias, the Brewers have a mix of guys who either are safe but unexciting, or are exciting but have gone through bouts of being absolutely terrible. Burnes represents the latter. He cruised through the Brewers' minor-league system and performed well in his big-league debut out of the bullpen in 2018, posting a 2.61 ERA with a 3.39 DRA. The right-hander followed that up with a dumpster fire of a season, in which he served up 17 homers in just 49 innings and had an 8.82 ERA. His performance raised questions about his repertoire, particularly his fastball and its spin, to the point that the Brewers sent him to their "pitching lab" in Maryvale during the summer to work things out. He's a massive question mark heading into 2020 and beyond.

Brice Turang and Eric Lauer are your safe-but-unexciting guys. They have useful, high floors, but come with physical limitations that will be difficult to overcome. Turang hasn't posted an ISO above .090—ya know, in case you thought the questions about his power are overstated—while Lauer is your quintessential back-end lefty who doesn't throw hard and doesn't miss many bats. He's the left-handed version of Zach Davies, for those who regret Davies' move to San Diego. Safe but unexciting.

Lutz perhaps offers the best impact potential amongst the Brewers' bats in the upper reaches of the organization's minor-league system, but he's a 21-year-old power-hitting corner outfielder who has never hit more than 13 homers in a season. He also has holes in his swing. Ashby is a left-handed curveball specialist who saw his strikeout rate nosedive upon reaching High-A, which makes one wonder if his dynamic deuce is good enough on its own to overcome control issues. Hitters at the upper levels might just force him to throw strikes with his fastball. As for Small, he's a Trackman Superstar who seemingly finds way more success than his raw stuff would otherwise indicate. If you're looking for a potential breakout, Small is your guy. The lefty just has no professional track record to quiet those who raised an eyebrow when the Brewers popped him in the first round.

Peralta has been a volatile pitcher for the Brew Crew. He tossed eight shutout innings and struck out 11 against the Pirates on April 3 and subsequently coughed up seven earned runs in 3 1/3 innings his next time out against the Angels. After moving to the bullpen late in 2019, though, Peralta may have found his role. His fastball velocity jumped to 96.22 mph, and he struck out 52.6 percent of the batters he faced in September. The righty followed up that performance by striking out 23 batters in 6 2/3 innings down in the Dominican Winter League, reportedly hitting 98 mph on the gun. If the Brewers commit to him as a reliever, he could be a multi-inning weapon to pair with Hader as early as 2020. The small sample and aforementioned volatility, though, keep him low on the list. After all, we've done this song and dance with Peralta before many times.

Eyewitness Reports

Eyewitness Report: Brice Turang

Evaluator: Forest Stulting
Report Date: 11/15/2019
Dates Seen: 7/27/19-7/29/19
Risk Factor: Medium
Physical/Health: Medium frame, skinny upper and lower half, wiry, close to maxed out, quick-twitch, athletic, agile, plus body control, competes, gamer.

Tool	Future Grade	Report
Hit	60	Small leg kick, fairly straight with slight bend in knees, hands by shoulders, under control and in sync load, no bat wrap, swing stays through zone long time, level swing, stays balanced, plus barrel control, plus pitch selection, controls the zone extremely well, line-to-line approach, slightly above-average bat speed.
Power	40	Not strong enough to generate consistent over-the-fence power, contact hitter approach, level swing.
Baserunning/Speed	60	Runs like a deer, base stealing threat, easy speed, compact form, plus instincts, quick, agile, long strides
Glove	60	Plus range either way, smooth, under control, relaxed, fluid, soft hands, quick transfer, confident, plus instincts, jumps and reads.
Arm	55	Plays slightly above-average for short, velocity, accurate, quick release, small hitch at times.

Conclusion: Turang fits the mold of shortstops from years past with plus contact ability and speed but lacking power. However, that doesn't mean he won't be an everyday shortstop. Four plus tools in his belt give Turang a high floor and a chance to headline the next wave of Brewer prospects.

Minnesota Twins

The State of the System

The Twins system is deep enough now that I got legitimately annoyed I couldn't get a few of my favorite names on here.

The Top Ten

★ ★ ★ *2020 Top 101 Prospect* **#21** ★ ★ ★

1 **Royce Lewis** SS   OFP: 70   ETA: 2020/21
Born: 06/05/99   Age: 21   Bats: R   Throws: R   Height: 6'2"   Weight: 200   Origin: Round 1, 2017 Draft (#1 overall)

YEAR	TEAM	LVL	AGE	PA	R	2B	3B	HR	RBI	BB	K	SB	CS	AVG/OBP/SLG	DRC+	VORP	BABIP	BRR	FRAA	WARP	PF
2017	TWI	RK	18	159	38	6	2	3	17	19	17	15	2	.271/.390/.414	159	18.1	.292	4.6	SS(32) -0.9	1.7	103
2017	CDR	A	18	80	16	2	1	1	10	6	16	3	1	.296/.363/.394	111	6.5	.364	1.0	SS(17) 1.9	0.7	103
2018	CDR	A	19	327	50	23	0	9	53	24	49	22	4	.315/.368/.485	156	31.3	.349	3.7	SS(67) 0.8	3.7	105
2018	FTM	A+	19	208	33	6	3	5	21	19	35	6	4	.255/.327/.399	107	11.6	.291	1.7	SS(45) -4.8	0.7	97
2019	FTM	A+	20	418	55	17	3	10	35	27	90	16	8	.238/.289/.376	97	15.0	.281	-1.5	SS(84) 4.0	1.8	96
2019	PEN	AA	20	148	18	9	1	2	14	11	33	6	2	.231/.291/.358	67	7.8	.287	2.0	SS(28) -2.6, CF(1) 1.7	0.3	97
2020	MIN	MLB	21	251	25	12	1	7	28	19	62	6	2	.232/.296/.385	80	0.0	.288	0.3	SS 0, CF 0	0.2	100

Comparables: Cole Tucker, Alen Hanson, Jonathan Schoop

The Report: Don't scout the stat line is one of the older adages in prospect writing. It's generally good advice. But performance always needs to be explained, good or bad. Sometimes it's obvious, matching up to the tools and projection, like when Vlad Jr. hits .400 for a few months, or Ronald Acuña torches three levels of the minors. Sometimes there's an easy explanation for a mismatch of production and projection—a college arm spamming a fringy slider in the Appy League to video game K-rates, a teenaged bat struggling in cold Midwest League parks, a polished college slugger coming off a broken hamate.

Royce Lewis did not hit like a Top 10 national prospect this year. And yes, there's an explanation.

Lewis played another three-plus months of games—including a promotion to Double-A and an MVP Fall League campaign—since Keanan's piece detailing his swing issues. I saw the same issues at Futures, a needlessly long hand path, upper and lower halves constantly out of sync. I also saw premium hand speed once the bat starts moving forward, and top-of-the-scale athleticism. Ricky saw the same issues in Arizona, but his love of the athletic tools and the potential of the offensive profile won out.

I point all this out in a rather long preamble because Lewis might be the single most divisive prospect internally at BP, but we also all broadly agree on the All-Star OFP. Lewis has a chance to be a true five-tool player with 55s or better everywhere while playing a premium defensive position, perhaps a couple of them. But the difficulty level only ratchets up from here, and if the swing problems remain, Lewis could be putting up similarly puzzling stat lines in the majors. It should all work out. He has premium bat speed and body control, game-changing speed, plus raw power, defensive flexibility.

STEPHEN A: BUT!

Variance: High. Man, I'd almost be tempted to go extreme, which is a OFP/Variance combo I would normally only consider for generational IFA signees or post-TJ Lucas Giolito types. The athleticism is so good, Lewis can carve out a major league career even if the swing remains an endless work in progress. If he does sort things out...well, the OFP won't be light per se, but it might be a lot of all-star games.

Mark Barry's Fantasy Take: One might think that posting an OPS below .700 across two levels would create a buy-low opportunity for a top prospect. The fact that Lewis's stock hasn't really dropped all that much is a good indicator of how highly he's valued in the community. He's still a top 10-15 dynasty prospect, although the risk factor might be slightly higher than where it was this time last year.

★ ★ ★ *2020 Top 101 Prospect* **#32** ★ ★ ★

2 Brusdar Graterol   RHP   OFP: 70   ETA: 2019

Born: 08/26/98   Age: 21   Bats: R   Throws: R   Height: 6'1"   Weight: 265   Origin: International Free Agent, 2014

YEAR	TEAM	LVL	AGE	W	L	SV	G	GS	IP	H	HR	BB/9	K/9	K	GB%	BABIP	WHIP	ERA	DRA	WARP	PF
2017	TWI	RK	18	2	0	0	5	2	19^1	10	1	1.9	9.8	21	58%	.205	0.72	1.40	1.12	1.0	109
2017	ELZ	RK	18	2	1	0	5	5	20^2	16	1	3.9	10.5	24	59%	.300	1.21	3.92	2.38	0.8	104
2018	CDR	A	19	3	2	0	8	8	41^1	30	3	2.0	11.1	51	64%	.270	0.94	2.18	2.45	1.4	103
2018	FTM	A+	19	5	2	0	11	11	60^2	59	0	2.8	8.3	56	49%	.343	1.29	3.12	4.61	0.5	99
2019	PEN	AA	20	6	0	1	12	9	52^2	32	2	3.6	8.5	50	56%	.233	1.01	1.71	2.93	1.3	102
2019	MIN	MLB	20	1	1	0	10	0	9^2	10	1	1.9	9.3	10	52%	.346	1.24	4.66	3.44	0.2	101
2020	MIN	MLB	21	4	3	0	30	8	64	65	8	3.3	7.9	56	53%	.306	1.39	4.64	4.61	0.6	100

Comparables: Chris Tillman, Lucas Giolito, Jenrry Mejia

The Report: Graterol got off to a dominant start in the Pensacola rotation before going down with an shoulder impingement. He came back two months later and the Twins moved him to the bullpen for the rest of his season, which included a September cup of coffee with the big club. In the pen he showed an 80-grade sinker that routinely hit triple-digits and featured patently unfair movement. There's a slider that he ramps up into the low-90s and is a potential plus-plus offering as well. It's one of the best two-pitch combos you will find among prospect arms, and there's only a handful of major league arms that can boast something better.

So there's going to be a strong temptation to keep Braterol in the bullpen. 2019 only added to a bad injury track record that already includes a Tommy John surgery. However, Graterol is only 21, and he has shown feel for a potentially average change—although one of the three he threw in the majors per Brooks resulted in a very long Zack Collins home run. He's not quite as max effort with the delivery as a starter, but it's not exactly Greg Maddux either. The Twins have rotation spots to offer in 2020, and I'd be tempted to at least give him a shot firing bullets every fifth day. The upside could be worth it, and hey, that elite reliever fallback isn't going anywhere.

Variance: High. The durability track record isn't good and the reliever risk is significant.

Mark Barry's Fantasy Take: As a once silent-cowboy-turned-old-guy-yelling-at-an-empty-chair man once said, "You've got to ask yourself one question: Do I feel lucky?" The range of outcomes is huge with Graterol, and the most likely scenario isn't the most fun for fantasy purposes. Still, his ceiling is so high and the floor (non-injury version) is a very good closer, so he'll stay in the top-60 or so fairly easily.

★ ★ ★ *2020 Top 101 Prospect* **#85** ★ ★ ★

3 Trevor Larnach   OF   OFP: 55   ETA: 2020/21

Born: 02/26/97   Age: 23   Bats: L   Throws: R   Height: 6'4"   Weight: 223   Origin: Round 1, 2018 Draft (#20 overall)

YEAR	TEAM	LVL	AGE	PA	R	2B	3B	HR	RBI	BB	K	SB	CS	AVG/OBP/SLG	DRC+	VORP	BABIP	BRR	FRAA	WARP	PF
2018	ELZ	RK	21	75	10	5	0	2	16	10	11	2	0	.311/.413/.492	157	5.5	.340	-1.5	RF(14) 3.8	0.8	99
2018	CDR	A	21	102	17	8	1	3	10	11	17	1	0	.297/.373/.505	154	8.8	.338	0.7	RF(17) -1.5	0.7	101
2019	FTM	A+	22	361	33	26	1	6	44	35	74	4	1	.316/.382/.459	165	22.2	.389	-1.4	RF(59) -8.1, LF(9) -0.4	1.9	95
2019	PEN	AA	22	181	26	4	0	7	22	22	50	0	0	.295/.387/.455	146	13.9	.390	-0.3	RF(28) -2.2, LF(5) -0.1	0.8	96
2020	MIN	MLB	23	251	26	13	1	7	29	21	71	1	0	.258/.324/.409	96	0.0	.345	-0.3	RF -4, LF 0	0.3	100

Comparables: Zoilo Almonte, James Jones, Jordan Patterson

The Report: Larnach and Kirilofff are a matched pair in my mind, but that's harder to convey visually with all the biographic info on the top half of these lists. Both are polished corner bats that haven't hit for quite as much game power or quite as much in general as you might like given the defensive limitations in the profiles. Larnach was a college pick, Kiriloff a prep bat, but he's only nine months older and both ended the year in Double-A. So at this point it's a fairly dead rubber on age-relative-to-league.

Larnach has plus raw power and enough uppercut to his swing where you'd think it'd get into games more, but he struggles to consistently lift the ball as often as your typical prospect sluggers. He already makes a lot of hard line drive contact so it shouldn't take much of a tweak to turn some of those doubles into home runs, and he's strong enough to drive the ball to all fields. But it hasn't happened yet. Larnach can get passive and struggle with offspeed, but there's enough bat speed and he'll do enough damage on fastballs to project at least an average hit tool. That should allow the raw power to play enough to carry an otherwise nondescript corner outfield profile.

Variance: Medium. He's a high college pick that has performed well enough at every stop, but the defensive and athletic limitations means that will have to continue.

Mark Barry's Fantasy Take: Getting serious Nicholas Castellanos vibes (or like, prime Kole Calhoun) from Larnach, as he could be a guy that doesn't play much defense but launches maybe 25-30 homers and hits for a decent average. It's probably a better profile for fantasy than in real life, but luckily that's all we care about in this here blurb.

★ ★ ★ *2020 Top 101 Prospect* **#86** ★ ★ ★

4 **Alex Kirilloff OF**   OFP: 55   ETA: 2020/21

Born: 11/09/97   Age: 22   Bats: L   Throws: L   Height: 6'2"   Weight: 195   Origin: Round 1, 2016 Draft (#15 overall)

YEAR	TEAM	LVL	AGE	PA	R	2B	3B	HR	RBI	BB	K	SB	CS	AVG/OBP/SLG	DRC+	VORP	BABIP	BRR	FRAA	WARP	PF
2018	CDR	A	20	281	36	20	5	13	56	24	47	1	1	.333/.391/.607	169	27.2	.364	-0.8	RF(53) -4.0, CF(1) 0.0	1.9	104
2018	FTM	A+	20	280	39	24	2	7	45	14	39	3	2	.362/.393/.550	169	26.9	.399	-0.8	RF(51) 0.4, CF(3) 0.3	2.3	99
2019	PEN	AA	21	411	47	18	2	9	43	29	76	7	6	.283/.343/.413	121	10.5	.333	-3.3	RF(41) -4.0, 1B(35) 0.3	0.6	98
2020	MIN	MLB	22	251	26	14	1	8	31	14	58	0	0	.268/.315/.436	96	0.0	.325	-0.4	RF -3, 1B 0	0.4	100

Comparables: Tyler Austin, Justin Williams, Gabriel Guerrero

The Report: While Larnach's prospect profile has been slow and steady, a late first round college pick who climbs prospect rankings bit by bit as he hits at every stop, Kirilloff's has been a bit more of a yo-yo. He announced himself quickly after the draft, mashing in the Appy League and garnering better reports on the bat than you'd expect from a cold weather prep without much athletic projection. Tommy John surgery then cost him all of 2017, injecting a fair bit of uncertainty into the profile. 2018 came and he destroyed two A-ball levels, although the performance outpaced the tools and it started to look more likely he'd slide from a corner outfield spot to first base. 2019 was uneven at the plate, although you could easily point out that he was 21 in Double-A and missed the first month with a wrist injury. Those tend to linger. But he made some swing changes that geared him more for pull power and affected his plate coverage and ability to hit to all fields. He also played almost as much first base as outfield, and the cold corner may be his long term home. On the other hand, he did heat up and hit for more power towards the end of the year.

In conclusion, Alex Kirilloff is a land of contrasts.

He also remains a good prospect and not that far off from the potential plus hit/power guy you're still expecting.

Variance: Medium. If he slides to first base, that means he will really have to hit. The injuries can explain away the early season production issues, but he's also had a fair bit of injuries now, and they are of the type that can sap offensive skills.

Mark Barry's Fantasy Take: I'm targeting Kirilloff wherever I can. Sure, more injuries are troubling, but now is the time to pounce, especially since his shift to the cold corner likely means an expedited path to the big leagues. Despite the scrapes and bruises, Kirilloff still maintained above-average contact and even chipped in a handful of steals. He's still firmly in the top-15ish for me as far as dynasty prospects are concerned.

5 Jhoan Duran RHP   OFP: 60   ETA: 2020/21

Born: 01/08/98   Age: 22   Bats: R   Throws: R   Height: 6'5"   Weight: 230   Origin: International Free Agent, 2014

YEAR	TEAM	LVL	AGE	W	L	SV	G	GS	IP	H	HR	BB/9	K/9	K	GB%	BABIP	WHIP	ERA	DRA	WARP	PF
2017	DIA	RK	19	0	2	0	3	3	11¹	19	0	3.2	10.3	13	64%	.452	2.03	7.15	7.31	-0.1	94
2017	YAK	A-	19	6	3	0	11	11	51	44	5	3.0	6.4	36	54%	.253	1.20	4.24	4.19	0.6	94
2018	KNC	A	20	5	4	0	15	15	64²	69	6	3.9	9.9	71	52%	.346	1.50	4.73	4.49	0.5	106
2018	CDR	A	20	2	1	0	6	6	36	19	2	2.5	11.0	44	66%	.218	0.81	2.00	5.32	-0.1	101
2019	FTM	A+	21	2	9	0	16	15	78	63	5	3.6	11.0	95	53%	.317	1.21	3.23	4.39	0.6	97
2019	PEN	AA	21	3	3	0	7	7	37	34	2	2.2	10.0	41	64%	.349	1.16	4.86	6.27	-0.6	97
2020	MIN	MLB	22	2	2	0	33	0	35	34	5	3.6	9.0	35	50%	.303	1.38	4.70	4.71	0.2	100

Comparables: Huascar Ynoa, Joel Payamps, Alex Cobb

The Report: If you liked Brusdar Graterol, you'll like Jhoan Duran. It's the same type of power stuff. Duran can work his high-spin, four-seam fastball up over 100 and he complements it with a diving, mid-90s sinker/splitter hybrid. He also throws a power 11-5 breaker that he can run up into the upper-80s and will flash plus-plus. It's an ideal starter's fame, but not ideal starter's mechanics due to some late effort that causes him to fall off to the first base side. So it's not exactly easy velocity, and his command and control play on the fringe side of average.

If you think the second fastball look is enough of a change of pace, you could already give Duran credit for three plus major league pitches. Honestly even if you don't buy that taxonomy, the different fastball looks combined with the breaking ball might be enough to start anyway, but given the mechanics, and what he might be able to offer in short bursts, like with Graterol the temptation to unleash him at the end of games might be too great.

Variance: High. Limited upper minors experience, high relief risk.

Mark Barry's Fantasy Take: So, I'm not as high on Duran for fantasy, moreso because of the delivery as opposed to the arsenal. Even if he starts, it's hard to pencil him in as a guy that wades into the sixth and seventh innings with consistency. Like Graterol, Duran could be a lights out reliever, but that dramatically decreases his fantasy upside.

6 Keoni Cavaco SS   OFP: 55   ETA: 2023

Born: 06/02/01   Age: 19   Bats: R   Throws: R   Height: 6'2"   Weight: 195   Origin: Round 1, 2019 Draft (#13 overall)

YEAR	TEAM	LVL	AGE	PA	R	2B	3B	HR	RBI	BB	K	SB	CS	AVG/OBP/SLG	DRC+	VORP	BABIP	BRR	FRAA	WARP	PF
2019	TWI	RK	18	92	9	4	0	1	6	4	35	1	1	.172/.217/.253	28	-6.0	.275	-0.6	SS(20) 0.5	-0.3	92
2020	MIN	MLB	19	251	19	11	1	3	21	17	113	2	1	.194/.253/.293	43	0.0	.360	0.0	SS 0	-0.9	100

Comparables: Billy Hamilton, Isan Díaz, Gavin Cecchini

The Report: The Twins moved Cavaco from third base to shortstop full time after drafting him—he played a bit of both in high school and on the showcase circuit—and he certainly looks the part of a highly-touted SoCal prep shortstop. He has a left side arm and is a plus runner. If he does have to slide back to third as he enters his twenties and fills out, the quick twitch athleticism should make him comfortably above-average there. He has enough raw power for a corner spot too, although the swing can be a little stiff in the upper half at times to generate the pop. Cavaco was a pop-up name that only turned 18 right before draft day, so he is going to take some time to develop as a professional, but the speed/power combo will be intriguing wherever he ends up the diamond.

Variance: Very high. Complex-league resume, shorter amateur track record, hit tool questions. If he does stick at short and the bat comes good, however, Cavaco has the potential to make a few all-star games.

Mark Barry's Fantasy Take:

7 Jordan Balazovic RHP   OFP: 55   ETA: 2021
Born: 09/17/98   Age: 21   Bats: R   Throws: R   Height: 6'5"   Weight: 215   Origin: Round 5, 2016 Draft (#153 overall)

YEAR	TEAM	LVL	AGE	W	L	SV	G	GS	IP	H	HR	BB/9	K/9	K	GB%	BABIP	WHIP	ERA	DRA	WARP	PF
2017	TWI	RK	18	1	3	0	10	3	40¹	47	5	4.5	6.5	29	37%	.331	1.66	4.91	8.77	-1.3	97
2018	CDR	A	19	7	3	0	12	11	61²	54	5	2.6	11.4	78	48%	.327	1.17	3.94	3.53	1.2	105
2019	CDR	A	20	2	1	0	4	4	20²	15	1	1.7	14.4	33	42%	.318	0.92	2.18	1.97	0.8	98
2019	FTM	A+	20	6	4	0	15	14	73	52	3	2.6	11.8	96	45%	.283	1.00	2.84	3.23	1.6	95
2020	MIN	MLB	21	2	2	0	33	0	35	35	5	3.4	10.2	40	43%	.320	1.38	4.77	4.71	0.2	100

Comparables: German Márquez, Alex Reyes, Antonio Senzatela

The Report: Playing the entire season at 20, Balazovic blitzed two A-ball levels on the strength of his mid-90s fastball, which shows life up and sink down. He has two potentially average major league secondaries as well. The best of the two at present is a mid-80s slider that he can manipulate to spot in the zone, or to induce swings out of it. The latter version is preferable, firmer with good tilt. The changeup is more of a projection pitch at present, but he maintains his arm speed well, and it will flash average fade. The slider needs more consistent shape, the change more consistent location, but they should end up quality offerings to play off the plus fastball.

Balazovic has a good frame and while his uptempo delivery can occasionally get out of sync, he generally repeats his mechanics well. If he continues to refine his secondaries, he should be ready to step into the middle of the Twins rotation in a year or two.

Variance: Medium. Secondaries need further development, and he hasn't seen Double-A yet. If you believe the conventional wisdom that cold weather prep arms can pop later, well, Canada is pretty cold.

Mark Barry's Fantasy Take: I like Balazovic quite a bit more than Duran and Cavaco for fantasy, as he's a huge dude that could shoulder a relatively-full starter's workload. Also appealing: he punched out around a third of the guys he faced last season. Pair those two things together and you have a guy who could bust out of the dreaded "mid-rotation-starter" mold.

8 Lewis Thorpe LHP   OFP: 55   ETA: 2019
Born: 11/23/95   Age: 24   Bats: R   Throws: L   Height: 6'1"   Weight: 218   Origin: International Free Agent, 2012

YEAR	TEAM	LVL	AGE	W	L	SV	G	GS	IP	H	HR	BB/9	K/9	K	GB%	BABIP	WHIP	ERA	DRA	WARP	PF
2017	FTM	A+	21	3	4	0	16	15	77	62	3	3.6	9.8	84	39%	.304	1.21	2.69	4.02	1.1	101
2017	CHT	AA	21	1	0	0	1	1	6	5	2	3.0	10.5	7	19%	.214	1.17	6.00	4.12	0.1	96
2018	CHT	AA	22	8	4	0	22	21	108	105	13	2.5	10.9	131	38%	.327	1.25	3.58	4.14	1.5	105
2018	ROC	AAA	22	0	3	0	4	4	21²	20	3	2.5	10.8	26	45%	.321	1.20	3.32	3.94	0.4	95
2019	ROC	AAA	23	5	4	0	20	19	96¹	91	13	2.3	11.1	119	43%	.318	1.20	4.58	3.53	2.9	100
2019	MIN	MLB	23	3	2	0	12	2	27²	38	3	3.3	10.1	31	35%	.438	1.73	6.18	5.36	0.0	101
2020	MIN	MLB	24	4	3	0	30	8	64	60	9	3.0	8.7	62	38%	.288	1.27	4.15	4.22	0.9	100

Comparables: Anthony Banda, Jake Odorizzi, Zack Littell

The Report: It feels like we have been writing about Thorpe forever, but despite that—and despite missing two full seasons due to Tommy John—he only just turned 24. He's also made the majors now, and while the best hitters in the world weren't particularly kind to him during his debut, the stuff remains major-league-quality, if not particularly superlative.

Thorpe is a four-pitch lefty that likes to mix his full arsenal. The fastball is mostly low-90s and a little true—although he will occasionally cut it in to righties—but there's deception from his delivery, and the pitch can be effective when he spots it around the edges of the zone. The slider was his primary secondary in the majors and it's developed into a potential swing-and-miss offering in the mid-80s despite showing more cutterish action than two-plane break. The changeup got punished badly in the majors, and he hung too many of them, but it's had average action and projection in the past. There's a mid-70s lollipop curve for a different breaking ball look to round things out. Thorpe's command simply wasn't fine enough during his major league debut, but he continued to miss bats like he always has. If he can consistently get ahead of major league hitters and keep his stuff out of the middle of the zone, there's the potential for an above-average major league starter, but the likely outcome here is more of a backend guy that's a little too hittable.

Variance: Medium. Thorpe made the majors and at time of publication his main competition for an Opening Day 2020 rotation spot are Devin Smeltzer and Randy Dobnak. There's some downside risk here if the stuff just can't consistently get outs, but he's a lefty with a broad arsenal, he'll likely find a major league role of some sort.

Mark Barry's Fantasy Take: Thorpe is moderately more interesting if you're in the middle of your deep-league contention cycle, as he could help your rotation as early as this year. I don't know if there's much more than a fantasy SP4 on the high end, but he should tally a bunch of strikeouts, if underwhelming elsewhere.

9 Ryan Jeffers C   OFP: 55   ETA: 2021

Born: 06/03/97   Age: 23   Bats: R   Throws: R   Height: 6'4"   Weight: 230   Origin: Round 2, 2018 Draft (#59 overall)

YEAR	TEAM	LVL	AGE	PA	R	2B	3B	HR	RBI	BB	K	SB	CS	AVG/OBP/SLG	DRC+	VORP	BABIP	BRR	FRAA	WARP	PF
2018	ELZ	RK	21	129	29	7	0	3	16	20	16	0	1	.422/.543/.578	219	19.7	.482	-1.0	C(10) 0.7	1.9	103
2018	CDR	A	21	155	19	10	0	4	17	14	30	0	0	.288/.361/.446	149	10.3	.343	0.4	C(22) 0.2	1.4	102
2019	FTM	A+	22	315	35	11	0	10	40	28	64	0	0	.256/.330/.402	122	15.0	.297	-2.7	C(57) 0.7	1.6	95
2019	PEN	AA	22	99	13	5	0	4	9	9	19	0	0	.287/.374/.483	142	9.8	.328	1.4	C(16) -0.9	0.8	96
2020	MIN	MLB	23	251	28	12	0	9	32	19	64	0	0	.253/.320/.428	99	0.0	.313	-0.5	C -3	0.5	100

Comparables: Willson Contreras, Devin Mesoraco, Oscar Hernández

The Report: Jeffers made it to Double-A by the end of his first full professional season, that's moving pretty quickly for a second-round college catcher. The bat has really yet to be challenged by professional pitching and the power has continued to develop in games, which has paved his speedy path up the organizational ladder. There's a potential 50/55 hit/power combination here, and Jeffers has filled out his lean frame and improved his receiving. He has an above-average arm as well, so there's true two-way catcher upside in the profile now. If you want to find a potential breakout Top 101 name in the Twins system for next year, look no further.

Variance: High. Catchers are weird. Jeffers still has some strides to make defensively and the bat might be ready for the majors before the glove is.

Mark Barry's Fantasy Take: A bat-first catcher, you say? You have my attention. If you have roster space, and can stomach rolling the dice on a fantasy catcher, Jeffers is as good an under-the-radar name as any. There's risk he might have to move to first base, in which case he's less interesting, but Jeffers is an easy name for a flier in deep leagues.

10 Gilberto Celestino OF   OFP: 55   ETA: 2021/22

Born: 02/13/99   Age: 21   Bats: R   Throws: L   Height: 6'0"   Weight: 170   Origin: International Free Agent, 2015

YEAR	TEAM	LVL	AGE	PA	R	2B	3B	HR	RBI	BB	K	SB	CS	AVG/OBP/SLG	DRC+	VORP	BABIP	BRR	FRAA	WARP	PF
2017	GRV	RK	18	261	38	10	2	4	24	22	59	10	2	.268/.331/.379	102	14.1	.339	5.3	CF(43) 2.6, RF(8) 0.1	1.5	97
2018	ELZ	RK	19	117	13	4	1	1	13	6	16	8	2	.266/.308/.349	89	-0.8	.301	1.1	CF(23) -1.0	0.2	101
2018	TCV	A-	19	142	18	8	0	4	21	10	25	14	0	.323/.387/.480	175	15.2	.374	1.6	CF(16) 0.9, RF(12) 2.6	1.7	97
2019	CDR	A	20	503	52	24	3	10	51	48	81	14	8	.276/.350/.409	137	22.7	.317	-3.6	CF(82) 3.7, RF(25) -3.6	3.0	99
2019	FTM	A+	20	33	6	4	0	0	3	2	4	0	0	.300/.333/.433	124	3.5	.333	0.2	CF(4) -0.8, RF(3) -0.3	0.0	104
2020	MIN	MLB	21	251	23	13	1	5	25	17	59	5	1	.234/.291/.362	73	0.0	.293	0.0	CF 1, RF 0	0.1	100

Comparables: Brett Phillips, Dalton Pompey, Victor Robles

The Report: Celestino sticks in the number ten spot again this year, but that obscures some improvements in the profile. He's gotten a little more comfortable lifting the ball pull side, so while the approach remains mostly gap-to-gap, he could sneak 10-15 bombs over the left field fence as well. He's also added some good weight in his lower half which has stabilized the leg kick in his swing and given everything a bit more oomph offensively. Last year, we were still questioning how much Celestino would hit, and while a season in A-ball won't answer all concerns, we're more confident now in at least average hit tool here.

The center field profile remains no-doubt. He's an above-average runner whose speed plays up on the grass because of his excellent instincts. He picks out the landing spot, and then goes and gets it, rarely drifting to the ball. The defense remains the carrying tool, but the improving bat makes it more likely Celestino gets penciled into the lineup every day.

Variance: High. There's still a limited professional track record with the bat.

Mark Barry's Fantasy Take: Bret suggested Ender Inciarte as a nonzero outcome for Celestino, and with the improvements in his game, namely hitting for contact and stealing some bases, that still feels kinda right. It might not be sexy (or necessary to run out and roster him), but Inciarte was good for a bit, right?

The Next Ten

11 Devin Smeltzer LHP

Born: 09/07/95   Age: 24   Bats: R   Throws: L   Height: 6'3"   Weight: 195   Origin: Round 5, 2016 Draft (#161 overall)

YEAR	TEAM	LVL	AGE	W	L	SV	G	GS	IP	H	HR	BB/9	K/9	K	GB%	BABIP	WHIP	ERA	DRA	WARP	PF
2017	GRL	A	21	2	3	0	10	10	52¹	40	6	2.1	9.8	57	49%	.266	0.99	3.78	2.93	1.4	95
2017	RCU	A+	21	5	4	0	16	15	90	107	10	1.8	10.2	102	44%	.367	1.39	4.40	4.75	0.5	105
2018	TUL	AA	22	5	5	0	23	14	83²	94	9	2.0	7.2	67	39%	.321	1.35	4.73	4.70	0.5	110
2018	CHT	AA	22	0	0	4	10	0	12	14	0	1.5	12.0	16	36%	.389	1.33	3.00	3.60	0.2	100
2019	PEN	AA	23	3	1	0	5	5	30	19	0	0.9	9.9	33	42%	.268	0.73	0.60	2.66	0.8	103
2019	ROC	AAA	23	1	4	0	15	14	74¹	68	14	2.3	8.6	71	40%	.271	1.17	3.63	3.89	2.0	98
2019	MIN	MLB	23	2	2	1	11	6	49	50	8	2.2	7.0	38	39%	.294	1.27	3.86	5.59	0.0	101
2020	MIN	MLB	24	4	4	0	11	11	60	66	12	2.7	7.0	47	38%	.297	1.40	5.44	5.38	0.1	100

Comparables: Josh Rogers, Ranger Suárez, Andrew Heaney

It's not a secret I'm a sucker for a lefty sitting in the upper-80s with a good changeup, but usually those pitchers end up in the "Personal Cheeseball" section below. Bonus points if they have rec-specs and a questionable goatee. Smeltzer checks all those boxes, but his change has developed into a swing-and-miss pitch against righties at the highest level, with plus fade and sink and a deceptive arm action more than making up for less than ideal separation off the fastball. A mid-70s, big breaking, 1-7 curve is similarly deployed against lefties, an his low-three-quarters slot makes it look like the breaker starts at their ear flap.

Smeltzer will throw one of the above-average offspeeds about half the time, which makes sense given that the fastball merely touches 90. He's confident enough to throw it to either side of the plate, and he can sneak it by you if you are focused on the secondaries. It's a profile with thin margins, but Meltzer's arsenal and approach have yet to wobble against big league bats, and while there's not a ton of upside, he looks like a fairly safe backend starter or swingman. Minnesota's lineup might be mashing home runs by the bunches now, but it's nice to see that they still employ at least one extremely Twins Pitcher™.

12 Nick Gordon IF

Born: 10/24/95   Age: 24   Bats: L   Throws: R   Height: 6'0"   Weight: 160   Origin: Round 1, 2014 Draft (#5 overall)

YEAR	TEAM	LVL	AGE	PA	R	2B	3B	HR	RBI	BB	K	SB	CS	AVG/OBP/SLG	DRC+	VORP	BABIP	BRR	FRAA	WARP	PF
2017	CHT	AA	21	578	80	29	8	9	66	53	134	13	7	.270/.341/.408	118	32.7	.347	1.1	SS(104) 0.4, 2B(14) 0.4	3.7	100
2018	CHT	AA	22	181	22	10	3	5	20	11	27	7	2	.333/.381/.525	140	13.8	.366	-1.4	SS(34) 2.4, 2B(6) -0.3	1.6	106
2018	ROC	AAA	22	410	40	13	4	2	29	23	82	13	3	.212/.262/.283	48	-7.1	.264	2.8	SS(69) 2.6, 2B(30) 4.1	0.5	93
2019	ROC	AAA	23	319	49	29	3	4	40	18	65	14	4	.298/.342/.459	107	16.5	.364	-0.1	SS(40) 1.6, 2B(29) -1.4	1.5	100
2020	MIN	MLB	24	140	12	7	1	2	12	8	35	3	1	.234/.284/.343	64	2.0	.306	0.1	2B 1, SS 0	0.0	100

Comparables: Richard Ureña, Tim Beckham, Yairo Muñoz

In the beginning God created the heaven and the earth. Then he wrote up a Nick Gordon prospect blurb. When I wrote above that "[i]t feels like we have been writing about Thorpe forever," that's not nearly as long as we've been writing about Gordon, whose high school scouting report was the second thing to come off Gutenberg's press. Jokes aside, he's still just 24, and hit in Triple-A in a repeat engagement truncated at the front by acute gastritis and at the back by a leg bruise. Gordon is unlikely to hit the heights implied when drafted fifth overall as a prep shortstop, but he's come back around to perhaps being a bit underrated. He is high-waisted and athletic with a loose, contact-oriented swing, but he's never really developed much physicality and it's a smallish frame. There is sneaky doubles pop, and he's a pesky at-bat, but aggressive enough that walks aren't going to be a huge part of his game. There's an above-average hit tool here on balance, and Gordon can handle either middle infield spot. He's a better fit at second, so there's some Joe Panik in the profile, but Panik was a decent starter for a few years. It's not a smash hit from a top-five pick, but it's a pretty good prospect to have outside your top ten.

13 Brent Rooker OF/1B

Born: 11/01/94 Age: 25 Bats: R Throws: R Height: 6'3" Weight: 215 Origin: Round 1, 2017 Draft (#35 overall)

YEAR	TEAM	LVL	AGE	PA	R	2B	3B	HR	RBI	BB	K	SB	CS	AVG/OBP/SLG	DRC+	VORP	BABIP	BRR	FRAA	WARP	PF
2017	ELZ	RK	22	99	19	5	0	7	17	11	21	2	2	.282/.364/.588	134	10.3	.288	0.6	LF(17) 0.4	0.7	96
2017	FTM	A+	22	162	23	6	0	11	35	16	47	0	0	.280/.364/.552	171	13.3	.341	-1.5	LF(16) -2.6, 1B(11) -0.4	0.8	101
2018	CHT	AA	23	568	72	32	4	22	79	56	150	6	1	.254/.333/.465	117	13.2	.316	-4.7	1B(47) -5.7, LF(44) -8.2	0.0	103
2019	ROC	AAA	24	274	41	16	0	14	47	35	95	2	0	.281/.398/.535	123	22.6	.417	2.6	LF(56) -0.6	1.5	100
2020	MIN	MLB	25	70	7	4	0	2	8	6	26	0	0	.219/.299/.389	81	0.0	.331	-0.1	LF -1	-0.1	100

Comparables: Chris Shaw, Joe Benson, Jake Lamb

I wonder if Rooker feels a bit left out from the Twins offensive explosion in 2019. He's a perfect fit for the parade of bash brothers that rolled out in Target Field. Rooker was heating up and putting himself in contention for a MLB call up when a groin injury functionally ended his season in mid-July. He's an ideal hitter for our rabbit ball/launch angle era, and while strikeouts continue (and likely will continue) to be an issue there's enough pop and approach to get him above the Quad-A line and into the middle of a major league lineup for a few years. He's limited to left field, first base and designated hitter, all areas the Twins have plenty of MLB options, so it might take someone else's injury misfortune to open a spot for Rooker.

14 Matt Wallner OF

Born: 12/12/97 Age: 22 Bats: L Throws: R Height: 6'5" Weight: 220 Origin: Round 1, 2019 Draft (#39 overall)

YEAR	TEAM	LVL	AGE	PA	R	2B	3B	HR	RBI	BB	K	SB	CS	AVG/OBP/SLG	DRC+	VORP	BABIP	BRR	FRAA	WARP	PF
2019	ELZ	RK+	21	238	35	18	1	6	28	19	66	1	1	.269/.361/.452	133	12.2	.368	-0.8		1.2	99
2019	CDR	A	21	53	7	3	1	2	6	5	14	0	0	.205/.340/.455	114	1.9	.250	-0.4	RF(10) -1.8	-0.1	99
2020	MIN	MLB	22	251	21	13	1	5	23	15	91	2	1	.198/.264/.323	55	0.0	.303	0.0	RF -1	-0.7	100

Comparables: Luke Montz, Jabari Blash, Jaylin Davis

The Twins do like their corner guys with pop, and they added another one to the org with their Comp A pick. They might have gotten the biggest raw in the draft class, and Wallner gets there without a huge load or all that much length to the swing. He does like to get extended, and struggles to adjust his bat path once he commits so he could struggle with velocity inside or adjusting to breaking stuff. He'll be fine enough in right field, as he's athletic for his size and was up to 97 in college when he was still pitching. The present issues hit tool will likely limit how much the prodigious power plays, but the native Minnesotan has pop enough to spare.

15 Cole Sands RHP

Born: 07/17/97 Age: 22 Bats: R Throws: R Height: 6'3" Weight: 215 Origin: Round 5, 2018 Draft (#154 overall)

YEAR	TEAM	LVL	AGE	W	L	SV	G	GS	IP	H	HR	BB/9	K/9	K	GB%	BABIP	WHIP	ERA	DRA	WARP	PF
2019	CDR	A	21	2	1	0	8	8	41¹	41	0	2.4	10.7	49	41%	.373	1.26	3.05	4.03	0.6	98
2019	FTM	A+	21	5	2	0	9	9	52	36	4	1.2	9.2	53	39%	.254	0.83	2.25	2.64	1.5	96
2020	MIN	MLB	22	2	2	0	33	0	35	35	5	3.8	8.8	34	41%	.303	1.42	4.80	4.76	0.2	100

In his feature on gaming the draft, former BP Prospect staff member and current Pirates Quantitative Analyst, Grant Jones suggested Cole Sands as one of the prep prospects to target as a significantly overslot pick in later rounds. Sands ended up going to Florida State and was drafted in the fifth round in 2018 after an uneven college career. Grant was onto something though, as Sands pitched at three levels in 2019, finding success working off a fastball that he can dial up to 95 with late run. There's an average curve—that flashes higher when it shows true 12-6 action— and potentially average change-up. Sands has pretty much the ideal starting pitcher body, but the delivery is a bit upright and arm-heavy. He's yet to throw 100 innings in a season, but once that hurdle is cleared, the profile looks like a solid number four starter.

16 Misael Urbina OF

Born: 04/26/02   Age: 18   Bats: R   Throws: R   Height: 6'0"   Weight: 175   Origin: International Free Agent, 2018

One of the top prospects in the 2018 IFA class, Urbina is more polish than tools with an advanced approach and hit tool for a 17-year-old. The swing would look good at any age, balanced and able to drive the ball from line to line. He's far from a finished product, and could add 20 pounds or so without impacting his above-average speed and center field glove projection. How much power Urbina ultimately develops will determine if we are looking at a plus regular or more of a cromulent everyday guy, but he's advanced enough at present to handle a fairly aggressive stateside assignment in 2020 if the Twins were so inclined.

17 Randy Dobnak RHP

Born: 01/17/95   Age: 25   Bats: R   Throws: R   Height: 6'1"   Weight: 230   Origin: Undrafted Free Agent, 2017

YEAR	TEAM	LVL	AGE	W	L	SV	G	GS	IP	H	HR	BB/9	K/9	K	GB%	BABIP	WHIP	ERA	DRA	WARP	PF
2017	ELZ	RK	22	2	0	1	5	3	26¹	19	3	2.1	7.5	22	46%	.225	0.95	2.39	1.91	1.1	99
2017	CDR	A	22	0	0	0	1	1	7	6	0	1.3	1.3	1	56%	.240	1.00	2.57	4.57	0.1	106
2018	CDR	A	23	10	5	0	24	20	129	138	6	1.7	5.9	84	47%	.314	1.26	3.14	4.44	1.1	104
2019	FTM	A+	24	3	0	0	4	4	22¹	18	0	1.6	5.6	14	59%	.273	0.99	0.40	3.78	0.3	97
2019	PEN	AA	24	4	2	0	11	10	66²	58	6	0.8	8.2	61	60%	.278	0.96	2.57	3.67	1.0	97
2019	ROC	AAA	24	5	2	0	9	7	46	28	0	3.5	6.7	34	62%	.229	1.00	2.15	2.47	1.8	98
2019	MIN	MLB	24	2	1	1	9	5	28¹	27	1	1.6	7.3	23	54%	.302	1.13	1.59	4.60	0.3	101
2020	MIN	MLB	25	4	3	0	21	10	63	61	7	3.1	8.3	58	56%	.299	1.31	4.07	4.09	1.0	100

Comparables: Taylor Jordan, Brock Stewart, Phil Irwin

You know the story by now: Unfancied, undrafted, org guy strike-thrower makes good, makes the majors, starts in a playoff game. Dobnak didn't get his Hollywood ending against the Damn Yankees, but did put himself in position for a role on the 2020 Twins pitching staff. He's a real throwback, and it isn't just the *I Love the 90's* Rod Beck facial hair. In a high-spin, four-seam fastball up era, Dobnak pounds the bottom of the zone with a low-90s sinking fastball, and dares the launch angle superstars to try and lift it. It's an extreme groundball pitch with good sink and run. A mid-80s slider will show razor blade depth, but can get slurvy or back-up. There's a changeup as well, potentially average, and Dobnak will throw it to both righties and lefties. He's somewhat duplicative in profile with Devin Smeltzer, and they might be competing for the same spot in February. Dobnak doesn't have a pitch as good as Smeltzer's change. He doesn't have his left-handedness either, but he should get a shot at a heartwarming sequel this year.

18 Matt Canterino RHP

Born: 12/14/97   Age: 22   Bats: R   Throws: R   Height: 6'2"   Weight: 222   Origin: Round 2, 2019 Draft (#54 overall)

YEAR	TEAM	LVL	AGE	W	L	SV	G	GS	IP	H	HR	BB/9	K/9	K	GB%	BABIP	WHIP	ERA	DRA	WARP	PF
2019	CDR	A	21	1	1	0	5	5	20	6	0	3.2	11.2	25	49%	.146	0.65	1.35	2.03	0.7	101
2020	MIN	MLB	22	2	2	0	33	0	35	35	5	3.6	9.1	35	43%	.306	1.39	4.75	4.80	0.2	100

Comparables: Carl Edwards Jr., Michael Stutes, Jorge Alcala

The Twins second round pick, Canterino is a big, physically maxed college arm with average fastball velocity that plays up due to his advanced command of the pitch and the plane on it he generates from his high-three-quarters slot. He pairs it with a slider in the mid-80s that features late cut. The command of the slider lags behind the fastball at present, but the offering is a potential plus pitch with refinement. Canterino will also use a humpy, 11-6 curveball on occasion. Canterino isn't the most athletic specimen and his delivery can be a bit hitchy as well. So while there's no reason to move him to the bullpen yet, I wouldn't be surprised if he ends up a solid 95-and-a-slider setup type.

19   Blayne Enlow   RHP

Born: 03/21/99   Age: 21   Bats: R   Throws: R   Height: 6'3"   Weight: 170   Origin: Round 3, 2017 Draft (#76 overall)

YEAR	TEAM	LVL	AGE	W	L	SV	G	GS	IP	H	HR	BB/9	K/9	K	GB%	BABIP	WHIP	ERA	DRA	WARP	PF
2017	TWI	RK	18	3	0	0	6	1	20¹	10	1	1.8	8.4	19	56%	.176	0.69	1.33	1.16	1.0	97
2018	CDR	A	19	3	5	1	20	17	94	94	4	3.4	6.8	71	47%	.315	1.37	3.26	5.10	0.1	104
2019	CDR	A	20	4	3	0	8	8	41¹	42	4	3.3	9.6	44	61%	.317	1.38	4.57	4.72	0.2	97
2019	FTM	A+	20	4	4	0	13	12	69¹	61	4	3.0	6.6	51	46%	.275	1.21	3.38	4.76	0.2	93
2020	MIN	MLB	21	2	2	0	33	0	35	34	5	3.5	6.1	24	46%	.272	1.37	4.72	4.77	0.2	100

Comparables: Jonathan Hernández, Nate Adcock, Mike Foltynewicz

Enlow keeps on keeping on, not missing quite as many bats as you'd like with any of his five offerings. He can dial his fastball up into the mid-90s now, but fringy command makes it a bit too hittable. The cutter sits around 90, and flashes above-average, but can roll in a bit lazily too. He can be overly fond of trying to backdoor the low-80s slider, and the gloveside command isn't always there when he tries to back foot it to lefties. The curve and the change-up remain more show-me offerings, although the cutter is useful enough against as a crossover option. The frame's good. The delivery's fine. But we are going to have to wait a while longer for something to pop in the profile. The sum of the parts should get Enlow to a backend starter, but the math hasn't added up so far.

20   Edwar Colina   RHP

Born: 05/03/97   Age: 23   Bats: R   Throws: R   Height: 5'11"   Weight: 240   Origin: International Free Agent, 2015

YEAR	TEAM	LVL	AGE	W	L	SV	G	GS	IP	H	HR	BB/9	K/9	K	GB%	BABIP	WHIP	ERA	DRA	WARP	PF
2017	ELZ	RK	20	3	5	0	12	11	59¹	48	6	4.4	8.5	56	47%	.264	1.30	3.34	3.56	1.6	100
2018	CDR	A	21	7	4	0	19	18	98	71	4	4.6	8.7	95	50%	.261	1.23	2.48	3.84	1.6	103
2018	FTM	A+	21	0	1	0	2	2	11¹	13	1	2.4	8.7	11	34%	.353	1.41	3.97	5.23	0.0	97
2019	FTM	A+	22	4	2	0	10	10	61²	53	3	2.2	8.9	61	51%	.296	1.10	2.34	4.02	0.8	95
2019	PEN	AA	22	4	0	0	7	4	31	21	0	4.4	10.7	37	42%	.292	1.16	2.03	4.25	0.2	100
2020	MIN	MLB	23	2	2	0	33	0	35	35	5	4.1	8.0	31	39%	.294	1.45	4.90	4.79	0.2	100

Colina has mid-90s heat and can touch higher, but he prefers to throw his slider. Over and over and over again. He manipulates the pitch well, and it's a plus slider, but that's not an approach that is going to work long term as a starter. The fastball runs pretty true and batters seem pretty comfortable taking their hacks at it. The delivery has some effort, and the fastball command and control is below-average too. so let Colina loose in the pen where he can spam the breaker to either side of the plate, early in counts, behind in counts, to get ahead, for strikeouts, whatever.

Personal Cheeseball

PC   Gabriel Maciel   OF

Born: 01/10/99   Age: 21   Bats: B   Throws: R   Height: 5'10"   Weight: 170   Origin: International Free Agent, 2016

YEAR	TEAM	LVL	AGE	PA	R	2B	3B	HR	RBI	BB	K	SB	CS	AVG/OBP/SLG	DRC+	VORP	BABIP	BRR	FRAA	WARP	PF
2017	MSO	RK	18	245	40	14	1	3	25	24	34	9	8	.323/.389/.438	117	11.6	.368	-2.1	CF(25) 3.2, LF(25) -0.4	0.7	116
2018	KNC	A	19	313	44	10	0	1	16	30	50	14	5	.287/.362/.333	102	5.1	.346	0.2	CF(54) -7.1, RF(16) 0.0	0.3	107
2018	CDR	A	19	126	16	4	2	2	7	5	21	2	5	.263/.302/.381	102	3.1	.302	-1.2	CF(15) -0.8, RF(9) -0.2	0.1	101
2019	CDR	A	20	187	28	3	4	0	17	23	31	8	2	.309/.395/.377	135	15.6	.382	2.7	CF(24) -2.1, RF(16) -0.1	1.2	99
2019	FTM	A+	20	229	29	6	2	3	17	21	30	14	7	.261/.342/.357	117	10.9	.290	0.5	CF(31) 2.5, RF(16) -0.9	1.2	95
2020	MIN	MLB	21	251	22	10	1	3	22	17	52	5	3	.248/.304/.340	72	0.0	.308	-0.1	CF 0, RF 1	0.0	100

Comparables: Gorkys Hernández, Victor Reyes, Harold Ramirez

Maciel came to the Twins in the same deal Jhoan Duran, and while he hasn't broken out to the same level, he's an intriguing outfield prospect. Generously listed at 5-foot-10, Maciel knows his game, he's a burner that is never going to hit for much power. He needs to hit the ball on the ground, or on a line, and run. Despite a wide open stance and leg kick, Maciel is short to the ball, and shows solid barrel control. There's enough bat speed to shoot fastballs over the second baseman's head, but the lack of physicality means he might not drive the ball enough to develop a true plus hit tool. He'll mitigate some of that by bunting his way on a dozen times a year or so. Like I said, he knows his game. His plus-plus speed makes him a solid enough center fielder, and while the lack of pop might limit him to more to a bench outfielder role, it feels like we are about due for another Ben Revere. Not a surprise he would come back as a Twin again.

Low Minors Sleeper

LMS **Luis Rijo** **RHP**
Born: 09/06/98   Age: 21   Bats: R   Throws: R   Height: 6'1"   Weight: 200   Origin: International Free Agent, 2015

YEAR	TEAM	LVL	AGE	W	L	SV	G	GS	IP	H	HR	BB/9	K/9	K	GB%	BABIP	WHIP	ERA	DRA	WARP	PF
2017	YAN	RK	18	4	3	0	11	7	54	51	2	1.5	9.2	55	46%	.329	1.11	3.50	3.80	1.2	92
2018	PUL	RK	19	3	1	0	5	3	27	28	0	0.3	8.7	26	59%	.329	1.07	2.67	4.41	0.5	101
2018	ELZ	RK	19	2	0	0	5	5	21¹	15	1	1.7	7.2	17	52%	.237	0.89	1.27	5.13	0.2	101
2018	STA	A-	19	0	0	0	1	1	6	8	0	3.0	4.5	3	41%	.364	1.67	3.00	7.04	-0.1	118
2018	TAM	A+	19	1	0	0	1	1	6	6	0	0.0	4.5	3	33%	.286	1.00	3.00	4.11	0.1	105
2019	CDR	A	20	5	8	0	19	19	107	89	5	1.9	8.3	99	54%	.285	1.05	2.86	3.78	1.8	99
2020	MIN	MLB	21	2	2	0	33	0	35	34	5	3.0	6.8	26	47%	.276	1.29	4.17	4.27	0.4	100

The third of the Yankees prospect Luises was dealt for Lance Lynn last summer. He's never had the premium raw stuff of Medina or Gil, but Rijo has the most advanced pitchability of the troika, and the stuff is solid enough. His fastball has ticked up into an average velocity band, but he's close to physically maxed, so it's unlikely there's too many more ticks to come. He throws effective strikes with it, and it's a lively pitch. Rijo works a full four-pitch mix with decent feel for everything, and his-mid 70s curveball has turned into more of an upper-70s power slurve with sharp two-plane action. That might give him the out pitch he's been missing and make a backend rotation role more likely. Keep your eye on this space for further developments.

Top Talents 25 and Under (as of 4/1/2020)

1. Royce Lewis
2. Jose Berrios
3. Brusdar Graterol
4. Alex Kirilloff
5. Byron Buxton
6. Fernando Romero
7. Miguel Sano
8. Jorge Polanco
9. Trevor Larnach
10. Nick Gordon

Max Kepler is the only member of last year's 25-and-under list to age out, but last year's no. 1 (Byron Buxton) and no. 3 (Miguel Sano) young talents had miserable 2018 seasons that saw them demoted to the minors. That makes ranking this year's 25-and-under options tricky, which is similar to trying to figure out where the Twins stand in general right now. They still have plenty of young major-league talent, with plenty of long-term upside, but the current crop has failed to establish itself as a winning core and it's hard not to turn your attention to the next wave.

Royce Lewis is a top 10 global prospect, the gem of a vastly improved farm system, and the base around which the next title-contending Twins team could be built. That those same things were said about Buxton, and to a lesser extent Sano, just a couple years ago is a reminder that not every prospect build is structurally sound. That both Buxton and Sano still qualify for this list, and might still be potential building blocks for the Twins when Lewis arrives this year or next, is also a reminder that a wave of talent can hit the same beach more than once.

Jose Berrios is the only member of the current young core to fully live up to the hype, or at least to do so without incident. Still only 24, he's coming off his first All-Star season and is the anchor of the staff. Fernando Romero lost his "prospect" status by five innings, but he won't be 24 until later this month and ended 2018 at Triple-A. Whether you consider him a prospect or a young major-leaguer, and whether you view him as a future starter or reliever, long term he's probably still closer to Brusdar Graterol as the Twins' best non-Berrios pitching hope than many think.

Buxton is impossible to rank definitively, especially compared to Alex Kirilloff, who's yet to reach Double-A. Last year, Kirilloff topping Buxton would've seemed absurd, yet it's reasonable now and if anything Kirilloff has the stronger case to be higher. Buxton is 25. He's an amazing center fielder and runner, but he's also a .230/.285/.387 hitter who generally looks lost at the plate. Similarly, how do you compare Miguel Sano, with his various flaws now exposed, to Trevor Larnach or even Brent Rooker, for whom a positive outcome might look like… Sano?

There's still a timeline where Buxton and Sano get back on track, rejoining Berrios as building blocks, and the Lewis-led next wave turns the Twins into contenders. It's not even that difficult to picture. Lewis, Sano, Jorge Polanco, Nick Gordon, and Rooker in the infield. Buxton flanked by Kirilloff, Kepler, and Larnach in the outfield. Berrios, Graterol, and Romero atop the rotation. But there's also a timeline where this wave dissipates further, leaving only one or two long-term pieces, and Twins fans pin their new hopes on Lewis/Graterol/Kirilloff instead of Buxton/Berrios/Sano.

Eyewitness Reports

Eyewitness Report: Royce Lewis

Evaluator: Ricky Conti
Report Date: 09/26/2019
Dates Seen: 9/18, 9/19, 9/20
Risk Factor: Medium
Physical/Health: Super long legs and arms with strong core. Thin arms, definitely some room for muscle. High-end athleticism with solid explosive abilities.

Tool	Future Grade	Report
Hit	60	Super high handset that stays high with huge leg kick. Lands quickly and aggressively into a wide base. Long, but explosive downhill swing, but hits a lot of flyballs because he's looking to hit the ball out in front. The performance itself won't blow you away, but when you consider the speed of his development and the performance relative to age, a plus hit tool is very reasonable.
Power	55	Over the fence power is mainly to the pull side, but can still drive the ball opposite field without a problem. Chance it gets to 60 raw, but will probably play 55 in-game.
Baserunning/ Speed	60	Great accelerator who changes direction with ease. The tool makes centerfield is definitely an option. The excellent baseball IQ and instincts makes him a genuine threat on the bases.
Glove	55	Taking reps at all of SS, 3B, and CF. Top tier athleticism and above average speed allows him to get to plenty of balls. Does a great job of always keeping his feet moving.
Arm	55	Above arm pure strength, but still working on throwing accuracy. Might be able to hide the developing accuracy in the outfield.

Conclusion: Royce Lewis is so close, yet so far. He made an insane catch in centerfield, one that players at this stage of development simply don't make unless they're special. It came with little experience out there. Nonetheless, the defensive home is still a question, as it's not quite clear which position his tools play best at. The bat shows signs of being plus, but the swing is unorthodox with an abundance of moving parts. He hasn't posted the numbers that typically come with a prospect of this caliber, but nobody will be surprised once the numbers start to come. What really makes Lewis interesting is that there is an outside chance at 60 grade for all five tools. The question that remains is, with the exception of speed, which are going to develop to their peak.

Eyewitness Report: Trevor Larnach

Evaluator: Steven Givarz
Report Date: 06/18/2019
Dates Seen: 5/6-5/18/19; 6/10-6/12/19
Risk Factor: Moderate
Physical/Health: Large frame and body, physcial throughout, somewhat boxy build, mature.

Tool	Future Grade	Report
Hit	50	Hits from an open stance with a leg kick, pull-side hitter, shift candidate, saw a lot of soft rolled over ground balls in viewing, struggled with adjusting to pitches on the lower half, but punished balls that were left up in the zone, can hit some hard line drives, has definite strength in hands/wrists with above-average bat speed, did not miss fastballs but struggled with better breaking pitches in viewing, see as a future average hitter.
Power	60	70 raw power, has definite strength in body with above-average bat speed to take a ball out to all parts of the field, really only saw the power play in game to the pull side, but am confident the power will play to plus in game.
Baserunning/ Speed	30	Not a runner, slow first step out of the box, won't ever be fast as a straight-line runner. Not a base clogger, but also not a base stealing threat.
Glove	50	Slow first step in the OF and won't ever be known for his defense, but should provide average defense in a corner, good instincts make up for poor first step with accurate routes to the bal.
Arm	55	Above-average arm strength, weapon in the outfield, throws were firm while on a straight line and accurate.

Conclusion: See as an average major league starter. 22 y/o L/R corner outfielder, profiles best in right field with plus game power and above-average throwing arm, future average hitter but one that could make adjustments to hit the ball more in the air, strong interest.

New York Mets

The State of the System

The Mets system is improved at the top due to an aggressive 2019 draft strategy, but the overall talent is still very thin and most of these names are far away from Flushing.

The Top Ten

──────────────────────── ★ ★ ★ *2020 Top 101 Prospect* **#48** ★ ★ ★ ────────────────────────

1   Ronny Mauricio   SS   OFP: 60   ETA: 2021

Born: 04/04/01   Age: 19   Bats: B   Throws: R   Height: 6'3"   Weight: 166   Origin: International Free Agent, 2017

YEAR	TEAM	LVL	AGE	PA	R	2B	3B	HR	RBI	BB	K	SB	CS	AVG/OBP/SLG	DRC+	VORP	BABIP	BRR	FRAA	WARP	PF
2018	MTS	RK	17	212	26	13	3	3	31	10	31	1	6	.279/.307/.421	125	10.1	.310	-0.3	SS(45) 0.3	1.3	107
2018	KNG	RK	17	35	6	3	0	0	4	3	9	1	0	.233/.286/.333	78	1.9	.304	0.5	SS(8) -0.1	0.1	111
2019	COL	A	18	504	62	20	5	4	37	23	99	6	10	.268/.307/.357	100	24.4	.330	2.9	SS(106) -0.1	2.3	92
2020	NYN	MLB	19	251	22	12	1	3	23	20	66	1	1	.239/.303/.344	73	0.0	.322	-0.5	SS 1	0.0	92

Comparables: Amed Rosario, Andrew Velazquez, Leury García

The Report: This is what it's supposed to look like at 18 years old. There's real-deal, first-division ability here regardless of future position. Our confidence in that comes mostly from a potential plus hit tool, advanced feel for the barrel, and above-average-to-plus bat speed. It's a loose, easy stroke with good hands and commensurate feel for contact, and it's downright pretty when his lower half syncs and fires effectively. Mauricio relies on his raw feel at times, because he's overly aggressive and can get out of sync, especially if you bust him inside.

Mauricio's power is mostly projection right now, but there's a lot of room to grow into impact pop. A bat path tweak for increased loft paired with his feel to hit would mean plus game power. Mauricio's soft hands, smooth actions, and easy plus arm would work anywhere in the infield, but the book is still out on his range as he fills out. He's currently rangy enough to stay at shortstop, but dropping a tick there could signal a move to third, where his defensive profile could grade out as plus. He's a solid athlete and an average runner underway but is below-average down the line. Mauricio has the makings of a mashing infielder with four consistent tools and tons of projection. Although he's just 18, this is what an org's number one prospect looks like.

Variance: High. There's confidence that the bat will play and power will come, but an aggressive eye will present a challenge or two along the way, and he just finished his first full season.

Ben Carsley's Fantasy Take: Yes, please. Any time you can tease me with plus-power/plus-hit projection I'll pay attention, and that's doubly true when we're talking about an infielder. It's reasonable to have visions of a .280 hitter with 25-30 bombs dancing in your head. The only issue here is lead time; even if Mauricio does reach the aggressive MLB ETA cited above, I'd argue his true fantasy impact ETA is closer to 2022 or beyond. Still, we snuck Mauricio into the "Honorable Mentions" section of our Top 101 list a year ago, and I wish we'd been even more aggressive now. Basically, this is my way of saying "sorry, Bret (but now we're even for Robert Gsellman)."

★ ★ ★ *2020 Top 101 Prospect* **#88** ★ ★ ★

2 Francisco Alvarez C   OFP: 60   ETA: 2023

Born: 11/19/01 Age: 18 Bats: R Throws: R Height: 5'11" Weight: 220 Origin: International Free Agent, 2018

YEAR	TEAM	LVL	AGE	PA	R	2B	3B	HR	RBI	BB	K	SB	CS	AVG/OBP/SLG	DRC+	VORP	BABIP	BRR	FRAA	WARP	PF
2019	MTS	RK	17	31	8	4	0	2	10	4	4	0	1	.462/.548/.846	224	7.7	.500	-0.3	C(4) 0.3	0.4	102
2019	KNG	RK+	17	151	24	6	0	5	16	17	33	1	1	.282/.377/.443	128	9.1	.344	-1.4		0.9	102
2020	NYN	MLB	18	251	24	12	1	5	25	24	75	3	1	.232/.313/.358	82	0.0	.326	0.0	C 0	0.3	92

Comparables: Oscar Hernández, Gary Sánchez, Jefry Marte

The Report: One should always proceed with caution when projecting great things of a player just past most of the world's legal drinking age—and ranking him as such—but Álvarez was rated highly as an international signee and has done nothing but improve his standing early in his pro career. He put up very good numbers as a 17-year-old in the Appy League, which would be surprising if not for his natural hitting talent and advanced approach at the dish. Álvarez has an advanced, patient approach already and waits for his pitch to drive. There is a deadly controlled aggression to his swing, and power is already showing up in games thanks to well above-average bat speed and his strength, which is visible throughout his frame.

As for that frame, it is a stocky one and lacking in physical projection. To my eye, it's perfect for a catcher as long as he can maintain it where it is. Álvarez is very comfortable behind the plate, too, athletic enough to handle bad breakers in the dirt, and he shows a quick trigger out of the crouch that allows his above-average arm to play up. The receiving appears advanced for his age, and he takes charge with his pitchers. It is early yet but this is a very well-rounded and advanced catching profile that has the teenager living up to his hype.

Variance: High. Álvarez is about as safe a bet as there is among teenagers just off the complexes, but that really isn't saying much. There's still a lot of development in front of him, both behind the plate and next to it.

Ben Carsley's Fantasy Take: At the risk of being inflexible, I just refuse to buy in on teenage catching prospects anymore. Too much can go wrong, and even if things go right eventually, we tend to be way off in our fantasy impact ETAs. If you still believe in catching prospects then the time to get in on Álvarez is now. If you're like me, well, you'll hang a picture of Francisco Mejia next to your bed as a reminder not to get sucked in by toolsy guys like Álvarez. Unless he's Prime Buster Posey, Álvarez (and guys like him are) is just not worth punting a roster spot for four or five years before he starts returning any value.

★ ★ ★ *2020 Top 101 Prospect* **#90** ★ ★ ★

3 Andrés Giménez SS   OFP: 50   ETA: Late 2020

Born: 09/04/98 Age: 21 Bats: L Throws: R Height: 6'0" Weight: 161 Origin: International Free Agent, 2015

YEAR	TEAM	LVL	AGE	PA	R	2B	3B	HR	RBI	BB	K	SB	CS	AVG/OBP/SLG	DRC+	VORP	BABIP	BRR	FRAA	WARP	PF
2017	COL	A	18	399	50	9	4	4	31	28	61	14	8	.265/.346/.349	110	22.3	.310	0.7	SS(89) 6.6	2.9	92
2018	SLU	A+	19	351	43	20	4	6	30	22	70	28	11	.282/.348/.432	113	24.8	.343	3.4	SS(83) 14.2, 2B(2) -0.1	3.8	97
2018	BIN	AA	19	153	19	9	1	0	16	9	22	10	3	.277/.344/.358	102	8.4	.330	1.2	SS(36) -1.3, 2B(1) 0.2	0.7	100
2019	BIN	AA	20	479	54	22	5	9	37	24	102	28	16	.250/.309/.387	92	17.9	.306	-2.9	SS(111) -0.7	1.3	94
2020	NYN	MLB	21	35	3	1	0	1	3	2	9	1	0	.229/.287/.357	70	0.0	.289	0.0	SS 0	0.0	92

Comparables: Rougned Odor, Jake Bauers, Francisco Lindor

The Report: Giménez scuffled in a return engagement with the Eastern League. The Mets tweaked his swing for more power, and the results were less than ideal. He did scrape a few more over the fence, and he did flash another half grade of power at five o'clock, but at the cost of increased swing-and-miss and worse quality of contact overall. Giménez was routinely late on fastballs away, and struggled to deal with left-on-left spin. What was previously a plus hit tool projection now looks fringier, which could be a major blow to the overall profile. The staff reports on him from the Fall League were better, as he seems to at least be more comfortable with the tweaks, but I'm still concerned until I see it work somewhere else than the surface of the moon against gassed pitchers.

The good news is the speed and glove are still intact. Giménez is a present above-average shortstop, with more than enough arm for the left side of the diamond. More game reps could easily smooth things out further and make him plus there. He's a plus, borderline plus-plus runner, although his baserunning can be a bit rough at times. If he smooths out the swing, or goes back to what worked for him in 2020, this might all seem overly reactive. Sometimes you just have a year, but it was a bad year.

Variance: Medium. The glove gives Giménez a reasonable bench floor, but the hit tool variance is worrisome now for a player who can lack physicality at the plate at times.

Ben Carsley's Fantasy Take: Ehhhhh. I'm usually a sucker for speed-first infielders, but Giménez doesn't really do it for me. It's great that he's a lock to stick at short, and the relatively short lead time gives him an argument to still serve as a top-101 dynasty prospect. He should be at the very back of that list if he makes it at all, though, and I'm concerned enough that I get real Orlando Arcia vibes from the overall profile. It's reasonable to be higher on Giménez than I am given the previous aptitude he showed with the bat, but this is not exactly the Age of Reason.

4 Matthew Allan RHP   OFP: 50   ETA: 2022-23

Born: 04/17/01   Age: 19   Bats: R   Throws: R   Height: 6'3"   Weight: 225   Origin: Round 3, 2019 Draft (#89 overall)

YEAR	TEAM	LVL	AGE	W	L	SV	G	GS	IP	H	HR	BB/9	K/9	K	GB%	BABIP	WHIP	ERA	DRA	WARP	PF
2019	MTS	RK	18	1	0	0	5	4	8^1	5	0	4.3	11.9	11	32%	.263	1.08	1.08	2.36	0.3	101
2020	NYN	MLB	19	2	2	0	33	0	35	35	5	3.8	8.2	32	41%	.296	1.42	4.74	4.85	0.2	92

Comparables: Jake Thompson, Tyler Glasnow, Neftalí Feliz

The Report: Allan was widely considered one of the top prep pitchers in the 2019 class, but was floating a large bonus demand that caused him to fall. Jeff Passan of ESPN reported during the draft that the Cubs almost selected him with the 27th pick, but went elsewhere because of signability. (Their actual pick there, Ryan Jensen, later signed for a below-slot $2 million.) The Mets took him in the third round, and made room for his $2.5 million bonus by selecting a slew of extremely cheap senior signs in rounds 4-10.

Is Allan worth it? That'll take a solid four or five years to work out, but early signs are positive. He looked the part in his abbreviated pro debut, popping up in short-season Brooklyn for their Penn League title run and throwing a consistent 95-96. His out pitch is a plus curveball, and his changeup projects out to at least average. It's a strong mix of stuff and relative polish, and we like him enough that we have him ahead of actual first-rounder Brett Baty on the current organizational ranking and in the mix for the bottom of the 101. Yet the risk of investing this heavily in prep pitching is the same as it ever was.

Variance: Very high. He's an 18-year-old pitcher who has yet to pitch in full-season ball. Things can go in many, many, many directions from here.

Ben Carsley's Fantasy Take: Don't let Allan fall off your radar just because he was popped later than some of the other big-name prep arms from this draft class; he's got the goods. While I don't foresee him ranking anywhere near the dynasty version of our top-101, he's in the next, meaty glut of high-upside arms who essentially amount to shiny lottery tickets for our purposes. If you play with less seasoned dynasty leaguers who are likely to only look at first-round hitters in their supplemental drafts, Allan could provide you with some nice value late.

5 Brett Baty 3B   OFP: 55   ETA: 2023

Born: 11/13/99   Age: 20   Bats: L   Throws: R   Height: 6'3"   Weight: 210   Origin: Round 1, 2019 Draft (#12 overall)

YEAR	TEAM	LVL	AGE	PA	R	2B	3B	HR	RBI	BB	K	SB	CS	AVG/OBP/SLG	DRC+	VORP	BABIP	BRR	FRAA	WARP	PF
2019	MTS	RK	19	25	5	3	0	1	8	5	6	0	0	.350/.480/.650	148	4.1	.462	0.2	3B(4) -0.2	0.2	103
2019	KNG	RK+	19	186	30	12	2	6	22	24	56	0	0	.222/.339/.437	108	5.5	.302	-0.4		0.6	103
2020	NYN	MLB	20	251	21	12	1	4	21	25	92	2	1	.187/.276/.301	55	3.0	.298	0.0	3B 0	-0.6	92

Comparables: Carlos Peguero, Chris Carter, José Altuve

The Report: Baty's profile is the type that will create splits of opinion resulting in widely varied outcome projections and wildly controversial rankings. There are those who see an already advanced bat who will quickly conquer each level and alleviate concerns about other parts of his game. It is well known that Baty was on the older end of draft-eligible high-schoolers, and the importance of this fact is of course up for debate. Detractors might also point to his very developed body that leans toward negative physical projection more than anything else, or to his underwhelming athleticism and feel for the hot corner. I got a quick glance near the end of his Appy League campaign and noted roughly these same positives and negatives. He's a mature hitter with excellent plate discipline, and this held true even as he was struggling to find his footing following his promotion off the complex. His power is real too, plus to all fields. In fact, his approach the other way is quite good and he has an impressive ability to wait back on breaking stuff and drive it. It concerned me slightly that despite the bat speed he swung through some fastballs and I didn't really see him pull anything with authority, though it was eight or ten plate appearances and the latter part seemed mostly by design.

Variance: High. He really needs to hit and he hasn't yet, though that doesn't mean he won't. He'll have to hit even more if it ends up that he's a first baseman, which is a possibility.

Ben Carsley's Fantasy Take: I, too, have a "very developed body that leans toward negative physical projection," but at least writing with Craig keeps me from being old for my level. Anyway, Baty is a better dynasty prospect than real life prospect because he should move relatively quickly and because his bat is his best tool. That being said, he comes with just enough risk that he's a fringier dynasty asset than this draft position might indicate. It's a very Maikel Franco profile, for better and for worse.

6   Mark Vientos   3B   OFP: 55   ETA: 2022

Born: 12/11/99   Age: 20   Bats: R   Throws: R   Height: 6'4"   Weight: 185   Origin: Round 2, 2017 Draft (#59 overall)

YEAR	TEAM	LVL	AGE	PA	R	2B	3B	HR	RBI	BB	K	SB	CS	AVG/OBP/SLG	DRC+	VORP	BABIP	BRR	FRAA	WARP	PF
2017	MTS	RK	17	193	22	12	0	4	24	14	42	0	2	.259/.316/.397	108	8.2	.313	0.8	SS(19) -1.6, 3B(14) 0.1	0.7	98
2018	KNG	RK	18	262	32	12	0	11	52	37	43	1	0	.287/.389/.489	140	17.4	.312	-3.0	3B(54) -1.7	1.5	106
2019	COL	A	19	454	48	27	1	12	62	22	110	1	4	.255/.300/.411	122	16.3	.311	-5.2	3B(98) -3.0	1.5	91
2020	NYN	MLB	20	251	24	13	0	7	27	18	74	0	0	.225/.287/.376	74	3.0	.299	-0.6	3B 0, SS 0	0.0	92

Comparables: Franchy Cordero, Thairo Estrada, Dilson Herrera

The Report: Already a somewhat polarizing prospect, it can be hard to believe that Vientos is still only 19 and (age-appropriately) submerged in the low minors. Vientos has made a good impression with the bat all things considered, winning an organizational award this season despite tailing off as the campaign neared its conclusion. His best tool is his raw power, which is easily plus and already more than viable in game. The hit tool is a little more questionable, as there is some swing-and-miss in his long levers, and the approach is a little aggressive at present. There are positives though, like his all-fields approach and ability to wait back on and drive breaking stuff. Vientos has a wiry strong frame with some physical projection remaining in the upper body and possesses good overall athleticism. His arm is just shy of plus, the best feature of a defensive profile that is more or less fringe-average. How his story is written will largely depend on where he can get his hit tool, and how much of his power it allows him to tap into. Still young, Vientos has plenty of time to shape the narrative.

Variance: High. Questions about the hit tool still exist and as a corner bat who is only decent defensively he'll need it, even with the power.

Ben Carsley's Fantasy Take: Anyone else getting Michael Chavis flashbacks? Despite the flaws in his game, I actually like Vientos more than the two prospects listed above him in this non-dynasty list. The power is real, I think he can stick at third unless usurped by a much better option, and the ETA is fantasy-friendly. He's probably not a top-101 dude at this point, but you can make an argument for him as top-150. Don't let the prospect fatigue set in just yet.

7   Josh Wolf   RHP   OFP: 55   ETA: 2024

Born: 09/01/00   Age: 19   Bats: R   Throws: R   Height: 6'3"   Weight: 170   Origin: Round 2, 2019 Draft (#53 overall)

YEAR	TEAM	LVL	AGE	W	L	SV	G	GS	IP	H	HR	BB/9	K/9	K	GB%	BABIP	WHIP	ERA	DRA	WARP	PF
2019	MTS	RK	18	0	1	0	5	5	8	9	0	1.1	13.5	12	40%	.450	1.25	3.38	3.77	0.2	101

The Report: The Mets went back to the Texas prep arm well for their second round pick last summer, after popping Simeon Woods Richardson in 2018. The two are actually fairly comparable on their respective draft days, although Wolf is the more traditional tall, lean, projectable Lone Star arm. Both were velocity pop-up guys their senior year of high school, as Wolf came out touching 98. Both feature advanced, big breaking 11-6 curveballs. Wolf has gotten better marks for pitchability, but the delivery has more reliever markers, and he lacks Woods Richardson's plus athleticism on the mound. On the other hand, given his thin frame, Wolf might be more likely to sit mid 90s as a starter if he fills out and adds arm strength in his twenties. He'll need to stay healthy and develop a changeup and so on and so forth, but he is an intriguing power arm for a system sorely lacking in interesting pitching prospects.

Variance: Very high. The track record of prep righties taken outside of the first round is not amazing. There's the usual third pitch concerns at present.

Ben Carsley's Fantasy Take: Wolf is a bit too far away for me to get truly excited at this point, but I do like him a bit more than the plethora of righties with decent upsides who occupy the back halves of most of these lists. Maybe it's because I'm a sucker for curveballs? Or Wolves? Either way, he's a good one for your watch list.

8 David Peterson LHP   OFP: 50   ETA: Second half 2020
Born: 09/03/95   Age: 24   Bats: L   Throws: L   Height: 6'6"   Weight: 240   Origin: Round 1, 2017 Draft (#20 overall)

YEAR	TEAM	LVL	AGE	W	L	SV	G	GS	IP	H	HR	BB/9	K/9	K	GB%	BABIP	WHIP	ERA	DRA	WARP	PF
2018	COL	A	22	1	4	0	9	9	59¹	46	1	1.7	8.6	57	68%	.283	0.96	1.82	3.45	1.2	90
2018	SLU	A+	22	6	6	0	13	13	68²	74	1	2.5	7.6	58	64%	.335	1.35	4.33	4.89	0.4	97
2019	BIN	AA	23	3	6	0	24	24	116	119	9	2.9	9.5	122	54%	.340	1.34	4.19	5.65	-1.0	95
2020	NYN	MLB	24	2	2	0	6	6	32	30	4	3.6	7.9	29	49%	.282	1.33	4.19	4.48	0.5	92

Comparables: Nick Margevicius, Matt Hall, Matt Bowman

The Report: Peterson more or less held serve as a prospect in 2019. Double-A wasn't much of a test for his array of average-ish stuff, although he was occasionally too hittable due to his command being not fine enough. He's a tall, extra-large lefty with a tough angle due to his extension, crossfire, and three-quarters slot. His fastball sits in the low 90s and he can turn it over with some arm-side run, or bore it in to righties. His slider is his best secondary, a low-80s, two-plane breaker that he commands well. It's an above-average offering that flashes better, but lacks the true "hard slider" characteristics to be consistently plus. The changeup is the third pitch, inconsistent and often firm, but showing good sink in the low 80s when he pulls the string. Peterson has never really dominated to the level you'd expect from a first-round college arm, but he has a solid frame built to log innings, and enough stuff to get major league hitters out. It's just a very average profile overall.

Variance: Medium. He was fine in Double-A, and while there will be lingering concerns about a major league out pitch until he's getting major leaguers out, he's a polished lefty with a solid slider. That usually plays.

Ben Carsley's Fantasy Take: "What if Wade Miley, but taller?" just isn't a very enticing fantasy proposition. Peterson is a fine speculative grab if you need 2020 innings or if your league rosters 300-plus prospects. So are about 20 other dudes with this profile, and many of them at least have a hint of upside and/or guaranteed rotation spots.

9 Junior Santos RHP   OFP: 55   ETA: 2023-24
Born: 08/16/01   Age: 18   Bats: R   Throws: R   Height: 6'8"   Weight: 218   Origin: International Free Agent, 2018

YEAR	TEAM	LVL	AGE	W	L	SV	G	GS	IP	H	HR	BB/9	K/9	K	GB%	BABIP	WHIP	ERA	DRA	WARP	PF
2018	DME	RK	16	1	1	0	11	10	45	35	1	1.2	7.2	36	48%	.270	0.91	2.80	2.66	1.6	89
2019	KNG	RK+	17	0	5	0	14	14	40²	46	4	5.5	8.0	36	31%	.333	1.75	5.09	7.00	-0.3	104

The Report: Santos may be a young'un—he was born a month before *Yankee Hotel Foxtrot* came out—but the Mets have pushed him hard as a pro. After signing for 150k, he came stateside in 2018 as soon as he was 17, and spent almost the entire summer in Kingsport unable to legally purchase Marlboros (or I guess vape juice or whatever the kids are huffing now). Santos doesn't look like literally a child though, as he's already a huge human, probably at least 20 pounds bigger than his listed weight, but still physically projectable. The delivery is a little stiff at present, but he keeps all the limbs in mostly good order throughout. And when the baseball comes out of the child's hands it's mid-90s heat touching as high as 98—although the velo can be inconsistent. There's feel for a potentially above-average breaking ball as well. Look, Santos posted a 5+ ERA in the Appy, and this could go in a bunch of different directions in the coming years—many of them involving three spent eating fried seafood at Lola's in St. Lucie, a conversion to the pen, maybe a Tommy John surgery. But it's a quality frame with projection and better stuff and more polish than you'd expect from a teenager. In this system, grab every lottery ticket you can.

Variance: Extreme. He was 17 for most of the year and not particularly efficient in the Appy. He might never get out of A-ball, he might be the best pitching prospect in the system next year.

Ben Carsley's Fantasy Take: Check back in five years, at which point Santos might be in Low-A.

10 Thomas Szapucki LHP   OFP: 50   ETA: 2021

Born: 06/12/96   Age: 24   Bats: R   Throws: L   Height: 6'2"   Weight: 181   Origin: Round 5, 2015 Draft (#149 overall)

YEAR	TEAM	LVL	AGE	W	L	SV	G	GS	IP	H	HR	BB/9	K/9	K	GB%	BABIP	WHIP	ERA	DRA	WARP	PF
2017	COL	A	21	1	2	0	6	6	29	24	0	3.1	8.4	27	44%	.304	1.17	2.79	4.34	0.3	90
2019	COL	A	23	0	0	0	11	8	21²	14	1	4.2	10.8	26	37%	.260	1.11	2.08	3.62	0.4	99
2019	SLU	A+	23	1	3	0	9	9	36	33	1	3.8	10.5	42	48%	.314	1.33	3.25	4.69	0.1	98
2020	NYN	MLB	24	2	2	0	33	0	35	34	5	3.5	8.5	33	40%	.293	1.35	4.42	4.66	0.3	92

Comparables: *Domingo Germán, Jarlin García, Brad Mills*

The Report: Szapucki got a slow start to 2019, eighteen months off Tommy John surgery. Reports from St. Lucie in March suggested he wasn't really stretched out enough to break camp, but the Mets sent him north to Columbia anyway, where he topped out in the low 90s and quickly got a one-month breather. He's slowly built up arm strength since then and earned a July promotion to High-A. Later reports have the fastball touching 95, and Szapucki showing an improved curve, but this is still a ways off from the mid-90s and potential plus-plus breaker he showed in 2016. The changeup is still below average. Szapucki struggles to hold that stuff even 50 pitches into games and only threw 61 innings across 22 outings this season. This looks like a bad rehab at present, but even 75 percent of the stuff he used to have is an average fastball and above-average curveball in short bursts. You can play the waiting game a bit longer here—he's left-handed with a good frame—but the Mets have had enough bad TJ rehabs in recent years that it might not just be bad luck.

Variance: Very High. Szapucki's stuff hasn't fully come back now two-plus years off Tommy John, and there were durability questions about him before the UCL tear. He'll be 24 next year and has made one start above A-ball. We'd like to bet on the stuff that once made him a Top 101 arm, but we'll need to see it back in games first.

Ben Carsley's Fantasy Take: I know you might be tempted to want to buy low on Szapucki given his former rankings, but the risk-to-reward ratio here is all wrong. You can keep an eye on him for a quick pickup if the stuff looks like it's back, but right now Szapucki should be unowned in all but the very deepest of dynasty leagues. Odds are the Mets fan in your league still wants him, though!

The Next Ten

11 Shervyen Newton IF

Born: 04/24/99   Age: 21   Bats: B   Throws: R   Height: 6'4"   Weight: 180   Origin: International Free Agent, 2015

YEAR	TEAM	LVL	AGE	PA	R	2B	3B	HR	RBI	BB	K	SB	CS	AVG/OBP/SLG	DRC+	VORP	BABIP	BRR	FRAA	WARP	PF
2017	MET	RK	18	303	51	11	9	1	31	50	57	10	4	.311/.433/.444	161	33.0	.398	-2.0	SS(60) 7.7, 3B(5) 0.8	3.7	104
2018	KNG	RK	19	266	50	16	2	5	41	46	84	4	0	.280/.408/.449	124	24.5	.421	2.2	SS(49) 10.8, 2B(3) 0.3	3.0	105
2019	COL	A	20	423	35	15	2	9	32	37	139	1	4	.209/.283/.330	86	3.9	.303	-2.0	2B(53) -0.4, SS(27) -2.0	0.2	93
2020	NYN	MLB	21	251	22	12	1	5	23	23	96	0	0	.204/.282/.328	61	0.0	.330	-0.4	SS 1, 2B 0	-0.3	92

Comparables: *Luis Rengifo, Drew Robinson, Teoscar Hernández*

Newton's frame and tools are really loud. He looks the part with a high waist, present strength and tons of projection in a lengthy frame, but he's also a solid athlete with smooth actions in the field to help his tools translate. That feel shows at the plate, too, with a sound swing from the left side featuring excellent lift and separation with flashes of a solid eye and plus bat speed. The question is whether he can tone down the swing-and-miss and bouts of over-aggressiveness. He'll grow out of the middle infield to become a solid, athletic corner defender at third or right with a plus arm and potential double-plus raw power. The risk here is extreme as a boom-or-bust type who needs the hit tool to come along, but the ceiling is equally extreme with big projection, big pop and big athleticism.

12 Franklyn Kilomé RHP

Born: 06/25/95   Age: 25   Bats: R   Throws: R   Height: 6'6"   Weight: 175   Origin: International Free Agent, 2013

YEAR	TEAM	LVL	AGE	W	L	SV	G	GS	IP	H	HR	BB/9	K/9	K	GB%	BABIP	WHIP	ERA	DRA	WARP	PF
2017	CLR	A+	22	6	4	0	19	19	97¹	96	5	3.4	7.7	83	48%	.325	1.37	2.59	4.99	0.3	94
2017	REA	AA	22	1	3	0	5	5	29²	25	2	4.6	6.1	20	43%	.267	1.35	3.64	3.95	0.4	106
2018	REA	AA	23	4	6	0	19	19	102	96	7	4.5	7.3	83	46%	.305	1.44	4.24	4.92	0.5	105
2018	BIN	AA	23	0	3	0	7	7	38	31	3	2.4	9.9	42	41%	.289	1.08	4.03	5.65	-0.1	101
2020	NYN	MLB	25	1	1	0	10	0	11	10	2	3.8	7.2	9	42%	.278	1.38	4.53	4.72	0.1	92

Comparables: Adrian Houser, Bryan Mitchell, Nick Pivetta

Kilomé missed all of 2019 recovering from Tommy John surgery, and still comes in as the sixth-best pitching prospect in the Mets system. That says plenty about the pitching depth here, but also a little bit about Kilomé's upside. He flashed better command of his stuff at the end of 2018, and while a reliever outcome is far more likely now—Kilomé will be turning 25 next season and hasn't pitched above Double-A—there's near-term late-inning impact potential the Mets don't have anywhere else in the system. Kilomé could be 95+ with a 7 curveball from a tough angle for hitters. There's very high risk here, though, and the Mets don't have a great recent track record with Tommy John recoveries.

/gestures further up the list to Thomas Szapucki.

/pours one out for Marcos Molina.

13 Jaylen Palmer IF

Born: 07/31/00   Age: 19   Bats: R   Throws: R   Height: 6'3"   Weight: 195   Origin: Round 22, 2018 Draft (#650 overall)

YEAR	TEAM	LVL	AGE	PA	R	2B	3B	HR	RBI	BB	K	SB	CS	AVG/OBP/SLG	DRC+	VORP	BABIP	BRR	FRAA	WARP	PF
2018	MTS	RK	17	100	13	4	1	1	11	8	27	5	2	.310/.394/.414	110	5.2	.441	0.2	3B(9) -0.1, SS(6) -1.0	0.3	107
2019	KNG	RK+	18	276	41	12	2	7	28	31	108	1	3	.260/.344/.413	113	17.0	.434	0.3		1.5	102
2020	NYN	MLB	19	251	20	11	1	3	21	19	112	3	1	.203/.270/.302	49	3.0	.378	0.0	3B 0, SS 0	-0.8	92

"Next year's Shervyen Newton" had a very 2018 Shervyen Newton season in the Appy. So far, so good. Well, there's some bad in there, like significant swing-and-miss. Palmer generates good bat speed out of a lean, athletic frame, but the swing path is long and steep. As he fills out the power should come—and his seven bombs this summer is already a good showing for an 18-year-old outside of the complex—but how much of it plays in games will be an open question for, oh a half decade or so. He's played third base and short so far as a pro, but is likely to end up at third as he fills out, assuming he stays on the dirt—Palmer could be an interesting center field candidate at some point. There's a lot of *could be's* in the profile, and like with a lot of the Mets system—including Shervyen Newton still—you are betting on an athletic body and some loud tools. Worse parlays to make, one supposes, and often better than the alternatives on this list.

14 Kevin Smith LHP

Born: 05/13/97   Age: 23   Bats: R   Throws: L   Height: 6'5"   Weight: 200   Origin: Round 7, 2018 Draft (#200 overall)

YEAR	TEAM	LVL	AGE	W	L	SV	G	GS	IP	H	HR	BB/9	K/9	K	GB%	BABIP	WHIP	ERA	DRA	WARP	PF
2018	BRO	A-	21	4	1	0	12	3	23²	12	1	2.3	10.6	28	49%	.220	0.76	0.76	2.09	0.8	97
2019	SLU	A+	22	5	5	0	17	17	85²	83	5	2.5	10.7	102	45%	.359	1.25	3.05	4.32	0.7	104
2019	BIN	AA	22	3	2	0	6	6	31¹	25	1	4.3	8.0	28	40%	.289	1.28	3.45	5.60	-0.2	90
2020	NYN	MLB	23	2	2	0	33	0	35	34	5	3.4	8.7	34	40%	.300	1.36	4.37	4.49	0.4	92

Comparables: Jarlin García, Eric Lauer, Caleb Smith

If there was a breakout performance in the Mets system in 2019—at least among prospects they didn't trade away at the deadline—it might have been Kevin Smith. The 2018 seventh-round pick posted a solid ERA and strong K rates at two levels. The stuff doesn't match the numbers, though, as Smith sits either side of 90. Smith is, at least, a tall lefty with a long stride and good extension on the fastball, and it's a high spin offering. There's a slurvy breaker that's tough left-on-left due to the angle he creates, and the changeup will flash average fade. Smith generally keeps everything down in the zone despite fringe command, but we'll need to see a longer track record of success and quality strike throwing in the upper minors before we throw a backend starter OFP on him, since the profile is fringy overall.

15 Stephen Gonsalves   LHP

Born: 07/08/94   Age: 25   Bats: L   Throws: L   Height: 6'5"   Weight: 220   Origin: Round 4, 2013 Draft (#110 overall)

YEAR	TEAM	LVL	AGE	W	L	SV	G	GS	IP	H	HR	BB/9	K/9	K	GB%	BABIP	WHIP	ERA	DRA	WARP	PF
2017	CHT	AA	22	8	3	0	15	15	87¹	67	7	2.4	9.9	96	35%	.270	1.03	2.68	3.13	2.1	99
2017	ROC	AAA	22	1	2	0	5	4	22²	27	4	3.2	8.7	22	34%	.343	1.54	5.56	5.64	0.0	102
2018	CHT	AA	23	3	0	0	4	4	20¹	11	2	4.4	11.1	25	51%	.231	1.03	1.77	3.23	0.5	106
2018	ROC	AAA	23	9	3	0	19	18	100¹	65	6	4.9	8.5	95	40%	.237	1.20	2.96	3.38	2.4	94
2018	MIN	MLB	23	2	2	0	7	4	24²	28	2	8.0	5.8	16	40%	.321	2.03	6.57	8.22	-0.9	107
2019	TWI	RK	24	0	1	0	5	5	9	6	2	0.0	16.0	16	35%	.267	0.67	2.00	0.42	0.5	86
2020	NYN	MLB	25	1	2	0	13	3	27	30	6	5.0	5.9	18	38%	.288	1.67	6.26	6.01	-0.1	92

Comparables: Yohander Méndez, Lucas Sims, A.J. Cole

It's not a great sign when a 25-year-old waiver claim who missed almost all of 2019 with an elbow strain is making your prospect list. That said he fits right in with this tier of Mets prospect arms in that regard, and when healthy Gonsalves projected as a quality back-of-the-rotation option with four fringe-to-above-average pitches. It's overly simplistic to call him "Kevin Smith with better secondaries," but the deliveries and fastballs aren't that dissimilar. Gonsalves has a tick more velo if anything, touching 93 in his late season appearances, and has flashed an above-average change and slider/cutter thing at times. Smith is healthy, Gonsalves hasn't been—although he has a clean bill of health at the time of publication—and neither would be as high in even an average system. The Mets—as you may have gathered by now—are not an average system.

16 Freddy Valdez   OF

Born: 12/06/01   Age: 18   Bats: R   Throws: R   Height: 6'3"   Weight: 212   Origin: International Free Agent, 2018

YEAR	TEAM	LVL	AGE	PA	R	2B	3B	HR	RBI	BB	K	SB	CS	AVG/OBP/SLG	DRC+	VORP	BABIP	BRR	FRAA	WARP	PF
2020	NYN	MLB	18	251	22	11	1	4	22	23	89	3	1	.213/.292/.324	69	0.0	.331	0.0	RF 0	-0.2	92

Valdez was held back in the Dominican Summer League this summer and ended up playing the bulk of the season two levels behind Álvarez, his fellow seven-figure 2018 J2 signing. It's not like it's a true negative for a 17-year-old to spend the year in the international complex and come stateside for a late cameo, but it does indicate he's on a slower track. Frankly, he fits the criteria for high profile international signings who tend to be overrated in this period of their prospectdom. The scouting reports that would've gotten him said seven-figure bonus are years old now, and teams tend to pay for early physical development because of how early players are (illegally) agreeing to terms. Valdez has barely even been exposed to domestic complex level pitching yet, so it's hard to figure out what to make of him as a pro outside of generic "future power hitter" platitudes. Then again, he's just behind a waiver claim on this list, and just ahead of a back-end starter exposed to Rule 5 and a pitcher coming off two years off for Tommy John, so we'll call his placement an artifact of a very thin system.

17 Harol Gonzalez   RHP

Born: 03/02/95   Age: 25   Bats: B   Throws: R   Height: 6'0"   Weight: 160   Origin: International Free Agent, 2014

YEAR	TEAM	LVL	AGE	W	L	SV	G	GS	IP	H	HR	BB/9	K/9	K	GB%	BABIP	WHIP	ERA	DRA	WARP	PF
2017	COL	A	22	9	8	0	20	20	126¹	123	11	2.6	6.5	91	45%	.293	1.27	3.56	5.31	0.0	93
2017	SLU	A+	22	0	1	0	3	3	11¹	10	2	2.4	7.1	9	32%	.222	1.15	3.18	4.35	0.1	102
2018	SLU	A+	23	1	6	0	13	12	73¹	62	6	2.3	7.2	59	46%	.262	1.10	2.82	3.53	1.5	99
2018	BIN	AA	23	0	9	0	9	9	52	79	10	2.9	5.2	30	38%	.367	1.85	7.79	8.44	-1.9	98
2018	LVG	AAA	23	0	1	0	1	1	6	4	0	3.0	1.5	1	29%	.190	1.00	3.00	4.89	0.0	91
2019	BIN	AA	24	6	4	0	17	16	97¹	83	12	2.1	8.2	89	46%	.269	1.09	3.14	4.26	0.8	95
2019	SYR	AAA	24	6	0	0	8	7	40¹	33	8	2.2	5.1	23	44%	.214	1.07	2.68	3.69	1.2	96
2020	NYN	MLB	25	2	2	0	33	0	35	36	7	3.5	6.7	26	42%	.276	1.41	5.09	5.28	0.1	92

Comparables: Adonis Rosa, Tyler Wilson, Joel Payamps

I was fully expecting to pen a fun little riff on Harol Gonzalez in the personal cheeseball section below. My affinity for him dates back to the first piece I ever wrote for BP. If there is any prospect in baseball I root to outperform my projection, it's Harol. But the projection has never been all that rosy. The undersized righty has added some bulk and a few ticks on the fastball. He now sits low 90s with occasional cut or arm-side wiggle. I even got a report he touched 95. The curve has gotten to average, as he manipulates the shape and commands the pitch well, although it can roll into the lefty happy zone at times.

Harol's slider/cutter thing never really developed though, and the changeup has stagnated. It's a collection of fringe offerings with some pitchability and command, but long ball issues even before he got the Triple-A ball in his hands. Yet here he sits in the Next Ten, because this system is so shallow that being both reasonably close to the majors and with a shot to be a fifth starter or swingman made it challenging to find 20 prospects I preferred, even with my biases set aside. The Mets don't seem to agree, so I won't be shocked if he gets popped in the Rule 5 and ends up a bulk innings guy behind somebody's opener in 2021, although you'd prefer to be able to shuttle this profile back and forth from Triple-A.

18 Jordan Humphreys RHP

Born: 06/11/96   Age: 24   Bats: R   Throws: R   Height: 6'2"   Weight: 223   Origin: Round 18, 2015 Draft (#539 overall)

YEAR	TEAM	LVL	AGE	W	L	SV	G	GS	IP	H	HR	BB/9	K/9	K	GB%	BABIP	WHIP	ERA	DRA	WARP	PF
2017	COL	A	21	10	1	0	11	11	69²	41	2	1.2	10.3	80	40%	.241	0.72	1.42	2.36	2.4	88
2017	SLU	A+	21	0	0	0	2	2	11	17	1	2.5	2.5	3	30%	.348	1.82	4.09	7.03	-0.2	113
2020	NYN	MLB	24	2	2	0	33	0	35	34	5	3.2	8.0	31	34%	.288	1.33	4.28	4.59	0.3	92

Comparables: Ryan Helsley, Josh Lindblom, Merandy Gonzalez

Speaking of problematic Tommy John rehabs, Humphreys missed two full seasons after mid-2017 surgery, popping up once in June and once in August for complex appearances. Seems bad. He looked fine in the AFL, sitting low 90s and touching 96 and flashing a decent slider and change, which jibes with our 2017 looks, albeit with a different breaker popping. There was fairly significant relief risk in the profile even then, and that's only increased with the lost development time. Humphreys will be 24 next year and has thrown 11 innings above the South Atlantic League. Nevertheless the Mets added him to the 40-man for Rule 5 protection. He could move quickly with a full-time shift to the pen in 2020, although there's an argument that he still needs starter's innings for development reasons, even if he's not too likely to be a long term rotation piece. There's setup potential as a reliever, but the variance here is, uh, significant.

19 Sebastian Espino IF

Born: 05/29/00   Age: 20   Bats: R   Throws: R   Height: 6'2"   Weight: 176   Origin: International Free Agent, 2016

YEAR	TEAM	LVL	AGE	PA	R	2B	3B	HR	RBI	BB	K	SB	CS	AVG/OBP/SLG	DRC+	VORP	BABIP	BRR	FRAA	WARP	PF
2017	DME	RK	17	269	36	16	9	2	35	22	60	6	5	.267/.338/.433	109	11.5	.344	-1.3	SS(63) 3.1	1.6	104
2018	MTS	RK	18	169	20	13	1	0	18	15	39	4	3	.267/.329/.367	96	3.1	.354	-1.2	2B(43) -4.3, SS(4) -0.3	-0.1	107
2019	KNG	RK+	19	202	26	7	1	2	12	12	61	3	2	.251/.303/.332	73	0.4	.363	-0.1		0.2	101
2020	NYN	MLB	20	251	19	13	1	3	21	16	93	1	1	.210/.264/.315	49	0.0	.335	0.0	SS 0, 2B -1	-0.9	92

There are probably dudes with a higher floor who could fill this slot, but there are enough positive traits here to elevate Espino into the discussion. A mid-level international signing a few years ago now, the 19-year-old shortstop has put up mediocre offensive numbers that I would argue are not commensurate with his talents. The stats basically reflect weaknesses that are easy to pick up in a couple looks. He's long, lean, and very physically projectible but the power just isn't there yet, although of course it isn't guaranteed to ever get there. But he is quick to the ball in spite of his long arms, and can jump a fastball in his zone. He will swing and miss, one might say too much, at breaking stuff especially. While he might be a work in progress at the plate, his defensive work is quite impressive. He is silky at the six, with good action and reactions and more than enough range and arm. A lot of what I like here is tangled up in offensive production, but there are worse prospects to have in the corner of your eye.

20 Daison Acosta RHP

Born: 08/24/98   Age: 21   Bats: R   Throws: R   Height: 6'2"   Weight: 160   Origin: International Free Agent, 2016

YEAR	TEAM	LVL	AGE	W	L	SV	G	GS	IP	H	HR	BB/9	K/9	K	GB%	BABIP	WHIP	ERA	DRA	WARP	PF
2017	MTS	RK	18	0	2	0	6	4	22	18	0	2.9	7.8	19	48%	.305	1.14	3.27	3.26	0.6	100
2018	KNG	RK	19	2	5	0	10	9	42¹	38	8	3.8	9.8	46	39%	.278	1.32	4.46	4.18	0.9	102
2019	BRO	A-	20	1	0	0	4	3	18¹	9	0	2.9	12.3	25	56%	.250	0.82	0.98	2.27	0.6	95
2019	COL	A	20	1	4	0	11	11	52¹	50	4	4.5	8.4	49	44%	.303	1.45	3.78	5.66	-0.3	93
2020	NYN	MLB	21	2	2	0	33	0	35	36	6	4.1	7.5	29	42%	.291	1.48	5.24	5.28	0.1	92

A great example of the type of prospect who can pop up when you have room for a few extra in your lower minors (he signed for only $70K in 2016), Acosta is lean and projectible at 6-foot-2 and a listed 160. He's 92-94 from a low-effort three-quarters motion and complements the fastball with a strong slider around 80 mph that has late, sharp bite. Interestingly, the night I saw him he seemed to be experimenting with a cutter-like pitch around 86-88 that turned out to be very effective. It was a dark and stormy night and difficult to tell what sort of effect the mound conditions were having on pitch selection, but it appeared to be an interesting wrinkle in between his two bread and butter offerings. He's probably ready to begin his age-21 season at High-A, and in a system such as this he's worth following. If the cutter is a mirage he's more likely a two-pitch guy and quite possibly a reliever, but if he's in that role and making noise at the upper levels in a couple years the Mets will definitely be able to use him.

Personal Cheeseball

PC Stephen Villines RHP

Born: 07/15/95   Age: 24   Bats: R   Throws: R   Height: 6'2"   Weight: 175   Origin: Round 10, 2017 Draft (#307 overall)

YEAR	TEAM	LVL	AGE	W	L	SV	G	GS	IP	H	HR	BB/9	K/9	K	GB%	BABIP	WHIP	ERA	DRA	WARP	PF
2017	KNG	RK	21	2	1	0	8	0	8¹	10	0	0.0	11.9	11	57%	.476	1.20	1.08	4.03	0.1	100
2017	BRO	A-	21	1	1	1	11	0	19	13	1	0.5	14.2	30	52%	.308	0.74	1.89	2.38	0.6	100
2018	COL	A	22	2	4	6	24	0	33¹	33	2	1.4	14.6	54	46%	.413	1.14	4.86	3.30	0.6	100
2018	SLU	A+	22	2	0	4	16	0	22	7	0	2.5	10.2	25	44%	.152	0.59	0.41	1.53	0.9	100
2018	BIN	AA	22	1	0	0	7	0	11¹	6	1	1.6	13.5	17	39%	.227	0.71	3.18	2.87	0.3	100
2019	BIN	AA	23	2	1	7	28	0	45	34	1	2.8	8.4	42	41%	.268	1.07	1.20	3.68	0.5	100
2019	SYR	AAA	23	0	0	0	13	0	16	23	4	4.5	6.8	12	28%	.339	1.94	6.75	7.87	-0.3	100
2020	NYN	MLB	24	2	2	0	33	0	35	35	5	3.3	8.0	31	37%	.295	1.35	4.46	4.60	0.3	92

There was a serial comic that ran in *SI for Kids* in the 1990s. I only half-remember most of it, and there's a non-zero chance it's part of some odd Mandela Effect. I think it was set in the 1950s—I recall a bunch of deep V-neck cricket sweaters—but I do distinctly remember one story arc that featured a nerdy kind of sports fan who discovered he was a very good junkballing pitcher. He leads his team to the state championship or something where he faces some jockish lout from their rival in the ninth inning. Our protagonist thinks to himself, "If he's going to beat me he's going to have to hit my best fastball." The next panel narration announces, "And he does, for a HOME RUN!" Steve Villines' ethos on the mound was to throw his best fastball and dare minor league batters to hit it. His fastball, mind you, is mid 80s from a sidearm slot. Up until a midseason promotion to Triple-A, no one could. But our humble 90s comics narrator came for Villines as he gave up 23 hits and four home runs in 16 innings for Syracuse. Villines does throw a short frisbee slider, and his change has flashed at times, although not for a while. But mostly he just tries to beat guys with that fastball. I appreciate the *joie de vivre* inherent in just shoving 86 mph in the faces of the best hitters on the planet and daring them to mash it, but that didn't even work long in the funny pages

Low Minors Sleeper

LMS **Jordany Ventura RHP**
Born: 07/06/00   Age: 19   Bats: R   Throws: R   Height: 6'0"   Weight: 162   Origin: International Free Agent, 2018

YEAR	TEAM	LVL	AGE	W	L	SV	G	GS	IP	H	HR	BB/9	K/9	K	GB%	BABIP	WHIP	ERA	DRA	WARP	PF
2018	MET	RK	17	0	1	0	3	1	6²	7	0	9.4	4.1	3	46%	.318	2.10	0.00	9.51	-0.3	93
2019	MTS	RK	18	2	1	0	9	7	33	27	2	2.2	9.3	34	47%	.287	1.06	4.36	2.76	1.1	100
2019	KNG	RK+	18	0	1	0	2	2	8	3	0	6.8	10.1	9	62%	.188	1.12	1.12	3.55	0.2	98

Ventura wasn't a big name out of the Dominican Republic and sort of came out of nowhere last year as a 19-year-old to begin blurring the edges of the radar. He was just up from Florida when I saw him on the August Appy circuit sitting low 90s with a well-developing curve in the upper 70s with an interesting change trailing behind. The breaker has sharp bite and is pretty true, around 11-5, and he can throw it for strikes. I said the change was trailing behind but that is due more to the strength of the curve than the weakness of his third pitch, which has some nice split action and drew some rough passes. The heater might not sound overpowering but there's some natural cut to it and the broad-shouldered Ventura is very physically projectible. Listed at 6-foot but looking taller up on the mound, he has a solid motion with a very high three-quarters release point that he repeats well enough for an average to above command projection. It will be interesting to see if the Mets push him to full season ball when next season begins, because there is a fair amount to like here.

Top Talents 25 and Under (as of 4/1/2020)

1. Pete Alonso
2. Amed Rosario
3. Dominic Smith
4. Ronny Mauricio
5. Francisco Alvarez
6. Andrés Giménez
7. Matthew Allan
8. Brett Baty
9. Mark Vientos
10. Luis Guillorme

One glance at this list and the top-heavy nature of the Mets' young talent becomes immediately apparent. Occupying the top three positions are the reigning National League Rookie of the Year, a solid, everyday regular major league shortstop, and a player who had a breakout season in 2019 and proved he belonged at the big league level.

What more is there to write about Pete Alonso that hasn't already been written? Expectations were high for his rookie season and yet it's safe to say he exceeded them and then some. He blasted 53 home runs in 2019, the most by a rookie in baseball history. He drove in 120 runs and posted a 141 DRC+. There were concerns about his ability to connect consistently on offspeed pitches. He dispelled them quickly. There were reservations about his defense at first base. Those were cast aside as well. Not only is Alonso easily the best player on the Mets under 25 years of age, he is arguably the best player on the Mets period not named Jacob deGrom.

Amed Rosario's big league journey has been more circuitous than Alonso's, despite the more prestigious prospect pedigree at the time of his debut. In fact, the hype led many to cry "bust" before his age-24 season. But he quietly took a step forward in 2019, more than doubling his 2018 WARP total. A free swinger, Rosario's selectivity at the plate has markedly improved. While his speed and athleticism are undeniable, his highlight-reel-worthy plays in the field often belied his missteps on routine plays. But extra work with his coaching staff paid off for the young shortstop to the tune of a much better defensive performance in the second half of the season. A solid .287/.323/.432 slash line combined with continued improvements defensively made Rosario an above-average regular at shortstop in 2019.

Dominic Smith capped off his 2019 season with a moment befitting its magic—a walk-off home run to lift the Mets to victory in the bottom of the 11th in the final game of the season. This season saw Smith elevate himself from a prospect who never lived up to his potential to folk hero status. Though it's hard to imagine now, entering spring training in 2019, it was unclear whether Alonso or Smith would be the Opening Day first baseman for the Mets. Alonso hit himself into the starting lineup and never left, but Smith produced in a way that made him impossible to ignore—so much so that the Mets conducted an ill-fated experiment playing Smith in the outfield. While his defense there was horrid, his performance with the bat was not. He slashed .282/.355/.525 with a 112 DRC+ in 89 games, far eclipsing the underwhelming numbers he had posted in his short big league career prior to 2019. Unfortunately, his breakout season was cut short by a stress reaction in his left foot. His improbable walk-off home run in the season's waning hour was his first plate appearance in over two months. But with Alonso already a franchise cornerstone, Smith's future with the Mets remains uncertain, despite the massive strides he made in 2019.

Just below this tier of major leaguers is the consensus top prospect in the Mets' system, but, like many guys on this list, he is far away from the major leagues. The 5-10 spots here are virtually interchangeable and all but one of this group of players has yet to play above the Double-A level. Notably absent from this list are all of the young arms the Mets have shuttled back and forth between Triple-A and the majors over the past couple of seasons, mostly products of trades made in an attempt to bolster organizational pitching depth that never panned out. A player who has been shuttled back and forth between the big leagues and the minors a fair amount in his professional career and rounds out this list is Luis Guillorme, a glove-first middle infielder. He posted an 85 DRC+ over 70 plate appearances for the Mets in 2019, but there remains enough hope in his offensive upside to earn him an appearance here, buoyed by his elite skills in the field. The fact that all but two of the players on this list, outside of the top three established major leaguers, are not just 25 or younger, but 20 or younger, speaks volumes about the state of the Mets organization.

Eyewitness Reports

Eyewitness Report: Ronny Mauricio

Evaluator: David Lee
Report Date: 06/19/2019
Dates Seen: 4/4-6/19; 6/3-4/19
Risk Factor: High
Physical/Health: Extreme length and projection with a high waist. Tons of room to fill out a lean frame. He'll remain lean but will grow into a solid body with strength. Quick, athletic motions despite his length. Slows the game down well for his age.

Tool	Future Grade	Report
Hit	60	Shows an advanced feel for the barrel. Loose stroke generates easy above-average bat speed that cranks up to plus. Consistent actions at the plate. Can settle for line-drive plane and cut himself off at times, but hands are loose and he has knack for adjustments. Attributes are here for plus hit tool, but his eye is overly aggressive at times and his length means constant challenges inside.
Power	60	Power is mostly projection right now. Considerable room to grow into impact strength. Combine projection with above-average to plus bat speed and adjusted loft to produce future plus power.
Baserunning/ Speed	40	Below-average runner down the line. Closer to an average runner when he hits second gear with long strides. Will settle and remain a below-average runner despite good athleticism.
Glove	50	Enough glove for any infield position. Smooth actions and soft hands at shortstop. Occasional lapse chalked up to youth. Future limited range holds him back to average shortstop potential, but sticking is a real possibility. This grade could bump a tick with a move to third.
Arm	60	Easy plus arm. Quick, compact release with easy plus carry and good accuracy. His arm will play anywhere.

Conclusion: Mauricio's overall grade reaches 60 because of the likelihood he makes an impact in the major leagues, no matter the position. There's real-deal, first-division-regular ability here. He shows an advanced feel for the bat beyond his years and has the athleticism and aptitude to adjust for increased power. The bat profiles as a masher that will play at any position, with an aggressive eye being the one knock. He shows the feel and actions to stick at shortstop, but his filled-out frame will ultimately make that decision. The ability to stay at short would be an org's dream considering the bat's potential, but a move to third would give an org a corner masher with at least an above-average glove and plus arm.

Eyewitness Report: Mark Vientos

Evaluator: Ben Spanier
Report Date: 08/28/2019
Dates Seen: 7/5, 7/31, 8/1, 8/2
Risk Factor: Medium
Physical/Health: Wiry strong, athletic frame. Still room for a some more good weight in the upper body especially.

Tool	Future Grade	Report
Hit	50	Easy swing and excellent all-fields approach, often waits back and looks to drive ball the other way; good approach on spin. Can look a bit grooved at times though; definitely the swing of a power hitter. Better high-ball than low-ball hitter in my looks and tries to lift. There's some swing and miss with his fairly long levers and he could probably work the count more.
Power	60	Real pop to all fields that already plays in game; has natural strength and good bat speed along with some loft to the swing. This is his main asset that he will need to maximize as he refines his hit tool. He will be able to tap into his power even more with improved plate discipline.
Baserunning/ Speed	40	Average at-best runner despite frame and the athleticism he shows elsewhere.
Glove	50	No real worries with his defense, even if he doesn't wow you with it. Makes all the routine plays.
Arm	55	Definitely strong enough to handle third, and the most impressive asset he has defensively.

Conclusion: It is possible I'm overstating the case a bit, but I believe some of the ambient handwringing around Vientos is unnecessary. He is fine at third base, and he has at least plus power and should grow into more. He will need to refine the hit tool, preferably lowering strikeouts slightly and improving his selectivity at the plate which would add to his overall offensive value in multiple ways. Excited to see how he adjusts to the higher levels, where he will still be on the young side.

New York Yankees

The State of the System

It's your typical Yankees system. They have arms that jumped in Double-A, arms that will jump sometime in the next two years in Double-A, and Estevan Florial again.

The Top Ten

★ ★ ★ *2020 Top 101 Prospect* **#24** ★ ★ ★

1 Deivi Garcia RHP OFP: 70 ETA: mid 2020

Born: 05/19/99 Age: 21 Bats: R Throws: R Height: 5'9" Weight: 163 Origin: International Free Agent, 2015

YEAR	TEAM	LVL	AGE	W	L	SV	G	GS	IP	H	HR	BB/9	K/9	K	GB%	BABIP	WHIP	ERA	DRA	WARP	PF
2017	DYA	RK	18	1	1	0	3	3	15¹	10	1	1.2	10.6	18	58%	.281	0.78	1.17	1.77	0.7	114
2017	YAT	RK	18	3	0	0	4	2	16²	9	3	2.2	13.0	24	32%	.194	0.78	3.24	1.42	0.8	104
2017	PUL	RK	18	2	1	0	6	5	28	23	3	4.2	13.8	43	32%	.370	1.29	4.50	3.01	0.9	98
2018	CSC	A	19	2	4	0	8	8	40²	31	5	2.2	13.9	63	31%	.302	1.01	3.76	3.14	1.0	85
2018	TAM	A+	19	2	0	0	5	5	28¹	19	0	2.5	11.1	35	37%	.292	0.95	1.27	2.69	0.9	100
2019	TAM	A+	20	0	2	0	4	4	17²	14	0	4.1	16.8	33	50%	.438	1.25	3.06	3.55	0.3	98
2019	TRN	AA	20	4	4	0	11	11	53²	43	2	4.4	14.6	87	44%	.360	1.29	3.86	4.30	0.4	93
2019	SWB	AAA	20	1	3	0	11	6	40	39	8	4.5	10.1	45	38%	.307	1.48	5.40	5.12	0.6	105
2020	NYA	MLB	21	2	2	0	15	5	30	30	5	3.6	11.7	39	40%	.339	1.40	4.79	5.01	0.1	101

Comparables: Sean Reid-Foley, David Holmberg, Alex Reyes

The Report: Start with a deceptive fastball that he can get regularly into the mid 90s. Add a plus-plus curveball. Sprinkle in an average change that flashes higher. Stir with a plus slider…wait, Deivi García has a plus slider now?

A lot of things came together in 2019. García threw 111 1/3 innings, setting a new career high by over 35 and reducing concerns that he might end up in relief because of his slight frame and low innings counts in the low-minors. His velocity bumped up a little. His curveball command tightened. His changeup consistency improved. He got an awful lot of swings and misses from high-minors hitters. He nearly earned a September call-up from a pennant contender. He did it all during a year in which he didn't turn 20 until a month-and-a-half into the season.

The addition of a slider during the season is the most intriguing development in 2019 for his future profile, and it was a plus pitch for him almost immediately. Nick Stellini spoke to García about the emergence of the pitch this past summer. In short, it's a key addition to an arsenal that now looks a lot more like an upper-rotation starter than it did at this time last year.

Variance: Medium. There's relief risk due to his size and inconsistent command, but he's pretty close to MLB-ready and inched closer to a full workload this season.

Ben Carsley's Fantasy Take: Concerns about size be damned; García is a fantasy stud in the making. It'd be nice if he were headed for greener pitching pastures than Yankee Stadium, to be sure, but he should pile up wins and strikeouts in pinstripes. Plus, as discussed above, he's pretty much ready now. It's possible that the Yankees don't call him up until mid-season and use him in more of a spot-start or hybrid role, but I think by early 2021, at the latest, we'll have a bona fide fantasy SP3 with upside here. Buy, buy, buy.

———————————— ★ ★ ★ *2020 Top 101 Prospect* **#46** ★ ★ ★ ————————————

2 Jasson Dominguez   OF   OFP: 70   ETA: 2023-2026
Born: 02/07/03   Age: 17   Bats: B   Throws: R   Height: 5'10"   Weight: 190   Origin: International Free Agent, 2019

The Report: The primary basis for our list products is our own in-person staff looks. We don't have staff looks at *every* player on every list, although we strive to and came pretty close this year. We supplement that with background discussion with a fairly large network of industry sources—primarily pro scouts who base *their* opinions on *their* in-person looks.

This presents a recurring problem for players who have yet to make their stateside debut. Much to my eternal dismay, we don't have live staff coverage in the Dominican Republic at the moment. Teams are starting to scout the DSL and the informal Tricky League instructs more than they used to, but their coverage is incomplete. Therefore, our access to scout opinions out of there is a lot more uneven than it is for any level of stateside baseball. And, of course, many of the highest-profile J2 signees have been hidden from sight for some time before signing because they agreed to illegal early deals, so the period in which they're available to opposing scouts after being signed is short.

Jasson Dominguez has yet to make his pro debut. We know a lot about him anyway. He's one of the highest-profile J2 signees ever, a potential five-tool center fielder touted as the next Mike Trout or Mickey Mantle. The Yankees made an early deal for him and blew their entire pool to do it. He did play in the Tricky League and fall instructs this summer, and reviews were universally positive.

It would be a silly exercise to omit Dominguez from this list. He's obviously one of the best prospects in this system. There was some early internal support for him to make the 101, and we ultimately placed him in the top 50. But we have live looks at all 21 other players on this list, plus the ability to get industry reports backchecking them. We *don't* have that for Dominguez, and all we'd be doing writing a scouting report on him is repeating low-confidence second/third-hand information about a 16-year-old that hasn't yet made his pro debut.

Variance: Extreme. Kevin Maitan was the last J2 to make the 101 the following offseason.

Ben Carsley's Fantasy Take: Were dynasty baseball an endeavor for sane people, guys like Dominguez would not be valued quite so highly out of the chute. Sure, there's a chance that he's the next Ronald Acuña Jr., but there's also a chance that he's the next [INSERT FAILED J2 PROSPECT HERE]. Despite the insane volatility, the prospect of a franchise-changing player is just too alluring for most, and guys like Dominguez end up being valued way more than immediate contributors with lower ceilings. Essentially, I *wish* that I could say it's a year too early to buy in on Dominguez. But the reality is this: if you don't buy now, you'll never get the chance. It's up to you if you want to take on the risk/eat the roster spot for a half-decade, but the upside is certainly there.

3 Albert Abreu   RHP   OFP: 60   ETA: 2020
Born: 09/26/95   Age: 24   Bats: R   Throws: R   Height: 6'2"   Weight: 175   Origin: International Free Agent, 2013

YEAR	TEAM	LVL	AGE	W	L	SV	G	GS	IP	H	HR	BB/9	K/9	K	GB%	BABIP	WHIP	ERA	DRA	WARP	PF
2017	CSC	A	21	1	0	0	3	2	14²	9	1	1.8	13.5	22	61%	.296	0.82	1.84	2.92	0.4	89
2017	TAM	A+	21	1	3	0	9	9	34¹	33	2	3.9	8.1	31	48%	.316	1.40	4.19	4.60	0.3	100
2018	TAM	A+	22	4	3	0	13	13	62²	54	9	4.2	9.3	65	45%	.274	1.32	4.16	4.07	0.9	102
2019	TRN	AA	23	5	8	0	23	20	96²	103	9	4.9	8.5	91	43%	.336	1.61	4.28	6.77	-2.2	95
2020	NYA	MLB	24	1	1	0	10	0	11	11	2	3.7	7.1	9	41%	.282	1.40	4.73	4.96	0.0	101

Comparables: Sandy Alcantara, Merandy Gonzalez, Hunter Wood

The Report: Abreu bounced back from an injury-marred 2017 and 2018 to have a, uh, slightly less injury-marred 2019. Look, when he's on the mound and right, the stuff is electric. Abreu features an explosive high-90s fastball that touched 99 for me and has reportedly hit triple digits. It's a high-spin pitch with late life up in the zone, and he can change eye levels with it despite only average overall command due to some weird timing stuff in his delivery. It's a plus-plus fastball as a starter, and it's not impossible that the heater could be a true 8 out of the pen. His curveball is an easy plus projection, a power breaker that he can manipulate, and he shows better command of the breaking ball than the fastball. Like most Yankees pitching prospects in the upper minors, Abreu has added a slider. Although it flashes, it is well behind his curveball at present. The change is also fringy. It's firm and he can struggle to turn it over at times, but the pitch has flashed more than changeups normally do for pitchers with his profile. Abreu ultimately possesses the ingredients to start, if both his command and his right arm cooperate over the long term.

Variance: High. Abreu has thrown 100 innings only once in a season, and that happened back in 2016. This year it was a bicep issue that sidelined him for a bit—another injury that just adds to the worrying cornucopia of arm issues that have plagued him over the years. If you were confident that he could take the ball 30 times a year, the overall profile is only a whisker off Deivi. We're not that confident, so he's here.

Ben Carsley's Fantasy Take: The Yankees sure do have a lot of dudes with this fantasy profile! Standard caveats about investing in fantasy pitchers aside, there's a lot to like about Abreu, who has insane strikeout upside and who is very close to the majors. That being said, there are a few scenarios that one can envision in which Abreu's fantasy production won't match his stuff. The Yankees could use him in a quasi-opener role as they attempt to build up his innings, preventing him from earning wins. Likewise, Abreu could end up serving as a non-closing, high-leverage relief arm that's only usable in the very deepest of leagues. The uncertainty about his future role knocks his top-50-type talent down to a likely back-of-the-top-101 ranking for me.

4 Luis Medina RHP   OFP: 60   ETA: 2022
Born: 05/03/99 Age: 21 Bats: R Throws: R Height: 6'1" Weight: 175 Origin: International Free Agent, 2015

YEAR	TEAM	LVL	AGE	W	L	SV	G	GS	IP	H	HR	BB/9	K/9	K	GB%	BABIP	WHIP	ERA	DRA	WARP	PF
2017	DYA	RK	18	1	1	0	4	3	15²	17	0	5.7	9.8	17	61%	.370	1.72	5.74	5.25	0.1	113
2017	PUL	RK	18	1	1	0	6	6	23	14	1	5.5	8.6	22	56%	.217	1.22	5.09	2.16	0.9	99
2018	PUL	RK	19	1	3	0	12	12	36	32	3	11.5	11.8	47	43%	.337	2.17	6.25	6.93	-0.3	102
2019	CSC	A	20	1	8	0	20	20	93	86	9	6.5	11.1	115	47%	.339	1.65	6.00	7.09	-2.1	93
2019	TAM	A+	20	0	0	0	2	2	10²	7	0	2.5	10.1	12	71%	.250	0.94	0.84	3.52	0.2	88
2020	NYA	MLB	21	2	2	0	33	0	35	35	6	4.9	8.5	33	45%	.298	1.54	5.25	5.36	-0.1	101

Comparables: Huascar Ynoa, Brad Keller, Lucas Giolito

The Report: Medina began this year as he had in most others—wowing sparse crowds with radar-gun readings that touched triple digits while walking well over a batter an inning. The overall stat line for the season isn't great. It suffers from too many free passes from when he couldn't find the zone, as well as hard contact from when he found too much of it. Something seemed to click around early July, though, when he began a dominant run that resulted in a late-August promotion to Tampa, something that didn't seem likely back in April and May. Medina went at least five innings in each of his final six Sally League starts, allowing three or more runs only once and never striking out fewer than seven. He posted double-digit strikeouts three times in that stretch.

Medina's stuff has always been great, beginning, of course, with an upper-90s fastball that has both late life and plane. It is especially effective up and above the zone. Less talked about are the two secondaries, both of which regularly flash plus. His low- to mid-80s curve has a couple different looks to it. It can be 11-5 with strong vertical action on the lower end, while being more of a power slurve at the upper. Both variations show good, late bite.

His high-80s change is advanced, given the overall stage of his development, and it features convincing arm speed and real fade. Medina is athletic, and his frame is filling out nicely. He also looks taller than his listed height. If you want to nitpick, his delivery could be more fluid, but the control and command seem to be improving as he grows into his body. Next year will be an important one for Medina. He will try to consolidate the gains he has made with his control, while continuing to refine his command, as he works toward the realization of his plus potential.

Variance: High, and this works in both directions. It is possible that the recent gains in control regress, and the command doesn't get to where it needs to be, which pushes him to the pen. It is also possible that Medina really has flipped a switch, and the stuff could be top-of-the-rotation level.

Ben Carsley's Fantasy Take: The Yankees sure do have a lot of dudes with this fantasy profile! While Abreu may have slightly higher upside and a better ETA, I actually prefer Medina, who I think has a better shot to start long-term. He's already owned in deeper dynasty leagues, of course, but if you play in a shallower one, you'll need to buy now. As soon as his 2019 improvements prove to be real, he will skyrocket up the rankings. Whenever I make dynasty top-101 predictions this early in the process, I tend to regret it, but I think he should make our upcoming edition of the list.

5 Luis Gil   RHP   OFP: 55   ETA: 2022

Born: 06/03/98   Age: 22   Bats: R   Throws: R   Height: 6'3"   Weight: 176   Origin: International Free Agent, 2015

YEAR	TEAM	LVL	AGE	W	L	SV	G	GS	IP	H	HR	BB/9	K/9	K	GB%	BABIP	WHIP	ERA	DRA	WARP	PF
2017	DTW	RK	19	0	2	0	14	14	41²	31	2	4.3	10.6	49	54%	.287	1.22	2.59	3.01	1.4	125
2018	PUL	RK	20	2	1	0	10	10	39¹	21	1	5.7	13.3	58	35%	.256	1.17	1.37	1.74	1.8	98
2018	STA	A-	20	0	2	0	2	2	6²	11	1	8.1	13.5	10	39%	.455	2.55	5.40	8.07	-0.2	87
2019	CSC	A	21	4	5	0	17	17	83	60	1	4.2	12.1	112	50%	.304	1.19	2.39	3.89	1.3	94
2019	TAM	A+	21	1	0	0	3	3	13	11	0	5.5	7.6	11	40%	.297	1.46	4.85	5.60	-0.1	104
2020	NYA	MLB	22	2	2	0	33	0	35	34	5	4.5	9.6	37	44%	.308	1.47	4.71	4.93	0.1	101

Comparables: Dylan Cease, Devin Williams, Domingo Germán

The Report: Traded to the Yankees from the Twins in 2018, Gil has quickly made a name for himself within the organization. He features a dominant fastball-curveball combination that helped him strike out 123 batters in 96 innings between both A-ball levels. His 95-98 mph fastball is a plus one. It has ride and is also aided by Gil's ability to create downhill plane. The delivery was effortless, suggesting that he may be able to add a tick with further physical growth. But the fastball is already a swing-and-miss pitch.

Gil's best secondary offering is an 81-84 slurvy curveball that has sweeping action and plus depth. Although the command of this pitch can waver, the shape stays steady, and it's his go-to out pitch. His third pitch is a 90-92 mph power changeup. It's fairly new for Gil, which is evident because it still lacks movement or even average command. His biggest issue is consistency. He can be erratic and lose the strike zone at times. He also has a tendency to overthrow his fastball, especially when behind in the count. Despite the control issues, Gil has potentially high-end stuff and intriguing upside.

Variance: High. Throwing strikes and repeating his delivery remain concerns for the 21-year-old. There is also a chance that he will wind up as a high-leverage reliever instead of a starter, if he can't develop a third pitch.

Ben Carsley's Fantasy Take: The Yankees sure do have a lot of dudes with this fantasy profile! He's my least-favorite arm among the Abreu/Medina/Gil trio, yet Gil still has a reasonable argument to rank among the top-150-or-so dynasty prospects. If you feel as though you have a solid grasp of which of these three arms is gonna end up in the rotation versus the bullpen, please let us know, because to be honest it's anyone's guess right now.

6 Anthony Volpe   SS   OFP: 55   ETA: 2023

Born: 04/28/01   Age: 19   Bats: R   Throws: R   Height: 5'11"   Weight: 180   Origin: Round 1, 2019 Draft (#30 overall)

YEAR	TEAM	LVL	AGE	PA	R	2B	3B	HR	RBI	BB	K	SB	CS	AVG/OBP/SLG	DRC+	VORP	BABIP	BRR	FRAA	WARP	PF
2019	PUL	RK+	18	150	19	7	2	2	11	23	38	6	1	.215/.349/.355	100	8.5	.289	0.3		0.7	99
2020	NYA	MLB	19	251	24	11	1	5	24	28	87	3	1	.210/.307/.340	78	0.0	.322	0.0		0.1	101

The Report: Volpe doesn't exactly fit the mold of your traditional first-round prep shortstop. The tools don't really pop like they do with Bobby Witt or CJ Abrams, but he's a very well-rounded player with a decent shot to stick at short. He's more polished than quick-twitch at the six, too, with solid hands, solid actions, and enough arm for the left side. He'd be an asset defensively if he had to slide to second or third.

He looks the part at the plate as well. His hands and hips work well, helping to generate above-average bat speed. His sturdy frame stays balanced throughout the swing, although he can get a little wrap at times, which adds length to the bat path. The swing is fairly flat at present, and there's minimal physical projection left in his frame, so the ultimate power ceiling remains an open question. He's a strong kid, though, so I wouldn't be shocked if he unlocks average game power with a bit more lift.

Volpe offers a broad base of skills, but you'd struggle to find anything higher than a 55 on the scouting sheet. Sometimes those profiles play up, but if one of the offensive tools—or the shortstop glove—fall short of projection, it's a quick slide from above-average regular to bench piece.

Variance: High. He's more polished than your usual prep shortstop, but he's just as far away and no less risky.

Ben Carsley's Fantasy Take: Volpe reads as more well-rounded than special, and while the potential shortstop eligibility is intriguing, not much in the rest of the package is. He could sneak onto the back of some top-101 lists once he's much closer to the majors, but at three-plus seasons out, the relative lack of upside doesn't justify a heavy dynasty investment at this point. Between being a Yankee and a first-rounder, he's likely to be overvalued.

7 Estevan Florial OF   OFP: 55   ETA: 2021

Born: 11/25/97   Age: 22   Bats: L   Throws: R   Height: 6'1"   Weight: 185   Origin: International Free Agent, 2015

YEAR	TEAM	LVL	AGE	PA	R	2B	3B	HR	RBI	BB	K	SB	CS	AVG/OBP/SLG	DRC+	VORP	BABIP	BRR	FRAA	WARP	PF
2017	CSC	A	19	389	64	21	5	11	43	41	124	17	7	.297/.373/.483	134	31.8	.431	-0.7	CF(62) -2.1, LF(13) 2.9	2.4	96
2017	TAM	A+	19	87	13	2	2	2	14	9	24	6	1	.303/.368/.461	125	7.4	.404	0.7	CF(18) 0.4	0.6	102
2018	TAM	A+	20	339	45	16	3	3	27	44	87	11	10	.255/.354/.361	103	10.5	.353	-0.9	CF(59) 1.8, RF(6) -0.2	1.1	103
2019	TAM	A+	21	301	38	10	3	8	38	24	98	9	5	.237/.297/.383	92	4.2	.335	1.0	CF(62) 2.9	1.1	102
2020	NYA	MLB	22	35	3	2	0	1	4	2	13	1	0	.222/.280/.370	72	0.0	.344	0.0	CF 0	0.0	101

Comparables: Lewis Brinson, Byron Buxton, Daniel Fields

The Report: Florial made his unofficial Double-A debut in the 2017 Eastern League playoffs, capping off a season in which he rose from toolsy sleeper to top outfield prospect. We expected him to spend most of 2018 for real at Double-A and even projected 2019 as his major-league ETA. The stats above will tell you that not only did he not make his major-league debut in 2019, but also that he spent the entire season in the Florida State League and struggled all the while. What on earth happened?

A series of hand and wrist injuries is a good place to start. Florial has missed nearly half a year in each of the last two seasons, with the bulk of that time coming from two breaks in his right hamate area. Hamate injuries are notorious for sapping hitting ability, especially power, for some time after the player returns to action. That's a partial explanation for Florial's offensive struggles over the past two years, but he has also just not mastered pitching in the way that we had hoped two years ago. His approach simply has never improved much.

We aren't entirely getting off the bandwagon here. He still has outstanding underlying tools: the bat speed, the raw power, and the overall athleticism. We're just becoming less sure of the hit-tool development as each year passes where we don't see it.

Variance: High. He needs to get it going, but there's significant upside beyond the OFP if the tools finally click.

Ben Carsley's Fantasy Take: I'm mad at Florial. He made me love him, and he's given me nothing in return. I understand that the tools remain, and you're not at all crazy if you value him as a top-101 prospect still. Personally, I don't. Perhaps I'm just being a spiteful ex-lover, but I don't think Florial is worth the risk now that we understand the ceiling is lower.

8 Ezequiel Duran 2B   OFP: 55   ETA: Late 2022

Born: 05/22/99   Age: 21   Bats: R   Throws: R   Height: 5'11"   Weight: 185   Origin: International Free Agent, 2017

YEAR	TEAM	LVL	AGE	PA	R	2B	3B	HR	RBI	BB	K	SB	CS	AVG/OBP/SLG	DRC+	VORP	BABIP	BRR	FRAA	WARP	PF
2017	DYA	RK	18	65	12	5	4	3	11	3	15	4	1	.393/.415/.754	158	10.9	.477	1.1	2B(9) -1.5, SS(4) -0.9	0.4	115
2018	PUL	RK	19	235	34	8	2	4	20	9	65	7	0	.201/.251/.311	32	-4.2	.265	4.4	2B(51) -1.2, SS(1) -0.2	-0.7	101
2019	STA	A-	20	277	49	12	4	13	37	25	77	11	4	.256/.329/.496	160	21.3	.314	0.6	2B(56) 7.6	3.0	98
2020	NYA	MLB	21	251	23	11	2	8	28	13	89	2	1	.211/.257/.372	62	2.0	.301	0.2	2B 2, SS 0	-0.1	101

Comparables: Zoilo Almonte, Abraham Toro, Billy Hamilton

The Report: I wrote an entire column earlier this year about my decision to stuff Ezequiel Duran, so it should be no surprise that he ended up highly-ranked even in a very deep Yankees system. Most important is the combination of plus raw power and a potential plus glove at second. Duran has above-average bat speed with loft. He can cover major-league-quality velocity, turning on it inside and using the big part of the park when it's away. I wasn't sure, at the time, how quickly it would play in games because he liked to drive the gaps, but then he went and led the Penn League in home runs, so...

In the infield, he's a polished, rangy fielder, with good hands and actions. He probably doesn't have quite enough range or arm to slide over to short in non-emergency situations, but the arm and range are both above-average for the keystone. He's a smooth defender, and there's no weakness. I know we don't usually gush about second-base defense, but he's fun to watch in a Robinson Canó kind of way.

The overall approach at the plate is still a little raw. You could lock him up front door with breaking balls, and he'd expand up more than you'd like for fastballs. Both of those are fixable with reps, but given the grip-it-and-rip-it style, I can't project more than an average hit tool at present. That should be enough to get the power into games and make him a nice everyday guy at second. There's more in the tank here, too, as he doesn't have a ton of pro reps and was banged up for much of 2018.

Variance: High. He has no full-season track record, and it might be a fringe hit tool if he doesn't make adjustments to his approach (specifically spin). He might grow off the middle infield, but I suspect we are going to be less concerned about that than other sources. He also might be a Top 101 guy next year with a good campaign in Charleston (and not a back-end guy).

Ben Carsley's Fantasy Take: Anyone else getting a Jonathan Schoop vibe from that report? There's plenty of value in a guy like Schoop in deeper leagues, of course, but not so much that you'd want to roster the prospect version of him unless your league stored roughly 200 minor leaguers. Duran is an interesting add, for sure, but don't get too carried away.

9 Clarke Schmidt RHP   OFP: 50   ETA: 2020/21

Born: 02/20/96   Age: 24   Bats: R   Throws: R   Height: 6'1"   Weight: 200   Origin: Round 1, 2017 Draft (#16 overall)

YEAR	TEAM	LVL	AGE	W	L	SV	G	GS	IP	H	HR	BB/9	K/9	K	GB%	BABIP	WHIP	ERA	DRA	WARP	PF
2018	YAT	RK	22	0	0	0	3	3	7^1	4	0	2.5	9.8	8	69%	.250	0.82	1.23	5.74	0.0	104
2018	YAN	RK	22	0	2	0	3	2	7^2	8	1	2.3	14.1	12	50%	.412	1.30	7.04	5.16	0.1	104
2018	STA	A-	22	0	1	0	2	2	8^1	4	0	2.2	10.8	10	37%	.211	0.72	1.08	2.89	0.2	87
2019	TAM	A+	23	4	5	0	13	12	63^1	59	2	3.4	9.8	69	57%	.331	1.31	3.84	4.13	0.7	99
2019	TRN	AA	23	2	0	0	3	3	19	14	1	0.5	9.0	19	45%	.260	0.79	2.37	3.84	0.3	99
2020	NYA	MLB	24	2	2	0	33	0	35	34	5	3.7	8.9	34	42%	.302	1.40	4.58	4.68	0.2	101

Comparables: Erick Fedde, Troy Scribner, Bruce Billings

The Report: In his first full year back on the field since his 2017 Tommy John surgery, Schmidt showed the power stuff that made him a first-round pick. He offers a mid-90s fastball that is an above-average offering, a plus slider, and a solid frame. Schmidt did miss time this year with the flu and with right forearm soreness that kept him out of action for nearly a month. The changeup isn't great, more of a show-me pitch that he telegraphs, and the overall fastball command leaves a lot to be desired. Given these concerns, it is more likely that he ends up in the bullpen long term.

Variance: Medium. The stuff is good no matter the role, but the injury history is cause for concern.

Ben Carsley's Fantasy Take: Nah. The upside isn't high enough, and in an organization this loaded with pitching talent, it's tough to see how Schmidt remains a long-term starter anyway. You can pass.

10 Kevin Alcantara OF   OFP: 55   ETA: 2023

Born: 07/12/02   Age: 17   Bats: R   Throws: R   Height: 6'6"   Weight: 188   Origin: International Free Agent, 2018

YEAR	TEAM	LVL	AGE	PA	R	2B	3B	HR	RBI	BB	K	SB	CS	AVG/OBP/SLG	DRC+	VORP	BABIP	BRR	FRAA	WARP	PF
2019	YAN	RK	16	128	19	5	2	1	13	3	27	3	3	.260/.289/.358	108	2.0	.326	0.5	CF(27) -1.3	0.4	92
2020	NYA	MLB	17	251	21	11	1	4	22	18	86	3	1	.220/.284/.325	63	0.0	.335	0.0	CF 0	-0.3	101

Comparables: Yorman Rodriguez, Carlos Tocci, Adalberto Mondesi

The Report: Alcantara oozes projection. He played half the season at 16 years old, turning 17 in July. It looks like he could add 30-plus pounds of good weight, which makes the profile even more exciting, given his current tool set. He has plus speed, present above-average raw power, and plus arm strength. He could grow into even more power as he matures and will most likely not face a pitcher younger than him until he is 18 years old. In the outfield he tracks balls well with long graceful strides, but he might have to settle into a corner spot as his body matures and he loses a step or two. He struggled against better velocity and offspeed stuff simply because he has never seen it before. There is boom-or-bust potential, but the boom would require industrial-strength ear protection.

Variance: Is there a grade higher than Extreme? He is very young and didn't light the world on fire in his stateside debut. There is a wide range of outcomes.

Ben Carsley's Fantasy Take: If you enjoyed betting on Florial, you'll love the sequel in Alcantara: 2 Fast 2 Florial. That's not entirely fair, of course—they're different players despite the similarities in skill sets—but you can treat Florial's trials as a cautionary tale of sorts as to what might happen with Alcantara. Still, we can't fully ignore his upside. If you're filling out the bottom of your roster in a TDGX-sized (200-plus prospects rostered) league, it's reasonable to gamble on Alcantara.

The Next Ten

11 Roansy Contreras RHP

Born: 11/07/99   Age: 20   Bats: R   Throws: R   Height: 6'0"   Weight: 175   Origin: International Free Agent, 2016

YEAR	TEAM	LVL	AGE	W	L	SV	G	GS	IP	H	HR	BB/9	K/9	K	GB%	BABIP	WHIP	ERA	DRA	WARP	PF
2017	DYA	RK	17	0	3	0	6	6	22	25	2	2.0	7.0	17	57%	.311	1.36	3.68	4.48	0.4	112
2017	YAN	RK	17	4	1	0	8	5	31²	35	2	3.4	4.8	17	43%	.297	1.48	4.26	6.13	0.0	93
2018	STA	A-	18	0	0	0	5	5	28²	15	1	2.8	10.0	32	49%	.219	0.84	1.26	1.79	1.2	88
2018	CSC	A	18	0	2	0	7	7	34²	29	4	3.1	7.3	28	34%	.255	1.18	3.38	4.59	0.3	84
2019	CSC	A	19	12	5	0	24	24	132¹	105	10	2.4	7.7	113	42%	.255	1.07	3.33	3.94	1.9	94
2020	NYA	MLB	20	2	2	0	33	0	35	35	6	3.7	6.4	25	38%	.278	1.42	4.85	4.95	0.1	101

Comparables: Seranthony Domínguez, Mike Soroka, Pedro Payano

He's a small pitcher in the Deivi García mold rather than the power builds of Luises Gil and Medina, and Contreras does not have their explosiveness or upside of any of those three. Even so, he shouldn't go unmentioned in a discussion about the Yanks' collection of young arms. Listed six-foot and 175 pounds, the Dominican righty is athletic with a smooth enough delivery to project above-average command. Contreras is mainly a two-pitch guy at present, with a fastball sitting low-to-mid 90s that has touched 96. This is an above-average pitch that could be plus with command refinement, as it features some late life and run.

His most intriguing offering is his curve, which shows tight 11-5 shape and finishes with late and sharp break. He can throw it for strikes but wastes it in the dirt too much at present. Still, this should be a future plus pitch. His upper-80s change comes in pretty firm and is a distant third in the present arsenal, but it flashes some dive and fade and could become at least average in time. After performing very well as a teenager in the Sally League, Contreras will hit High-A Tampa in 2020.

12 Yoendrys Gomez RHP

Born: 10/15/99   Age: 20   Bats: R   Throws: R   Height: 6'3"   Weight: 175   Origin: International Free Agent, 2016

YEAR	TEAM	LVL	AGE	W	L	SV	G	GS	IP	H	HR	BB/9	K/9	K	GB%	BABIP	WHIP	ERA	DRA	WARP	PF
2017	DYA	RK	17	0	3	0	10	8	32	36	2	3.4	9.0	32	43%	.358	1.50	4.78	6.19	-0.1	115
2018	DYA	RK	18	1	0	0	2	2	9	2	0	7.0	7.0	7	63%	.105	1.00	1.00	3.69	0.2	119
2018	YAN	RK	18	3	1	0	10	9	38²	27	1	3.5	10.0	43	42%	.271	1.09	2.33	2.46	1.5	101
2019	PUL	RK+	19	4	2	0	6	6	29²	26	1	3.0	8.5	28	45%	.309	1.21	2.12	3.68	0.8	101
2019	CSC	A	19	0	3	0	6	6	26²	28	2	3.0	8.4	25	43%	.353	1.39	6.07	5.78	-0.2	108
2020	NYA	MLB	20	2	2	0	33	0	35	35	6	4.2	7.5	29	40%	.292	1.48	5.17	5.16	0.0	101

Comparables: Mauricio Cabrera, Luke Jackson, Chris Flexen

Gomez has slowly grown on me from a good org arm to a nice developmental project to one of the next good major league arms they'll churn out of this organization. He's grown into his lanky body and now fires plus fastballs which are tough to square up when he's spotting it up in the zone. Gomez can tend to overthrow his pitches and miss spots, which doesn't allow the fastball to play as high as the velocity grade at present. He pairs the heater with a potential plus changeup and average curveball. The *cambio* is his go-to pitch, as it has late split-finger-like action and can generate a fair amount of weak contact. The curve is inconsistent. It can get slurvy and roll into the zone, or be vulnerable to hard contact when it rides up. Next season could be a breakout year for Gomez, and he might be in the mix with the top arms in the system on our 2021 list.

13 Michael King   RHP
Born: 05/25/95   Age: 25   Bats: R   Throws: R   Height: 6'3"   Weight: 210   Origin: Round 12, 2016 Draft (#353 overall)

YEAR	TEAM	LVL	AGE	W	L	SV	G	GS	IP	H	HR	BB/9	K/9	K	GB%	BABIP	WHIP	ERA	DRA	WARP	PF
2017	GRB	A	22	11	9	0	26	25	149	141	14	1.3	6.4	106	57%	.285	1.09	3.14	4.24	1.8	105
2018	TAM	A+	23	1	3	0	7	7	40¹	33	1	2.2	10.0	45	61%	.302	1.07	1.79	3.24	1.0	104
2018	TRN	AA	23	6	2	0	12	11	82	65	4	1.4	8.3	76	46%	.276	0.95	2.09	2.85	2.3	93
2018	SWB	AAA	23	4	0	0	6	6	39	20	3	1.4	7.2	31	54%	.167	0.67	1.15	1.79	1.7	99
2019	TRN	AA	24	0	1	0	3	2	12²	20	1	1.4	5.7	8	51%	.396	1.74	9.95	6.92	-0.3	101
2019	SWB	AAA	24	3	1	0	4	3	23²	20	3	2.3	10.6	28	48%	.293	1.10	4.18	2.99	0.8	98
2019	NYA	MLB	24	0	0	0	1	0	2	2	0	0.0	4.5	1	38%	.250	1.00	0.00	5.19	0.0	116
2020	NYA	MLB	25	1	1	0	12	2	17	19	4	2.8	6.3	12	47%	.293	1.43	5.31	5.45	0.0	101

Comparables: Kyle McPherson, Brandon Workman, Tyler Duffey

It was a weird season for King. He was one of the "shut down in February with vague elbow problems while ramping up" guys from this spring. He wouldn't show up on the mound until July, and didn't get stretched out until August, so it was an extremely abbreviated MiLB season for him. We got a bunch of staff looks on him, and his velocity was varied wildly from start-to-start, but at times he was the 91-93 mph sinkerballer with plus command from 2018 that projected as a mid-rotation starter. He was then a very delayed September call-up for emergency innings, and got into one relief outing in late September, where he pitched well. King mixes in a four-seam, change, slider, and cutter with the sinker, but none of them currently project as above-average; it's the sinker that's going to make or break his career. We are concerned about the durability now given a five month elbow-injury-wrecked his season, but a No. 3/4 innings-eater type starting outcome is still quite plausible here. A ground-ball specialist out of the pen isn't a bad fallback.

14 T.J. Sikkema   LHP
Born: 07/25/98   Age: 21   Bats: L   Throws: L   Height: 6'0"   Weight: 221   Origin: Round 1, 2019 Draft (#38 overall)

YEAR	TEAM	LVL	AGE	W	L	SV	G	GS	IP	H	HR	BB/9	K/9	K	GB%	BABIP	WHIP	ERA	DRA	WARP	PF
2019	STA	A-	20	0	0	0	4	4	10²	6	0	0.8	11.0	13	52%	.240	0.66	0.84	2.02	0.4	98
2020	NYA	MLB	21	2	2	0	33	0	35	35	5	4.0	8.5	33	43%	.300	1.45	4.89	4.96	0.1	101

Comparables: Tyler Alexander, Brett Cecil, Clay Buchholz

A polished Mizzou arm who had a career 2.38 ERA in the SEC as well as a 1.72 ERA on the Cape, Sikkema wasn't talked about as much as other top arms in that conference. It isn't for a lack of stuff, though, as his fastball is up to 95 from a variety of angles and he features a deceptive crossfire delivery. The breaking balls all flash above-average, and come in from a variety of angles. There's a potentially average changeup as well. Sikkema might have gotten overlooked because he doesn't have an ideal frame—it's a thick, barrel chested, 6-foot-even—and the delivery isn't ideal either given the crossfire and angle. But sometimes the results speak for themselves, and in a system known for developing arms this is an arm that can jump.

15 Frank German   LHP
Born: 09/22/97   Age: 22   Bats: R   Throws: R   Height: 6'2"   Weight: 195   Origin: Round 4, 2018 Draft (#127 overall)

YEAR	TEAM	LVL	AGE	W	L	SV	G	GS	IP	H	HR	BB/9	K/9	K	GB%	BABIP	WHIP	ERA	DRA	WARP	PF
2018	STA	A-	20	1	3	1	10	4	28¹	22	0	1.9	12.1	38	44%	.314	0.99	2.22	2.45	0.8	92
2019	TAM	A+	21	4	4	0	16	15	76	70	9	4.1	9.7	82	46%	.314	1.38	3.79	5.94	-0.9	101
2020	NYA	MLB	22	2	2	0	33	0	35	35	6	3.7	8.3	32	42%	.297	1.41	4.77	4.93	0.1	101

Comparables: Adrian Sampson, Justin Dunn, Robert Dugger

One of the Yankees favorite types of draft pick—a day two, Directional Florida arm—German dealt with elbow soreness late in spring, and a shoulder strain which cost him the month of July. We already had reliever concerns here, and the 2019 durability issues won't do much to assuage those. When he was on the mound, though, German maintained his velocity gains from 2018, pumping mid-90s heat and pairing the fastball with a pair of potentially average secondaries. The arsenal and the frame is a starting pitcher, but we've still never seen him stretched out as a pro, so he more or less holds serve within the Yankees system. But as we have to write for basically every arm in this range, German is a guy who could jump in 2020. And all he really has to do is stay healthy.

16 Antonio Cabello   RHP
Born: 11/01/00   Age: 19   Bats: R   Throws: R   Height: 5'10"   Weight: 160   Origin: International Free Agent, 2017

It was a year to forget for Cabello, who has struggled to show the same loud tools since dislocating his shoulder in late 2018. Last year this was an all-star profile—a potential plus hitter with plus speed and arm strength who profiled well in center field. Since the injury Cabello has looked lost at the plate, flailing at pitches and not driving the ball with the same authority he showed in the complex. He has also lost a step out on the grass, moving him to a corner outfield spot. He is still young—he spent the whole season at age 18—so you hope that with more time away from his injury the tools can come back.

17 Anthony Seigler   C
Born: 06/20/99   Age: 21   Bats: B   Throws: S   Height: 6'0"   Weight: 200   Origin: Round 1, 2018 Draft (#23 overall)

YEAR	TEAM	LVL	AGE	PA	R	2B	3B	HR	RBI	BB	K	SB	CS	AVG/OBP/SLG	DRC+	VORP	BABIP	BRR	FRAA	WARP	PF
2018	YAT	RK	19	42	7	2	0	1	4	6	7	0	0	.333/.429/.472	175	4.7	.393	-0.3	C(10) -0.2	0.4	103
2018	PUL	RK	19	53	4	1	0	0	5	8	5	0	0	.209/.340/.233	94	0.4	.231	0.1	C(11) 0.0	0.2	104
2019	CSC	A	20	120	10	3	0	0	6	20	28	1	0	.175/.328/.206	73	1.1	.246	-0.2	C(23) 0.4	0.2	92
2020	NYA	MLB	21	251	23	11	0	4	23	27	68	1	0	.214/.306/.325	73	0.0	.289	-0.5	C 0	-0.1	101

Comparables: Danny Jansen, Adrian Nieto, Josmil Pinto

Last year's first-rounder had a lost season in his first full year of pro ball. He debuted for the River Dogs in mid-June following a quad strain and 30 games later was done for the season after suffering a patella fracture. Seigler didn't show much offensively during his brief stint on the field, though his approach was very solid and he drew his fair share of walks. The first impression is of a mature hitter with an opposite-field mindset and an eye towards contact, though upon further examination this gives way to concern about a somewhat timid hitter who currently struggles to drive the ball. He is slight of frame and not very projectible, which won't alleviate concerns about his future power output. Still, Seigler just turned twenty and should get a fresh shot at the level next spring.

It is a completely different story defensively, where the Georgia prep's athleticism is obvious watching him move around behind the plate. His better-than-plus arm stands out more than anything, and while he has a quick pop and release he doesn't always need it—I saw him casually gun down a runner from his knees. How he performs next year when fully healthy will say a lot about his trajectory as a prospect.

18 Josh Stowers   OF
Born: 02/25/97   Age: 23   Bats: R   Throws: R   Height: 6'0"   Weight: 200   Origin: Round 2, 2018 Draft (#54 overall)

YEAR	TEAM	LVL	AGE	PA	R	2B	3B	HR	RBI	BB	K	SB	CS	AVG/OBP/SLG	DRC+	VORP	BABIP	BRR	FRAA	WARP	PF
2018	EVE	A-	21	244	32	15	0	5	28	37	57	20	4	.260/.380/.410	136	12.1	.336	0.5	CF(47) -2.8	1.3	109
2019	CSC	A	22	460	61	24	2	7	40	64	123	35	16	.273/.386/.400	146	33.1	.383	0.6	RF(65) -1.5, CF(31) 0.1	2.9	97
2020	NYA	MLB	23	251	24	12	1	6	26	18	84	8	2	.223/.285/.362	71	0.0	.322	0.0	CF 0, RF 1	0.1	101

Shed Long was acquired for Sonny Gray and spent about thirty seconds in the Yankees organization before he was flipped to Seattle for Stowers, a 2018 second-round pick whom New York had reportedly been high on prior to the draft. The 22-year-old outfielder flashed some tools this year in Low-A, though the overall profile sends mixed messages. Stowers is athletic, but a bit brawnier than one might expect of someone who took a third of his reps in center field. His speed is comfortably above-average but not plus, although his range in the field plays up due to his instincts and flair. He has a quick bat and a good approach but there's some swing-and-miss. He's shown some over-the-fence power, but it is more gap-to-gap at present, and there's not a lot of room for projection here. Stowers's path to the majors could take a couple different routes: he could find a way to tap into some more pop and make his way as a corner bat, or he could prove his wares in center and try to hit his way into a fourth-outfielder outcome. He'll likely start next season in High-A and could move quickly if warranted, but for now it's a tweener profile.

19 Josh Smith SS

Born: 08/07/97 Age: 22 Bats: L Throws: R Height: 5'10" Weight: 172 Origin: Round 2, 2019 Draft (#67 overall)

YEAR	TEAM	LVL	AGE	PA	R	2B	3B	HR	RBI	BB	K	SB	CS	AVG/OBP/SLG	DRC+	VORP	BABIP	BRR	FRAA	WARP	PF
2019	STA	A-	21	141	17	6	1	3	15	25	17	6	3	.324/.450/.477	207	15.3	.355	0.7	SS(24) -1.3	1.7	98
2020	NYA	MLB	22	251	24	11	1	6	26	17	55	2	1	.231/.289/.369	76	0.0	.276	0.0	SS -1	0.0	101

Comparables: Tommy Edman, Garrett Hampson, Chris Taylor

The Yankees seem to have a lot of middle infield prospects who can make contact, draw walks and play good defense. The lefty-hitting, 5-foot-10 Smith is no exception. He was one of the most patient hitters in the New York-Penn League, as evidenced by his 17 percent walk rate. He complemented this with impressive bat-to-ball skills, as well as a knack for elevating the ball at a somewhat surprising rate, especially to the pull side. The power is more gap-to-gap, though, and it's most likely going to stay that way thanks to his already maxed-out frame and average bat speed. With good range and hands but a questionable arm, his best defensive fit is at second, but he could play anywhere on the diamond in a pinch. Greg Garcia is the major league comp here, as Smith is a tweener with some attractive offensive characteristics and sufficient defensive versatility.

20 Alexander Vizcaino RHP

Born: 05/22/97 Age: 23 Bats: R Throws: R Height: 6'2" Weight: 160 Origin: International Free Agent, 2016

YEAR	TEAM	LVL	AGE	W	L	SV	G	GS	IP	H	HR	BB/9	K/9	K	GB%	BABIP	WHIP	ERA	DRA	WARP	PF
2017	PUL	RK	20	3	5	0	12	11	51¹	69	9	4.0	8.6	49	51%	.377	1.79	5.79	7.17	-0.6	101
2018	PUL	RK	21	3	3	0	11	11	54	49	7	3.5	9.2	55	52%	.290	1.30	4.50	3.43	1.5	101
2019	CSC	A	22	5	5	0	16	16	87²	80	6	2.8	10.4	101	48%	.323	1.22	4.41	5.51	-0.3	98
2019	TAM	A+	22	1	1	0	5	5	27¹	33	2	3.6	8.9	27	53%	.403	1.61	4.28	6.90	-0.6	106
2020	NYA	MLB	23	2	2	0	33	0	35	37	7	3.9	7.9	31	45%	.295	1.49	5.48	5.48	-0.1	101

Compared to his fellow young Dominican arms–Luis Medina, Roansy Contreras and Luis Gil–Vizcaino doesn't have the same hullabaloo surrounding him. Still, he has nearly as much upside as the others. His pitchability and sequencing are impressive with his three-pitch arsenal. His fastball sits mid 90s and features arm-side tail. Command for this pitch can be lacking, but it played as an above-average pitch when thrown in the zone. Vizcaino's 88-90 mph power changeup is by far his best offering. The arm action doesn't slow down, making it a true swing-and-miss pitch, especially paired with his fastball. Displaying hard downward action and late tail, he is able to throw it to both right- and left-handed batters with success. Vizcaino's third offering is an 80-83 mph slider that lacks consistency. When he is able to snap off a good one it shows plus tilt with late bite. But feel for this pitch is still a work in progress. Due to his high-waisted, long-levered physicality, and a similar arsenal, Vizcaino reminds me a lot of Domingo German. There are no mechanical concerns, just the ability to throw strikes consistently.

Personal Cheeseball

PC Nick Nelson RHP

Born: 12/05/95 Age: 24 Bats: R Throws: R Height: 6'1" Weight: 195 Origin: Round 4, 2016 Draft (#128 overall)

YEAR	TEAM	LVL	AGE	W	L	SV	G	GS	IP	H	HR	BB/9	K/9	K	GB%	BABIP	WHIP	ERA	DRA	WARP	PF
2017	CSC	A	21	3	12	0	22	22	100²	103	5	4.5	9.8	110	47%	.356	1.52	4.56	5.88	-0.7	94
2018	CSC	A	22	1	1	0	5	5	24²	18	1	2.6	12.8	35	56%	.304	1.01	3.65	2.57	0.8	98
2018	TAM	A+	22	7	5	0	18	17	88¹	69	1	4.8	10.1	99	46%	.301	1.31	3.36	3.95	1.4	100
2018	TRN	AA	22	0	0	0	3	3	8²	10	1	9.3	10.4	10	50%	.360	2.19	5.19	7.28	-0.2	103
2019	TRN	AA	23	7	2	0	13	12	65	48	4	4.8	11.5	83	31%	.308	1.28	2.35	4.62	0.3	94
2019	SWB	AAA	23	1	1	0	4	4	21	20	2	3.0	10.3	24	45%	.321	1.29	4.71	2.75	0.8	106
2020	NYA	MLB	24	0	0	0	5	0	5	5	1	4.0	10.1	6	37%	.316	1.40	4.47	4.67	0.0	101

Comparables: Scott Barlow, Luis Escobar, Nick Pivetta

Jarrett and Jeffrey giggled when I jokingly ("jokingly" – j.p) clamored for Nelson to be in the Yankees Top 10. I knew that wasn't going to happen, but it got the point across: I was impressed by Nelson. Set to be a Rule 5 Draft-eligible prospect this offseason, the firm-bodied righty has three average or better pitches in his fastball, curve and change. The fastball was mid-90s, touching 97 in my look, and he maintained it throughout the entire start. The curve had really nice shape, going 11-5 and getting whiffs consistently. He left some of them in the middle of the zone, but the command of the pitch improved as the game progressed. The change was less impressive, as it was a little firm. It occasionally flashed impressive tumble, though, and I'm confident there's further projection for the pitch. Nelson's age, inconsistent feel for the change and command profile would suggest he's a future reliever, but he's also relatively new to pitching and has made strides on the mound every year. He has a major league future of some sort coming—perhaps I'm the lone advocate on the staff in thinking there's a potential mid-to-backend starter—and Nelson's three pitch mix shouldn't go unnoticed.

Low Minors Sleeper

LMS **Anderson Munoz** **RHP**
Born: 08/04/98   Age: 21   Bats: R   Throws: R   Height: 5'8"   Weight: 158   Origin: International Free Agent, 2017

YEAR	TEAM	LVL	AGE	W	L	SV	G	GS	IP	H	HR	BB/9	K/9	K	GB%	BABIP	WHIP	ERA	DRA	WARP	PF
2018	YAN	RK	19	1	5	0	11	9	36¹	38	4	6.4	9.4	38	48%	.327	1.76	5.20	7.83	-0.7	102
2019	STA	A-	20	7	2	0	13	10	62¹	46	1	3.3	9.1	63	45%	.278	1.11	2.60	4.18	0.7	98
2019	CSC	A	20	1	1	0	6	0	22	20	2	5.7	12.7	31	53%	.340	1.55	6.14	5.80	-0.3	100
2020	NYA	MLB	21	2	2	0	33	0	35	35	5	3.6	7.7	30	42%	.290	1.40	4.74	4.87	0.1	101

Like Deivi Garcia, Munoz is an undersized righty with plus arm strength. His fastball sits in the low-to-mid 90s and has gotten up to 99 as a starter. He has a hard slider that lacks consistent shape and acts more like a cutter at times but will flash average with good tilt. He also has a change that serves as a change-of-pace pitch but not much else, although it's better than the average changeup you will see in the Penn League. I like Munoz because he has a very repeatable delivery and has made significant strides in his strike-throwing ability (6.44 BB/9 in 2018 vs. 3.32 in 2019 NYPL). There is a fair bit of reliever risk because of the frame and mediocre secondaries, but he's made enough strides in key areas where we're at least keeping our eyes on him.

Top Talents 25 and Under (as of 4/1/2020)

1. Gleyber Torres
2. Deivi Garcia
3. Miguel Andujar
4. Clint Frazier
5. Jasson Dominguez
6. Albert Abreu
7. Luis Medina
8. Luis Gil
9. Anthony Volpe
10. Estevan Florial

Gleyber Torres is a star. He took a small step forward with the bat, as more of his raw power started to play in games—the baseballs probably didn't hurt there either—and he was top-five in DRC+ for a second baseman. He can pitch in at shortstop adequately as well, as he did during Didi Gregorius's absence, and he still has two more years of eligibility for this 25U list. He's the overwhelming favorite to be number one in 2021 and 2022 as well and the best may be yet to come.

Garcia has the best outside shot to unseat him. If it all comes together as a front-of-the-rotation starter, he'll have a case, but Torres is already approaching his OFP 70 projection as a prospect. Garcia still has a ways to go. Andujar lost the season to a right labrum injury that eventually required surgery. He was already likely to slide across the infield, and this might accelerate the process. After his strong rookie campaign with the bat in 2018 he's likely to have a spot waiting for him, though, unlike Clint Frazier. Frazier was fine at the plate in 2019, but had some high profile defensive miscues and equally high profile spats with the notoriously easygoing NYC baseball media. He's a prime change of scenery candidate for playing time if nothing else, although he looks more like an average regular in a corner nowadays than a future star.

Tyler Wade is a useful super-utility type on a team a bit worse than the Yankees, although the hit tool never developed as well as we'd hoped against major league arms. Chance Adams has struggled to regain his velocity or command after arm issues. Pitchers, man. The Yankees have graduated a lot of top prospect talent in recent seasons, much of which currently forms the core of their 100-win division winner. It's still a strong system overall, but there's less immediate help on the farm and some uncertainty with the Andujars and Severinos of the world at the moment.

Eyewitness Reports

Eyewitness Report: Albert Abreu

Evaluator: Jeffrey Paternostro
Report Date: 05/28/2019
Dates Seen: 5/19/19
Risk Factor: High
Delivery: Semi-wind up, breaks at his hip, average arc to three-quarters slot with plus arm speed. Minimal lower half engagement with hitch/hesitiation. Athletic and repeats okay despite the weird timing stuff, but lost the delivery/command a bit deeper in the outing.

Pitch Type	Future Grade	Sitting Velocity	Peak Velocity	Report
FB	70	95-98	99	Average command, occasional run, worked up in the zone with the four-seam. High spin offering with late life up. Could change eye levels when needed. More 93-95 later in the start, but kept the top end velocity.
CU	60	79-82	82	Better command of the curve than the fastball, can manipulate the shape and show some different looks to it. Power breaker, will manipulate it between 11-5 and 11-6, but consistently tight, very polished pitch, potential plus with refinement, half-grade or so shy of that at present. Command wavered late but kept at it, would throw 3-2
CH	45		0	Struggled to turn it over, would cut, firm, but flashed a half dozen good ones. Clearly a point of in-game emphasis. Enough here to 5 if you really wanted to, but it's a ways off that at present. Should be enough change to start if the rest of the profile cooperates

Conclusion: There's a 7 outcome here, change flashes better than your typical 6/high backend top 101 guy, but injuries and durability issues keep the risk factor high enough to keep the OFP there for me. Could be a two starter, could be in the MLB pen by August, could get hurt again. Checkered injury history along with some mechanical/command questions makes a late-inning reliever outcome more likely than mid-rotation starter for me.

Eyewitness Report: Ezequiel Duran

Evaluator: Jeffrey Paternostro
Report Date: 07/30/2019
Dates Seen: 7/24-7/25
Risk Factor: High
Physical/Health: Frame is a little rectangular with a long trunk. Minimal projection, but already a strong kid. More athletic than you'd expect, but I'd expect him to fill out a bit more in his twenties and lose a bit of flexibility and foot speed.

Tool	Future Grade	Report
Hit	50	Even stance, medium leg kick. Hands start high, drop and go, above-average bat speed with some loft. Can be vulnerable up, still adjusting to spin from college arms, but there is a semblance of an approach. Hard contact, can drive the ball to all fields. Sacrifices some barrel control for power at present, but doesn't get pull-happy and uses the big part of the park well. Average projection but high risk.
Power	55	Plus raw, power already plays to the opposite field gap. Strong kid and I'd expect him to get stronger and lose some of the occasional stiffness in the swing to get to the power. 20-home-run potential.
Baserunning/Speed	45	4.3 dig, sub-12 first-to-third, but I expect he'll slow down a bit in his twenties. Range at second will be fine.
Glove	60	Everything is smooth. He moves well laterally, soft hands, good actions. Comfortable around the bag both giving and receiving double play feeds. Nothing stands out as amazing, but more than the sum of his tools defender at second.
Arm	55	Above-average arm strength, accurate from a variety of angles and on the move. Can get it out in a hurry when needed, but I enjoy the casual flair he shows as well.

Conclusion: Duran projects as an above-average second baseman who could offer you some pop towards the bottom of the lineup of a first division team. There's significant risk in the hit tool until we see him against better arms, but the raw power and defensive tools give him a utility fallback position even if he's more of a .230-.240 hitter. There's also some positive risk if something clicks in the approach/swing mechanics with further pro instruction.

Oakland Athletics

The State of the System

We aren't sure yet, but this is potentially the most average system in baseball.

The Top Ten

★ ★ ★ *2020 Top 101 Prospect* **#9** ★ ★ ★

1 Jesus Luzardo   LHP   OFP: 70   ETA: 2019

Born: 09/30/97   Age: 22   Bats: L   Throws: L   Height: 6'0"   Weight: 209   Origin: Round 3, 2016 Draft (#94 overall)

YEAR	TEAM	LVL	AGE	W	L	SV	G	GS	IP	H	HR	BB/9	K/9	K	GB%	BABIP	WHIP	ERA	DRA	WARP	PF
2017	NAT	RK	19	1	0	0	3	3	13²	14	1	0.0	9.9	15	33%	.342	1.02	1.32	3.00	0.4	106
2017	ATH	RK	19	0	1	0	4	3	11²	9	0	0.8	10.0	13	58%	.290	0.86	1.54	2.17	0.5	100
2017	VER	A-	19	1	0	0	5	5	18	12	1	2.0	10.0	20	53%	.250	0.89	2.00	2.75	0.5	104
2018	STO	A+	20	2	1	0	3	3	14²	6	0	3.1	15.3	25	56%	.240	0.75	1.23	1.88	0.6	93
2018	MID	AA	20	7	3	0	16	16	78²	58	5	2.1	9.8	86	46%	.268	0.97	2.29	2.70	2.4	108
2018	NAS	AAA	20	1	1	0	4	4	16	25	2	3.9	10.1	18	51%	.469	2.00	7.31	7.75	-0.4	91
2019	STO	A+	21	1	0	0	3	1	10	6	1	0.0	16.2	18	50%	.294	0.60	0.90	2.19	0.3	98
2019	LVG	AAA	21	1	1	0	7	7	31	29	3	2.3	9.9	34	56%	.302	1.19	3.19	2.57	1.2	109
2019	OAK	MLB	21	0	0	2	6	0	12	5	1	2.2	12.0	16	42%	.160	0.67	1.50	3.32	0.3	103
2020	OAK	MLB	22	9	7	0	43	21	128	109	18	3.7	10.9	156	48%	.293	1.25	3.69	3.98	2.2	96

Comparables: Luiz Gohara, Alex Reyes, Tyler Skaggs

The Report: A southpaw with three potential plus pitches. That's it, man. That's the report.

It's all you need, but we here at the Baseball Prospectus Prospect Team aren't exactly known for restraint when it comes to describing the best prospects in baseball. So with that in mind…

The fastball is easy mid 90s as a starter. There wasn't any more noticeable effort when he was dialing it up to 98-99 out of the major league bullpen late last season. Luzardo can run it into righties, or turn it over with some arm-side wiggle. The command is plus. He keeps the pitch down where it shows some sink. He can elevate it for Ks. The curveball is a power breaker with slider velocity and big lateral break. If you want to nitpick, it doesn't always show ideal depth from his three-quarters slot, but the velocity and command of the pitch should get it to plus regardless. The change comes in even harder, but still has around 10 mph of separation from the fastball and above-average dive. It's the pitch here most in need of refinement, but we are only talking about refinement.

Luzardo is a shorter lefty with a bad injury track record, and looked so good in the pen that you'd be tempted to make him your modern fireman, but he should get every chance to start in 2020, and as long as he has a shot to start, he's one of the best starting pitching prospects in baseball.

Variance: Medium. Luzardo has had arm issues recently. He had a Tommy John surgery right out of high school. He's never thrown more than 109 1/3 innings in a season. There's some risk he might just be one of the better late inning arms in baseball. There's also some risk he gets hurt again and never reaches his enormous potential. On the other hand if he puts it all together, he's one of the few arms I'll throw the "ace upside" tag on.

Mark Barry's Fantasy Take: With all due respect to dudes like MacKenzie Gore or Casey Mize, Luzardo is my favorite dynasty pitching prospect in the game. Sure, I would've preferred if he tossed a few more innings in 2019, and the injuries aren't fun (feels like I'm trying to talk myself out of this, but I promise you, I'm not), but Luzardo should start the season in the rotation, and the domination should shortly follow. Mid-90's heat with two solid secondaries and plus command? Yes, I will sign up for that.

★ ★ ★ *2020 Top 101 Prospect* **#17** ★ ★ ★

2 A.J. Puk LHP   OFP: 70   ETA: 2019
Born: 04/25/95   Age: 25   Bats: L   Throws: L   Height: 6'7"   Weight: 238   Origin: Round 1, 2016 Draft (#6 overall)

YEAR	TEAM	LVL	AGE	W	L	SV	G	GS	IP	H	HR	BB/9	K/9	K	GB%	BABIP	WHIP	ERA	DRA	WARP	PF
2017	STO	A+	22	4	5	0	14	11	61	44	1	3.4	14.5	98	42%	.336	1.10	3.69	2.35	2.0	105
2017	MID	AA	22	2	5	0	13	13	64	64	2	3.5	12.1	86	48%	.380	1.39	4.36	3.51	1.3	108
2019	STO	A+	24	0	0	0	3	3	6	5	2	6.0	13.5	9	33%	.300	1.50	6.00	5.31	0.0	96
2019	MID	AA	24	0	0	0	6	1	8¹	9	2	3.2	14.0	13	58%	.412	1.44	4.32	5.92	-0.1	69
2019	LVG	AAA	24	4	1	0	9	0	11	7	3	2.5	13.1	16	45%	.222	0.91	4.91	2.25	0.4	100
2019	OAK	MLB	24	2	0	0	10	0	11¹	10	1	4.0	10.3	13	45%	.321	1.32	3.18	3.44	0.2	99
2020	OAK	MLB	25	7	6	0	43	16	110	97	17	3.3	10.4	127	44%	.292	1.25	3.78	4.11	1.6	96

Comparables: José De León, Sean Newcomb, Brian Matusz

The Report: Hey it's another lefty with no-shit power stuff. Puk started rehab from his 2018 Tommy John surgery in June, and stormed to the majors by the end of August. His fastball sits a tick higher than even Luzardo's, regularly registering upper 90s on your Stalker. An upper-90s fastball would rarely be described as sneaky fast, as it's just fast-fast, but Puk's length and long stride creates a nightmare angle and release point for batters. 98 gets on you fast regardless, but Puk's gets on you even faster. The long levers have led to control and command issues, and the fastball can run a little true at times, but it's still an easy 70 with elite potential if he corrals the command even a bit more.

Puk's slider is another potential plus-plus weapon in his holster. It routinely touches 90 and tunnels well off the fastball. It's not a big breaker, but the firmness and tilt make it a true swing-and-miss offering. The changeup will flash plus, but doesn't have much fade to it and here the firmness—it also hovers near 90—can sometimes make it seem like just a below-average fastball. At other times there's enough sink and velo separation to make it a real asset. Puk also offers a "slower" curveball in the low 80s for a different breaking ball look. It can get a bit lazy at times, but it's a useful change of pace offering in light of his other three pitches.

Puk's main issue has been the fineness of the command and the control profile, and a guy that size is never going to be Bob Tewksbury. The stuff is good enough he can be a top-of-the-rotation arm with a 10% walk rate, but it's a fine line between effectively wild and inefficiently wild. His late-season cameo could be a preview of what he could look like as a lights out closer, but like with Luzardo, give him every chance to start. And coming off Tommy John, he needs the innings anyway.

Variance: Medium. Puk was functionally still on Tommy John rehab while blowing guys away in the majors in September. On the one hand, the recent elbow issues are a red flag. On the other, he might get more comfortable with the breaking stuff and command when he's another six months out from the surgery date. On the, uh, third hand, he hasn't really answered the question of whether he will throw enough strikes to start yet.

Mark Barry's Fantasy Take: Top-shelf stuff, gaudy strikeout numbers, cringe-inducing WHIP potential, debut stints in the bullpen, uh, long hair—sounds a lot like the Josh Hader recipe for bullpen stud-ness. To be fair, I like Puk quite a bit more than I liked Hader at this point in their respective careers, but the similarities are stark. Anecdotally, the control is the last thing to come back after Tommy John surgery, so maybe Puk will refine some of the mechanical issues that lead to high charitability. If the walks persist, he's probably a reliever. A very, very good reliever, mind you, but a reliever nonetheless.

★ ★ ★ *2020 Top 101 Prospect* **#44** ★ ★ ★

3 Sean Murphy C OFP: 60 ETA: 2019

Born: 10/10/94 Age: 25 Bats: R Throws: R Height: 6'3" Weight: 232 Origin: Round 3, 2016 Draft (#83 overall)

YEAR	TEAM	LVL	AGE	PA	R	2B	3B	HR	RBI	BB	K	SB	CS	AVG/OBP/SLG	DRC+	VORP	BABIP	BRR	FRAA	WARP	PF
2017	STO	A+	22	178	22	11	0	9	26	11	33	0	0	.297/.343/.527	132	15.1	.323	0.2	C(40) -0.3	1.3	100
2017	MID	AA	22	217	25	7	0	4	22	21	34	0	0	.209/.288/.309	58	2.1	.232	0.6	C(51) 3.8	0.6	106
2018	MID	AA	23	289	51	26	2	8	43	23	47	3	0	.288/.358/.498	137	22.5	.324	2.1	C(65) 14.5	4.2	111
2019	AGO	RK	24	32	8	2	0	1	1	4	4	0	0	.214/.313/.393	122	0.0	.217	0.2	C(8) -0.1	0.2	100
2019	LVG	AAA	24	140	25	6	1	10	30	15	31	0	1	.308/.386/.625	122	13.4	.329	-1.3	C(27) 1.5	1.0	111
2019	OAK	MLB	24	60	14	5	0	4	8	6	16	0	0	.245/.333/.566	98	2.9	.273	1.1	C(18) -1.6	0.2	100
2020	OAK	MLB	25	385	43	18	1	16	50	31	98	1	0	.227/.297/.421	90	0.0	.268	-0.6	C -4	0.7	96

Comparables: J.T. Realmuto, Chris Parmelee, Ty France

The Report: Murphy dealt with knee issues on and off all year, eventually requiring surgery for a torn meniscus. Once he got back on the field, though, he mashed in Triple-A and won the lion's share of the A's catching job in September. Murphy is one of the best defensive catchers in the minors, and should quickly become one of the better ones in the majors. It's a large frame by backstop standards, but he's athletic and a solid receiver. He gets out of his crouch well and combines it with a well above-average, accurate arm. He also gets high marks for working with pitchers.

The glove alone would make him a viable starting catcher, but Murphy has some juice in his bat as well. He's a big, strong kid who swings hard, and while it isn't the easiest plus raw you'll see, there's 20+ bombs in the stroke due to plus bat speed and loft. The swing does get long and can be a little one-gear, so swing-and-miss is going to be the trade off for the dingers. The plate approach is strong as well, though, and there's the outline of a Three True Outcomes power bat here, which is more than enough to make him a plus regular behind the plate given the rest of the profile. And if Murphy finds a way to hit .270 now and again, he will make some all-star games.

Variance: Medium. Catchers are weird, but Murphy's defense is good enough that he could give you only .240 with 15 home runs and be a perfectly reasonable starter. There's more upside than that in the bat. He's also a 25-year-old catcher already dealing with knee problems.

Mark Barry's Fantasy Take: Murphy wasn't a trainwreck in his first stint behind the dish in Oakland, which is, you know, good (How's that for faint praise?). To be honest, I like Murphy. In a vacuum he has the skills to be a top-10 dude behind the plate, and the defensive skills to get plenty of chances. However, he's hurt more than the dude from the Operation game, and donning the tools of ignorance isn't typically conducive to preserving one's health. I'd have Murphy in the top-five (maybe even the top-three) dynasty catching prospects, but I'll also be holding my breath any time he hits or catches or when someone looks at him the wrong way.

4 Nick Allen SS OFP: 55 ETA: 2021

Born: 10/08/98 Age: 21 Bats: R Throws: R Height: 5'9" Weight: 166 Origin: Round 3, 2017 Draft (#81 overall)

YEAR	TEAM	LVL	AGE	PA	R	2B	3B	HR	RBI	BB	K	SB	CS	AVG/OBP/SLG	DRC+	VORP	BABIP	BRR	FRAA	WARP	PF
2017	ATH	RK	18	154	26	3	2	1	14	13	28	7	3	.254/.322/.326	99	6.8	.312	1.1	SS(33) 2.5	1.0	98
2018	BLT	A	19	512	51	17	6	0	34	34	85	24	8	.239/.301/.302	74	15.2	.289	3.7	SS(121) 5.2	1.8	101
2019	STO	A+	20	328	45	22	5	3	25	28	52	13	5	.292/.363/.434	135	17.6	.348	-4.4	SS(45) 4.7, 2B(24) -1.6	2.1	101
2020	OAK	MLB	21	251	20	11	1	3	21	15	56	5	2	.222/.277/.320	57	0.0	.281	0.2	SS 3, 2B 0	-0.2	96

Comparables: Ehire Adrianza, Tyler Wade, Jose Pirela

The Report: After selecting Allen in the third round of the 2017 amateur draft, Oakland convinced the SoCal prep infielder to forego his USC commitment. Long saddled with a reputation as a glove-over-bat shortstop, Allen was just as impressive offensively during an injury-limited campaign in the 2019 Cal League season. The 21-year-old infielder continues to mature physically and add strength to his listed 5-foot-9, 166-pound physique. Often batting at the top of the lineup, Allen's offensive profile works best as a tablesetter; he works counts, gets on base, and scores runs with a little help from his friends. The swing is compact and quick, and quality bat-to-ball supplements his patience to help the hit tool play up. Once aboard, Allen uses quickness and cunning to steal bases and be a general nuisance to opposing pitchers and defenses. A shortstop by nature, he logged a couple dozen games at second base as part of a semi-platoon with Stockton teammate Jeremy Eierman this past season. Allen's foundation of athleticism, adept fielding actions, and capable arm strength provide a path to above-average or better play at the six, and ensure he will thrive at any position in the infield if deployed in a utility role. Ultimately, his advanced baseball instincts and acumen should accelerate his offensive progression and have him ready to contribute at the big league-level by 2021.

Variance: Medium. The sturdy base of 'good defensive middle infielder' limits risk, however stalled offensive progress could result in a replaceable, light-hitting infielder a la Rafael Belliard.

Please don't confuse this guy with the Nick Allen that spent time behind the plate for the Cincinnati Reds in 1920, because rest assured, this is not that Nick Allen. He wasn't all that interesting heading into last season as a glove-first middle infielder, but a strong season with the stick surely perked up my ears. He's not going to hit for much, if any, power, but Allen could be a threat to steal 20 bags with a strong batting average, which means he needs to be on your radar.

5 Austin Beck OF   OFP: 55   ETA: Early 2022
Born: 11/21/98   Age: 21   Bats: R   Throws: R   Height: 6'1"   Weight: 200   Origin: Round 1, 2017 Draft (#6 overall)

YEAR	TEAM	LVL	AGE	PA	R	2B	3B	HR	RBI	BB	K	SB	CS	AVG/OBP/SLG	DRC+	VORP	BABIP	BRR	FRAA	WARP	PF
2017	ATH	RK	18	174	23	7	4	2	28	17	51	7	1	.211/.293/.349	59	2.7	.294	1.8	CF(33) 1.2	0.2	99
2018	BLT	A	19	534	58	29	4	2	60	30	117	8	6	.296/.335/.383	105	14.9	.377	-4.8	CF(113) 2.0	1.6	101
2019	STO	A+	20	367	40	22	4	8	49	24	126	2	2	.251/.302/.411	92	7.5	.372	-0.1	CF(69) -0.3, RF(10) 2.7	1.1	99
2020	OAK	MLB	21	251	20	12	1	3	22	16	95	1	1	.216/.270/.325	55	0.0	.347	-0.3	CF -2, RF 0	-0.8	96

Comparables: Willy García, Trayvon Robinson, Gabriel Guerrero

The Report: Oakland used the sixth-overall pick of the 2017 Draft to select Beck, a high school outfielder from North Carolina, before other notable first-round picks Keston Hiura and Jo Adell. The 20-year-old outfielder's 2019 Cal League campaign was interrupted by injury on multiple occasions, limiting him to just 85 games with inconsistent production when he was on the field. When healthy, the lean 6-foot-1, 200-pound athlete roams center field, showing plus range, efficient routes, and an above-average throwing arm. He could easily shift to either corner outfield position, but is suited for center thanks to his natural athleticism.

Offensively, Beck employs a gap-to-gap hitting approach and a level swing that limits the game utility of his strength-driven raw power, but does promote hard contact. His swing can still get lengthy, leading to inconsistent rates and quality of contact. The approach remains unrefined and aggressive; his 126 strikeouts and 24 walks in 338 at-bats this past season reflect his free-swinging mentality and inconsistent bat-to-ball skills. After contact, Beck's 60-grade speed allows him to hustle into plenty of extra bases, although he's yet to refine his base-stealing abilities. With advanced outfield defense and baserunning, it will be Beck's offensive progression that will dictate his big league ETA. The upside here is a plus-defending outfielder with a run-producing bat, though the latter half of that equation will take some time to flesh out even in a best-case scenario. At his current rate, the athletic center fielder should be ready to contribute at the big league level by late-2021 or the spring of 2022.

Variance: High. The hit tool is always difficult to handicap due to its blatant unpredictability. Beck's foundation of raw athleticism provides a certain degree of comfort, but his baseball-specific skills need further nurturing and cultivation.

Mark Barry's Fantasy Take: A defense-first athletic that just needs to learn how to hit. Where do I sign up? Kidding.

Beck struck out over 34 percent of the time at High-A last season, which leaves me bearish on his ability to hit enough to put his athleticism to work, especially in a fantasy sense. I don't typically have a penchant for giving up on 20-year-old, top-10 picks, but I'm kinda close on Beck.

6 Jorge Mateo SS   OFP: 55   ETA: 2020

Born: 06/23/95   Age: 25   Bats: R   Throws: R   Height: 6'0"   Weight: 192   Origin: International Free Agent, 2012

YEAR	TEAM	LVL	AGE	PA	R	2B	3B	HR	RBI	BB	K	SB	CS	AVG/OBP/SLG	DRC+	VORP	BABIP	BRR	FRAA	WARP	PF
2017	TAM	A+	22	297	39	16	8	4	11	16	79	28	3	.240/.288/.400	87	15.6	.321	7.6	SS(42) 2.9, CF(22) -0.8	1.8	98
2017	TRN	AA	22	140	26	9	3	4	26	15	32	11	7	.300/.381/.525	127	16.7	.372	1.6	SS(17) 1.1, CF(7) -0.4	1.3	95
2017	MID	AA	22	147	25	5	7	4	20	9	33	13	3	.292/.333/.518	105	14.8	.356	2.2	SS(30) 0.8	1.0	105
2018	NAS	AAA	23	510	50	17	16	3	45	29	139	25	10	.230/.280/.353	61	3.7	.316	1.1	SS(123) -0.8, 2B(4) -0.5	-0.1	91
2019	LVG	AAA	24	566	95	29	14	19	78	29	145	24	11	.289/.330/.504	81	27.8	.366	3.2	SS(100) 16.6, 2B(14) -0.2	2.9	110
2020	OAK	MLB	25	105	10	5	1	2	10	5	31	6	2	.228/.273/.372	67	0.0	.312	0.5	CF 0, 2B 0	0.1	96

Comparables: Abiatal Avelino, Andrew Velazquez, Yairo Muñoz

The Report: I have been writing about Jorge Mateo so long that I'm half-sure I made a shoebox diorama of him stealing second base in the Tampa complex for a sixth grade class project. You might look at the 19 home runs this year—more than his 2017 and 2018 combined—and give credit to the new Triple-A ball and move from Nashville to Las Vegas for his 2019 home games. That probably explains some of the power bump, but Mateo has gotten stronger and added loft to his swing, so fringe or maybe even average game power isn't out of the realm of possibility now. How much the newfound pop plays in the majors remains an open question as his overaggressive approach is still here and may get exploited by the best arms in the world. The Yankees experimented with Mateo in the outfield, but the A's have essentially made him their Triple-A starting shortstop, with the occasional reps at second mixed in. He remains a passable if rough fit there, but he's not displacing Marcus Semien anyway. His speed remains a true weapon, although he's not the volume base-stealer he was in the low minors—possibly because he's not on base as much. Overall, it was a bounce back year for Mateo and he's basically ready for a superutility or fifth infield role on a good team.

Variance: Medium. That's high for a guy with two seasons of Triple-A under his belt but there are still unanswered questions about the hit tool utility against better stuff. The other part of the variance here is Mateo is the type of profile that might be significantly impacted by which baseballs Rawlings decides to put on the assembly line next year. Projecting that is out of my purview.

Mark Barry's Fantasy Take: It would be awesome if you could take, like, five percentage points from Mateo's strikeout rate and tack them on to his walk rate, but alas, we don't have the technology for that yet. The increase of power this season is encouraging, but his fantasy relevance is, and always will be, tied to his ability to get on base to utilize his blazing speed. Let's welcome Mateo back to the top-150ish and cross our fingers that he can get on base more than 30 percent of the time.

7 Robert Puason SS   OFP: 60   ETA: 2024ish

Born: 09/11/02   Age: 17   Bats: B   Throws: R   Height: 6'3"   Weight: 165   Origin: International Free Agent, 2019

The Report: I first wrote about Robert Puason back in 2017, almost two years before he was eligible to sign with a major-league organization. By that time, his agent had already agreed to an illegal deal with the Atlanta Braves that involved international cap circumvention. The Braves were subsequently barred from signing him, and general manager John Coppolella was banned for life as part of the greater scandal. According to ESPN's Jeff Passan, Robert Puason was just 13 when that deal was struck.

A short time after Atlanta was barred from signing Puason, word started spreading throughout the industry that he had a deal for similar money with Oakland. As it almost always does with high profile July 2 signings, the word turned out to be correct, and the A's spent the vast majority of their pool on him earlier this year.

In the intervening time since Puason became a prominent prospect and agreed to these deals and when they were actually signed, Jasson Dominguez has passed him as a prospect. He's still generally considered the second-best player from the 2019-20 J2 talent pool, a projectable and toolsy infielder. Like with Dominguez, we just really don't have a whole lot to go on here because he hasn't seen real game action quite yet, although he did play in instructs. We do think he probably deserves to be ranked somewhere, and this is our best guess as to where that is.

But we simply cannot ignore the elephant in the room here, either. It is inherently wrong to be locking 13-year-olds up in handshake agreements years in advance of when you can actually sign them, with no protections and the burden entirely on the player. It's just wrong, and MLB has chosen to turn the other way on this and only care about pool manipulation instead. And that is a big part of Puason's story.

Variance: Extreme. There's nothing here that's all that different from Kevin Maitan at the same age—right down to the illegal early deal with Atlanta—and you probably know how that turned out.

Mark Barry's Fantasy Take: Like many J2 teenagers, lots of Puason's skills have been shrouded in secrecy, or at least grainy YouTube clips and vague "I Love How He Plays" statements from the team. Also like J2 teenagers, his value is bound to be artificially goosed. I'd have him in the first 8-10 picks for first year player drafts this winter, but not in the top five.

8. Daulton Jefferies RHP   OFP: 55   ETA: Late 2020

Born: 08/02/95   Age: 24   Bats: L   Throws: R   Height: 6'0"   Weight: 182   Origin: Round 1, 2016 Draft (#37 overall)

YEAR	TEAM	LVL	AGE	W	L	SV	G	GS	IP	H	HR	BB/9	K/9	K	GB%	BABIP	WHIP	ERA	DRA	WARP	PF
2017	STO	A+	21	0	0	0	2	1	7	7	0	1.3	7.7	6	67%	.292	1.14	2.57	4.07	0.1	101
2019	STO	A+	23	1	0	0	5	3	15	10	1	1.2	12.6	21	44%	.273	0.80	2.40	2.57	0.4	96
2019	MID	AA	23	1	2	0	21	12	64	63	7	1.0	10.1	72	42%	.327	1.09	3.66	3.39	1.1	102
2020	OAK	MLB	24	1	1	0	22	0	23	23	3	3.0	9.4	24	40%	.308	1.32	4.27	4.63	0.1	96

Comparables: Michael King, Daniel Gossett, Brandon Workman

The Report: Jefferies finally got back on the mound after a 2017 Tommy John surgery followed by rehab issues in 2018. Durability questions were present even before the Tommy John, as he's a shorter, leaner righty who had shoulder issues in college. The volume has only been turned up there after missing almost two full seasons, but the good news is the stuff has come back. The fastball sits mid 90s in short bursts. It can run a little true, but occasionally flashes a bit of arm-side hop. The command profile isn't great either due to his short arm action and crossfire delivery.

Jeffries best secondary is a hard cutter that will flash slider-like two-plane action. He also mixes in a 11-6 curve around 80, which can be a bit of an up-and-under, humpy offering, but shows decent depth and gives a different breaking ball look and a different velo band for hitters to deal with. He rounds out the four-pitch mix with a firm changeup which lacks ideal velocity separation—it routinely hits 90—but offers wiffle-ball-like hard fade and dive when he turns it over.

Jeffries has a squint-and-you-can-see-it arsenal of four average-or-better pitches, but the likelihood is they don't all actually get there, and the injury track record might mean he's better suited to shorter outings. For now he needs more healthy innings, period. We'll check back after 2020, but 2019 was a success, albeit qualified.

Variance: Very high. His last healthy season was 2015, his sophomore year at Cal. There are reliever markers in the delivery and frame, and the fastball can run a little true and play down from the plus velo it shows. But if he's actually healthy and puts it together in 2020, the stuff isn't all that dissimilar from your backend 101 type.

Mark Barry's Fantasy Take: Jeffries flashes some decent skills and has certainly posted impressive strikeout numbers. But the whole "Only Pitched 20 1/3 innings from 2016-2018" thing makes him a risk I'm not taking. His proximity could keep him in the Top-200 range, but he's not there for me.

9. Sheldon Neuse 3B   OFP: 50   ETA: 2019

Born: 12/10/94   Age: 25   Bats: R   Throws: R   Height: 6'0"   Weight: 218   Origin: Round 2, 2016 Draft (#58 overall)

YEAR	TEAM	LVL	AGE	PA	R	2B	3B	HR	RBI	BB	K	SB	CS	AVG/OBP/SLG	DRC+	VORP	BABIP	BRR	FRAA	WARP	PF
2017	HAG	A	22	321	40	19	3	9	51	25	66	12	5	.291/.349/.469	147	26.7	.347	-1.9	SS(43) -2.9, 3B(33) 6.6	3.0	101
2017	STO	A+	22	94	21	3	0	7	22	9	25	2	0	.386/.457/.675	217	17.0	.490	0.4	3B(10) -1.5, SS(8) -0.4	1.3	100
2017	MID	AA	22	75	9	4	0	0	6	6	21	0	0	.373/.427/.433	142	4.9	.532	0.3	3B(18) 1.4, 1B(1) -0.4	0.7	109
2018	NAS	AAA	23	537	48	26	3	5	55	32	172	4	1	.263/.304/.357	77	11.4	.385	-0.4	3B(130) -3.1, 2B(1) 0.0	0.2	91
2019	LVG	AAA	24	560	99	31	2	27	102	56	132	3	3	.317/.389/.550	117	39.2	.384	0.3	3B(96) 12.3, 2B(15) 0.6	4.4	109
2019	OAK	MLB	24	61	3	3	0	0	7	4	19	0	0	.250/.295/.304	70	-0.4	.368	0.3	2B(20) -1.4, 3B(5) -0.3	-0.2	100
2020	OAK	MLB	25	175	17	8	1	5	19	12	52	1	0	.245/.302/.388	81	2.0	.333	-0.2	2B -1, SS 0	0.1	96

Comparables: Cody Asche, Preston Tucker, Trea Turner

The Report: The A's acquired Neuse in 2017 and aggressively assigned him to Triple-A the following season after he'd logged just a dozen and a half games in the Texas League, and it didn't work out so well at the time. The former second-rounder promptly got exposed by better velocity and guile, and offensive struggles snowballed for the better part of the year before a late surge in the second half. And lo, the moon ball cameth; Neuse was able to get his approach development back on track last season while tapping into zero-gravity power. It's a relatively compact swing with a minimal load and quick hips that produce some bat speed, and while he still puts the ball on the ground too much he's learned to better leverage himself in hitting counts, so there's cause for hope that last year's over-the-fence outburst wasn't entirely context-driven. He's a solid if unspectacular third baseman, and the club started to move him around a bit last season with reps at second, short (where he played in college), and even a couple glimpses in left. The versatility can only help his quest to carve out a regular role, and the best-case scenario has him contributing average defensive value across a couple spots, hitting some bombs, and playing a solid, everyday role. In the meantime, he can plug in for the A's whenever they need him next season and try again to slow down big-league pitching and get his career rolling in The Show.

Variance: Medium. It's not that there's a huge amount of volatility here, it's just not the most unique of profiles or dynamic of skill sets for the role. He's ready to roll, but the downside is an up-and-down guy.

Mark Barry's Fantasy Take: Lazy teammate comp time! I get some Chad Pinder vibes from Neuse (with maybe slightly higher upside). If that leaves you cold, that's ok, I'm a little chilly too. The potential positional flexibility makes Neuse an AL-only stash, but I'm not running out to grab him elsewhere.

10 Logan Davidson SS   OFP: 50   ETA: 2022

Born: 12/26/97   Age: 22   Bats: B   Throws: R   Height: 6'3"   Weight: 185   Origin: Round 1, 2019 Draft (#29 overall)

YEAR	TEAM	LVL	AGE	PA	R	2B	3B	HR	RBI	BB	K	SB	CS	AVG/OBP/SLG	DRC+	VORP	BABIP	BRR	FRAA	WARP	PF
2019	VER	A-	21	238	42	7	0	4	12	31	55	5	0	.239/.345/.332	133	16.0	.308	1.5	SS(49) 11.8	3.0	93
2020	OAK	MLB	22	251	22	11	0	5	24	16	80	2	1	.214/.268/.334	59	0.0	.300	0.0	SS 4	-0.1	96

Comparables: Tyler Greene, Taylor Featherston, Trea Turner

The Report: The draft day consensus pegged Davidson as a tall, switch-hitting shortstop with some athleticism and pop but a questionable hit tool. The current consensus is he's a tall, switch-hitting shortstop with some athleticism and pop but a questionable hit tool. He struggled badly in the Penn League outside of a torrid week and a half stretch, and at the time some scouts were hypothesizing his long season and small Vermont crowds might be the culprit. I'm personally a bit skeptical of that reasoning, as Davidson's issues are more related to his timing and long swing. He utilizes a quiet load which likely isn't ideal for his long-limbed body, as the body can get stiff as the pitcher begins his throwing motion. His underwhelming professional debut only serves as a continuation of poor wood bat performance spanning back to his Cape Cod days.

All this said, we'd be doing a disservice by not highlighting the attractive characteristics in the profile, characteristics which are first round-worthy: there is above-average raw power from both sides of the plate, and he plays an adequate defensive shortstop. He drove the ball to all fields in the ACC, and doing so in pro ball will be key as he moves up the ladder.

Variance: High. There are real concerns about the hit tool that could require a swing adjustment. That's easier said than done for switch-hitters.

Mark Barry's Fantasy Take: After questions about his hit tool, Davidson posted a .239 batting average in his first 238 trips to the plate. He did walk a lot though, and the potential power/speed combo is fun to dream on. That said, it's a little like buying the body of a race car with a Ford Escort engine (might be harsh, but whatever). A league needs 250+ prospects for me to take a flier on Davidson.

The Next Five

11 Lazaro Armenteros OF

Born: 05/22/99   Age: 21   Bats: R   Throws: R   Height: 6'0"   Weight: 182   Origin: International Free Agent, 2016

YEAR	TEAM	LVL	AGE	PA	R	2B	3B	HR	RBI	BB	K	SB	CS	AVG/OBP/SLG	DRC+	VORP	BABIP	BRR	FRAA	WARP	PF
2017	DAT	RK	18	26	6	0	0	0	1	3	9	2	2	.167/.385/.167	39	1.8	.300	0.9	CF(6) 1.5	0.2	89
2017	ATH	RK	18	181	24	9	4	4	22	16	48	10	1	.288/.376/.474	110	14.5	.387	2.8	LF(28) 4.2, CF(2) -0.5	1.1	99
2018	BLT	A	19	340	43	8	2	8	39	36	115	8	6	.277/.374/.401	121	21.6	.427	2.1	LF(69) -0.7	1.6	101
2019	STO	A+	20	538	65	22	5	17	61	73	227	22	6	.222/.336/.403	102	18.0	.395	2.4	LF(112) -1.3, CF(7) -0.1	1.4	100
2020	OAK	MLB	21	251	20	11	1	4	21	19	113	2	1	.191/.264/.295	46	0.0	.357	0.0	LF 1, CF 0	-0.7	96

Comparables: Tyler O'Neill, Ryan McMahon, Nick Williams

On one hand, Armenteros drips strength and physicality; at 20 he's already filled out plenty, and it's just one of those bodies that was built to grow more and more muscle through his 20s. He's got some quicker-twitch aesthetics to his movements now, though he's likely to stiffen some as he matures into the gobs of top-half strength left to come, and his presently above-average straight line speed should fade a bit. His age also earns him some slack for the year's performance, as he was one of the younger regulars in his High-A league. Caveats notwithstanding, though, it was a really rough year to watch. The swing mechanics are often disjointed, with a high back shoulder that can create awkward angles into the zone when he's slightly off-time, and a tight bottom hand that'll get too strong and leave the barrel dragging under balls on the regular. There are significant swaths of the zone in which he's currently vulnerable, and he also showed plenty of willingness to expand above and below it without much improvement as the season wore on. Despite his strength the throw tool isn't great, so it's a left field profile, and he wasn't especially consistent at reading contact or judging trajectory in that corner this year. All of this is to say that he's still really, really raw. The physicality is such that it could very well click and turn into an impressive package. But that's unlikely to happen quickly, and his will be one of the more interesting developmental journeys in the system next year.

12 Grant Holmes   RHP

Born: 03/22/96   Age: 24   Bats: L   Throws: R   Height: 6'0"   Weight: 224   Origin: Round 1, 2014 Draft (#22 overall)

YEAR	TEAM	LVL	AGE	W	L	SV	G	GS	IP	H	HR	BB/9	K/9	K	GB%	BABIP	WHIP	ERA	DRA	WARP	PF
2017	MID	AA	21	11	12	0	29	24	148¹	149	15	3.7	9.1	150	46%	.328	1.42	4.49	4.54	1.0	106
2018	STO	A+	22	0	0	0	2	2	6	4	1	3.0	12.0	8	47%	.214	1.00	4.50	2.62	0.2	94
2019	MID	AA	23	6	5	0	22	16	81²	71	9	3.0	8.4	76	52%	.281	1.20	3.31	4.78	0.1	102
2020	OAK	MLB	24	2	2	0	31	3	43	43	7	3.6	7.7	37	46%	.288	1.40	4.73	4.96	0.2	96

Comparables: Jesse Biddle, Lucas Sims, Raúl Alcántara

Holmes at 12 in this system represents the prospect version of a waystation. Injuries have plagued the righty, but 2019 also included more flashes of his first-round talent. His recovery from rotator cuff surgery included spending most of his time in Double-A Midland, where he came out innings-limited and gradually worked his way up to more robust outings before finishing up with a single Triple-A Las Vegas start. The velocity and pitch quality at season's open looked wonky, but as time went on and the surgery fell further into the rearview Holmes began to find it a little more regularly. When it's working it's the same moving fastball/okay cutter/downer curve combo that propelled his early career, but he made impressive strides in keeping that arsenal in the zone—an issue that has long limited his when-healthy development. Injuries will be a valid risk factor to consider at every step on his path, but the sum total of this age-23 season was a large and encouraging one in the right direction. Next season will be about maintaining his consistency gains, staying on the bump long enough to improve on them, and potentially seeing how it plays against major leaguers. It's hard to imagine Holmes doesn't start his 2020 campaign in Las Vegas, and with Oakland's seemingly fearless nature about advancement, Holmes could see the big leagues sooner than later. It's also been long enough into this writeup to tell you that Holmes has amazing hair, if you didn't already know. The #flow is an easy 7, and the best of Holmes' tools without question. If he can ride the waves on his scalp, he's never gonna fail.

13 Alfonso Rivas   1B/OF

Born: 09/13/96   Age: 23   Bats: L   Throws: L   Height: 6'0"   Weight: 188   Origin: Round 4, 2018 Draft (#113 overall)

YEAR	TEAM	LVL	AGE	PA	R	2B	3B	HR	RBI	BB	K	SB	CS	AVG/OBP/SLG	DRC+	VORP	BABIP	BRR	FRAA	WARP	PF
2018	VER	A-	21	257	33	16	1	1	28	36	44	7	4	.285/.397/.383	167	16.8	.351	-2.6	1B(40) -2.4, LF(4) -0.3	1.2	100
2019	STO	A+	22	509	60	24	3	8	55	66	113	2	2	.283/.383/.408	135	24.8	.362	-1.5	1B(98) -0.7, LF(7) -0.8	1.9	101
2019	LVG	AAA	22	34	2	2	1	1	5	2	7	0	0	.406/.441/.625	103	0.1	.500	-2.4	1B(7) -0.3, LF(1) 0.1	-0.2	117
2020	OAK	MLB	23	251	23	12	1	4	24	18	69	1	0	.239/.300/.358	74	1.0	.321	0.0	1B 0, LF 0	0.0	96

The A's fourth-round selection in the 2018 Draft out of the University of Arizona, Rivas' polished skill set and high baseball IQ establish a high floor for the first baseman/outfielder. Rivas slashed .292/.387/.423 across two-levels in the 2019 season, including eight late-season games with the Triple-A Las Vegas Aviators where he went 13-for-32 (.406 AVG). The fast-twitch athleticism and manual dexterity that make him a plus-defending first baseman also allowed him to play 11 games in left field this season, adding defensive versatility to his resume. Offensively, Rivas has plus bat-to-ball abilities and a line-to-line approach that enabled him to accumulate 39 extra-base hits, nine of which were long balls. Equipped with his newfound defensive versatility and advanced offensive acumen, Rivas should continue to rapidly matriculate through the Oakland farm system. Considering Matt Olson's current Gold Glove-occupation of first base, Rivas' versatility is vital within the A's organization. Capable of providing quality left-handed at-bats and playing multiple positions, he'd be a valuable contributor off the bench or in a potential trade.

14 James Kaprielian RHP
Born: 03/02/94 Age: 26 Bats: R Throws: R Height: 6'3" Weight: 210 Origin: Round 1, 2015 Draft (#16 overall)

YEAR	TEAM	LVL	AGE	W	L	SV	G	GS	IP	H	HR	BB/9	K/9	K	GB%	BABIP	WHIP	ERA	DRA	WARP	PF
2019	STO	A+	25	2	2	0	11	10	36¹	35	6	2.0	10.7	43	32%	.319	1.18	4.46	4.47	0.2	103
2019	MID	AA	25	2	1	0	7	5	27²	18	2	2.6	8.5	26	41%	.232	0.94	1.63	3.01	0.6	108
2020	OAK	MLB	26	3	3	0	32	5	52	51	8	3.1	8.7	50	39%	.301	1.34	4.46	4.72	0.4	96

Comparables: Joe Musgrove, Glenn Sparkman, David Phelps

Kaprielian's stock has had a steady slide over the last few years. Once upon a time, he was flashing top-of-the-rotation stuff, and so much so that he made the 2017 101 despite difficulty staying on the mound. He had Tommy John surgery that spring and was included in the Sonny Gray trade later that year while rehabbing. He proceeded to miss not only all of 2017, but all of 2018 with rehab complications and shoulder troubles. When he finally got back into games this past May, he was still somewhat limited; he only pitched five innings twice all season, and capped out at 73 pitches. He's now more low 90s with occasional bursts into the mid 90s instead of mid-90s-flashing-higher, and the slider is now ahead of the other offspeeds. He's also entering his age-26 season with less than 100 official pro innings after spending the majority of his age-25 campaign pitching truncated outings in High-A. There's still, somehow, an obvious mid-rotation talent level here if he ever can pitch 150 healthy innings in a season, and there's also late-innings potential if he takes to short relief as a fastball/slider type.

15 Luis Barrera CF
Born: 11/15/95 Age: 24 Bats: L Throws: L Height: 6'0" Weight: 205 Origin: International Free Agent, 2012

YEAR	TEAM	LVL	AGE	PA	R	2B	3B	HR	RBI	BB	K	SB	CS	AVG/OBP/SLG	DRC+	VORP	BABIP	BRR	FRAA	WARP	PF
2017	BLT	A	21	301	41	13	7	3	22	16	61	13	7	.277/.320/.406	94	6.8	.341	0.4	RF(38) -2.3, CF(23) 1.0	0.4	102
2017	STO	A+	21	124	15	2	0	4	16	8	25	3	1	.228/.276/.351	67	-1.6	.256	0.7	LF(16) -1.3, RF(12) 0.6	-0.1	101
2018	STO	A+	22	351	51	18	7	3	46	32	63	10	4	.284/.354/.415	117	21.4	.345	1.3	CF(39) 5.1, RF(37) 3.7	2.6	96
2018	MID	AA	22	144	24	8	4	0	18	9	18	13	3	.328/.378/.450	110	11.1	.377	3.5	CF(22) 3.1, RF(6) -0.5	1.2	110
2019	MID	AA	23	240	35	9	11	4	24	12	48	9	7	.321/.357/.513	136	19.5	.393	-1.0	CF(36) -5.5, RF(14) 3.0	1.1	104
2020	OAK	MLB	24	251	22	11	3	4	24	13	67	5	2	.244/.287/.367	74	0.0	.324	0.3	CF 0, RF 1	0.1	96

Comparables: Zoilo Almonte, Erik González, Aaron Altherr

The A's threw a big pile of money at Barrera out of the Dominican way back in 2012, and he has travelled through just about every nook and cranny of Oakland's minor league landscape in the years since. Most recently, he's hit .324 in 90 games at Double-A over the past two seasons. He throws arms at pitches, with a handsy left-handed swing that doesn't typically feature a whole lot of plane to it. He clips 200 pounds as a 6-footer, and at 24 he's now filled out considerably over the years. It's conceivable there's some latent power here, though the swing definition isn't really conducive for it at all at present, and he'll be on the comeback from a season-ending shoulder injury when next we see him. He struggled to steal bases last year against advanced batteries, but the speed has held at least plus as he's matured physically, and he tracks balls well in center. He's on the 40-man roster now, and should see a chance to break in during the 2020 season.

16 Tyler Baum RHP
Born: 01/14/98 Age: 22 Bats: R Throws: R Height: 6'2" Weight: 195 Origin: Round 2, 2019 Draft (#66 overall)

YEAR	TEAM	LVL	AGE	W	L	SV	G	GS	IP	H	HR	BB/9	K/9	K	GB%	BABIP	WHIP	ERA	DRA	WARP	PF
2019	VER	A-	21	0	3	0	11	11	30²	29	4	2.1	10.0	34	40%	.306	1.17	4.70	4.42	0.3	91
2020	OAK	MLB	22	2	2	0	33	0	35	35	6	3.3	8.0	31	38%	.294	1.38	4.67	4.84	0.1	96

Comparables: Joel Carreno, Pat Light, Jensen Lewis

Your typical second-round college arm generally falls into one of two categories: i) Good stuff, but not as much polish as you'd expect; and ii) good polish and performance, but not as much stuff as you'd hope. Baum doesn't quite fit in either basket. He was a three year-starter in the ACC, but never really dominated and the stuff is more of the 50-55 variety. You'd expect that arm to have more success in college than he did, and maybe there is some untapped potential with pro instruction, although North Carolina has a reputation as one of the more analytically-minded college programs out there. There's feel for four pitches here and the fastball can touch 95, but the delivery is uptempo with some late effort, so relief risk looms.

17 Skye Bolt OF

Born: 01/15/94 Age: 26 Bats: B Throws: R Height: 6'2" Weight: 187 Origin: Round 4, 2015 Draft (#128 overall)

YEAR	TEAM	LVL	AGE	PA	R	2B	3B	HR	RBI	BB	K	SB	CS	AVG/OBP/SLG	DRC+	VORP	BABIP	BRR	FRAA	WARP	PF
2017	STO	A+	23	496	76	24	7	15	66	53	134	9	8	.243/.327/.435	98	22.8	.314	-0.4	CF(107) -2.3, LF(3) 0.1	1.2	101
2018	STO	A+	24	209	28	8	4	9	32	31	47	9	3	.266/.382/.521	137	26.7	.308	2.1	CF(45) -8.1, LF(4) -0.6	0.8	100
2018	MID	AA	24	315	41	18	3	10	37	27	75	10	1	.256/.325/.446	107	10.8	.315	1.7	CF(50) -3.1, RF(19) 0.8	1.0	112
2019	LVG	AAA	25	347	57	19	3	11	61	37	94	7	5	.269/.350/.459	81	4.8	.351	-0.3	RF(39) 8.5, CF(37) 1.1	1.1	110
2019	OAK	MLB	25	11	1	1	0	0	0	1	3	0	0	.100/.182/.200	77	0.0	.143	-0.1	CF(3) 0.0, RF(1) 0.0	0.0	97
2020	OAK	MLB	26	35	3	1	0	1	4	3	11	0	0	.204/.273/.354	67	0.0	.279	0.0	RF 1	0.0	96

Comparables: Blake Tekotte, Ryan Cordell, Melky Mesa

It's been tough to know quite what to do with Bolt for a long time now, as his is the quintessential case of the early-blooming toolsy kid who never quite actualizes any of those tools in any kind of linear progression. He's battled general inconsistency for much of his professional career, though there have been a bunch of flashes of interesting game talent along the way, including both a huge finishing run to his 2018 season and a monstrous open to this past year, with the latter forcing a big-league debut. There have been and remain across-the-board tools here, and also a lot of caveats. He's a switch-hitter, but the splits are heavily weighted in favor of a left-handed swing that provides a solid rate of line-drive contact and occasional pull-side carry. He's fast, but he hasn't quite developed consistency as a base-stealer or center field route-runner. There's arm strength for right, but even a best-case scenario for the bat's outcome may leave him a little light for the position. The safe bet on the outcome remains that of a fourth- or fifth-outfielder, with second-division upside for stretches if and when the bat's clicking.

18 Greg Deichmann OF

Born: 05/31/95 Age: 25 Bats: L Throws: R Height: 6'2" Weight: 190 Origin: Round 2, 2017 Draft (#43 overall)

YEAR	TEAM	LVL	AGE	PA	R	2B	3B	HR	RBI	BB	K	SB	CS	AVG/OBP/SLG	DRC+	VORP	BABIP	BRR	FRAA	WARP	PF
2017	VER	A-	22	195	31	10	4	8	30	28	40	4	1	.274/.385/.530	168	18.3	.316	0.8	RF(34) 3.1, LF(1) -0.1	1.9	99
2018	ATH	RK	23	43	9	2	2	1	7	5	8	0	0	.289/.372/.526	124	3.3	.345	-0.1	RF(11) -0.4	0.1	104
2018	STO	A+	23	185	18	14	0	6	21	17	63	0	1	.199/.276/.392	67	-0.7	.276	-0.1	RF(28) 0.7, LF(8) -0.8	-0.3	97
2019	MID	AA	24	340	42	10	2	11	36	34	103	19	5	.219/.300/.375	91	4.6	.289	2.7	RF(69) 0.0, CF(3) 0.2	0.7	106
2020	OAK	MLB	25	251	25	12	1	9	30	19	89	0	0	.211/.275/.385	71	0.0	.299	0.1	RF 0, LF 0	-0.1	96

Comparables: David Washington, Scott Cousins, Donald Lutz

IThe A's made a tough decision to keep their former second-rounder on an age-appropriate development curve in Double-A last season after an injury-curtailed and unproductive 2018 season at Stockton, and things didn't go so hot. He continues to show a decent awareness of the strike zone, and the swing is mechanically pretty simple. But there's also some stiffness to it, and he struggled to extend on fastballs and do much damage for most of the year. The arm's fine for right, and he gets moving reasonably well, to where he should be able to hold his own defensively. He's unlikely to add much positive value with the leather, however, so he's really going to need to tap into just about all of his 5:00 o'clock power to make the profile work. He showed flashes of what that looks like against the tired arms of the AFL, but he'll be 25 next year and it'll become increasingly incumbent on him to show it in-season.

19 Jonah Heim C

Born: 06/27/95 Age: 25 Bats: B Throws: R Height: 6'4" Weight: 220 Origin: Round 4, 2013 Draft (#129 overall)

YEAR	TEAM	LVL	AGE	PA	R	2B	3B	HR	RBI	BB	K	SB	CS	AVG/OBP/SLG	DRC+	VORP	BABIP	BRR	FRAA	WARP	PF
2017	BGR	A	22	321	45	17	1	9	53	27	57	0	1	.268/.327/.426	111	17.4	.303	-2.1	C(61) 3.1	1.8	104
2017	PCH	A+	22	61	3	3	0	0	8	3	17	1	0	.218/.262/.273	43	0.2	.300	0.4	C(15) 0.4	0.0	101
2018	STO	A+	23	348	41	21	1	7	49	29	60	3	1	.292/.353/.433	116	21.9	.337	-0.9	C(55) -0.1	1.7	97
2018	MID	AA	23	154	16	4	0	1	11	10	22	0	0	.182/.238/.234	17	-6.4	.205	-0.9	C(38) 1.6	-0.4	111
2019	MID	AA	24	208	20	12	0	5	34	24	27	0	1	.282/.370/.431	137	12.9	.307	-1.6	C(43) 7.7	2.3	108
2019	LVG	AAA	24	119	22	9	0	4	19	11	18	0	0	.358/.412/.557	125	10.0	.395	-0.5	C(28) 2.2	1.0	110
2020	OAK	MLB	25	105	10	5	0	2	11	7	22	0	0	.229/.288/.361	73	0.0	.272	-0.2	C 2	0.3	96

Comparables: Martín Maldonado, Steven Lerud, Alfredo González

Originally drafted by the Baltimore Orioles in the fourth round of the 2013 Draft, the switch-hitting catcher is now with his third organization and was recently added to the Athletics' 40-man roster. A plus defender behind the plate, Heim apprehended 52-percent (26-of-50) of attempted base-burglars in 2019 with the help of a rocket throwing arm, often deployed from his knees. After a disastrous Double-A debut with the bat in 2018, the switch-hitting Heim rebounded to hit well at the level before pounding the Triple-A moon ball all around the Mojave Desert. He displays a catcher's approach at the dish and advanced baseball instincts all over the place, and is the most polished out of a nice batch of solid backup catching prospects scattered throughout this system.

20 Jeremy Eierman SS

Born: 09/10/96 Age: 23 Bats: R Throws: R Height: 6'0" Weight: 205 Origin: Round 2, 2018 Draft (#70 overall)

YEAR	TEAM	LVL	AGE	PA	R	2B	3B	HR	RBI	BB	K	SB	CS	AVG/OBP/SLG	DRC+	VORP	BABIP	BRR	FRAA	WARP	PF
2018	VER	A-	21	267	36	8	2	8	26	13	70	10	4	.235/.283/.381	74	5.6	.294	-0.1	SS(56) 0.3, 2B(2) 0.9	0.6	100
2019	STO	A+	22	552	57	29	7	13	64	39	177	11	3	.208/.270/.357	68	11.5	.289	3.7	SS(90) -8.6, 2B(33) 1.1	0.1	100
2020	OAK	MLB	23	251	23	11	1	8	27	15	95	4	2	.202/.255/.355	57	0.0	.301	0.0	SS -2, 2B 0	-0.6	96

Comparables: Jaycob Brugman, Kevin Cron, Chase d'Arnaud

Oakland's second-round pick out of Missouri State in 2018, Eierman displayed a unique power and speed combination for a shortstop in college, but it has yet to translate to his professional career. It's a durable, athletic frame at 6-feet and 205 pounds, and he swung between both middle-infield positions over the course of the year. He displayed quality lateral quickness and above-average range on both sides of second base, while a big-time arm produces throws with excellent carry through the bag. He shows an advanced internal clock that allows him to slow the game down, and his footwork around the bag is another defensive strength.

Offensively, Eierman has plus raw power and consistently displays it in batting practice. He generates good loft, and can spray the ball gap-to-gap. Far too often he sells out to try and find it in game, however, and there is stiffness and length into the zone off a very deep hand load and little early momentum to the swing. It all works to compromise his timing, and he struggled consistently to catch up to velocity all year. Swing adjustments and some corresponding growth in the offensive projection can bump him up this list a good bit next year, but the hit tool concerns cloud the profile for now.

Personal Cheeseball

PC Alexander Pantuso RHP

Born: 10/14/95 Age: 24 Bats: L Throws: R Height: 6'6" Weight: 235 Origin: Round 31, 2018 Draft (#923 overall)

YEAR	TEAM	LVL	AGE	W	L	SV	G	GS	IP	H	HR	BB/9	K/9	K	GB%	BABIP	WHIP	ERA	DRA	WARP	PF
2018	ATH	RK	22	0	0	0	15	0	24¹	15	0	4.8	12.9	35	52%	.288	1.15	3.33	2.43	0.8	100
2019	AGO	RK	23	1	2	3	14	0	19¹	11	0	5.6	15.4	33	21%	.324	1.19	2.33	2.00	0.8	100
2020	OAK	MLB	24	2	2	0	33	0	35	35	5	3.6	11.6	45	42%	.337	1.38	4.49	4.61	0.2	96

Pantuso is a 24-year-old former 31st-rounder who just logged his first four innings of short-season ball at the end of the season. Are you not entertained? Well, you will be if he can find any semblance of command, because the stuff is almost as huge as his frame now. He leverages every inch of his 6-foot-6, long-levered body with a way, way, over-the-top release point that creates obscene plane and a very difficult angle for barrels to find. His gas now checks in high 90s, while the slider's shape is both weird from the slot and late in showing. Pitch-to-pitch repetition is as spotty as you may imagine coming from that kind of length, but the club will have every incentive to push him quickly, and it'll be neat if it works.

Low Minors Sleeper

LMS Marcus Smith OF
Born: 09/11/00   Age: 19   Bats: L   Throws: L   Height: 5'11"   Weight: 190   Origin: Round 3, 2019 Draft (#104 overall)

YEAR	TEAM	LVL	AGE	PA	R	2B	3B	HR	RBI	BB	K	SB	CS	AVG/OBP/SLG	DRC+	VORP	BABIP	BRR	FRAA	WARP	PF
2019	AGO	RK	18	119	21	6	1	0	14	20	29	1	1	.361/.466/.443	164	12.9	.507	0.9	CF(20) -5.1, LF(7) 0.6	0.6	102
2020	OAK	MLB	19	251	22	12	1	3	21	24	84	3	1	.235/.311/.328	73	0.0	.362	0.0	CF -2, LF 0	-0.2	96

Comparables: Jake Smolinski, Juan Soto, Jesse Winker

It's cheating a little bit to throw a club's third-rounder into this slot, but the Kansas City prep pick debuted for all of 29 games in the AZL after signing, and he's a fun player, so he counts. He's the kind of 5-foot-11 that has really strong legs and builds muscle mass well, and he's a 70-grade runner who gets off the blocks and up to speed efficiently in center. It's raw out there, in both his reads and his efforts to harness solid arm strength, but the speed will give him ample opportunity to grow into the leather, and there's potential to eventually add a good chunk of value there. His swing is armsy and quick, with very little lower-half engagement or ability to impact the ball, but he showed ability to take pitches and stay in the zone pretty well while finding the barrel consistently in his debut. Whether he can translate physical strength into any semblance of game thump will be the $400,000 question, and it'll take some evolution to the swing to get there.

Top Talents 25 and Under (as of 4/1/2020)

1. Jesus Luzardo
2. Ramon Laureano
3. Matt Olson
4. A.J. Puk
5. Sean Murphy
6. Franklin Barreto
7. Dustin Fowler
8. Nick Allen
9. Austin Beck
10. Jorge Mateo

This year's 25U looks very similar to last year's. There is still a good amount of young, controllable talent in the system which should make an impact with the big-league club in 2020.

With Matt Chapman graduating and his health returning, Jesús Luzardo claims the top spot in this iteration. Nipping at his heels, though, Ramon Laureano followed up his breakout 2018 debut with a similarly outstanding 2019 campaign. Although Laureano missed about six weeks with a stress fracture in his right shin, he was still highly productive in all phases when healthy, running up 4.2 WARP to rank fourth among all AL center fielders. Laureano's true claim to fame comes from his arm and his ability to throw runners out, but after a tough start to the year he also continued rounding into a solid offensive player with the ability to drive the ball, get on base, and add runs on the basepaths.

Matt Olson has been a mainstay on this list and returns for the 2020 season, making the cut by a matter of days. He also missed 34 games after injuring his hand in the second A's-Mariners game in Japan in March, but when he returned in May he looked productive as ever and appeared to have no lingering effects from the injury. Olson posted a 134 DRC+ over 127 games while winning a Gold Glove at first, confirming that the A's have the corners of their infield taken care of for the foreseeable future.

It feels like Franklin Barreto has been around (and failing against big-league pitching) forever, but he's still only 23 and has logged all of 208 career plate appearances over the past three seasons. Barreto spent the majority of 2019 at Triple-A Las Vegas where he amassed an above-average 108 DRC+ which includes a heavy penalty for the environment, before finally getting another call up in September. He's firmly in the Daulton Pompey zone as a post-prospect guy, but there's still upside as a starting middle infielder and he should get a crack at the Opening Day roster in 2020.

Dustin Fowler can spin a similar yarn after spending all of 2019 in Triple-A a year removed from playing in 69 nice games for the A's the season prior. The A's acquired Fowler in 2017 from the Yankees, the same year in which he ruptured his patellar tendon. It looks more like a tweener profile at this point, and both his offensive and defensive performance stagnated in the desert last season. There's still big league-caliber (and -ready) value to be found here, though.

Eyewitness Reports

Eyewitness Report: Nick Allen

Evaluator: Brandon Williams
Report Date: 06/11/2019
Dates Seen: 5/11 ; 5/19 ; 5/24 - 5/26
Risk Factor: Low
Physical/Health: Allen is a high-energy athlete with exceptional coordination and quickness. His physique and athleticism are similar to that of a soccer or tennis player.

Tool	Future Grade	Report
Hit	60	An efficient, compact swing and a high-rate of hard contact ensure Allen will hit for a good average. His plus-speed and willingness to use the entire field allow him to procure hits at a rapid pace.
Power	40	Physical limitations will limit Allen's HR Derby nominations, although his fast-twitch athleticism is capable of jolting the baseball on occasion. He will generate plenty of doubles and triples with gap power and plus-speed.
Baserunning/ Speed	60	More quick than fast, Allen's first step burst and rapid acceleration allow him to take extra-bases and swipe plenty of bags.
Glove	60	Quick feet, outstanding balance, and exceptional hand-eye coordination contribute to Allen's plus fielding abilities. The natural shortstop is capable of providing above-average defense at any infield position and possesses the athleticism to play center field.
Arm	55	A quick release and fielding instincts/timing developed with thousands of repetitions enable Allen's arm to play better than its natural velocity.

Conclusion: Already a highly-skilled and experienced player at the age of 20, Allen's energetic athleticism and high baseball IQ make him the prototypical table-setting, plus-defending shortstop that championship-caliber teams covet.

Eyewitness Report: Logan Davidson

Evaluator: David Lee
Report Date: 06/01/2019
Dates Seen: 3/1-3/2019
Risk Factor: High
Physical/Health: Typical big-bodied shortstop and good athlete for size. Lengthy with projection for impact strength. Good actions. Leader type with bloodlines.

Tool	Future Grade	Report
Hit	45	More consistent stroke from right side with good, quick path to zone and slight lift. He covers the plate from the right side. Power-based stroke from the left side with a deeper hand load with lift. Clearer hot zones from the left side. Overall swing-and-miss concerns. Solid-average bat speed. Feel to walk but in-zone miss is there.
Power	55	Projects for overall consistent gap power and solid pull-side pop. Occasional opposite, over-the-fence carry. Left-handed stroke geared for impact pull-side power. Hit could prevent max utilization.
Baserunning/ Speed	50	Likely to slow a tick as he ages. He'll remain a solid runner with an occasional stolen bag. Good athlete but not impactful home to first.
Glove	50	Solid actions carry his defensive profile. Soft glove. Strong first step and footwork. Range could slow a tick and prevent permanent shortstop future. Does everything right at short but time will tell future. More than enough athleticism for third.
Arm	55	Solid-average release and carries well. Not a weapon from left side but more than enough.

Conclusion: Davidson is a first-round talent based on the frame and array of tools. He doesn't have a clear carrying tool, but he does pretty much everything well and does it from the left side of the infield. It's a solid frame with height, length and athleticism, and there's room for added muscle to tap into good power projection. There are swing-and-miss concerns and he's likely to rack up strikeouts, but he walks and will hit for power while playing short or third down the road. An organization will probably have a decision to make regarding his defensive home in the future, but he's a serviceable shortstop and will remain one for at least a while. There's a lot to like with the potential in this profile.

Philadelphia Phillies

The State of the System

The Phillies farm system has steadily diminished as they transition to win-now mode, but they may have a few more cards to play in 2020.

The Top Ten

★ ★ ★ 2020 Top 101 Prospect **#36** ★ ★ ★

1 **Spencer Howard** **RHP**   OFP: 60   ETA: 2020
Born: 07/28/96   Age: 23   Bats: R   Throws: R   Height: 6'2"   Weight: 205   Origin: Round 2, 2017 Draft (#45 overall)

YEAR	TEAM	LVL	AGE	W	L	SV	G	GS	IP	H	HR	BB/9	K/9	K	GB%	BABIP	WHIP	ERA	DRA	WARP	PF
2017	WPT	A-	20	1	1	0	9	9	28^1	22	0	5.7	12.7	40	48%	.349	1.41	4.45	4.13	0.4	100
2018	LWD	A	21	9	8	0	23	23	112	101	6	3.2	11.8	147	40%	.349	1.26	3.78	3.87	1.8	91
2019	CLR	A+	22	2	1	0	7	7	35	19	1	1.3	12.3	48	44%	.261	0.69	1.29	2.25	1.2	102
2019	REA	AA	22	1	0	0	6	6	30^2	20	2	2.6	11.2	38	42%	.242	0.95	2.35	2.93	0.8	105
2020	PHI	MLB	23	2	2	0	33	0	35	34	5	3.3	10.8	42	41%	.327	1.35	4.33	4.46	0.4	103

Comparables: Dylan Cease, Hunter Wood, José De León

The Report: Spencer Howard had a breakout at the end of the 2018 season, leading to anticipation about how quickly he could move through the organization during the 2019 season. The Phillies conservatively did not double-jump him past Clearwater. Instead, an early season arm injury cost him two months and delayed his promotion to Double-A until late July. In addition to the missed time, it meant that it was over four months into the season until the late 2018 version of Howard took the mound.

Once he did get fully healthy to end the season Howard was back to sitting mid 90s, touching 99. Howard did lose velocity during his starts, but that could potentially be attributed to his conditioning being thrown off by the injury. His top secondary pitch is his changeup, a future plus pitch with good arm-side fade that took a large step forward late in the season. Howard's slider gives him a second plus pitch. It is a two-plane breaker, that can sometimes get a bit long and loopy. He still leans too much on his humpy curveball, which is at best an average pitch. It has been effective in the minors based on the velocity separation from the fastball, but advanced hitters will be able to read it out of his hand.

Howard repeats his delivery well, and has made big strides with consistency in pro ball. Like many young pitchers he is still working to fully make the move from control to command, but he has shown the ability to work his fastball up and his changeup to the outside of the zone.

The arm injury could have set back Howard's timetable for the majors, but the Phillies made sure he got plenty of innings in Double-A and the AFL to close the gap. He will compete for a spot out of the Phillies rotation to open the season, but the team has expressed a desire for him to get some work in with the major league ball in Triple-A before reaching the majors.

Variance: Medium. Howard has the stuff right now to step right into a major league rotation on Opening Day. The biggest knock against him is the lack of a sustained track record, and it is likely that early in the 2020 season the Phillies decide the stuff is too good to wait on the track record to develop.

Ben Carsley's Fantasy Take: Howard is exactly the type of fantasy pitching prospect you should be willing to get aggressive on. He's got legitimate SP3 upside, he figures to make an impact within the next season, and the scouting reports and numbers match up. Howard's arm injury and relatively limited track record of projecting as a dominant pitcher keep him out of the upper echelon of minor league fantasy arms, but he's firmly entrenched in the next group.

★ ★ ★ *2020 Top 101 Prospect* **#40** ★ ★ ★

2 Alec Bohm 3B   OFP: 60   ETA: 2020

Born: 08/03/96   Age: 23   Bats: R   Throws: R   Height: 6'5"   Weight: 225   Origin: Round 1, 2018 Draft (#3 overall)

YEAR	TEAM	LVL	AGE	PA	R	2B	3B	HR	RBI	BB	K	SB	CS	AVG/OBP/SLG	DRC+	VORP	BABIP	BRR	FRAA	WARP	PF
2018	PLL	RK	21	27	8	1	1	0	3	2	0	2	0	.391/.481/.522	147	2.1	.391	-1.6	3B(5) 1.3	0.2	98
2018	WPT	A-	21	121	9	5	1	0	12	10	19	1	0	.224/.314/.290	89	-0.4	.273	-0.9	3B(20) -2.7	-0.2	95
2019	LWD	A	22	93	13	9	0	3	11	12	14	3	0	.367/.441/.595	213	14.3	.406	-0.8	3B(14) -0.8, 1B(5) -0.1	1.1	88
2019	CLR	A+	22	177	25	10	3	4	27	17	21	1	2	.329/.395/.506	173	18.1	.358	0.8	3B(25) 1.1, 1B(7) 0.6	2.0	102
2019	REA	AA	22	270	38	11	1	14	42	28	38	2	2	.269/.344/.500	154	16.4	.265	-0.7	3B(43) 0.0, 1B(12) -0.8	2.1	104
2020	PHI	MLB	23	280	31	13	1	10	35	21	54	1	0	.256/.317/.433	97	3.0	.290	-0.4	3B -1	0.5	103

Comparables: *Matt Antonelli, Carlos Asuaje, Adam Duvall*

The Report: We have a tendency as evaluators to make connections between prospects in the form of comparisons or comps. Players tend to be comped to others who look or feel the same, often in ways that show subtle (or not so subtle) biases. I try to stay away from comps as much as possible, but sometimes you just make a connection in your head.

So, with that disclaimer, Alec Bohm reminds me a lot of Maikel Franco as a prospect. It's not a visual comp; Bohm is a tall white kid from the Great Plains and Franco is a stout Dominican. It is a skill set comp in that they are both right-handed third basemen with limited range. Bohm's calling card is raw power that he hasn't quite translated into game power yet, and a potential plus hit tool that is far from locked in as plus. That looks a lot like Franco at the same stage. And, of course, Bohm is also seeking to replace the released Franco as the third baseman of the Philadelphia Phillies.

Franco has had enough of a major-league career that it's a bit much to call him a total bust, but he certainly never turned into the first-division regular that the Phillies hoped for. The similarities end at a certain point. Bohm already has a better plate approach than Franco ever developed, and Bohm's bat path is conducive to the adjustments that Franco never made. But Franco was once just about as touted a prospect as Bohm is now in a broadly similar form, and if nothing else it shows that there's some risk to the profile.

Variance: Medium. We believe in him as a major league regular, but there's a fair bit of variability in exactly how much power he hits for. He's also at some long-term risk of sliding off of third base to first or an outfield corner.

Ben Carsley's Fantasy Take: It would appear as though I'm more bullish on Bohm than my colleagues who know a lot more about him than I do. A normal human might take that as a sign he should recalibrate, but this is 2019, friends, and there's no time like the present to double down. Bohm is easily the best dynasty prospect in this org for my money, and while there's some risk attached to his profile in terms of future positional eligibility, I firmly believe he'll hit. We might not get truly star-level production out of Bohm, but I think he can get to .270 with 30-plus bombs and 3B eligibility at least into his late 20s. That'd make him a top-15 third baseman a la the 2019 iteration of Josh Donaldson.

3 Francisco Morales RHP   OFP: 60   ETA: Late 2021

Born: 10/27/99   Age: 20   Bats: R   Throws: R   Height: 6'4"   Weight: 185   Origin: International Free Agent, 2016

YEAR	TEAM	LVL	AGE	W	L	SV	G	GS	IP	H	HR	BB/9	K/9	K	GB%	BABIP	WHIP	ERA	DRA	WARP	PF
2017	PHL	RK	17	3	2	0	10	9	41¹	34	1	4.4	9.6	44	44%	.308	1.31	3.05	5.16	0.4	99
2018	WPT	A-	18	4	5	0	13	13	56¹	54	6	5.3	10.9	68	42%	.324	1.54	5.27	6.11	-0.6	93
2019	LWD	A	19	1	8	1	27	15	96²	82	8	4.3	12.0	129	46%	.325	1.32	3.82	4.39	0.7	94
2020	PHI	MLB	20	2	2	0	33	0	35	36	6	4.0	9.4	37	40%	.313	1.47	5.11	5.10	0.1	103

Comparables: *JC Ramírez, Joel Payamps, Fabio Castillo*

The Report: The Phillies have done very well with five- and six-figure international free agent arms over the past decade. Morales is on the high side of that bonus range, but he's developing all the same. The projectability we've noted over the past few years finally manifested, as he was slinging it at 94-96 and bumping a tick or two higher in looks throughout the season. There might be a little projectability there left as a starter, and I'd expect the fastball to end up consistently in the high 90s if he moved to short relief. The slider is a plus pitch bordering on plus-plus, a true slider and a true out pitch. Those two weapons alone are enough to throw him into the 60 OFP conversation.

The usual concerns for the high-variance 60 OFP A-ball power pitcher profile are here too, of course. The changeup has developed faster than we thought it would a year or two ago, but that only gets it from fringy to fringe-average. Fringe-average is right on the border of being enough to give him a viable third pitch for a rotation, and a half-grade either way could make or break that. His delivery gives him some deception but also lends to repeatability problems. Because the Phillies employed a tandem system at Lakewood this year he never turned over the heart of the lineup a third time.

We could see the Phillies moving Morales to the bullpen as a fastball/slider guy, and we expect that he would be a quick mover with dominant late-game potential if they do. But the upside in the rotation might be too tantalizing...for the time being.

Variance: High, albeit typical. Adonis Medina had this sort of profile a few years ago and has stagnated a touch as he's moved up the chain. The changeup or command might never quite get all the way there. He just turned 20 and has yet to crack a hundred innings in a season.

Ben Carsley's Fantasy Take: For as special as Morales' arm can appear if you catch him on the right night, this is actually a fairly common dynasty prospect profile: Great Stuff (TM), but with substantial reliever risk and a so-so ETA. If you decide Morales is your dude among the glut of pitchers with similar profiles, that's totally reasonable. It's also reasonable to view him as a fringe-101 guy, as players with Morales' skill set bust in fantasy more often than they click.

4 Bryson Stott SS   OFP: 55   ETA: Late 2021

Born: 10/06/97 Age: 22 Bats: L Throws: R Height: 6'3" Weight: 200 Origin: Round 1, 2019 Draft (#14 overall)

YEAR	TEAM	LVL	AGE	PA	R	2B	3B	HR	RBI	BB	K	SB	CS	AVG/OBP/SLG	DRC+	VORP	BABIP	BRR	FRAA	WARP	PF
2019	WPT	A-	21	182	27	8	2	5	24	22	39	5	3	.274/.370/.446	149	17.7	.336	1.1	SS(33) -1.0, 2B(2) -0.1	1.4	97
2020	PHI	MLB	22	251	24	12	1	7	27	16	71	2	1	.227/.282/.377	73	0.0	.296	0.0	SS 0, 2B 0	0.0	103

Comparables: Tyler Greene, Brent Lillibridge, J.D. Davis

The Report: The Phillies have taken a college hitter in the first round of the last three drafts, opting for safety over upside. In many ways Stott is similar to the first player of that group, Adam Haseley. Stott put up very good numbers in college, showing power, contact, and approach. The collection of tools are not overwhelming. His swing can get a bit long, and his bat speed is just average, leading to some questions about his long term ability to make contact at a high level. He has average power, mostly to his pull side. He may fill out and grow into more strength, but it is unlikely he will ever be much more than a 20-home-run-a-year hitter.

Stott's abilities in the field are similar to his abilities at the plate, more a collection of solid tools than anything stand out. He has enough range to stick at shortstop, and his hands are perfectly fine there. He has a bit of an awkward throwing motion that makes everything look not quite right, and his arm strength is slightly questionable, but still playable for the position. If he can't play shortstop full time, he could easily slide to second or third base and be a good defender at either.

The Phillies have been decently aggressive with their college players recently, and given Stott's polish he should start the year for High-A Clearwater, and should end the year in Double-A. His lack of upside means that he is probably that infielder that will move to a team's position of need than having a spot opened up for him.

Variance: Medium. Stott's collection of tools gives him a lot of safety, even if the tools don't all play to their ceiling. He does lose some value and ceiling if he has to move off of shortstop, but he should have plenty of glove, and just enough bat for second or third base.

Ben Carsley's Fantasy Take: First of all, this is a terrible name. Second of all, this is a weird-ass fantasy profile. I'm getting a hint of Jed Lowrie with...I think there are some notes of Paul DeJong? Then again, there's something about the aftertaste that denotes trace amounts of Joe Panik. Basically, Stott's value will hinge entirely on whether he can force his way into enough playing time to serve as an accumulator. That makes him an awfully tough dude to value from a dynasty standpoint, but tells you that you can stay away from popping Stott particularly early in your supplemental drafts.

5 Adonis Medina RHP   OFP: 55   ETA: 2021

Born: 12/18/96   Age: 23   Bats: R   Throws: R   Height: 6'1"   Weight: 185   Origin: International Free Agent, 2014

YEAR	TEAM	LVL	AGE	W	L	SV	G	GS	IP	H	HR	BB/9	K/9	K	GB%	BABIP	WHIP	ERA	DRA	WARP	PF
2017	LWD	A	20	4	9	0	22	22	119²	103	7	2.9	10.0	133	49%	.306	1.19	3.01	4.29	1.4	84
2018	CLR	A+	21	10	4	0	22	21	111¹	103	11	2.9	9.9	123	51%	.316	1.25	4.12	4.73	0.8	99
2019	REA	AA	22	7	7	0	22	21	105²	103	11	3.5	7.0	82	47%	.287	1.36	4.94	5.99	-1.3	102
2020	PHI	MLB	23	1	2	0	5	5	24	25	4	3.9	6.4	17	44%	.278	1.45	5.31	5.24	0.2	103

Comparables: Yennsy Diaz, Miguel Almonte, Paul Blackburn

The Report: With the Phillies shipping off Sixto Sanchez and Franklyn Kilomé, 2019 was supposed to be Adonis Medina's year to ascend to the top of the Phillies' pitching rankings. While the jump to Double-A is hard for most, it was particularly difficult for Medina. He regressed across the board, and his small frame seemingly struggled under the demands of a full-season workload.

If you gather the best of every Medina start, you can see the pitcher we projected him to be last year. However, he is now sitting in the lower end of his 91-96 fastball range, though he still shows the mid 90s. His changeup was trending towards plus, but it lacked sharpness and command. Starting in 2017, Medina had been phasing out a loopy curveball, for a sharp, hard slider, but it seems the two have mixed again into a loopy slider lacking bite. In addition to each individual pitch regressing, Medina's command has not improved, causing him to leave a lot of hittable pitches in the strike zone.

Medina still has mid-rotation upside if the Phillies can get him back to his pre-2019 path, and because of that they will likely return him to the Reading rotation to open the 2020 season. If the Medina's frame cannot hold up to the rigors of starting and maintain plus stuff, the Phillies may explore moving him to the bullpen where he may profile as a late-inning reliever.

Variance: High. The Adonis Medina that was on the mound for much of the 2019 season showed very ordinary stuff. If he cannot recapture his former stuff, he is just an ordinary reliever. However, Medina just finished his age-22 season and has some time still recapture his former prospect pedigree.

Ben Carsley's Fantasy Take: I'm too scared, basically. I wouldn't mind so much if Medina were just short, or just had some reliever risk, or was just coming off a down year. But combine all three and I think we've reached the point where Medina has more name value than actual value in dynasty formats right now. That's not to suggest you should sell low, but I wouldn't be diving into Medina stocks right now either.

6 Luis Garcia SS   OFP: 55   ETA: 2023-24

Born: 10/01/00   Age: 19   Bats: B   Throws: R   Height: 5'11"   Weight: 170   Origin: International Free Agent, 2017

YEAR	TEAM	LVL	AGE	PA	R	2B	3B	HR	RBI	BB	K	SB	CS	AVG/OBP/SLG	DRC+	VORP	BABIP	BRR	FRAA	WARP	PF
2018	PLL	RK	17	187	33	11	3	1	32	15	21	12	8	.369/.433/.488	196	22.6	.418	-0.1	SS(43) -2.1	2.2	99
2019	LWD	A	18	524	36	14	3	4	36	44	132	9	8	.186/.261/.255	58	-9.8	.247	-5.0	SS(71) -0.2, 2B(55) -5.3	-1.4	91
2020	PHI	MLB	19	251	20	11	1	3	21	18	71	4	2	.208/.271/.305	53	0.0	.285	-0.3	SS -1, 2B -1	-0.9	103

Comparables: Jefry Marte, Carson Kelly, Cheslor Cuthbert

The Report: We're not going to sugarcoat this: it was a rough season for Garcia. Playing the entire season at age-18, he jumped from complex ball all the way to full-season and he struggled badly. The switch-hitter was nearly pitcher-level useless from the left side, and only barely passable from the right side. He was overmatched, physically and developmentally. He'd probably have been better served spending the rainy months in Florida before heading to the Appy League, if only the Phillies *had* an Appy League affiliate.

Yet it wasn't a total loss. Surviving as an 18-year-old in full-season ball is, itself, an accomplishment. Garcia showed plus barrel control and a general feel for hitting even while not actually hitting much. There was a touch of bat speed on both sides, enough to project out that he's probably not going to be overmatched forever. He has keen defensive instincts and actions at the six spot and is likely to stay there or excel somewhere else on the dirt. It'll take some time, but there are still the makings of a regular shortstop here despite the ugly topline.

Variance: Very high. We don't know if he can hit yet. It's likely to be a few years before we know. He's very, very far away. Yet even if it takes a half-decade to sort everything out, he'll only be 23 during the 2024 season.

Ben Carsley's Fantasy Take: My issue is less with Garcia's full-season performance than it is that he was always a better real life prospect than a dynasty one. But between the long lead time, modest fantasy upside and recent track record, it's hard to make a case for Garcia as anything more than a prospect who'd rank in the 250-ish range at present. The Nationals' one is better.

7 Mickey Moniak OF   OFP: 55   ETA: Late 2020

Born: 05/13/98 Age: 22 Bats: L Throws: R Height: 6'2" Weight: 185 Origin: Round 1, 2016 Draft (#1 overall)

YEAR	TEAM	LVL	AGE	PA	R	2B	3B	HR	RBI	BB	K	SB	CS	AVG/OBP/SLG	DRC+	VORP	BABIP	BRR	FRAA	WARP	PF
2017	LWD	A	19	509	53	22	6	5	44	28	109	11	7	.236/.284/.341	84	12.6	.292	-0.1	CF(115) -9.8	-0.3	86
2018	CLR	A+	20	465	50	28	3	5	55	22	100	6	5	.270/.304/.383	84	6.5	.334	-0.1	CF(99) -7.3, LF(9) -0.3	-0.1	100
2019	REA	AA	21	504	63	28	13	11	67	33	111	15	3	.252/.303/.439	97	20.9	.307	1.4	CF(93) -2.2, RF(24) 0.5	1.3	103
2020	PHI	MLB	22	251	21	13	2	5	25	14	68	2	1	.221/.269/.358	61	0.0	.290	0.0	CF -2, RF 0	-0.6	103

Comparables: Xavier Avery, Dustin Fowler, Rey Fuentes

The Report: Prospect lists are an exercise in many things. One of those is expectations. When you draft a prep bat first overall amidst whispers of a plus or plus-plus hit tool, and he shows up and puts up a string of below-average offensive performances with muted scouting reports, it's a disappointment.

Moniak is not on track to develop an above-average hit tool, let alone a plus-plus one. He has subpar pitch recognition and ends up taking far too many off-balance hacks at spin that he can't hit. The plus barrel control that once spawned the lofty hit tool projections has let him survive through all of this, but it's hard to project major development there now. It's a long swing, and he hasn't shown many markers for future high averages since entering pro ball. What was once projected as his greatest strength is now a major weakness.

However, Moniak is still a solid prospect if you ignore his draft position and accept what he is now. He's grown into some thump, and we expect him to grow into at least average game power. He's a good athlete that runs well and can handle center. There's a very plausible outcome—indeed, it is the one we are giving him as his OFP—where he lands with a bunch of tools starting with the number 5 and ends up being a regular starting major league outfielder. It's not exactly what you want out of a 1-1, but it's not *bad*.

Variance: Medium. Moniak has a broad base of secondary skills that make him a likely reserve outfielder even if he misses a reasonable upside projection. It's been long enough that we're not assigning his former draft status much weight at all for potential positive variance, but your mileage may vary.

Ben Carsley's Fantasy Take: Few prospects in recent memory have had such wild fluctuations in dynasty value as Moniak. First, he was a top-50 dude based on his hit tool and draft position. Not too long after, every scouting report indicated you should drop him. And now, well, I wouldn't exactly call him a "buy low" candidate, but I think he has more value than you'd assume given the perception that he's a total bust. In fact, I'd argue that Moniak is probably a top-150 dynasty prospect; he's just got a very different profile than the one we hoped he'd have post-draft.

8 Johan Rojas OF   OFP: 55   ETA: 2023

Born: 08/14/00 Age: 19 Bats: R Throws: R Height: 6'1" Weight: 165 Origin: International Free Agent, 2018

YEAR	TEAM	LVL	AGE	PA	R	2B	3B	HR	RBI	BB	K	SB	CS	AVG/OBP/SLG	DRC+	VORP	BABIP	BRR	FRAA	WARP	PF
2018	DPH	RK	17	292	42	12	4	2	31	18	37	19	8	.320/.376/.421	147	33.2	.360	2.3	CF(68) 6.1	3.1	98
2019	PLL	RK	18	84	13	6	5	0	4	9	12	3	2	.311/.393/.527	147	7.7	.371	-0.6	CF(16) 4.8, LF(1) -0.1	1.0	93
2019	WPT	A-	18	172	17	5	6	2	11	5	29	11	4	.244/.273/.384	82	2.9	.284	-0.6	CF(17) -3.1, RF(13) 0.9	-0.1	97
2020	PHI	MLB	19	251	22	12	3	3	23	16	59	5	2	.235/.291/.353	71	0.0	.301	0.4	CF 1, RF 0	0.1	103

Comparables: Victor Robles, Eddie Rosario, Jason Martin

The Report: At some point I really want to write 3,000 words or so on MLB's plan for the minors. Unfortunately, I am in the midst of shepherding 30 team prospect lists, et. al., so it's going to be a while. And my thoughts on the plan are far more wide-reaching than "there'd have been no room for Johan Rojas under it," but I guess this will be my first salvo. Are the Phillies really making room for a diminutive, 17-year-old Johan Rojas as one of their 125 or 150 allowed contracted players? Are they dumping a 23-year-old, role 3 Double-A outfielder, one with enough speed-and-glove to have some up-and-down utility for a project like Rojas? Maybe, maybe not. They didn't have to make that calculation or one like it, and have developed a very nice outfield prospect as a result.

Rojas is a pure joy in center, a plus-plus runner who goes and gets it. He plays the outfield like a marauding strong safety, and he's built like one too, although in miniature. That frame will add good weight and he's already flashing plus raw in batting practice. The hit tool is raw, but he more than held his own as an 18-year-old in the Penn League, and was capable of the occasionally spectacular at the plate too. He's aggressive and the swing can get noisy generally or choppy against offspeed stuff, so the hit tool will take some time to develop. Fortunately, he has plenty of it, and the Phillies system is the better for it.

Variance: Extreme. There's hit tool questions here and he hasn't even reached full-season ball yet. As polished as the speed/glove part of the profile is at present, he may not end up with a true carrying tool.

Ben Carsley's Fantasy Take: Speed is relatively hard to come by in today's fantasy landscape, and that alone makes Rojas a decent add to your watch list. I'd be okay taking a flyer on him in leagues that roster 300-plus dudes, but anything shallower and you can probably wait and monitor for improvement. The hit tool risk and lead time are pretty big negatives for our purposes.

9 Damon Jones LHP   OFP: 55   ETA: 2020

Born: 09/30/94 Age: 25 Bats: L Throws: L Height: 6'5" Weight: 225 Origin: Round 18, 2017 Draft (#533 overall)

YEAR	TEAM	LVL	AGE	W	L	SV	G	GS	IP	H	HR	BB/9	K/9	K	GB%	BABIP	WHIP	ERA	DRA	WARP	PF
2017	WPT	A-	22	2	3	3	13	0	26	23	0	6.9	13.2	38	52%	.377	1.65	4.85	5.67	-0.2	100
2018	LWD	A	23	10	7	0	23	22	113¹	105	7	4.0	9.8	123	58%	.326	1.37	3.41	4.82	0.5	88
2019	CLR	A+	24	4	3	0	11	11	58¹	38	3	3.7	13.6	88	61%	.310	1.06	1.54	3.12	1.4	98
2019	REA	AA	24	1	0	0	4	4	22	9	0	3.7	12.7	31	52%	.225	0.82	0.82	2.63	0.6	99
2019	LEH	AAA	24	0	1	0	8	8	34	27	4	6.9	8.7	33	52%	.258	1.56	6.62	5.03	0.6	96
2020	PHI	MLB	25	2	2	0	33	0	35	34	5	4.0	10.6	41	46%	.322	1.42	4.74	4.68	0.3	103

Comparables: Anthony Kay, Wei-Chieh Huang, Rico Garcia

The Report: We first flagged Jones as a sleeper very early in the 2018 season, when he was an interesting three-pitch pop-up lefty in Low-A. At the time, he was throwing 91-94 as a starter, although he'd thrown in the mid 90s previously in relief. In 2019, he was 93-96 in the rotation, which, along with a sharpening changeup and improved command, kicked him into a higher gear as a prospect. Jones dominated early on for High-A and blitzed through Double-A before running into the unfriendly Triple-A environment at the end of the season.

Jones is overaged for a 2017 college pick; he was drafted as a redshirt junior and turned 25 shortly after the 2019 season ended. We tend to care about age-relative-to-level less for talented arms than we do for bats, and his quick progress this past season certainly helps. But we do have to temper expectations some given that he's on the old side, and he's still a bit on the wild side, too.

Variance: Medium. There's a bit of risk in role, and there's a bit of further late development upside potential.

Ben Carsley's Fantasy Take: Jones is *probably* just a reliever, but the eye-popping strikeout numbers above tell me there's no harm in at least putting Jones on your watch list on the off chance the Phillies deploy him as a starter. There's pretty much zero buzz on Jones in dynasty circles as far as I can tell right now, so you should be able to take a wait-and-see approach without losing much sleep.

10 Rafael Marchan C   OFP: 55   ETA: 2023-24

Born: 02/25/99 Age: 21 Bats: B Throws: R Height: 5'9" Weight: 170 Origin: International Free Agent, 2015

YEAR	TEAM	LVL	AGE	PA	R	2B	3B	HR	RBI	BB	K	SB	CS	AVG/OBP/SLG	DRC+	VORP	BABIP	BRR	FRAA	WARP	PF
2017	PHL	RK	18	93	10	5	0	0	10	4	8	1	0	.238/.290/.298	85	0.7	.256	-0.5	C(29) -0.7	0.2	98
2018	WPT	A-	19	210	28	8	2	0	12	11	18	9	6	.301/.343/.362	139	14.5	.330	0.3	C(47) 2.7	1.9	93
2019	LWD	A	20	265	21	16	0	0	20	24	31	1	3	.271/.347/.339	130	15.2	.311	0.7	C(48) 1.8	2.1	89
2019	CLR	A+	20	86	6	4	0	0	3	6	8	1	2	.231/.291/.282	84	0.6	.254	-0.4	C(21) -0.3	0.2	102
2020	PHI	MLB	21	251	21	12	0	3	21	14	40	2	1	.240/.288/.332	64	0.0	.279	-0.5	C 1	-0.3	103

Comparables: Thairo Estrada, Isiah Kiner-Falefa, Abiatal Avelino

The Report: Yes, the Phillies declined to protect Marchan from the Rule 5 Draft. No, that doesn't mean we're going to drop him out of our top ten prospects.

We repeatedly say that the primary basis of our prospect coverage is our live looks. We do actually mean that. We have many, many live looks at Marchan. I live close enough to Lakewood that I go to a couple dozen games a year there, and we had multiple full looks from other team members. All of our live looks on him were positive, and we got positive industry feedback on him too. He showed natural feel for hitting from both sides of the plate with potential for gap power. We like his defensive tools, although he's still inexperienced at the position and will need a good deal of work and time to develop.

The totality of that information would probably warrant a ranking a spot or two higher on this list. We aren't completely oblivious to the Rule 5 part of this, and this section of the list was tight enough that the protection information shaded Marchan down a spot or two. We also recognize that he's unprotected because he's a raw catcher with less than 100 games of full-season ball, and that is very tough to carry on an MLB roster unless you're egregiously tanking. (It wouldn't shock us at all to see one of those tanking teams take Marchan, actually.) We certainly think he's a better prospect than, say, Mauricio Llovera, but it's much easier to stick Llovera in an MLB bullpen right now than it is to carry Marchan as a reserve catcher. It's also much less of a big deal for the Phillies to start Llovera's option clock than Marchan's.

Variance: Extreme. He's an A-ball catcher and he's raw even by those standards.

Ben Carsley's Fantasy Take: You know how I feel about catching prospects by now, so you can probably guess how I feel about those described as "raw even by those standards." A hard pass for me.

The Next Ten

11 Simon Muzziotti   OF

Born: 12/27/98   Age: 21   Bats: L   Throws: L   Height: 6'1"   Weight: 175   Origin: International Free Agent, 2015

YEAR	TEAM	LVL	AGE	PA	R	2B	3B	HR	RBI	BB	K	SB	CS	AVG/OBP/SLG	DRC+	VORP	BABIP	BRR	FRAA	WARP	PF
2017	PHL	RK	18	141	20	4	6	0	14	7	8	8	3	.269/.305/.388	85	3.7	.286	1.4	CF(26) 2.2, LF(1) 0.0	0.6	98
2018	LWD	A	19	299	33	12	2	1	20	14	40	18	4	.263/.299/.331	83	6.2	.303	1.7	CF(66) 4.6, RF(1) 0.0	1.1	90
2019	CLR	A+	20	465	52	21	3	3	28	32	60	21	12	.287/.337/.372	108	15.7	.327	2.1	CF(79) 0.0, RF(16) 0.8	2.2	102
2020	PHI	MLB	21	251	21	11	1	3	22	13	43	7	3	.242/.283/.335	62	0.0	.284	0.2	CF 1, RF 0	-0.3	103

Comparables: Abiatal Avelino, Rey Fuentes, José Peraza

Muzziotti is one of the group of players signed by the Red Sox but then made free agents by MLB as a penalty for the Red Sox bundling of players to circumvent their bonus limit in 2016. Signed by the Phillies, he's made consistent progress as he has moved through the system.

At High-A Clearwater in 2019, the 20-year-old Muzziotti showed a quick and quiet swing and above-average plate discipline. He recognizes pitches well and uses the whole field. While his raw power is just average, Muzziotti finds gaps often enough to keep pitchers honest.

Muzziotti seems to understand the type of player he has to be in order to have success. He has an extreme ground ball approach, trying to take advantage of his plus speed. He is learning how to put that speed to use once he gets on base as well, improving his reads and jumps on the bases and creating enough distraction that pitchers have to be aware of him. He is becoming more comfortable stealing bases, though he still needs to improve his success rate.

Muzziotti uses his speed to his advantage in the field as well. He covers ground efficiently in center field and takes good routes to balls. His arm is strong and accurate enough to easily handle the position. Muzziotti is on a path—assuming continued improvement—to be a regular in center field.

12 Enyel De Los Santos   RHP

Born: 12/25/95   Age: 24   Bats: R   Throws: R   Height: 6'3"   Weight: 170   Origin: International Free Agent, 2014

YEAR	TEAM	LVL	AGE	W	L	SV	G	GS	IP	H	HR	BB/9	K/9	K	GB%	BABIP	WHIP	ERA	DRA	WARP	PF
2017	SAN	AA	21	10	6	0	26	24	150	131	12	2.9	8.3	138	45%	.290	1.19	3.78	4.21	1.7	92
2018	LEH	AAA	22	10	5	0	22	22	126²	104	12	3.1	7.8	110	42%	.264	1.16	2.63	3.60	2.8	99
2018	PHI	MLB	22	1	0	0	7	2	19	19	2	3.8	7.1	15	51%	.309	1.42	4.74	4.97	0.0	89
2019	LEH	AAA	23	5	7	0	19	19	94	81	16	3.4	7.9	83	39%	.256	1.23	4.40	3.99	2.5	100
2019	PHI	MLB	23	0	1	0	5	1	11	13	4	4.1	7.4	9	41%	.321	1.64	7.36	4.75	0.1	101
2020	PHI	MLB	24	3	4	0	24	8	57	57	10	3.1	7.6	48	40%	.286	1.35	4.71	4.78	0.6	103

Comparables: Jake Odorizzi, Brandon Maurer, Reynaldo López

The scouting report on Enyel De Los Santos has been pretty consistent for a few years now. At his best he will throw a fastball that spans the 90s, reaching up to 98, and back it up with an above-average to plus changeup and a collection of mediocre breaking balls. That seemed to be the report for most of the 2019 season, as De Los Santos continued to struggle to find a good breaking ball to step forward as a usable third pitch. His fastball command wavered, and at times his velocity fell more into the lower 90s. His struggles in Triple-A ultimately meant the Phillies didn't call him up as part of their September roster.

There is still a path forward where De Los Santos finds a slider or curveball that allows him to be a back end starting pitcher, but he has stagnated on the doorstep of that upside. At some point early in the 2020 season the Phillies are going to need to decide if they just want to move him to the bullpen and have him focus on being a fastball/changeup reliever.

13 Kendall Simmons 2B

Born: 04/11/00   Age: 20   Bats: R   Throws: R   Height: 6'2"   Weight: 180   Origin: Round 6, 2018 Draft (#167 overall)

YEAR	TEAM	LVL	AGE	PA	R	2B	3B	HR	RBI	BB	K	SB	CS	AVG/OBP/SLG	DRC+	VORP	BABIP	BRR	FRAA	WARP	PF
2018	PHL	RK	18	113	21	7	0	3	11	9	30	2	4	.232/.345/.400	102	4.8	.302	-1.3	SS(32) -3.9	0.0	105
2019	WPT	A-	19	205	31	7	3	12	34	20	54	5	6	.234/.333/.520	126	19.3	.255	0.1	2B(23) -2.0, 3B(16) -0.9	0.7	96
2020	PHI	MLB	20	251	24	11	1	7	26	18	85	2	2	.197/.273/.345	63	0.0	.280	0.0	SS -1, 2B 0	-0.4	103

Kendall (who went by Logan before changing it during the season) Simmons has a lot of positive traits going for him. The body is exactly what you like to see from a young high school draftee, lean with present muscle mass, but one you can still dream on adding more without losing his twitchiness. Present raw pop from above-average bat speed that can drive baseballs all over the field. The feel to hit is eh, the approach is very aggressive and can be exposed against arms with better sequencing. Defensively you don't really want him on the left side of the diamond given his lack of arm strength and first step quickness. He should be fine at second base, especially with all this shifting and such. This is kind of a boom or bust profile, one that might not work and get horribly exposed in full-season ball.

14 Cristopher Sanchez LHP

Born: 12/12/96   Age: 23   Bats: L   Throws: L   Height: 6'5"   Weight: 165   Origin: International Free Agent, 2013

YEAR	TEAM	LVL	AGE	W	L	SV	G	GS	IP	H	HR	BB/9	K/9	K	GB%	BABIP	WHIP	ERA	DRA	WARP	PF
2017	PRI	RK	20	1	6	0	13	7	38^2	61	8	3.7	7.0	30	51%	.384	1.99	10.01	8.39	-1.0	106
2018	PRI	RK	21	3	2	0	10	10	43	53	3	4.6	7.1	34	53%	.368	1.74	4.60	5.52	0.3	116
2018	HUD	A-	21	1	0	0	2	2	9	9	0	5.0	11.0	11	56%	.391	1.56	4.00	5.51	0.0	93
2019	BGR	A	22	3	1	2	11	4	40^1	28	3	2.5	8.3	37	56%	.231	0.97	2.01	3.02	0.9	104
2019	PCH	A+	22	1	0	0	12	6	34	28	0	3.4	9.5	36	55%	.322	1.21	1.85	4.68	0.1	98
2020	PHI	MLB	23	2	2	0	21	5	41	41	7	3.7	6.9	32	44%	.280	1.40	4.73	4.78	0.4	103

Comparables: Jesen Therrien, Wander Suero, Yefry Ramírez

Back in early May, Sanchez was an intriguing arm in Extended Spring Training for the Rays, albeit as a 22-year-old who had spent three years in the DSL and was yet to crack full-season ball. Fast forward three months and Sanchez torched both A-ball levels and even earned a cameo appearance in Triple-A. So what happened? For one, the Rays have been notoriously aggressive in pushing guys if they believe they will hold their own and learn. Second, some guys just take longer to develop, especially taller kids. The fastball is plus at 92-94, the slider is firm with tilt, and the change has a chance to be plus with quality separation from his heater and big sink. Tampa Bay had too many quality prospects to protect everyone in December's Rule 5 draft, so they dealt Sanchez to the Phillies who had the 40-man space to protect this intriguing arm.

15 Victor Santos RHP

Born: 07/12/00   Age: 19   Bats: R   Throws: R   Height: 6'1"   Weight: 191   Origin: International Free Agent, 2016

YEAR	TEAM	LVL	AGE	W	L	SV	G	GS	IP	H	HR	BB/9	K/9	K	GB%	BABIP	WHIP	ERA	DRA	WARP	PF
2017	DPH	RK	16	4	2	0	12	9	49	52	1	0.9	7.0	38	65%	.325	1.16	2.57	3.89	1.1	106
2018	PHL	RK	17	6	1	0	11	11	59^1	63	4	0.6	9.9	65	39%	.355	1.13	3.03	3.09	1.9	104
2019	LWD	A	18	5	10	0	27	13	105^1	106	11	1.5	7.6	89	43%	.310	1.18	4.02	5.28	-0.3	88
2020	PHI	MLB	19	2	2	0	33	0	35	35	6	3.5	6.4	25	40%	.278	1.40	4.79	4.91	0.2	103

I like Santos more than this ranking. Despite not turning 19 until July, he was one of the best A-ball pitchers I saw in 2019, an advanced arm with pitchability who hardly ever walked anyone. He throws a split-change that is already above-average and should end up at plus. He mixes in a usable slider. The fastball comes in with strong run. The hitters usually tell you how effective a pitcher currently is, and Santos was consistently hard to square up in the Sally. Most of the individual pieces for future rotation success are already present.

The fastball velocity is missing, however. He sits around 90 and he was most often in the 88-91 band for me in Lakewood this year. That's teetering on the edge of not having enough velocity to be a serious prospect as a righty, and Santos looks close to maxed out. If he had a swing-and-miss breaking ball, I could probably justify blowing him up anyway, but he doesn't. I just don't know how many bats he's going to miss at higher levels. As precocious as he is, unless there's another trick up his sleeve he looks headed for fourth or fifth starter type of future.

16 JoJo Romero LHP

Born: 09/09/96   Age: 23   Bats: L   Throws: L   Height: 5'11"   Weight: 190   Origin: Round 4, 2016 Draft (#107 overall)

YEAR	TEAM	LVL	AGE	W	L	SV	G	GS	IP	H	HR	BB/9	K/9	K	GB%	BABIP	WHIP	ERA	DRA	WARP	PF
2017	LWD	A	20	5	1	0	13	13	76²	61	2	2.5	9.3	79	60%	.299	1.07	2.11	3.77	1.4	90
2017	CLR	A+	20	5	2	0	10	10	52¹	43	2	2.6	8.4	49	52%	.289	1.11	2.24	4.00	0.8	98
2018	REA	AA	21	7	6	0	18	18	106²	97	13	3.5	8.4	100	53%	.286	1.29	3.80	4.23	1.4	105
2019	REA	AA	22	4	4	0	11	11	57²	58	4	1.9	8.1	52	50%	.321	1.21	4.84	4.99	0.0	104
2019	LEH	AAA	22	3	5	0	13	13	53²	68	8	5.9	6.7	40	50%	.345	1.92	6.88	7.96	-0.6	100
2020	PHI	MLB	23	3	3	0	10	10	49	48	8	3.6	6.5	35	47%	.273	1.38	4.60	4.67	0.6	103

Comparables: Steve Garrison, Yohander Méndez, Brock Burke

Romero entered 2019 on the verge of majors, but his season got off to trouble from the start. His velocity was down in Spring Training, pitching more in the 89-91 range, and not his typical 93-94 when he was at his best in 2018. The Phillies still aggressively pushed him to Triple-A where he struggled mightily. He was eventually demoted to Double-A where he struggled less, and saw his command return some. At his diminished velocity and control, Romero projected more as an up-and-down starter than the low-end No. 3 starter upside he flashed at times.

The Phillies moved Romero to the bullpen for the Arizona Fall League, and while his strikeouts weren't up, he was dominant and his velocity was back near his peak, leading to the Phillies protecting him on the 40-man roster. At his best, Romero has an above-average fastball, a plus changeup, and two average breaking balls. None of that projects to be a dominant reliever, but he should be able to handle a multi-inning role and provide a similar impact as Ranger Suarez did in 2019. If he manages to get most of his stuff back together, he could still be a back end starting pitcher.

17 Connor Seabold RHP

Born: 01/24/96   Age: 24   Bats: R   Throws: R   Height: 6'2"   Weight: 190   Origin: Round 3, 2017 Draft (#83 overall)

YEAR	TEAM	LVL	AGE	W	L	SV	G	GS	IP	H	HR	BB/9	K/9	K	GB%	BABIP	WHIP	ERA	DRA	WARP	PF
2017	WPT	A-	21	2	0	0	5	0	10	5	0	1.8	11.7	13	50%	.227	0.70	0.90	2.36	0.3	100
2018	CLR	A+	22	4	4	0	12	12	71²	57	6	1.8	8.5	68	47%	.260	0.99	3.77	2.91	2.0	100
2018	REA	AA	22	1	4	0	11	11	58²	55	10	2.9	9.8	64	36%	.290	1.26	4.91	3.92	1.0	104
2019	CLR	A+	23	1	0	0	2	1	9	4	1	1.0	10.0	10	55%	.158	0.56	1.00	2.82	0.2	98
2019	REA	AA	23	3	1	0	7	7	40	35	2	2.2	8.1	36	47%	.300	1.12	2.25	4.12	0.4	104
2020	PHI	MLB	24	2	2	0	33	0	35	35	6	3.5	8.5	33	41%	.299	1.40	4.78	4.88	0.2	103

The Phillies have turned to the Cal State Fullerton well many times in the draft or trades during recent years. Seabold has more stuff than most of his college rotation mates, but he is not going to blow hitters away either. The Phillies smoothed over his delivery in late 2018, ditching a Bronson Arroyo-esque leg kick for a more repeatable and consistent motion. An oblique injury delayed the beginning of Seabold's season until June 25, and it was August before he was throwing full starts, causing the Phillies to send him to the Arizona Fall League to get him to 73 1/3 innings.

Seabold's fastball sits in the low 90s, and can get it up to 94-95. He backs it up with a solid curveball and an average changeup. He has above-average control and solid command, allowing his full arsenal to play up. His ceiling is still fairly modest, as he projects more as a solid No. 4 starter, but he should open the year in Triple-A and could see the major leagues before the end of the 2020 season.

18 Nick Maton SS

Born: 02/18/97   Age: 23   Bats: L   Throws: R   Height: 6'1"   Weight: 165   Origin: Round 7, 2017 Draft (#203 overall)

YEAR	TEAM	LVL	AGE	PA	R	2B	3B	HR	RBI	BB	K	SB	CS	AVG/OBP/SLG	DRC+	VORP	BABIP	BRR	FRAA	WARP	PF
2017	WPT	A-	20	246	34	9	1	2	13	30	47	10	5	.252/.350/.333	116	13.4	.311	2.7	SS(57) 8.1	2.5	103
2018	LWD	A	21	466	52	26	5	8	51	43	103	5	3	.256/.330/.404	103	33.8	.318	1.6	SS(110) 7.4, 2B(3) -0.3	3.1	90
2019	CLR	A+	22	384	35	14	3	5	45	41	71	11	8	.276/.358/.380	127	14.7	.335	-5.9	SS(65) -2.0, 2B(14) -0.1	1.6	102
2019	REA	AA	22	72	6	3	0	2	6	9	14	1	1	.210/.306/.355	94	1.6	.234	0.1	2B(11) -0.1, SS(8) -0.2	0.2	104
2020	PHI	MLB	23	251	23	12	1	5	25	20	65	2	1	.229/.294/.359	72	0.0	.295	-0.3	SS 1, 2B 0	0.1	103

Comparables: Alex Blandino, Derek Dietrich, Richie Martin

Maton is likely not a future all-star, but he is becoming an interesting player. He has soft hands, good range, and good footwork. His arm would play anywhere in the infield. While he looks to be able to handle a regular gig at shortstop, his future is more likely that of an up-the-middle utility guy with solid defense and good on-base skills.

Offensively, Maton is patient and disciplined with a short swing that is quick to the ball and allows for a lot of contact. He starts from an open stance and uses a toe tap to get his timing and squares himself up and he reacts well to offspeed pitches. He doesn't project for a lot of power and he hits a lot of balls on the ground to make use of his speed, but he would help himself if he looked to use more of the field as he currently hits too many balls to the pull side.

Maton has better than average speed and can steal a base. While he does seem like a utility player long-term, whether that is an old school utility guy or more of a modern, everyday utility guy will likely depend on how much he can wring out of that hit tool.

19 Kyle Glogoski RHP

Born: 01/06/99   Age: 21   Bats: R   Throws: R   Height: 6'2"   Weight: 183   Origin: International Free Agent, 2018

YEAR	TEAM	LVL	AGE	W	L	SV	G	GS	IP	H	HR	BB/9	K/9	K	GB%	BABIP	WHIP	ERA	DRA	WARP	PF
2018	PLL	RK	19	4	0	0	10	8	39	30	2	2.5	10.8	47	39%	.283	1.05	2.31	2.63	1.4	99
2019	LWD	A	20	3	1	0	8	3	27²	14	1	2.6	14.6	45	46%	.255	0.80	1.30	2.10	1.0	85
2019	CLR	A+	20	2	2	0	11	11	52²	37	2	3.4	7.7	45	40%	.241	1.08	1.88	3.44	1.0	102
2020	PHI	MLB	21	2	2	0	33	0	35	35	5	3.8	8.8	34	40%	.304	1.42	4.75	4.81	0.2	103

Going into 2019, the only reason you might've come across Glogoski would be that he is from New Zealand, one of the Phillies' diverse international signees (this includes players from Russia, Taiwan, China, France and Saudi Arabia). He was fine in my 2018 looks. He commanded a fastball, big loopy curveball and a changeup that was his most effective swing-and-miss pitch. In 2019, he started in Extended Spring Training but then finished making 11 starts in High-A Clearwater. As part of the Phillies carousel of piggybacked arms in Lakewood, Glogoski was called up and proceeded to dominate the level, forcing a move to face stiffer competition. The fastball doesn't light up the gun, settling in at average, but he knows where to put it, consistently going inside and getting awkward swings. The curveball is still not especially sharp, but he can mix it in as a change of pace offering. The changeup jumped over the last year and is now his best offspeed pitch. It mirrors his fastball and has late dive, almost like a split, and he uses it to both sides of the plate. Without a swing-and-miss breaker at present, Glogoski can be vulnerable against better hitters as he climbs, but for now, as the ambassador for New Zealand baseball, he is fun.

20 Erik Miller LHP

Born: 02/13/98   Age: 22   Bats: L   Throws: L   Height: 6'5"   Weight: 240   Origin: Round 4, 2019 Draft (#120 overall)

YEAR	TEAM	LVL	AGE	W	L	SV	G	GS	IP	H	HR	BB/9	K/9	K	GB%	BABIP	WHIP	ERA	DRA	WARP	PF
2019	WPT	A-	21	0	0	0	6	4	20	13	0	3.2	13.1	29	54%	.283	1.00	0.90	2.34	0.6	101
2019	LWD	A	21	1	0	0	3	2	13	10	0	4.2	11.8	17	32%	.323	1.23	2.08	4.31	0.1	96
2020	PHI	MLB	22	2	2	0	33	0	35	35	5	3.8	9.7	38	41%	.314	1.42	4.80	4.87	0.2	103

Comparables: Radhames Liz, Michael Stutes, Adonis Rosa

Miller was the Phillies fourth-round pick in the 2019 draft, and it is easy to see why some viewed him as a steal. In college, Miller was up to 97 with a plus slider from the left side, but it is also easy to see why he fell to where he did. His velocity was often inconsistent, and his command was poor. In professional ball, the Phillies have worked on cleaning up his delivery to improve his control. The result has been that Miller has been working more comfortably in the 90-94 range, but with a much higher strike rate. He backs the fastball up with a slider that, when consistent, is a plus pitch. His changeup has also shown as an above-average pitch in the past.

The Phillies have had luck building big pitchers with arm strength back up in the past, and Miller could experience a jump like Damon Jones did this year, at which point his ceiling is mid-rotation starting pitcher. If the control issues come back, the Phillies may be forced to move Miller to the bullpen and hope the velocity comes back and he can work as a two-pitch reliever.

Personal Cheeseball

PC **Deivy Grullon** C
Born: 02/17/96   Age: 24   Bats: R   Throws: R   Height: 6'1"   Weight: 180   Origin: International Free Agent, 2013

YEAR	TEAM	LVL	AGE	PA	R	2B	3B	HR	RBI	BB	K	SB	CS	AVG/OBP/SLG	DRC+	VORP	BABIP	BRR	FRAA	WARP	PF
2017	CLR	A+	21	286	31	14	0	8	24	12	61	0	1	.255/.287/.395	107	10.8	.299	0.8	C(69) -0.9	1.5	94
2017	REA	AA	21	89	10	3	0	4	13	5	19	0	0	.229/.270/.410	66	1.1	.246	-1.9	C(23) -7.3	-0.9	105
2018	REA	AA	22	353	36	14	1	21	59	18	81	0	0	.273/.310/.515	108	20.9	.296	-2.9	C(87) -20.0	-0.4	104
2019	LEH	AAA	23	457	55	24	0	21	77	45	133	1	0	.283/.354/.496	115	23.8	.367	-0.9	C(85) -18.6, 1B(7) -0.3	0.9	99
2019	PHI	MLB	23	9	0	1	0	0	1	0	2	0	0	.111/.111/.222	93	0.4	.143	0.0	C(2) -0.1	0.0	104
2020	PHI	MLB	24	70	7	4	0	3	9	4	22	0	0	.233/.284/.408	77	0.0	.308	-0.2	C -3	-0.2	103

Comparables: Darrell Johnson, Francisco Mejía, John Ryan Murphy

We flagged Grullon as a potential Rule 5 pick last year as a major-league-ready catcher with a simple swing and surprising pop. He didn't get popped then, but he did get added to the Philadelphia 40-man as a September call-up off a strong Triple-A campaign. He's hit 21 homers in each of the last two seasons, though the 2019 homer output was just as assisted by the juiced Triple-A ball as the 2018 output was by Reading's generous confines. Grullon brings along a strong defensive reputation fueled by a rocket throwing arm, but he hasn't graded out well by our upper-minors framing metrics. He profiles as a fun backup catcher with power upside, and could take over that role for the Phillies in 2020.

Low Minors Sleeper

LMS **Starlyn Castillo** RHP
Born: 02/24/02   Age: 18   Bats: R   Throws: R   Height: 6'0"   Weight: 210   Origin: International Free Agent, 2018

YEAR	TEAM	LVL	AGE	W	L	SV	G	GS	IP	H	HR	BB/9	K/9	K	GB%	BABIP	WHIP	ERA	DRA	WARP	PF
2019	PHL	RK	17	0	2	0	5	4	9¹	9	0	7.7	9.6	10	56%	.333	1.82	7.71	5.11	0.1	92

Signed for a $1.6M bonus in the '18 signing period, Castillo's stateside debut was unspectacular and marred by false starts. He didn't pitch much during Extended Spring Training or in the GCL due to a myriad of ailments and injuries. When he did pitch, the results weren't great, but that can likely be chalked up to rust and inconsistency. You can see why he got so much money, with clean arm action, arm speed, a big heater, and swing-and-miss breaker. There are present signs of concern, given that the body has already softened up, he wasn't that "projectable" to begin with, he missed time in his first pro year, and he lacks feel for the strike zone. But, this is a 17-year-old kid with stuff that gets your attention and who still has a long developmental path in front of him.

Top Talents 25 and Under (as of 4/1/2020)

1. Scott Kingery
2. Spencer Howard
3. Alec Bohm
4. Adam Haseley
5. Zach Eflin
6. Francisco Morales

7. Bryson Stott
8. Seranthony Dominguez
9. Adonis Medina
10. Luis Garcia

The Phillies are a win-now team, with most of their core either in their traditional prime years, or 30ish free agent signings. Scott Kingery is eligible by a month, and followed up a disastrous rookie campaign with a solid sophomore bounceback. He's traded off some hit for power, but the pop plays—baseball contingent I suppose—and he's a quality defender at several spots, and passable at several more. He may only settle in as a solid-average regular, but that kind of production with that much defensive flexibility is a valuable piece in 2020 baseball.

As a prospect, Adam Haseley never really popped as much as you'd want an eighth-overall pick to. There's strong tweenerish markers in the profile, but he's useful at three outfield spots—although how useful depends a lot on your defensive metric of choice—and there's average hit/power projection in the bat. There's strong fourth outfielder/Role 45 vibes so far, but he's MLB-ready with upside past that, which is something the prospect names behind him can't really say.

Zach Eflin is the pitcher version of that profile and slots in right behind Haseley. He's league averageish the past two seasons, although DRA likes him less than RA or FIP metrics, and he's not quite durable/efficient enough or quite good enough to pencil him into your Opening Day rotation. There's a good chance he ends up there anyway though.

Seranthony Dominguez would be ahead of Haseley and Eflin if he weren't dealing with a small UCL tear. He's a potential dominant late inning reliever if healthy. His offseason should be normal, but elbow injuries are…well, not what you want.

Eyewitness Reports

Eyewitness Report: Spencer Howard

Evaluator: Steve Givarz
Report Date: 10/06/2019
Dates Seen: 10/4/19
Risk Factor: Moderate
Delivery: Large frame but well-proportioned. Pitches from a semi-wind-up, high lead arm, long arm action with average arm speed to a higher 3/4 slot. Slight crossfire as he lands towards third base, mild deception.

Pitch Type	Future Grade	Sitting Velocity	Peak Velocity	Report
Fastball	70	96-98	99	Was more 95-96 later but was strong pitch in outing, plus ride, hitters struggled to stay on top of it, consistently got under hands, commanded well. Worked north/south primarily, see as a plus-plus offering.
Curveball	45	77-79	79	More a change of pace option, not sharp but showed average 11-5 depth. Easily seen out of hand, effective as a steal a strike pitch but isn't his out pitch, fringe-average offering.
Slider	60	84-85	85	Plus offering with quality depth and tilt, late action that got swings and misses. Was out pitch in viewing, kept down in the zone, could flatten if left up but hitters struggled to time it up, plus pitch.
Changeup	60	81-83	84	Large velo separation, parachutes out of his hand, used to both sides to mess with hitters timing, late drop that almost acted like a soft split-finger, kept down in the zone, plus offering.

Conclusion: See as a mid-rotation starter with upside beyond that. 23 y/o RHP, missed time with right shoulder soreness, Plus-plus fastball with plus slider/change, and fringe curvevball that he can all drop for strikes. Plus control. Strong interest would acquire.

Eyewitness Report: Francisco Morales

Evaluator: Jarrett Seidler

Report Date: 11/25/2019

Dates Seen: 3x 2019

Risk Factor: High

Delivery: Tall righty with a high-3/4 arm slot. Comes through late with the back leg and lands with a bit of violence in the foot strike. This creates deception and makes him hard to pick up, but also lends to consistency/repeatability issues.

Pitch Type	Future Grade	Sitting Velocity	Peak Velocity	Report
Fastball	60	94-96	97	Mid-90s from a pitching prospect seems almost rote now, but Morales throws it with consistency and riding life. He's been ticking up as a pro and he could certainly have a tick or two left given physical projectability, and perhaps more than that if he ends up airing it out in relief eventually.
Slider	60	85-89	89	Advanced true slider with tight two-plane break. Locates the pitch well. Far too much for most A-ball hitters. Current and future out pitch and on the borderline of projecting to plus-plus instead of plus.
Changeup	50	86-88	88	Flashed better than I expected based on past reports. It's got some dive to it, and works well in concert with the fastball in a similar velocity band. Not likely to develop into an out pitch, but as a third offering it gives him a chance to stick in the rotation.

Conclusion: Morales is something of the prototypical high variance 60 OFP arm. It's a big fastball/slider combination, and there's a case to throw a 7 on either (or both) of the pitches. Recent development of his change gives him a better chance to stay in the rotation, and he has the makings of a power closer type if he shifts to the bullpen.

Pittsburgh Pirates

The State of the System
The NL Central is not exactly loaded with good systems. The Pirates Top Ten runs a little deeper in interesting names than their division rivals, but this out quickly after that.

The Top Ten

─────────────── ★ ★ ★ *2020 Top 101 Prospect* **#53** ★ ★ ★ ───────────────

1 **Mitch Keller** **RHP**   OFP: 60   ETA: 2019
Born: 04/04/96   Age: 24   Bats: R   Throws: R   Height: 6'2"   Weight: 210   Origin: Round 2, 2014 Draft (#64 overall)

YEAR	TEAM	LVL	AGE	W	L	SV	G	GS	IP	H	HR	BB/9	K/9	K	GB%	BABIP	WHIP	ERA	DRA	WARP	PF
2017	BRD	A+	21	6	3	0	15	15	77¹	57	5	2.3	7.4	64	55%	.248	1.00	3.14	3.14	1.9	99
2017	ALT	AA	21	2	2	0	6	6	34²	25	2	2.9	11.7	45	48%	.280	1.04	3.12	2.41	1.1	97
2018	ALT	AA	22	9	2	0	14	14	86	64	7	3.3	8.0	76	55%	.251	1.12	2.72	3.55	1.8	89
2018	IND	AAA	22	3	2	0	10	10	52¹	59	3	3.8	9.8	57	35%	.366	1.55	4.82	6.93	-0.8	93
2019	IND	AAA	23	7	5	0	19	19	103²	94	9	3.0	10.7	123	46%	.315	1.24	3.56	3.38	3.3	95
2019	PIT	MLB	23	1	5	0	11	11	48	72	6	3.0	12.2	65	41%	.475	1.83	7.12	4.18	0.8	99
2020	PIT	MLB	24	7	7	0	23	23	113	108	13	3.3	10.0	127	43%	.315	1.32	4.00	4.14	2.1	101

Comparables: Jake Faria, Zack Littell, Lucas Sims

The Report: We said last year in this space that Keller's fastball/curve combination was "one of the best in the minors." That remains true on raw stuff. The fastball was still sitting in the mid-90s and touching 98. The curveball still flashed plus-plus. But—and this is a pretty big "but" even for prospect writing—Keller's fastball got absolutely tattooed in the majors, like Ted Williams in his prime opposing line tattooed, and he only threw the curveball just a little over 16 percent of the time. Instead, he favored a recently-added hard slider, and while that pitch showed individual promise and was effective in a small sample, the overall package just didn't look like it was working. That slider virtually replaced Keller's change, which he'd been trying to develop for years and just wasn't getting past fringe. That leaves him with a fastball/breaking ball/breaking ball arsenal, which is a tough package to stick as a starter with, especially given sometimes wavering fastball command.

If it feels like you've heard this story before...well, the Pirates have certainly had promising young pitchers stagnate and then turn into top of the rotation arms elsewhere a few times recently. More troublingly, it seems to be immediate changes when moved to teams that are strong in pitch design, which infers that the Pirates are not maximizing incumbent talent as part of the player development process. We have no choice but to build that into Keller's report at this point, because it's already manifesting as stagnation while he's still technically prospect-eligible.

Variance: High, unusually so for a healthy player so close to graduating.

Mark Barry's Fantasy Take: Not sure if you remember, but Keller wasn't particularly good in his first taste of the big leagues. That said, he got swinging strikes a little better than league average, and even though opposing hitters treated him like a slow-pitch pitching machine, he was still a *tad* unlucky as far as his BABIP and strand rates were concerned. The ceiling might be lower, but I think there's a buying opportunity as it's likely Keller managers have quite the bitter taste lingering in their respective mouths.

★ ★ ★ *2020 Top 101 Prospect* **#55** ★ ★ ★

2 **Oneil Cruz** **SS** OFP: 60 ETA: 2021
Born: 10/04/98 Age: 21 Bats: L Throws: R Height: 6'7" Weight: 175 Origin: International Free Agent, 2015

YEAR	TEAM	LVL	AGE	PA	R	2B	3B	HR	RBI	BB	K	SB	CS	AVG/OBP/SLG	DRC+	VORP	BABIP	BRR	FRAA	WARP	PF
2017	GRL	A	18	375	51	9	1	8	36	28	110	8	7	.240/.293/.342	83	13.9	.323	3.2	3B(47) -9.3, SS(30) 0.2	-0.1	97
2017	WVA	A	18	63	9	2	1	2	8	8	22	0	0	.218/.317/.400	78	3.4	.323	1.0	3B(15) 0.6, SS(1) 0.0	0.2	102
2018	WVA	A	19	443	66	25	7	14	59	34	100	11	5	.286/.343/.488	130	37.7	.346	2.5	SS(102) -5.9	2.9	99
2019	BRD	A+	20	145	21	6	1	7	16	8	38	7	3	.301/.345/.515	152	14.8	.374	0.1	SS(35) 2.2	1.6	99
2019	ALT	AA	20	136	14	8	3	1	17	15	35	3	1	.269/.346/.412	121	10.1	.365	1.1	SS(34) 2.9	1.3	97
2020	PIT	MLB	21	251	24	12	1	7	27	18	80	3	1	.234/.291/.381	76	0.0	.327	-0.2	SS 1, 3B 0	0.2	101

Comparables: Yorman Rodriguez, Alex Liddi, Andrew Velazquez

The Report: Cruz is a unicorn amongst baseball prospects, a huge young man who is far too big to play shortstop who not only plays short but still excels there. He's nimble, with good reactions and a cannon for an arm. If dropped into the majors tomorrow, he wouldn't look out of place at the position, except that he's 6-foot-7 and has substantially filled out since his listed/signing weight. Because of the unprecedented nature of his physique relative to his present defensive skills, we still have no clue where he lands defensively; he runs well enough and is agile enough that nearly anywhere in the infield or outfield is reasonably in play depending on the body development.

There's exciting upside with the stick. Cruz has monster raw power that he hasn't fully tapped into yet, but we think he's getting there. He also has unexpectedly good bat-to-ball skills given his size and aggressive MiLB assignments, which allowed him to look perfectly in place as a 20-year-old in Double-A in the second half of 2019. His levers are long and he takes a healthy cut, so there's always going to be swing-and-miss concerns present, yet they're manageable for his size and overall skill set. It's within his range of projections that he combines the feel for the bat with the raw power and turn into an offensive force.

Variance: Medium, although on the higher side of medium. It's a weird, weird group of skills and there's a lot of variance in the shape of things to come, but less in whether or not he's going to be a decent MLB regular of some form.

Mark Barry's Fantasy Take: There's not really a good comp for Cruz, because he's basically Aaron Judge minus 100 pounds, and he plays shortstop. It's not quite Judge power, but it's not-not Judge power potential. He struck out more than you'd like as he moved up the ladder, and he's still not super close, but he's an easy back-end, top-100 guy for me.

★ ★ ★ *2020 Top 101 Prospect* **#63** ★ ★ ★

3 **Ke'Bryan Hayes** **3B** OFP: 60 ETA: 2020
Born: 01/28/97 Age: 23 Bats: R Throws: R Height: 6'1" Weight: 210 Origin: Round 1, 2015 Draft (#32 overall)

YEAR	TEAM	LVL	AGE	PA	R	2B	3B	HR	RBI	BB	K	SB	CS	AVG/OBP/SLG	DRC+	VORP	BABIP	BRR	FRAA	WARP	PF
2017	BRD	A+	20	482	66	16	7	2	43	41	76	27	5	.278/.345/.363	124	18.8	.331	0.8	3B(108) 20.7	4.9	99
2018	ALT	AA	21	508	64	31	7	7	47	57	84	12	5	.293/.375/.444	133	38.7	.344	-0.8	3B(116) 9.0	4.5	92
2019	IND	AAA	22	480	64	30	2	10	53	43	90	12	1	.265/.336/.415	96	14.6	.311	2.3	3B(103) 8.2	2.3	94
2020	PIT	MLB	23	42	4	2	0	1	4	3	10	1	0	.231/.298/.357	72	3.0	.290	0.0	3B 1	0.0	101

Comparables: Jefry Marte, Miguel Andújar, Rio Ruiz

The Report: Ke'Bryan Hayes had a perfectly normal Ke'Bryan Hayes season as a 22-year-old in Triple-A and it feels…disappointing. He played to the profile and held serve as a national prospect. There's still excellent third base defense, a solid approach, good feel for contact, and plenty of doubles. Did he know they were using new baseballs? It feels like we have been waiting for the power breakout here for a while. It's easy plus raw power when he wants to show it off, he's just never consistently lifted the ball in games. I'm sure there will be other places on the list for us to grouse about Pirates prospect development, and those complaints are usually directed towards the pitching side anyway, and it seems needlessly snarky to blame them, Hayes is still a good prospect with a potential plus hit tool and plus defense. And all those laser beam doubles to left field will add up anyway.

Variance: Medium. Hayes is pretty much ready to man the hot corner in PNC Park, but how his major league game power plays out will determine if the Pirates are looking to upgrade in a few years, or if they are selling a few All-Star jerseys with "Hayes" on the back.

Mark Barry's Fantasy Take: Hayes was a dude that I long targeted as an "OMG, wait 'til he gets the to juiced balls"-type dude. Well, that didn't go particularly well. Hayes still makes a lot of contact and has a knack to get on base, but unless he adds some loft he could be a little more Brian Anderson-y as opposed to anything more interesting. That's still not bad, though.

4 Quinn Priester RHP   OFP: 60   ETA: 2023
Born: 09/15/00   Age: 19   Bats: R   Throws: R   Height: 6'3"   Weight: 195   Origin: Round 1, 2019 Draft (#18 overall)

YEAR	TEAM	LVL	AGE	W	L	SV	G	GS	IP	H	HR	BB/9	K/9	K	GB%	BABIP	WHIP	ERA	DRA	WARP	PF
2019	PIR	RK	18	1	1	0	8	7	32²	29	1	2.8	10.2	37	58%	.318	1.19	3.03	5.66	0.1	97
2020	PIT	MLB	19	2	2	0	33	0	35	35	5	3.8	7.7	30	48%	.289	1.42	4.77	4.92	0.2	101

Comparables: Domingo Germán, Sandy Baez, Alex Reyes

The Report: You may have read this a few times by this point, but Priester had a case as the best prep pitcher in the 2019 draft. A cold weather arm with a good mix of projection and present stuff, Priester generally sits low-90s with his fastball at present, but with a frame that should add some good weight and a couple ticks in coming years. The pitch will flash some good sink and run, although the command can be inconsistent. The party piece here is a power 11-5, upper-70s breaking ball that consistently flashes plus. It can get a bit lazy or loopy, but we are looking at refinement here more than projection. There's the usual prep arm change, in that it exists, but it's pretty firm. You are betting on some developmental leaps once Priester gets into a professional development program, but there's also a lot to like already. You might prefer the present stuff and mid-rotation starter frame of Matt Allan. You might lean for arm strength and take Daniel Espino. Perhaps you go for what's behind door number three—the polish of Brennan Malone—but Priester is right there with all of them.

Variance: High. Leaning towards extreme given the lack of mound reps. The track record of prep righties is not great, and the command and change need grade jumps. Maybe more than one. You know the drill.

Mark Barry's Fantasy Take: You guys, it gets pretty rough pretty quickly. Priester is intriguing (especially if you play in a league that rewards Dope Names) but he's too far away and too raw to be anything more than a deep-league dart throw.

5 Cal Mitchell RF   OFP: 55   ETA: 2021
Born: 03/08/99   Age: 21   Bats: L   Throws: L   Height: 6'0"   Weight: 209   Origin: Round 2, 2017 Draft (#50 overall)

YEAR	TEAM	LVL	AGE	PA	R	2B	3B	HR	RBI	BB	K	SB	CS	AVG/OBP/SLG	DRC+	VORP	BABIP	BRR	FRAA	WARP	PF
2017	PIR	RK	18	185	17	11	0	2	20	24	35	2	3	.245/.351/.352	123	4.8	.303	-0.9	LF(35) 2.6, CF(3) 0.5	0.9	98
2018	WVA	A	19	495	55	29	3	10	65	41	109	4	5	.280/.344/.427	127	20.4	.347	-4.4	RF(100) 0.5, LF(11) -1.6	1.7	98
2019	BRD	A+	20	493	54	21	2	15	64	32	142	1	1	.251/.304/.406	104	8.5	.328	0.0	RF(110) -0.4	1.0	98
2020	PIT	MLB	21	251	25	12	1	7	28	20	81	0	0	.234/.300/.391	81	0.0	.328	-0.4	RF 0, LF 0	0.2	101

Comparables: Dalton Pompey, Willy García, Yorman Rodriguez

The Report: Bradenton is an absolutely brutal place to hit, so if you were wondering that slash line above actually comes out to a bit above-average by DRC+. Yes, yes, don't scout the statline, and a bit above average isn't going to be all that special given Mitchell's limited athletic tools and corner outfield profile, but he can hit. Mitchell's swing is compact and quick, designed more for hard line drives than booming home runs, but he'll run into plenty of those as well. He can get aggressive against offspeed, but he makes enough adjustments with the barrel to project a plus hit tool, and he's strong enough to bop 20 home runs here and there along the way. He's not going to offer a ton of defensive or baserunning value, but he's perfectly fine in a corner. It's a bat-first profile that will get tested in Double-A, but so far he's handled everything pro ball has thrown at him while rarely facing a pitcher younger than him.

Variance: High. Double-A will be a stern test of the bat.

Mark Barry's Fantasy Take: To continue a long-standing tradition in these parts—can I interest you in a Jay Bruce with more strikeouts, less power and fewer walks (or say, Hunter Renfroe with way less power)?

6 Travis Swaggerty CF   OFP: 55   ETA: 2021

Born: 08/19/97 Age: 22 Bats: L Throws: L Height: 5'11" Weight: 180 Origin: Round 1, 2018 Draft (#10 overall)

YEAR	TEAM	LVL	AGE	PA	R	2B	3B	HR	RBI	BB	K	SB	CS	AVG/OBP/SLG	DRC+	VORP	BABIP	BRR	FRAA	WARP	PF
2018	WEV	A-	20	158	22	9	1	4	15	15	40	9	3	.288/.365/.453	151	12.5	.379	0.9	CF(36) -0.6	1.2	96
2018	WVA	A	20	71	6	1	1	1	5	7	18	0	0	.129/.225/.226	40	-1.2	.159	-0.6	CF(16) 0.7	-0.2	93
2019	BRD	A+	21	524	79	20	3	9	40	57	116	23	8	.265/.347/.381	124	25.2	.334	-0.2	CF(120) 7.4	3.7	98
2020	PIT	MLB	22	251	23	11	1	5	25	17	74	3	1	.223/.281/.348	65	0.0	.303	0.2	CF 2	0.0	101

Comparables: Daniel Fields, Zoilo Almonte, Kirk Nieuwenhuis

The Report: If you were wondering, DRC+ likes Swaggerty's 2019 even more than Mitchell's. I have my concerns, so it's man versus machine, let's go Deep Blue. I assume Judge's torquetem sees that Swaggerty is walking more than Mitchell and striking out less, and that jibes with his amateur profile that praised his approach and bat control. I wonder if he will be too passive against better pitching, and am not a huge fan of the double toe tap timing mechanism in his swing. When Swaggerty is right, he can spray line drives from gap-to-gap and there's potential average home run power as well. And he's maintained his plus speed so far and should stick in center. It remains a rather unexciting profile that might lack a carrying tool, but a good approach, plus an average hit/power combo and a center field glove. Well you don't need Deep Blue to crunch those numbers.

Variance: Medium. In contrast to Mitchell, Swaggerty does offer some defense and baserunning value, so even if he doesn't hit a ton, there's a bench outfielder role waiting for him. By the same token, he doesn't offer Garrett-Anderson-type upside with the bat either.

Mark Barry's Fantasy Take: For fantasy, I like Swaggerty more than Mitchell and Priester. He makes contact and gets on base at a solid clip, freeing him up to use his carrying fantasy tool—those sweet, sweet wheels. More power would be nice, sure, but gimme 25-plus steals, and I'll be more than happy.

7 Cody Bolton RHP   OFP: 55   ETA: 2021

Born: 06/19/98 Age: 22 Bats: R Throws: R Height: 6'3" Weight: 185 Origin: Round 6, 2017 Draft (#178 overall)

YEAR	TEAM	LVL	AGE	W	L	SV	G	GS	IP	H	HR	BB/9	K/9	K	GB%	BABIP	WHIP	ERA	DRA	WARP	PF
2017	PIR	RK	19	0	2	0	9	9	25²	23	1	2.8	7.7	22	44%	.286	1.21	3.16	2.84	0.9	95
2018	WVA	A	20	3	3	0	9	9	44¹	43	6	1.4	9.1	45	43%	.308	1.13	3.65	4.28	0.5	102
2019	BRD	A+	21	6	3	0	12	12	61²	39	1	2.0	10.1	69	48%	.245	0.86	1.61	2.73	1.7	97
2019	ALT	AA	21	2	3	0	9	9	40	37	6	3.6	7.4	33	35%	.277	1.33	5.85	4.31	0.3	98
2020	PIT	MLB	22	2	2	0	33	0	35	35	6	3.8	8.1	32	37%	.296	1.43	4.78	4.91	0.2	101

Comparables: Tyler Mahle, Edwin Díaz, Kyle Drabek

The Report: Bolton got a couple extra ticks on his fastball this year, and boy did the rest of the profile pop with the radar gun readings. The fastball sits mid-90s with some plane and he can bore it into lefties effectively. His cutterish slider in the upper-80s plays well off the fastball, and he can manipulate the offering as well, taking a little off to get a bit more depth on it. It's a potential plus two-pitch combo of power stuff. His change lags a fair bit behind at present, too firm and he struggles to turn it over. He also tired a bit late in the season despite being used fairly conservatively within his outings. So there's a chance he's a better fit in the late innings rather than taking the ball every fifth day, but the top two pitches here will play in any role.

Variance: Medium. The fastball/slider combo will get major league hitters out, but he really hasn't worked a real starter's routine/workload yet, and the change and command still need refinement.

Mark Barry's Fantasy Take: There's nothing too exciting about Bolton in a fantasy sense. Pass.

8   Tahnaj Thomas   RHP   OFP: 55   ETA: 2023/24

Born: 06/16/99   Age: 21   Bats: R   Throws: R   Height: 6'4"   Weight: 190   Origin: International Free Agent, 2016

YEAR	TEAM	LVL	AGE	W	L	SV	G	GS	IP	H	HR	BB/9	K/9	K	GB%	BABIP	WHIP	ERA	DRA	WARP	PF
2017	CLE	RK	18	0	3	0	13	10	33	35	4	6.8	7.9	29	48%	.330	1.82	6.00	7.41	-0.5	107
2018	CLE	RK	19	0	0	0	8	6	19²	13	2	4.6	12.4	27	60%	.275	1.17	4.58	2.13	0.8	98
2019	BRI	RK+	20	2	3	0	12	12	48¹	40	5	2.6	11.0	59	42%	.292	1.12	3.17	3.77	1.3	102

The Report: The Bahamian bats get most of the press around these parts—and to be honest I really enjoyed Trent Deveaux's recent home run derby performance—but Thomas gives the island a pretty good prospect arm to call its own. He seems like he's almost all legs. It's a high-waisted, very projectable frame that generates mid-90s heat, up to 99. The fastball barrels down on hitters from a high-three-quarters slot with good plane, and Thomas has a bit of feel for a power curve, although it's not a tight spinner yet and can get slurvy. He's athletic on the mound, but the delivery has a bit of effort and there's relief risk generally. But as projectable arm strength bets go, Thomas is one to circle at the top of your watch list.

Variance: Extreme. Thomas is a raw, Appy league arm that's mostly arm strength at present. This can go in any number of directions.

Mark Barry's Fantasy Take: Thomas is super, super raw and super, super far away, but I'd be more likely to take a chance on him putting it together than your run-of-the-mill SP5ish dude that will become a middle reliever.

9   Sammy Siani   OF   OFP: 50   ETA: 2023/24

Born: 12/14/00   Age: 19   Bats: L   Throws: L   Height: 6'0"   Weight: 195   Origin: Round 1, 2019 Draft (#37 overall)

YEAR	TEAM	LVL	AGE	PA	R	2B	3B	HR	RBI	BB	K	SB	CS	AVG/OBP/SLG	DRC+	VORP	BABIP	BRR	FRAA	WARP	PF
2019	PIR	RK	18	164	21	3	3	0	9	26	41	5	0	.241/.372/.308	95	2.5	.340	-1.1	CF(21) -3.0, LF(16) 1.4	0.1	102
2020	PIT	MLB	19	251	21	11	1	3	20	23	85	3	1	.209/.287/.303	60	0.0	.322	0.0	CF -1, LF 0	-0.5	101

Comparables: Derrick Robinson, Brett Phillips, Jason Martin

The Report: The younger brother of Michael Siani in the Reds system, Sammy shares a few familial traits on the field. He's a speedy outfielder with a loose, sweet left-handed swing that features plus bat speed and advanced barrel control. It's a hit-first profile given both his size and relative lack of loft in the swing plane, but he should make plenty of hard line drive content. He's not as advanced defensively as his older sibling, but he should be able to stick in center. There is limited physical projection here and somewhat limited upside, but outside of the lack of pop, there isn't a real weakness in Siani's game either.

Variance: High. Complex-league resume, hit-tool driven profile that hasn't seen better pitching yet. The bat really needs to be a center field profile and not a left field profile.

Mark Barry's Fantasy Take: If you want to toss Siani on your watchlist and hope he ultimately turns into Oscar Mercado with less power in a couple of years, that's perfectly respectable.

10   Lolo Sanchez   OF   OFP: 50   ETA: 2022

Born: 04/23/99   Age: 21   Bats: R   Throws: R   Height: 5'11"   Weight: 168   Origin: International Free Agent, 2015

YEAR	TEAM	LVL	AGE	PA	R	2B	3B	HR	RBI	BB	K	SB	CS	AVG/OBP/SLG	DRC+	VORP	BABIP	BRR	FRAA	WARP	PF
2017	PIR	RK	18	234	42	11	2	4	20	21	19	14	7	.284/.359/.417	126	14.9	.295	-0.9	CF(49) 7.6	1.9	98
2018	WVA	A	19	441	57	18	1	4	34	41	72	30	13	.243/.322/.328	97	14.2	.287	2.7	CF(88) 8.4, LF(19) -2.1	2.1	98
2019	GRB	A	20	263	43	10	6	4	26	17	28	20	10	.301/.377/.451	142	25.5	.327	2.1	CF(40) -3.7, LF(14) 0.5	1.8	96
2019	BRD	A+	20	195	21	3	3	1	9	18	31	13	5	.196/.300/.270	63	1.1	.233	2.4	LF(41) 0.3, CF(4) -0.8	-0.1	97
2020	PIT	MLB	21	251	21	11	1	3	21	18	46	7	4	.218/.287/.315	61	0.0	.260	0.0	CF 1, LF -1	-0.3	101

Comparables: Abiatal Avelino, Abraham Almonte, Jason Martin

The Report: Sanchez is the sort of prospect that on a good day might look like a future table-setter at the top of a big league order, and on a bad one might look like he hasn't a prayer of escaping Double-A. His 2019 season could be split into two clean halves; one in which he tears up the Sally League and another in which he failed to find his footing down in Florida. So yes, he is like many prospects. Sanchez does have some skills in rare abundance, though. He's a natural centerfielder whose plus speed translates effortlessly into range and whose sure glove and good reads allow him to complete most plays on an easy glide. He can easily cover left and the arm should be just good enough that he can fill in at right. The speed plays well on the bases as well, and he'll steal a handful of bags. He's a very good athlete with some twitch, though he's small framed and compact without a lot of physical projection. His above-average bat speed allows him some unexpected gap power, which is augmented by his ability to take the extra base. The approach isn't terrible but he's close to a dead pull hitter who sits on pitches on the inner part of the plate, and the swing isn't the most beautiful you'll see. He has shown the ability to make adjustments in the past, however, and will flip a breaking ball the other way from time to time. Sanchez is an exciting player to watch, but his ultimate outcome will depend on how well he can continue to make those adjustments against high-level pitching.

Variance: High. Doubts abound when it comes to the hit tool, and he'll need to answer some questions even to hit his fallback role as a fourth outfielder.

Mark Barry's Fantasy Take: If you want to toss Sanchez on your watchlist and hope he ultimately turns into Oscar Mercado with less hit-tool in a couple of years, that's perfectly respectable.

The Next Ten

11 Jared Oliva OF

Born: 11/27/95   Age: 24   Bats: R   Throws: R   Height: 6'3"   Weight: 203   Origin: Round 7, 2017 Draft (#208 overall)

YEAR	TEAM	LVL	AGE	PA	R	2B	3B	HR	RBI	BB	K	SB	CS	AVG/OBP/SLG	DRC+	VORP	BABIP	BRR	FRAA	WARP	PF
2017	WEV	A-	21	254	30	10	7	0	17	17	57	15	4	.266/.327/.374	97	9.3	.353	-0.4	CF(42) 0.6, LF(6) -0.2	0.7	108
2018	BRD	A+	22	454	75	24	4	9	47	40	91	33	8	.275/.354/.424	129	28.7	.332	4.3	CF(101) -7.6	2.4	104
2019	ALT	AA	23	507	70	24	6	6	42	42	104	36	10	.277/.352/.398	128	34.4	.347	4.2	CF(113) -1.2, LF(1) -0.1	3.4	96
2020	PIT	MLB	24	251	24	12	2	5	24	16	67	9	3	.236/.298/.362	75	0.0	.314	1.0	CF 0, LF 0	0.1	101

Comparables: Bryan Reynolds, Jake Marisnick, Tyler Naquin

Oliva's skillset isn't going to wow you. He was a Day 2 college pick from a major college program. He shared a lineup card at Arizona with Kevin Newman, Scott Kingery, Bobby Dalbec and J.J. Matijevic. Scouts probably weren't there to see him most weekends. This is the first time he's made one of our Pirates lists. He's had to prove it every level, and he's mostly been fine. But now he's spent a season in Double-A. He's one phone call away from the majors and you start to shift your focus to what a player can do for you major league ball club. And Oliva offers a little bit of everything.

He has a patient approach and knows how to make good contact. He picks his spots and can drive the ball the other way. There's below-average over-the-fence power, due to merely average bat speed and an emphasis on contact, but he'll hit some doubles. He can spot you in three outfield spots. He's only an average runner, but his instincts and routes play in center, and he'd be above average in a corner. You might not want him starting every day, but he can fill in for a month if someone goes down and keep the lineup moving. He's going to have to keep proving it at every level, but he's pretty close to the majors now, and surety has value too.

12 James Marvel RHP

Born: 09/17/93   Age: 26   Bats: R   Throws: R   Height: 6'4"   Weight: 205   Origin: Round 36, 2015 Draft (#1087 overall)

YEAR	TEAM	LVL	AGE	W	L	SV	G	GS	IP	H	HR	BB/9	K/9	K	GB%	BABIP	WHIP	ERA	DRA	WARP	PF
2017	WVA	A	23	6	8	0	20	20	94²	92	10	2.8	7.1	75	48%	.288	1.28	3.99	4.62	0.7	102
2017	BRD	A+	23	1	0	0	4	4	24	19	0	1.9	6.0	16	63%	.253	1.00	1.50	3.08	0.6	87
2018	BRD	A+	24	9	6	0	22	21	134¹	132	10	2.1	6.7	100	49%	.305	1.21	3.68	4.75	0.9	103
2018	ALT	AA	24	3	1	0	5	5	33	29	1	2.5	6.0	22	50%	.272	1.15	3.00	3.58	0.7	97
2019	ALT	AA	25	9	5	0	17	17	101²	85	6	2.1	7.3	83	51%	.273	1.07	3.10	4.51	0.5	96
2019	IND	AAA	25	7	0	0	11	11	60²	46	4	3.3	7.9	53	49%	.258	1.12	2.67	3.02	2.2	92
2019	PIT	MLB	25	0	3	0	4	4	17¹	25	4	3.1	4.7	9	54%	.333	1.79	8.31	5.86	0.0	98
2020	PIT	MLB	26	1	1	0	3	3	15	16	3	3.5	6.0	10	49%	.289	1.50	5.69	5.65	0.0	101

Comparables: Sean Poppen, Daniel Ponce de Leon, Mark Leiter Jr.

A major-league endgame was a long time coming for Marvel. He missed his entire junior year at Duke recovering from Tommy John surgery and ended up a 36th round pick. He was always old for his level of competition, and the stuff never popped on the scouting sheet, but he kept pounding the zone with a good sinker and he beat a path to Pittsburgh while opposing hitters beat the ball into the ground. Marvel's fastball sits around 90, and shows really good late sink. It will get groundballs as long as he commands it down in the zone. He'll pop a four-seam up for a change of pace now and again too. Marvel's curve comes in either side of 80, and while he commands it well, it can lack ideal depth to get whiffs, running down barrels instead. There's also a sinking change that can run a bit too close to the sinker in both velocity and movement. Marvel's never going to rack up a ton strikeouts with his averageish stuff, but that's not really his game either. Major league hitters punished him badly when he wasn't down in the zone with everything, so he will have to tighten up his command next time around in the majors, but he should remain a backend starter candidate for Pittsburgh.

13 Jared Triolo 3B/SS

Born: 02/08/98 Age: 22 Bats: R Throws: R Height: 6'3" Weight: 212 Origin: Round 2, 2019 Draft (#72 overall)

YEAR	TEAM	LVL	AGE	PA	R	2B	3B	HR	RBI	BB	K	SB	CS	AVG/OBP/SLG	DRC+	VORP	BABIP	BRR	FRAA	WARP	PF
2019	WEV	A-	21	264	30	19	5	2	34	27	49	3	1	.239/.314/.389	100	10.4	.290	1.8	3B(40) -3.3, SS(17) -0.1	0.8	104
2020	PIT	MLB	22	251	20	13	1	4	23	16	68	2	1	.198/.253/.321	50	3.0	.260	0.0	3B -1, SS 0	-0.8	101

The Pirates Comp B pick out of Houston looks like he should be a power hitter, but the bat speed can be a bit on the fringy side and he tends to use his feel for the barrel to favor contact rather than try and lift the ball. He's sneaky athletic and quick for his size, so the Pirates decided to give him some reps at shortstop in the Penn League. It's an interesting experiment, and he grinds when he's there, but the skill set is a much better fit for the hot corner. He has plenty of arm for either spot and the range is above-average at third, but defensive flexibility can't hurt especially since both the hit and power tools might end up fringy.

14 Braxton Ashcraft RHP

Born: 10/05/99 Age: 20 Bats: L Throws: R Height: 6'5" Weight: 195 Origin: Round 2, 2018 Draft (#51 overall)

YEAR	TEAM	LVL	AGE	W	L	SV	G	GS	IP	H	HR	BB/9	K/9	K	GB%	BABIP	WHIP	ERA	DRA	WARP	PF
2018	PIR	RK	18	0	1	0	5	5	17²	16	2	2.5	6.1	12	52%	.259	1.19	4.58	3.27	0.5	98
2019	WEV	A-	19	1	9	0	11	11	53	49	4	3.7	6.6	39	45%	.273	1.34	5.77	5.18	0.0	103
2020	PIT	MLB	20	2	2	0	33	0	35	35	6	3.6	5.1	20	40%	.266	1.40	4.80	4.97	0.2	101

Comparables: Alex Cobb, Jake Brigham, Peter Lambert

Ashcraft was drafted in the second round in 2018 as a projectable prep righty. The fastball hasn't popped yet, as he still mostly sits in the low-90s. The frame remains lean, and Ashcraft repeats his uptempo delivery pretty well. There's developing feel for a low-to-mid-80s slider. It's inconsistent in both shape and velocity but he will flash an above-average at the upper end of the velo band. The changeup is a work in progress but he will occasionally show one with good sink in the mid-80s. That would be decent velo separation if he could get a couple more ticks on the fastball, but we will have to wait another year for that, as the overall prospect profile remains quite raw.

15 Rodolfo Castro 2B

Born: 05/21/99 Age: 21 Bats: B Throws: R Height: 6'0" Weight: 200 Origin: International Free Agent, 2015

YEAR	TEAM	LVL	AGE	PA	R	2B	3B	HR	RBI	BB	K	SB	CS	AVG/OBP/SLG	DRC+	VORP	BABIP	BRR	FRAA	WARP	PF
2017	PIR	RK	18	211	27	12	4	6	32	16	47	4	3	.277/.344/.479	120	18.1	.338	0.5	SS(19) 1.3, 3B(17) -4.4	0.9	98
2018	WVA	A	19	426	47	19	4	12	50	26	100	6	3	.231/.278/.395	82	10.9	.276	2.9	2B(89) 4.3, SS(12) 1.6	1.4	98
2019	GRB	A	20	246	33	13	2	14	46	18	68	6	5	.242/.306/.516	127	20.7	.271	2.1	2B(34) -0.2, SS(17) -0.9	1.6	97
2019	BRD	A+	20	215	26	13	1	5	27	13	54	1	0	.243/.288/.391	105	8.0	.308	0.3	2B(36) 1.9, SS(16) -1.2	0.9	96
2020	PIT	MLB	21	251	22	13	1	6	26	17	81	1	0	.206/.265/.353	61	2.0	.286	-0.3	2B 1, SS 0	-0.3	101

Comparables: Dilson Herrera, Abiatal Avelino, Michael Chavis

The sort who seems to find himself posted up stubbornly on the back end of these lists year in and year out, Castro lacks a huge ceiling but is still interesting enough to warrant some words. A switch-hitter who is much more proficient from the right side, the Dominican has a loose, whippy swing that at its best sprays line drives all about the field and generates above-average gap power and decent over the fence pop. There are things that he'll have to iron out in order to improve his results from the long side of the platoon, such as his propensity to chase breaking stuff in the dirt and a tendency to pull off the ball that leaves him susceptible to hard stuff away. Well-built but sinewy with long limbs that belie his listed height of six even, Castro is more than capable at both middle-infield positions and has the arm for third if he needs it. The range is good enough and he comes in on the ball well, but his strongest trait defensively is a plus arm that plays from all sorts of angles.

16 Will Craig 1B

Born: 11/16/94   Age: 25   Bats: R   Throws: R   Height: 6'3"   Weight: 212   Origin: Round 1, 2016 Draft (#22 overall)

YEAR	TEAM	LVL	AGE	PA	R	2B	3B	HR	RBI	BB	K	SB	CS	AVG/OBP/SLG	DRC+	VORP	BABIP	BRR	FRAA	WARP	PF
2017	BRD	A+	22	542	59	26	1	6	61	62	106	1	3	.271/.373/.371	144	11.7	.335	-7.8	1B(93) 9.4	2.9	98
2018	ALT	AA	23	549	73	30	3	20	102	42	128	6	3	.248/.321/.448	111	28.6	.288	0.6	1B(122) 8.8	2.4	92
2019	IND	AAA	24	556	69	23	0	23	78	44	146	2	3	.249/.326/.435	94	3.2	.304	-0.4	1B(110) 0.7, RF(13) -1.1	0.2	94
2020	PIT	MLB	25	251	25	12	0	8	28	16	75	1	0	.223/.291/.382	77	1.0	.296	-0.5	1B 2, RF 0	0.3	101

Comparables: Travis Shaw, Christian Walker, Tyler Collins

Craig is a tricky prospect to actually rank when you sit down to do a list. The projection here is inevitably bifurcated. He has to either hit enough to be a regular or there isn't much major league utility. There aren't gradations like there would be with, say Lolo Sanchez, a sliding scale of value. The Pirates gave Craig a handful of outfield reps in Triple-A this year, perhaps a nod to his needing positional flexibility, but he's unlikely to have the requisite speed and athleticism to play on the grass. The offensive profile remains broadly the same. There's pop, and he'll take a walk, but a stiff, long swing leads to too much swing-and-miss in the zone. Occasionally this profile hits .240, and gets on-base enough, gets enough of the power into games. But you are wishcasting for CJ Cron, and there's no room to fall short. I suppose if the Pirates really want to get creative, Craig was a solid college reliever for Wake Forest, so you might be able to carve out a Jared-Walsh-like role for him. It would certainly be more fun than watching him play right field.

17 Fabricio Macias OF

Born: 03/11/98   Age: 22   Bats: R   Throws: R   Height: 6'0"   Weight: 188   Origin: International Free Agent, 2018

YEAR	TEAM	LVL	AGE	PA	R	2B	3B	HR	RBI	BB	K	SB	CS	AVG/OBP/SLG	DRC+	VORP	BABIP	BRR	FRAA	WARP	PF
2018	WEV	A-	20	83	9	4	2	0	5	6	12	2	3	.325/.373/.429	122	4.5	.385	-1.6	CF(11) -1.3, RF(4) -0.9	0.0	100
2018	WVA	A	20	148	22	6	2	1	19	14	42	5	1	.222/.315/.325	77	4.2	.318	0.8	LF(27) -2.6, RF(9) -0.4	-0.3	99
2019	GRB	A	21	515	72	25	3	8	79	28	90	18	11	.280/.330/.396	140	35.1	.327	4.0	CF(51) 1.6, LF(40) -3.5	3.5	98
2020	PIT	MLB	22	251	22	12	1	3	22	17	61	3	1	.237/.299/.341	73	0.0	.309	0.0	LF -1, CF 0	-0.1	101

Macias is essentially a less dynamic version of Lolo Sanchez, who you'll have been acquainted with earlier on in this list. He's an aggressive hitter with quick hands and a pull-heavy approach. He has the low-minors speed and power combination going, slashing and yanking hard stuff on the inner half and feasting on hanging curves. He'll steal you a base and he's managed thus far to keep his strikeouts at a reasonable clip. He's well capable of covering all three outfield positions given his good range and great arm. A sleeper prospect out of México, Macias can open some more eyes if he keeps this up against stiffer competition.

18 Mason Martin 1B

Born: 06/02/99   Age: 21   Bats: L   Throws: R   Height: 6'0"   Weight: 201   Origin: Round 17, 2017 Draft (#508 overall)

YEAR	TEAM	LVL	AGE	PA	R	2B	3B	HR	RBI	BB	K	SB	CS	AVG/OBP/SLG	DRC+	VORP	BABIP	BRR	FRAA	WARP	PF
2017	PIR	RK	18	166	37	8	0	11	22	32	41	2	2	.307/.457/.630	216	23.3	.368	-2.2	1B(26) 1.5, RF(9) -1.2	1.5	98
2018	BRI	RK	19	269	42	10	1	10	40	42	87	2	2	.233/.357/.422	109	8.1	.328	1.4	1B(52) -1.7	0.5	102
2018	WVA	A	19	173	16	8	0	4	18	18	62	1	1	.200/.302/.333	80	0.8	.310	0.0	1B(43) -3.0	-0.5	100
2019	GRB	A	20	355	58	19	3	23	83	46	103	8	2	.262/.361/.575	163	33.3	.311	-1.5	1B(77) 4.1	2.9	96
2019	BRD	A+	20	201	32	13	1	12	46	22	65	0	1	.239/.333/.528	130	8.8	.303	-0.8	1B(46) 3.4	1.1	97
2020	PIT	MLB	21	251	24	12	1	7	26	26	93	0	0	.190/.282/.341	65	1.0	.288	-0.3	1B 2, RF 0	-0.1	101

Comparables: Tyler O'Neill, Matt Olson, Travis Demeritte

Martin may be a late-round first base only prospect but in the interest of fairness it must be noted that he is young, and he is a lefty swinger. He's performed admirably against older competition, performing well enough in the Sally to earn a mid-season promotion. The most impressive thing about Martin is his approach at the plate, which allows him to consistently work favorable counts that allow him to flex his above-average pop. The swing looks fairly rigid to me, but he nonetheless shows an ability to adjust to varying speeds, breaks, and location in order to drive the ball to all fields. He'll look weak at times against good heat up in the zone, but he's off to a promising start despite carrying an unfavorable profile.

19 Luis Escobar RHP

Born: 05/30/96   Age: 24   Bats: R   Throws: R   Height: 6'1"   Weight: 205   Origin: International Free Agent, 2013

YEAR	TEAM	LVL	AGE	W	L	SV	G	GS	IP	H	HR	BB/9	K/9	K	GB%	BABIP	WHIP	ERA	DRA	WARP	PF
2017	WVA	A	21	10	7	0	26	25	131²	97	9	4.1	11.5	168	44%	.282	1.19	3.83	3.42	2.9	100
2018	BRD	A+	22	7	6	0	17	16	92²	76	9	3.7	8.3	85	48%	.272	1.23	3.98	4.04	1.4	105
2018	ALT	AA	22	4	0	0	7	7	35²	30	4	5.3	6.3	25	43%	.248	1.43	4.54	5.21	0.1	87
2019	BRD	A+	23	0	0	3	10	0	13¹	6	0	4.1	10.1	15	58%	.194	0.90	0.00	3.34	0.2	100
2019	IND	AAA	23	2	1	1	24	5	55	54	7	5.2	9.3	57	48%	.329	1.56	4.09	5.36	0.6	93
2019	PIT	MLB	23	0	0	0	4	0	5²	10	1	6.4	3.2	2	46%	.429	2.47	7.94	4.72	0.0	97
2020	PIT	MLB	24	2	2	0	33	0	35	41	7	5.1	7.3	28	43%	.317	1.75	6.75	6.21	-0.3	101

Comparables: Merandy Gonzalez, Dylan Cease, Kendry Flores

The Pirates finally converted Escobar to relief in 2019 to mixed results. The fastball did pop into the mid-90s with some sink out of the pen, but the extra effort to ramp it up made him ineffectively wild at times. The bigger issue is he might not have a bat-missing secondary option. He tends to lean on his change more than his breaking ball and while it gets plenty of separation from the fastball, it only shows good fade in flashes. The curve has been even more inconsistent, although he can occasionally rips off a decent 11-5 yakker. We write a lot at the back of these team lists about 95-and-a-slider guy. Those guys can pitch in the seventh and eighth inning. Escobar needs to become a 95-and-a-something-else guy to be more than a middle reliever.

20 Matt Gorski OF

Born: 12/22/97   Age: 22   Bats: R   Throws: R   Height: 6'4"   Weight: 198   Origin: Round 2, 2019 Draft (#57 overall)

YEAR	TEAM	LVL	AGE	PA	R	2B	3B	HR	RBI	BB	K	SB	CS	AVG/OBP/SLG	DRC+	VORP	BABIP	BRR	FRAA	WARP	PF
2019	WEV	A-	21	202	32	9	2	3	22	19	48	11	3	.223/.297/.346	85	6.5	.282	2.2	CF(21) 0.2, LF(19) 2.9	0.8	103
2020	PIT	MLB	22	251	20	12	1	4	22	15	80	2	1	.200/.250/.312	47	0.0	.283	0.0	CF 1, LF 1	-0.6	101

Comparables: Skye Bolt, Adam Haseley, Ryan Cordell

The Pirates second-round pick out of Indiana, Gorski has the kind of body that wouldn't look out of place in a major league outfield right now. It's close to the ideal baseball body, tall, athletic, lean and well-proportioned. He's a good runner and shouldn't fill out or slow down all that much more. There's plus raw power that can play from line-to-line. So the speed/power combo is intriguing, but the speed might not be enough to keep Gorski up the middle, and he struggles to get the power in game. There's decent bat speed, but the swing is long, and he likes to get extended. He's never really hit with wood bats and can struggle with spin. So this is more of a low-floor project than you might prefer in your college bat popped on Day One.

Personal Cheeseball

PC Stephen Alemais SS/2B

Born: 04/12/95   Age: 25   Bats: R   Throws: R   Height: 5'11"   Weight: 190   Origin: Round 3, 2016 Draft (#105 overall)

YEAR	TEAM	LVL	AGE	PA	R	2B	3B	HR	RBI	BB	K	SB	CS	AVG/OBP/SLG	DRC+	VORP	BABIP	BRR	FRAA	WARP	PF
2017	PIR	RK	22	31	6	3	0	0	2	4	5	0	0	.259/.355/.370	117	2.3	.318	0.8	SS(8) -1.2	0.1	96
2017	WVA	A	22	131	14	6	2	3	12	5	32	5	3	.223/.266/.380	69	0.1	.279	-0.8	SS(26) -1.5, 2B(1) 0.0	-0.1	103
2017	BRD	A+	22	122	10	6	0	1	20	14	14	5	2	.317/.393/.406	165	10.2	.352	0.7	SS(29) -1.2	1.1	100
2018	ALT	AA	23	463	56	16	4	3	34	44	69	16	9	.279/.346/.346	102	20.8	.326	2.4	2B(114) 8.3, SS(7) 1.7	2.8	92
2019	ALT	AA	24	46	4	0	0	0	2	1	9	2	0	.267/.283/.267	87	0.3	.333	1.0	SS(11) 0.0	0.3	93
2020	PIT	MLB	25	251	21	11	1	3	22	15	58	6	3	.231/.283/.330	61	2.0	.293	0.0	2B 2, SS 0	-0.2	101

Alemais' season barely got started before he injured his shoulder on a slide. The injury would eventually require surgery and end his 2019 season after just 12 games. You hope there's no lingering effects for him, because boy is he fun to watch in the field. He's been a plus glove since college, and checks every box defensively—hands, actions, arm. The offensive profile is extremely Brendan Ryanish, and while the glove is good, it isn't THAT good. Alemais might even have less power than Ryan too. Don't ever bet against a good shortstop making the majors, but I also won't be complaining too much if I get a look at Alemais' slick glovework around the Eastern or International League circuit in 2020.

Low Minors Sleeper

LMS **Colin Selby** **RHP**
Born: 10/24/97 Age: 22 Bats: R Throws: R Height: 6'1" Weight: 218 Origin: Round 16, 2018 Draft (#474 overall)

YEAR	TEAM	LVL	AGE	W	L	SV	G	GS	IP	H	HR	BB/9	K/9	K	GB%	BABIP	WHIP	ERA	DRA	WARP	PF
2018	BRI	RK	20	1	3	0	11	11	47²	43	4	3.0	7.7	41	55%	.289	1.24	4.15	3.91	1.1	105
2019	GRB	A	21	6	3	0	17	17	88	71	8	2.8	8.8	86	40%	.266	1.11	2.97	4.12	1.1	98
2020	PIT	MLB	22	2	2	0	33	0	35	36	6	3.7	7.2	28	38%	.287	1.44	4.98	5.09	0.1	101

A 16th-rounder last year out of D-III Randolph-Macon, Selby put up good numbers backed up by good stuff and at 21 was age-appropriate for the Sally League. Listed at 6-foot-1, the righty is sturdily built without much projection remaining. This is fine, as he already holds his velo at 94 mph late into outings and can hit as high as 97 early. He also has a nascent four-pitch mix, with secondary offerings of varying efficacy. He looks to have both a slider and a curve, in the mid and low 80s, respectively, but they do blend at times. The former doesn't have a whole lot of bite, though he can drop it in for strikes especially to the gloveside against right-handed hitters. The latter is effective as a chase pitch in the dirt, at least at this level. He also throws a change that often comes in firm around 90 but occasionally shows split action. Long way to go but could end up a steal considering where they got him, even if he ends up a middle reliever.

Top Talents 25 and Under (as of 4/1/2020)

1. Mitch Keller
2. Oneil Cruz
3. Ke'Bryan Hayes
4. Bryan Reynolds
5. Cole Tucker
6. Quinn Priester
7. Travis Swaggerty
8. Cody Bolton
9. Tahnaj Thomas
10. Sammy Siani

There's all of two players on this list who have exhausted their prospect eligibility. A year ago, Reynolds checked in at No. 9 in the Pirates' system, while Tucker was No. 6. In their respective rookie seasons, Reynolds put up a 110 DRC+ that shows his .317 batting average wasn't entirely fluky despite an obscene .387 BABIP. He's hit at every level, including now the majors, and while his ceiling is probably what we saw in 2019, that's an above-average corner outfielder by any stretch of the imagination.

Tucker didn't see as much playing time as Reynolds and scuffled in a 159-plate appearance cup of coffee, but we're still talking about someone who is likely to stick at shortstop as something resembling a second-division starter.

Neither Reynolds nor Tucker have quite the upside of the trio that dots the top of the list, but as the Pirates enter what's looking like a painful couple of years, they're likely to both be quality major leaguers the other youngsters will meet in Pittsburgh in the coming years.

Eyewitness Reports

Eyewitness Report: Oneil Cruz

Evaluator: Ricky Conti
Report Date: 09/25/2019
Dates Seen: 9/18, 9/20
Risk Factor: High
Physical/Health: Sticks for arms, with just a touch of meat on the legs. Extra trim frame and body. Genuine chance to add 40 pounds and still be in great shape. All of 6'7" and definitely looks the part. Long arms and legs. Excellent coordination and athleticism for someone of his height.

Tool	Future Grade	Report
Hit	45	The body gives him a big zone to be responsible for. He has the length in the arms to reach any pitch, but since there's so much zone, his discipline is reasonable fringe-average. There is some swing and miss to the game, but he handles velo well. The swing is short, as he keeps his hands close to his body at load, then they naturally get long during the swing. Good ability to go opposite field. The discipline will need to be perfect for him to be better than average. Struggles with timing at the moment, even in batting practice
Power	70	Best raw power I saw at the AFL. Had no trouble displaying plus plus strength to all fields using a minimal effort swing. Really impressed that the power is to the opposite field as well. Doesn't always show up in games because of timing. Scary potential if he figures it out.
Baserunning/ Speed	50	Strides are actually not that long for someone of his height. Above average speed at present, but no chance it stays there given how much physical development is left.
Glove	45	His transfers and footwork are both smooth, something that will allow him to turn double pays quickly. You can tell he struggles to get low to the ground because of his long frame. This might really limit his range, as he hands now have even farther to travel than before. The hands and feet can pay at short, but if the speed regresses, I doubt he has enough range.
Arm	70	Plus-plus, so much that he was very timid on shorter throws. He has the arm for any position on the field, and he knows it. The accuracy is very average, but the pure strength is impressive. The strength can be found at any angle, balanced or off-balance.

Conclusion: Two plus-plus tools with a chance to stick at short isn't something to joke about. The power is somewhere in between plus and plus-plus at the moment. If he decides to go all out in his physical development, it could get close to 80 grade (and maybe the arm could, too).

Eyewitness Report: Rodolfo Castro

Evaluator: Ben Spanier
Report Date: 06/05/2019
Dates Seen: April/May 2019
Risk Factor: High
Physical/Health: Athletic, rangy, and somewhat lean but solidly built with a bit of room for projection. Long arms and legs make it appear to the naked eye that he is taller than listed.

Tool	Future Grade	Report
Hit	50	Loose, whippy swing with a two-hand finish. Makes loud contact when he stays through the ball but has a tendency to pull off of it, especially from the left side, which leads to vulnerability on good breaking balls and pitches on the outer part of the plate. Pretty swing with a natural uppercut, but can get loopy at times. Approach isn't terrible but he strikes out a bit too much and has spots where he can be exploited.
Power	55	Primarily gap-to-gap doubles type power but has tapped into previously un-evidenced home run pop this year in a league not known for yielding strong power numbers. When he is going well he sends screaming high line-drives around the field, and the ball carries the other way as well as pull-side.
Baserunning/ Speed	50	Average speed with long strides; won't add or subtract a lot of value on the base-paths.
Glove	55	Primarily a second baseman but also shows good actions at shortstop. Is smoother than you might think looking at him, especially coming in on the ball and finishing the play. Didn't notice exceptional range, but has a long reach and solid reactions.
Arm	60	Strong and accurate arm that plays better at short than second, where he generally adopts a side-arm motion. Arm plays well when turning double plays, is effective form multiple angles, and is strong enough for third.

Conclusion: Has the ceiling of a starting middle-infielder, but a utility outcome is more likely. Even that carries some risk, as it is possible his hit tool never completely comes together and he fizzles out at the upper levels of the minors. Still, there is an intriguing package of tools and skills here.

San Diego Padres

The State of the System

It's almost unfair that the Padres system could graduate two rookie-of-the-year candidates and still be this good.

The Top Ten

★ ★ ★ *2020 Top 101 Prospect* **#5** ★ ★ ★

1 MacKenzie Gore LHP OFP: 70 ETA: 2020
Born: 02/24/99 Age: 21 Bats: L Throws: L Height: 6'3" Weight: 195 Origin: Round 1, 2017 Draft (#3 overall)

YEAR	TEAM	LVL	AGE	W	L	SV	G	GS	IP	H	HR	BB/9	K/9	K	GB%	BABIP	WHIP	ERA	DRA	WARP	PF
2017	PDR	RK	18	0	1	0	7	7	21¹	14	0	3.0	14.3	34	69%	.333	0.98	1.27	0.48	1.3	100
2018	FTW	A	19	2	5	0	16	16	60²	61	5	2.7	11.0	74	41%	.354	1.30	4.45	4.11	0.8	105
2019	LEL	A+	20	7	1	0	15	15	79¹	36	4	2.3	12.5	110	38%	.211	0.71	1.02	1.70	3.2	94
2019	AMA	AA	20	2	1	0	5	5	21²	20	3	3.3	10.4	25	40%	.308	1.29	4.15	4.20	0.2	116
2020	SDN	MLB	21	2	3	0	8	8	38	37	6	4.1	11.6	49	40%	.335	1.43	4.83	4.93	0.4	94

Comparables: Bryse Wilson, José Berríos, Henry Owens

The Report: There's not much we can say here that we haven't said many times over this year. Gore will enter 2020 as the top pitching prospect in baseball after thoroughly decimating the hitter-friendly California League last season before dipping his 20-year-old toes in Double-A water in the second half. Blisters derailed his 2018 season and limited him to 60 innings, so the club took a mindful approach to his workload, limiting him to just five appearances and 20ish innings after his July 2nd promotion to park him smooth and tidy at 100 for the year, with a presumable eye towards tacking on another 40 or so again next year. I wrote at mid-season that Gore made just about the strongest case an A-ball pitcher could make to be considered the top prospect in all of baseball, and nothing about his abbreviated Double-A stint changed that at all.

It's four above-average-or-better pitches, highlighted by a fastball that'll work into the mid 90s with rare explosiveness and finish. His curve's a nasty yakker, he can land a tight slider below either side of the zone, and the change moves late with plus velocity separation. If you want to pick nits the control can wander around a little when the delivery disjoints, but, well, he's 20 and that happens.

Variance: Moderate; or, put another way, as low as it can get for a 20-year-old prep arm.

Mark Barry's Fantasy Take: Well it's no longer even a lukewarm take to peg Gore as the best pitching prospect in the game, but still, to reiterate, Gore is the best pitching prospect in the game. He's still a pitcher, though, which brings some risk, but his ceiling is top-10 starter in baseball. Me likey (are people still saying "me likey"? Were they ever? Nevermind, this isn't the place for that. Moving on).

★ ★ ★ *2020 Top 101 Prospect* **#15** ★ ★ ★

2 Luis Patiño RHP   OFP: 70   ETA: 2021

Born: 10/26/99   Age: 20   Bats: R   Throws: R   Height: 6'0"   Weight: 192   Origin: International Free Agent, 2016

YEAR	TEAM	LVL	AGE	W	L	SV	G	GS	IP	H	HR	BB/9	K/9	K	GB%	BABIP	WHIP	ERA	DRA	WARP	PF
2017	DPA	RK	17	2	1	0	4	4	16	11	0	1.1	8.4	15	58%	.256	0.81	1.69	1.90	0.7	99
2017	PDR	RK	17	2	1	0	9	8	40	32	2	3.6	9.7	43	50%	.286	1.20	2.47	2.60	1.5	101
2018	FTW	A	18	6	3	0	17	17	83^1	65	1	2.6	10.6	98	45%	.320	1.07	2.16	2.87	2.3	104
2019	LEL	A+	19	6	8	0	18	17	87	61	4	3.5	11.7	113	40%	.278	1.09	2.69	2.71	2.4	89
2019	AMA	AA	19	0	0	0	2	2	7^2	8	0	4.7	11.7	10	19%	.381	1.57	1.17	4.52	0.0	125
2020	SDN	MLB	20	2	2	0	33	0	35	34	5	3.6	9.8	38	37%	.315	1.37	4.44	4.49	0.4	94

Comparables: Mike Soroka, Taijuan Walker, Jordan Lyles

The Report: The entire package isn't quite as advanced, nor is the stuff quite as impressive, as Gore's. But which one has the higher upside is a legitimate conversation to have, and Patiño is eight months younger. That should tell you all you need to know about just how good this kid was this year, and could become in years future. As a right-hander who barely scrapes 6-feet, he's exactly the kind of archetype who would've been vulnerable to institutional biases and corresponding whispers of an inevitable bullpen future in days past, but there wasn't much of anything in his stuff, performance, or countenance this year that pointed even faintly in that direction. The delivery mirrors Gore's from the right side, with a similar high leg kick though with a more deliberate turn downhill, and while he lacks the lefty's elite athleticism he's got more than enough to hold the delivery together. There's some crossfire to it that'll wobble the command at times, but the deception he creates is a helpful cake-topper for what is on its own a nasty combination of pitches.

It's high-end stuff; as with Gore, there are four pitches here that present at least above-average, including three I hung 6s or better on at mid-season. A high three-quarters slot with the aforementioned crossfire creates a fun angle for him to impart horizontal action on his pitches, though he'll need to further refine his change and a developing cut look on his fastball to eat into some present split issues with left-handed hitters. There may be some ongoing control issues that crop up while he finishes growing into an adult body, but we're reasonably confident his physicality and extremely mature approach to his craft will be enough to overcome those concerns and that he'll develop enough command to allow for near-full utility of the impressive raw stuff.

Variance: Moderately High; or, put another way, pretty damn low for a kid who pitched his way to Double-A at 19.

Mark Barry's Fantasy Take: If you think it's unfair that the Padres can back up Gore with Patiño in their system, well, I agree. The righty answered any questions about his pop-up status by fanning 123 dudes in 94 2/3 innings, getting to Double-A as a 19-year-old. All of those things are good. While he finished at the same level as Gore, his age and volatility probably keep him from the immediate doorstep to the big league rotation, knocking him down a bit, but he's still a top-50 dynasty name for me.

★ ★ ★ *2020 Top 101 Prospect* **#33** ★ ★ ★

3 CJ Abrams SS   OFP: 60   ETA: 2022

Born: 10/03/00   Age: 19   Bats: L   Throws: R   Height: 6'2"   Weight: 185   Origin: Round 1, 2019 Draft (#6 overall)

YEAR	TEAM	LVL	AGE	PA	R	2B	3B	HR	RBI	BB	K	SB	CS	AVG/OBP/SLG	DRC+	VORP	BABIP	BRR	FRAA	WARP	PF
2019	PDR	RK	18	156	40	12	8	3	22	10	14	14	6	.401/.442/.662	199	24.1	.425	-0.7	SS(28) 6.9	2.5	108
2020	SDN	MLB	19	251	22	13	2	4	23	17	46	3	1	.240/.297/.361	76	0.0	.286	0.0	SS 2	0.3	94

Comparables: J.P. Crawford, Juan Soto, Justin Williams

The Report: Fresh out of the draft, you'd expect someone with the skills of CJ Abrams taken in the top 10 to automatically rest atop his organization's rankings. Slotting Abrams third isn't an indictment of his ability, but speaks to the depth of the Padres system as it currently stands. A premium athlete playing a premium position, the upside potential is sky high. His quick movements in short bursts, along with speed in longer distances every bit as impressive, combine to give him range at shortstop. He's a top-of-the-scale runner who can take just a ton of extra bases. His first foray into pro ball at the complex level was impressive, and he emphatically answered some of the questions that rumbled prior to the draft about the thump he'd be able to generate. The swing is explosive, and he generates loud contact, though he'll leak to the front-side at present.

He'd be physically capable of playing pretty much anywhere, though he currently lacks for arm strength. He's still much thinner right now than he will be, and his frame will support a big transformation in the coming years that will challenge his balance between heavy strength or lean quickness. That leaves the biggest question to his ultimate potential resting on his hitting coaches and his desire to listen and make adjustments.

Variance: Very high. There are players all around the big leagues who hang their hat on running and playing defense. If he can grow offensively in keeping with his potential, he will be a top-of-the-order menace for years.

Mark Barry's Fantasy Take: We didn't see much of Abrams outside of the AZL, but what we did see was, uh, good. He just turned 19 years old, so he's still a little raw, but we're looking at a guy that could hit 15-20 homers and snag 30 bases while not killing you with the batting average. There's even upside for a little more if it all clicks.

★ ★ ★ *2020 Top 101 Prospect* **#67** ★ ★ ★

4   Luis Campusano   C   OFP: 60   ETA: 2021

Born: 09/29/98   Age: 21   Bats: R   Throws: R   Height: 5'10"   Weight: 215   Origin: Round 2, 2017 Draft (#39 overall)

YEAR	TEAM	LVL	AGE	PA	R	2B	3B	HR	RBI	BB	K	SB	CS	AVG/OBP/SLG	DRC+	VORP	BABIP	BRR	FRAA	WARP	PF
2017	PDR	RK	18	98	3	4	0	1	13	6	14	0	1	.278/.327/.356	110	0.0	.316	-1.7	C(17) -0.3	0.3	101
2017	SDP	RK	18	53	5	0	0	3	12	9	11	0	1	.250/.377/.455	110	5.0	.267	0.3	C(10) -0.3	0.4	102
2018	FTW	A	19	284	26	11	0	3	40	19	43	0	1	.288/.345/.365	118	6.1	.335	-1.1	C(38) -0.8, 1B(4) 0.2	1.2	104
2019	LEL	A+	20	487	63	31	1	15	81	52	57	0	0	.325/.396/.509	168	44.6	.340	-4.4	C(76) -2.6, 1B(2) 0.0	3.9	97
2020	SDN	MLB	21	251	26	12	0	7	28	17	46	0	0	.255/.311/.401	88	0.0	.292	-0.5	C 0, 1B 0	0.4	94

Comparables: Chance Sisco, Christian Vázquez, Gorkys Hernández

The Report: The Georgia high school product was the 39th-overall pick, and the first catcher selected in the 2017 draft. That kind of pedigree is rare air for a prep catcher, and Campusano responded last year by winning a batting title and sharing an MVP in the California League as a 20-year-old. The right-handed hitter was a doubles machine, swatting 31 of 'em while walking nearly as often as he struck out. Campusano's exceptional strike zone awareness and selectivity results in consistent, professional at-bats. He attacks pitches you want a hitter to attack and frequently finds barrel when he does. His gap-to-gap approach is really mature, and natural strength can produce plenty of extra-base hits.

Meanwhile, his athleticism and mobility provide a strong defensive foundation behind the plate. His blocking, receiving, and throwing abilities are all solid, although he'll need to further refine his catch-and-release to improve upon last season's inconsistent throwing game. He'll pop 1.8s and 1.9s, though, and he has the physical tools and arm strength to improve.

Campusano's leadership qualities and gritty competitiveness are evident when you watch him play. His advanced offensive ability is extremely valuable from the catcher position, and he could force DH or first base starts when getting a break from catching. Continued improvement of his defensive abilities could make Campusano a primary big league backstop. His floor may be the offensive side of a catching platoon.

Variance: Moderate; he's a prep catcher, and they take time and often random routes. But Campusano is an all-around, everyday catcher for a good baseball team with first-division upside.

Mark Barry's Fantasy Take: Sure, I could take the lazy way out and say "Dynasty catcher, no thanks lol", but a) I would never not give you my all and b) I actually really like Campusano. His patience and contact-oriented approach at the dish raise his floor, and his prowess behind said dish should satisfy the requisite defensive threshold. The only drawback on Campusano is that he's currently behind defensive wizard Austin Hedges and the enigmatic Francisco Mejia on the depth chart. As far as drawbacks go, that's not too bad, as these things tend to work themselves out.

★ ★ ★ *2020 Top 101 Prospect* **#69** ★ ★ ★

5 Taylor Trammell OF OFP: 55 ETA: 2020/21

Born: 09/13/97 Age: 22 Bats: L Throws: L Height: 6'2" Weight: 215 Origin: Round 1, 2016 Draft (#35 overall)

YEAR	TEAM	LVL	AGE	PA	R	2B	3B	HR	RBI	BB	K	SB	CS	AVG/OBP/SLG	DRC+	VORP	BABIP	BRR	FRAA	WARP	PF
2017	DYT	A	19	571	80	24	10	13	77	71	123	41	12	.281/.368/.450	127	43.1	.345	3.1	LF(104) -3.7, CF(17) -0.9	2.8	101
2018	DAY	A+	20	461	71	19	4	8	41	58	105	25	10	.277/.375/.406	128	26.4	.358	-0.8	CF(60) -1.7, LF(29) 4.5	2.6	103
2019	CHT	AA	21	381	47	8	3	6	33	54	86	17	4	.236/.349/.336	110	11.6	.299	2.1	LF(91) -0.7, CF(1) 0.1	1.5	111
2019	AMA	AA	21	133	14	4	1	4	10	13	36	3	4	.229/.316/.381	89	-0.9	.295	-0.6	CF(30) -1.4	0.1	117
2020	SDN	MLB	22	35	4	1	0	1	4	3	10	1	0	.226/.305/.364	83	0.0	.307	0.0	CF 0	0.1	94

Comparables: Jesse Winker, Clint Frazier, Trent Grisham

The Report: I'll be honest at the outset and admit that I don't know if our staff looks this year really justify holding the line to this extent on Trammell. A year ago we filed him as a potential plus hit/plus power center fielder and ranked him as the 11th-best prospect in baseball despite the top-line performance being merely okay. He was internally divisive even then, and reports on his swing went backwards during his time with the Reds in 2019. Despite the swing issues, the underlying hit tool remains intact, with plus bat speed and good feel for the barrel. The approach is still a bit raw even after three full professional seasons focusing solely on baseball, and he often prioritizes contact over getting his raw power into games. The plus raw power is still there and will flash. The athleticism is unquestioned, he's a plus runner with excellent body control with the closing speed for center, but his present outfield instincts might limit him to a corner, likely left since his arm strength is fringy at best.

Trammell is in some ways both high variance and low. The baseline offensive and defensive skills for a solid fourth outfielder are here, so there's not a ton of downside risk in the profile. I can't help but think there is still a switch to be flipped, and he'll end up a plus regular for a few years. It's getting harder and harder to see it though, but sometimes you stay on a guy for an extra year just in case.

Variance: Medium. The hit tool and athleticism will likely get him a major league role, but he's never really gotten his plus raw power into games and might end up in left field.

Mark Barry's Fantasy Take: It's hard to look at Trammell's progress in 2018 and not think last season was somewhat of a disappointment. He struck out more, was inefficient in his base thievery, and hit .234 in 514 trips to the plate across two organizations. Still, despite a turbulent year for the 22-year-old, sometimes you just need to bet on the skills and underlying tools. Trammell still got on base at a nice clip, and the athleticism that we loved heading into last season is certainly still there. Maybe he slides a couple of spots on the dynasty-101, but he shouldn't plummet.

★ ★ ★ *2020 Top 101 Prospect* **#75** ★ ★ ★

6 Adrian Morejon LHP OFP: 60 ETA: 2019

Born: 02/27/99 Age: 21 Bats: L Throws: L Height: 6'0" Weight: 175 Origin: International Free Agent, 2016

YEAR	TEAM	LVL	AGE	W	L	SV	G	GS	IP	H	HR	BB/9	K/9	K	GB%	BABIP	WHIP	ERA	DRA	WARP	PF
2017	TRI	A-	18	2	2	0	7	7	35¹	37	2	0.8	8.9	35	41%	.337	1.13	3.57	4.30	0.4	94
2017	FTW	A	18	1	2	0	6	6	27²	28	2	4.2	7.5	23	34%	.321	1.48	4.23	5.57	-0.1	101
2018	LEL	A+	19	4	4	0	13	13	62²	54	6	3.4	10.1	70	55%	.302	1.24	3.30	3.49	1.3	98
2019	AMA	AA	20	0	4	0	16	16	36	29	3	3.8	11.0	44	51%	.292	1.22	4.25	2.75	1.0	116
2019	SDN	MLB	20	0	0	0	5	2	8	15	1	3.4	10.1	9	37%	.483	2.25	10.12	5.09	0.0	94
2020	SDN	MLB	21	1	2	0	15	3	29	31	5	3.6	7.8	25	42%	.308	1.47	5.23	5.31	0.1	94

Comparables: Tyler Skaggs, Jenrry Mejia, Chris Tillman

The Report: In just about any other system save for a couple, Morejon is probably the top pitching prospect and a definite top-fiver. He made his major league debut at 20 this year, after all. AJ Preller and company, however, have tapped into some sort of arcane sorcery, evil or otherwise, that blesses the south tip of the Golden Coast with enough young talent that Morejon falls just outside those tiers for San Diego. He's a three-pitch pitcher with two at-least above-average pitches and the third with the potential to join them. Morejon's fastball sat 92-94 for most of the year, and he ticked it up to 96 (t98) in short big-league bursts. He commands the pitch well and gets aggressive with it early in counts to draw contact. That plan of attack worked well in the Texas League, not so much above it. He pairs the gas with a harder changeup at 83-86 that has a good amount of drop, and a curveball at 79-81. The breaker has an inconsistent shape, but when it's on it works 12-5 in a hurry to generate swings and misses.

He doesn't always repeat the delivery efficiently, and his arm was really dragging over the summer, leading to a stressed shoulder and forcing an early shutdown in August. The talent has never been Morejon's problem, but a tricep injury cost him a chunk of 2017 and he managed just 44 innings last season before looking reasonably healthy in a brief AFL cameo. Durability will drive the role, there's a higher bullpen risk now.

Variance: Higher than ideal for an already-debuted prospect. A healthy Morejon is going to be good at something in the majors, the question is what. At his highest ceiling he could be a high No. 3 starter, though command and health questions cloud that path significantly.

Mark Barry's Fantasy Take: We all know that pitching prospects are health risks, and Morejon especially has battled nagging injuries for the better part of his career. But I can't help but think now is a decent time to buy low on the lefty, who seems to be buried in this system by buzzier guys. Morejon struck dudes out at every level, including a five-game stint in the big leagues (just don't look at the ERA), and still has a starter's profile despite debuting from the bullpen. He's got SP2-3 upside, but you know, injuries and stuff.

★ ★ ★ *2020 Top 101 Prospect* **#94** ★ ★ ★
---

7 **Gabriel Arias SS**   OFP: 60   ETA: Late 2021

Born: 02/27/00 Age: 20 Bats: R Throws: R Height: 6'1" Weight: 201 Origin: International Free Agent, 2016

YEAR	TEAM	LVL	AGE	PA	R	2B	3B	HR	RBI	BB	K	SB	CS	AVG/OBP/SLG	DRC+	VORP	BABIP	BRR	FRAA	WARP	PF
2017	SDP	RK	17	168	18	6	3	0	13	10	51	4	6	.275/.329/.353	77	5.8	.408	-1.1	SS(33) 1.4, 3B(2) 0.1	0.4	102
2017	FTW	A	17	64	8	1	0	0	4	2	16	1	0	.242/.266/.258	62	-2.9	.326	0.3	SS(14) -0.2, 3B(2) 0.1	0.0	108
2018	FTW	A	18	504	54	27	3	6	55	41	149	3	3	.240/.302/.352	84	8.8	.340	-0.5	SS(111) 6.2, 3B(6) 0.2	1.9	103
2019	LEL	A+	19	511	62	21	4	17	75	25	128	8	4	.302/.339/.470	122	51.6	.378	1.5	SS(103) -11.4, 3B(10) 1.4	2.1	95
2020	SDN	MLB	20	251	24	11	1	7	27	16	81	1	1	.247/.298/.388	80	0.0	.349	-0.3	SS -1, 3B 0	0.1	94

Comparables: Gleyber Torres, Franklin Barreto, Andrew Velazquez

The Report: The third of many 2016 J2 alums dotting this list, and one of almost as many who couldn't buy a drink in Riverside County, Arias showed up to the California League as a 19-year-old with an overmatched bat. He spent the first couple months fishing at every predictable piece of spin he saw, and he saw a lot of it. That turned out to be a good thing in the long run, as he made some nice strides in advancing his approach and becoming more disciplined around the zone as the year went on. It's the second straight season he's made successful in-season adjustments across a full season.

Arias is a strong, physical kid with excellent hand speed that shows up on both sides of the ball. The glove is sweet at the six, with a baseline fluidity to his movements that allows for quick reactions and a graceful attack on the ball. He's not especially fast, but his movements are quick and efficient, and he anticipates his contact points very well. It's at least a plus arm, and he controls his body consistently well into his throws.

Even with the strides he made in the box, he's still an aggressive swinger in the zone, and he'll get himself out on pitchers' pitches early in counts. He generates solid bat speed, and there's above-average raw power that he's shown an ability to find in games once he settles in to his league.

Variance: Moderately high; he's going to be a very good defender at shortstop with at least some offensive utility, so the floor here is high. But so is the range in value between a first-division shortstop and, like, 2016 Zack Cozart.

Mark Barry's Fantasy Take: Oh cool, a defense-first prospect that learned how to hit and now could be really good. This system just keeps on giving. Arias doesn't walk and still strikes out more than you'd like, but his breakout 2019 probably puts him in the top-200ish for dynasty prospects.

8 Michel Baez RHP   OFP: 55   ETA: 2019

Born: 01/21/96 Age: 24 Bats: R Throws: R Height: 6'8" Weight: 220 Origin: International Free Agent, 2016

YEAR	TEAM	LVL	AGE	W	L	SV	G	GS	IP	H	HR	BB/9	K/9	K	GB%	BABIP	WHIP	ERA	DRA	WARP	PF
2017	FTW	A	21	6	2	0	10	10	58²	41	8	1.2	12.6	82	36%	.264	0.84	2.45	2.30	2.0	106
2018	LEL	A+	22	4	7	0	17	17	86²	73	5	3.4	9.6	92	37%	.297	1.22	2.91	3.01	2.3	96
2018	SAN	AA	22	0	3	0	4	4	18¹	22	4	5.9	10.3	21	31%	.375	1.85	7.36	7.00	-0.4	103
2019	AMA	AA	23	3	2	1	15	0	27	22	1	3.7	12.7	38	38%	.333	1.22	2.00	3.42	0.4	100
2019	SDN	MLB	23	1	1	0	24	1	29²	25	3	4.2	8.5	28	40%	.265	1.31	3.03	5.75	-0.1	97
2020	SDN	MLB	24	1	2	0	26	8	19	17	3	4.0	8.1	17	38%	.280	1.36	4.40	4.59	0.2	94

Comparables: Jorge Alcala, Vince Velasquez, Ryan Helsley

The Report: Part of the Padres' heralded 2016 international haul, Baez pitched professionally in Cuba before signing with San Diego as a 20-year-old. The 6-foot-8 monster pitched exclusively as a starter in his first two minor league seasons, but after missing seven weeks with shoulder inflammation to begin the 2019 season, Baez worked out of the bullpen at Double-A Amarillo, where he dominated and earned a promotion to the big leagues in late July.

The right-hander maintains an efficient and athletic delivery despite his size, allowing him to adequately command his 96-98 mph fastball. A promising 85-87 mph changeup has been effective at the big league level, separating nicely from the high-90s heat. Baez has utilized an above-average-flashing 84-86 mph slider as his primary breaker in the past, though he consolidated to an occasional 76-79 mph curveball to round out his bullpen repertoire last year.

Baez proved generally effective in his first work out of the big league bullpen last season, but the Padres plan to return him to the rotation next spring, where he'll be part of a deep stable of young, exciting arms competing for big league innings. As his teammate Chris Paddack proved last season, a quality fastball-changeup combo can be a great foundation, but Baez will have to further groom his breaking-balls, if he's to last deep into ballgames and hang onto a coveted rotation spot.

Variance: Moderate; he showed the stuff can get big leaguers out last year, but health and role questions still swirl.

Mark Barry's Fantasy Take: The Padres are treating Baez as a starter, which makes sense, but I'd have a hard time envisioning the big guy holding up after spending the entirety of the 2019 campaign using the bullpen cart. He could be a stud closer, but relying on a prospect as closer-in-waiting is a little like rolling the dice on sun-baked potato salad (read: bad, it's bad).

9 Tirso Ornelas OF   OFP: 55   ETA: 2022

Born: 03/11/00 Age: 20 Bats: L Throws: R Height: 6'3" Weight: 200 Origin: International Free Agent, 2017

YEAR	TEAM	LVL	AGE	PA	R	2B	3B	HR	RBI	BB	K	SB	CS	AVG/OBP/SLG	DRC+	VORP	BABIP	BRR	FRAA	WARP	PF
2017	SDP	RK	17	238	46	11	3	3	26	40	61	0	0	.276/.399/.408	137	18.2	.383	0.5	CF(32) -1.4, RF(19) -2.3	1.1	102
2018	FTW	A	18	355	45	13	3	8	40	40	68	5	1	.252/.341/.392	106	9.3	.297	1.2	RF(63) -1.8, CF(5) 1.8	0.9	103
2019	PDR	RK	19	97	6	2	0	0	11	9	22	4	0	.205/.278/.227	51	-5.5	.273	0.7	RF(19) -0.7, CF(1) 0.0	-0.2	109
2019	LEL	A+	19	379	41	11	5	1	30	44	91	3	1	.220/.309/.292	67	-5.0	.296	-1.8	RF(75) -2.9, CF(3) 0.2	-0.9	98
2020	SDN	MLB	20	251	21	10	1	4	22	24	73	0	0	.214/.292/.317	63	0.0	.300	-0.3	RF 0, CF -1	-0.4	94

Comparables: Victor Robles, Cheslor Cuthbert, Engel Beltre

The Report: The 19-year-old corner outfielder appeared overwhelmed during much of the 2019 California League season, scuffling to a .203 batting average before being reassigned to Arizona's development league to regain some confidence. That didn't really work, either, at least in terms of his production, as he continued to struggle mightily in the box in Arizona. He picked it up after returning to Lake Elsinore in August, hitting .280 with eight extra-base hits down the stretch, but it was a tough year pretty much start to finish.

Ornelas is an impressive physical specimen with plenty of natural strength and power, though neither his current swing nor his approach generates much lift or backspin at all. His coordination and bat-to-ball ability are among his strengths, and he's patient at times to a fault right now. He's currently at his best with a middle-of-the-field hitting approach, though eventually he's going to have to start to learn how to get more aggressive in hitting counts and turn on pitches with some semblance of authority. For now, in-game power production remains very much a figment of our collective imagination. Ornelas runs well for his size and has good mobility in the outfield, even making four starts in center field last season. His strong and accurate throwing arm is best-suited for right, however, where he could be an above-average defender.

It's an impressive collection of extremely raw tools, and the eventual package can be that of an all-around corner outfielder with a plus hit tool and above-average power potential, even if the tool and role grades remain entirely projection at this stage.

Variance: Extreme; last season's struggles seemed to affect his confidence at times, and there's just an enormous gulf between his present and potential future selves.

Mark Barry's Fantasy Take: A guy that doesn't run, get to power in games or hit for average? Where do I sign up? Admittedly that's a little mean to Ornelas, but the 19-year-old is almost 100 percent projection right now, and needs to take a slight step in the right direction in any of these areas before I'd feel good about rostering him.

10 Ryan Weathers LHP OFP: 55 ETA: 2022

Born: 12/17/99 Age: 20 Bats: R Throws: L Height: 6'1" Weight: 230 Origin: Round 1, 2018 Draft (#7 overall)

YEAR	TEAM	LVL	AGE	W	L	SV	G	GS	IP	H	HR	BB/9	K/9	K	GB%	BABIP	WHIP	ERA	DRA	WARP	PF
2018	SDP	RK	18	0	2	0	4	4	9¹	8	2	2.9	8.7	9	69%	.222	1.18	3.86	3.31	0.3	104
2018	FTW	A	18	0	1	0	3	3	9	11	0	1.0	9.0	9	58%	.355	1.33	3.00	4.54	0.1	92
2019	FTW	A	19	3	7	0	22	22	96	101	6	1.7	8.4	90	46%	.347	1.24	3.84	5.46	-0.3	106
2020	SDN	MLB	20	2	2	0	33	0	35	35	6	3.6	6.8	27	43%	.281	1.40	4.85	4.91	0.2	94

Comparables: John Lamb, Darwinzon Hernandez, Kolby Allard

The Report: Weathers is a slightly shorter, wider, left-handed clone of his father, which is a thing to be. The body type and arm action are real mirrors, with junior taking a quick, short arm stroke that makes his pitches jump on hitters. He burst out of the gate in the Midwest League to rule April, but he never really looked quite right after that, laboring through outings with flagging velocity.

He's a very good athlete, with major league bloodlines and a state basketball championship on his resume, and the stuff is very good, too. Healthy Weathers rolls 94-95 with that aforementioned jump, a product of tight spin and ride, and he'll work in a curve and change that both grade out as solid complements. He's shown the ability to execute sequencing with all three, and the compact delivery gives him consistency and command. You can see why the club drafted him where they did.

He hasn't developed any dominant finishing pitches yet, and the arm slot limits his options for creating new ones. But he can thrive off and around enough barrels to be a highly effective rotation member with his current arsenal.

Variance: High; there's a good amount of pedigree here, but prep arms are prep arms, and balky shoulders don't know anyone's bonus number.

Mark Barry's Fantasy Take: Weathers seems like a pretty safe bet for a pretty safe pitcher, but the middling strikeout numbers and injury history produce real questions about his ultimate upside. I'd keep him on the radar in leagues with 250-300 prospects..

The Next Ten

11 Tucupita Marcano INF

Born: 09/16/99 Age: 20 Bats: L Throws: R Height: 6'0" Weight: 170 Origin: International Free Agent, 2016

YEAR	TEAM	LVL	AGE	PA	R	2B	3B	HR	RBI	BB	K	SB	CS	AVG/OBP/SLG	DRC+	VORP	BABIP	BRR	FRAA	WARP	PF
2017	DPA	RK	17	209	17	4	2	0	15	34	15	10	3	.206/.337/.253	96	4.4	.222	1.6	2B(41) 6.1, SS(3) -0.5	1.2	98
2018	SDP	RK	18	160	33	4	1	0	17	26	10	10	7	.395/.497/.444	195	25.4	.419	1.8	SS(18) 1.6, 2B(18) 0.6	2.4	99
2018	TRI	A-	18	77	12	1	2	1	9	4	6	5	0	.314/.355/.429	165	9.3	.328	2.1	2B(11) -0.4, SS(6) 1.0	1.0	90
2019	FTW	A	19	504	55	19	3	2	45	35	45	15	16	.270/.323/.337	92	7.6	.293	-2.9	3B(42) -1.1, SS(40) -5.6	0.3	107
2020	SDN	MLB	20	251	22	10	1	2	21	21	35	4	2	.244/.311/.329	73	2.0	.279	-0.3	2B 0, SS -1	-0.1	94

Comparables: Luis Arraez, Enrique Hernández, José Peraza

Marcano's named for his home, and after signing with the Padres in 2016 for $320,000 the Tucupita, Venezuela native made his way stateside in 2018. He spent the entirety of the 2019 regular season in the Midwest League before being promoted to High-A for a postseason run, and thus finished the year as yet another 19-year-old in Lake Elsinore. Marcano inspires comps to former system-mate Luis Urias, as their skill sets are nearly identical. Marcano is a plus athlete with a plus hit tool, and he shows advanced skills as a smooth defender at second base. The club has worked him in at short and third as well, but while his reactions and hands can play at either spot, the arm's light for the left side. He's very thin at present, and will need to develop physically, but even with added strength the power potential will be limited if the bat path remains flat. He's fun to watch and a really intelligent player in all facets of the game, which yields a higher degree of confidence in the growth and development to come. If Marcano were a part of any other organization he would be a slam dunk top-10 prospect, but alas, even his 80-grade name wasn't enough to push him over the hump here in this crazy-deep system.

12 Owen Miller INF

Born: 11/15/96   Age: 23   Bats: R   Throws: R   Height: 6'0"   Weight: 190   Origin: Round 3, 2018 Draft (#84 overall)

YEAR	TEAM	LVL	AGE	PA	R	2B	3B	HR	RBI	BB	K	SB	CS	AVG/OBP/SLG	DRC+	VORP	BABIP	BRR	FRAA	WARP	PF
2018	TRI	A-	21	216	22	8	3	2	20	15	24	4	4	.335/.395/.440	160	19.0	.369	-2.5	SS(44) 3.3	2.1	103
2018	FTW	A	21	114	18	11	0	2	13	4	17	0	0	.336/.368/.495	138	10.0	.382	0.9	3B(13) -2.8, SS(7) -0.4	0.6	101
2019	AMA	AA	22	560	76	28	2	13	68	46	86	5	5	.290/.355/.430	112	23.0	.328	1.3	SS(70) 5.1, 2B(48) 0.5	3.4	116
2020	SDN	MLB	23	251	24	13	1	5	26	15	51	1	0	.258/.311/.388	85	0.0	.310	-0.4	SS 1, 2B 0	0.4	94

Comparables: Danny Worth, Drew Jackson, Trea Turner

IThe club's third-rounder in 2018, Miller skipped High-A last year and jumped straight from the Midwest League to Texas. He looked no worse for the wear after the aggressive promotion, posting an above-average offensive season while adding up-the-middle defensive value at second and short. The offensive package is solid all around, as he pairs above-average bat speed with a good feel to hit. He understands the zone well and attacks strikes, and while it's below-average raw he should be able to bring a modest amount of pop into games. He moves well at short, turning plus speed into solid range, though the arm is borderline for the left side. It's a solid utility profile, and he has the athleticism and baseball IQ to potentially add some outfield into the mix to further bolster his chances of impacting a 25-man roster down the line.

13 Jeisson Rosario CF

Born: 10/22/99   Age: 20   Bats: L   Throws: L   Height: 6'1"   Weight: 191   Origin: International Free Agent, 2016

YEAR	TEAM	LVL	AGE	PA	R	2B	3B	HR	RBI	BB	K	SB	CS	AVG/OBP/SLG	DRC+	VORP	BABIP	BRR	FRAA	WARP	PF
2017	PDR	RK	17	224	31	10	0	1	24	33	36	8	6	.299/.404/.369	141	12.8	.362	0.0	CF(51) -9.7	0.6	101
2018	FTW	A	18	521	79	17	5	3	34	66	108	18	12	.271/.368/.353	97	25.9	.347	3.5	CF(113) -1.2, RF(1) -0.2	1.7	103
2019	LEL	A+	19	525	67	14	4	3	35	87	114	11	4	.242/.372/.314	118	31.5	.322	4.3	CF(110) 0.6, LF(5) 1.7	3.3	96
2020	SDN	MLB	20	251	21	10	1	3	20	23	66	3	2	.220/.296/.306	62	0.0	.300	-0.2	CF 0, RF 0	-0.4	94

Comparables: Jake Bauers, Victor Robles, Cheslor Cuthbert

Yes, he too was in the 2016 haul, and the Dominican is a plus-defending outfielder with exceptional athleticism. Playing as a 19-year-old in High-A last season, Rosario led the California League with 87 walks, though the patience came at a cost, as the deep counts he routinely worked resulted in a lot of hittable pitches passing by and sub-optimal contact quality. His is a lean wiry strength, and while he'll show occasional gap power, he rarely seeks to drive the ball and most of his extra-base hits are the product of his plus-or-better speed. He shows some baseline aptitude for swiping bags, and positive baserunning value should be a part of his game. Rosario possesses the arm strength to play right field, but his expansive range and predatorial closing speed are best utilized in center, where he's capable of growing into a true plus defender. While the hit tool looks like it may be a slower burn in refinement, Rosario's blend of dynamic play-making and graceful athleticism gives him a lot to build on and should afford him all the time he needs to round into a valuable player.

14 Edward Olivares CF

Born: 03/06/96　Age: 24　Bats: R　Throws: R　Height: 6'2"　Weight: 186　Origin: International Free Agent, 2014

YEAR	TEAM	LVL	AGE	PA	R	2B	3B	HR	RBI	BB	K	SB	CS	AVG/OBP/SLG	DRC+	VORP	BABIP	BRR	FRAA	WARP	PF
2017	LNS	A	21	464	82	26	9	17	65	22	82	18	7	.277/.330/.500	131	28.3	.306	4.9	RF(43) 5.5, CF(41) 0.3	3.7	109
2017	DUN	A+	21	77	11	1	1	0	7	8	17	2	2	.221/.312/.265	86	0.5	.294	1.0	CF(17) -1.3	0.1	108
2018	LEL	A+	22	575	79	25	10	12	62	29	102	21	8	.277/.321/.429	103	27.6	.319	2.8	CF(115) 0.6, RF(7) 0.5	2.6	100
2019	AMA	AA	23	551	85	25	2	18	77	43	98	35	10	.283/.349/.453	114	25.3	.317	3.7	RF(104) 5.5, CF(19) -0.1	2.9	117
2020	SDN	MLB	24	35	4	2	0	1	4	2	8	1	0	.236/.299/.398	86	0.0	.287	0.0	CF 0	0.1	94

Comparables: Zoilo Almonte, Alfredo Marte, Ramón Torres

Olivares is one of the poster children for the depth of this system. A year after cracking our top 20 as a physical toolsy guy, he went out and put up a 114 DRC+ in the Texas League while improving offensively pretty much across the board at a higher level, and he only managed to nudge his way up a half-dozen spots on the list. He's started to grow into some of the physical projection he's long threatened, and it wasn't a fluke that a bunch of his doubles and triples turned into homers. There's some inconsistency in the barrel delivery still, but he's continued to make a bunch of contact against better arms. He's gained a bit of explosiveness to his stride with added strength, and, provided he continues to hone his route-running, he can become a value-adding center fielder. He'll be 24 this year with a full, successful season at Double-A under his belt, and he should factor into the mix for big-league at-bats at some point in 2020.

15 Ronald Bolaños RHP

Born: 08/23/96　Age: 23　Bats: R　Throws: R　Height: 6'3"　Weight: 220　Origin: International Free Agent, 2016

YEAR	TEAM	LVL	AGE	W	L	SV	G	GS	IP	H	HR	BB/9	K/9	K	GB%	BABIP	WHIP	ERA	DRA	WARP	PF
2017	FTW	A	20	5	2	0	16	11	69¹	65	3	4.4	6.6	51	46%	.301	1.43	4.41	5.38	-0.1	103
2018	LEL	A+	21	6	9	0	25	23	125	138	13	3.6	8.5	118	44%	.341	1.50	5.11	5.11	0.3	103
2019	LEL	A+	22	5	2	0	10	10	53²	37	4	3.9	9.1	54	50%	.244	1.12	2.85	3.37	1.1	94
2019	AMA	AA	22	8	5	0	15	13	76²	71	7	3.5	10.3	88	48%	.335	1.32	4.23	4.88	0.0	113
2019	SDN	MLB	22	0	2	0	5	3	19²	17	3	5.5	8.7	19	41%	.264	1.47	5.95	6.03	-0.1	97
2020	SDN	MLB	23	2	2	0	15	3	29	28	4	4.3	7.9	26	43%	.293	1.46	4.99	5.03	0.2	94

Comparables: Chris Flexen, Robert Dugger, T.J. Zeuch

Bolaños is the eighth and final member of San Diego's 2016 J2 crew to crack our top 15, and his arm is as electric as any name above or below him. He's a big, physical right-hander who has grown a bunch since his days as Michel Baez's teammate in Cuba. His big-league debut last year came shortly before he turned 23 and was earned largely on the back of an excellent fastball that sits mid 90s and will touch 98. He generates plenty of life and ride with the pitch crossfiring from a three-quarters slot, though his fine command of the pitch is below-average, as his arm will show up late and sail balls arm-side. Behind the fastball is a kitchen sink full of a slider with flashes of two-plane action, a show-me change, and a deep curveball he'll throw whenever and mess around with the velocity and trajectory. The delivery is aggressive and up-tempo, and he'll rush through checkpoints and get out of sync. Fringy command and control will make him less consistent as a rotation option, but he can fill starts and log multiple middle innings a pop in 2020.

16 Reggie Lawson RHP

Born: 08/02/97　Age: 22　Bats: R　Throws: R　Height: 6'4"　Weight: 205　Origin: Round 2, 2016 Draft (#71 overall)

YEAR	TEAM	LVL	AGE	W	L	SV	G	GS	IP	H	HR	BB/9	K/9	K	GB%	BABIP	WHIP	ERA	DRA	WARP	PF
2017	FTW	A	19	4	6	0	17	17	73	65	8	4.3	11.0	89	42%	.317	1.37	5.30	3.88	1.2	104
2018	LEL	A+	20	8	5	0	24	22	117	130	11	3.9	9.0	117	43%	.348	1.55	4.69	5.46	-0.2	99
2019	AMA	AA	21	3	1	0	6	6	27²	28	4	4.2	11.7	36	39%	.353	1.48	5.20	4.99	0.0	119
2020	SDN	MLB	22	2	2	0	33	0	35	36	6	3.8	8.8	34	40%	.304	1.44	5.07	5.03	0.2	94

Comparables: Jonathan Hernández, Jason Adam, Lance McCullers Jr.

It's easy to lose Lawson in the depth of the Padres' system after he was limited to just six starts last year, but he's still just 22 years old and showed flashes in the Arizona Fall League of the talent that prompted San Diego to select him 71st-overall in 2016. The fastball sits in the mid 90s with life, and he complements it well with a curve that generates plenty of swing-and-miss. The changeup is not as advanced, but it does show promise of eventually turning into an average pitch. Prior to injuring his elbow last spring there were times the control would waver, but the delivery is easy and he's athletic enough to eventually clean up some of those issues. If he can stay healthy, the stuff is there for Lawson to eventually sneak his way onto the back of the rotation, and there's a healthy fallback route where he cranks up the heat in short bursts to evolve into a lights-out reliever.

17 Hudson Potts 3B

Born: 10/28/98 Age: 21 Bats: R Throws: R Height: 6'3" Weight: 205 Origin: Round 1, 2016 Draft (#24 overall)

YEAR	TEAM	LVL	AGE	PA	R	2B	3B	HR	RBI	BB	K	SB	CS	AVG/OBP/SLG	DRC+	VORP	BABIP	BRR	FRAA	WARP	PF
2017	FTW	A	18	522	67	23	4	20	69	23	140	0	1	.253/.293/.438	90	10.3	.312	-0.5	3B(116) -6.9, SS(2) 0.2	0.4	105
2018	LEL	A+	19	453	66	35	1	17	58	37	112	3	1	.281/.350/.498	145	36.7	.348	0.3	3B(99) 0.7, 1B(8) 0.1	3.6	100
2018	SAN	AA	19	89	5	0	0	2	5	10	33	1	0	.154/.258/.231	39	-2.9	.233	-0.2	3B(21) 0.3	-0.2	102
2019	AMA	AA	20	448	56	23	1	16	59	32	128	3	1	.227/.290/.406	58	0.2	.288	-1.7	3B(85) -6.4, 2B(19) -0.7	-1.2	117
2020	SDN	MLB	21	251	24	13	1	7	28	16	80	1	0	.222/.277/.378	70	3.0	.304	-0.3	3B -2, 2B 0	-0.3	94

Comparables: Matt Dominguez, Jake Bauers, Rafael Devers

One of the things they teach us here when we're brand new members of the BP prospect team is an important axiom: "Someone is paying this person to play professional baseball; it's up to you to figure out why." Potts is one of the prospects that tested this axiom in 2019. The 2016 first-rounder from Southlake, Texas was quite young for the level at 20, and he showed power with 17 homers. But they came at an expensive cost of poor patience and a lot of swing-and-miss, and he was frequently overmatched at the level. The glove at the hot corner stalled some, and now looks more okay than great, so the bat needs to do a good bit of work to drive the profile. We'll chalk this year up to a young player in over his head against much more advanced competition, and see if he can't answer us the original question a little more clearly in what figures to be a repeat engagement at Amarillo.

18 Joey Cantillo LHP

Born: 12/18/99 Age: 20 Bats: L Throws: L Height: 6'4" Weight: 220 Origin: Round 16, 2017 Draft (#468 overall)

YEAR	TEAM	LVL	AGE	W	L	SV	G	GS	IP	H	HR	BB/9	K/9	K	GB%	BABIP	WHIP	ERA	DRA	WARP	PF
2017	SDP	RK	17	1	0	0	7	0	8	5	0	6.8	15.8	14	47%	.333	1.38	4.50	1.35	0.4	100
2018	SDP	RK	18	2	2	0	11	9	45¹	33	0	2.4	11.5	58	59%	.300	0.99	2.18	1.93	2.0	102
2019	FTW	A	19	9	3	0	19	19	98	58	3	2.5	11.8	128	46%	.264	0.87	1.93	2.18	3.5	106
2019	LEL	A+	19	1	1	0	3	3	13²	12	2	4.6	10.5	16	38%	.270	1.39	4.61	3.75	0.2	107
2020	SDN	MLB	20	2	2	0	33	0	35	34	5	3.8	10.3	40	42%	.320	1.40	4.62	4.54	0.3	94

Comparables: Adrian Morejon, Noah Syndergaard, Brusdar Graterol

Many pitchers in the Midwest League had better stuff, but none dominated hitters the way that Cantillo did last season. The former 16th-round selection struck out 128 in just 98 innings and held opposing hitters to a .173 average. The arsenal is underwhelming on the surface, with a fastball that sits in the mid to upper 80s and a big, soft curve, but he gets the job done with feel and deception. The changeup is the best secondary; it looks like the fastball out of his hand and he's confident enough to throw it in any situation. He gets good downhill plane and some velocity will come as he physically matures, but there will always be a dependence on pitchability. It will be interesting to see how that profile fares against the more hitter-friendly stops in the upper minors.

19 Blake Hunt C

Born: 11/10/98   Age: 21   Bats: R   Throws: R   Height: 6'3"   Weight: 215   Origin: Round 2, 2017 Draft (#69 overall)

YEAR	TEAM	LVL	AGE	PA	R	2B	3B	HR	RBI	BB	K	SB	CS	AVG/OBP/SLG	DRC+	VORP	BABIP	BRR	FRAA	WARP	PF
2017	PDR	RK	18	32	7	2	0	1	4	3	13	0	0	.214/.313/.393	68	0.8	.357	0.4	C(3) 0.0	-0.3	100
2017	SDP	RK	18	98	14	7	2	1	15	5	29	1	0	.250/.316/.409	71	2.6	.356	1.1		-0.1	101
2018	TRI	A-	19	245	34	13	0	3	25	27	56	2	1	.271/.371/.377	116	15.8	.351	-1.0	C(47) -0.7	1.2	99
2019	FTW	A	20	376	40	21	3	5	39	35	67	4	1	.255/.331/.381	118	11.4	.303	-5.2	C(76) -1.0, 1B(9) -0.4	1.6	107
2020	SDN	MLB	21	251	22	13	1	5	25	15	69	1	0	.219/.275/.350	63	0.0	.289	0.0	C -1, 1B 0	-0.4	94

The Padres saw a future above-average defender with a bit of pop when they went overslot to lure Hunt away from a Pepperdine commitment in 2017. He hasn't disappointed behind the dish since signing, blocking well and showing quality lateral movement for someone his size. He's also tough to run on, as he is quick to transfer and has a strong, accurate arm. Offensively, he's still a work in progress. The bat speed is average and there's length to the swing, though he does control the zone well. Fringe-average power should eventually play in-game, mostly based on his raw strength. There's still a ways to go for the bat, but Hunt's strong defense will give him plenty of opportunity to figure it out, and should eventually lead him to a sustained big-league role.

20 Hudson Head CF

Born: 04/08/01   Age: 19   Bats: L   Throws: L   Height: 6'1"   Weight: 180   Origin: Round 3, 2019 Draft (#84 overall)

YEAR	TEAM	LVL	AGE	PA	R	2B	3B	HR	RBI	BB	K	SB	CS	AVG/OBP/SLG	DRC+	VORP	BABIP	BRR	FRAA	WARP	PF
2019	PDR	RK	18	141	19	7	3	1	12	15	29	3	3	.283/.383/.417	125	8.9	.363	-0.3	CF(26) -5.9	0.1	110
2020	SDN	MLB	19	251	22	12	1	4	22	22	79	3	1	.217/.295/.326	68	0.0	.318	0.0	CF -2	-0.4	94

Comparables: Trent Grisham, Che-Hsuan Lin, Ronald Acuña Jr.

Head popped up last spring as a late-rising Texas prep bat, and San Diego made an aggressive play for him, grabbing him in the third round and signing him for the slot value of the 23rd-overall pick in the draft to buy him out of a strong commitment to Oklahoma. He's a five-tool player with just the kind of projectable frame to support such a towering draft commitment. He's thin and wiry at present, and while he's never going to grow into a ton of bulk, there's ample room to add lean muscle and pack on strength. There's an arm bar and some rigidity to the present load, but the swing is fluid on trigger, with quality bat speed and whip. He generates excellent extension and already gets into his legs well, which bodes well for his ability to grow into raw power that should reach at least above-average, with the potential for a tick more depending on how full he fills out. He's an efficient runner with a gliding gait, and the speed translates pretty well in the outfield already. It's not a no-doubt center field profile, but the raw fundamentals are there, and when all's said and done he could very well wind up with above-average tools all the way across the board. Given how aggressive the org is, he's likely to see plenty of full-season reps next season and could move up this list right quick.

Personal Cheeseball

PC Eguy Rosario INF

Born: 08/25/99   Age: 20   Bats: R   Throws: R   Height: 5'9"   Weight: 150   Origin: International Free Agent, 2015

YEAR	TEAM	LVL	AGE	PA	R	2B	3B	HR	RBI	BB	K	SB	CS	AVG/OBP/SLG	DRC+	VORP	BABIP	BRR	FRAA	WARP	PF
2017	SDP	RK	17	234	36	12	7	1	33	24	43	16	7	.282/.363/.422	96	15.9	.350	1.9	2B(27) 1.7, 3B(26) 2.0	1.2	101
2017	FTW	A	17	204	15	9	2	0	13	20	51	17	5	.206/.296/.278	73	-4.2	.287	1.1	2B(22) 0.6, 3B(18) -0.7	0.0	104
2018	LEL	A+	18	505	60	28	1	9	45	38	119	9	8	.239/.307/.363	83	6.7	.302	-0.7	2B(101) -8.0, 3B(14) 0.2	-0.3	99
2019	LEL	A+	19	512	60	25	8	7	72	37	103	21	9	.278/.331/.412	97	18.3	.338	1.0	3B(68) -0.3, SS(20) -0.5	1.3	97
2020	SDN	MLB	20	251	23	12	1	4	23	18	67	8	4	.227/.290/.346	67	2.0	.303	0.0	2B -1, 3B -1	-0.4	94

Contrary to what I wrote in my Eyewitness Report on Rosario, it turned out that he wasn't Rule 5-eligible this winter after all. Hence he'll benefit from another year of development without needing to be on anyone's 40-Man roster. On the dirt, he displays enough glove, arm, and athleticism to handle all three infield positions to the left of first base. At the plate, he combines above-average bat-to-ball skills with advanced discipline, though he struggles to catch up with plus stuff. At present, he hits the majority of his batted balls on the ground, but his strong lower half implies that the game power could play up to below-average if he learns how to lift the ball without sacrificing too much contact. The likely outcome is a fifth infielder rounding out a first-division roster, but there's a chance he'll grow into a full-time player. Despite having spent each of the last two seasons in High-A, he only turned 20 in late August. Eguy (pronounced egg-y) is well-cooked beyond his age, and salmonella-free! (editing note: Wilson, don't you dare cut the last pun out).

Low Minors Sleeper

LMS Joshua Mears   OF

Born: 02/21/01   Age: 19   Bats: R   Throws: R   Height: 6'3"   Weight: 230   Origin: Round 2, 2019 Draft (#48 overall)

YEAR	TEAM	LVL	AGE	PA	R	2B	3B	HR	RBI	BB	K	SB	CS	AVG/OBP/SLG	DRC+	VORP	BABIP	BRR	FRAA	WARP	PF
2019	PDR	RK	18	195	30	4	3	7	24	23	59	9	1	.253/.354/.440	100	5.8	.343	0.4	RF(29) 2.1, LF(9) -1.6	0.5	109
2020	SDN	MLB	19	251	21	11	1	3	21	23	101	3	1	.205/.284/.305	60	0.0	.353	0.0	RF 2, LF 0	-0.3	94

It's not cheating to take last summer's second-rounder in this slot, because in most other systems he'd probably crack the top 20 on pedigree alone. He was an underslot pick to clear space for Head, but he's a sight to behold all the same. He's an enormous kid, standing 6-foot-3 and 230 as an 18-year-old on draft day, and there is corresponding strength for days. There is also a corresponding sluggishness to his swing progression right now. The hands drift forward off a shallow load to choke off some of his torque, and he got eaten alive by velocity after signing, whiffing more than 30-percent of the time in the AZL. The raw power is sick, though, and the frame could tighten and grow into elite full-body strength. He runs well for his size, and showed good instincts on the bases as well as some tracking ability in right. It's not the highest-probability profile, but it's a fun bat to dream on actualizing down the line.

Top Talents 25 and Under (as of 4/1/2020)

1. Fernando Tatis, Jr.
2. Chris Paddack
3. MacKenzie Gore
4. Luis Patiño
5. CJ Abrams
6. Francisco Mejia
7. Luis Campusano
8. Taylor Trammell
9. Cal Quantrill
10. Adrian Morejon

A pulled hammy put Tatito on the shelf in May, and then a back injury ultimately ended his season in the middle of August, and those were both huge bummers because it sure was a lot of fun to watch him play in between those extended absences. The list of 20-year-olds to put up three-and-a-half win seasons is a real short one, and while his offensive production surely punched above its weight – .410 BABIPs and 30-percent strikeout rates don't tend to be all that sustainable – we can forgive those shortcomings some since, you know, the whole he's-20-years-old thing. He's a franchise cornerstone player in an organization that appears flush with those sorts.

On the other side of the ball, Chris Paddack sure did look like a front-of-the-rotation starter for an organization that also, somehow, appears flush with those sorts. The 23-year-old's four-WARP debut was by and large the sustainable-looking kind according to his under-the-hood metrics, though the arsenal's probably going to need more refinement if he's going to stay in that rarefied air. He's fastball-heavy, which is just a fine thing to be in light of his fastball being very, very good, but hitters started making a bit more contact against his cambio as the season progressed, and he's still not great at spinning the ball. He's very good, though, and should help anchor a resurgent rotation for the first half of the decade to come.

Francisco Mejia continued to remind everyone that catcher development isn't linear, but he flashed a bunch of reasons for optimism that his is progressing solidly in the right direction. The bat slogged early, but it warmed up late with glimpses of a long-heralded plus hit tool, and the glove true to form, performed okay enough behind the dish. It remains an offense-first profile that yangs nicely with Hedges' glovely yin, and another step forward in the box next year in his age-24 season can check a big box for the franchise.

Paul Quantrill's son hasn't quite fulfilled the lofty expectations that come with a top-ten draft pedigree, but his big-league debut last year was absolutely fine. There were some warning signs, however, notably that his vaunted changeup didn't actually fool hitters nearly as much as he needs it to, and after an initial bout of effectiveness his slider missed fewer and fewer bats as the season progressed and hitters adjusted. But hey, if a true No. 4 starter's the 10th guy on your organization's 25U list you're in pretty good shape, and that's where it appears things are right now in San Diego.

Beyond the top 10 here there's also a deep trove of useful pieces for good measure; it's unclear what exactly we should expect from Manuel Margot going forward after another sub-one WARP season in more or less full playing time, but there are still fun underlying skills and sometimes guys like him'll pop a few years into their careers. Josh Naylor flashed some of the barrel skills that got him drafted at the top of a first round, along with a good chunk of his defensive deficiencies, and Andrés Muñoz breathed enough fire in his debut to inspire confidence that the club is deep in the process of developing yet another back-of-the-bullpen stalwart to complement its embarrassing riches of forthcoming starting pitching.

All of this is to confirm that after years of terrible, terrible big-league play, San Diego has triangulated an awfully exciting young core that should finally be able to give their neighbors to the north a run for their NL West money in the 2020s.

Eyewitness Reports

Eyewitness Report: MacKenzie Gore

Evaluator: Wilson Karaman
Report Date: 04/30/2019
Dates Seen: Spring 2019
Risk Factor: Moderate

Delivery: Athletic, projectable frame, extremely fluid physicality, elasticity, excellent balance and body control; calm and composed, takes time between warm-up tosses, controls game tempo; flowing, elegant delivery, huge leg kick with hard but contained drive, channels energy efficiently, consistent down hill, extension and deception, lunging effect, perceived velocity plays up

Pitch Type	Future Grade	Sitting Velocity	Peak Velocity	Report
FB	70	93-95	96	Commands it well, shows ability to elevate, gets at hands and generates late swings, swing-and-miss in and above zone, will tease a cut on it and hold velo band, projection for another couple ticks at peak; plays above radar with life and explosion
CB	60	75-79	79	Advanced pitch, mostly works it ball-to-strike, consistently lands it into the zone, best flash tight two-plane action, will take a little off of it for a different look; plays well off fastball line, quality tunnel; arm angle will dip on some, casts it on occasion
SL	55	82-83	85	Short action, tight spinner, will flash depth, finishes well, will throw through the pack door or draw it out as a chaser, less consistent present feel, plenty of flashes; lacks ceiling of the curve, but a similarly advanced, quality pitch
CH	55	80-83	85	Tight fade with some bottom below the zone, can struggle to find release and sail it, competitive efforts flash late action, plus velo separation, plays well in arsenal, elements to grow into above-average pitch

Conclusion: Gore is an elite pitching prospect, with top-shelf athleticism and command of his physicality. The raw stuff is outstanding. It's a deep arsenal of pitches that play well together. He's balanced and consistent with his mechanics and pitch execution. This is what a front-of-the-rotation arm looks like.

Eyewitness Report: Luis Patiño

Evaluator: Wilson Karaman
Report Date: 07/10/2019
Dates Seen: 6/28/19
Risk Factor: High
Delivery: Strong, durable frame, some slope to the shoulders, width to add a touch more strength through maturity; good hips and lower half, powerful drive; Gore-style mechanics, slightly less fluid, some stop-and-start to it, more deliberate at the top & through the turn can lead to slips in timing and sync; plus-plus athlete, efficient movements; higher three-quarter slot, elite arm speed; crossfire adds deception, occasional jangle at foot strike; low-effort delivery, steady head with quick and controlled deceleration

Pitch Type	Future Grade	Sitting Velocity	Peak Velocity	Report
FB	70	93-96	97	Explosive pitch, ball has carry to beat barrels in and above zone, swing-and-miss offering when he elevates; natural ride, will throw a cut on it; confidence in pitch, strong glove-side command when he's synced downhill, angle from high slot/crossfire can leave it vulnerable against lefties; top-end velo likely maxed
CB	55	78-81	83	11-5 shape, hard vertical action with finish below the zone; will cast it, gets steeper trying to come up and over to create angle, issue should improve with reps, average movement plays up off FB line, above-average utility with anticipated gains in consistency
SL	60	84-87	90	Plus horizontal action, mild vertical, late movement, darting action misses bats; feel to keep spin tight, can occasionally get sweepy but command to pull it out of danger zones; confidence to throw ball-to-strike early in counts, will front- and back-door it
CH	60	85-88	89	Plus lateral movement, quality tumble, will disappear off FB line when he turns it over; feel to land it in the zone, solid present and projectable future command, pitch works to generate swing-miss below the zone when ahead; confidence isn't quite there yet, will baby it when he's trying to land it; projection pitch with impact potential

Conclusion: Patino's an extremely advanced pitcher for his age, pitching with the confidence and maturity of a much older arm. He engages with his catcher and coaches and works through advanced sequencing with a consistency born of excellent strength and athleticism in the delivery. The athleticism offsets some command concern related to his crossfire delivery. A nascent cut look with the fastball can combine with continued advancement with his changeup to counter current issues with left-handed hitters. He's a teenaged arm in A-ball, and the risk is inherently high, though it is lower than most with that pedigree. The ceiling is that of a No. 2 starter.

San Francisco Giants

The State of the System

The Giants' system is more fun—if not all that appreciatively deeper—than it's been in recent years.

The Top Ten

★ ★ ★ *2020 Top 101 Prospect* **#14** ★ ★ ★

1. Marco Luciano SS   OFP: 70   ETA: 2022

Born: 09/10/01   Age: 18   Bats: R   Throws: R   Height: 6'2"   Weight: 178   Origin: International Free Agent, 2018

YEAR	TEAM	LVL	AGE	PA	R	2B	3B	HR	RBI	BB	K	SB	CS	AVG/OBP/SLG	DRC+	VORP	BABIP	BRR	FRAA	WARP	PF
2019	GNT	RK	17	178	46	9	2	10	38	27	39	8	6	.322/.438/.616	195	26.5	.378	1.2	SS(31) 1.6	2.4	101
2019	SLO	A-	17	38	6	4	0	0	4	5	6	1	0	.212/.316/.333	97	1.0	.259	-0.2	SS(9) -0.8	0.0	102
2020	SFN	MLB	18	251	22	12	1	4	22	26	77	3	1	.210/.300/.320	69	0.0	.304	0.0	SS 1	-0.1	86

Comparables: Gary Sánchez, Nomar Mazara, Oscar Hernández

The Report: If you were building a high-dollar, high-upside, teenaged IFA prospect from scratch it would look a lot like Luciano. It's an ideal frame, medium build with some projection but also present strength. There's enough athleticism to maybe stick at short despite thicker waist and thighs that portend near-term strength gains. Plus bat speed, controlled violence with loft. Present plus raw with more to come. A solid runner at present, who's likely to bleed some speed as he ages, but could remain average underway. A true left side arm if he does have to move off of shortstop. It's the total package, a potential hit/power/speed combo with impact wherever he ends up.

Obviously at present there is some rawness. Luciano's actions at short are merely average, and his throwing mechanics can get loose or rushed. His approach can get overly aggressive early in counts, although he has enough control over the swing to make contact even when fooled, it's just not always good quality contact. While he grades out somewhat similarly to Wander Franco as a 17-year-old at roughly the same level of competition, he's not nearly as polished or likely to move as quickly. That's hardly a damning criticism though, and the offensive upside isn't far off regardless.

Variance: Highish. All in all, Luciano has a very traditional risk profile for a high-end, low minors prospect. He might grow off shortstop, putting pressure on the offensive profile. We also haven't seen him in full-season ball yet against more advanced arms. However, we believe in the bat enough that we don't even consider him a particularly high risk prospect at present, even coming off an age-17 season spent mostly in the complex.

Mark Barry's Fantasy Take: There isn't a next Wander Franco, to be clear. However, if there were, Luciano would be a good bet to take the mantle. He's super young, but the combination of lightning-quick hands, samurai-esque discipline and projectable power is certainly a top-10 prospect starter kit.

───────── ★ ★ ★ *2020 Top 101 Prospect* **#25** ★ ★ ★ ─────────

2 Joey Bart C   OFP: 60   ETA: 2020/21

Born: 12/15/96   Age: 23   Bats: R   Throws: R   Height: 6'3"   Weight: 235   Origin: Round 1, 2018 Draft (#2 overall)

YEAR	TEAM	LVL	AGE	PA	R	2B	3B	HR	RBI	BB	K	SB	CS	AVG/OBP/SLG	DRC+	VORP	BABIP	BRR	FRAA	WARP	PF
2018	GNT	RK	21	25	3	1	1	0	1	1	7	0	0	.261/.320/.391	85	0.6	.375	-0.1	C(4) -0.1	0.0	101
2018	SLO	A-	21	203	35	14	2	13	39	12	40	2	1	.298/.369/.613	149	21.6	.318	1.2	C(32) -1.0	1.7	118
2019	SJO	A+	22	251	37	10	2	12	37	14	50	5	2	.265/.315/.479	112	17.2	.291	1.0	C(50) -1.9	1.2	98
2019	RIC	AA	22	87	9	4	1	4	11	7	21	0	2	.316/.368/.544	164	8.0	.382	-1.2	C(15) 0.2	0.8	92
2020	SFN	MLB	23	251	29	12	1	11	35	14	69	1	0	.245/.296/.450	94	0.0	.300	-0.3	C -4	0.3	86

Comparables: Kevin Cron, Devin Mesoraco, Travis d'Arnaud

The Report: Bart had a bit of an abbreviated pro debut due to a pair of hand injuries—one in April and one in Fall Ball—but when on the field, he looked every bit of one of the top catching prospects in baseball. Much was made pre-draft of Bart being one of the rare catchers to call his own game in college. We can't really offer much insight into how those soft skills are translating to the pro game yet, but the more concrete defensive tools all look good. He's on the larger side for a catcher, but shows solid athleticism behind the plate. He's a strong receiver with a quiet glove hand. Bart also offers an easy plus arm and shows good footwork and actions getting out of the crouch. The overall defensive profile gives him a floor as a major league catcher even before we talk about the bat. And his bat more than pulls its own weight in the profile. It's power-over-hit due to an upright, at times stiff swing with a long stride, but he has plus raw that he can get to most of already given his strong approach at the plate. Bart needs a season of healthy reps for skill consolidation purposes, and we can offer the usual caveats about catcher development being weird and Young Catcher Stagnation Syndrome, but ultimately we can only find minor quibbles with the profile here.

Variance: Medium. The hand injuries are a little concerning, but freak enough that it's more in a "lost development time" way than a "not durable enough for catcher" way. It's possible the hit tool plays to fringe or below-average and the power plays more around 15-20 home runs, and the package ends up more solid regular.

Mark Barry's Fantasy Take: A late-season stint at Double-A Richmond in his second season as a pro is definitely a good sign. An even better sign—he mashed in said stint, carrying an OPS north of .900 in 87 trips to the plate. As you may have heard, catchers are a different animal, man. There is so much that goes into donning the tools of ignorance that sometimes offense takes a back seat (as if you hadn't noticed based on most catcher stat lines). Bart is promising and a no-doubt top-3 catching prospect. That said, I don't have confidence that his status will translate to an effective fantasy backstop soon enough to justify his likely lofty price tag.

───────── ★ ★ ★ *2020 Top 101 Prospect* **#34** ★ ★ ★ ─────────

3 Heliot Ramos OF   OFP: 60   ETA: 2021

Born: 09/07/99   Age: 20   Bats: R   Throws: R   Height: 6'0"   Weight: 188   Origin: Round 1, 2017 Draft (#19 overall)

YEAR	TEAM	LVL	AGE	PA	R	2B	3B	HR	RBI	BB	K	SB	CS	AVG/OBP/SLG	DRC+	VORP	BABIP	BRR	FRAA	WARP	PF
2017	GIA	RK	17	151	33	11	6	6	27	10	48	10	2	.348/.404/.645	163	21.0	.500	2.2	CF(29) -2.3	1.3	99
2018	AUG	A	18	535	61	24	8	11	52	35	136	8	7	.245/.313/.396	107	21.5	.319	1.8	CF(113) -4.5	1.7	96
2019	SJO	A+	19	338	51	18	0	13	40	32	85	6	7	.306/.385/.500	143	32.4	.385	0.1	CF(70) -5.1	1.7	98
2019	RIC	AA	19	106	13	6	1	3	15	10	33	2	3	.242/.321/.421	120	3.5	.339	-1.6	CF(19) -1.5	0.2	92
2020	SFN	MLB	20	251	25	13	1	7	28	18	83	2	1	.236/.301/.391	83	0.0	.338	-0.4	CF -3	-0.1	86

Comparables: Ronald Acuña Jr., Jesus Montero, Justin Upton

The Report: The 19th selection of the 2017 draft, the Puerto Rican center fielder's five tools and frenetic energy are straight off the sandlot. The free-swinger utilized the whole field and natural bat-to-ball abilities to slash .306/.385/.500 with 13 homers and 18 doubles as a teenager in the High-A California League last season. His elongated swing is susceptible to the strikeout (118 K in 389 AB last season), but also generates impressive power from his otherwise everyman 6-foot physique. Ramos' raw speed, athleticism, and plus-arm make him a potential center fielder with further refinement of his reads and routes. He could win a gold glove in a corner. His 4.05-second home-to-first time in the Arizona Fall League was among the best according to Statcast, although he's yet to adapt that speed to base thievery (8 SB / 10 CS in '19). The newly turned 20-year-old will begin next season at Double-A most likely, and seemingly has a clear runway to the big league outfield job.

With continued development of his raw tools, primarily his bat-to-ball skill, Ramos could be a dynamic, middle-of-the-order, two-way player in the mold of Kirby Puckett. He should be the opening day center fielder in 2021, with a chance to roam San Francisco's outfield as soon as next season.

Variance: Medium. He just turned 20 and struggled in limited exposure versus older Double-A/AFL competition in 2019.

Mark Barry's Fantasy Take: When Ramos stole 10 bases with a 1.049 OPS in his first 35 games after being drafted, we were all tantalized by the power/speed combo. He's swiped just 16 bags in 226 games since, leaving a trail of strikeouts in his wake. He can still be good and useful, no doubt, but the likelihood of him being National League Teoscar Hernandez is growing by the day. Is that too harsh?(

★ ★ ★ *2020 Top 101 Prospect* **#68** ★ ★ ★

4 Hunter Bishop OF OFP: 60 ETA: 2020/21

Born: 06/25/98 Age: 22 Bats: L Throws: R Height: 6'5" Weight: 210 Origin: Round 1, 2019 Draft (#10 overall)

YEAR	TEAM	LVL	AGE	PA	R	2B	3B	HR	RBI	BB	K	SB	CS	AVG/OBP/SLG	DRC+	VORP	BABIP	BRR	FRAA	WARP	PF
2019	GNT	RK	21	29	4	3	0	1	3	9	11	2	0	.250/.483/.550	113	3.6	.500	0.4	CF(4) -1.0	0.0	103
2019	SLO	A-	21	117	21	1	1	4	9	29	28	6	2	.224/.427/.400	177	9.2	.278	-0.3	CF(21) -2.2	0.7	107
2020	SFN	MLB	22	251	23	11	1	6	24	25	87	2	1	.199/.287/.329	65	0.0	.298	0.0	CF -1	-0.4	86

Comparables: Dansby Swanson, Nolan Reimold, Christin Stewart

The Report: Bishop, younger brother of Braden, didn't look all that different as a baseball player coming into his junior year at ASU. He looked different physically for sure—a tall, strong, projectable frame—but he had played more as the speedy outfielder type despite plus raw pop. He then promptly went out and slugged 22 home runs in 57 games, playing himself into a top 10 pick. Bishop is likely to grow into a right fielder's body, and despite his present above-average speed, he's on the raw side in center. It's an intriguing power/speed combo even in a corner. Bishop generates big bat speed with minimal extra motion in setup or load, and his swing features the kind of loft and game power you'd expect from a typical right field masher. The approach can be overly aggressive and geared for power—although he knows the zone well enough—so there will be questions about swing-and-miss as he moves up the professional ladder. The power and athleticism are worth betting on, however.

Variance: Medium. The usual college corner bat questions: lack of pro experience, swing-and-miss, and if the overall bat will be good enough at the highest level to carry a middle-of-the-order profile.

Mark Barry's Fantasy Take: After the draft, our fearless leader comped Bishop's profile (if not necessarily his upside) to that of George Springer. After a season of pro experience, the profile hasn't really changed, as Bishop flashed bouts of power and speed across two levels. He'll need to cut down on the strikeouts, but his profile and pedigree alone probably keeps him in the 150-200 range for dynasty prospects.

5 Will Wilson SS OFP: 55 ETA: Late 2021

Born: 07/21/98 Age: 21 Bats: R Throws: R Height: 6'0" Weight: 184 Origin: Round 1, 2019 Draft (#15 overall)

YEAR	TEAM	LVL	AGE	PA	R	2B	3B	HR	RBI	BB	K	SB	CS	AVG/OBP/SLG	DRC+	VORP	BABIP	BRR	FRAA	WARP	PF
2019	ORM	RK+	20	204	23	10	3	5	18	14	47	0	0	.275/.328/.439	94	5.3	.343	-0.8		0.6	108
2020	SFN	MLB	21	251	18	11	1	3	20	14	81	2	1	.205/.253/.298	44	0.0	.299	0.0		-0.9	86

The Report: Wilson is the epitome of a polished college bat; he hit all three years in college, and he held his own in the Pioneer League after signing despite being dinged up for much of the experience. The swing features good balance and strong hands that attack the baseball, and he's shown an adaptive stroke that can lay a barrel on pitches in all quadrants. The body is already pretty mature, and he's got some sneaky strength that couples well with his contact ability to generate average power. The run tool checks in around that range as well, perhaps a tick below, and he lacks for a ton of twitch in his reactions or explosiveness in his movements. It's likely a second base profile down the line, and he already received about a third of his reps there after signing, but he's got the offensive tools to profile there and he's a high-effort player who is a better bet than most to max out his potential.

Variance: Moderate. There's a bunch of good pedigree here, and he's earned some believe-it-until-it-isn't slack. He'll make his full-season debut next year, and should be expected to show well out of the gate.

Mark Barry's Fantasy Take: It's not Wilson's fault that he follows four uber-exciting and toolsy prospects, but his placement makes the dichotomy between his (lack of) upside and the gaudy ceilings we've discussed so far especially stark. Yes, guys like Wilson sometimes turn out to be Gavin Lux, but more often than not they're, like, C.J. Chatham. There are worse dudes to take fliers on if your league rosters 250-plus prospects, but there are plenty of more exciting ones, too.

6 Alexander Canario OF   OFP: 60   ETA: 2023

Born: 05/07/00   Age: 20   Bats: R   Throws: R   Height: 6'1"   Weight: 165   Origin: International Free Agent, 2016

YEAR	TEAM	LVL	AGE	PA	R	2B	3B	HR	RBI	BB	K	SB	CS	AVG/OBP/SLG	DRC+	VORP	BABIP	BRR	FRAA	WARP	PF
2017	DGI	RK	17	274	42	17	4	5	45	33	40	18	10	.294/.391/.464	162	22.3	.335	-1.0	RF(50) 4.0, CF(7) 0.7	2.6	98
2018	GIA	RK	18	208	36	5	2	6	19	27	51	8	5	.250/.357/.403	113	13.2	.317	-0.5	CF(44) 1.0	1.0	97
2019	GNT	RK	19	46	13	3	1	7	14	2	9	1	0	.395/.435/1.000	285	11.7	.370	-0.3	CF(8) -0.7	0.8	99
2019	SLO	A-	19	219	38	17	1	9	40	18	71	3	1	.301/.365/.539	158	17.9	.419	-1.0	CF(26) -8.1, RF(16) -1.1	0.5	105
2020	SFN	MLB	20	251	22	13	1	4	23	19	86	5	2	.212/.279/.333	62	0.0	.319	-0.2	CF -2, RF 0	-0.6	86

Comparables: José Martínez, Teoscar Hernández, Ronald Acuña Jr.

The Report: If you enjoy the controlled violence of Marco Luciano's swing, you will love the max effort blur that is Canario's. He doesn't load the bat, so much as coil himself in a bow-legged, open stance before exploding the barrel through the zone. That does create a fair bit of length—especially when he is trying to get the barrel on pitches down in the zone, but also some serious whip and power. He has better barrel control than that description implies, and he can do some damage even when he doesn't square the ball, but you can beat him down and out of the zone pretty consistently at present. If you don't get your stuff down or out, he can hit it out, and to just about any part of any ballpark. While everything here is raw, the upside in the bat is tremendous.

Canario is splitting time between right and center field at present, but to put it delicately, that is not the butt of a future center fielder. He chugs a bit even in right, but is an average runner and should be fine in a corner. Ultimately this will come down to how much the power plays, but it's a whole lot of potential power.

Variance: Extreme. Unlike with Luciano, we do have some worries about the bat. Canario doesn't have Luciano's easy quick twitch or projectable frame, and everything is very effortful. He struck out 32 percent of the time in short-season, so it could blow up at higher levels. And not in a good way. On the other hand, if he continues to refine his approach it could blow up at higher levels in a good way too.

Mark Barry's Fantasy Take: Canario finally graduated from the complex leagues and did nothing to dispel his reputation as a high-risk/high-reward, raw dude. You typically have to get in early on these types, because when things click, they click quickly. Right now, though, he's a top-250ish guy.

7 Mauricio Dubón IF   OFP: 50   ETA: 2019

Born: 07/19/94   Age: 25   Bats: R   Throws: R   Height: 6'0"   Weight: 160   Origin: Round 26, 2013 Draft (#773 overall)

YEAR	TEAM	LVL	AGE	PA	R	2B	3B	HR	RBI	BB	K	SB	CS	AVG/OBP/SLG	DRC+	VORP	BABIP	BRR	FRAA	WARP	PF
2017	BLX	AA	22	304	34	14	0	2	24	25	42	31	9	.276/.338/.351	101	6.0	.319	0.3	SS(53) 5.4, 2B(20) 3.0	2.3	102
2017	CSP	AAA	22	244	40	15	0	6	33	14	34	7	6	.272/.320/.420	76	0.4	.297	-0.4	SS(30) -1.0, 2B(27) 3.5	0.4	121
2018	CSP	AAA	23	114	18	9	2	4	18	2	19	6	3	.343/.348/.574	107	10.6	.379	1.5	SS(23) 0.3, 2B(4) 0.6	0.8	114
2019	SAC	AAA	24	112	23	4	0	4	9	10	9	1	2	.323/.391/.485	103	8.4	.326	0.6	SS(17) -0.1, 2B(6) 0.3	0.9	101
2019	SAN	AAA	24	427	59	22	1	16	47	18	59	9	6	.297/.333/.475	103	22.9	.316	-0.9	SS(83) 4.1, 2B(12) 0.7	2.4	94
2019	MIL	MLB	24	2	0	0	0	0	0	0	1	0	0	.000/.000/.000	84	0.1	.000	0.0	SS(1) 0.0	0.0	97
2019	SFN	MLB	24	109	12	5	0	4	9	5	19	3	1	.279/.312/.442	88	2.4	.309	1.1	2B(22) 3.8, SS(9) -0.4	0.7	92
2020	SFN	MLB	25	385	37	15	1	9	40	18	68	13	4	.250/.290/.375	76	2.0	.286	0.4	2B 9, SS 0	1.5	86

Comparables: Yairo Muñoz, Marwin Gonzalez, Didi Gregorius

The Report: Dubón bounced back from his 2018 ACL tear without missing much of a beat. He made good use of the new Triple-A ball—and will flash some sneaky power pull side no matter the seam height—and held his own in the majors with San Francisco after a deadline deal sent him West. He will be 26 next May, and the profile hasn't really changed or added all that much upside since his days with the Red Sox. Dubón is also ready to be a major league starter in San Francisco, and despite a big leg kick and a swing that can get mechanical at times, he's an effective all-fields hitter that could play three different infield spots well for the Giants. The game power probably won't play as well in the Bay as it did in the PCL, but those are big inviting gaps for Dubón to hit to, and he might be able to sneak a few down the left field line to go with a .270 batting average and above-average defense.

Variance: Low. Dubón looked pretty serviceable at the plate in his major league debut, and the defensive skills alone up the middle should keep him employed for a bit.

Mark Barry's Fantasy Take: Dubón debuted in San Francisco and was, uh, fine? He's penciled in as a starter at the keystone for 2020, but that says more about the Giants' depth chart than it does about Dubón. He needs to be rostered in NL-only leagues, and he won't kill you in deep-mixed formats, but he's not terribly exciting elsewhere.

8 Seth Corry LHP   OFP: 55   ETA: 2022

Born: 11/03/98   Age: 21   Bats: L   Throws: L   Height: 6'2"   Weight: 195   Origin: Round 3, 2017 Draft (#96 overall)

YEAR	TEAM	LVL	AGE	W	L	SV	G	GS	IP	H	HR	BB/9	K/9	K	GB%	BABIP	WHIP	ERA	DRA	WARP	PF
2017	GIA	RK	18	0	2	0	13	10	24¹	14	1	8.1	7.8	21	46%	.203	1.48	5.55	4.03	0.5	95
2018	GNT	RK	19	3	1	0	9	9	38	38	1	4.0	9.9	42	46%	.349	1.45	2.61	5.01	0.5	100
2018	SLO	A-	19	1	2	0	5	5	19²	14	1	6.9	7.8	17	54%	.245	1.47	5.49	4.42	0.2	118
2019	AUG	A	20	9	3	0	27	26	122²	73	4	4.3	12.6	172	47%	.265	1.07	1.76	3.32	2.7	96
2020	SFN	MLB	21	2	2	0	33	0	35	35	5	4.2	10.2	40	44%	.321	1.45	4.52	4.82	0.2	86

Comparables: Darwinzon Hernandez, Matt Moore, Neftalí Feliz

The Report: Corry led the South Atlantic League in both K% and BB% in 2019. The former came about on the strength of an above-average fastball/curve combo from the left side. Corry can ramp his fastball up to 95 and he gets good extension and deception on it. The curve can vacillate—occasionally on purpose—between a humpy downer to spot, and a tighter, slurvier 1-7 offering to get swings and misses. The inconsistencies in the hook will need to be ironed out, but it consistently flashes plus. There's a straight change he sells all right, but it doesn't fade much and he's pretty limited to working it away to righties at present.

The culprit for the walk rate isn't hard to spot either. The same funky mechanics that lend him some deception can get out of sync, and Corry doesn't consistently repeat his arm stroke, which can lead to him overthrowing to the gloveside. There's a balance between deception and command/control here. I expect some of it to get smoothed out as Corry is a good athlete, but it limits the upside at present.

Variance: High. Third-pitch and control/command questions. Moderate reliever risk. Could also be something like a 6/6/5 starter if a switch flips.

Mark Barry's Fantasy Take: It's hard to get too excited about a dude who walks more than 11 percent of opposing hitters. It's a little easier when that dude strikeouts out more than 12 guys per nine. The control will need to get better to quell bullpen rumblings, but Corry is a great watch-list add while you wait.

9 Sean Hjelle RHP   OFP: 50   ETA: 2021

Born: 05/07/97   Age: 23   Bats: R   Throws: R   Height: 6'11"   Weight: 225   Origin: Round 2, 2018 Draft (#45 overall)

YEAR	TEAM	LVL	AGE	W	L	SV	G	GS	IP	H	HR	BB/9	K/9	K	GB%	BABIP	WHIP	ERA	DRA	WARP	PF
2018	SLO	A-	21	0	0	0	12	12	21¹	24	4	1.7	9.3	22	49%	.317	1.31	5.06	4.10	0.3	115
2019	AUG	A	22	1	2	0	9	9	40²	41	3	2.0	9.7	44	63%	.333	1.23	2.66	5.32	-0.1	98
2019	SJO	A+	22	5	5	0	14	14	77²	73	2	2.2	8.6	74	69%	.326	1.18	2.78	4.11	0.9	97
2019	RIC	AA	22	1	2	0	5	5	25¹	38	1	3.2	7.5	21	48%	.430	1.86	6.04	7.44	-0.8	91
2020	SFN	MLB	23	2	2	0	33	0	35	35	5	3.6	7.2	28	43%	.285	1.40	4.48	4.93	0.2	86

Comparables: David Phelps, Mike Wright, Shane Carle

The Report: Hjelle's listed vitals are not an exaggeration. It's well-documented by this point that the Kentucky product stands at an incredible height on the mound. He uses it to his advantage by allowing a mostly low-90s fastball to play up with extreme extension and a tough angle that makes stepping in against him an uncomfortable challenge. The fastball is also heavy down in the zone with sink and late arm-side movement. Hjelle's two secondaries don't stand out but are enough thanks to advanced command of both. The curveball is the better secondary with average potential and the occasional flash of above-average. It comes out slurvy at times but it's mostly a consistent two-plane breaker with downward action and just enough bite to get whiffs. His changeup also flashes above-average but is a tick below the curve in command, sitting mid-to-upper-80s with average fade. There's no standout, plus pitch in Hjelle's arsenal, but he gets average or better grades from all three with an above-average command profile. It's an easy, repeatable delivery, and he has a durable frame and the arm to eat innings. It's not a thrilling profile despite the listed height, but he's a safe No. 4 starter.

Variance: Medium. The low grade on Hjelle will question the effectiveness of the stuff at the major-league level, but he knows how to command what he has and get the most from it based on his size and repeatability. He should get his chance soon.

Mark Barry's Fantasy Take: If your league rewards guys who look more like basketball players, then Hjelle is your guy. If your league is literally anything else, then I'll pass.

10 Jaylin Davis OF   OFP: 50   ETA: 2019
Born: 07/01/94   Age: 25   Bats: R   Throws: R   Height: 6'1"   Weight: 190   Origin: Round 24, 2015 Draft (#710 overall)

YEAR	TEAM	LVL	AGE	PA	R	2B	3B	HR	RBI	BB	K	SB	CS	AVG/OBP/SLG	DRC+	VORP	BABIP	BRR	FRAA	WARP	PF
2017	CDR	A	22	272	36	13	3	12	41	16	77	9	2	.267/.316/.486	105	13.6	.335	1.1	RF(60) 7.4	1.5	102
2017	FTM	A+	22	233	26	8	2	3	25	12	70	1	1	.237/.288/.335	65	-6.0	.333	-0.5	RF(45) 4.4, LF(10) 2.3	0.3	103
2018	FTM	A+	23	227	23	10	0	5	19	23	57	3	2	.271/.354/.397	126	12.4	.355	4.1	RF(50) -6.2, LF(2) -0.2	0.7	98
2018	CHT	AA	23	267	30	14	2	6	34	21	69	5	2	.275/.341/.425	111	7.9	.359	-0.2	RF(50) 2.5, CF(1) -0.1	1.1	103
2019	PEN	AA	24	251	34	9	0	10	25	36	64	7	3	.274/.382/.458	156	18.3	.345	-0.2	RF(42) -2.0, LF(8) 0.8	1.8	102
2019	SAC	AAA	24	117	21	6	0	10	27	14	28	1	1	.333/.419/.686	138	13.6	.375	0.9	RF(15) 3.1, CF(7) 0.6	1.2	98
2019	ROC	AAA	24	173	39	11	1	15	42	15	46	2	0	.331/.405/.708	160	19.0	.387	0.3	RF(32) 2.8, CF(6) 0.5	1.8	101
2019	SFN	MLB	24	47	2	0	0	1	3	3	11	1	2	.167/.255/.238	68	-0.8	.200	-0.7	RF(15) -0.5	-0.2	90
2020	SFN	MLB	26	105	11	4	0	4	12	9	34	1	0	.223/.297/.383	83	0.0	.305	-0.2	RF 0	-0.1	86

Comparables: Brad Komminsk, Aaron Altherr, Johnny Lewis

The Report: Davis is another swing change success story, although his came from his lower body, rather than an upper body launch angle tweak. He always had plus raw power, but he turned that into monstrous game power across three levels, the final of his 36 bombs a walkoff shot to dead center for the Giants, his first pro home run. The power will come at a cost, as it's still a length and strength swing that may struggle to consistently square better velocity, but Davis has improved his approach at well. He's a good runner and should be at least an average defender even in the cavernous corners of Oracle Park.

Variance: Medium. While he's made the majors and clearly has nothing left to prove in Triple-A, there are some Quad-A markers in the swing until we see it work over a longer stretch against major league arms. However, The speed/pop combo should make him a useful bench outfielder if he can even hit a little bit.

Mark Barry's Fantasy Take: Davis hit 36 homers last season across three levels for two organizations. That alone should keep him on your radar. He could be an end-game option in redraft leagues as early as this season, depending on how the Giants construct their roster.

The Next Ten

11 Luis Matos OF
Born: 01/28/02   Age: 18   Bats: R   Throws: R   Height: 5'11"   Weight: 160   Origin: International Free Agent, 2018

YEAR	TEAM	LVL	AGE	PA	R	2B	3B	HR	RBI	BB	K	SB	CS	AVG/OBP/SLG	DRC+	VORP	BABIP	BRR	FRAA	WARP	PF
2020	SFN	MLB	18	251	23	11	1	3	22	23	75	3	1	.224/.308/.326	77	0.0	.321	0.0	CF -1	0.0	86

Comparables: Manuel Margot, Victor Robles, José Altuve

The other big signing of the Giants' 2018 July 2 class, the 17-year-old is at present a frame and a swing. It's a very good frame and a very good swing, mind you, the kind that will have you dreaming on a five-tool center fielder. Matos shows good balance, bat speed, and loft in the batter's box, and has a good shot to stick up-the-middle. Check back in four years on all of this, but the upside is comparable to the names towards the top of this list.

12 Tristan Beck RHP

Born: 06/24/96　Age: 24　Bats: R　Throws: R　Height: 6'4"　Weight: 165　Origin: Round 4, 2018 Draft (#112 overall)

YEAR	TEAM	LVL	AGE	W	L	SV	G	GS	IP	H	HR	BB/9	K/9	K	GB%	BABIP	WHIP	ERA	DRA	WARP	PF
2019	BRA	RK	23	0	0	0	2	2	9	9	0	4.0	14.0	14	52%	.429	1.44	4.00	2.23	0.4	101
2019	SJO	A+	23	3	2	0	6	6	35²	33	1	3.3	9.3	37	44%	.337	1.29	2.27	4.38	0.3	96
2019	BRV	A+	23	2	2	0	8	8	36²	45	2	3.4	9.6	39	53%	.413	1.61	5.65	7.05	-0.9	96
2020	SFN	MLB	24	2	2	0	33	0	35	34	5	3.4	8.1	32	45%	.291	1.34	3.92	4.42	0.4	86

Comparables: Marco Estrada, Brock Stewart, Jeff Brigham

Acquired from the Braves in the Mark Melancon trade last season, the former fourth round pick is a 6-foot-4 right-hander with good athleticism and an efficient delivery. In six starts and 35 ⅔ innings pitched post-trade with the Giants' High-A California League affiliate, Beck posted a 2.27 ERA with 37 strikeouts and 13 walks allowed. His well-crafted repertoire consists of a mid-90s fastball, a plus curveball whose shape and velocity he can manipulate between the mid-70s and upper-80s, and a developing mid-80s changeup. The 23-year-old Stanford product's advanced command, pitching acumen, and durability should allow him to navigate the minor league waters swiftly. He could have a role in the back-end of the Giants starting rotation by 2021, possibly contributing as a spot starter or from the bullpen prior to that.

13 Logan Webb RHP

Born: 11/18/96　Age: 23　Bats: R　Throws: R　Height: 6'2"　Weight: 220　Origin: Round 4, 2014 Draft (#118 overall)

YEAR	TEAM	LVL	AGE	W	L	SV	G	GS	IP	H	HR	BB/9	K/9	K	GB%	BABIP	WHIP	ERA	DRA	WARP	PF
2017	SLO	A-	20	2	0	0	15	0	28	26	1	2.2	10.0	31	68%	.325	1.18	2.89	3.49	0.5	100
2018	SJO	A+	21	1	3	0	21	20	74	54	2	4.4	9.0	74	48%	.274	1.22	1.82	3.10	1.9	98
2018	RIC	AA	21	1	2	0	6	6	30²	30	4	3.2	7.6	26	52%	.289	1.34	3.82	5.29	0.0	93
2019	AUG	A	22	1	0	0	2	1	10	4	0	2.7	8.1	9	62%	.167	0.70	0.90	3.02	0.2	91
2019	RIC	AA	22	1	4	0	8	7	41¹	41	2	2.6	10.2	47	66%	.333	1.28	2.18	4.35	0.3	94
2019	SAC	AAA	22	0	0	0	1	1	7	7	0	0.0	9.0	7	63%	.368	1.00	1.29	3.15	0.2	91
2019	SFN	MLB	22	2	3	0	8	8	39²	44	5	3.2	8.4	37	48%	.333	1.46	5.22	4.17	0.7	94
2020	SFN	MLB	23	5	7	0	18	18	89	94	12	3.5	7.7	76	52%	.309	1.45	4.40	4.95	0.9	86

Comparables: Tyler Mahle, Joe Ross, Zack Littell

Last year's Annual pegged Webb for a seventh inning role, however he had other ideas when he joined the starting rotation in mid August. Webb's season didn't go as most expected as he got off to a strong start in Double-A before receiving an 80 game suspension for PEDs. He returned to the minors, completing a start at every level, primed to prove he didn't need them to reach the majors. In 39 innings at the MLB level, he relied mostly on his fastball, using a curveball and changeup as secondaries while developing a sinker he used occasionally. He finished with 3.2 BB/9 and 8.4 K/9, displaying good command of his arsenal. He will need to produce similar results to retain his role in the majors as the fifth starter. Webb will be relied upon to go deep into his outings next year and be able to turn over the lineup multiple times.

14 Jake Wong RHP

Born: 09/03/96　Age: 23　Bats: R　Throws: R　Height: 6'2"　Weight: 215　Origin: Round 3, 2018 Draft (#80 overall)

YEAR	TEAM	LVL	AGE	W	L	SV	G	GS	IP	H	HR	BB/9	K/9	K	GB%	BABIP	WHIP	ERA	DRA	WARP	PF
2018	SLO	A-	21	0	2	0	11	11	27¹	28	1	2.0	8.9	27	53%	.329	1.24	2.30	4.16	0.3	114
2019	AUG	A	22	2	1	0	8	8	40²	26	2	2.4	7.5	34	50%	.226	0.91	1.99	3.43	0.8	98
2019	SJO	A+	22	3	2	0	15	15	72¹	76	6	3.0	8.3	67	43%	.345	1.38	4.98	5.78	-0.7	95
2020	SFN	MLB	23	2	2	0	33	0	35	35	5	3.7	6.8	26	43%	.280	1.40	4.34	4.81	0.2	86

Comparables: Daniel Mengden, Bryan Price, Corey Kluber

Wong is a case study in the value and limitations of average projection. He's a polished college arm who works a fastball, mostly 92-93—the average velo band—down in the zone. It will show a bit of sink, but the command and movement are merely average, so it can be hittable up. His curveball is likewise average. Slurvy at times, but showing solid, if short, 12-6 drop at others. He can spot it, or dive it out of the zone. The change requires some projection to get to average, but he sells it well with his arm action. The frame is sturdy if on the shorter side, and there's not much in the way of physical projection left. There's certainly an outcome here where Wong has three average pitches—and major league average is nothing to sneeze at—where he gets enough ground balls with the fastball, and enough swings and misses with the curve to be a backend starter. We often talk about the fine margins with this profile, and that's where the limitations come into play. If any of these projections fall even a half-grade short, major-league hitters will knock you around the park. And High-A hitters already had a bit of a good time against Wong, admittedly in the Cal League. The Cal League is an offensive paradise, but it's also a long way from the majors. The stuff is average, but the variance isn't.

15 Logan Wyatt 1B

Born: 11/15/97   Age: 22   Bats: L   Throws: R   Height: 6'4"   Weight: 230   Origin: Round 2, 2019 Draft (#51 overall)

YEAR	TEAM	LVL	AGE	PA	R	2B	3B	HR	RBI	BB	K	SB	CS	AVG/OBP/SLG	DRC+	VORP	BABIP	BRR	FRAA	WARP	PF
2019	GIA	RK	21	29	7	1	0	0	9	4	6	0	1	.375/.448/.417	113	2.8	.474	0.4	1B(6) 0.8	0.2	95
2019	SLO	A-	21	78	10	2	0	2	12	10	9	0	1	.284/.385/.403	175	4.5	.304	-0.5	1B(16) -0.5	0.4	113
2019	AUG	A	21	76	9	3	0	1	9	12	14	0	0	.233/.368/.333	108	0.8	.277	-1.4	1B(14) -0.4	-0.1	97
2020	SFN	MLB	22	251	22	11	1	4	22	20	62	3	1	.228/.296/.330	68	1.0	.297	0.0	1B -2	-0.3	86

Comparables: Ty France, Christian Walker, Adam Haseley

Wyatt is a case study in the value and limitations of a good approach. The Giants' second-round pick out of Louisville walked significantly more than he struck out his sophomore and junior seasons and posted a near 1:1 rate in his pro debut. He has an obvious knowledge of the strike zone and won't expand at present, and his swing is geared to make high levels of contact. It's a very hit-over-power swing though, with a flat plane and minimal lower-half engagement. It can get slashy and a bit opposite-field geared as well. Wyatt has shown plus raw power, and he's a strong, well-built fellow, but it's very difficult to maintain this kind of walk-rate driven profile up the organizational ladder. The bat speed is only average, and while the hit tool should play above, at present it's hard to see enough total offense to carry a major-league first base profile unless everything goes right.

16 Prelander Berroa RHP

Born: 04/18/00   Age: 20   Bats: R   Throws: R   Height: 5'11"   Weight: 170   Origin: International Free Agent, 2016

YEAR	TEAM	LVL	AGE	W	L	SV	G	GS	IP	H	HR	BB/9	K/9	K	GB%	BABIP	WHIP	ERA	DRA	WARP	PF
2017	DTW	RK	17	2	0	0	9	3	17²	26	0	5.6	8.2	16	55%	.419	2.09	5.60	7.91	-0.4	122
2018	TWI	RK	18	2	0	0	9	8	39¹	31	0	3.4	8.7	38	41%	.290	1.17	2.29	3.34	1.1	97
2019	ELZ	RK+	19	2	1	0	7	7	31²	29	4	4.5	10.5	37	40%	.312	1.42	4.55	4.00	0.7	101
2019	SLO	A-	19	0	1	0	4	4	16	17	2	5.1	6.2	11	49%	.294	1.62	9.56	5.83	-0.1	109
2020	SFN	MLB	20	2	2	0	33	0	35	35	5	4.5	7.0	27	43%	.285	1.50	4.74	5.07	0.1	86

Another piece of the Sam Dyson deal, Berroa is much further away from the majors than Jaylin Davis, but there's some interesting upside in the profile. Most of that is due to an explosive mid-90s fastball that can touch as high as 98. Berroa is on the shorter and stocky side, and there's some effort to ramp it up, but the pitch is a potential plus-plus weapon with command refinement. Berroa also offers a slurvy slider that he commands fairly well around the zone, although it can lack late two-plane movement out of the zone and a potentially average change. Berroa doesn't turn 20 until April, but give the lack of projection and current secondaries, he's more likely to be a good late-inning reliever than a long term starter.

17 Luis Toribio 3B

Born: 09/28/00   Age: 19   Bats: L   Throws: R   Height: 6'1"   Weight: 165   Origin: International Free Agent, 2017

YEAR	TEAM	LVL	AGE	PA	R	2B	3B	HR	RBI	BB	K	SB	CS	AVG/OBP/SLG	DRC+	VORP	BABIP	BRR	FRAA	WARP	PF
2018	DGI	RK	17	274	44	13	1	10	39	51	62	4	1	.270/.423/.479	155	23.9	.333	-1.8	3B(47) -5.6	1.6	99
2019	GNT	RK	18	234	45	15	3	3	33	45	54	4	5	.297/.436/.459	166	24.2	.400	-0.3	3B(41) -6.4	1.4	100
2020	SFN	MLB	19	251	22	13	1	3	22	27	85	0	0	.210/.302/.320	69	3.0	.324	-0.4	3B -3	-0.5	86

Comparables: Victor Robles, Ronald Acuña Jr., Daniel Robertson

One of a large group of 300k signings from the Giants' 2017 J2 class, Toribio has the prospect pole position early in their pro careers. Despite just being 19-years-old, you can already see the outline of a power-hitting third baseman. His swing generates good bat speed, whip, and loft, and it isn't a grooved, grip-it-and-rip-it type stroke. Toribio is aggressive at the plate at present and looks particularly lost against offspeed stuff. Given his age and experience level that's not too surprising, but it's something that could impact the hit tool long term. Despite a rather stout lower half, Toribio moves fairly well at third, and has more than enough arm for the hot corner. His hands and actions are a bit rough at present though, and the frame may require some maintenance in his 20s. If he can bump the hit tool and glove past fringy, there's a shot at a solid regular at third, but the marinating is going to take a while.

18 Conner Menez LHP

Born: 05/29/95   Age: 25   Bats: L   Throws: L   Height: 6'3"   Weight: 205   Origin: Round 14, 2016 Draft (#425 overall)

YEAR	TEAM	LVL	AGE	W	L	SV	G	GS	IP	H	HR	BB/9	K/9	K	GB%	BABIP	WHIP	ERA	DRA	WARP	PF
2017	SJO	A+	22	7	7	0	23	22	114¹	127	5	3.9	7.8	99	43%	.347	1.55	4.41	5.59	-0.4	100
2018	SJO	A+	23	2	5	0	11	11	50¹	48	2	3.8	12.5	70	46%	.368	1.37	4.83	3.44	1.1	93
2018	RIC	AA	23	6	4	0	15	15	74	73	1	4.1	11.2	92	39%	.375	1.45	4.38	4.72	0.5	94
2018	SAC	AAA	23	1	1	0	2	2	11	6	0	4.1	7.4	9	50%	.214	1.00	3.27	3.10	0.3	106
2019	RIC	AA	24	3	3	0	11	11	59²	37	5	3.0	10.6	70	39%	.237	0.96	2.72	3.47	1.1	91
2019	SAC	AAA	24	3	1	0	12	11	61¹	60	12	4.4	12.3	84	33%	.340	1.47	4.84	3.82	1.7	103
2019	SFN	MLB	24	0	1	0	8	3	17	13	4	6.4	11.6	22	31%	.257	1.47	5.29	4.07	0.3	86
2020	SFN	MLB	25	3	3	0	33	5	53	47	10	4.1	9.3	55	34%	.273	1.35	4.19	4.81	0.5	86

Comparables: Matt Hall, Jeff Manship, Wes Parsons

The southpaw made 11 starts at both Double-A and Triple-A, with a few spot starts in the majors before being called up for good in September. Menez has become a workhorse in the organization, throwing more than 400 innings, mostly as a starter, with only one trip to the injured list since being drafted in 2016. In his major league appearances his fastball lost a few ticks, averaging 91 mph, and he also struggled with his command, something that was not an issue for him in the minors. His secondary pitches include an average changeup, an above average curveball and a slider that he recently developed. His arsenal should give him the opportunity to compete for a spot in the starting rotation, however, if he continues to struggle with his command in spring training he will find himself among several lefty arms competing for a bullpen spot.

19 Melvin Adon RHP

Born: 06/09/94   Age: 26   Bats: L   Throws: R   Height: 6'3"   Weight: 235   Origin: International Free Agent, 2015

YEAR	TEAM	LVL	AGE	W	L	SV	G	GS	IP	H	HR	BB/9	K/9	K	GB%	BABIP	WHIP	ERA	DRA	WARP	PF
2017	AUG	A	23	3	11	0	23	19	99¹	110	5	3.2	8.1	89	56%	.343	1.46	4.35	5.73	-0.6	92
2018	SJO	A+	24	2	5	0	16	15	77²	82	6	3.9	8.2	71	57%	.338	1.49	4.87	6.13	-0.7	101
2019	RIC	AA	25	2	6	14	36	0	45	38	2	5.2	11.8	59	52%	.356	1.42	2.60	5.04	-0.2	100
2019	SAC	AAA	25	0	1	0	12	0	10¹	16	1	7.0	15.7	18	50%	.517	2.32	13.94	5.19	0.1	100
2020	SFN	MLB	26	1	1	0	11	0	12	11	2	4.0	9.6	13	46%	.308	1.41	4.13	4.72	0.1	86

Comparables: Kyle Dowdy, Félix Peña, Jairo Asencio

Adon lit up the radar gun at the Eastern League Double-A All-Star game last year which had heads turning to see his 80 grade fastball. He spent the beginning of the season in Richmond, working to refine his slider and determine his role in the bullpen, before being promoted to Sacramento where he finished the season. He struggled a bit with the juiced ball, giving up 16 earned runs and eight walks in 10 innings in the PCL. Going into spring training, Adon should have the opportunity to compete for a backend bullpen role with the major league team. He will need to rely on his fastball to get hitters out, while also being able to command his slider and limit his walks.

20 Camilo Doval RHP

Born: 07/04/97 Age: 22 Bats: R Throws: R Height: 6'2" Weight: 180 Origin: International Free Agent, 2015

YEAR	TEAM	LVL	AGE	W	L	SV	G	GS	IP	H	HR	BB/9	K/9	K	GB%	BABIP	WHIP	ERA	DRA	WARP	PF
2017	GIA	RK	19	1	2	1	17	0	32¹	23	0	3.6	14.2	51	65%	.348	1.11	3.90	1.91	1.3	100
2018	AUG	A	20	0	3	11	44	0	53	40	2	4.6	13.2	78	42%	.322	1.26	3.06	3.23	1.0	100
2019	SJO	A+	21	3	5	0	45	0	56¹	41	2	5.4	12.8	80	52%	.315	1.33	3.83	4.02	0.4	100
2020	SFN	MLB	22	2	2	0	33	0	35	34	5	4.3	10.8	42	44%	.328	1.46	4.41	4.77	0.3	86

Doval is a potential power relief arm. He has a long, max effort arm action, and a low-three-quarters slot that will be tough for righties to deal with. The late torque and effort in his delivery mean the control/command profile is going to struggle to even be fringy, but Doval's fastball is mid-90s with cut and can touch 100. He pairs it with a power slider around 90 that doesn't always get ideal depth given the slot. If the slider refines some in the upper minors he could be a 97-and-a-slider guy, which is a little bit better than being a 95-and-a-slider guy.

Personal Cheeseball

PC Rico Garcia RHP

Born: 01/10/94 Age: 26 Bats: R Throws: R Height: 5'11" Weight: 190 Origin: Round 30, 2016 Draft (#890 overall)

YEAR	TEAM	LVL	AGE	W	L	SV	G	GS	IP	H	HR	BB/9	K/9	K	GB%	BABIP	WHIP	ERA	DRA	WARP	PF
2017	BOI	A-	23	0	4	0	8	8	41	50	2	2.4	7.7	35	45%	.369	1.49	3.95	5.57	-0.1	116
2017	ASH	A	23	2	2	0	8	4	28	27	2	2.2	9.6	30	49%	.316	1.21	2.57	3.97	0.4	115
2018	LNC	A+	24	7	7	0	16	15	100	99	12	2.0	9.1	101	46%	.315	1.21	3.42	3.54	2.1	108
2018	HFD	AA	24	6	2	0	11	11	67	54	8	2.7	8.2	61	44%	.264	1.10	2.28	4.07	1.0	105
2019	HFD	AA	25	8	2	0	13	13	68	41	4	3.0	11.5	87	49%	.261	0.94	1.85	2.95	1.7	109
2019	ABQ	AAA	25	2	4	0	13	13	61¹	77	14	4.1	7.5	51	37%	.330	1.71	6.90	5.95	0.5	108
2019	COL	MLB	25	0	1	0	2	1	6	9	3	7.5	3.0	2	44%	.300	2.33	10.50	7.29	-0.1	139
2020	SFN	MLB	26	1	2	0	33	0	35	61	15	4.4	7.2	28	40%	.385	2.24	11.17	7.01	-0.6	86

Comparables: Wei-Chieh Huang, Mike Bolsinger, Daniel Wright

At 37, I still have recurring nightmares that I am back in high school. Sometimes I've forgotten to do a class project that was due that day, other times someone has discovered that I was actually a few credits short of graduating and have to make up a class. Occasionally, they end with my falling down stairs. I wonder if Rico Garcia dreams of being back at Coors, or Albuquerque, or Hartford, or Lancaster. The Giants claimed him off waivers, and he may end up going from one of the most extreme hitters parks to one of the most extreme pitchers parks. It of course doesn't change the underlying skill set, which is fringy at best—low-90s fastball, average change, little dipsy doodle curve—but as I said about Garcia in a chat this year, Coors eats that profile alive. The PCL does too, and he may find his way back there to open 2020, but so does a big outfield at sea level in Oracle Park if he can ward off the nightmares in the minors for a little while.

Low Minors Sleeper

LMS Kai-Wei Teng RHP

Born: 12/01/98 Age: 21 Bats: R Throws: R Height: 6'4" Weight: 260 Origin: International Free Agent, 2017

YEAR	TEAM	LVL	AGE	W	L	SV	G	GS	IP	H	HR	BB/9	K/9	K	GB%	BABIP	WHIP	ERA	DRA	WARP	PF
2018	TWI	RK	19	3	3	0	10	9	42²	36	0	3.2	9.9	47	54%	.319	1.20	3.59	3.22	1.3	97
2019	CDR	A	20	4	0	0	9	8	50²	40	1	2.5	8.7	49	56%	.277	1.07	1.60	3.33	1.1	100
2019	AUG	A	20	3	0	0	5	5	29	16	0	2.2	12.1	39	46%	.262	0.79	1.55	2.47	0.9	97
2020	SFN	MLB	21	2	2	0	33	0	35	34	5	3.4	8.2	32	48%	.293	1.34	3.99	4.43	0.4	86

Comparables: Miguel Almonte, Neftalí Feliz, Rob Whalen

The Twins parted with another interesting low minors arm in the Sam Dyson trade in Teng. He doesn't have close to Berroa's fastball, sitting more low-90s, but Teng shows above-average command of the pitch, moving it all to all four quadrants from a very easy delivery. He has advanced feel for his full four-pitch mix. The changeup is the best of the present secondaries, showing good fade and occasional dive, despite not having ideal velocity separation in the mid-80s. He shows two different breaking ball looks, a potentially average 11-5 curve and a sweepier slider. Teng mixes his stuff well, and his command and pitchability proved far too much for A-ball hitters. I do wonder if there's enough stuff here to be more than a swingman/long relief type, but the frame and delivery are built to log innings.

Top Talents 25 and Under (as of 4/1/2020)

1. Marco Luciano
2. Joey Bart
3. Heliot Ramos
4. Hunter Bishop
5. Will Wilson
6. Alexander Canario
7. Mauricio Dubón
8. Shaun Anderson
9. Seth Corry
10. Sean Hjelle

And now for an exercise in redundancy.

A 25 and Under talent list for the Giants tells a stark tale of why so many long time members of the front office have lost jobs or authority the last two years—the team simply stopped producing young talent. Top prospects of recent vintage who are still seeking to solidify major league futures for themselves (Tyler Beede or Steven Duggar, say) are too old for this list. Even prospects on this year's list barely qualify as 25 year olds (Mauricio Dubón and Jaylin Davis both turn 26 in July).

Amazingly, the Giants have just one player in their entire organization who is eligible for the 25 and Under list, but NOT eligible for the prospect list. And if you're a Where's Waldo adept, you will have spotted him by now: Shaun Anderson who entered last year as the club's top starting pitching prospect and enters this year as a potential candidate for their closer or setup roles or potentially some piggyback/swing starter position.

Anderson started 16 games for the 2019 Giants, but struggled to miss bats with any of his four pitches or show precise enough control to get by with the stuff. After a late season move back to the bullpen (his college role at the University of Florida) he showed slightly sharper stuff and attacked hitters more aggressively, though command issues remained. Slotting Anderson onto the list at all was somewhat painful, as it costs the intriguing potential of Davis, but Anderson should be able to help the pitching-starved Giants in some capacity for the next several years, even if the impact is relatively low. That sets him just after Dubón, who is certain to play a significant role in the daily lineup in 2020 and potentially down the road as well.

Eyewitness Reports

Eyewitness Report: Joey Bart

Evaluator: Steve Givarz
Report Date: 10/06/2019
Dates Seen: 10/1/19 + 10/4/19
Risk Factor: Moderate
Physical/Health: Large frame with a thick, physical body, barrel-chested, definite catcher frame, strength throughout, mature.

Tool	Future Grade	Report
Hit	55	Hits from a tall, slightly open stance with a small load to even. Plus bat speed with definite strength in wrists/hands to drive even mishit balls. Primarily pull hitter when going for power but can work all over the field, tracks balls out of pitchers hand, can be aggressive early in count, but has made adjustments in viewing to wait guys out, see as a future above-average hitter.
Power	60	Plus-plus raw power, strength in body with plus bat speed to take a ball out to any part of the park. Batted balls have significant carry and drive, can sell out for power and get too aggressive, but should play to plus.
Baserunning/ Speed	30	Not a runner, not fleet of foot, catcher, doesn't matter.
Glove	60	Quality defender behind the plate, blocks pitches to both sides as well as in front, receives well, sets up on the inner half but can move the glove and give a good target for the umpire, leader on the field and takes control, plus defender.
Arm	60	Plus arm strength with quick hands and smooth transfer, 1.94-1.98 to 2B, throws were accurate to the 2B side.

Conclusion: See as a quality regular behind the plate, chance for all-star seasons at a premium positon. 22 y/o R/R catcher, future above-average hitter with plus-plus raw, plus game pop and plus arm/glove. One of the top prospects in baseball, strong interest, would acquire.

Eyewitness Report: Sean Hjelle

Evaluator: David Lee
Report Date: 06/19/2019
Dates Seen: 4/20/19; 5/18/19
Risk Factor: Medium

Delivery: Extreme length from a frame that would tie major-league records for height. He's filled out well for his length and has present strength and durability. Framework is here for a durable workhorse because of strength and consistency in his actions. Delivery creates difficult angles for hitters. Extreme extension causes discomfort at the plate. Comes from three-quarters angle with some crossfire. Motion is shockingly consistent for size and he repeats well with average arm speed.

Pitch Type	Future Grade	Sitting Velocity	Peak Velocity	Report
Fastball	55	91-94	94	Comes easy with plus-plus plane and extension. The pitch sinks and runs arm-side late with above-average movement. Profiles as a heavy pitch with above-average command.
Curveball	50	80-82	83	Comes out slurvy at times. Flashes two-plane action with 11/5 tilt when he gets on top of it. Lacks the hard bite of a plus breaker but can consistently show an average offering that flashes above-average multiple times. Above-average command potential.
Changeup	50	85-87	88	Good arm speed with average fade. Flashes above-average when he replicates fastball movement with the right arm speed. Needs further refinement with feel, as he sometimes casts and slows his actions. Average command potential.

Conclusion: It's not at all out of the question that Hjelle could bump a grade on one or two of these pitches. A little more fastball velocity could turn the pitch into a true weapon, while the breaking ball could tighten a little more and start showing enough bite to profile consistently above-average. There's maybe a little more here because Hjelle has above-average command potential. He repeats exceptionally well for his size, which creates tough angles and huge extension. Put these factors together and he's a safe no. 4 with a 3/4 ceiling.

Seattle Mariners

The State of the System

The…Mariners system…is good?

The Top Ten

★ ★ ★ *2020 Top 101 Prospect* **#7** ★ ★ ★

1 Jarred Kelenic OF   OFP: 70   ETA: 2020-21

Born: 07/16/99   Age: 20   Bats: L   Throws: L   Height: 6'0"   Weight: 196   Origin: Round 1, 2018 Draft (#6 overall)

YEAR	TEAM	LVL	AGE	PA	R	2B	3B	HR	RBI	BB	K	SB	CS	AVG/OBP/SLG	DRC+	VORP	BABIP	BRR	FRAA	WARP	PF
2018	MTS	RK	18	51	9	2	2	1	9	4	11	4	0	.413/.451/.609	183	8.0	.514	-0.1	CF(9) 2.0	0.7	106
2018	KNG	RK	18	200	33	8	4	5	33	22	39	11	1	.253/.350/.431	120	15.2	.300	2.5	CF(43) 5.8	1.9	105
2019	WVA	A	19	218	33	14	3	11	29	25	45	7	4	.309/.394/.586	181	25.6	.356	-0.5	CF(33) -1.8, RF(8) -0.1	2.3	99
2019	MOD	A+	19	190	36	13	1	6	22	17	49	10	3	.290/.353/.485	138	17.7	.368	1.4	CF(32) 1.1, RF(8) -1.2	1.3	95
2019	ARK	AA	19	92	11	4	1	6	17	8	17	3	0	.253/.315/.542	134	9.0	.246	0.6	CF(12) 0.6, RF(5) 0.6	0.7	95
2020	SEA	MLB	20	251	29	12	1	11	34	19	69	3	1	.246/.308/.454	100	0.0	.304	0.3	CF -1, RF -1	0.6	94

Comparables: Ronald Acuña Jr., Byron Buxton, Corey Seager

The Report: Mets fans, don't read this…

Mariners fans, hello.

Kelenic's stock started shooting up early in the season when he showed off an improved swing path while dominating the Low-A South Atlantic League. He was promoted to High-A shortly after Memorial Day and performed quite well. He was promoted again to Double-A less than a month after his 20th birthday for the August stretch run and Texas League playoffs, and he kept hitting against upper-minors pitching too. So much for the draft-time concerns about being on the older side for a prep bat.

Kelenic has a chance to be a five-tool player. Not one of those dudes who has a bunch of 5s and a 55 run who occasionally gets called a five-tool player, but an actual five-tool star that collects black ink and awards. He projects for plus hit and plus power from a sweet, classic lefty swing. He's a present plus runner with a plus arm. The weakest projection at the moment is defensive. The routes and closing ability aren't quite there for a sure-shot bet in center yet, and we could easily see a team preferring him in a corner, especially if he slows down as he moves through his 20s. But it's not out of the question that he ends up as a net positive in center down the road.

Variance: Medium. Our degree of confidence that he ends up as a good regular is high, but the positional risk that he'll slide to a corner is significant, and that would put a lot of pressure on the bat. Getting to a 70 OFP as a corner outfielder means you have to hit.

Mark Barry's Fantasy Take: Quibble about the order of the top two here if you'd like, but for now, in the year of the pig, Kelenic gets the narrow nod mostly thanks to proximity. It's not just because of the timetable, though. Kelenic snagged 20 bags in 2019 in addition to hitting for power and average. That, as they say, is very good. If Kelenic isn't a top-10 dynasty guy right now, he's definitely beating down the doors. I'm really sorry, Mets fans, but at least you'll always have the Edwin Díaz memories to fall back on.

★ ★ ★ *2020 Top 101 Prospect* **#10** ★ ★ ★

2 **Julio Rodriguez** OF   OFP: 70   ETA: 2021
Born: 12/29/00 Age: 19 Bats: R Throws: R Height: 6'4" Weight: 225 Origin: International Free Agent, 2017

YEAR	TEAM	LVL	AGE	PA	R	2B	3B	HR	RBI	BB	K	SB	CS	AVG/OBP/SLG	DRC+	VORP	BABIP	BRR	FRAA	WARP	PF
2018	DMR	RK	17	255	50	13	9	5	36	30	40	10	0	.315/.404/.525	163	34.0	.364	0.6	RF(45) 8.1, CF(6) -0.1	2.9	96
2019	WVA	A	18	295	50	20	1	10	50	20	66	1	3	.293/.359/.490	160	27.7	.353	0.0	RF(40) 4.7, CF(22) -0.2	2.8	95
2019	MOD	A+	18	72	13	6	3	2	19	5	10	0	0	.462/.514/.738	254	17.2	.528	0.5	CF(13) -3.4, RF(3) -0.5	0.9	90
2020	SEA	MLB	19	251	26	13	2	7	29	19	65	1	0	.254/.322/.416	99	0.0	.328	-0.2	RF 1, CF -1	0.8	94

Comparables: Nomar Mazara, Vladimir Guerrero Jr., Jon Singleton

The Report: Signed by the Mariners in July of 2017, Rodriguez has one of the higher-end offensive packages in all of the minors. Just 18 years old during his first full season in the states, he showed an extremely advanced approach at the plate. He controls the zone well and routinely finds his pitch to hit. His swing is compact, quick and showcases an ability to hit line-to-line. Rodriguez hit 12 homers in 84 games this year, but he has yet to fully tap into his power stroke. Once he matures, 25-plus home runs will not be out of the question.

Rodriguez is sneaky fast on the basepaths. He isn't a burner but displays the wheels to be a slightly above-average stolen base threat. In early looks defensively he looked like an average fielder at best. But on second inspection he has the potential to play a slightly above-average center field. Additionally, his plus arm can play anywhere on the grass.

Variance: Medium. Rodriguez is still very young and has not played a full slate of games yet, with that comes a little uncertainty. Also uncertain is his ability to tap into his power tool as he grows. That will be the key to him reaching his full potential.

Mark Barry's Fantasy Take: The second part of a one-two punch rarely seen outside of time-traveling bro duos from the 80s and 90s, Rodriguez offers one of the highest ceilings in the minor leagues, laying waste to two levels in 2019 before turning 19 years old. I kinda love this guy. If you want to go crazy and dream on .300/35/10, you're not going to get much pushback from me.

★ ★ ★ *2020 Top 101 Prospect* **#39** ★ ★ ★

3 **Logan Gilbert** RHP   OFP: 60   ETA: 2021-22
Born: 05/05/97 Age: 23 Bats: R Throws: R Height: 6'6" Weight: 225 Origin: Round 1, 2018 Draft (#14 overall)

YEAR	TEAM	LVL	AGE	W	L	SV	G	GS	IP	H	HR	BB/9	K/9	K	GB%	BABIP	WHIP	ERA	DRA	WARP	PF
2019	WVA	A	22	1	0	0	5	5	22²	9	2	2.4	14.3	36	22%	.184	0.66	1.59	1.53	1.0	103
2019	MOD	A+	22	5	3	0	12	12	62¹	52	3	1.7	10.5	73	47%	.320	1.03	1.73	3.20	1.4	94
2019	ARK	AA	22	4	2	0	9	9	50	34	2	2.7	10.1	56	33%	.271	0.98	2.88	3.57	0.8	83
2020	SEA	MLB	23	2	2	0	33	0	35	35	5	3.4	10.0	39	36%	.319	1.37	4.56	4.62	0.2	94

Comparables: Ryan Helsley, Matt Harvey, Ben Lively

The Report: Drafted in the first round in 2018, Gilbert dominated across three levels in his first pro season in 2019. The first thing that stands out when watching Gilbert is his confidence and mound presence–both resembling that of a seasoned vet. He backed it up with a solid four-pitch mix. The Stetson product's fastball sits in the low 90s but can touch 95 when needed. It's a straight pitch that plays up due to his command and extension. Gilbert's best secondary is a 12-6, mid-70s curveball that features late bite. This pitch is a plus swing-and-miss offering, whether he throws it in the zone or buries it in the dirt. His third pitch is a slider that sits 80-82 mph. It doesn't have hard bite but shows slightly above-average sweeping action. Gilbert added a mid-80s changeup this year which dives out of the zone with some fade and he seems to have a decent feel for it. Gilbert is able to mix and command all four offerings, attacking the zone without fear and with an understanding of how to sequence his arsenal.

Variance: Medium. With sound mechanics, an ability to consistently throw strikes and a solid four-pitch mix, Gilbert has set himself a fairly high floor.

Mark Barry's Fantasy Take: I'm of two minds with Gilbert. I, like our venerable leader, Bret Sayre, mentioned last year, have a hard time trusting super tall guys to repeat their mechanics enough to be effective for the duration of an outing. There are just a lot of moving parts to account for. That said, Gilbert just barely crept above a 1.00 WHIP during his time in Modesto, and stayed below that benchmark in his two other stops—maybe it's much ado about nothing. I'd like his slider and changeup to garner a few more whiffs, but I'd also like Manny Machado money to write these comments, so I guess the lesson is we can't always get what we want. Gilbert has SP3 upside, but will probably settle in as a SP5-6.

★ ★ ★ *2020 Top 101 Prospect* **#62** ★ ★ ★

4 Evan White 1B   OFP: 55   ETA: Late 2020
Born: 04/26/96 Age: 24 Bats: R Throws: L Height: 6'3" Weight: 205 Origin: Round 1, 2017 Draft (#17 overall)

YEAR	TEAM	LVL	AGE	PA	R	2B	3B	HR	RBI	BB	K	SB	CS	AVG/OBP/SLG	DRC+	VORP	BABIP	BRR	FRAA	WARP	PF
2017	EVE	A-	21	55	6	1	1	3	12	6	6	1	1	.277/.345/.532	122	3.7	.250	-0.1	1B(8) -0.6	0.1	104
2018	MOD	A+	22	538	72	27	7	11	66	52	103	4	3	.303/.375/.458	143	38.4	.363	-0.5	1B(106) 5.5	3.5	94
2019	ARK	AA	23	400	61	13	2	18	55	29	92	2	0	.293/.350/.488	153	32.0	.346	1.1	1B(88) -5.3	1.9	89
2020	SEA	MLB	24	385	45	17	2	17	53	23	105	0	0	.261/.310/.457	103	1.0	.323	-0.6	1B -1	0.7	94

Comparables: Matt Clark, Rhys Hoskins, Kevin Cron

The Report: White carried his late 2018 power surge over into 2019, setting a career high for home runs in just over half a season. He's filled out with good weight since college and added enough loft to his swing to project at least average game power. He hasn't added much in the way of length to his stroke, and it remains a compact swing with above-average bat speed. White's hit tool and glove have never been concerns. He will likely have seasons where he hits .300, and it's an easy plus projection otherwise. His defense at first is gold glove caliber. While there was talk of his playing the outfield off and on over his pro career, he's been first-base-only, but not with the pessimistic connotation that usually carries. It's an unusual first base profile—the bats-right-throws-left thing is still truly bizarre—but the bat is good enough now that it's a fairly safe one.

Variance: Medium. White is a weird profile at first base—there were thoughts he could handle center—and he's been a slow burn of marginal improvement or consolidation year-over-year. That makes him already 23 and only in Double-A, but the developments have all been positive. There's somewhat limited upside here, but if the power gains in Double-A continue to carry over, there's no reason he can't be a plus regular. We just need to see it for a bit longer.

Mark Barry's Fantasy Take: I've heard Cody Bellinger and Paul Goldschmidt fantasy comps for White, and I think if you expect anything approaching that level of production, you'll be sorely disappointed. There's a chance he could be good-Eric Hosmer, though, which is not that bad, if a touch less sparkly.

5 Justin Dunn RHP   OFP: 55   ETA: 2019
Born: 09/22/95 Age: 24 Bats: R Throws: R Height: 6'2" Weight: 185 Origin: Round 1, 2016 Draft (#19 overall)

YEAR	TEAM	LVL	AGE	W	L	SV	G	GS	IP	H	HR	BB/9	K/9	K	GB%	BABIP	WHIP	ERA	DRA	WARP	PF
2017	SLU	A+	21	5	6	0	20	16	95¹	101	5	4.5	7.1	75	44%	.322	1.56	5.00	6.27	-1.2	106
2018	SLU	A+	22	2	3	0	9	9	45²	43	2	3.0	10.1	51	42%	.325	1.27	2.36	3.66	0.9	97
2018	BIN	AA	22	6	5	0	15	15	89²	85	7	3.7	10.5	105	47%	.345	1.36	4.22	4.68	0.7	101
2019	ARK	AA	23	9	5	0	25	25	131²	118	13	2.7	10.8	158	38%	.314	1.19	3.55	4.61	0.6	88
2019	SEA	MLB	23	0	0	0	4	4	6²	2	0	12.1	6.8	5	44%	.125	1.65	2.70	5.32	0.0	96
2020	SEA	MLB	24	6	9	0	23	23	113	121	25	4.5	7.5	94	38%	.288	1.57	6.10	5.83	-0.3	94

Comparables: Robert Dugger, Ronald Bolaños, Hunter Wood

The Report: The shape of Dunn's profile has changed fairly significantly from when he was drafted in the first round out of Boston College. He's bled a bit of fastball velocity and now sits more in the low 90s, touching 95, but he has developed a full complement of average-or-better secondaries. The fastball command is still fringy, but he's more consistently showing the kind of late arm-side run that he only flashed as a Mets prospect. The changeup development has been key here, as the pitch is now above-average despite less-than-ideal command and velocity separation. Dunn sells the pitch well and it has above-average tumble and fade. The mid-80s slider has been his best offspeed historically, and continues to be a potential plus pitch. It's sharp enough to backfoot to lefties, and Dunn commands the pitch well. He started working a curveball in more often in 2018 as a different breaking ball look. It's a useful addition to the arsenal, although more of a spot than chase pitch, and does bleed into the slider at times.

Dunn probably isn't actually 6-foot-2 and has gotten stockier, although he's still able to repeat an athletic delivery with good arm speed. In some ways there is a lot less reliever risk here than there was coming out of the draft, but he also doesn't have a late inning fallback anymore if the command isn't fine enough against major league hitters as a starter. However, he looks more like a rotation cog now than he has in years past, with the potential for four above-average offerings. His pitchability and confidence in the secondary stuff has improved as well. Dunn has different ways to beat you each time through the order now and looks like a major-league-ready mid-rotation starter.

Variance: Low. The Mariners tried to keep Dunn out of the PCL which led to him repeating Double-A as a 23-year-old, where he wasn't as dominant as you'd like. I don't read much into the wildness in his MLB cup of coffee, but if there is something that will undo him in the majors, it's the command and control profile, so that's worth monitoring. Overall though, the broad arsenal gives him a lot of options. Dunn could win a 2020 major league job out of camp.

Mark Barry's Fantasy Take: Dunn is sort of like plain toast. It's not the good stuff that you really want, but it's not bad either. I think he'll be better as a mid-rotation starter in real life than fantasy, but he could have some SP4-5 good years ahead. He'll be useful. I'm really sorry, Mets fans, but at least you'll always have the Edwin Díaz memories to fall back on.

6 George Kirby RHP   OFP: 55   ETA: 2021
Born: 02/04/98   Age: 22   Bats: R   Throws: R   Height: 6'4"   Weight: 201   Origin: Round 1, 2019 Draft (#20 overall)

YEAR	TEAM	LVL	AGE	W	L	SV	G	GS	IP	H	HR	BB/9	K/9	K	GB%	BABIP	WHIP	ERA	DRA	WARP	PF
2019	EVE	A-	21	0	0	0	9	8	23	24	1	0.0	9.8	25	48%	.355	1.04	2.35	3.50	0.5	118
2020	SEA	MLB	22	2	2	0	33	0	35	35	5	3.5	7.4	29	42%	.286	1.38	4.65	4.77	0.2	94

Comparables: Andrew Moore, Joe Musgrove, Pat Light

The Report: Lacking the typical "wow" stuff you find in first-round pitchers, what Kirby does have as a carrying tool is plus-plus command of a four-pitch repertoire. In the 2019 calendar year between starting games at Elon University and his professional debut for the Mariners in the Northwest League, Kirby walked just SIX batters in 111 1/3 innings while striking out 132 along the way. It's not just fastball command, either, as he is able to land each of his pitches for strikes while also making in-game adjustments when he knows a pitch is slightly off.

The fastball sits comfortably in the low 90s but there is enough arm strength to ramp into the mid 90s when he wants to reach back for it. It's used relentlessly the first time through the order, peppering every quadrant of the zone. In two-strike counts and the second time through both a curveball and slider can be deployed to get hitters off balance. There are also signs of a good changeup that could be an average-to-better pitch. The awareness of his abilities and body control are unteachable qualities and, with some room still left to fill out, Kirby could jump several levels in 2020.

Variance: Low. No history of injuries, a developed college pitcher, and the command/control ability that he can lean on throughout his career gives him a high floor, even if there is a limited ceiling.

Mark Barry's Fantasy Take: It's hard not to fall in love with Kirby's control. He's walked zero dudes in his professional career, which is equal parts awe-inspiring and hilarious. His fantasy usefulness will rest almost solely on his ability to strike guys out. Sometimes these extreme control guys yield Shane Bieber and sometimes they yield Josh Tomlin. I'd jump on Kirby in a 200ish prospect league hoping for the former, while ready to cut bait on the latter.

7 Juan Then RHP   OFP: 60   ETA: 2022
Born: 02/07/00   Age: 20   Bats: R   Throws: R   Height: 6'1"   Weight: 155   Origin: International Free Agent, 2016

YEAR	TEAM	LVL	AGE	W	L	SV	G	GS	IP	H	HR	BB/9	K/9	K	GB%	BABIP	WHIP	ERA	DRA	WARP	PF
2017	DMR	RK	17	2	2	0	13	13	61¹	50	3	2.2	8.2	56	54%	.278	1.06	2.64	1.91	2.7	97
2018	YAN	RK	18	0	3	0	11	11	50	38	2	2.0	7.6	42	48%	.259	0.98	2.70	2.07	2.1	102
2019	EVE	A-	19	0	3	0	7	6	30¹	24	1	2.7	9.5	32	36%	.299	1.09	3.56	3.17	0.7	122
2019	WVA	A	19	1	2	0	3	3	16	7	1	2.2	7.9	14	32%	.150	0.69	2.25	2.90	0.4	91
2020	SEA	MLB	20	2	2	0	33	0	35	35	5	3.8	7.5	29	34%	.291	1.42	4.81	4.86	0.1	94

Comparables: Felix Jorge, Jose Suarez, Huascar Ynoa

The Report: Then has taken a more circuitous route to full-season baseball than most of his West Virginia Power teammates. He was traded from the Mariners to the Yankees before coming stateside, and then back to the Mariners in exchange for Edwin Encarnacion last summer. After the return trade, and a few weeks in rookie ball, he made his full-season debut in mid-August of this year. You'll undoubtedly hear more about those deals in the future, and Then's route will be offered as a microcosm of Jerry Dipoto's tenure in Seattle.

But let's talk about Then the prospect, and he's developed into a good one. He has a thin, athletic frame with narrow hips, which means he should always be on the slight side. He fields his position well and looks cat-like coming off the mound. At present the mechanics are a bit inconsistent, but he's athletic enough that those issues should be ironed out down the road. He has a very quick arm with a short path and topped out at 96 with sharp arm-side run in my look. All three pitches are above-average, but the curveball will likely be his best offering when it's all said and done. The change is a bit firm right now, but it's still advanced for his age. He should be able to throw all his pitches with confidence and get plenty of swing-and-miss both in the zone and out of it. Then's mound presence is something that could use some work—he looks anxious at times, but seems to benefit from mound visits and make adjustments in-game. Expect a bump in velocity as he gets stronger and adds mass to his lower half.

Variance: High. Then only has three full-season starts under his belt. He's athletic, but there are issues that need to be worked out. He's a small righty. Added strength will go a long way with Then, and he has all the right pieces to turn into solid piece in any big-league rotation.

Mark Barry's Fantasy Take: Then is an intriguing prospect, both for his work on the bump and the fun we could have with his surname in tweets. He's pretty young and far away, though. I wouldn't argue if you're the gambling sort and want to take a flier, but I probably wouldn't roster Then outside of the deepest, 350-plus prospect leagues.

8 Noelvi Marte SS   OFP: 60   ETA: 2024ish
Born: 10/16/01   Age: 18   Bats: R   Throws: R   Height: 6'1"   Weight: 181   Origin: International Free Agent, 2018

The Report: I had a discussion on our podcast Discord recently (Ed. Become a patron and join today!) about what counts as useful data when it comes to IFA guys with little or no stateside experience. Bonus numbers end up out of date fast. Sure, there were a few prospects in our Top 25 who were seven-figure bonus babies, but for every Wander Franco there's a Gilbert Lara. For every Vlad Jr., a Kevin Maitan. And there's five-figure bonus guys right behind them as well. The bonus figures might have been a decent approximation of talent at the time of agreeing to them, but things change quickly for teenage baseball players, and the deals aren't being magically agreed to on the morning of July 2nd anyway.

Complex-league stats are mostly useless—I honestly wish they didn't keep them—but how quickly a player gets assigned stateside might not be? Eh, I'm not convinced. I don't think Marte is necessarily a worse prospect solely because he spent the summer mashing in the Dominican instead of Peoria. Acculturation isn't just about adjusting to the level of competition stateside, so I don't particularly read anything into Marte being in the DSL while, say, Kevin Alcantara and Orelvis Martinez came stateside.

What that does mean though, is our staff has less info on Noelvi Marte. So he falls more into the Jasson Dominguez or Robert Puason bucket than the Marco Luciano one. But we don't have any reason to think he isn't still a potential plus shortstop so...

Variance: Extreme.

Mark Barry's Fantasy Take: Ah, a teenager who dominated the DSL, flashing power, speed and average—what could possibly go wrong? Age and proximity aside, Marte is a hot name in the fantasy community right now, so you're going to have to take the plunge early if you want any shares. If Marte hits in Everett like he did in 2019, people will lose their damn minds and he'll be untouchable. Get in early, whether you want to or not.

9 Justus Sheffield LHP   OFP: 55   ETA: 2018
Born: 05/13/96   Age: 24   Bats: L   Throws: L   Height: 6'0"   Weight: 200   Origin: Round 1, 2014 Draft (#31 overall)

YEAR	TEAM	LVL	AGE	W	L	SV	G	GS	IP	H	HR	BB/9	K/9	K	GB%	BABIP	WHIP	ERA	DRA	WARP	PF
2017	TRN	AA	21	7	6	0	17	17	93¹	94	14	3.2	7.9	82	48%	.293	1.36	3.18	5.33	-0.2	95
2018	TRN	AA	22	1	2	0	5	5	28	16	1	4.5	12.5	39	44%	.259	1.07	2.25	3.54	0.6	91
2018	SWB	AAA	22	6	4	0	20	15	88	66	3	3.7	8.6	84	46%	.264	1.16	2.56	3.41	2.1	95
2018	NYA	MLB	22	0	0	0	3	0	2²	4	1	10.1	0.0	0	55%	.300	2.62	10.12	6.56	-0.1	111
2019	ARK	AA	23	5	3	0	12	12	78	62	4	2.1	9.8	85	44%	.293	1.03	2.19	3.77	1.1	87
2019	TAC	AAA	23	2	6	0	13	12	55	59	12	6.7	7.9	48	54%	.292	1.82	6.87	4.99	0.9	103
2019	SEA	MLB	23	0	1	0	8	7	36	44	5	4.5	9.2	37	54%	.375	1.72	5.50	5.81	0.0	96
2020	SEA	MLB	24	9	10	0	62	24	161	167	23	4.2	9.2	164	47%	.320	1.50	5.01	4.94	1.0	94

Comparables: Jake Thompson, Zack Littell, Robert Stephenson

The Report: Sheffield had a nice run of three straight years in the 50s on the 101, which was the inspiration for me to write his prospect blurb as Alanis Morissette song verse in last year's Annual, as if a child of the 90s needs such inspiration. He will, uh, not be in the 50-59 band of this year's 101. Even including caveats about the ball, he looked so bad in Triple-A that he was sent back to Double-A in June. He pitched well enough after the demotion to earn another September call-up, but he should have given that he originally mastered the level in 2017.

This is Sheffield's sixth eligible list cycle (for context, the first BP top ten he was on was headlined by Francisco Lindor). Suffice to say, we have a lot of priors and comfort with him as a staff. He most typically works 92-94 as a starter, touching 96, and he's shown a bit higher out of the bullpen in the past. The slider is the potential out pitch here, a tight mid-80s offering that he threw over 35 percent of the time in the majors in 2019. He also mixes in a changeup that has flashed but still lacks consistency. His command has come and gone for most of his pro career, and continued to be evasive in 2019. While he pitched a nice combined 169 innings last season, he's had durability questions linger for most of his prospectdom, and he's still short.

We've tipped for years because of all this that Sheffield's future might be in the bullpen, and the needle certainly moved a bit further in that direction in 2019. At the same time, Seattle's not likely to be competitive anytime real soon, so they're likely to keep running Sheffield out there as a starter in the fading hopes that he can replicate James Paxton, the pitcher he was most recently traded for.

Variance: High. As noted, he's been a 60 OFP and a 101 guy for us with some regularity recently, and the arm talent is certainly still there. We're just giving him a lower chance to reach the higher outcomes in his band because he stalled out this year, basically.

Mark Barry's Fantasy Take: Boy, was that a 2019 season for Sheffield, huh? I haven't seen a lefty with such promise suffer that kind of fall from grace since, well, nevermind. Sheffield should still be useful in AL-only leagues or deep-mixed formats, but it's hard to imagine he'll ever reach that SP2 upside and might be relegated to a back-of-the-rotation guy.

10 Jake Fraley OF   OFP: 55   ETA: 2019

Born: 05/25/95   Age: 25   Bats: L   Throws: L   Height: 6'0"   Weight: 195   Origin: Round 2, 2016 Draft (#77 overall)

YEAR	TEAM	LVL	AGE	PA	R	2B	3B	HR	RBI	BB	K	SB	CS	AVG/OBP/SLG	DRC+	VORP	BABIP	BRR	FRAA	WARP	PF
2017	PCH	A+	22	105	6	3	1	1	12	7	24	1	3	.170/.238/.255	36	-5.0	.211	-0.6	CF(26) -3.6	-0.7	100
2018	PCH	A+	23	260	39	19	7	4	41	26	44	11	8	.347/.415/.547	169	26.4	.407	-2.2	LF(31) 2.6, CF(21) 2.1	2.7	100
2019	ARK	AA	24	259	40	15	2	11	47	23	55	16	5	.313/.386/.539	191	35.6	.370	-0.3	RF(21) -1.3, LF(12) -1.1	2.1	85
2019	TAC	AAA	24	168	28	12	3	8	33	11	34	6	2	.276/.333/.553	103	11.2	.304	-1.3	CF(21) 0.9, RF(9) -0.7	0.5	94
2019	SEA	MLB	24	41	3	2	0	0	1	0	14	0	0	.150/.171/.200	64	-0.6	.231	-0.7	CF(11) -1.5, RF(1) 0.0	-0.3	100
2020	SEA	MLB	25	350	39	14	3	13	43	22	92	14	7	.234/.292/.413	87	0.0	.287	0.7	CF 0, RF 1	0.4	94

Comparables: Rip Repulski, Roy Sievers, Anthony Gose

The Report: Before 2019, Fraley was generally regarded as a toolsy bat with potential, but his issues staying on the field left him a bit lost in the shuffle in a very deep Rays system. He found a new home in Seattle via one of Dipoto's fourteen-hundred trades and promptly put together a breakout season in his new organization. Fraley is a plus athlete with plus, whippy, bat speed and the ability to find the barrel in every quadrant of the zone. He certainly enjoyed his brief time mashing the Triple-A ball, but the overall game power projection is more average than plus. He can also have issues with spin, which is something that got exposed in his first taste of major league action.

In the field—despite above-average speed—Fraley is best-suited to a corner, and likely left field due to fringe arm strength, although he can cover center for you. The profile can look a bit tweenerish at times, but we think there is enough bat and baserunning here to give Fraley a decent shot at being an everyday player somewhere on the outfield grass.

Variance: Medium. Fraley has conquered the upper minors, but there's a track record of durability issues and still lingering questions about the hit tool against major league offspeed stuff.

Mark Barry's Fantasy Take: Fraley might be a rare case of "better in fantasy than real life." He offers a little power, a little speed and he should see plenty of playing time this season in Seattle. The upside might be limited, but he could be an OF4 as soon as 2020 in standard formats (OBP leagues might be rough because Fraley literally didn't walk once in a 12-game cup of coffee in September).

The Next Ten

11 Kyle Lewis OF

Born: 07/13/95   Age: 24   Bats: R   Throws: R   Height: 6'4"   Weight: 210   Origin: Round 1, 2016 Draft (#11 overall)

YEAR	TEAM	LVL	AGE	PA	R	2B	3B	HR	RBI	BB	K	SB	CS	AVG/OBP/SLG	DRC+	VORP	BABIP	BRR	FRAA	WARP	PF
2017	MRN	RK	21	46	9	2	1	1	7	4	14	1	0	.263/.348/.447	80	4.0	.360	1.4	CF(8) -1.0	0.1	102
2017	MOD	A+	21	167	20	4	0	6	24	15	38	2	1	.255/.323/.403	110	1.9	.299	-1.5	CF(13) 0.1	0.3	99
2018	MOD	A+	22	211	21	18	0	5	32	11	55	0	0	.260/.303/.429	104	9.0	.333	0.3	CF(23) -3.1, RF(11) -0.7	0.2	96
2018	ARK	AA	22	152	18	8	0	4	20	17	32	1	0	.220/.309/.371	91	0.2	.255	-2.0	CF(29) -2.6, RF(1) 0.0	-0.2	103
2019	ARK	AA	23	517	61	25	2	11	62	56	152	3	2	.263/.342/.398	111	21.4	.367	-3.3	LF(48) 0.1, CF(36) -4.0	0.8	89
2019	SEA	MLB	23	75	10	5	0	6	13	3	29	0	0	.268/.293/.592	84	0.3	.351	0.8	RF(17) 0.0, CF(2) 0.1	0.1	98
2020	SEA	MLB	24	455	48	20	1	17	56	35	159	1	0	.230/.293/.404	84	0.0	.327	-0.7	LF -3, RF 0	-0.2	94

Comparables: Zoilo Almonte, Bubba Starling, Trayce Thompson

Lewis's power surge in the majors in September was a great story. After a catastrophic knee injury during his pro debut back in 2016 it wasn't clear if he'd make it at all, let alone have a run like that. While he hit the ball incredibly hard across 75 major-league plate appearances, the overall profile hasn't changed all that much, and the September run frankly looks like a bit of an outlier given that he slugged under .400 in Double-A. There's plus raw and an uppercut conducive to power here, but the swing requires a lot of effort to unlock that pop and the approach isn't great. Those factors led to a 38.7 percent strikeout rate in the majors, after he struck out 29.3 percent of the time in Double-A. The knee injury sapped his speed, and he's best suited to a corner now. There might be enough boom in the profile to carry the offensive burden of a corner spot, and his OFP is the same as Evan White's up at number four in the system. We just see higher risk here given the swing-and-miss and overall approach issues.

12 Cal Raleigh C

Born: 11/26/96   Age: 23   Bats: B   Throws: R   Height: 6'3"   Weight: 215   Origin: Round 3, 2018 Draft (#90 overall)

YEAR	TEAM	LVL	AGE	PA	R	2B	3B	HR	RBI	BB	K	SB	CS	AVG/OBP/SLG	DRC+	VORP	BABIP	BRR	FRAA	WARP	PF
2018	EVE	A-	21	167	25	10	1	8	29	18	29	1	1	.288/.367/.534	141	11.7	.309	0.3	C(25) -0.2	1.2	112
2019	MOD	A+	22	348	48	19	0	22	66	33	69	4	0	.261/.336/.535	151	33.4	.267	0.8	C(55) 0.9	3.1	95
2019	ARK	AA	22	159	16	6	0	7	16	14	47	0	0	.228/.296/.414	108	7.5	.286	-0.6	C(26) 0.0	0.6	89
2020	SEA	MLB	23	251	31	12	0	14	39	17	71	1	0	.239/.295/.480	101	0.0	.279	-0.5	C -3	0.5	94

Comparables: Chris Shaw, Josh Donaldson, Travis Shaw

The Mariners have a lot of potential above-average bats in the organization now, and Raleigh rounds out that tier. You could argue for him several spots higher as he's perhaps the best bet to play in the majors for a while given the positive developments behind the plate and with the bat. It's a pretty traditional stocky catcher's frame, but he shows solid athleticism both in receiving and blocking, and his receiving has improved to the point where he's a good bet to be at least an average glove. While his arm isn't the strongest, he will at least keep would-be base stealers honest.

Raleigh has flashed plus raw from both sides of the plate and brought that pop into games this year. Yes, most of that season was spent as an advanced college bat in the Cal League, but regardless, there's the potential for 20-homer power in the majors. He has above-average bat speed although the swing can get a bit mechanical at times. The hit tool might end up a bit fringy, but he's a true two-way catching prospect now, and a strong Double-A campaign could fire him up this list next year and onto national radars.

13 Brandon Williamson   LHP
Born: 04/02/98   Age: 22   Bats: L   Throws: L   Height: 6'6"   Weight: 210   Origin: Round 2, 2019 Draft (#59 overall)

YEAR	TEAM	LVL	AGE	W	L	SV	G	GS	IP	H	HR	BB/9	K/9	K	GB%	BABIP	WHIP	ERA	DRA	WARP	PF
2019	EVE	A-	21	0	0	0	10	9	15¹	9	0	2.9	14.7	25	55%	.310	0.91	2.35	2.25	0.5	113
2020	SEA	MLB	22	2	2	0	33	0	35	35	5	3.8	10.1	39	44%	.319	1.42	4.82	4.85	0.1	94

Comparables: Radhames Liz, A.J. Puk, Caleb Smith

A big lefty who signed underslot as a second-round pick out of TCU, Williamson offers an intriguing combination of the present and the projectable. Not as dominant his junior year as you'd expect given the size and stuff, Williamson showed off a four-pitch arsenal as a pro that overwhelmed Northwest League hitters. The fastball is low 90s, but his height and high-three-quarters slot makes it a tough angle for batters. He showed two different breaking ball looks: a slider he could bury to get chases and a big breaking curve to spot. Both are potentially average offerings. The change is the fourth pitch and will need to develop to keep him on pace for a back-of-the-rotation destination, but the size and delivery look the part of an innings eater. It's a lean body so you could dream on him adding some strength and velocity, but Williamson's frame is on the narrow side, so I don't know how much more fastball you are actually going to wring out here.

14 Isaiah Campbell   RHP
Born: 08/15/97   Age: 22   Bats: R   Throws: R   Height: 6'4"   Weight: 225   Origin: Round 2, 2019 Draft (#76 overall)

Campbell was one of the better college arms available—granted not a banner year for that cohort—so the Mariners were likely thrilled he slipped to their Comp B pick. He's a big, physically mature righty who features a potentially above-average fastball/slider combo. The fastball has some plane from a high-three-quarters slot and can touch 95, while the slider at its best is a mid-80s hard breaker with good shape and depth. There's better feel for a changeup than you'd expect, but it's not so advanced that there isn't a fair bit of reliever risk here. But whatever role he makes the majors in, when he does he will be the first Portuguese-born major leaguer since Frank Thompson who played for the 1875 incarnation of the Washington Nationals. Campbell pitched deep into the summer with the Razorbacks; the Mariners kept him off short-season mounds and throwing sim games for the balance of 2019, so we will have to wait and see how he adjusts to pro ball.

15 Sam Carlson   RHP
Born: 12/03/98   Age: 21   Bats: R   Throws: R   Height: 6'4"   Weight: 195   Origin: Round 2, 2017 Draft (#55 overall)

One of my least-favorite types of dart throws during list season is the "prospect arm who has missed significant time due to Tommy John surgery before throwing significant pro innings." Carlson threw…uh…/checks notes…three innings in 2017. Some of this is just the vagaries of timing. Carlson had his surgery in the summer of 2018 while in extended. So there's nothing unusual about his recovery so far. That all said, we won't have any real, actionable information about where to rank him until he steps back on a professional mound next year. What we do know is he was an OFP 55 for us coming out of the draft based on the projectability and present fastball/slider combo. So if that's all in its proper place in April, there's an argument he should be up with Dunn and Kirby. But the variance here is extreme, and until we see it, we are going to be cautious.

16 Ljay Newsome   RHP
Born: 11/08/96   Age: 23   Bats: R   Throws: R   Height: 5'11"   Weight: 210   Origin: Round 26, 2015 Draft (#785 overall)

YEAR	TEAM	LVL	AGE	W	L	SV	G	GS	IP	H	HR	BB/9	K/9	K	GB%	BABIP	WHIP	ERA	DRA	WARP	PF
2017	CLN	A	20	8	9	0	25	25	129²	131	14	1.1	7.7	111	34%	.302	1.13	4.10	4.25	1.6	100
2018	MOD	A+	21	6	10	0	26	26	138²	169	24	0.8	8.0	123	32%	.337	1.31	4.87	5.79	-0.7	95
2019	MOD	A+	22	6	6	0	18	18	100²	105	11	0.8	11.1	124	27%	.357	1.13	3.75	4.26	0.9	95
2019	ARK	AA	22	3	4	0	9	9	48²	41	4	1.3	6.5	35	37%	.270	0.99	2.77	4.08	0.5	89
2020	SEA	MLB	23	4	5	0	15	15	61	65	13	2.8	8.5	58	38%	.301	1.37	5.00	5.14	0.3	94

Comparables: Liam Hendriks, Gabriel Ynoa, José Ureña

Newsome always had plus command and major-league-quality secondaries, but even in the recent era of much shallower Mariners systems, it was tough to get on board with ranking a dude sitting in the mid-to-upper 80s with his fastball. But his velocity "spike" in 2019 has taken the profile from undesirable to undeniable. Well undeniably a back-end starter prospect, but hey, that's something. Newsome now sits around 90 and touches as high as 94. There's not much life on it, but he commands it well down in the zone. He'll have to. Now that he can at least establish the heater, the above-average slider and change play up. The secondaries were far too much for Cal League hitters, and got enough swings and misses against upper minors ones to portend good—or at least average—things in the majors. Newsome throws a lot of strikes, and the fastball is still below-average for a right-hander. It remains to be seen if he can live in the zone with this arsenal against major league bats. The Mariners seem unsure as they left him off the 40-man and unprotected in the Rule 5 draft, but given the improved fastball and how close to the majors he is now, he makes our list.

17 Braden Bishop OF

Born: 08/22/93 Age: 26 Bats: R Throws: R Height: 6'1" Weight: 190 Origin: Round 3, 2015 Draft (#94 overall)

YEAR	TEAM	LVL	AGE	PA	R	2B	3B	HR	RBI	BB	K	SB	CS	AVG/OBP/SLG	DRC+	VORP	BABIP	BRR	FRAA	WARP	PF
2017	MOD	A+	23	412	71	25	3	2	32	45	65	16	4	.296/.385/.400	124	23.3	.356	0.8	CF(70) -1.8, LF(14) 2.1	2.3	99
2017	ARK	AA	23	145	18	9	1	1	11	15	15	6	1	.336/.417/.448	176	15.1	.373	-1.5	CF(31) 1.5	1.5	91
2018	ARK	AA	24	394	70	20	0	8	33	37	68	5	2	.284/.361/.412	142	17.1	.331	-1.9	CF(81) -0.9, RF(2) -0.1	2.5	101
2019	MOD	A+	25	29	7	1	1	0	3	2	9	0	0	.240/.345/.360	56	2.3	.375	1.4	CF(3) 0.6	0.2	92
2019	TAC	AAA	25	211	29	15	0	8	31	23	44	2	2	.276/.360/.486	92	10.7	.321	-0.2	CF(34) 0.7, RF(6) 1.0	0.6	103
2019	SEA	MLB	25	60	3	0	0	0	4	3	21	0	0	.107/.153/.107	45	-2.2	.171	0.2	CF(20) -0.6, LF(4) 0.2	-0.2	101
2020	SEA	MLB	26	105	10	4	0	2	10	8	28	1	0	.223/.291/.332	67	0.0	.292	-0.1	CF 0, LF 1	-0.1	94

Comparables: Alex Presley, Travis Jankowski, Abraham Almonte

Bishop has suffered through pretty bad injury luck the last two seasons. His 2018 was cut short by a broken forearm, and he missed a chunk of time this year with a lacerated spleen, the result of a hit by pitch. When on the field, though, he has remained indubitably Braden Bishop. He struggled badly across intermittent playing time with the big club, but hit in Triple-A and made good use of the new baseballs. Even when the bat isn't performing Bishop is a quality defender at all three outfield spots, so if he does manage to hit even a little bit he should have a long career as a bench outfielder.

18 Art Warren RHP

Born: 03/23/93 Age: 27 Bats: R Throws: R Height: 6'3" Weight: 230 Origin: Round 23, 2015 Draft (#695 overall)

YEAR	TEAM	LVL	AGE	W	L	SV	G	GS	IP	H	HR	BB/9	K/9	K	GB%	BABIP	WHIP	ERA	DRA	WARP	PF
2017	MOD	A+	24	3	1	8	43	0	64²	58	5	3.5	9.3	67	45%	.312	1.28	3.06	4.50	0.3	100
2018	ARK	AA	25	1	2	2	14	0	15²	10	0	8.0	12.6	22	39%	.303	1.53	1.72	4.44	0.1	100
2019	ARK	AA	26	2	1	15	29	0	31²	23	1	3.7	11.7	41	60%	.310	1.14	1.71	3.41	0.5	100
2019	SEA	MLB	26	1	0	0	6	0	5¹	2	0	3.4	8.4	5	29%	.143	0.75	0.00	5.56	0.0	100
2020	SEA	MLB	27	1	1	0	25	0	26	28	5	4.7	6.9	20	45%	.292	1.58	5.81	5.63	-0.1	94

Comparables: Kyle Dowdy, Jon Meloan, Brad Wieck

After another season missing plenty of bats in Arkansas, Warren got his first cup of coffee in the majors. His brief success in September followed the same formula that has made him an intriguing relief prospect the past couple years. He throws a plus—flashing plus-plus—slider a lot. It's the very model of a modern major pen arm. The slider sits mid 80s with big downward bite. When on, it's basically unhittable. The slide piece can show a little bit more like a power slurve at times, which is the only thing keeping it from a straight 7 on our sheets. There's plenty of fastball, as well, as Warren sits 95 and touches higher. Even the good systems still have their 95-and-a-slider guys, but Warren's slider is good enough to play in the eighth or ninth.

19 Joey Gerber RHP

Born: 05/03/97   Age: 23   Bats: R   Throws: R   Height: 6'4"   Weight: 215   Origin: Round 8, 2018 Draft (#238 overall)

YEAR	TEAM	LVL	AGE	W	L	SV	G	GS	IP	H	HR	BB/9	K/9	K	GB%	BABIP	WHIP	ERA	DRA	WARP	PF
2018	EVE	A-	21	1	0	6	13	0	14	9	0	3.9	13.5	21	59%	.333	1.07	1.93	3.10	0.3	100
2018	CLN	A	21	0	0	2	9	0	11²	9	0	3.9	17.0	22	35%	.450	1.20	2.31	2.83	0.3	100
2019	MOD	A+	22	0	2	8	25	0	26	17	0	4.2	13.5	39	39%	.304	1.12	3.46	2.41	0.7	100
2019	ARK	AA	22	1	2	0	19	0	22²	21	2	2.8	11.9	30	41%	.352	1.24	1.59	4.30	0.1	100
2020	SEA	MLB	23	2	2	0	33	0	35	34	5	3.7	11.1	43	40%	.331	1.40	4.59	4.64	0.2	94

Comparables: Akeel Morris, Nick Wittgren, Heath Hembree

When you go twenty deep on systems you start to realize that even the better systems tend to thin out in similar ways. So we've reached the reliever-only section of the Mariners list. Gerber is an eighth-round college closer made good, as his mid-90s fastball and mid-80s slider have dominated at every stop so far on Seattle's organizational ladder. You see the fastball pretty late out of the hand and the slider has hard, late tilt. Gerber has a violent delivery and below-average command of both his pitches, but the stuff is setup man quality.

20 Damon Casetta-Stubbs RHP

Born: 07/22/99   Age: 20   Bats: R   Throws: R   Height: 6'4"   Weight: 225   Origin: Round 11, 2018 Draft (#328 overall)

YEAR	TEAM	LVL	AGE	W	L	SV	G	GS	IP	H	HR	BB/9	K/9	K	GB%	BABIP	WHIP	ERA	DRA	WARP	PF
2018	MRN	RK	18	0	2	0	6	5	6²	15	0	5.4	9.4	7	46%	.536	2.85	13.50	10.37	-0.3	103
2019	EVE	A-	19	3	3	0	15	15	70	52	7	3.5	8.6	67	61%	.247	1.13	4.11	3.52	1.4	113
2019	WVA	A	19	3	5	0	10	10	44¹	61	4	2.6	7.5	37	48%	.393	1.67	7.11	7.46	-1.2	99
2020	SEA	MLB	20	2	2	0	33	0	35	35	6	3.9	6.3	25	49%	.278	1.45	5.31	5.25	0.0	94

We had Casetta-Stubbs 11th last year out of the draft as an overslot prep. He's not that much worse of a prospect this time around, which points to a generally improved system, although he struggled mightily as a 19-year-old aggressively assigned to full-season ball. He was more low 90s than mid 90s for me in April, and the slider is miles ahead of the changeup at present even though both lack consistency. He showed useful command, and I intuitively liked him a little more than I should've. He's got projectability left and the variance on both sides for where he's going to be even two years from now is extremely high, but there's the outline of a useful starter or reliever here. In short, he's an interesting live arm.

Personal Cheeseball

PC Wyatt Mills RHP

Born: 01/25/95   Age: 25   Bats: R   Throws: R   Height: 6'3"   Weight: 175   Origin: Round 3, 2017 Draft (#93 overall)

YEAR	TEAM	LVL	AGE	W	L	SV	G	GS	IP	H	HR	BB/9	K/9	K	GB%	BABIP	WHIP	ERA	DRA	WARP	PF
2017	EVE	A-	22	0	1	2	7	0	7	3	0	3.9	14.1	11	50%	.214	0.86	2.57	1.70	0.3	100
2017	CLN	A	22	0	1	4	11	0	13¹	5	0	4.1	12.1	18	57%	.179	0.82	1.35	2.36	0.4	100
2018	MOD	A+	23	6	0	11	35	0	42¹	29	1	1.9	10.4	49	54%	.277	0.90	1.91	2.55	1.2	100
2018	ARK	AA	23	0	2	0	9	0	10²	18	0	3.4	8.4	10	42%	.450	2.06	10.12	7.79	-0.4	100
2019	ARK	AA	24	4	2	8	41	0	52²	43	2	2.9	11.3	66	55%	.320	1.14	4.27	4.29	0.2	100
2020	SEA	MLB	25	2	2	0	33	0	35	34	5	3.3	9.7	38	46%	.310	1.33	4.31	4.37	0.3	94

Comparables: Pedro Araujo, Ryan Reid, Montana DuRapau

Mills has struggled some in Double-A, which is not an unusual spot for your typical mid-round college sidearmer to run aground. Mills has a fair bit more stuff than that genus, though. He has average fastball velocity, regularly hitting 94, although it takes a lot of effort to dial it up, and he lacks the finer command you associate with a polished sidewinder. The slider flashes short, late frisbee action in the mid 80s, but it can have inconsistent shape or back up some. Everything is a bit too hittable for Mills to sneak onto the back of the list this year with Warren and Gerber, but nothing says personal cheeseball here at BP like a low-slot dude throwing bullets.

Low Minors Sleeper

LMS **Austin Shenton** 3B
Born: 01/22/98   Age: 22   Bats: L   Throws: R   Height: 6'0"   Weight: 195   Origin: Round 5, 2019 Draft (#156 overall)

YEAR	TEAM	LVL	AGE	PA	R	2B	3B	HR	RBI	BB	K	SB	CS	AVG/OBP/SLG	DRC+	VORP	BABIP	BRR	FRAA	WARP	PF
2019	EVE	A-	21	92	16	10	1	2	16	8	15	0	0	.367/.446/.595	193	12.7	.429	0.1	3B(14) -0.7, RF(1) 0.2	1.0	111
2019	WVA	A	21	134	13	7	1	5	20	11	29	0	0	.252/.328/.454	108	4.6	.291	-1.0	2B(8) -1.2, 3B(7) 0.1	0.2	94
2020	SEA	MLB	22	251	24	13	1	7	27	16	68	2	1	.230/.291/.381	77	3.0	.297	0.0	3B -1, 2B 0	0.0	94

The Mariners' fifth-round pick this year, Shenton offers a bit more projection than you usually find in a Day Two college bat. He isn't raw, either, taking to pro ball immediately and showing a viable hit tool. Shenton is short to the ball, with enough physical strength and bat speed to drive it. He's started to tap into some raw power as well, and he will need to continue to do so, as he's only passable at third, and might end up seeing time at first or an outfield corner. He could add further strength and power, allowing the bat to carry whatever defensive spot he mans. Shenton is worth keeping an eye on in full-season ball for sure.

Top Talents 25 and Under (as of 4/1/2020)

1. Jarred Kelenic
2. Julio Rodriguez
3. J.P. Crawford
4. Logan Gilbert
5. Evan White
6. Justin Dunn
7. George Kirby
8. Juan Then
9. Noelvi Marte
10. Justus Sheffield

The primary difference between art and sport is that sports have a predefined goal, a victory condition. Sports have one expression. The Seattle Mariners, therefore, are art.

The defining characteristic of this 25U isn't that it's good or bad—it's both good, and bad—but that it's nearly identical to the prospect list up top. Only Crawford is guaranteed a job in the majors this season, while Sheffield and Dunn may be pressed into service not out of merit but because of the contractual obligations of fielding a full roster. Not that it matters. Those games will have happened, technically, but they won't really happen. The 2020 Seattle Mariners won't really exist.

Come October, we'll agree that they couldn't have, that it was all some collective fever dream, an Out of the Park simulation retconned into the box scores. It won't have made sense for so much effort, so many millions of dollars and billions of hours to be pooled into the creation of something so thoroughly pointless as the 2020 Seattle Mariners, a product of planned obsolescence. Did they really stand in line to file through the metal detectors to watch the lineup get dissected by Justin Verlander? Did they really cheer for a Clayton Richard slider that caught a batter napping and stranded runners on the corners? No. It's not possible.

Jerry Dipoto has planted his flag in 2021 as the point in which the Mariners officially resume their pursuit of winning baseball games. (It was actually mid-2020, but that was before Sheffield's fall from grace, so he'd probably prefer we all forget that.) So the real #1 to look out for in the city of Seattle isn't Crawford, or even the team's playoff drought, nine months younger than Julio Rodriguez. It's the cognitive dissonance that goes into producing, consuming, and particularly selling this cardboard facade of a baseball team, ready to topple at the first gust of wind. Sports may be about winning and losing, but the acceptance and the rationalization of sports is an artistic expression. The good news: if, as Orson Welles said, "the enemy of art is the absence of limitation," 2020 will provide Mariners fans with so much art.

Eyewitness Reports

Eyewitness Report: Jarred Kelenic

Evaluator: Jarrett Seidler
Report Date: 05/07/2019
Dates Seen: 4/30/2019, 5/1/2019, 5/2/2019
Risk Factor: Medium
Physical/Health: Athletic frame, but looks pretty close to fully developed already.

Tool	Future Grade	Report
Hit	60	Classic, smooth lefty swing. Swing path and setup has noticeably improved compared to 2018 video. Keeps the bat in the zone for awhile with strong bat speed. Showed off precocious barrel control all series, including beating a typical shift by doubling over the third base bag. Does sometimes still get out of sync with lower half. Overall plate approach was very strong for age and level, with slight questions about breaking ball recognition against lefties and chasing when behind in the count. Moderately open stance with small leg kick as timing mechanism.
Power	60	Consistently hit the ball very hard to all fields in my viewings, including a long home run to RF and multiple balls that went just short of going out. Swing is geared for significant power output, especially given current era of baseball. Ball just absolutely jumps off his bat.
Baserunning/ Speed	55	No dig time, because he didn't have a hard run to first all series. Visual interpretation matched Jeffrey Paternostro's 2018 report: "11.4 on a triple, good second gear, looks like a present plus runner, would expect him to give some of that back in his 20s, but the frame looks close to a finished product."
Glove	50	Generally showed good instincts and routes in the outfield, and runs well enough to handle center. Got a good jump on the ball. Closed noticeably poorly on one shallow flyball in front of him that dropped. Expect him to be able to handle center competently enough if team needs so warrant, but could see a team preferring him in the corner depending on organizational needs.
Arm	60	Jeffrey's 2018 report seemed accurate with limited throws: "Plus arm strength, good carry, accurate. Didn't get to see him really air it out, and have heard plus-plus thrown on him here."

Conclusion: Kelenic has rare 6 hit/6 power future potential, along with athletic secondary skills and a shot to remain in CF. Likely first-division regular outfielder with a chance to be a perennial All-Star.

Eyewitness Report: Julio Rodriguez

Evaluator: Forest Stulting
Report Date: 10/15/2019
Dates Seen: April 4-7 and Oct. 10-12
Risk Factor: Medium
Physical/Health: XL frame, athletic, muscular, quick-twitch, strong lower half, excellent body control.

Tool	Future Grade	Report
Hit	60	High hands, small leg kick with stride, easy compact swing, quick bat, plus barrel control, line-to-line hitter, bat stays through the zone a long time, slight uppercut, good extension, advanced approach, controls the zone.
Power	60	Raw power at present, will come with age and maturity. 25+ home run ability yearly, future power to all fields.
Baserunning/ Speed	50	Not a burner but can steal bases, heady baserunner, long strides, no mechanical issues.
Glove	55	Moves well, takes solid routes, goes back to wall well, can make highlight-reel catches. Has ability to play a slightly above-average center field.
Arm	60	Cannon for an arm, accurate, high velocity, carry. Plays plus in right field, knows situations.

Conclusion: Rodriguez has one of the more high-end packages in all of the minors. When you watch Rodriguez play his tools are easy to spot. What also stands out are his intangibles–grit, determination, confidence, and love for the game. His floor is very high with his ability to control the zone, find the barrel and play right field at an above-average level. But Rodriguez sure looks like he is on the path of perennial All-Star.

St. Louis Cardinals

The State of the System

The Cardinals system is below-average on balance, but there are a couple impact bats at the top of the list, and some depth in potential MLB arms.

The Top Ten

───────────────────── ★ ★ ★ *2020 Top 101 Prospect* **#18** ★ ★ ★ ─────────────────────

1 **Dylan Carlson** **OF** OFP: 70 ETA: 2020
Born: 10/23/98 Age: 21 Bats: B Throws: L Height: 6'3" Weight: 205 Origin: Round 1, 2016 Draft (#33 overall)

YEAR	TEAM	LVL	AGE	PA	R	2B	3B	HR	RBI	BB	K	SB	CS	AVG/OBP/SLG	DRC+	VORP	BABIP	BRR	FRAA	WARP	PF
2017	PEO	A	18	451	63	18	1	7	42	52	116	6	6	.240/.342/.347	98	14.6	.323	2.6	RF(79) 0.8, CF(24) 0.1	1.4	96
2018	PEO	A	19	57	5	3	0	2	9	10	10	2	0	.234/.368/.426	137	1.4	.257	-0.7	RF(10) 2.3, CF(4) -0.3	0.5	101
2018	PMB	A+	19	441	63	19	3	9	53	52	78	6	3	.247/.345/.386	115	18.2	.286	1.7	RF(50) 4.7, LF(37) -0.1	2.1	94
2019	SFD	AA	20	483	81	24	6	21	59	52	98	18	7	.281/.364/.518	151	40.3	.315	3.1	CF(86) -10.2, RF(9) -0.3	2.7	105
2019	MEM	AAA	20	79	14	4	2	5	9	6	18	2	1	.361/.418/.681	142	10.9	.429	0.1	CF(8) -0.5, LF(7) 0.0	0.6	93
2020	SLN	MLB	21	287	32	13	1	11	37	25	77	1	0	.238/.312/.427	96	0.0	.297	-0.1	RF -1, LF 1	0.5	87

Comparables: Nomar Mazara, Victor Robles, Yorman Rodriguez

The Report: There's breakout prospects and then there's breakout prospects. Carlson is the latter. He had spent the last couple years flashing big tools while putting up fine, but unspectacular performance, albeit while relatively young for his leagues. In 2019 he finally started tapping into his raw power, and a move to center field went well enough—stupid Cardinals Devil Magic—and he's gone from an good org name with some tweener tendencies to a potential five-tool center fielder and national darling. It's not a lock he sticks up-the-middle. Although he's a good baserunner, he's not a true burner. He's filled out in his upper body and has maintained his loose, athletic swing. He has plus bat speed from both sides of the plate and gets to his plus raw power without sacrificing any barrel control. Some .290, 25 HR seasons are likely, and if he can actually handle center in the majors, All-Star games will follow.

Variance: Medium. There's a chance he continues his growth and there's a bit more in the tank at the plate. There's also the risk he's more of a .270, 20 HR corner outfielder that plays center once or twice a week. That's still a very nice major leaguer, but not a star.

Mark Barry's Fantasy Take: While it's not groundbreaking to be enamored with Carlson, I'll go a bit further and say he's one of my five-favorite dynasty prospects, in the land.

★ ★ ★ *2020 Top 101 Prospect* **#23** ★ ★ ★

2 **Nolan Gorman** **3B**   OFP: 60   ETA: 2021/22
Born: 05/10/00 Age: 20 Bats: L Throws: R Height: 6'1" Weight: 210 Origin: Round 1, 2018 Draft (#19 overall)

YEAR	TEAM	LVL	AGE	PA	R	2B	3B	HR	RBI	BB	K	SB	CS	AVG/OBP/SLG	DRC+	VORP	BABIP	BRR	FRAA	WARP	PF
2018	JCY	RK	18	167	41	10	1	11	28	24	37	1	3	.350/.443/.664	191	25.2	.411	-0.7	3B(33) 7.6	2.7	109
2018	PEO	A	18	107	8	3	0	6	16	10	39	0	2	.202/.280/.426	76	2.3	.255	-0.5	3B(25) 3.9	0.5	102
2019	PEO	A	19	282	41	14	3	10	41	32	79	2	0	.241/.344/.448	129	16.9	.312	0.4	3B(51) 8.4	2.6	102
2019	PMB	A+	19	230	24	16	3	5	21	13	73	0	1	.256/.304/.428	107	6.7	.365	-2.1	3B(48) -5.9	0.0	97
2020	SLN	MLB	20	251	26	12	1	8	29	24	86	1	0	.223/.303/.394	84	3.0	.321	-0.4	3B 1	0.4	87

Comparables: Miguel Sanó, Austin Riley, Gary Sánchez

The Report: The questionable hit tool projection that caused Gorman to slide down draft boards in 2018 crept back into the conversation about his profile this year. The holes in his swing were exposed a bit during his second half stint in the Florida State League with his strikeout rate spiking to over 30%. He's still a teenager and possesses some of the best left-handed power in all of minor league baseball. It's easy power, generated by his raw strength and a quick swing that makes the ball jump off his bat. He also proved to be a capable defender at third this year, showing solid instincts and a strong accurate arm. The Cardinals have aggressively pushed him in his assignments, making him one of the youngest players at each of his stops. That sink-or-swim approach is going to give Gorman the opportunity to make adjustments at the plate and fully tap into his power. If he does, he still profiles as a middle of the order slugging third baseman.

Variance: High. There's the risk that the bat never develops enough to become more than a low average, slugging corner infielder.

Mark Barry's Fantasy Take: The drop in walk rate concerns me more than all of the strikeouts, but Gorman was over three years younger than his High-A counterparts, so growing pains were more or less inevitable. The power is what keeps us coming back, and 30+ dinger seasons are still there to dream on. Bret and Ben had Gorman listed as their 23rd best dynasty prospect in their midseason writeup, and while I might not go that high, it's hard to quibble too much with their expertise.

3 **Zack Thompson** **LHP**   OFP: 55   ETA: 2021
Born: 10/28/97 Age: 22 Bats: L Throws: L Height: 6'2" Weight: 225 Origin: Round 1, 2019 Draft (#19 overall)

YEAR	TEAM	LVL	AGE	W	L	SV	G	GS	IP	H	HR	BB/9	K/9	K	GB%	BABIP	WHIP	ERA	DRA	WARP	PF
2019	PMB	A+	21	0	0	0	11	0	13^1	16	0	2.7	12.8	19	48%	.455	1.50	4.05	6.71	-0.3	100
2020	SLN	MLB	22	2	2	0	33	0	35	35	5	3.8	8.9	35	43%	.305	1.42	4.75	4.90	0.2	87

Comparables: Tony Cingrani, Roman Mendez, Chasen Shreve

The Report: Thompson pushed himself into the first round of the draft with a dominant junior year at Kentucky. His frame is right off the "mid-rotation pitching prospect" assembly line— good height, sturdy build. He maintains his low-90s fastball deep into games, and it's a bit of a funky arm action, so the heater sneaks up on you. Both his slider and curve are potentially above-average, and the change is already enough to cross over. He's had multiple arm injuries in the last few years and was used heavily at Kentucky, so while he has the frame to start, we'll have to monitor his durability as he gets stretched out in the pros. I hesitate to call Thompson a safe arm, but health permitting, he has a fairly high floor due to the broad repertoire

Variance: Medium. Thompson has had injury issues in the somewhat recent past, but needs merely refinement in the pros and could move quickly.

Mark Barry's Fantasy Take: I like Thompson about as much you can like an oft-injured, high-usage college arm, which is to say—I like him some. It's cliche at this point in the exercise to say that pitchers are all risky, so I'll spare you here, but I could see Thompson as a SP3 pretty quickly, you know, health permitting.

4 Ivan Herrera C   OFP: 55   ETA: 2023

Born: 06/01/00   Age: 20   Bats: R   Throws: R   Height: 6'0"   Weight: 180   Origin: International Free Agent, 2016

YEAR	TEAM	LVL	AGE	PA	R	2B	3B	HR	RBI	BB	K	SB	CS	AVG/OBP/SLG	DRC+	VORP	BABIP	BRR	FRAA	WARP	PF
2017	DCA	RK	17	201	21	15	0	1	27	18	36	2	2	.335/.425/.441	144	19.5	.415	-0.5	C(49) 0.7	1.9	107
2018	CRD	RK	18	130	23	6	4	1	25	11	20	1	1	.348/.423/.500	154	11.6	.409	-1.9	C(20) 0.6	1.0	107
2019	PEO	A	19	291	41	10	0	8	42	35	56	1	1	.286/.381/.423	138	21.7	.337	-0.1	C(64) -1.0	2.4	103
2019	PMB	A+	19	65	7	0	0	1	5	5	16	0	0	.276/.338/.328	117	2.5	.357	-1.1	C(17) -0.1	0.3	98
2020	SLN	MLB	20	251	26	11	1	6	27	19	66	1	0	.258/.325/.393	93	0.0	.339	-0.3	C -1	0.5	87

Comparables: Victor Robles, J.P. Crawford, César Puello

The Report: It's just like Ben Franklin said: There are only three certainties in life: Death, taxes, and the Cardinals developing a good catching prospect who will inevitably be blocked by Yadi Molina. In Herrera's case, another aphorism may be appropriate: Timing is everything. The 19-year-old may end up ready for a major-league job right about when Molina is ready to retire—assuming that actually ever happens. Herrera's bat took a step forward last season, as he showed a quick stroke that was short to the ball. Despite the compact swing, he flashes some pullside raw already and the power could play average in games at maturity. Herrera can handle good velocity, but is a bit raw against spin, often out in front. It's nothing too concerning for a teenager seeing full-season arms for the first time, but it's something to keep an eye on going forward.

Herrera moves well behind the plate and has an above-average arm. The receiving should get to at least average as well. There isn't a standout tool here yet, and the bat will need to continue to develop, but a collection of average tools makes you a heckuva prospect when one of them is catcher defense.

Variance: High. Catchers are weird. Teenage catchers are weirder.

Mark Barry's Fantasy Take: Logline: A team of Cardinals back-up catchers and catching prospects team up for a heist to steal Yadier Molina's glove, in a plot to, you know, actually play.

5 Andrew Knizner C   OFP: 55   ETA: 2019

Born: 02/03/95   Age: 25   Bats: R   Throws: R   Height: 6'1"   Weight: 200   Origin: Round 7, 2016 Draft (#226 overall)

YEAR	TEAM	LVL	AGE	PA	R	2B	3B	HR	RBI	BB	K	SB	CS	AVG/OBP/SLG	DRC+	VORP	BABIP	BRR	FRAA	WARP	PF
2017	PEO	A	22	191	18	10	1	8	29	9	22	1	1	.279/.325/.480	124	13.5	.282	0.5	C(26) -0.3, 1B(3) -0.1	1.1	95
2017	SFD	AA	22	202	27	13	0	4	22	14	27	0	1	.324/.371/.462	145	18.7	.355	0.5	C(49) -3.5	1.5	101
2018	SFD	AA	23	313	39	13	0	7	41	23	40	0	1	.313/.365/.434	133	21.9	.339	-1.4	C(74) -7.3	1.6	105
2018	MEM	AAA	23	61	3	5	0	0	4	4	8	0	0	.315/.383/.407	115	3.8	.370	-0.1	C(16) 1.8	0.6	92
2019	MEM	AAA	24	280	41	10	0	12	34	24	37	2	0	.276/.357/.463	112	21.8	.281	-0.8	C(61) -17.2	0.2	94
2019	SLN	MLB	24	58	7	2	0	2	7	4	14	2	0	.226/.293/.377	82	1.7	.270	0.5	C(16) -4.4, 1B(1) 0.0	-0.2	96
2020	SLN	MLB	25	182	19	7	0	6	21	12	34	0	0	.242/.305/.388	87	0.0	.274	-0.4	C -10	-0.5	87

Comparables: AJ Hinch, Randy Knorr, Hal King

The Report: Knizner on the other hand, might be stuck behind Yadier Molina for a bit longer. He got a chance midseason when Molina hit the IL for a bit and didn't exactly seize the day. Despite the rough debut, there's good reason to think Knizner will hit going forward. He's short to the ball, and strong enough to drive it to all fields. He's happy to hit the ball where it's pitched, and goes the other way well. Major League spin gave him some trouble, but I'd expect him to make the necessary adjustments to be an above-average hitter overall. He's not generally looking to hit the ball over the fence, but he's strong enough to run into 15ish home runs a year. That's a nice little offensive package for an everyday catcher—assuming there's a job opening soon, I wouldn't exactly be waiting for the Monster.com email.

The defensive side is going to be more problematic and not just by way of comparison to Molina. Knizner is a converted third baseman, and the glove skills are still a bit rough. You could argue the lack of experience just means there's more room for improvement, but while the bat is major-league-ready, Knizner graded out as one of the worst framers in Triple-A and he wasn't any better in the majors. He controls the running game all right despite fringy arm strength, and he's athletic enough you'd like to think he can get the receiving up to acceptable. But there's a ceiling for the glove here, and it's a far cry from the Cards current backstop.

Variance: Low. He's likely to break camp as the backup, I'd expect him to post an above-average offensive line given semi-regular MLB reps, but the glove might limit how many reps the Cardinals want to give him, barring improvements.

Mark Barry's Fantasy Take: If you're looking for a second catcher in an only league or deeper redraft format, Knizner might be a decent bet. For dynasty, value Knizner much like you would have valued Carson Kelly pre-trade. He's a good talent that should hit enough to be one of the 10-15 best catchers in fantasy, if he ever gets a chance to play.

6 Randy Arozarena OF   OFP: 55   ETA: 2019

Born: 02/28/95   Age: 25   Bats: R   Throws: R   Height: 5'11"   Weight: 170   Origin: International Free Agent, 2016

YEAR	TEAM	LVL	AGE	PA	R	2B	3B	HR	RBI	BB	K	SB	CS	AVG/OBP/SLG	DRC+	VORP	BABIP	BRR	FRAA	WARP	PF
2017	PMB	A+	22	295	38	22	3	8	40	13	53	10	4	.275/.333/.472	144	24.3	.313	-2.5	LF(47) 4.3, CF(13) -0.5	2.2	91
2017	SFD	AA	22	195	34	10	1	3	9	27	34	8	3	.252/.366/.380	114	9.0	.299	2.7	LF(40) 0.1, CF(4) -0.9	0.9	99
2018	SFD	AA	23	102	22	5	0	7	21	6	25	9	3	.396/.455/.681	200	15.4	.492	1.0	RF(12) 1.6, CF(6) -0.4	1.5	103
2018	MEM	AAA	23	311	42	16	0	5	28	28	59	17	5	.232/.328/.348	83	9.3	.278	0.8	LF(49) -2.7, RF(18) 0.2	-0.1	90
2019	SFD	AA	24	116	14	7	2	3	15	13	23	8	5	.309/.422/.515	160	10.9	.380	-0.5	CF(13) 0.9, LF(5) 0.0	0.9	101
2019	MEM	AAA	24	283	51	18	2	12	38	24	48	9	7	.358/.435/.593	154	34.3	.404	-1.2	CF(25) -3.4, RF(20) 4.6	2.7	95
2019	SLN	MLB	24	23	4	1	0	1	2	2	4	2	1	.300/.391/.500	84	0.3	.333	-1.7	RF(6) -0.1, CF(5) 0.5	-0.1	98
2020	SLN	MLB	25	140	16	8	1	5	17	11	32	5	2	.260/.340/.440	111	0.0	.316	0.0	LF 0, CF 0	0.6	87

Comparables: Jack Daniels, Jordan Luplow, Joe Lefebvre

The Report: In 2018, Arozarena bounced between Double-A and Triple-A, mashing at the former, while struggling at the latter. In 2019 he crushed both levels and earned a late-season promotion to St. Louis, finally. He's always had good pop for his size, but the new Triple-A balls were particularly welcoming to his above-average bat speed. Arozarena's swing might be a little bit too line-drive oriented at present to project average game power, but he should create enough hard contact pull side to dump a dozen or so fliners over the left field fence. And sure, I wouldn't be shocked if he's the kind of guy who hits 20 bombs eventually after some "swing tweak," although that's not something you can or should project.

Arozarena has good feel for contact as well, and despite an overly aggressive approach, he doesn't get pull-happy. He won't walk a ton, which is unfortunate given his plus-plus speed, but he should hit .270-.280 generally. Arozarena is a true burner but he's not a true center fielder. I suspect he'd end up average there if he got more reps, but he's a better fit in a corner where he's spent most of his outfield time as a pro. The 2019 performance has mostly disposed of the "tweener" tag, but there's still some risk his approach gets exposed as the league gets more info on him.

Variance: Low. He's probably not quite THIS good, but he has the ability to man all three outfield positions, hit a little bit, run a little bit. Even if he falls short of being an everyday regular, Arozarena is the kind of player that hangs around on major league rosters for the better part of a decade.

Mark Barry's Fantasy Take: Arozarena could do no wrong in 2019, and if you only looked at his three-stop, 2019 sample, you'd probably think he was a top-10ish fantasy guy. He's not, though. And that's not to say he isn't good, or can't be serviceable, but it's more likely that the skillset plays like a fantasy OF4-5 as opposed to a stud.

7 Johan Oviedo RHP   OFP: 55   ETA: 2021

Born: 03/02/98   Age: 22   Bats: R   Throws: R   Height: 6'6"   Weight: 210   Origin: International Free Agent, 2016

YEAR	TEAM	LVL	AGE	W	L	SV	G	GS	IP	H	HR	BB/9	K/9	K	GB%	BABIP	WHIP	ERA	DRA	WARP	PF
2017	JCY	RK	19	2	1	0	6	6	27²	22	0	5.9	10.1	31	51%	.306	1.45	4.88	3.79	0.7	98
2017	SCO	A-	19	2	2	0	8	8	47¹	53	3	3.4	7.4	39	58%	.340	1.50	4.56	6.65	-0.8	109
2018	PEO	A	20	10	10	1	25	23	121²	108	6	5.8	8.7	118	38%	.304	1.54	4.22	5.11	0.1	102
2019	PMB	A+	21	5	0	0	6	5	33²	29	1	3.2	9.4	35	48%	.308	1.22	1.60	4.23	0.3	96
2019	SFD	AA	21	7	8	0	23	23	113	120	9	5.1	10.2	128	44%	.366	1.63	5.65	6.32	-1.9	104
2020	SLN	MLB	22	2	2	0	33	0	35	34	5	4.1	8.0	31	42%	.294	1.43	4.55	4.73	0.3	87

Comparables: Yennsy Diaz, Keury Mella, Dennis Santana

The Report: Oviedo is a massive human, a looming presence on the mound. The fastball sits mid-90s and can touch higher, and with a long stride and high-three-quarters slot, it gets on you quickly and from a steep angle that is difficult to elevate. The command and control are still below-average. He has a fairly short, simple arm action to go with the leg kick and long stride, and can struggle with the timing/syncing the delivery. The secondaries are inconsistent as well. Oviedo tends to slow his arm down on a soft 12-6 curve in the upper-70s. His mid-80s slider is a bit more projectable, although the shape can vary.

There's also a firmish change with some tail to it. He'll need to tighten up the mechanics and the offspeed stuff to stick as a starter, and the overall profile is pretty raw for someone with 100+ innings in Double-A, but the frame and arm strength are worth betting on.

Variance: High. It's mostly a fastball at present, and he doesn't consistently throw strikes with...well, anything. It's an ideal frame and the secondaries will flash enough that if he does put it together with more reps, he could blow past this projection. I wouldn't put the mortgage on that bet though.

Mark Barry's Fantasy Take: The fastball is nice, but that's kind of it right now for Oviedo, which super screams reliever to me. Until he gets a little control or adds reliability to the arsenal, I'm not all that interested.

8 Trejyn Fletcher OF   OFP: 55   ETA: 2024
Born: 04/30/01 Age: 19 Bats: R Throws: R Height: 6'2" Weight: 200 Origin: Round 2, 2019 Draft (#58 overall)

YEAR	TEAM	LVL	AGE	PA	R	2B	3B	HR	RBI	BB	K	SB	CS	AVG/OBP/SLG	DRC+	VORP	BABIP	BRR	FRAA	WARP	PF
2019	CRD	RK	18	42	6	3	0	2	8	4	17	0	0	.297/.357/.541	92	2.1	.474	0.0	CF(7) 2.2	0.3	108
2019	JCY	RK+	18	133	9	4	1	2	18	7	59	7	1	.228/.271/.325	63	-3.3	.406	-0.2		-0.1	101
2020	SLN	MLB	19	251	21	11	1	4	22	19	128	2	1	.201/.267/.311	52	0.0	.426	0.0	CF 1	-0.5	87

Comparables: Colby Rasmus, Addison Russell, Bo Bichette

The Report: Fletcher hasn't played a lot of pro ball yet, so there are a lot of things that could happen and a lot of directions this could go in the future. When I saw him near the end of the Appy League season I was struck by a few things. Most obvious was the body. Though he's got a lot of development ahead of him, there isn't much physical projection left and there doesn't need to be. He's very athletic, sturdy and muscular with burst and twitch that show up both sides of the ball. Fletcher has the range and quick first step to handle center, and though I didn't see the arm tested, I've heard great things about that tool as well.

One can easily see where the power will come from after witnessing just one of his incredibly quick and explosive cuts. Unfortunately there is a catch and it is, of course, the hit tool. He actually looked quite lost at the plate and appeared to be lacking in confidence and conviction, constantly caught in between on velocity and flailing at breaking stuff down and away. There's a lot happening mechanically, with some loud hand movement and a big leg kick hindering his ability to stay on time and causing a sort of spiraling effect. Back in September I wrote of Fletcher that he's the type of player whom you can watch strike out three times in four trips to the plate and still walk away fascinated. I believe this will continue to be the case. What does that mean for his career? We'll see.

Variance: Extreme. He's very young and the hit tool is very questionable.

Mark Barry's Fantasy Take: So how do you feel about a mystery box? Inside could be anything—a five-tool stud or a guy that strikes out almost half the time in rookie league en route to a middling and unspectacular minor-league run. Giving up on this sort of profile is obviously silly, but it would take a 300ish-prospect sized league for me to invest.

9 Kodi Whitley RHP   OFP: 55   ETA: 2020
Born: 02/21/95 Age: 25 Bats: R Throws: R Height: 6'4" Weight: 220 Origin: Round 27, 2017 Draft (#814 overall)

YEAR	TEAM	LVL	AGE	W	L	SV	G	GS	IP	H	HR	BB/9	K/9	K	GB%	BABIP	WHIP	ERA	DRA	WARP	PF
2017	CRD	RK	22	0	0	2	12	0	14²	15	0	1.8	11.7	19	47%	.441	1.23	1.84	3.46	0.3	100
2018	PEO	A	23	4	2	9	41	2	71²	67	2	3.3	8.5	68	48%	.319	1.30	2.51	4.34	0.4	98
2019	SFD	AA	24	1	4	7	31	0	39¹	31	3	3.0	10.5	46	43%	.275	1.12	1.83	2.80	0.9	100
2019	MEM	AAA	24	2	0	2	16	0	23²	21	0	1.5	10.3	27	28%	.323	1.06	1.52	2.21	0.9	100
2020	SLN	MLB	25	1	1	0	16	0	17	16	2	3.0	8.7	16	38%	.297	1.28	3.83	4.23	0.2	87

Comparables: Ryan Meisinger, Jesen Therrien, Brock Stewart

The Report: And here is this year's first true Cardinals Devil Magic entry. Whitley was a Division II arm that didn't even get full pool on Day 3 of the 2017 draft. Now in 2019, he's got among the easier upper-90s velocity you will see. It can look like he's just playing catch with his backstop, and the fastball is a lively enough pitch to be swing-and-miss offering on it's own. Whitley also has the requisite potential plus slider, a mid-80s offering with tilt, and even has a better change-up than you'd expect from your typical late-inning two-pitch power arm. He dominated the minors this year and could be ready to step into the late innings for the Cardinals pen as soon as Opening Day.

Variance: Low. Whitley needs to refine the breaking ball some more to have true late-inning stuff, but the fastball is good enough to keep him employed as a major league reliever for a while.

Mark Barry's Fantasy Take: A career minor-league reliever is likely headed for a decently long major-league career as a, well, you get it. Whitley's role will be determined by his breaker, and his fantasy value will dutifully follow. We should see him this season, but his real value will likely be put to the test in 2021 and beyond, based on how many saves he can wrestle away from whomever dons the closer cap in St. Louis.

10 Elehuris Montero 3B   OFP: 50   ETA: 2021
Born: 08/17/98   Age: 21   Bats: R   Throws: R   Height: 6'3"   Weight: 215   Origin: International Free Agent, 2014

YEAR	TEAM	LVL	AGE	PA	R	2B	3B	HR	RBI	BB	K	SB	CS	AVG/OBP/SLG	DRC+	VORP	BABIP	BRR	FRAA	WARP	PF
2017	CRD	RK	18	208	30	16	1	5	36	22	33	0	2	.277/.370/.468	141	10.8	.305	-0.5	3B(41) 2.8	1.5	108
2018	PEO	A	19	425	68	28	3	15	69	33	81	2	0	.322/.381/.529	169	39.7	.372	0.3	3B(77) 2.7	4.6	101
2018	PMB	A+	19	106	13	9	0	1	13	5	22	1	0	.286/.330/.408	118	5.7	.355	0.6	3B(20) 0.8	0.6	95
2019	SFD	AA	20	238	23	8	0	7	18	14	74	0	1	.188/.235/.317	34	-5.4	.245	-0.4	3B(51) -6.2	-1.4	104
2020	SLN	MLB	21	251	23	13	0	7	27	14	81	0	0	.221/.272/.370	69	3.0	.307	-0.4	3B -3	-0.4	87

Comparables: Jorge Polanco, Miguel Andújar, Jonathan Schoop

The Report: After a breakout in 2018, the 2019 campaign was more muted for Montero. Wrist injuries limited his time on the field and surely played a role in his poor performance in the Texas League as well. The bat didn't quite pop as much, although he remains fairly quick to the ball. Montero will still show the ability to drive the ball authoritatively to the opposite field, and you'd imagine the above-average raw will still be there when he's fully healthy again. He has begun to fill out a bit more, and is a below-average runner now. His first step and hands at third are all right, and he has plenty of arm, but there's continued risk he will have to move across the diamond if he gets much bigger/less rangy. You're hoping he can battle third base to more or less of a draw, and that the above-average hit/power combination does more than flash in a healthy 2020 season back in the Texas League. That's a lot of ifs, even though Montero is only 21-year-old.

Variance: High. Hey, lost seasons happen. And Montero dealt with wrist injuries and was 20-years-old for almost the entire Double-A season. But the injuries inject more risk into the profile as does the more filled out frame.

Mark Barry's Fantasy Take: Montero's 2019 was a big fat yikes. Sure, a lot of that can be attributed to injuries, but it's hard not to view the Potential Flags as at least orange. There's still a lot to like, offensively, but a David Freese-y upside doesn't really set the fantasy world on fire.

The Next Ten

11 Mateo Gil SS
Born: 07/24/00   Age: 19   Bats: R   Throws: R   Height: 6'1"   Weight: 180   Origin: Round 3, 2018 Draft (#95 overall)

YEAR	TEAM	LVL	AGE	PA	R	2B	3B	HR	RBI	BB	K	SB	CS	AVG/OBP/SLG	DRC+	VORP	BABIP	BRR	FRAA	WARP	PF
2018	CRD	RK	17	194	27	6	1	1	20	20	51	2	2	.251/.340/.316	85	4.8	.353	0.9	SS(41) 2.9	0.9	108
2019	JCY	RK+	18	225	42	8	2	7	30	17	56	1	3	.270/.324/.431	112	14.8	.333	2.5		1.5	99
2020	SLN	MLB	19	251	21	11	1	4	22	19	85	0	0	.217/.281/.322	59	0.0	.327	0.0	SS 0	-0.5	87

The Cardinals 2018 third-round shortstop was known more for his glove as a draft prospect— unsurprising as the son of slick-fielding infielder Benji Gil—but his bat showed some surprising pop in the Appy League last Summer (that was not really part of his father's game). Gil has a prototypical shortstop's build, lean and athletic, with plenty of arm for the 6—he was a half-decent pitching prospect as a prep as well. As a 19-year-old shortstop who wasn't an elite draft prospect, there can be fits and starts on both sides of the ball, and full-season ball in 2020 will ramp up the game speed for him both offensively and defensively, but there's a potential above-average two-way shortstop lurking in the tools profile.

12 Junior Fernandez RHP

Born: 03/02/97   Age: 23   Bats: R   Throws: R   Height: 6'1"   Weight: 180   Origin: International Free Agent, 2014

YEAR	TEAM	LVL	AGE	W	L	SV	G	GS	IP	H	HR	BB/9	K/9	K	GB%	BABIP	WHIP	ERA	DRA	WARP	PF
2017	PMB	A+	20	5	3	0	16	16	90¹	82	5	3.9	5.8	58	45%	.281	1.34	3.69	4.91	0.4	94
2018	PMB	A+	21	1	0	3	8	0	9²	9	0	1.9	6.5	7	43%	.321	1.14	0.00	4.69	0.0	100
2018	SFD	AA	21	0	0	0	16	0	21	19	1	6.9	7.3	17	36%	.295	1.67	5.14	6.42	-0.4	100
2019	PMB	A+	22	0	0	4	9	0	11²	8	0	6.2	8.5	11	45%	.258	1.37	1.54	4.57	0.0	100
2019	SFD	AA	22	1	1	5	18	0	29	18	0	3.4	13.0	42	48%	.295	1.00	1.55	3.03	0.6	100
2019	MEM	AAA	22	2	1	2	18	0	24¹	17	0	4.1	10.0	27	63%	.274	1.15	1.48	2.36	0.9	100
2019	SLN	MLB	22	0	1	0	13	0	11²	9	2	4.6	12.3	16	50%	.269	1.29	5.40	3.34	0.3	93
2020	*SLN*	*MLB*	*23*	*2*	*2*	*0*	*32*	*0*	*34*	*27*	*4*	*5.4*	*13.6*	*51*	*47%*	*.321*	*1.40*	*4.03*	*4.20*	*0.4*	*87*

Comparables: Touki Toussaint, Jonathan Hernández, Tyrell Jenkins

Fernandez shook off two injury-marred seasons and pitched his way into the Cardinals bullpen at the end of 2019. I wouldn't call his upper-90s fastball as easy as Whitley's, but it's plus-plus velocity all the same. He can sink it or cut it a bit down in the zone, although it can flatten out at times up when he's overthrowing. An upper-80s change-up is the best present secondary, and he'll throw it to both righties and lefties. The pitch flashes plus tumble and fade when he successfully pulls the string on it. A slider sits in the same velo band as the change. It's a little less consistent and can get cutterish, although he will show some with power tilt as well. The delivery is high effort and Fernandez may never throw enough strikes where you'll feel comfortable with him closing games, but the stuff is high leverage, and he could end up with two above-average secondaries to go with his 70-grade fastball.

13 Justin Williams OF

Born: 08/20/95   Age: 24   Bats: L   Throws: R   Height: 6'2"   Weight: 215   Origin: Round 2, 2013 Draft (#52 overall)

YEAR	TEAM	LVL	AGE	PA	R	2B	3B	HR	RBI	BB	K	SB	CS	AVG/OBP/SLG	DRC+	VORP	BABIP	BRR	FRAA	WARP	PF
2017	MNT	AA	21	409	53	21	3	14	72	37	69	6	2	.301/.364/.489	147	18.6	.334	-2.0	RF(80) -4.8, LF(7) 1.2	2.1	102
2018	DUR	AAA	22	386	41	18	0	8	46	25	81	4	3	.258/.313/.376	97	-4.9	.315	-2.7	RF(80) 13.7, LF(2) 1.0	1.8	98
2018	MEM	AAA	22	76	8	3	0	3	11	5	17	0	1	.217/.276/.391	86	-0.6	.240	-1.1	LF(10) 4.2, RF(7) 0.9	0.5	86
2018	TBA	MLB	22	1	0	0	0	0	0	0	0	0	0	.000/.000/.000	83	-0.5	.000	0.0	RF(1) 0.0	0.0	98
2019	SFD	AA	23	61	7	1	0	1	3	4	17	1	0	.193/.246/.263	56	-2.3	.256	-0.1	LF(12) -0.7, RF(2) -0.1	-0.2	105
2019	MEM	AAA	23	119	20	5	0	7	26	16	30	0	0	.353/.437/.608	146	14.2	.439	-0.5	RF(24) 3.9	1.2	93
2020	*SLN*	*MLB*	*24*	*112*	*11*	*4*	*0*	*3*	*13*	*7*	*31*	*1*	*0*	*.240/.293/.388*	*78*	*0.0*	*.308*	*-0.2*	*RF 1*	*0.1*	*87*

Comparables: Xavier Avery, Gabriel Guerrero, Yorman Rodriguez

We paired Arozarena and Williams on last year's list, and Williams didn't have quite the same upper minors breakout as his outfield mate. He got a late start to 2019 recovering from a fractured hand he suffered in the offseason after punching a TV, and then missed another month over the summer after a promotion to Triple-A. Williams did absolutely rake during his time in Memphis and has always had the potential for plus offensive tools, he's just never put it together for a sustained period of time. The above-average regular ceiling is still there if healthy, and with Ozuna leaving as a free agent, and the subsequent trade of Jose Martinez and Arozarena, there might be a clearer path to a major league role in 2020.

14 Génesis Cabrera LHP

Born: 10/10/96   Age: 23   Bats: L   Throws: L   Height: 6'2"   Weight: 190   Origin: International Free Agent, 2013

YEAR	TEAM	LVL	AGE	W	L	SV	G	GS	IP	H	HR	BB/9	K/9	K	GB%	BABIP	WHIP	ERA	DRA	WARP	PF
2017	PCH	A+	20	4	5	0	13	12	69²	45	3	3.2	7.8	60	39%	.230	1.00	2.84	2.83	2.0	96
2017	MNT	AA	20	5	4	0	12	12	64²	75	6	3.8	7.1	51	37%	.332	1.58	3.62	5.63	-0.4	102
2018	MNT	AA	21	7	6	0	21	20	113²	90	11	4.5	9.8	124	35%	.282	1.29	4.12	4.27	1.4	92
2018	SFD	AA	21	1	3	0	5	5	24²	24	3	4.7	7.7	21	37%	.300	1.50	4.74	5.19	0.0	105
2019	MEM	AAA	22	5	6	0	20	18	99	107	20	3.5	9.6	106	42%	.330	1.47	5.91	5.11	1.5	95
2019	SLN	MLB	22	0	2	1	13	2	20¹	23	2	4.9	8.4	19	39%	.323	1.67	4.87	5.53	0.0	92
2020	SLN	MLB	23	3	4	0	38	6	63	65	10	3.8	7.1	49	38%	.296	1.47	4.87	5.06	0.4	87

Comparables: Eduardo Rodriguez, Jake Thompson, Lucas Giolito

Cabrera remains equal parts prospecty and frustrating. He's a lefty with a fastball that regularly hits the upper-90s. It'd be an easy plus-plus offering if the command and control were just a little bit better. He ditched his pretty good slider/cutter thing to focus primarily on his slower—although certainly not slow—12-6 curve in the low-80s. It's potentially pretty good although it's not all the way there yet. He also has a firm change-up in the upper 80s. It has just enough fade and he commands it just well enough on the outer half to righties to make it potentially average. The Cardinals seem to have settled on him as a reliever—which is the right call—and if he tightens up the command (we write this every year) and re-introduces the cutter, he could have late-or-multi-inning utility.

15 Jhon Torres OF

Born: 03/29/00   Age: 20   Bats: R   Throws: R   Height: 6'4"   Weight: 199   Origin: International Free Agent, 2016

YEAR	TEAM	LVL	AGE	PA	R	2B	3B	HR	RBI	BB	K	SB	CS	AVG/OBP/SLG	DRC+	VORP	BABIP	BRR	FRAA	WARP	PF
2017	DIN	RK	17	226	25	7	3	5	35	28	41	4	4	.255/.363/.408	112	13.0	.290	-0.3	RF(29) -0.8, CF(22) -4.6	0.2	88
2018	CLT	RK	18	111	16	3	0	4	16	11	24	3	0	.273/.351/.424	123	2.6	.324	-0.3	RF(24) 5.6, CF(1) -0.1	1.0	107
2018	CRD	RK	18	75	11	6	0	4	14	8	13	1	1	.397/.493/.683	206	12.5	.457	0.2	RF(15) 5.2	1.3	108
2019	JCY	RK+	19	133	24	9	0	6	17	19	36	0	2	.286/.391/.527	151	11.8	.366	0.8		1.1	100
2019	PEO	A	19	75	4	3	0	0	8	7	29	0	1	.167/.240/.212	49	-4.5	.282	-0.6	RF(20) 3.8	0.1	104
2020	SLN	MLB	20	251	22	12	1	5	23	23	89	0	0	.211/.291/.330	66	0.0	.326	-0.4	RF 4, CF 0	0.1	87

Comparables: José Martínez, Abraham Almonte, Dilson Herrera

The Cardinals plucked Torres out of Cleveland's complex at the 2018 trade deadline as part of the return for Oscar Mercado. They then jumped him to the Midwest League a month into the 2019 season, and he predictably struggled during his three weeks on the roster. He was overmatched by full-season arms, especially when they threw their offspeed stuff, but a more age appropriate assignment to Johnson City once the Appy League opened went far better.

Torres just looks like a good right field prospect, tall and lean, strong but still projectable. He has plus bat speed and generates good hand/hip separation. He couldn't really lift the ball against Midwest League arms as he was mostly trying to just stay afloat, but the plus raw power got into games more against age-appropriate pitching. He played right field exclusively for Peoria, but they got him the occasional center field rep in Johnson City. That's ambitious, as Torres is a well-below-average runner and takes short strides that limit his range even in right field. There's going to be a ton of pressure on the bat, but there's markers in here that suggest he can make consistent hard contact with more pro experience.

16   Luken Baker   1B

Born: 03/10/97   Age: 23   Bats: R   Throws: R   Height: 6'4"   Weight: 265   Origin: Round 2C, 2018 Draft (#75 overall)

YEAR	TEAM	LVL	AGE	PA	R	2B	3B	HR	RBI	BB	K	SB	CS	AVG/OBP/SLG	DRC+	VORP	BABIP	BRR	FRAA	WARP	PF
2018	CRD	RK	21	28	10	2	0	1	7	3	4	0	0	.500/.536/.708	212	3.9	.550	-0.7	1B(5) 0.1	0.2	109
2018	PEO	A	21	156	16	9	0	3	15	16	31	0	0	.288/.359/.417	148	2.7	.349	-1.4	1B(20) 0.3	0.8	101
2019	PMB	A+	22	496	47	32	1	10	53	52	112	1	1	.244/.327/.390	118	4.7	.304	-6.1	1B(96) -3.6	0.3	95
2020	SLN	MLB	23	251	25	13	0	8	29	17	71	1	0	.230/.287/.394	77	1.0	.297	-0.5	1B -1	-0.1	87

Comparables: Mark Trumbo, Nate Lowe, Matt Thaiss

Last year we noted that given Baker's significant defensive limitations—he's a fringy first baseman—"The bat better be great." Admittedly, Palm Beach is an absolutely brutal home park if you are a slugger, but .244 and 10 home runs against Florida State League pitching isn't great, and you could argue is in fact a big flashing red light for a polished college power bat. There weren't huge strikeout issues, as Baker knows what to hack at—although given how long it takes him to uncoil his beer league softball swing, there will be swing-and-miss in the zone—and the plus-plus raw power remains. It's length and strength pop, but Baker is plenty strong—his build is best described as "Scandanavian Wife Carrying Champion." The profile here is pretty all or nothing, and his issues timing High-A arms are more concerning to me than the underlying stat line, but Baker's potential 70 power keeps him on my radar for now.

17   Tony Locey   RHP

Born: 07/29/98   Age: 21   Bats: R   Throws: R   Height: 6'3"   Weight: 239   Origin: Round 3, 2019 Draft (#96 overall)

YEAR	TEAM	LVL	AGE	W	L	SV	G	GS	IP	H	HR	BB/9	K/9	K	GB%	BABIP	WHIP	ERA	DRA	WARP	PF
2019	PEO	A	20	1	2	0	10	0	15	15	1	6.0	16.8	28	37%	.483	1.67	6.00	5.21	-0.1	100
2020	SLN	MLB	21	2	2	0	33	0	35	35	6	4.1	10.6	41	39%	.328	1.46	4.85	5.00	0.2	87

Comparables: Juan Jaime, Rhiner Cruz, Jaye Chapman

The Cardinals third-round pick out of Georgia, Locey is a hefty righty with a big fastball. He sits mid-90s with good sink and shows a potentially above-average slider as well. He could struggle with his control both in college and in his pro debut, and his uptempo, full-wind-up delivery can have a lot going on, but he repeats it well enough to project improvements w/r/t throwing strikes. Nonetheless he might be a better fit in the bullpen than the rotation, and only really started full-time his Junior year with the Bulldogs. Locey's curveball shows a pronounced hump in the mid-70s, and his split-change is still inconsistent, so he may not have that pesky third pitch evaluators like to see for starting pitching prospects. He certainly looks the part of an innings eating starter, and I imagine the Cardinals will keep him stretched out for the foreseeable future, but Locey could have the most impact as a power sinker/slider setup man.

18   Jake Woodford   RHP

Born: 10/28/96   Age: 23   Bats: R   Throws: R   Height: 6'4"   Weight: 220   Origin: Round 1, 2015 Draft (#39 overall)

YEAR	TEAM	LVL	AGE	W	L	SV	G	GS	IP	H	HR	BB/9	K/9	K	GB%	BABIP	WHIP	ERA	DRA	WARP	PF
2017	PMB	A+	20	7	6	0	23	21	119	128	7	2.9	5.4	72	47%	.313	1.40	3.10	5.72	-0.7	92
2018	SFD	AA	21	3	8	0	16	16	81	94	13	3.9	6.2	56	48%	.309	1.59	5.22	6.02	-0.6	104
2018	MEM	AAA	21	5	5	0	12	12	64	64	5	3.8	6.3	45	38%	.292	1.42	4.50	4.85	0.5	93
2019	MEM	AAA	22	9	8	0	26	26	151²	124	22	4.5	7.8	131	37%	.242	1.31	4.15	3.38	4.9	95
2020	SLN	MLB	23	1	1	0	3	3	15	15	2	3.9	7.0	11	38%	.284	1.45	4.90	5.16	0.1	87

Comparables: Jeanmar Gómez, Kohl Stewart, Peter Lambert

The scouting report on Woodford hasn't really changed much since he was a first round pick in 2015. He features a low-90s heater that can get up to 95 with occasional sink. He'll also show a cut fastball as well. When Woodford is hitting his spots and changing eye levels, he doesn't need much in the way of secondaries, and none of the secondaries are going to jump off the page here anyway. There's a slurvy slider that he works mostly gloveside and off the plate, and a big yakker of a mid-70s curve. He'll use a change-up sparingly as well. None of the offspeed pitches really project as even average, more fringy but useful, as Woodford mixes them in enough to keep hitters off the fastball and cutter. The stuff really hasn't taken as big a step forward as you might have hoped, but given his size and repeatable delivery, Woodford should be able to eat innings in the back of the rotation or the bullpen. He's got a less fastball than Locey, but perhaps a little better shot to start, and he's certainly closer. Pick 'em.

19 Angel Rondon RHP

Born: 12/01/97 Age: 22 Bats: R Throws: R Height: 6'2" Weight: 185 Origin: International Free Agent, 2016

YEAR	TEAM	LVL	AGE	W	L	SV	G	GS	IP	H	HR	BB/9	K/9	K	GB%	BABIP	WHIP	ERA	DRA	WARP	PF
2017	CRD	RK	19	3	3	0	11	8	47²	46	2	3.2	7.7	41	43%	.317	1.32	2.64	3.89	1.1	110
2018	SCO	A-	20	0	4	0	5	5	29	29	3	2.2	7.1	23	38%	.302	1.24	3.72	5.26	0.0	95
2018	PEO	A	20	3	2	0	10	10	59	49	7	2.6	8.7	57	42%	.259	1.12	2.90	4.04	0.8	102
2019	PMB	A+	21	5	1	0	8	8	45	26	3	3.4	9.4	47	41%	.209	0.96	2.20	2.99	1.1	96
2019	SFD	AA	21	6	6	0	20	20	115	99	11	3.3	8.8	112	37%	.283	1.23	3.21	4.33	0.9	102
2020	SLN	MLB	22	2	2	0	33	0	35	36	6	3.9	8.0	31	37%	.297	1.46	4.99	5.15	0.1	87

Like Woodford, Rondon doesn't have big stuff, but mixes everything well enough to project as a potential major league piece. His fastball sits in the low-90s with a bit of armside run, although it can be hittable in the zone. His change-up is potentially above-average. It doesn't always have a ton of fade, but the significant velocity difference—it tops out around 80—can induce swings out of a Bugs Bunny cartoon. Rondon also sells the change well with consistent arm speed. The breaking ball is below-average, a short, slurvy slider either side of 80. If Rondon can tighten up the breaker to give him a gloveside option, he could slot in to the Cardinals pitching staff quickly as a fifth starter or long reliever.

20 Alvaro Seijas RHP

Born: 10/10/98 Age: 21 Bats: R Throws: R Height: 6'1" Weight: 175 Origin: International Free Agent, 2015

YEAR	TEAM	LVL	AGE	W	L	SV	G	GS	IP	H	HR	BB/9	K/9	K	GB%	BABIP	WHIP	ERA	DRA	WARP	PF
2017	JCY	RK	18	4	3	0	12	12	63¹	79	2	2.8	9.0	63	52%	.393	1.56	4.97	5.89	0.1	98
2018	PEO	A	19	5	8	1	25	22	129¹	149	14	4.2	5.8	84	41%	.332	1.62	4.52	6.92	-2.7	100
2019	PEO	A	20	4	5	0	14	14	80	73	6	3.2	8.0	71	46%	.300	1.26	2.92	5.67	-0.5	103
2019	PMB	A+	20	4	1	0	10	10	54¹	54	2	4.3	7.1	43	48%	.313	1.47	2.65	5.98	-0.6	95
2020	SLN	MLB	21	2	2	0	33	0	35	34	5	3.8	5.9	23	40%	.271	1.41	4.61	4.92	0.2	87

Comparables: Chris Flexen, Ronald Herrera, Jonathan Hernández

Seijas struggled during his first taste of full-season ball 2018 in Peoria, but a return engagement last year went better and he carried over his success to the Florida State League after a midseason promotion. Seijas is a shorter righty, and the stuff won't wow you, but there's three potentially average pitches in the arsenal. His fastball sits mostly low-90s but can touch 95 and there's some sink and run from his three-quarters slot. Given the arm slot, the low-80s curveball will show surprising depth, and while it's not a huge downer, there's tight, late break, and he commands the pitch well. He also shows a potentially average sinking change, although he can use the curve as an out pitch against lefties as well. Seijas has an uptempo delivery with some effort, and he can have bouts of wildness and command issues due to that. He's also on the slimmer side, so command and durability might force him to the pen despite the well-rounded arsenal.

Personal Cheeseball

PC Merandy Gonzalez RHP

Born: 10/09/95 Age: 24 Bats: R Throws: R Height: 6'0" Weight: 216 Origin: International Free Agent, 2013

YEAR	TEAM	LVL	AGE	W	L	SV	G	GS	IP	H	HR	BB/9	K/9	K	GB%	BABIP	WHIP	ERA	DRA	WARP	PF
2017	COL	A	21	8	1	0	11	11	69²	50	3	1.7	8.4	65	43%	.253	0.90	1.55	3.14	1.7	90
2017	SLU	A+	21	4	2	0	6	6	36¹	33	1	2.0	5.9	24	43%	.271	1.13	2.23	4.64	0.2	106
2017	JUP	A+	21	1	0	1	5	3	24¹	18	0	1.8	5.2	14	56%	.247	0.95	1.11	5.25	0.0	95
2018	JAX	AA	22	3	6	0	14	14	73	68	7	4.1	5.8	47	41%	.282	1.38	4.32	4.93	0.4	94
2018	MIA	MLB	22	2	1	0	8	1	22	31	4	3.3	7.8	19	34%	.375	1.77	5.73	7.39	-0.6	97
2019	CRD	RK	23	0	0	0	5	2	6	4	0	3.0	15.0	10	33%	.444	1.00	0.00	2.20	0.2	111
2019	SFD	AA	23	2	3	4	34	1	40²	54	5	6.9	8.6	39	50%	.383	2.09	6.64	7.58	-1.5	110
2020	SLN	MLB	24	2	2	0	33	0	35	38	6	3.6	7.6	30	41%	.303	1.48	5.26	5.30	0.0	87

Merandy Gonzalez's player card tells a very familiar story. He dominated the low minors off of above-average fastball velocity and feel for a below-average, but projectable, curve. He wasn't a non-prospect by any means. He was the kind of OFP 50 with significant relief risk that dots the next ten of lesser systems, but you could picture him sitting 95 in short bursts, and the curve would flash 55 when he got it up into the low-80s. These prospects can hit a wall in Double-A and sure enough Gonzalez struggled as a starter in Jacksonville in 2018. Nevertheless, as he was on the 40-man roster, the Marlins called him up early that year to throw a few innings out of their bullpen because they needed a healthy, fresh arm. As you'd expect, that didn't go any better.

Miami tried to get him through waivers before 2019. He was still prospecty enough that the Giants claimed him and tried to sneak him through themselves, and that's how he ended up with the Cardinals. St. Louis did get him through waivers midseason in the midst of more struggles in Double-A, this time as a reliever. The fastball is low-90s now—and he never got much extension. The curve doesn't look as sharp either, still that below-average one from the low minors. He is—if you want to be technical and a prospect list is inherently littered with weird technicalities—not even part of the Cardinals system at the moment, as he has "elected minor league free agency." Although that might put the agency, so to speak, on the wrong party.

Overall future potential is just that, and it often goes unrealized. I saw a couple Merandy Gonazlez outings back in 2016 when he was in the Penn League with Brooklyn. I saw the possibilities. They weren't lofty, but there was major league utility in his right arm. He didn't end up in the greatest situation for his development, and there were injuries along the way. This story is among the more common in the minor leagues, but definitionally we rarely get to see such denouement within the column inches of a prospect list.

Low Minors Sleeper

LMS Patrick Romeri OF
Born: 06/29/01 Age: 19 Bats: R Throws: R Height: 6'3" Weight: 195 Origin: Round 12, 2019 Draft (#365 overall)

YEAR	TEAM	LVL	AGE	PA	R	2B	3B	HR	RBI	BB	K	SB	CS	AVG/OBP/SLG	DRC+	VORP	BABIP	BRR	FRAA	WARP	PF
2019	CRD	RK	18	162	23	6	3	6	20	19	46	4	0	.246/.346/.464	110	7.5	.318	0.6	RF(37) 1.7, CF(1) 0.1	0.7	106
2020	SLN	MLB	19	251	21	11	1	4	22	23	96	2	1	.201/.280/.310	58	0.0	.330	0.0	RF 0, CF 0	-0.5	87

The Cardinals paid a little bit overslot to sign Romeri in the 12th round of last year's draft. He was just 17 on draft day and has a plus power/speed combination that could prove worth every penny—with some surplus value to spare. There's ferocious bat speed for a Day 3 prep, but the swing really only has one gear, and there could be a fair bit of swing-and-miss both in and out of the zone. Romeri has a right field profile as well, and while the power, speed, and arm all fit that mold, the hit tool is raw enough to keep him off the list proper for now.

Top Talents 25 and Under (born 4/1/93 or later)

1. Jack Flaherty
2. Dylan Carlson
3. Nolan Gorman
4. Dakota Hudson
5. Zack Thompson
6. Tommy Edman
7. Tyler O'Neill
8. Ivan Herrera
9. Andrew Knizner
10. Jordan Hicks

Carlson has the potential to be a five-tool outfielder who can play center and may have multiple All-Star appearances in his future. The fact that he only ranks second on this list says a whole lot about the type of pitcher Flaherty has turned into. The right-hander just put together a 7.1 WARP season, just missing out on 200 innings and from about the All-Star break through the end of the season, was arguably the most dominant pitcher in baseball. The slider, curve, and sinker are all plus, and he has mid-90s heat that moves. With still another year of eligibility for this list after this year, he's likely to anchor the Cardinals' rotation for the foreseeable future.

The drop-off from Flaherty to Hudson is stark, but while Carlson and Gorman split the two because of the prospect pair's respective ceilings, the other young arm has all the makings of a solid mid-rotation piece. DRA insists his 2019 numbers were a bit lucky, but the sinkerballer avoided the long ball among the best of 'em, and despite pedestrian strikeout numbers, that's a pretty big deal in today's game.

Hudson profiles similarly to Thompson, not so much in terms of stuff or repertoire but in the fact that the latter profiles as a mid-rotation piece once he makes his way to St. Louis. That potential is enough for him to slot in ahead of a trio of major leaguers. Edman is the most surprising name, as the Cardinal Devil Magic Factory got him off the assembly line just in time for him to make a difference down the stretch, whether it was spelling the aging Matt Carpenter at third or the offensively-inept Harrison Bader in center. Edman played five positions for the Cardinals and was worth 2.3 WARP in a little more than a half-season's worth of action. This is probably what he is, but it's pretty danged good.

Edman represents the end of the "polished major leaguer or high-upside prospect" portion of the list. O'Neill is still all potential. It's impressive and powerful potential, to be clear, but until he puts it all together in games he'll still be but a dream. Then there's Hicks, who is an erratic but electric hurler who underwent Tommy John surgery in June 2019. Elite, back-end reliever is still the ceiling there, but we're a ways away from finding out if he can put it all together.

Eyewitness Reports

Eyewitness Report: Nolan Gorman

Evaluator: Nathan Graham
Report Date: 07/16/2019
Dates Seen: 5/10/19; 6/19/19
Risk Factor: High
Physical/Health: Large frame, athletic and muscular build with a strong lower half; projection remains for additional upper body growth.

Tool	Future Grade	Report
Hit	50	Slightly open stance, quiet pre-swing with a leg kick timing mechanism. Swing can get a little stiff, lacking fluidity at times, length in the swing; above average bat speed with very quick hands. Recognizes pitches well but will still get out front on secondaries occasionally. There's always going to be some swing and miss in his game but the hit tool will improve with increased experience and exposure to more advanced pitching.
Power	70	Double plus raw power generated from strong frame and above average bat speed; gets loft in the swing, ball jumps off the bat, easy power to all fields. Currently plays down in game due to contact issues.
Baserunning/ Speed	45	4.20 clock home to first from the left side; will play fringe average with maturity.
Glove	50	Unspectacular, yet solid at third base. Lacks the range to be anything more than average, but has the instincts and hands to stick at the hot corner.
Arm	60	Above average arm strength, accurate and shows good carry, more than enough for third base.

Conclusion: Gorman has all the tools to eventually become a future all-star. He's still raw at the plate and will need to continue to make adjustments to his swing and approach if he's going to maximize his power. The arm and glove are solid enough to allow him to stick at third but the bat is strong enough to handle a move across the diamond if needed. The high ceiling comes with a strong amount of risk due to his youth but it's an exciting profile due to the exceptional power.

Tampa Bay Rays

The State of the System

It's not quite as deep or quite as good as last year's version, but the Rays still have an extremely strong system topped by the best prospect in baseball.

The Top Ten

1 Wander Franco SS   OFP: 70   ETA: 2021

Born: 03/01/01   Age: 19   Bats: B   Throws: R   Height: 5'10"   Weight: 189   Origin: International Free Agent, 2017

YEAR	TEAM	LVL	AGE	PA	R	2B	3B	HR	RBI	BB	K	SB	CS	AVG/OBP/SLG	DRC+	VORP	BABIP	BRR	FRAA	WARP	PF
2018	PRI	RK	17	273	46	10	7	11	57	27	19	4	3	.351/.418/.587	166	35.4	.346	-0.4	SS(53) -5.3	2.4	115
2019	BGR	A	18	272	42	16	5	6	29	30	20	14	9	.318/.390/.506	158	29.3	.318	0.1	SS(53) -1.0	2.6	103
2019	PCH	A+	18	223	40	11	2	3	24	26	15	4	5	.339/.408/.464	175	30.9	.346	4.3	SS(44) 8.1	3.9	97
2020	TBA	MLB	19	251	27	12	2	6	27	25	31	2	1	.271/.348/.414	108	0.0	.294	-0.3	SS 2	1.3	88

Comparables: Vladimir Guerrero Jr., Mike Trout, Manny Machado

The Report: The Rays signed Franco for nearly $4 million back in 2017, and that is going to end up looking like a bargain. "El Patrón" was the best hitter in both the Midwest and Florida State League this year, putting up excellent numbers against much older competition. The bat is elite, reminiscent of Vlad Jr., a rare combination of contact and power. Blessed with a superb eye and plus bat speed, Franco commands the zone, gladly taking walks, but also punishing mistakes. This summer at Bowling Green the unparalleled bat control was on display as Franco went nearly two weeks without a swing and miss. The raw power is plus and will play plus in-game as he continues to mature physically.

The rest of the tools are not nearly as sexy. Lacking the arm strength for short, he'll eventually find a home at second base where he will be an above-average defender. On the bases, he's extremely aggressive to the point of recklessness, at times, but with continued experience he should become an average baserunner. Neither of these limitations should be much of a concern with a bat that looks to eventually become one of the best in the league.

Variance: Medium. Inherent risk due to the fact that he's still a teenager and yet to play above High-A but watch him hit and your worries will be put to rest.

Mark Barry's Fantasy Take: It's hard to read Franco's write up and not get Tex Avery vibes (no, I didn't have to google that as opposed to just writing "the wolf cartoon with the bulging eyes"). The home run numbers don't look great, but the slugging numbers sure do, and there's plenty of time for that raw power to manifest itself in the form of dingers. Even Franco's limitations (might move to second base) don't really matter in a fantasy context, so there really aren't any nits to pick here. Last season, Nostra-Carsley predicted that Franco "could rank 1-1 a year from now". Turns out he knows some stuff some of the time. The 18-year-old is a top-30ish dynasty player for me, and could be awfully Javy Baez-y except without strikeouts (read: really, really good).

★ ★ ★ *2020 Top 101 Prospect* **#28** ★ ★ ★

2 Brendan McKay LHP

Born: 12/18/95 Age: 24 Bats: L Throws: L Height: 6'2" Weight: 212 Origin: Round 1, 2017 Draft (#4 overall)

YEAR	TEAM	LVL	AGE	PA	R	2B	3B	HR	RBI	BB	K	SB	CS	AVG/OBP/SLG	DRC+	VORP	BABIP	BRR	FRAA	WARP	PF
2017	HUD	A-	21	149	16	4	1	4	22	21	33	2	0	.232/.349/.376	120	3.7	.281	-1.3	1B(21)-1.1, P(6)0.1	0.2	93
2018	BGR	A	22	91	12	2	0	1	16	28	13	0	0	.254/.484/.333	180	1.0	.306	-3.1	1B(9)-0.3, P(6)0.1	0.5	101
2018	PCH	A+	22	139	19	6	1	5	21	16	38	0	0	.210/.317/.403	97	1.5	.260	0.5	1B(18)-0.4, P(11)-0.3	0.1	101
2019	MNT	AA	23	90	8	2	0	0	8	7	27	0	1	.167/.256/.192	50	-4.2	.245	0.3	P(8)0.5	-0.3	99
2019	DUR	AAA	23	78	11	2	0	5	11	10	24	1	0	.239/.346/.493	94	1.3	.289	-0.3	P(7)-0.2	0.0	100
2019	TBA	MLB	23	11	2	0	0	1	1	1	2	0	0	.200/.273/.500	57	0.2	.143	-0.1	P(13)-0.1	0.0	92
2020	TBA	MLB	24	35	3	2	0	1	4	4	11	0	0	.207/.298/.351	76	1.0	.290	0.0	1B 0	-0.1	88

Comparables: Chris McGuiness, Chris Shaw, Pete Alonso

YEAR	TEAM	LVL	AGE	W	L	SV	G	GS	IP	H	HR	BB/9	K/9	K	GB%	BABIP	WHIP	ERA	DRA	WARP	PF
2017	HUD	A-	21	1	0	0	6	6	20	10	3	2.2	9.4	21	53%	.159	0.75	1.80	2.68	0.6	93
2018	RAY	RK	22	0	0	0	2	2	6	2	0	1.5	13.5	9	58%	.167	0.50	1.50	0.71	0.3	101
2018	BGR	A	22	2	0	0	6	6	24²	8	1	0.7	14.6	40	63%	.167	0.41	1.09	1.44	1.1	103
2018	PCH	A+	22	3	2	0	11	9	47²	45	2	2.1	10.2	54	39%	.350	1.17	3.21	3.90	0.7	99
2019	MNT	AA	23	3	0	0	8	7	41²	25	2	1.9	13.4	62	44%	.280	0.82	1.30	2.51	1.2	95
2019	DUR	AAA	23	3	0	0	7	6	32	17	1	2.5	11.2	40	49%	.229	0.81	0.84	1.54	1.6	102
2019	TBA	MLB	23	2	4	0	13	11	49	53	8	2.9	10.3	56	37%	.331	1.41	5.14	5.79	0.0	96
2020	TBA	MLB	24	5	5	0	18	18	77	73	12	2.9	8.6	73	39%	.287	1.27	4.15	4.44	1.0	88

Comparables: Dan Straily, Rogelio Armenteros, Joe Musgrove

The Report: After dominating the upper minors in the first half of 2019, McKay just barely qualifies for this list, having tossed 49 innings for the Rays. It was an uneven major-league debut for the polished lefty. His fastball actually ticked up in the majors, sitting 93-94 and touching 96. He spots it well to both sides, although there isn't a ton of wiggle. In the majors, he leaned heavily on his potential plus curveball. Uncle Chuck is a low-90s, sharp 1-7 breaker at its best, but will roll or flatten out some when he's spamming it. McKay mostly eschewed his change—which has had average projection in the past—for a fringy cutter against righties. He has an ideal frame and delivery for a starting pitcher, but his plus command didn't show up consistently, and McKay's fastball and cutter got punished in the zone by major league hitters.

We still list McKay as a two-way player, but it's fairly clear at this point that his future is on the mound. His arm got him to the majors faster than his bat could develop, but it was always a bit of a longshot that the offensive profile would play as a DH even with full-time hitting development. He may have some Michael Lorenzenish utility if the Rays want to get creative, but a solid number three starter is valuable enough on its own.

Variance: Low. McKay has about as much major-league experience as you can have while still being eligible for this list, and he was a polished lefty even in college. He needs to tighten up his command to hit this OFP, but there have always been positive markers there.

Mark Barry's Fantasy Take: McKay is a tricky one (there's the top-level analysis you came for). The lefty enjoyed some success strikeout-wise in a late-season cup of coffee, but didn't get a ton of swinging strikes, which could signal trouble for sustainability. Having said that, a hilariously low strand rate and a hilariously high BABIP wreaked havoc on his ERA, so we could see some positive regression on that front. It's unlikely McKay will be a star, but if the Rays allow him to log some innings, we could see a handful of SP3 seasons scattered on his otherwise around-average resume. I do not think we'll see much offense, so don't count on it.

★   ★   ★ *2020 Top 101 Prospect* **#30** ★   ★   ★

3 **Shane Baz** **RHP**   OFP: 60   ETA: 2022
Born: 06/17/99   Age: 21   Bats: R   Throws: R   Height: 6'2"   Weight: 190   Origin: Round 1, 2017 Draft (#12 overall)

YEAR	TEAM	LVL	AGE	W	L	SV	G	GS	IP	H	HR	BB/9	K/9	K	GB%	BABIP	WHIP	ERA	DRA	WARP	PF
2017	PIR	RK	18	0	3	0	10	10	23²	26	2	5.3	7.2	19	51%	.348	1.69	3.80	7.48	-0.4	95
2018	BRI	RK	19	4	3	0	10	10	45¹	45	2	4.6	10.7	54	64%	.344	1.50	3.97	6.79	-0.3	98
2018	PRI	RK	19	0	2	0	2	2	7	11	1	7.7	6.4	5	48%	.417	2.43	7.71	7.16	-0.1	111
2019	BGR	A	20	3	2	0	17	17	81¹	63	5	4.1	9.6	87	39%	.279	1.23	2.99	3.88	1.2	102
2020	TBA	MLB	21	2	2	0	33	0	35	35	6	4.0	7.8	30	37%	.294	1.45	4.99	5.02	0.1	88

Comparables: Drew Anderson, Elvin Ramirez, Yennsy Diaz

The Report: The trade with the Pirates that brought Baz to Tampa Bay in 2018 is looking more and more like highway robbery. Austin Meadows and Tyler Glasnow have already made their mark, and it looks as though Baz will do the same after a successful year with Low-A Bowling Green. The tall and slender righty has easy gas, pumping 96-98, and he locates the heat well in the upper half of the zone. Add a deceptive three-quarters arm slot and his fastball is a true swing-and-miss pitch. He does have a tendency to overthrow at times, which results in loss of command, but it doesn't seem to be a mechanical issue. Baz also employs a sharp, plus slider, sitting mid-80s and touching 88, featuring excellent tilt. That's a second out-pitch in his arsenal. A mid-80s changeup is a work in progress, but it shows some potential with solid arm-side fade. There is a lot to like in Baz's profile. He has quick arm action, he's athletic, and has already shown that he has an idea of how to pitch. The ceiling is quite high with his lethal fastball/slider combination alone.

Variance: High. With any young flame-thrower, the risk of future arm issues will always be present, and his shorter arm action adds to the injury risk. Additionally, he will need to start filling up the strike zone a little more to ease command concerns.

Mark Barry's Fantasy Take: Man, that Chris Archer trade is just the gift that keeps on giving (well, for the Rays, at least). If it's ceiling you seek, might I interest you in a little Baz? While McKay offers the stability of a high floor, Baz is all upside baby. His charitability has been troubling this season, dishing out a small village worth of free passes, but the improvement of his changeup as a legit third pitch has me dreaming on an SP2 flirting with that top tier of fantasy aces.

★   ★   ★ *2020 Top 101 Prospect* **#50** ★   ★   ★

4 **Matthew Liberatore** **LHP**   OFP: 60   ETA: 2022
Born: 11/06/99   Age: 20   Bats: L   Throws: L   Height: 6'5"   Weight: 200   Origin: Round 1, 2018 Draft (#16 overall)

YEAR	TEAM	LVL	AGE	W	L	SV	G	GS	IP	H	HR	BB/9	K/9	K	GB%	BABIP	WHIP	ERA	DRA	WARP	PF
2018	RAY	RK	18	1	2	0	8	8	27²	16	0	3.6	10.4	32	45%	.258	0.98	0.98	2.03	1.2	98
2019	BGR	A	19	6	2	0	16	15	78¹	70	2	3.6	8.7	76	58%	.311	1.29	3.10	4.78	0.4	104
2020	TBA	MLB	20	2	2	0	33	0	35	34	5	4.0	7.2	28	52%	.281	1.40	4.41	4.65	0.3	88

Comparables: Brad Hand, Jake Thompson, Eduardo Rodriguez

The Report: A first-round pick in 2018, Liberatore has quickly risen through the prospect ranks. The lefty throws from a high-three-quarters slot, creating excellent extension and downhill plane with his tall, wiry frame. He offers a four-pitch mix, although none are true swing-and-miss offerings currently. Liberatore's fastball sits 93-94 mph with occasional, slight tail and the command isn't there yet so hitters can square it up more than you'd like. His best pitch is an 11-6, upper-70s curveball that comes in on a high angle and features late bite. It has the makings of a potential plus pitch. A mid-80s changeup with hard dive also shows potential, but consistent feel and command still are issues. His fourth pitch is a below-average slider in the low 80s. Given his age and limited pro experience, Liberatore showed a lot of poise on the mound, which is a positive marker for his development. The profile isn't electric, but it offers potential along with a relatively high floor for a prep arm.

Variance: High. Without a true swing-and-miss pitch at the moment to lean heavily on, Liberatore will need to fine-tune his command at each step in the minors.

Mark Barry's Fantasy Take: No shots at Liberatore. He's a good, if not great, pitching prospect. I'm just a little concerned about the lack of strikeouts in the minors. He got a ton of groundballs in 2019, but his lack of a true swing-and-miss pitch doesn't bode well for his ability to be a strikeout asset in the big leagues. Sometimes these low-K, high-GB guys turn into Dallas Keuchel. Other times they're late-career Andrew Cashner. The boring and hedging answer is that Liberatore will probably wind up as something in the middle, with a Jalen Beeks-type future of bulking after an opener potentially in his future.

★ ★ ★ *2020 Top 101 Prospect* **#71** ★ ★ ★

5 Shane McClanahan LHP OFP: 60 ETA: 2021

Born: 04/28/97 Age: 23 Bats: L Throws: L Height: 6'1" Weight: 200 Origin: Round 1C, 2018 Draft (#31 overall)

YEAR	TEAM	LVL	AGE	W	L	SV	G	GS	IP	H	HR	BB/9	K/9	K	GB%	BABIP	WHIP	ERA	DRA	WARP	PF
2019	BGR	A	22	4	4	0	11	10	53	38	3	5.3	12.6	74	48%	.304	1.30	3.40	3.83	0.8	103
2019	PCH	A+	22	6	1	0	9	8	49¹	33	1	1.5	10.8	59	44%	.250	0.83	1.46	2.48	1.5	98
2019	MNT	AA	22	1	1	0	4	4	18¹	30	3	2.9	10.3	21	43%	.450	1.96	8.35	7.93	-0.7	96
2020	TBA	MLB	23	2	2	0	33	0	35	34	5	3.4	9.4	37	41%	.308	1.36	4.38	4.50	0.3	88

Comparables: Greg Smith, Gregory Soto, Steven Matz

The Report: McClanahan teamed with fellow first-rounders Baz and Liberatore to anchor a formidable rotation in Bowling Green. But, while his teammates spent the entire summer in Kentucky, McClanahan breezed through two levels before finishing up in the Southern League. His fastball is electric, sitting in the high 90s with deception. It's the type of pitch that makes hitters uncomfortable. He features two secondaries, a 12-6 curve, and a change that sits in the high 80s. Neither is perfected yet. While he still struggles with consistency with the breaker, the curve can be a knee-buckler when he gets it right. On the mound, he's an extremely quick worker, with some moderate effort in the delivery. This causes him to get out of sync at times, and negatively impacts his command projection. The future might eventually be in the bullpen, but for now the Rays seem committed to using his high-ceiling arm in a starting role.

Variance: Medium. The lack of consistency in the secondaries and command are a concern, but the plus-plus fastball makes up for a lot.

Mark Barry's Fantasy Take: I am a very large fan of strikeouts. McLahahan punched out 154 dudes in 120 2/3 innings this season and has a premium, plus heater. If the breaker gets consistent, good lord, look out. In addition, while his former rotation-mates Baz and Liberatore topped out in Bowling Green, McLanahan made it to Double-A for four starts, making a 2020 big-league look more of a realistic possibility. Blah blah blah TINSTAAPP (I'm just as guilty of this by the way) blah blah. There's a bullpen risk, sure, but the pure upside makes McLanahan a fringe-101 guy at the very worst.

★ ★ ★ *2020 Top 101 Prospect* **#73** ★ ★ ★

6 Vidal Brujan 2B OFP: 60 ETA: 2020

Born: 02/09/98 Age: 22 Bats: B Throws: R Height: 5'9" Weight: 155 Origin: International Free Agent, 2014

YEAR	TEAM	LVL	AGE	PA	R	2B	3B	HR	RBI	BB	K	SB	CS	AVG/OBP/SLG	DRC+	VORP	BABIP	BRR	FRAA	WARP	PF
2017	HUD	A-	19	302	51	15	5	3	20	34	36	16	8	.285/.378/.415	155	20.4	.321	-3.7	2B(65) 14.9	3.4	92
2018	BGR	A	20	434	86	18	5	5	41	48	53	43	15	.313/.395/.427	144	41.0	.351	8.2	2B(88) 4.4	4.6	100
2018	PCH	A+	20	114	26	7	2	4	12	15	15	12	4	.347/.434/.582	172	13.8	.380	1.0	2B(24) 4.5	1.7	101
2019	PCH	A+	21	196	28	8	3	1	15	17	26	24	5	.290/.357/.386	131	18.2	.333	5.5	2B(29) 0.7, SS(14) 0.7	2.0	96
2019	MNT	AA	21	233	28	9	4	3	25	20	35	24	8	.266/.336/.391	95	4.8	.304	-2.6	2B(33) 2.7, SS(14) -0.1	0.6	98
2020	TBA	MLB	22	35	3	2	0	1	3	3	6	1	1	.243/.305/.358	79	2.0	.284	0.0	2B 1	0.1	88

Comparables: Luis Valbuena, Corban Joseph, Thairo Estrada

The Report: It is hard to crack the top five in this organization, as illustrated well by Brujan, who earned two double-plus grades off a look last season. His speed is plus-plus out of the box as he accelerates quickly and reaches his top speed in a flash. It forces infielders to work quickly and helps him to get infield hits. The hit tool could be 70-grade. He shows quality bat speed and control of the barrel, rarely swinging and missing in our looks. Brujan works the whole field, attacks fastballs, recognizes offspeed and knows what he can swing at and drive. While he won't ever be known as a home-run hitter (we think, baseballs and such), there is enough strength here to hit a lot of doubles and triples.

Defensively, he has primarily played second and short, showing quality range and a quick first step. His hands are fringe and he has had troubles with his throwing accuracy, leading this author to speculate that he could see time in the outfield, where his speed would be a true asset.

Variance: Medium. The quality of the hit tool and speed gives him major-league value even if the defense forces a move to another position. Being the Rays, he might be playing elsewhere soon, especially since he is Rule 5 eligible.

Mark Barry's Fantasy Take: I'm not sure if you're aware of this, but steals are rare in fantasy, and in baseball writ large. Brujan is fast, oh so fast, not only stealing tons of bases, but stealing them relatively efficiently. Last season he paired the speed with a double-digit walk rate and slugged nearly .460. That's an Adalberto Mondesi-type, no-doubt top-30 dynasty guy. This year the walks took a step back, and he slugged under .400. The speed and contact rate still plays, to be sure, but if he doesn't at least feign power, that's more Mallex Smith—still valuable, but not unequivocally elite.

─────────────── ★ ★ ★ *2020 Top 101 Prospect* **#95** ★ ★ ★ ───────────────

7 Xavier Edwards 2B/SS   OFP: 55   ETA: Late 2021/Early 2022

Born: 08/09/99   Age: 20   Bats: B   Throws: R   Height: 5'10"   Weight: 175   Origin: Round 1, 2018 Draft (#38 overall)

YEAR	TEAM	LVL	AGE	PA	R	2B	3B	HR	RBI	BB	K	SB	CS	AVG/OBP/SLG	DRC+	VORP	BABIP	BRR	FRAA	WARP	PF
2018	PDR	RK	18	88	19	4	1	0	11	13	10	12	1	.384/.471/.466	187	13.5	.438	1.9	SS(15) 3.1	1.5	105
2018	TRI	A-	18	107	21	4	0	0	5	18	15	10	0	.314/.438/.360	181	9.9	.380	-0.3	SS(19) -1.1, 2B(5) 0.0	1.1	93
2019	FTW	A	19	344	44	13	4	1	30	30	35	20	9	.336/.392/.414	141	24.6	.371	0.2	2B(51) 4.1, SS(21) 3.1	3.4	106
2019	LEL	A+	19	217	32	5	4	0	13	14	19	14	2	.301/.349/.367	102	15.3	.331	3.5	2B(35) 0.2, SS(9) -1.2	0.9	100
2020	TBA	MLB	20	251	24	11	1	2	22	21	38	10	2	.278/.341/.367	92	2.0	.325	0.6	2B 2, SS 0	0.9	88

Comparables: José Ramírez, J.P. Crawford, Victor Robles

The Report: Edwards has borderline elite, game-changing speed. That's the top line summary—and by this point in the report the dynasty players have already put him near the top of their draft boards—but he's not a mere burner. He has a potential plus hit tool as well. Edwards knows the zone well and sprays the ball line-to-line with his quick hands and wrists. The swing is not geared to elevate, and the power projection is well-below-average, but the speed should allow him to grab an extra base or two when he shoots one in to the gaps.

Edwards split his time between second and shortstop this year, but second base is his likely long term home due to fringy arm strength. The hands and actions work well on the right side of the infield, and he has good instincts on grounders, so while I'd consider handing him an outfield glove to see if the speed could play in center as well, he'd be above-average overall at the keystone if you just want to stick him there for 150 games a year. The lack of power projection or premium defensive position limits the upside in the profile a little bit, but the hit tool and speed give him a good shot to have some sort of a bench role even if the bat is a little light at the highest level. We think he will hit enough to play everyday though.

Variance: Medium. The athletic tools should get him to the majors, but hit-tool-driven profiles in A-ball aren't the safest.

Mark Barry's Fantasy Take: Edwards stole 34 bases in his first full season as a pro, and has yet to hit below .300. That's pretty much all you need to know, mostly because that's all there is. In today's fantasy landscape, that's still super useful, however, and in Edwards's case specifically, it makes him a top-50 dynasty prospect.

8 Greg Jones SS   OFP: 55   ETA: 2022

Born: 03/07/98   Age: 22   Bats: B   Throws: R   Height: 6'2"   Weight: 175   Origin: Round 1, 2019 Draft (#22 overall)

YEAR	TEAM	LVL	AGE	PA	R	2B	3B	HR	RBI	BB	K	SB	CS	AVG/OBP/SLG	DRC+	VORP	BABIP	BRR	FRAA	WARP	PF
2019	HUD	A-	21	218	39	13	4	1	24	22	56	19	8	.335/.413/.461	174	25.2	.467	4.2	SS(21) 2.2	2.6	98
2020	TBA	MLB	22	251	22	12	1	4	23	16	84	3	1	.239/.295/.348	71	0.0	.358	0.0	SS 1	0.1	88

Comparables: Mark Hamilton, J.D. Martinez, Alex Dickerson

The Report: Jones continued his torrid hitting with Hudson Valley after he was drafted from UNC Wilmington with the 22nd-overall pick in the 2019 draft. Jones has an exciting collection of tools ranging from his 70 or 80-grade speed (depending on the day) to his impressive bat control. The strikeouts were up from college, but that was more a result of being too patient at the plate, similar to what Yoan Moncada struggled with pre-2019. The swing is actually quite nice. It's flat but he generates above-average bat speed and regularly drives the ball to the gaps. The bat and barrel control are good enough where he could hit for 10-15 home runs if he had more loft in the swing. Defensively, he has the physical tools to be a regular at shortstop. The range is undoubtedly there, though the footwork can get messy and he occasionally rushes throws. The arm strength is fine, and the reports on his defense have improved over time. If he did have to move off shortstop, his speed could play well in center field. The collection of tools at either premium position means Jones's path to the bigs is clearer than most other prospects.

Variance: Medium. He can play up the middle and has some feel to hit, so Jones has a solid shot of having some sort of major league career.

Mark Barry's Fantasy Take: Though his name is a little boring, Jones's profile is anything but. Much like Brujan, Jones is a high-contact, high-speed guy, with plate discipline to boot. He currently hits for less power than a decent-hitting pitcher, so you can really only rely on him for a max of four categories. Even so, he's a top-150 fantasy prospect, for sure.

9 Ronaldo Hernandez C   OFP: 55   ETA: 2021
Born: 11/11/97   Age: 22   Bats: R   Throws: R   Height: 6'1"   Weight: 185   Origin: International Free Agent, 2014

YEAR	TEAM	LVL	AGE	PA	R	2B	3B	HR	RBI	BB	K	SB	CS	AVG/OBP/SLG	DRC+	VORP	BABIP	BRR	FRAA	WARP	PF
2017	PRI	RK	19	246	42	22	1	5	40	16	39	2	2	.332/.382/.507	150	24.4	.379	2.5	C(43)1.1	2.6	107
2018	BGR	A	20	449	68	20	1	21	79	31	69	10	4	.284/.339/.494	136	39.2	.292	-0.8	C(85)1.2	3.5	100
2019	PCH	A+	21	427	43	19	3	9	60	17	65	7	0	.265/.299/.397	105	20.3	.290	1.8	C(81)1.9	2.3	97
2020	TBA	MLB	22	251	27	13	1	9	32	13	52	1	0	.255/.300/.435	94	0.0	.290	-0.5	C 0	0.6	88

Comparables: Meibrys Viloria, Abiatal Avelino, Dom Nuñez

The Report: Hernandez was an infielder when the Rays originally signed him. They moved him behind the dish in his first pro season, so he has had a lot of work to do to learn the nuances of catching. The defensive part of his game is coming along, as he does show some aptitude for blocking and receiving, though he still lacks consistency in those areas. Hernandez has always had the arm to be successful, and he has made progress with his transfer and footwork to improve his overall catch-and-throw skills. With continued refinement, Hernandez should be able to develop into at least an average defensive catcher.

At the plate, Hernandez still shows flashes of plus raw power, but his approach leaves him struggling to get to that pop into games. He is a very aggressive hitter who makes a lot of contact, but he needs to learn to be more selective. He tends to swing at every pitch he can make contact with rather than being focused on those he can drive. Unsurprisingly, Hernandez is also very pull-oriented. The overall approach leaves him making too much weak contact. The foundational tools are there if he can find some patience and not be afraid to let his power play the other way at times.

Hernandez will face a tough test in Double-A and how he handles the offensive part of his development will make all the difference in determining his prospect trajectory.

Variance: High, especially given the work still remaining on defense.

Mark Barry's Fantasy Take: Though Hernandez is moving up from his 2018 spot on this list, it's hard to imagine anything other than a drop in his fantasy standing. He snagged seven bases without being caught, which is cool, but Hernandez hit just nine homers, down from 21 in 2018. That's less cool. Learning to catch is hard. Learning plate discipline is hard. Trying to learn them both at the same time: Priceless (wait that doesn't even make sense). Since fantasy catcher is still, and will likely always be, a barren wasteland, Hernandez is still one of the top-five catching prospects in fantasy, but his 2019 wasn't a step in the right direction.

10 Brent Honeywell Jr. RHP   OFP: 60   ETA:
Born: 03/31/95   Age: 25   Bats: R   Throws: R   Height: 6'2"   Weight: 180   Origin: Round 2, 2014 Draft (#72 overall)

YEAR	TEAM	LVL	AGE	W	L	SV	G	GS	IP	H	HR	BB/9	K/9	K	GB%	BABIP	WHIP	ERA	DRA	WARP	PF
2017	MNT	AA	22	1	1	0	2	2	13	4	1	2.8	13.8	20	45%	.158	0.62	2.08	1.98	0.5	99
2017	DUR	AAA	22	12	8	0	24	24	123²	130	11	2.3	11.1	152	42%	.366	1.30	3.64	4.26	2.0	99
2020	TBA	MLB	25	3	3	0	29	5	47	46	7	3.3	9.5	50	38%	.308	1.34	4.35	4.55	0.4	88

Comparables: Mitch Keller, Zack Littell, Stephen Gonsalves

The Report: The backbone of these lists are our staff's live looks. You may be tired of us writing that by now. Usually there is a greater rhetorical point we are making, but in this case, it's a preamble to throwing up our hands. While rehabbing from Tommy John surgery this Summer, Honeywell fractured a bone in his elbow. There was no further ligament damage, but the former top-20 prospect hasn't thrown a pitch in a pro game in two years now. We've dealt with this situation before. Jameson Taillon was shut down during TJ rehab, but that was a hernia, and he's not exactly been a sterling example of pitcher health since then anyway. The comp for this kind of injury is Jeremy Hefner, who never pitched again after breaking his arm on rehab, although that injury necessitated a second surgery.

Like I wrote in the 2016 Annual for Taillon, I have no idea if this Honeywell ranking will look high or low in a year. But we have to put him somewhere. The rules are the rules.

Variance: Extreme. The stuff is front-of-the-rotation. He also might literally never pitch professionally again.

Mark Barry's Fantasy Take: I'm so mad ¯_(ツ)_/¯ got used for Honeywell before I had the chance. He's the ultimate lottery ticket where if you win, you get a stud, ace-level starter and if you lose you get punched in the face.

The Next Ten

11 Joe Ryan   RHP

Born: 06/05/96   Age: 24   Bats: R   Throws: R   Height: 6'1"   Weight: 185   Origin: Round 7, 2018 Draft (#210 overall)

YEAR	TEAM	LVL	AGE	W	L	SV	G	GS	IP	H	HR	BB/9	K/9	K	GB%	BABIP	WHIP	ERA	DRA	WARP	PF
2018	HUD	A-	22	2	1	0	12	7	36¹	26	3	3.5	12.6	51	38%	.303	1.10	3.72	3.61	0.6	91
2019	BGR	A	23	2	2	0	6	6	27²	19	2	3.6	15.3	47	29%	.315	1.08	2.93	2.91	0.7	105
2019	PCH	A+	23	7	2	0	15	13	82²	47	3	1.3	12.2	112	38%	.244	0.71	1.42	2.02	3.0	96
2019	MNT	AA	23	0	0	0	3	3	13¹	11	2	2.7	16.2	24	27%	.375	1.12	3.38	4.14	0.1	96
2020	TBA	MLB	24	2	2	0	33	0	35	35	5	3.2	11.9	46	38%	.346	1.36	4.55	4.64	0.2	88

Comparables: Jaime Schultz, Erick Fedde, Daniel Ponce de Leon

The Report: Did the Rays do it again? Ryan comes aggressively to the plate with a three-quarters slot and smooth delivery. At 6-foot-1, Ryan isn't the most intimidating presence on the mound, but he is fairly consistent in his release and exudes supreme confidence throwing his dart of a fastball. The pitch has natural sink and projects for future plus command. It sits in the low 90s and has topped out at 96. The curveball comes in in the low 70s and flashes above-average. The shape isn't as tight as one may like at the moment, but used in combination with his impressive fastball it's an effective change of pace.

Ryan also has a cutter that's nothing to write home about yet, and a low-80s changeup that also needs work. But guess what? It's the Rays. As a traditional starter, this probably won't work, but as a mid-game three-to-four inning pitcher that fastball-curve mix would play.

Variance: High. Ryan is a thin four-pitch pitcher with two-and-a-half pitches at present.

Mark Barry's Fantasy Take: I kinda like this guy. Sure he might be a reliever. Sure he might be a tiny bit too old for High-A. Sure pumping low-90s fastballs as your primary pitch is probably better out of the bullpen. Wait, where was I? Ryan seems like the kind of guy that gets tossed into a spot start and then saves your season for like three months. It might not be until 2021, but a saved season is still a saved season. Additionally, it's hard to bet against a Cal State Stanislaus alum, because as we all know, nothing bad has ever come to a Stannis-ian.

12 Seth Johnson   RHP

Born: 09/19/98   Age: 21   Bats: R   Throws: R   Height: 6'1"   Weight: 200   Origin: Round 1, 2019 Draft (#40 overall)

YEAR	TEAM	LVL	AGE	W	L	SV	G	GS	IP	H	HR	BB/9	K/9	K	GB%	BABIP	WHIP	ERA	DRA	WARP	PF
2019	RAY	RK	20	0	0	0	5	5	10	7	0	1.8	6.3	7	43%	.233	0.90	0.00	2.02	0.4	107
2019	PRI	RK+	20	0	1	0	4	4	7	10	0	1.3	11.6	9	40%	.500	1.57	5.14	6.47	0.0	97

From anonymity to a top-40 pick in the draft, Johnson went from a light-hitting JuCo shortstop to Campbell University No. 1 starter to legitimate pitching prospect in just over a year's time. You can see the former infielder's athleticism in the delivery, as he stays balanced over his front-side with easy effort in the arm action. Johnson is still very raw in terms of developing his pitches and learning to pitch, but with a fastball bumping 97-98 and the makings of a plus slider, there is a very talented base to build on. There were some durability concerns as the year wore on, and he came out of the bullpen for the Camels in the NCAA Tournament instead of starting. Building up a starter's endurance will be among the first tasks as he approaches his first full year in pro ball with the Rays.

13 Josh Lowe OF

Born: 02/02/98 Age: 22 Bats: L Throws: R Height: 6'4" Weight: 205 Origin: Round 1, 2016 Draft (#13 overall)

YEAR	TEAM	LVL	AGE	PA	R	2B	3B	HR	RBI	BB	K	SB	CS	AVG/OBP/SLG	DRC+	VORP	BABIP	BRR	FRAA	WARP	PF
2017	BGR	A	19	507	60	26	2	8	55	42	144	22	8	.268/.326/.386	101	22.1	.369	2.3	CF(112) 3.4	2.3	104
2018	PCH	A+	20	455	62	25	3	6	47	47	117	18	6	.238/.322/.361	95	14.7	.318	1.1	CF(102) 4.1	1.8	99
2019	MNT	AA	21	519	70	23	4	18	62	59	132	30	9	.252/.341/.442	128	38.1	.316	5.6	CF(110) -7.0, RF(8) 2.2	3.3	98
2020	TBA	MLB	22	251	28	12	1	9	30	25	81	4	2	.232/.310/.408	89	0.0	.321	0.2	CF 0, RF 0	0.5	88

Comparables: Clint Frazier, Byron Buxton, Jordan Schafer

Going into the 2016 draft, Nate Lowe was referred to as the brother of Josh. Fast forward to the present day and now Josh is known as Nate Lowe's brother. That's mostly because of Nate's rather quick ascendance than the development of Josh, who could still end up being a better major leaguer. The younger Lowe oozes athleticism, tools and physicality, and seeing him in Arizona after a poor showing in 2018 reaffirmed the upside here. There are a lot of tools here: plus speed, plus raw pop, plus throwing arm and quality outfield defense. The power improved in 2019, as he added strength over last year and drove the ball to all fields more effectively. He still struggles against better breaking stuff and might always be vulnerable against lefties, lowering his overall ceiling. Still, when there are this many tools in the profile, I will always be a believer.

14 Nick Schnell OF

Born: 03/27/00 Age: 20 Bats: L Throws: R Height: 6'3" Weight: 180 Origin: Round 1C, 2018 Draft (#32 overall)

YEAR	TEAM	LVL	AGE	PA	R	2B	3B	HR	RBI	BB	K	SB	CS	AVG/OBP/SLG	DRC+	VORP	BABIP	BRR	FRAA	WARP	PF
2018	RAY	RK	18	82	8	4	1	1	4	14	23	2	6	.239/.378/.373	115	2.8	.349	-2.7	CF(13) -1.3, RF(5) -0.7	-0.1	96
2019	PRI	RK+	19	166	28	11	3	5	27	18	51	5	2	.286/.361/.503	118	11.4	.402	0.2		0.8	101
2019	BGR	A	19	60	7	3	1	0	3	2	24	0	1	.236/.271/.327	50	1.9	.406	1.2	CF(12) 1.8	0.2	106
2020	TBA	MLB	20	251	22	12	2	5	24	20	103	4	3	.206/.273/.340	62	0.0	.344	0.0	CF 1, RF 0	-0.2	88

Another toolsy athlete with upside. Schnell keeps his hands low pre-pitch and slightly moves his load up to get to the baseball. It's not a rip-through-the-ball swing, but it's pretty clean. Nothing is really too loud at that plate, but he probably projects as a 50 hit, 50 power guy. Still raw as hell, but a Ross-Adolph-type profile with a touch more speed and a better arm fits this 2018 first-round selection.

15 Lucius Fox SS

Born: 07/02/97 Age: 22 Bats: B Throws: R Height: 6'1" Weight: 180 Origin: International Free Agent, 2015

YEAR	TEAM	LVL	AGE	PA	R	2B	3B	HR	RBI	BB	K	SB	CS	AVG/OBP/SLG	DRC+	VORP	BABIP	BRR	FRAA	WARP	PF
2017	BGR	A	19	345	45	13	3	2	27	33	80	27	10	.278/.362/.361	110	13.5	.371	0.2	SS(71) -3.8	1.4	105
2017	PCH	A+	19	131	19	3	0	1	12	12	33	3	3	.235/.321/.287	79	1.7	.317	-0.6	SS(29) 4.4	0.7	98
2018	PCH	A+	20	404	54	17	1	2	30	42	79	23	7	.282/.371/.353	126	22.3	.358	2.1	SS(79) -1.5	2.7	99
2018	MNT	AA	20	120	14	3	1	1	9	8	20	6	2	.221/.284/.298	69	1.3	.259	0.6	SS(26) -0.7	0.1	94
2019	MNT	AA	21	431	60	16	8	3	33	53	89	37	11	.230/.340/.342	106	16.6	.293	0.6	SS(79) -3.9, 2B(12) 1.4	2.0	98
2019	DUR	AAA	21	49	6	0	1	0	1	6	15	2	0	.143/.250/.190	47	0.1	.222	0.6	SS(12) 0.4, 2B(1) -0.1	0.0	101
2020	TBA	MLB	22	35	3	1	0	0	3	3	10	1	0	.209/.289/.307	61	0.0	.289	0.1	SS 0	0.0	88

Comparables: Cole Tucker, Tyler Wade, J.P. Crawford

Fox projects for little power from either side of the plate with a pretty weak swing. It has a one-handed release with a toe tap and a bit of a timid approach—30 game power with very little room for projection. However, the swing is not carrying Fox in the majors (or minors for that matter). The Bahamanian is a 70 runner and possesses high-end athleticism. He still looks raw in pretty much all facets of the game except on the basepaths— but there is some projectability in the game and the glove. We *pretty* much know what he is by now, but if the athleticism allows him to get to above-average at shortstop, he could be a fringe starter.

16 Anthony Banda LHP
Born: 08/10/93   Age: 26   Bats: L   Throws: L   Height: 6'2"   Weight: 225   Origin: Round 10, 2012 Draft (#335 overall)

YEAR	TEAM	LVL	AGE	W	L	SV	G	GS	IP	H	HR	BB/9	K/9	K	GB%	BABIP	WHIP	ERA	DRA	WARP	PF
2017	RNO	AAA	23	8	7	0	22	22	122	125	15	3.8	8.6	116	43%	.317	1.44	5.39	4.15	2.1	115
2017	ARI	MLB	23	2	3	0	8	4	25²	26	1	3.5	8.8	25	39%	.329	1.40	5.96	4.21	0.4	97
2018	DUR	AAA	24	4	3	0	8	8	42	43	3	3.9	10.5	49	40%	.360	1.45	3.64	5.21	0.2	97
2018	TBA	MLB	24	1	0	0	3	1	14²	12	1	1.8	6.1	10	49%	.262	1.02	3.68	4.75	0.1	99
2019	DUR	AAA	25	2	3	0	9	4	28¹	28	7	3.5	8.6	27	41%	.284	1.38	6.04	4.75	0.5	108
2019	TBA	MLB	25	0	0	0	3	0	4	6	0	0.0	4.5	2	25%	.375	1.50	6.75	5.51	0.0	95
2020	TBA	MLB	26	1	1	0	3	3	13	15	3	3.4	6.3	9	39%	.298	1.52	6.03	5.91	0.0	88

Comparables: Jake Faria, Blake Snell, Dana Eveland

Banda stepped back on a complex-league mound a shade over a year after his 2018 Tommy John surgery. He rehabbed at a fairly quick pace, and the results were good enough to find himself back in the majors after rosters expanded in September. Banda was mostly fastball/slider/change in 2019. The fastball can hit 93-94 with regularity and there's some deception, but not a ton of movement. The slider is averageish as well. It's a firm, mid-80s offering that he can front door to lefties or backfoot to righties, but it can lack ideal depth. The change remains a bit of a work in progress. He's still close enough to his surgery date that you can hope for the stuff to tick back up a bit more, but he's also major-league-ready enough to be a useful utility arm for the 2020 Rays.

17 JJ Goss RHP
Born: 12/25/00   Age: 19   Bats: R   Throws: R   Height: 6'3"   Weight: 185   Origin: Round 1, 2019 Draft (#36 overall)

YEAR	TEAM	LVL	AGE	W	L	SV	G	GS	IP	H	HR	BB/9	K/9	K	GB%	BABIP	WHIP	ERA	DRA	WARP	PF
2019	RAY	RK	18	1	3	0	9	8	17	19	1	1.1	8.5	16	46%	.353	1.24	5.82	4.59	0.3	108

Goss isn't your traditional big ol' Day One Texas prep arm. He's a projectable 6-foot-3, mostly because he's pretty doggone skinny, but he generates average fastball velocity at present from a short, quick arm action. There might be more in the tank there as well given the present frame. Goss has a very advanced low-80s breaking ball for a prep arm, and the requisite developing changeup. It's going to be interesting to see how he grows into his body, but there are positive markers in his delivery to stick as a starter if the third pitch develops.

18 Kevin Padlo 3B
Born: 07/15/96   Age: 23   Bats: R   Throws: R   Height: 6'2"   Weight: 205   Origin: Round 5, 2014 Draft (#143 overall)

YEAR	TEAM	LVL	AGE	PA	R	2B	3B	HR	RBI	BB	K	SB	CS	AVG/OBP/SLG	DRC+	VORP	BABIP	BRR	FRAA	WARP	PF
2017	PCH	A+	20	259	28	13	3	6	34	35	60	4	5	.223/.324/.391	109	10.3	.272	-1.5	3B(60) -1.1	0.8	96
2018	PCH	A+	21	449	54	26	0	8	54	47	119	5	0	.223/.318/.353	94	9.4	.295	-0.1	3B(87) -2.5, 1B(18) -1.0	0.6	100
2019	MNT	AA	22	277	39	20	0	12	35	47	70	11	4	.250/.383/.505	167	30.9	.299	0.2	3B(57) 7.1, 1B(6) -0.4	3.5	96
2019	DUR	AAA	22	155	25	11	1	9	27	21	46	1	0	.290/.400/.595	128	11.7	.382	1.0	3B(30) 3.5, 2B(3) 0.2	1.3	102
2020	TBA	MLB	23	35	4	2	0	1	5	4	11	1	0	.222/.322/.435	101	3.0	.297	0.0	3B 0	0.1	88

Comparables: Jeimer Candelario, Nicky Delmonico, Andrew Velazquez

After two middling campaigns in A-ball where Padlo struggled to get his raw power into games, a swing adjustment may have unlocked something for him in the upper minors. Padlo starts with his hands back now, almost at a full arm bar, and explodes at pitches with loft. You have to be pretty strong to pull that off, but Padlo looks the part in short sleeves, and he smashed 21 home runs in 110 upper minors games. The quality of contact isn't always going to be great and he'll pop a fair bit of high fastballs up, but he has a strong enough approach to perhaps make the offensive profile work overall. It might look a bit like post-peak Todd Frazier, although the glove at third base is more average than plus. Doing enough damage on contact with this kind of swing can be tricky against major league arms, so there's a wide range of uncertainty on the hit tool, but Padlo is very much a hitter of his times. Well, assuming the ball stays juiced.

19 Niko Hulsizer OF

Born: 02/01/97   Age: 23   Bats: R   Throws: R   Height: 6'2"   Weight: 225   Origin: Round 18, 2018 Draft (#554 overall)

YEAR	TEAM	LVL	AGE	PA	R	2B	3B	HR	RBI	BB	K	SB	CS	AVG/OBP/SLG	DRC+	VORP	BABIP	BRR	FRAA	WARP	PF
2018	OGD	RK	21	202	47	13	0	9	32	30	52	12	2	.281/.426/.531	153	25.1	.360	3.7	RF(33) -1.2, LF(6) -0.4	1.0	110
2019	GRL	A	22	256	46	17	1	15	49	37	75	4	1	.268/.395/.574	186	28.8	.339	-3.3	LF(29) 4.2, RF(4) 1.0	2.9	98
2019	PCH	A+	22	39	4	2	0	1	4	4	11	0	1	.235/.308/.382	96	1.6	.304	-0.1	LF(5) 0.1, RF(3) 0.3	0.1	95
2019	RCU	A+	22	98	15	6	0	5	18	9	33	3	2	.259/.327/.506	100	7.2	.340	1.1	LF(15) 1.6	0.5	105
2020	TBA	MLB	23	251	25	13	0	8	28	19	93	2	1	.202/.276/.368	69	0.0	.301	-0.4	LF 2, RF 1	0.0	88

Comparables: Jake Lamb, Peter O'Brien, Todd Frazier

As an 18th-round draft choice out of Morehead State in 2018, Hulsizer wasn't on many prospect radars to begin the year. Then he was traded to the Rays, and being traded to the Rays seems to guarantee improvements these days. Hulsizer is a tank—from top to bottom he is as solidly built as they come. He's an average runner with an average glove and an average arm, but his power is very much not average. The raw is an easy 70. He's as strong as an ox, shows plus bat speed, and generates loft from his swing plane. According to the Rancho Cucamonga Quakes one of his home runs left the bat at 116 mph.

Hulsizer's hit tool might reach average if everything goes right developmentally, and if that happens you have a plus regular. He shows good pitch recognition and a nice approach at the plate. Still, at present there are some issues, the biggest of which is significant swing-and-miss. I always find it promising when hitters with swing-and-miss issues can still earn walks at a healthy clip, and Hulsizer definitely does that (12.9 percent walk rate). For as bulky as he is, he's a good athlete which should make reaching his OFP more likely than average. He is an immediate eye-catcher on the field and if he continues to put up the numbers he did in 2019 expect him to fly up prospect rankings at midseason.

20 Simon Rosenblum-Larson RHP

Born: 02/11/97   Age: 23   Bats: R   Throws: R   Height: 6'3"   Weight: 202   Origin: Round 19, 2018 Draft (#570 overall)

YEAR	TEAM	LVL	AGE	W	L	SV	G	GS	IP	H	HR	BB/9	K/9	K	GB%	BABIP	WHIP	ERA	DRA	WARP	PF
2018	HUD	A-	21	1	1	5	9	0	21	11	0	1.7	14.1	33	52%	.275	0.71	0.00	1.50	0.8	100
2018	BGR	A	21	0	2	3	9	0	17²	8	1	2.5	14.8	29	33%	.219	0.74	2.55	2.19	0.6	100
2019	PCH	A+	22	2	3	8	37	2	60¹	44	4	5.1	11.0	74	40%	.276	1.29	3.13	4.19	0.4	96
2020	TBA	MLB	23	2	2	0	33	0	35	35	5	3.6	9.6	37	38%	.316	1.41	4.89	4.94	0.1	88

The Harvard draftee has a fastball that sits 88-91 with plenty of running action. The delivery features a big drop and drive. The arm slot is sidearm, but it doesn't feature the shoulder drop in the back that traditional sidearms and submariners have. His upper-70s slider features incredible sweeping action, and plays well off the fastball that moves arm-side. The red flag here is the command, as Rosenblum-Larson really slings it, causing both the fastball and slider to miss outside the zone too often. He's the type of arm you throw out there if you really need a strikeout, but have to pull him quickly if the command isn't there that day.

Personal Cheeseball

PC Drew Strotman RHP

Born: 09/03/96   Age: 23   Bats: R   Throws: R   Height: 6'3"   Weight: 195   Origin: Round 4, 2017 Draft (#109 overall)

YEAR	TEAM	LVL	AGE	W	L	SV	G	GS	IP	H	HR	BB/9	K/9	K	GB%	BABIP	WHIP	ERA	DRA	WARP	PF
2017	HUD	A-	20	2	3	0	11	7	50²	29	0	1.6	7.5	42	60%	.216	0.75	1.78	2.24	1.8	94
2018	BGR	A	21	3	0	0	9	9	46	40	0	3.5	8.4	43	47%	.320	1.26	3.52	4.90	0.2	98
2019	RAY	RK	22	0	1	0	4	4	8	9	0	3.4	12.4	11	56%	.391	1.50	3.38	4.24	0.2	101
2019	PCH	A+	22	0	2	0	5	5	16	20	3	5.1	7.3	13	43%	.354	1.81	5.06	7.56	-0.5	100
2020	TBA	MLB	23	2	2	0	33	0	35	34	5	3.3	6.8	27	46%	.277	1.33	4.24	4.40	0.3	88

I liked Strotman coming out of the 2017 draft as a four-pitch small college guy who mixed his stuff pretty well, even if he lacked a standout, or even above-average offering. Tommy John surgery cost him most of 2018 and 2019, but he's back on the mound now and was working at the upper end of his velocity range in the AFL. That's a borderline plus fastball, but it doesn't move a ton and the command projection is only average. Strotman also has two potentially average breaking balls, and a below-average change. He's lost a fair bit of development time to injury already, but during his time on the shelf, the Rays have popularized a role for this kind of pitcher as a bulk innings guy behind an opener. So he's got that going for him.

Low Minors Sleeper

LMS **Neraldo Catalina RHP**
Born: 06/21/00   Age: 20   Bats: R   Throws: R   Height: 6'6"   Weight: 202   Origin: International Free Agent, 2018

YEAR	TEAM	LVL	AGE	W	L	SV	G	GS	IP	H	HR	BB/9	K/9	K	GB%	BABIP	WHIP	ERA	DRA	WARP	PF
2019	RAY	RK	19	3	3	0	11	1	21	20	0	3.9	9.9	23	64%	.345	1.38	2.14	5.49	0.1	113

Much of this list is an ode to the Rays' pro scouting and player development teams. We don't want to puff them up too too much, but it was kind of unfair that they were allowed to trade with the Mets this season. Catalina—the return for roughly two months of Wilmer Font—was a $150k, overage, but still quite projectable, IFA that popped some in Extended Spring Training. The 6-foot-6 righty sits mid-90s, touching higher, with a potentially average curve. He's a two-pitch guy at present, but there's a lot of raw material to work with here. He would have made the Mets list comfortably.

Top Talents 25 and Under (as of 4/1/2020)

1. Wander Franco
2. Austin Meadows
3. Brendan McKay
4. Shane Baz
5. Brandon Lowe
6. Matthew Liberatore
7. Willy Adames
8. Vidal Brujan
9. Nate Lowe
10. Greg Jones

The fact that Franco ranks ahead of a 25-year-old outfielder coming off an All-Star season speaks to the type of generational talent he's projected to become. Meadows is no slouch himself, of course, as his 135 DRC+ ranked 18th in the majors, tied with top-three MVP finisher Marcus Semien. His power-speed combo should be something the Rays can rely on for the next half-decade at least, and while he won't be confused for Mookie Betts in right field, he can hold his own out there and masquerade in center if the situation called for it. Brandon Lowe acclimated himself well in his first extended look at playing time and also made the All-Star team, at which point he suffered a shin injury that shut him down for most of the rest of the season. When he did play, the swing change that landed him on the radar a year ago played up and he exhibited solid power that more than made up for the swing-and-miss in his approach. It was an impressive enough season to boost him ahead of Adames, whose 3.8 WARP season was thanks almost entirely to his glove which FRAA said was the best—or at least the most consistent—in all of baseball. Adames's bat was unreliable, but the power many hoped he'd develop was there, at least in this juiced-up-baseball world. The only other player not eligible for the prospect list to grace our Top 10 is Lowe No. 2, Nate, whose TTO routine translated to the majors in a 50-game audition—40 percent of his plate appearances ended in either a home run, walk, or strikeout. Tampa had a glut of 1B/DH types on their roster in 2019—Ji-Man Choi, Yandy Diaz, Jesus Aguilar—but he should get an extended look if and when circumstances surrounding the position change.

Eyewitness Reports

Eyewitness Report: Wander Franco

Evaluator: Nathan Graham
Report Date: 06/25/2019
Dates Seen: 3X May/June 2019
Risk Factor: High
Physical/Health: Medium frame; compact and athletic with a thick lower half. Has room to carry some additional good weight.

Tool	Future Grade	Report
Hit	70	Upright stance with hands starting high; Appears more comfortable and natural from the left side; utilizes a toe tap timing mechanism from the right side and bigger leg kick from the left. Expect the right side to catch up with more at-bats versus lefties. Elite bat control with a short, quick swing. Plus bat speed, stays balanced, recognizes spin well.
Power	60	Plus raw, mostly pull-side presently. Advanced hit tool will allow him to attack in hitters' counts. Power will play above-average with maturity.
Baserunning/ Speed	50	4.19 home to first clock from the left, 4.26 from the right. Raw speed will play average at maturity. Currently very aggressive on the bases to the point of recklessness, will make needless mistakes running into outs or getting picked off; will improve with more experience.
Glove	50	Quick first step and adequate hands. Shows solid range.
Arm	45	Fringe-average arm strength for SS, has to step into throws from short. Will likely necessitate a move to 2B, where the arm will play as average.

Conclusion: Franco's an elite hitting prospect who will have above average power with maturity. He will likely find a home at second, but the bat is strong enough to handle a move to any position. Profiles as a perennial All-Star, impact player.

Eyewitness Report: Shane McClanahan

Evaluator: Nathan Graham
Report Date: 07/30/2019
Dates Seen: 6/5/19
Risk Factor: High
Delivery: Large frame with an athletic build, has room for potential growth; works extremely fast, high energy. Plus arm speed, 3/4 armslot, moderate effort in the delivery and some recoil upon landing.

Pitch Type	Future Grade	Sitting Velocity	Peak Velocity	Report
FB	70	95-97	99	Electric pitch, has life, makes hitters look uncomfortable; has some arm side run, allows him to stay off barrels. Delivery can get a little out of sync at times causing the command to waver.
CB	60	81-82	82	12-6 shape, has bite and will buckle knees when he's got a good feel for it; struggles with consistency and will lose his release point. Anticipated plus offering with future gains in consistency.
CH	55	86-89	89	Only showed a handful, good velocity separation, will play well off the fastball; looks to be a future above-average offering.

Conclusion: McClanahan, a former first round pick, has nasty stuff. The type that, when he's got everything right, it makes hitters look uncomfortable. He needs to find consistency with the secondaries and command but with his athleticism and three pitch mix he's got a fairly high floor. Profiles as a no. 3 starter or a high leverage bullpen arm if the change does not fully develop.

Texas Rangers

The State of the System

Shockingly, the Rangers are once again loaded with low minors, high upside talent. As usual, Hickory and Down East will be must-see in 2020.

The Top Ten

★ ★ ★ *2020 Top 101 Prospect* **#37** ★ ★ ★

1 **Leody Taveras** **OF**   OFP: 60   ETA: 2020

Born: 09/08/98   Age: 21   Bats: B   Throws: R   Height: 6'1"   Weight: 171   Origin: International Free Agent, 2015

YEAR	TEAM	LVL	AGE	PA	R	2B	3B	HR	RBI	BB	K	SB	CS	AVG/OBP/SLG	DRC+	VORP	BABIP	BRR	FRAA	WARP	PF
2017	HIC	A	18	577	73	20	7	8	50	47	92	20	6	.249/.312/.360	98	16.8	.287	3.3	CF(125) -3.7, LF(3) -0.1	1.6	101
2018	DEB	A+	19	580	65	16	7	5	48	51	96	19	11	.246/.312/.332	90	4.2	.292	0.3	CF(123) 7.0, RF(3) 0.0	2.0	101
2019	DEB	A+	20	290	44	7	4	2	25	31	62	21	5	.294/.368/.376	124	14.6	.378	-0.4	CF(34) -0.6, RF(23) 4.0	1.7	97
2019	FRI	AA	20	293	32	12	4	3	31	23	60	11	8	.265/.320/.375	97	9.2	.327	0.5	CF(64) 8.1	1.8	102
2020	TEX	MLB	21	70	6	3	1	1	6	5	18	1	1	.239/.291/.350	65	0.0	.310	0.1	CF 0	0.0	116

Comparables: Engel Beltre, Carlos Tocci, Cheslor Cuthbert

The Report: Movement quality, general athleticism, premium baseball instincts, and an athlete's build give Taveras one of the most "pleasing to the eye" games in minor-league baseball. Taveras bursts into action at the plate or in the field, showing plus bat speed or quick 0-100 closing speed on fly balls. Taveras makes quick reads and decisions on the bases or the grass, and his plus-plus athleticism takes care of the rest of the job.

His impressive bat speed generates plus raw power, although an inconsistent plan of attack at the plate keeps him from tapping into it. Despite that, he generally makes good contact and has enough pitch recognition and patience for a respectable OBP-first profile with flashes of impact upside. If he doesn't tap into it, he could see seasons on offense somewhere in between Leonys Martin and Ender Inciarte, but if he does make the needed adjustment he could provide above-average production with the bat. The right-handed swing has lagged behind the left, but Taveras is making good adjustments with tracking the lefty breaking ball and started to show a similar power profile from both sides.

He is a plus runner who makes excellent reads, takes good routes, and flashes an above-average arm. Taveras makes the kind of 50/50 plays that many center fielders require max effort to get to without breaking into a full sprint due to quick jumps and seemingly instant acceleration.

Overall, Taveras profiles as an above-average regular with impact defensive value in center field and an AVG/OBP profile in the lineup. There's significant upside in his power projection, and if he can just tap into some of it, he could be a plus regular.

Variance: Medium. There's a high floor with the speed/glove up the middle, but the ultimate outcome in the bat could put Taveras anywhere from bench outfielder to All-Star.

Ben Carsley's Fantasy Take: I might need to go into Witness Protection if Jeff reads this, but I think Taveras is a substantially better real life prospect than fantasy prospect. The speed is nice of course, as is the fact that Taveras' glove should keep him in the lineup. But the power is mostly projection at this point, and I'm not a big believer in his ability to hit from the right. His upside remains very attractive, and because of the speed his floor is high enough that Taveras is definitely a top-101 dude. I'm just not betting on fantasy stardom, though I'll be pleasantly surprised if he makes it happen.

★ ★ ★ *2020 Top 101 Prospect* **#70** ★ ★ ★

2 Josh Jung 3B OFP: 60 ETA: 2022

Born: 02/12/98 Age: 22 Bats: R Throws: R Height: 6'2" Weight: 215 Origin: Round 1, 2019 Draft (#8 overall)

YEAR	TEAM	LVL	AGE	PA	R	2B	3B	HR	RBI	BB	K	SB	CS	AVG/OBP/SLG	DRC+	VORP	BABIP	BRR	FRAA	WARP	PF
2019	HIC	A	21	179	18	13	0	1	23	16	29	4	1	.287/.363/.389	137	13.7	.341	0.6	3B(35) 2.5	1.5	99
2020	TEX	MLB	22	251	22	12	1	4	23	15	60	3	1	.233/.288/.344	68	3.0	.297	0.0	3B 4	0.3	116

Comparables: Zelous Wheeler, Ty Kelly, Paul DeJong

The Report: The hit tool is explosive. Jung's well-muscled build generates impact bat speed and he can cover any portion of the zone. Batting practice sees him scorching hard contact pull-side or up the middle from a compact swing. The righty has the physical markers for a plus hit tool at the major league level, and it wouldn't take much to get him there. Unfortunately his approach is often tailored for opposite field contact as he tries to go with the ball instead of focusing on doing damage. He rarely gets on plane with the ball, even on inside pitches, and as such he sees a significant number of low line drives and ground balls. Jung has plus raw power and possibly could tap into more if there was intent to do damage when he swings. A "go with the ball" mentality is wasted on someone with Jung's physical abilities. The former Raider will also need to iron out some issues with his ability to pick up spin, specifically low and outside breakers.

Defensively, Jung flashes good hands and has an above-average arm, but he attacks the ball standing almost straight up and the change in eye height going to meet the ball can cause some predictable miscues. The physical traits suggest he should be able to provide average value at the hot corner with some adjustments to how he approaches groundballs.

Jung should find himself fitting on a major league team as a regular at third where his batting average, mid-teens home run power, and average glove will make him a clear contributor. Jung's hit tool and plus raw power give him significant upside if he changes his approach and improves his spin recognition.

Variance: Medium. Much like with Taveras, the ultimate power output will shape the profile, as the hit tool and glove at third give Jung a likely major league future of some sort.

Ben Carsley's Fantasy Take: Honestly, I can't be trusted with this profile. Hit tool-first third baseman who go the other way and have potential power? Be still, my heavily-taxed heart. Jung should move fast given his pedigree as a first-round college bat and his advanced approach at the plate, which means I'm going to push for him to rank as a top-50ish dynasty league prospect already. If it all really clicks, I think he could get most of the way to a Justin Turner-esque fantasy profile. We'll see how good Bret, Mark and co. are at tempering my excitement.

★ ★ ★ *2020 Top 101 Prospect* **#74** ★ ★ ★

3 Nick Solak IF OFP: 55 ETA: 2019

Born: 01/11/95 Age: 25 Bats: R Throws: R Height: 5'11" Weight: 190 Origin: Round 2, 2016 Draft (#62 overall)

YEAR	TEAM	LVL	AGE	PA	R	2B	3B	HR	RBI	BB	K	SB	CS	AVG/OBP/SLG	DRC+	VORP	BABIP	BRR	FRAA	WARP	PF
2017	TAM	A+	22	406	56	17	4	10	44	53	76	13	4	.301/.397/.460	173	39.3	.357	2.5	2B(92) 1.4	4.0	99
2017	TRN	AA	22	132	16	9	1	2	9	10	24	1	1	.286/.344/.429	108	8.1	.340	0.5	2B(30) 2.0	0.8	93
2018	MNT	AA	23	565	91	17	3	19	76	68	112	21	6	.282/.384/.450	141	46.4	.330	-0.5	2B(61) -6.9, LF(40) -3.3	2.9	93
2019	NAS	AAA	24	128	23	6	0	10	27	6	25	2	0	.347/.386/.653	135	14.6	.369	0.7	2B(21) 0.4, RF(4) 0.3	1.0	93
2019	DUR	AAA	24	349	56	13	1	17	47	39	80	3	2	.266/.353/.485	108	10.3	.303	-3.6	2B(61) -7.5, LF(17) 0.4	0.3	103
2019	TEX	MLB	24	135	19	6	1	5	17	15	29	2	0	.293/.393/.491	109	5.1	.354	1.3	3B(11) -0.1, 2B(5) -0.7	0.6	110
2020	TEX	MLB	25	525	66	22	2	23	73	44	126	6	2	.267/.340/.469	112	3.0	.319	-0.2	3B -2, 2B -1	1.5	116

Comparables: Preston Tucker, Brandon Lowe, Logan Forsythe

The Report: We never really had much doubt Nick Solak would hit, even going back two orgs ago to his time with the Yankees. The term "professional hitter" was all but invented for him. That usually implies something about the player's defense, and here, yeah I mean it fits. Solak played second base primarily in the minors, but he was never all that good there, and his arm is probably a little short for third. He has some corner outfield experience as well, so you have options to get his bat in the lineup. The Rangers will want to, because Solak has added power year-over-year, and while his 31 homers at three levels this year is too rich to project for him in the majors, something like .280 with low-20s bombs is certainly in play now. He's gotten to his power without lengthening his compact swing, and he gets on-base at a good clip and can run well. He's not quite the the Hubie Brooks "F to a C+" wherever you put him, but C- is a passing grade when you hit like Solak.

Variance: Low. He's already conquered the upper minors and had a solid major league cup of coffee. He's barely eligible for this list, and we have little doubt he will hit enough to outpace the defensive issues, even if they will also limit his upside.

Ben Carsley's Fantasy Take: Seriously, what is it with the Rangers and small, positionless dudes who can rake? I think the biggest danger with Solak is that his glove will keep him off the field more than we'd care for, making him a dude who earns more like 400 at-bats a year than 600 when the Rangers are competitive. But no one doubts that he can hit, he's ready to play now, and he should offer multi-position eligibility for a bit. It's a weird-ass fantasy profile to be sure, but also a very intriguing one.

4 Joe Palumbo LHP OFP: 60 ETA: 2019

Born: 10/26/94 Age: 25 Bats: L Throws: L Height: 6'1" Weight: 168 Origin: Round 30, 2013 Draft (#910 overall)

YEAR	TEAM	LVL	AGE	W	L	SV	G	GS	IP	H	HR	BB/9	K/9	K	GB%	BABIP	WHIP	ERA	DRA	WARP	PF
2017	DEB	A+	22	1	0	0	3	3	13²	4	0	2.6	14.5	22	58%	.167	0.59	0.66	1.48	0.6	100
2018	DEB	A+	23	1	4	0	6	6	27	24	3	2.0	11.3	34	42%	.304	1.11	2.67	4.07	0.4	102
2018	FRI	AA	23	1	0	0	2	2	9¹	6	0	2.9	9.6	10	39%	.261	0.96	1.93	3.31	0.2	102
2019	FRI	AA	24	0	0	0	11	10	53²	43	5	4.2	11.6	69	41%	.309	1.27	3.19	3.60	0.9	99
2019	NAS	AAA	24	3	0	0	6	6	27	13	4	3.3	13.0	39	40%	.188	0.85	2.67	1.78	1.3	93
2019	TEX	MLB	24	0	3	0	7	4	16²	21	7	4.3	11.3	21	36%	.326	1.74	9.18	5.67	0.0	112
2020	TEX	MLB	25	2	3	0	34	3	45	47	9	3.4	7.9	39	38%	.294	1.42	5.39	5.12	0.1	116

Comparables: Thomas Pannone, Antonio Bastardo, Jarlin García

The Report: It's hard to find a lefty with a better three-pitch mix in the minors than Joe Palumbo. On good nights he flashes a mid-90s high-spin four-seamer, a plus two-plane curveball, and a plus changeup with both tumble and fade. He throws enough strikes and misses plenty of bats, but unfortunately inconsistency can ruin otherwise stellar outings. Palumbo's fastball command comes and goes at the best of times, which can put him into problem counts too often. His curveball can at times flatten out and get hammered when left in the zone. Even on bad nights he will still miss bats thanks to his changeup, which has become a consistent offering, but hitters can sit fastball and do damage.

Palmubo is only a season and change removed from coming back from Tommy John surgery, so it's possible that his command inconsistencies will lessen with a bit more time. Regardless, it creates the risk that he won't find enough command or consistency to stick in a rotation, but will be forced into a pen role.

As it is, Palumbo's stuff still warrants a projection as middle-of-the-rotation arm, but with significant risk that he ends up in the bullpen before long. Conversely, he also has one of the higher upsides in the Rangers system, and could end up as a high-end third starter if he can iron out the command.

Variance: High. The command will dictate the eventual role here, and there are health and durability red flags as well.

Ben Carsley's Fantasy Take: Sub out "curveball" for "slider" above and it would sure feel like you were reading an Eduardo Rodriguez scouting report, no? That's the type of upside Palumbo possesses; a good fantasy SP4/5 who racks up strikeouts, but who doesn't always perform consistently from year-to-year (or, uh, start-to-start, or inning-to-inning). I'd like Palumbo more were he in an organization with a better track record of developing pitching, but even so he's a borderline top-101 guy thanks to his proximity.

5 Sam Huff C OFP: 55 ETA: 2022

Born: 01/14/98 Age: 22 Bats: R Throws: R Height: 6'4" Weight: 230 Origin: Round 7, 2016 Draft (#219 overall)

YEAR	TEAM	LVL	AGE	PA	R	2B	3B	HR	RBI	BB	K	SB	CS	AVG/OBP/SLG	DRC+	VORP	BABIP	BRR	FRAA	WARP	PF
2017	RNG	RK	19	225	34	9	2	9	31	24	66	3	2	.249/.329/.452	97	14.6	.320	0.7	C(30) -0.5	0.7	100
2018	HIC	A	20	448	53	22	3	18	55	23	140	9	1	.241/.292/.439	97	14.0	.317	-0.1	C(56) 1.9, 1B(11) -0.4	1.3	99
2019	HIC	A	21	114	22	5	0	15	29	6	37	4	1	.333/.368/.796	217	22.7	.375	0.8	C(14) 0.9	1.8	99
2019	DEB	A+	21	405	49	17	2	13	43	27	117	2	5	.262/.326/.425	110	18.4	.347	-2.7	C(50) 1.9, 1B(4) 0.1	1.5	99
2020	TEX	MLB	22	251	24	12	1	7	27	16	92	1	0	.219/.277/.365	67	0.0	.328	-0.3	C 1, 1B 0	-0.2	116

Comparables: Eric Haase, Isan Díaz, Chris Carter

The Report: Without a doubt the highest riser in the Rangers system this year, Huff went from someone on some people's radars to the middle of everyone's. After a good year in Hickory, Huff repeated his results at both A-ball levels. He is definitely a bat-first catcher, with plus power and a solid hit tool. One thing holding Huff back offensively is his decision making at the dish; better pitch recognition and a more patient approach is something he'll want to work on going forward.

Huff's defense behind the plate isn't awe inspiring, but does show good athleticism and a willingness to hustle and improve. Catchers are notoriously slow-developing players, but Huff has accelerated his development and become the top backstop in the Texas system. With his size there will always be questions about whether his long term future is in the crouch or at, say, first base. For now, Huff's abilities and skills can keep him catching without being a defensive liability. With no one blocking Huff on the depth chart, his performance next season and beyond is the only thing limiting his future.

Variance: MHigh. Catchers, man. They're always a little hard to predict. In Huff's case the questions come about whether he can hold up behind the plate long term. His future changes if he is forced into a corner infield or outfield position. Time will tell, but it's something to keep in mind.

Ben Carsley's Fantasy Take: I know this might not be a popular take, but I'm letting others go all-in on Huff while I watch from a distance. He's far from a lock to stay at catcher, and even if he does manage to stay behind the plate for a bit, then we get to worry about the horrendous track record for fantasy catching prospects at large. Yes, there's a chance he's Mitch Garver, but there's also a chance he's…Tom Murphy? Jacob Nottingham? Fancy Dog Zack Collins? Huff should be owned in leagues that roster 200-plus prospects, but odds are he'll be showing up on some dynasty top-100 lists this winter, and I won't agree with those rankings.

6 Hans Crouse RHP   OFP: 55   ETA: 2022

Born: 09/15/98   Age: 21   Bats: L   Throws: R   Height: 6'4"   Weight: 180   Origin: Round 2, 2017 Draft (#66 overall)

YEAR	TEAM	LVL	AGE	W	L	SV	G	GS	IP	H	HR	BB/9	K/9	K	GB%	BABIP	WHIP	ERA	DRA	WARP	PF
2017	RNG	RK	18	0	0	0	10	6	20	7	1	3.2	13.5	30	60%	.176	0.70	0.45	0.00	1.3	102
2018	SPO	A-	19	5	1	0	8	8	38	25	2	2.6	11.1	47	36%	.253	0.95	2.37	2.18	1.4	106
2018	HIC	A	19	0	2	0	5	5	16²	18	1	4.3	8.1	15	40%	.333	1.56	2.70	5.31	0.0	104
2019	HIC	A	20	6	1	0	19	19	87²	86	12	2.0	7.8	76	34%	.297	1.20	4.41	5.12	0.1	98
2020	TEX	MLB	21	2	2	0	33	0	35	36	6	3.3	7.0	27	33%	.288	1.40	5.08	5.02	0.1	116

Comparables: Joe Ross, Nate Adcock, Mike Foltynewicz

The Report: Crouse has a lot of the traits you look for in a big-time pitcher. He's got the height and frame typically desired, as well as a competitive fire that often manifests itself visibly on the field. Not only is it evident in how he owns the mound during his starts, or in his reactions after a big out, but Crouse pitched roughly the last half of this season with a bone spur in his elbow and performed admirably anyway.

It's not just empty bluster on the mound, either. Crouse has a pair of pitches that project plus in a fastball that sits in the mid 90s and a low-80s curve that he manipulates and is good for plenty of swings and misses. There is also a considerable amount he has to improve on, and there are aspects to the profile that will be of concern until they aren't, so to speak. The command isn't a strength at this point, and there's a lot of violence in the delivery, so a starting outcome is far from a guarantee. His current injury will be taken care of in the offseason, but elbow issues are always worrisome. He hasn't really had a third pitch declare itself yet, either. The high-80s change is pretty firm but shows enough fade that it holds some promise, though he doesn't use it much at present.

Variance: Medium. A lot of what is outlined in the report points to significant reliever risk, but the stuff and overall package is enough to be comfortable projecting a productive big leaguer of some kind.

Ben Carsley's Fantasy Take: Crouse belongs near the top of that big, mushy group of 20-or-so potential mid-rotation starters who generally just make the tail end or barely miss our top-101 dynasty list every season. He's got size and stuff on his side, but organizational weakness and reliever risk against him. That third pitch will be pretty important for his fantasy value, so keep an eye on his development in shallow leagues; in deeper ones, he's rightfully already owned.

7 Brock Burke LHP   OFP: 50   ETA: 2019

Born: 08/04/96   Age: 23   Bats: L   Throws: L   Height: 6'4"   Weight: 180   Origin: Round 3, 2014 Draft (#96 overall)

YEAR	TEAM	LVL	AGE	W	L	SV	G	GS	IP	H	HR	BB/9	K/9	K	GB%	BABIP	WHIP	ERA	DRA	WARP	PF
2017	BGR	A	20	6	0	0	10	10	57¹	37	0	3.1	9.3	59	35%	.253	0.99	1.10	2.69	1.7	103
2017	PCH	A+	20	5	6	0	13	13	66	75	6	2.2	6.7	49	47%	.329	1.38	4.64	5.46	-0.2	98
2018	PCH	A+	21	3	5	0	16	13	82	85	4	3.3	9.5	87	48%	.343	1.40	3.84	4.77	0.5	100
2018	MNT	AA	21	6	1	0	9	9	55¹	39	2	2.3	11.5	71	37%	.282	0.96	1.95	2.91	1.6	93
2019	FRI	AA	22	3	5	0	9	9	45¹	34	2	2.4	9.7	49	50%	.262	1.01	3.18	2.73	1.2	95
2019	NAS	AAA	22	0	0	0	2	2	8	12	1	6.8	12.4	11	50%	.478	2.25	7.88	6.74	0.0	95
2019	TEX	MLB	22	0	2	0	6	6	26²	30	6	3.7	4.7	14	52%	.276	1.54	7.43	6.82	-0.3	110
2020	TEX	MLB	23	1	2	0	5	5	22	26	4	3.4	4.8	12	46%	.297	1.57	6.22	5.72	0.0	116

Comparables: Stephen Gonsalves, Robbie Ray, Lucas Sims

The Report: A solid three-pitch mix helped the big lefty carve up the Texas League when he was healthy. Burke features a good fastball that sat low 90s but could pop higher on occasion, a firm changeup in the low 80s with good sink, and a curveball that wasn't fully developed, but had enough consistent shape and command that Double-A hitters weren't able to handle it. By the end of the season, he had added a slider which became his primary breaking pitch. Part of that is due to the slider revolution across the game and part of it was Burke's blister issues, which made the curve a less than ideal option. Burke having the ability to throw both only helps him, assuming he can find a way to throw the curve without pain. His development is still ongoing, but when right Burke has shown the tools and knowledge to get hitters back into the dugout, and given the dearth of starting pitching options in Texas at the moment, he may have spent his last year in the minors.

Variance: High. The injury factor is the big player here; with blister and shoulder issues already on the board, Burke is a high risk to spend time on the injured list going forward. If those issues are non-factors, Burke could pitch for a decade and maybe bump up a half grade on the OFP. Until he shows major league durability, Burke's projection remains somewhat cloudy.

Ben Carsley's Fantasy Take: Nope. Between the lack of upside, the injury risk and this org's track record, I'm all set. You should be too.

8 Sherten Apostel 3B   OFP: 55   ETA: 2022

Born: 03/11/99   Age: 21   Bats: R   Throws: R   Height: 6'4"   Weight: 200   Origin: International Free Agent, 2018

YEAR	TEAM	LVL	AGE	PA	R	2B	3B	HR	RBI	BB	K	SB	CS	AVG/OBP/SLG	DRC+	VORP	BABIP	BRR	FRAA	WARP	PF
2017	DPI	RK	18	259	43	12	4	9	48	56	49	4	5	.258/.422/.495	158	37.7	.296	-0.6	3B(59) 8.9	2.9	86
2018	BRI	RK	19	175	28	7	0	7	26	32	42	3	1	.259/.406/.460	148	12.7	.319	-0.9	3B(35) 3.6	1.7	103
2018	SPO	A-	19	49	7	1	0	1	10	9	8	0	1	.351/.469/.459	203	9.0	.400	0.0	3B(8) -0.6	0.5	101
2019	HIC	A	20	319	38	13	1	15	43	28	71	2	1	.258/.332/.470	119	13.7	.290	-3.0	3B(70) 1.6, 1B(12) 0.0	1.4	98
2019	DEB	A+	20	159	18	5	1	4	16	23	49	0	0	.237/.352/.378	117	9.9	.341	1.6	3B(40) 1.4	1.1	98
2020	TEX	MLB	21	251	27	11	1	8	30	26	82	0	0	.228/.315/.398	87	3.0	.320	-0.4	3B 2, 1B 0	0.6	116

Comparables: Yairo Muñoz, Brett Phillips, Drew Robinson

The Report: Apostel has big tools, and he's translated enough of them into on-field performance to have gotten to the Carolina League as a 20-year-old. He has a well-filled out, strong and athletic frame. The two notable tools for the Curaçaoan are big power and an exceptional arm. The present hit tool could inspire a wide range of opinions depending on what day you see him. There is plus bat speed and Apostel makes very satisfying contact when he squares it up. He will whiff a fair bit though, which is not a surprise given the long levers and corresponding length in his swing. That contributes to a high strikeout rate at present, but he also has excellent plate discipline. The approach can border on passiveness though, and put him behind in counts as often as it gets him ahead. This is obviously beneficial to him when he gets a good pitch in a hitter's count, but the early selectivity can dig a hole which accounts for some of the strikeouts.

Apostel's offensive profile is ideal for third base, but there are already questions about whether he'll stick at the hot corner long term. I think he's fine there at present. While he isn't the smoothest or most natural-looking defender, his range, instincts, and first step are good enough. Still, he's not going to get any quicker, and if he fills out any more he might be a first baseman.

Variance: High. There's development that needs to happen with the hit tool and he'll probably need to sharpen up his defense as well, but time is on his side. A move to first base would put significant pressure on the bat, though.

Ben Carsley's Fantasy Take: Apostel already started to get some buzz in dynasty leagues last season, and it's easy to see why. I wish we could be slightly more confident in his ability to stay at third long term, but Apostel has the power and approach required to potentially be fantasy-relevant even if he does move to the cold corner. He should be owned in any league that rosters 125-plus prospects. If you're the type who bases your team name off your roster, Apostel is arguably a top-2 dude.

9 Cole Winn RHP   OFP: 55   ETA: 2022

Born: 11/25/99   Age: 20   Bats: R   Throws: R   Height: 6'2"   Weight: 190   Origin: Round 1, 2018 Draft (#15 overall)

YEAR	TEAM	LVL	AGE	W	L	SV	G	GS	IP	H	HR	BB/9	K/9	K	GB%	BABIP	WHIP	ERA	DRA	WARP	PF
2019	HIC	A	19	4	4	0	18	18	68²	59	5	5.1	8.5	65	48%	.290	1.43	4.46	5.47	-0.2	99
2020	TEX	MLB	20	2	2	0	33	0	35	35	6	4.1	6.7	26	44%	.280	1.45	5.04	4.96	0.1	116

Comparables: Luke Jackson, Tyler Chatwood, Mauricio Cabrera

The Report: As a first-round prep arm receiving plaudits for his command, Winn came out of last year's draft saddled with high expectations. Early struggles following this year's aggressive assignment to full-season ball have seen him slip in some quarters, but he finished the campaign well and will enter next season as a strong bounceback candidate. The command didn't live up to expectations early on, but it improved as time went on and projects as potential plus with his clean and repeatable delivery. Winn sits mid 90s with the heater, flashing life up in the zone where it can be a swing-and-miss offering. There is an easy plus fastball here when he commands it. The curveball is his best secondary and also projects plus. The hook is a high-70s, 12-to-6 breaker coming with good bite that he can spot for strikes or put away hitters out of the zone. The low-80s slider and mid-80s change flash above-average, and it certainly looks like there is a legitimate four-pitch mix developing.

Variance: Medium. Risk is inherent with prep arms and Winn didn't set the world on fire in his debut season. There aren't many red flags here though, and what he may lack in upside he should make up for in polish.

Ben Carsley's Fantasy Take: Although they're very different pitchers, Winn doesn't rank too differently than Crouse will in my eyes. He lacks some of Crouse's upside, but he's also a safer bet to remain a starter long-term. At a certain point, this really just comes down to your preference in pitcher profile.

10 Bubba Thompson OF   OFP: 50   ETA: 2022

Born: 06/09/98   Age: 22   Bats: R   Throws: R   Height: 6'1"   Weight: 180   Origin: Round 1, 2017 Draft (#26 overall)

YEAR	TEAM	LVL	AGE	PA	R	2B	3B	HR	RBI	BB	K	SB	CS	AVG/OBP/SLG	DRC+	VORP	BABIP	BRR	FRAA	WARP	PF
2017	RNG	RK	19	123	23	7	2	3	12	6	28	5	5	.257/.317/.434	83	4.0	.317	0.8	CF(27) -4.0	-0.1	101
2018	HIC	A	20	363	52	18	5	8	42	23	104	32	7	.289/.344/.446	118	26.0	.396	6.1	CF(67) 1.1, LF(17) 0.7	2.6	99
2019	DEB	A+	21	228	24	8	2	5	21	21	72	12	3	.178/.261/.312	55	-2.9	.246	2.6	LF(33) 1.5, CF(20) -1.8	-0.2	97
2020	TEX	MLB	22	251	23	12	1	6	25	14	91	9	3	.206/.259/.344	55	0.0	.307	0.9	CF -1, LF 2	-0.4	116

Comparables: Dexter Fowler, Keon Broxton, Darren Ford

The Report: It was an up and down year for Thompson, starting down before ending up. A hamate bone injury cost him time early in the season, while draining a lot of his offensive capabilities later in the season. Thompson got sent to the Arizona Fall League where he posted an .861 OPS in 16 games, looking closer to the highly-rated prospect he was coming into the 2019 season. That said, the road ahead for Thompson is long. At the plate, Thompson struggles with pitch recognition, and has yet to show the game power to make up for a hefty strikeout rate, as he's more of a line drive hitter at present.

When he does get on base, Thompson has good wheels that also serve him well in the outfield. He lacks the elite profile of fellow prospect Leody Taveras, but his work in the field is far from a liability. Thompson is entering his fourth year of organized baseball at just 21, so the door is still wide open. The concerning part is entering that fourth year without showing much refinement at the plate. Without that, Thompson's future will remain hazy even with all the potential in the world.

Variance: High. The lack of consistency in his approach limits the ceiling on Thompson. There is significant upside past the OFP if something clicks, but there is little evidence of that happening so far.

Ben Carsley's Fantasy Take: I'm not quite ready to give up yet. We viewed Thompson as a top-50 dynasty league prospect not too long ago, and while the reports about his trouble with pitch recognition are discouraging, I won't hold a hamate injury against him. He's definitely a high-risk prospect, but Thompson still has the speed, athleticism, and ability to make hard contact that I'm inclined to gamble on. I view this as a good time to buy low on Thompson, even if I acknowledge that the odds of him paying off for you seem lower than they did a year or two ago.

The Next Ten

11 Tyler Phillips RHP

Born: 10/27/97 Age: 22 Bats: R Throws: R Height: 6'5" Weight: 191 Origin: Round 16, 2015 Draft (#468 overall)

YEAR	TEAM	LVL	AGE	W	L	SV	G	GS	IP	H	HR	BB/9	K/9	K	GB%	BABIP	WHIP	ERA	DRA	WARP	PF
2017	SPO	A-	19	4	2	0	13	13	73	78	6	1.4	9.6	78	52%	.338	1.22	3.45	3.60	1.4	98
2017	HIC	A	19	1	2	0	7	4	25¹	28	2	3.2	5.3	15	47%	.302	1.46	6.39	5.99	-0.3	99
2018	HIC	A	20	11	5	0	22	22	128	117	4	1.0	8.7	124	54%	.308	1.02	2.67	3.48	2.6	97
2019	DEB	A+	21	2	2	0	6	6	37²	28	1	1.4	6.7	28	57%	.260	0.90	1.19	3.46	0.7	96
2019	FRI	AA	21	7	9	0	18	16	93¹	95	15	1.9	7.1	74	52%	.292	1.23	4.72	5.29	-0.4	103
2020	TEX	MLB	22	1	1	0	12	2	17	17	3	3.8	6.7	13	47%	.284	1.45	5.09	4.88	0.1	116

Comparables: Zack Littell, Duane Underwood Jr., Logan Webb

Phillips has an athletic build on a 6-foot-5 frame with broad shoulders, a high waist, and a strong lower half. He has a clean delivery with a loose whippy arm action from a high three-quarters arm slot.

He works with two fastballs, a four-seamer that sits 93-94 and a two-seamer at 90-93 with heavy sink and arm-side action. His primary secondary is a plus changeup with excellent arm speed, plus tumble, and some fade. Phillips also includes an average curveball with a slurvy shape that occasionally will flash above average. He has solid feel for both of his secondaries and can locate them fairly consistently. Phillips likes to lean heavily on his fastball mix and when he's able to command the zone he works in all four quadrants effectively before utilizing a tunnel to get whiffs on the changeup. He mixes in the breaking ball for a change of speed or to try and catch a hitter off balance, but his changeup is his primary out pitch. Phillips has excellent control of all three offerings, but his fastball command can come and go, leading to bursts of hard contact from the opposition. Without improving consistency there, he's going to have enough bad innings to limit his effectiveness as a starting pitcher, but if he irons that out he could slot himself into the back of a major league rotation.

12 Davis Wendzel 3B

Born: 05/23/97 Age: 23 Bats: R Throws: R Height: 6'0" Weight: 205 Origin: Round 1, 2019 Draft (#41 overall)

YEAR	TEAM	LVL	AGE	PA	R	2B	3B	HR	RBI	BB	K	SB	CS	AVG/OBP/SLG	DRC+	VORP	BABIP	BRR	FRAA	WARP	PF
2020	TEX	MLB	23	251	21	11	1	5	23	18	83	2	1	.209/.271/.326	59	3.0	.304	0.0	3B 0	-0.5	116

Comparables: Austin Meadows, Tyler White, Johnny Monell

It was a bit of a surprise when the Rangers selected Wendzel in the comp round of 2019 draft. Wendzel's shorter, stocky build doesn't match the body type of traditional Rangers draft picks—who tend to look more like say, Bubba Thompson—but you could argue that their upside seeking has persisted here despite the feel of a "safe college bat" pick. Perhaps the Rangers are merely adjusting which upside traits they prioritize; here, approach, quickness, and coordination over a projectable frame and foot speed. Wendzel has coordination, plus bat speed, and a top-tier approach at the plate, but his swing is currently tooled to always make contact way out in front of his body. As a result there is a smaller window to create quality contact, and when he does it's almost always to the pull side. With adjustments to swing mechanics, Wendzel could better tap into his innate quality hit-tool markers while maintaining his raw power.

Defensively Wendzel has impressive hands, reactions, and instincts. He plays both third base and short, although his fringy foot speed and lateral range will likely limit him to a corner infield or outfield position. He flashes plus arm strength to complete the profile of a player who could step into any corner and be an asset defensively.

All in all, Wendzel paints the picture of a future four-corners bench player who has more upside than you'd expect from a late-first-round college bat, but has significant issues to iron out before he's there. If swing adjustments happen while his body and approach hold steady, there's a potential above-average regular here down the line.

13 David Garcia C
Born: 02/06/00   Age: 20   Bats: B   Throws: R   Height: 5'11"   Weight: 170   Origin: International Free Agent, 2016

YEAR	TEAM	LVL	AGE	PA	R	2B	3B	HR	RBI	BB	K	SB	CS	AVG/OBP/SLG	DRC+	VORP	BABIP	BRR	FRAA	WARP	PF
2017	DRN	RK	17	222	27	7	1	1	26	25	49	1	0	.215/.321/.280	78	3.2	.279	1.8	C(41) 0.9	0.6	104
2018	RNG	RK	18	129	10	8	0	1	20	9	26	0	1	.269/.320/.361	99	4.0	.337	0.2	C(33) 0.0	0.6	102
2019	SPO	A-	19	210	33	14	0	5	29	21	42	1	1	.277/.351/.435	127	15.0	.331	-0.6	C(37) -0.3	1.2	101
2020	TEX	MLB	20	251	22	12	0	5	24	18	73	1	0	.219/.281/.343	64	0.0	.298	0.0	C 0	-0.3	116

At the Texas Rangers Futures Camp held in Frisco, Garcia saw his stock rise more than any other player on the field. Coming in with a reputation as a small-bodied catcher with quality defensive markers, Garcia showed up with a reasonably mature build with good muscle both on his upper and lower halves. There's still room for more, but he's well on his way.

Garcia was even better than advertised defensively. His hands glided to receive the ball and strong wrists stopped it dead in its tracks after contact with the glove. He worked it well to all corners of the plate with natural movements. Footwork on blocks were second nature and he took a group of bad pitches in the dirt without one getting away from him. He popped 1.89 to second, showing a quick transfer and plus arm strength. The switch-hitter has above-average bat speed and quality hand-eye, portenting good contact abilities.

His pitch recognition wasn't nearly as raw as you'd expect for a hitter off the bus from short-season, and Garcia flashed gap-to-gap power, but his teenaged frame only produces below-average raw power, although that should bump up with further strength gains.

Garcia currently profiles as a tandem defense-first catcher with above-average regular upside if he can continue to add raw strength and get some power to transfer into games.

14 Anderson Tejeda SS
Born: 05/01/98   Age: 22   Bats: B   Throws: R   Height: 5'11"   Weight: 160   Origin: International Free Agent, 2014

YEAR	TEAM	LVL	AGE	PA	R	2B	3B	HR	RBI	BB	K	SB	CS	AVG/OBP/SLG	DRC+	VORP	BABIP	BRR	FRAA	WARP	PF
2017	HIC	A	19	446	68	24	9	8	53	36	132	10	7	.247/.309/.411	93	21.4	.343	2.0	SS(82) -2.0, 2B(30) 0.0	1.4	101
2018	DEB	A+	20	522	76	17	5	19	74	49	142	11	4	.259/.331/.439	122	29.5	.330	3.0	SS(105) 2.9, 2B(12) 1.6	4.1	102
2019	DEB	A+	21	181	22	10	1	4	24	17	58	9	4	.234/.315/.386	84	11.5	.333	1.3	SS(39) 2.4	0.8	98
2020	TEX	MLB	22	251	24	12	2	8	29	15	92	2	1	.220/.271/.393	68	0.0	.323	0.0	SS 0, 2B 1	-0.1	116

Comparables: Trevor Story, Yu Chang, Junior Lake

Another victim of the evil curse placed upon Rangers infield prospects, Tejeda only played 43 games in Kinston before a subluxed shoulder ended his 2019. Tejeda is an enigmatic player who has yet to put it all together. His arm in the field is strong enough for shortstop and third base, he showed a power surge in 2018 with 18 bombs, and won't be 22 until next May. Not unlike a couple players on the list above him, Tejeda would do well to work on being more patient at the plate. Combining a more refined eye for what to lay off with his prowess for driving balls would vault him up the list in a system that has an assortment of shortstops below Double-A. The shoulder injury is worrisome, but indications are that Tejeda will make a full recovery in time for next season.

15 Jonathan Ornelas SS
Born: 05/26/00   Age: 20   Bats: R   Throws: R   Height: 6'1"   Weight: 178   Origin: Round 3, 2018 Draft (#91 overall)

YEAR	TEAM	LVL	AGE	PA	R	2B	3B	HR	RBI	BB	K	SB	CS	AVG/OBP/SLG	DRC+	VORP	BABIP	BRR	FRAA	WARP	PF
2018	RNG	RK	18	203	34	10	4	3	28	25	41	15	5	.302/.389/.459	137	16.4	.371	1.7	3B(31) 1.1, SS(12) -1.3	1.5	102
2019	HIC	A	19	472	61	24	3	6	38	42	103	13	4	.257/.333/.373	116	23.6	.322	-1.7	SS(61) -4.0, 2B(34) -0.3	1.7	99
2020	TEX	MLB	20	251	23	12	1	4	23	21	69	6	2	.226/.297/.339	70	0.0	.309	0.0	SS -2, 2B 0	-0.3	116

Ornelas is definitely closer to 10 than 20 on this list and a strong candidate for a breakout next season. He didn't put up huge numbers this season, but held his own as a teenager in full-season ball and showed off a wide array of skills. Ornelas is an excellent defender, mainly at shortstop but he also showed well in stints at second and third. He's got the range, arm, and instincts for the six, and those tools play well at the other spots too. He's promising at the plate as well, with a quick bat, plus hands and strong wrists that consistently produce very hard contact. Mainly pull-oriented, Ornelas has shown the ability to adjust to and slice offspeed pitches the other way when necessary. Solid and wiry strong, the former third-rounder projects for a bit of power as he continues to acclimate himself to pro ball. Good utility types who can hit and play quality defense are always nice pieces to have.

16 Julio Pablo Martinez   OF
Born: 03/21/96   Age: 24   Bats: L   Throws: L   Height: 5'9"   Weight: 174   Origin: International Free Agent, 2018

YEAR	TEAM	LVL	AGE	PA	R	2B	3B	HR	RBI	BB	K	SB	CS	AVG/OBP/SLG	DRC+	VORP	BABIP	BRR	FRAA	WARP	PF
2018	DRG	RK	22	33	10	1	1	1	3	9	7	2	3	.409/.606/.682	158	11.5	.571	2.2	CF(5) 0.4, RF(1) 0.0	0.5	94
2018	SPO	A-	22	273	49	9	5	8	21	34	69	11	6	.252/.351/.436	103	16.4	.323	0.5	CF(55) 1.5, LF(2) 0.1	1.1	105
2019	HIC	A	23	44	7	1	1	1	5	3	12	4	1	.250/.295/.400	112	1.0	.321	-0.7	CF(7) -0.7, LF(3) 0.1	0.0	95
2019	DEB	A+	23	456	59	21	4	14	58	39	144	28	12	.248/.319/.423	111	29.5	.344	6.0	CF(65) -5.0, LF(38) -3.0	1.6	98
2020	TEX	MLB	24	251	26	11	1	8	29	18	92	4	2	.223/.284/.390	76	0.0	.331	0.2	CF 0, LF 0	0.1	116

Comparables: Justin Maxwell, Kevin Mattison, Mike Yastrzemski

The Cuban defector arrived to the Rangers system with a lot of hype. Some of that has been well-deserved; 15 homers between Low and High-A last season paired with borderline elite speed gave Martinez the base for a strong center field profile. The downside to that power was significant swing-and-miss issues as he struck out 156 times in 500 plate appearances. An aggressive approach paired with pitch recognition politely described as "has room to improve" keeps Martinez from reaching his full potential as a prospect. With year three of affiliated ball on deck, Martinez's ability to get on base more will be crucial to his development and advancement. There's a good chance Martinez will also see more games in the corner outfield positions in 2020, as it's likely that he'll share a roster with Rangers top prospect Leody Taveras for some of the season. A 24-year-old who hasn't cracked Double-A would be running out of prospect time normally, but Martinez's background makes it less of an issue here. Still 2020 is a big year for Martinez, who needs to take a step forward with the bat to maintain his prospect status.

17 Keithron Moss   IF
Born: 08/20/01   Age: 18   Bats: B   Throws: R   Height: 5'11"   Weight: 165   Origin: International Free Agent, 2017

YEAR	TEAM	LVL	AGE	PA	R	2B	3B	HR	RBI	BB	K	SB	CS	AVG/OBP/SLG	DRC+	VORP	BABIP	BRR	FRAA	WARP	PF
2018	DRG	RK	16	204	29	11	1	0	23	35	62	8	7	.196/.350/.276	89	7.9	.314	1.4	2B(30) -6.8, SS(17) -2.0	-0.3	93
2019	RNG	RK	17	147	27	4	3	2	14	21	40	8	2	.308/.425/.442	171	12.6	.443	0.3	2B(17) 0.2, 3B(11) 2.1	1.5	108
2020	TEX	MLB	18	251	23	11	1	4	22	27	102	4	3	.219/.312/.329	75	2.0	.388	0.0	2B -2, SS 0	-0.1	116

Many years ago my father had a Lebanese roommate in Hartford or New Britain, I forget which. He had just gotten out of the service. I should remember, because I've heard this story many times. He always brings up the lamb tartare his roommate's mother made, and how it was one of the best dishes he ever had. Moss is rawer than that kibbeh nayyeh. There's the potential for a power over hit corner bat here. Not as tasty an outcome, but not too bad either.

18 Taylor Hearn   LHP
Born: 08/30/94   Age: 25   Bats: L   Throws: L   Height: 6'5"   Weight: 210   Origin: Round 5, 2015 Draft (#164 overall)

YEAR	TEAM	LVL	AGE	W	L	SV	G	GS	IP	H	HR	BB/9	K/9	K	GB%	BABIP	WHIP	ERA	DRA	WARP	PF
2017	BRD	A+	22	4	6	0	18	17	87¹	65	8	3.8	10.9	106	50%	.281	1.17	4.12	3.88	1.4	99
2018	ALT	AA	23	3	6	0	19	19	104	75	6	3.3	9.3	107	41%	.256	1.09	3.12	3.02	2.8	92
2018	FRI	AA	23	1	2	0	5	5	25	29	5	3.2	11.9	33	36%	.375	1.52	5.04	5.68	-0.1	114
2019	NAS	AAA	24	1	3	0	4	4	20	14	3	4.5	11.7	26	29%	.262	1.20	4.05	2.90	0.7	91
2019	TEX	MLB	24	0	1	0	1	1	0¹	3	0	108.0	0.0	0	50%	.750	21.00	108.00	1.88	0.0	94
2020	TEX	MLB	25	0	0	0	2	2	5	6	1	4.2	5.1	3	37%	.281	1.57	6.05	5.59	0.0	116

Comparables: Eric Skoglund, Taylor Rogers, Sean Nolin

Murphy's Law hit the 25-year-old lefty hard this year. After four games for Triple-A Nashville, Hearn got called up for his major league debut against Seattle. Hearn threw a third of an inning, gave up five runs, and left with an elbow injury never to be seen again for the rest of 2019. Barring an unannounced setback, Hearn will be able to resume his career in 2020, and he was a top-flight pitching prospect before the mysterious elbow ailment. It's hard to know what we'll see from Hearn when he retakes the diamond, but pre-injury Hearn had a fastball around 93-94 with a good changeup and fringey breaking ball. After almost a full year on the shelf, however, it'll be good to see Hearn do anything involving throwing a baseball.

19 Ronny Henriquez RHP

Born: 06/20/00 Age: 20 Bats: R Throws: R Height: 5'10" Weight: 155 Origin: International Free Agent, 2017

YEAR	TEAM	LVL	AGE	W	L	SV	G	GS	IP	H	HR	BB/9	K/9	K	GB%	BABIP	WHIP	ERA	DRA	WARP	PF
2018	DRN	RK	18	5	0	0	11	11	58	37	2	1.2	12.3	79	50%	.269	0.78	1.55	1.13	3.1	112
2019	HIC	A	19	6	6	0	21	19	82	91	6	3.0	10.9	99	39%	.384	1.44	4.50	5.91	-0.7	99
2020	TEX	MLB	20	2	2	0	33	0	35	35	5	3.7	8.8	34	37%	.304	1.40	4.76	4.74	0.2	116

Comparables: Pedro Avila, Joe Wieland, José Berríos

Possessed of a fast arm on a small body, Henríquez is likely to strike many as a future reliever as he climbs the ladder and gains more exposure. It's an understandable assumption, as he really is short—listed at 5-foot-10 and not convincingly so—and to this point hasn't consistently made it deep into outings. It is far too early to give up on him as a starter, though, because he has a pair of interesting secondaries and he made strides with his command as a teenager in full-season ball. He has a plus fastball that holds velocity late into outings, sitting mid 90s and touching 97 with flashes of life up and sink down. His slider and split-change are both future above-average offerings, though he's not entirely consistent with either at present. He is a work in progress; his effectiveness will swing wildly from one start to the next, getting knocked around one week and looking dominant the next. But he's advanced for his age, and though he'll fly under-the-radar as far as right-handed pitching prospects in this organization are concerned, he's worth your attention.

20 Curtis Terry 1B

Born: 10/06/96 Age: 23 Bats: R Throws: R Height: 6'3" Weight: 264 Origin: Round 13, 2015 Draft (#378 overall)

YEAR	TEAM	LVL	AGE	PA	R	2B	3B	HR	RBI	BB	K	SB	CS	AVG/OBP/SLG	DRC+	VORP	BABIP	BRR	FRAA	WARP	PF
2017	SPO	A-	20	244	26	12	0	12	30	7	60	3	0	.258/.303/.467	98	7.6	.299	-1.4	1B(54) -6.6	-0.6	96
2018	SPO	A-	21	290	51	17	2	15	60	32	64	1	1	.337/.434/.606	187	30.5	.405	-0.6	1B(38) -1.1	2.5	105
2019	HIC	A	22	259	39	24	0	15	47	14	67	0	1	.263/.328/.560	130	16.8	.301	-0.6	1B(58) 0.1	0.9	100
2019	DEB	A+	22	271	35	12	2	10	33	23	50	0	1	.322/.395/.515	166	19.0	.370	-0.9	1B(57) 0.0	1.9	99
2020	TEX	MLB	23	251	28	14	1	10	33	13	75	0	0	.238/.292/.435	88	1.0	.305	0.0	1B -1	0.4	116

Guys like Curtis Terry don't often make top prospect lists in any form or fashion. A large man at 6-foot-3 and 246 pounds, he doesn't look the part of a baseball player in the modern era. He's—as the kids would say—thicc from his head to his toes. Yet, he does the thing you have to do: produce. Terry is a power hitter, swatting 25 home runs this year between two A-ball stops. The 2015 13th-round pick has blossomed into a fearsome bat, and earned his place on this list. You'll never see anything save for 1B or DH by his name on a lineup card, though his abilities at first base are underrated, but he hits and that's what teams care about these days. Terry has earned a chance to start 2020 at Double-A Frisco, and with no established starter at first base above him in the system Terry's ascent could take him further than anyone imagined.

Personal Cheeseball

PC Kyle Cody RHP

Born: 08/09/94 Age: 25 Bats: R Throws: R Height: 6'7" Weight: 245 Origin: Round 6, 2016 Draft (#189 overall)

YEAR	TEAM	LVL	AGE	W	L	SV	G	GS	IP	H	HR	BB/9	K/9	K	GB%	BABIP	WHIP	ERA	DRA	WARP	PF
2017	HIC	A	22	6	6	0	18	18	95¹	77	4	3.1	9.5	101	47%	.286	1.15	2.83	3.54	1.9	99
2017	DEB	A+	22	3	0	0	5	5	30²	25	0	2.9	10.3	35	51%	.325	1.14	2.05	3.79	0.5	92
2020	TEX	MLB	25	2	2	0	33	0	35	35	5	3.7	8.9	35	45%	.308	1.43	4.93	4.74	0.2	116

Comparables: Shaun Anderson, Christian Garcia, Alex Meyer

We had Cody pegged for this spot even before he was surprisingly added to the 40-man, but given that nugget he might be the team's cheeseball too. He went unsigned as a 2015 Minnesota second-rounder out of Kentucky, and then was drafted the following year as a $150,000 sixth-round senior sign by Texas. The big Wisconsinite was one of our favorite rising pitching prospects in 2017, pairing a mid-90s fastball with plus sink and plane with a changeup and curveball that both flashed above-average to plus. It was a tantalizing arsenal, and he looked like he might move fast as a mid-rotation type…right up until his 2018 Tommy John surgery, which wiped out nearly all of his last two seasons. He's 25 with limited pro experience and none above A-ball, but it's a very interesting arm if he's healthy, and the Rangers thought enough of him to protect him from Rule 5. At the very least, he's a worthwhile 2020 follow.

Low Minors Sleeper

LMS **Pedro Gonzalez** OF

Born: 10/27/97   Age: 22   Bats: R   Throws: R   Height: 6'5"   Weight: 190   Origin: International Free Agent, 2014

YEAR	TEAM	LVL	AGE	PA	R	2B	3B	HR	RBI	BB	K	SB	CS	AVG/OBP/SLG	DRC+	VORP	BABIP	BRR	FRAA	WARP	PF
2017	GJR	RK	19	209	28	16	6	3	28	18	53	11	6	.321/.388/.519	96	13.7	.432	0.9	CF(41) -3.9	-0.1	120
2018	HIC	A	20	371	47	17	5	12	46	28	110	9	5	.234/.296/.421	92	11.7	.307	1.7	CF(60) 4.7, LF(20) -1.1	1.7	100
2019	HIC	A	21	459	69	13	5	23	67	39	129	14	6	.248/.317/.471	119	24.2	.300	-0.1	RF(55) 0.3, CF(37) -0.8	1.6	99
2020	TEX	MLB	22	251	23	11	2	7	27	13	94	3	2	.205/.253/.361	56	0.0	.306	0.0	CF 1, RF 0	-0.5	116

Comparables: Carter Kieboom, Drew Robinson, Isan Díaz

González has hovered near the back of prospect lists ever since he signed for a pretty hefty bonus a few years back, which he earned with qualities that jump out on first look. He's tall and lean, strong and athletic, with big raw power and a good arm. It is true that he has all of these virtues, and that they are just enough to keep him hanging around. He did have a solid age-21 season, making the Sally League All-Star Game in his second year at the level while pacing the circuit in homers. He covers all three outfield positions ably. Although he improved his approach a bit in his second pass at the league, he is still haunted by the demons that beset many a tools-driven prospect—swing-and-miss. And it is a lot of swing-and-miss. Long arms and difficulty picking up spin will do that, and it is hard to see these issues fading away when he faces higher levels of pitching. Still, who am I to bet against tools? He's worth stashing somewhere on this list just in case.

Top Talents 25 and Under (as of 4/1/2020)

1. Willie Calhoun
2. Leody Taveras
3. Josh Jung
4. Nick Solak
5. Joe Palumbo
6. Sam Huff
7. Hans Crouse
8. Nomar Mazara
9. Brock Burke
10. Sherten Apostel

Not unlike the Rangers themselves, the 25U list features potential ruling the day over the current reality. It's been the situation since the teardown of the major league team that began in 2017. The future is the focus, in the hope that it one day becomes a strong present.

Willie Calhoun tops the list in his final year of eligibility; the Yu Darvish trade's crown jewel overcame the warped meritocracy of modern baseball becoming a top half of the lineup hitter in the second half of the season. It was a victory for talent and resilience in the face of unnecessary obstacles.

It gets complicated behind him, but complicated in the delightful way of deciding between favorite dishes at a fabulous restaurant. The lower rankings of a major leaguer like Mazara likely raises eyebrows, but understand it's not without consideration. Mazara has plateaued as league-average, a major leaguer, yes, but one who doesn't stand out.

Taveras has an elite defensive profile, good enough to play in the majors right now. The ceiling is high on the 20-year-old conjuring All-Star dreams in the minds of fans and evaluators alike. Jung turns 22 soon, but has shown as more the 1b to Taveras' 1a after being taken in the top ten this past draft. On a team desperate for a franchise third baseman, Jung is a few steps away from seizing the position that Texas attempted to patch using a combination of Asdrubal Cabrera, Logan Forsythe, Isiah Kiner-Falefa, and Solak.

Huff, as noted above, is the high riser this season, riding a hot bat and competent behind the plate defense to becoming a top prospect. Catchers are odd and rare birds, with potential stars being worth their weight in gold. Huff occupies that status now for Texas, who is projected to run Jeff Mathis and Jose Trevino as a platoon for 2020.

Then there's the enigmatic gasoline-bringer Crouse. The 21-year-old has stuff for days, but durability concerns abound with the wiry righty. Those fears weren't alleviated with Crouse needing elbow surgery in October for bone spur removal. Crouse's ceiling is the sky, but don't look down because the floor might give you vertigo.

Mix in a major leaguer with injury concerns in Burke with young phenoms who had stellar 2019s in Apostel and Winn, and the Rangers' future is bright. With other names like Ronny Henriguez, Ricky Vanasco, Jonathan Ornelas, and many other baby Rangers bubbling under the surface this list is going to be one worth reading for the next half decade in the Lone Star State.

Eyewitness Reports

Eyewitness Report: Leody Taveras

Evaluator: Kevin W Carter
Report Date: 07/17/2019
Dates Seen: 7/9/2019 - 7/11/2019
Risk Factor: Medium
Physical/Health: Right at list height and maybe 5-10 lbs heavier than listed 171 lbs. Lean muscle throughout lower body with a slim, but lean torso. Frame could support 15 lbs comfortably. Taveras is an excellent athlete, loose with explosive, twitchy actions and graceful body control. Good traditional athleticism with quick acceleration and bendy flexibility.

Tool	Future Grade	Report
Hit	60	Excellent coordination and quickness currently key to his offensive skillset. Left-handed hitting: Plus bat speed, plus feel for barrel, adjusts swing well to location and can adjust breaking ball. Gets on plane well and sprays hard line drives around the field. Righth-handed hitting: Average bat speed with contact first swing. Moderate feel for barrel with contact oriented swing. Swing much more flat from right side and produces more grounders. Usually aggressive on early fastballs, but can be a little too passive. Still struggles with above average breaking/off speed at times.
Power	40	Above average raw power. Approach currently limits power from both sides as he defaults to contact approach too often. Right handed swing doesn't tap into raw power at all and currently plays down to true 20 game power.
Baserunning/ Speed	60	Plus speed with plus acceleration and top speed. Reads pitchers well and should be a plus base stealer at the MLB level. Good instincts on the basepaths as well.
Glove	60	Good reads off the bat with plus closing speed. Routes can be a bit inconsistent, but he makes up for a bit by good tracking skills at full speed.
Arm	55	Above-average arm strength and regularly makes strong, accurate throws. Will play at an above-average level in center field.

Conclusion: Leody Taveras profiles as a first division regular in center where his plus defensive profile and speed will allow him to provide significant value that will offset a slightly below-average bat. Taveras is an excellent athlete with quality body control and will likely provide enough contact and OBP to allow his base stealing abilities and premium defense to play every day at the MLB level. It's possible that poor power from the right side will limit him to a long side platoon role if he is unable to bring his righty swing closer to his left side. Taveras has the athletic ability, raw power, feel for hit, and patience for plus regular 75th percentile upside if he's able to tie the tools together and refine his swing/approach to get more out of his natural abilities.

Eyewitness Report: David Garcia

Evaluator: Kevin Carter
Report Date: 10/07/2019
Dates Seen: 9/29, 10/1, 10/4, 10/6
Risk Factor: High
Physical/Health: 5'11", 185 lbs with sloped shoulders and a sturdy catcher's lower half. Still has room for 10-15 pounds more. Good athlete with excellent coordination, some quick twitch, and a lean frame.

Tool	Future Grade	Report
Hit	55	Excellent hands allow him to get the bat on the ball often. Above average bat speed. Gets out of sync a bit with the lower half and loses power when fooled a bit, leading to weak flies to the opposite field. Approach advanced for age and recognizes above average breaking stuff, but still a bit over-aggressive on stuff slightly outside the zone.
Power	40	Fringy raw power, but Garcia gets to a surprising amount of it with an XBH driven-approach. Gap powers to the opposite field from both sides of the plate and home run power pullside.
Baserunning/ Speed	30	"Fast for a catcher" is a backhanded compliment and it rings true here. Currently a 40 runner, but won't be for long as he continues to put muscle on his lower half and play catcher 100 games per season.
Glove	60	Premium hands with strong wrists and fluid controlled actions. Hands glide to ball and stick when the ball meets the glove. Good footwork and blocking abilities.
Arm	60	1.89 pop time to 2nd. Quick efficient footwork with plus arm strength and excellent accuracy.

Conclusion: David Garcia is a good athlete with advanced catching abilities and quality offensive markers that should allow him to project as a tandem catcher at the MLB level. Garcia's quality hit tool and approach along with a "drive the ball" mentality will likely let him provide enough value with the bat to allow his quality defensive profile to shine through. If playing catcher and the grind stiffens Garcia's swing up as he ages, his carrying tool on the offensive side will be limited and he would likely be relegated to a up/down role. If Garcia maintains his athleticism and improves his approach moving through the system and carrying a heavy workload, he could be a solid regular on a first division team.

Toronto Blue Jays

The State of the System

Well, graduating two of the best prospects in baseball is going to leave a mark, but there's more depth here than you might have thought.

The Top Ten

─────────────── ★ ★ ★ *2020 Top 101 Prospect* **#19** ★ ★ ★ ───────────────

1   **Nate Pearson   RHP**   OFP: 70   ETA: 2020

Born: 08/20/96   Age: 23   Bats: R   Throws: R   Height: 6'6"   Weight: 245   Origin: Round 1, 2017 Draft (#28 overall)

YEAR	TEAM	LVL	AGE	W	L	SV	G	GS	IP	H	HR	BB/9	K/9	K	GB%	BABIP	WHIP	ERA	DRA	WARP	PF
2017	VAN	A-	20	0	0	0	7	7	19	6	0	2.4	11.4	24	40%	.158	0.58	0.95	1.01	0.9	103
2019	DUN	A+	22	3	0	0	6	6	21	10	2	1.3	15.0	35	35%	.229	0.62	0.86	1.59	0.9	105
2019	NHP	AA	22	1	4	0	16	16	62²	41	4	3.0	9.9	69	40%	.250	0.99	2.59	3.16	1.4	100
2019	BUF	AAA	22	1	0	0	3	3	18	12	2	1.5	7.5	15	44%	.208	0.83	3.00	3.61	0.5	102
2020	TOR	MLB	23	3	3	0	14	8	46	46	8	3.7	10.0	52	40%	.314	1.40	4.73	4.73	0.4	98

Comparables: Clay Buchholz, Marco Gonzales, Daniel Hudson

The Report: There hasn't been a pitching prospect since Noah Syndergaard that features this combination of overpowering stuff and physical imposition on the mound. After missing nearly the entire 2018 season, Pearson eclipsed the 100-inning mark for the first time in his career across three separate levels. It all starts with a top-of-the scale fastball that routinely touched triple-digits. Once the batter starts to cheat to catch up with 100+, he does a good job of reading swings and switching to the "slow" stuff. With the fastball having all the makings of a 70+ grade, his secondaries don't have to be perfect to be effective. His slider has very good late bite in the mid-to-upper 80s, while the changeup is very firm and still a work-in-progress. His power curveball comes from a tough release point, but is inconsistent.

The 2019 season couldn't have gone better for Pearson, whose innings were heavily monitored until the last month of the season. He proved he could ramp up his workload and stay healthy—even though previous injuries were more of the freak kind—and the stuff he displayed multiple times through the order put to bed the idea that a move to the bullpen was imminent. The next step is to continue working on his secondary pitches in 2020. There is effort to the delivery that could be cut down, but the overall physicality and strength of Pearson gives the appearance of a future workhorse in the top half of a rotation.

Variance: Medium. The stuff could play in the majors now, but there is always inherent risk with guys who throw as hard as Pearson.

Ben Carsley's Fantasy Take: Normally this would be the part of the program where I warn you against investing in fantasy pitching prospects, but Pearson is one of my dudes, and I'm in love. Yes, the risk is high, but Pearson offsets it by providing sky-high potential as well. It's all but a lock that Pearson will miss more than a bat per inning in whatever role he occupies, and despite his injury history, Pearson has the frame and athleticism required to log innings. If it all breaks right, we're looking at a bona fide SP1 who notches 200-plus Ks in 180-plus innings. But even a more moderate outcome should see Pearson rack up a ton of strikeouts. Sometimes you gotta jump in headfirst: I have Pearson as a top-25 dynasty prospect.

★ ★ ★ *2020 Top 101 Prospect* **#43** ★ ★ ★

2 Jordan Groshans SS   OFP: 60   ETA: 2022
Born: 11/10/99   Age: 20   Bats: R   Throws: R   Height: 6'3"   Weight: 205   Origin: Round 1, 2018 Draft (#12 overall)

YEAR	TEAM	LVL	AGE	PA	R	2B	3B	HR	RBI	BB	K	SB	CS	AVG/OBP/SLG	DRC+	VORP	BABIP	BRR	FRAA	WARP	PF
2018	BLJ	RK	18	159	17	12	0	4	39	13	29	0	0	.331/.390/.500	147	14.7	.387	-0.8	3B(16) -1.2, SS(15) 0.6	1.1	103
2018	BLU	RK	18	48	4	1	0	1	4	2	8	0	0	.182/.229/.273	46	-0.6	.194	0.1	SS(6) 0.9, 3B(5) 0.0	0.0	102
2019	LNS	A	19	96	12	6	0	2	13	13	21	1	1	.337/.427/.482	169	10.6	.433	-0.4	SS(20) -1.8	0.9	106
2020	TOR	MLB	20	251	23	12	0	5	25	19	70	1	0	.238/.301/.364	77	0.0	.319	-0.5	SS 0, 3B 0	0.1	98

Comparables: Trevor Story, Brendan Rodgers, Alen Hanson

The Report: A foot injury limited Groshans to 23 games in the Midwest League this season. Prior to going down, he was on his way to a breakout season slashing .337/.427/.482 in 83 at-bats. Big and strong, Groshans projects as a plus bat with above-average contact ability and power. He has a quick trigger at the plate that allows him to catch up to velocity and the power plays in-game to all fields. The Jays will continue to give him reps at shortstop, where he's average as a defender, but his defensive future is likely at third. He has the arm strength and instincts to be solid at the hot corner.

There wasn't much time to catch Groshans in action this year, but when he was on the field it was easy to forget he was a teenager in his first full professional season. Rather, he looked more like a polished, college bat. And he's already showing the kind of hit/power combo you'd look for in a middle-of-the-order hitter.

Variance: High. Groshans has fewer than 100 games under his belt and is likely to begin 2020 back in Low-A. He'll need to prove that he can hit against more advanced pitching, and that foot issues won't be a recurring problem in the pros.

Ben Carsley's Fantasy Take: The Blue Jays start off their list with two personal favorites of mine. I don't believe in Groshans' ability to stick at short, but I like pretty much everything else about the package, and the Jays have a strong track record when it comes to developing this type of talent. He got a ton of buzz last year so he's unlikely to be available in deeper dynasty leagues, but if you play in a shallower format or your leaguemates were asleep, now is the time to buy. He's already a very legitimate top-101 candidate.

★ ★ ★ *2020 Top 101 Prospect* **#83** ★ ★ ★

3 Alek Manoah RHP   OFP: 60   ETA: Late 2021
Born: 01/09/98   Age: 22   Bats: R   Throws: R   Height: 6'6"   Weight: 260   Origin: Round 1, 2019 Draft (#11 overall)

YEAR	TEAM	LVL	AGE	W	L	SV	G	GS	IP	H	HR	BB/9	K/9	K	GB%	BABIP	WHIP	ERA	DRA	WARP	PF
2019	VAN	A-	21	0	1	0	6	6	17	13	1	2.6	14.3	27	30%	.379	1.06	2.65	3.15	0.4	97
2020	TOR	MLB	22	2	2	0	33	0	35	36	6	3.7	9.9	38	36%	.320	1.43	4.96	4.96	0.1	98

Comparables: Radhames Liz, Michael Stutes, Jeremy Hefner

The Report: You might be able to drop Manoah in a big league pen right now on the strength of his fastball/slider combo. The fastball sits mid 90s and routinely bumps higher in short bursts. He also gets extension from his height and stride, so the pitch gets on batters in a hurry and makes for an uncomfortable experience in the box. You can't sit fastball here either, as Manoah's slider was one of the better breaking balls in the NCAA, a mid-80s two-plane beast. It should easily end up plus and that might even be a grade light when the smoke clears. His change remains a work-in-progress, with the usual caveat that he hasn't needed even an average one as an amateur.

Manoah is a large human and can struggle with his command at times due to his size and arm action. The delivery will need to be cleaned up some to keep him as a starter long term, as will the command and changeup. Hmm, this might be a true backend Top 101, mid-rotation starter or late inning reliever prospect.

Variance: Medium. Manoah arguably had the best present stuff in the 2019 draft class, and the fastball/slider combo gives him a reasonably attainable major league relief fallback. However, the profile comes with a fair bit of relief risk as well.

Ben Carsley's Fantasy Take: Anyone else getting big-time Alex Meyer vibes? I am getting big-time Alex Meyer vibes. You're better off taking a shot on a dude like Manoah than you are a safer back-end type with low upside, but in most cases you're probably better off taking a position player than Manoah. He'll be in the big mishmosh of pitchers we end up dropping off the top-101, listing in the honorable mentions, or referencing as "he'd be in the next 50" come formal rankings time. He should absolutely be owned if your league rosters 150-plus prospects, but I still think there's considerable reliever risk here.

4 Eric Pardinho RHP   OFP: 55   ETA: 2022

Born: 01/05/01   Age: 19   Bats: R   Throws: R   Height: 5'10"   Weight: 155   Origin: International Free Agent, 2017

YEAR	TEAM	LVL	AGE	W	L	SV	G	GS	IP	H	HR	BB/9	K/9	K	GB%	BABIP	WHIP	ERA	DRA	WARP	PF
2018	BLU	RK	17	4	3	0	11	11	50	37	5	2.9	11.5	64	47%	.274	1.06	2.88	1.45	2.5	108
2019	LNS	A	18	1	1	0	7	7	33²	29	1	3.5	8.0	30	44%	.304	1.25	2.41	4.68	0.2	104
2020	TOR	MLB	19	2	2	0	33	0	35	35	6	4.0	7.9	31	41%	.293	1.45	4.92	4.93	0.1	98

Comparables: Jordan Lyles, Pedro Avila, Lewis Thorpe

The Report: It's been over three years now since Pardinho was the toast of baseball as the 15-year-old Brazilian dominating the WBC qualifying round. He remains largely the same—preternaturally advanced for his age, but with a frame that limits his projectability. The Blue Jays handled him extraordinarily carefully after a spring elbow injury, holding off his debut until late June, limiting his pitch counts, giving him extra rest, and ultimately shutting him down a few weeks early. Unsurprisingly, he wasn't entirely sharp in the six weeks he was on the mound. There is plenty of time though, because Pardinho is an 18-year-old who already made it to full-season ball.

When right, he is about as advanced a teenager as you'll find. At his best, he'll slings the fastball in the low 90s, touching the mid 90s, although he was generally below peak velocity in his 2019 stint. His primary offspeed is a plus curve, and he's been working on improving his changeup and sharpening and distinguishing his slider. The command and pitchability profile is unusually strong for a teenager. This season raised some serious durability concerns in addition to the ones which were already present due to his slight size and frame. Pardinho might end up as something less than a full starting pitcher, but that's less of a knock than it used to be.

Variance: High. He's an 18-year-old who just missed half the season with an elbow injury, so the risk is pretty significant no matter how developed and advanced he is.

Ben Carsley's Fantasy Take: Pardinho is a fun story, but that doesn't necessarily make him a great fantasy prospect. In fact, he represents a subset of pitcher that I find is often overvalued in our game; the dreaded "advanced teenage arm." That's great and all, but people often tend to bake in further improvement for these types even though the primary thing that makes them special is their advanced pitchability for their age. None of this is to say Pardinho is devoid of upside, but he doesn't have enough of it for me to go all-in given the risks associated with the profile. Only proceed if your league rosters 200-plus prospects.

5 Simeon Woods Richardson RHP   OFP: 55   ETA: 2022

Born: 09/27/00   Age: 19   Bats: R   Throws: R   Height: 6'3"   Weight: 210   Origin: Round 2, 2018 Draft (#48 overall)

YEAR	TEAM	LVL	AGE	W	L	SV	G	GS	IP	H	HR	BB/9	K/9	K	GB%	BABIP	WHIP	ERA	DRA	WARP	PF
2018	MTS	RK	17	1	0	1	5	2	11¹	9	0	3.2	11.9	15	50%	.321	1.15	0.00	1.39	0.6	101
2018	KNG	RK	17	0	0	0	2	2	6	6	1	0.0	16.5	11	38%	.417	1.00	4.50	1.97	0.3	114
2019	COL	A	18	3	8	0	20	20	78¹	78	5	2.0	11.1	97	50%	.356	1.21	4.25	5.04	0.1	89
2019	DUN	A+	18	3	2	0	6	6	28¹	18	1	2.2	9.2	29	38%	.254	0.88	2.54	3.05	0.7	113
2020	TOR	MLB	19	2	2	0	33	0	35	35	5	4.1	9.2	36	44%	.306	1.44	4.78	4.85	0.1	98

Comparables: Jordan Lyles, Lewis Thorpe, Mike Soroka

The Report: Woods Richardson looks the part as a big power righty from the state of Texas and he has the stuff to match. He fires from a high slot with plus arm speed and goes right after hitters. The delivery has some effort, but he repeats it pretty well because of his premier athleticism. The fastball and curveball are potential plus pitches. The heater sits mid 90s in short bursts and can tick higher while settling low-to-mid 90s in longer outings. The pitch shows good life up and down the zone.

Woods Richardson pairs the fastball with a sharp, 12-to-6 breaking ball that spins tight and features strong bite, playing well off the high-slot fastball. The changeup is well behind, currently a show-me pitch with firmness and lack of feel. Arm speed is on his side with the changeup, and it could take big steps forward with further reps, but it'll be difficult to project too much by way of gains given his current release point. The safe call is late-inning reliever with two knockout pitches, but those who especially like Woods Richardson see a mid-rotation starter with a third pitch of some kind. Either way, it's obvious that he has the frame and stuff for impactful major-league innings.

Variance: High. The value can shoot upward with the development of a third pitch, but there's the strong likelihood of a reliever outcome.

Ben Carsley's Fantasy Take: Woods Richardson (seriously, how is there not a hyphen) is in the same general tier of prospect as Pardinho, but I actually prefer him for our purposes. The odds may be greater that he's a reliever, but they're also greater that he'll make an impact if he does stick as a starter, or that he'll close if shifted to the bullpen. Essentially, this isn't a terribly unique profile, but as far as guys with it go, I like Woods Richardson a fair amount.

6 Anthony Kay LHP   OFP: 55   ETA: 2019

Born: 03/21/95   Age: 25   Bats: L   Throws: L   Height: 6'0"   Weight: 218   Origin: Round 1, 2016 Draft (#31 overall)

YEAR	TEAM	LVL	AGE	W	L	SV	G	GS	IP	H	HR	BB/9	K/9	K	GB%	BABIP	WHIP	ERA	DRA	WARP	PF
2018	COL	A	23	4	4	0	13	13	69¹	73	6	2.9	10.1	78	45%	.356	1.37	4.54	5.46	-0.2	95
2018	SLU	A+	23	3	7	0	10	10	53¹	51	1	4.6	7.6	45	41%	.321	1.46	3.88	5.52	-0.1	94
2019	BIN	AA	24	7	3	0	12	12	66¹	38	2	3.1	9.5	70	36%	.224	0.92	1.49	2.66	1.9	95
2019	BUF	AAA	24	2	2	0	7	7	36	33	3	5.5	9.8	39	42%	.323	1.53	2.50	6.22	0.2	99
2019	SYR	AAA	24	1	3	0	7	7	31¹	40	7	3.2	7.5	26	33%	.355	1.63	6.61	5.87	0.3	95
2019	TOR	MLB	24	1	0	0	3	2	14	15	0	3.2	8.4	13	55%	.341	1.43	5.79	4.76	0.1	98
2020	TOR	MLB	25	4	4	0	17	11	63	59	11	3.8	7.7	54	39%	.274	1.37	4.71	4.68	0.6	98

Comparables: Pedro Figueroa, Pat Light, Amir Garrett

The Report: Now almost three full years off his post-draft Tommy John, Kay started to put it all together in 2019 and pitched well enough in the upper minors to get a cup of coffee with his new Canadian team. The fastball sits in the low 90s, bumping 95+ early in his outings. It will show hard, late run at times, but the overall command profile is a bit too much "wild in the zone." The changeup was his signature pitch in college, but it has been inconsistent post-surgery. Kay sells the offering well, but it's inconsistent and can show more as a straight change rather than as a true bat-misser. It will flash almost Wiffle ball arm-side movement at times, though, and should play as at least an average major league offering.

Kay has developed a much better curveball in the pros, a tight 1-7 yakker that tunnels well off the fastball. He also manipulates the speed of the pitch effectively—running from the mid 70s all the way up to 80—and can spot it to either side of the plate. The breaker can get a bit lazy at times, or show as more of a chase offering. More advanced hitters were able to lay off the curve once Kay got out of the Eastern League, but it still projects as an above-average offering that could get to plus with a bit more refinement.

Kay has three average-or-better pitches, more than enough to stick in the middle of a rotation, but he can struggle with both efficiency and strike-throwing. He may lack a true putaway pitch in the majors, and has had issues bleeding stuff after 50-60 pitches or so. But overall, he's a major-league-ready, polished lefty starting pitcher.

Variance: Low. There's some risk the breaker doesn't play as well in the majors as it did in Double-A and Kay is more of a five-and-dive fifth starter, but he's already seen big league time and has three average-or-better pitches in his arsenal.

Ben Carsley's Fantasy Take: Kay is a good name to file away if you're looking for some under-the-radar 2020 contributions in your very deep mixed or AL-only league. There's nothing in front of him in Toronto's rotation at present, and he's got enough skill to stick around as a No. 4/5 starter on a decent team. If you're hunting for a high-upside prospect, however, you can move along.

7 Gabriel Moreno C   OFP: 55   ETA: 2022

Born: 02/14/00   Age: 20   Bats: R   Throws: R   Height: 5'11"   Weight: 160   Origin: International Free Agent, 2016

YEAR	TEAM	LVL	AGE	PA	R	2B	3B	HR	RBI	BB	K	SB	CS	AVG/OBP/SLG	DRC+	VORP	BABIP	BRR	FRAA	WARP	PF
2017	DBL	RK	17	135	9	4	1	0	17	6	5	5	4	.248/.274/.296	86	2.1	.250	-0.9	C(24) 0.0	0.2	101
2018	BLJ	RK	18	101	14	12	2	2	22	4	7	1	1	.413/.455/.652	210	15.2	.429	-2.1	C(17) 0.1	1.2	102
2018	BLU	RK	18	66	10	5	0	2	14	3	13	1	0	.279/.303/.459	95	2.6	.313	-0.8	C(15) 0.0	0.2	103
2019	LNS	A	19	341	47	17	5	12	52	22	38	7	1	.280/.337/.485	130	23.6	.282	0.4	C(54) 1.0	2.5	109
2020	TOR	MLB	20	251	27	13	1	9	31	13	41	2	1	.250/.297/.430	91	0.0	.269	-0.2	C 0	0.5	98

Comparables: Jason Martin, Miguel Andújar, Jorge Polanco

The Report: Moreno is one of my favorite Midwest League bats of the year. He's slight—and is likely shorter than his listed height, but he's a big ball of energy on the field. His teammates seem to like him and feed off that energy, which is exactly what you want from a catcher. For me, he's more impressive at the plate than behind it, and the hit tool leads the way. The bat-to-ball skills are all there and the barrel control is impressive. His stance and swing are atypical with almost no weight transfer, but Moreno manages to show respectable power, and the ball jumps off his bat. As he advances, it will be interesting to see if he adds some weight transfer to his swing and how that affects his power and bat-to-ball skills. If the latter doesn't suffer with added lower-half movement, he may eventually tap into above-average game power.

Moreno is raw behind the plate and his arm is merely average. He does have a quick transfer though, so it is unlikely that the arm will force him out from behind the plate. At present he isn't a great receiver, but he's athletic and moves well behind the plate. Glovework for a catcher seems to be a teachable skill, so we will check on Moreno's progression in that dimension of his game down the road. There are decent foundational tools here already, though.

Variance: High. If he has to move from behind the plate, it's uncertain if the bat will carry the profile. If there is more power without sacrificing the hit tool, he might top that OFP.

Ben Carsley's Fantasy Take: Friends don't let friends draft fantasy catching prospects. That's especially true when said prospects aren't guaranteed to stick at catcher.

8 Orelvis Martinez SS   OFP: 55   ETA: 2023

Born: 11/19/01   Age: 18   Bats: R   Throws: R   Height: 6'1"   Weight: 188   Origin: International Free Agent, 2018

YEAR	TEAM	LVL	AGE	PA	R	2B	3B	HR	RBI	BB	K	SB	CS	AVG/OBP/SLG	DRC+	VORP	BABIP	BRR	FRAA	WARP	PF
2019	BLJ	RK	17	163	20	8	5	7	32	14	29	2	0	.275/.352/.549	140	18.2	.296	1.1	SS(26) -3.2, 3B(11) -2.0	0.8	92
2020	TOR	MLB	18	251	21	12	2	4	22	20	72	2	1	.203/.273/.318	58	0.0	.277	0.0	SS -1, 3B 0	-0.6	98

Comparables: Franklin Barreto, Engel Beltre, Juan Lagares

The Report: The Blue Jays' biggest bonus baby in their 2018 J2 Class, Martinez looked the seven-figure part. At the plate he shows quality bat speed and uses the whole field to his advantage, showing advanced feel for hitting for someone so young. He is lean now but already shows average raw power, which should grow into potential plus raw power as he further matures, and he already shows big exit velocity with loft for a 17-year-old.

Defensively he may lose a step as he enters his twenties, pushing him off shortstop, but for now he combines good actions with plus arm strength and plus hands. He can be overly aggressive and flashy on the field, but these are things that iron out over time. The defensive tools would fit well at third base long term, and if the game power gets at least to plus, that bat will be more than enough to carry a corner.

Variance: High. While still young and having an impressive debut year, he could fill out the wrong way or see his aggression limit the hit tool. If/when he loses a step he could lose athleticism as well, moving him down the defensive spectrum.

Ben Carsley's Fantasy Take: Martinez is a total flier, but he's a fairly fun one as fliers go. Plus, he reminded me of Runelvys Hernandez, so overall I see this as a total win.

9 Josh Winckowski RHP   OFP: 55   ETA: 2021

Born: 06/28/98   Age: 22   Bats: R   Throws: R   Height: 6'4"   Weight: 202   Origin: Round 15, 2016 Draft (#462 overall)

YEAR	TEAM	LVL	AGE	W	L	SV	G	GS	IP	H	HR	BB/9	K/9	K	GB%	BABIP	WHIP	ERA	DRA	WARP	PF
2017	BLU	RK	19	2	2	0	12	11	54	61	8	4.0	7.5	45	58%	.317	1.57	5.33	5.82	0.1	96
2018	VAN	A-	20	4	5	0	13	13	68	68	2	2.0	9.4	71	55%	.338	1.22	2.78	4.48	0.6	103
2019	LNS	A	21	6	3	0	13	13	73²	62	3	3.2	8.7	71	56%	.299	1.19	2.32	3.74	1.3	108
2019	DUN	A+	21	4	5	1	11	10	53²	48	5	2.9	6.2	37	50%	.259	1.21	3.19	3.98	0.7	110
2020	TOR	MLB	22	2	2	0	33	0	35	35	6	3.8	6.4	25	49%	.274	1.41	4.79	4.89	0.1	98

Comparables: Nick Tropeano, Ricardo Pinto, Hunter Wood

The Report: Winckowski has been steadily moving up the organizational ladder since being drafted in 2016, but had a breakout season this year in A-ball. He gets good extension on his heavy fastball, which sits in the mid 90s with late life. The changeup works well off of the heater and is a potential swing-and-miss pitch. Winckowski replicates his arm action well and the pitch shows good arm-side fade. His slider is inconsistent and can lack depth, but has an average projection. Physically, he's got the classic starter's build and if the secondaries develop he would profile as an innings eater at the back of the rotation.

Variance: High. Needs to get a bit more out of the breaking ball to reach his OFP and hasn't pitched in the upper minors yet.

Ben Carsley's Fantasy Take: A low-ceiling pitcher with high risk who's not ready right now: sign me up! Just kidding. Please do not sign me up. In fact, please remove me from your email list.

10   Griffin Conine   OF   OFP: 50   ETA: 2022

Born: 07/11/97   Age: 22   Bats: L   Throws: R   Height: 6'1"   Weight: 200   Origin: Round 2, 2018 Draft (#52 overall)

YEAR	TEAM	LVL	AGE	PA	R	2B	3B	HR	RBI	BB	K	SB	CS	AVG/OBP/SLG	DRC+	VORP	BABIP	BRR	FRAA	WARP	PF
2018	VAN	A-	20	230	24	14	2	7	30	19	63	5	0	.238/.309/.427	92	2.2	.304	-1.5	RF(46) 10.1	1.1	103
2019	LNS	A	21	348	59	19	2	22	64	38	125	2	0	.283/.371/.576	155	32.8	.405	2.8	RF(73) 6.2	3.7	108
2020	TOR	MLB	22	251	21	13	1	6	25	16	103	0	0	.202/.259/.338	54	0.0	.332	-0.3	RF 3	-0.3	98

Comparables: Austin Hays, Xavier Scruggs, Kennys Vargas

The Report: After missing the first 50 games of the season due to a positive test for a banned stimulant, Conine arrived in the Midwest League, showing off the plus raw power that made him a potential first-round pick in 2018. The power does come with a cost at the plate, though, as his strikeout rate in Low-A was over 35 percent. Defensively, he's limited to a corner spot where he makes up for below-average range with good instincts. He'll be able to hold down right field with an arm that's accurate and strong. Conine has the makings of a classic power hitting right-fielder but he'll need to tighten up the approach at the plate to reach that profile.

Variance: High. There are questions about whether the hit tool will play and Conine has yet to face advanced pitching.

Ben Carsley's Fantasy Take: On the one hand, Conine doesn't have a terribly exciting fantasy profile. On the other hand, he's the son of a former big leaguer in Toronto's system, so he's probably at least a role-60 player in disguise. Add him to your watch list, but don't pounce yet.

The Next Ten

11   Adam Kloffenstein   RHP

Born: 08/25/00   Age: 19   Bats: R   Throws: R   Height: 6'5"   Weight: 243   Origin: Round 3, 2018 Draft (#88 overall)

YEAR	TEAM	LVL	AGE	W	L	SV	G	GS	IP	H	HR	BB/9	K/9	K	GB%	BABIP	WHIP	ERA	DRA	WARP	PF
2019	VAN	A-	18	4	4	0	13	13	64¹	47	4	3.2	9.0	64	61%	.262	1.09	2.24	3.03	1.6	101
2020	TOR	MLB	19	2	2	0	33	0	35	35	6	4.4	7.7	30	52%	.288	1.48	5.08	5.04	0.1	98

Comparables: Jenrry Mejia, Arodys Vizcaíno, Jamie Callahan

Kloffenstein wasn't all that different a draft prospect from his now org-mate Woods Richardson. He went a round later last summer, but commanded a bigger bonus to buy him out of his college commitment. He's your more traditional "everything's bigger in Texas" prep arm, a towering, physically mature 6'5" even while playing almost the entire year at age 18. But while Woods Richardson's stuff popped in A-ball, Kloffenstein sat more low 90s—as opposed to the mid 90s he flashed his draft year—and the profile looked more strike-thrower than big stuff guy. As mentioned, he just turned 19, and it's an ideal starter's frame, but he might not be as safe a prep arm as we posited last year, which is still risky, but now riskier.

12   Alejandro Kirk   C

Born: 11/06/98   Age: 21   Bats: R   Throws: R   Height: 5'9"   Weight: 220   Origin: International Free Agent, 2016

YEAR	TEAM	LVL	AGE	PA	R	2B	3B	HR	RBI	BB	K	SB	CS	AVG/OBP/SLG	DRC+	VORP	BABIP	BRR	FRAA	WARP	PF
2018	BLU	RK	19	244	31	10	1	10	57	33	21	2	0	.354/.443/.558	174	28.3	.354	-2.4	C(32) 3.2	2.7	107
2019	LNS	A	20	96	15	6	1	3	8	18	8	1	0	.299/.427/.519	162	10.4	.299	0.9	C(17) 0.1	1.1	110
2019	DUN	A+	20	276	26	25	0	4	36	38	31	2	0	.288/.395/.446	154	18.4	.317	-3.4	C(67) 0.8	2.4	108
2020	TOR	MLB	21	251	26	13	1	6	27	25	39	1	0	.244/.325/.392	92	0.0	.271	-0.3	C 0	0.6	98

Comparables: Rowdy Tellez, Mookie Betts, Jacob Nottingham

Kirk will undoubtedly draw comparisons to Willians Astudillo for a handful of reasons. They are both international catchers with rather large, not jean-modeling frames, they rarely swing and miss, they get on base, and while the former had been overlooked for some time, that is not the case with Kirk anymore. It isn't pretty sometimes. The bat speed doesn't wow you, the power isn't over the fence variety, he can't run, and you wouldn't be remiss if you didn't like the overall athleticism. He just gets on base and hits and hits. The swing works. It is short and direct to the ball, he recognizes pitches well, and he doesn't often force himself to swing at pitches out of the zone. The defense is better than you would imagine, as he blocks well, has tick-above-average arm strength, and has worked hard to improve his receiving. The overall outcome is a hit over power, on-base driven catcher. The risk here is that if he stops getting on-base there isn't anything else to carry the load, but hey was this even a profile you would have banked on even just a few years ago?

13 T.J. Zeuch   RHP

Born: 08/01/95   Age: 24   Bats: R   Throws: R   Height: 6'7"   Weight: 225   Origin: Round 1, 2016 Draft (#21 overall)

YEAR	TEAM	LVL	AGE	W	L	SV	G	GS	IP	H	HR	BB/9	K/9	K	GB%	BABIP	WHIP	ERA	DRA	WARP	PF
2017	BLJ	RK	21	0	2	0	3	3	7	9	1	2.6	6.4	5	60%	.333	1.57	5.14	2.68	0.3	93
2017	DUN	A+	21	3	4	0	12	11	58²	63	3	2.6	7.1	46	64%	.312	1.36	3.38	4.85	0.3	102
2018	DUN	A+	22	3	3	0	6	6	36¹	34	4	2.2	5.9	24	63%	.273	1.18	3.47	3.99	0.6	102
2018	NHP	AA	22	9	5	0	21	21	120	120	7	2.3	6.1	81	56%	.298	1.26	3.08	4.37	1.4	105
2019	DUN	A+	23	0	0	0	2	2	8²	7	0	2.1	12.5	12	43%	.143	1.04	4.15	2.19	0.3	90
2019	BUF	AAA	23	4	3	0	13	13	78	70	6	3.7	4.5	39	58%	.256	1.31	3.69	3.95	2.1	98
2019	TOR	MLB	23	1	2	0	5	3	22²	22	2	4.4	7.9	20	48%	.303	1.46	4.76	5.30	0.1	99
2020	TOR	MLB	24	2	2	0	31	3	46	46	6	3.8	7.5	38	53%	.296	1.44	4.82	4.78	0.3	98

Comparables: Chad Kuhl, Ricardo Pinto, José Ureña

Zeuch is probably going to pitch in the majors for a long time. It's a bushel of average or slightly-above pitches. He leads off with a sinker that typically sits 91-94, topping out at 95, and rides in with plus movement especially against righties. He'll also show you a slider, a curve, and a change that all come in around average and flash higher. That stuff from a 6'7" pitcher with a classic delivery explains the "former first-round pick" part pretty easily. Yet the sum as a professional pitcher has, to date, been less than the sum of his parts. He just hasn't fooled enough batters to strike anyone out despite being an advanced college pitcher with, what is on paper, pretty good stuff. He came up for September and was fine, used as both a back-end starter and the bulk guy behind an opener. He currently profiles as, well, pretty much that moving forward, with an asterisk denoting that tall pitchers with good stuff are more likely to suddenly put it together quite late in the development cycle.

14 Kendall Williams   RHP

Born: 08/24/00   Age: 19   Bats: R   Throws: R   Height: 6'6"   Weight: 205   Origin: Round 2, 2019 Draft (#52 overall)

YEAR	TEAM	LVL	AGE	W	L	SV	G	GS	IP	H	HR	BB/9	K/9	K	GB%	BABIP	WHIP	ERA	DRA	WARP	PF
2019	BLJ	RK	18	0	0	0	6	5	16	6	0	3.9	10.7	19	36%	.167	0.81	1.12	1.93	0.7	89

In yesteryear's baseball, a player like Williams probably gets drafted much higher, and ends up much higher on prospect lists. Who doesn't like a 6'6" right-hander who showed an above-average fastball and potential plus curveball? He was simply too much for young hitters in the complex given his size, angle, strike throwing, and stuff. The stuff is still inconsistent and the fastball dropped later in the year as he wore down, which was partially why he was still on the board at 52. Williams's stuff should be ready for a full-season roster next year, but they will most likely keep him in extended to add strength to his wiry frame.

15 Dasan Brown   OF

Born: 09/25/01   Age: 18   Bats: R   Throws: R   Height: 6'0"   Weight: 185   Origin: Round 3, 2019 Draft (#88 overall)

YEAR	TEAM	LVL	AGE	PA	R	2B	3B	HR	RBI	BB	K	SB	CS	AVG/OBP/SLG	DRC+	VORP	BABIP	BRR	FRAA	WARP	PF
2019	BLJ	RK	17	63	8	2	2	0	5	9	17	6	2	.222/.444/.356	106	6.1	.357	-0.5	CF(11) -1.3, RF(1) 2.1	0.2	91
2020	TOR	MLB	18	251	24	11	1	4	23	24	93	3	1	.213/.319/.335	83	0.0	.349	0.0	CF 0, RF 0	0.3	98

A local kid whom the Jays drafted out of an Ontario high school, Brown displays a collection of loud tools. At the plate, he shows plus raw power. While his understanding of the zone is advanced for the age, his pitch recognition is undeveloped and, consequently, there are a lot of whiffs, especially against offspeed stuff. The swing itself comes with length. The arm and speed (which is plus to plus-plus) are sufficient for him to stick in center, though he may have to slide to a corner at physical maturity. There's a major-league regular ceiling here, but his road to The Show will be longer than a Dream Theater song.

16 Miguel Hiraldo   IF

Born: 09/05/00   Age: 19   Bats: R   Throws: R   Height: 5'11"   Weight: 170   Origin: International Free Agent, 2017

YEAR	TEAM	LVL	AGE	PA	R	2B	3B	HR	RBI	BB	K	SB	CS	AVG/OBP/SLG	DRC+	VORP	BABIP	BRR	FRAA	WARP	PF
2018	DBL	RK	17	239	41	18	3	2	33	23	30	15	6	.313/.381/.453	168	22.9	.355	2.8	SS(46) 2.9, 3B(4) -0.3	3.1	102
2018	BLJ	RK	17	40	3	4	0	0	3	1	12	3	0	.231/.250/.333	50	-1.7	.333	-0.3	3B(5) 0.0, SS(4) -0.8	-0.1	103
2019	BLU	RK+	18	256	43	20	1	7	37	14	36	11	3	.300/.348/.481	125	20.5	.328	1.3		1.7	97
2020	TOR	MLB	19	251	22	14	1	4	24	15	58	6	2	.232/.282/.354	68	0.0	.291	0.2	SS 1, 3B 0	-0.1	98

Comparables: Thairo Estrada, Enrique Hernández, Franchy Cordero

Hiraldo, a $750k bonus baby out of the Dominican in 2017, has some thunder in his stick. The bat is going to have to carry the profile here, as he's already playing a lot of second base, and his arm is likely to limit him there in the medium-to-long term, and the glove isn't much more than average even at the keystone. There might be enough juice in the offensive profile to make it work though, as a potential average hit/solid-average power combo isn't hard to see. And Hiraldo will spend all of next season as a 19-year-old. He's definitely a potential breakout Blue Jays name for 2020.

17 Otto Lopez   SS

Born: 10/01/98   Age: 21   Bats: R   Throws: R   Height: 5'10"   Weight: 160   Origin: International Free Agent, 2016

YEAR	TEAM	LVL	AGE	PA	R	2B	3B	HR	RBI	BB	K	SB	CS	AVG/OBP/SLG	DRC+	VORP	BABIP	BRR	FRAA	WARP	PF
2017	BLJ	RK	18	203	30	6	3	1	15	19	23	7	3	.275/.361/.360	122	9.7	.312	2.4	2B(19) -0.2, 3B(10) 0.0	0.9	92
2018	BLU	RK	19	34	8	5	2	0	6	0	5	1	0	.364/.382/.636	129	5.4	.429	0.4	2B(3) 0.4, SS(2) -0.3	0.2	101
2018	VAN	A-	19	206	31	7	4	3	22	26	21	13	6	.297/.390/.434	137	16.7	.320	0.8	3B(14) 0.8, 2B(13) 0.4	1.7	103
2019	LNS	A	20	492	61	20	5	5	50	34	63	20	15	.324/.371/.425	137	34.8	.365	-0.9	SS(81) -2.4, 2B(19) 3.5	3.8	109
2020	TOR	MLB	21	251	23	11	2	4	24	14	46	5	2	.261/.309/.370	80	0.0	.312	0.0	SS 0, 2B 1	0.2	98

The Jays seem to be grooming Lopez for a super utility role. This year most of his reps came at short, but he has played everywhere but first and catcher during his professional career. He is more than capable at short, but that position may be occupied in Toronto for a while. Lopez is a clean, smooth defender with good footwork, hands, and body control. At the plate he's balanced and takes confident swings. He doesn't strike out much thanks to quick hands, a simple, smooth swing, and a flat bat path that's relatively short to the ball. He really doesn't do anything poorly, but he's not flashy and aside from the hit tool, lacks any other loud aspect to his game. He's never going to be a top prospect, but expect him to continue putting up strong batting averages until he cracks the majors. If things go well developmentally he may wind up an everyday player. There isn't a lot of variance in his profile, so the floor is high here.

18 Riley Adams   C

Born: 06/26/96   Age: 24   Bats: R   Throws: R   Height: 6'4"   Weight: 225   Origin: Round 3, 2017 Draft (#99 overall)

YEAR	TEAM	LVL	AGE	PA	R	2B	3B	HR	RBI	BB	K	SB	CS	AVG/OBP/SLG	DRC+	VORP	BABIP	BRR	FRAA	WARP	PF
2017	VAN	A-	21	227	26	16	1	3	35	18	50	1	1	.305/.374/.438	136	15.5	.391	0.0	C(34) -0.6	1.5	101
2018	DUN	A+	22	409	49	26	1	4	43	50	93	3	0	.246/.352/.361	123	19.6	.323	-1.3	C(93) 4.3, 1B(1) 0.0	3.1	102
2019	DUN	A+	23	83	12	3	0	3	12	14	18	1	0	.277/.434/.462	168	10.5	.341	0.4	C(19) 0.1	1.0	102
2019	NHP	AA	23	332	46	15	2	11	39	32	105	3	1	.258/.349/.439	131	26.3	.362	1.0	C(56) -2.5	2.1	98
2020	TOR	MLB	24	35	4	2	0	1	4	3	12	0	0	.233/.306/.400	87	0.0	.334	0.0	C -1	0.0	98

A third-round pick in the 2017 draft, Adams conquered the Florida State League on his second go-around and was perfectly fine over a half-season-plus in New Hampshire. The profile behind the plate is a bit nondescript if I'm honest. He's much taller and a bit narrower than your average catcher, but he's reasonably quiet and athletic behind the dish, although he can snatch for the low strike. There's a solid approach at the plate, but some stiffness to the swing that leads to swing-and-miss in the zone, although it gives him potential above-average pop as well. This was the kind of catcher that was a backup for a decade in the late-90s or early-00s. A passable glove that could run into a bomb for you. With the modern emphasis on receiving, Adams might have a tougher time getting major league per diems, but the profile is still solid backup catcher on balance.

19 Patrick Murphy   RHP
Born: 06/10/95   Age: 25   Bats: R   Throws: R   Height: 6'4"   Weight: 220   Origin: Round 3, 2013 Draft (#83 overall)

YEAR	TEAM	LVL	AGE	W	L	SV	G	GS	IP	H	HR	BB/9	K/9	K	GB%	BABIP	WHIP	ERA	DRA	WARP	PF
2017	BLJ	RK	22	1	0	0	3	2	9	7	0	1.0	15.0	15	72%	.389	0.89	0.00	1.66	0.4	109
2017	LNS	A	22	4	3	0	15	15	88²	87	5	3.3	5.8	57	50%	.299	1.35	2.94	4.95	0.3	107
2017	DUN	A+	22	0	1	0	2	2	9	14	0	3.0	5.0	5	50%	.389	1.89	7.00	7.58	-0.2	108
2018	DUN	A+	23	10	5	0	26	26	146²	126	5	3.1	8.3	135	60%	.297	1.20	2.64	4.10	2.1	102
2018	NHP	AA	23	0	0	0	1	1	6	4	0	4.5	9.0	6	56%	.250	1.17	3.00	3.73	0.1	110
2019	NHP	AA	24	4	7	0	18	18	84	75	7	2.9	9.2	86	53%	.285	1.21	4.71	4.44	0.5	99
2020	TOR	MLB	25	1	1	0	11	0	12	11	2	3.7	7.5	10	48%	.279	1.35	4.34	4.45	0.1	98

Comparables: Tobi Stoner, Tyler Wilson, Dylan Covey

The early part of Murphy's pro career was routinely interrupted by injuries, but he was healthy and showing progress throughout 2018 and early 2019. That all came to a screeching halt last summer when his delivery was deemed illegal by the Major League Baseball Umpires Association, and he was sent back to the drawing board to craft a new set of mechanics that removed his key timing mechanism—a toe tap just before he began his drive toward the plate. Prior to that revelation, Murphy was consistently showing a plus fastball and plus curveball with potential for impact in the middle-to-late innings out of the bullpen. Now, after only throwing 20 innings in the season's final three months following news of his illegal delivery, Murphy's future is decidedly up in the air. Any challenges finding consistency with his new mechanics could hasten an already-likely move to the bullpen, and the timeline for his big league debut could be pushed back beyond 2020.

20 Kevin Smith   SS
Born: 07/04/96   Age: 23   Bats: R   Throws: R   Height: 5'11"   Weight: 188   Origin: Round 4, 2017 Draft (#129 overall)

YEAR	TEAM	LVL	AGE	PA	R	2B	3B	HR	RBI	BB	K	SB	CS	AVG/OBP/SLG	DRC+	VORP	BABIP	BRR	FRAA	WARP	PF
2017	BLU	RK	20	283	43	25	1	8	43	16	70	9	0	.271/.312/.466	95	18.6	.337	3.9	SS(58) 8.3	2.2	100
2018	LNS	A	21	204	36	23	4	7	44	17	33	12	1	.355/.407/.639	196	33.7	.397	3.1	SS(24) 1.7, 3B(21) 0.7	3.5	104
2018	DUN	A+	21	371	57	8	2	18	49	23	88	17	5	.274/.332/.468	128	23.3	.319	4.6	SS(63) 6.9, 2B(13) 1.0	3.8	102
2019	NHP	AA	22	468	49	22	2	19	61	29	151	11	6	.209/.263/.402	91	9.8	.269	1.4	SS(86) 0.4, 3B(18) -1.1	1.5	99
2020	TOR	MLB	23	251	27	13	1	11	34	13	89	4	1	.226/.271/.433	79	0.0	.307	0.3	SS 3, 3B 0	0.5	98

Comparables: Ryan O'Hearn, Lane Thomas, Zach Walters

We ranked Smith in the top five of last year's list based on his quick hands and above-average bat speed. We had hope for a good offensive outcome despite some continuing pitch recognition and approach issues, and he performed well at the A-ball levels. He proceeded to hit .209 with a 32 percent strikeout rate in Double-A in 2019, and then followed it up by performing about as well as your random American League pitcher in interleague at the plate in the Arizona Fall League. Worse, he looked just as lost as those numbers indicate. There's enough of an excuse with a failed swing change that tried to tap into his raw—and help him deal better with the high fastballs that he's always struggled against—to hope that some of this comes back around. And there's always the utility fallback for a versatile player who can handle the 6, of course. But we really didn't see or hear a single good thing on his bat out of the Eastern League or the Arizona Fall League all year.

Personal Cheeseball

PC   Jordan Romano   RHP

Born: 04/21/93   Age: 27   Bats: R   Throws: R   Height: 6'4"   Weight: 200   Origin: Round 10, 2014 Draft (#294 overall)

YEAR	TEAM	LVL	AGE	W	L	SV	G	GS	IP	H	HR	BB/9	K/9	K	GB%	BABIP	WHIP	ERA	DRA	WARP	PF
2017	DUN	A+	24	7	5	0	28	26	138	141	2	3.5	9.0	138	38%	.344	1.41	3.39	5.30	-0.1	105
2018	NHP	AA	25	11	8	0	25	25	137¹	122	15	2.7	8.2	125	38%	.279	1.19	4.13	3.82	2.4	103
2019	BUF	AAA	26	2	2	5	24	3	37²	37	8	3.3	12.7	53	40%	.333	1.35	5.73	4.27	0.8	100
2019	TOR	MLB	26	0	2	0	17	0	15¹	17	4	5.3	12.3	21	51%	.351	1.70	7.63	4.07	0.2	101
2020	TOR	MLB	27	2	2	0	33	0	35	31	6	4.0	9.8	38	40%	.274	1.32	4.42	4.41	0.3	98

Comparables: Seth Lugo, Phillips Valdez, Mike Bolsinger

I've liked Romano for some time as a late-blooming arm of interest, in that sort of way that you like 45 OFP future relievers sometimes. I wasn't surprised to see him get a shot with the Rangers in last year's Rule 5 Draft; arms who can both potentially contribute now and have some projection are the prototypical Rule 5 picks. He was returned to the Toronto system late in spring training, but got called up in June and promptly touched 100 in his major league debut. That's a bit above where he typically pitches, and surely he was jazzed up for his first game in the majors, but he does sit 94-96 regularly. He pairs the fastball with a decent little hard slider, having dropped a not-so-hot change since becoming a reliever. He's definitionally a 95-and-a-slider pen guy, but it's always fun to see a random arm out of nowhere who you pegged at that outcome actually get there.

Low Minors Sleeper

LMS   Alejandro Melean   RHP

Born: 10/11/00   Age: 19   Bats: R   Throws: R   Height: 6'0"   Weight: 175   Origin: International Free Agent, 2017

YEAR	TEAM	LVL	AGE	W	L	SV	G	GS	IP	H	HR	BB/9	K/9	K	GB%	BABIP	WHIP	ERA	DRA	WARP	PF
2018	BLJ	RK	17	1	3	0	9	7	32²	36	5	6.1	8.5	31	41%	.320	1.78	4.68	5.97	0.0	105
2019	BLU	RK+	18	1	1	0	7	6	21	20	2	6.4	10.7	25	51%	.327	1.67	5.57	6.25	0.0	99

Part of the '17 J2 class, Melean doesn't have ideal size as he is smaller than the 6-foot, 175 pounds listed on his player card, but he still has quality stuff. Melean features a fastball that sits in the low 90s, touching higher with quality sink, and a slider that has flashed for me in the past. This past season was a bit of a lost one for the right-hander, though, as he battled various injuries and had control issues. On the positive side he finished his second year of pro ball and got out of the complex before turning 19. Look for this young arm to rebound next season with improved health.

Top Talents 25 and Under (as of 4/1/2020)

1. Vladimir Guerrero Jr.
2. Bo Bichette
3. Nate Pearson
4. Jordan Groshans
5. Cavan Biggio
6. Alek Manoah
7. Eric Pardinho
8. Danny Jansen
9. Simeon Woods Richardson
10. Anthony Kay

Guerrero Jr. didn't light the world aflame during his much-anticipated debut. He merely sparked a match, putting up league-average offense while oftentimes giving us a taste of his prodigious power (the Home Run Derby doesn't count but, ya know, it was still cool). He did it at the age of 20 and will play the entirety of his sophomore season at the age of 21. Nothing he did or did not do in his first season leads us to believe he's anything less than what was expected of him when he was the No. 1 prospect in all of baseball a year ago.

The player Vladito is expected to stand next to on the infield for the next half-decade or so came up later in the season but was arguably just as impressive. Bichette's raw power played up in games and he showed an advanced hit tool. He's not likely to contend for any fielding awards at the 6 but can hold his own over there. So much of the Blue Jays' future depends on Guerrero Jr. and Bichette living up to expectations, and they're off to a solid start.

The third and least-heralded of the Major League Sons, Biggio, was actually the most productive in his 430-plate appearance sample after ranking just 11th in the system a year ago. Biggio looked the part of the TTO utility infielder many projected him to be, showing an advanced eye that led to an OBP 130 points higher than his batting average. All told, he homered, walked, or struck out in 49 percent of his plate appearances and his 112 DRC+ was the best of the trio. Biggio's the oldest of the three by a good three years and has the lowest ceiling, thus his ranking a few spots down, but he proved at the very least to be a competent major leaguer.

Jansen was Example #206,754 that catchers are weird, as the bespectacled one came up as a potential bat-first power threat with a questionable glove and looked…like a solid defender with a questionable hit tool. He finished with the seventh best CDA (Catcher Defensive Adjustment) in baseball, which was almost entirely the reason behind his 2.2 WARP. Catching development remains unpredictable, but the defense at the very least should afford him more opportunities to snatch the starting gig long term.

Eyewitness Reports

Eyewitness Report: Jordan Groshans

Evaluator: Nathan Graham
Report Date: 04/30/2019
Dates Seen: 2X April 2019
Risk Factor: High
Physical/Health: Large frame with a thin build and high waist. Plenty of projection remaining with the ability to add good weight.

Tool	Future Grade	Report
Hit	55	Quiet pre-swing, mild load with a leg kick used for timing. Above-average bat speed and plus barrel control. Stays balanced through swing. Has a quick trigger that can catch up to velocity.
Power	60	Plus raw power, ball jumps off of the bat. Has the ability to hit with power to all fields. Power will play more in game with physical maturity.
Baserunning/ Speed	40	Current average foot speed, will play down to fringe-average with maturity. Possesses a choppy, upright running style. Athletic and with good instincts, can be a decent base runner in the future but speed will not be part of his game. 4.33 clock on home to first.
Glove	50	Jays will keep him at shortstop as long as they can but will eventually find a home at third base. Lacks lateral quickness to excel at the six. Good instincts and soft hands, will be a capable defender at the hot corner.
Arm	55	Plenty of arm strength for either position on the left side.

Conclusion: Groshans has the look of an older, more polished college bat not a teenager playing in his first full season assignment. He's big and strong with plenty of projection left in the tank. The bat has potential to be a middle of the lineup type that is a rare mix of contact and power. That offensive potential will allow for an eventual move off the six. Profiles as a plus starter at the major league level that is an occasional All-Star.

Eyewitness Report: Griffin Conine

Evaluator: Nathan Graham
Report Date: 08/28/2019
Dates Seen: 6/11, 8/22/19
Risk Factor: High
Physical/Health: Extra large build, athletic frame with wide shoulders; minimal projection remaining.

Tool	Future Grade	Report
Hit	45	Conine utilizes an open stance with hands held high and explodes through the zone with above average bat speed. Strikeouts will always be part of his game but are elevated due to his aggressive approach and current lack of pitch recognition. The ability to see spin will improve as he matures and is exposed to more secondaries.
Power	60	Physically strong with plus bat speed and natural loft to the swing make for plus power. It plays well in game to all fields as he knows how to attack fastballs in hitters counts and punish mistakes.
Baserunning/ Speed	40	Current average foot speed (4.18 home-to-first clock) but will play below-average as he ages. Will not be a base clogger but speed is not part of his game.
Glove	50	Below-average range due to lack of foot speed but possesses solid instincts and takes a good first step. Conine will not be spectacular in the field but will not be a liability.
Arm	60	Strong arm, throws are accurate and show good carry. Big enough arm to handle any outfield spot but grades out as plus even for right field.

Conclusion: Drafted in the second round out of Duke in 2018, Conine has the tools and pedigree to be a solid everyday corner outfielder. The approach at the plate needs to become more disciplined but the power will play at the highest level. Profiles as a solid everyday right fielder.

Washington Nationals

The State of the System

The Nats won't be flying any "Number One Org Ranking" flags anytime soon. The other flag is better anyway, and it flies forever.

The Top Ten

1   Carter Kieboom   SS   OFP: 70   ETA: 2019

Born: 09/03/97   Age: 22   Bats: R   Throws: R   Height: 6'2"   Weight: 190   Origin: Round 1, 2016 Draft (#28 overall)

YEAR	TEAM	LVL	AGE	PA	R	2B	3B	HR	RBI	BB	K	SB	CS	AVG/OBP/SLG	DRC+	VORP	BABIP	BRR	FRAA	WARP	PF
2017	AUB	A-	19	29	4	1	0	1	4	1	2	1	0	.250/.276/.393	101	0.2	.240	0.2	SS(6) 1.1	0.2	109
2017	HAG	A	19	210	36	12	0	8	26	28	40	2	2	.296/.400/.497	163	20.0	.344	-0.7	SS(45) 1.4	2.3	101
2018	POT	A+	20	285	48	15	0	11	46	36	50	6	1	.298/.386/.494	159	31.4	.332	0.5	SS(56) -0.4	2.9	101
2018	HAR	AA	20	273	36	16	1	5	23	22	59	3	1	.262/.326/.395	108	13.3	.324	0.5	SS(62) 2.6	1.8	100
2019	FRE	AAA	21	494	79	24	3	16	79	68	100	5	2	.303/.409/.493	126	43.7	.362	1.4	SS(62) -3.7, 2B(40) 3.2	3.5	102
2019	WAS	MLB	21	43	4	0	0	2	2	4	16	0	0	.128/.209/.282	62	0.0	.143	0.1	SS(10) -1.0	-0.1	105
2020	*WAS*	*MLB*	*22*	*385*	*42*	*17*	*1*	*13*	*46*	*35*	*104*	*1*	*1*	*.239/.315/.406*	*88*	*3.0*	*.305*	*-0.6*	*3B -3*	*0.0*	*108*

Comparables: Corey Seager, Dilson Herrera, Victor Robles

The Report: In most ways, Carter Kieboom had a very successful 2019. He hit over .300 at Triple-A as a 21-year-old. He continued to show a well-rounded offensive skill set, with the potential for plus hit and above-average power. He's becoming more selective at the plate, which we targeted as an area for him to improve. And he did, briefly, reach the majors.

The major league stint probably received more ink than the rest of it combined. Kieboom was called up in April to replace an injured Trea Turner. He promptly went into a massive offensive slump, wasn't great at shortstop, and got sent down about two weeks later. It was bad, but he continued chugging along for the rest of the Triple-A season, despite strangely being bypassed for a September call-up.

Kieboom's future defensive home is the biggest mystery at the moment. He's more likely to stay at shortstop than he was in the low-minors in a vacuum, but capable if unspectacular defense isn't going to unseat Trea Turner. The Nationals exposed him to a good deal of second base and a little bit of third base last season, and he projects as more than capable at both. Where he lands will be as much determined by team needs that are themselves not yet clear, and he'll likely be in the mix for a job out of spring training.

Variance: Low. We're reasonably sure he's going to be a long-term regular, even if he doesn't hit his star upside.

Mark Barry's Fantasy Take: In all likelihood, had Kieboom spent the entirety of his 2019 campaign in the minors, he'd probably be a top-fiveish dynasty prospect, hitting .303 with an OPS approaching .900 at Triple-A Fresno. But alas, he joined the big club for 11 games early in the season and was Very Not Good. If that dampens his dynasty value in your league, though, that's great for enterprising managers. He's not going to run, so his fantasy ceiling will be capped. He's not a star, but we're still looking at a dude who should flirt with a .300 average and decent pop up the middle, which is nice.

2 Luis Garcia SS   OFP: 60   ETA: 2021

Born: 05/16/00   Age: 20   Bats: L   Throws: R   Height: 6'2"   Weight: 190   Origin: International Free Agent, 2016

YEAR	TEAM	LVL	AGE	PA	R	2B	3B	HR	RBI	BB	K	SB	CS	AVG/OBP/SLG	DRC+	VORP	BABIP	BRR	FRAA	WARP	PF
2017	NAT	RK	17	211	25	8	3	1	22	9	32	11	2	.302/.330/.387	97	7.5	.353	1.7	2B(25) -3.0, SS(17) 0.7	0.6	104
2018	HAG	A	18	323	48	14	4	3	31	19	49	8	5	.297/.335/.402	110	16.4	.343	0.7	3B(36) -4.6, SS(27) 0.4	1.0	98
2018	POT	A+	18	221	34	7	2	4	23	12	33	4	1	.299/.338/.412	118	9.8	.337	-0.3	SS(40) -2.7	0.9	101
2019	HAR	AA	19	553	66	22	4	4	30	17	86	11	5	.257/.280/.337	69	6.7	.299	3.1	SS(92) -3.9, 2B(38) 0.4	0.5	99
2020	WAS	MLB	20	251	21	11	1	4	23	11	50	2	1	.243/.280/.347	63	0.0	.294	-0.1	SS 0, 2B 0	-0.4	108

Comparables: Jake Bauers, Mike Trout, Elvis Andrus

The Report: The Nationals have a knack for finding young untapped talent and putting them in the best position to succeed. Luis Garcia is the current prospect being aggressively promoted through the system, showcasing a wise-beyond-his-years baseball IQ despite his young age and lack of professional experience. There's room for growth in his frame, and he already has the confidence of a major leaguer. Probably because he's extremely close to being one.

He's a dream with the glove; swift movements, quick hands and great range. There's a natural tendency for splashy plays and his abilities at shortstop translate just as well to second and third. Versatility is Garcia's best friend, as the Nats are fully stocked in the middle infield, and while they're sticking to developing him as a shortstop, that may not be where he lands once he makes it to the big club.

At the plate, he's aggressive and contact-heavy, often jumping on the first pitch he sees. His bat-to-ball skills are there, with great barrel control, and he hits it all over the park. The approach wasn't nearly as effective in Double-A as it was at previous levels. Patience is a virtue, and it's something Garcia will have to bring to his game if he really wants to improve his hit tool. The same aggressiveness at the plate is a weapon on the basepaths; he has above-average speed and utilizes it to swipe bags whenever he can. The one weakness in his offensive profile is he's unlikely to ever hit for much power.

Variance: Medium. There were some offensive struggles, albeit minor ones, that will likely be improved upon with more experience in higher levels.

Mark Barry's Fantasy Take: Looking at Garcia's profile and production gives me strong Jean Segura vibes. Last year in this very space, Ben labeled him as a guy that could go 20/20 while sticking at shortstop, and nothing really has changed, except that Garcia is now a guy who could go 20/20 with positional eligibility all over the infield.

3 Jackson Rutledge RHP   OFP: 60   ETA: 2022

Born: 04/01/99   Age: 21   Bats: R   Throws: R   Height: 6'8"   Weight: 250   Origin: Round 1, 2019 Draft (#17 overall)

YEAR	TEAM	LVL	AGE	W	L	SV	G	GS	IP	H	HR	BB/9	K/9	K	GB%	BABIP	WHIP	ERA	DRA	WARP	PF
2019	AUB	A-	20	0	0	0	3	3	9	4	2	3.0	6.0	6	42%	.091	0.78	3.00	3.55	0.2	99
2019	HAG	A	20	2	0	0	6	6	27¹	14	0	3.6	10.2	31	46%	.222	0.91	2.30	3.40	0.6	95
2020	WAS	MLB	21	2	2	0	33	0	35	35	5	3.8	7.8	30	41%	.292	1.43	4.77	4.93	0.2	108

Comparables: Parker Markel, José Castillo, Keyvius Sampson

The Report: Rutledge is a big JuCo arm in every sense, his hulking frame oozing intimidation with a double-plus fastball cashing the checks. Sitting 94-96 and touching 98 for me, the pitch is extremely lively up in the zone where he gets plenty of swings and misses as well as weak contact. There's also some deception here, as Rutledge employs surprisingly short arm action before releasing from a lowish three-quarters slot. I saw him tear up right-handed hitters, pounding his number one inside to begin counts and finishing them off with his plus slider. Easily his best secondary at present, this pitch comes in hard mid-to-upper 80s with late, tight break. But wait, there's more! His 11-5 curve could be future plus as well with a little refinement, as he can already throw it for strikes with some snap. He throws a change as well but it lags behind the rest of the arsenal. Rutledge runs into issues with his motion from time to time, unsurprisingly given his size, and does have bouts of trouble with his control and command. He's far from devoid of athleticism though, and showed me an ability to adjust when necessary and retain strength late in an outing.

Variance: High. There is give both ways; if the command and pitch mix don't develop as desired, Rutledge could be destined for the pen. If everything comes together, with his stuff he's a No. 2 or better.

Mark Barry's Fantasy Take: Yeesh. So this list gets rough in a hurry. Rutledge is a big dude with a power arm and two great pitches. His tippy-top ceiling of an SP2 will depend on his control and the development of a third pitch. He's a top 200ish guy as it stands.

4 Wil Crowe RHP   OFP: 50   ETA: 2020
Born: 09/09/94   Age: 25   Bats: R   Throws: R   Height: 6'2"   Weight: 240   Origin: Round 2, 2017 Draft (#65 overall)

YEAR	TEAM	LVL	AGE	W	L	SV	G	GS	IP	H	HR	BB/9	K/9	K	GB%	BABIP	WHIP	ERA	DRA	WARP	PF
2017	AUB	A-	22	0	0	0	7	7	20²	18	3	1.3	6.5	15	52%	.250	1.02	2.61	3.71	0.4	107
2018	POT	A+	23	11	0	0	16	15	87	71	6	3.1	8.1	78	47%	.267	1.16	2.69	4.17	1.2	101
2018	HAR	AA	23	0	5	0	5	5	26¹	31	4	5.5	5.1	15	44%	.325	1.78	6.15	7.17	-0.6	99
2019	HAR	AA	24	7	6	0	16	16	95¹	85	8	2.1	8.4	89	50%	.294	1.12	3.87	4.50	0.5	99
2019	FRE	AAA	24	0	4	0	10	10	54	66	7	4.3	6.8	41	42%	.337	1.70	6.17	6.16	0.3	98
2020	WAS	MLB	25	2	2	0	33	0	35	36	6	3.7	6.9	27	44%	.286	1.44	4.92	4.84	0.2	108

Comparables: *Erick Fedde, Dillon Tate, Mike Parisi*

The Report: Crowe has a big, durable, starter's frame, but a high-effort reliever's delivery. There's crossfire and head whack, deception and below-average command. The fastball can get to 95 in short bursts, but sits more low 90s with the occasional distinct two-seam a tick below that. Crowe's best secondary is a power, mid-80s slider with good tilt. He commands it better than the fastball, and you could see it playing up in a role where he can throw it two out of five times or so. Crowe rounds out the arsenal with a slurvy curveball around 80 with inconsistent 11-5 shape. He can flash a tighter one for a different look both in velocity and break. The change is firm and he struggles to turn it over or get it down. Crowe very much looks the part of a major league reliever still starting in the minors, although if he can squeeze out a bit more command and improve the changeup, he could be a backend innings eater, although that's a role that doesn't really exist anymore for modern orgs.

Variance: Medium. Crowe is still starting and has been durable despite the health concerns coming out of the draft. They haven't been great or efficient starter's innings though, and he's a better fit in the pen.

Mark Barry's Fantasy Take: If Crowe sticks in the rotation, he's not going to strike out enough guys to be relevant. If he's an "average setup" guy, then uh, he's an average setup guy, which also isn't particularly of interest.

5 Mason Denaburg RHP   OFP: 55   ETA: 2023
Born: 08/08/99   Age: 20   Bats: R   Throws: R   Height: 6'4"   Weight: 195   Origin: Round 1, 2018 Draft (#27 overall)

YEAR	TEAM	LVL	AGE	W	L	SV	G	GS	IP	H	HR	BB/9	K/9	K	GB%	BABIP	WHIP	ERA	DRA	WARP	PF
2019	NAT	RK	19	1	1	0	7	4	20¹	23	1	6.2	8.4	19	48%	.361	1.82	7.52	8.54	-0.6	104

The Report: Drafted just a short year ago, Denaburg has not had much game experience to justify his first round status. Towards the end of his senior prep season, he was shutdown due to arm soreness, which perhaps allowed him to fall slightly to the Nationals at the end of the round. He was treated very cautiously after the draft, failing to appear in any official games while working out at their complex in West Palm Beach. In 2019, he pitched sparsely before a shoulder injury ended his season.

For someone who hasn't seen the field much in almost two years there is still plenty to dream on. The young righty has an athletic body and delivery that allows for very good movement on his pitches. Prior to being hurt, his fastball sat in the low 90s with sink, he possessed a slurvy breaking ball with two-plane break, and feel for a developing changeup. The key for now is simply getting healthy. If that's in place, he still has plenty of time to develop the tools that made him one of the top arms drafted in 2018.

Variance: Extreme. When you don't pitch, it's tough to gauge which direction you're headed in. Health questions continue to remain a theme in his evaluation, and until we see some sustained success on the mound his projection is as much a question mark as any.

Mark Barry's Fantasy Take: After getting drafted, Denaburg paid off his parents' loans with his signing bonus. That's really cool. And for that act of magnanimousness, I will press pause on the snarkiness for one spot.

6 Tim Cate LHP   OFP: 50   ETA: 2021

Born: 09/30/97   Age: 22   Bats: L   Throws: L   Height: 6'0"   Weight: 185   Origin: Round 2, 2018 Draft (#65 overall)

YEAR	TEAM	LVL	AGE	W	L	SV	G	GS	IP	H	HR	BB/9	K/9	K	GB%	BABIP	WHIP	ERA	DRA	WARP	PF
2018	AUB	A-	20	2	3	0	9	8	31	34	1	2.9	7.5	26	45%	.333	1.42	4.65	5.74	-0.2	101
2018	HAG	A	20	0	3	0	4	4	21	23	4	2.6	8.1	19	44%	.306	1.38	5.57	5.20	0.0	106
2019	HAG	A	21	4	5	0	13	13	70¹	61	2	1.7	9.3	73	57%	.309	1.05	2.82	3.63	1.3	93
2019	POT	A+	21	7	4	0	13	13	73¹	71	4	2.3	8.1	66	61%	.324	1.23	3.31	5.29	-0.3	101
2020	WAS	MLB	22	2	2	0	33	0	35	34	5	3.8	7.0	27	50%	.277	1.39	4.37	4.58	0.3	108

Comparables: Ranger Suárez, Jeff Locke, Patrick Sandoval

The Report: Businesslike and incisive on the mound, Cate has one clear plus pitch and does very well to get the most from the rest of his arsenal. His true 12-to-6 curve is the money pitch, coming in around 80 with late and sharp break. When I saw him he seemed to have a well-constructed plan of attack against right-handed hitters, which was to pound his 90-ish fastball in on the hands to generate weak contact or set up the curve as a chase pitch down or in the dirt. The pitch flashes glove-side cut which increases the intended effect and allows him to mix in his third pitch, a changeup with some decent fade. The delivery is low effort and he repeats it well; he hardly walks anyone and his fastball command is very good already. He'll need it, of course.

Variance: Low. He's a command lefty with a well-developed curve; there's not much more ceiling but he should be fine. Worst case, he ekes out a career as a middle reliever where the fastball should play up in shorter stints.

Mark Barry's Fantasy Take: I don't know, maybe like a worse-2019 Jose Quintana? Does that do anything for you?

7 Matt Cronin LHP   OFP: 50   ETA: Late 2020

Born: 09/20/97   Age: 22   Bats: L   Throws: L   Height: 6'2"   Weight: 195   Origin: Round 4, 2019 Draft (#123 overall)

YEAR	TEAM	LVL	AGE	W	L	SV	G	GS	IP	H	HR	BB/9	K/9	K	GB%	BABIP	WHIP	ERA	DRA	WARP	PF
2019	HAG	A	21	0	0	1	17	0	22	11	1	4.5	16.8	41	20%	.345	1.00	0.82	2.34	0.6	100
2020	WAS	MLB	22	2	2	0	33	0	35	36	6	3.8	12.1	47	34%	.350	1.44	4.78	4.85	0.2	108

Comparables: Craig Kimbrel, Bryan Abreu, Donnie Veal

The Report: Yeah, we're stuffing a fourth-round college reliever here. It's that kind of system, but Cronin is also a pretty interesting prospect. The Arkansas closer made a seamless transition to pro ball, continuing to dominate hitters after being assigned straight to full-season ball. He pairs a fastball that gets into the mid 90s with a high-spin curveball that already grades out as plus. Cronin has a very high-effort delivery, but he repeats it well enough, and he's been extremely difficult for hitters to pick up in both college and his brief pro experience. With two plus pitches, he has a chance to be an impact relief arm. He could also move very fast; we think he has the potential to be an in-season 2020 add for the Nats if things work out well.

Variance: Medium. The track record of college relief arms is quite mixed, which keeps it from being low. Cronin himself has an obvious lefty specialist sort of fallback as a fastball/curve lefty, but anti-LOOGY rulemaking could nerf that a bit.

Mark Barry's Fantasy Take: A college reliever who could see his destiny as a LOOGY halted by crazy anti-LOOGY laws? Where do I sign up!?

8 Drew Mendoza 1B   OFP: 50   ETA: 2021/22

Born: 10/10/97   Age: 22   Bats: L   Throws: R   Height: 6'5"   Weight: 230   Origin: Round 3, 2019 Draft (#94 overall)

YEAR	TEAM	LVL	AGE	PA	R	2B	3B	HR	RBI	BB	K	SB	CS	AVG/OBP/SLG	DRC+	VORP	BABIP	BRR	FRAA	WARP	PF
2019	HAG	A	21	239	23	12	0	4	25	34	57	3	0	.264/.377/.383	127	12.6	.348	0.8	1B(44) -3.5, 3B(6) 1.2	0.8	95
2020	WAS	MLB	22	251	21	12	1	5	23	16	79	2	1	.212/.269/.329	57	1.0	.299	0.0	1B -2, 3B 0	-0.7	108

Comparables: Kyle Kubitza, Ji-Man Choi, Steven Souza Jr.

The Report: Mendoza is a typical long and strong corner college slugger. He played mostly third base at FSU, and while the Nats still rolled him out there occasionally for Hagerstown, his large frame is bound for the colder corner as a professional. He might have the bat to play there, as Mendoza generates plus raw power despite a stiff swing and merely average bat speed.

His track record with wood isn't outstanding, and there's significant swing-and-miss concerns at the plate, but he generally knows what to swing at, and could profile as a three true outcomes second-division first baseman. The margins are very fine with this profile however. Normally, I'd tee up a C.J. Cron reference here, but Mark is on fantasy comments, so...

Variance: High. The usual hit tool questions for a length and strength first base slugger, and Mendoza doesn't have much of a professional track record yet.

Mark Barry's Fantasy Take: I see your C.J. Cron reference and I'm not playing.

9 Seth Romero LHP

OFP: 55   ETA: 2021

Born: 04/19/96   Age: 24   Bats: L   Throws: L   Height: 6'3"   Weight: 240   Origin: Round 1, 2017 Draft (#25 overall)

YEAR	TEAM	LVL	AGE	W	L	SV	G	GS	IP	H	HR	BB/9	K/9	K	GB%	BABIP	WHIP	ERA	DRA	WARP	PF
2017	AUB	A-	21	0	1	0	6	6	20	19	0	2.7	14.4	32	40%	.404	1.25	5.40	3.16	0.5	108
2018	HAG	A	22	0	1	0	7	7	25¹	20	3	2.8	12.1	34	45%	.279	1.11	3.91	2.93	0.7	98
2020	WAS	MLB	24	2	2	0	33	0	35	35	6	3.6	9.4	36	39%	.311	1.41	4.72	4.89	0.2	108

Comparables: Matt Hall, Caleb Smith, Steven Matz

The Report: Probably the best thing that happened with Seth Romero this year is that we just didn't hear about him. The talented but troubled lefty underwent Tommy John surgery late in the 2018 season, and missed the entirety of 2019. His rehab seems to be going well, and he should return in 2020.

Before the surgery, Romero would flash three plus pitches from the left side. He would also get in trouble constantly; he was dismissed from college and sent home from his first pro spring training, both for personal misbehavior. He hasn't been on the mound all that much in the last three seasons between injuries and suspensions, and correspondingly his command profile had yet to develop much. Suffice to say, there's very substantial relief and complete flame-out risk here.

Variance: Xtreme, for many of the same reasons Jeffrey laid out in the Jay Groome report.

Mark Barry's Fantasy Take: Romero didn't punch anyone this season and he didn't get suspended. I think that should be considered an unequivocal win.

10 Yasel Antuna SS

OFP: 55   ETA: 2023

Born: 10/26/99   Age: 20   Bats: B   Throws: R   Height: 6'0"   Weight: 170   Origin: International Free Agent, 2016

YEAR	TEAM	LVL	AGE	PA	R	2B	3B	HR	RBI	BB	K	SB	CS	AVG/OBP/SLG	DRC+	VORP	BABIP	BRR	FRAA	WARP	PF
2017	NAT	RK	17	199	25	8	3	1	17	23	29	5	5	.301/.382/.399	138	10.7	.352	-1.9	SS(21) -0.7, 3B(15) 1.4	1.2	105
2018	HAG	A	18	362	44	14	2	6	27	32	79	8	7	.220/.293/.331	83	2.4	.269	-0.6	SS(67) -8.8, 2B(9) 0.2	-0.2	97
2020	WAS	MLB	20	251	23	11	1	6	25	20	66	2	1	.220/.286/.348	69	0.0	.284	-0.4	SS -3, 3B 0	-0.5	108

Comparables: Abiatal Avelino, José Rondón, Leury García

The Report: Antuna was out until late-June following late-2018 Tommy John surgery. He played three games in the GCL and was promptly shut down again until instructs. It was a totally lost season for the infielder, albeit one he could afford better than most in his age-19 season given that he got over 350 plate appearances in Low-A at age-18. Going back to our 2018 looks, he'd shown wide-ranging potential, with athletic and smooth actions and the potential to hit for both average and power. The switch-hitter couldn't actualize much yet, though. His bat was nearly useless from the port side and not all that much better from the starboard, and he wasn't consistent defensively. We're hoping a mostly lost year doesn't knock him too far off the track, because he's projectable as all hell.

Variance: Extreme, which is lower than Xtreme. Antuna doesn't have a lot of experience and hasn't hit anywhere yet.

Mark Barry's Fantasy Take: Antuna basically redshirted 2019, so if you liked him last year, nothing about this season should change your mind. He's still a top-150 or 200 dynasty guy.

The Next Ten

11 Eddy Yean RHP
Born: 06/25/01   Age: 19   Bats: R   Throws: R   Height: 6'1"   Weight: 180   Origin: International Free Agent, 2017

YEAR	TEAM	LVL	AGE	W	L	SV	G	GS	IP	H	HR	BB/9	K/9	K	GB%	BABIP	WHIP	ERA	DRA	WARP	PF
2018	DWA	RK	17	1	2	0	11	10	43²	57	1	4.7	6.6	32	51%	.381	1.83	5.98	8.20	-1.0	100
2019	NAT	RK	18	1	2	0	8	8	35¹	30	3	3.1	9.2	36	52%	.293	1.19	3.82	3.48	1.0	101
2019	AUB	A-	18	1	1	0	2	2	11	7	0	4.1	5.7	7	44%	.219	1.09	2.45	4.35	0.1	91
2020	WAS	MLB	19	2	2	0	33	0	35	35	5	3.9	6.4	25	41%	.278	1.43	4.74	4.91	0.2	108

Comparables: Ronald Herrera, German Márquez, Mauricio Cabrera

So the 11th-best prospect here is a young Latin arm whose first mention within the pages of Baseball Prospectus will be in this list. Originally signed for $100K in the '17 J2 class, Yean has bulked up very quickly, with evaluators guesstimating he is around 6-foot with 210 pounds of muscle. This is a good frame, but meh at the same time, as we usually like young guys with stuff and projection, and Yean lacks that projection. The fastball is the main attraction, a potential plus offering with above-average life from a tick above three-quarters slot. The slider is the obvious out pitch, with late action that he locates well against right-handers. He does get hit harder than you expect, with his pitches finding barrels way too much for your liking. Improved command should come with more reps though, and at 18 years old, Yean has plenty of time to get those reps. It is unlikely Yean gets sent straight to full-season ball next year, and some more polish in Extended Spring could help further refine this muscular ball of clay.

12 Sterling Sharp RHP
Born: 05/30/95   Age: 25   Bats: R   Throws: R   Height: 6'3"   Weight: 170   Origin: Round 22, 2016 Draft (#664 overall)

YEAR	TEAM	LVL	AGE	W	L	SV	G	GS	IP	H	HR	BB/9	K/9	K	GB%	BABIP	WHIP	ERA	DRA	WARP	PF
2017	HAG	A	22	4	9	0	18	17	92²	100	8	1.4	6.7	69	57%	.310	1.23	3.69	5.18	0.1	99
2017	POT	A+	22	2	2	0	6	5	32	39	4	3.7	7.3	26	62%	.354	1.62	4.78	6.46	-0.5	101
2018	POT	A+	23	5	3	0	14	14	79²	82	4	2.4	6.6	58	62%	.310	1.29	3.16	4.90	0.4	100
2018	HAR	AA	23	6	3	0	13	13	68²	72	6	3.4	6.2	47	57%	.301	1.43	4.33	5.12	0.2	101
2019	AUB	A-	24	0	1	0	2	2	7	4	0	1.3	6.4	5	76%	.235	0.71	1.29	4.83	0.0	91
2019	HAR	AA	24	5	3	0	9	9	49²	56	1	2.5	8.2	45	64%	.362	1.41	3.99	5.91	-0.6	100
2020	WAS	MLB	25	2	2	0	33	0	35	34	5	3.5	6.5	25	54%	.276	1.37	4.28	4.59	0.3	108

Comparables: Tobi Stoner, David Buchanan, Drew Gagnon

One of the more entertaining prospects on social media, Sharp is a bit of a throwback as a prospect. He's a sinkerballer who has put up strong ground-ball and home run rates while being generally effective despite only throwing around 88-90. He also mixes in a slider, changeup, and two-seam fastball, and all of those come in around the fringe-average to average ratio. There's no out pitch projection amongst those at present, but sometimes that can actually work for a sinkerballer. For an extreme example, Steve Givarz comped him to Aaron Cook during the Fall League, and Cook once made an All-Star team. Sharp has already vastly exceeded expectations for a 22nd-rounder out of Division II baseball, at the very least. We expect he'll be somewhere in the utility to back-of-the-rotation arm spectrum soon, with sneaky upside if he can keep getting hitters to pound it into the ground.

13 Israel Pineda C

Born: 04/03/00   Age: 20   Bats: R   Throws: R   Height: 5'11"   Weight: 190   Origin: International Free Agent, 2016

YEAR	TEAM	LVL	AGE	PA	R	2B	3B	HR	RBI	BB	K	SB	CS	AVG/OBP/SLG	DRC+	VORP	BABIP	BRR	FRAA	WARP	PF
2017	NAT	RK	17	65	10	5	2	0	12	4	13	0	0	.288/.323/.441	104	6.0	.354	0.3	C(16) -0.1	0.3	104
2018	AUB	A-	18	185	25	7	0	4	24	12	35	0	0	.273/.341/.388	113	8.6	.320	-1.2	C(30) 0.2	0.7	102
2019	HAG	A	19	411	48	12	0	7	35	30	102	1	2	.217/.278/.305	68	4.1	.276	0.9	C(83) 1.6	0.7	95
2020	WAS	MLB	20	251	23	11	0	6	25	18	74	1	0	.219/.280/.346	65	0.0	.295	-0.5	C 0	-0.3	108

Comparables: Deivy Grullon, Francisco Mejía, Pedro Severino

Pineda was higher on this list last year, and a very brief glance at his season line is illustrative as to why. A big part of his prospect profile is his bat, and while he still seems to possess his underlying talents there they did not manifest themselves in games in what turned out to be a lost season in the Sally League. He's still very young, though, not turning 20 until around Opening Day, and trying to realize a hit tool projection while dealing with the various tasks of ignorance behind the dish can't be easy. He's decent enough back there already and at the plate he shows the ability to keep the bat in the zone a while and barrel up all sorts of pitches. The power isn't there yet and it is unclear whether it will ever be, but let's have him repeat the level and see where it takes us.

14 Joan Adon RHP

Born: 08/12/98   Age: 21   Bats: R   Throws: R   Height: 6'2"   Weight: 185   Origin: International Free Agent, 2016

YEAR	TEAM	LVL	AGE	W	L	SV	G	GS	IP	H	HR	BB/9	K/9	K	GB%	BABIP	WHIP	ERA	DRA	WARP	PF
2017	DWA	RK	18	2	1	1	13	0	28	24	1	2.9	10.0	31	46%	.329	1.18	3.54	3.67	0.6	100
2018	NAT	RK	19	2	0	2	13	0	19²	20	0	5.9	13.3	29	51%	.377	1.68	2.29	7.53	-0.4	100
2018	AUB	A-	19	1	1	0	7	0	11	13	2	7.4	9.0	11	46%	.355	2.00	7.36	7.63	-0.4	100
2019	HAG	A	20	11	3	0	22	21	105	93	8	3.8	7.7	90	46%	.289	1.30	3.86	5.27	-0.1	96
2020	WAS	MLB	21	2	2	0	33	0	35	35	6	4.1	6.5	25	42%	.281	1.47	5.06	5.14	0.1	108

Comparables: Elvin Ramirez, Yennsy Diaz, Jeff Ferrell

At some point in some barely-remembered time I decided that regardless of system depth we would go 20-deep on every team with a personal cheeseball and a low minors sleeper. It allows for a certain amount of streamlining within the list process, but realistically it underplays the Rays and the Padres where we could go 30 deep without much issue, and overplays…well, the Nats system, where Jarrett yelled at me for making him come up with more than ten names. He's not wrong, and although Adon is a perfectly cromulent 95-and-a-slider guy out of the pen…perhaps, he is currently a struggling, physically maxed A-ball starter. It's a solid frame, and he'd be a neat little low minors sleeper for every other team in the NL East—eh, well he might make the Mets list, too—but it's not a prospect you should feel the need to spend a full blurb on given the high-effort delivery and the command issues. Inevitably some of this job is make-work, and Nats fans would like to read about 22 prospects too, or maybe not now, because who cares about the 14th-best prospect in a bottom-five system when you just won the World Series. Must be nice. Adon might be a seventh inning guy, but he's a ways away. We'll move on swiftly now.

15 Nick Banks OF

Born: 11/18/94   Age: 25   Bats: L   Throws: L   Height: 6'0"   Weight: 215   Origin: Round 4, 2016 Draft (#124 overall)

YEAR	TEAM	LVL	AGE	PA	R	2B	3B	HR	RBI	BB	K	SB	CS	AVG/OBP/SLG	DRC+	VORP	BABIP	BRR	FRAA	WARP	PF
2017	HAG	A	22	483	52	24	4	7	58	31	90	14	7	.252/.303/.373	87	2.8	.300	2.4	RF(58) 0.6, LF(34) -1.8	0.3	100
2018	HAG	A	23	215	25	9	0	6	27	13	45	10	4	.260/.307/.395	99	3.1	.307	0.6	RF(42) 1.5, LF(6) -0.2	0.5	98
2018	POT	A+	23	253	27	11	2	4	30	14	52	1	0	.263/.310/.379	98	2.9	.318	-0.8	CF(21) 4.2, LF(21) 1.4	1.3	100
2019	POT	A+	24	304	41	21	0	9	35	19	54	2	2	.271/.327/.443	131	13.8	.309	0.4	LF(30) 3.9, RF(28) 1.9	2.2	103
2019	HAR	AA	24	173	19	12	2	1	21	15	41	6	0	.288/.358/.410	110	7.8	.386	0.3	RF(24) 3.2, LF(16) 0.9	1.0	99
2020	WAS	MLB	25	251	24	13	1	6	26	16	66	3	1	.237/.290/.376	74	0.0	.306	0.0	RF 1, LF 2	0.4	108

Banks keeps making these lists, and I keep writing him. I'm not altogether happy about it. There's a little more there this year than in the past; he's made positive swing changes over the last year. We've spotted more power than we used to as well, and he's flashing above-average to plus raw now. He's added a lot of loft to his swing. All of this portends a possibility of an outcome where everything comes together late and he starts hitting the ball with authority around the ballpark. At present, he's still not quite there, and he's also a year older with only incremental gains to show for it. We're talking about the mere potential for big gains from a polished college bat who just turned 25 and has barely made it out of A-ball yet. It's not a high-percentage outcome, is it?

16 Steven Fuentes RHP

Born: 05/04/97   Age: 23   Bats: R   Throws: R   Height: 6'2"   Weight: 175   Origin: International Free Agent, 2011

YEAR	TEAM	LVL	AGE	W	L	SV	G	GS	IP	H	HR	BB/9	K/9	K	GB%	BABIP	WHIP	ERA	DRA	WARP	PF
2017	HAG	A	20	4	3	2	25	1	63¹	80	9	1.8	7.5	53	52%	.351	1.47	4.41	6.35	-1.1	87
2018	HAG	A	21	2	1	3	9	0	23	17	0	0.8	10.6	27	57%	.283	0.83	2.35	2.69	0.6	100
2018	POT	A+	21	3	3	3	24	0	45	33	1	3.2	8.6	43	54%	.258	1.09	3.00	3.54	0.7	100
2019	POT	A+	22	1	1	1	8	0	17	8	0	3.7	13.8	26	46%	.242	0.88	0.53	2.36	0.5	100
2019	HAR	AA	22	5	4	0	15	11	63²	63	1	2.1	8.9	63	58%	.326	1.23	2.69	4.61	0.2	100
2020	WAS	MLB	23	2	2	0	33	0	35	34	5	3.5	8.5	33	50%	.294	1.36	4.30	4.50	0.4	108

Comparables: Ryan Kelly, Jake Newberry, Abel De Los Santos

Fuentes is a filled-out sinker/slider righty with a low arm slot who got a 50-game ban for using a banned stimulant towards the end of the 2019 season. That wasn't the best life choice. Neither was going 20-deep in this system, but we have covered that already. Fuentes has an uptempo delivery with a tough angle and slot for righties, which are nice things we write about a pitching prospect with clear relief markers. There isn't a clear bat-misser here, which might limit the relief upside, but he's a fairly safe relief prospect given his frame, Double-A success, and low-90s sinker.

17 Jeremy De La Rosa OF

Born: 01/16/02   Age: 18   Bats: L   Throws: L   Height: 5'11"   Weight: 160   Origin: International Free Agent, 2018

YEAR	TEAM	LVL	AGE	PA	R	2B	3B	HR	RBI	BB	K	SB	CS	AVG/OBP/SLG	DRC+	VORP	BABIP	BRR	FRAA	WARP	PF
2019	NAT	RK	17	99	14	1	2	2	10	12	29	3	2	.232/.343/.366	85	0.6	.321	-0.8	RF(12) -0.2, LF(10) -0.2	-0.1	102
2020	WAS	MLB	18	251	22	11	1	3	21	27	104	3	1	.210/.303/.314	69	0.0	.379	0.0	RF 0, LF 0	-0.1	108

Comparables: Ronald Acuña Jr., Nomar Mazara, Andrew Velazquez

Signed for 300k as part of the Nationals' 2018 July 2nd class, De La Rosa came stateside quickly, due to his present physicality and bat control. He's already spending most of his time in corner outfield spots, and with a likely long-term landing spot in left, the pressure on his bat is already strong. There's some present pop, although the swing can get slashy and play as hit over power. Check back in a couple years, when he will probably still be on these lists regardless.

18 Tyler Dyson RHP

Born: 12/24/97   Age: 22   Bats: R   Throws: R   Height: 6'3"   Weight: 210   Origin: Round 5, 2019 Draft (#153 overall)

YEAR	TEAM	LVL	AGE	W	L	SV	G	GS	IP	H	HR	BB/9	K/9	K	GB%	BABIP	WHIP	ERA	DRA	WARP	PF
2019	AUB	A-	21	2	1	0	8	8	31²	20	1	2.3	4.0	14	50%	.209	0.88	1.14	4.11	0.4	100
2020	WAS	MLB	22	2	2	0	33	0	35	35	5	3.7	5.0	19	43%	.263	1.39	4.62	4.85	0.2	108

Comparables: Trevor Williams, Joe Colòn, Peter Fairbanks

I certainly admire the Nationals for taking big swings on talent every now and again. It does contribute to the system weakness, sure, but one of the ways you're going to dig out of that hole is by hitting on the Tyler Dysons of the world. The Nats drafted Dyson in June after a college career where he was often injured or not that good (although he did super-shove as a freshman in the College World Series clincher), and signed him for $500,000, well-above slot for the fifth round. He's a three-pitch righty who gets into the mid 90s and even a little higher, which is a lot better than you're usually getting from a fifth-round SEC starting pitcher. There's substantial fastball/slider reliever vibes in the profile, and he was repeating the trick of not really striking anyone out despite the stuff in pro ball, but at least there's some real upside here.

19 Nick Raquet LHP

Born: 12/12/95   Age: 24   Bats: R   Throws: L   Height: 6'0"   Weight: 215   Origin: Round 3, 2017 Draft (#103 overall)

YEAR	TEAM	LVL	AGE	W	L	SV	G	GS	IP	H	HR	BB/9	K/9	K	GB%	BABIP	WHIP	ERA	DRA	WARP	PF
2017	AUB	A-	21	3	2	0	11	11	51¹	56	2	1.2	3.9	22	62%	.307	1.23	2.45	5.78	-0.3	105
2018	HAG	A	22	4	6	0	12	12	67²	68	1	2.4	7.4	56	61%	.327	1.27	2.79	5.03	0.1	95
2018	POT	A+	22	5	3	0	12	12	55	72	3	3.4	5.9	36	53%	.365	1.69	4.91	6.69	-0.9	101
2019	POT	A+	23	11	9	0	25	25	130¹	129	12	3.0	8.4	122	56%	.314	1.32	4.07	5.54	-0.8	104
2020	WAS	MLB	24	2	2	0	33	0	35	34	5	3.7	6.6	26	53%	.272	1.37	4.31	4.56	0.3	108

A former third-rounder, Raquet had a good enough time repeating High-A this year, but he's already 23 and how he does in Double-A first time around will be instructive. The stuff isn't terrible with a fastball sitting low 90s, touching higher, and a low-80s slider that has nice tight break when it's right. He's inconsistent with the slider, though, and can be inconsistent in general. His change and curve aren't too reliable either and on my look he appeared to begin tiring at around 70 pitches. The delivery is a high-effort crossfire deal and his command can suffer because of it. He's a reliever to my eye but he could make it. Being a lefty always helps.

20 Jackson Tetreault RHP

Born: 06/03/96   Age: 24   Bats: R   Throws: R   Height: 6'5"   Weight: 189   Origin: Round 7, 2017 Draft (#223 overall)

YEAR	TEAM	LVL	AGE	W	L	SV	G	GS	IP	H	HR	BB/9	K/9	K	GB%	BABIP	WHIP	ERA	DRA	WARP	PF
2017	AUB	A-	21	2	2	0	11	6	38¹	32	1	3.8	8.5	36	47%	.277	1.25	2.58	3.98	0.5	107
2018	HAG	A	22	3	8	0	20	20	110	108	10	2.8	9.7	118	39%	.320	1.29	4.01	4.50	0.9	99
2018	POT	A+	22	1	1	0	4	4	22²	21	2	2.8	7.9	20	31%	.288	1.24	4.37	4.53	0.2	98
2019	POT	A+	23	4	2	0	7	7	37²	29	0	3.1	6.9	29	40%	.269	1.12	1.91	3.80	0.6	106
2019	HAR	AA	23	4	5	0	18	18	85²	98	8	4.2	6.6	63	38%	.335	1.61	4.73	6.90	-2.0	99
2020	WAS	MLB	24	2	2	0	33	0	35	35	5	4.0	6.0	23	38%	.274	1.44	4.71	4.82	0.2	108

So we are probably about done waiting for the lean, 7th-round JuCo draftee to become a backend starting pitcher now. Tetreault is still on the skinny side, with command and change issues. The fastball still sits either side of 90, touching 94 or so, with good sink and occasional, possibly accidental, cut. There's a short, tight curve around 80, and a too-firm change. It more or less is what it is now, and what it is is the 20th best prospect in a bottom five system. There might be some middle relief utility here, and it's still a good frame, but that means more when you are 21 instead of 23. Life comes at you fast. Faster if you are a pitching prospect.

Personal Cheeseball

PC Cole Freeman 2B/OF

Born: 09/27/94   Age: 25   Bats: R   Throws: R   Height: 5'9"   Weight: 175   Origin: Round 4, 2017 Draft (#133 overall)

YEAR	TEAM	LVL	AGE	PA	R	2B	3B	HR	RBI	BB	K	SB	CS	AVG/OBP/SLG	DRC+	VORP	BABIP	BRR	FRAA	WARP	PF
2018	HAG	A	23	522	78	32	3	3	43	47	59	26	8	.266/.354/.371	132	28.7	.298	5.1	2B(101) 4.3, 3B(7) 1.3	4.3	99
2019	POT	A+	24	534	82	27	3	3	49	53	60	31	6	.311/.394/.404	150	44.7	.351	6.9	2B(54) -2.6, CF(46) -0.2	4.5	103
2020	WAS	MLB	25	251	22	13	1	3	22	16	43	6	2	.243/.304/.339	73	2.0	.288	0.4	2B 1, CF 0	0.2	108

Comparables: Will Rhymes, Nate Orf, Dean Anna

In some ways, the cheeseball spot was made for players like Freeman. He was a 2017 fourth-round priority senior sign out of LSU. He's listed at 5-foot-9 and 175 pounds, likely generously. He's a slap-and-dash hitter. He's a second baseman who has picked up the outfield. He put up good offensive numbers in the Carolina League, but he was 24 in the Carolina League. He went to the Arizona Fall League, but as we've been discussing for many thousands of words already, the Nationals don't really have the type of prospect depth that you'd usually send to the AFL. As the prospect world's resident hype man on both Jeff McNeil and Nick Madrigal I certainly have an affinity for this general profile, hence the cheeseball designation. Freeman absolutely has a path to the majors as a utility type as long as he keeps hitting singles, but it's a tough route, and it's hard to realistically project him as a regular when you're already 25 and haven't seen the high minors yet. Perhaps he'll prove us wrong yet again.

Low Minors Sleeper

LMS   Viandel Pena   IF
Born: 11/22/00   Age: 19   Bats: B   Throws: R   Height: 5'8"   Weight: 148   Origin: International Free Agent, 2017

YEAR	TEAM	LVL	AGE	PA	R	2B	3B	HR	RBI	BB	K	SB	CS	AVG/OBP/SLG	DRC+	VORP	BABIP	BRR	FRAA	WARP	PF
2018	DWA	RK	17	295	49	13	5	1	24	47	51	4	2	.250/.386/.358	121	18.2	.314	1.6	2B(37) 0.3, SS(31) -1.1	1.8	99
2019	NAT	RK	18	154	27	10	3	0	15	21	31	6	3	.359/.455/.481	188	19.4	.470	2.1	2B(16) -2.0, SS(15) 0.7	1.8	102
2020	WAS	MLB	19	251	22	12	1	3	23	22	74	0	0	.233/.307/.344	74	2.0	.332	-0.3	2B 0, SS 0	0.0	108

Comparables: Dilson Herrera, Luis Rengifo, Jason Martin

What do you do for a low-minors sleeper in a system where the guys we originally pegged for this ended up fairly high up the list? We had two options for this spot: Pena, who put up a shiny average in complex league ball, but is a tiny dude who correspondingly doesn't hit the ball very hard yet, or J2 pitcher Andry Lara, which would basically be a blind shot based on his signing bonus. We went with Pena. Honestly, our feedback on Pena was that he's probably a utility guy prospect, but that's better than Lara, for whom we have more or less nothing. Be forewarned that Pena could get the bat blown out of his hands in the Penn League or the Sally this year given his frame and swing, and his spot here is a complete indictment of the system.

Top Talents 25 and Under (as of 4/1/2020)

1. Juan Soto
2. Victor Robles
3. Carter Kieboom
4. Luis Garcia
5. Jackson Rutledge
6. Wil Crowe
7. Mason Denaburg
8. Tim Cate
9. Matt Cronin
10. Drew Mendoza

The Nationals packed a lot of narrative into their historic 2019 season, but perhaps the thing that they'll be most remembered for is being *old*. Old as the hills. Old as the Pixies "Doolittle" album. Organizationally, being this old is a problem, an indication of the farm system's weakness, particularly when injuries early in the season highlighted their vulnerability in replacing key players. It's also a problem–one that speaks to our relationship to professional athletes, and the commodification of their bodies–that it's considered normal to act like anyone over 30 is a breath away from crumbling into dust. Noted *viejo* Max Scherzer has explicitly tied that tendency to teams devaluing older players–and not wanting to pay free agents their worth.

The Nationals won the World Series with a roster whose average age was 30, with Howie Kendrick and Aníbal Sánchez and Fernando Rodney, and with two young players likely familiar to everyone reading this. So, without further ado, meet two guys you probably already know:

If you're going to have a team that's older than the Appalachians and only have two young players, be glad one is Juan Soto. Soto is everything his 2018 ROY-caliber season promised he'd be. Last season, his two main weaknesses were hitting breaking pitches and his defense in left field, a position he learned while in the majors having only played a handful of games in the minors there. This season, he responded by continuing to hit fastballs with a vigor that will surely haunt Josh Hader (and Gerrit Cole, and Justin Verlander, and and and…), and improved his ability to hit everything but sliders, including going from struggling against changeups to demolishing them. (It should perhaps soothe Kershaw to know Soto hits sliders off southpaws somewhat better than righties.) Defensively, he benefited from the mentoring of the many older players on the Nats, most notably Gerardo Parra, going from a defensive liability to an asset, all while keeping his elite offensive numbers.

Victor Robles would be the young outfielder on the Nats everyone was talking about...if not for Juan Soto. Robles struggled a bit more at the plate this year than he did during his September call-up last season, hitting respectably, stealing the number of bases one would expect from a guy with 95th-percentile speed, and getting hit with an Utley-ian, Espinosa-esque number of pitches. His defensive numbers are consistently elite, including a league-leading number of outfield assists and putouts.

Eyewitness Reports

Eyewitness Report: Jackson Rutledge

Evaluator: Ben Spanier
Report Date: 11/12/2019
Dates Seen: 8/28/2019
Risk Factor: High

Delivery: Huge dude, XL frame to go with the height. More athletic than some with this body type (ex. Dellin Betances) but will carry with him slight to moderate mechanical concerns. Kicks leg almost to letters, not the most fluid but he hides the ball well before releasing from a lowish three-quarters slot with a surprisingly short-armed release. All of that helps create deception to pair with his elite stuff, though extension can be somewhat inconsistent. Command isn't great at the moment (will likely never be his calling card) and he'll have bouts with his control as well. Outwardly competitive and can appear volatile at times. Makes adjustments when necessary and got stronger later into outing.

Pitch Type	Future Grade	Sitting Velocity	Peak Velocity	Report
Fastball	70	94-96	98	Easy future double-plus, he'll live on the heater and have everything else play off of it. Jumps on hitters due to quick release and gets great life, especially up in the zone. Extremely effective on the inner third against same-sided hitters, sets up the slider beautifully. Enough action get weak contact and swing/miss even when command gets spotty.
Slider	60	85-86	87	At least a future plus and possibly better, the hard slider is his second-best pitch and rivals his fastball for swings and misses. Has short, tight, break. A little more lateral than horizontal but the downward bite is late, sharp, and disappearing. Especially effective in the lower glove-side quadrant.
Curveball	55	77-78	79	Tempting to call this a future plus, was also a consideration to mark it lower than I did. No real command of it at present, but can generally drop it in for an early strike. Mostly landed it in the upper-middle part of the zone when it was unexpected. True 11-5 shape with some good snap, it has potential.
Changeup	40	87-88	89	Didn't see it much, didn't do much when I did. Weakest offering at present.

Conclusion: There's real risk here; he's a big guy who will have to stay on top of his command, which isn't overly advanced at present. The stuff is top-shelf though, and there is an easily apparent reliever fall-back plan if the command and pitch mix don't quite make it. The ceiling is quite high, 2 or 3 starter at least if they do. Low-A is a waltz for dudes with talent like this; Rutledge will look to avoid the pitfalls stalking his profile (see: Alec Hansen) as he hits High-A and beyond.

Organization Rankings

by Jeffrey Paternostro

Tier 9: It's not what you want

30. Milwaukee Brewers

29. Washington Nationals

28. Boston Red Sox

27. Colorado Rockies

If you are going to have a shallow system, it's nice to have some juice at the top. But outside of the Nationals with Carter Kieboom, all of our bottom tier organizations lack for both impact talent and depth of potential regulars. Brice Turang and Triston Casas—the best prospects for Milwaukee and Boston—both fell a bit outside our Top 101. Brendan Rodgers—Colorado's number one name—clocked in at #56, but is coming off of a labrum tear, and hasn't shown sustained dominance in the upper minors.

There's no pennant for topping our org rankings, but the lack of system depth will have impact on the major league side for all these clubs. The Brewers will struggle to add to a squad that's in the middle of a contention cycle, as most of their top talent behind Turang is years away, and there isn't a trade piece in there you could see headlining a major deal. The Nats are in a similar place, although one imagines they care about it, uh, less than the Brewers do, as they already have one of the flags that fly forever.

The Red Sox of 2020 are caught between two MBTA stops. They still have the same core that won a World Series in 2018, but may be sailing towards the siren's song of "sustainable success." I expect they will be ranked higher on our 2021 org rankings.

I've often said in the pages of Baseball Prospectus that the Rockies are the most personally confounding organization to me. The whys and hows of many of their moves feel like a particularly complex parlor room mystery, see: possibly trading Nolan Arenado by the time you read this.

Tier 8: Slump? I'm not in a slump. I'm just not hitting.

26. Pittsburgh Pirates

25. Houston Astros

24. Chicago Cubs

23. New York Mets

22. Toronto Blue Jays

These are your generically below-average systems. There's some premium talent at the top—all of these orgs have at least three Top 101 prospects—but they also tend to tail off quickly. This seems like a good spot to discuss how I weight value up and down a system for the purposes of these rankings. Premium talent is going to carry a lot of juice for me—the impact talent you find towards the top of national lists, the clear plus regulars. It's hard to find those players if you don't develop them. You have to pay a heavy price in trade or a lot of money in free agency.

You can find the kind of Role 45 extra outfielders, or back end starters, or seventh inning guys that comprise the "depth" of most of these team lists much more cheaply. That said, depth is valuable, because it's always there exactly when you need it. And if you collect enough of those types of players, one here or there will probably turn into an above-average regular for you. These five organizations don't have those guys in bulk.

The Pirates have seen a lot of their top talent from last year stagnate. Cole Tucker got enough at-bats to graduate off prospect lists, but didn't put his stamp on the everyday shortstop gig for 2020. Mitch Keller has gone backwards, and if you haven't already heard jokes on twitter about him winning the 2022 Cy Young with the Rays, they are surely coming. Ke'Bryan Hayes still didn't have the power breakout we've been expecting for years. You'd hope as bad as the MLB team has been in recent years that the farm system would contain more hope for the future, but alas.

Given the draft pick forfeitures the Astros are facing—the first two picks in both 2020 and 2021—and the impending graduations of Forrest Whitley and Jose Urquidy, this might be a high-water mark for a bit.

The Mets and Cubs always seem to get paired up on these rankings recently. They once again feel like similarly shaped systems. A strong top five, a couple interesting names past that, and then a very thin 11-20. The Mets top names are mostly in A-ball or below, and this system would probably be top ten if they hadn't made the Edwin Díaz/Robinson Cano and Marcus Stroman deals. Would that make the team better from 2019-2021. It's less clear to me than it is Mets fans on the internet I think, but perhaps new owner Steve Cohen's billions will patch all the minor and major league holes regardless.

The Blue Jays graduated three top 101 prospects from a top-five system, including last year's number one prospect, Vladimir Guerrero Jr. That's how you end up down here. Again, premium talent is important.

Tier 7: The great thing about baseball is there is a crisis every day

21. **Philadelphia Phillies**
20. **St. Louis Cardinals**
19. **Cincinnati Reds**
18. **Chicago White Sox**

The Phillies have cycled back up into contention and converted a formerly top-ten farm system into some pretty good major league pieces, through both promotion and trade. Alec Bohm and Spencer Howard give them two more pretty good pieces to play, but there's a gap to the next wave of help after them. And they are suddenly thin in arms from the major league on down.

The Cardinals will no doubt turn some generic name on the backend of their list into a Top 101 prospect next year. I'd place my crafty quid on Jhon Torres.

The Reds are a better version of the teams in Tier 8 with a strong top five and then some depth issues. Their 2019 draft class is interesting though.

The White Sox are even stronger at the top than the Reds, with Nick Madrigal, Andrew Vaughn, and Michael Kopech topping their list, but they might have even less depth.

Tier 6: You can win, or you can lose, or it can rain

17. **Detroit Tigers**
16. **Cleveland Indians**
15. **Los Angeles Angels**
14. **Baltimore Orioles**
13. **San Francisco Giants**
12. **Kansas City Royals**

Our mushball middle is mostly made up of teams in the midst of deep tanks rebuilds. You could reorder this tier in a bunch of different ways and I wouldn't quibble much. To wit:

You could have Detroit higher if...you think Casey Mize's shoulder is fine, that Tarik Skubal has enough stuff and durability to start, and Isaac Paredes has an above-average bat.

You could have Cleveland higher if...you believe in the projection of Valera, Rocchio, and Bracho over the lack of proximity and really, *really* like high-end relief prospects.

You could have the Angels higher if...you think Jeremiah Jackson, D'Shawn Knowles, and Trent Deveaux are all potential stars (and after watching the Bahamian Home Run Derby this year, I'm sympathetic).

You could have the Orioles lower if...you don't get why we keep ranking Ryan Mountcastle this high every year and aren't as sold on their plethora of backend pitching prospects.

You could have the Giants lower if...wait you guys ranked Marco Luciano how high? Sure seems like a lot of risky short-season bats around here.

You could have the Royals lower if...you're not sold on their 2018 draft class as starters.

Tier 5: The Texas Rangers

11. **Texas Rangers**

It seems we often end up the high source on the Rangers system. You'd think this would be the year that would end, but the staff reports on Leody Taveras matched the mush notes I've been writing since 2017. They have a bevvy of interesting arms, depth in toolsy international teenagers—as always—and I could easily pick out five names I was annoyed I had to leave off their Top 20. You can point out that this happens every year and they've struggled to develop all that prospect talent into MLB help, but the clay is still really, really good.

Tier 4: Juuuuuuuuuust a bit outside

10. **Oakland Athletics**
9. **New York Yankees**
8. **Miami Marlins**

We are into the good systems now, although each has a flaw that holds them back from being a bit higher. Oakland might have the best one-two pitching prospect punch in baseball with Jesus Luzardo and A.J. Puk. There really isn't much in the way of impact talent past those two though.

The Yankees—as usual—have depth for days, but their two best prospects are a 5-foot-9 right-hander, and a 2019 July 2nd signing that won't be able to drink until the next New Hampshire primary.

The Marlins are a fun system, loaded with talent. But they are all high risk profiles, and Miami hasn't had much luck with developing their last batch of toolsy athletes.

Tier 3: I got a Porsche already. I got a 911 with a quadraphonic Blaupunkt

7. Minnesota Twins
6. Los Angeles Dodgers
5. Atlanta Braves

The Twins have one of the deepest systems in baseball, and they aren't hurting at the top either with four Top 101 prospects. The pitchers here have a lot of relief risk, but nowadays whose pitchers don't?

The Dodgers have thinned out a bit from recent seasons when they routinely checked in among the top five systems in baseball. The top end talent is still there though. It's mostly close to the majors though, so the Dodgers might continue to slide down our org rankings without an infusion of more prospect talent.

The Braves system is still very good. It feels like it's the exact same pitching prospects every year and they never actually graduate. Most of this next wave will probably be up in 2021, so they could have another nice little wave ready to follow Acuña, Albies and Soroka.

Tier 2: The Upwardly Mobile Prospect Seekers

4. Seattle Mariners
3. Arizona Diamondbacks

If you want to know how to jump up these rankings quickly, here are two options:

(1) Trade for a high first-round draft pick. Tweak his setup and swing and watch him become a top ten prospect in baseball. Oh yeah, also have your top IFA from two years ago breakout and look like a top-ten prospect in baseball.

(That's an oversimplification of how the Mariners did it. They've gotten general improvements around the system as well, but the two elite prospects at the top don't hurt.)

(2) End up with seven draft picks in the first three rounds of a reasonably deep draft. Don't do what the Rays did in 2011, instead end up with a half-dozen really good prospects.

(Oh yeah, also have your top IFA from two years ago breakout and look like a Top-20 prospect in baseball.)

Tier 1: Organizational Ranking Flags Fly Forever

2. San Diego Padres
1. Tampa Bay Rays

The top two orgs from last year flip spots. It's a testament to the Padres obscene depth that they graduated Fernando Tatis, Jr, Chris Paddack, Francisco Mejia, and Luis Urias and only dropped to the second spot.

The Rays are just as deep though, and have the best prospect in baseball, two more top-30 prospects, and run into their next ten for Top 101 candidates. All they really need though is Wander Franco to work out honestly. ▪

—*Jeffrey Paternostro is an author of Baseball Prospectus.*

The View From Behind the Backstop: No One Reads Your Gamer in 2019

by Jeffrey Paternostro

*A*lternatively, *"So you want to be a prospect writer?"* *Or perhaps, "OFP: Long Relief"*

Sen. Thomas J. Dodd Memorial Stadium is around an hour from my house, depending on traffic. It's a bucolic drive along CT-2, through the (mostly) woods of Eastern Connecticut. I'm making the jaunt more often this year since the Penn League is the more interesting coverage area for me. The trip is just long enough to be annoying, it's also about one album's length of driving, so I've taken to re-listening to old LPs, usually from around 2001-2005, that I remember liking at some point, but have more or less bobbed along, unplayed in my iTunes since three Macs ago.

Here's notes on some of what I've listened to so far:

1. As a white teenager who grew up in Connecticut in the late 90s, I owned exactly the four hip-hop albums you would suspect,[1] so I am not remotely qualified to discuss the genre. As a white twenty-something who read too much Pitchfork, at some point I ended up downloading a bunch of Busdriver albums. They hold up well, *Roadkillovercoat* is good driving music for the way down, *Fear of a Black Tangent* works well for the more contemplative drives back, heat lightning in the July night skies. At 37 I don't need much more than that. I also think we have similar views on creativity and content creation, which I appreciate.

2. I am plenty qualified to discuss Beirut's *Gulag Orkestar* which exists as a perfect time capsule of 2005 indy music. Part David Byrne, part Neutral Milk Hotel, a weird and perhaps pretentious nod to Béla Bartók. This is what we listened to, I guess. It's all mid-tempo, the production is warm, but not hi-fi, and there's no hooks.[2]

3. I have three Animal Collective albums on my phone. I got nothing here. One of them's even an EP.

4. When it was released I found *Sound of Silver* to be a bit twee and lightweight. Now that I am actually an aging hipster? "Big mood," as the young millennials say.

This was a two-album trip because of traffic, an accident on the two-lane highway. My occasionally-mentioned minivan is still running[3], despite a fuel line scare before Futures.[4] The air conditioning can't really keep up with the kind of heat we had in the northeast last weekend, but I'm going to be sweating for the first couple hours of this 6:05 p.m. game anyway, so whatever.

I'm primarily here to see Riley Greene, recently promoted. I've written this year about the dangers of post-draft looks, but you will still make the drive every day to see the fifth overall pick. I'm only two games into the report, so you won't get that yet. You've probably figured that out by now. "Obsequious banter is protocol."

The first piece I wrote for Baseball Prospectus, almost (f**k) four years ago now, was titled "The Pitchers You Meet in the Appy League." Reading it back right now…it's okay, although a bit disjointed narratively. The reports were fine at least. Consider this a bit of a companion piece.

"The Games You Watch in the Penn League."

It didn't have to be this way. Chavez Fernander got the start for Connecticut. This was my third look at him—vagaries of the schedule—and he's very much a pitcher you meet in the Penn League: a late-round JuCo flyer with some arm strength and feel for secondaries. He's close to physically maxed but bumps 93, and the breaker and change aren't awful. He generally throws strikes and works at a decent pace. He probably gets to Double-A, maybe the stuff pops a little in the pen.

Anyway, he's a decent benchmark to judge an opposing lineup against at this level, even if that opposing lineup is the 2019 Brooklyn Cyclones, whose average age is roughly "Jamie Murphy when he wrote *Sounds of Silver*."

Other than Greene, I've got fairly thorough notes on this Tigers team[5] by now. I don't even bother chalking up a sheet for Fernander today. I'm instead planning on full coverage on this Brooklyn team. I had some fragments and half-formed thoughts for an article about the Mets' 2019 senior sign strategy, comparing it to their failures on Day 2 and 3 with more traditional junior year college dudes and overslot prep arms in recent draft classes. The thesis would amount to, "Well, if you aren't hitting on those guys, might as well go cheap and get more top-end talent."

I perhaps write about the Mets more than I should as a "national prospect writer," but they are a Wittgenstein's ladder for drafting and player development, and that is often useful for rhetorical purposes.

The first three innings were perfectly fine. I got a good feel for Jake Mangum's left-handed swing, Riley Greene barreled a couple balls, and we got it all done in under an hour. When it comes to Penn League game times though, past results extremely do not guarantee future performance. Fernander left with the trainer after a strikeout to start the top of the fourth. This is not an actual gamer, so if you are looking for an injury report, you won't get that. You've probably figured that out by now.

He's replaced by Cristhian Tortosa who is exactly the kind of pitcher you'd expect to elicit a "he kind of had his shit together in extended spring training" comment in Slack. He's also exactly the kind of pitcher that is gonna get multiple chances to get his shit together because it's 95 from the left side and the breaker flashes on the scant occasions he actually gets ahead with the fastball. Saturday night was not one of those occasions. A parade of walks and mound visits began. It happens.

I should note that behind home plate in Norwich is usually pretty quiet even on the weekends, but somehow I had staked out a seat with people on three sides of me. I'm very good at blocking out the din from the different degrees of drunken dialogues around me at the park. So I ignored the stereotypical Boomer grousing about snowflakes and yelling "swing" intermittently on pitches.[6] I was oblivious to the woman next to me patiently explaining why you don't bunt with two outs to a young child. Honestly, the closest I came to losing my cool in the RealFeel® 105 degree heat was a discussion happening back and to my right. Connecticut—like many minor league clubs—occasionally runs alternate jersey/team nights representing local foodstuffs. So tonight they were the New England Lobster Rolls.

"But do you have them cold or warm?"

It took every ounce of my sweaty being to not snap back, "Warm, drawn butter, squeeze of lemon, split-top roll, you rube. This is Connecticut."

I don't even really like lobster. Or, often, Connecticut.

Let's talk about the fifth inning. If you've read my work, you know I am not a fan of brevity. If you've never read anything of mine before this article, you've already teased that out. Dashiell Hammett is lovely to read, admirable in his restraint, but that's not my palette. A picture's worth a thousand words? Eh, I can find the 1k. Show don't tell? Yeah, Hemingway made a great daiquiri. I'm not big on murdering my darlings, either, which is how "they are a Wittgenstein's ladder for drafting and player development" made it into the CMS. But in this instance, I can add nothing to these images:

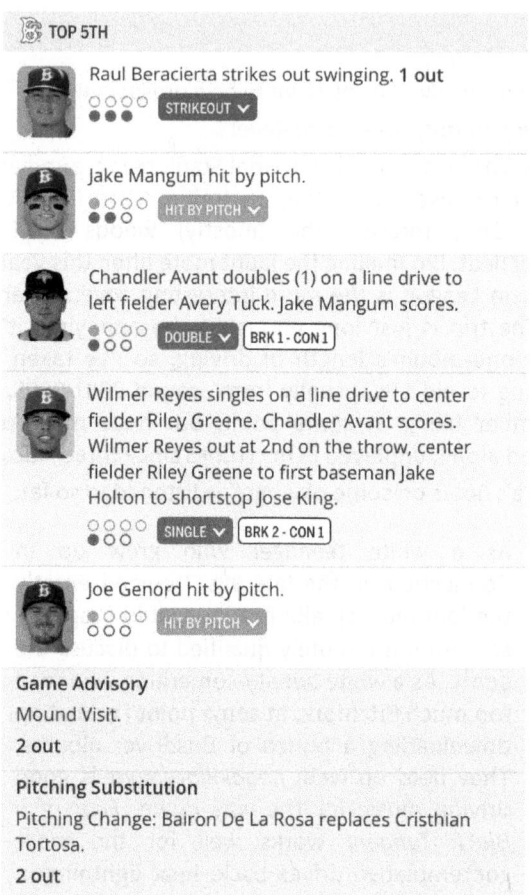

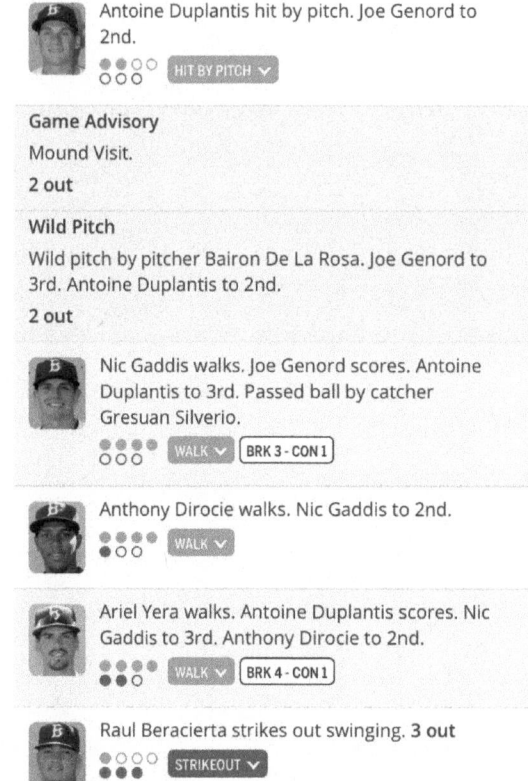

Antoine Duplantis hit by pitch. Joe Genord to 2nd.

● ● ○ ○
○ ○ ○   HIT BY PITCH ∨

Game Advisory
Mound Visit.
2 out

Wild Pitch
Wild pitch by pitcher Bairon De La Rosa. Joe Genord to 3rd. Antoine Duplantis to 2nd.
2 out

Nic Gaddis walks. Joe Genord scores. Antoine Duplantis to 3rd. Passed ball by catcher Gresuan Silverio.

● ● ● ●
○ ○ ○   WALK ∨   BRK 3 - CON 1

Anthony Dirocie walks. Nic Gaddis to 2nd.

● ● ● ●
● ○ ○   WALK ∨

Ariel Yera walks. Antoine Duplantis scores. Nic Gaddis to 3rd. Anthony Dirocie to 2nd.

● ● ● ●
● ● ○   WALK ∨   BRK 4 - CON 1

Raul Beracierta strikes out swinging. 3 out

● ○ ○ ○
● ● ●   STRIKEOUT ∨

Okay, that's not entirely true.

1. There was an additional delay during Jake Mangum's at-bat as he fouled a fastball off his instep or ankle and was down for a good bit. He naturally got hit on the very next pitch.

2. Now I have no reason to believe that the stringer in the press box missed a mound visit (or three) that inning, but I can tell you that it felt like many more. The umpire would go to his little note pad to mark off each mound visit. And by the seventh inning: "He must just be making a grocery list now, because they should be out of visits, right?"

3. Oh, and I don't remember which mound visit it was, but it came before a 2-0 pitch. The next one went to the backstop.

At some point later we got a fun side-arming undrafted free agent from Johns Hopkins[7] who is built like me, down to the sport specs that suggest he would also enjoy some Neutral-Milk-Hotel-referencing[8] bands.

We get two verses of "God Bless America." This is the darndest thing I've ever seen at a baseball game. I don't know if it was strictly the longest version I've heard. I have fond memories of an acapella trio that did it in Lakewood. They included a rigorous orchestration of the full spoken intro. It ran over two minutes on Jarrett's Accusplit.

This was just confusing. She came out and sang the normal version, but instead of the second "my home sweet home" she just went back to the start and sang the same verse again. I wondered for a moment what would have happened if she had just kept going, dal segno after dal segno. At what point would someone stop her?

We were three hours into the game at this point.

The Lobster Roll Guy is now complaining about how long the in-between inning time is. Yes, that is the issue here, sir. It is not the combined 11 walks, nine mound visits, four hit-by-pitches, four mid-inning pitching changes, two verses of "God Bless America" and one argument about a fair/foul bunt.

Other stuff happened, I have notes. I was doing full coverage on Brooklyn for a column that somehow turned into this.

I got home around 11:00 p.m. I drank half of a local Strawberry Pale Ale and at some point fell asleep on my couch.

"How do you feel?"

"Terrible. I must've gone to bed sober." ▪

—Jeffrey Paternostro is an author of Baseball Prospectus.

1. *Marshall Mathers LP, 2001, Ready to Die, 36 Chambers*

2. The peak of this "genre" was of course, Clap Your Hands Say Yeah.

3. 218,000 miles now and possibly a hood latch/car alarm problem. It's a known issue as I found out googling at 2:00 a.m. this week.

4. Turned out it was a combo of being parked on a steep incline and A/C condensation. My next podcast will not be a Car Talk reboot.

5. I'll need a couple more games on Eliezer Alfonzo behind the plate and Ryan Kreidler at shortstop too, but I don't expect the needle to move much

6. He was drunk enough that he began (mostly jovially) arguing with his partner over whether a song on the PA in between innings was The Eagles or Huey Lewis. They danced during "Sweet Caroline" in the seventh, her standing (swaying) on the plastic seat.

7. Go, Fighting…Erlenmeyer Flasks?.

8. No, I don't know how I have made two separate NMH references and neither were about literally Jake Mangum.

Catching the Outliers

by Wilson Karaman

Scouting only works because it is a collaborative endeavor. Scouting is a lot like hitting, because every scout misses on a ton of players. Predicting the future is really hard, especially when basing those predictions off a few clumps of days and at-bats over the course of a long season…in what is an arduous run through the gauntlet of many seasons a given prospect will play as he works his way up towards the majors. The whole process of collaborative scouting dilutes the value of one scout's information dramatically, and we all benefit because of it.

⚾   ⚾   ⚾

Jacob Nottingham's first Bernie ball reminded me of that time he auditioned to be Johnny Bench's stunt double. I saw a bunch of Nottingham both with Lancaster before he got traded to Oakland and then Stockton before he got traded to Milwaukee for Khris Davis in what has to this point played out as an unfortunate trade for Milwaukee.

The Nottingham I saw was a big-bodied catcher, slower than ideal for the position and lacking in lateral quickness. But he used his size very effectively and absolutely wolfed a bunch of splitters and spiked sliders in all directions from an A-ball lifer in one of the games I saw. And across the rest of them he continued to move around pretty well behind the dish, with intent that played as physical skill and an odd sort of agility. He looked like he could become at least adequate as a blocker despite being big and slow.

The framing wasn't great at the time, but he had a very strong wrist and seemed to track the ball pretty well on all of those dirtballs and other, better pitches as well. His pops were slower because of the "big and slow" thing, but he had solid arm strength and it all looked like it should be able to come together and create at least a passable arm tool.

At the dish he just pounded the ball in my looks. Yeah, the swing was pretty muscled and a little stiff and sluggish against the better velocity, but he was eating every damn time I saw him across three non-consecutive series. He let the ball travel deep and showed big in-game power oppo and straight-away. I saw him hit Piazza homers and scald balls off the opposite-field wall so hard he jogged it out to first because he knew he wouldn't have time to stretch it into a deserved double. And yeah, some of it was in Lancaster, but the balls he was hitting could've split the Chatham air on a soggy June night. He stayed in the zone, hunted pitches to extend on, and crushed lasers all over the yard. Even took some walks along the way.

There were at least some defensive building blocks there, even though they still required "ample projection." That was enough for me. I put a 6 on the OFP, 50 Realistic.

I sort of had no choice but to buy in on the bat. He got his barrel to about a dozen different pitches of various types, speeds, and locations across my looks. He showed a catcher's eye for the zone, seeing spin out of the hand and staying off of it for the most part. He let fastballs travel and relied on his natural strength to bully his hits on the off occasions he didn't barrel one. I was sure there were weaknesses—potentially glaring ones—but the player I saw looked like a 50 hit/60 power catcher with average defense. And that's a 60/50 role catcher.

Nottingham promptly went on to struggle a bunch at the Double-A level, which is not an uncommon thing for young catchers. Reports about the strides of his glove nigh-on started outpacing those about his bat, and while our catching metrics weren't as optimistic as those reports, he seemed indeed to be playing himself up into respectability. Then he started to mash in the high minors in 2018, and here we are.

That ceiling I saw is unlikely. My report on him definitely came in high relative to the vast majority of reports on him. If you averaged together all of the reports out there on him in all the front offices and corners of the internet, dollars to donuts you'd have yourself a 50/45 prospect. And that's not a half-bad place for a sixth-round prep catcher at this stage of his career, mind you. Shout out to all the Day Two prep catchers who'll be big leaguers some day.

It's not what I saw, though. And it's important to have outlying reports on guys when scouts see them at both their best and their worst. It's all part of the context for understanding who a young player is and what he might become if it all works out one way or another.

⚾   ⚾   ⚾

Austin Allen's a guy I wish I'd written more about. I managed this blurb about his power in a wrap column for the Cal League two years ago, but I saw more than enough of him to write up a full report. We didn't mention him among San Diego's top prospects that winter. Nor did he crack this most recent accounting of the franchise's youth, despite a very good 2018 season after leaving Elsinore. Both of these things are San Diego's fault. He was getting better in the middle of a stacked system. A solid start at Triple-A this spring positioned him for the call when Mejia went down.

I didn't really see his 2018 season coming at Double-A, nor did I see him debuting as a big-league catcher this soon. He had massive power, there was no denying that. He's a big beefy boy, broad and strong, with catching legs he keeps under him when he swings in hitting counts. It's a strength-driven swing, but one that's driven by a lot of strength.

I probably caught 10 games of Allen across four series looks at Elsinore, six or seven of 'em when he donned the tools of ignorance. And for his part he probably hit about a buck-twelve in those games. I talked in that lone write-up about being cautiously optimistic about him getting to power in games, but honestly I'm just a sucker for the profile and it took an awful lot of projection off of what I saw firsthand.

In my looks, velocity up exposed a swing that could get grooved and too upper-cutting for its own good, and he struggled to adapt and catch up against some of the better velocity he saw. He had a hard time staying back on changeups, too, frequently losing those fabled legs against more advanced sequencing and execution. Lots of rollovers, lots of unenthusiastic fly balls. He was patient, but in that bad way where he watched a bunch of hittable strikes go by, worked deep counts, then pulled off something soft or got under hot cheddar. It looked like a 4 hit tool, maybe, that would pull 6 power down into solid-average range.

That's more than enough stick if you can catch, but Allen didn't look like he could catch. At all. He was noisy and lumbering behind the plate, his glove hand danced around like he was tasting Hate Street's hanging tree, and his pops were too slow. I would've written him up as a 40/30, noting the potential for some occasional pop but emphasizing hit tool concern and realistically a first base-only defensive projection. That description's a thin line to 25-man relevance in the present day, and a fringe big-leaguer only if the bat works out enough.

And that report definitely would've come in low relative to the vast majority of reports on him. He, too, is probably a 50/45. The power has kept on playing, he's shown the hit tool can stack up okay against better pitching, and for what little it's worth he even managed to wow the computers with a pretty solid little defensive season in the Texas League in 2018. He's not going to come for Pudge any time soon, but it might just be workable back there after all, especially if the bat's all that it has been.

⚾   ⚾   ⚾

If the end goal of scouting is to figure out the likeliest path for a prospect's development—and I think that is indeed a primary end goal—then it is important to have reports at the outlying extremes for each prospect, just the same as it's important to have (plenty) of looks that cluster more towards the mean. Establishing the bookends of that range is an important exercise. And because of it, scouting is a profession in which there's value in the error bars. Consensus requires serving all kinds, and that's good news for scouts: They can be so hip, even their errors are correct. ▪

—Wilson Karaman is an author of Baseball Prospectus.

Dynasty Top 101

by Ben Carsley, Jesse Roche and Bret Sayre

How many data points does a trend make? We think a lot about this at Baseball Prospectus in general, but there's a general movement in the fantasy community when it comes to prospect evaluation that is rooted both in recency bias and just plain old FOMO. More than a handful of the recent wave of elite prospects, some of whom have already turned into elite performers in the majors, share a common thread: extreme youth. It started with the likes of Vladimir Guerrero Jr., Juan Soto and Fernando Tatis, Jr., and it has continued with current elite dynasty prospects like Wander Franco and Julio Rodriguez.

It's caused a shift in the landscape when it comes to dynasty prospect rankings and evaluation that has become hyper aggressive and feels particularly unsustainable. In order to get in on who might be the next elite prospect, you now need to jump in head first as soon as they're signed in international free agency—or at the very least when they make their stateside debut. But this isn't just siloed with J2 signees, it shows up any time a teenager gets flagged as a five-category contributor or rocks and impressive strikeout-to-walk rate when they are notably younger than their peers.

And it all leads to uncomfortable decisions based less information than we want to have, though some people with greater risk appetites will stick their necks out further. In fact, on this list even your relatively conservative rankers have two players on the list proper who were signed as part of the 2019 J2 class (and another in the Honorable Mention section), but the biggest points of consternation come when looking at actual upper-level performers who just don't have that "top-half-of-first-round-redrafts" hype. Not every prospect needs to have that level of ceiling—and plenty of players who aren't supposed to have that ceiling reach it anyway. Christian Yelich, Trevor Story, Cody Bellinger, Nolan Arenado—none of these players were hyped as potential elite-elite fantasy studs, and yet they are living the life fantastic as top-10 players in 2019 with projections to keep them there in 2020.

So who are some of these players that will get overlooked for the next 17-year-old who might get so elite that he just spontaneously combusts into championship trophies? You'll have to read on to find out, but don't let the recent sugar rush fool you into overlooking prospects with high probabilities and upper-minors performance. If you missed out on Wander Franco, at least take off your oversized FOMO sunglasses before you jump all over Jasson Dominguez. If you missed out on Juan Soto, grabbing George Valera isn't going to make that pain go away. You don't chase whiskey with whiskey unless you're John Bonham.

And with that out of the way, let's get to everyone's favorite part of this exercise: the fine print!

As always, there are a few list-specific disclaimers to go over before we jump in. These rankings are for fantasy purposes only, and do not directly take into account things like an outfielder's ability to stick in center or a catcher's pop time. That being said, these factors matter indirectly as they affect a player's ability to either stay in the lineup or maintain eligibility. Additionally, we factor in home parks and organizational strengths, just as when we are talking about a major-league player. We can't pretend that these prospects operate in a vacuum, unaffected by park factors. Of course, there's no guarantee that they will reach the majors with their current organization, so while it is reflected, it's not a heavy ranking factor. Most importantly, the intention of this list is to balance the upside, probability, and proximity of these players to an active fantasy lineup.

Within the list below, you'll find important information about each prospect, including their potential fantasy value (in dollars) at their peak and the risk factor associated with reaching their projected output. Also, you will find a fantasy overview, which summarizes how many categories each player will be useful in, along with any that carry impact. For this exercise, we defined "impact" has having the potential to be in the top 15-20 players in a given category. For instance, impact in home runs roughly equates to the potential to hit 30, impact in steals is 25, and impact for strikeouts is the potential to punch out 200. Then you'll see a realistic ceiling and floor for each prospect, purely in terms of rotisserie value. Because we're nothing but timely at Baseball Prospectus, the ceiling is labeled as "A.J. Hinch's Apology," while the floor is labeled as "Jeff Luhnow's Apology." The Astros: the gifts that keep on giving. The comments are brief because we've already written fantasy-specific comments on each of these players in the individual top-10 lists.

Previous Rank correlates to where repeat entrants placed on the 2019 Top 101. The "NR" key means the player was not ranked, while "N/A" means they were not eligible. Ages listed are as of 4/1/2020.

So let's pull back the curtain and see what's behind door number one. We hope you enjoy!

1. Jo Adell, OF, Los Angeles Angels (Age: 20, Previous Rank: 5)

Potential Earnings: $35+
Risk Factor: Low
Fantasy Overview: Five-category contributor; Impact potential in R, HR, RBI, SB
Fantasy Impact ETA: Conveniently by late April 2020
A.J. Hinch's Apology: A top-5 redraft pick for a decade
Jeff Luhnow's Apology: Justin Upton's career. Yeah, we really like him.

2. Wander Franco, SS, Tampa Bay Rays (Age: 19, Previous Rank: 10)

Potential Earnings: $35+
Risk Factor: Low
Fantasy Overview: Five-category contributor; Impact potential in AVG, R, HR, RBI
Fantasy Impact ETA: 2021
A.J. Hinch's Apology: How about Javy Baez with better plate discipline?
Jeff Luhnow's Apology: "Only" a top-7ish second baseman

3. Gavin Lux, 2B/SS, Los Angeles Dodgers (Age: 22, Previous Rank: 77)

Potential Earnings: $30-35
Risk Factor: Low
Fantasy Overview: Five-category contributor; Impact potential in AVG, R, RBI
Fantasy Impact ETA: Right now
A.J. Hinch's Apology: Ketel Marte without the outfield eligibility
Jeff Luhnow's Apology: So about that above-average power we thought he had...

4. Luis Robert, OF, Chicago White Sox (Age: 22, Previous Rank: 24)

Potential Earnings: $35+
Risk Factor: Medium
Fantasy Overview: Five-category contributor; Impact potential in R, RBI, HR, SB
Fantasy Impact ETA: Opening Day
A.J. Hinch's Apology: Legally speaking, you can't make us stop using "properly appreciated Starling Marte"
Jeff Luhnow's Apology: The Rich Man's Ender Inciarte

5. Julio Rodriguez, OF, Seattle Mariners (Age: 19, Previous Rank: NR)

Potential Earnings: $30-35
Risk Factor: Medium
Fantasy Overview: Four-category contributor; Impact potential in AVG, R, HR, RBI
Fantasy Impact ETA: 2021

A.J. Hinch's Apology: What if J.D. Martinez could run a little bit?
Jeff Luhnow's Apology: Closer to an Eddie Rosario-type OF3

6. Jarred Kelenic, OF, Seattle Mariners (Age: 20, Previous Rank: 79)

Potential Earnings: $25-30
Risk Factor: Low
Fantasy Overview: Five-category contributor; Impact potential in AVG, R
Fantasy Impact ETA: 2021
A.J. Hinch's Apology: He's got the Charlie Blackmon starter kit, basically
Jeff Luhnow's Apology: Even someone this talented can't outrun Mets *and* Mariners curses

7. Andrew Vaughn, 1B, Chicago White Sox (Age: 21, Previous Rank: N/A)

Potential Earnings: $30-35
Risk Factor: Medium
Fantasy Overview: Four-category contributor; Impact potential in AVG, R, HR, RBI
Fantasy Impact ETA: 2021
A.J. Hinch's Apology: A top-five first baseman who's especially strong in OBP leagues
Jeff Luhnow's Apology: A top-12 first baseman who's especially strong in OBP leagues

8. Drew Waters, OF, Atlanta Braves (Age: 21, Previous Rank: 42)

Potential Earnings: $25-30
Risk Factor: Low
Fantasy Overview: Five-category contributor; Impact potential in RBI
Fantasy Impact ETA: Mid 2020
A.J. Hinch's Apology: What if David Dahl could stay healthy?
Jeff Luhnow's Apology: Kole Calhoun, maybe?

9. Kristian Robinson, OF, Arizona Diamondbacks (Age: 19, Previous Rank: 59)

Potential Earnings: $35+
Risk Factor: High
Fantasy Overview: Five-category contributor; Impact potential in R, HR, RBI, SB
Fantasy Impact ETA: Mid 2022
A.J. Hinch's Apology: An Acuna-esque OF1
Jeff Luhnow's Apology: The cause of many angry letters to Bret

10. Adley Rutschman, C, Baltimore Orioles (Age: 22, Previous Rank: N/A)

Potential Earnings: $30-35
Risk Factor: Medium
Fantasy Overview: Four-category contributor; Impact potential in AVG, R, HR, RBI

Fantasy Impact ETA: 2021
A.J. Hinch's Apology: Fantasy's top catcher for a decade. No, really.
Jeff Luhnow's Apology: An elite Orioles catching prospect would *never* fail to pan out

11. MacKenzie Gore, LHP, San Diego Padres (Age: 21, Previous Rank: 35)

Potential Earnings: $30-35
Risk Factor: Medium
Fantasy Overview: Four-category contributor; Impact potential in W, K, ERA, WHIP
Fantasy Impact ETA: Late 2020
A.J. Hinch's Apology: A no-doubt fantasy ace
Jeff Luhnow's Apology: Just making it to SP3 status as a starting pitching prospect is still a success

12. Marco Luciano, SS, San Francisco Giants (Age: 18, Previous Rank: HM)

Potential Earnings: $35+
Risk Factor: High
Fantasy Overview: Five-category contributor; Impact potential in AVG, R, HR, RBI
Fantasy Impact ETA: 2023
A.J. Hinch's Apology: The next Gleyber Torres
Jeff Luhnow's Apology: The next Starlin Castro

13. Carter Kieboom, SS, Washington Nationals (Age: 22, Previous Rank: 21)

Potential Earnings: $20-25
Risk Factor: Low
Fantasy Overview: Four-category contributor; Impact potential in AVG, RBI
Fantasy Impact ETA: 2020
A.J. Hinch's Apology: Off-Peak Xander Bogaerts
Jeff Luhnow's Apology: A suped-up Jed Lowrie

14. Dylan Carlson, OF, St. Louis Cardinals (Age: 21, Previous Rank: NR)

Potential Earnings: $20-25
Risk Factor: Low
Fantasy Overview: Five-category contributor; Impact potential in R
Fantasy Impact ETA: Early 2020
A.J. Hinch's Apology: A Ramon Laureano type OF2
Jeff Luhnow's Apology: A slightly worse Ramon Laureano type OF3

15. Nick Madrigal, 2B, Chicago White Sox (Age: 23, Previous Rank: 22)

Potential Earnings: $20-25
Risk Factor: Low
Fantasy Overview: Three-category contributor; Impact potential in AVG, R, SB
Fantasy Impact ETA: Early 2020

A.J. Hinch's Apology: Winner of batting titles who steals you 30 bases
Jeff Luhnow's Apology: Fancy Dog Jose Peraza

16. Royce Lewis, SS, Minnesota Twins (Age: 20, Previous Rank: 11)

Potential Earnings: $30-35
Risk Factor: High
Fantasy Overview: Five-category contributor; Impact potential in R, SB
Fantasy Impact ETA: 2021
A.J. Hinch's Apology: Prime Ian Desmond
Jeff Luhnow's Apology: Current Ian Desmond

17. Jesus Luzardo, LHP, Oakland Athletics (Age: 22, Previous Rank: 18)

Potential Earnings: $25-30
Risk Factor: Medium
Fantasy Overview: Four-category contributor; Impact potential in W, K, ERA, WHIP
Fantasy Impact ETA: Right now
A.J. Hinch's Apology: A left-handed Walker Buehler
Jeff Luhnow's Apology: Something closer to Robbie Ray

18. Dustin May, RHP, Los Angeles Dodgers (Age: 22, Previous Rank: 69)

Potential Earnings: $20-25
Risk Factor: Low
Fantasy Overview: Four-category contributor; Impact potential in W, ERA, WHIP
Fantasy Impact ETA: Right now
A.J. Hinch's Apology: Mike Soroka with better hair
Jeff Luhnow's Apology: A perfectly average SP4 (with great hair)

19. CJ Abrams, SS, San Diego Padres (Age: 19, Previous Rank: N/A)

Potential Earnings: $30-35
Risk Factor: High
Fantasy Overview: Five-category contributor; Impact potential in AVG, R, SB
Fantasy Impact ETA: 2023
A.J. Hinch's Apology: Have you had the luxury of rostering Trea Turner?
Jeff Luhnow's Apology: Career written by J.J. Abrams

20. Brendan Rodgers, 2B/SS, Colorado Rockies (Age: 23, Previous Rank: 13)

Potential Earnings: $30-35
Risk Factor: High
Fantasy Overview: Four-category contributor; Impact potential in AVG, HR, RBI
Fantasy Impact ETA: 2020
A.J. Hinch's Apology: It's not too late for him to do his best

Tulo impression

Jeff Luhnow's Apology: It's not too late for him to do his best Ryan McMahon impression

21. Vidal Brujan, 2B, Tampa Bay Rays (Age: 22, Previous Rank: 46)

Potential Earnings: $25-30
Risk Factor: Medium
Fantasy Overview: Three-category contributor; Impact potential in AVG, R, SB
Fantasy Impact ETA: 2021
A.J. Hinch's Apology: Dee Gordon
Jeff Luhnow's Apology: Mallex Smith

22. Casey Mize, RHP, Detroit Tigers (Age: 22, Previous Rank: 64)

Potential Earnings: $25-30
Risk Factor: Medium
Fantasy Overview: Four-category contributor; Impact potential in W, K, ERA, WHIP
Fantasy Impact ETA: Late 2020
A.J. Hinch's Apology: The platonic ideal of a Fantasy SP2
Jeff Luhnow's Apology: Hurt again

23. Forrest Whitley, RHP, Houston Astros (Age: 22, Previous Rank: 23)

Potential Earnings: $25-30
Risk Factor: Medium
Fantasy Overview: Four-category contributor; Impact potential in W, K, ERA, WHIP
Fantasy Impact ETA: 2020
A.J. Hinch's Apology: The platonic ideal of a Fantasy SP2
Jeff Luhnow's Apology: Hurt or suspended again

24. Heliot Ramos, OF, San Francisco Giants (Age: 20, Previous Rank: 73)

Potential Earnings: $25-30
Risk Factor: Medium
Fantasy Overview: Four-category contributor; Impact potential in HR, RBI
Fantasy Impact ETA: 2021
A.J. Hinch's Apology: Aren't the good Yasiel Puig years super fun?
Jeff Luhnow's Apology: Aren't most Yasiel Puig years incredibly frustrating?

25. Nate Pearson, RHP, Toronto Blue Jays (Age: 23, Previous Rank: 70)

Potential Earnings: $25-30
Risk Factor: Medium
Fantasy Overview: Four-category contributor; Impact potential in W, K, ERA, WHIP
Fantasy Impact ETA: 2020
A.J. Hinch's Apology: Noah Syndergaard's career
Jeff Luhnow's Apology: Nate Eolvadi's career

26. Jasson Dominguez, OF, New York Yankees (Age: 17, Previous Rank: N/A)

Potential Earnings: $35+
Risk Factor: Extreme
Fantasy Overview: Five-category contributor; Impact potential in R, HR, RBI, SB
Fantasy Impact ETA: 2024
A.J. Hinch's Apology: The best player in MLB history
Jeff Luhnow's Apology: Never makes it out of Double-A

27. George Valera, OF, Cleveland Indians (Age: 19, Previous Rank: 60)

Potential Earnings: $30-35
Risk Factor: High
Fantasy Overview: Five-category contributor; Impact potential in AVG, R, HR, RBI
Fantasy Impact ETA: 2023
A.J. Hinch's Apology: What if Michael Brantley could stay healthy?
Jeff Luhnow's Apology: We felt this way about Nomar Mazara once, too

28. Bobby Witt Jr., SS, Kansas City Royals (Age: 19, Previous Rank: N/A)

Potential Earnings: $30-35
Risk Factor: High
Fantasy Overview: Four-category contributor; Impact potential in R, HR, RBI, SB
Fantasy Impact ETA: 2023
A.J. Hinch's Apology: Trevor Story II: 2 Trevor 2 Story
Jeff Luhnow's Apology: Those early Marcus Semien years

29. Alec Bohm, 3B, Philadelphia Phillies (Age: 23, Previous Rank: 50)

Potential Earnings: $20-25
Risk Factor: Low
Fantasy Overview: Four-category contributor; Impact potential in AVG, R, RBI
Fantasy Impact ETA: Mid 2020
A.J. Hinch's Apology: The player everyone wanted Maikel Franco to be
Jeff Luhnow's Apology: The world's worst Philly accent pun

30. Trevor Larnach, OF, Minnesota Twins (Age: 23, Previous Rank: 30)

Potential Earnings: $20-25
Risk Factor: Low
Fantasy Overview: Four-category contributor; Impact potential in AVG, R, RBI
Fantasy Impact ETA: 2021
A.J. Hinch's Apology: Do we really appreciate Trey Mancini enough?
Jeff Luhnow's Apology: There's a reason we no longer care about Nomar Mazara

31. Cristian Pache, OF, Atlanta Braves (Age: 21, Previous Rank: 45)

Potential Earnings: $15-20
Risk Factor: Low
Fantasy Overview: Five-category contributor
Fantasy Impact ETA: Late 2020
A.J. Hinch's Apology: Victor Robles, minus some batting average
Jeff Luhnow's Apology: Brett Gardner with a better glove

32. Alex Kirilloff, 1B/OF, Minnesota Twins (Age: 22, Previous Rank: 14)

Potential Earnings: $20-25
Risk Factor: Medium
Fantasy Overview: Four-category contributor; Impact potential in HR, RBI
Fantasy Impact ETA: 2021
A.J. Hinch's Apology: A power-driven OF2 in his best years
Jeff Luhnow's Apology: A borderline top-20 first baseman in his best years

33. Luis Patiño, RHP, San Diego Padres (Age: 20, Previous Rank: HM)

Potential Earnings: $25-30
Risk Factor: High
Fantasy Overview: Four-category contributor; Impact potential in W, K, ERA, WHIP
Fantasy Impact ETA: 2021
A.J. Hinch's Apology: The top-rated pitcher on this list next year
Jeff Luhnow's Apology: Even the most exciting pitchers are pitchers

34. Taylor Trammell, OF, San Diego Padres (Age: 22, Previous Rank: 9)

Potential Earnings: $25-30
Risk Factor: High
Fantasy Overview: Five-category contributor; Impact potential in AVG, R, SB
Fantasy Impact ETA: 2021
A.J. Hinch's Apology: The statistical successor to Carl Crawford
Jeff Luhnow's Apology: The statistical successor to Cameron Maybin

35. Alek Thomas, OF, Arizona Diamondbacks (Age: 19, Previous Rank: 92)

Potential Earnings: $20-25
Risk Factor: Medium
Fantasy Overview: Five-category contributor; Impact potential in R
Fantasy Impact ETA: 2022
A.J. Hinch's Apology: Adam Eaton if he hit 25 homers a year
Jeff Luhnow's Apology: Adam Eaton if he didn't

36. Nolan Gorman, 3B, St. Louis Cardinals (Age: 19, Previous Rank: 49)

Potential Earnings: $20-25
Risk Factor: Medium
Fantasy Overview: Three-category contributor; Impact potential in HR, RBI
Fantasy Impact ETA: 2022
A.J. Hinch's Apology: The good Mike Moustakas
Jeff Luhnow's Apology: Renato Nunez, basically

37. A.J. Puk, LHP, Oakland Athletics (Age: 24, Previous Rank: 37)

Potential Earnings: $20-25
Risk Factor: Medium
Fantasy Overview: Four-category contributor; Impact potential in W, K, ERA
Fantasy Impact ETA: 2020
A.J. Hinch's Apology: Patrick Corbin with a few more walks
Jeff Luhnow's Apology: Brad Hand with a few more walks

38. J.J. Bleday, OF, Miami Marlins (Age: 22, Previous Rank: N/A)

Potential Earnings: $20-25
Risk Factor: Medium
Fantasy Overview: Four-category contributor; Impact potential in AVG, RBI
Fantasy Impact ETA: 2021
A.J. Hinch's Apology: Jay Bruce, before he became a punchline
Jeff Luhnow's Apology: An utterly unremarkable OF4

39. Ryan Mountcastle, 1B, Baltimore Orioles (Age: 23, Previous Rank: 26))

Potential Earnings: $15-20
Risk Factor: Low
Fantasy Overview: Four-category contributor; Impact potential in RBI
Fantasy Impact ETA: Right now
A.J. Hinch's Apology: A Nick Castellanos who's even worse with the glove, if you can imagine that
Jeff Luhnow's Apology: How does he already have "future A's waiver claim" energy?

40. Brennen Davis, OF, Chicago Cubs (Age: 20, Previous Rank: NR)

Potential Earnings: $25-30
Risk Factor: High
Fantasy Overview: Five-category contributor; Impact potential in HR, RBI
Fantasy Impact ETA: 2022
A.J. Hinch's Apology: Cubs fans will think he should bring back Mookie in a trade
Jeff Luhnow's Apology: Cubs fans will be pissed he replaces Bryant in the lineup

41. Luis Garcia, SS, Washington Nationals (Age: 19, Previous Rank: 29)

Potential Earnings: $20-25
Risk Factor: Medium
Fantasy Overview: Five-category contributor; Impact potential in AVG, R
Fantasy Impact ETA: 2021
A.J. Hinch's Apology: Jean Segura minus a few steals but with multi-position eligibility
Jeff Luhnow's Apology: Tommy Edman's 2019, basically

42. Spencer Howard, RHP, Philadelphia Phillies (Age: 23, Previous Rank: HM)

Potential Earnings: $20-25
Risk Factor: Medium
Fantasy Overview: Four-category contributor; Impact potential in W, K, ERA
Fantasy Impact ETA: Late 2020
A.J. Hinch's Apology: A strikeout-laden, high-end SP3
Jeff Luhnow's Apology: Vince Velazquez, right down to his durability

43. Jazz Chisholm, SS, Miami Marlins (Age: 22, Previous Rank: 65)

Potential Earnings: $20-25
Risk Factor: Medium
Fantasy Overview: Four-category contributor; Impact potential in HR, RBI
Fantasy Impact ETA: Late 2020
A.J. Hinch's Apology: Eugenio Suarez with shortstop eligibility
Jeff Luhnow's Apology: Rougned Odor with shortstop eligibility

44. Hunter Bishop, OF, San Francisco Giants (Age: 21, Previous Rank: N/A)

Potential Earnings: $25-30
Risk Factor: High
Fantasy Overview: Five-category contributor; Impact potential in R, HR
Fantasy Impact ETA: 2022
A.J. Hinch's Apology: Faster Michael Conforto
Jeff Luhnow's Apology: Faster Mark Canha

45. Sixto Sanchez, RHP, Miami Marlins (Age: 21, Previous Rank: 27)

Potential Earnings: $20-25
Risk Factor: Medium
Fantasy Overview: Four-category contributor; Impact potential in W, ERA, WHIP
Fantasy Impact ETA: Mid 2020
A.J. Hinch's Apology: HDMH
Jeff Luhnow's Apology: TINSTAAPP

46. Jordan Groshans, SS/3B, Toronto Blue Jays (Age: 20, Previous Rank: NR)

Potential Earnings: $20-25
Risk Factor: Medium
Fantasy Overview: Four-category contributor; Impact potential in AVG, R, RBI
Fantasy Impact ETA: 2022
A.J. Hinch's Apology: A well-rounded top-12 third baseman
Jeff Luhnow's Apology: Closer to the Asdrubal Cabrera tier of infielders

47. Matt Manning, RHP, Detroit Tigers (Age: 22, Previous Rank: HM)

Potential Earnings: $20-25
Risk Factor: Medium
Fantasy Overview: Four category contributor; Impact potential in W, K
Fantasy Impact ETA: Late 2020
A.J. Hinch's Apology: He keeps inching closer and closer to a true fantasy SP3 projection
Jeff Luhnow's Apology: He still has far more relieve risk than you'd like

48. Oneil Cruz, ¯_(ツ)_/¯, Pittsburgh Pirates (Age: 21, Previous Rank: 52)

Potential Earnings: $20-25
Risk Factor: Medium
Fantasy Overview: Four-category contributor; Impact potential in HR, RBI
Fantasy Impact ETA: 2021
A.J. Hinch's Apology: Yao Ming
Jeff Luhnow's Apology: Shawn Bradley

49. Ronny Mauricio, SS, New York Mets (Age: 18, Previous Rank: HM))

Potential Earnings: $25-30
Risk Factor: High
Fantasy Overview: Four-category contributor; Impact potential in AVG, HR, RBI
Fantasy Impact ETA: 2022
A.J. Hinch's Apology: We would never overrate a Mets shortstop prospect!
Jeff Luhnow's Apology: We would NEVER overrate a Mets shortstop prospect!

50. Riley Greene, OF, Detroit Tigers (Age: 19, Previous Rank: N/A)

Potential Earnings: $25-30
Risk Factor: High
Fantasy Overview: Five-category contributor; Impact potential in AVG, HR, RBI
Fantasy Impact ETA: 2022
A.J. Hinch's Apology: He'll do a lovely Andrew Benintendi

impression
Jeff Luhnow's Apology: He'll do a lovely impression of a fourth outfielder

51. Michael Kopech, RHP, Chicago White Sox (Age: 23, Previous Rank: 38)

Potential Earnings: $25-30
Risk Factor: High
Fantasy Overview: Four-category contributor; Impact potential in W, K, ERA, WHIP
Fantasy Impact ETA: Early 2020
A.J. Hinch's Apology: Worth the hit to your WHIP thanks to the Ks
Jeff Luhnow's Apology: A right-handed Josh Hader, but not in a closing role

52. Corbin Carroll, OF, Arizona Diamondbacks (Age: 19, Previous Rank: N/A)

Potential Earnings: $25-30
Risk Factor: High
Fantasy Overview: Five-category contributor; Impact potential in AVG, R, SB
Fantasy Impact ETA: 2022
A.J. Hinch's Apology: He'll do a lovely Adam Eaton impression
Jeff Luhnow's Apology: He'll do a lovely impression of a fourth outfielder

53. Jordyn Adams, OF, Los Angeles Angels (Age: 20, Previous Rank: 58)

Potential Earnings: $25-30
Risk Factor: High
Fantasy Overview: Five-category contributor; Impact potential in R, SB
Fantasy Impact ETA: 2022
A.J. Hinch's Apology: Starling Marte with a touch more speed
Jeff Luhnow's Apology: Jake Marisnick with a touch more speed

54. Deivi Garcia, RHP, New York Yankees (Age: 20, Previous Rank: NR)

Potential Earnings: $20-25
Risk Factor: Medium
Fantasy Overview: Four-category contributor; Impact potential in ERA, K
Fantasy Impact ETA: Early 2020
A.J. Hinch's Apology: If you liked Luis Severino, you'll enjoy the slightly worse sequel!
Jeff Luhnow's Apology: If you liked Adam Ottavino, you'll enjoy the slightly better sequel!

55. Shane Baz, RHP, Tampa Bay Rays (Age: 20, Previous Rank: NR)

Potential Earnings: $25-30
Risk Factor: High
Fantasy Overview: Four-category contributor; Impact potential in W, K, ERA, WHIP
Fantasy Impact ETA: 2022
A.J. Hinch's Apology: A top-15 fantasy prospect at this time next year
Jeff Luhnow's Apology: A reliever

56. Xavier Edwards, 2B/SS, Tampa Bay Rays (Age: 20, Previous Rank: 87)

Potential Earnings: $25-30
Risk Factor: High
Fantasy Overview: Three-category contributor; Impact potential in AVG, R, SB
Fantasy Impact ETA: 2021
A.J. Hinch's Apology: He hits exactly three homers in his career, but one comes off a 41-year-old Ivan Nova in Coors Field so I guess that one gets an asterisk
Jeff Luhnow's Apology: A really good pinch runner

57. Brandon Marsh, OF, Los Angeles Angels (Age: 22, Previous Rank: 71)

Potential Earnings: $15-20
Risk Factor: Medium
Fantasy Overview: Four-category contributor; Impact potential in RBI
Fantasy Impact ETA: 2021
A.J. Hinch's Apology: Kole Calhoun feels too apt not to use
Jeff Luhnow's Apology: It kinda fits here too

58. Nico Hoerner, 2B/SS, Chicago Cubs (Age: 22, Previous Rank: 97)

Potential Earnings: $15-20
Risk Factor: Low
Fantasy Overview: Four-category contributor; Impact potential in AVG
Fantasy Impact ETA: Mid 2020
A.J. Hinch's Apology: A .290-hitting middle infielder with 15 bombs and little else
Jeff Luhnow's Apology: A .270-hitting middle infielder with 15 bombs and little else

59. Brendan McKay, LHP, Tampa Bay Rays (Age: 24, Previous Rank: HM)

Potential Earnings: $15-20
Risk Factor: Medium
Fantasy Overview: Four-category contributor; Impact potential in W, WHIP
Fantasy Impact ETA: Right Now
A.J. Hinch's Apology: Off-Peak Jon Lester
Jeff Luhnow's Apology: Fancy Dog Wade Miley

60. Joey Bart, C, San Francisco Giants (Age: 23, Previous Rank: 84)

Potential Earnings: $15-20
Risk Factor: Medium
Fantasy Overview: Four-category contributor
Fantasy Impact ETA: 2021
A.J. Hinch's Apology: "Kill, Bart! Kill, Bart! Kill, Bart!"
Jeff Luhnow's Apology: "Kill Bart! Kill Bart! Kill Bart!"

61. Ian Anderson, RHP, Atlanta Braves (Age: 21, Previous Rank: 47)

Potential Earnings: $15-20
Risk Factor: Medium
Fantasy Overview: Four-category contributor; Impact potential in ERA
Fantasy Impact ETA: Mid 2020
A.J. Hinch's Apology: We'll stick with "the middle class Aaron Nola" from last year
Jeff Luhnow's Apology: Michael Wacha's career

62. Nolan Jones, 3B, Cleveland Indians (Age: 21, Previous Rank: 99)

Potential Earnings: $15-20
Risk Factor: Medium
Fantasy Overview: Four-category contributor; Impact potential in R
Fantasy Impact ETA: Late 2020
A.J. Hinch's Apology: Matt Chapman (remember, this is offense only)
Jeff Luhnow's Apology: A more patient Maikel Franco

63. Noelvi Marte, SS, Seattle Mariners (Age: 18, Previous Rank: NR)

Potential Earnings: $25-30
Risk Factor: Extreme
Fantasy Overview: Five-category contributor; Impact potential in AVG, R, SB
Fantasy Impact ETA: 2024
A.J. Hinch's Apology: This year's Marco Luciano
Jeff Luhnow's Apology: This year's Kevin Maitan

64. Nick Solak, 2B, Texas Rangers (Age: 25, Previous Rank: NR)

Potential Earnings: $10-15
Risk Factor: Low
Fantasy Overview: Four-category contributor
Fantasy Impact ETA: 2019
A.J. Hinch's Apology: An eligibility lord who covers you at three or four spots
Jeff Luhnow's Apology: The glove is bad enough that he only gets ~300 PA a year

65. Jeter Downs, SS, Los Angeles Dodgers (Age: 21, Previous Rank: NR)

Potential Earnings: $15-20
Risk Factor: Medium
Fantasy Overview: Four-category contributor
Fantasy Impact ETA: 2021
A.J. Hinch's Apology: A bat-first middle infielder in a great org? Yeah Jeets!
Jeff Luhnow's Apology: He could wind up a utility infielder. And during Jeter Week, no less …

66. Evan White, 1B, Seattle Mariners (Age: 23, Previous Rank: NR)

Potential Earnings: $10-15
Risk Factor: Low
Fantasy Overview: Four-category contributor; Impact potential in RBI
Fantasy Impact ETA: Right now
A.J. Hinch's Apology: Eric Hosmer, before he turned into a pumpkin
Jeff Luhnow's Apology: Mark Kotsay, maybe?

67. Jose Urquidy, RHP, Houston Astros (Age: 24, Previous Rank: NR)

Potential Earnings: $15-20
Risk Factor: Medium
Fantasy Overview: Four-category contributor; Impact potential in W, WHIP
Fantasy Impact ETA: Right now
A.J. Hinch's Apology: Yonny Chirinos with an extra strikeout every other game
Jeff Luhnow's Apology: Yonny Chirinos

68. Jesús Sánchez, OF, Miami Marlins (Age: 22, Previous Rank: 32)

Potential Earnings: $15-20
Risk Factor: Medium
Fantasy Overview: Four-category contributor
Fantasy Impact ETA: 2021
A.J. Hinch's Apology: Marcell Ozuna
Jeff Luhnow's Apology: Still good enough to start for the Marlins

69. Mitch Keller, RHP, Pittsburgh Pirates (Age: 23, Previous Rank: 36)

Potential Earnings: $15-20
Risk Factor: Medium
Fantasy Overview: Four-category contributor; Impact potential in WHIP, K
Fantasy Impact ETA: Right now
A.J. Hinch's Apology: A very nice SP3
Jeff Luhnow's Apology: The literal definition of anchoring

70. Greg Jones, SS, Tampa Bay Rays (Age: 21, Previous Rank: N/A)

Potential Earnings: $20-25
Risk Factor: High
Fantasy Overview: Four-category contributor; Impact potential in R, SB
Fantasy Impact ETA: 2022
A.J. Hinch's Apology: 80 percent of Jonathan Villar
Jeff Luhnow's Apology: 80 percent of Everth Cabrera

71. Josh Jung, 3B, Texas Rangers (Age: 22, Previous Rank: N/A)

Potential Earnings: $15-20
Risk Factor: Medium
Fantasy Overview: Four-category contributor; Impact potential in AVG, RBI
Fantasy Impact ETA: 2022
A.J. Hinch's Apology: Who we still think Ryan McMahon can be
Jeff Luhnow's Apology: Fancy Dog Colin Moran

72. Geraldo Perdomo, SS, Arizona Diamondbacks (Age: 20, Previous Rank: NR)

Potential Earnings: $15-20
Risk Factor: Medium
Fantasy Overview: Five-category contributor; Impact potential in AVG, R
Fantasy Impact ETA: 2022
A.J. Hinch's Apology: A .380-OBP table setter who can steal 25 bags
Jeff Luhnow's Apology: Kevin Newman with a few hits traded for walks

73. Logan Gilbert, RHP, Seattle Mariners (Age: 22, Previous Rank: NR)

Potential Earnings: $15-20
Risk Factor: Medium
Fantasy Overview: Four-category contributor; Impact potential in W, WHIP
Fantasy Impact ETA: Late 2020
A.J. Hinch's Apology: What if Mike Soroka but tall
Jeff Luhnow's Apology: Lmao I can't believe we actually ranked a Mariners pitcher

74. Daulton Varsho, C, Arizona Diamondbacks (Age: 23, Previous Rank: NR)

Potential Earnings: $20-25
Risk Factor: High
Fantasy Overview: Five-category contributor
Fantasy Impact ETA: Late 2020
A.J. Hinch's Apology: Peak Russell Martin
Jeff Luhnow's Apology: Scott Kingery

75. Brusdar Graterol, RHP, Minnesota Twins (Age: 21, Previous Rank: 62)

Potential Earnings: $20-25
Risk Factor: High
Fantasy Overview: Four-category contributor; Impact potential in ERA, K
Fantasy Impact ETA: Mid 2020
A.J. Hinch's Apology: A Top-5 closer
Jeff Luhnow's Apology: An on-again/off-again starter without a valuable role

76. Josiah Gray, RHP, Los Angeles Dodgers (Age: 22, Previous Rank: NR)

Potential Earnings: $15-20
Risk Factor: Medium
Fantasy Overview: Four-category contributor; Impact potential in W, ERA
Fantasy Impact ETA: 2021
A.J. Hinch's Apology: He's a Dodger, so he'll somehow be a borderline SP2 in another 6 months
Jeff Luhnow's Apology: He's a Dodger, so his usage will be incredibly maddening

77. Grayson Rodriguez, RHP, Baltimore Orioles (Age: 20, Previous Rank: NR)

Potential Earnings: $20-25
Risk Factor: High
Fantasy Overview: Four-category contributor; Impact potential in W, ERA, K
Fantasy Impact ETA: 2022
A.J. Hinch's Apology: Next year's Matt Manning or Spencer Howard on this list
Jeff Luhnow's Apology: Lmao I can't believe we actually ranked an Orioles pitcher

78. Triston Casas, 1B, Boston Red Sox (Age: 20, Previous Rank: NR)

Potential Earnings: $20-25
Risk Factor: High
Fantasy Overview: Three-category contributor; Impact potential in R, HR, RBI
Fantasy Impact ETA: 2022
A.J. Hinch's Apology: Matt Olson
Jeff Luhnow's Apology: This isn't a joke for once; C.J. Cron

79. Tyler Freeman, 2B/SS, Cleveland Indians (Age: 20, Previous Rank: NR)

Potential Earnings: $15-20
Risk Factor: Medium
Fantasy Overview: Four-category contributor; Impact potential in AVG, R
Fantasy Impact ETA: 2021
A.J. Hinch's Apology: Once upon a time we thought Gavin Lux

had this profile, too!
Jeff Luhnow's Apology: He might just be Brock Holt with worse hair

80. Alexander Canario, OF, San Francisco Giants (Age: 19, Previous Rank: NR)

Potential Earnings: $20-25
Risk Factor: High
Fantasy Overview: Four-category contributor; Impact potential in HR, RBI
Fantasy Impact ETA: 2023
A.J. Hinch's Apology: The next Jorge Soler
Jeff Luhnow's Apology: Remember how long it took Jorge Soler to click?

81. Brett Baty, 3B, New York Mets (Age: 20, Previous Rank: N/A)

Potential Earnings: $20-25
Risk Factor: High
Fantasy Overview: Four-category contributor; Impact potential in HR, RBI
Fantasy Impact ETA: 2023
A.J. Hinch's Apology: Most of the way to Joey Gallo
Jeff Luhnow's Apology: Most of the way to Will Middlebrooks

82. Leody Taveras, OF, Texas Rangers (Age: 21, Previous Rank: 57)

Potential Earnings: $15-20
Risk Factor: Medium
Fantasy Overview: Five-category contributor
Fantasy Impact ETA: 2021
A.J. Hinch's Apology: There's still a chance it clicks and he's a star!
Jeff Luhnow's Apology: Offensively, he's looking more like, uh, Kevin Pillar?

83. Jonathan India, 3B, Cincinnati Reds (Age: 23, Previous Rank: 51)

Potential Earnings: $15-20
Risk Factor: Medium
Fantasy Overview: Five-category contributor
Fantasy Impact ETA: 2021
A.J. Hinch's Apology: 80 percent of Nick Senzel
Jeff Luhnow's Apology: Forever Eugenio Suarez's understudy

84. Tarik Skubal, LHP, Detroit Tigers (Age: 23, Previous Rank: NR)

Potential Earnings: $15-20
Risk Factor: Medium
Fantasy Overview: Four-category contributor; Impact potential in K
Fantasy Impact ETA: Late 2020
A.J. Hinch's Apology: The good version of The Eduardo Rodriguez Experience
Jeff Luhnow's Apology: King of Skubals Mountain

85. Orelvis Martinez, SS, Toronto Blue Jays (Age: 19, Previous Rank: NR)

Potential Earnings: $25-30
Risk Factor: Extreme
Fantasy Overview: Five-category contributor; Impact potential in AVG, HR, RBI
Fantasy Impact ETA: 2023
A.J. Hinch's Apology: This year's Marco Luciano
Jeff Luhnow's Apology: This year's Kevin Maitan

86. Erick Pena, OF, Kansas City Royals (Age: 17, Previous Rank: N/A)

Potential Earnings: $25-30
Risk Factor: Extreme
Fantasy Overview: Five-category contributor; Impact potential in AVG, HR, RBI
Fantasy Impact ETA: 2024
A.J. Hinch's Apology: The next Juan Soto/Julio Rodriguez/Kristian Robinson, etc
Jeff Luhnow's Apology: As an industry, we've really gone off the rails when it comes to valuations for teenagers

87. Daniel Lynch, LHP, Kansas City Royals (Age: 23, Previous Rank: NR)

Potential Earnings: $15-20
Risk Factor: Medium
Fantasy Overview: Four-category contributor; Impact potential in W, ERA
Fantasy Impact ETA: 2021
A.J. Hinch's Apology: A reasonable SP3
Jeff Luhnow's Apology: A frustrating SP5

88. Adrian Morejon, LHP, San Diego Padres (Age: 21, Previous Rank: 75)

Potential Earnings: $20-25
Risk Factor: High
Fantasy Overview: Four-category contributor; Impact potential in ERA, K
Fantasy Impact ETA: 2021
A.J. Hinch's Apology: There's plenty of valuable in a No. 4/5 Fantasy SP!
Jeff Luhnow's Apology: It's just not that hard to replace a No. 4/5 Fantasy SP!

89. Khalil Lee, OF, Kansas City Royals (Age: 21, Previous Rank: 43)

Potential Earnings: $15-20
Risk Factor: Medium
Fantasy Overview: Three-category contributor; Impact potential in SB
Fantasy Impact ETA: Mid 2020
A.J. Hinch's Apology: Lorenzo Cain's prime without the AVG
Jeff Luhnow's Apology: Lorenzo Cain's 2019

90. Andrés Giménez, SS, New York Mets (Age: 21, Previous Rank: 33)

Potential Earnings: $15-20
Risk Factor: Medium
Fantasy Overview: Five-category contributor
Fantasy Impact ETA: 2021
A.J. Hinch's Apology: He'll run his way into being a top-15 shortstop
Jeff Luhnow's Apology: Maybe we should just sit out ranking Mets prospects for a while.

91. Bryson Stott, SS, Philadelphia Phillies (Age: 22, Previous Rank: N/A)

Potential Earnings: $20-25
Risk Factor: High
Fantasy Overview: Five-category contributor; Impact potential in R, SB
Fantasy Impact ETA: 2022
A.J. Hinch's Apology: Elvis Andrus's stat line
Jeff Luhnow's Apology: Eric Sogard's stat line

92. Seth Beer, 1B, Arizona Diamondbacks (Age: 23, Previous Rank: NR)

Potential Earnings: $15-20
Risk Factor: Medium
Fantasy Overview: Three-category contributor; Impact potential in HR, RBI
Fantasy Impact ETA: Late 2020
A.J. Hinch's Apology: A Treehouse IPA canned just three days ago
Jeff Luhnow's Apology: The line at Treehouse

93. Ethan Hankins, RHP, Cleveland Indians (Age: 19, Previous Rank: NR)

Potential Earnings: $20-25
Risk Factor: High
Fantasy Overview: Four-category contributor; Impact potential in W, K
Fantasy Impact ETA:
A.J. Hinch's Apology: A legit SP2, when healthy
Jeff Luhnow's Apology: A frustrating setup man, when healthy

94. Brayan Rocchio, SS, Cleveland Indians (Age: 19, Previous Rank: NR)

Potential Earnings: $20-25
Risk Factor: High
Fantasy Overview: Five-category contributor; Impact potential in AVG, R
Fantasy Impact ETA: 2023
A.J. Hinch's Apology: Jean Segura, minus a few steals (which maybe makes him Luis Garcia???)
Jeff Luhnow's Apology: More of a Kevin Newman type

95. Matthew Liberatore, LHP, St. Louis Cardinals (Age: 20, Previous Rank: NR)

Potential Earnings: $20-25
Risk Factor: High
Fantasy Overview: Four-category contributor; Impact potential in W, ERA
Fantasy Impact ETA: 2022
A.J. Hinch's Apology: The most valuable asset in baseball, if you believe MLB Trade Twitter
Jeff Luhnow's Apology: A fairly generic SP5/6

96. Ke'Bryan Hayes, 3B, Pittsburgh Pirates (Age: 23, Previous Rank: 63)

Potential Earnings: $10-15
Risk Factor: Low
Fantasy Overview: Five-category contributor
Fantasy Impact ETA: Early 2020
A.J. Hinch's Apology: Remember Bill Mueller?
Jeff Luhnow's Apology: Functionally not all that different from Colin Moran

97. Aaron Bracho, 2B, Cleveland Indians (Age: 18, Previous Rank: NR)

Potential Earnings: $20-25
Risk Factor: High
Fantasy Overview: Five-category contributor; Impact potential in AVG, R
Fantasy Impact ETA: 2023

A.J. Hinch's Apology: A reason to name your team Aaron Bracho-vich
Jeff Luhnow's Apology: Whatever, it wasn't that great of a name anyway

98. Sherten Apostel, 3B, Texas Rangers (Age: 21, Previous Rank: NR)

Potential Earnings: $20-25
Risk Factor: High
Fantasy Overview: Four-category contributor; Impact potential in HR, RBI
Fantasy Impact ETA: 2022
A.J. Hinch's Apology: Who Yankees fans think Miguel Andujar is
Jeff Luhnow's Apology: Folks, call us "Jesus" because we're about to be let down by an Apostel

99. Jordan Balazovic, RHP, Minnesota Twins (Age: 21, Previous Rank: NR)

Potential Earnings: $20-25
Risk Factor: High
Fantasy Overview: Four-category contributor; Impact potential in W, K, ERA
Fantasy Impact ETA: 2021
A.J. Hinch's Apology: A well-rounded SP3 in the Zack Wheeler

mold

Jeff Luhnow's Apology: Insert your favorite failed tall pitching prospect here ... Alex Meyer?

100. Travis Swaggerty, OF, Pittsburgh Pirates (Age: 22, Previous Rank: 66)

Potential Earnings: $20-25

Risk Factor: High

Fantasy Overview: Four-category contributor; Impact potential in R, SB

Fantasy Impact ETA: 2021

A.J. Hinch's Apology: A 20/20 type who won't hurt you too much in batting average

Jeff Luhnow's Apology: Even Danny Santana got his shit together for one season

101. Misael Urbina, OF, Minnesota Twins (Age: 17, Previous Rank: NR)

Potential Earnings: $25-30

Risk Factor: Extreme

Fantasy Overview: Five-category contributor; Impact potential in AVG, R, SB

Fantasy Impact ETA: 2024

A.J. Hinch's Apology: Whit Merrifield

Jeff Luhnow's Apology: A whit of value

Honorable Mention

Francisco Alvarez, C, NYM; Keoni Cavaco, SS, MIN; Bobby Dalbec, 3B, BOS; Estevan Florial, OF, NYY: Jake Fraley, OF, SEA; Hunter Greene, RHP, CIN; DL Hall, LHP, BAL; Austin Hays, OF, BAL; Kody Hoese, 3B, Brent Honeywell, RHP, TB; LAD; Gilberto Jimenez, OF, BOS; James Karinchak, RHP, CLE; D'Shawn Knowles, OF, LAA; Nick Lodolo, LHP, CIN; Brailyn Marquez, RHP, CHC; Luis Matos, OF, OAK; Jorge Mateo, SS/OF, OAK; Robert Puason, SS, OAK; Keibert Ruiz, C, LAD; Kyle Wright, RHP, ATL; Ryan Vilade, SS/3B, COL

—Ben Carsley, Jesse Roche and Bret Sayre are authors of Baseball Prospectus.

Top 50 Signees

by Bret Sayre and Jesse Roche

Commercials and lite radio stations will tell you that Christmas is the most wonderful time of the year. Don't get us wrong, it's very enjoyable to celebrate with friends and family and get all kinds of presents you don't really need, but dynasty draft season is truly what the song is about. It's the opportunity to turn those precious draft picks into future cogs of the team that ultimately helps you dominate your leaguemates in a way that makes random bystanders want to jump in and break up the fight.

The 2020 draft class presents a number of such opportunities. Unlike some of the last few years, it's a very good one to have a top-end pick. The first five players on the list to come all rank within the top-30 dynasty prospects globally, including three in the top-20, with a second tier not too far behind them. This is a pretty stark comparison to last year when there were zero in the top-20 and just two in the top-30. It means that it's one of those draft years where trading up can actually make a notable difference in your team's outlook. The depth of this class isn't bad, but it's slightly below average overall, and odds are that you're not really going to miss that third- or fourth-rounder.

There are a couple of reasons for the shape of talent in dynasty drafts this year. First, it's a very fantasy-flavored MLB Draft crop. With pitching and defense diminished, it may not have been a particularly vaunted group for IRL value, but we don't particularly care about that, do we? There will always be high-end shortstops in any draft, but corner outfielders and corner infielders don't get us any less excited than center fielders and middle infielders. A strong group of college hitters and an overall dearth of pitching talent? Sign us up.

The second is the rise of the IFA impact on dynasty drafts. We've seen it creep in over the last couple of years, and while it may have gotten out of control in some places, there has definitely been more safety in the most elite J2 players during the last half-decade than we've seen historically. The meteoric rises of Vladimir Guerrero Jr. and Wander Franco are impossible to ignore, and they do fundamentally change the way these players are mixed in with the Rule 4 draftees. Even the initial success of Marco Luciano colors this. However, we can't forget that the biggest and slam-dunkiest J2 prospect of the last decade was Kevin Maitan, and he's been an abject failure. The incentives of teams do not align with the public getting quality information about these players from the time they actually sign (hint: it's not July 2nd) to when they arrive in the U.S. and get properly scouted. It means there are many rumors and incendiary reports—we just have to be realistic about how much we should believe and how we should value it.

Before we get to the most exciting part, it's the paragraph that frames the list and its utility. The below is intended for dynasty leagues of approximately 14-16 teams, with one catcher. It assumes a separate farm team, and if your league does not have a separate farm team, feel free to bump up the players with faster timetables. If you're in a deeper league, prioritize safety. If you're in a shallower league, load up on risk. And, finally, each player's situation is factored into their values. This can mean organizational history of developing players and/or future home ballpark (though the latter is discounted a bit since these players are generally pretty far away and park factors are not constants). You know your league best, and now you know how to translate what is about to come to your individual circumstances. And if you're not sure, this is why we have comments.

We appreciate your patience as you let us rumble through the non-ordinal portion of this journey. Please make sure your arms and legs are inside the vehicle at all times, and that your safety restraint is secure. Now, may we present the 50 best players who entered professional baseball during the 2019 calendar year.

1. Andrew Vaughn, 1B, Chicago White Sox, Age: 21.99

Vaughn is a special talent at the plate and arguably the best college hitter since Kris Bryant. He possesses a plus-or-better hit tool with a polished, all-fields approach and advanced plate discipline. In addition, he has big raw power, the kind capable of making the 12-year-olds in the second half of the bleachers pay extra attention when he's up. Given his nearly impeccable track record, it is difficult to find faults with Vaughn, though detractors will note his less-than-ideal size and athleticism. They might also point to the fact that he did not blow the doors off the low minors in his debut, hitting just .253/.367/.411 between the South Atlantic and Carolina Leagues.

2. Adley Rutschman, C, Baltimore Orioles, Age: 22.15

If any college hitter can challenge Vaughn as the top college bat, it is Rutschman. Part of the 2018 National Champion Oregon State team, he formed a modern-day murderers' row with Nick Madrigal and Trevor Larnach. Rutschman profiles as the rarest of birds: a high-end catching prospect with both an extreme floor and ceiling. At the plate, his discipline is extremely advanced and showcases the potential for a plus-hit, plus-power package. Meanwhile, he is a superb defender and is not a current risk to leave the position. Rutschman is the best catching prospect since Buster Posey (2008) and Matt Wieters (2007), and there's a fair argument to make that he's even better. Nevertheless, catchers carry more limited value in most fantasy formats, given the real-life demands of the position and the fewer games they play by nature. With that said, if you play in a two-catcher format, go get your dude.

3. C.J. Abrams, SS, San Diego Padres, Age: 19.49

Abrams is arguably the fastest player in this draft class, regularly clocking 80-grade home-to-first times. In addition to the blazing speed, he has advanced bat control, allowing him to profile as a high-contact, top-of-the-order hitter. However, he surprised even his most ardent supporters by displaying more in-game power and less overall rawness in his spectacular debut (.393/.436/.647). The speed is what put him on the radar as a strong dynasty draft target, but the potential to hit for average and push 20 homers is what makes him a potential fantasy superstar.

4. Jasson Dominguez, OF, New York Yankees, Age: 17.15

There's probably not a single player about whom we talked more while making this list than Dominguez, who is purely a hypothetical at this point—much more than anyone else in this range. How you feel about Dominguez likely has to do with your risk aversion and how much you anchor to the recent J2 prospect explosions of Vladimir Guerrero Jr., Wander Franco, Julio Rodríguez, and Marco Luciano. Whispers of the tools are intense, but just because those top-rated IFA prospects were developmental successes doesn't mean Dominguez will be. Plus, we don't know enough about him as a prospect to suggest otherwise. So put stock in grainy video and unreliable sources at your own risk. Sure, it's easy to dream on a 30/30 stud, but it's not yet grounded in enough reality. Even Ronald Acuña wasn't supposed to be Ronald Acuña, after all.

Ultimately, this is a hedge and a compromise. One of us (Jesse) has him inside the top-three, while one of us (Bret) doesn't have him inside the top-five players. The reality is, though, that he's unlikely to be around with the third pick of most dynasty drafts anyway. For those who would take him over everyone else on this list, you may ultimately be right, but bad process turns into poor outcomes more often than not.

5. Bobby Witt Jr., SS, Kansas City Royals, Age: 19.80

Witt Jr. has plus raw power and speed, but questions surrounding his hit tool keep him out of the elite group at the top of this list. A near lock to stick at shortstop, the ceiling is Trevor Story-ish and as high, from a fantasy standpoint, as anyone else in the draft class. Part of Witt Jr.'s issue is that he's been on the radar for so long from his prep days that he's just not as exciting as the new breakout guys. Don't fall into that trap.

6. J.J. Bleday, OF, Miami Marlins, Age: 22.39

The Division I leader in home runs (26), Bleday has a leveraged and powerful left-handed swing from a well-built 6-foot-3 frame. He's not just a power hitter, either. He shows an excellent feel for hitting, driving the ball to all fields and hitting it where it is pitched. Bleday has the potential to hit .280-.290 with 25-30 homers, and he should move quickly through the minors.

7. Hunter Bishop, OF, San Francisco Giants, Age: 21.77

The younger brother of Braden Bishop, a speedy outfielder for the Mariners, Hunter has the same plus speed and high-end athleticism. However, the comparisons end there, as he inherited nearly all the power in the Bishop family. His large, 6-foot-5 frame portends both easy pop to all fields and elevated swing-and-miss, which could lead to an average in the .260 and below range at peak. Bishop comes into pro ball more raw than most high-end college bats and lacks much of an extended track record of success against advanced pitching, but few prospects possess his 30-homer/20-steal potential.

8. Riley Greene, OF, Detroit Tigers, Age: 19.51
9. Corbin Carroll, OF, Arizona Diamondbacks, Age: 19.61

This pair of prep hitters share the ability to hit for average—both could potentially push .300 at peak—but the rest of their profiles diverge from there. Greene displays a silky smooth swing and an uncanny feel for line drive-contact, but he has enough strength to flirt with 25-30 homers down the road. On the other side of the ledger, speed will likely never be a big part of his game, though he has the athleticism to notch five-to-10 steals while he's still spry. Carroll is an all-fields, line-drive hitter, who smartly utilizes his double-plus speed. Despite his smaller stature, his wiry strength could help him rack up doubles and triples, while being able to put 12-15 or so over the fence. Notably, he has worked diligently to add weight and strength to his frame, and he receives high accolades for his makeup and work ethic. Regardless of how the power develops, anyone who has a shot to hit for average and steal 30 bases is a potential fantasy star.

10. Greg Jones, SS, Tampa Bay Rays, Age: 22.07

The younger brother of Braden Bishop, a speedy outfielder for the Mariners, Hunter has the same plus speed and high-end athleticism. However, the comparisons end there, as he inherited nearly all the power in the Bishop family. His large, 6-foot-5 frame portends both easy pop to all fields and elevated swing-and-miss, which could lead to an average in the .260 and below range at peak. Bishop comes into pro ball more raw than most high-end college bats and lacks much of an extended track record of success against advanced pitching, but few prospects possess his 30-homer/20-steal potential.

11. Josh Jung, 3B, Texas Rangers, Age: 22.12

Jung looks like he should have more power than he does, mostly because he relies on a contact-oriented approach. So while he might look like a guy who hits .260-30, the output is more likely to be .290-20. Anyone can sell out for power these days, but if it happens with the former Texas Tech third baseman, the average will likely sink to a point where the overall value proposition won't change much from a fantasy perspective.

12. Brett Baty, 3B, New York Mets, Age: 20.37

A prodigious power hitter, Baty possesses potential 40-homer pop. It comes in the form of a sweet, left-handed swing with an advanced ability to work counts. Notably, his poor defense and athleticism have improved dramatically, and he should stick at third base, where his big arm will play. There's not a whole lot separating Baty from what Nolan Gorman was last year out of the draft.

13. Erick Peña, OF, Kansas City Royals, Age: 17.11

A darling of fall instructs, Peña currently carries a ton of helium that has been generated by increased coverage and recency bias. There is, however, a lot to like. He boasts a sweet, left-handed swing, which already generates impressive raw power with tons of room for growth on his 6-foot-3 frame. His load is simple, and his bat explodes through the zone. Despite his youth, Peña displays an advanced plate discipline and a feel for all-fields contact. He even has some present speed, though, as he fills out, he projects to be an average-to-below runner. Regardless, Peña's precocious hitting ability and power potential give him as much upside as nearly any player in this class, though it also comes with the risk associated with all 17-year-old prospects prior to their pro debut.

14. Bryson Stott, SS, Philadelphia Phillies, Age: 22.49
15. Kody Hoese, 3B, Los Angeles Dodgers, Age: 22.72
16. Nick Lodolo, LHP, Cincinnati Reds, Age: 22.16

Heading into 2019, Stott was on the radar as a potential .290-hitting shortstop with 20-25 stolen-base upside, but he added more game power last spring. He could now could hit 15-20 homers to boot. He's been getting overlooked in drafts this winter, but he has more upside than you think. The landing spot is a strong one, too. Hoese had a true breakout in his junior season and was one of the top college hitters last year (.391/.486/.779 with 23 home runs). Large and strong, he has the potential to hit 30 homers without hurting you in batting average despite his long levers. Lodolo is the first arm to show up on this list. It's both a product of this being a poor class for pitching, both at the prep and college levels, and our general distaste for pitching prospects in the early stages of dynasty drafts. He's tall (6-foot-6 to be exact) and could end up with above-average command of an arsenal that includes a mid-90s fastball and two secondary pitches that can miss bats. All of that makes him a relatively high-confidence SP3-4, at least as far as pitching prospects go.

17. Shogo Akiyama, OF, Cincinnati Reds, Age: 31.96
18. Keoni Cavaco, SS, Minnesota Twins, Age: 18.83
19. Robert Puason, SS, Oakland Athletics, Age: 17.56

Regarding Akiyama, Kazuto Yamazaki provided a detailed report in October. Since then, he signed a lucrative, three-year deal with the Reds. While it is a crowded outfield situation in Cincinnati, he likely will receive everyday playing time (at least against righties) based on his contract, defense, and hitting ability. Akiyama has sneaky 20/20 upside in, well, 2020. Cavaco is a pure upside play, as his amateur track record was more limited than his peers and he'll get poo-pooed because he flatlined in his pro debut. That is a terrible reason to look past a prep hitter who has the potential to be a five-category contributor and push 30 homers. Puason is another highly-regarded J2 signing from last summer, but unlike Dominguez and Peña, his profile is more speed-over-power and average. That doesn't make it any more comfortable to bet on, nor does it make him any safer than the rest, but at least there's 30-steal upside to go with a supposed five-tool profile.

20. Jackson Rutledge, RHP, Washington Nationals, Age: 21.00
21. Kameron Misner, OF, Miami Marlins, Age: 22.23
22. Yoshitomo Tsutsugo, OF, Tampa Bay Rays, Age: 28.35

Rutledge is a big dude, and he can hit 100 on the radar gun. Despite the fact that he's got injury risk, reliever risk, and basically every other kind of risk of which you can think, he also has the most upside of any pitcher available in dynasty drafts this year. Go big or go home. Speaking of going big, Misner possesses mammoth power and pairs it with speed that could nab him 15-20 steals as well. The question is whether he can hit, and that is as significant of a question as there is in dynasty circles. Indeed, Misner was nearly nonexistent in SEC action (.222/.353/.315) and powerless in his debut (.092 ISO), but the tools are there. Tsutsugo landed in an extremely crowded situation in Tampa, with fellow lefties Ji-Man Choi and Nate Lowe vying for playing time at first base and designated hitter. How much he actually plays is uncertain, as is how much he will hit. While Tsutsugo has lauded power, he also has substantial swing-and-miss tendencies, including 141 strikeouts (a 25-percent rate) just last year.

23. Michael Toglia, 1B, Colorado Rockies, Age: 21.63
24. Michael Busch, 2B, Los Angeles Dodgers, Age: 22.15
25. George Kirby, RHP, Seattle Mariners, Age: 22.15

Toglia and his big-time power landed in a dream fantasy spot with the Rockies. He'll have to fight through some real swing-and-miss concerns, but a Three True Outcomes bat in Colorado still carries tons of fantasy upside—and a shot at 40 dingers. Busch possesses a quick left-handed swing, with all-fields power and excellent discipline to go along with a long track record of success. Kirby's profile is one based on command and control, rather than raw stuff, but his four-pitch mix is still impressive enough to miss bats and achieve an SP4 future. If that kind of pitching prospect is your jam, he's probably the top arm for you. He's not for us, though.

26. Matthew Allan, RHP, New York Mets, Age: 18.96
27. Alek Manoah, RHP, Toronto Blue Jays, Age: 22.23
28. Trejyn Fletcher, OF, St. Louis Cardinals, Age: 18.92
29. Quinn Priester, RHP, Pittsburgh Pirates, Age: 19.54
30. Braden Shewmake, SS, Atlanta Braves, Age: 22.37

Allan is every top prep righty you've met. He's got a good frame, a mid-90s fastball, and a curve that should be able to miss plenty of bats in the majors. He's outside the top-25 draftees partially because the profile is particularly risky and partially because prep pitchers were down overall in last year's draft, but there's SP2 upside here. Large and imposing, Manoah understandably throws mid-to-upper-90s gas with a lethal power-slider. His size, unrefined change-up, and so-so command make him an extreme relief risk. Fletcher was a late reclassification from the 2020 to the 2019 class and a raw, cold-weather prospect all the way up in Maine. Still, he possesses a tantalizing blend of plus tools (power, speed, and arm strength). Priester was a late-rising, cold-weather prep arm, and he may even still be underrated despite his first-round draft pedigree. Unlike the others in this section, Shewmake is a low-risk, consistent college performer with defensive versatility and a strong hit tool, but he has limited power/speed upside. His ceiling is not too dissimilar from what Dansby Swanson has become.

31. Tyler Callihan, 3B/2B, Cincinnati Reds, Age: 19.78
32. Luis Rodríguez, OF, Los Angeles Dodgers, Age: 17.54
33. Hudson Head, OF, San Diego Padres, Age: 19.00
34. Kwang-hyun Kim, LHP, St. Louis Cardinals, Age: 31.69
35. Noah Song, RHP, Boston Red Sox, Age: 22.84

Few doubt Callihan's ability to hit, as he could reach .290 with 25 homers at peak, but he's somewhat position-less as well. Think of him as 90 percent of Willie Calhoun's bat with 110 percent of Calhoun's defensive chops. Rodríguez lacks the standout tools of fellow top J2 signees, but he profiles as a five-category contributor like the rest. An over-slot third-round pick ($3 million!), Head is a potential five-category performer who impressed in his debut, showcasing excellent bat speed, budding power, and some footspeed. Kim is a likely back-end starter with a little bit of "they haven't seen me yet" overperformance potential in 2020, and he'll be more impactful in ratios than strikeouts. Song would be 20 spots higher on this list without the cloud around his military commitment, as he's a college arm with SP2 upside if you squint. Unfortunately, he's a pure game-theory exercise in drafts this year given the uncertainty.

36. Daniel Espino, RHP, Cleveland Indians, Age: 19.24
37. Will Wilson, SS/2B, San Francisco Giants, Age: 21.69
38. Zach Thompson, LHP, St. Louis Cardinals, Age: 22.432
39. Brennan Malone, RHP, Arizona Diamondbacks, Age: 19.56
40. Gunnar Henderson, SS, Baltimore Orioles, Age: 18.76

Espino has high-end stuff, but he lacks ideal size and is a worse bet than the prep arms ahead of him—even if he has a similar SP2 ceiling. Wilson has already changed uniforms as part of a salary-dump trade from the Angels to the Giants. A poor defender, he is a strong bet to move to second base, where he carries a lot of fantasy value as a potential .260 hitter with 20-home run pop, even in San Francisco. Injuries plagued Thompson's college career, but his four-pitch arsenal and a deceptive delivery made him a first-round pick. Unfortunately, it also limits his upside compared to his peers. Henderson is a tall, projectable shortstop with a promising hit tool and substantial power potential. As he fills out, he may require a move to third base, but then again what player with his profile hasn't had that said about him?

41. Anthony Volpe, SS, New York Yankees, Age: 18.93

42. Matthew Lugo, SS, Boston Red Sox, Age: 18.89

43. Josh Lindblom, RHP, Milwaukee Brewers, Age: 32.79

44. Bayron Lora, OF, Texas Rangers, Age: 17.51

45. Rece Hinds, 3B, Cincinnati Reds, Age: 19.57

Two prep middle infielders without overly dynamic tools headline this group. Volpe is a rarity: a polished, prep shortstop with a high floor but limited power/speed upside. Meanwhile, Lugo is extremely raw with a feel to hit, good speed, and an athletic frame. A former major-league journeyman, Lindblom reinvigorated his career in the KBO, leading the league last year in nearly every pitching category. The development of a splitter and improved spin rate of his mediocre fastball (90.3 mph average) has elevated his otherwise pedestrian repertoire. He'll likely settle in as a boring SP6/7. We end this group with two powerful behemoths with questionable hit tools and defensive value. Lora signed for nearly $4 million and is already a massive human at 17 years old. IS THAT JAIRO BERAS' MUSIC?? (Man, we hope not.) Hinds showcases crazy power in home run derbies and sometimes in games, but he does little else reliably.

46. Blake Walston, LHP, Arizona Diamondbacks, Age: 18.76

47. Logan Davidson, SS, Oakland Athletics, Age: 22.26

48. Nasim Nuñez, SS, Miami Marlins, 19.62

49. Jordan Brewer, OF, Houston Astros, Age: 22.67

50. Maximo Acosta, SS, Texas Rangers, Age: 17.42

Walston is all dream at this point, relying on frame and a potentially dominant curve. Davidson is a switch-hitter with power and speed, but he's unlikely to hit even .250 and has historically struggled with wood bats. Nuñez is an excellent defensive shortstop with a huge arm and the potential to steal 40-plus bases, if he can figure out how to get on base regularly. Brewer has tools for days and showcased them during Michigan's run in the College World Series; however, he is as raw as college juniors come at the plate. While Texas doled out a hefty bonus to Bayron Lora, Acosta may be the better dynasty prospect. He boasts a tantalizing blend of speed, projectable power, and a promising line-drive stroke.

Honorable Mention (in alphabetical order)

- Benyamin Bailey, OF, Chicago White Sox, Age: 18.54
- Bryce Ball, 1B, Atlanta Braves, Age: 21.73
- Peyton Burdick, OF, Miami Marlins, Age: 23.10
- Brenton Doyle, OF, Colorado Rockies, Age: 21.88
- JJ Goss, RHP, Tampa Bay Rays, Age: 19.27
- Tommy Henry, LHP, Arizona Diamondbacks, Age: 22.67
- Seth Johnson, RHP, Tampa Bay Rays, Age: 21.53
- Shea Langeliers, C, Atlanta Braves, Age: 22.37
- Brady McConnell, SS, Kansas City Royals, Age: 21.85
- Luis Medina, OF, Milwaukee Brewers, Age: 17.10
- Ismael Mena, OF, San Diego Padres, Age: 17.34
- Bryant Packard, OF, Detroit Tigers, Age: 22.49
- Kyren Paris, SS, Los Angeles Angels, Age: 18.39
- Reginald Preciado, SS, San Diego Padres, Age: 16.88
- Nick Quintana, 3B, Detroit Tigers, Age: 22.47
- Emmanuel Rodriguez, OF, Minnesota Twins, Age: 17.09
- Aaron Schunk, 3B, Colorado Rockies, Age: 22.69
- Sammy Siani, OF, Pittsburgh Pirates, Age: 19.30
- Ethan Small, LHP, Milwaukee Brewers, Age: 23.13
- Kyle Stowers, OF, Baltimore Orioles, Age: 22.25
- Matt Wallner, OF, Minnesota Twins, Age: 22.30
- Davis Wendzel, 3B, Texas Rangers, Age: 22.86
- Josh Wolf, RHP, New York Mets, Age: 19.58
- Arol Vera, SS, Los Angeles Angels, Age: 17.55
- Shun Yamaguchi, RHP, Toronto Blue Jays, Age: 32.72

—Bret Sayre and Jesse Roche are authors of Baseball Prospectus.

The Top 31 Dynasty Players Outside U.S. Pro Ball

by Jesse Roche

Mining the Minors for future dynasty talent is a regular job for most dynasty owners. For those owners in open universe leagues, the breadth of available talent expands to high school freshmen and sophomores, even to pre-pubescent precocious stars, and overseas to Nippon Professional Baseball (NPB), the Korea Baseball Organization (KBO), and the Cuban National Series, among others. Sifting through this expansive talent pool can be confusing and burdensome. Luckily, we did the work for you! This article details the top 31 amateur and international dynasty league players entering the 2019/2020 off-season.

1. Spencer Torkelson, 1B, Arizona State, Age: 20

"Tank for Tork" will be a common refrain across dynasty leagues this coming year. The slugging first baseman not only obliterated the freshman home run record at Arizona State set by Barry Bonds, but led all Division I with 25 home runs in 2018. Then, Torkelson decimated the Cape Cod Baseball League (CCBL), hitting .333/.472/.704 with 7 home runs in 25 games. While his power numbers slightly slumped during his sophomore campaign, he still launched 23 home runs and paced teammate Hunter Bishop, the tenth overall pick in the 2019 MLB Draft. Following the season, Torkelson again impressed with wooden bats in both the CCBL and for the 2019 Collegiate National Team (CNT).

Remarkably, the 2020 MLB Draft should mark the second time in two years in which an undersized, right-handed hitting and throwing first baseman is a top three selection (Andrew Vaughn). Like Vaughn, to which comparisons will inevitably be drawn, Torkelson possesses mammoth, and arguably more raw power. Further, he effortlessly taps into his power with a simple, quick swing. Torkelson also exhibits a disciplined, all-fields approach, though with enough swing-and-miss to warrant some trepidation regarding his future hit tool. Still, he profiles as an elite fantasy performer with a potential average-to-above hit tool and double-plus game power. Our advice to dynasty owners: "TANK FOR TORK!"

2. Austin Martin, UTL, Vanderbilt, Age: 21

The leadoff hitter for the National Champions, Martin enjoyed a breakout campaign this past year, leading the SEC in batting average by an astounding 34 points! To cap off his spectacular season, he singlehandedly provided the only offense in Vanderbilt's opening win against Louisville in the College World Series with two home runs.

A pure hitter, Martin demonstrates advanced plate discipline and utilizes a quick, compact swing to consistently spray line drives to all fields. In fact, his renowned hit tool has even garnered some double-plus grades. Further, his ability to regularly barrel balls and turn on mistakes allows him to maximize his average raw power. Meanwhile, Martin has above-average speed, quick-twitch athleticism, and strong instincts, making him a threat on the bases. All told, he has sneaky 20/20 upside, despite more modest tools.

In the field, Martin has no clear home, although he mainly played at third base during his sophomore year. Regardless of position, he has the requisite infield actions and arm strength to be serviceable anywhere, and MLB teams likely will prize his defensive versatility.

3. Emerson Hancock, SP, Georgia, Age: 21

The premier arm in the 2020 MLB Draft, Hancock is an early favorite to be the first overall pick. As a sophomore, he was nearly unhittable until uncharacteristic struggles during the postseason. Over his first 12 starts, including 8 in the difficult Southeastern Conference (SEC), Hancock allowed just 43 hits and 12 earned runs in 82 2/3 innings (1.31/0.74 ERA/WHIP)!

Hancock's success is no surprise given his deep, electric arsenal, headlined by a potential double-plus, lively, mid-to-upper-90s fastball, touching 99 mph. In addition to his heater, he utilizes three promising secondaries, including a sweeping, low-80s slider, a diving, mid-80s change-up, and an improved, upper-70s curveball. At his best, Hancock flashes four plus-or-better offerings with above-average command.

Hancock, however, missed over three weeks due to a lat strain and struggled with consistency and command over his final starts. Further, he declined an invitation by the CNT this summer, presumably to rest and rehabilitate. This year, Hancock will look to quell these concerns and cement his status as the top player in the draft class, while headlining a lethal Friday/Saturday rotation at Georgia with Cole Wilcox (below).

4. Nick Gonzales, 2B, New Mexico State, Age: 21

Gonzales is an enigma. A walk-on at New Mexico State, he impressed as a freshman and dominated as a sophomore, leading Division I in hitting (.432/.532/.773). This elite performance, however, must be taken in context. Presly Askew Field is a well-known hitter's park, located at an elevation of 3,980 feet in the dry New Mexico air. Simply, balls fly there. In fact, the Aggies hit .356/.469/.573 as a team, and his teammate Tristan Peterson similarly hit .400/.510/.769. Further, Gonzales plays in the non-elite, Western Athletic Conference, where he only hit .349/.486/.585 following a weak out-of-conference schedule. Consequently, many question whether his performance was a product of his hitting environment and competition.

With that said, Gonzales answered many doubts about his bat in the CCBL following the season. There, he earned MVP honors, hitting .351/.451/.630 with 7 home runs and 6 stolen bases. Most importantly, he exhibited elite bat speed, quick hands, and a short stroke to generate tons of hard contact. While Gonzales possesses only average raw power, he taps into every ounce with an excellent feel for the barrel. In addition, he has above-average speed, which he is learning to utilize on the base paths. In the field, his poor arm strength likely limits him to second base, where he should provide solid defense. The whole package, including his size, tools, and small school background, is slightly reminiscent of Keston Hiura. Target in dynasty leagues accordingly!

5. Tetsuto Yamada, 2B, Yakult Swallows (NPB), Age: 27

Yamada is one of the stars of NPB, earning the Central League MVP in 2015 and posting 30/30 campaigns in four of the last five years. The difficulty with projecting NPB players is determining when, and if, they will play in the MLB. Following the 2020 season, Yamada will be an international free agent, but it is unclear if he will leave NPB, and, unlike other recent Japanese imports, he has not expressed a strong desire to play in the MLB.

As such, Yamada carries substantial risk as an open universe asset. Regardless, he also possesses immense offensive upside with second base eligibility. Kaz Yamazaki provided his observations of Yamada in June, noting:

> [Yamada] displays a stellar combination of power and approach at the plate. He stands slightly crouched, hands high above his head, and fires up a remarkably quick swing that's geared towards elevating the ball. Despite his big, pronounced leg kick and a gargantuan finish, the stroke is short enough to allow him to catch up with fastballs

to the inner-third; he pulled one inside pitch on the black for a long ball over the left field fence in my look. Listed at 5-foot-11 and 168 pounds, he does well to translate most of his weight into game power.

> He pairs top-shelf pitch recognition with elite plate discipline – he boasts the lowest chase rate in the league at present – but while he's among the least-frequent swingers he isn't passive. He'll jump first pitches when he's challenged in the zone early in the count, and he'll make excellent mid-at-bat adjustments to spoil tough pitches.

> Yamada's home-to-first times undersell his raw speed on account of the aforementioned huge finish to his swing, but once he reaches base, he shows great instincts and gets consistently good jumps on base-stealing attempts. Over his career he has swiped 151 bags in 172 attempts, and he hasn't been caught yet this season. He takes quality angles on his first-to-third stretches, as well.

Should Yamada decide to take his talents across the Pacific, he likely will be a highly coveted free agent. For fantasy purposes, he promises alluring 20/20 upside and an immediate impact if, and it is a big "if," he arrives in the MLB.

6. Blaze Jordan, 1B/3B, DeSoto Central HS (MS), Age: 17

Jordan arguably possesses the most raw power in the 2020 MLB Draft class, and he is one of the youngest following his reclassification in May. His well-known power prowess has been on display for years. As a 13-year-old, he infamously launched two 500-foot home runs at Globe Life Park during the Power Showcase home run derby. Since then, Jordan has only cemented his standing as a top amateur prospect, continually impressing at showcase events and displaying elite exit velocities. In addition to the power, he has a promising hit tool, showing a feel to hit, hard contact to all fields, and a short and simple, but powerful, swing. Meanwhile, Jordan has improved his physique, athleticism, and defense to the point some believe he has a future at third base or right field, where his strong arm will play.

7. Seiya Suzuki, OF, Hiroshima Carp (NPB), Age: 25

At just 25 years old, Suzuki has quickly developed into an international superstar. This past year, he won the Central League batting title (.335/.453/.565) and a Gold Glove in right field while leading NPB in OPS. After the season, he starred in the 2019 WBSC's Premier 12 for the tournament champion Samurai Japan national team (12-for-27, 3 HR, 9 R, 13 RBI). Looking forward, Suzuki will again be able to showcase his impressive bat on the world stage during the 2020 Summer Olympics in Toyko. That bat is the main draw and potentially special, with above-to-plus hitting ability and raw power.

Unfortunately, Suzuki is eligible to be posted for the first time following the 2020 season, and unlikely to arrive in the MLB for some time.

8. Garrett Mitchell, OF, UCLA, Age: 21

A top-50 prospect heading into the 2017 MLB Draft, Mitchell fell to the 14th round due to concerns about his hit tool and a strong commitment to UCLA. After an up-and-down, powerless freshman year (.280/.337/.331), he impressed in the CCBL, flashing a feel to hit with some power and speed. As a sophomore, Mitchell built on his summer performance, hitting .349/.418/.566 while cutting his K%-BB% by 11.62%. Notably, he showcased his blazing, double-plus speed with 18 stolen bases and 12 triples, and regularly clocked sub-4-second home-to-first times. In addition, he has begun to tap into his raw power while displaying improved pitch recognition and plate discipline. With continued progress, Mitchell profiles as an exciting, five-tool talent and a potential fantasy force.

9. Jordan Walker, 3B, Decatur HS (GA), Age: 18

The Player of the Game in the 2019 MLB High School All-Star Game, Walker has seen his draft stock skyrocket this past summer, and for good reason. A large and physical specimen, he possesses immense power potential emanating from his extremely projectable, 6-foot-5 frame. Walker already exhibits easy raw power, double-digit exit velocities, and plus bat speed. Double-plus raw power at peak is well within his range of outcomes. While power is his calling card, he also has a feel to hit with a balanced and fluid swing, though his long levers likely will lead to some swing-and-miss. A plus athlete, Walker has excellent mobility and agility for his size, flashing surprising long speed with more limited acceleration. Long-term, speed likely will not be a part of his game, but this athleticism should allow him to stick at third base, where his strong arm is a perfect fit.

10. Brady House, SS, Winder-Barrow HS (GA), Age: 17

The top dynasty prospect in the 2021 MLB Draft class, House is a gifted, two-way player with massive offensive upside. At just 16 years old, he is already launching long home runs during games with impressive exit velocities. Incredibly, even more power is to come. With a large, broad-shouldered frame, House is, quite literally, built like a house. He hits from a wide base with a short stride and compact stroke, and yet generates elite bat speed. Further, House has a lauded feel to hit, spraying hard contact to all fields. Currently a shortstop, he likely is destined for third base as he continues to fill out due to his size and limited athleticism. Nonetheless, House has three potential plus tools in his power, arm, and hitting ability, and likely will come with even more fanfare than recent prep third baseman, Nolan Gorman.

11. Austin Hendrick, OF, West Allegheny HS (PA), Age: 19

Hendrick epitomizes a prototypical, slugging, right field prospect, with a lightning-quick, leveraged swing that generates huge exit velocities and easy plus raw power. Further, he is strong and athletic with above-average speed once he gets going and a big arm. Unfortunately, Hendrick also suffers plenty of swing-and-miss, largely stemming from an unorthodox stance and load. A high hand set up, pre-load movement, and a bat wrap have caused timing issues and inconsistency. After dominating showcase events early in the summer, Hendrick began struggling during MLB's Prospect Development Pipeline (PDP) League. Later, while playing for Team USA in the WBSC U-18 Baseball World Cup, he went 1-18 with 6 strikeouts and 5 walks, including a golden sombrero, and retreated to the bench for the final 5 games. When he is in sync, however, he is a dynamic force at the plate.

12. Zac Veen, OF, DeSoto Central HS (MS), Age: 17

Tall, lanky, and athletic, Veen is a classic, projectable outfielder in the mold of Kyle Tucker. Already, he flashes substantial raw power with impressive exit velocities, including a 105.6 mph single in the 2019 Under Armour All-America Game. It is easy to envision Veen adding weight and muscle without sacrificing fluidity or speed. Further, he has a quick, smooth swing and balanced, all-fields approach, and repeatedly impressed on the showcase circuit. Veen also has plus speed underway and profiles well at all three outfield positions.

13. Masataka Yoshida, OF, Orix Buffaloes (NPB), Age: 26

Although a diminutive 5-foot-8, Yoshida packs a punch, tallying 55 home runs over the last two years. He generates plus raw power from a lightning quick and leveraged swing. Meanwhile, he has a feel to hit with advanced plate discipline, resulting in a 64-to-79 strikeout-to-walk ratio last year. Due to injury-shortened seasons, Yoshida has only accrued approximately three years of service time. As such, he likely is not even eligible to be posted until after the 2022 season. Still, his bat should be worth the wait and a hold in open universe formats.

14. Kumar Rocker, SP, Vanderbilt, Age: 20

A projected first-round pick in the 2018 MLB Draft, Rocker had lofty bonus demands and ultimately honored his commitment to Vanderbilt. The decision to forego the pros likely will pay off as he is an early favorite to be the first overall pick in the 2021 MLB Draft after leading Vanderbilt to the National Championship. Indeed, Rocker was named the Most Outstanding Player of the 2019 College World Series as a freshman. During the NCAA Tournament, he was incredible, winning all four of his starts, allowing just 3 earned runs, 15 hits, and 5 walks in 28 innings with 44 strikeouts, including a 19-strikeout no-hitter in the Super Regional.

An imposing figure on the mound, Rocker is physically mature with no remaining projection. No matter, he already throws steady, mid-90s gas with an elite, double-plus, mid-80s slider that falls off the table and elicits boatloads of swings and misses. In addition, he displays advanced command of both his fastball and slider, which proved too much for most college bats. Moving forward, Rocker will need to keep his weight in check and further develop his change-up in order to reach his frontline starter potential.

15. Dylan Crews, OF, Lake Mary HS (FL), Age: 18

Crews is a well-known member of the 2020 prep class, having played for the 2018 18-U National Team as a rising junior. Although lacking much remaining projection, he already flashes above-average tools across the board. Notably, he generates elite bat speed with an easy load and quick hands. Crews also demonstrates solid plate discipline and uses the whole field. His extensive track record of success against advanced prep pitching provides further confidence in his hitting ability. Most observers believe he will hit for both average and power. In addition, Crews is a gifted athlete with above-average speed and quick acceleration.

16. Jared Kelley, SP, Refugio HS (TX), Age: 18

A flamethrower, Kelley normally sits around 95-96 mph and registered the fastest velocity (99 mph) at the 2019 Perfect Game National Showcase. He generates this velocity with ease and little effort from a simple, repeatable delivery. Kelley chiefly pairs his heater with a similarly effective, fading change-up, which he uses liberally and with great confidence. This change-up is thrown from the same arm angle as his fastball with impressive separation (low-80s). His breaking ball, a low-80s, sweeping slurve, lacks much bite, and may benefit from being thrown with greater velocity. Still, Kelley shows advanced command of all three pitches within the zone for a prep arm. With further development and tightening of his breaking ball, Kelley has all the traits of a frontline starter.

17. Kodai Senga, SP, Fukuoka Softbank Hawks (NPB), Age: 27

Senga has been one of the most dominant pitchers in NPB since 2016. This past year, he led NPB in strikeouts (227) by 39. His raw stuff matches his elite performance, with a mid-to-upper-90s fastball, a double-plus, diving splitter, and a power cutter/slider. Indeed, many consider his forkball splitter to be one of the best splitters in the world. However, Senga has struggled with inconsistent command at times and elevated walk rates over the past two years. In addition, he is unlikely to be posted and not eligible for international free agency until 2022. With that said, Senga has legitimate frontline starter upside, especially if he refines his command.

18. Casey Martin, SS, Arkansas, Age: 21

Martin offers an unparalleled blend of power and speed in the 2020 MLB Draft class. In fact, he receives top-of-the-scale grades for his speed, though he is still learning to utilize it effectively on the bases. While he lacks much size, he possesses incredible bat speed and a violent, upper-cut stroke designed to inflict damage. As such, Martin punches above his weight in the batter's box, amassing 28 home runs and a .235 isolated slugging percentage over his first two years at Arkansas. Unfortunately, he has also totaled 138 strikeouts (22.85%), and this penchant to swing-and-miss casts doubt on his hit tool. Martin is ultimately a high-variance prospect with very similar offensive tools and production to former SEC standout, Jeren Kendall. Proceed with caution!

19. Robert Hassell III, OF, Independence HS (TN), Age: 18

As a standout two-way player, Hassell III earned the Gatorade Player of the Year for Tennessee as a high school junior. At the plate, however, is where most believe he possesses the highest upside. Hassell III has a sweet, left-handed swing with plus bat speed and a patient, disciplined approach. Meanwhile, he is also a plus runner with a high-waisted, projectable frame that portends future average-to-above, raw power. Hassell III's offensive potential was on full display for Team USA in the WBSC U-18 Baseball World Cup. There, Hassell III shined, hitting .472/.524/.806 over 9 games and earning WBSC's International Baseball Player of the Year award.

20. Ed Howard, SS, Mount Carmel HS (IL), Age: 18

Few amateur prospects had a better summer showing than Howard. The well-rounded shortstop impressed at the plate and in the field. Offensively, he flashes a promising hit tool with simple and repeatable swing mechanics, electric, double-plus bat speed, and advanced zone awareness and patience. Notably, Howard already generates explosive, hard contact to all fields, which projects to impact raw power as he fills out his athletic and muscular frame. Further, he is a highly regarded defender with excellent range, actions, and hands. The only blemish on his outlook is his modest speed and limited acceleration, though this does not hinder him defensively.

21. Cole Wilcox, SP, Georgia, Age: 20

A highly regarded prospect prior to the 2018 MLB Draft, Wilcox was thought to be a mid-first-round pick but opted to honor his commitment to Georgia. After a poor start to the season, in which he allowed 12 earned runs and 9 walks in his first 12 1/3 innings, he settled down, impressing in SEC play and flashing top-of-the-rotation upside. Large and imposing, Wilcox can touch triple digits with his fastball in short stints, while sitting in the mid-90s during starts. His two secondaries (power slider and fading change-up) both sit in the mid-80s and flash plus. While it is hard to question his raw stuff, his command is wildly inconsistent, resulting an elevated walk rate (5.73 BB/9). In addition, his delivery is violent with a long arm action, leading to the dreaded relief-risk designation. Regardless, Wilcox is a special talent who is a potential high-upside fantasy option, be it in the rotation or the bullpen.

22. Luke Leto, SS, Portage Central HS (MI), Age: 17

The epitome of a well-rounded athlete, Leto can do it all. He can hit, hit for power, run, field, and pitch. Meanwhile, he also plays both football and basketball, showcasing his versatile athleticism. However, Leto truly shines on the diamond, where he has dominated showcases and international competition for years. A well-built left-handed hitter, he has a balanced stance with a quick stroke and a feel to hit. While his power is still developing, Leto flashes impressive exit velocities for his age. His best offensive tool is his easy plus speed, which he aggressively utilizes on the basepaths, stealing tons of bases and legging out triples.

23. Braylon Bishop, OF, Arkansas HS (AR), Age: 17

Like Luke Leto (above), Bishop is a special athlete, who moonlights as the starting quarterback for his high school team. A speedster, he registers easy plus run times with the type of fast-twitch athleticism scouts fawn over. Bishop also has a chiseled physique with a projectable, broad-shouldered and high-waisted frame. At the plate, he exhibits solid bat speed, fast hands, and budding power, though some pre-swing movement can cause timing issues. Still, Bishop has immense, five-tool upside with plus speed and power potential.

24. Pete Crow-Armstrong, OF, Harvard-Westlake HS (CA), Age 18

A staple of USA Baseball since 2014, Crow-Armstrong may have suffered some prospect fatigue within the industry. Regardless, he is a steady, elite performer with undeniable hitting ability. A polished bat, Crow-Armstrong is a high-contact hitter with a mature approach and quick, compact stroke. His best tool, however, is his plus speed, which plays even faster due to his instinctual feel for the game, on the bases and in the field. Crow-Armstrong also has some pop with plenty of remaining physical projection, but his approach is geared for low, hard contact at present. While he lacks much power, he profiles similarly to recent, underrated hit/speed prep outfielders, Alek Thomas and Corbin Carroll.

25. Heston Kjerstad, OF, Arkansas, Age: 21

Along with Casey Martin (above), Kjerstad has similarly excelled over his first two years with Arkansas, helping to carry the Razorbacks to back-to-back College World Series appearances. Further, he was the top performing hitter for the 2019 CNT (.395/.426/.651). Strong and powerful, he can drive the ball out to any part of the park with plus raw power and a leveraged swing. Like Martin, however, Kjerstad suffers plenty of swing-and-miss and there are questions surrounding his hit tool and swing. In particular, he utilizes a lot of pre-swing hand movement, which may lead to timing and balance issues, though this bizarre load has a remarkably consistent finish. Nevertheless, Kjerstad is a promising, slugging, corner outfield prospect with tons of success against more advanced pitching.

26. Alex Binelas, 3B, Louisville, Age: 21

A cold-weather prospect from Wisconsin, Binelas flew a bit under the radar prior to the 2018 MLB Draft, and a commitment to Louisville caused him to fall to the 35th round. Last year, he was one of the most impressive freshmen in the country, flashing prodigious power (.321 ISO) and earning unanimous Freshman All-American honors. Binelas also has quieted concerns about his hit tool, showing a feel to hit, solid plate discipline, and the ability to adjust. At third base, he remains a work-in-progress, but he has the athleticism and arm strength to profile at the hot corner long-term.

27. Robby Martin, OF, Florida State, Age: 20

Martin was a solid, but far from a spectacular, prospect entering the 2018 MLB Draft with a strong commitment to Florida State. Understandably, he fell to the 37th round and decided to go to school. As a freshman, he was a standout performer, leading Florida State in hitting (.345) before struggling in the post-season. Martin is a tall, broad-shouldered slugger with improving strength and burgeoning raw power. In the box, he has a wide base and quietly rests his bat on his shoulder with a brief load and kick. Notably, he exhibits excellent bat control and plate discipline, often driving the ball where it is pitched and using the whole field. Limited to a corner defensively due to below-average speed, Martin will need to continue to hit and begin to more fully tap into his plus raw power.

28. Mick Abel, SP, Jesuit HS (OR), Age: 18

Abel has a tall, long, and lanky frame, affording plenty of physical projection and possibly more future velocity. That is not to say he lacks for velocity, regularly sitting in the mid-90s, and as high as 97 mph, with good downhill plane and late life. Further, Abel throws a mid-80s, power slider with sharp, late break that profiles as a potential plus, swing-and-miss offering. His firm, upper-80s change-up, however, remains a work-in-progress, but flashes promising diving action. Arguably, Abel is the highest upside prep arm in the 2020 MLB Draft class should he grow into even more velocity and refine his change-up and command.

29. Asa Lacy, SP, Texas A&M, Age: 21

A pair of lefties, Lacy and John Doxakis, a second-round pick in the 2019 MLB Draft, arguably were the best Friday-Saturday combo in college baseball last year. Indeed, they combined to start 31 games while allowing just 45 earned runs and striking out 245 batters. Lacy was particularly unhittable, leading Division I in H/9 (4.97) while also finishing among the leaders in K/9 (13.20). He confounds hitters with a four-pitch mix, headlined by a low-to-mid-90s mph fastball and low-80s curveball. Further, Lacy's pitches play up due to solid downhill plane from his high three-quarter delivery. With that said, he has shaky command and control, often missing his spots and issuing plenty of walks. A strong junior year with improved command and sharpened secondaries likely would make Lacy a lock for the top-5 in the 2020 MLB Draft.

30. Chase Davis, OF, Franklin HS (CA), Age: 18

A strong performance during the summer showcase circuit has vaulted Davis up draft boards and expect him to climb even further. The right field archetype, he checks nearly all the boxes with potential plus raw power, a cannon for an arm, and sneaky above-average speed. Davis, however, has some timing issues at plate, likely stemming from a bat wrap and inconsistent mechanics. Nevertheless, he flashes a solid hit tool with good plate discipline and bat control. A big spring should cement Davis in the first-round discussion.

31. Jack Leiter, SP, Vanderbilt, Age: 20

The son of former major league pitcher Al Leiter, Jack was a projected first-round pick in the 2019 MLB Draft, but advised teams prior to the draft that he would honor his commitment to Vanderbilt. Now, he is set to join Kumar Rocker in one of the most exciting college rotations in 2020. Leiter is as polished as a prep arm comes, with advanced pitchability and excellent command. While he lacks prototypical size, he possesses a deep, four-pitch arsenal, including a low-to-mid-90s fastball and a potential plus (or better), knee-buckling curveball.

—Jesse Roche is an author of Baseball Prospectus.

Index of Names